G000292337

STREET ATLAS
Surrey

Contents

III	Key to map symbols
IV-V	Key to map pages
VI-VII	Route planning
VIII	Administrative and post code boundaries
1	Street maps
219	Extra-large-scale maps of town centres

219	Dorking
219	Epsom
220	Guildford
220	Kingston upon Thames
221	Leatherhead
221	Woking

222	Index of hospitals, industrial estates, railway stations, schools, shopping centres, street names and universities

First published 1996 by

Philip's, a division of
Octopus Publishing Group Ltd
2-4 Heron Quays, London E14 4JP

Second colour edition 2000
Fourth impression 2002

ISBN 0-540-07794-1 (hardback)
ISBN 0-540-07795-X (spiral)

© Philip's 2000

Digital Data

The exceptionally high-quality mapping found in this atlas is available as digital data in TIFF format, which is easily convertible to other bit-mapped (raster) image formats.

The index is also available in digital form as a standard database table. It contains all the details found in the printed index together with the National Grid reference for the map square in which each entry is named.

For further information and to discuss your requirements, please contact Philip's on 020 7531 8439 or george.philip@philips-maps.co.uk

22a	Motorway (with junction number)
	Primary route (dual carriageway and single)
	A road (dual carriageway and single)
	B road (dual carriageway and single)
	Minor road (dual carriageway and single)
	Other minor road (dual carriageway and single)
	Road under construction
	Pedestrianised area
DY7	Postcode boundaries
	County and Unitary Authority boundaries
	Railway
	Tramway, miniature railway
	Rural track, private road or narrow road in urban area
	Gate or obstruction to traffic (restrictions may not apply at all times or to all vehicles)
	Path, bridleway, byway open to all traffic, road used as a public path
	The representation in this atlas of a road, track or path is no evidence of the existence right of way
126 / 94 / 164	Adjoining page indicators
	The map area within the pink band is shown at a larger scale on the page indicated by the red block and arrow

■ The dark grey border on the inside edge of some pages indicates that the mapping does not continue onto the adjacent page
■ The small numbers around the edges of the maps identify the 1 kilometre National Grid lines

Walsall	Railway station
	London Underground station
	Croydon Tramlink
	Private railway station
	Bus, coach station
	Ambulance station
	Coastguard station
	Fire station
	Police station
	Accident and Emergency entrance to hospital
H	Hospital
	Places of worship
i	Information Centre (open all year)
P P&R	Parking, Park and Ride
PO	Post Office
Prim Sch	Important buildings, schools, colleges, universities and hospitals
River Medway	Water name
	Stream
	River or canal (minor and major)
	Water
	Tidal water
	Woods
	Houses
House	Non-Roman antiquity
VILLA	Roman antiquity

Acad	Academy	Ent	Enterprise	LC	Level Crossing	Obsy	Observatory	Sch	School
Crem	Crematorium	Ex H	Exhibition Hall	Liby	Library	Pal	Royal Palace	Sh Ctr	Shopping Centre
Cemy	Cemetery	Ind Est	Industrial Estate	Mkt	Market	PH	Public House	TH	Town Hall/House
C Ctr	Civic Centre	Inst	Institute	Meml	Memorial	Recn Gd	Recreation Ground	Trad Est	Trading Estate
CH	Club House	Ct	Law Court	Mon	Monument	Resr	Reservoir	Univ	University
Coll	College	L Ctr	Leisure Centre	Mus	Museum	Ret Pk	Retail Park	YH	Youth Hostel

The scale of the maps is 5.52 cm to 1 km (3½ inches to 1 mile)

0	¼	½	¾	1 mile
0	250 m 500 m 750 m	1 kilometre		

The scale of the maps on pages numbered in red is 11.04 cm to 1 km (7 inches to 1 mile)

0	220 yards	440 yards	660 yards	½ mile
0	125 m 250 m	375 m ½ kilometre		

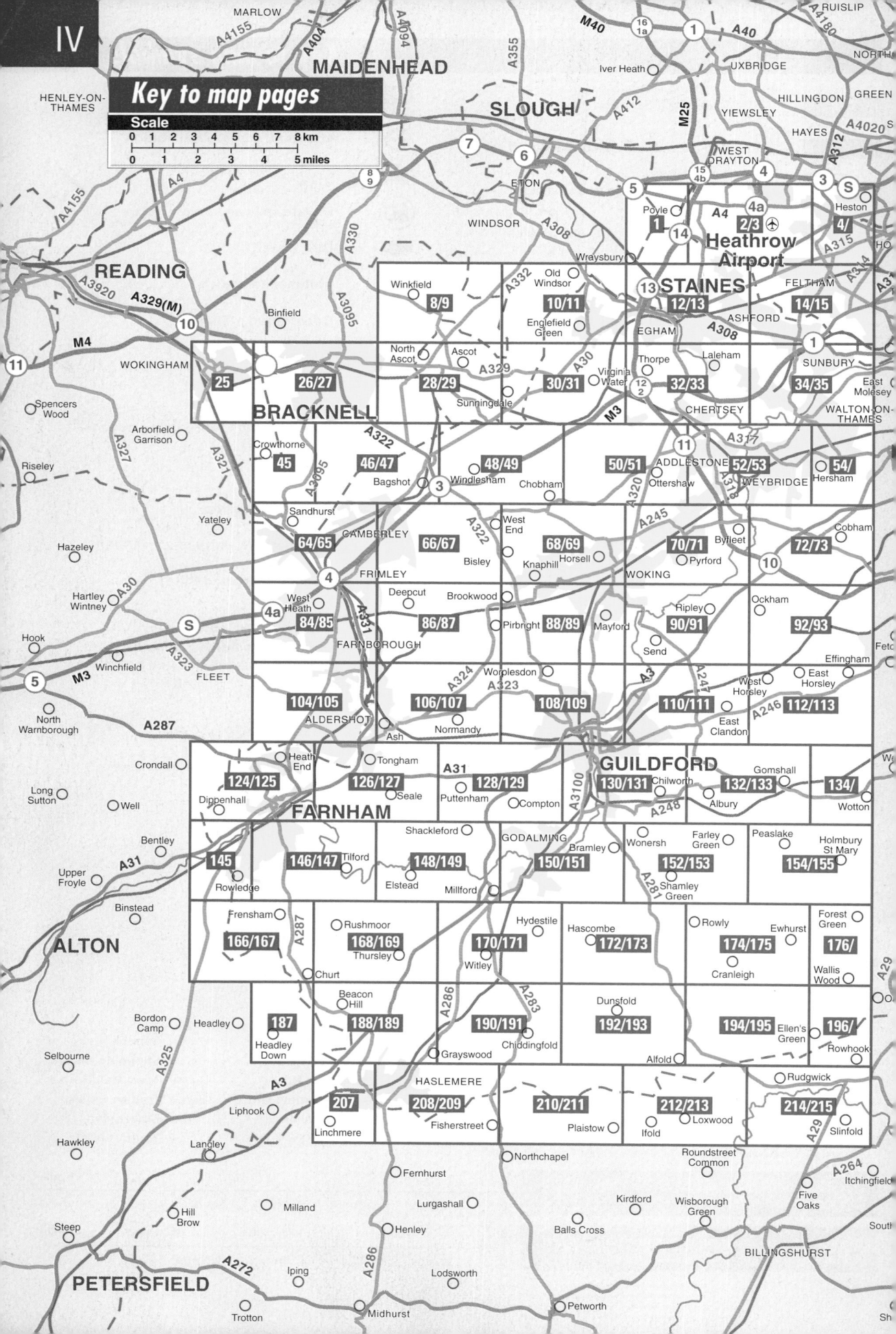

IV

Key to map pages

Scale

0 1 2 3 4 5 6 7 8 km
0 1 2 3 4 5 miles

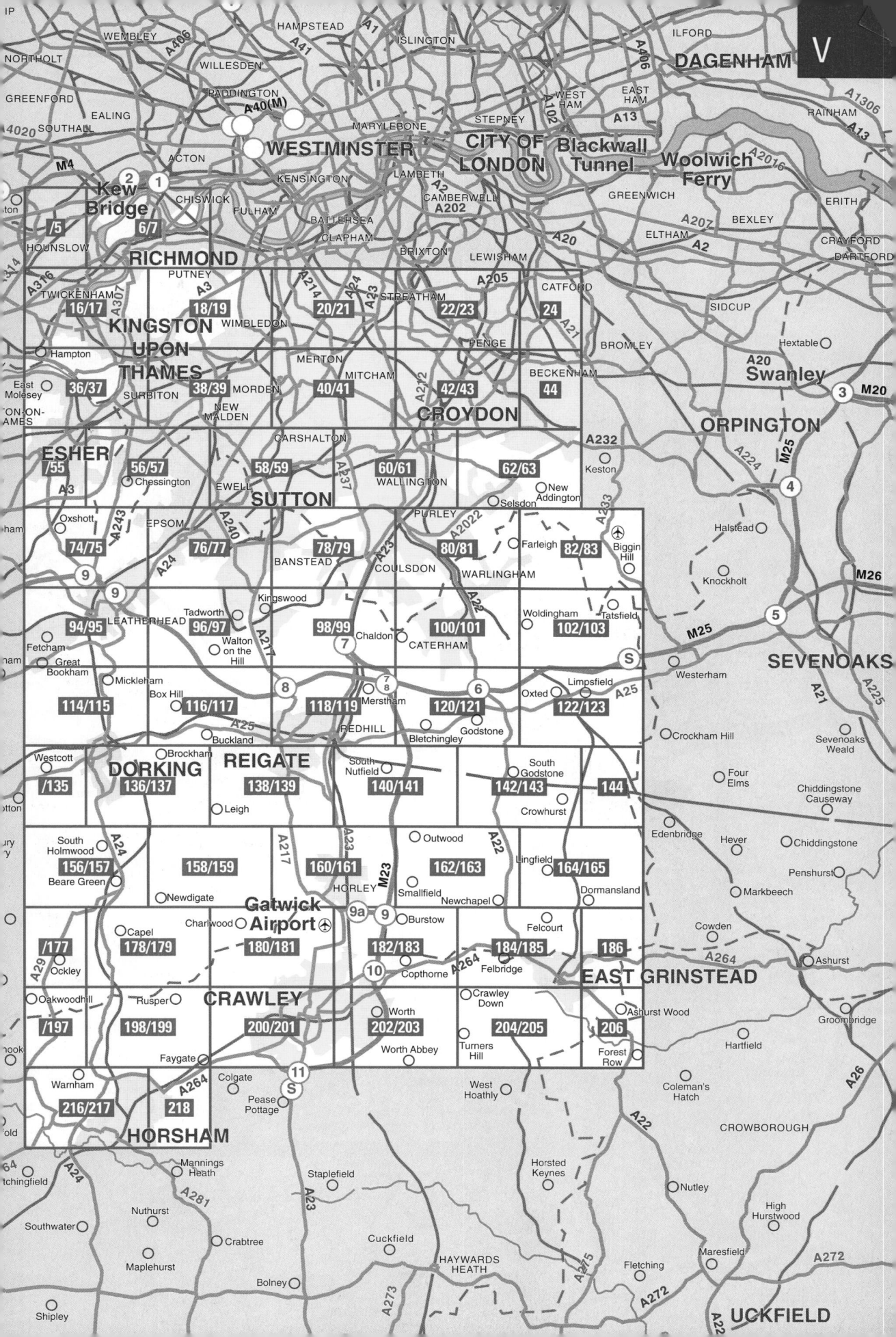

Route planning

Scale

0 1 2 3 4 5 6 7 8 km

0 1 2 3 4 5 miles

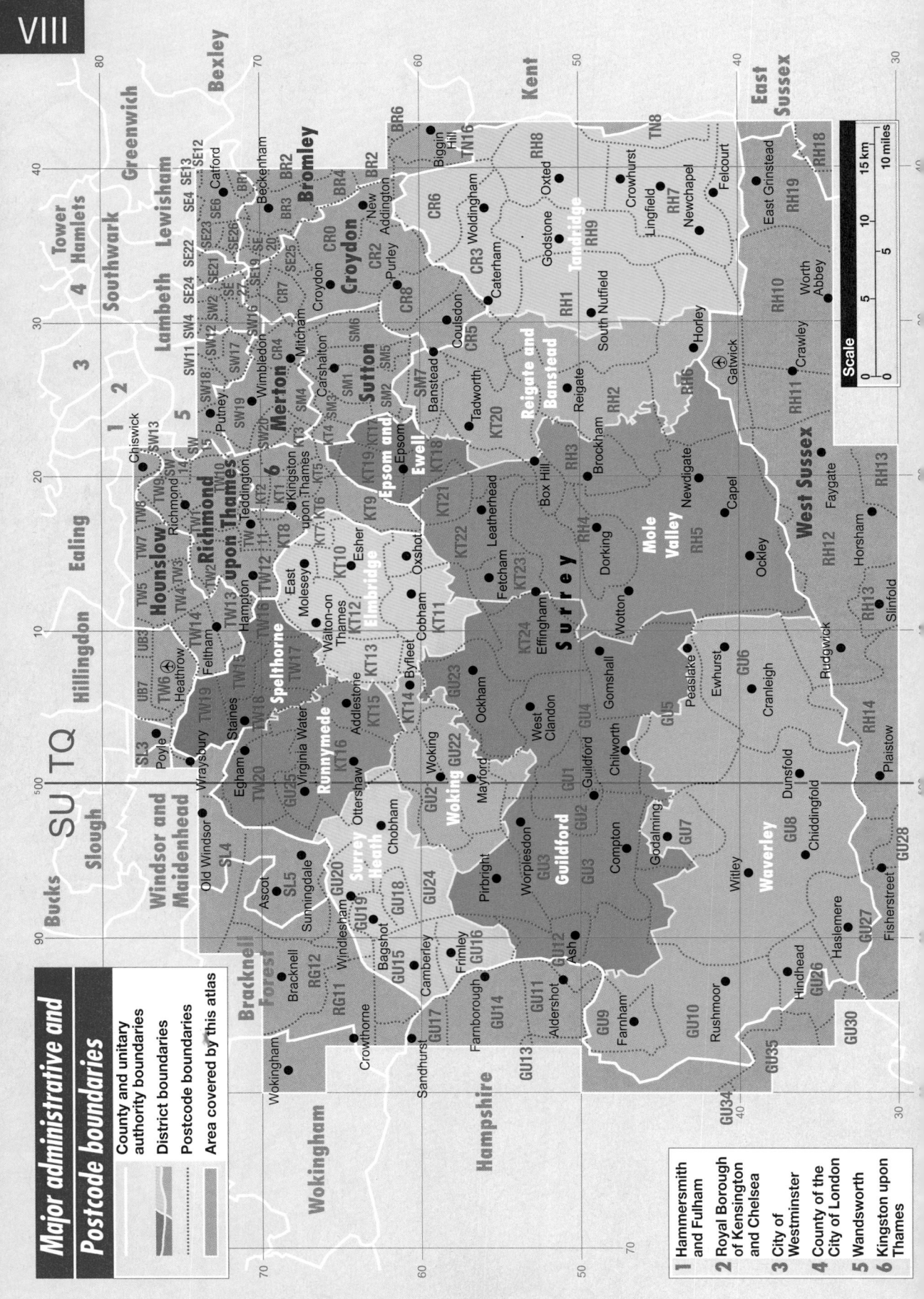

Major administrative and Postcode boundaries

- County and unitary authority boundaries
- District boundaries
- Postcode boundaries
- Area covered by this atlas

1 Hammersmith and Fulham
2 Royal Borough of Kensington and Chelsea
3 City of Westminster
4 County of the City of London
5 Wandsworth
6 Kingston upon Thames

Scale

0   5   10   15 km
0   5   10 miles

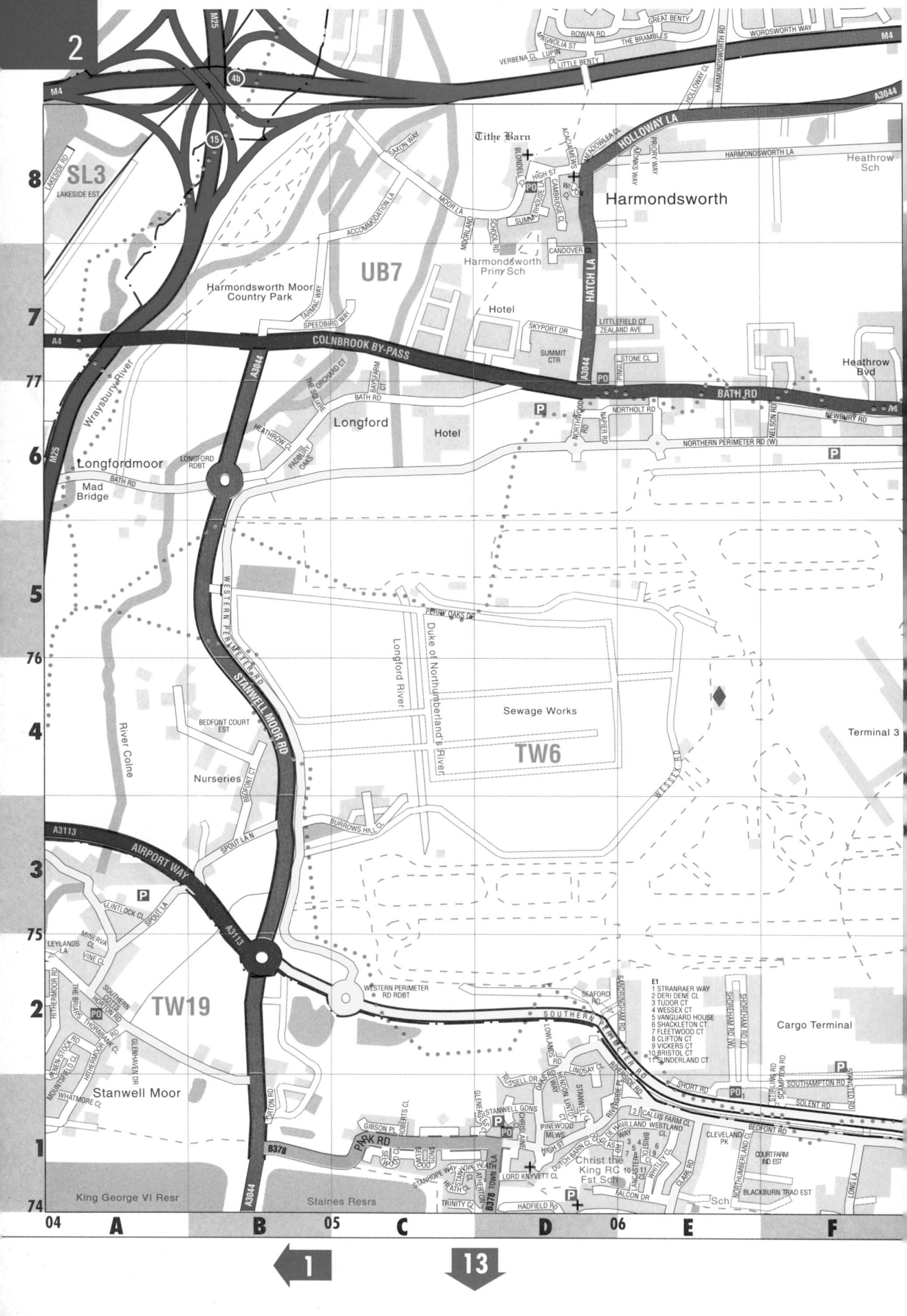

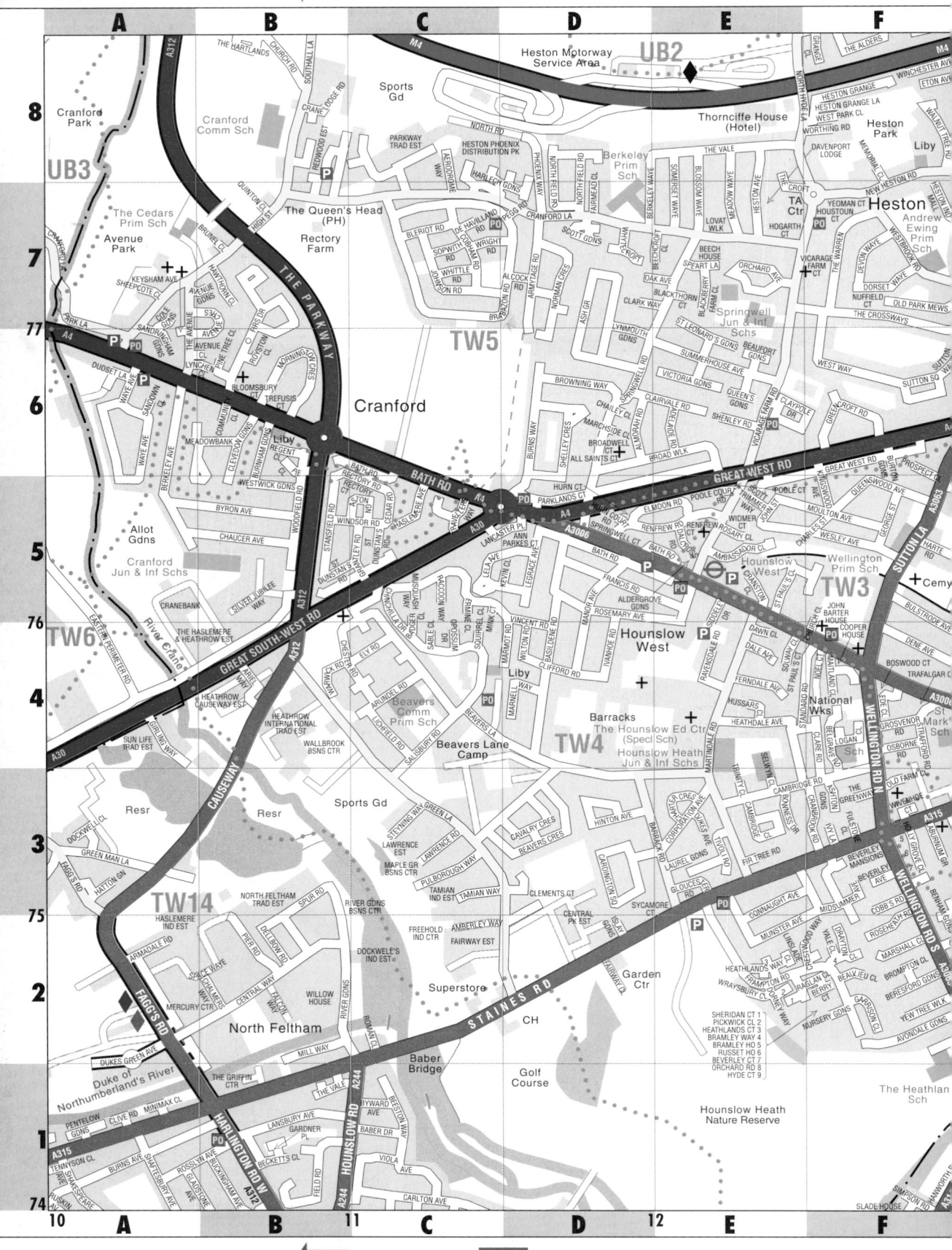

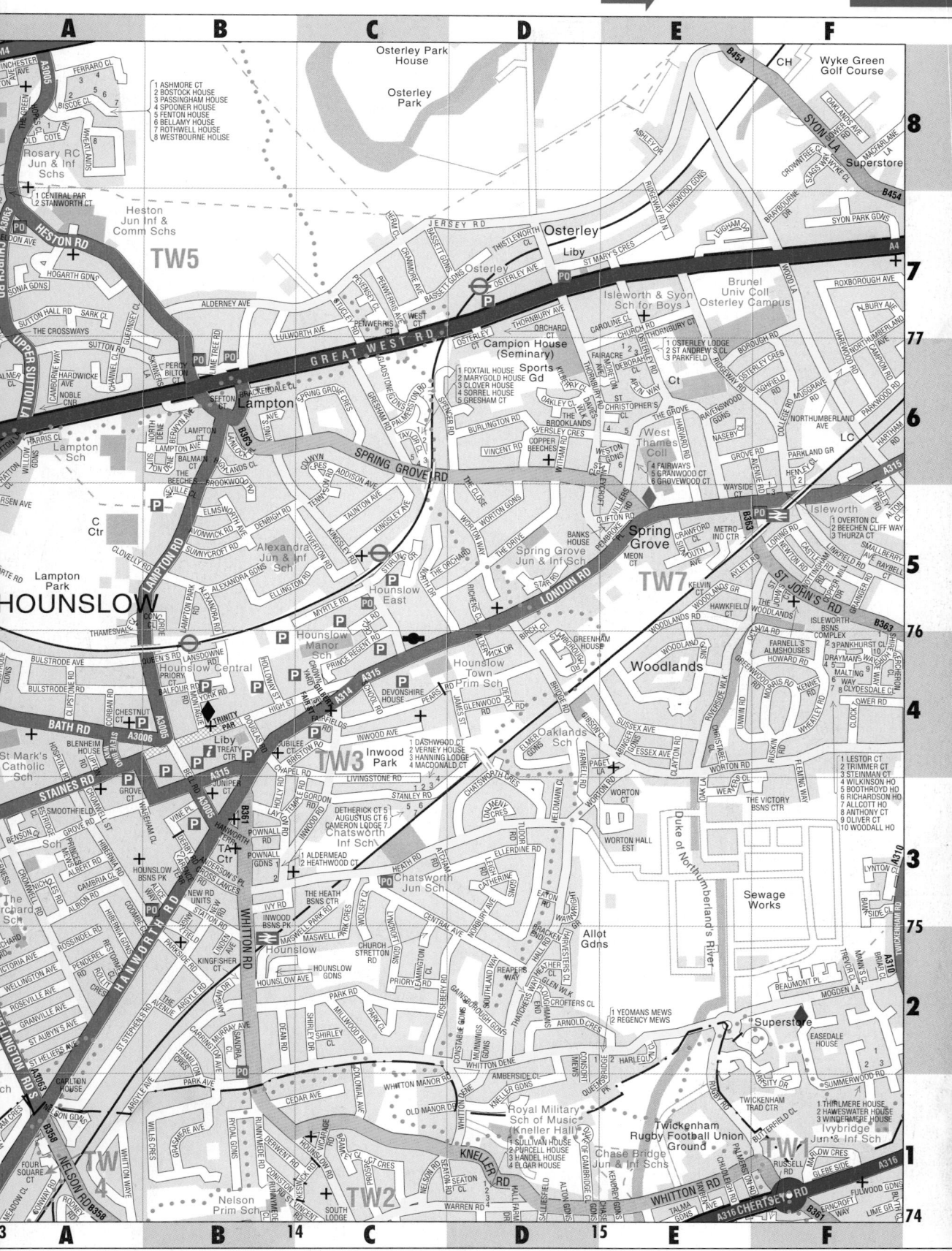

D8
1 BROCKSHOT CL
2 WESTBURY PL
3 BROOK LA N
4 BROOK LA BNS CTR
5 BREAMAR CT
6 BROOK CT
7 CLIFDEN HOUSE
8 CEDAR CT
9 CRANBROOK CT
10 ALEXANDRA RD
11 BERKELEY HOUSE
12 WATERMANS CT

E8
1 FERRY SQ
2 WATERMANS CT
3 WILKES RD
4 ALBANY PAR
5 CHARLTON HOUSE
6 ALBANY HOUSE
7 ALMA HOUSE
8 GRIFFIN CT
9 CRESSAGE HOUSE
10 TUNSTALL WLK
11 TRIMMER WLK
12 RUNNING HORSE YD
13 MISSION SQ
14 DISTILLERY WLK
15 COATES WLK
16 PERRAN WLK

D7
1 GALBA CT
2 SERVIUS CT
3 MAURICE CT
4 LEO CT
5 OTHO CT
6 ROMULUS CT

F6
1 PRIMROSE HOUSE
2 LAWMAN CT
3 ROYSTON CT
4 GARDEN CT
5 CAPEL LODGE
6 DEVONSHIRE CT
7 CELIA CT
8 ROSSLYN HOUSE
9 BRANSTONE CT
10 KEW LODGE
11 DUNRAVEN HOUSE
12 STONELEIGH LODGE
13 TUNSTALL CT
14 VOLTAIRE

A4
1 BREWERY MEWS BSNS CTR
2 TOLSTON HOUSE
3 PERCY GDNS
4 WYNNE CT
5 WISDOM CT
6 SWANN CT
7 SHREWSBURY WLK
8 KING'S TERR

F3
1 THE TOWERS
2 LONGS CT
3 SOVEREIGN CT
4 ROBINSON CT
5 CALVERT CT
6 BEDFORD CT
7 HICKEY'S ALMSHOUSES
8 CHURCH ALMSHOUSES

WOBURN CT 2
BLENHEIM CT 1
FINUCANE CT 3
TRINITY COTTS 4

D2
1 GARRICK CL
2 OLD PALACE YD
3 THE WARDROBE
4 MAIDS OF HONOUR ROW
5 HUNTERS CT
6 QUEENSBERRY HOUSE
7 THE GREEN
8 OLD PALACE TERR
9 PAVED CT
10 GOLDEN CT
11 BREWERS LA
12 THE SQUARE
13 LOWER GEORGE ST
14 ST JAMES'S COTTS
15 CHURCH WLK
16 VICTORIA PL
17 CASTLE YD
18 LEWIS RD
19 WAKEFIELD RD
20 CHURCH TERR
21 WARRINGTON RD
22 ORMOND AVE
23 ST HELENA TERR
24 WHITTAKER PL
25 HERON SQ
26 NORTHUMBERLAND PL

E3
1 ST JOHN'S GR
2 MICHEL'S ROW
3 MICHELSDALE DR
4 BLUE ANCHOR ALLEY
5 CLARENCE ST
6 SUN VALLEY
7 THAMES LINK HOUSE

THE GATEWAYS 1
FITZWILLIAM HOUSE 2
PORTLAND TERR 3
PEMBROKE VILLAS 4

B1
1 THE GROVE
2 CUMBERLAND CL
3 WESTMORLAND CL
4 SUSSEX CL
5 NORFOLK CL
6 NICOL CL
7 OLD LODGE PL
8 KELVIN CT
9 ST MARGARET'S CT
10 PARK COTTS
11 ST MARGARETS BSNS CTR
12 AMYAND COTTS

C1
1 HOWMIC CT
2 SEFTON LODGE
3 RAVENSBOURNE
4 ARLINGTON CT
5 GEORGINA CT
6 TREVELYAN HOUSE
7 CARADON CT
8 GREEN HEDGES
9 OLD HOUSE
10 QUEENS KEEP
11 BERESFORD CT
12 LANGHAM CT
13 POPLAR CT

D1
1 RICHMOND BRIDGE MANSIONS
2 HEATHERDENE MANSIONS
3 AROSA RD
4 ROSELEIGH CL
5 BEAULIEU CL
6 RICHMOND MANSIONS
7 MALLARD CT

E1
1 LANCASTER COTTS
2 LANCASTER MEWS
3 LICHFIELD TERR
4 UNION CT
5 CARRINGTON RD
6 WILTON CT
7 EGERTON CT
8 BEVERLEY LODGE
9 FRIARS STILE PLACE
10 SPIRE CT
11 RIDGEWAY
12 MATTHIAS

F1
1 CHESTER CL
2 GROSVENOR CT
3 QUEEN'S CT
4 RUSSELL WLK
5 CHARLOTTE SQ
6 JONES WLK
7 BISHOP DUPPA'S ALMSHOUSES
8 REGENCY WLK
9 TEMPLE CT
10 ONSLOW AVENUE MANSIONS
11 MICHELS ALMSHOUSES

F2
1 BEATRICE RD
2 LORNE RD
3 YORK RD
4 CONNAUGHT RD
5 ALBANY TERR
6 KINGSWOOD CT
7 SELWYN CT
8 BROADHURST CT
9 GROVE RD

E2
1 LICHFIELD TERR
2 UNION CT
3 CARRINGTON RD
4 WILTON CT
5 EGERTON CT
6 BEVERLEY LODGE
7 HILDITCH HOUSE
8 ISABELLA CT
9 DAMER HOUSE
10 ELIOT HOUSE
11 FITZHERBERT HOUSE
12 REYNOLDS PL
13 CHISHOLM RD
14 HOBART PL

A6
1 CLARENDON CT
2 QUINTOCK HOUSE
3 BROOME CT
4 LONSDALE MEWS
5 ELIZABETH COTTS
6 SANDWAYS
7 VICTORIA COTTS
8 NORTH AVE
9 GROVEWOOD
10 HAMILTON HOUSE
11 MELVIN CT

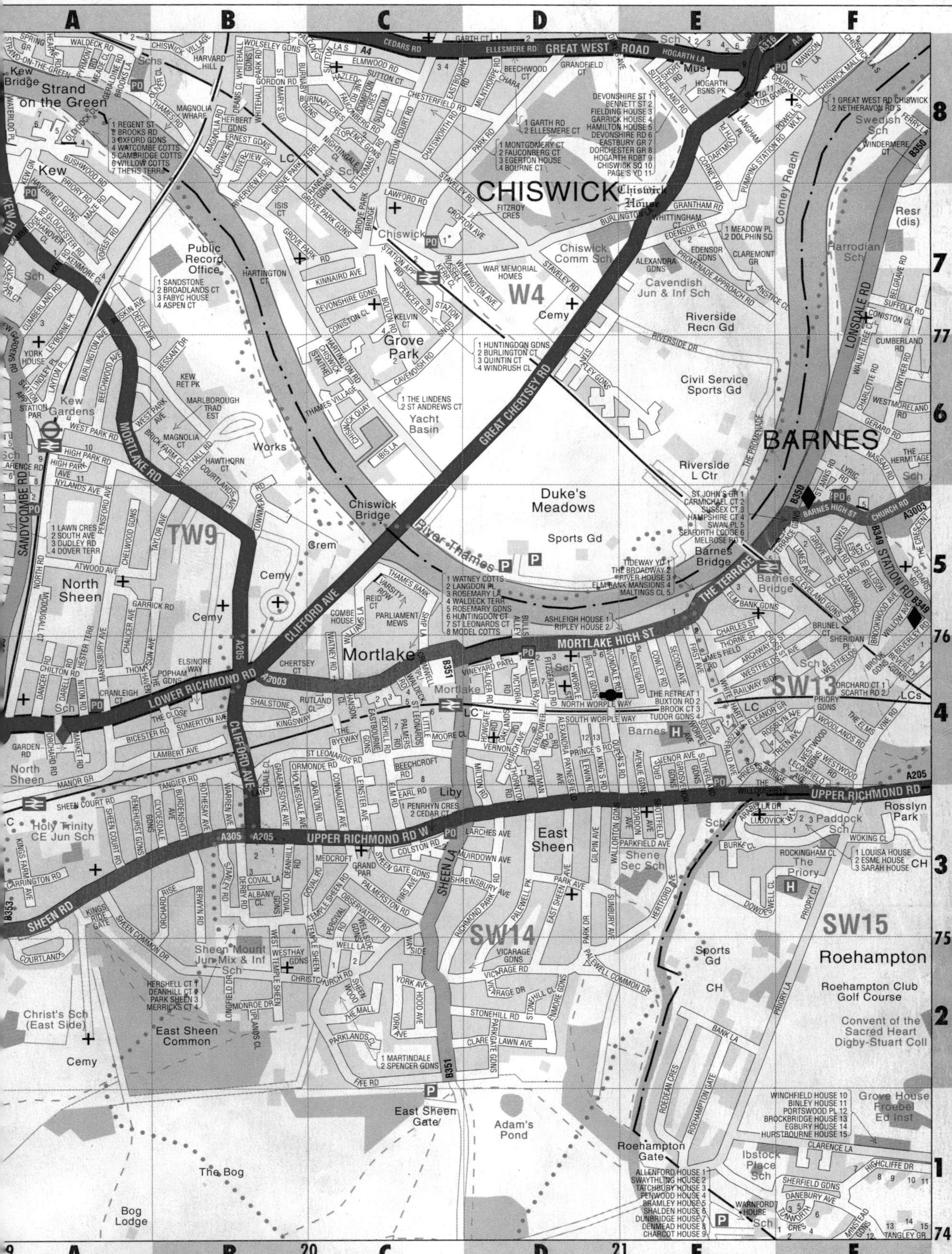

Strand on the Green

1 REGENT ST
2 BROOKS RD
3 OXFORD GDNS
4 WATCOMBE COTTS
5 CAMBRIDGE COTTS
6 WILLOW COTTS
7 THEIS TERR

1 SANDSTONE
2 BROADLANDS CT
3 FABYC HOUSE
4 ASPEN CT

Public Record Office

Kew Gardens

1 LAWN CRES
2 SOUTH AVE
3 DUDLEY RD
4 DOVER TERR

TW9

North Sheen

CHISWICK

Chiswick House

1 GARTH CT
2 ELLESMERE CT

1 MONTGOMERY CT
2 FAUCONBERG CT
3 EGERTON HOUSE
4 BOURNE CT

DEVONSHIRE ST 1
BENNETT ST 2
FIELDING HOUSE 3
GARRICK AVE 4
HAMILTON HOUSE 5
DEVONSHIRE RD 6
EASTBURY GR 7
DORCHESTER GR 8
HOGARTH RDBT 9
CHISWICK SQ 10
PAGE'S YD 11

1 GREAT WEST RD CHISWICK
2 NETHERAVON RD

1 MEADOW PL
2 DOLPHIN SQ

W4

Chiswick Comm Sch

Cavendish Jun & Inf Sch

1 HUNTINGDON GDNS
2 BURLINGTON CT
3 QUINTIN CT
4 WINDRUSH CL

1 THE LINDENS
2 ST ANDREWS CT

Grove Park

Yacht Basin

Riverside Recn Gd

Civil Service Sports Gd

BARNES

1 WATNEY COTTS
2 LANGDON PL
3 ROSEMARY LA
4 WALDECK TERR
5 ROSEMARY GDNS
6 HUNTINGDON CT
7 ST LEONARDS CT
8 MODEL COTTS

ST JOHN'S GR 1
CARMICHAEL CT 2
HAMPSHIRE CT 3
SWAN PL 4
SEAFORTH LODGE 6
MELROSE RD 5

Duke's Meadows

Sports Gd

Chiswick Bridge

Barnes Bridge

THE TERRACE

SW13

1 ORCHARD CT
2 SCARTH RD

Mortlake

MORTLAKE HIGH ST

THE RETREAT 1
BUXTON RD 2
BROOK CT 3
TUDOR GDNS 4

Barnes

SW14

East Sheen

Shene Sec Sch

UPPER RICHMOND RD

Rosslyn Park

Paddock Sch

Woking Cl

1 LOUISA HOUSE
2 ESME HOUSE
3 SARAH HOUSE

The Priory

SW15

Roehampton

Sheen Mount Jun Mix & Inf Sch

HERSHELL CT 1
DEANHILL CT 2
PARK SHEEN 3
MERRICKS CT 4

Christ's Sch (East Side)

East Sheen Common

1 MARTINDALE
2 SPENCER GDNS

East Sheen Gate

Adam's Pond

Roehampton Gate

Roehampton Club Golf Course

Convent of the Sacred Heart Digby-Stuart Coll

WINCHFIELD HOUSE 10
BINLEY HOUSE 11
PORTSWOOD PL 12
BROCKBRIDGE HOUSE 13
EGBURY HOUSE 14
HURSTBOURNE HOUSE 15

Grove House Froebel Ed Inst

Ibstock Place Sch

ALLENFORD HOUSE 1
SWAYTHLING HOUSE 2
TATCHBURY HOUSE 3
PENWOOD HOUSE 4
BRAMLEY HOUSE 5
SHALDEN HOUSE 6
DUNBRIDGE HOUSE 7
DENMEAD HOUSE 8
CHARCOT HOUSE 9

The Bog

Bog Lodge

D4
1 RANN HOUSE
2 CRAVEN HOUSE
3 JOHN DEE HOUSE
4 KINDELL HOUSE
5 MONTGOMERY HOUSE
6 AVONDALE HOUSE
7 ADDINGTON CT
8 DOVECOTE GDNS
9 FIRMSTON HOUSE
10 GLENDOWER GDNS
11 CHESTNUT AVE
12 TREHERN RD
13 ROCK AVE

18

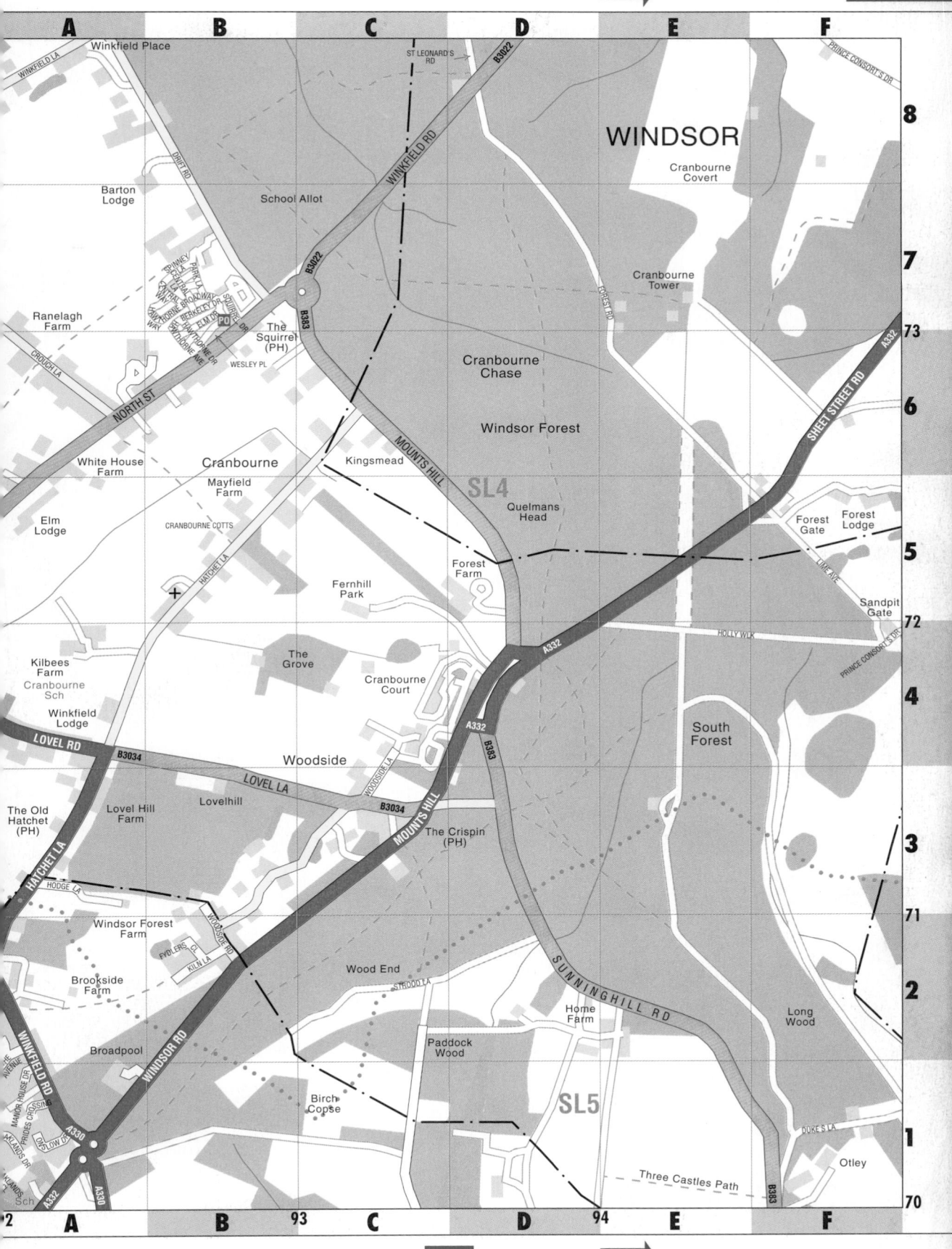

A B C D E F

8

Flemish Farm

A332

SHEET STREET RD

Pickleherring
Pond

Ranger's
Lodge

Beehive
Hill

PRINCE CONSORT'S DR

7

73

Fiddle
Covert

Russel's
Pond

Seymours
Plantation

Battle Bourne

The Gallop

Prince of Wales
Pond

Rush
Pond

THE LONG WLK

Bear's
Rails

Cemy

BEARS RAIL
PK

CRIMP HILL

Bear's Rails
Pond

6

Statue

Snow
Hill

Spring
Hill

Cookes Hill

SL4

Richardson's
Lawn

RICHARDSON'S LAWN COTTS

THE VILLAGE

QUEEN ANNE'S CL

PO

Isle of
Wight Pond

The
Village

Poets
Lawn

Deepstrood

Three Castles Path

Royal
Lodge

+

Windsor Great Park

BISHOPSGATE RD

The Fox &
Hounds
(PH)

5

72

Queen Anne's Ride

4

Dark
Wood

Royal
School

Cow
Pond

Bishopsgate

Chapel
Wood

PARK CLOSE
COTTS

DUKE'S LA

MEZEL HILL
COTTS

CUMBERLAND
LODGE

RHODODENDRON RIDE

The Sun
(PH)

WICK LA

Park
Close

3

Hilton's
Covert

Mezel
Hill

Wilderness

71

Square
Covert

Leiper
Hill

Slans
Hill

Great
Meadow
Pond

The Savill
Gardens

Parkside
House

2

Temple
Hill

Mill
Pond

Statue

Smith's
Lawn

TW20

P

Obelisk

SL5

Norfolk
Plantation

Norfolk
Farm

Obelisk
Pond

1

Rosy
Bottom

Polo Gds

70

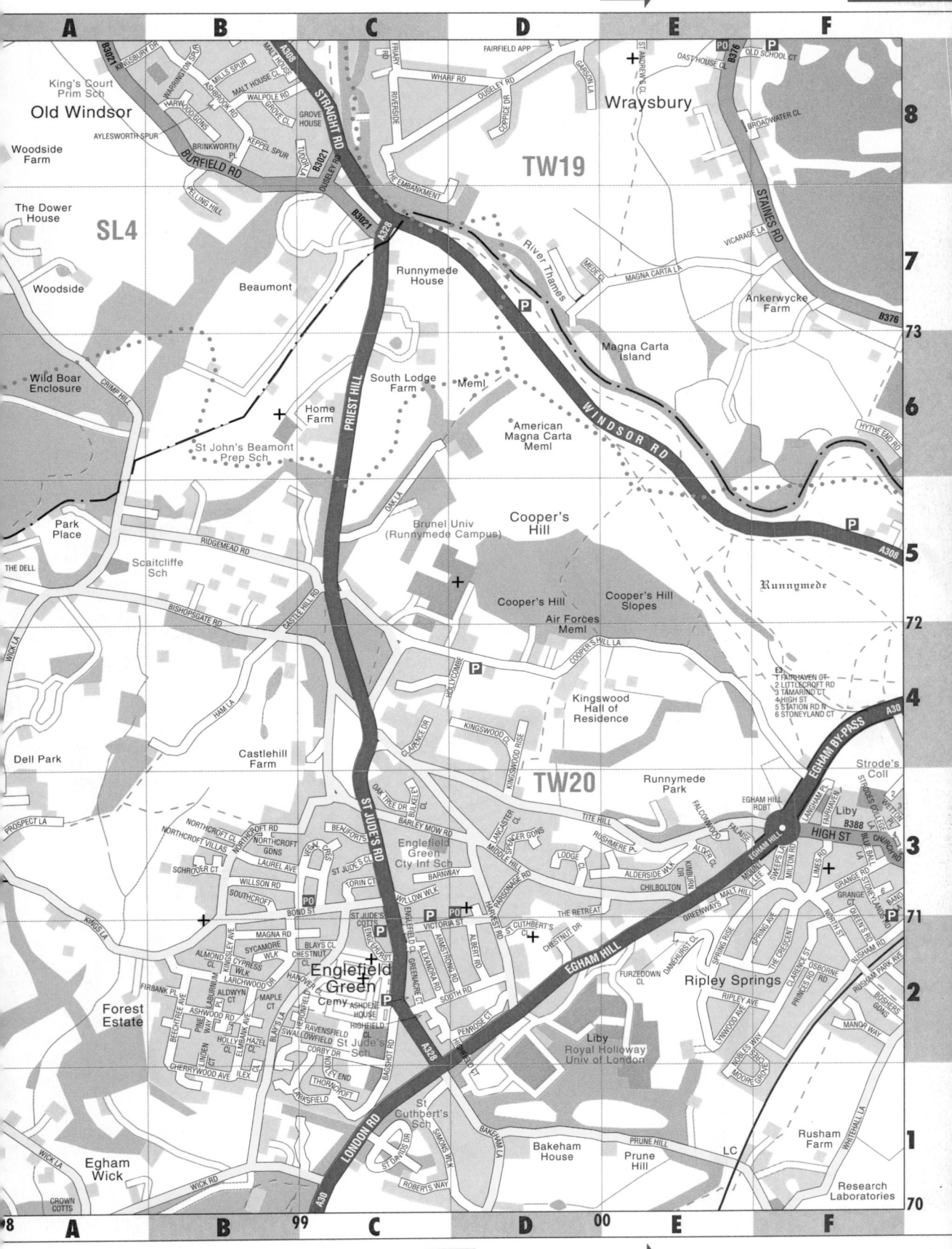

A B C D E F

8
7
73
6
5
72
4
3
71
2
1
70

'8 A B 99 C D 00 E F

A　B　C　D　E　F

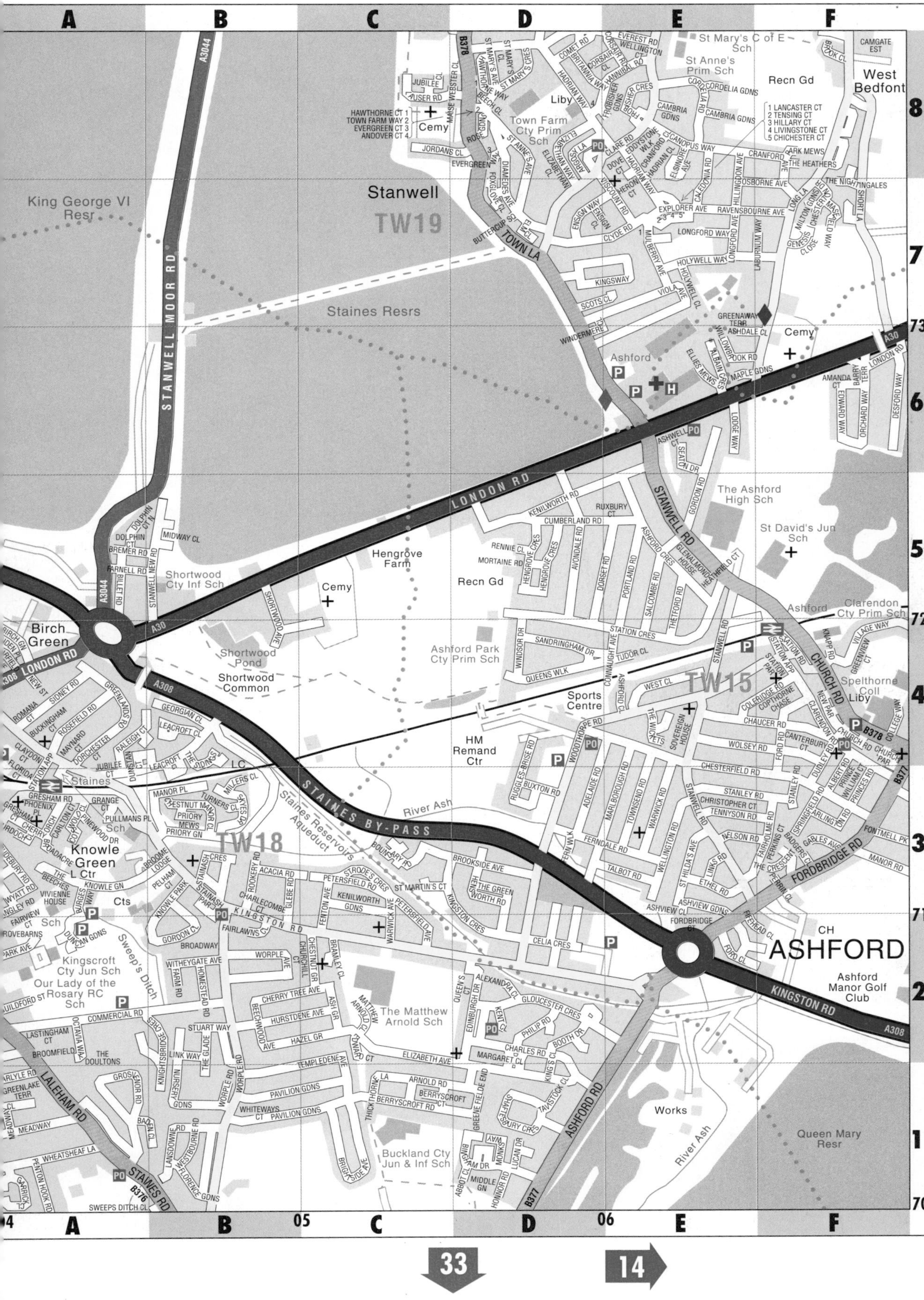

Stanwell
TW19

King George VI Resr

Staines Resrs

St Mary's C of E Sch
St Anne's Prim Sch
Recn Gd
West Bedfont
CAMGATE EST

Liby
Town Farm Cty Prim Sch
Cemy

1 LANCASTER CT
2 TENSING CT
3 HILLARY CT
4 LIVINGSTONE CT
5 CHICHESTER CT

The Heathers
The Nightingales

HAWTHORNE CT 1
TOWN FARM WAY 2
EVERGREEN CT 3
ANDOVER CT 4

TOWN LA

Cemy

Ashford

ASHWELL
Greenaway Terr
Ashdale Cl

The Ashford High Sch
St David's Jun Sch

Ashford Cty Prim Sch
Clarendon Cty Prim Sch

LONDON RD

Hengrove Farm

Shortwood Cty Inf Sch
Cemy
Recn Gd

Birch Green
A30
A308

Shortwood Pond
Shortwood Common

Ashford Park Cty Prim Sch

STANWELL RD
CHURCH RD
Spelthorne Coll
Liby

TW15

Sports Centre
HM Remand Ctr

Staines
STAINES BY-PASS
Staines Reservoirs Aqueduct
River Ash

TW18
Knowle Green L Ctr
FORDBRIDGE RD

ASHFORD
CH
Ashford Manor Golf Club
KINGSTON RD
A308

Kingscroft Cty Jun Sch
Our Lady of the Rosary RC Sch

Sweep's Ditch
LALEHAM RD
STAINES RD
B376

The Matthew Arnold Sch

Buckland Cty Jun & Inf Sch

Works
Queen Mary Resr
River Ash

B377

TW19
TW6
TW14
East Bedfont
Bedfont Lakes Country Park
TW13
Lower Feltham
Feltham Hill Jun & Inf Schs
The Sawyers Arms (PH)
HM Young Offender Ctr
Vineyard Nurseries
TW15
Chattern Hill
TW16
Ashford Common
Sunbury Common
Spelthorne Sports Club
Queen Mary Resr
Littleton Common

F1
1 BISHOPS CT
2 ASH LODGE
3 LIME LODGE
4 OAK LODGE
5 ELM CT
6 WILLOW LODGE
7 SYCAMORE LODGE
8 PRISCILLA HOUSE
9 SUNBURY CROSS CTR

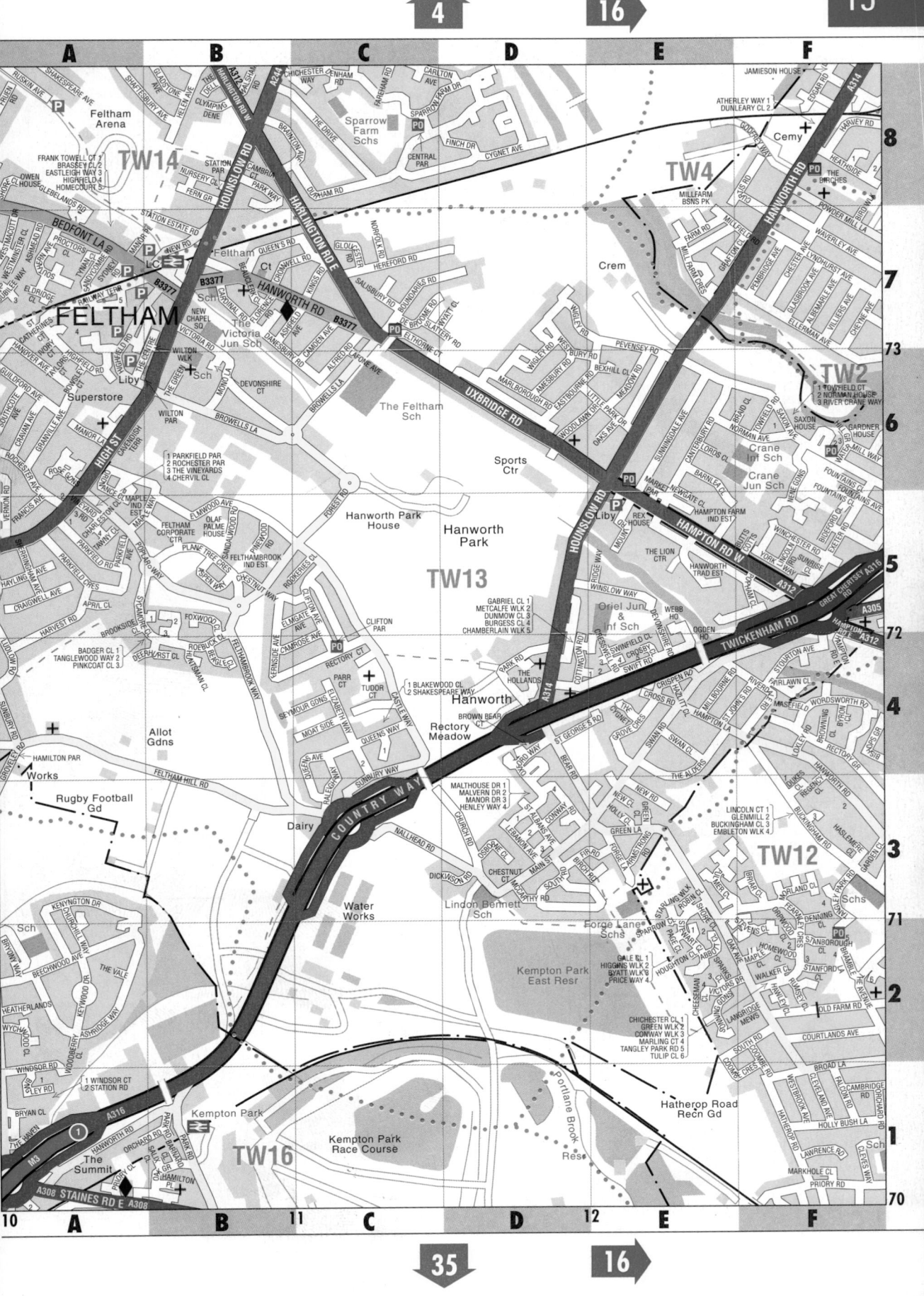

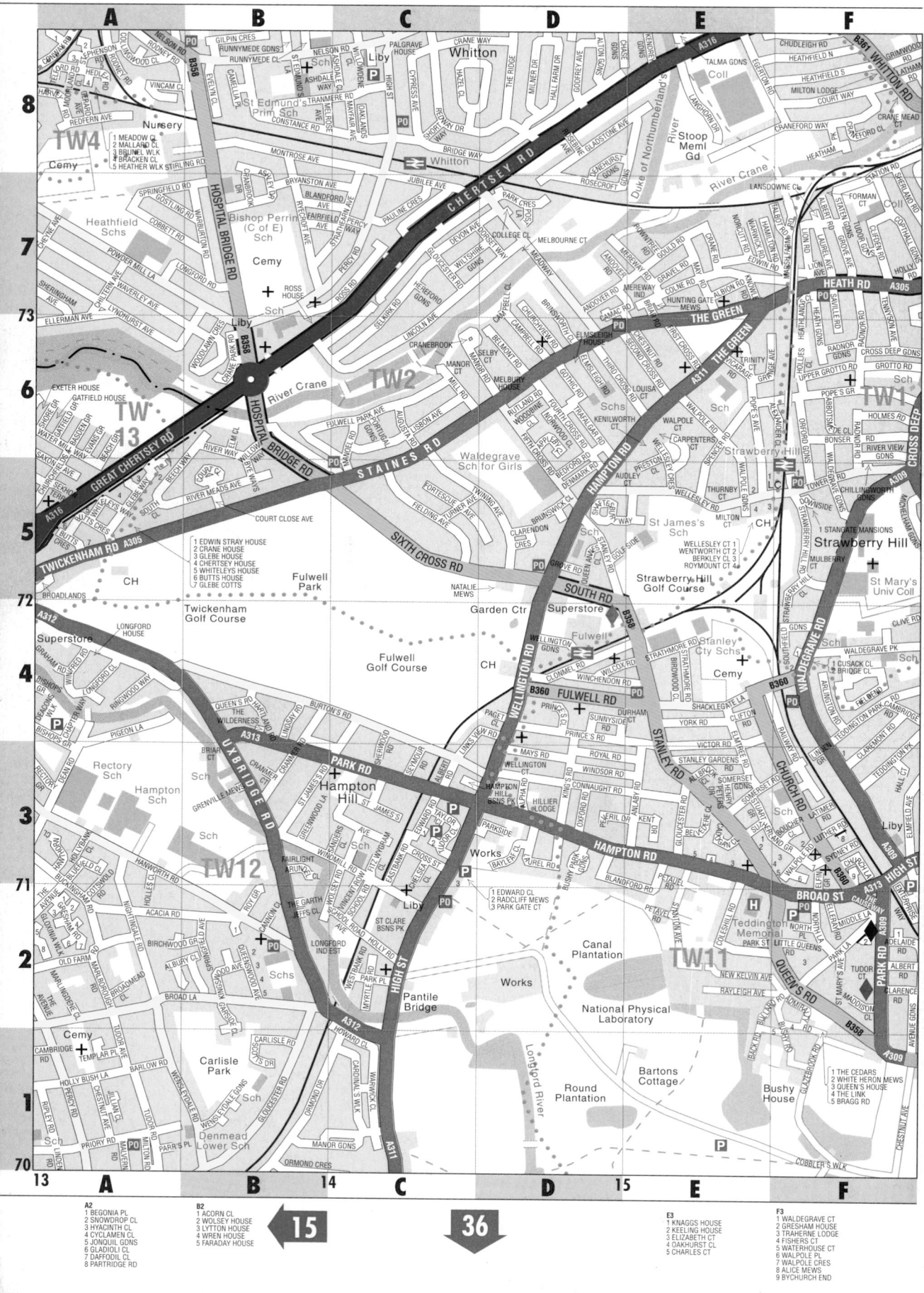

SW14

Polo Field

Old House

Bog Lodge

Sch

PORTSWOOD PL 1
FINCHDEAN HOUSE 2
HOLMSLEY HOUSE 3
OVERTON HOUSE 4
TANGLEY GR 5
REDENHAM HOUSE 6
MOUNT ANGELUS RD 7

SAWYER'S HILL

Saw Pit
Plantation

Sidmouth
Wood

White Lodge
The Royal Ballet
Sch

Golf
Course

SW15

Deer Park

Pen Ponds

TW10

Spankers Hill
Wood

Beverley Brook

Pond
Plantation

Pond
Slade

Richmond Park

FLORENCE TERR 1
EBOR COTTS 2

Robin Hood
Gate

ROEHAMPTON VALE

A3

Kingston Univ
Roehampton Vale
Ctr

War
Meml

Hamcross
Plantation

Isabella
Plantation

ROBINWOOD CL

BEVERLEY COTTS

KINGSTON VALE

A308

ROBIN HOOD
RDBT

STROUD CRES

FRIARS AVE

High
Wood

IAM GATE AVE

WOODVIEW CL

KINGSTON HILL PL

CEDAR DR

ULLSWATER CL

ULLSWATER CRES

Kingston
Vale

GRASMERE AVE

DERWENT AVE

WINDERMERE RD

ROBIN HOOD LA

Playing
Fields

VALE CRES

QUEEN'S RD

Thatchedhouse
Lodge

Walkden Hall
(Hall of Residence)

Combe Martin
Coll

Combe Hurst

Kingston
Univ

Sch

BORRANS CRES

RYDAL GDNS

ROBIN HOOD WAY

KINGSTON BY PASS

SW19

PARK GDNS

King
Clump

COOMBE WOOD RD

RANDOLPH CL

COOMBE PK

KESWICK AVE

Mill
Corner

Coombe Hill
Golf Course

B2
1 GODSTONE HOUSE
2 HAMBLEDON HOUSE
3 KINGSWOOD HOUSE
4 LEIGH HOUSE
5 MILTON HOUSE
6 NEWDIGATE HOUSE
7 FARLEIGH HOUSE
8 OCKLEY HOUSE
9 EFFINGHAM HOUSE
10 DUNSFOLD HOUSE
11 PIRBRIGHT HOUSE
12 CLANDON HOUSE
13 RIPLEY HOUSE

COESCOMBE CL

COOMBE RIDINGS

KT2

Coombe Hill
Golf Course

SW20

WARBOYS APP

WARBOYS RD

KINGSTON HILL

ASTOR CL

FAIRLAWN CL

PAGET PL

Warren
House

THE
WATERGARDENS

WARREN PK

WARREN RD

HIGH COOMBE PL

HENCROFT

GREENWOOD PK

COOMBE HILL
GLADE

WINGFIELD RD

BOCKHAMPTON RD

BERTRAM RD

WYNDHAM RD

UPPER PARK RD

KELVEDON CL

HEATHERDALE CL

HAYGREEN CL

KINGSTON HILL

DUTCH GDNS

MAGNOLIA CT

RISE

COTSWOLD CL

WINCHESTER CL

MOWBRAY RD

RENFREW RD

BEVEREN RD

WARREN CUTTING

Coombe Wood
Golf Course

COOMBE NEVILLE

EDGECOMBE CL

GOLF CLUB DR

CH

BEVERLEY LA

BEVERLEY AVE

A3

ROBIN HOOD WAY

PARK RD

KING'S RD

LIVERPOOL RD

NEW RD

TUDOR RD

ROSEWOOD WAY

THORNWOOD RD

CRESCENT RD

DEER PARK RD

BOYD CL

EATON RD

GALSWORTHY RD

CUMBERLAND
HOUSE

BERYSTEDE

BLENHEIM GDNS

CH

MOWCOMBE CL

WINDSOR RD

STOKE
RD

GEORGE RD

THE DRIVE

GATEHOUSE CL

Holy Cross
Prep RC
Sch

Schs

COOMBE END

BALLARD CL

A238

Coombe

COOMBE LA W

A238

PRESTON RD

PO

ELM RD

PRINCES RD

Schs

ALEXANDRA RD

QUEEN'S RD

A3082

Kingston

B351

20

A238

B283

21

A3

A1
1 QUEEN'S CT
2 ST GEORGES RD
3 PARK ROAD HOUSE
4 DAGMAR RD
5 TAPPING CL
6 ARTHUR RD
7 BOROUGH RD
8 BELVEDERE CT

9 BRAYWICK CT
10 DEAN CT
11 ROWAN CT
12 RICHMOND CT
13 SUNNINGDALE CT
14 HAWKER CT
15 CROMWELL CT
16 KINGS CT

B1
1 BRAMLEY HOUSE
2 ABINGER HOUSE
3 THURSLEY HOUSE
4 RIDGE HOUSE
5 THE CLONE
6 MOUNT CT
7 HILLSIDE CT
8 HILL CT
9 ROYAL CT

10 LAKESIDE
11 HIGH ASHTON

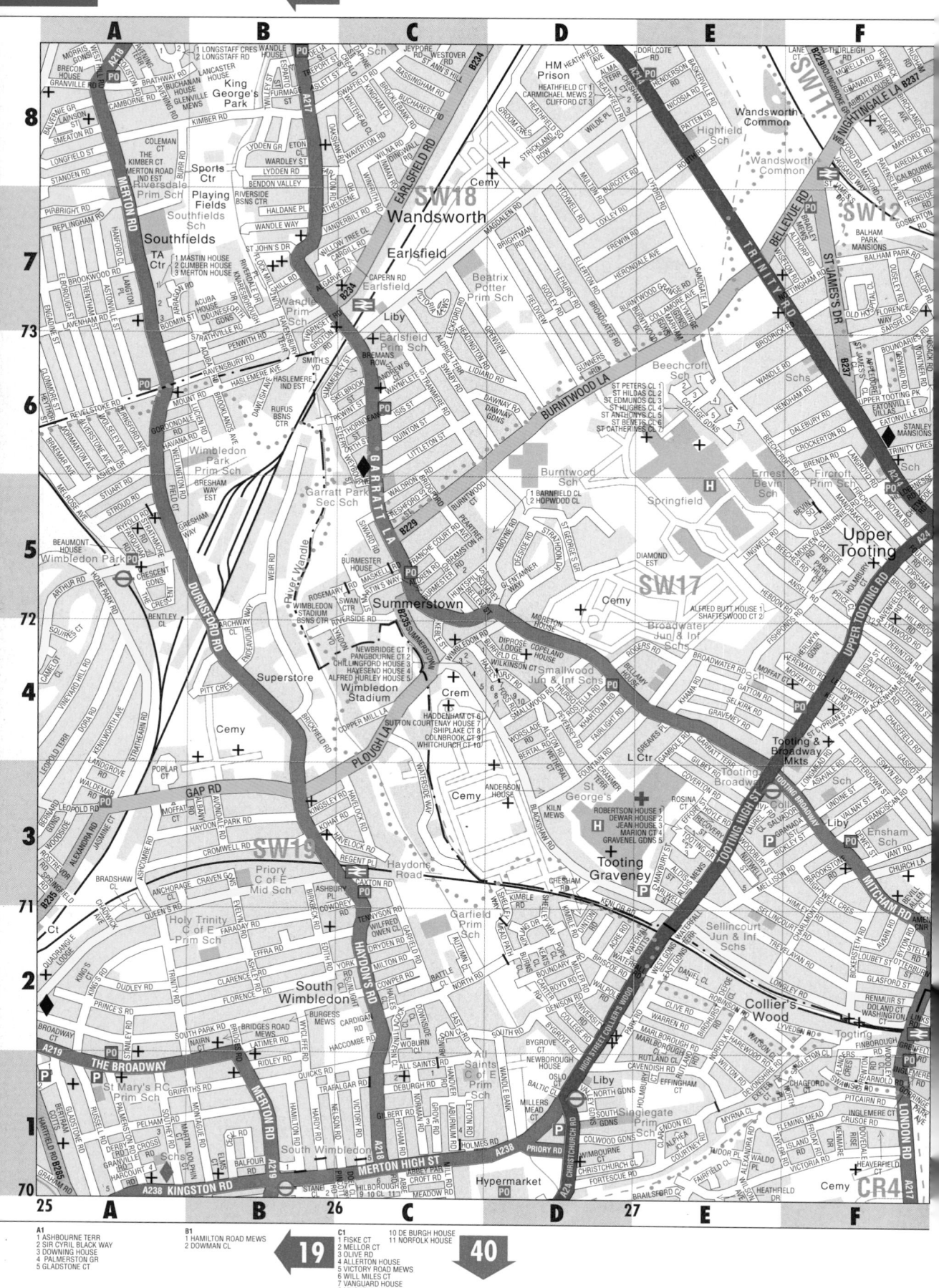

A1
1 ASHBOURNE TERR
2 SIR CYRIL BLACK WAY
3 DOWNING HOUSE
4 PALMERSTON GR
5 GLADSTONE CT

B1
1 HAMILTON ROAD MEWS
2 DOWMAN CL

C1
1 FISKE CT
2 MELLOR CT
3 OLIVE RD
4 ALLERTON HOUSE
5 VICTORY ROAD MEWS
6 WILL MILES CT
7 VANGUARD HOUSE
8 MYCHELL HOUSE
9 MERTON PL

10 DE BURGH HOUSE
11 NORFOLK HOUSE

8	7 PRENDERGAST HOUSE	E8	7 PEARCE HOUSE	14 NEW PARK PAR	21 PARSONS HOUSE	F8	7 DUNSFOLD HOUSE	14 BROCKHAM HOUSE

RILEY HOUSE   7 PRENDERGAST HOUSE   E8   7 PEARCE HOUSE   14 NEW PARK PAR   21 PARSONS HOUSE   F8   7 DUNSFOLD HOUSE   14 BROCKHAM HOUSE

RILEY HOUSE
BENNETT HOUSE
WHITE HOUSE
RODGERS HOUSE
DUMPHREYS HOUSE
HOMAN HOUSE

7 PRENDERGAST HOUSE
8 HUTCHINS HOUSE
9 WHITELEY HOUSE
10 TRESSIDER HOUSE
11 PRIMROSE CT
12 ANGUS HOUSE
13 CURRIE HOUSE

E8
1 PICTON HOUSE
2 RIGG HOUSE
3 WATSON HOUSE
4 MACARTHUR HOUSE
5 SANDON HOUSE
6 THOROLD HOUSE

7 PEARCE HOUSE
8 MUDIE HOUSE
9 MILLER HOUSE
10 LYCETT HOUSE
11 LAFONE HOUSE
12 LUCRAFT HOUSE
13 FREEMAN HOUSE

14 NEW PARK PAR
15 ARGYLL CT
16 DUMBARTON CT
17 KINTYRE CT
18 COTTON HOUSE
19 CROSSMAN HOUSE
20 CAMEFORD CT

21 PARSONS HOUSE
22 BRINDLEY HOUSE
23 ARKWRIGHT HOUSE
24 PERRY HOUSE
25 BRUNEL HOUSE
26 NEW PARK CT
27 TANHURST HOUSE

F8
1 HYPERION HOUSE
2 SOMERS HOUSE
3 ARCHBISHOP'S PL
4 LEANDER CT
5 WITLEY HOUSE
6 OUTWOOD HOUSE

22 →

7 DUNSFOLD HOUSE
8 DEEPDENE LODGE
9 WARNHAM HOUSE
10 ALBURY LODGE
11 TILFORD HOUSE
12 ELSTEAD HOUSE
13 THURSLEY HOUSE

14 BROCKHAM HOUSE
15 CAPEL LODGE
16 LEITH LODGE
17 FAIRVIEW HOUSE
18 WEYMOUTH HOUSE
19 ASCALON CT

21

6
UPPER TOOTING PARK MANS
CECIL MANS
MARIUS MANS
THE BOULEVARD
ELMFIELD MANS
HOLDERNESSE RD
:7
HESLOP CT
ST JAMES'S TERR

3 BOUNDARIES MANS
4 STATION PAR
A8
1 ST ANTHONY'S CT
2 HOLLIES WAY
3 ENDLESHAM CT
B8
1 MEYER HOUSE
2 FARADAY HOUSE
3 HALES HOUSE

4 FRANKLAND HOUSE
5 GRAHAM HOUSE
6 GIBBS HOUSE
7 DALTON HOUSE
8 ANSLIE WLK
9 ROKEBY HOUSE
10 CAISTER HOUSE
11 IVANHOE HOUSE
12 CATHERINE BAIRD CT
13 MARMION HOUSE

14 DEVONSHIRE HOUSE
C8
1 LIMERICK CT
2 HOMEWOODS
3 JEWELL HOUSE
4 GLANVILLE HOUSE
5 DAN BRYANT HOUSE
6 OLDING HOUSE
7 QUENNEL HOUSE
8 WEIR HOUSE

41 ↓

E5
1 DE MONTFORT PAR
2 LEIGHAM HALL PAR
3 LEIGHAM HALL
4 ENDSLEIGH HOUSE
5 JOHN KIRK HOUSE
6 RAEBARN CT
7 WAVEL CT
8 HOMELEIGH CT
9 WEST HOUSE
10 NEVILLE CT

10 BEAUCLERK HOUSE
11 BERTRAND HOUSE
12 DREW HOUSE
13 DOWES HOUSE
14 DUNTON HOUSE
15 RAYNALD HOUSE
16 SACKVILLE HOUSE
17 THURLOW HOUSE
18 ASTORIA MANS

E6
1 WYATT PARK MANS
2 BROADLANDS MANS
3 STONEHILL'S MANS
4 STREATLEIGH PAR
5 DORCHESTER CT
E7
1 BEAUMONT HOUSE
2 CHRISTCHURCH HOUSE
3 STAPLEFIELD CL
F7
1 CHARLWOOD HOUSE

4 CHIPSTEAD HOUSE
5 COULSDON HOUSE
6 CONWAY HOUSE
7 TELFORD AVE MANS
8 TELFORD PAR MANS
9 GWYNNE HOUSE
10 HARTSWOOD HOUSE
11 WRAY HOUSE

2 EARLSWOOD HOUSE
3 BALCOMBE HOUSE
4 CLAREMONT CL
5 HOLBROOK HOUSE
6 GWYNNE HOUSE
7 KYNASTON HOUSE
8 TILLMAN HOUSE
9 REGENT LODGE
10 HAZELMERE CT
11 DYKES CT

A3
1 BELLTREES GR
2 ASH CT
3 ALDER CT
4 BEECH CT
5 ACACIA CT
6 BLACKTHORN CT
7 CYPRESS CT
8 HAWTHORN CT
9 HAZEL CT
10 SYCAMORE CT
11 MAPLE CT
12 LABURNAM CT
13 FERN LODGE

A4
1 JAMES BOSWELL
2 ST ALBANS HOUSE
3 SUFFOLK CT
4 STRODE HOUSE
5 DELPHIAN CT

A7
1 VALENS HOUSE
2 LOVEDAY HOUSE
3 ETHELWORTH CT
4 HARBIN HOUSE
5 BROOKS HOUSE
7 GODOLPHIN HOUSE
8 SHEPPARD HOUSE
9 McCORMICK HOUSE
10 TAYLOR HOUSE
11 SAUNDERS HOUSE
12 TALCOTT PATH
13 DERRICK HOUSE
14 WILLIAMS HOUSE
15 BALDWIN HOUSE
16 BERKELEY CT
17 CHURSTON CL
18 NEIL WATES CRES
19 BURNELL HOUSE
20 PORTLAND HOUSE

A8
1 ELLACOMBE HOUSE
2 BOOTH HOUSE
3 HATHERSLEY HOUSE
4 BRERETON HOUSE
5 HOLDSWORTH HOUSE
6 DEARMER HOUSE
7 CHERRY CL
8 GREENLEAF CL
9 LONGFORD WLK
10 SCARLETTE MANOR WLK
11 CHANDLERS WAY
12 UPGROVE MANOR WAY
13 ROPERS WLK
14 TEBBS HOUSE
15 BELL HOUSE
16 WORTHINGTON HOUSE
17 COURIER HOUSE
18 MACKIE HOUSE
19 HAMERS HOUSE
20 KELYWAY HOUSE

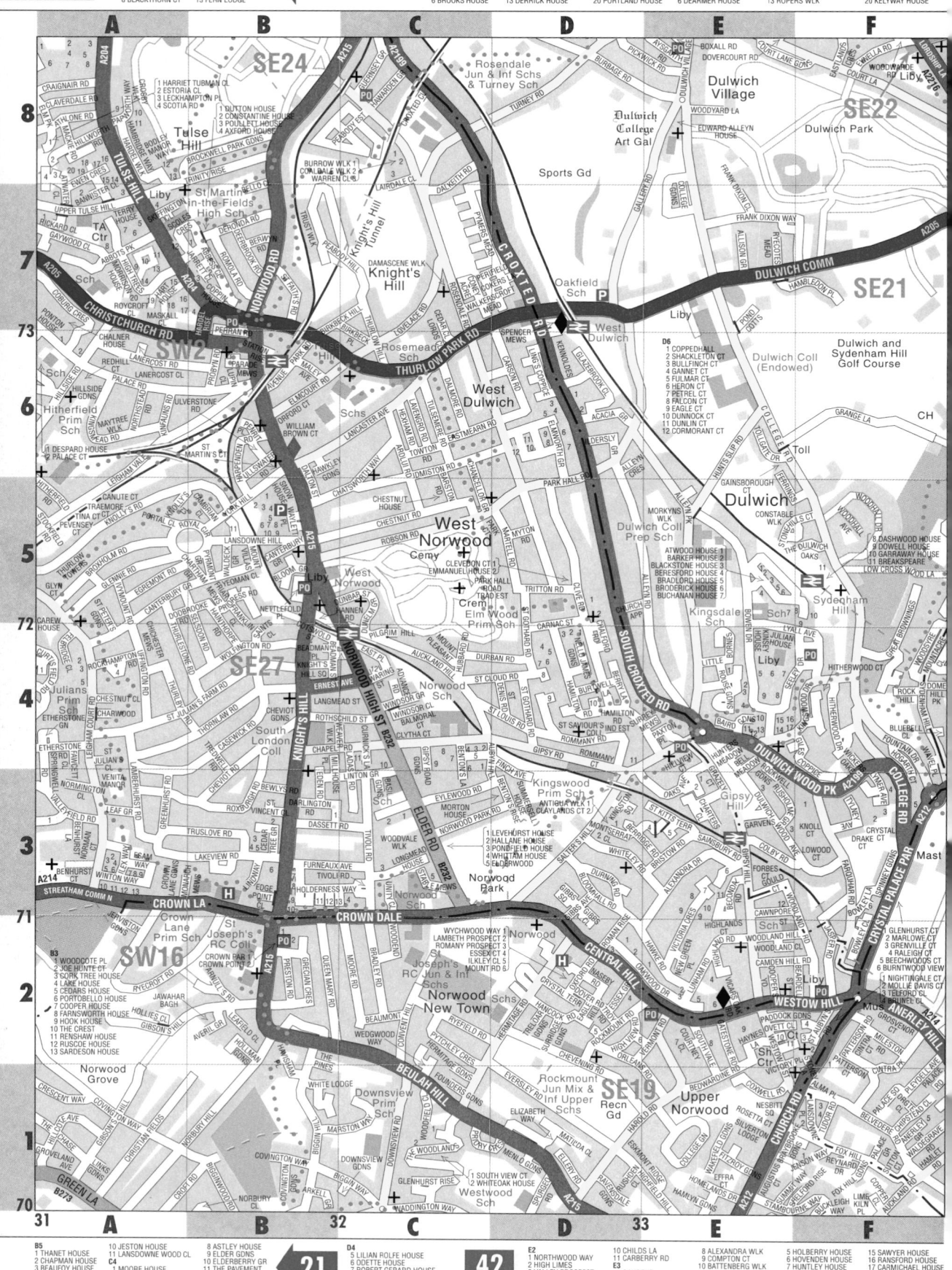

21

42

21

B5
1 THANET HOUSE
2 CHAPMAN HOUSE
3 BEAUFOY HOUSE
4 EASTON HOUSE
5 ROBERTS HOUSE
6 LLOYD CT
7 KERSHAW HOUSE
8 WAKELING HOUSE
9 EDRIDGE HOUSE
10 JESTON HOUSE
11 LANSDOWNE WOOD CL

C4
1 MOORE HOUSE
2 CHAUCER HOUSE
3 BUSHELL HOUSE
4 BLIGH HOUSE
5 HOBBS HOUSE
6 HOGARTH HOUSE
7 GOODBEHERE HOUSE
8 ASTLEY HOUSE
9 ELDER GDNS
10 ELDERBERRY GR
11 THE PAVEMENT
12 DUNKIRK ST

D4
1 JOSEF PERRIN HOUSE
2 JEAN HUMBERT HOUSE
3 CHARLES STAUNTON HOUSE
4 VIOLETTE SZABO HOUSE

D4
1 LILIAN ROLFE HOUSE
2 ODETTE HOUSE
3 ROBERT GERARD HOUSE
4 ST BERNARDS CL
5 CHAMPNESS CL
6 PENNINGTON CL
7 QUEENSWOOD CT

E2
1 NORTHWOOD WAY
2 HIGH LIMES
3 VALLEY PROSPECT
4 PLANE TREE WLK
5 CITY PROSPECT
6 BANKSIDE WAY
7 ROCHDALE
8 BARRINGTON WLK
9 GATESTONE CT

E2
1 NORTHWOOD WAY

E3
1 OAKDENE
2 THORSDEN WAY
3 OAKFIELD GDNS
4 GEORGETOWN CL
5 BRIDGETOWN CL
6 MOUNTBATTEN CL
7 BRABOURNE CL

E4
1 LINLEY CT
2 MELLOR HOUSE
3 WHITFIELD CT
4 MICHAELSON HOUSE

10 CHILDS LA
11 CARBERRY RD
8 ALEXANDRA WLK
9 COMPTON CT
10 BATTENBERG WLK
11 BURMA TERR
12 WISEMAN CT
5 HOLBERRY HOUSE
6 HOVENDEN HOUSE
7 HUNTLEY HOUSE
8 TELFEI HOUSE
9 MARKHAM HOUSE
10 OLDHAM HOUSE
11 PARNALL HOUSE
12 PIERSON HOUSE
13 ROPER HOUSE
14 ROUNDELL HOUSE
15 SAWYER HOUSE
16 RANSFORD HOUSE
17 CARMICHAEL HOUSE

F1
1 HETLEY GDNS
2 HIGHLAND LODGE
3 MASON CT
4 KENDALL CT
5 HIGH VIEW

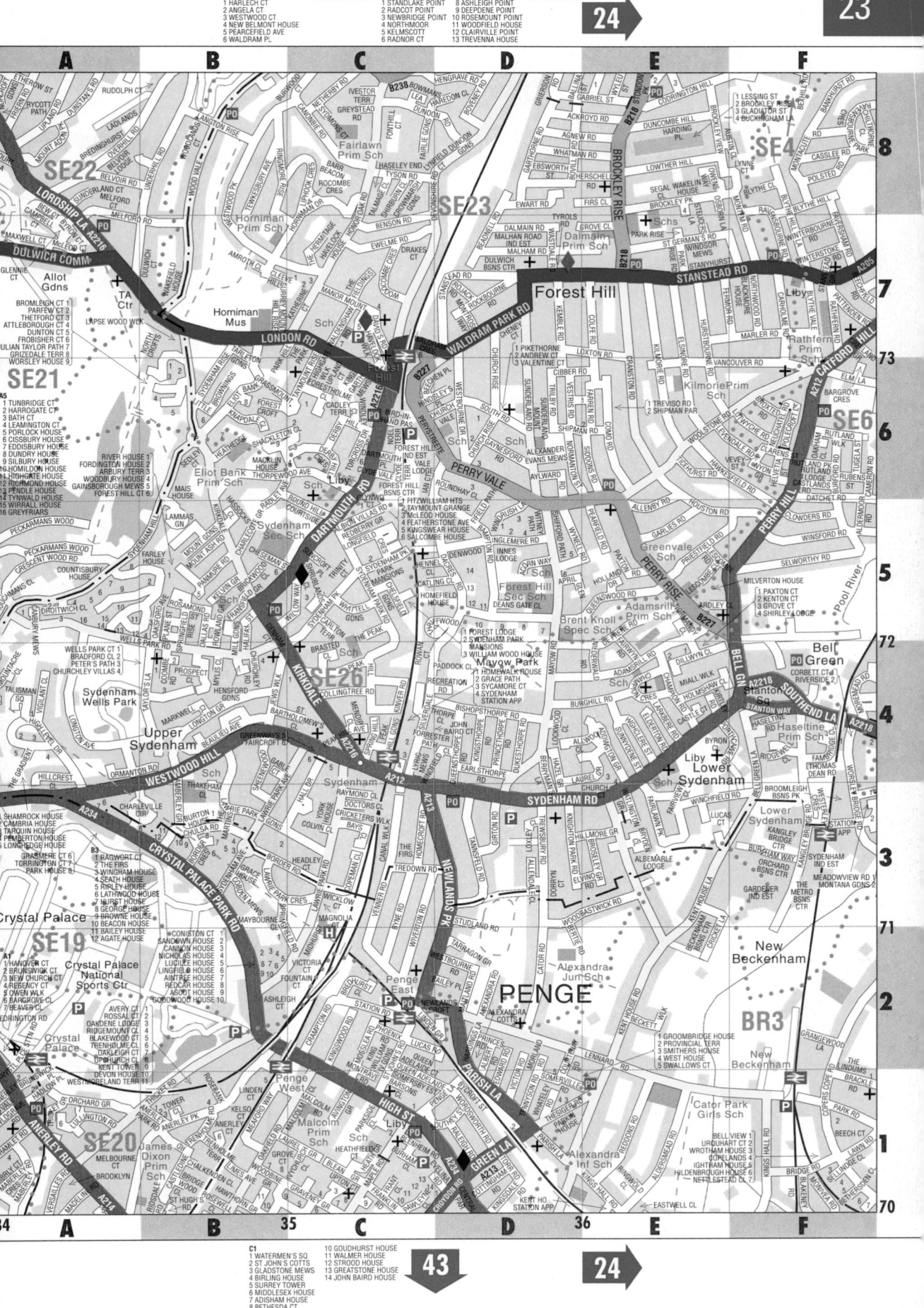

C7
1 HARLECH CT
2 ANGELA CT
3 WESTWOOD CT
4 NEW BELMONT HOUSE
5 PEARCEFIELD AVE
6 WALDRAM PL

7 HORNIMAN GRANGE

D5
1 STANDLAKE POINT
2 RADCOT POINT
3 NEWBRIDGE POINT
4 NORTHMOOR
5 KELMSCOTT
6 RADNOR CT

7 HEATHWOOD POINT
8 ASHLEIGH POINT
9 DEEPDENE ST
10 ROSEMOUNT POINT
11 WOODFIELD HOUSE
12 CLAIRVILLE POINT
13 TREVENNA POINT

14 HYNDEWOOD

C1
1 WATERMEN'S SQ
2 ST JOHN'S COTTS
3 GLADSTONE MEWS
4 BIRLING HOUSE
5 SURREY TOWER
6 MIDDLESEX HOUSE
7 ADISHAM HOUSE
8 BETHESDA CT
9 OSPRINGE CL

10 GOUDHURST HOUSE
11 WALMER HOUSE
12 STROOD HOUSE
13 GREATSTONE HOUSE
14 JOHN BAIRD HOUSE

B8
1 SILVERMERE RD
2 BROOKDALE RD
3 SCROOBY ST

23

E8
1 BEAUMONT TERR
2 LITTLEBOURNE
3 VERDANT CT

A1
1 GARDENIA CT
2 BRACKENDALE CT
3 DANIEL CT
4 MOLINER CT
5 CHARTWELL LODGE
6 RANDMORE CT
7 DOVER HOUSE
8 LUCERNE CT
9 MALLING HOUSE
10 WESTERHAM LODGE
11 BRASTED LODGE
12 MILTON HOUSE
13 BRADSOLE HOUSE
14 SANDGATE HOUSE
15 ADELAIDE CT
16 NETTLESTEAD CL
17 COPERS COPE RD
18 WARREN CT
19 ALTON CT
20 ROCKINGHAM CT
21 CAMELLIA CT
22 SINCLAIR CT
23 REGENTS CT
24 MINSHULL PL
25 SOUTH PARK CT

F1
1 HOMECOPPICE HOUSE
2 INGLEWOOD CT
3 MAVERY CT
4 GLEN CT
5 CAWSTON CT
6 HIGHLAND RD
7 MOORELAND RD

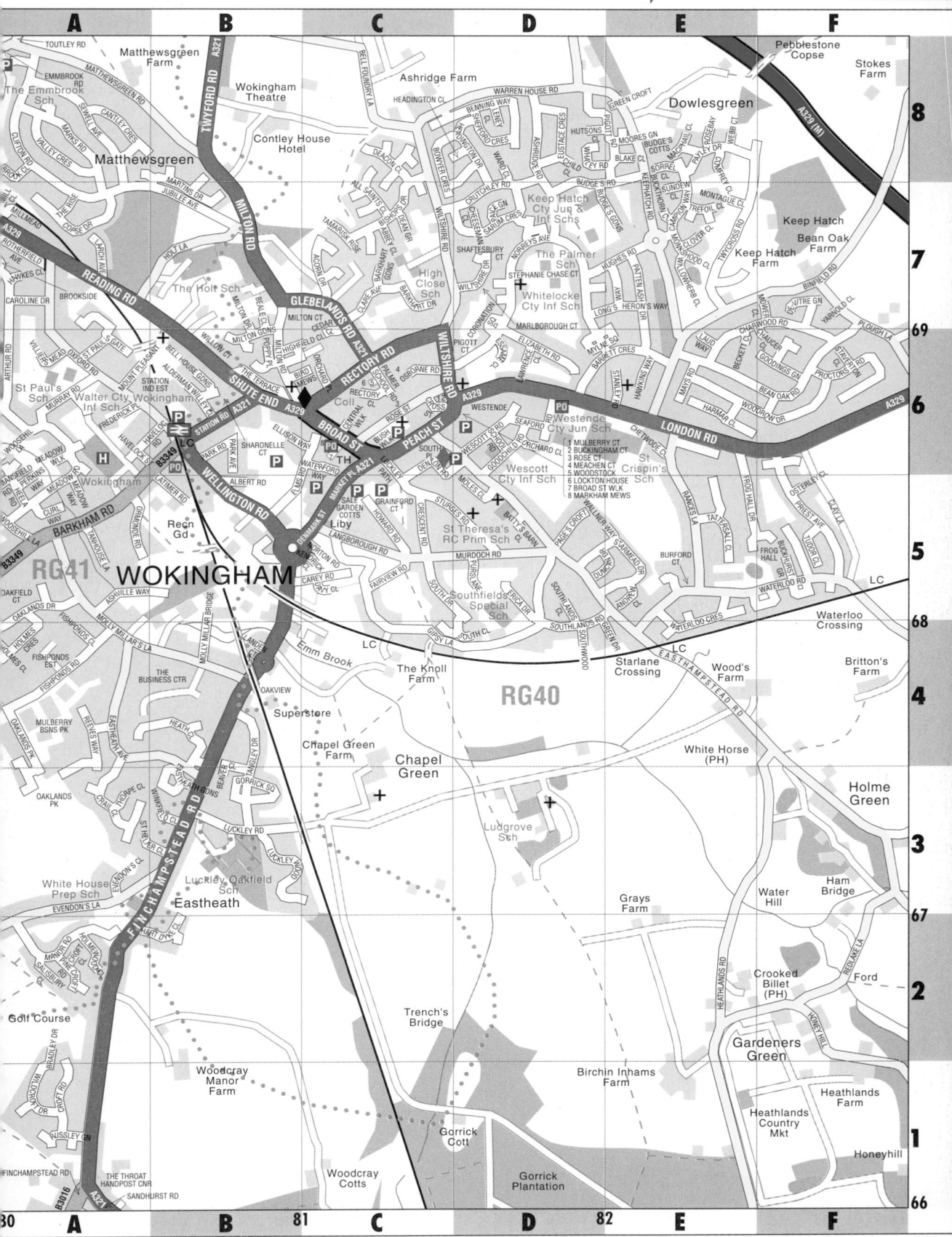

25

A8
1 PRIESTWOOD SQ
2 SALTIRE GDNS
3 WINDLEBROOK GN
4 APPLETREE PL
5 PORTMAN CL

B8
1 HART CL
2 BIRCHETTS CL
3 ASHRIDGE GN

C8
1 LYNWOOD CHASE
2 DENE CL
3 LAKESIDE
4 EDMONDS CT

F5
1 THE WILLOWS
2 CEDARS
3 MAPEL CT
4 GREENWOOD
5 LARCHWOOD
6 THE FIRS

7 CHARLBURY CL
8 HOLTON HEATH
9 BLOXWORTH CL

28

F4
1 MULBERRY CT
2 ROWAN
3 LINDEN
4 LYTCHET MINSTER CL
5 STOKEFORD CL
6 FROXFIELD DOWN

27 8

27 47

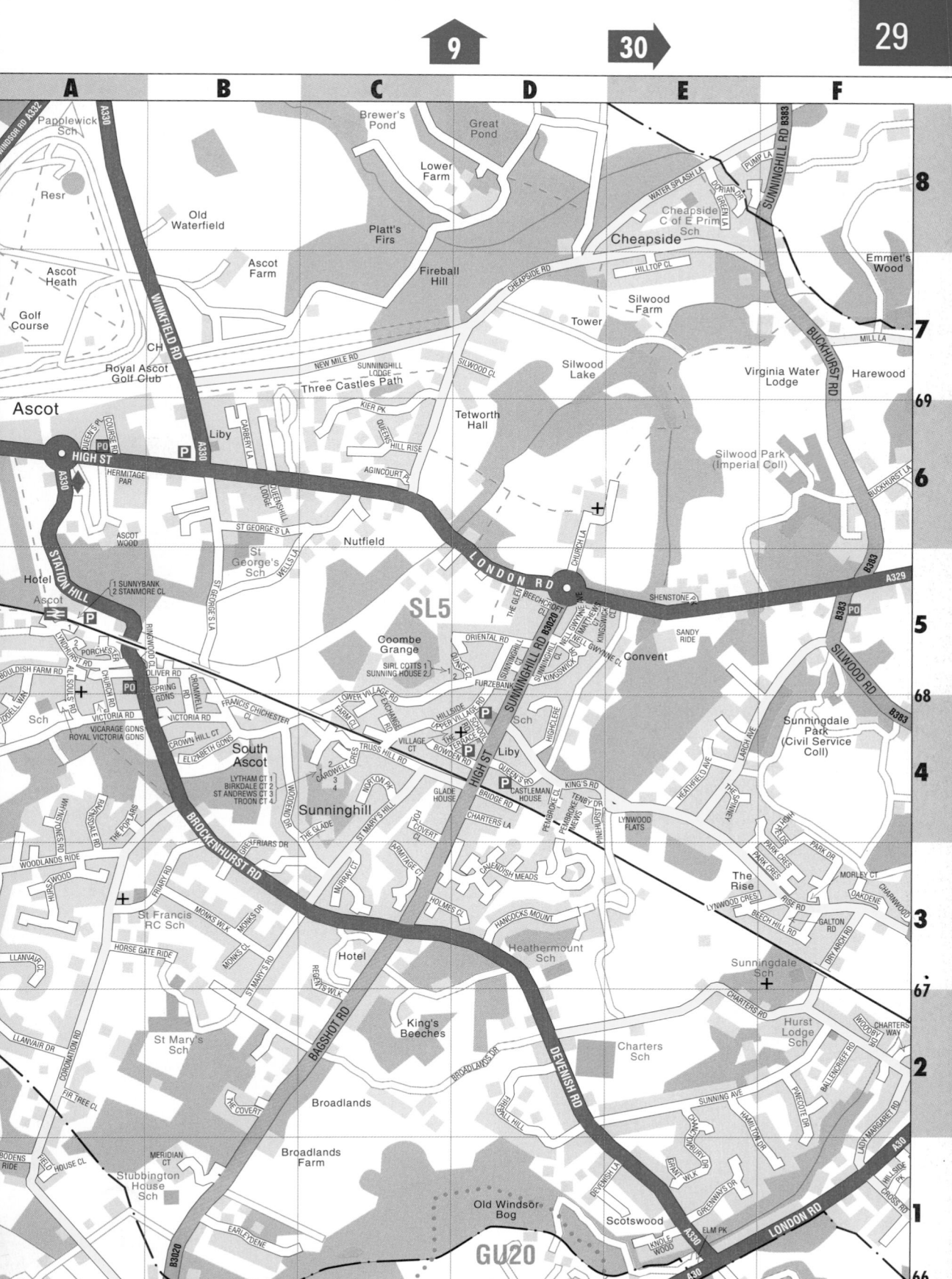

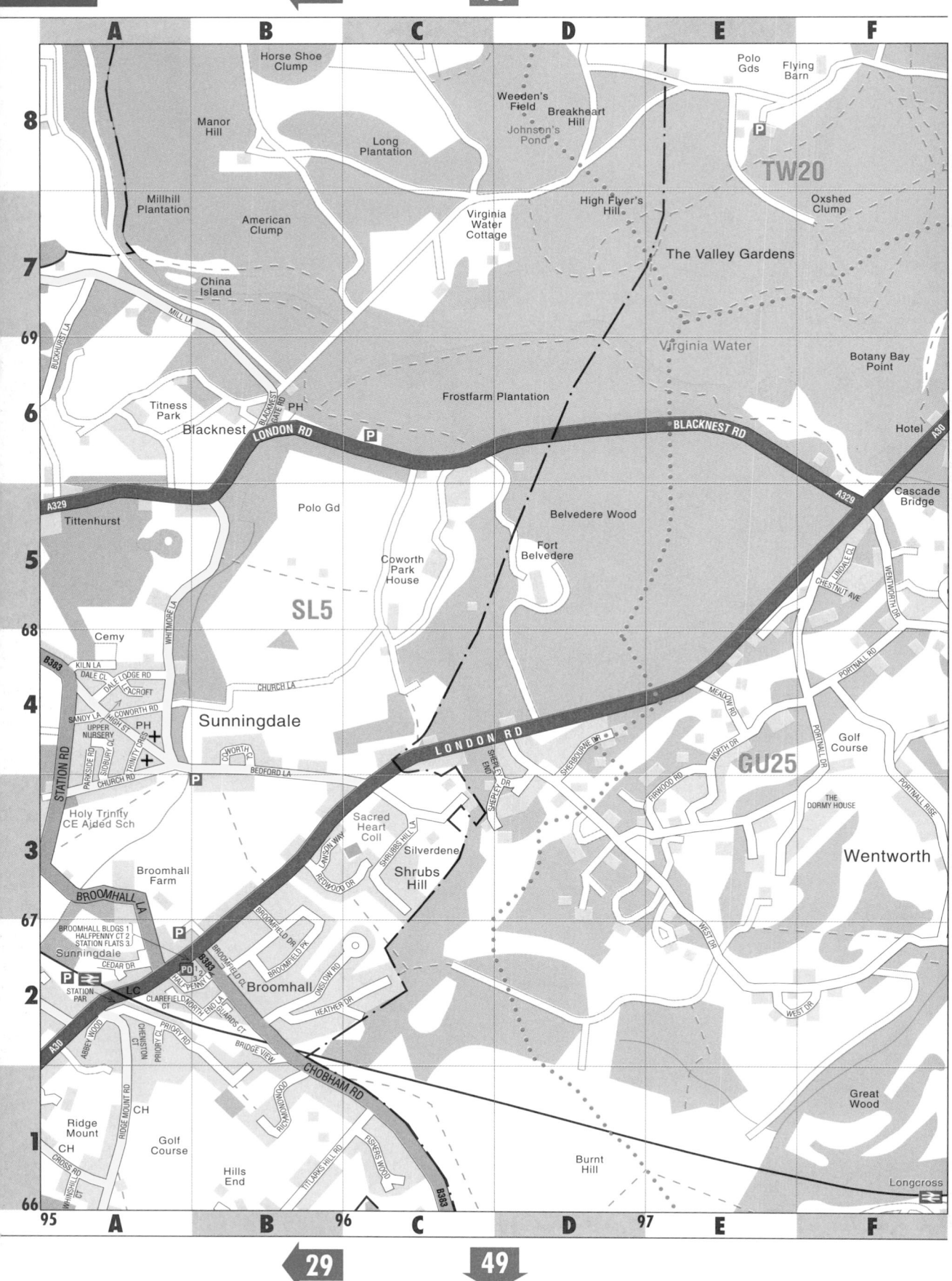

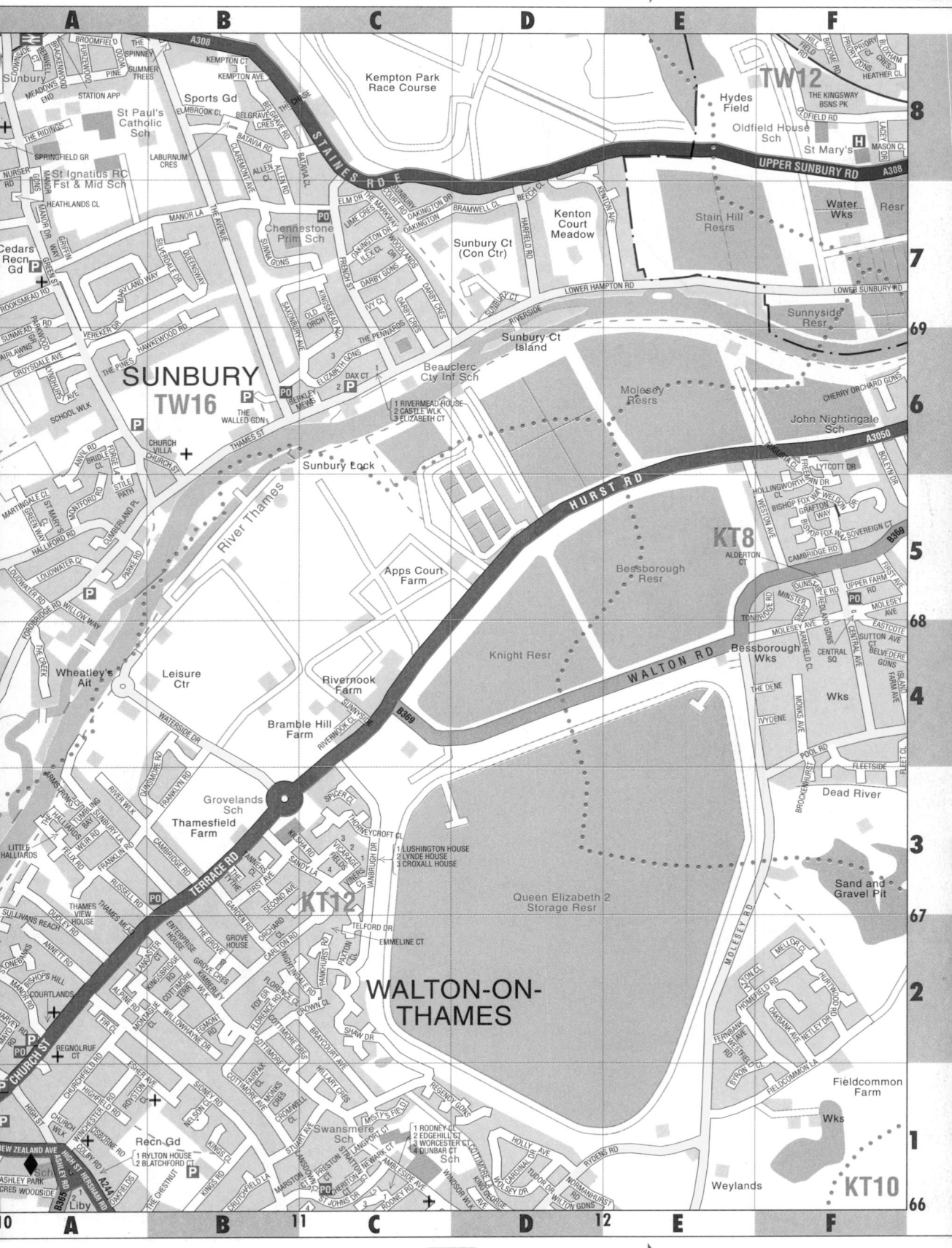

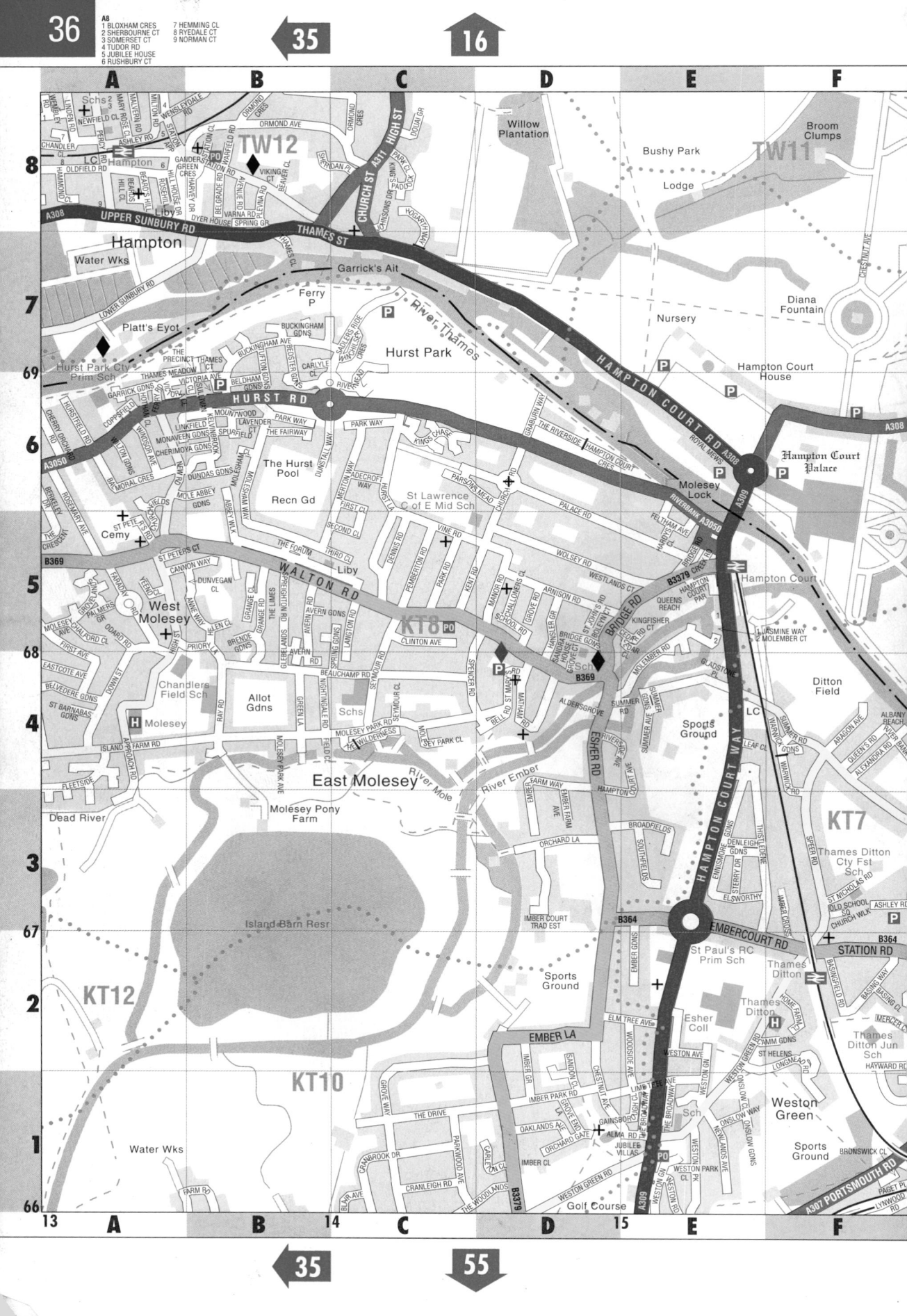

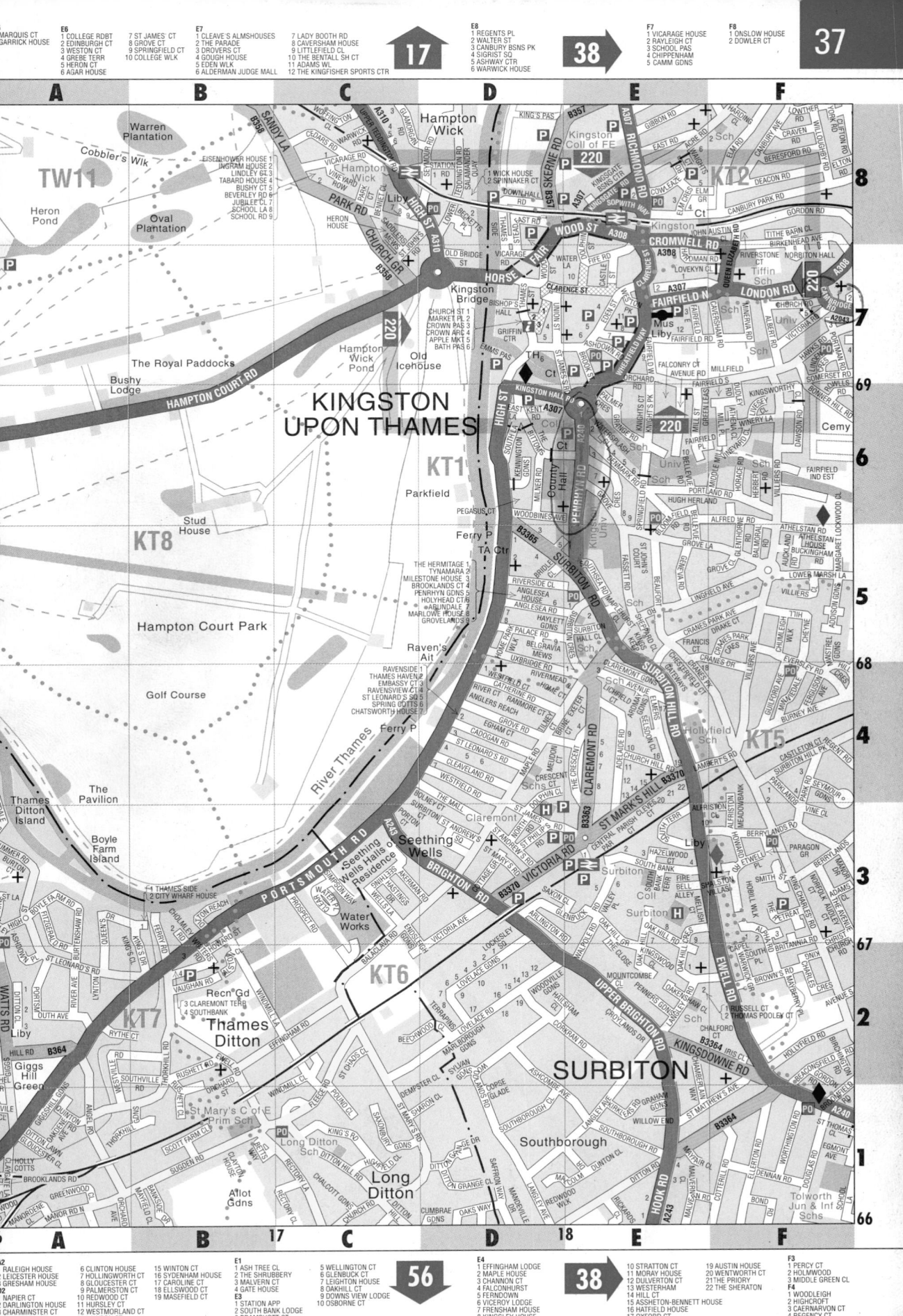

E6	**E7**		**F7**	**F8**

E6
MARQUIS CT
GARRICK HOUSE

1 COLLEGE RDBT
2 EDINBURGH CT
3 WESTON CT
4 GREBE TERR
5 HERON CT
6 AGAR HOUSE

7 ST JAMES' CT
8 GROVE CT
9 SPRINGFIELD CT
10 COLLEGE WLK

E7
1 CLEAVE'S ALMSHOUSES
2 THE PARADE
3 DROVERS CT
4 GOUGH HOUSE
5 EDEN WLK
6 ALDERMAN JUDGE MALL

7 LADY BOOTH RD
8 CAVERSHAM HOUSE
9 LITTLEFIELD CL
10 THE BENTALL SH CT
11 ASHWAY CL
12 THE KINGFISHER SPORTS CTR

E8
1 REGENTS PL
2 WALTER ST
3 CANBURY BSNS PK
4 SIGRIST SQ
5 ASHWAY CT
6 WARWICK HOUSE

F7
1 VICARAGE HOUSE
2 RAYLEIGH CT
3 CHIPPENHAM
4 SCHOOL PAS
5 CAMM GDNS

F8
1 ONSLOW HOUSE
2 DOWLER CT

37

17 ↑   38 →

1 RALEIGH HOUSE
2 LEICESTER HOUSE
3 GRESHAM HOUSE

1 NAPIER CT
2 DARLINGTON HOUSE
3 CHARMINSTER CT
4 MULBERRY CT
5 LEANDER CT

6 CLINTON HOUSE
7 HOLLINGWORTH CT
8 GLOUCESTER CT
9 PALMERSTON CT
10 REDWOOD CT
11 HURSLEY CT
12 WESTMORLAND CT
13 LAWSON CT
14 ALEXANDER CT

15 WINTON CT
16 SYDENHAM HOUSE
17 CAROLINE CT
18 ELLSWOOD CT
19 MASEFIELD CT

E1
1 ASH TREE CL
2 THE SHRUBBERY
3 MALVERN CT
4 GATE HOUSE

E3
1 STATION APP
2 SOUTH BANK LODGE
3 BRAMSHOTT CT
4 PANDORA CT

5 WELLINGTON CT
6 GLENBUCK CT
7 LEIGHTON HOUSE
8 OAKHILL CT
9 DOWNS VIEW LODGE
10 OSBORNE CT

E4
1 EFFINGHAM LODGE
2 MAPLE HOUSE
3 CHANNON CT
4 FALCONHURST
5 FERNDOWN
6 VICEROY LODGE
7 FRENSHAM HOUSE
8 KINGSLEY HOUSE
9 RANNOCH CT

10 STRATTON CT
11 MORAY HOUSE
12 DULVERTON CT
13 WESTERHAM
14 HILL
15 ASSHETON-BENNETT HOUSE
16 HATFIELD HOUSE
17 OXFORD CT
18 PENNINGTON LODGE

19 AUSTIN HOUSE
20 WENTWORTH CT
21 THE PRIORY
22 THE SHERATON

F3
1 PERCY CT
2 HOLMWOOD
3 MIDDLE GREEN CL

F4
1 WOODLEIGH
2 HIGHCROFT
3 CAERNARVON CT
4 EGMONT CT

56   38 →

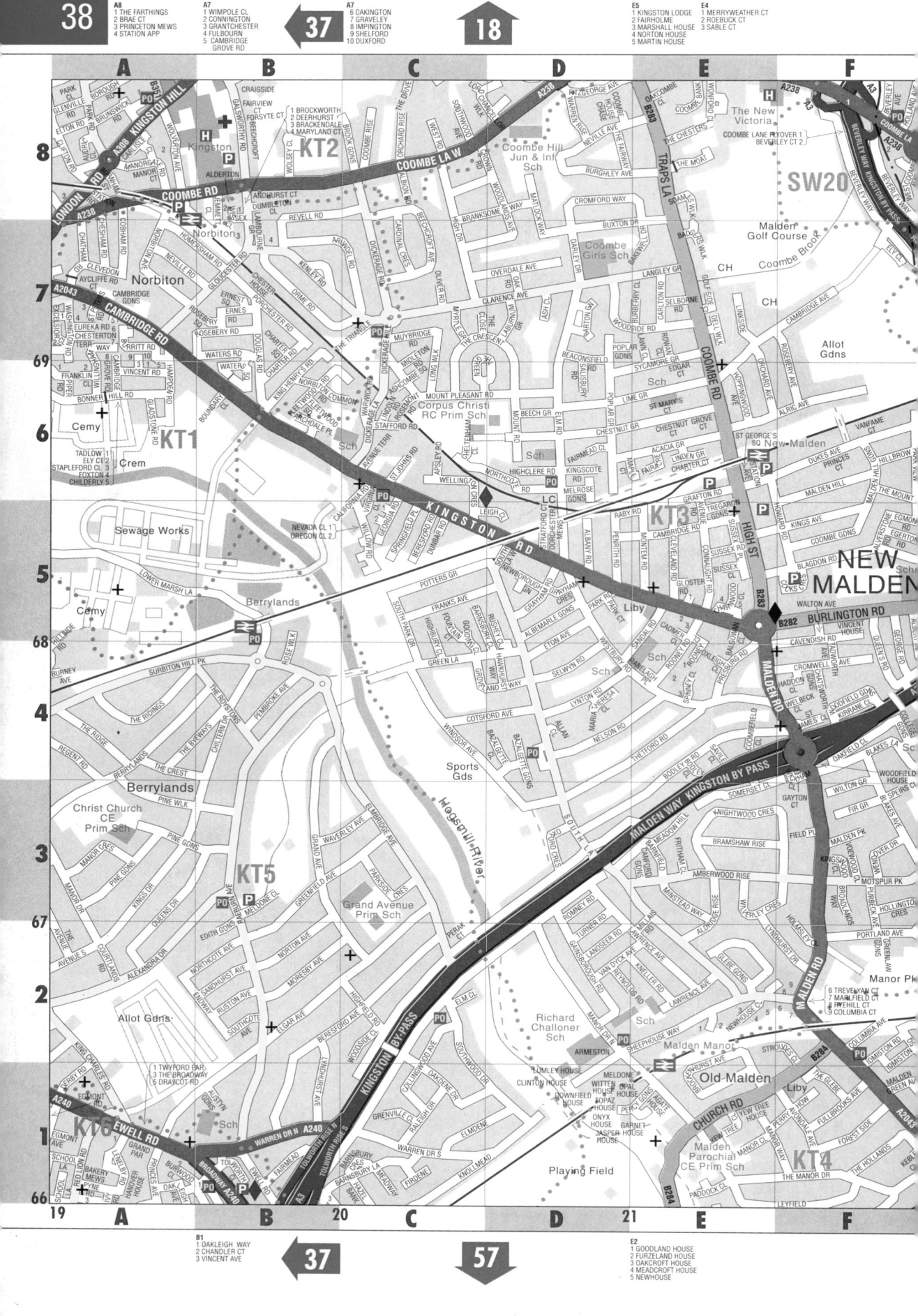

B8
1 GILBERT CL
2 BECKET CL
3 PRIORY CL
4 HUDSON CT
5 RYDER HOUSE
6 ELEANOR HOUSE
7 RAMSEY HOUSE

39

C8
1 TANNER HOUSE
2 MAY CT
3 MARSH CT
4 LOVELL HOUSE

20

F6
1 FAIR GREEN CT
2 REGAL CT
3 LEWES CT

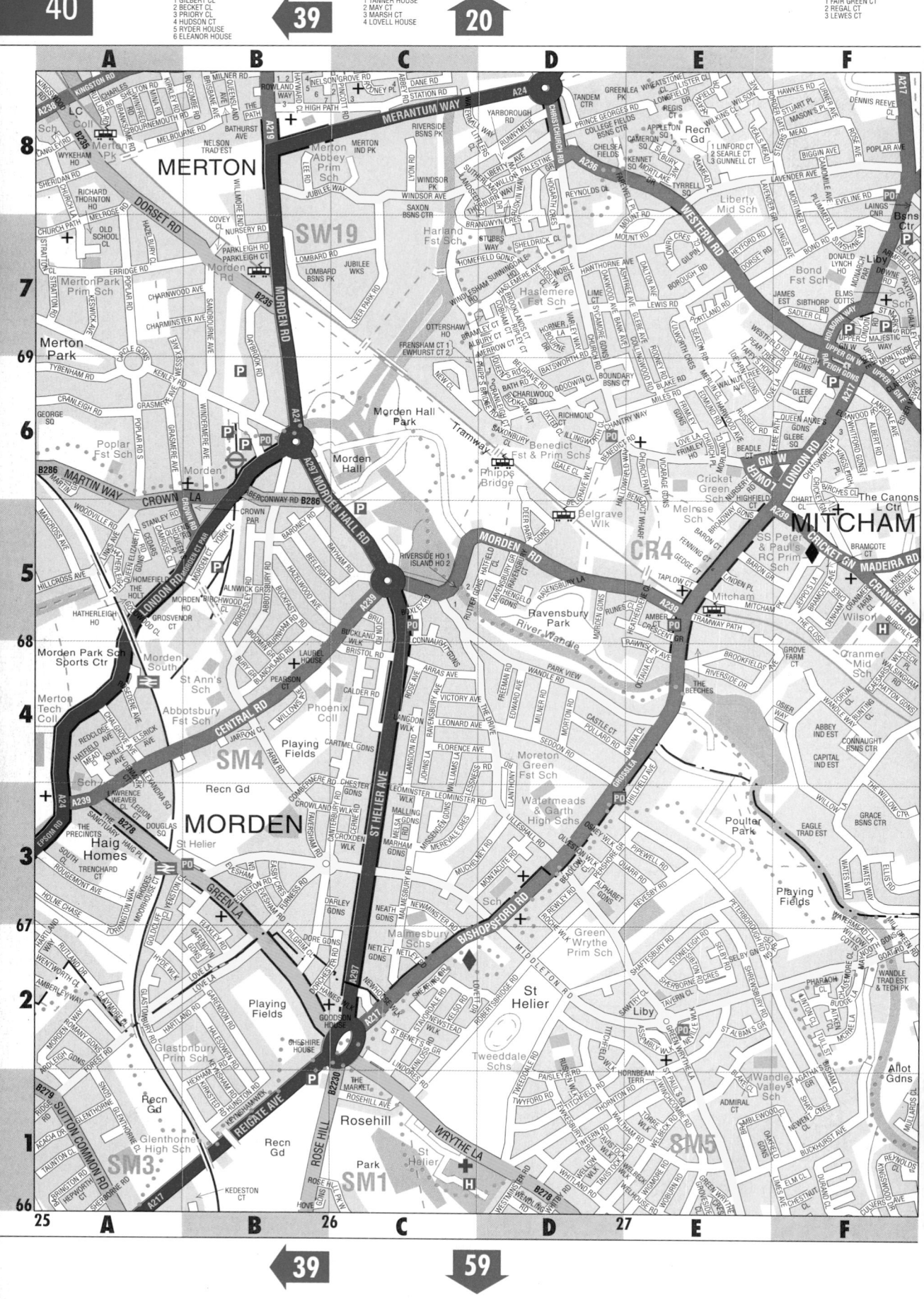

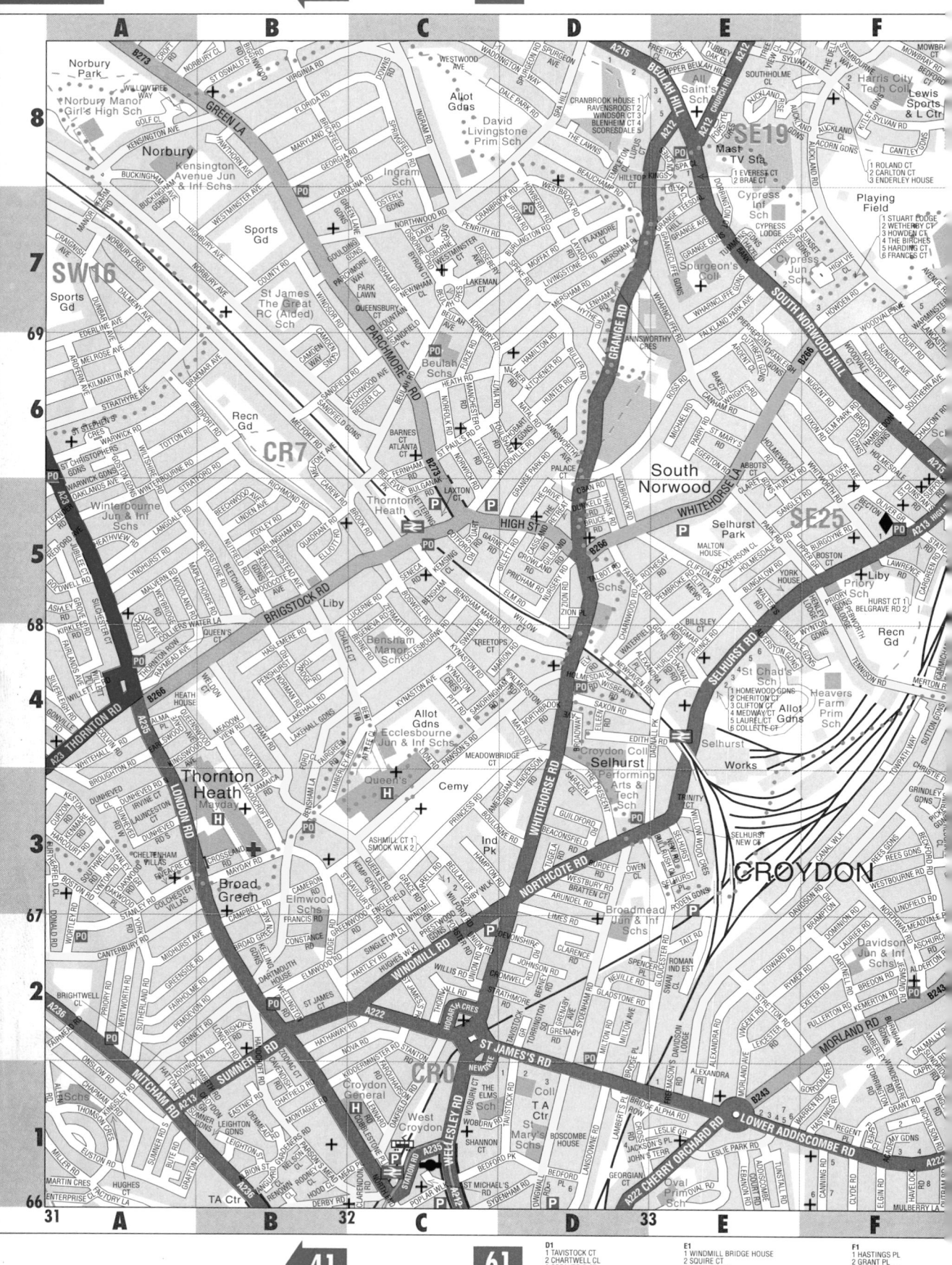

D1
1 TAVISTOCK CT
2 CHARTWELL CL
3 SPEAKER'S CT
4 CUMBERLAND CT
5 VICEROY CT
6 ORIEL CT

E1
1 WINDMILL BRIDGE HOUSE
2 SQUIRE CT
3 HOUSTON CT
4 ST JAMES'S LODGE
5 KENDAL HOUSE
6 WARREN CT
7 KENDAL CT

F1
1 HASTINGS PL
2 GRANT PL
3 CLIVE HOUSE
4 HAVELOCK HOUSE
5 BELLMORE CT
6 HEREFORD CT
7 CHEQUERS CT
8 HAVELOCK HALL

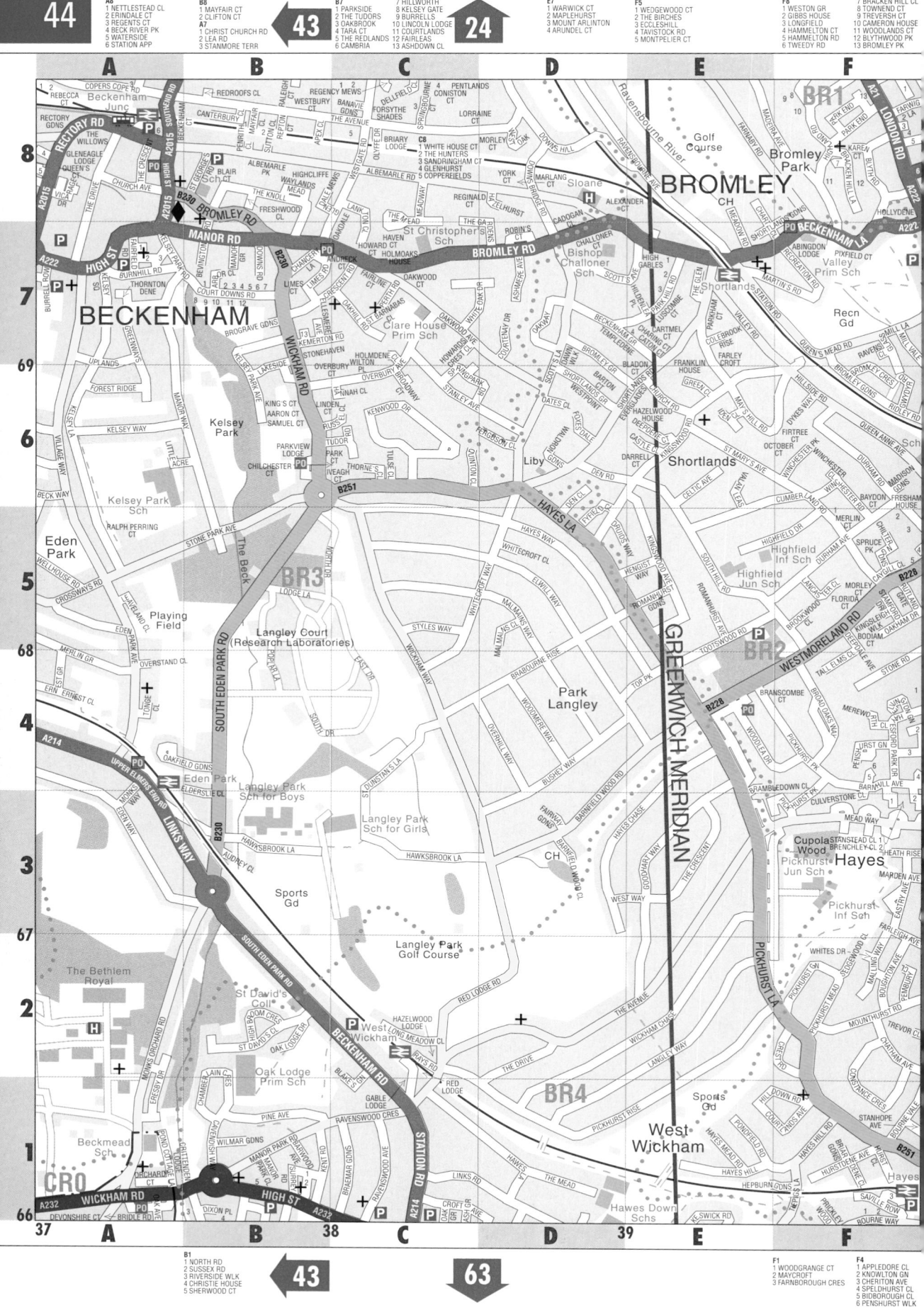

A8
1 NETTLESTEAD CL
2 ERINDALE CT
3 REGENTS CT
4 BECK RIVER PK
5 WATERSIDE
6 STATION APP

B8
1 MAYFAIR CT
2 CLIFTON CT
A7
1 CHRIST CHURCH RD
2 LEA RD
3 STANMORE TERR

B7
1 PARKSIDE
2 THE TUDORS
3 OAKBROOK
4 TARA CT
5 THE REDLANDS
6 CAMBRIA

7 HILLWORTH
8 KELSEY GATE
9 BURRELLS
10 LINCOLN LODGE
11 COURTLANDS
12 FAIRLEAS
13 ASHDOWN CL

E7
1 WARWICK CT
2 MAPLEHURST
3 MOUNT ARLINTON
4 ARUNDEL CT

F5
1 WEDGEWOOD CT
2 THE BIRCHES
3 ECCLESHILL
4 TAVISTOCK RD
5 MONTPELIER CT

F8
1 WESTON GR
2 GIBBS HOUSE
3 LONGFIELD
4 HAMMELTON CT
5 HAMMELTON RD
6 TWEEDY RD

7 BRACKEN HILL CL
8 TOWNEND CT
9 TREVERSH CT
10 CAMERON HOUSE
11 WOODLANDS CT
12 BLYTHWOOD CT
13 BROMLEY PK

B1
1 NORTH RD
2 SUSSEX RD
3 RIVERSIDE WLK
4 CHRISTIE HOUSE
5 SHERWOOD CT

43

63

F1
1 WOODGRANGE CT
2 MAYCROFT
3 FARNBOROUGH CRES

F4
1 APPLEDORE CL
2 KNOWLTON GN
3 CHERITON AVE
4 SPELDHURST CL
5 BIDBOROUGH CL
6 PENSHURST WLK

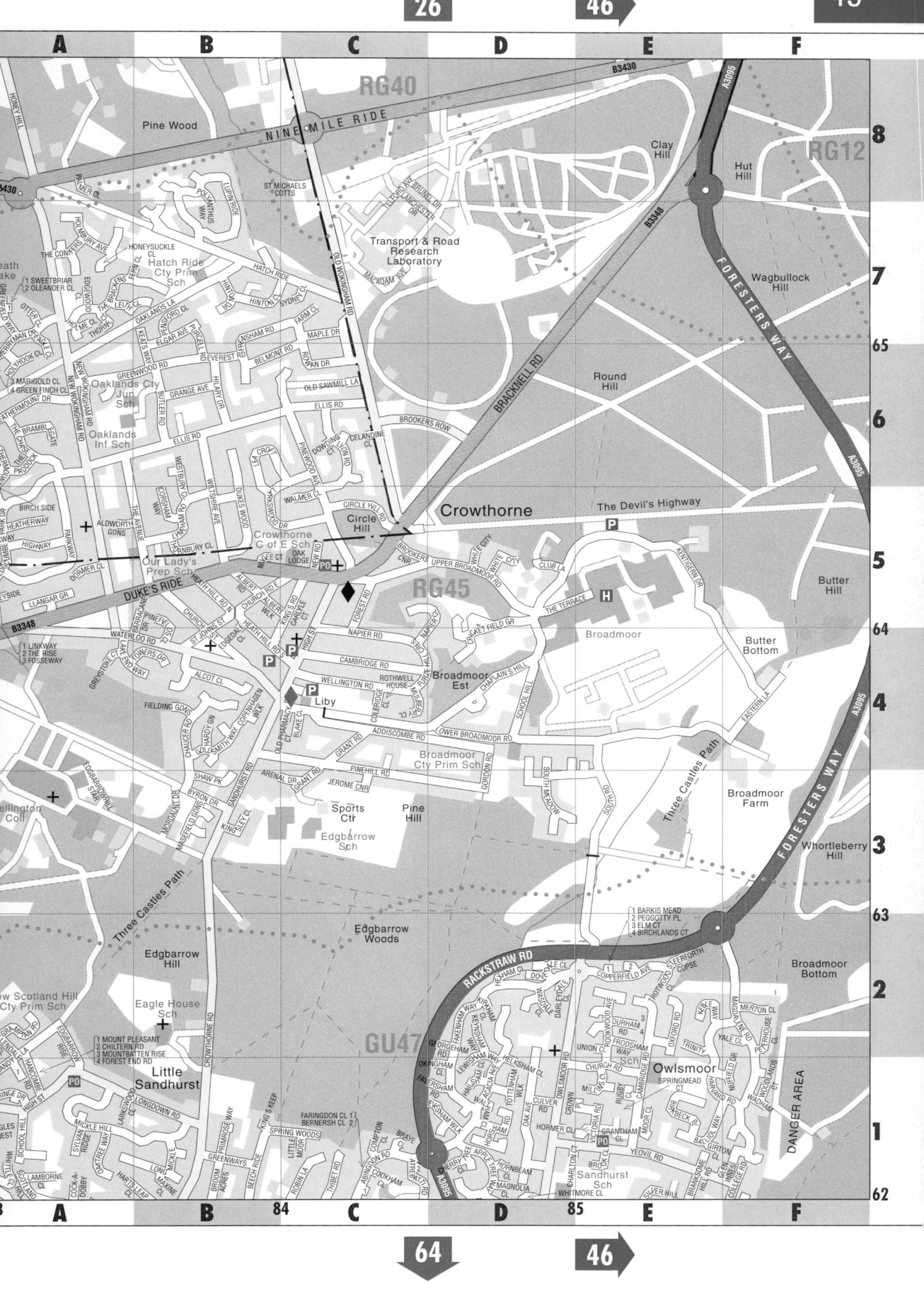

45
27

A **B** **C** **D** **E** **F**

8

Caesar's Camp

Gormoor Farm

Gravel Hill

Penny Hill

A322

Mill Pond

7

Pudding Hill

RG12

65

Wickham Bushes

New England Hill

6

Roman Star or Upper Star Post

The Devil's Highway

DANGER AREA

FORESTERS WAY

A3095

5

DANGER AREA

Windsor Ride

GU19

64

Lower Star Post

RG45

4

DANGER AREA

Wishmoor Cross

Poppy Hills

3

DANGER AREA

Deer Rock Hill

GU15

63

2

GU47

Wishmoor Bottom

Paschal Wood

Olddean Common

DANGER AREA

1

The Devil's Pound

WINDSOR RIDE

MATTHEWS RD

KING'S RIDE

QUEEN ELIZABETH RD

DUKE OF CORNWALL AVE

Saddleback Hill

P

HIGH VIEW CPES

WIMBLEDON CL

BRACKNEL CL

BERKSHIRE RD

Sch

62

A **B** **C** **D** **E** **F**

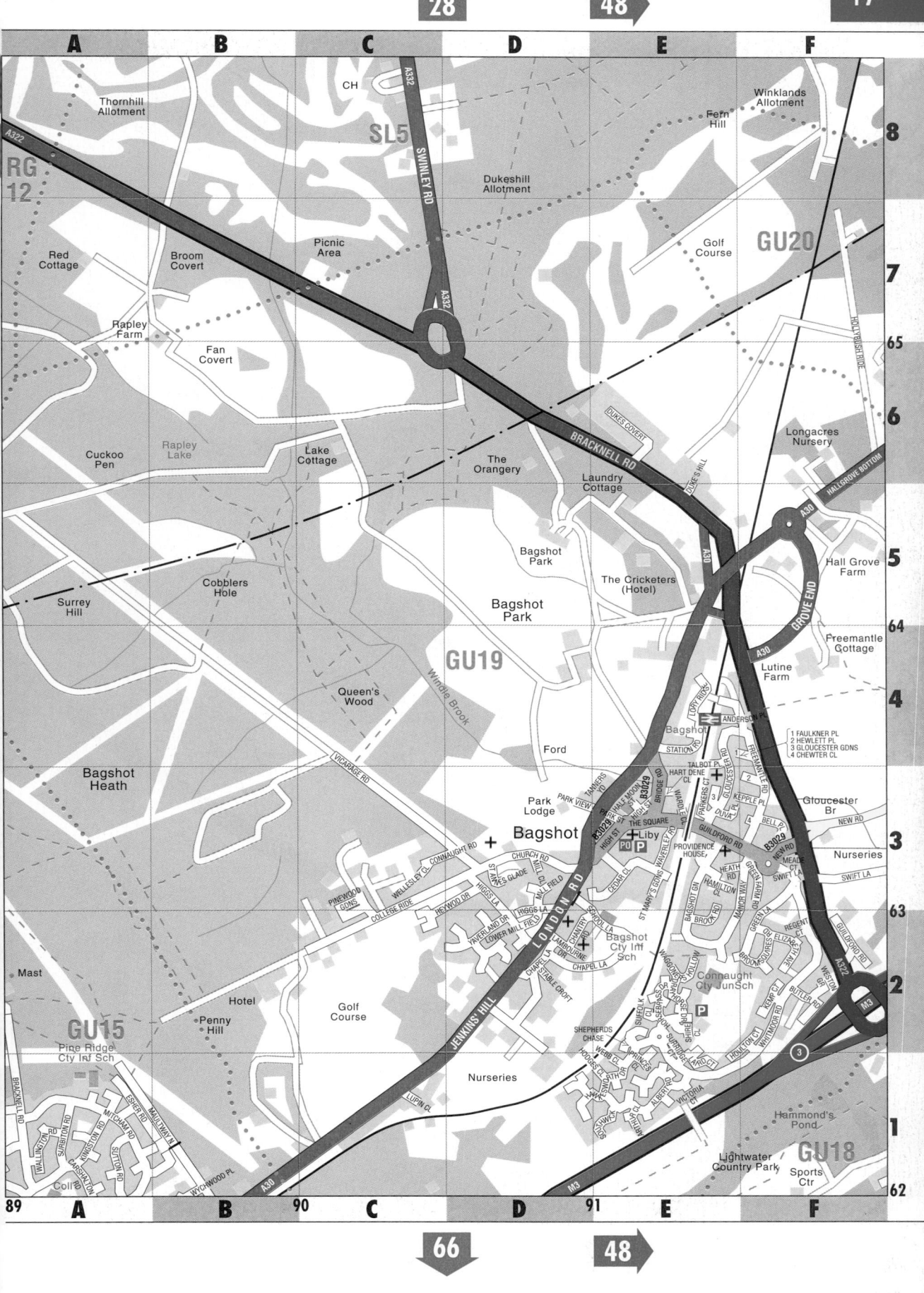

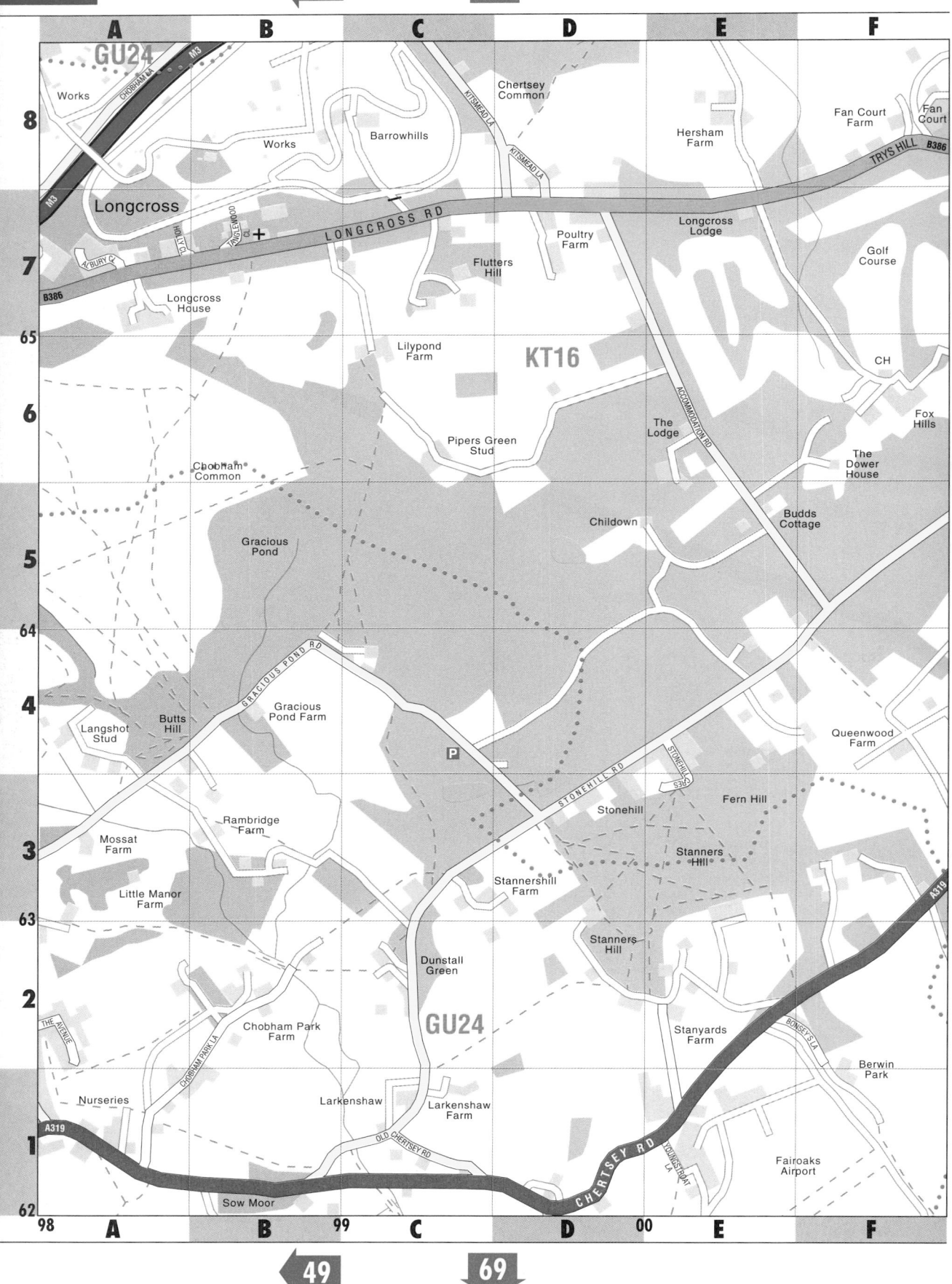

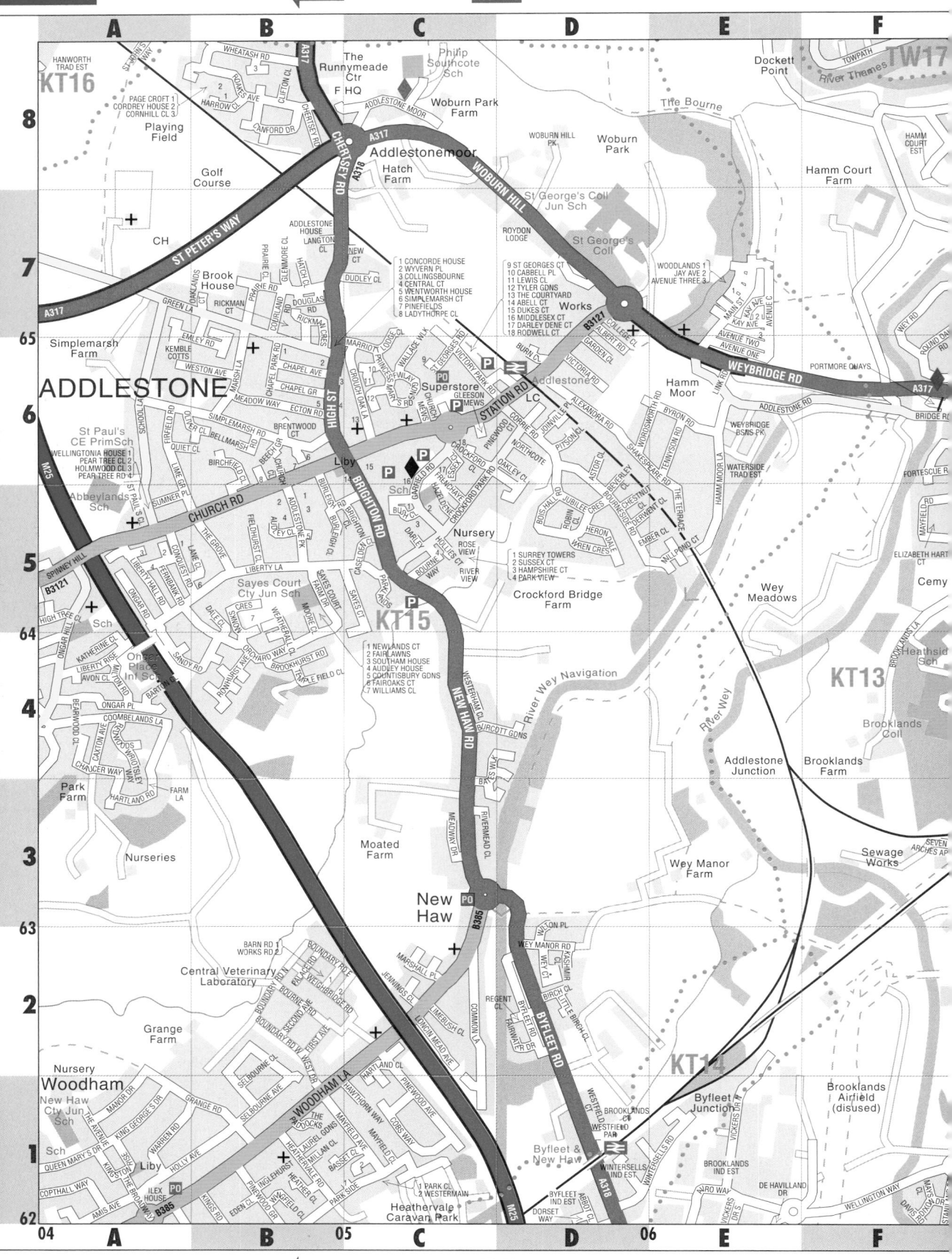

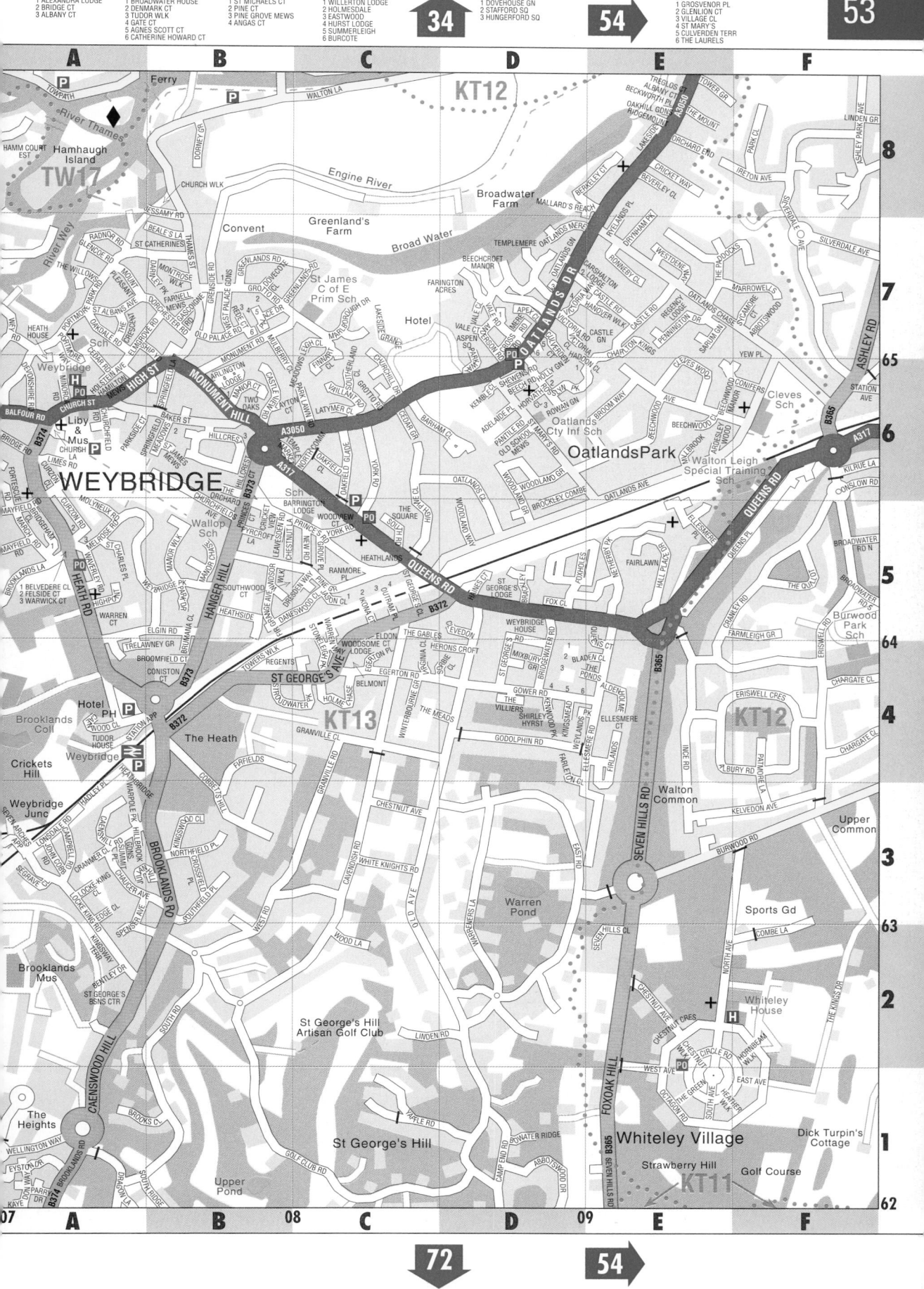

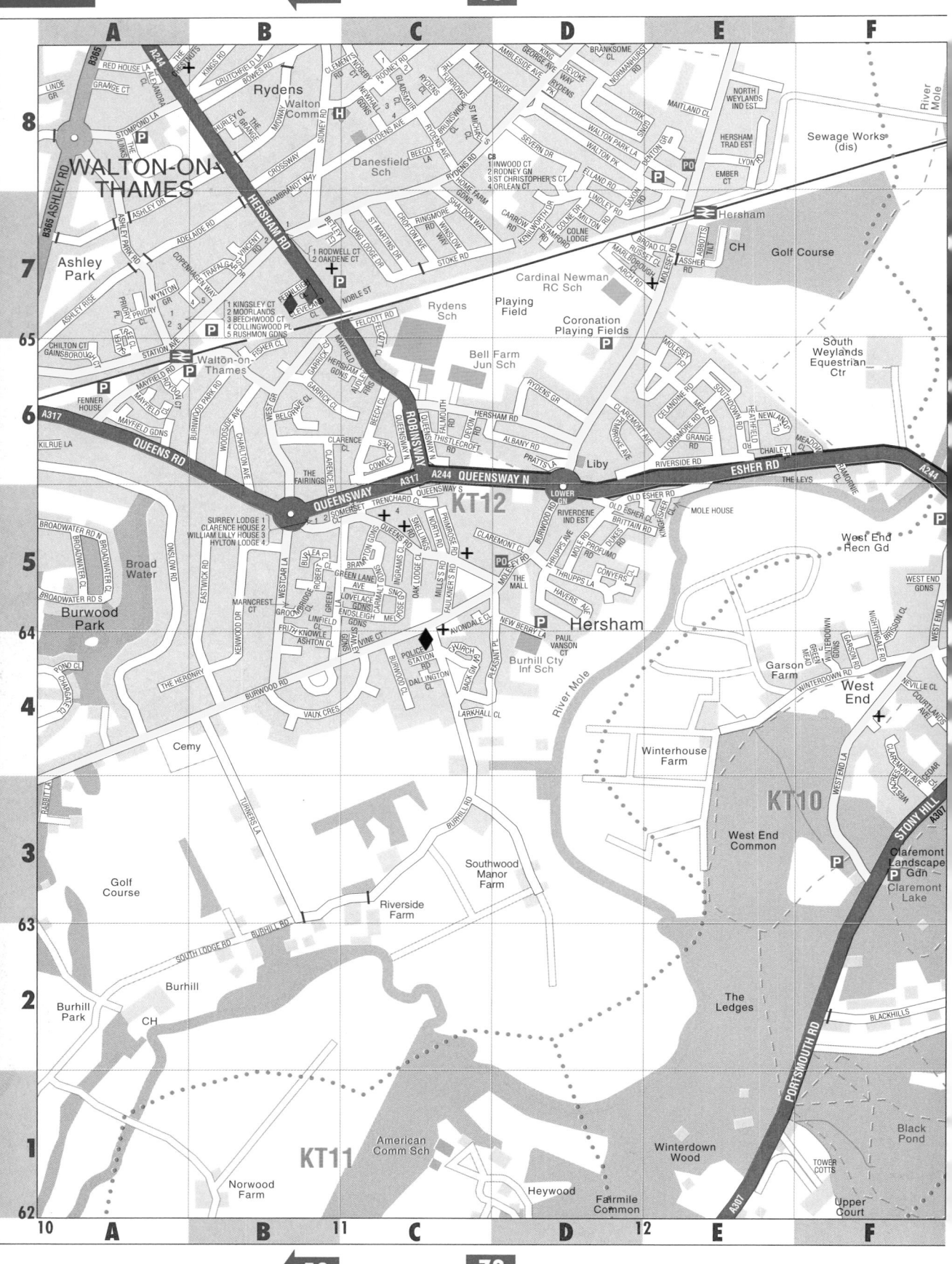

← 55   ↑ 37

8

KT7
Hinchley Wood Sch
Hinchley Wood Prim Sch
Hill Park Nurseries
Cemy
Manor House
Ditton Hill Nurseries
KT6
Sch
Sports Gd
Southborough Sch
PO
Tolworth Girls' Sch

7

Hinchley Way
KINGSTON BY-PASS
A309
A3
HOOK UNDERPASS
HOOK RISE N
Allot Gdns
King Edward Dr
Kelvin Gr
Kingston Bsns Ctr
Red Lion Bsns Ctr

E8
1 CULSAC RD
2 SUNNINGDALE CL
3 ARKLOW MEWS
4 SOUTH VALE RD
5 EDWARD PINNER CT

65

The Waffrons
Sports Gd Nursery (dis)
CH
Hawkhurst Gdns 1
Rosemary Gdns 2
Green End 3
Fourth Cl 4
Cecil Lodge 1
Bramham Gdns 2
St Paul's CE Prim Sch

6

Surbiton Golf Course
CH
Hook
Liby
Buckland Inf Sch

5

KT10
Manor Farm
Elm Farm
CH
Holsworthy Way
Lovelace Prim Sch
Whitehall Cres 1
Trewenna Dr 2
Chessington Par 3
Chessington N
Moor Lane Jun Sch

64

Denman Dr
Red La
Lower Wood
Merling Cl 1
Golding Cl 2
Nichols Cl 3
Withers Cl 4
Mitford Cl 5
Vidler Cl 6
Smeaton Cl 7
Mansfield Rd
St Mary's C of E Prim Sch

4

Hermitage Cl
Rosehill
Oakhill
Ray Cl
Simmons Pl
Ashlyns Way
St Philips Sch
Ellingham Prim Sch
Chessington
Coxwold Path 1
Wetherby Way 2

3

Claygate Common
Barwell
KT9
Fleetwood Cl
Burton Cl
Chessington Comm Coll
Chessington Golf Ctr
Golf Course

63

Barwell Bsns Ctr

2

Winey Hill
LEATHERHEAD RD
Park Farm
Pond Wood

1

Great Oaks
Sixty Acre Wood
Chessington World of Adventures
A243
KT19
Horton Country Pk

62

KT22

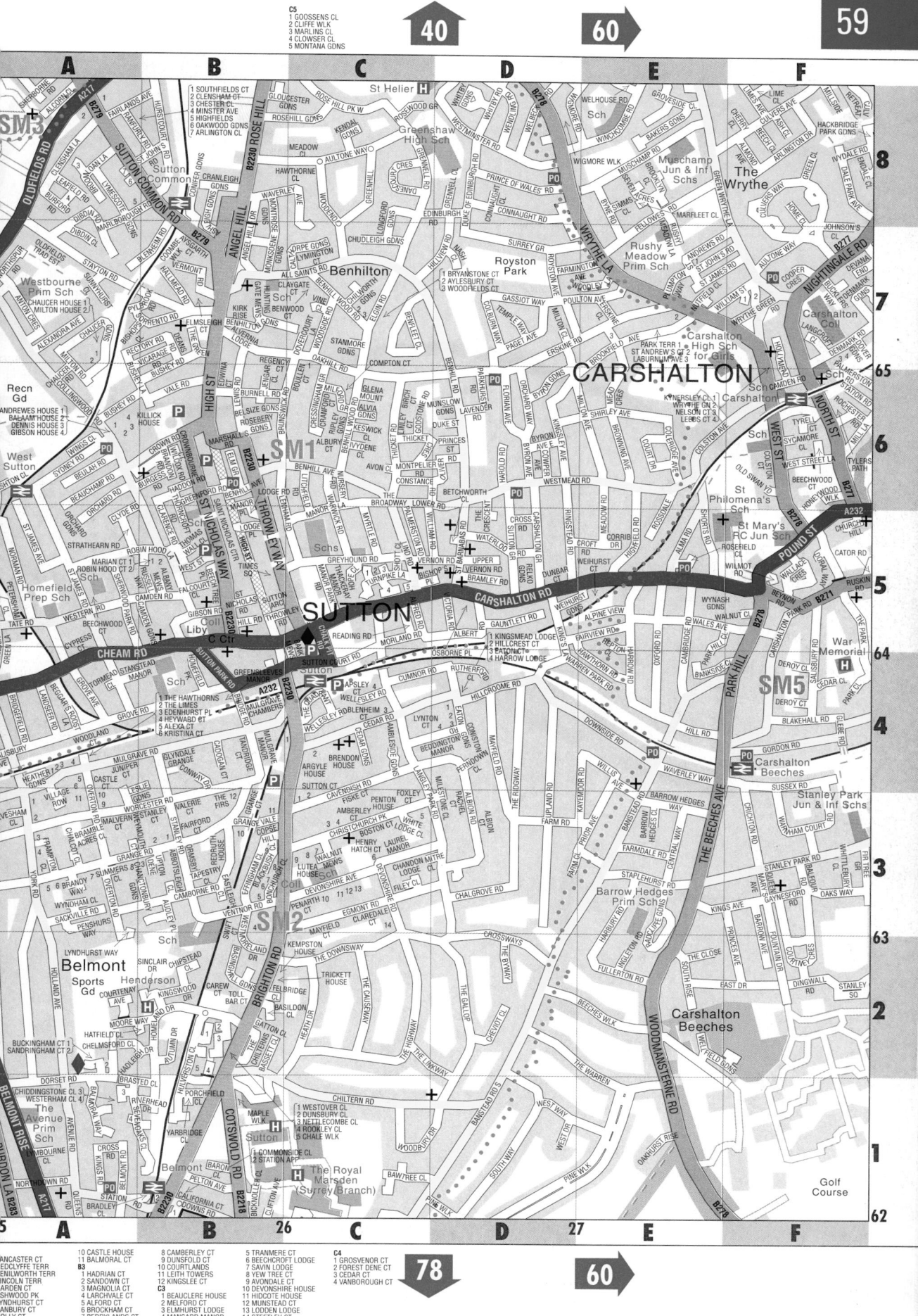

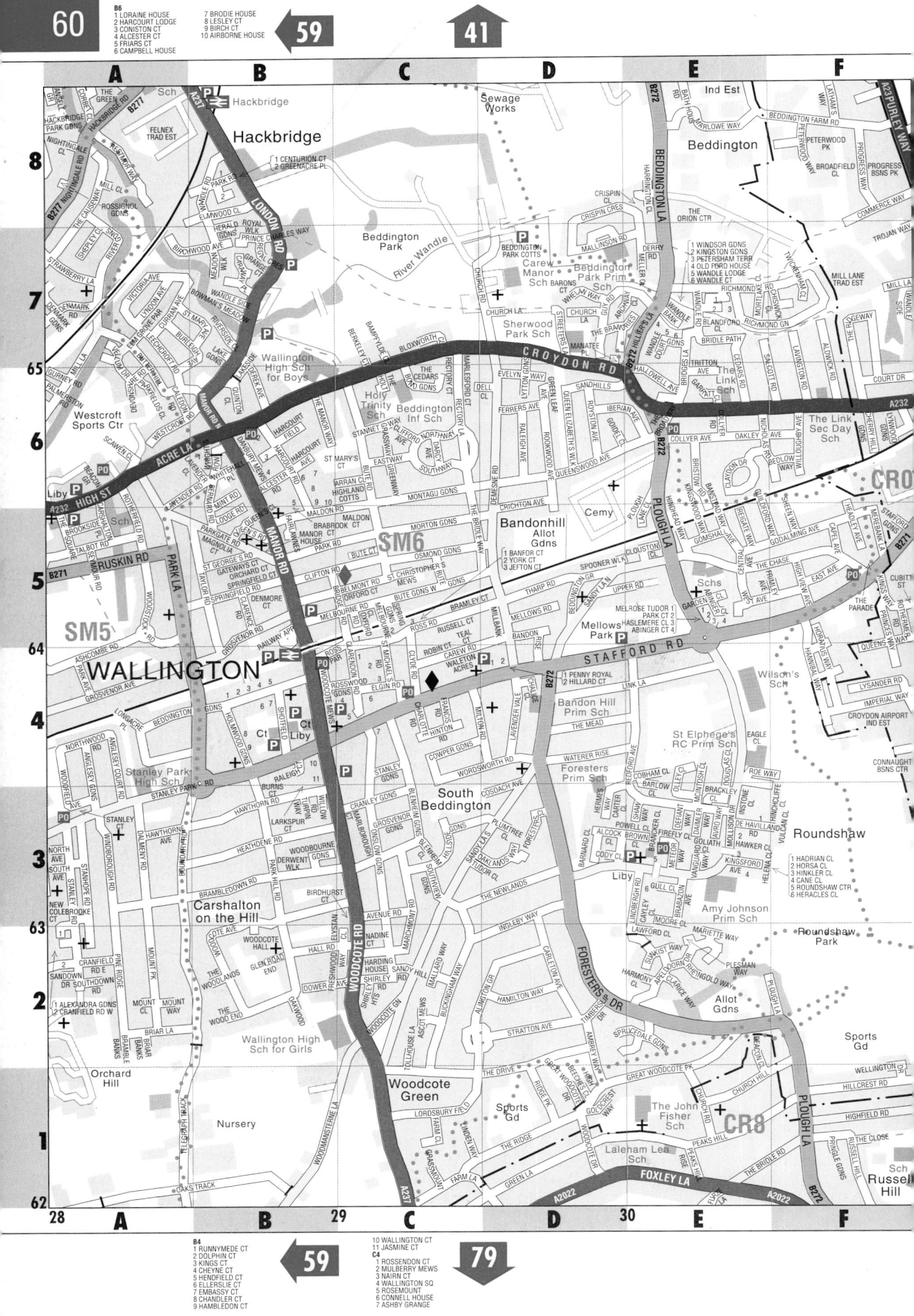

60

B6
1 LORAINE HOUSE
2 HARCOURT LODGE
3 CONISTON CT
4 ALCESTER CT
5 FRIARS CT
6 CAMPBELL HOUSE

7 BRODIE HOUSE
8 LESLEY CT
9 BIRCH CT
10 AIRBORNE HOUSE

59

41

B4
1 RUNNYMEDE CT
2 DOLPHIN CT
3 KINGS CT
4 CHEYNE CT
5 HENDFIELD CT
6 ELLERSLIE CT
7 EMBASSY CT
8 CHANDLER CT
9 HAMBLEDON CT

10 WALLINGTON CT
11 JASMINE CT
C4
1 ROSSENDON CT
2 MULBERRY MEWS
3 NAIRN CT
4 WALLINGTON SQ
5 ROSEMOUNT
6 CONNELL HOUSE
7 ASHBY GRANGE

59

79

C6
1 WEST STREET PL
2 MAPLE CT
3 ST ANDREW'S RD
4 ALBURY CT
5 CHESTNUT CT
6 ELGIN CT

7 BEECHFIELD CT

C8
1 OTTERBOURNE RD
2 CHARRINGTON RD
3 TAMWORTH PL
4 PRIDDY'S YD
5 HOSPITAL OF THE HOLY TRINITY
(ALMSHOUSES)

D8
1 WELLESLEY COURT RD
2 NORFOLK HOUSE
3 STATION APP
4 SUFFOLK HOUSE
5 ESSEX HOUSE
6 CHERRY ORCHARD GDNS

D8
7 HARRINGTON CT
F8
1 TIERNEY CT
2 SINCLAIR CT
3 GUINNESS CT
4 MAYFAIR CT

F8
5 GLOUCESTER LODGE
6 BISHOPSCOURT
7 BEVERLEY HYRST
8 MELTON CT
9 CECIL CT
10 NAPIER CT

42   62   **61**

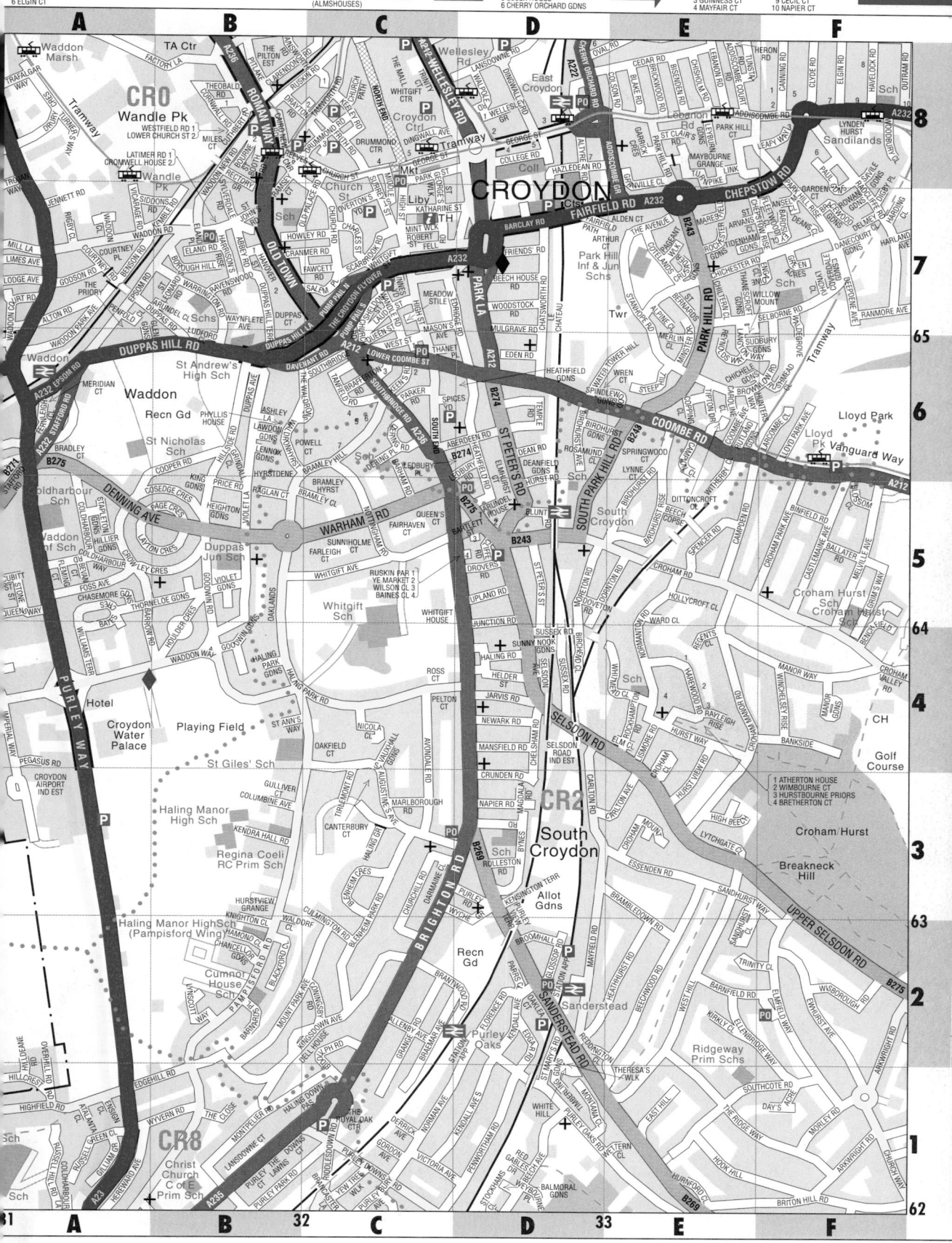

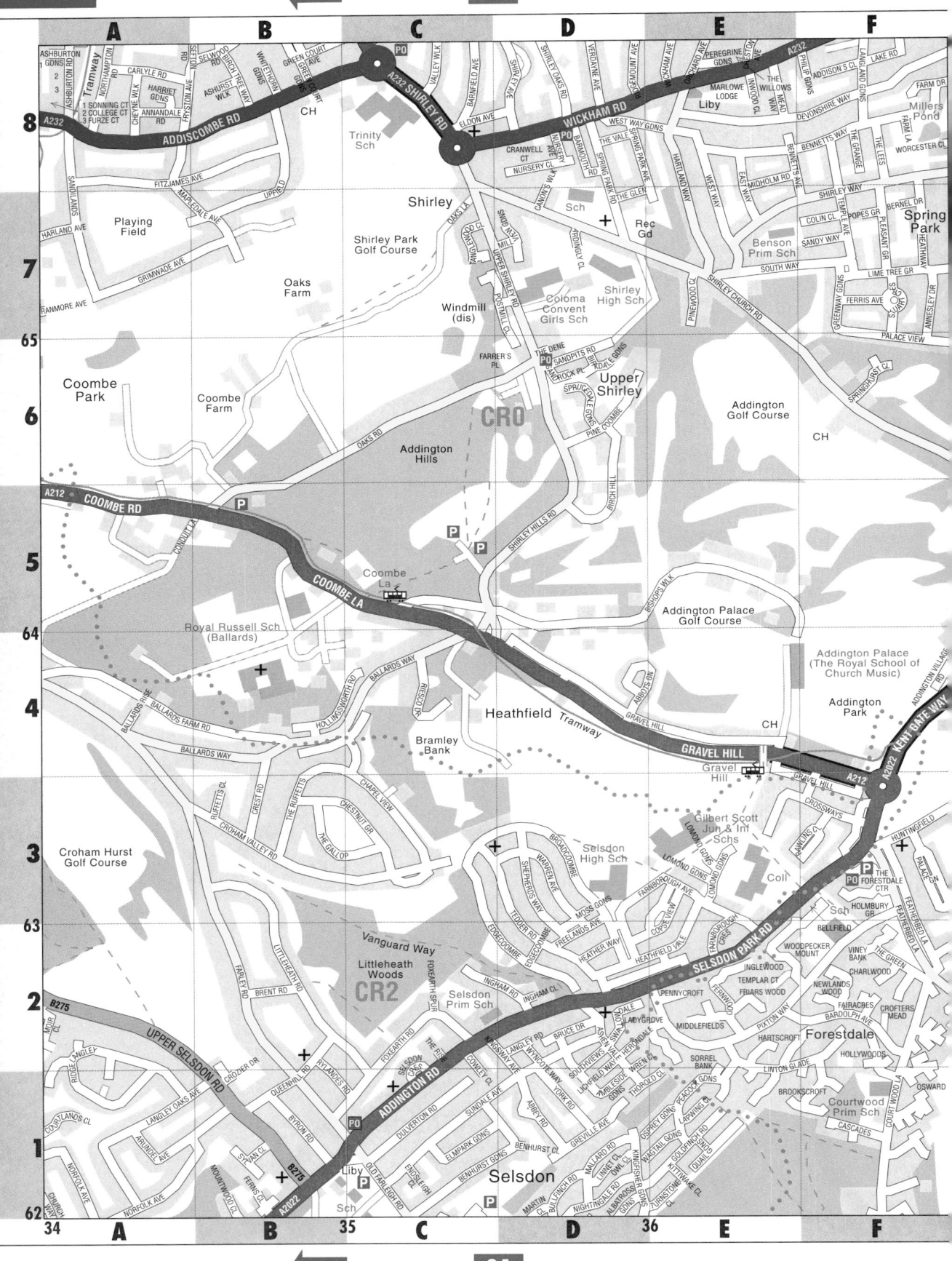

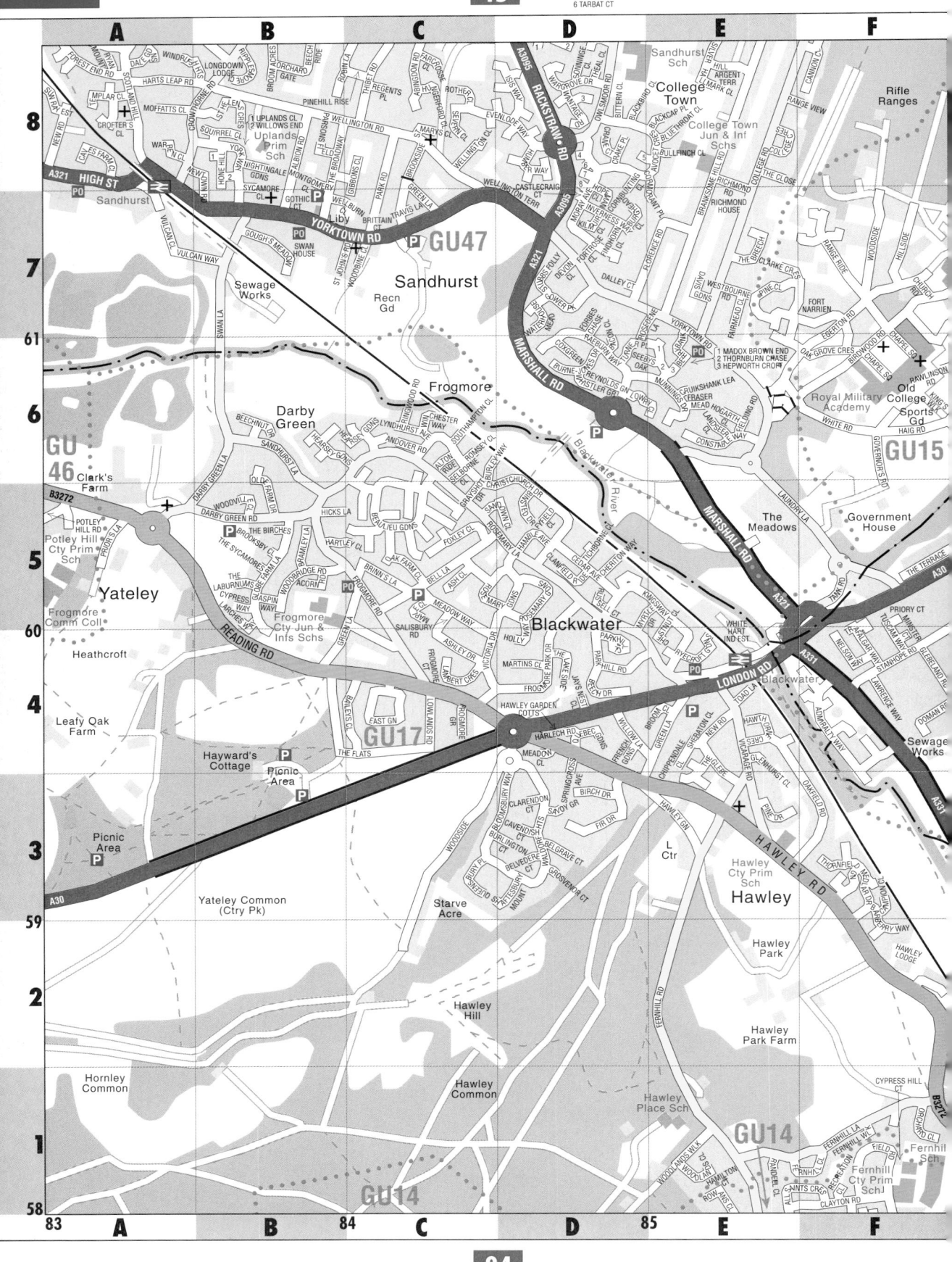

D8
1 MULBERRY CL
2 MAY CL
3 SHRIVENHAM CL
4 CENTURION CL
5 CHAFFINCH CL
6 TARBAT CT
7 ROCKFIELD WAY
8 BALINTORE CT

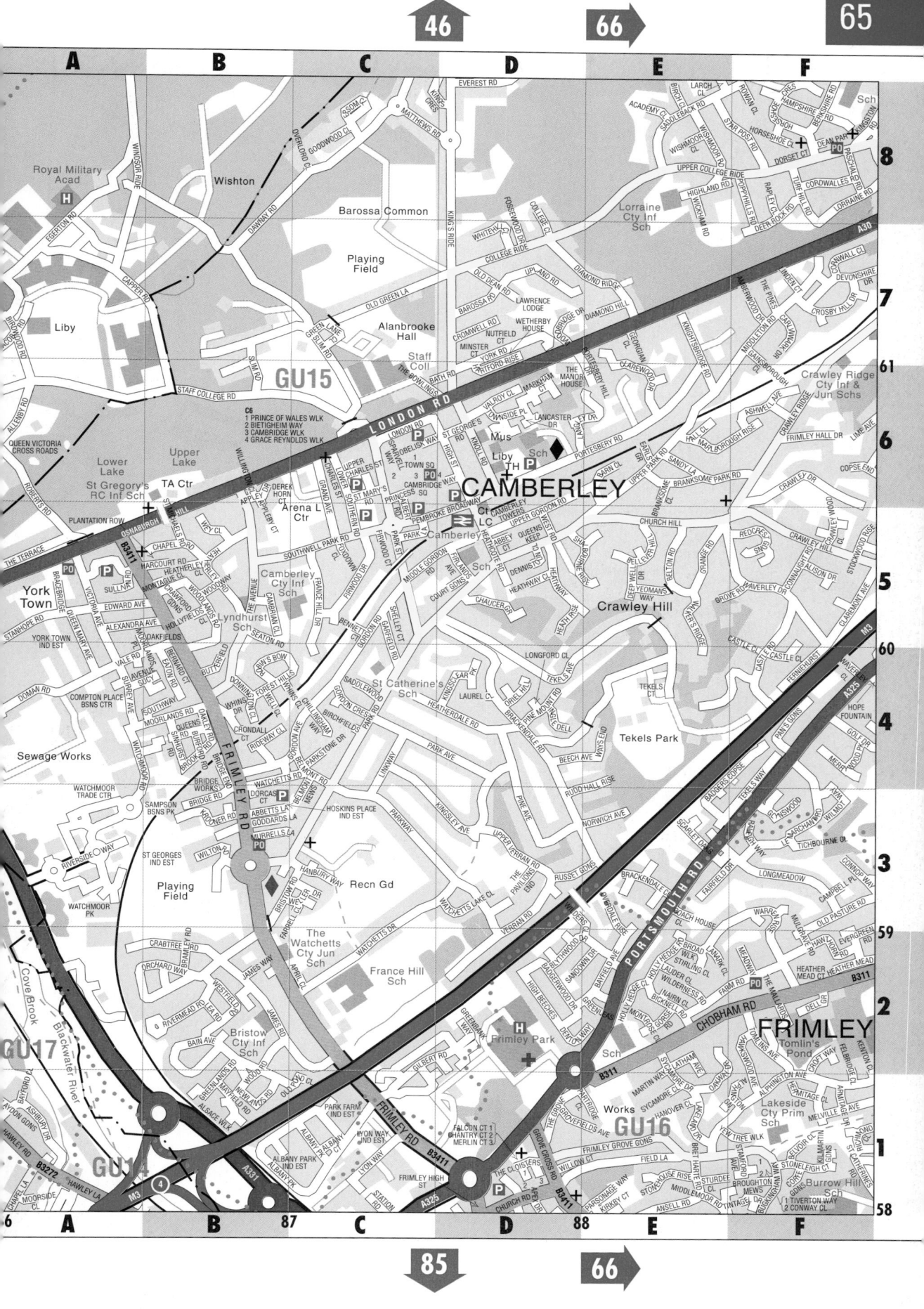

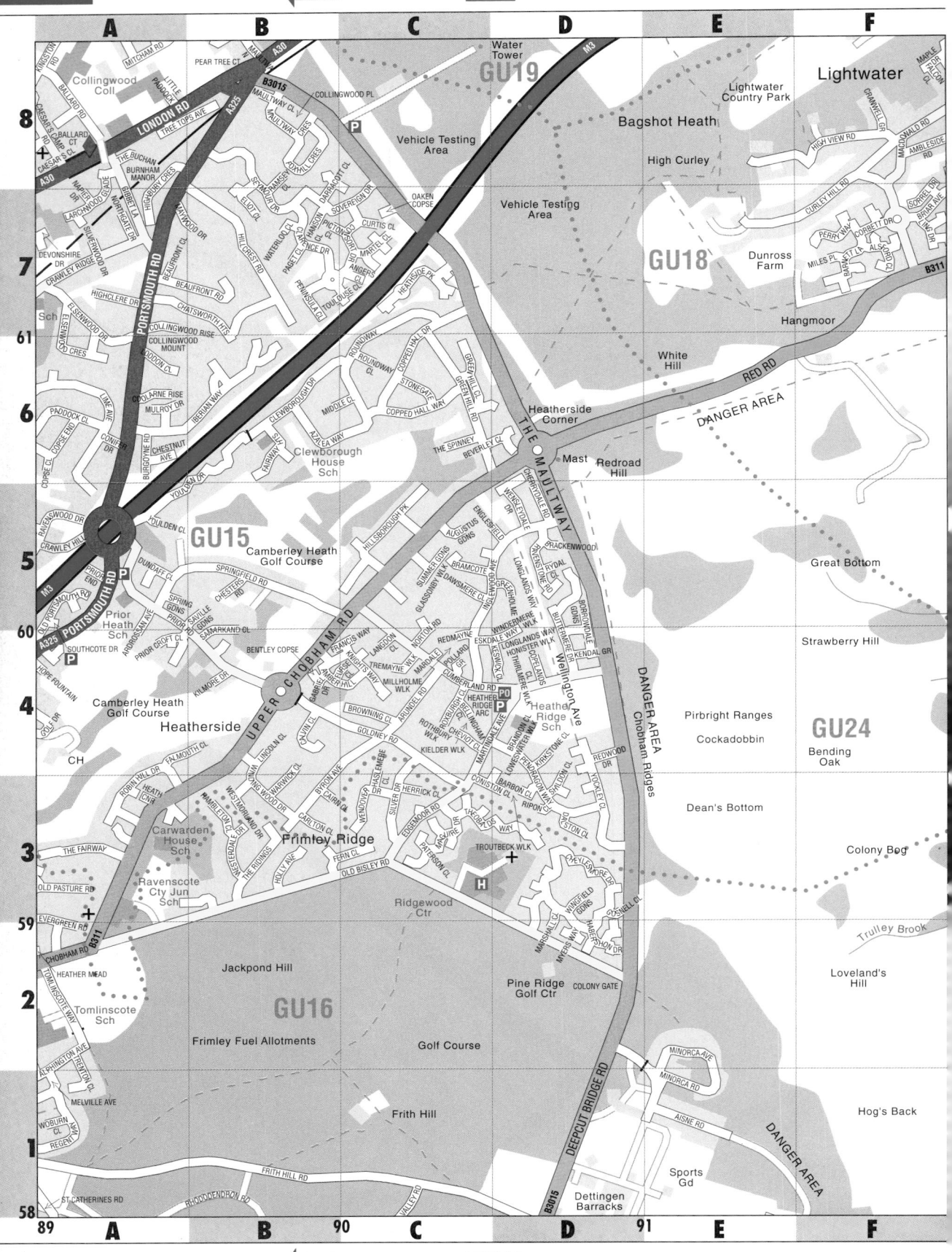

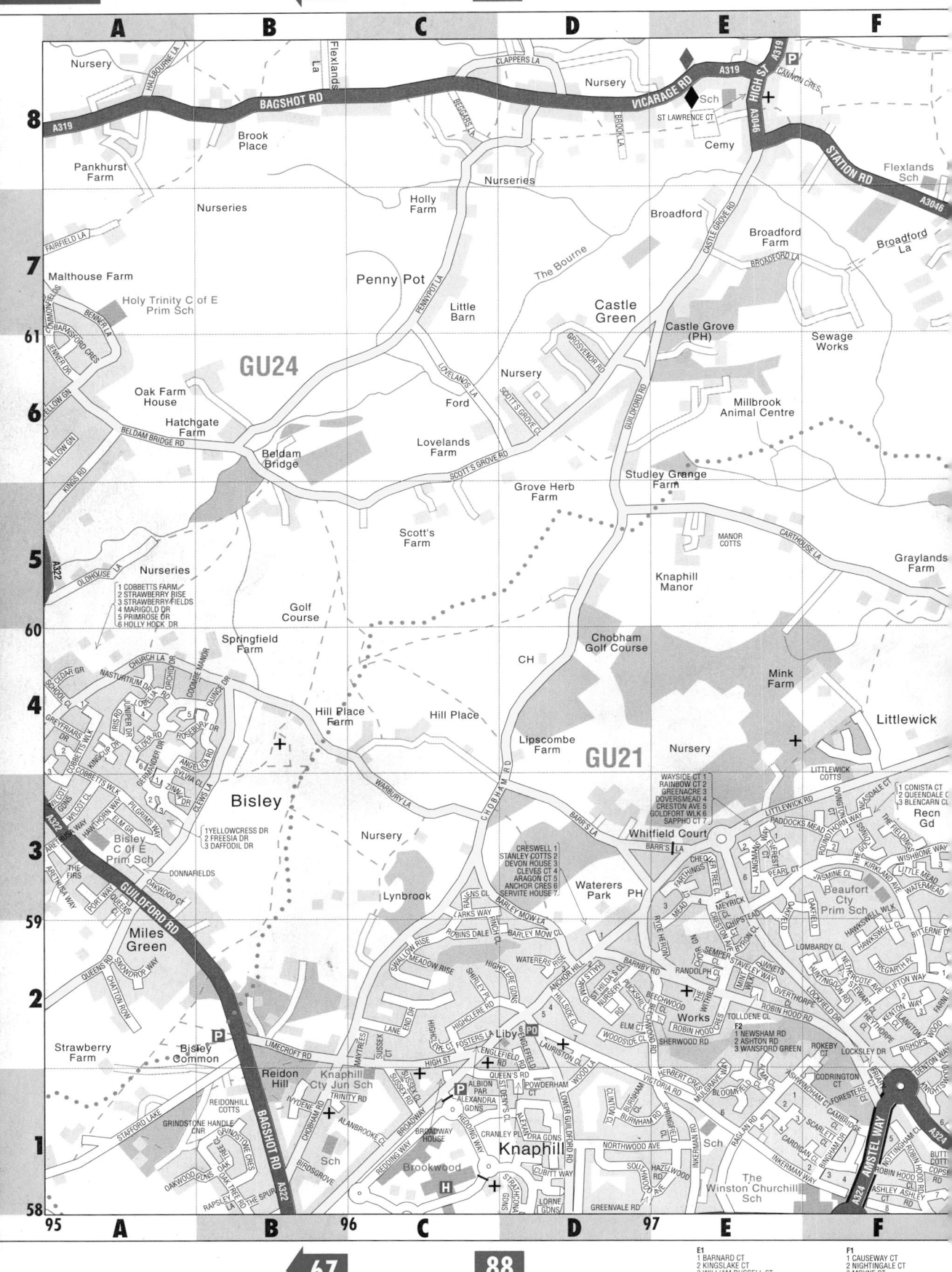

E1
1 BARNARD CT
2 KINGSLAKE CT
3 WILLIAM RUSSELL CT
4 SAYER CT
5 ROBERTSON CT
6 WELLINGTON TERR

F1
1 CAUSEWAY CT
2 NIGHTINGALE CT
3 MOYNE CT
4 GUINNESS CT
5 NOTTINGHAM CT
6 CRANFIELD CT
7 CAPSTANS WHARF
8 BARRACK PATH

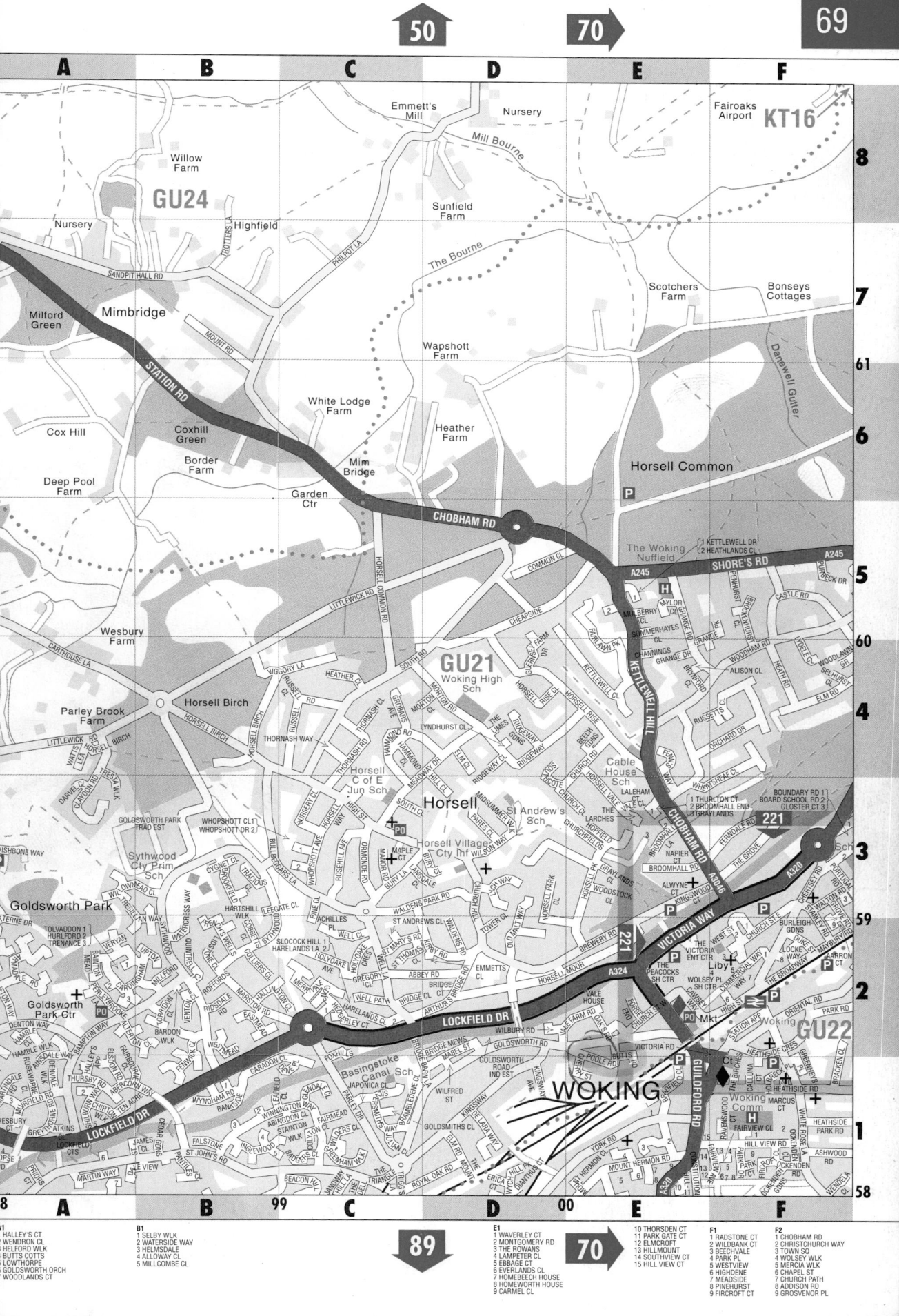

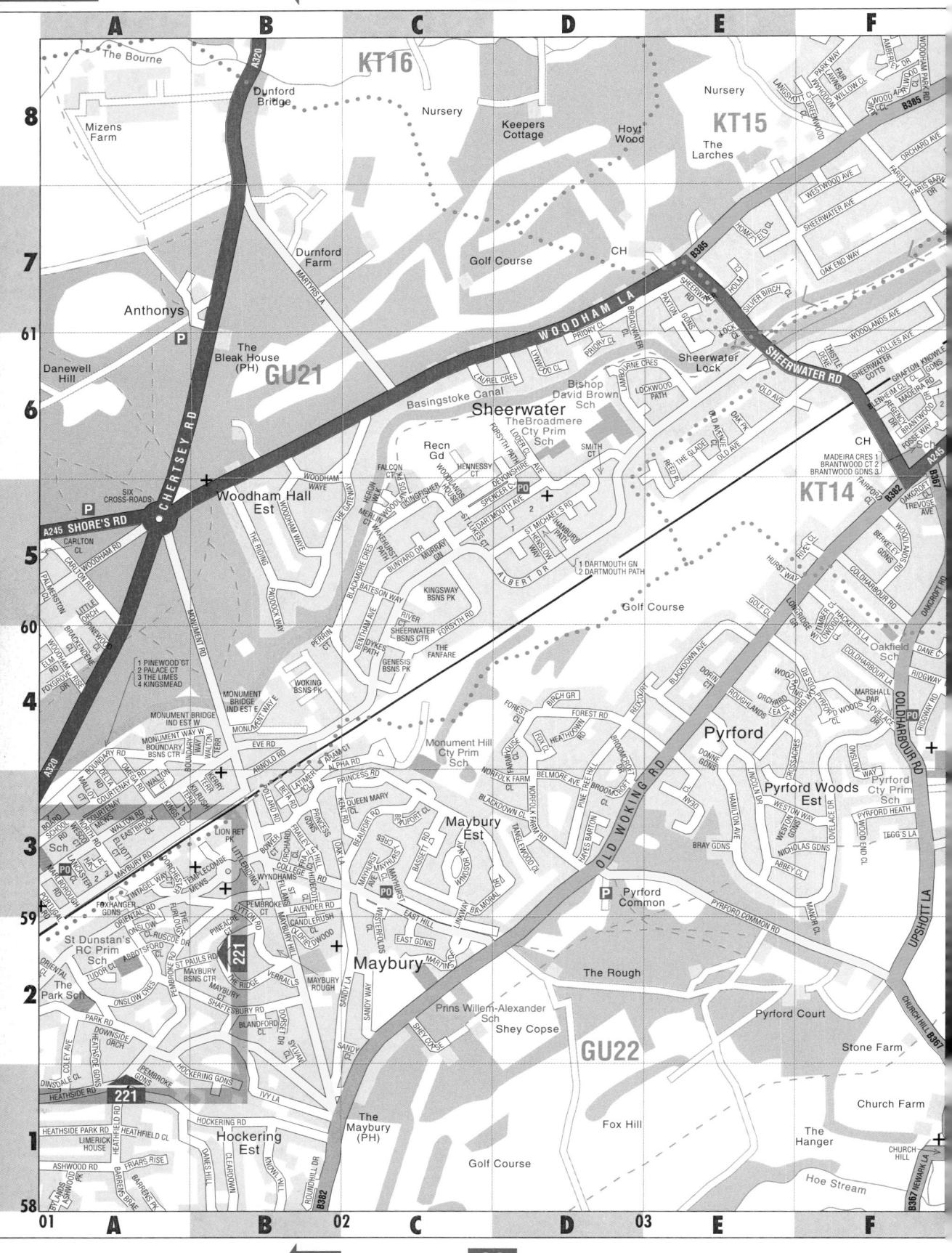

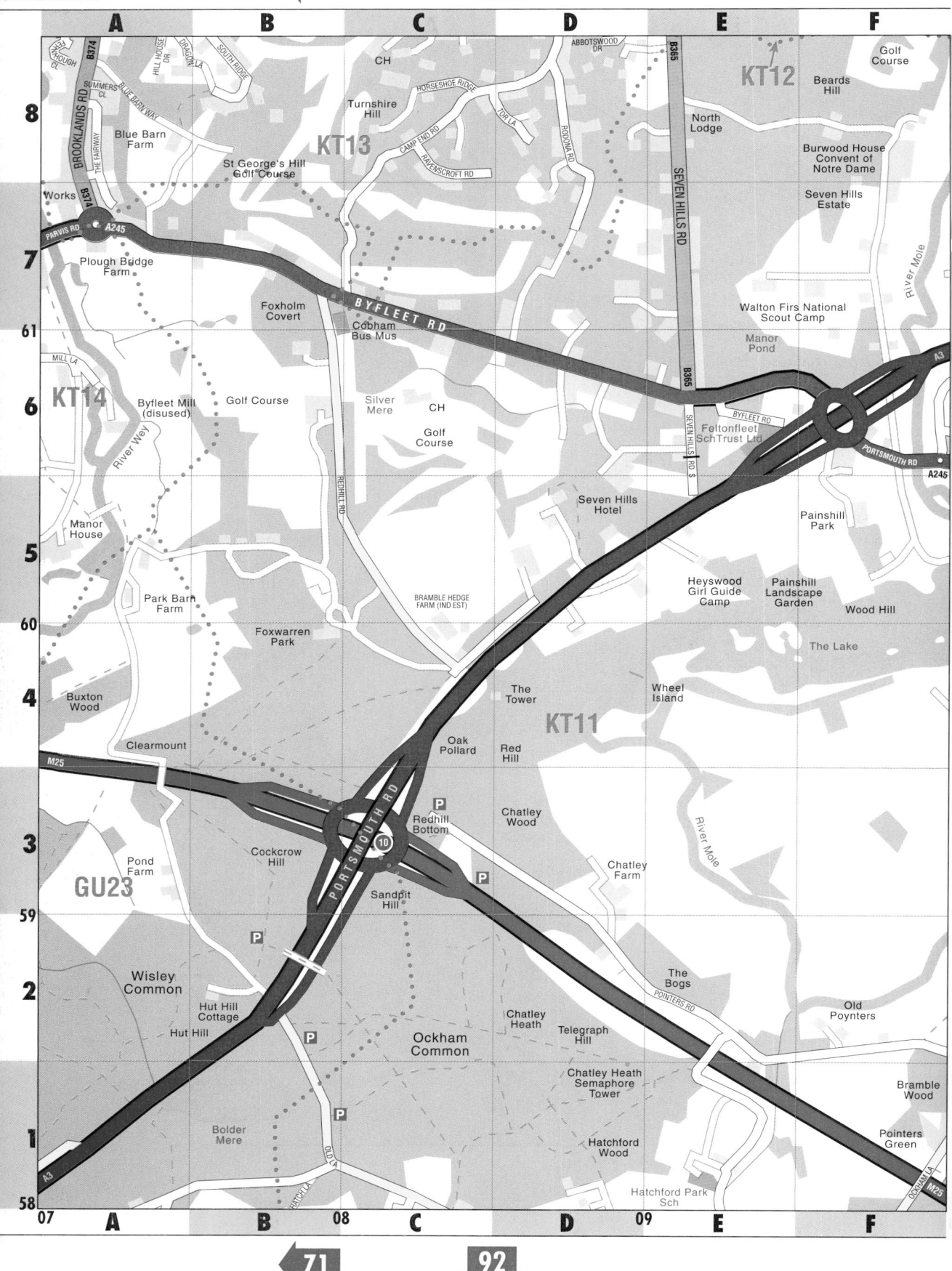

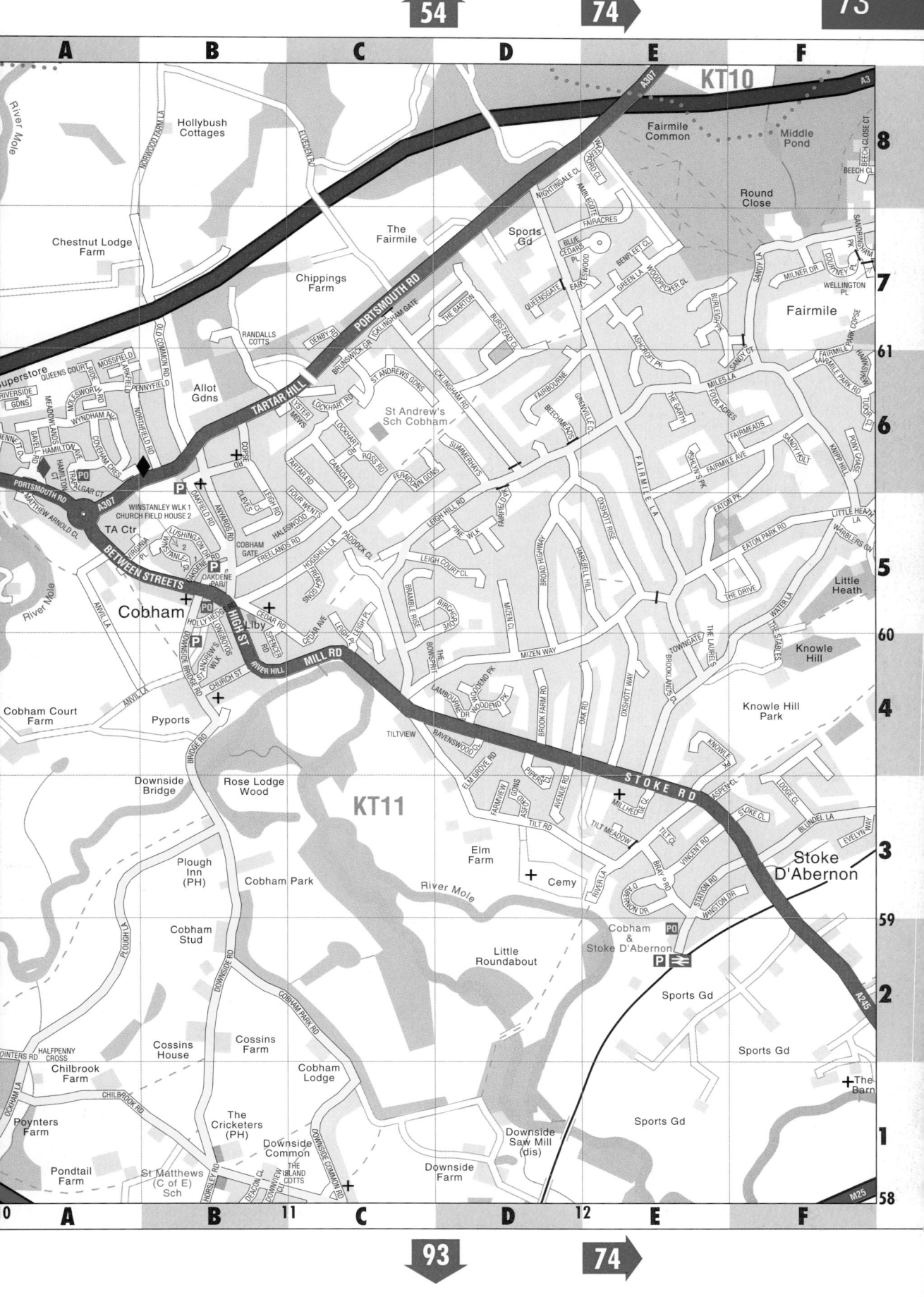

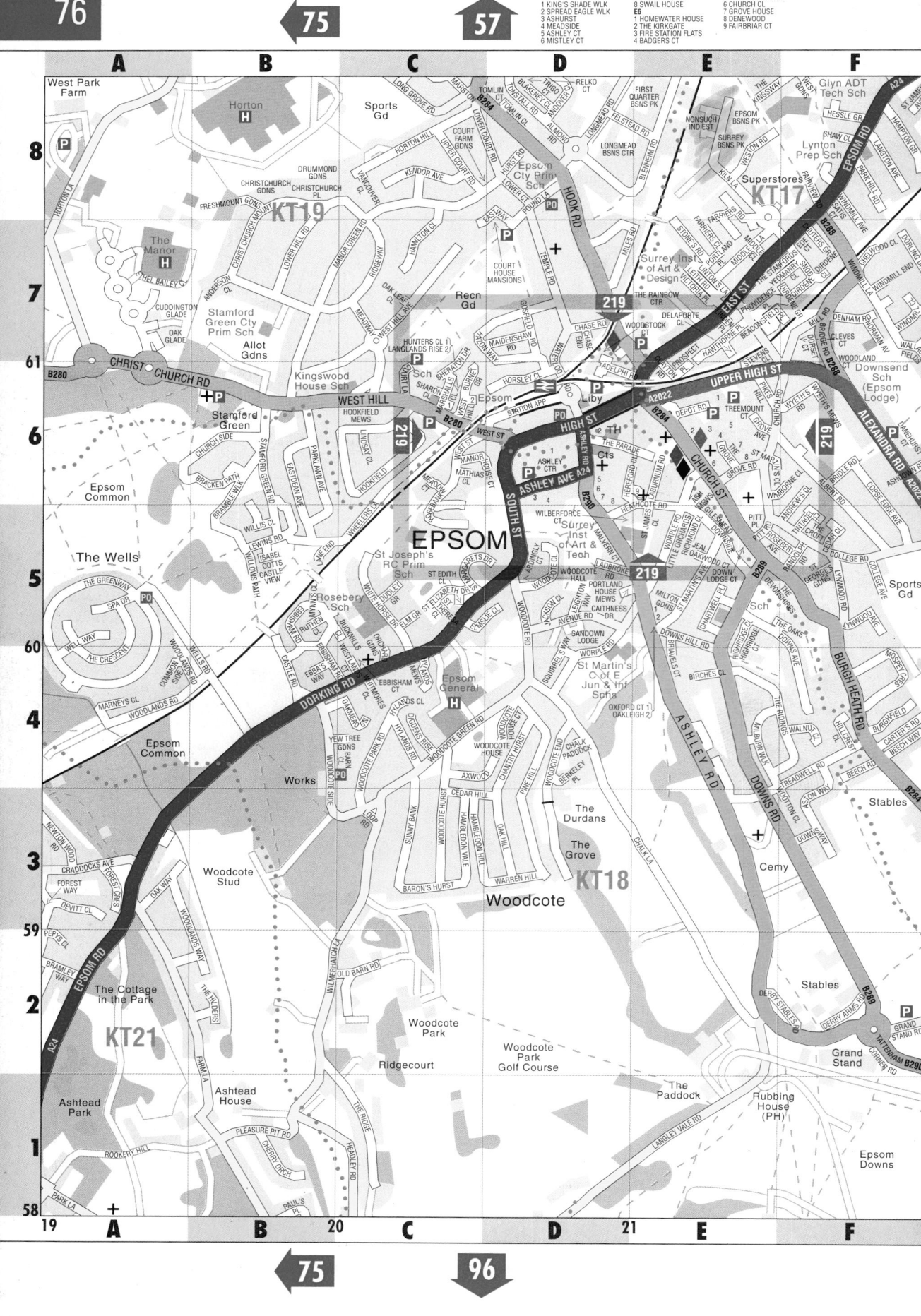

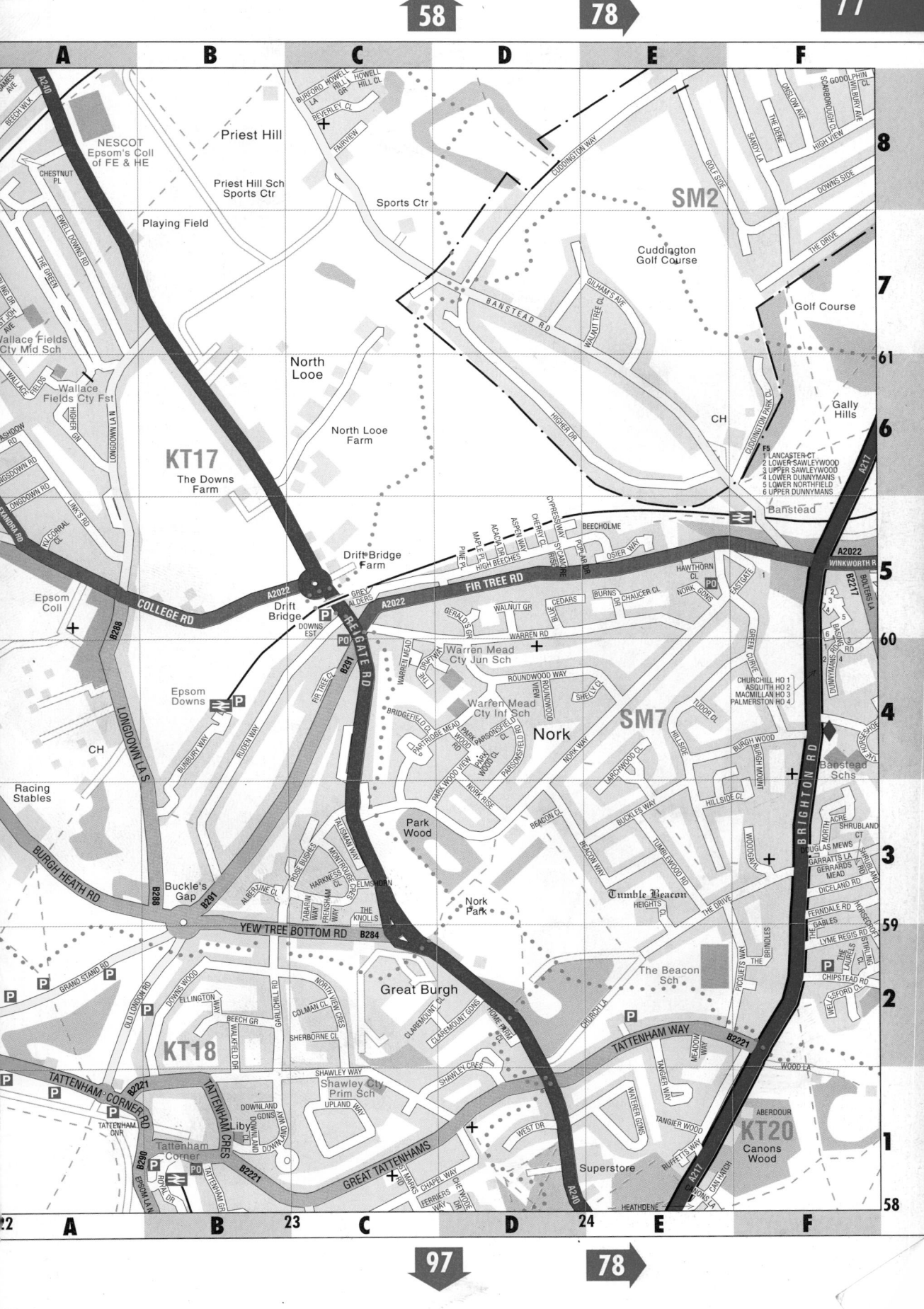

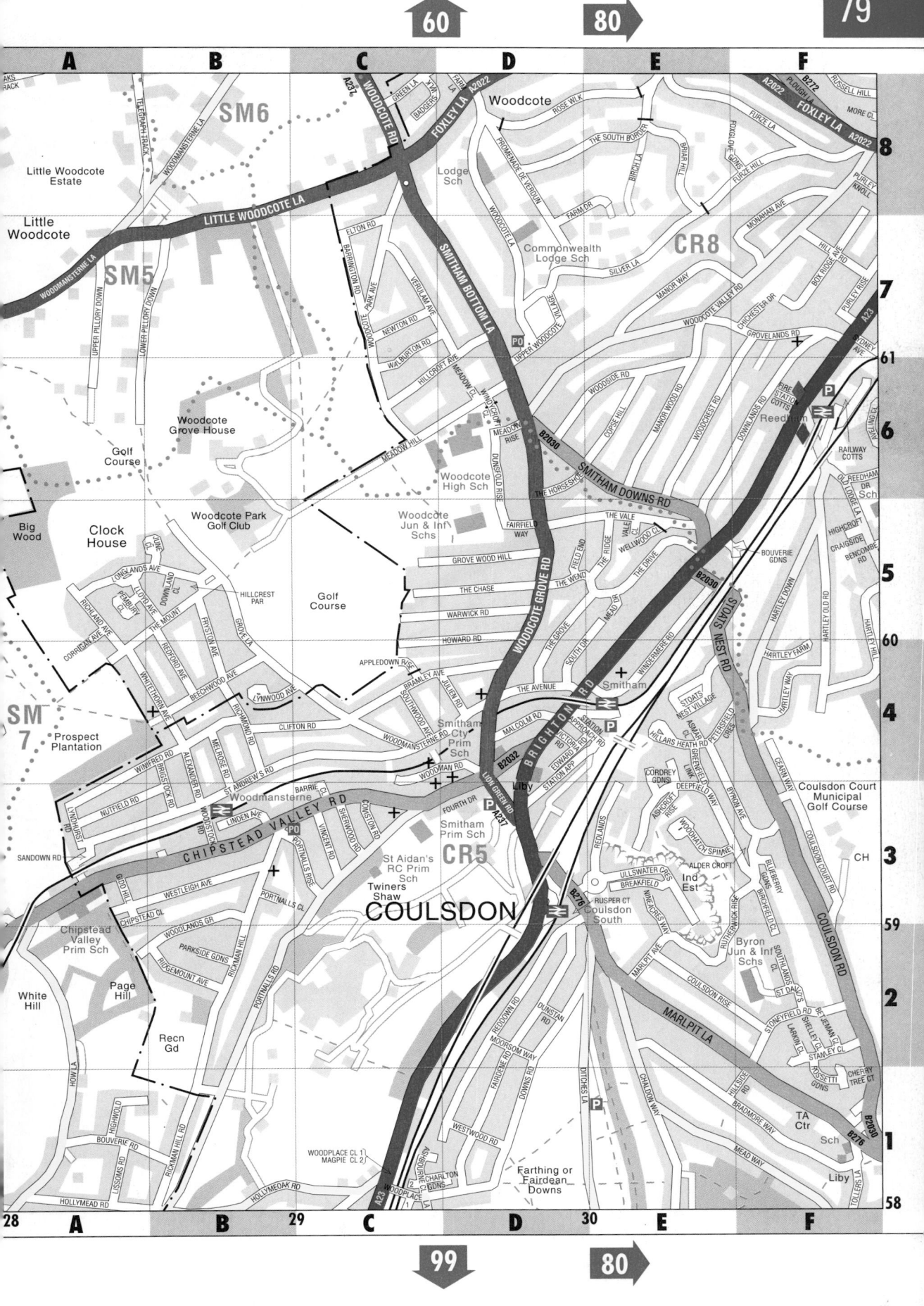

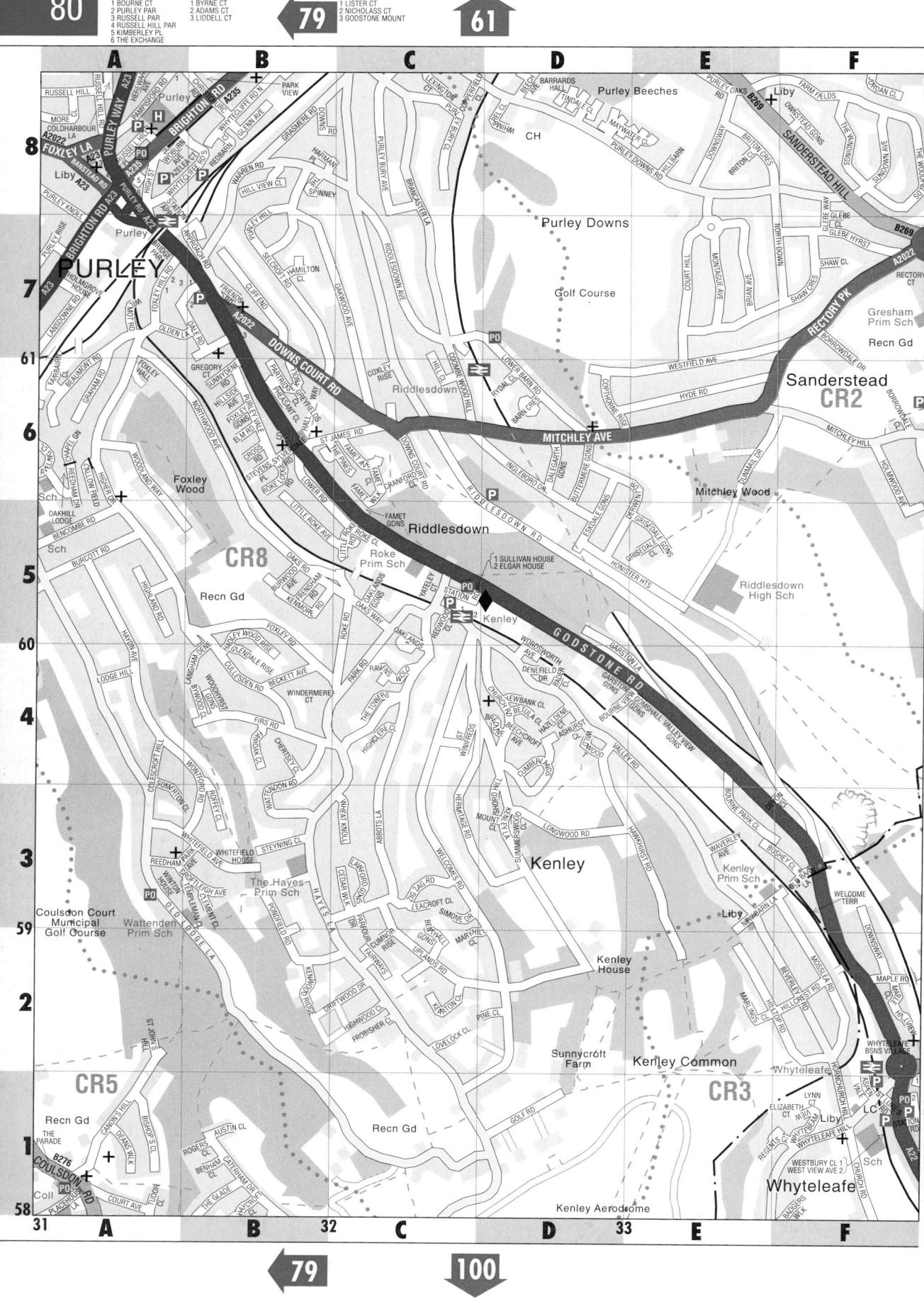

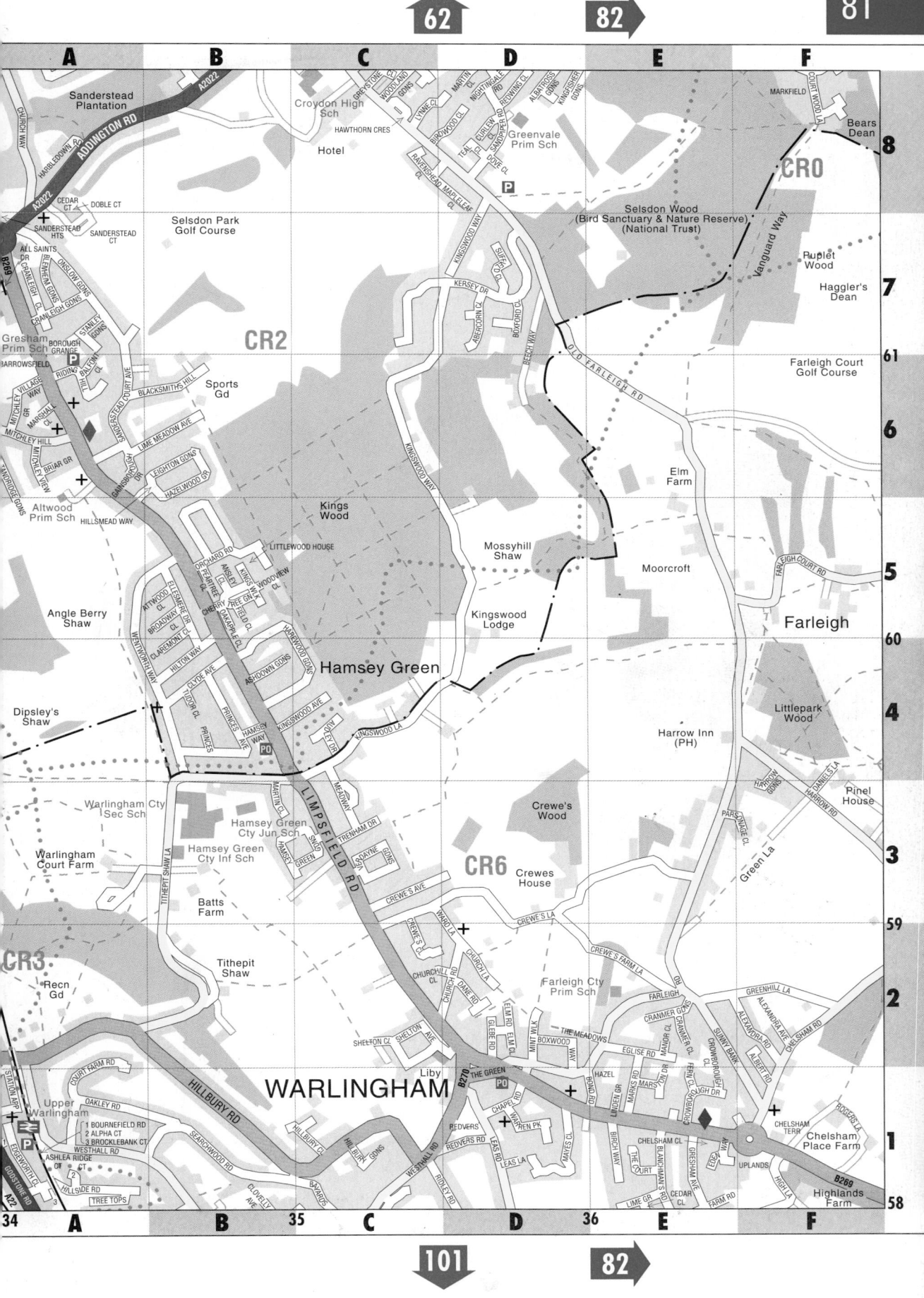

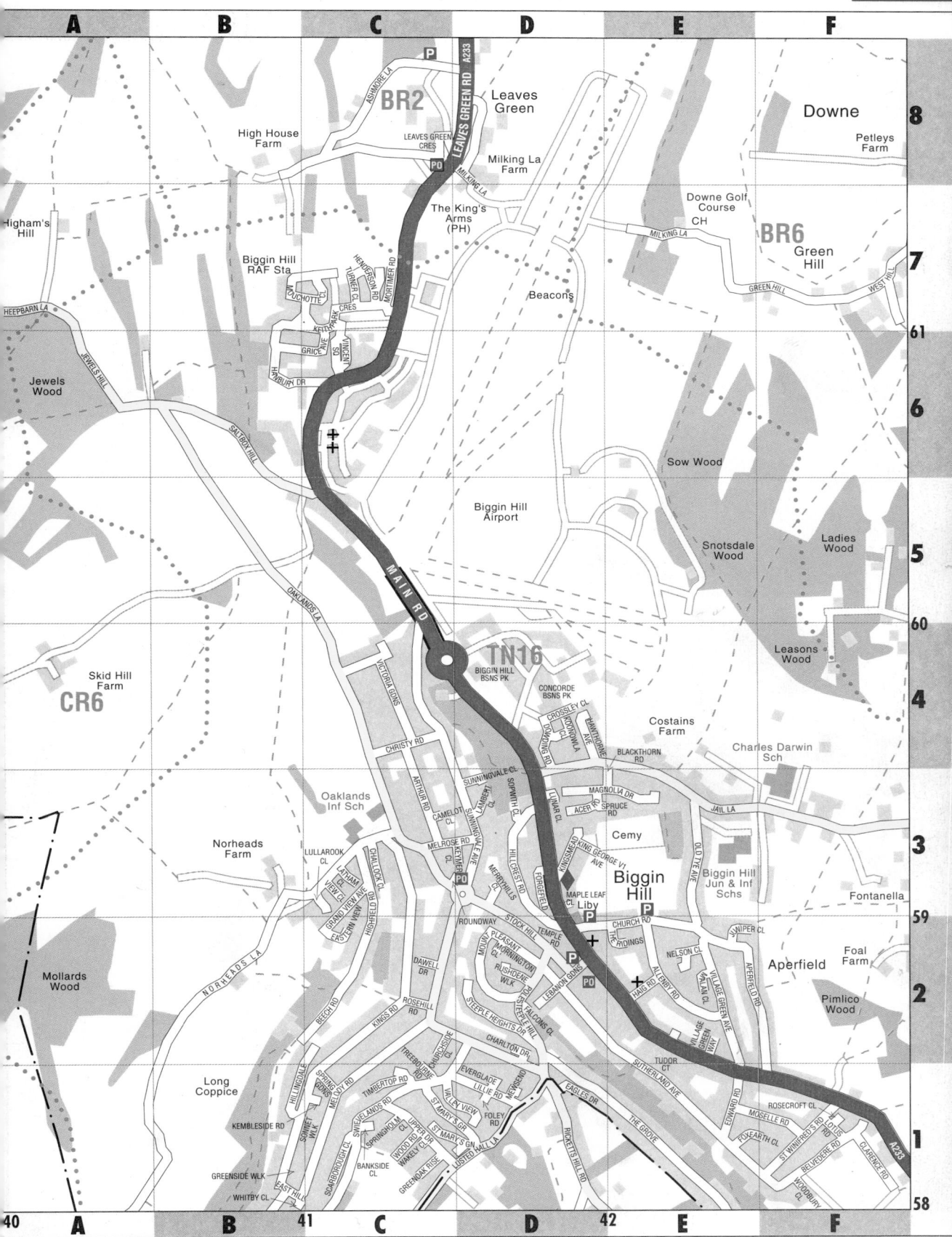

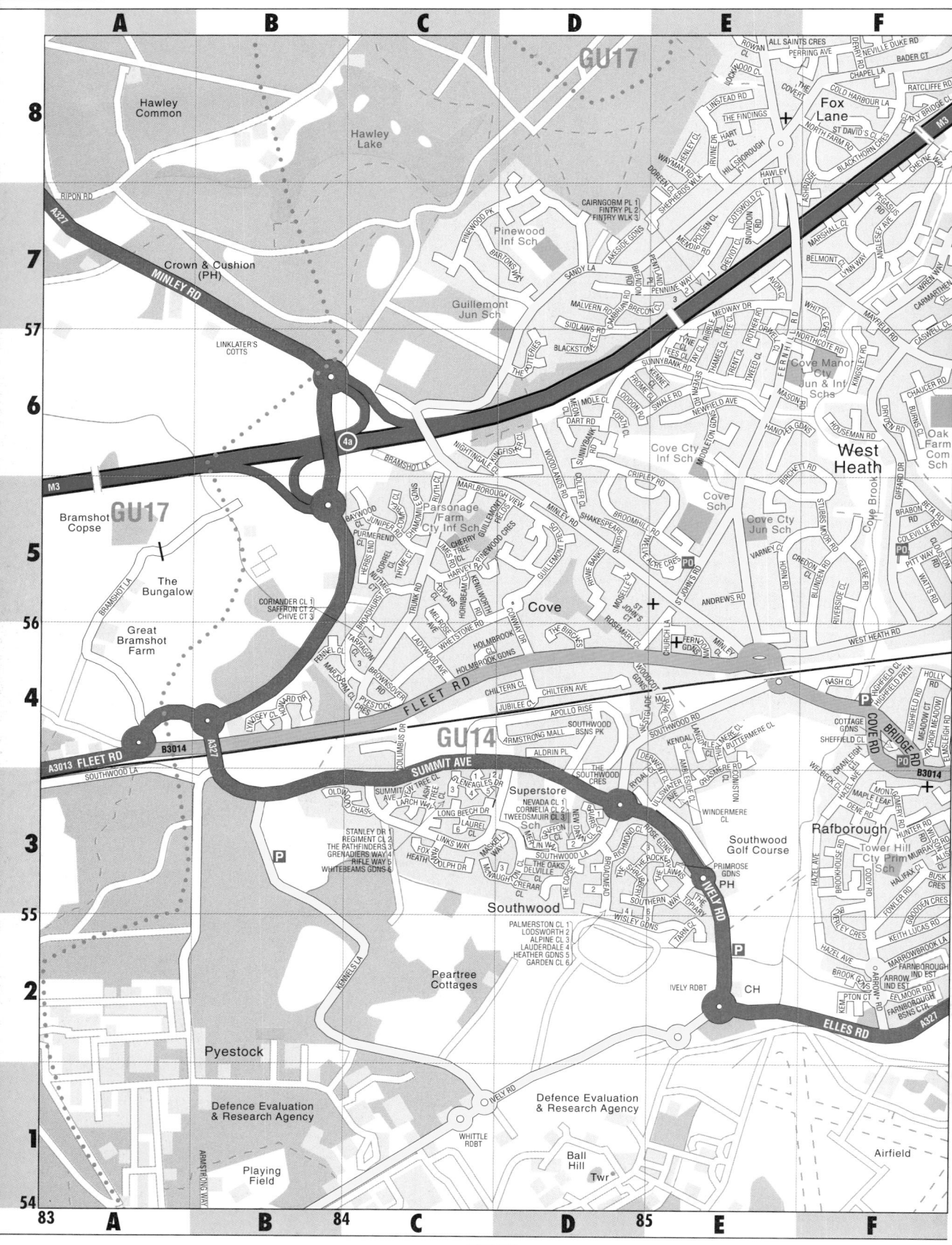

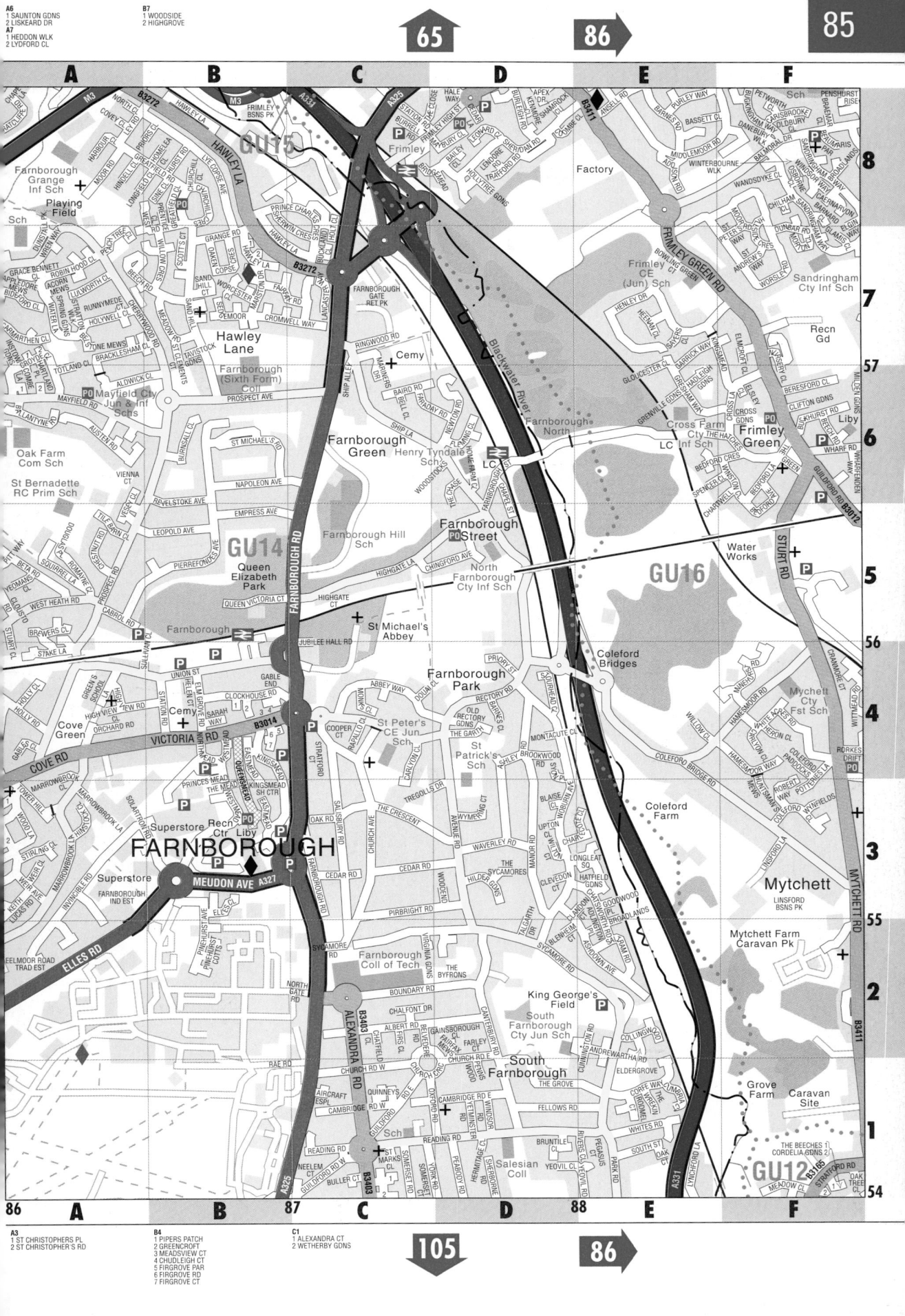

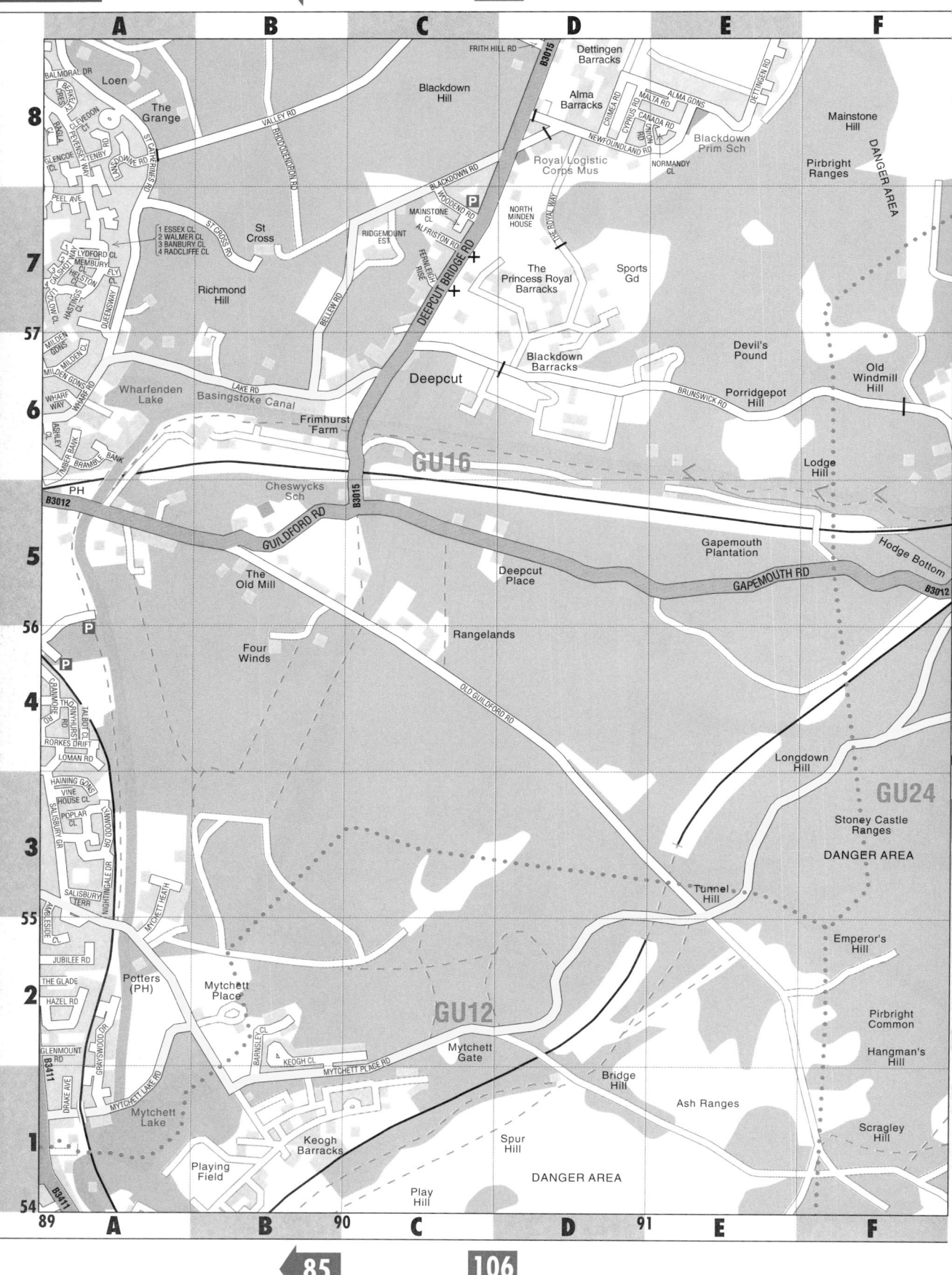

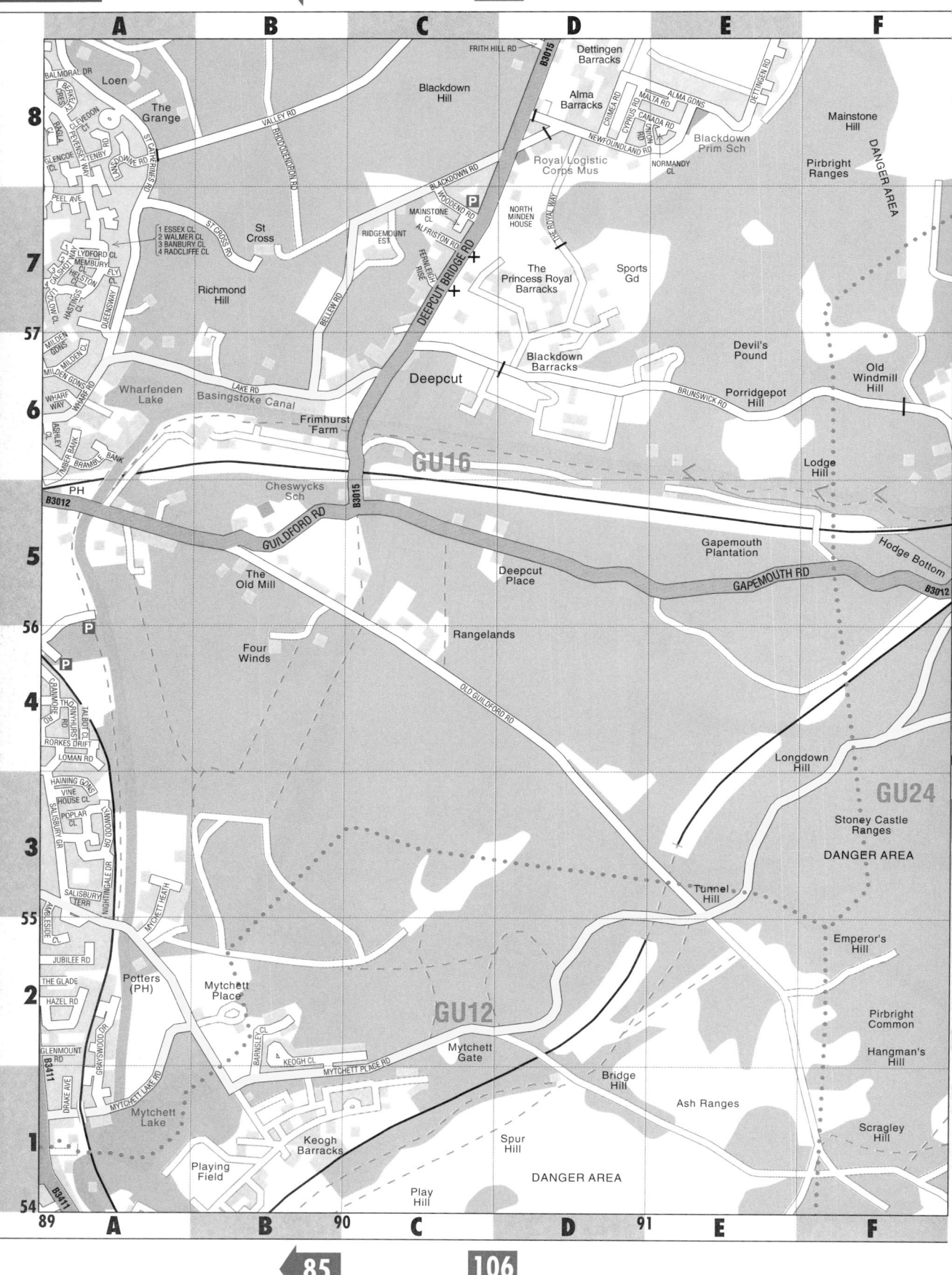

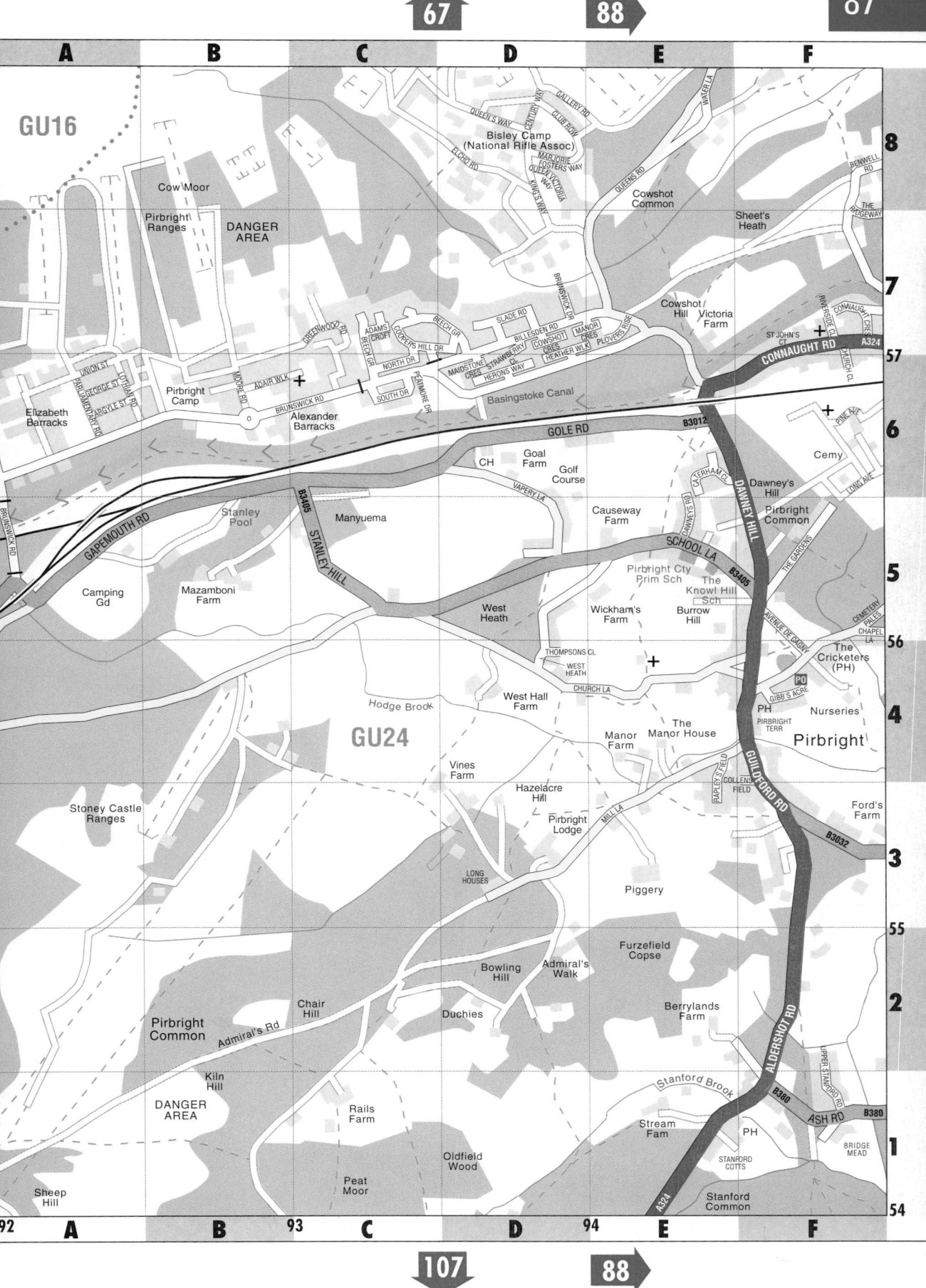

A B C D E F

GU16

8

Cow Moor

Pirbright
Ranges

DANGER
AREA

Bisley Camp
(National Rifle Assoc)

QUEEN'S WAY
CENTURY WAY
GALLERY RD
CLUB ROW

ECHO RD

MARJORIE
FOSTERS WAY
QUEEN VICTORIA
KING'S WAY

Cowshot
Common

QUEENS RD
WATER LA

Sheet's
Heath

BENWELL
RD

THE
RIDGEWAY

7

BRUNSWICK DR

SLADE RD
BILLESDEN RD
COWSHOT
CRES
MANOR
CRES
HEATHER WLK
PLOVERS RISE

Cowshot /
Hill
Victoria
Farm

ST JOHN'S
CT

RIVERSIDE CL
CONNAUGHT CRES
CHURCH CL
A324
CONNAUGHT RD

57

Elizabeth
Barracks

UNION ST
GEORGE ST
LOTHIAN RD
PARLIAMENTARY RD
ARGYLE ST

Pirbright
Camp

MOORE RD
ADAIR WLK

GREENWOOD RD

BEECH GR

ADAMS
CROFT
CLOCKERS HILL DR
NORTH DR
SOUTH DR

MAIDSTONE
CRES
STRAWBERRY CL
HERONS WAY

Alexander
Barracks

BRUNSWICK RD
PELHAM DR

PINE AVE

57

Basingstoke Canal

GOLE RD
B3012

Cemy

PINE AVE
LONG AVE

6

BRUNSWICK RD

GAPEMOUTH RD

Stanley
Pool

B3405
STANLEY HILL

Manyuema

CH

Goal
Farm
Golf
Course

VAPERY LA

Causeway
Farm

CATERHAM CL
DAWNEY'S CL

DAWNEY'S RD

Dawney's
Hill
DAWNEY HILL

Pirbright
Common

THE GARDENS

5

Camping
Gd

Mazamboni
Farm

West
Heath

SCHOOL LA
B3405

Pirbright Cty
Prim Sch
The
Knowl Hill
Sch

Wickham's
Farm
Burrow
Hill

AVENUE DE CAGNY

CEMETERY
PALES
CHAPEL
LA

56

THOMPSONS CL
WEST
HEATH
CHURCH LA

PO
GIBB'S ACRE
PH
PIRBRIGHT
TERR

The
Cricketers
(PH)

Nurseries

4

GU24

Hodge Brook

West Hall
Farm

Manor
Farm
The
Manor House

RAPLEY'S FIELD
COLLENS
FIELD

Pirbright

GUILDFORD RD

Ford's
Farm

Stoney Castle
Ranges

Vines
Farm

Hazelacre
Hill

Pirbright
Lodge

MILL LA

B3032

3

LONG
HOUSES

Piggery

55

Furzefield
Copse

ALDERSHOT RD

2

Pirbright
Common

ADMIRAL'S RD

Chair
Hill

Bowling
Hill

Admiral's
Walk

Duchies

Berrylands
Farm

UPPER STANFORD RD

Kiln
Hill

DANGER
AREA

Rails
Farm

Stanford Brook

Stream
Fam

PH

B380
ASH RD
B380

BRIDGE
MEAD

1

Sheep
Hill

Peat
Moor

Oldfield
Wood

STANFORD
COTTS

Stanford
Common

A324

54

A B 93 C D 94 E F

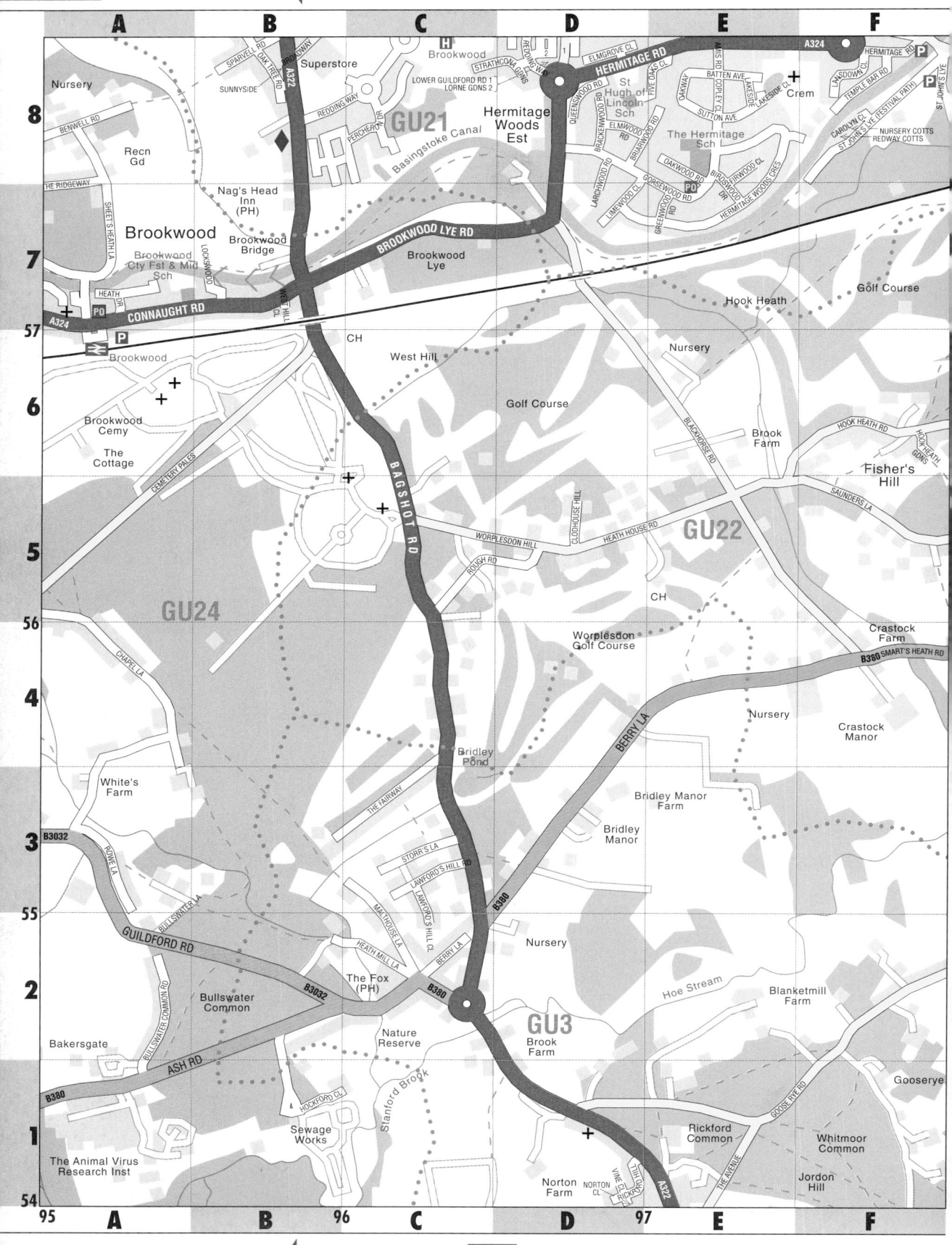

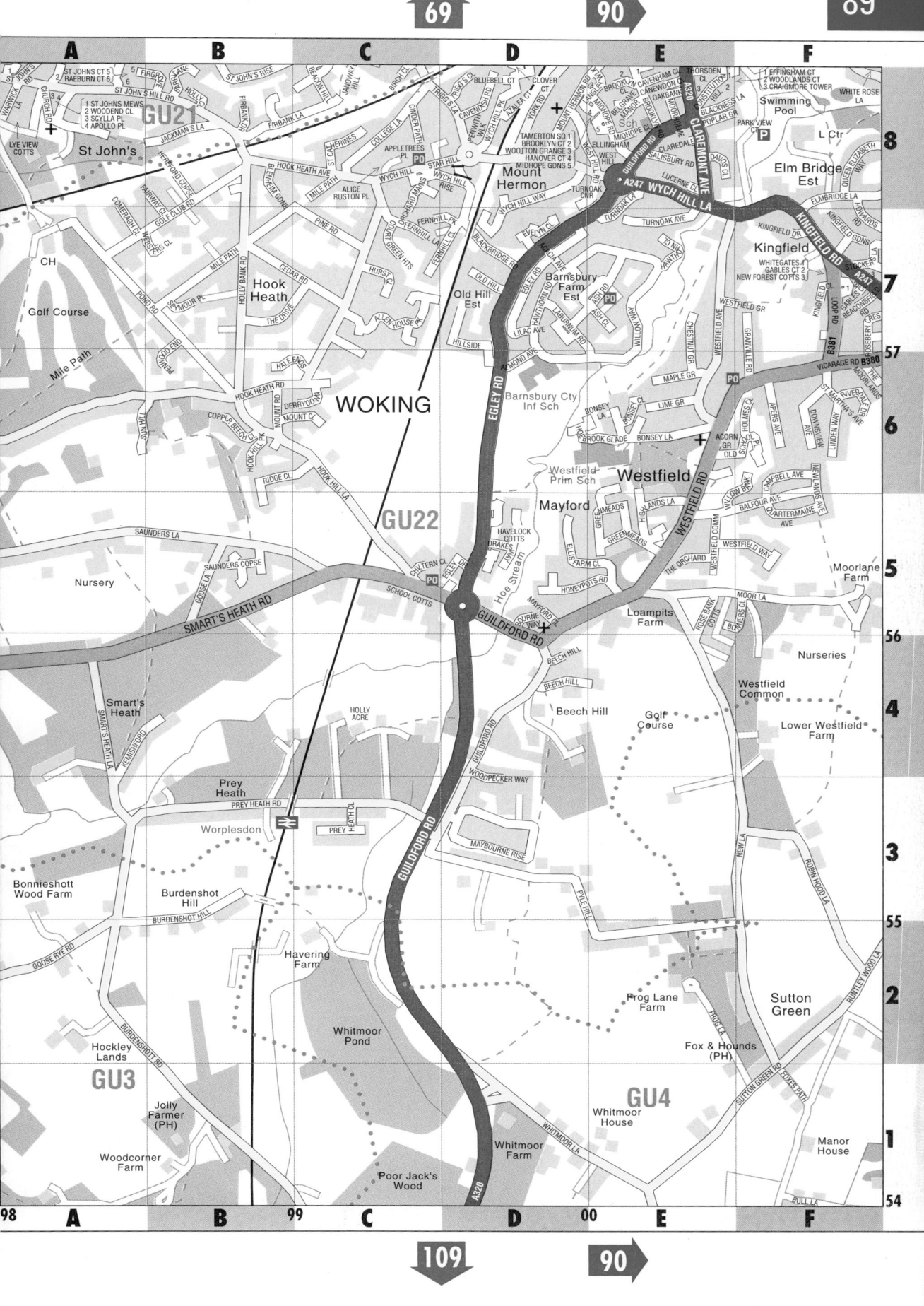

A   B   C   D   E   F

8
7
57
6
5
56
4
55
3
2
1
54

GU21

St John's

1 ST JOHNS CT 5
RAEBURN CT 6
St John's Rise
St John's Hill

LYE VIEW COTTS

1 ST JOHNS MEWS
2 WOODEND CL
3 SCYLLA PL
4 APOLLO PL

CH

Golf Course

Mile Path

Hook Heath Ave

Hook Heath

WOKING

GU22

SMART'S HEATH RD

Nursery

Saunders La

Saunders Copse

Smart's Heath

Holly Acre

Prey Heath

Worplesdon

Bonnieshott Wood Farm

Burdenshot Hill

Havering Farm

Hockley Lands

Jolly Farmer (PH)

Woodcorner Farm

GU3

Whitmoor Pond

Poor Jack's Wood

Whitmoor Farm

Mount Hermon

GUILDFORD RD

A320

WYCH HILL LA

A247

Egley Rd

Barnsbury Farm Est

Barnsbury Cty Inf Sch

Westfield Prim Sch

Mayford

Hoe Stream

School Cotts

Woodpecker Way

Maybourne Rise

Beech Hill

Golf Course

Guildford Rd

Whitmoor House

GU4

Manor House

Swimming Pool

L Ctr

Elm Bridge Est

Kingfield

WYCH HILL LA

Kingfield Rd

A247

B381

VICARAGE RD

B380

Westfield

Westfield Common

Westfield Comm

Loampits Farm

Moorlane Farm

Nurseries

Lower Westfield Farm

Sutton Green

Frog Lane Farm

Fox & Hounds (PH)

98   99   00

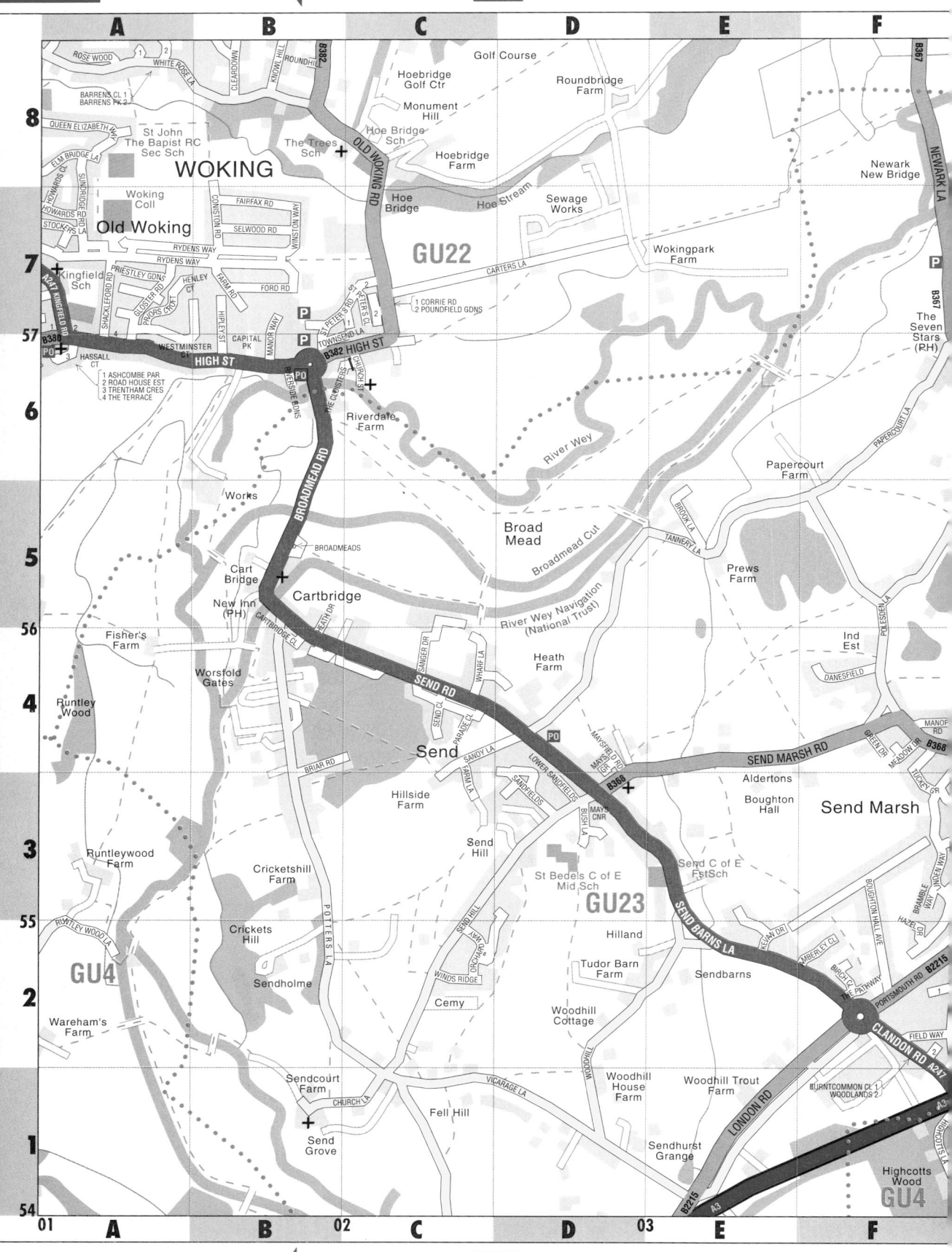

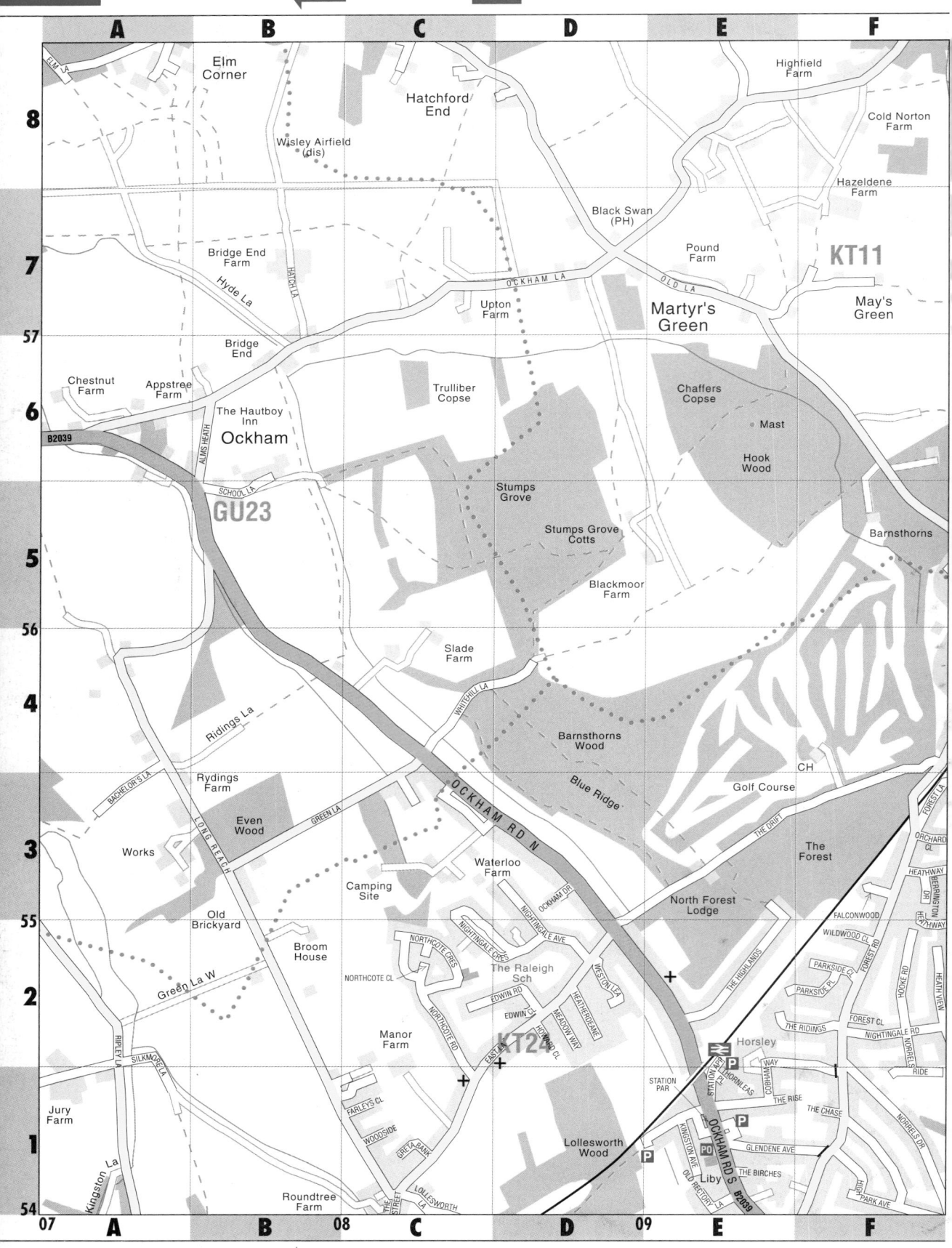

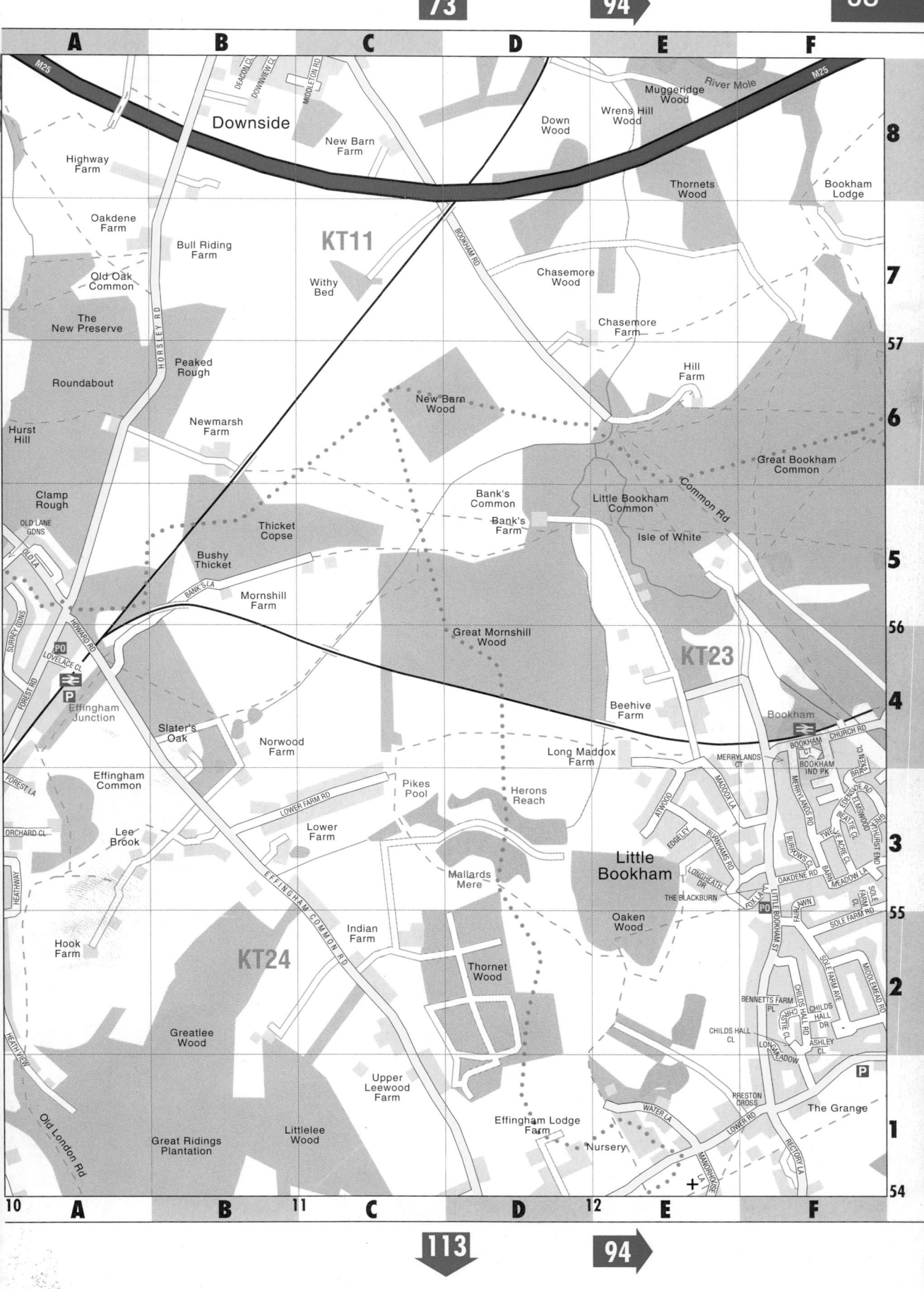

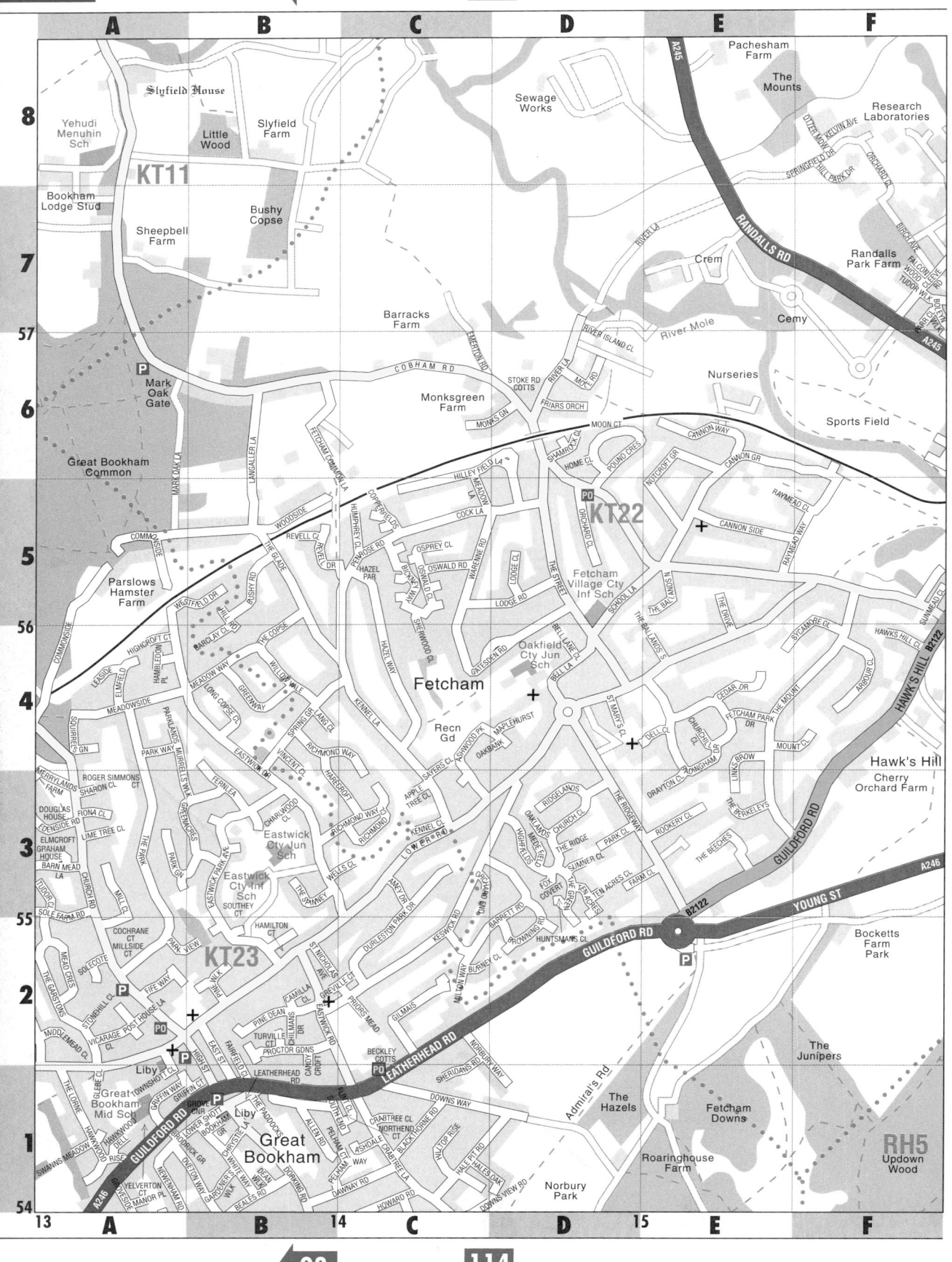

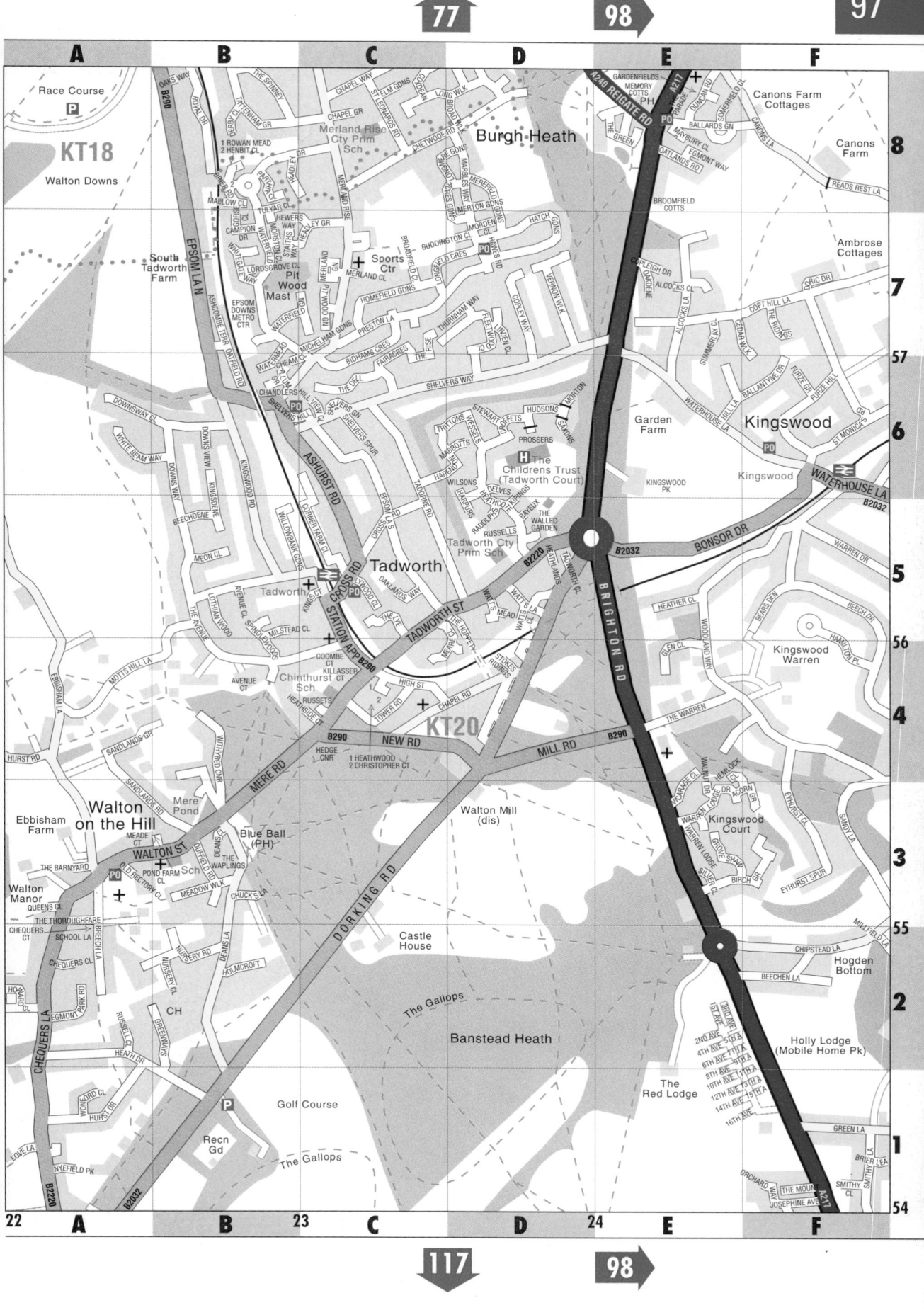

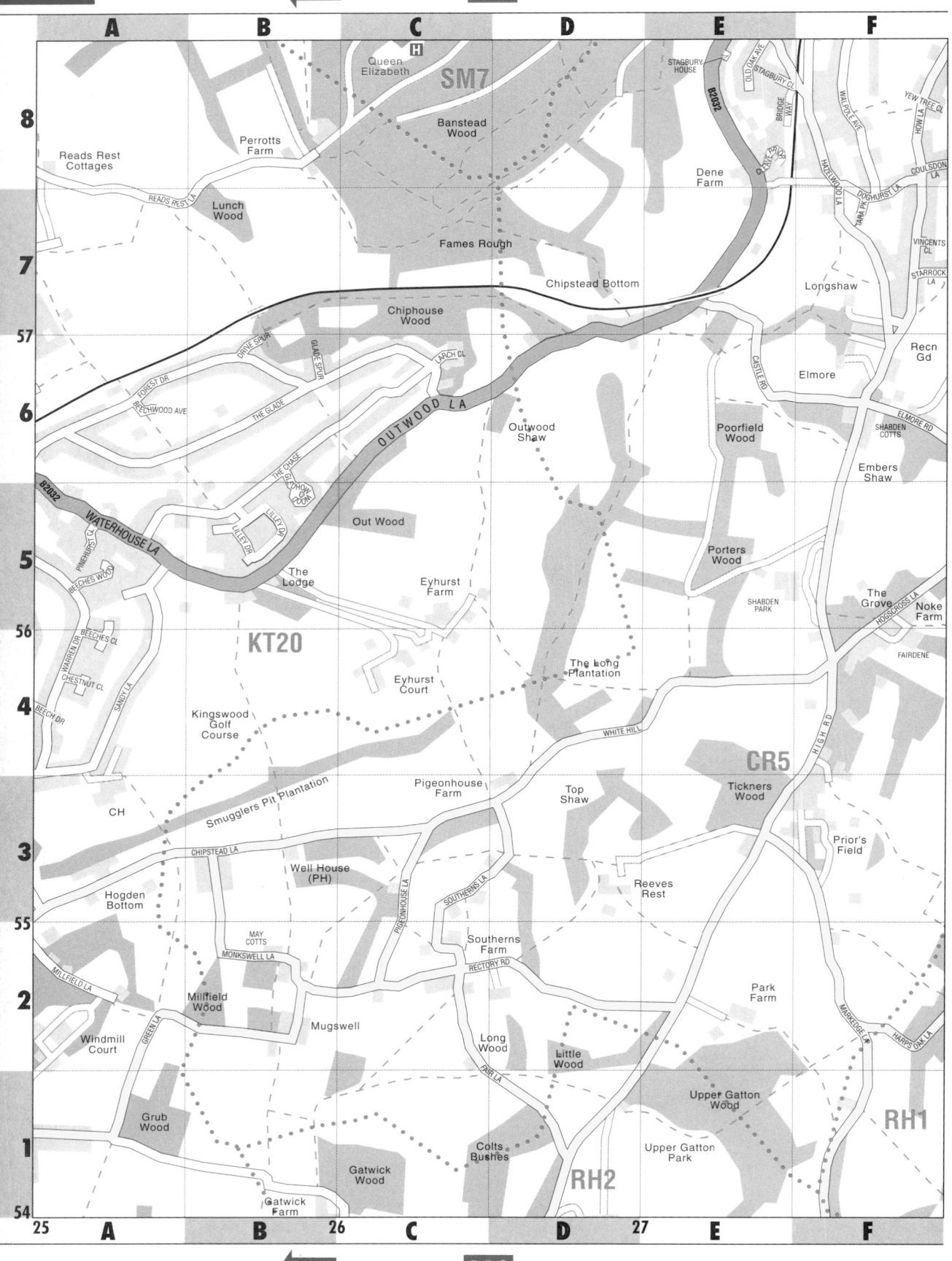

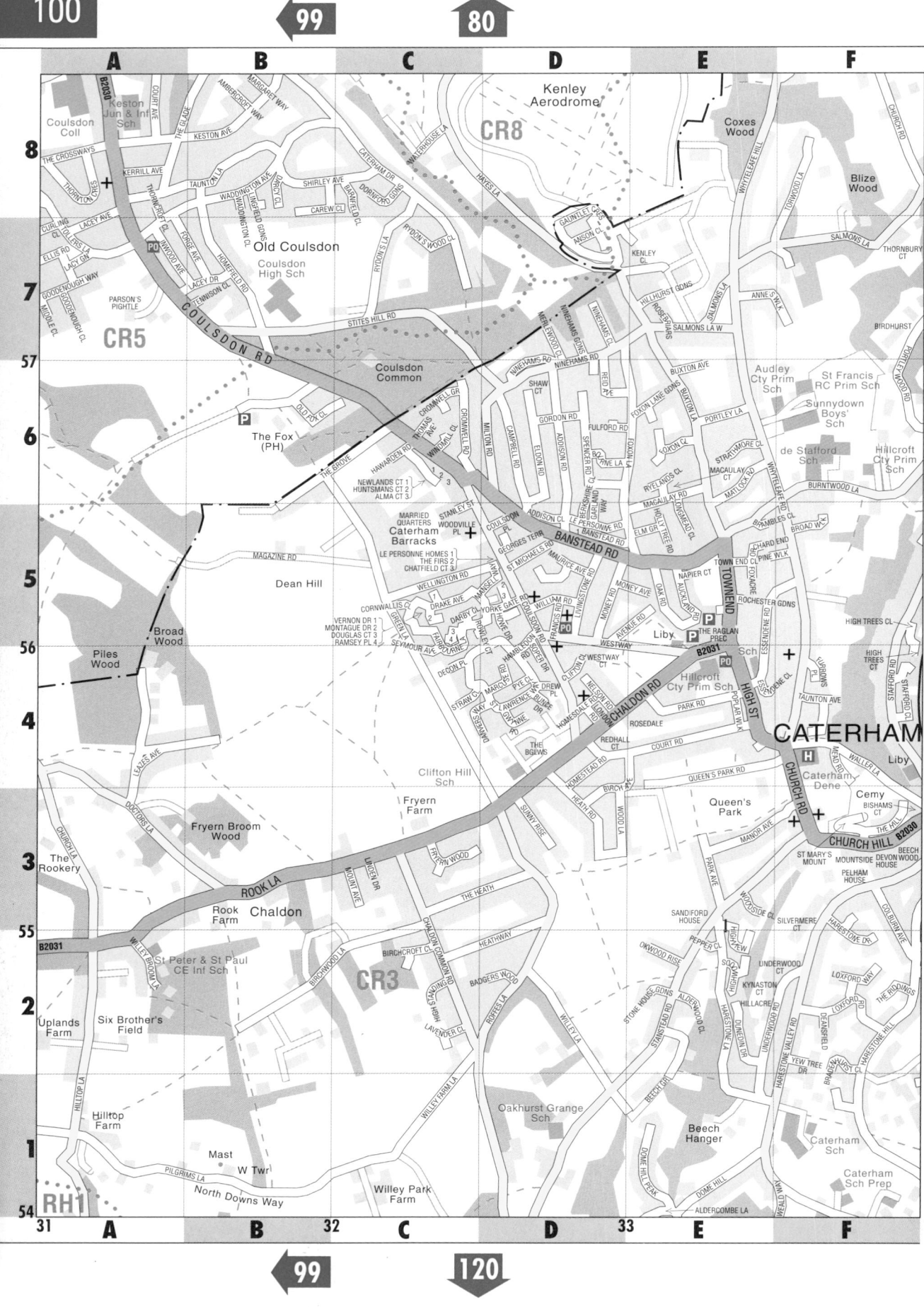

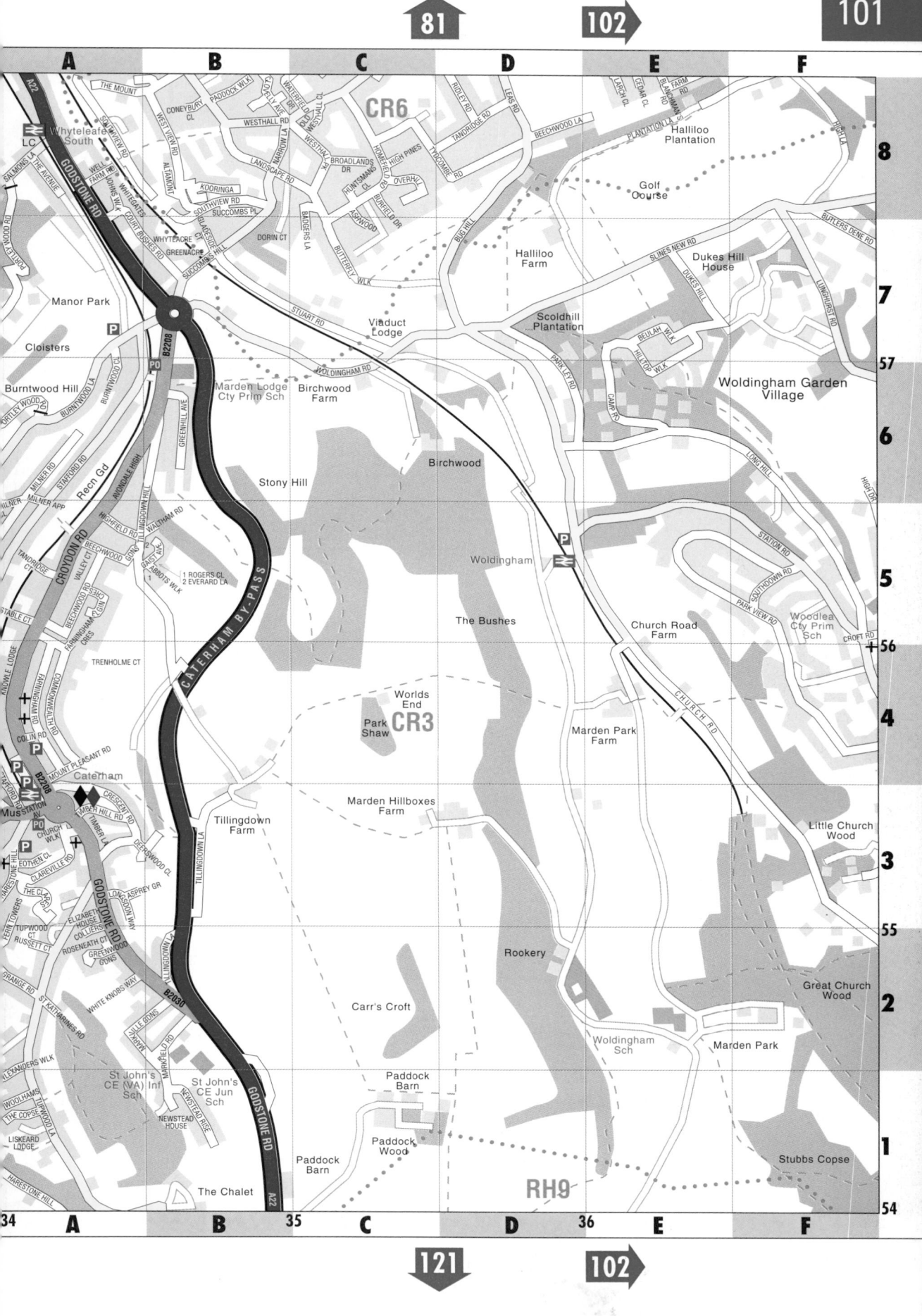

107 88

107 129

E1
1 BARGATE CT
2 FARLEIGH CT
3 ANSTON CT
4 PURBECK CT
5 EGERTON CT

F1
1 WEALDON CT
2 FRANKLIN CT
3 COACHLADS AVE

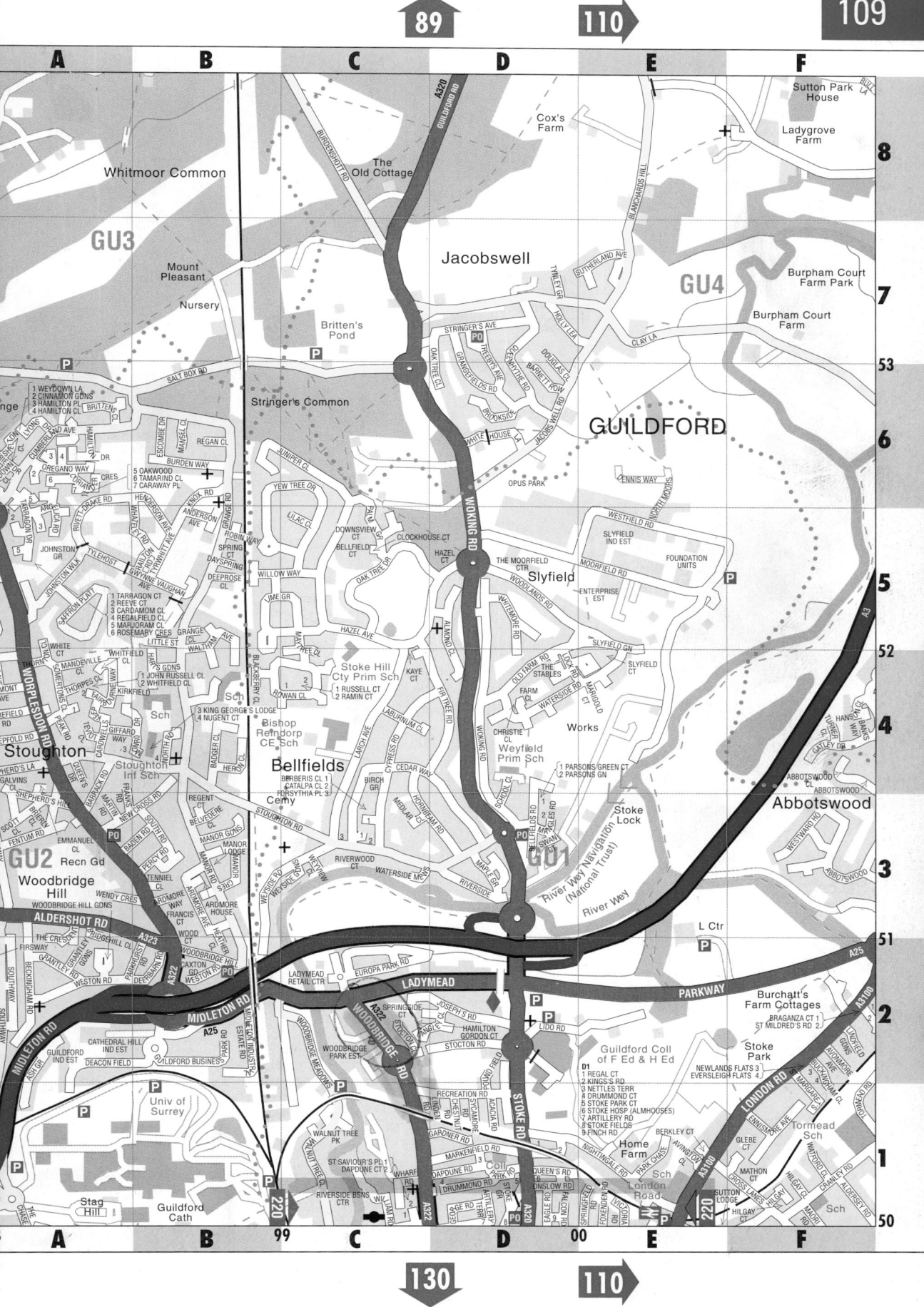

109
90

A B C D E F

8 Sutton Park
Sutton Boxes
GU23
Three Fords
Nutbourne Fruit Farm

Sutton Place
Whitehouse Farm
Nuthill Farm

7 Broadoak Bridge
River Wey Navigation
Frithys Wood

53 GUERNSEY CL 1
WATERSMEET CL 2
BOWERS CL 3
CHURCHFIELDS 4
ABINGER WAY 5
TYTHEBARN DR 6
WHIPLEY CL 7
NEWARK CL 8
SHETLAND CL 9
River Wey

6 Bowers Mill
CLAY LA
A3100
Gosden Hill Farm House
Cotts Wood

Burpham Prim Sch
Superstore
A3100
Oak Hill
GREAT OAKS PK
MEAD WAY
MERROW LA
Dillon Cottages

5 A3
Burpham
Burpham La
ORCHARD RD
GOSDEN HILL RD
GU4
Merrow Depot

52 ALFORD CL
LONDON RD
B2234
GROSVENOR
NEW INN LA
Merrow BSNS CTR
KEEPERS CL
MERROW BSNS CTR

4 Bridge Wks
Merrow Common
1 PLATT MEADOW
2 BURLINGHAM CL
3 DANSES CL
4 KIMBER CT
5 MULBERRY CT
Clandon Park

George Abbot Sch
MERROW WOODS
Temple Court

3 Bushy Hill
Sch
Park La
1 POND HOUSE
2 PADDOCK HOUSE
3 STILE HOUSE
4 MARES FIELD HOUSE
5 MEADOW HOUSE
6 POYLE HOUSE
7 BROWELL HOUSE
8 ORCHARD HOUSE

51 A3100
A25
BROCKWAY LA
Bushy Hill Jun Sch
B2234
EPSOM RD
A2

2 BOXGROVE RD
St Peter's RC Comp Sch
Merrow
EPSOM RD
A25
P PO

GU1
Boxgrove Cty Prim Sch
EPSOM RD
GUILDFORD

1 A25
Guildford Golf Club
MERROW CT
Golf Course

50 HILLIER MEWS
A246
A246
A25

01 A B 02 C D 03 E F

109
131

A   B   C   D   E   F

8

LOLLESWORTH LA

Lollesworth Farm

Parkrow Copse

East Horsley

West Horsley

PH

Lollesworth Wood

OAKWOOD DR

OAKWOOD DR

B2039

FOREST RD

WOODLAND DR

WOODLAND CL

WOODLAND

FRENCHLANDS HATCH

PENNYMEAD DR

PENNYMEAD DR RISE

Pennymead Lake

FRANGATE

HIGHER DR

LYNX HILL

7

Lower Hammond's Farm

RIPLEY LA

SKIMORE LA

THE STREET

TINTELLS LA

KENYONS

PICKSONS LA

FAIRWELL LA

PARK CORNER DR

Lower Pervers

MANOR CL

BISHOPSMEAD CL

HOLMWOOD CT

OCKHAM RD S

PINE WLK

FARM LA

HIGHFIELDS

FARM CL

House Pond

53

Dene Place

Pincott Farm

Barcombe Farm

PINCOTT LA

OVERBROOK

LITTLE CRANMORE LA

West Horsley Place

Fangate Manor Farm

St Martins CT

ST MARTINS CL

BISHOPSMEAD DR

FEARN CL

PO

BISHOPSMEAD PAR

GUILDFORD LODGE DR

Horsley Towers

6

Upper Hammonds Farm

OLD ST MARY'S

SCHOOL LA

MOUNT PLEASANT

CRANMORE LA

Britains Farm

Cranmore Sch

Nursery

EPSOM RD

P

B2039

Wellington Cotts

A24

Great Wix Wood

BUTLERS HILL

PO

Wix Farm

Poultry Farm

KT24

LONGHURST RD

ROWBARNS WAY

THE WARREN

GU4

52

A246

BLAKES LA

Wix Hill

JEFFRIES RD

Weston Wood

Angel Clump

CHALK LA

LARK RISE

LONDON CROSS

5

4

Woolgars Farm

Wix Hill House

Wix Hill Stables

The Sheepleas

SHERE RD

Green Dene Plantation

GREEN DENE

CROCKNORTH RD

Coles Copse

3

GU4

51

Daws Dene

P

Pebblehill Farm

PEBBLE HILL

Hillside Farm

P

Sheep Leas (Forest Walk)

HONEYSUCKLE BOTTOM

Dick Focks Common

2

Hook Wood

Fullers Farm

FULLERS FARM RD

Woodcote Lodge

SHERE RD

Mountain Wood

Troy Bridge

SHEEPWALK LA

1

GU5

Woodcote Farm

Upper Weston Wood

King's Hills

RH5 →

50

113
94

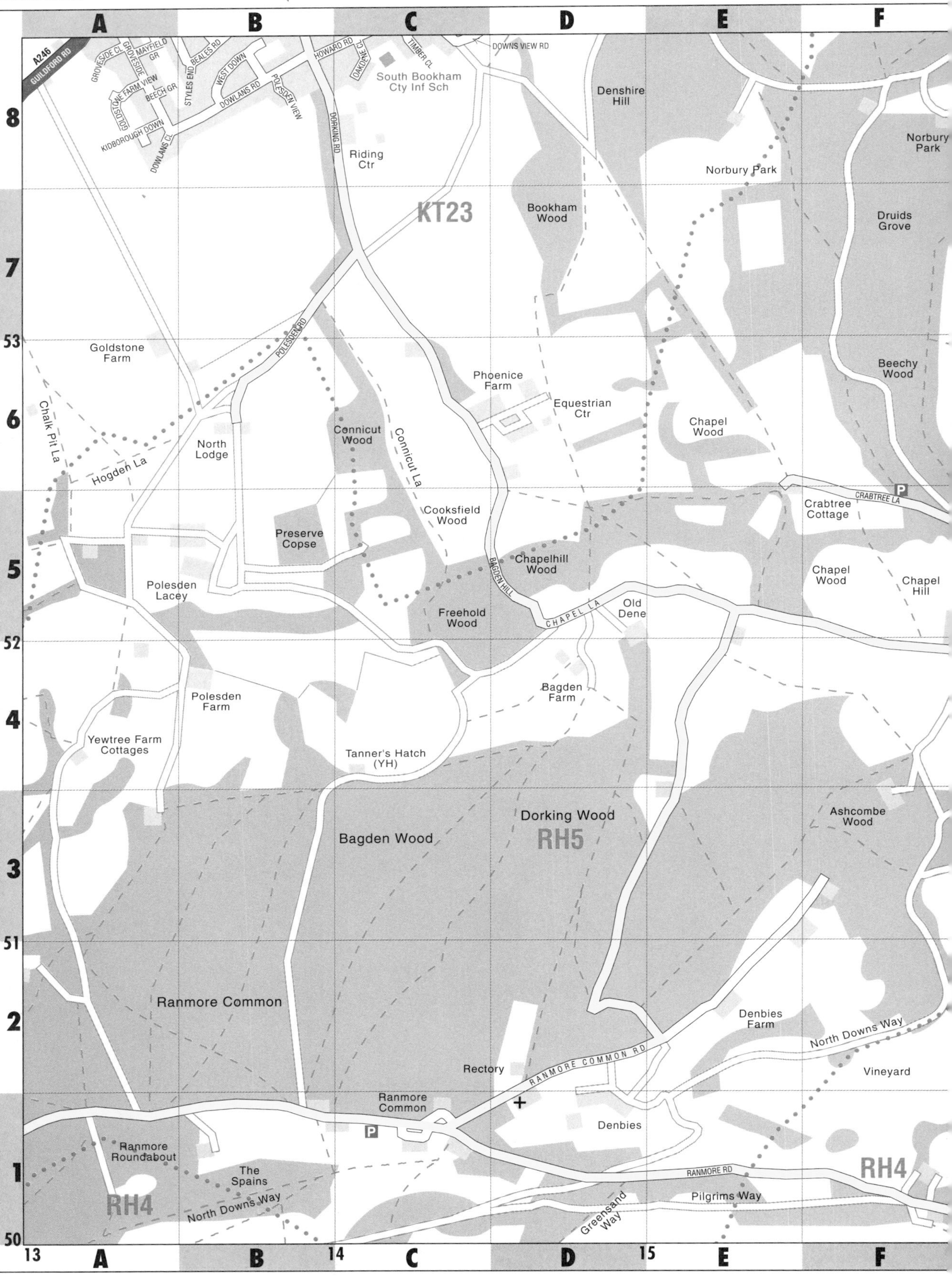

A246
GUILFORD RD

GROVESIDE CL
GROVESIDE
MAYFIELD GR
GOLDSTONE FARM VIEW
BEECH GR
KIDBOROUGH DOWN
DOWLANS CL
STYLES END
WEST DOWN
BEALES RD
DOWLANS RD
HOWARD RD
DAKDEN CL
POLESDEN VIEW
DORKING RD
TIMBER CL
DOWNS VIEW RD

South Bookham Cty Inf Sch

Denshire Hill

Norbury Park

KT23

Riding Ctr

Bookham Wood

Norbury Park

Druids Grove

Goldstone Farm

POLESDEN RD

Phoenice Farm

Equestrian Ctr

Chapel Wood

Beechy Wood

Chalk Pit La

North Lodge

Connicut Wood

Connicut La

Cooksfield Wood

CRABTREE LA

Crabtree Cottage

P

Hogden La

Preserve Copse

BAGDEN HILL

Chapelhill Wood

Chapel Wood

Chapel Hill

Polesden Lacey

Freehold Wood

CHAPEL LA

Old Dene

Polesden Farm

Bagden Farm

Yewtree Farm Cottages

Tanner's Hatch (YH)

Dorking Wood

RH5

Ashcombe Wood

Bagden Wood

Ranmore Common

Denbies Farm

North Downs Way

Rectory

RANMORE COMMON RD

Vineyard

Ranmore Common

P

Denbies

Ranmore Roundabout

RANMORE RD

RH4

RH4

The Spains

North Downs Way

Pilgrims Way

Greensand Way

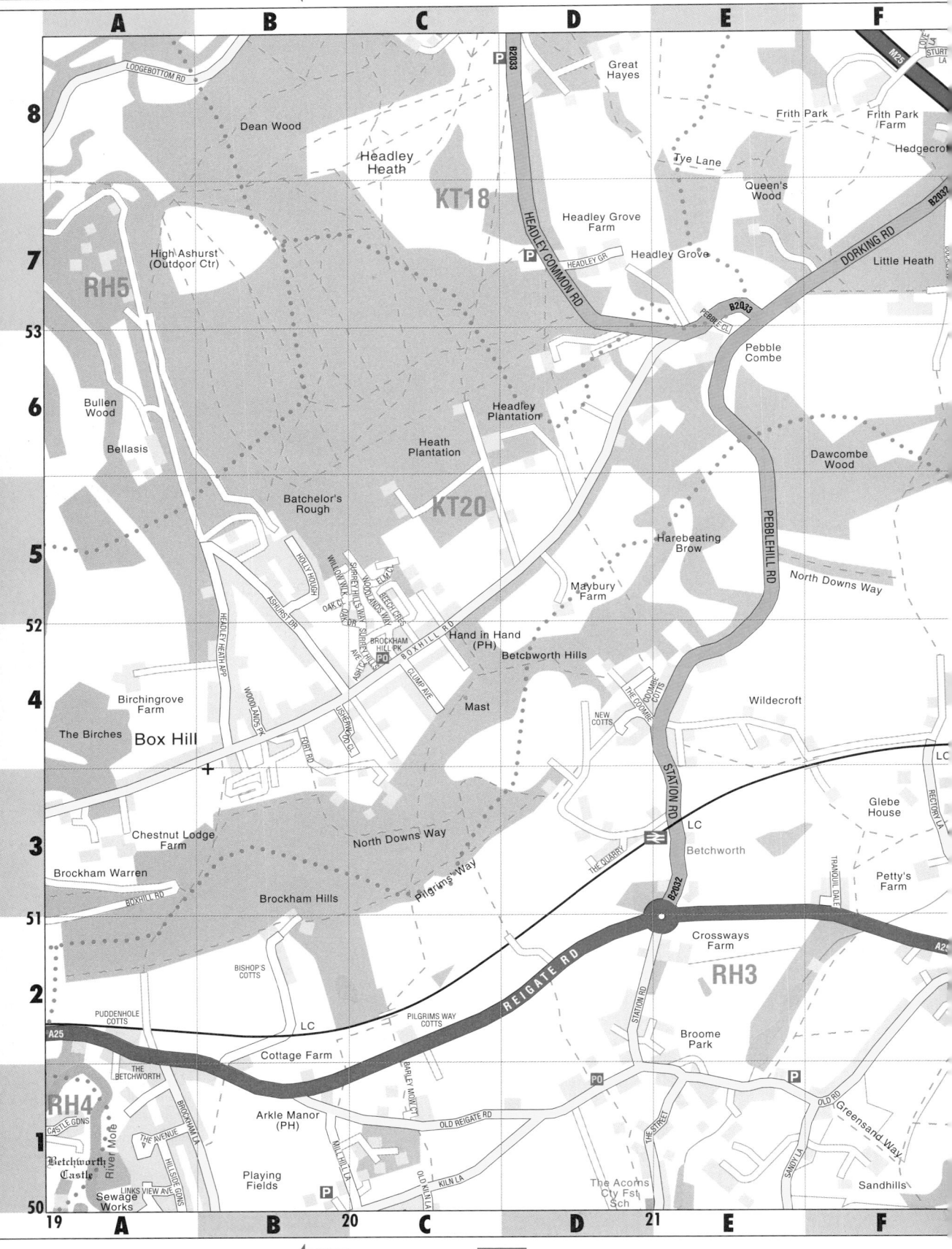

A2
1 SOMERS PL
2 FLANCHFORD HOUSE
3 CLAYHALL HOUSE
4 LITTLETON HOUSE

C1
1 VICTORIA ALMSHOUSES
2 EVERSFIELD CT
3 HILLBROW

D1
1 CLAIRVILLE CT
2 HIGHVIEW CT
3 TREEVIEW CT
4 HARLOW CT
5 WRAYMILL CT

F1
1 CROMWELL WLK
2 EDGEHILL HOUSE
3 MORRISS CT
4 OBSERVATORY WLK
5 WAVENEY HOUSE
6 GROVE HOUSE
7 ELY HOUSE
8 MAPLE HO
9 CHRISTCHURCH HTS
10 GLAMIS HO
11 ATHOLL HOUSE
12 DUNVEGAN HOUSE
13 STIRLING HOUSE
14 MARKETFIELD RD

F2
1 CHILMEAD
2 COLNE HOUSE
3 TAVY HOUSE
4 ROTHER HOUSE
5 WANDLE HOUSE
6 KENNET HOUSE
7 ORWELL HOUSE
8 WINDRUSH HOUSE
9 AVON HOUSE
10 HILLARY HOUSE
11 DOUGLAS HOUGHTON HOUSE
12 SQUIRRELS GN
13 CHILWORTH CT

1 PRINCESS HOUSE
2 LADBROKE COTTS
3 QUEENS CT
4 DIAMOND CT
5 ST ANNES WAY
6 CLEEVES CT
7 ST ANNES MOUNT
8 NIGHTINGALE CT
9 GABLE CT

10 HATHAWAY CT
11 BOLEYN CT
12 TUDOR CT
13 LENNOX CT
14 BRONTE CT
15 OAKLEY CT
16 STUART CT
17 CLYDE CT
18 LANCELOT HO
19 GIUNEVERE HO

20 GALAHAD HO
21 KNIGHTS PL
22 WARWICK QUADRANT
A3
1 ALTON HOUSE
2 SWALE HOUSE
3 BOVEY HOUSE
4 FRENCHES CT
5 PENRYN HOUSE
6 NASH DR

7 LADBROKE CT
8 PEBWORTH CT
9 BARFIELD CT
A4
1 RINGWOOD LODGE
2 DOWNS CT
3 LYNDALE CT
4 VICTORIA ALMSHOUSES
5 SPEEDWELL HOUSE
6 CAMPION HOUSE

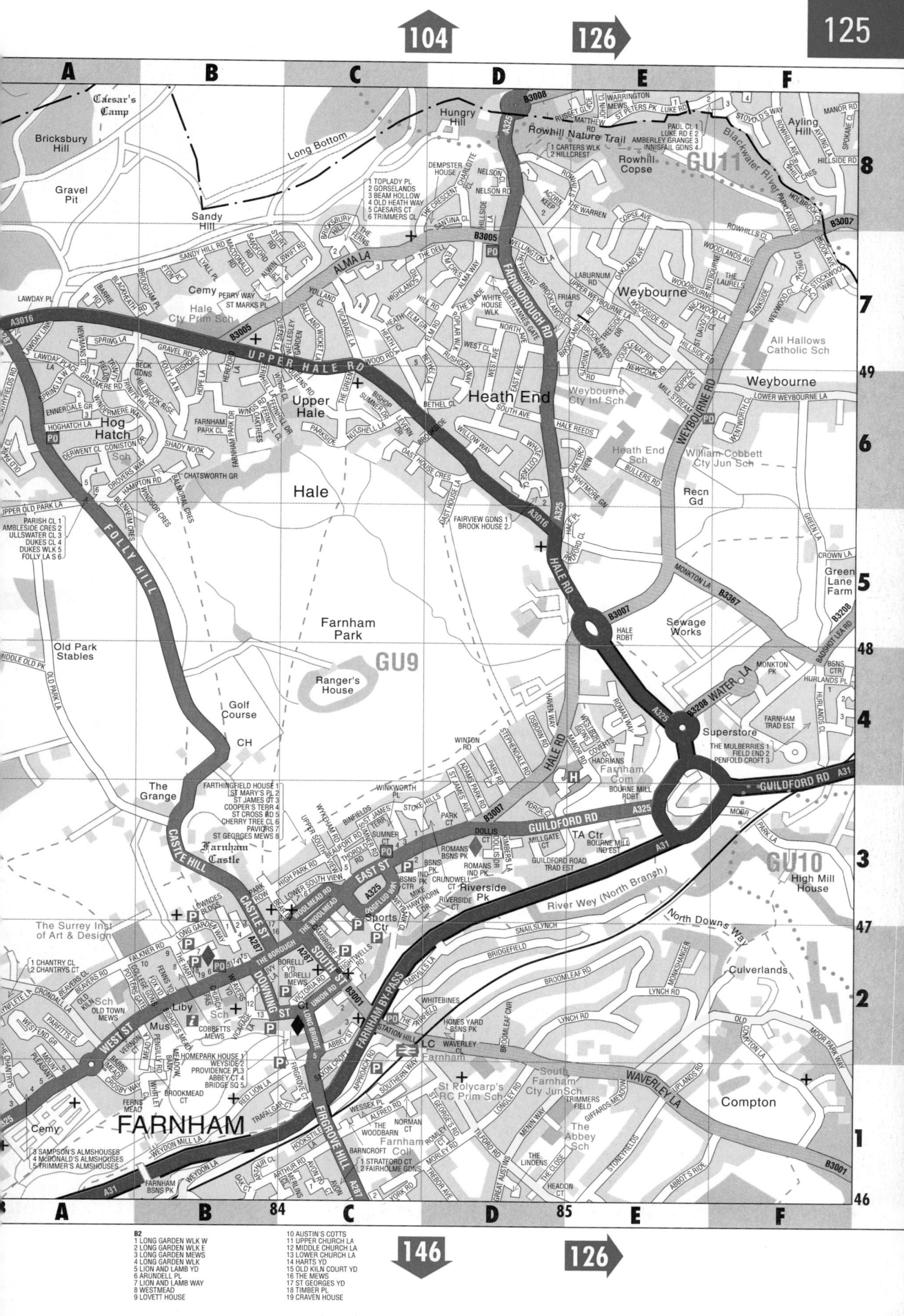

125
105

A B C D E F

GU3

Ash Green

Pound Farm

POUND FARM LA

Week Wood

8

Bin Wood

ASH GREEN LA W

ASH GREEN LA E

GU12

GREEN LA W

Rickwood Farm

NORTH SIDE

EAST RING

St Paul's CE/Inf Sch

SOUTH SIDE

Poyle Farm

POYLE RD

PILGRIMS VIEW

HAZEL RD

WHITE LA

Grubground Copse

7

49

Poyle Park

Whitegrass Copse

6

White Lane Farm

Inwood Farm

Hog's Back Hotel

A31

5

Nature Reserve

WOOD LA

P

Downlands

Great Down

Stony Hill

MANOR FIELDS

Manor Farm Craft Ctr

Seale

Eastend Farm

Williams Copse

48

SEALE LA

Shoelands Farm

SEALE LA

4

SCHOOL HILL

Seale CE Fst Sch

PUTTENHAM RD

GU10

North Downs Way

TOTFORD LA

Little Common

Payn's Firs

ELSTEAD RD

Totford Wood

Totford Hatch

Long Bottom

Lascombe Farm

3

47

Binton Wood

The Roughs

Trout Pond

Hillbury

GU3

2

Owlshatch

Hampton

Hampton Park

Long Pond

Puttenham Common

Picnic Area

P

The Ridge

General's Pond

1

LITTLEWORTH RD

Coach Bottom

Warren Pond

SUFFIELD LA

46

9 A B 90 C D 91 E F

A   B   C   D   E   F

8

Christmaspie

BEECH LA

ORCHARD CL

CHRISTMASPIE AVE

FLEXFORD RD

LAURELDENE

GREEN LA E

Long
Common

WEST FLEXFORD LA

West Flexford
Farm

Homestead
Farm
Pond Hill

WESTWOOD LA

Broadmead
Row

Greencut
Copse

EAST FLEXFORD LA

**GU
12**

Wanborough
Wood

7

49

Wanborough
Manor

+

GU3

6

Wanborough

Manor
Farm

Flexford
House

WANBOROUGH HILL

GU10

Hog's Back

A31

A31

Greyfriars

5

P   Picnic
Area

B3000

Puttenham Hill

Greyfriars
Farm

PUTTENHAM HILL

48

Puttenham Sch
CE (VA)

Clear
Barn

Monkgrove
Copse

4

SEALE LA   DARK

MUNDAY'S BORO

SCHOOL LA

THE STREET

+

Priory

P

P

CH

Cemy

North Downs Way
Puttenham Heath

MUNDAY'S BORO RD

LASCOMBE LA

Jolly
Farmer
(Inn)

Golf Course
Wanborough Common

Little
Common

Little
Lascombe

Puttenham

Suffield
Farm

PUTTENHAM HEATH RD

3

HIGHFIELD LA

HOOK LA

Hurlands

B3000

A3

47

Gore's
Farm

Westbur
Barn

2

SUFFIELD LA

Church
Croft

Lone
Barn

PRIORSFIELD LA

PRIORS WOOD

PUTTENHAM LA

New
Barn

1

GU8

GU7

A3

Prior's
Wood

Lydling
Farm

Abbot's
Wood

PRIORS HATCH LA

46

92   A   B   93   C   D   94   E   F

A B C D E F

Wildfield Copse

Misley Copse

Strawberry Grove

The Surrey Research Pk

Nugent Rd
McLaurin Rd
Priestley Rd
Occam Rd
Huxley Rd
Gill Ave

Rosalind Franklin Cl

Royal Surrey County

Egerton Rd

Dennisville

Downing Ave
Raymond Cres
Penreath Ave

Frederick Sanger Rd

The Priestley Ctr

The Philip Henman Sports Gd

Hotel

Queen Eleanor's Rd
West Meads
The Orchard Rd
Ellis Ave
Wilderness Rd
Windsor Cl
Powell Cl

Blackwell Farm

Manor Copse

GUILDFORD

GU2

8

Down Place

Manor Farm

Wilderness Ct
Onslow Cty Inf Sch

Onslow Village

Barnster's Rd
Litchfield Way
The Square
PO

7

Chalkpit Wood

Wellington Place

GUILDFORD AND GODALMING BY-PASS RD

The Crossways

49

Beechcroft Dr

High View Rd

Manor Way

Abbot's Cl

A31

FARNHAM RD

6

A31

A3

Compton Hts

Sunnydown Plantation

Mast

B3000

Down La

North Downs Way

The Watts Gallery

West Warren

East Warren

48

5

East Flexford La

Hurt Hills

GU3

4

Coneycroft Farm

Polsted Manor

Losley Park

Cemy

Bummoor Copse

Polsted La

Loseley House

3

Angel Ct
Eastbury La

Compton

Spiceall

Almsgate
Fowlerscroft

Withies La

Ashen Copse

47

Eastbury Manor

THE STREET

Compton Common

The Withies (PH)

Mellersh Farm

Grove Cottage

2

Field Place

The Avenue

The Grange

New Pond Rd

GU7

Green Lane Cty Inf Sch

1

Eastbury Park

Fox Hanger

Binscombe

Copse Side
Squirrels Cl
Green La
Long Gore
Woodland View

Binscombe Jun Sch

New Pond Farm

B3000
Furze La

Priors Field Sch

GU7

Priors Hatch La

A B C D E F

129
109

C8
1 MANGLES CT
2 BAYLISS CT
3 BEDFORD HO
4 FRIARY HO
5 THE FRIARY
6 THE MALL

F8
1 FRESHBOROUGH CT
2 TELFORD CT
3 SHELDON CT
4 BEECH CT
5 GRAYLANDS CT
6 EDGEBOROUGH CT
7 COMPTON CT
8 GROSVENOR HO
9 ST LUKE'S SQ
10 KNIGHTSBRIDGE HO
11 CADOGAN HO
12 ALEXANDRA LODGE
13 LYNNE HO

14 CHESHAM MEWS

GUILDFORD

GU2

GU1

GU3

GU4

GU5

Henley Fort School Camp

Piccard's Farm

Mount Browne Pol HQ

Orange Grove

Littleton

Orange Court Farm

Brickfields Farm

Stakescorner Cottage

Peas Marsh

Peasmarsh

Artington

Braboeuf Manor (Coll of Law)

Broadford Bridge

Broadford

Stone Bridge

Shalford Park

Chantry Wood Nature Trail

Pewley Down

Holy Trinity Sch

St Luke's

Shalford

Tilehouse Farm
Shalford Mill

North Downs Way

Pilgrims' Way

Wey-South Path

River Wey

Wey Way Navigation

Tilling Bourne

Downs Link

1 BLOOMSBURY CT
2 EATON HO
3 ST BARTHOLOMEW'S CT
4 ST CATHERINE'S PK
5 ST THOMAS'S MEWS
6 ALEXANDRA CT

Queen Eleanor's CE Jun Sch

Guildford Park

Guildford Cty Sch

Wherwell Lodge

FARNHAM RD

OLD PORTSMOUTH RD

PORTSMOUTH RD

SHALFORD RD

THE STREET

HORSHAM RD

BROADFORD RD

LONDON RD

EPSOM RD

HIGH ST

NEW POND RD

B3000

A3100

A248

A281

A31

A246

A320

A322

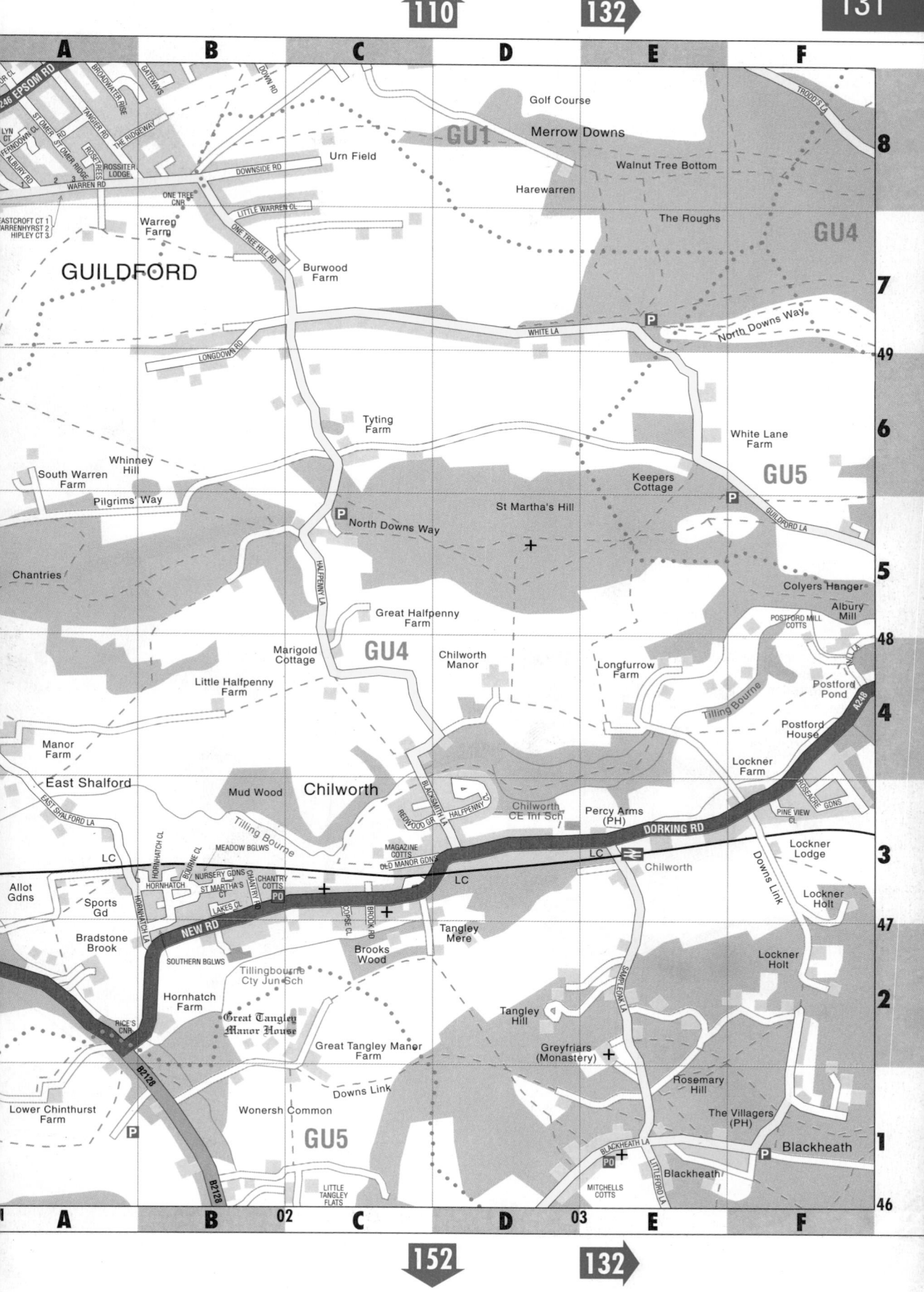

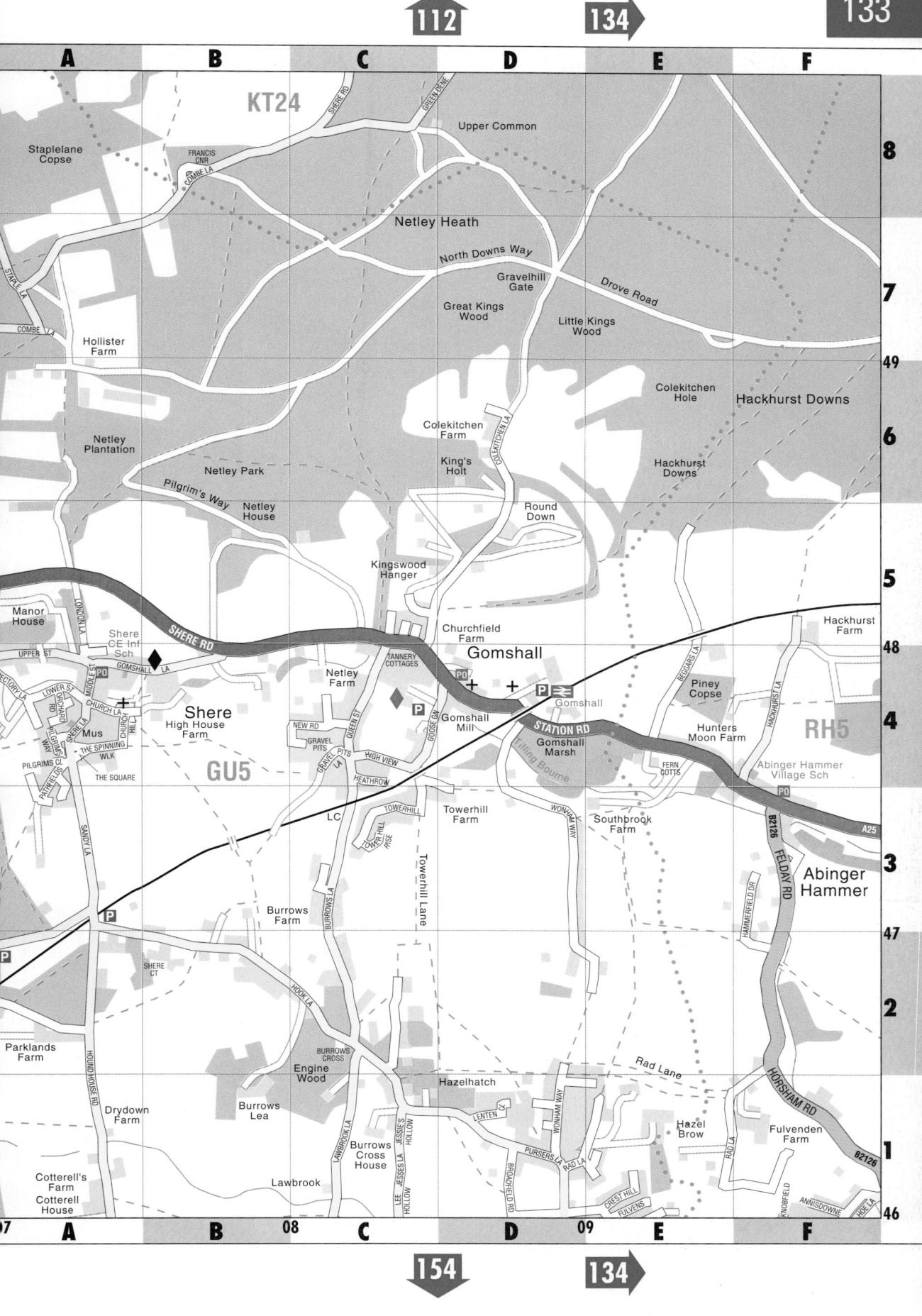

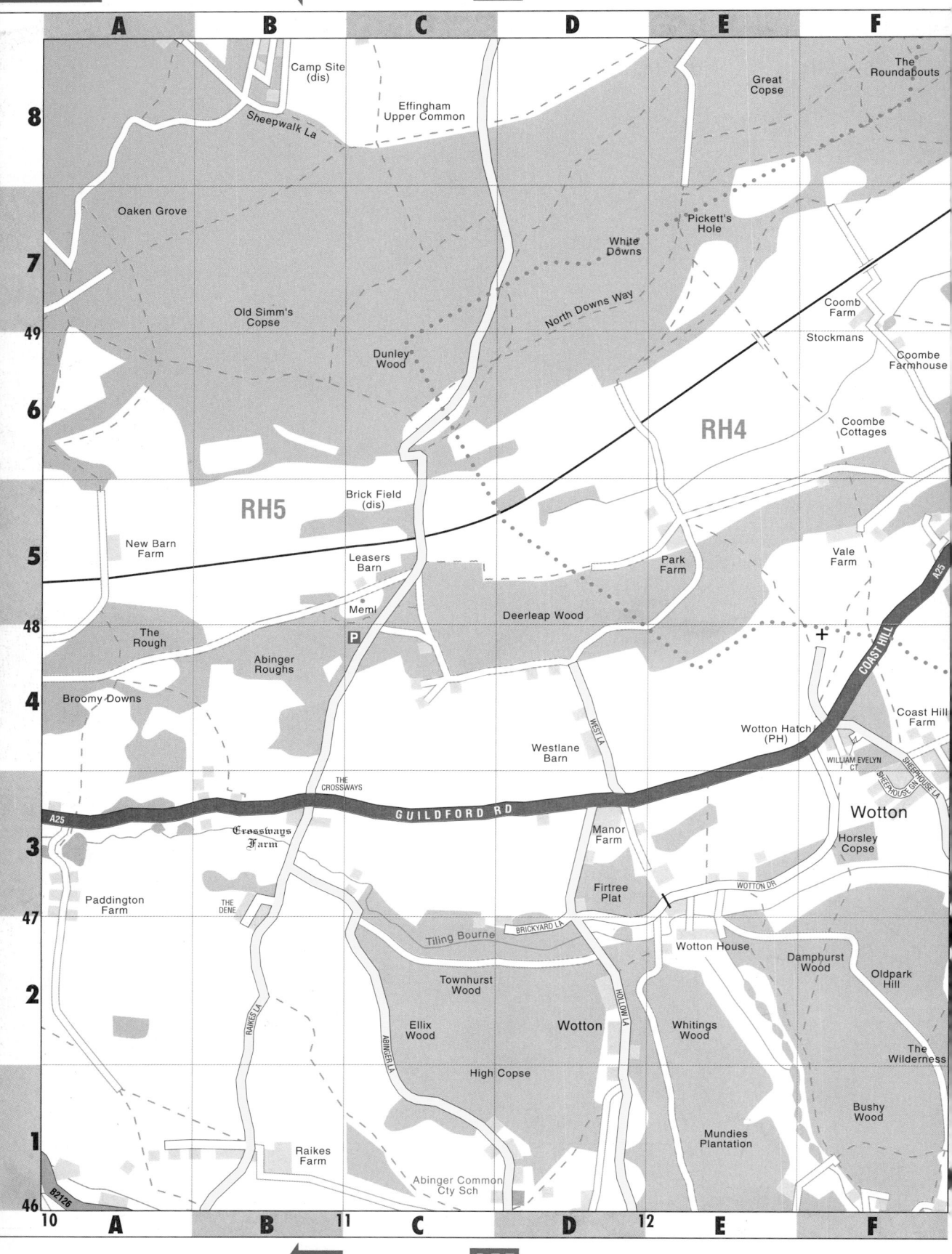

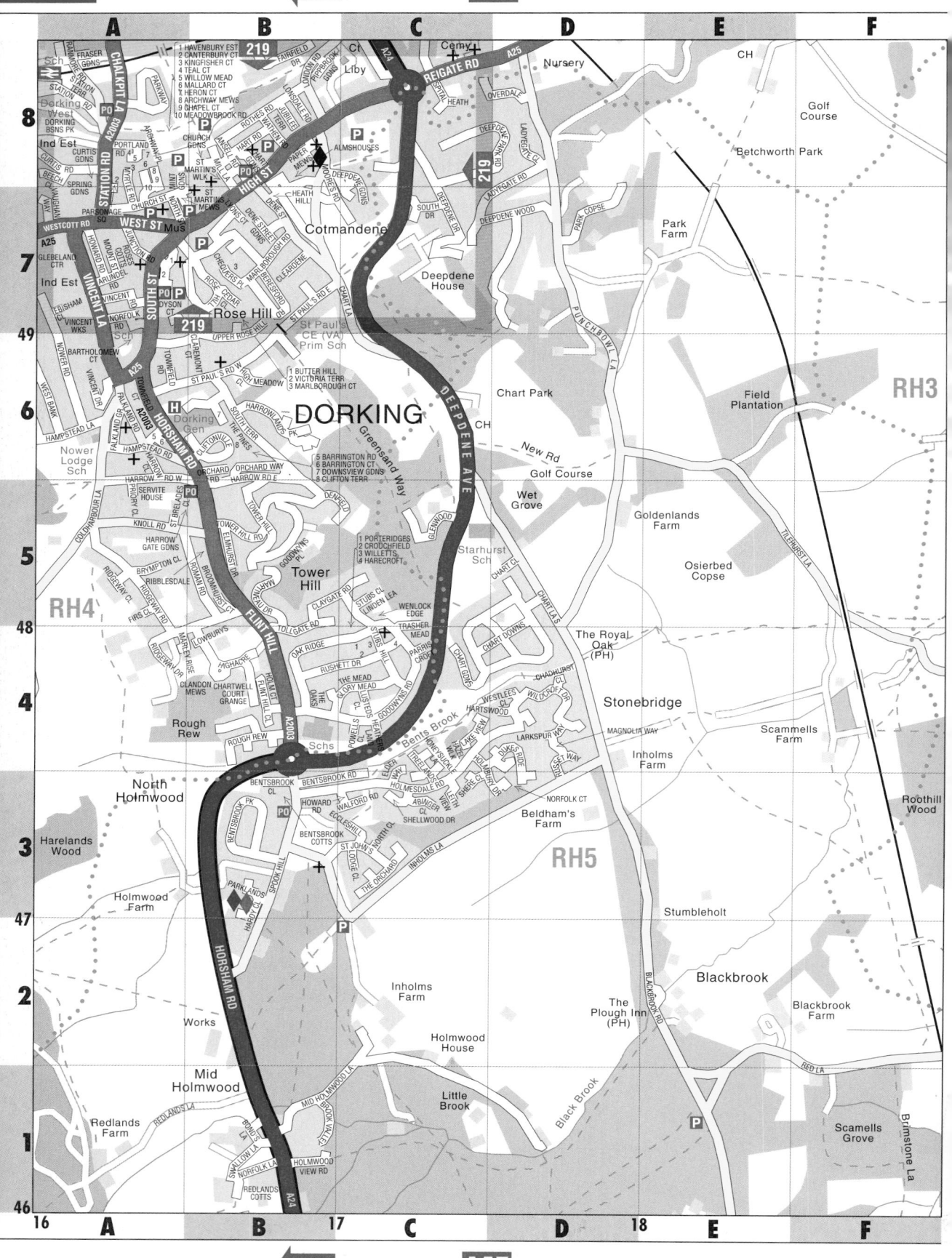

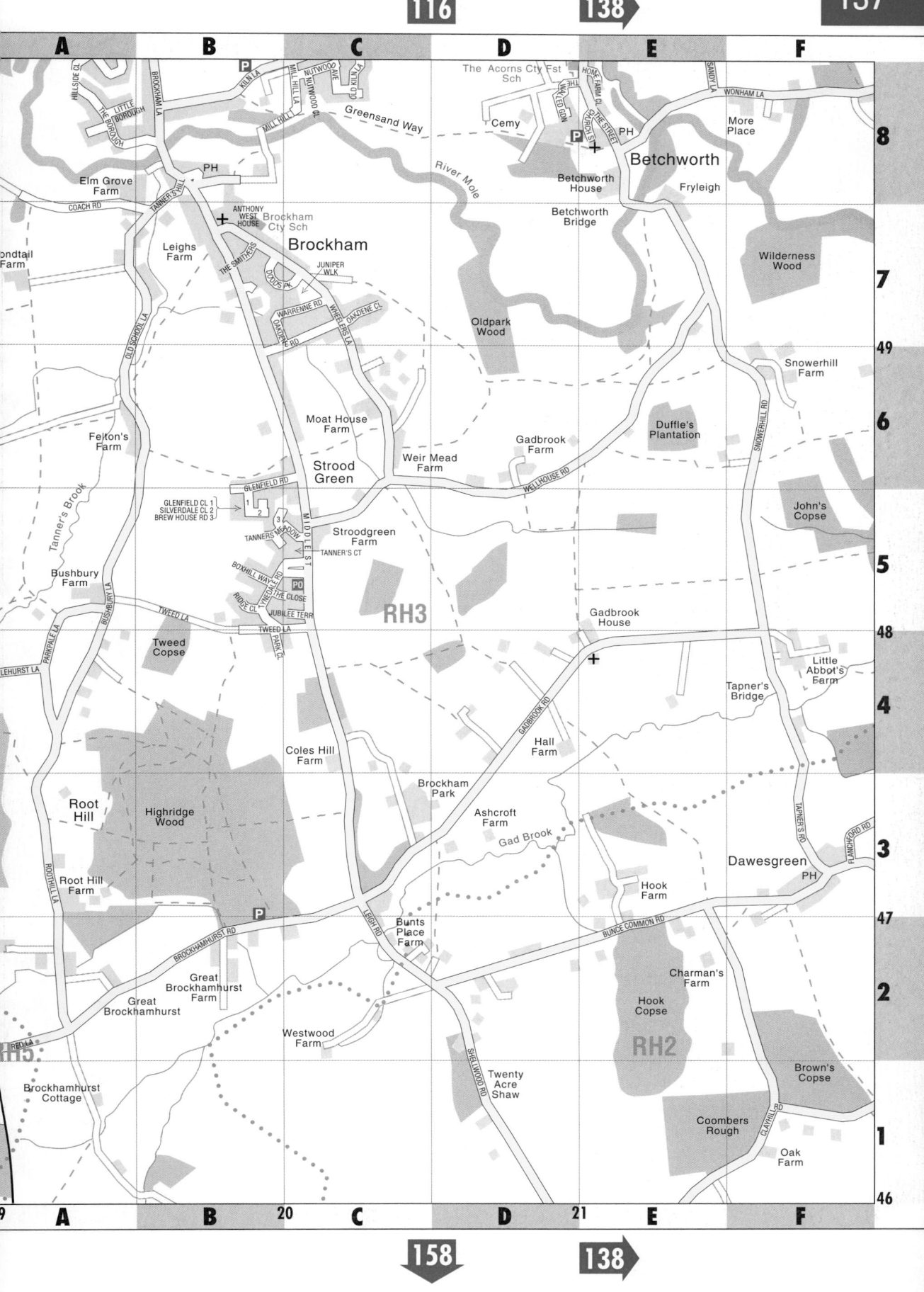

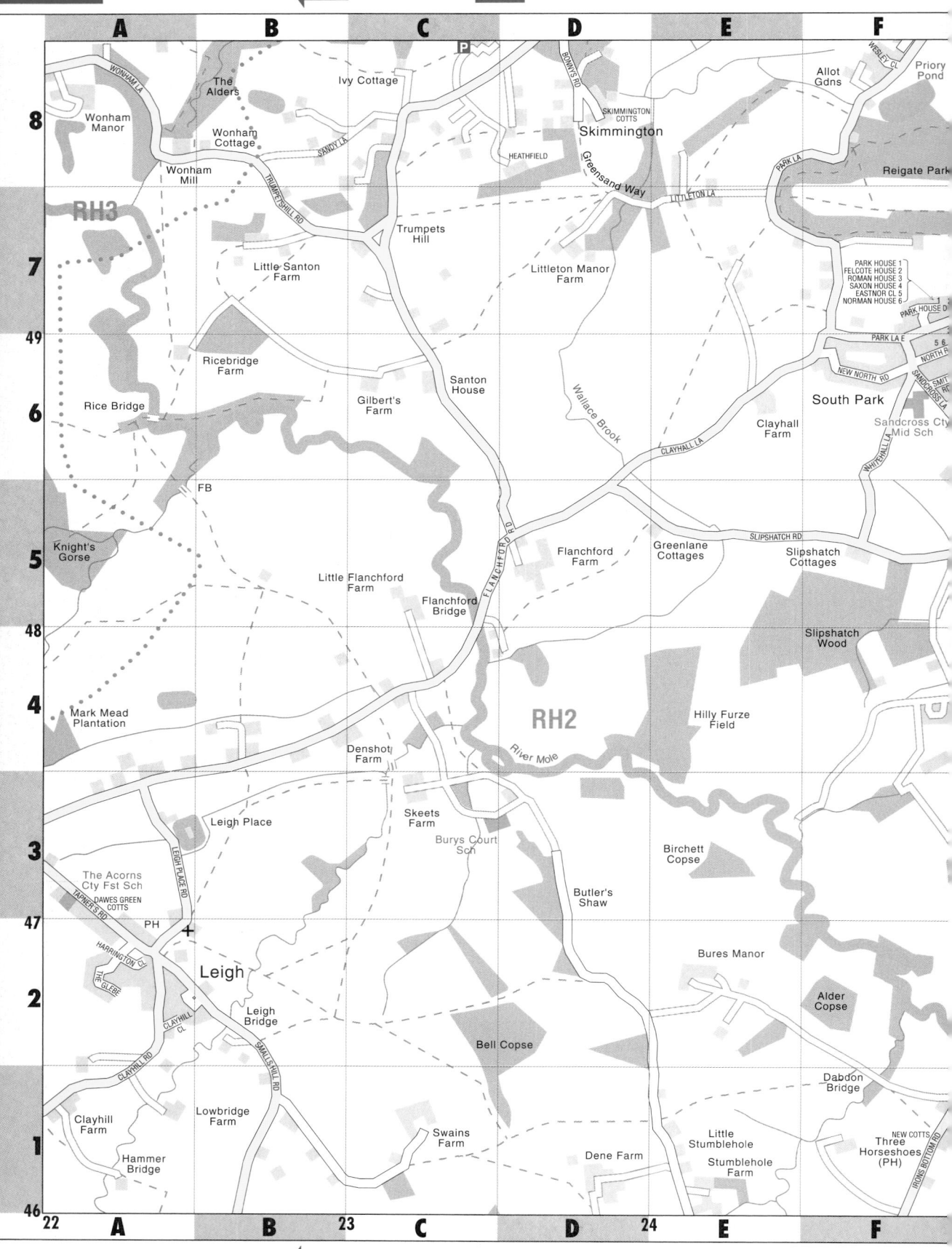

A B C D E F

8
Wonham Manor
Wonham LA
The Alders
Ivy Cottage
SKIMMINGTON COTTS
Skimmington
Allot Gdns
Priory Pond
WESLEY CL
Wonham Cottage
Wonham Mill
SANDY LA
HEATHFIELD
BONNYS RD
Greensand Way
PARK LA
Reigate Park

RH3

7
Little Santon Farm
TRUMPET SHILL RD
Trumpets Hill
Littleton Manor Farm
LITTLETON LA
PARK HOUSE 1
FELCOTE HOUSE 2
ROMAN HOUSE 3
SAXON HOUSE 4
EASTNOR CL 5
NORMAN HOUSE 6
PARK HOUSE D

49
Ricebridge Farm
PARK LA E
NEW NORTH RD
NORTH R
5 6
SANDCROSS LA SMIT

6
Rice Bridge
Gilbert's Farm
Santon House
Wallace Brook
CLAYHALL LA
Clayhall Farm
South Park
Sandcross Cty Mid Sch
WHITEHALL L

FB
Knight's Gorse
Little Flanchford Farm
Flanchford Bridge
FLANCHFORD RD
Flanchford Farm
Greenlane Cottages
SLIPSHATCH RD
Slipshatch Cottages

5

48
Slipshatch Wood

4
Mark Mead Plantation
RH2
Hilly Furze Field

Denshot Farm
River Mole

3
Leigh Place
Skeets Farm
Burys Court Sch
Birchett Copse

The Acorns Cty Fst Sch
LEIGH PLACE RD
DAWES GREEN COTTS
TAPNER'S RD
PH
Butler's Shaw

47
HARRINGTON CT
THE GLEBE
Leigh
Bures Manor

2
CLAYHILL CL
Leigh Bridge
SMALLS HILL RD
Alder Copse

CLAYHILL RD
Bell Copse
Dabdon Bridge

1
Clayhill Farm
Lowbridge Farm
Swains Farm
Dene Farm
Little Stumblehole
Stumblehole Farm
Three Horseshoes (PH)
NEW COTTS
IRONS BOTTOM RD

Hammer Bridge

46
22 A B 23 C D 24 E F

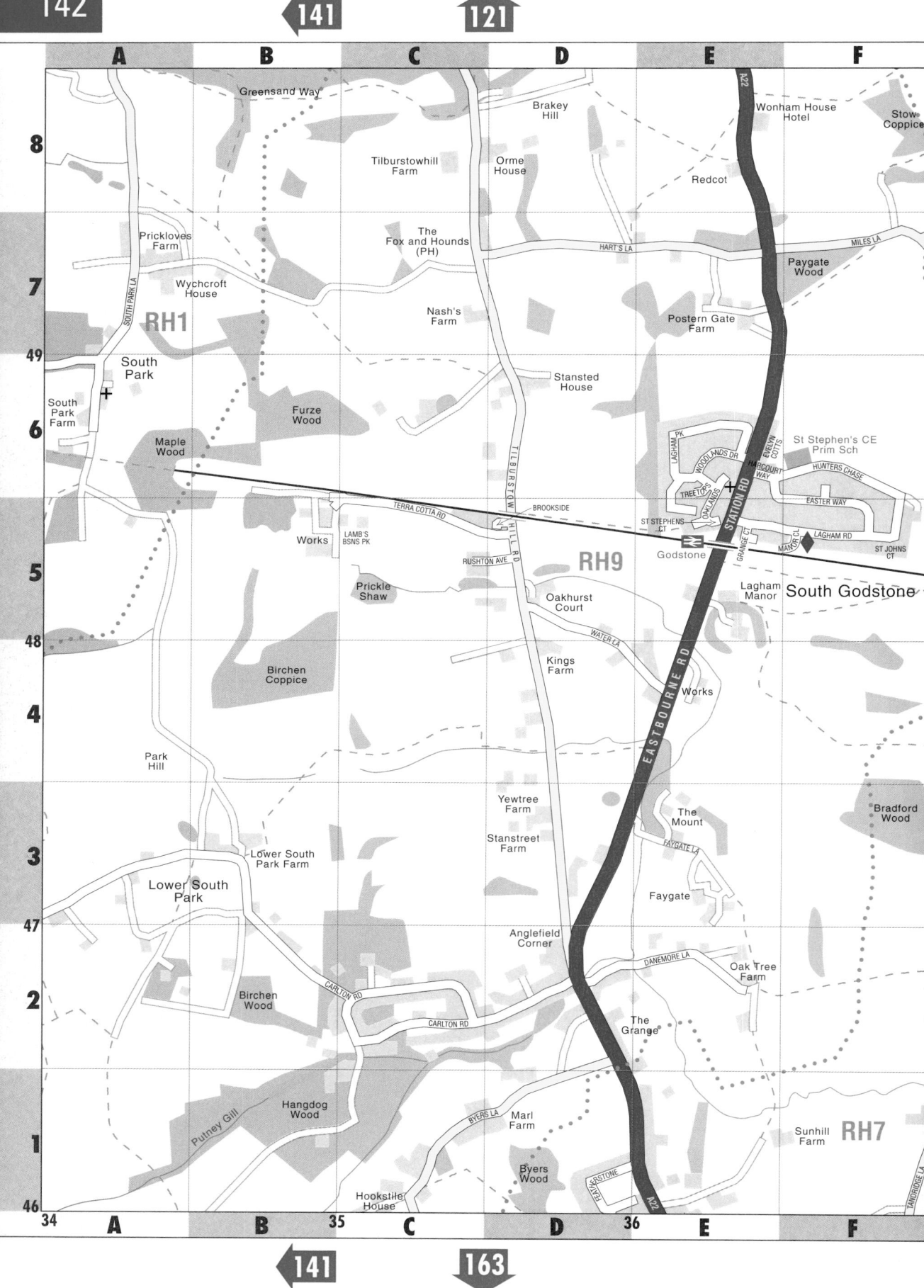

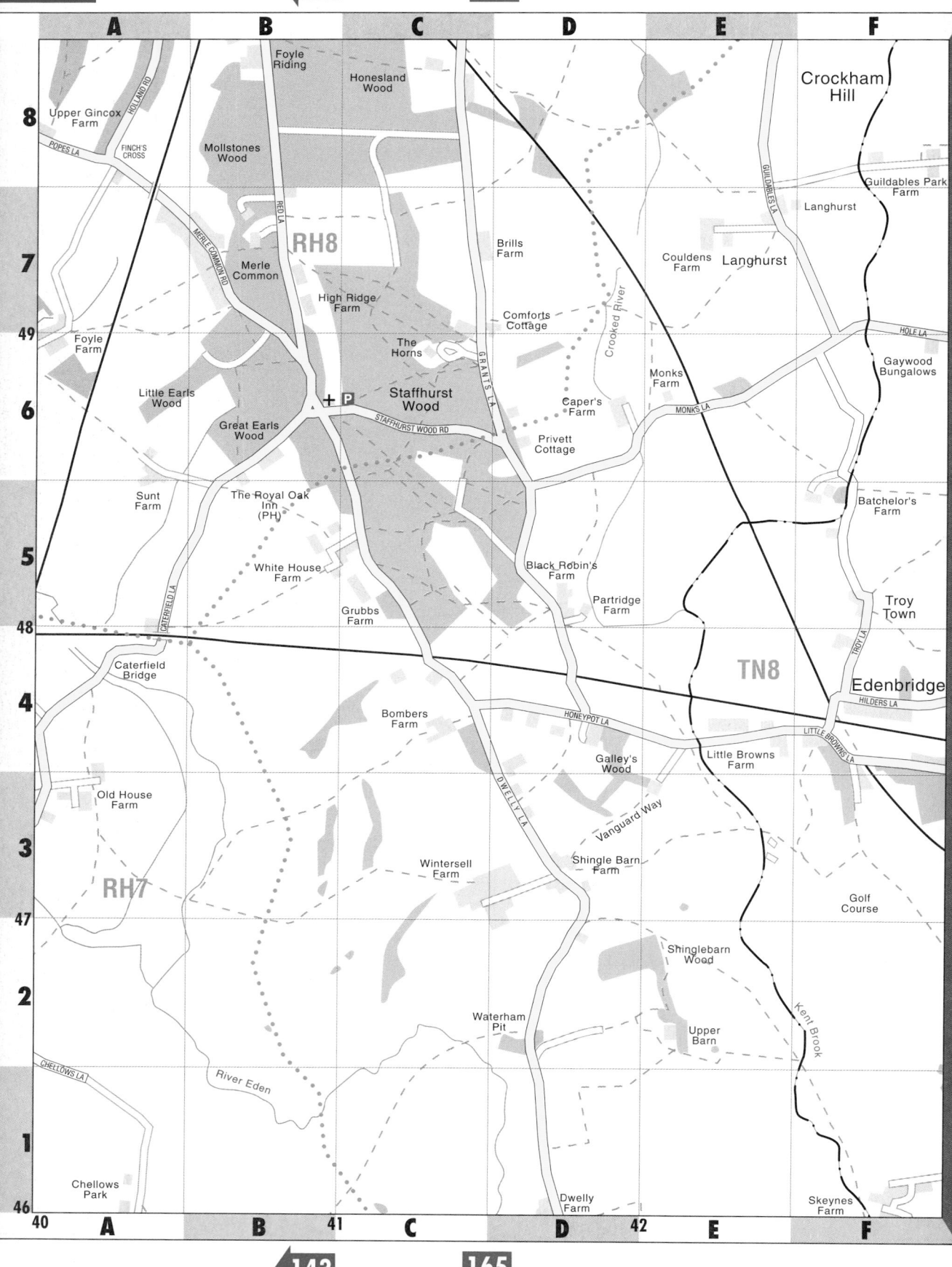

143
123
143
165

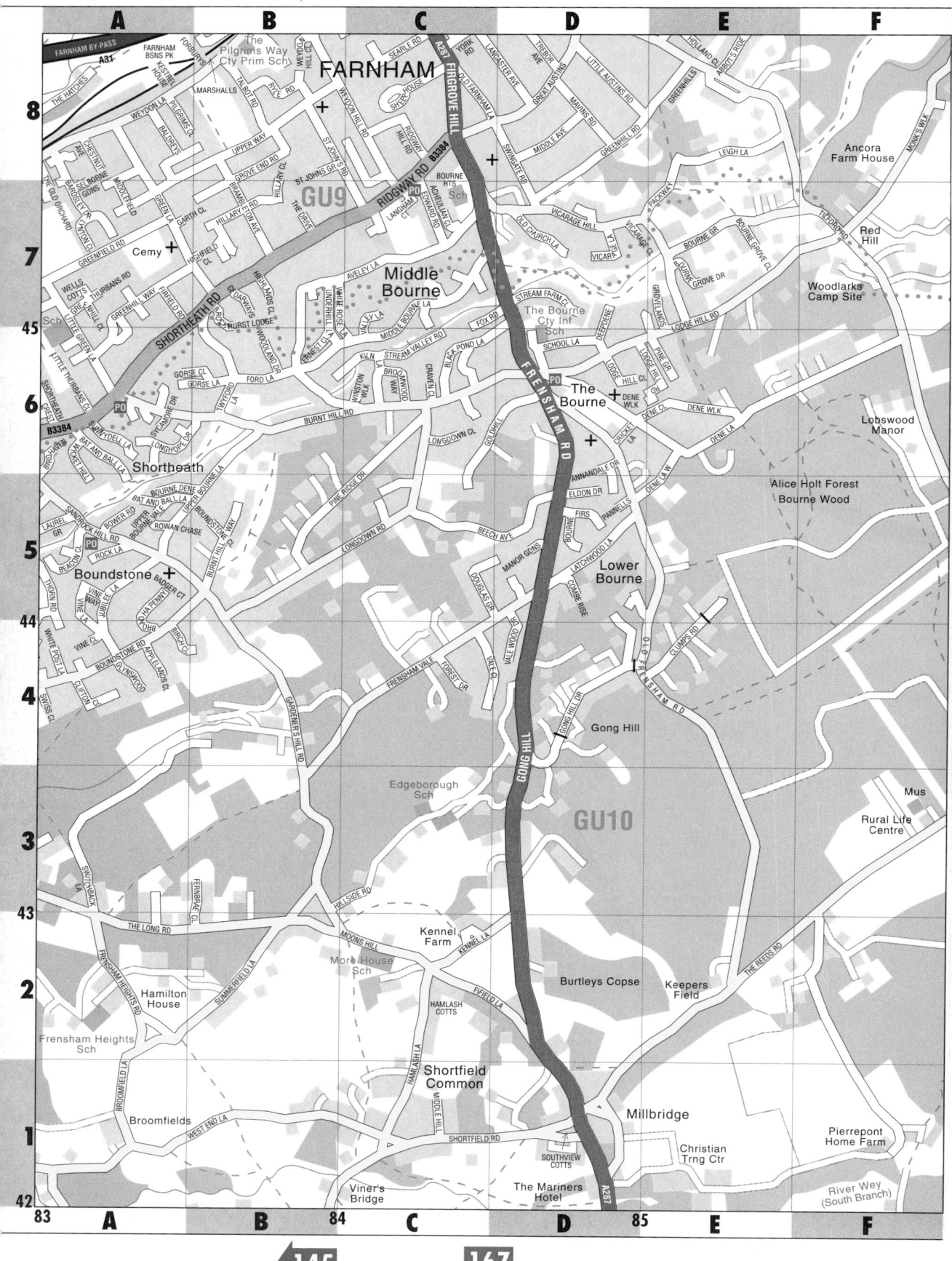

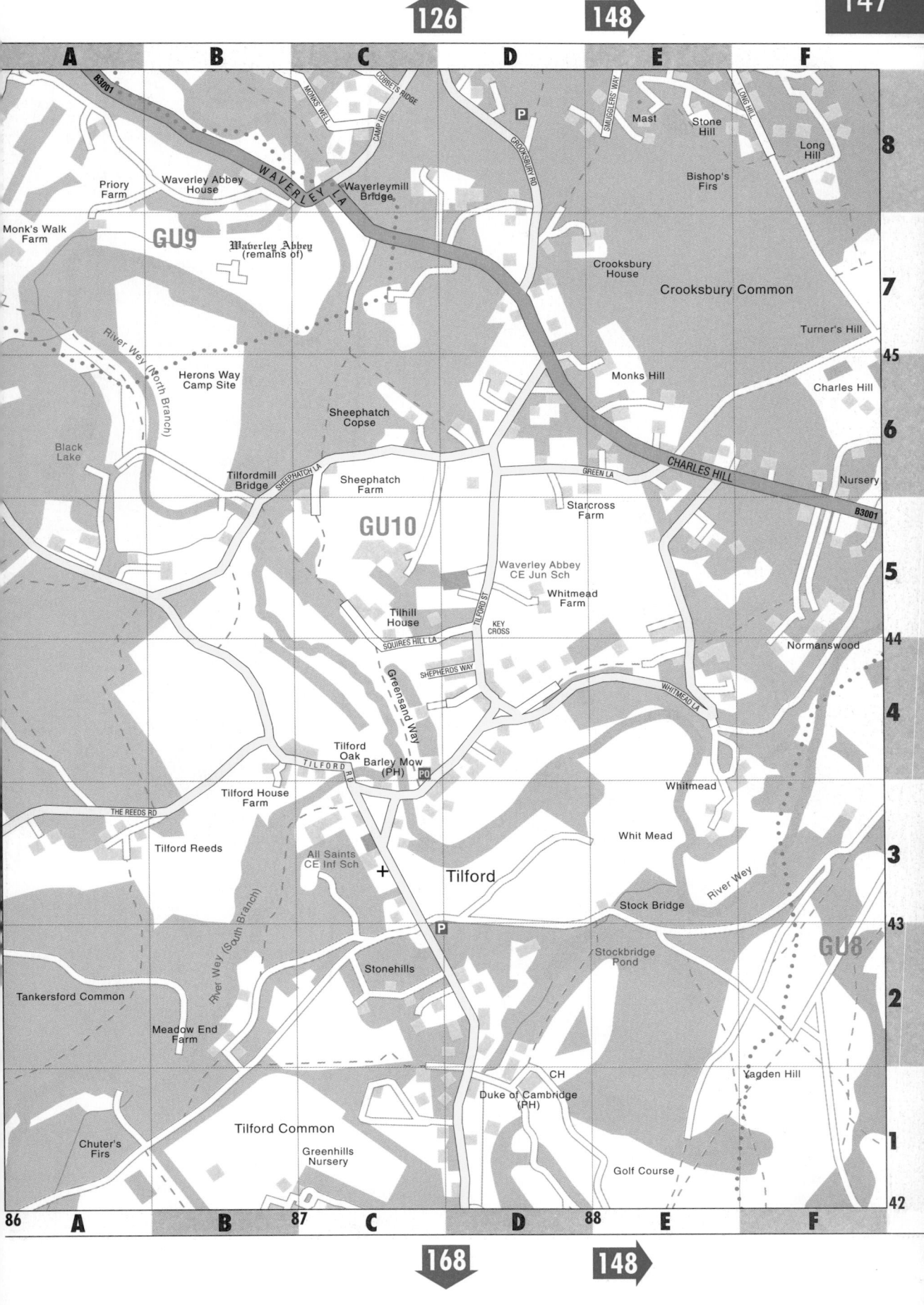

126
148
168
148

A B C D E F

8
7
45
6
5
44
4
3
43
2
1
42

86 A B 87 C D 88 E F

B3001
WAVERLEY LA
MONKS WELL
CORBET'S RIDGE
CAMP HILL
CROOKSBURY RD
SMUGGLERS WAY
LONG HILL

Mast
Stone Hill
Long Hill
Bishop's Firs

Priory Farm
Waverley Abbey House
Waverleymill Bridge
Monk's Walk Farm
GU9
Waverley Abbey (remains of)

Crooksbury House
Crooksbury Common

River Way (North Branch)
Herons Way Camp Site
Turner's Hill
Charles Hill

Black Lake
Sheephatch Copse
Monks Hill

Tilfordmill Bridge
SHEEPHATCH LA
Sheephatch Farm
GREEN LA
CHARLES HILL
Nursery
B3001

GU10
Starcross Farm
Waverley Abbey CE Jun Sch
Whitmead Farm
Normanswood

Tilhill House
TILFORD ST
KEY CROSS
SQUIRES HILL LA
SHEPHERDS WAY
Greensand Way
WHITMEAD LA

Tilford Oak
TILFORD RD
Barley Mow (PH)
PO
Whitmead

Tilford House Farm
THE REEDS RD
Whit Mead

Tilford Reeds
All Saints CE Inf Sch
River Wey (South Branch)
River Wey
Tilford
Stock Bridge

P
Stockbridge Pond
GU8

Tankersford Common
Stonehills

Meadow End Farm
CH
Duke of Cambridge (PH)
Yagden Hill

Chuter's Firs
Tilford Common
Greenhills Nursery
Golf Course

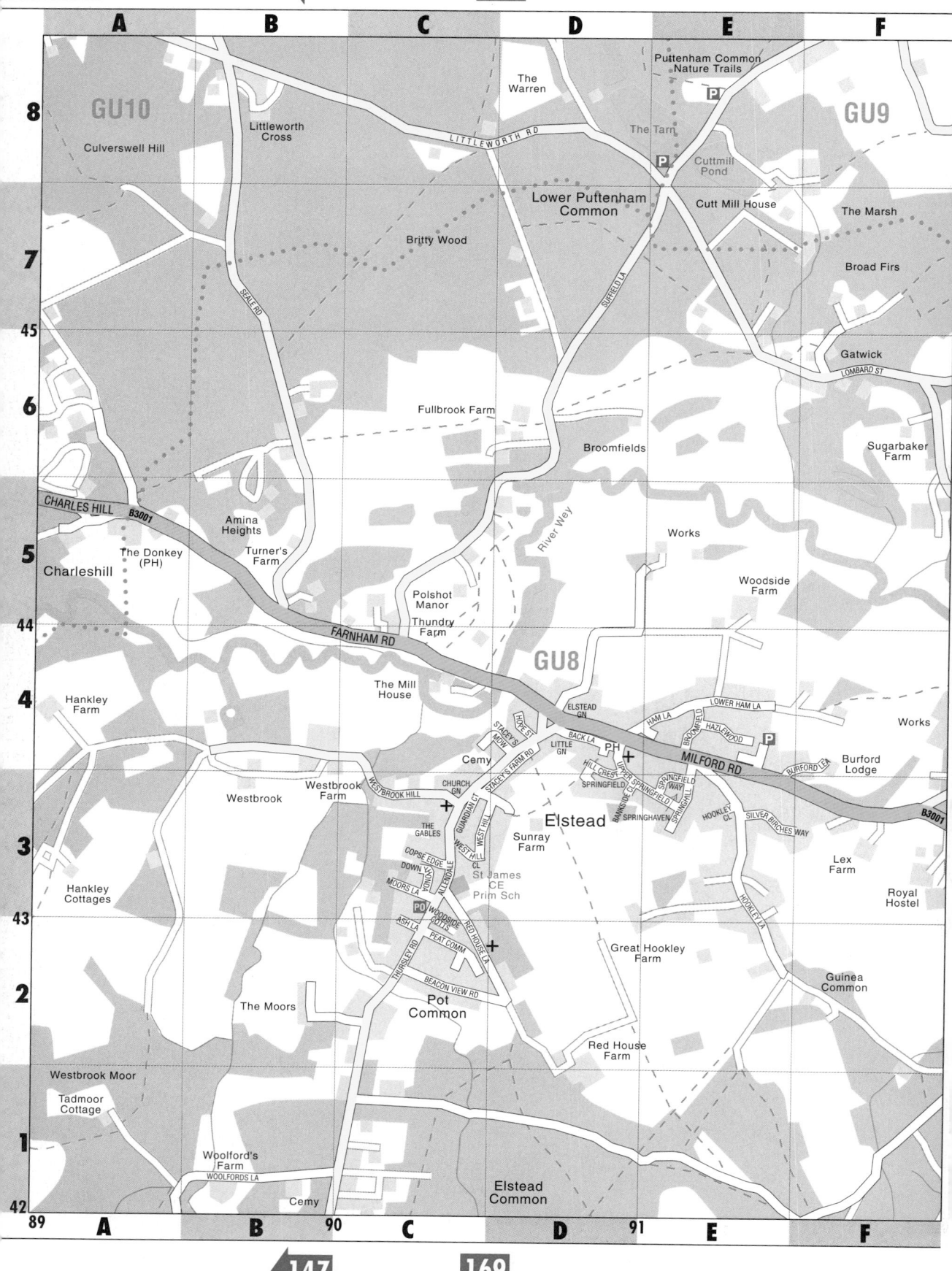

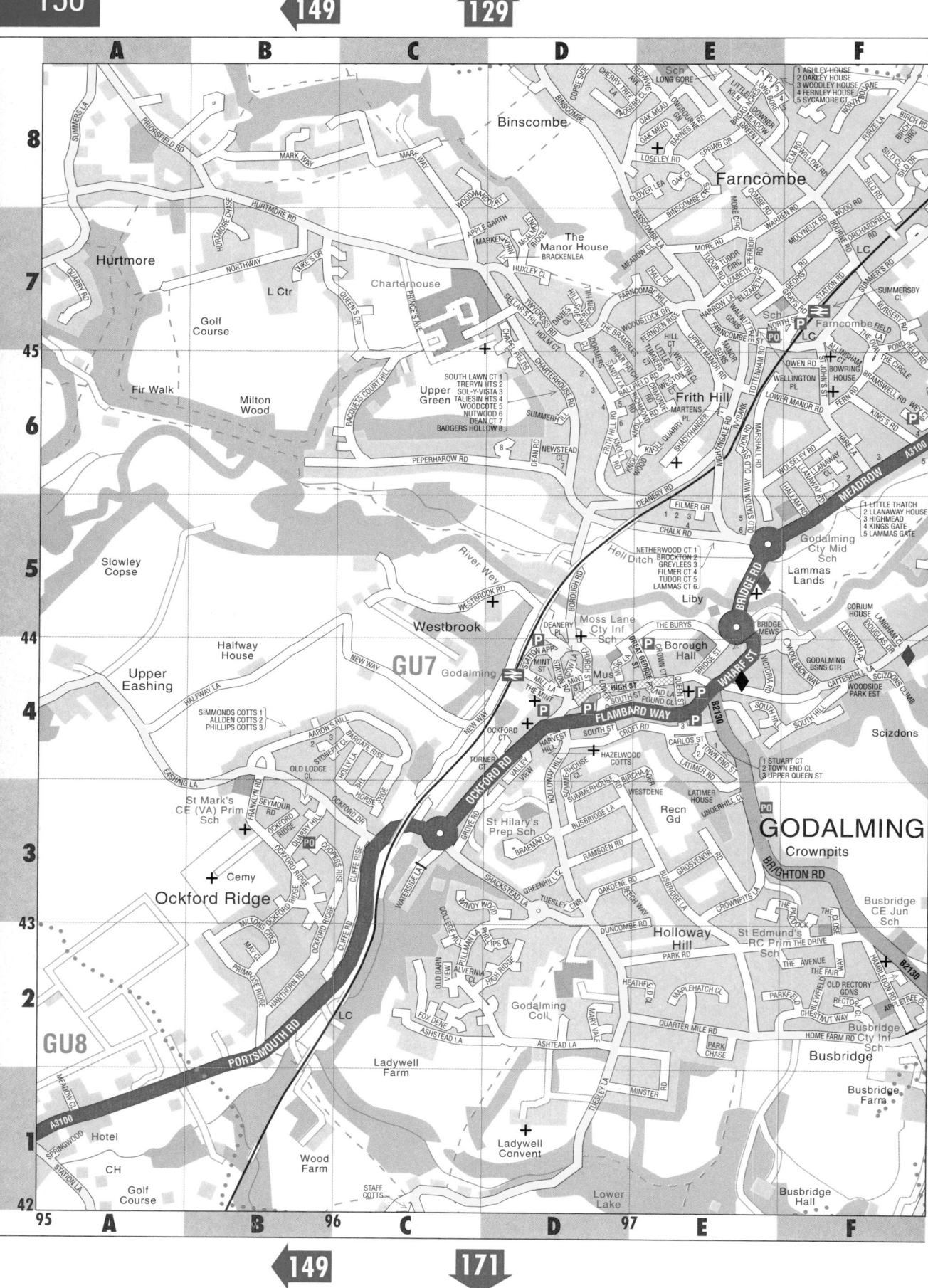

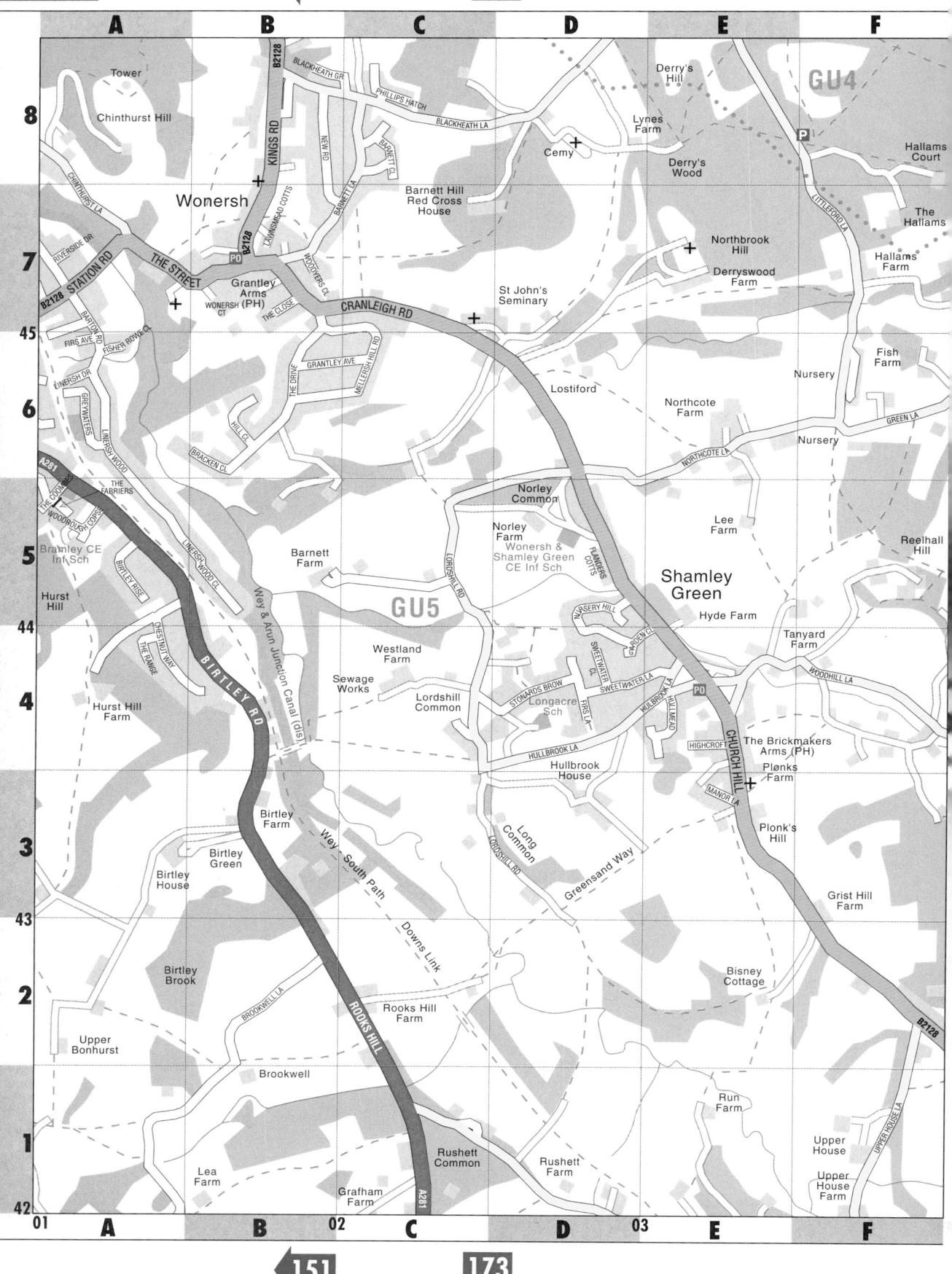

A   B   C   D   E   F

8
7
45
6
5
44
4
3
43
2
1
42

GU4

Mustard
Copse

Candleford
Cottage

Foxholes
Wood

Edgeley
Caravan Park

Dilton
Farm

Farley
Green

BROOK HILL

AUGUST LA

Darbyn's
Brook

Jelley's
Copse

Farley
Heath

Farley Green
Hall Farm

RIDE LA

Kingsfield

Caravan
Site

PONDS LA

7

Rompin
Downs

GREEN LA

Haldish
Farm

45

Greenlane
Farm

Far
Plantation

Mayorhouse
Holt

Mardons

SHOPHOUSE LA

LOCKHURSTHATCH LA

Lockhurst Hatch
Farm

6

Shophouse
Farm

Dick's
Hill

Sheepwalk

FARLEY HEATH RD

Sandhurst
Copse

Mayorhouse
Farm

Ride La

GU5

ROW LA

Treetops
Caravan
Park

5

44

Kiln
Hanger

Upper
Woodhill Farm

Reelhall
Farm

Woodhill
Manor

Woodhill

Woodlands

WOODHILL LA

Helmet
Copse

Winterfold
Forest

4

MADGEHOLE LA

Madgehole
Copse

Pithouse
Copse

Stroud
Farm

Franklin's
Farm

STROUD LA

Madgehole

Madgehole
Farm

Winterfold
Cottage

3

43

Great
Copse

Greensand Way

Winterfold
Heath

Winterfold
Hill

2

Willinghurst
Farm

Barn
Plaits

Ash Tree
Lake

Willinghurst
House

Rock
Copse

P

GU6

Winterfold
Heath

Alderbrook
Copse

Sandy
Hill

Jelleys
Hollow

Stroud
Common

GUILDFORD RD

B2128

South
Copse

Willinghurst
Lake

Lapscombe
Farm

THE
COURTYARD

Alderbrook

1

42

04   A   B   05   C   D   06   E   F

A **B** **C** **D** **E** **F**

8

Dilton
Copse

7

45

6

5

44

4

3

43

2

1

42

Knowle
Farm

Hound
House
Farm

Hound
House

Kiln Platt
Cottage

HOUND HOUSE RD

Wickham's
Copse

Bentlys

Lane End
Farm

LANGBROOK LA

Hazel
Hall

POND LA

Peaslake
House

JESSES LA

BURCHETS HOLLOW

Smoky
Hole

MACKIES HILL

PEASLAKE LA

The
Hurtwood
Inn

P

PO

P
PLANS HILL

Ridge
Hill

Cemy

WALKING BOTTOM

GU5

P

Hurt Wood

P

Gasson
Copse

P

Ewhurst
Windmill

GU6

Pitch
Hill

RIDE WAY

Windmill
Inn
(PH)

Hurtwood
Edge

Reynards
Hill

The
Warren

P

Greensand Way

Gasson
Farm

Duke of Kent
Sch

Woolpit
Farm

EWHURST RD

Coverwood
Farm

Coverwood

RADMOR RD

Lake
House

Isemongers
Farm

Woolpit
Wood

Holt Copse

RH5

Sherborne Lane

BROADFIELD RD

PURSERS HOLTON

PURSERS LA

SWEET LA

St Martha's

HOE LA

HOE COTTS

Pursers
Farm

Hoe

Hoe
Farm

FRANKSFIELD

FRANKSFIELD

Peaslake
Sch

DALMANS

HILL

Peaslake

Colman's
Hill

Riding
Bottom

Spurfold
Copse

Riding
Copse

Horse
Shoes
Farm

KNOBFIELD

WESTFIELD

SUTTON PL

HOE LA

Tenningshook
Wood

RH5

Hurtwood
Chase

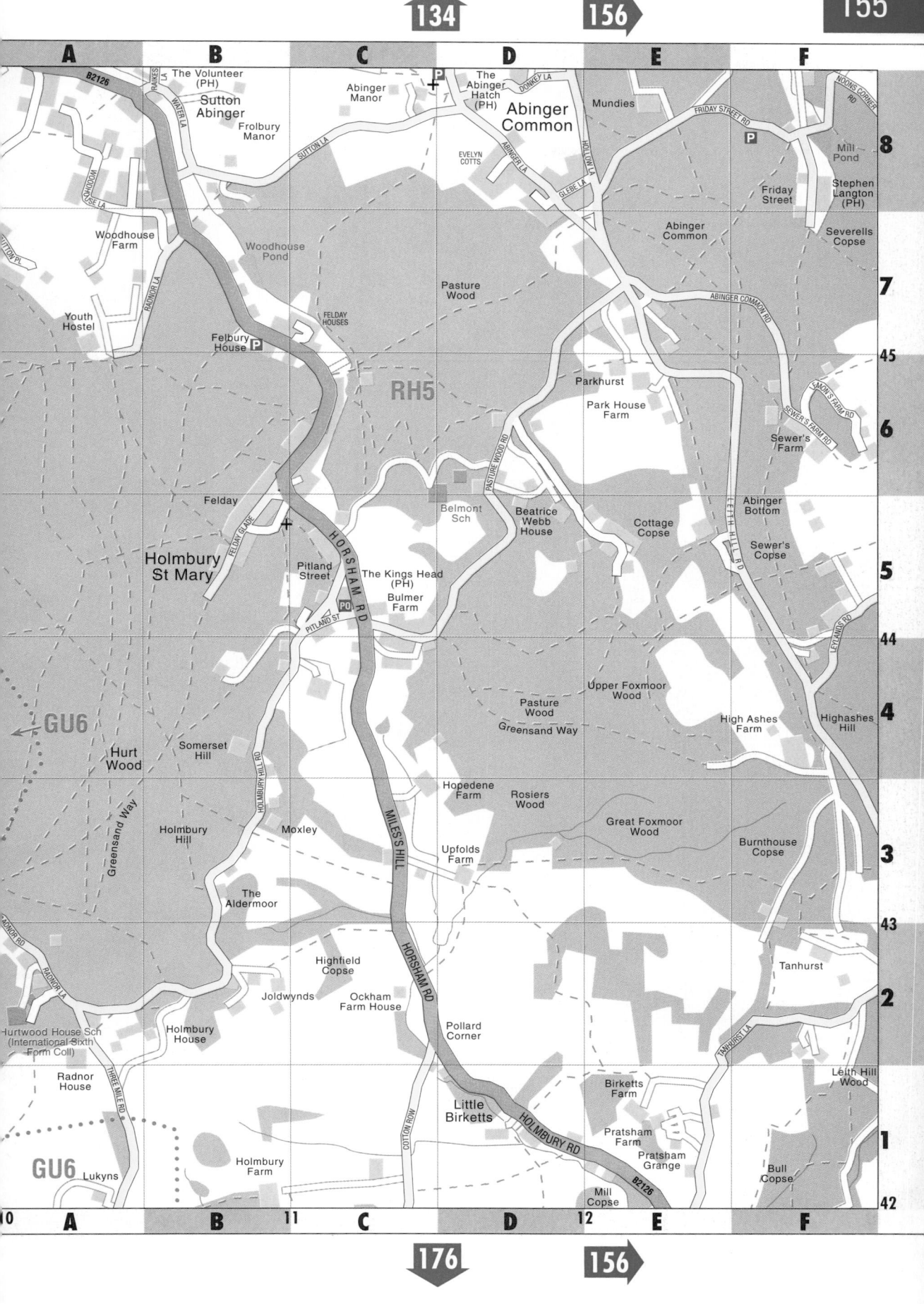

A   B   C   D   E   F

B2126

RAIKES LA

The Volunteer
(PH)

Sutton
Abinger

Abinger
Manor

P

The Abinger
Hatch (PH)

DONKEY LA

Mundies

Abinger
Common

NOONS CORNER RD

FRIDAY STREET RD

P

Mill
Pond

8

Frolbury
Manor

WATER LA

SUTTON LA

Friday
Street

Stephen
Langton
(PH)

Severells
Copse

WOODHOUSE LA

Woodhouse
Farm

RADNOR LA

Woodhouse
Pond

EVELYN
COTTS.

ABINGER LA

HOLLOW LA

GLEBE LA

Abinger
Common

7

Youth
Hostel

FELDAY
HOUSES

Pasture
Wood

ABINGER COMMON RD

45

Felbury
House

P

RH5

Parkhurst

Park House
Farm

PASTURE WOOD RD

Sewer's
Farm

CANON'S FARM RD

SEWER'S FARM RD

6

Felday

FELDAY GLADE

Belmont
Sch

Beatrice
Webb
House

Cottage
Copse

Abinger
Bottom

Sewer's
Copse

Holmbury
St Mary

HORSHAM RD

Pitland
Street

The Kings Head
(PH)

Bulmer
Farm

LEITH HILL RD

5

PITLAND ST

PO

44

Pasture
Wood

Upper Foxmoor
Wood

LEYLANDS RD

4

Hurt
Wood

Somerset
Hill

Greensand Way

High Ashes
Farm

Highashes
Hill

GU6

Greensand Way

HOLMBURY HILL RD

Holmbury
Hill

Moxley

Hopedene
Farm

Rosiers
Wood

Great Foxmoor
Wood

Burnthouse
Copse

3

The
Aldermoor

MILES'S HILL

Upfolds
Farm

43

RADNOR RD

Highfield
Copse

HORSHAM RD

Tanhurst

2

Joldwynds

Ockham
Farm House

Pollard
Corner

TANHURST LA

Leith Hill
Wood

Hurtwood House Sch
(International Sixth
Form Coll)

THREE MILE RD

Holmbury
House

Birketts
Farm

Radnor
House

COTTON ROW

Little
Birketts

HOLMBURY RD

Pratsham
Farm

Pratsham
Grange

Bull
Copse

1

GU6   Lukyns

Holmbury
Farm

Mill
Copse

B2126

42

A   B   C   D   E   F

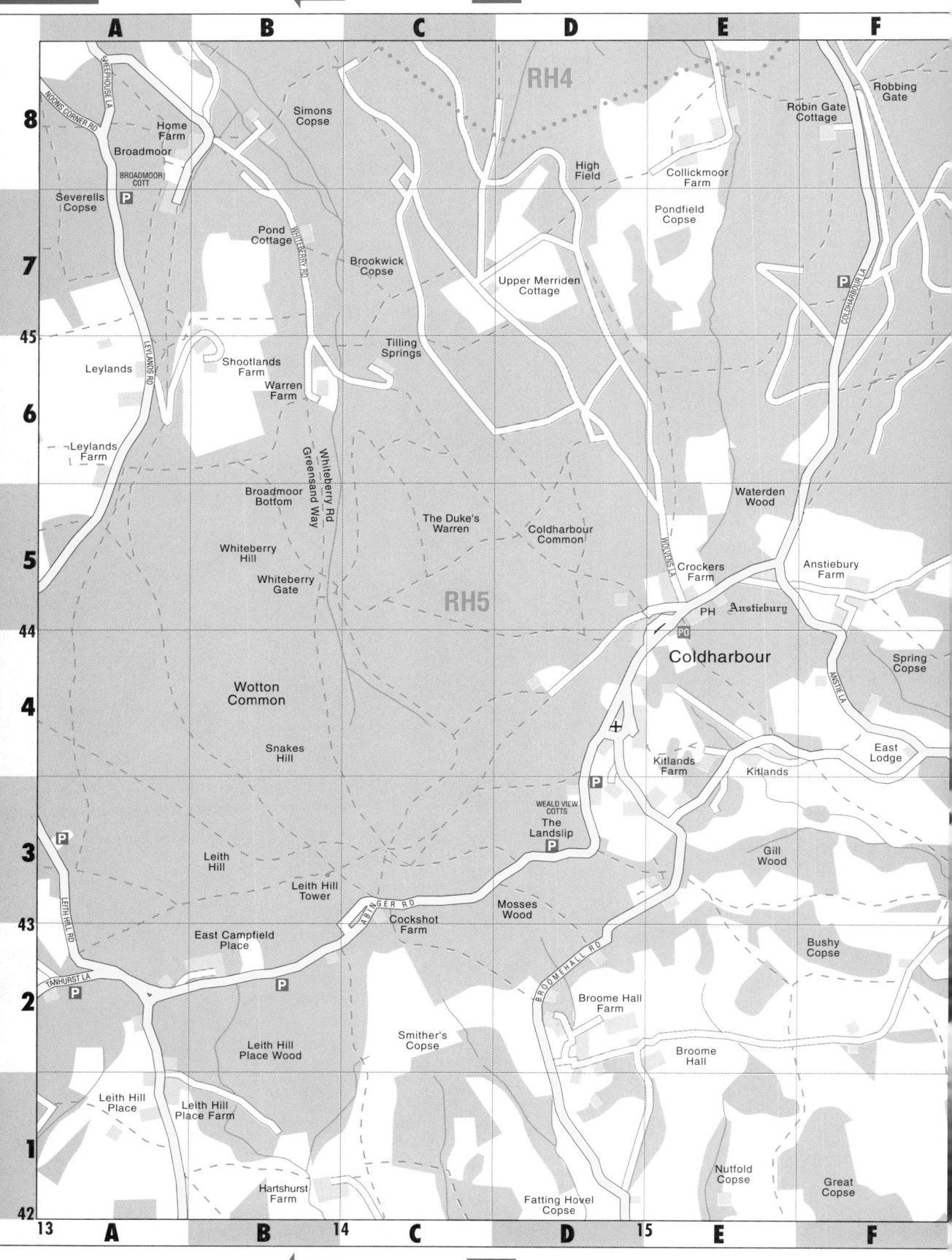

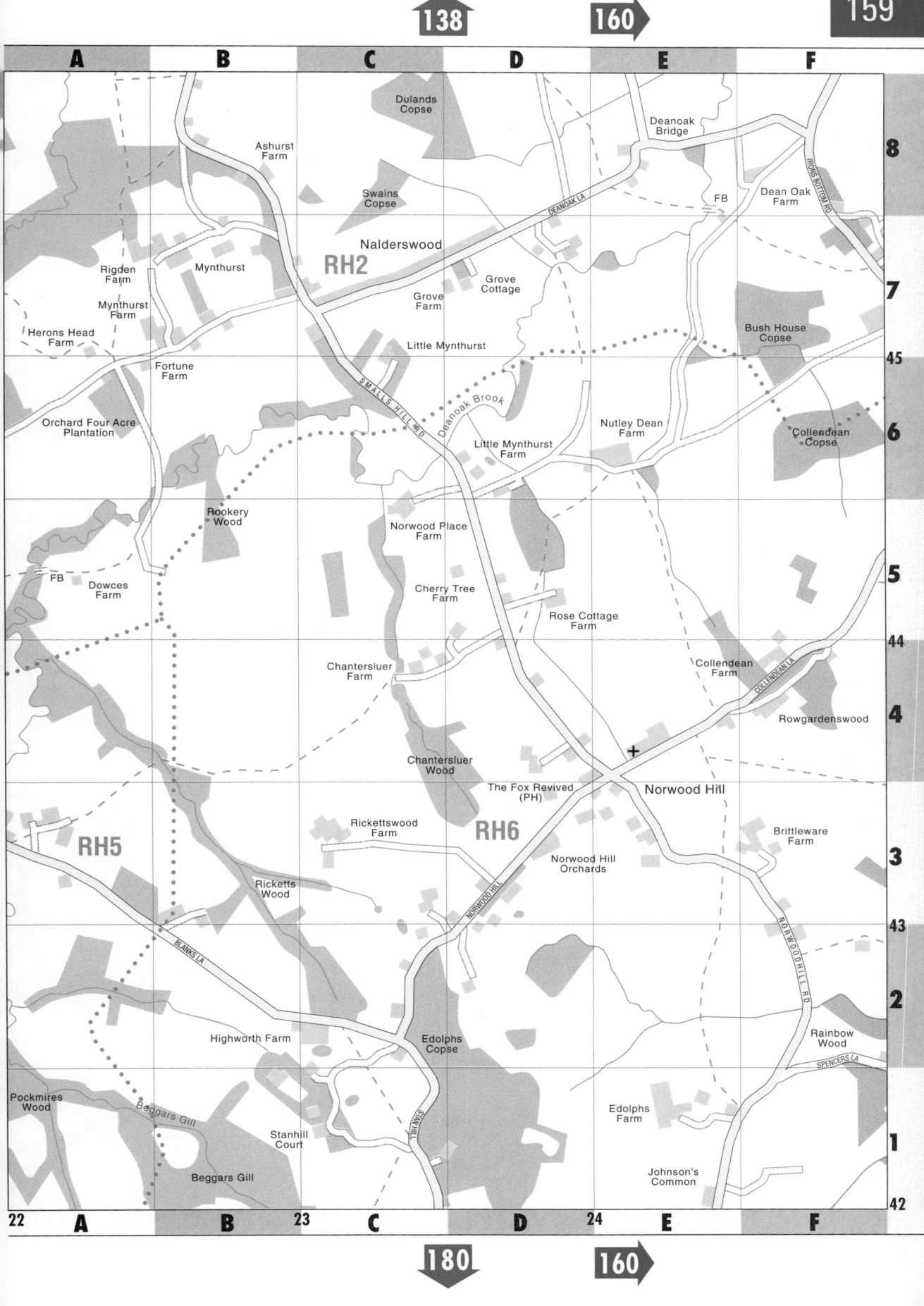

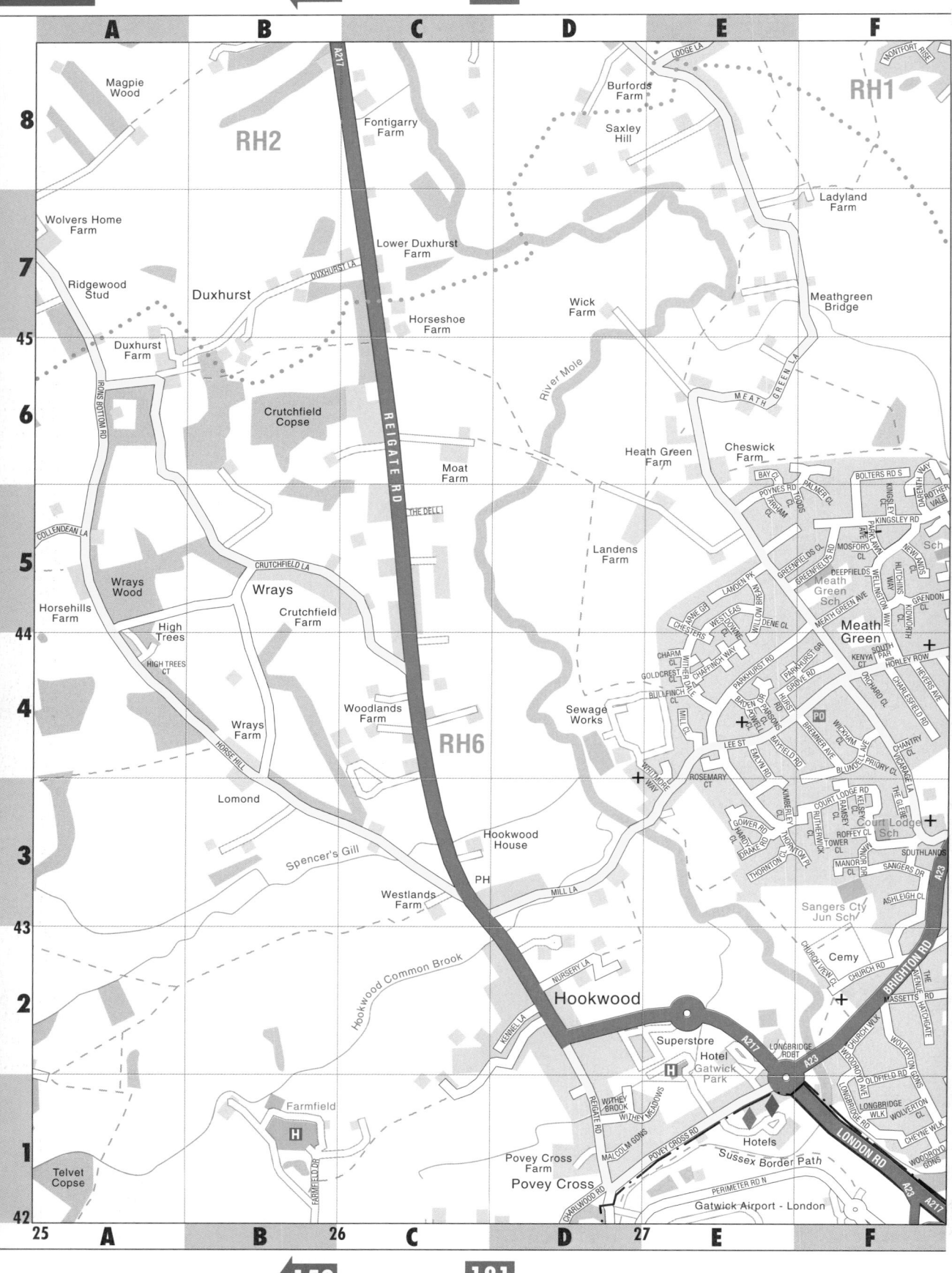

140
162

A B C D E F

8

7

45

6

5

44

4

3

43

2

1

42

RH1

Horley Lodge La
Wood Pk
Harwood Pk
Pear Tree Hill
Redhill Distribution Ctr.
The Orchard B&NS Ctr
Astra Bsns Ctr
Beechwood Villas
Empire Villas

Perry Wood

Picketts

Pickets La

Job's Farm

Woolborough Farm

Orchard Farm

New House La

M23

La Houdon Row

Cross Oak La

Lake Cottage

Hunters Moon Farm

Hathersham La

Bonehurst Farm

Bonehurst Rd

Bonehurst Bridge

Willow Ct
The Grange
Burstow House
Skipton Way
Sariel Way
Brookwood House
Longyard House
Haversham House

Lake La

Littlelake Farm

Hathersham Farm

Burstow Stream

Greatlake Farm

Longyards Shaw

Kingsley Rd
Avondale Ct
The Spinney
Butlers Rd
Ballard Rd
Branrary Kiln La
Bak
Kiln La
Fern Down Cl
Yew Tree Cl
Horley Row
Chequers Cl
Chequers Dr

Carlton Ct
Bemham's Cl
Waterside
Chestnut Rd
The Chestnuts
Ladbroke
Cranbourne

The Farmhouse (PH)

1 Fallowfield Way
2 Fairstone Ct
3 Harrowsley Ct
4 Fieldview
5 Woodhayes
6 Rickwood
7 Hayfields
8 Ryelands
9 Whitecroft
10 Brookwood
11 Barleymead
12 Meadowside

Tanyard Farm

Brook Wood

Sewage Works

Weatherhill Common

Weatherhill Cl

Southlands Ave
Brighton Rd
Heuers Ave
Le May Cl
Lumley Ct
Oakwood Rd
The Fell
B2036
Yattendon Jun Sch

Thatchers Cl
Smithbarn
Cartersmead
Tanyard
Collingwood
Woodcote
The Frodings
Heritage Lawn
Birch
West
Langshott

Thatchers Cl
Homefield Cl
Greatlake Ct
Herons Wood Ct
Larksfield
Brackenside
Cl Overfield
Gatwick Metro Ctr
Windmill La

Grassmere
Wheatfield Way
Honeysuckle La
Dovern
Woodlands
Maize Croft
Stokes
Firlands
The Meadway
Langshott
Newbury
Keep

Tawney
Side La
Twyner Cl
Lambeth Cl
Meridian Ctr
Broad Mead
Oaklands
Acorn
Carlton Tye
Bramley Wlk
Longchamp
Grays Wood
Clarence
Ct
Hilton Ct
Clarence Ct
Water View

Langshott Wood

Langshott

Harrowsley Green Farm

Park View
Victoria Rd
Albert Rd
St Hilda's Cl
Kings Rd
Queen's Rd
Magnolia
Liby
Pine Gdns
Ringley Ave
Church Rd

P

Horley Cty Inf Sch

Station Rd
St Georges Cl
Crewton Rd
Rosemary La
Belgravia Ct
Roslan Ct

Smallmead

Langshott Cty Inf Sch

Oakwood Sch

Wilgers Farm

RH6

HORLEY

Massetts Rd
Hampton Lodge
Russells Cres
Lincoln Rd
Upford Cl
Delta
Michael Cres
Crescent Way
Upfield Cl
The Ridgeway
The Crescent
Riverside
Garwick Stream
A217

1 Delta House
2 Delta Bglws
Atkinson Ct
Horley
Stocks Cl
Limes Ave

The Group
Victoria Rd
Aurum Cl
Fairlawns
Fairfield Ave
Cheyne Wlk

Silverlea Gdns
Avenue Gdns
Balcombe Gdns
Castle Dr
Bayhorn La
The Coronet
Bayhorne La
Warltersville Way
The Close
B2036
The Spiers Way

Balcombe Rd
Station App
Primrose Ave
Hyperion Wlk
The Drive

Newstead Hall

Haroldslea Poultry Farm

Haroldslea

Haroldslea Dr

Newstead Hall

Haroldslea House

Burstow Stream

Peeks Brook La

The Roughs

M23

Smallfield Rd

28 A 29 B C 30 D E F

182
162

161
141
161
183

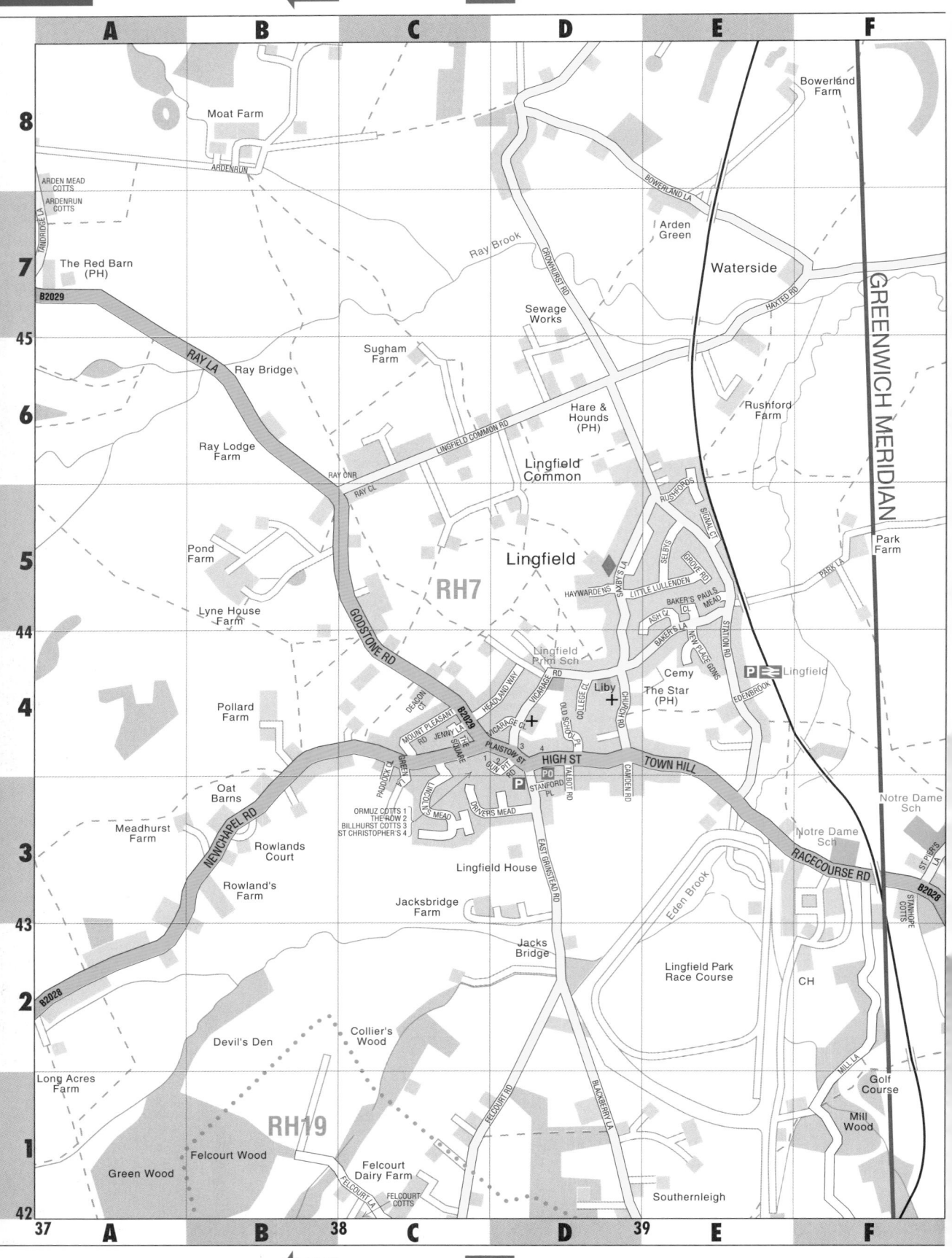

LINGFIELD RD

Haxted Hill

West Haxted Farm

East Haxted Farm

Haxted

8

DWELLY LA

Puttenden Manor

Haxted Mead

NORMANS LA

Barrow Green Farm

HAXTED RD

Haxted Mead Farm

Haxted Mill Mus

7

WATER LA

River Eden

Eden Brook

45

6

RH7

Cernes Farm

Eden Valley Walk

Vanguard Way

TN8

Dencher Wood

Jesmor Farm

Starborough Farm

STARBOROUGH RD

Starborough Castle

5

Billeshurst Wood

St Pier's Farm

ST PIER'S LA

44

Margaret's Hill

Furze Wood

Margaret's Wood

Bottoms Wood

4

Lingfield Hospital Sch

YOUNGMAN

ORCHARD COTTS

Moor Farm

Skitts Farm House

Old Forge

B2028

Carewell Wood

Windermere

MOOR LA

3

Carewell Farm

Skitts Farm

43

RACECOURSE RD

Woodgate

CLANDERS MEAD

DORMANS RD

FORD MANOR RD

Hoopers Farm

2

The Plough (PH)

PLAYFORD

CLARIDGE

DORMANS AVE

GUNS

PLOUGH RD

JEDDERE COTTS

BASSETTS HILL

Greathed Manor

Dormansland

MAYFIELD

SWALLOWFIELD

KINNIBRUGH DR

NEWHACHE

DORMANS HIGH ST

HOLLOW LA

ST CLAIRE COTTS

MEARES CL

THE MEADES

Home Farm

Reynolds Wood

1

WEST ST

COLES MEADOW

LAUDRE CL

HURST

PO

BARNFIELD COTTS

WEBB

FORD MANOR COTTS

Ford Manor

Dairy Wood

Old Plantation

Sussex Border Path

MOON'S LA

42

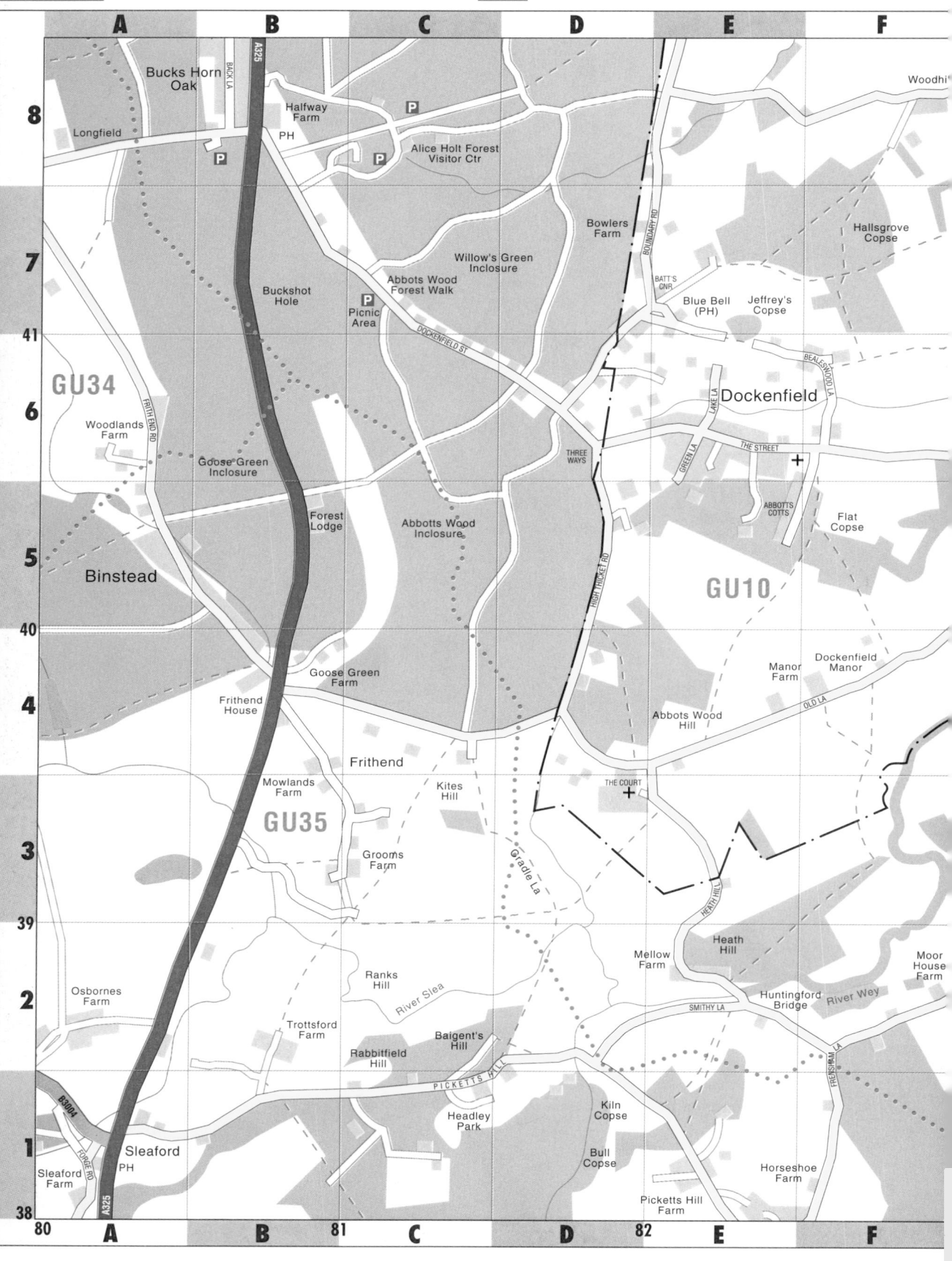

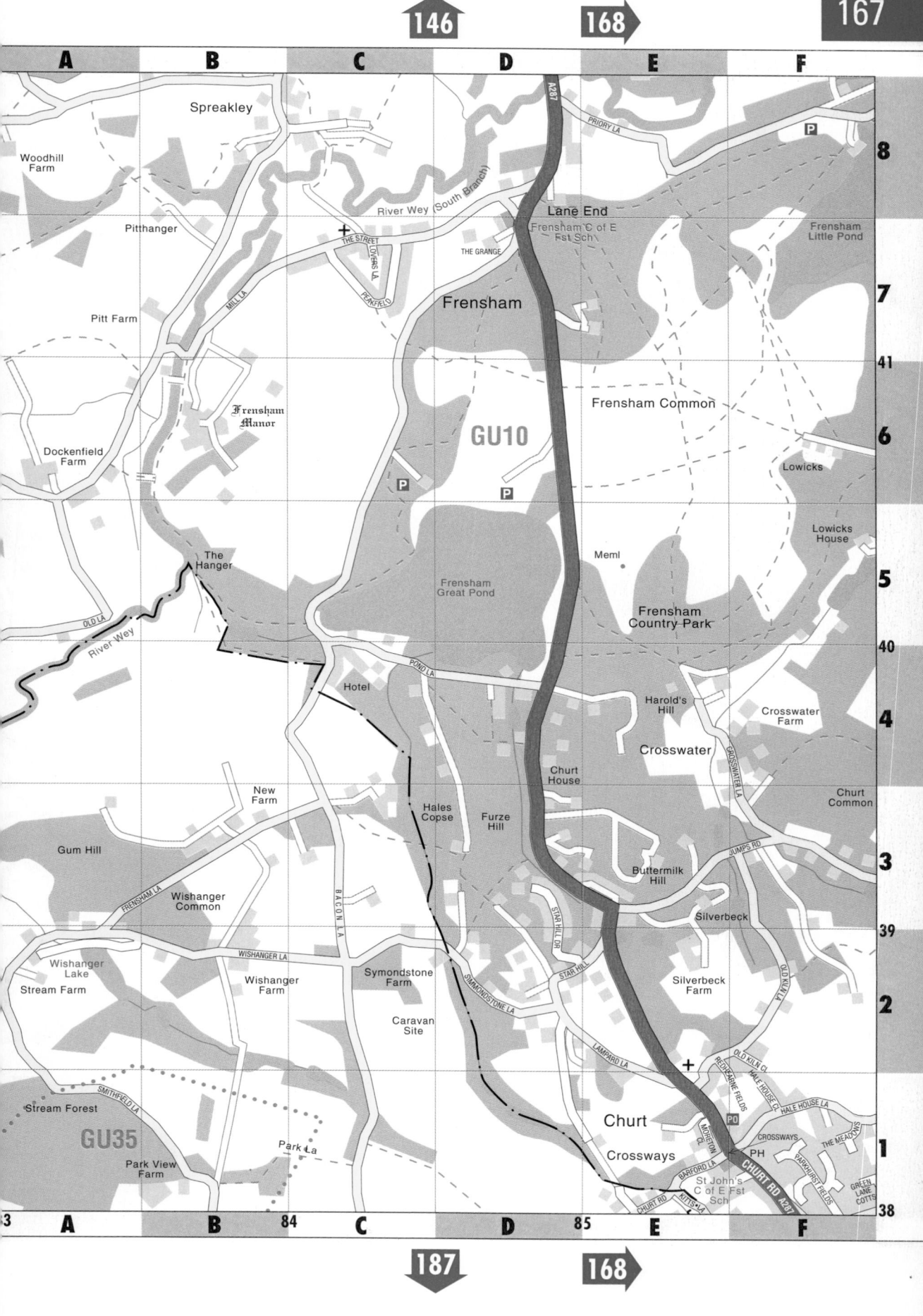

A B C D E F

Chuter's Cottage

Green Hill

Abbot's Lodge

Greensand Way

Lion's Mouth

8

Frensham Little Pond

Greenhills Farm

GRANGE RD

The Grange

7

WINCHESTER RD

EGLINTON RD

41

CARLISLE RD

Hankley Common

WELLESLEY RD

6

LOWICKS RD

Kettlebury Hill

Grey Walls

SANDY LA

GLEBE LA

Rushmoor

GU10

GU8

5

PO

40

The Flashes

TILFORD RD

Gold Hill

4

The Devil's Jumps

Wychmoor Copse

THURSLEY RD

Kettlebury Farm

3

The Miravalle (PH)

JUMPS RD

Churt Place Farm

Pitch Place Farm

39

Churt Lea

CRABTREE LA

Old Kiln Farm

2

HALE HOUSE LA

Hillside Farm

Hyde Farm

Hyde Copse

SALOIS LA

GREEN CROSS LA

Avalon

OLD BARN LA

Hyde LA

Glenhead Farm

Fair View Farm

Upper Ridgeway Farm

1

Green Cross Farm

Green Cross

Green Farm

Stock Farm House

Marchants Farm

38

GREEN LA

GREEN LA

86 A B 87 C D 88 E F

A   B   C   D   E   F

8

Pudmore
Pond

The
Moat

Ockley
Common

7

Forked
Pond

41

Truxford
Wood
Farm

6

Will
Reeds

Warren
Mere

Silkmill
Pond

Thursley
Common

New
Pond

Houndown
Bottom

Nature
Reserve

GU8

Hammer
Pond

5

40

Houndown

Sewage
Works

Dye
House

Thursley

Foldsdown

OLD PORTSMOUTH RD

French
Hill

LAKE
COTTS

4

GREENSAND WAY

THE LANE

Three
Horse
Shoes
(PH)

Milhanger

Smallbrook

STREETFIELD

+

The
Grove

3

THE STREET

PORTSMOUTH RD

39

Haybarn

Pitch
Place

HOMEFIELD

Hedge
Farm

HIGHFIELD LA

Cosford
House

Heath
Hall

2

Ridgeway
Farm

Little
Cowdray
Farm

Lower
Highfield
Farm

Bedford
Farm

Heath Hall
Farm

FRENCH LA

LOWER HOUSE RD

Punchbowl
Farm

Upper
Highfield
Farm

Mount
Pleasant

Bowlhead
Green

BOWLHEAD GREEN RD

BEECH HILL

Bedford and
Hole Farm

HUTTON HILL RD

Bowlhead
Green
Farm

1

38

A3

A3

89   A   B   90   C   D   91   E   F

171 151

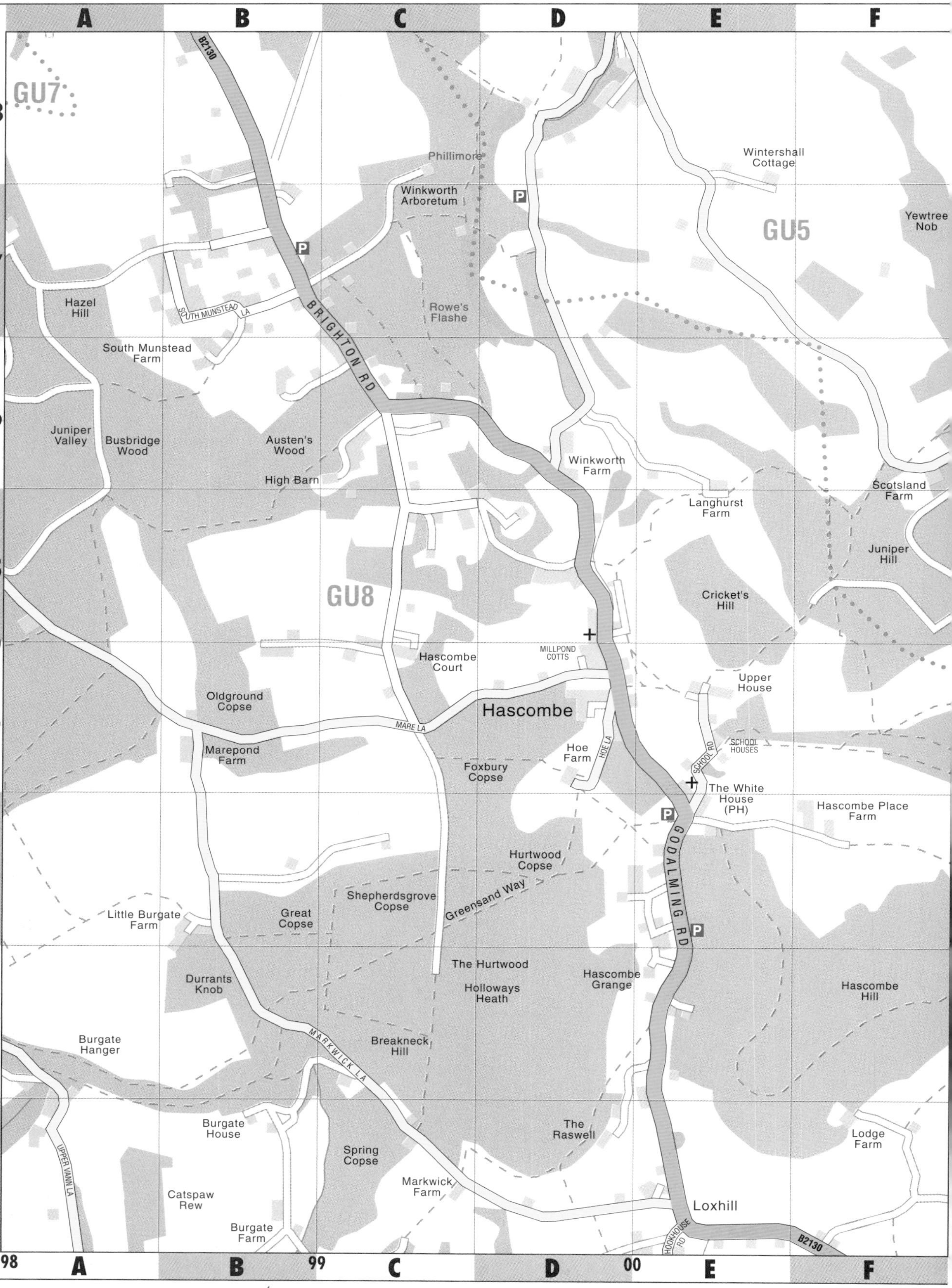

GU7

B2130

GU5

Wintershall Cottage

Phillimore

Winkworth Arboretum

Yewtree Nob

P

Hazel Hill

SOUTH MUNSTEAD LA

P

BRIGHTON RD

Rowe's Flashe

41

South Munstead Farm

Juniper Valley

Busbridge Wood

Austen's Wood

Winkworth Farm

Langhurst Farm

Scotsland Farm

High Barn

Juniper Hill

GU8

Cricket's Hill

Hascombe Court

MILLPOND COTTS

Upper House

Oldground Copse

MARE LA

Hascombe

SCHOOL HOUSES

SCHOOL RD

The White House (PH)

Hascombe Place Farm

Marepond Farm

Hoe Farm

HOE LA

Foxbury Copse

P

GODALMING RD

Hurtwood Copse

Shepherdsgrove Copse

Greensand Way

P

Little Burgate Farm

Great Copse

The Hurtwood

Hascombe Grange

Hascombe Hill

Durrants Knob

Holloways Heath

MARKWICK LA

Burgate Hanger

Breakneck Hill

UPPER VANN LA

Burgate House

Spring Copse

The Raswell

Lodge Farm

Catspaw Rew

Markwick Farm

Loxhill

Burgate Farm

HOOKHOUSE RD

B2130

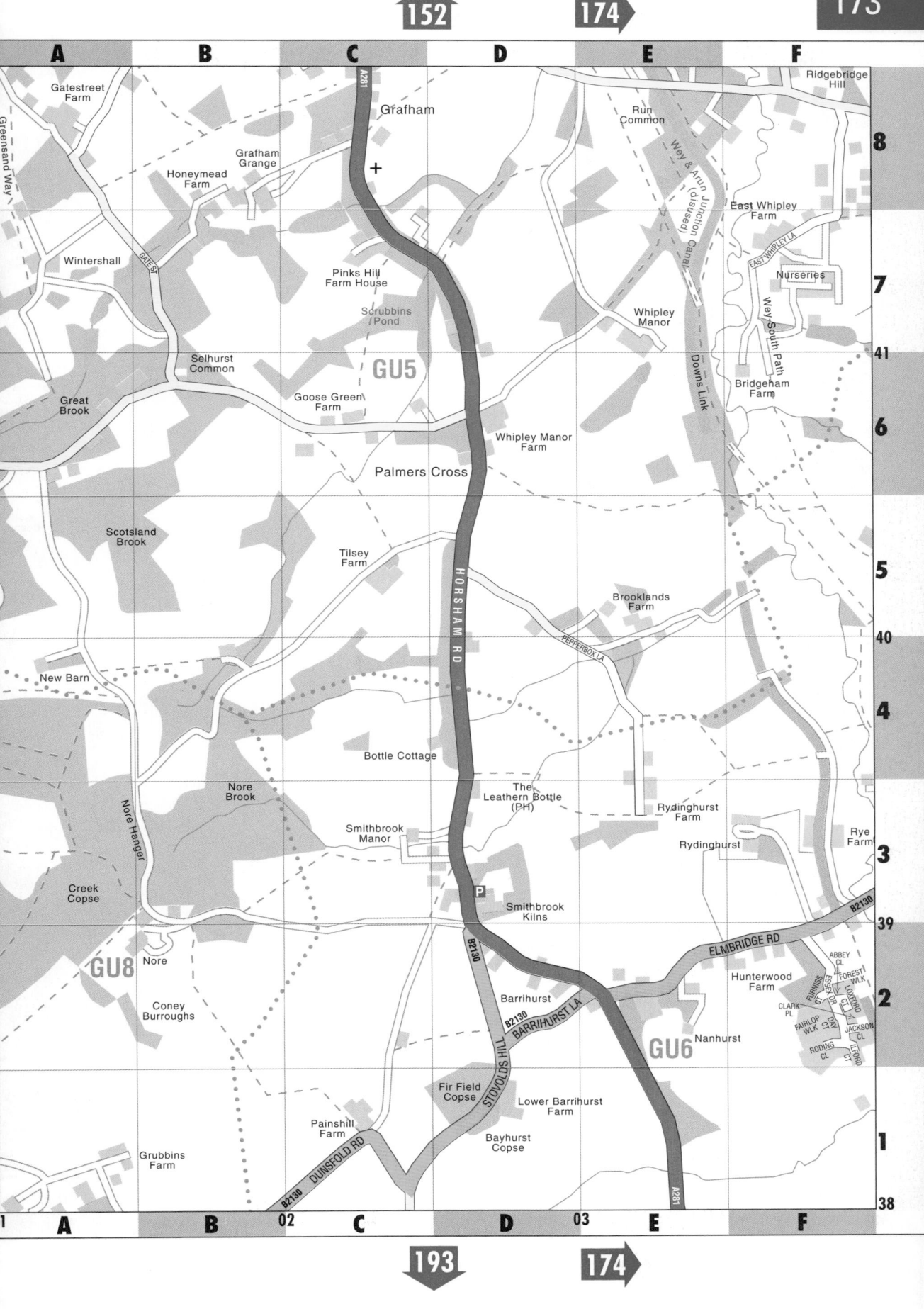

A B C D E F

Winterfold House
High Wethersell Wood
Rapsley Farm
RIDE WAY
EWHURST RD
Ewhurst Place
Radnor Place Farm
8

CONEYHURST LA
Cornhill Manor (Training Ctr)
Path Four Acres
Bramblehurst Farm
High Canfold Stud
Wykehurst Farm
Coneyhurst House
Gulls Isle
7
Coneyhurst Gill
SHERE RD
41
The Bull's Head (PH)
OCKLEY RD
B2127
High Copse
Shippen Hill
LINKS CL
DOWNHURST RD
THE AVENUE
FARTHINGHAM LA
6
CH
High Wykehurst
Wykehurst Lodge
THE STREET
THE GLEBE
Westland Farm
Golf Course
+
THE MOUNT
RECTORY CL
MAPLEDRAKES RD
Lemans Barn Farm
Ewhurst C of E Prim Sch
+
MAPLEDRAKES CL
Ewhurst
GU6
MOUNT CL
PO
WILLIAMS CL
5
Ashen Copse
Sayers Croft Rural Ctr
BROOMERS LA
HAZEL BANK
GRANSDEN CL
THE GREEN
40
Upper Canfold Wood
LILYFIELDS CHASE
LARKFIELD
THE PADDOCK
Campions
CRANLEIGH RD
GADBRIDGE LA
THE GREEN
Ewhurst Green
4
CANFOLD COTTS
Gadbridge Farm
PLOUGH LA
Park Mead Schs
BOOKHURST HILL
BOOKHURST RD
Rumbeams Farm
WANBOROUGH LA
LORETTO CL
CASTLE CL
DOVER CT
BLOXHAM RD
STUDWAY'S CL
FETTES RD
Lower Canfold Wood
Slythehurst
HORSHAM RD
3
Book Hurst
Thornhurst Brook
THE RIDGEWAY
HOMEWOOD
RIDGEWAY CL
Parliament Farm
39
CRANLEIGH MEAD
Bowles Farm
Old House
2
TURNSFORD WAY
Coxland
New Park Farm
SOMERSBURY LA
Galley Wood
Bowles Rough
Great Copse
1
Rowgardens Copse
Whitehall Copse
38

07 A B 08 C D 09 E F

A B C D E F

8

Luykins
Farm

Brookhurst
Grange

Brookhurst
Farm

COTTON ROW

Wickland
Farm

Forest Green
Farm

Etherley
Farm

Etherley
Copse

7

Losely

South Lodge
Farm

Coophurst
Farm

Stubbetts

Lyefield
Lodge

OCKLEY RD

Forest
Green

Forest
Green

The
Parrot
Inn

Gosterwood
Manor

B2126
PANTHURST LA
HOLMBURY RD
B2127
MILL LA

41

Woodlands
Farm

Woodlands
Place

B2127

6

Eastland
Farm

North Breache
Manor

Cobbetts
Farm

Waterland
Farm

Sewage
Works

NEW RD

Jordan's
Farm

Ives
Farm

POND HEAD LA

Bullcroft
Farm

Pisley
Farm

PISLEY LA

5

Yard
Farm

PLOUGH LA

GU6

Lyefield
Farm

LYEFIELD LA

Bridgham
Farm

RH5

Pisley
Copse

40

4

Plough
Farm

Lower Breache
House

LOWER BREACHE RD

Pond Head
Farm

Pond Head
Farm

HORSHAM RD

Holden Brook

Pisley
Copse

3

Cobbler's Brook

Lowerhouse
Farm

Mayes
Court

POND HEAD LA

Wollards
Farm

Mayes
Green

Parklands

Holden
Wood

Golf
Course

Gatton Manor
(Hotel &
Country Club)

Golf
Course

39

2

Buildings
Wood

Northlands

Stonehouse
Wood

TRAP LA

Okewood
Cottage

STANDON LA

Hutchings
Copse

1

Somersbury
Manor

HORSHAM RD

FROGGETTS LA

Froggetts

Walliswood
Farm

Wallis
Wood

The
Scarlett Arms
(PH)

Kiln
Copse

Pollingfold

CHURCH LA

38

Works

A | B | C | D | E | F

8
Etherley Copse
ABINGER RD
Church Wood
New Barn House
Meares Copse
Buckinghill Farm
Lodgelands Farm
BOGNOR RD
A29

ETHERLEY HILL
COX CNR
Pennsylvania Copse
BROOMEHALL RD
Highfield Wood

7
Goster Wood
OCKLEY RD
Sheep Green
Aviary Barn
Aviary Copse
BURYWOOD HILL
Square Copse
Holms Gill
PARK LA

41
High Woods
Wellspring Pond
Hatch Park

6
Woodstock House
Volvens Farm
Kissing Copse
Home Farm
Jayes Park
Jayes Park
LAKE RD
COLE'S LA
Ockley Court
Courtbottom Wood
B2126

5
MOLE ST
Castle Copse
RH5
Weavers Pond
B2126
Red Lion Inn
PO
Kings Arms Inn
Church Copse

40
PISLEY LA
Fishfold Farm
Parkland Farmhouse
The Scott-Broadwood CE Inf Sch
Sewage Works
CRICKETERS CL
Ockley
Vann Farm
Wickney Holt
VANN FARM RD

4
ELMERS RD
The Cricketers Arms (PH)
Elmers Farm
STANE ST
FRIDAY'S
Vann House
Vann Lake
VANN LAKE
BRICKYARD COPSE
RECTORY CL

3
Golf Course
NEW BARN LA
CATHILL LA
New Barn
Cathill Wood
VANN LAKE RD

39
LEITH VALE COTTS
Standon Homestead
STANDON LA
Birches Wood

2
Leith Vale
Hannah Peschar Gall & Gdn
Fir Copse
Sewage Works
Eversheds Farm
MEARE'S

1
A29
Oakwood Mill Farm
WALEY'S
Waleys La
Hopgardens Rue
Waleys

38

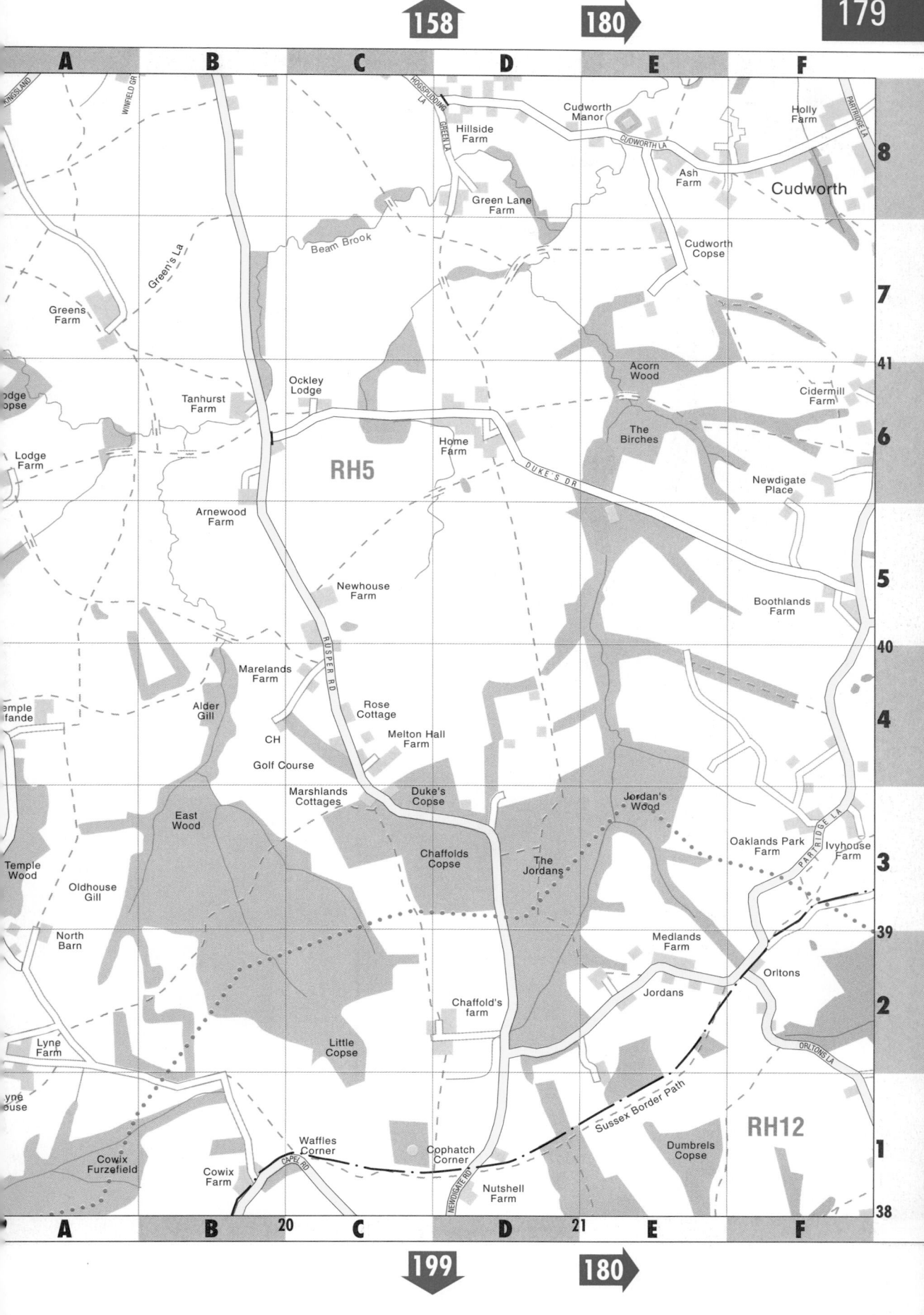

A B C D E F

WINFIELD GR

KINGSLAND

HOGSPUDDING LA

GREEN LA

Cudworth
Manor

Holly
Farm

PARTRIDGE LA

Hillside
Farm

CUDWORTH LA

Ash
Farm

Cudworth

8

Green Lane
Farm

Green's La

Beam Brook

Cudworth
Copse

7

Greens
Farm

Acorn
Wood

41

Ockley
Lodge

odge
opse

Tanhurst
Farm

Cidermill
Farm

The
Birches

6

Lodge
Farm

RH5

Home
Farm

DUKE'S DR

Newdigate
Place

Arnewood
Farm

Newhouse
Farm

Boothlands
Farm

5

40

emple
fande

Marelands
Farm

Alder
Gill

Rose
Cottage

RUSPER RD

Temple
Wood

CH

Melton Hall
Farm

Golf Course

4

Marshlands
Cottages

Duke's
Copse

East
Wood

Jordan's
Wood

Oaklands Park
Farm

Ivyhouse
Farm

PARTRIDGE LA

3

Oldhouse
Gill

Chaffolds
Copse

The
Jordans

39

North
Barn

Medlands
Farm

Orltons

Chaffold's
farm

Jordans

2

Lyne
Farm

Little
Copse

yne
ouse

ORLTONS LA

Sussex Border Path

Dumbrels
Copse

RH12

1

Cowix
Furzefield

Waffles
Corner

CAPEL RD

Cophatch
Corner

NEWDIGATE RD

38

Cowix
Farm

Nutshell
Farm

A B 20 C D 21 E F

179   159

A   B   C   D   E   F

Gildings Farm

Beggarshouse La

Beggarshouse La

STAN HILL

8

Greenings Farm

Greenings

Little Greenings

Barfield Farm

Charlwood Place

NORWOODHILL RD

PUDDING LA

Spottles Farm

Charlwood Cty Inf Sch

7

Furzefield Farm

PARTRIDGE LA

Pagewood

RECTORY LA

Charlwood

ROSEMARY LA

FIR TREE RD

SWAN LA

CHAPEL RD

WIDGW CNR

PO

PH

SEWILL CL

PERRY LA

ORCHARD COTTS

41

Welland Gill

RH5

GLOVER'S RD

GLENFIELD COTTS

THE STREET

DOLBY TERR

CHALMERS CT

HORLEY RD

Charlwood Place Farm

Gatwick Zoo Windmill

Spicer's Bridge

6

Glover's Plantation

Glover's Wood

Welling Barn Farm

Betchworth Works

Tifter's Farm

Sussex Border Path

RH6

COUNCIL COTTS

IFIELD RD

LOWFIELD HEATH RD

5

RUSS HILL

CHARLWOOD LA

Mountnoddy Wood

Russ Hill Farm

40

Gatwick Wena Hotel

Westlands

Waggoners Farm

Birchfield

4

Westlands Farm

Upper Prestwood Farm

Great Burlands

Little Park Farm

LITTLE PARK ENTERPRISES

Prestwood Copse

Burlands

Furze Field

Man's Brook

Water Hall

3

Scrag Copse

Burlands Copse

Naldretts Farm

Red Gables

PRESTWOOD LA

39

CHARLWOOD RD

Orltons Copse

Lower Prestwood Farm

RH11

Ifield Wood

Cophall Wood

2

Gotwick Farm

Oak Tree Farm

Tilgate

HILLYBARN RD

Ifield Court Farm

Ifield Court Hotel

RH12

IFIELD WOOD

ORLTONS LA

LANGHURST LA

Langhurst Farm

THE MOUNT

The Mount Farm

Hilly Barn Farmhouse

Ifieldwood

The Druids

Pockney's Farm

TWEED LA

38

22   A   B   23   C   D   24   E   F

183
163

RH6

Nevergood Wood

Leighfurze Field

Quarry Farm

B2028

Churchill Stud

8

Homewood

Eastpark Farm

WEST PARK RD

The Plantation

Laylands Farm

HOBBS IND EST

RH7

7

STUBPOND LA

Sewage Works

Woodcock Bridge

The Woodcock (PH)

HEATHERWAY

Wire Mill LA

Wire Mill Lake

EASTBOURNE RD

A22

West Park

41

B2028

Baker's Wood

Moat Wood

Cooper's Moors

WOODCOCK HILL

6

Perry Farm

Hedgecourt

Hedgecourt Lake

Park Farm

A22

Domewood

HERONS CL

Park Wood

5

HERONS LEA

COPTHORNE RD

MILL LA

HEDGECOURT PL

TANGLE OAK

Felbridge

40

SNOW HILL BSN & CTR

B2037

SNOW HILL

B2037

Felbridge Cty Prim Sch

LYNDHURST PARK CL

A264

Snow Hill

Fellcot Farm

TWITTEN LA

4

A264

SNOW HILL

Kenward's Farm

LAKE VIEW RD

FELLCOT RD

CHESTERFIELD CL

Furnace Wood

Michaelmas Farm

WHEELERS WAY

ROWPLATT LA

MARDELL CL

MOVER CL

TITHE ORCH

CRAWLEY DOWN RD

Gibbshaven Farm

Felbridge RD

RH19

Nurseries

Felbridge Water

The Birches

3

RH10

Furnace Wood

FURNACE RD

39

Furnace Pond

Nurseries.

2

Stubbits Wood

CUTTINGLYE RD

Cuttinglye Wood

HOPHURST HILL

Greenfield Shaw

Gulledge

Down Park Farm

Parkfields Farm

Hophurst Farm

Worth Way

Sussex Border Path

1

CUTTINGLYE LA

FERNHILL CL

HAVEN GDNS

HOPHURST LA

TILLWOOD DR

GAGE CL

AVIARY WAY

The Larches

Railway Shaw

38

34

35

36

C1
1 THE BROWNINGS
2 BYRON GR
3 CHAUCER AVE
4 TENNYSON RISE
5 THE SAYERS
6 WORDSWORTH RISE

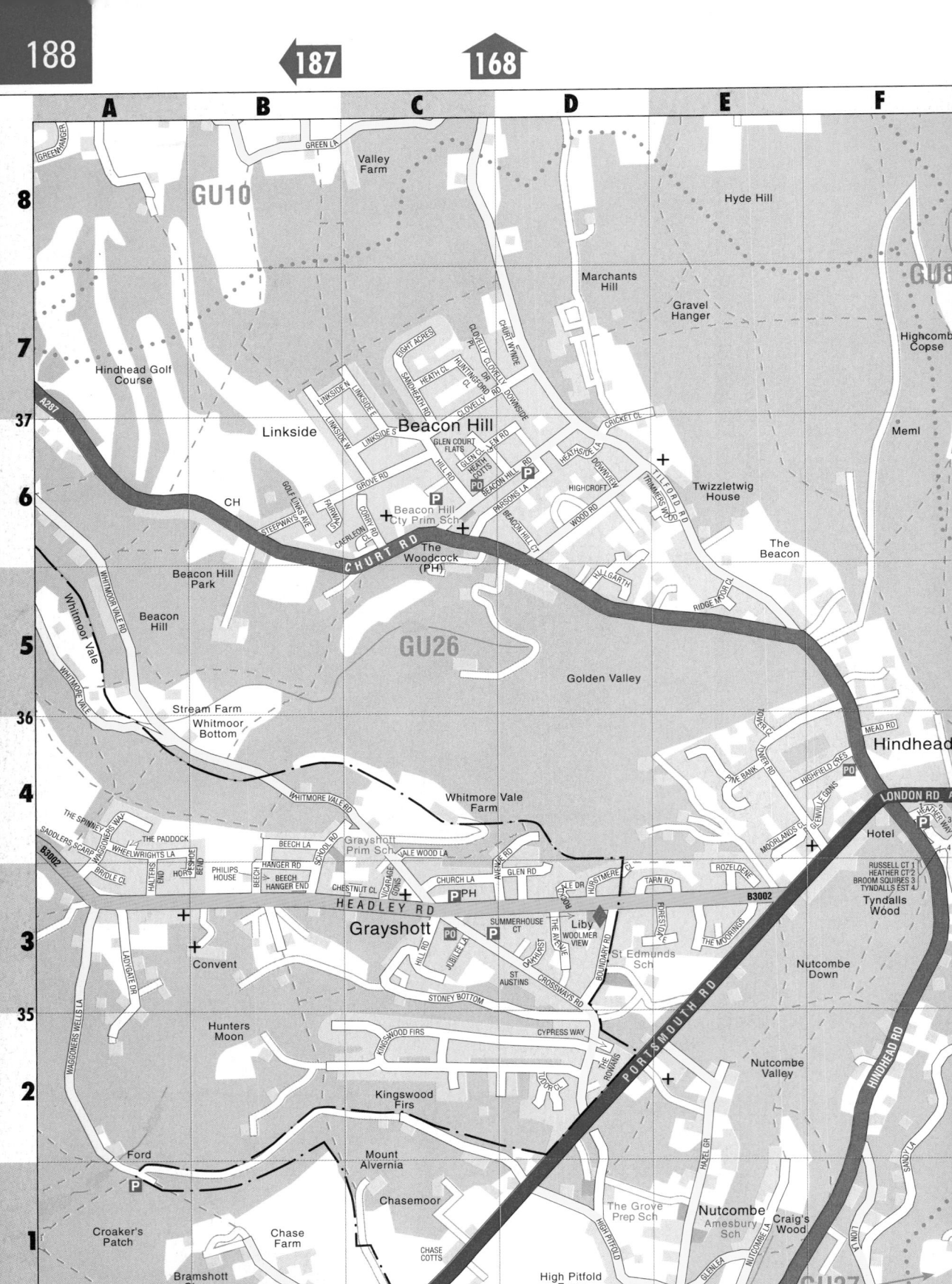

A B C D E F

8
7
37
6
5
36
4
3
35
2
1
34

Highcomb Bottom

A3
Black Hanger
Emley Farm
Beech Hanger
BEECH HILL
Black Hanger Farm
Rutton Hill
Hall's Cottage
Halnacker Copse
Harry's Holt
The Soaks
RUTTON HILL RD
PARK LA
Park House
GU8
Begley Farm
Sawpit Rew
Youth Hostel
PORTSMOUTH RD
Begley Copse
Highcombe Farm
Boundless Farm
The Roundles
Creedhole Farm
Witley Farm
Hindhead Common
Greensand Way
Boundless Copse
High Button
Devil's Punch Bowl
GU26
Nature Trail
Mon
Gibbet Hill
Hurthill Copse
P
Hind Head
Invall
South Park Farm
Lower Park Farm
Tuder's Copse
A286
Keffold's Copse
Grayswood Farm
Coombe Head
Keffolds
GU27
CHURCH LA
Grayswood Sch
The Royal Sch
Keffolds Farm
PH
LOWER RD
Nursery
Coombswell Copse
Weydown Common
Wispers Sch
GRAYSWOOD RD
Grayswood
THE MOUNT
Grayswood Common
UPPER MOUNT
Grayswood Hill
FARNHAM LA
BUNCH LA
WEYCOMBE RD
WHITFIELD CL
WHITFIELD RD
A286
SANDY LA
WILLIAMSON CL
WILDWOOD CL
CLAMMER HILL

39
90
91
34

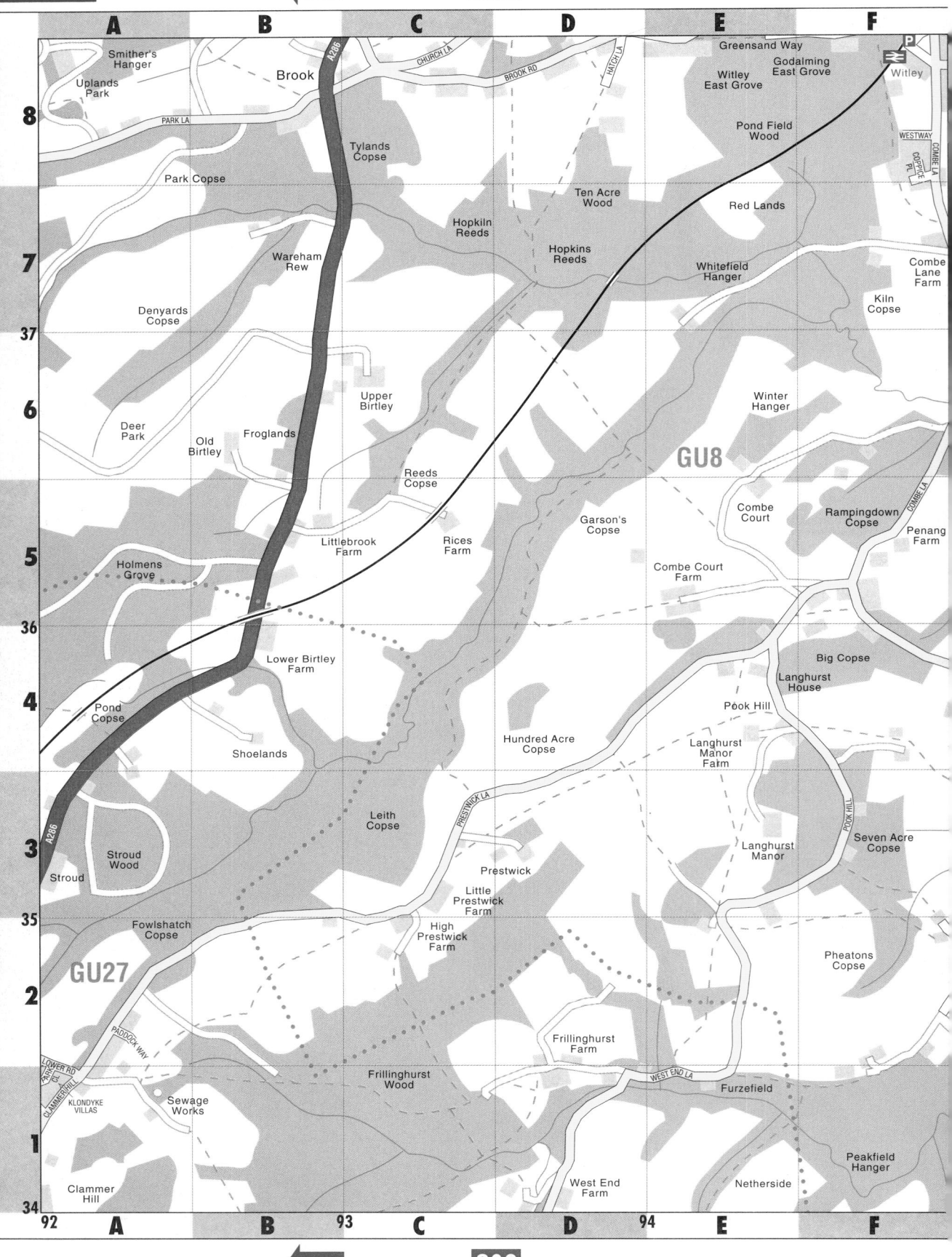

A B C D E F

HORSHAM RD
Whitehall
Norley Farm
Windgate Cott
8
Thornhurst Brook
Owlbarn Copse
Longhurst Hill
The Wind Break
SOMERSBURY LA
7
Vachery House
GU6
Home Wood
Brooklands Farm
37
Baynard's Park
Vachery Farm
6
Cobbler's Brook
Home Farm
Sharpe's Copse
Collins Farm
Baynard's Park
5
Tilthouse Farm
36
New Barn
Pollingfold Bridge
Massers Wood
LINACRE DR
Grub Copse
The Wheatsheaf (PH)
4
Ruet
FURZEN LA
STATION RD
North Wood
Maybanks Manor
Tolt Garth
3
LAWNS RD
Baynards Sta (dis)
35
HERMONGER LA
Starveall Copse
Downs Link
Woodthorpe
2
BAYNARDS RD
South Wood
RH12
COX GREEN RD
Great Inholms
Sussex Border Path
Little Hawks Hill
CHURCH ST
HAWKRIDGE
Cox Green
Little Inholms
Hobbs Copse
Street Copse
PO
The Kings Head (PH)
The Crickets
Works
LYNWICK ST
HIGHCROFT DR
Woodsomes Farm
Windacres Farm
B2128
34

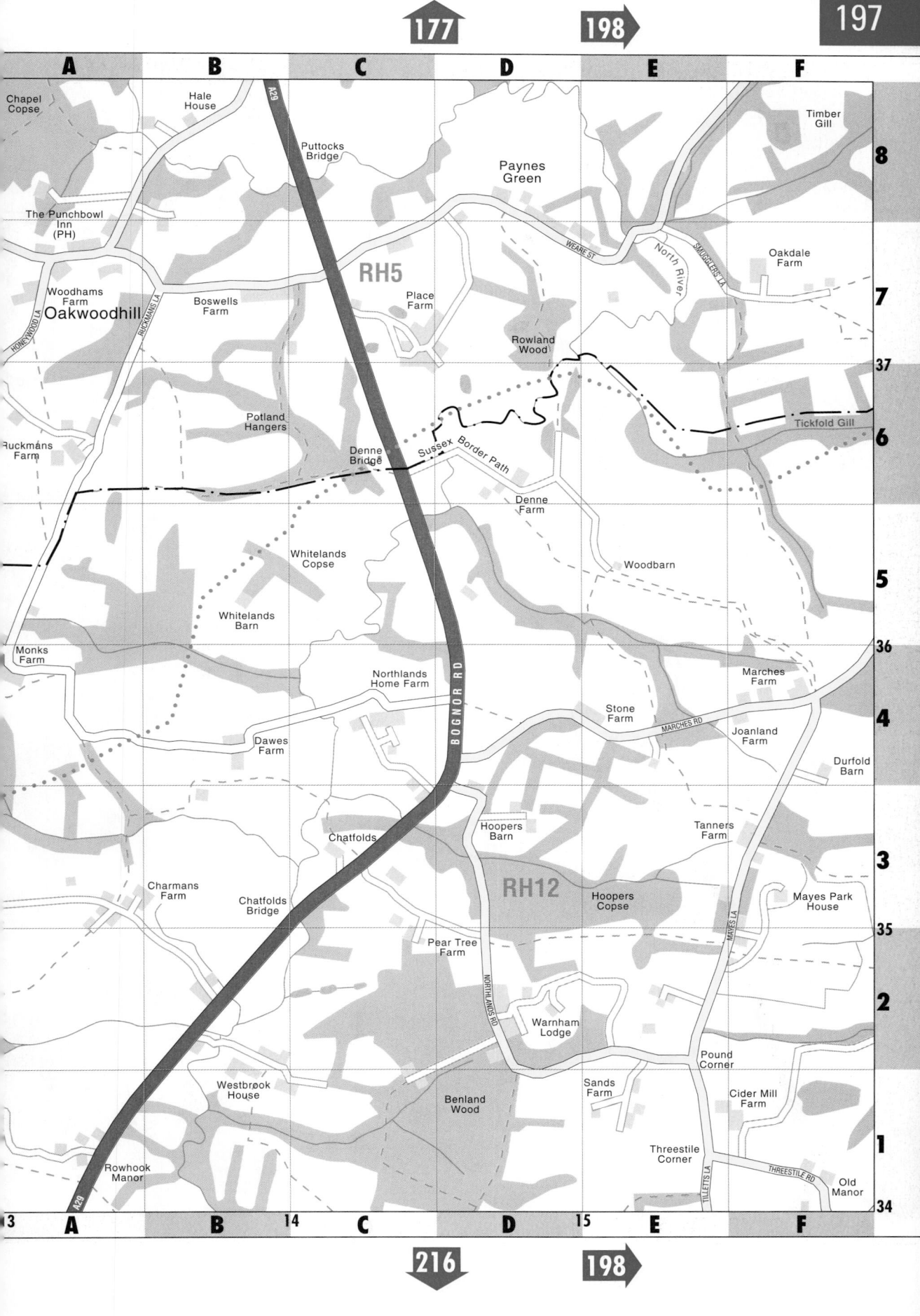

197
178

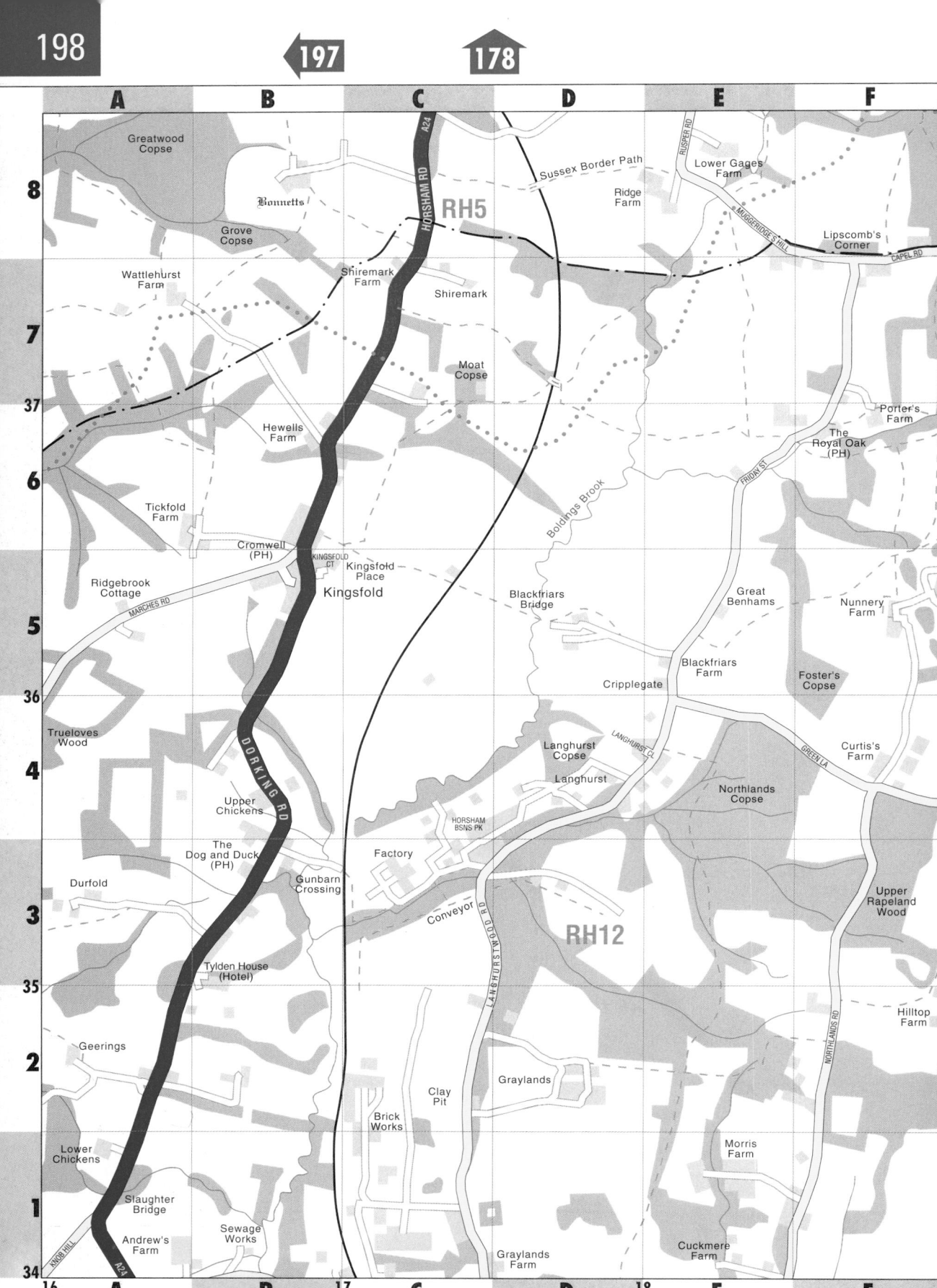

197
217

A B C D E F

8
Rome Wood
Highams
Furzefield Wood
Venters Farm
CAPEL RD
New Barn Farm
Yew Tree Cott
Rusper House
Venters
CAPEL RD
NEWDIGATE RD
Ghyll Manor (Hotel)
Chowles

7
Sussex Border Path
HIGH ST
Rusper
EAST ST
Rusper Cty Prim Sch
PO
PH
Normans
Cobnor
Horsegills Wood
COOKS MEAD
Millfields Farm
37
PEERS HILL
Pucks Croft
Lambs Green

6
ASHMORE LA
Baldhorns Copse
Kiln Copse
Nurseries
CANONBURY COTTS
PH
Dialpost Farm
GARDENERS GN
LAMBS GREEN RD
Axmas Farm
Ashfolds
Sewage Farm
Cow Wood
RH12
Rusper Court Farm

5
Nunnery
Nuns Wood
Manns Farm
Baldhorns Park Farm
Rusper Court House
Saykers
River Mole
HORSHAM RD
Baldhorns Park
36
Old Park Farm
Fay Cottages
Seers Croft

4
GREEN LA
The Lodge
WIMLAND RD
Faygate Wood Farm
Carylls Farm
Furze Field
FAYGATE LA
Sloughbrook Gill
Carylls Lodge

3
Holming Wood
Coombers Farm
Rusper Copse
North Grange Farm
KILNWOOD LA
Allingham Wood
WIMLANDS LA
35
Culross
Caryll's Lea Farm

2
Hurst Wood
Hurst Hill
Breakey Gill
Wimland Farm
Durrants Copse
Bakehouse Copse
WIMLAND HILL
RUSPER RD
Bush Copse
FAYGATE BSNS CTR
OAK WLK

1
Hawkesbourne Farm
Budd's Farm
Durrants
Holmbush Inn (PH)
Faygate
The Castle Earthwork
Benson's Cottage
Faygate
PARK RD
CLOVERS COTTS
CARYLLS COTTS
BENSON'S LA
CRAWLEY RD
A264
34

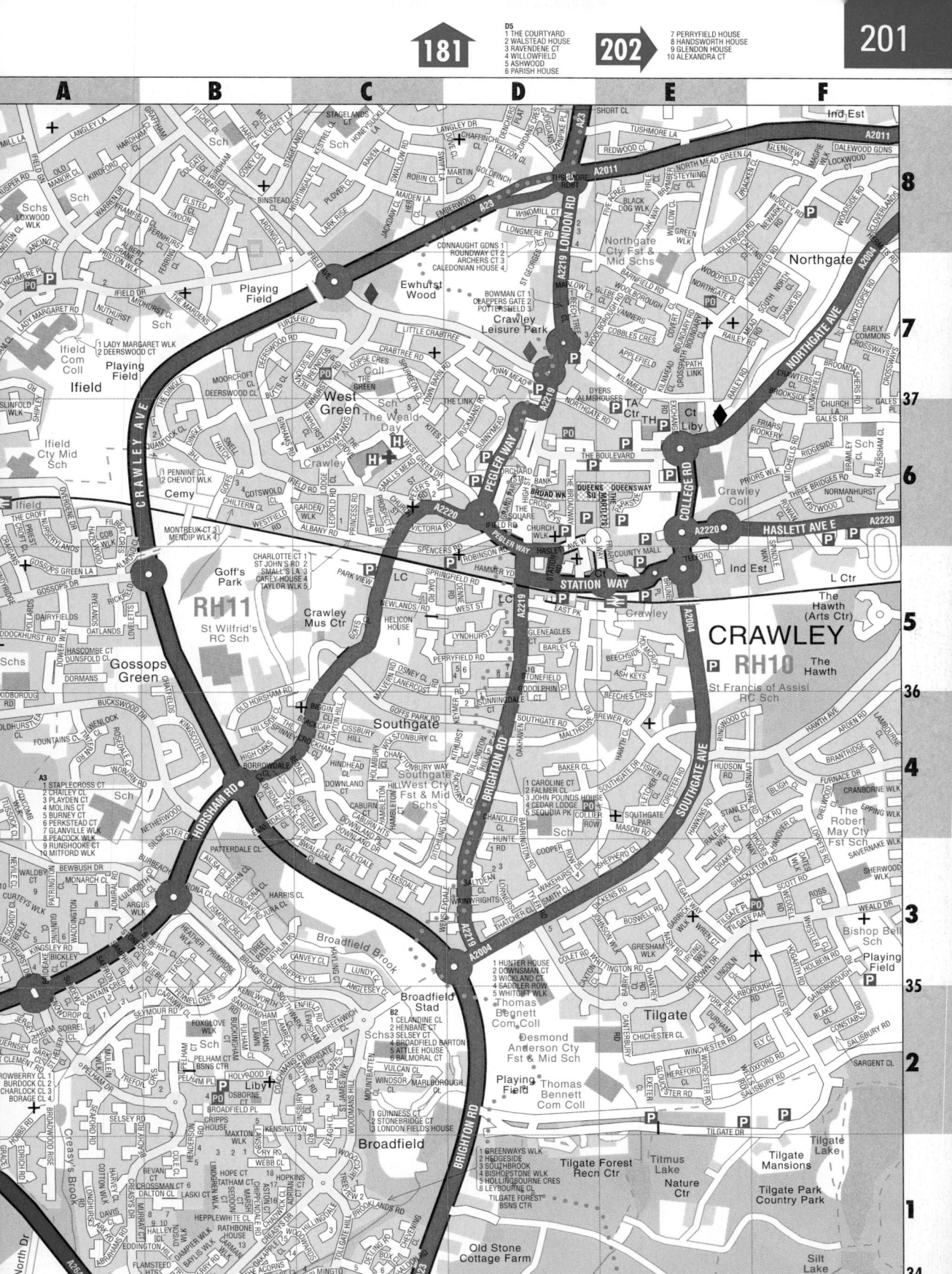

201
182

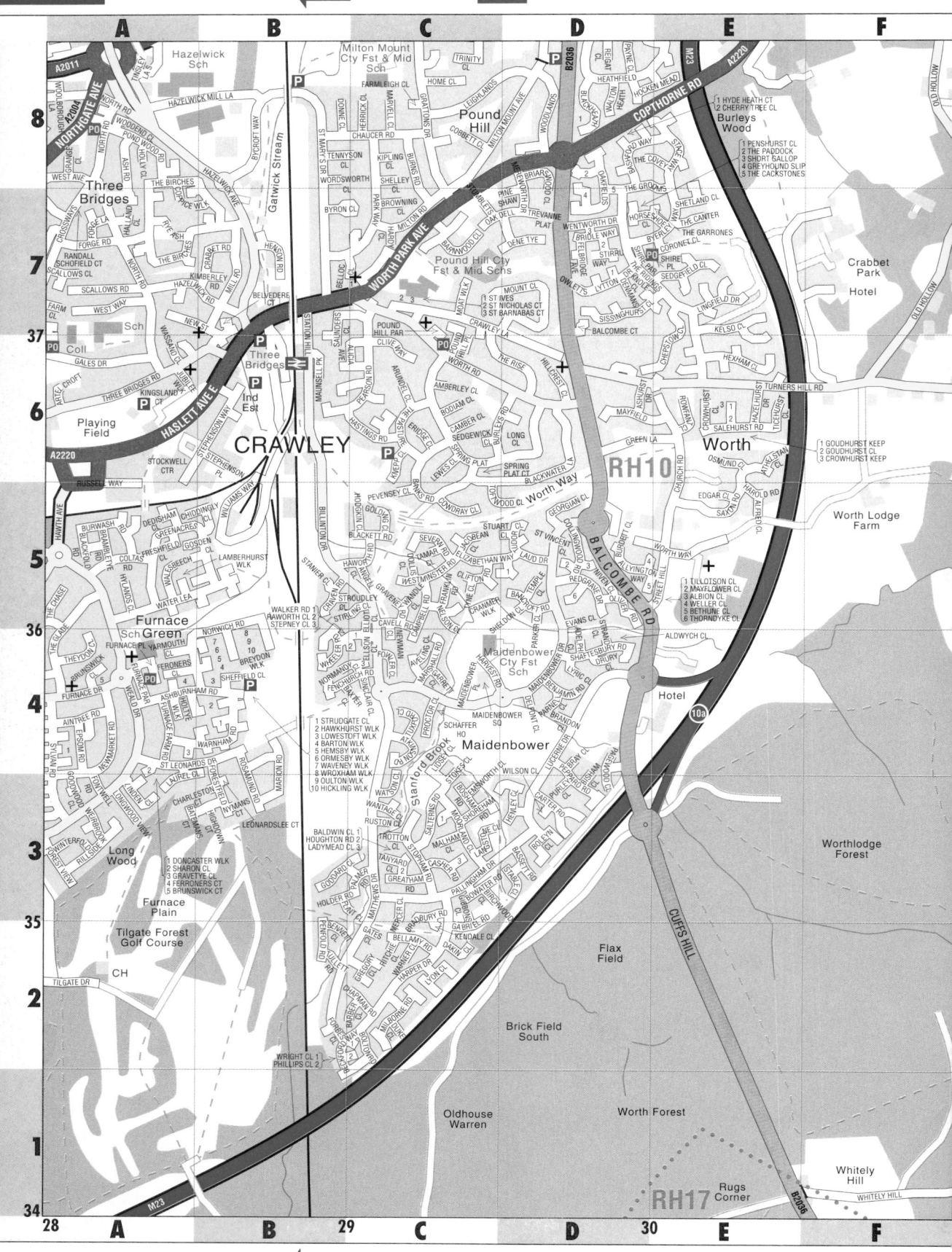

203

184

8

7

37

6

5

36

4

3

35

2

1

34

A B C D E F

34 35 36

Front Wood

SCHOLARS CT

Worth Way

B2028

RUFWOOD

WYN LA

SQUARES CL

SUNNY AVE

SANDY LA

GARDNER RD

LONG ACRE

BUCKLEY PL

SUNNYHILL CL

VICARAGE RD

BEECH GDNS

BEECH HOLME

STATION RD

BOWERS PL

OLD STATION CL

GRANGE RD

TURNERS HILL RD

GRANGE CRES

HOPHURST DR

HOPHURST CL

HILLSIDE

THE COPPICE

UNDERWOOD CL

BURLEIGH WAY

YORKE CT

BURLEIGH CL

ALDER CL

BRICKYARD LA 2

BRICKLANDS

KILN RD

WOODLANDS

SANDHILL LA

GRANGE RD

Schs

PO

HAWARDEN

SPINNEY CL

HAZEL WAY

HAZEL CL

COB CL

ASH CL

TILTWOOD DR

GRANSTON WAY

HALSELAND

THE MARTINS

ARCHWAY CL

BIRCH CL

COPSE

WOOD

The Grange

SUNNYMEAD 1
RIDGEDALE 2
AUCHINLECK CT 3
ROYAL OAK HOUSE 4

Grange Farm

Crawley Down

Worth Way

Rushetts Wood

BURLEIGH LA

Burleigh House Farm

Sussex Border Path

Gulledge Wood

French Wood

Tilkhurst Farm

RH10

Sandhill

Rainbow Shaw

Little Nobs

Warren Wood

Burleigh Arches Wood

Home Wood

Peartree Shaw

Fen Place Mill

River Medway

Moat Shaw

Hurley Farm

Ash Leigh Farm

Burleigh Oaks House

Alexander House

Mill Wood

MILLWOOD

Furze Field

TURNER'S HILL RD

RH19

MEDWAY

HILL HOUSE CL

B2028

EAST ST

Furzewood Farm

Castle Shaw

B2110

NORTH ST

Turners Hill

LION LA

PO

MAUDLIN LA

NEW COTTS LA

Burleigh Farm

Target Shaw

Tickeridge Farm

Kingscote

The Crown (PH)

WILLOW RIDGE

WITHYPITTS

Sch

CHURCH RD

Rashes Farm

Spring Wood

Rookery Wood

Holstein Wood

Tickeridge Shaw

Bluebell Rly

South Wood

Withypitts

Coomberdean Wood

Great Wildgoose Wood

Stone Wood

Vowels Forest Wlk

Minepit Wood

Mill Place Wood

Withy Pitts Farm

Thornhill Cottages

P

VOWELS LA

Vowels Gill

The Punch Bowl (PH)

SELSFIELD RD

Selsfield Common

Selsfield Place

Drive Shaw

Bushy Wood

Bramblehill

Selsfield Common

Moatlands

Home Farm

Warren's Wood

Pine Wood

Hastings Wood

Selsfield House

B2028

Ducknell's Wood

West Hoathly

Grauetye Manor

Lower Lake

185

206

205

F8
1 MIDDLE ROW
2 FOREST LODGE
3 SACKVILLE CT
4 GREAT HOUSE CT
5 PORTLAND HOUSE
6 CORNWALL GDNS
7 NORMANDY CL
8 WILLOW MEAD
9 KINGS COPSE
10 REGAL DR
11 BECKETT WAY

Great
Wood

Coles
Wood

Hill Place
Farm

Brook House
Farm

Brook
House

EAST
GRINSTEAD

High Grove

Crockshed
Wood

HAZLEDEN
CROSS

TURNER'S HILL RD

IMBERHORNE LA

SAINT HILL RD

Hazleden
Farm

The
Plantation

RH19

Greenfields
Sch

COOMBE HILL RD

Coombe Hall
Farm

Imberley

Dunning's
Wood

Bulrushes
Farm

The Meads
Cty Prim
Sch

Sunnyside

MILL COTTS

Dunnings Mill
L Complex

Tobias Sch
of Art

Eurythmy
Sch

The
Beechcroft
Towse

Rockwood
Park

Playing
Field

High
Wood

The
Rough

Saint Hill
Manor

Hen Robin
Wood

Playing
Field

Saint Hill
Farm

Saint Hill
Green

WEST HOATHLY RD

Rockingshill
Wood

Standen
Farm

Standen
(National Trust)

Jenkin's
Wood

Boyles
Farm

Rushett's
Shaw

Busses
Farm

Jenhurst
Wood

Busses
Wood

Cock Robin
Wood

Ridge Hill
Manor

Mary
Wood

River Medway

Mill Place
Farm

Bluebell Rly

Pit Shaw

Stone Hill
House

ADMIRAL'S BRIDGE LA

Sussex Border Path

Weir Wood Resr
(Nature Reserve)

RH18

Willet's
Bridge

GRINSTEAD LA

Admiral's Bridge
Wood

Charlwood
Farm

Alder
Moors

Birch Farm
Nursery

Neylands
Farm

LEGSHEATH LA

GREENWICH MERIDIAN

Herontye

F7
1 CROMWELL PL
2 CLARENCE DR
3 HARWOODS CL
4 COLLINGWOOD CL

B2110

FAIRFIELD RD

8

7

37

6

5

36

4

3

35

2

1

34

205
186

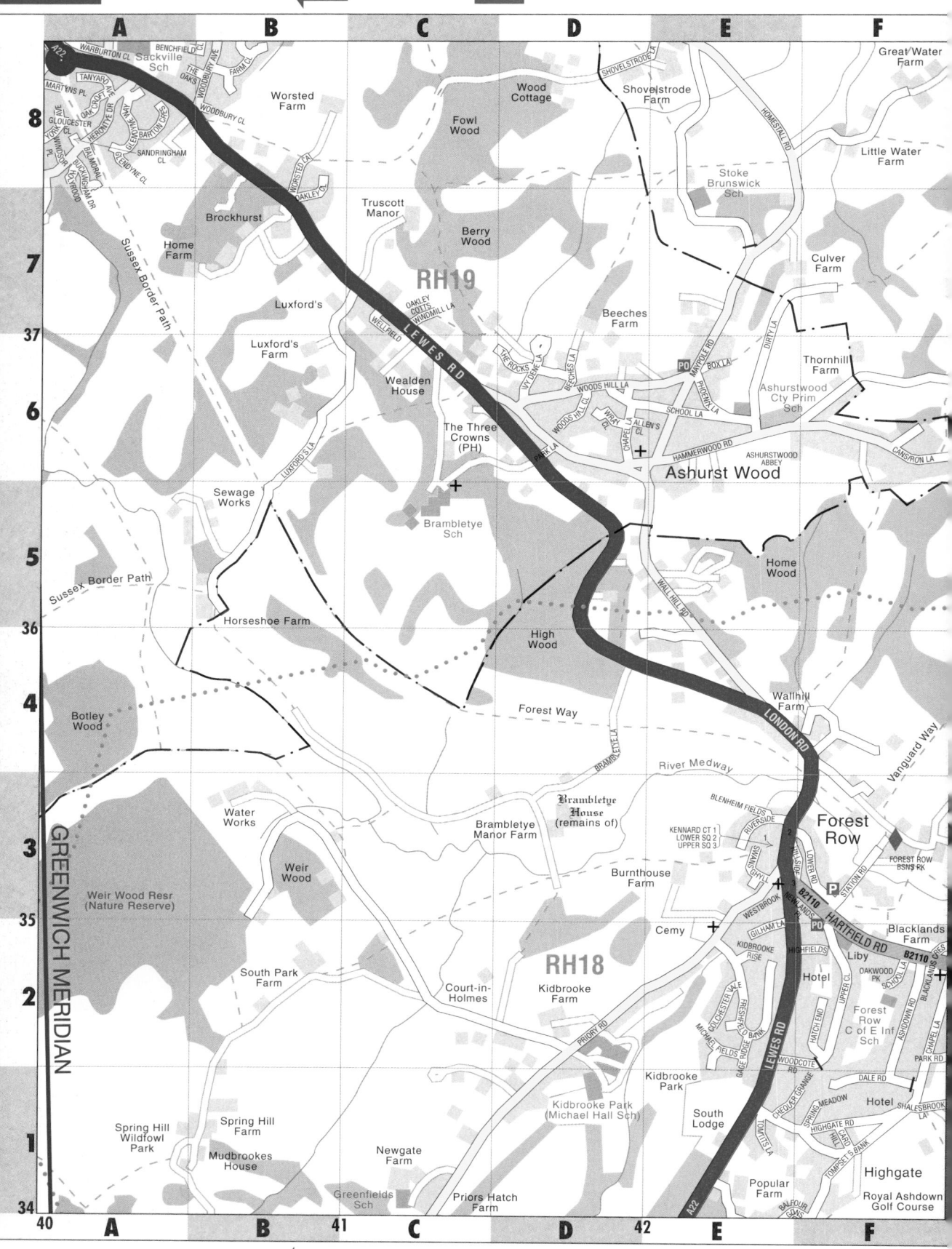

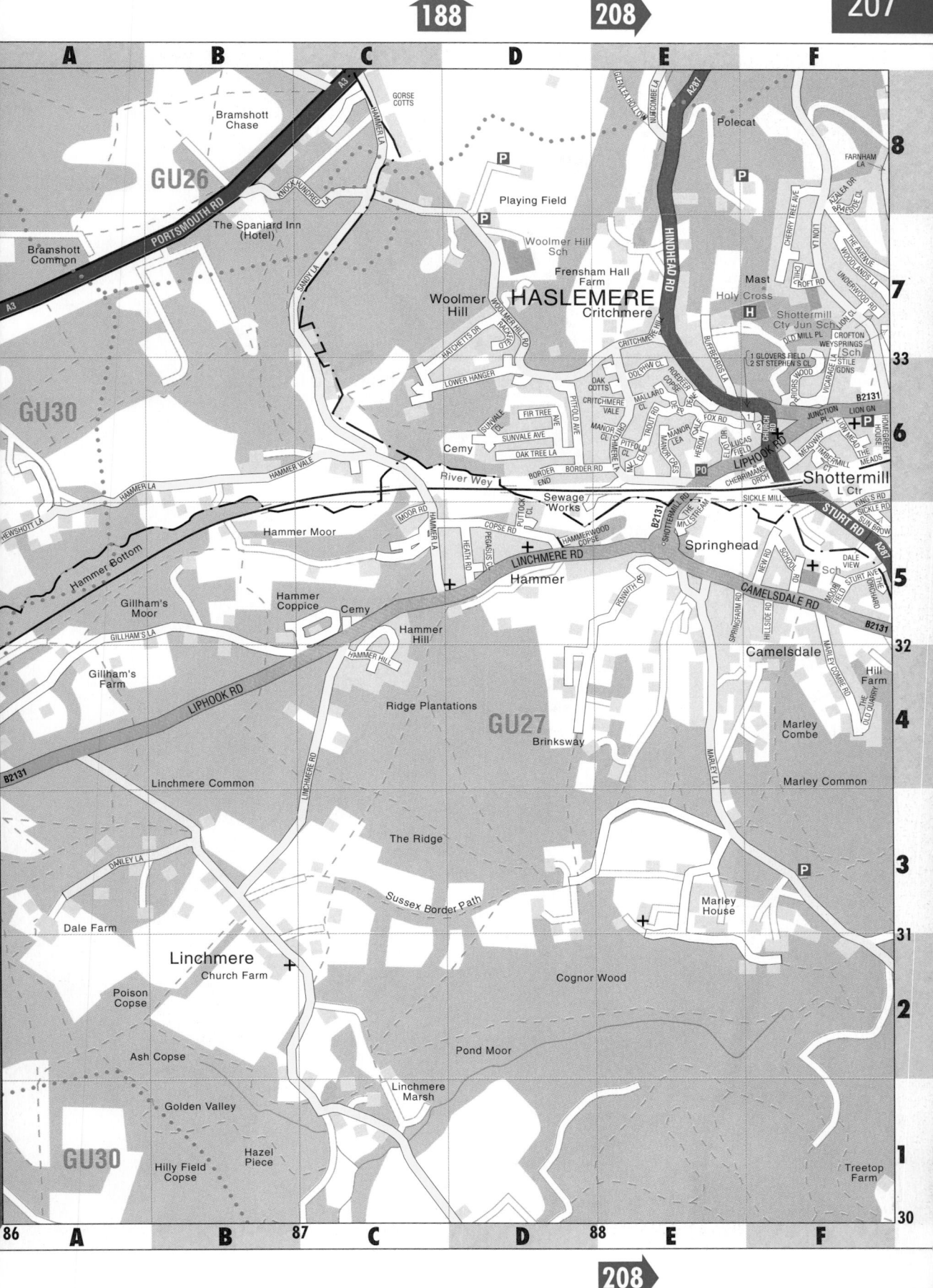

207
189

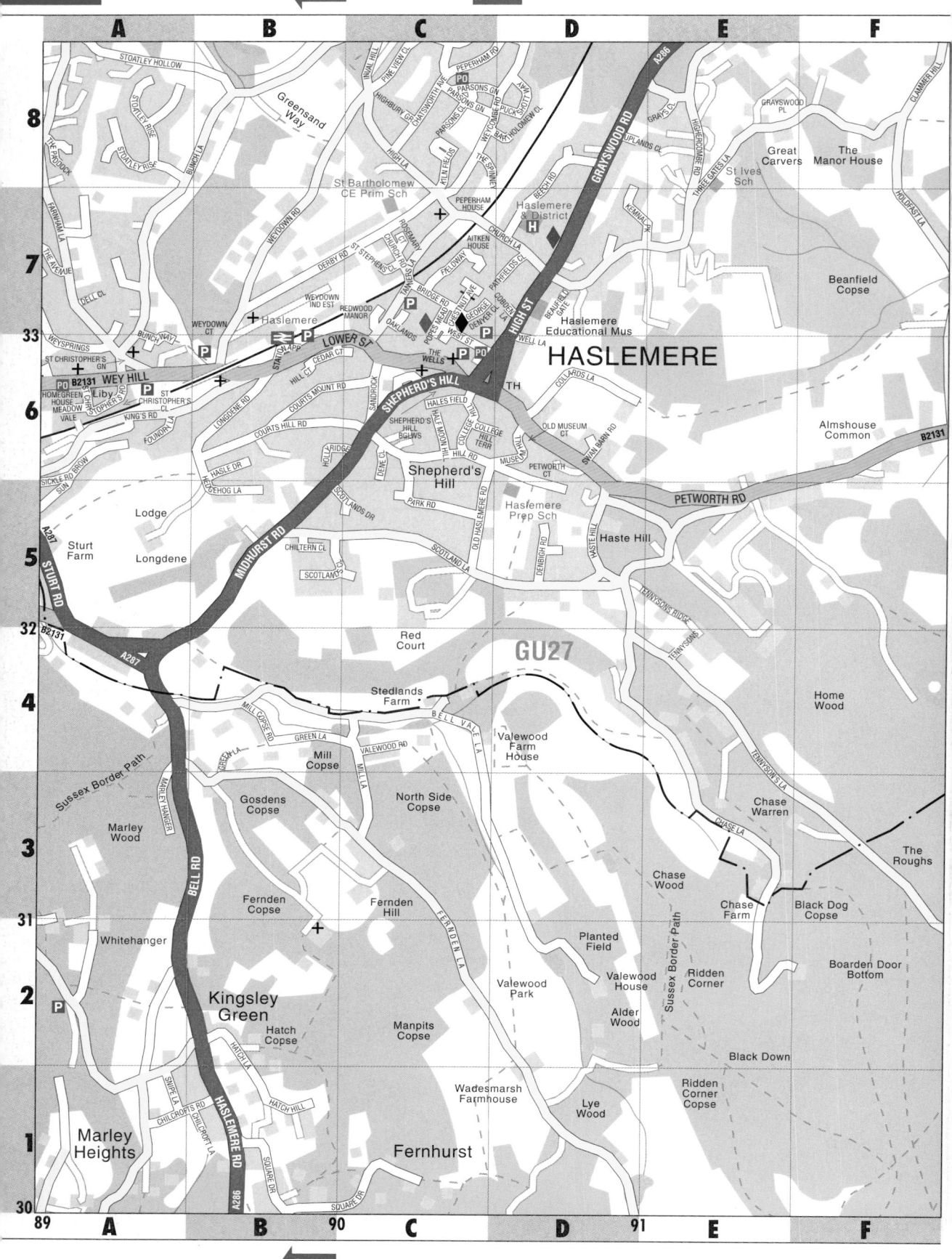

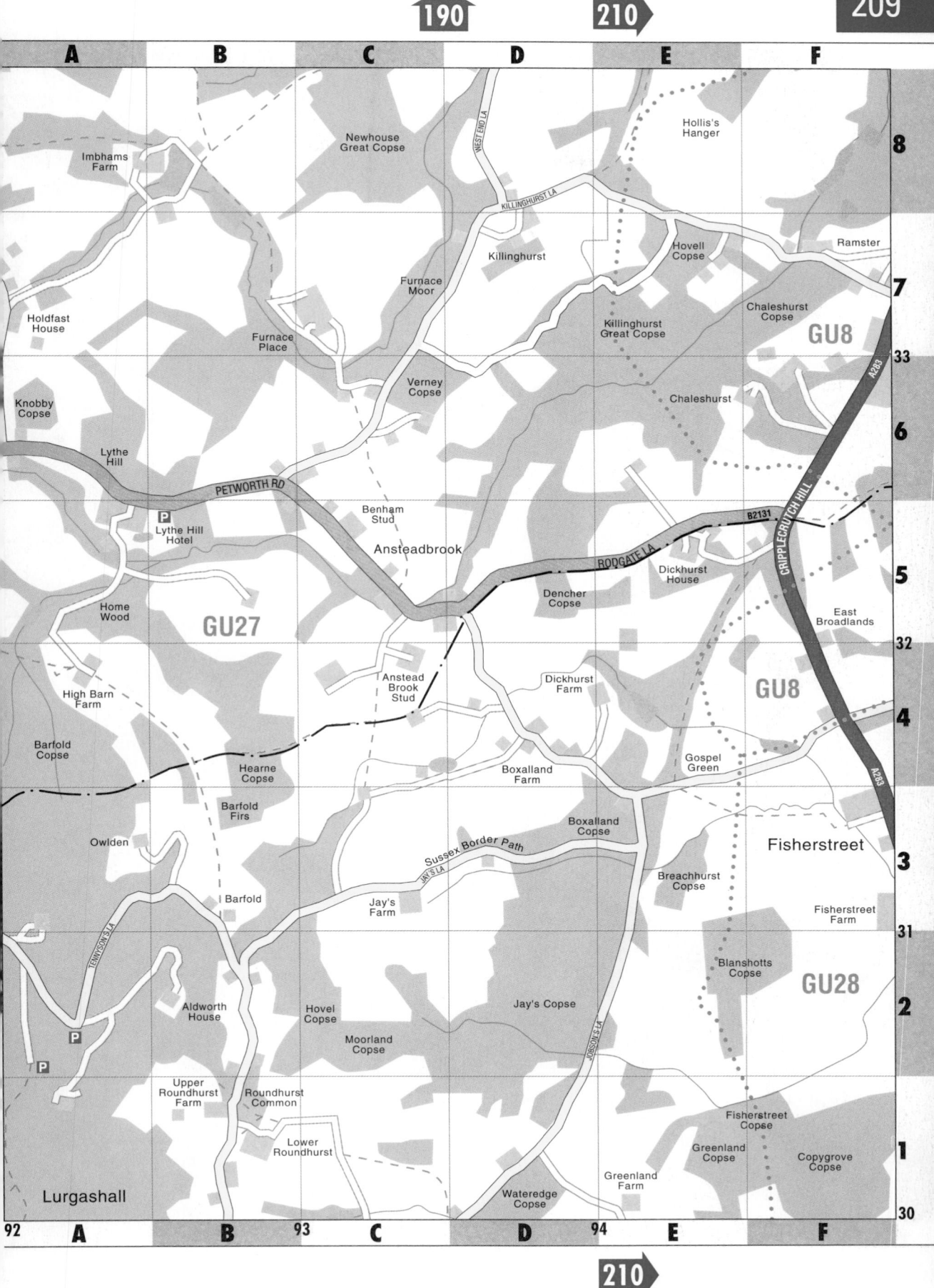

209
191

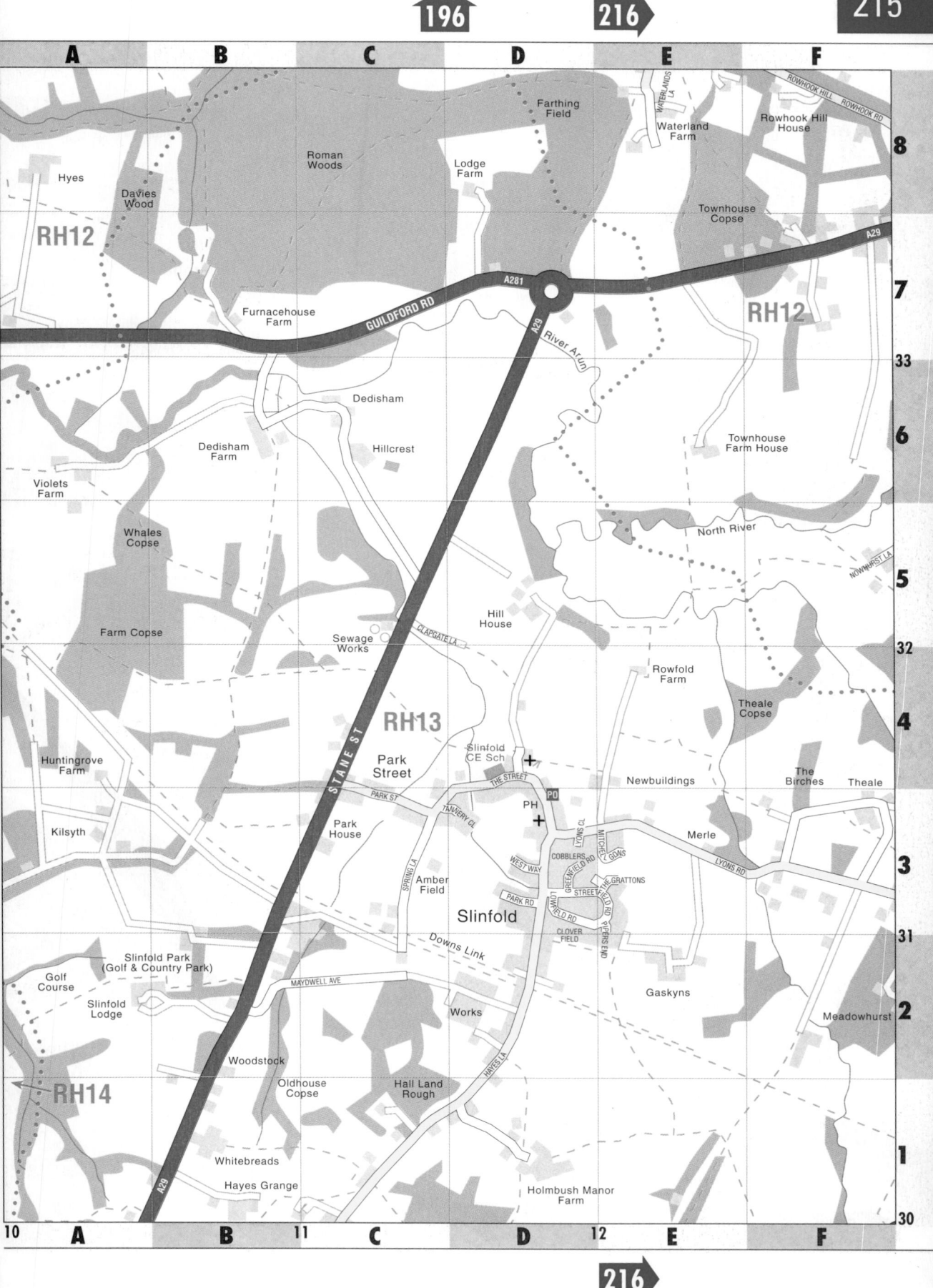

A B C D E F

8
7
33
6
5
32
4
3
31
2
1
30

RH12
Hyes
Davies Wood
Roman Woods
Farthing Field
Lodge Farm
Waterlands La
Waterland Farm
Rowhook Hill
Rowhook Hill House
Rowhook Rd
Townhouse Copse
A29
Furnacehouse Farm
GUILDFORD RD
A281
A29
RH12
River Arun
Dedisham
Hillcrest
Dedisham Farm
Townhouse Farm House
Violets Farm
Whales Copse
North River
Nowhurst La
Farm Copse
Sewage Works
CLAPGATE LA
Hill House
Rowfold Farm
Theale Copse
STANE ST
RH13
Park Street
Slinfold CE Sch
Newbuildings
The Birches
Theale
Huntingrove Farm
Park St
THE STREET
PO
Merle
Lyons Rd
Kilsyth
Park House
TANNERY CL
PH
LYONS CL
MITCHELL GDNS
SPRING LA
Amber Field
WEST WAY
COBBLERS
GREENFIELD RD
STREET
GRATTONS
PYPERS END
FIELD RD
Slinfold
PARK RD
LOWFIELD RD
CLOVER FIELD
Downs Link
Gaskyns
Golf Course
Slinfold Park (Golf & Country Park)
MAYDWELL AVE
Slinfold Lodge
Works
Meadowhurst
RH14
Woodstock
Oldhouse Copse
Hall Land Rough
HAYES LA
Whitebreads
Hayes Grange
A29
Holmbush Manor Farm

215
197

215

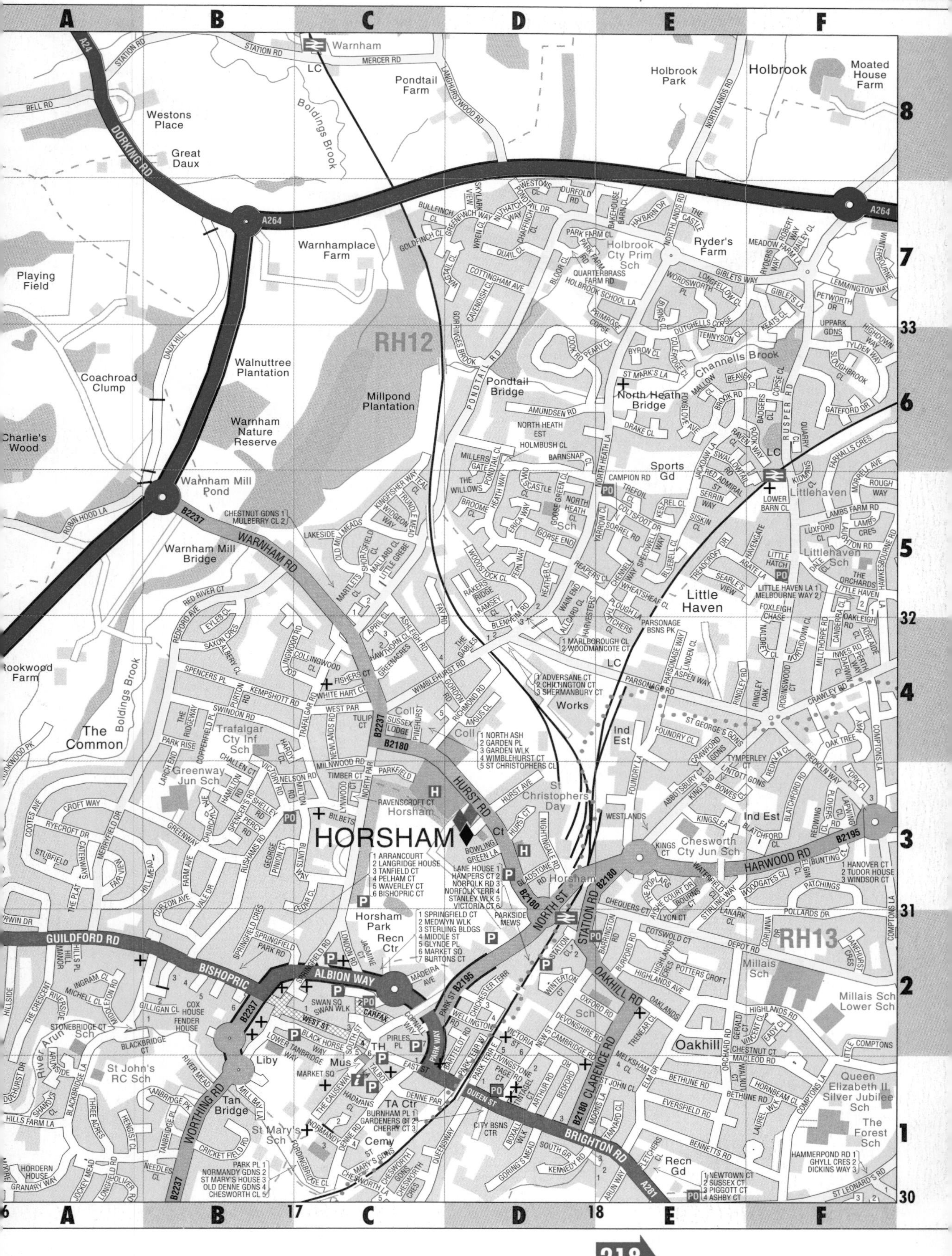

217
199

217

Scale: 7 inches to 1 mile

0 — 110 yards — 220 yards

0 — 125 m — 250 m

One-way Streets

House numbers

1 HIGH ST 59

Dorking (top map)

A2003

Dorking West

Sch

FRASER GDNS

RANMORE RD

STATION TERR

STATION RD

DORKING BSNS PK

CHALKPIT LA

PARKWAY

ARCHWAY PL

PORTLAND RD
TEAL CT

1 HAVENBURY EST
2 WILLOW MEAD
3 MALLARD CT
4 HERON CT
5 ARCHWAY MEWS
6 CHAPEL CT

RH4

FAIRFIELD DR

LONDON RD

PIPPBROOK GDNS

Ct

Liby

Cemy

REIGATE RD

A24

A25

OTTERDALE

SPITAL HEATH

8

Ind Est

CURTIS RD

BEECH

CT

CURTIS GDNS

SPRING GDNS

STATION RD

A2003

CANTERBURY CT

KINGFISHER CT

MYRTLE RD

MEADOWBROOK RD

MINT GDNS

MILL LA

MARTIN'S WLK

ANSELL RD

PO

HIGH ST

ROTHES RD

WATHEN RD

HART RD

HART GDNS

JUBILEE TERR

LONSDALE RD

PH
CHURCH GDNS

PAPER MEWS

ALMSHOUSES

MOORE RD

DEEPDENE GDNS

DEEPDENE PARK RD

DEEPDENE PARK RD

136

RH5

DEEPDENE DR

DEEPDENE WOOD

LADYGATE RD

495

PARSONAGE SQ

A2003

WESTCOTT RD

WEST ST

NORTH ST

CHURCH ST

Mus

ST MARTINS MEWS

HEATH HILL

DENE ST

LYONS CT

DENE STREET GDNS

PH

Cotmandene

DEEPDENE AVE

SOUTH DR

7

A25

GLEBELAND CTR

Ind Est

VINCENT LA

HOWARD RD

MOUNT ST

ARUNDEL RD

ROSES COTTS

JUNCTION RD

SOUTH ST

VICTORIA TERR

BUTTER HILL

PH

MARLBOROUGH CT

CHEQUERS PL

MARLBOROUGH RD

BERESFORD RD

CLEARDENE

CHART LA

Deepdene House

VAUGHAN WAY

EBISHAM CL

VINCENT WKS

ARUNDEL RD

NORFOLK RD

VINCENT RD

A25

PO

ROSE HILL

CEDAR CL

DYSON CT

Rose Hill

ST PAUL'S RD E

St Paul's CE (VA) Prim Sch

A25

136

490

Dorking

60 — 165 — 170

Epsom (bottom map)

Recn Gd

OAK LEAF AVE

WEST HILL AVE

KT19

HUNTERS CL 1
LANGLANDS RISE 2

COURT LA

B280

WEST HILL

SHARON CL
Sch

SHERATON DR

MARSHALLS CL

BURNET GR

WEST HILL

HAZON WAY

MAIDENSHAW RD

GOSFIELD RD

TEMPLE RD

CHASE RD

CHASE END

WOODSTOCK RD

HORSLEY CL

Epsom

STATION APP

HOOK RD

B284

76

THE RAINBOW CTR

A24

EAST ST

LINDEN PL

HAWTHORNE PL

DELAPORTE

PROVIDENCE PL

BEACONSFIELD PL

MILL RD

CLEVES CT

DORSET CT

BRIDGE RD

B288

7

STEVENS CL

CLAYTON RD

PROSPECT PL

UPPER HIGH ST

A2022

PIKES HILL

WYETH'S RD

WYETH'S MEWS

610

ADELPHI RD

Liby

PO PH

B284

A2022

DEPOT RD

HOMEWATER HOUSE

TREEMOUNT CT

CHURCH ST

KT17

76

6

HOOKFIELD

WHEELERS LA

WEST ST

B280

WEST ST

PH

Clock Tower

KING'S SHADE WLK

ASHLEY CTR

HIGH ST

SPREAD EAGLE WLK

TH

Cts

THE PARADE

ASHLEY RD

FIRE STATION FLATS

THE KIRKGATE

BADGERS LODGE

BADGERS CT

GROVE AVE

ST MARTIN'S CL

GROVE HOUSE

DENEWOOD

GROVE RD

THE GROVE

WIMBORNE CL

ALBERT RD

MEADOW CL

MANOR HOUSE CT

MATHIAS CL

Playhouse

ASHLEY AVE

A24

ASHURST MEADSIDE

ASHLEY CT

MISTLEY CT
STUART LODGE
SWAIL HOUSE

B290

HEREFORD CT

LABURNUM RD

FAIRBRIAR CT

ASH MEWS

HEATHCOTE RD

CHURCH CL

CHURCH ST

GILESMEAD

ANDREW'S CL

TINTAGEL CL

THE CROFT

CEDAR

COLLEGE RD

605

ROSEBANK

SOUTH ST

WILBERFORCE CT

ST JAMES CT

LITTLE ORCHARDS

WORPLE RD

RICHMOND CL

DOWNSIDE

DOWN LODGE CT

PITT PL

PITT RD

ROSEBERY AVE

RANDOLPH RD

5

EPSOM

St Joseph's RC Prim Sch

ST MARGARETS DR

A24

ASHLEY RD

MALVERN CT

Rosebery Park

WOODCOTE CL

ARDINGLY CT

WOODCOTE HALL

LADBROKE RD

B290

B284

Surrey Inst of Art & Tech

JEAL OAKWOOD CT

ST MARTIN'S AVE

B289

B284

76

Epsom

C — 205 — D — 210 — E — 215 — F

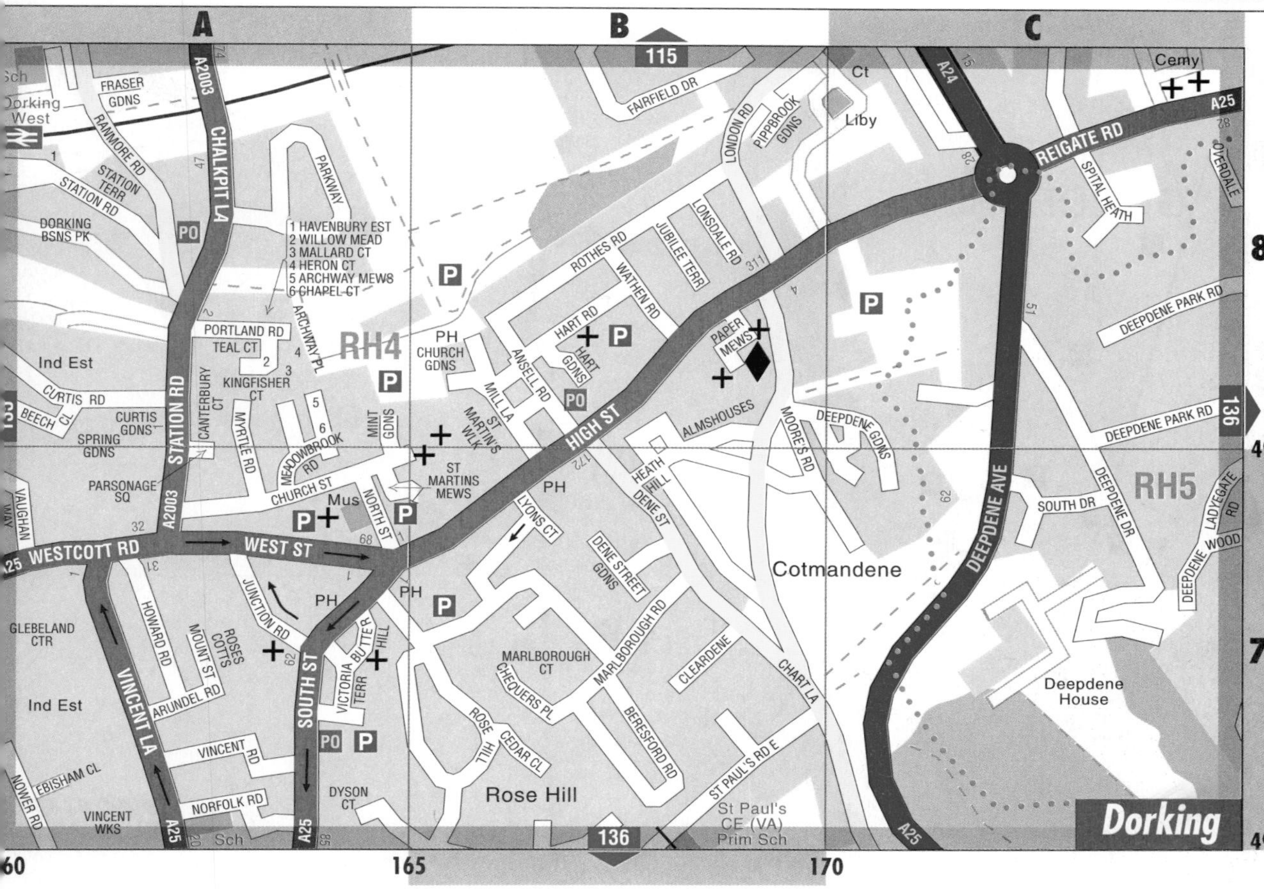

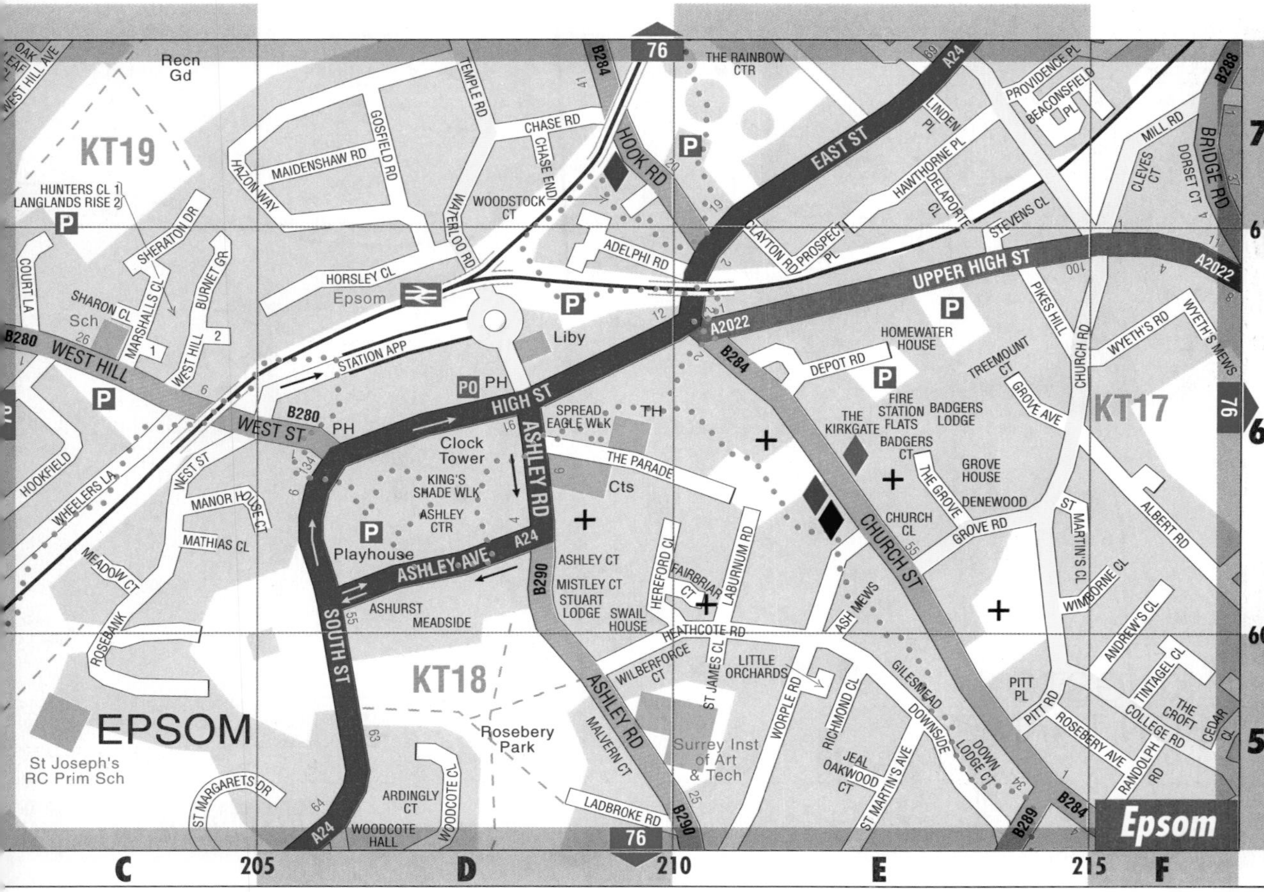

Scale: 7 inches to 1 mile

0   110 yards   220 yards
0   125 m   250 m

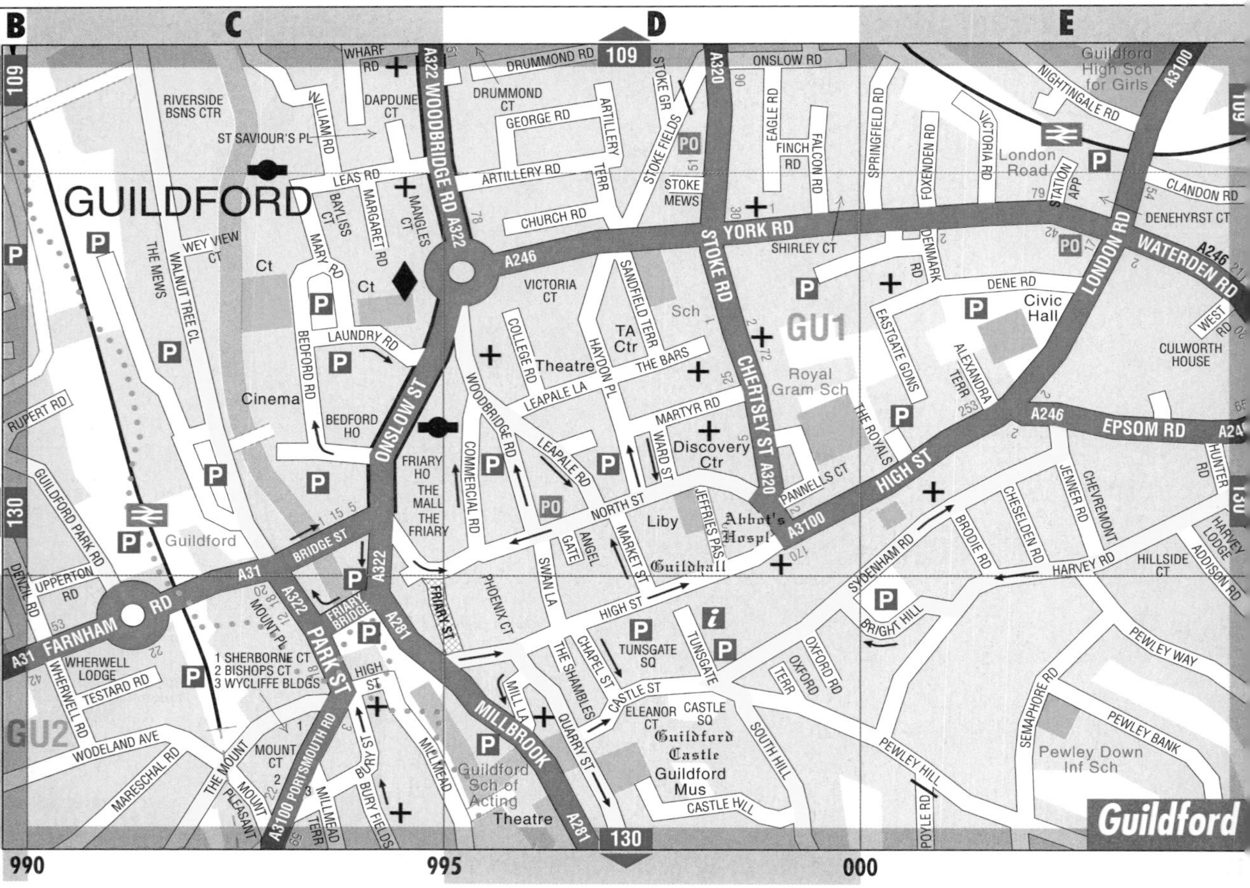

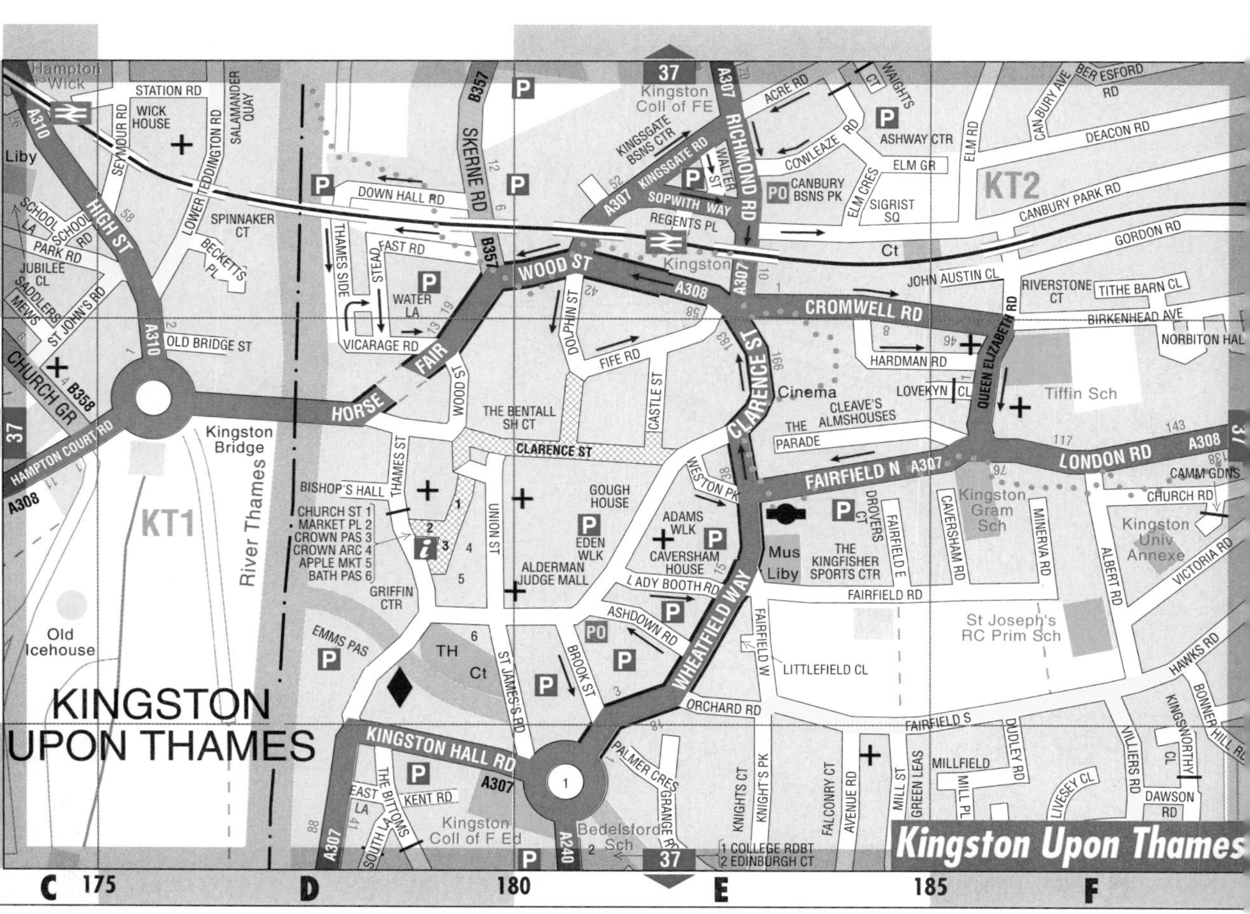

GUILDFORD

B   C   D   109   E

1

500

WHARF RD
DRUMMOND RD
DRUMMOND CT
GEORGE RD
ARTILLERY RD
ARTILLERY TERR
CHURCH RD
ONSLOW RD
STOKE GR
STOKE FIELDS
STOKE MEWS
EAGLE RD
FINCH RD
FALCON RD
SPRINGFIELD RD
FOXENDEN RD
VICTORIA RD
NIGHTINGALE RD
Guildford High Sch for Girls
A3100
London Road
STATION APP
CLANDON RD
DENEHYRST CT

RIVERSIDE BSNS CTR
WILLIAM RD
ST SAVIOUR'S PL
DAPDUNE CT
LEAS RD
MANGLES RD
MARGARET RD
MARY RD
WEY VIEW CT
WALNUT TREE CL
THE MEWS
BEDFORD RD
LAUNDRY RD
Ct   Ct
A322 WOODBRIDGE RD A322
ONSLOW ST
A246
VICTORIA CT
COLLEGE RD
SANDFIELD TERR
HAYDON PL
YORK RD
STOKE RD
CHERTSEY ST A320
TA Ctr
THE BARS
GU1
Royal Gram Sch
DENMARK RD
EASTGATE GDNS
ALEXANDRA TERR
DENE RD
Civic Hall
THE ROYALS
CULWORTH HOUSE
WEST
A246 EPSOM RD A24

8

Cinema
BEDFORD RD
BEDFORD HO
Theatre
LEAPALE LA
Friary HO THE MALL THE FRIARY
COMMERCIAL RD
LEAPALE RD
PO
NORTH ST
MARTYR RD
WARD ST
Discovery Ctr
Liby
Abbot's Hospl
JEFFRIES PAS
PANNELLS CT
HIGH ST
SYDENHAM RD
BRODIE RD
CHESELDEN RD
HARVEY RD
JENNER RD
CHEVREMONT
HUNTER RD
HILLSIDE CT
HARVEY RD
ADDISON RD
A24 130

130

495

RUPERT RD
GUILDFORD PARK RD
UPPERTON RD
DENZIL RD
Guildford
BRIDGE ST A31
A322 A281
FRIARY ST
MOUNT PL
FRIARY BRIDGE
FRIARY ST
PHOENIX CT
SWAN LA
ANGEL GATE
MARKET ST
Guildhall
HIGH ST
i
TUNSGATE SQ
TUNSGATE
OXFORD RD
OXFORD TERR
SOUTH HILL
BRIGHT HILL
PEWLEY HILL
PEWLEY WAY

7

FARNHAM RD
A31 FARNHAM RD A31
GU2
Wherwell Lodge
WHERWELL RD
TESTARD RD
WODELAND AVE
MARESCHAL RD
THE MOUNT
MOUNT PLEASANT
MOUNT CT
PARK ST
1 SHERBORNE CT
2 BISHOPS CT
3 WYCLIFFE BLDGS
HIGH ST
A3100 PORTSMOUTH RD
MILLMEAD TERR
BURY FIELDS
MILLMEAD
MILLBROOK
QUARRY ST
MILL LA
THE SHAMBLES
CHAPEL ST
CASTLE ST
ELEANOR CT
TUNSGATE SQ
CASTLE SQ
Guildford Castle
Guildford Mus
CASTLE HILL
SOUTH HILL
A281
Guildford Sch of Acting Theatre
POYLE RD
PEWLEY HILL
Pewley Down Inf Sch
PEWLEY BANK
SEMAPHORE RD
A281 130

Guildford

990   995   000

KINGSTON UPON THAMES

37

Hampton Wick
STATION RD
SALAMANDER QUAY
WICK HOUSE
B357
37
Kingston Coll of FE
A307
RICHMOND RD
KINGSGATE RD
KINGSGATE BSNS CTR
WATER ST
ACRE RD
WAIGHTS CT
COWLEAZE
ASHWAY CTR
ELM RD
ELM GR
CAN BURY AVE
BER ESFORD RD
DEACON RD
A310
Liby
HIGH ST
SCHOOL LA
PARK RD
JUBILEE CL
SADDLERS MEWS
ST JOHN'S RD
SEYMOUR RD
LOWER TEDDINGTON RD
SPINNAKER CT
BECKETT'S PL
DOWN HALL RD
THAMES SIDE
FAST RD
SKERNE RD
B357
WOOD ST
A308
SOPWITH WAY
REGENTS PL
Kingston
CANBURY BSNS PK
PO
ELM CRES
SIGRIST SQ
KT2
CANBURY PARK RD
GORDON RD

6

695

CHURCH GR
B358
OLD BRIDGE ST
Kingston Bridge
WATER LA
VICARAGE RD
FAIR ST
HORSE FAIR
THAMES ST
DOLPHIN ST
FIFE RD
WOOD ST
CASTLE ST
CLARENCE ST
Cinema
CLEAVE'S ALMSHOUSES
THE PARADE
LOVEKYN CL
JOHN AUSTIN CL
Ct
CROMWELL RD
HARDMAN RD
QUEEN ELIZABETH RD
RIVERSTONE CT
TITHE BARN CL
BIRKENHEAD AVE
NORBITON HALL
Tiffin Sch
HAMPTON COURT RD
A308
KT1
River Thames
Old Icehouse
BISHOP'S HALL
CHURCH ST 1
MARKET PL 2
CROWN PAS 3
APPLE MKT 5
BATH PAS 6
CROWN ARC 4
THAMES ST
UNION ST
THE BENTALL SH CTR
CLARENCE ST
i
GOUGH HOUSE
EDEN WLK
ALDERMAN JUDGE MALL
ADAMS WLK
CAVERSHAM HOUSE
CLARENCE ST
WESTON PK
Mus Liby
THE KINGFISHER SPORTS CTR
FAIRFIELD N A307
DROVERS
FAIRFIELD E
LONDON RD A308
CAMM GDNS
CHURCH RD
Kingston Gram Sch
MINERVA RD
CAVERSHAM RD
Kingston Univ Annexe
ALBERT RD
VICTORIA RD

5

690

KINGSTON UPON THAMES
GRIFFIN CTR
EMMS PAS
TH
Ct
ST JAMES'S RD
KINGSTON HALL RD
KENT RD
A307
EAST LA
THE BITTOMS
SOUTH LA
Kingston Coll of F Ed
PO
ASHDOWN RD
L ADY BOOTH RD
BROOK ST
A307
WHEATFIELD WAY
ORCHARD RD
1
PALMER CRES
A240
Bedelsford Sch
1 COLLEGE RDBT
2 EDINBURGH CT
KNIGHTS CT
GRANGE RD
KNIGHTS PK
FAIRFIELD W
LITTLEFIELD CL
FAIRFIELD RD
FALCONRY CT
AVENUE RD
FAIRFIELD S
St Joseph's RC Prim Sch
MILL ST
GREEN LEAS
MILLFIELD
DUDLEY RD
LIVESEY CL
HAWKS RD
VILLIERS RD
BONNER RD
KINGSNORTHY RD
HILL RD
DAWSON RD
37

Kingston Upon Thames

C   175   D   180   E   185   F

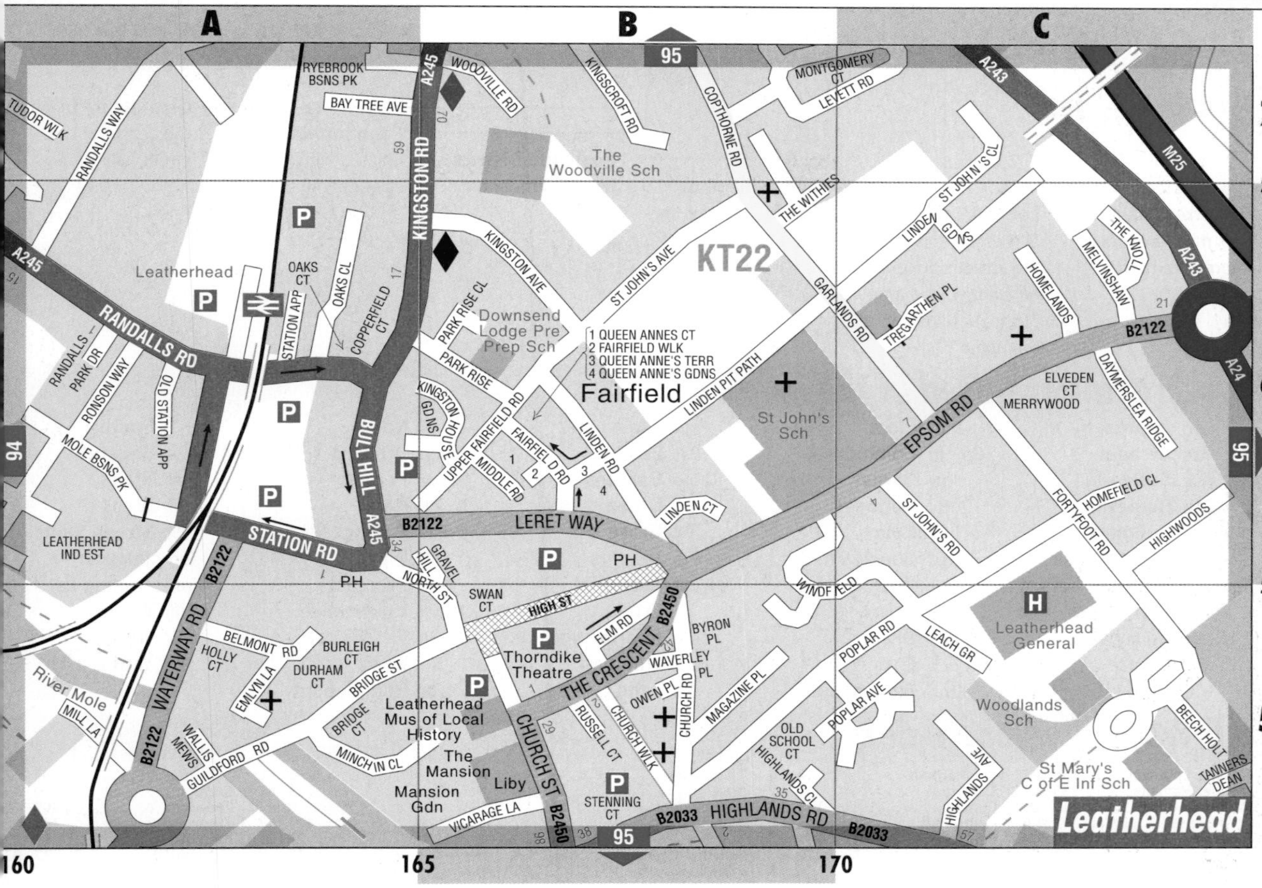

One-way Streets

House numbers
1 HIGH ST 59

Leatherhead

A | B | C

TUDOR WLK
RANDALLS WAY
RYEBROOK BSNS PK
BAY TREE AVE
WOODVILLE RD
KINGSCROFT RD
COPTHORNE RD
MONTGOMERY CT
LEVETT RD
A243
M25

7
570

A245
Leatherhead
OAKS CL
OAKS CT
COPPERFIELD CT 17
KINGSTON RD
KINGSTON AVE
ST JOHN'S AVE
The Woodville Sch
THE WITHIES
ST JOHN'S CL
LINDEN GDNS
TREGARTHEN PL
HOMELANDS
MELVINSHAW
THE KNOLL
A243
A24
B2122
21

KT22

6

STATION APP
PARK RISE CL
PARK RISE
Downsend Lodge Pre Prep Sch
KINGSTON HOUSE
GDNS LA
UPPER FAIRFIELD RD
FAIRFIELD RD
Fairfield
1 QUEEN ANNES CT
2 FAIRFIELD WLK
3 QUEEN ANNE'S TERR
4 QUEEN ANNE'S GDNS
LINDEN PIT PATH
St John's Sch
GARLANDS RD
EPSOM RD
ELVEDEN CT MERRYWOOD
FORTYFOOT RD
HOMEFIELD CL
HIGHWOODS
DAYMERSLEA RIDGE
95

94
MOLE BSNS PK
RANDALLS PARK DR
RONSON WAY
OLD STATION APP
BULL HILL
A245
UPPER MIDDLE RD
LINDEN RD
LINDEN CT
ST JOHN'S RD
WINDFIELD

LEATHERHEAD IND EST
B2122
STATION RD
B2122
LERET WAY

565

WATERWAY RD
PH
GRAVEL HILL RD
NORTH ST
SWAN CT
HIGH ST
ELM RD
THE CRESCENT
B2450
BYRON PL
WAVERLEY
POPLAR RD
LEACH GR
Leatherhead General
H

River Mole
MILL LA
B2122
WALLIS MEWS
EMLYN LA
BELMONT RD
HOLLY CT
BURLEIGH CT
DURHAM CT
BRIDGE ST
BRIDGE
MINCHIN CL
Thorndike Theatre
Leatherhead Mus of Local History
The Mansion
Mansion Gdn
Liby
RUSSELL CT
CHURCH WLK
OWEN PL
MAGAZINE PL
CHURCH PL
HIGHLANDS CL
OLD SCHOOL CT
POPLAR AVE
HIGHLANDS AVE
Woodlands Sch
St Mary's C of E Inf Sch
BEECH HOLT
TANNERS DEAN

5

GUILDFORD RD
CHURCH ST
B2450
VICARAGE LA
STENNING CT
HIGHLANDS RD
B2033
B2033

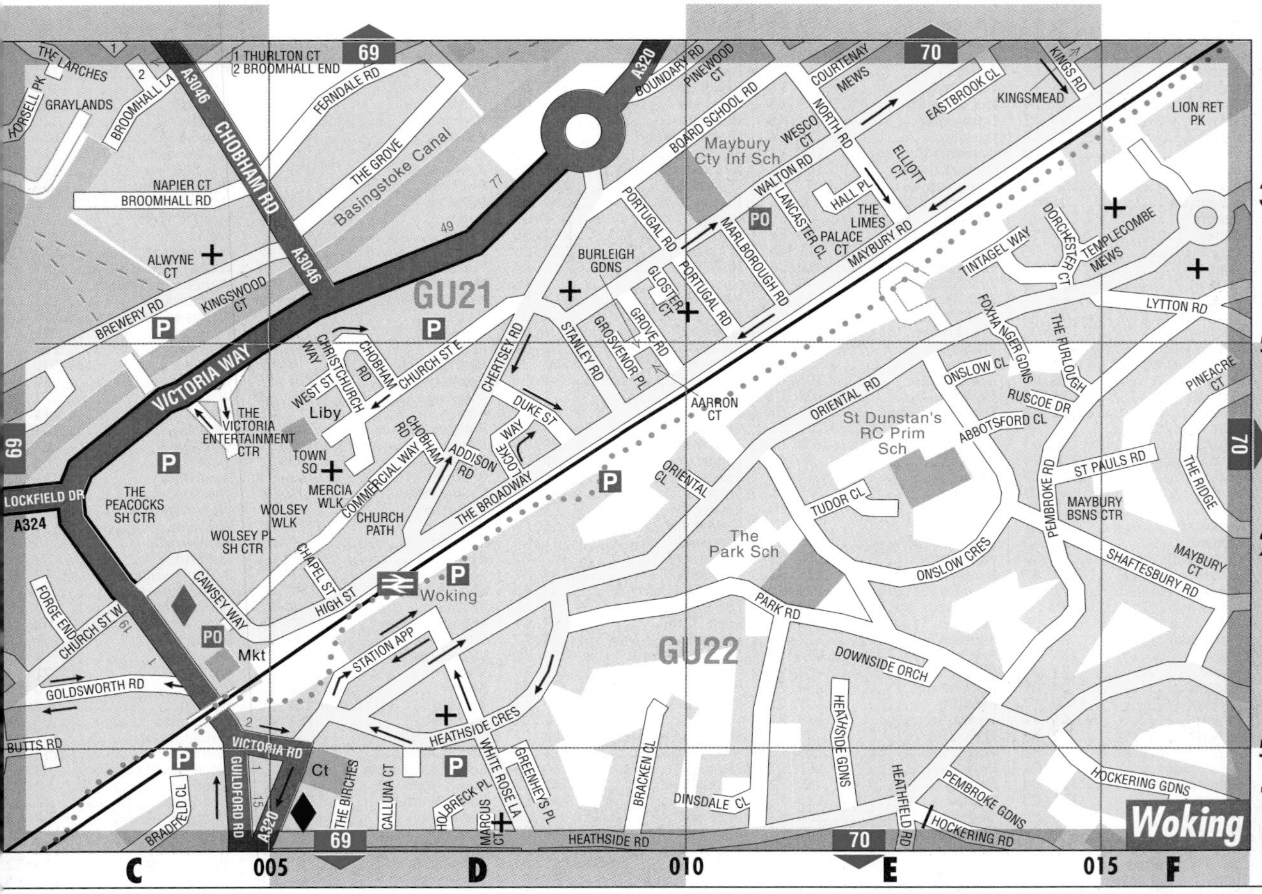

160 | 165 | 170
95

Woking

THE LARCHES
HORSELL PK
GRAYLANDS
BROOMHALL LA
A3046
1 THURLTON CT
2 BROOMHALL END
FERNDALE RD
69
A320
BOUNDARY RD
PINEWOOD
BOARD SCHOOL RD
COURTENAY MEWS
WESCO CT
NORTH RD
EASTBROOK CL
KINGSMEAD
KINGS RD
70
LION RET PK

NAPIER CT
BROOMHALL RD
CHOBHAM RD
THE GROVE
Basingstoke Canal
Maybury Cty Inf Sch
WALTON RD
LANCASTER CL
HALL PL
THE LIMES PALACE
MAYBURY RD
ELLIOTT CT
DORCHESTER CT
TINTAGEL WAY
TEMPLECOMBE MEWS
3
590

ALWYNE CT
KINGSWOOD CT
A3046
VICTORIA WAY
GU21
BURLEIGH GDNS
PORTUGAL RD
GLOSTER RD
GROVE RD
MARLBOROUGH RD
PO
AARRON CT
Oriental RD
St Dunstan's RC Prim Sch
ONSLOW CL
FOXHANGER GDNS
RUSCOE DR
ABBOTSFORD CL
THE FURLONGH
PINEACRE CT
LYTTON RD
70
THE RIDGE

BREWERY RD
69
LOCKFIELD DR
A324
THE VICTORIA ENTERTAINMENT CTR
THE PEACOCKS SH CTR
CHRISTCHURCH RD
WEST ST
Liby
CHOBHAM RD
CHURCH ST E
CHERTSEY RD
STANLEY RD
GROSVENOR PL
DUKE ST
WAY
ADDISON RD
CHOBHAM RD
COMMERCIAL WAY
THE BROADWAY
ORIENTAL CL
ORIENTAL RD
TUDOR CL
PEMBROKE RD
ST PAULS RD
MAYBURY BSNS CTR
MAYBURY CT
SHAFTESBURY RD

TOWN SQ
MERCIA WLK
WOLSEY WLK
WOLSEY PL SH CTR
CHURCH PATH
CHAPEL HIGH ST
CAWSEY WAY
PO
Mkt
Woking
STATION APP
The Park Sch
GU22
PARK RD
ONSLOW CRES
DOWNSIDE ORCH
2

FORGE END
CHURCH ST W
GOLDSWORTH RD
BUTTS RD
VICTORIA RD
GUILDFORD RD
A320
THE BIRCHES
CALLUNA CT
HOLBRECK PL
MACCOLL
WHITE ROSE LA
GREENHEY'S PL
BRACKEN CL
DINSDALE CL
HEATHSIDE CRES
HEATHSIDE GDNS
HEATHFIELD RD
PEMBROKE GDNS
HOCKERING RD
HOCKERING GDNS
585
1

BRADFIELD CL
69
HEATHSIDE RD
70

C | 005 | D | 010 | E | 015 | F

Index

Street names are listed alphabetically and show the locality, the Postcode District, the page number and a reference to the square in which the name falls on the map page

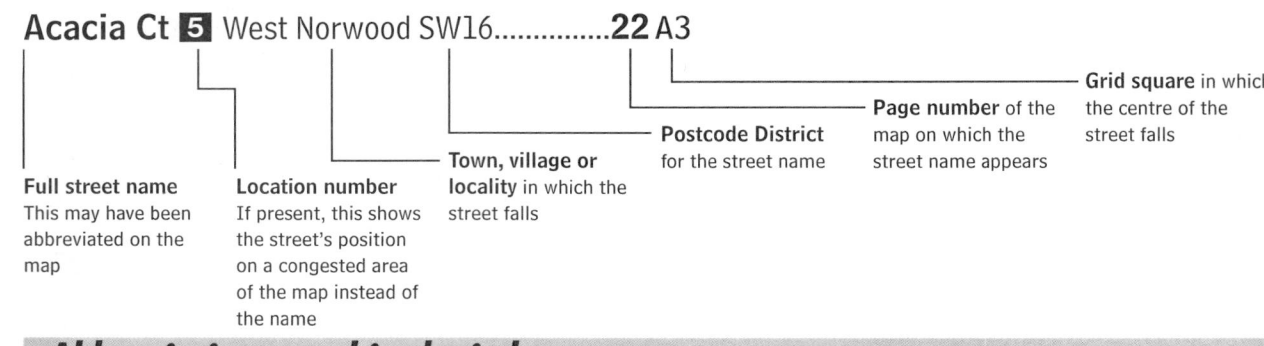

Acacia Ct **5** West Norwood SW16..............**22** A3

Grid square in which the centre of the street falls

Page number of the map on which the street name appears

Postcode District for the street name

Town, village or locality in which the street falls

Full street name
This may have been abbreviated on the map

Location number
If present, this shows the street's position on a congested area of the map instead of the name

Abbreviations used in the index

App	**Approach**	Cl	**Close**	Espl	**Esplanade**	N	**North**	S	**South**
Arc	**Arcade**	Comm	**Common**	Est	**Estate**	Orch	**Orchard**	Sq	**Square**
Ave	**Avenue**	Cnr	**Corner**	Gdns	**Gardens**	Par	**Parade**	Strs	**Stairs**
Bvd	**Boulevard**	Cotts	**Cottages**	Gn	**Green**	Pk	**Park**	Stps	**Steps**
Bldgs	**Buildings**	Ct	**Court**	Gr	**Grove**	Pas	**Passage**	St	**Street, Saint**
Bsns Pk	**Business Park**	Ctyd	**Courtyard**	Hts	**Heights**	Pl	**Place**	Terr	**Terrace**
Bsns Ctr	**Business Centre**	Cres	**Crescent**	Ind Est	**Industrial Estate**	Prec	**Precinct**	Trad	**Trading Est**
Bglws	**Bungalows**	Dr	**Drive**			Prom	**Promenade**	Wlk	**Walk**
Cswy	**Causeway**	Dro	**Drove**	Intc	**Interchange**	Ret Pk	**Retail Park**	W	**West**
Ctr	**Centre**	E	**East**	Junc	**Junction**	Rd	**Road**	Yd	**Yard**
Cir	**Circus**	Emb	**Embankment**	La	**Lane**	Rdbt	**Roundabout**		

Town and village index

Abinger Common 155 D8	Coldharbour 156 E4	Hackbridge 60 B8	Newchapel 163 F1	Surbiton 37 E2
Abinger Hammer ...133 F3	Colnbrook 1 D7	Hale 125 C6	Newdigate 158 B1	Sutton 59 C5
Addington 63 A5	Compton 129 B3	Hambledon 171 D2	Newell Green 8 A1	Tadworth 97 C5
Addlestone 52 A6	Coney Hall 63 F7	Hampton 36 A7	Normandy 107 A3	Tandridge 122 A2
Albury 132 C4	Copthorne 183 C3	Hamsey Green 81 C4	North Ascot 28 E8	Tatsfield 103 D7
Aldershot 105 B1	Coulsdon 79 D3	Harlington 3 C8	North Cheam 58 C8	Teddington 17 B3
Alfold 193 F1	Cranford 4 C6	Harmondsworth 2 E8	Nutfield 119 F2	Thames Ditton 37 B2
Alfold Crossways ...194 A3	Cranleigh 174 D2	Hascombe 172 D4	Oatlands Park 53 E6	The Chart 123 E5
Artington 130 C4	Crawley 201 E4	Haslemere 208 D6	Ockham 92 B6	The Sands 126 E2
Ascot 29 A6	Crawley Down 204 C7	Hatton 3 F2	Ockley 177 D5	Thornton Heath 42 B3
Ash 106 B3	Crondall 124 A5	Haxted 165 F8	Old Windsor 11 A8	Thorpe 32 C6
Ash Vale 106 B7	Crowhurst 143 E3	Hayes 44 F3	Old Woking 90 A7	Thorpe Lea 12 B1
Ashford 13 F2	Crowthorne 45 D5	Headley 96 C2	Ottershaw 51 D5	Thursley 169 C4
Ashstead 75 E1	Croydon 61 D7	Headley Down 187 B4	Outwood 162 B7	Tilford 147 D3
Ashurst Wood 206 E6	Cudworth 179 F8	Heath End 125 D6	Oxshott 74 C6	Titsey 103 B2
Bagshot 47 D3	Dockenfield 166 E6	Hersham 54 D5	Oxted 122 E5	Tolworth 57 B7
Balham 21 A7	Domewood 184 A5	Heston 4 F7	Parkgate 158 D4	Tongham 126 F6
Banstead 78 B3	Dorking 136 C6	Hinchley Wood 55 F8	Peaslake 154 D6	Turners Hill 204 A4
Barnes 7 F6	Dormans Park 185 E6	Hindhead 188 F4	Penge 23 D2	Twickenham 17 B8
Beacon Hill 188 C6	Dormansland 165 B1	Holmbury St Mary ..155 B5	Peper Harow 149 C5	Tyler's Green 121 C5
Beare Green 157 D3	Downside 93 B8	Hookwood 160 D2	Pirbright 87 F4	Upper Halliford 34 D5
Beckenham 44 A7	Dulwich 22 E5	Hooley 99 B5	Plaistow 211 F2	Upper Tooting 20 F5
Belmont 59 A2	Dunsfold 192 F5	Horley 161 C3	Poyle 1 D6	Virginia Water 31 C6
Bentley 145 A7	East Bedfont 14 E7	Horne 162 F5	Purley 80 A7	Wallington 60 A4
Betchworth 137 E8	East Clandon 111 E4	Horsham 217 C3	Putney 19 D7	Wallis Wood 176 E1
Biggin Hill 83 E3	East Ewell 58 D1	Horton 1 A4	Puttenham 128 C4	Walton on the Hill ..97 A3
Binstead 166 A5	East Grinstead 185 E2	Hounslow 5 A5	Pyrford 70 E4	Walton-On-Thames ...35 C2
Bisley 68 B3	East Horsley 112 E8	Hydestile 171 E6	Redhill 118 E2	Wanborough 128 C6
Blackwater 64 D4	East Molesey 36 C4	Ifold 212 D3	Reigate 118 B2	Wandsworth 20 C7
Bletchingley 120 D2	Edenbridge 144 F4	Isleworth 6 B4	Richmond 6 D2	Warlingham 81 C1
Blindley Heath 163 D8	Effingham 113 E8	Kenley 80 D3	Ripley 91 C6	Warnham 216 E7
Bowlhead Green ...169 E1	Egham 12 A4	Kingsley Green 208 B2	Roehampton 7 F2	Wentworth 30 F3
Box Hill 116 A4	Ellen's Green 196 A4	Kingston Upon Thames .37 C6	Rowhook 196 E1	West Barnes 39 C4
Bracknell 27 D6	Elstead 148 D3	Kingswood 97 F6	Rowledge 145 F3	West Byfleet 71 B6
Bramley 151 F6	Englefield Green 11 C2	Knaphill 68 D1	Rowly 174 B6	West Clandon 111 B6
Brands Hill 1 A8	Enton Green 171 B5	Laleham 33 C6	Rudgwick 214 C7	West End 67 F6
Brentford 6 D7	Epsom 76 C5	Lambs Green 199 F6	Rushmoor 168 C5	West Ewell 57 E3
Broadbridge Heath ...216 E4	Esher 55 C6	Langley Vale 96 D8	Rusper 199 D7	West Hoathly 204 D1
Brockham 137 C2	Ewell 58 A1	Leatherhead 95 D5	Salfords 140 B1	West Horsley 112 B8
Bromley 44 E8	Ewhurst 175 F5	Leigh 138 B2	Sanderstead 80 F6	West Norwood 22 C5
Brook 170 B1	Fairlands 108 C4	Lewisham 24 C8	Sandhurst 64 C7	West Wickham 44 E1
Brookwood 88 A7	Farley Green 153 E7	Lightwater 66 F8	Seale 127 B4	Westcott 135 D6
Buckland 117 A2	Farnborough 85 B3	Limpsfield 123 A6	Selsdon 62 D1	Westhumble 115 A4
Burgh Heath 97 D8	Farncombe 150 E8	Linchmere 207 B2	Send 90 C4	Weybridge 53 A6
Burstow 183 A7	Farnham 125 B1	Lingfield 164 D5	Send Marsh 90 F3	Whiteley Village 53 E1
Byfleet 71 D7	Faygate 199 F1	Little Bookham 93 E3	Shackleford 149 D7	Whyteleafe 80 F1
Camberley 65 D6	Felbridge 184 F4	Littleton 34 A6	Shalford 130 E2	Wimbledon 19 F2
Capel 178 C6	Felcourt 185 C8	Long Ditton 37 C1	Shamley Green 152 E5	Windlesham 48 C4
Carshalton 59 E6	Feltham 15 A7	Longcross 50 A7	Sheerwater 70 D6	Windsor 9 E3
Caterham 100 F4	Fetcham 94 C4	Lower Halliford 34 D2	Shepperton 34 C3	Winkfield 8 D4
Catford 24 A7	Fickleshole 82 E5	Lower Kingswood ...117 E8	Shere 133 B4	Wisley 71 E3
Charlton 34 D7	Fisherstreet 209 F3	Loxwood 212 F4	Sidlow 139 B2	Witley 170 F4
Charlwood 180 C1	Flexford 107 C1	Lurgashall 209 A1	Slinfold 215 D3	Woking 69 E1
Cheam 58 F5	Forest Green 176 B2	Lyne 32 B1	Smallfield 162 B2	Wokingham 25 B5
Chelsham 82 A2	Forest Hill 23 D7	Martyr's Green 92 E7	South Croydon 61 D3	Woldingham 102 A4
Chertsey 33 B2	Forest Row 206 F3	Merstham 119 D7	South Godstone 142 F5	Wonersh 152 B7
Chessington 56 E4	Frensham 167 D7	Merton 40 B8	South Holmwood ...157 C7	Wood Street Village ..108 B3
Chiddingfold 191 B4	Frimley 65 F2	Mickleham 115 C7	South Norwood 42 C5	Woodham 52 A1
Chilworth 131 C3	Gatton 118 F7	Milford 149 E1	South Nutfield 140 E7	Woodmansterne 78 E4
Chipstead 78 F1	Godalming 150 F3	Mitcham 40 F5	Staines 12 e4	Worcester Park 57 E6
Chiswick 7 D7	Godstone 121 B3	Morden 40 B3	Stanwell 13 C7	Wormley 170 F1
Chobham 49 F2	Gomshall 133 D4	Mortlake 7 C4	Stoke D'Abernon 73 F3	Worplesdon 108 D8
Church Crookham ...104 A7	Grayshott 188 C3	Mytchett 85 F3	Stoneleigh 58 A5	Wotton 134 F3
Churt 167 E1	Grayswood 189 F1	New Addington 63 D3	Streatham 21 E2	Wraysbury 11 B4
Claygate 55 F3	Great Bookham 94 B1	New Haw 52 C3	Sunbury 35 B6	Wrecclesham 145 E6
Cobham 73 B5	Guildford 130 B8	New Malden 38 C4	Sunningdale 30 B6	Yateley 64 A5

1

10th Ave KT20 . . . . .97 A1
11th Ave KT20 . . . . .97 F1
12th Ave KT20 . . . . .97 F1
13th Ave KT20 . . . . .97 F1
14th Ave KT20 . . . . .97 F1
15th Ave KT20 . . . . .97 F1
16th Ave KT20 . . . . .97 F1
1st Ave KT20 . . . . .97 E2

2

2nd Ave KT20 . . . . .97 E2

3

3rd Ave KT20 . . . . .97 E2

4

4th Ave KT20 . . . . .97 E2

5

5th Ave KT20 . . . . .97 E2

6

6th Ave KT20 . . . . .97 E2

7

7th Ave KT20 . . . . .97 F2

8

8th Ave KT20 . . . . .97 F2

9

9th Ave KT20 . . . . .97 F2

A

Aaron Ct BR3 . . . . .44 B6
Aaron's Hill GU7 . . . . .150 B4
Aarron Ct GU21 . . . . .69 F2
Abbess Cl SW2 . . . . .22 B7
Abbetts La GU15 . . . . .65 B3
Abbey Church The RH10 .203 B1
Abbey Cl Bracknell RG12 . . .27 D4
Crawley GU6 . . . . .173 F2
Pyrford GU22 . . . . .70 E3
Wokingham RG40 . . . . .25 F7
Abbey Ct Camberley GU15 . .65 D5
Chertsey KT16 . . . . .33 B2
Farnham GU9 . . . . .125 C2
Abbey Dr Laleham TW18 . . .33 C5
Upper Tooting SW17 . . . . . .21 A3
Abbey Gdns KT16 . . . . .33 A3
Abbey Gn SW19 . . . . .21 A3
Abbey Ind Est CR4 . . . . .40 F4
Abbey La BR3 . . . . .24 A1
Abbey Lodge TW18 . . . . . . .12 F3
Abbey Par SW19 . . . . .20 C1
Abbey Pk BR3 . . . . .24 A1
Abbey Rd
  Chertsey KT16 . . . . .33 B2
  Croydon CR0, CR9 . . . . . . .61 B7
  Lower Halliford TW17 . . . . .34 A1
  Merton SW19 . . . . .40 C8
  Selsdon CR2 . . . . .62 D1
  Virginia Water GU25 . . . . . .31 D5
  Woking GU21 . . . . .69 D2
Abbey River Cotts KT16 . . .33 C3
Abbey Sch The GU9 . . . . . .125 D1
Abbey St GU9 . . . . .125 C2
Abbey Way GU14 . . . . .85 C4
Abbey Wlk KT8 . . . . .36 B5
Abbey Wood SL5 . . . . .30 A2
Abbeylands Sch KT15 . . . . .52 A5
Abbot Byfleet KT14 . . . . . . .71 D8
  Staines TW18 . . . . .13 D1
Abbot Rd GU1 . . . . .130 D7
Abbot's Cl GU2 . . . . .129 F6
Abbot's Way GU1, GU4 . . . .110 D2
Abbots Ct SE25 . . . . .42 E6
Abbots Dr GU25 . . . . .31 C5
Abbots Gn CR0, CR2 . . . . . .62 D4
Abbots La CR8 . . . . .80 C3
Abbots Pk SW2 . . . . .22 A7
Abbots Way BR3 . . . . .43 E4
Abbots Wlk CR3 . . . . .101 B5
Abbots Wood Forest Wlk
  GU10 . . . . .166 C7
Abbotsbury RG12 . . . . .26 F4
Abbotsbury Ct RH13 . . . . . .217 E3
Abbotsbury Fst Sch SM4 . .40 B4
Abbotsbury Rd
  Coney Hall BR2, BR4 . . . . . .63 F8
  Morden SM4, SW19 . . . . . . .40 B5
Abbotsfield Rd RH11 . . . . .200 D4
Abbotsford Cl GU22 . . . . . . .70 A2
Abbotshall Rd SE6 . . . . .24 D6
Abbotsleigh Cl SM2 . . . . . . .59 B3
Abbotsleigh Rd SW16 . . . . .21 C3
Abbotsmede Cl TW1 . . . . . .16 F6

Abbotswood
  Guildford GU1 . . . . .109 F3
  Walton-on-T KT13 . . . . . . .53 F7
Abbotswood Cl GU1 . . . . . .109 F4
Abbotswood Dr KT13 . . . . . .53 D1
Abbotswood Rd SW16 . . . . .21 D5
Abbott Ave SW20 . . . . .39 D8
Abbott Cl TW12 . . . . .15 E2
Abbott House SW12 . . . . . . .20 F8
Abbotts Cotts GU10 . . . . . .166 E5
Abbotts Rd
  Cheam SM1, SM3 . . . . .58 E6
  Mitcham CR4, SW16 . . . . . .41 C5
Abbotts Rise RH1 . . . . .119 A3
Abbotts Tilt KT12 . . . . .54 E7
Abelia Cl GU24 . . . . .67 E6
Abell Ct KT15 . . . . .52 C6
Abercairn Rd SW16 . . . . . . .21 C1
Aberconway Rd SM4 . . . . . .40 B5
Abercorn Cl CR2 . . . . .81 D7
Abercorn Way GU21 . . . . . . .69 A1
Aberdare Cl BR4 . . . . .63 C8
Aberdeen Rd CR0 . . . . .61 D6
Aberdour KT20 . . . . .77 F1
Aberfoyle Rd SW16 . . . . . . .21 D2
Abingdon Cl Bracknell RG12 27 E4
  Merton SW19 . . . . .20 C2
  Woking GU21 . . . . .69 C1
Abingdon Lodge BR2 . . . . . .44 F7
Abingdon Rd
  Sandhurst GU47 . . . . .45 C1
  Thornton Heath SW16 . . . . .41 E8
Abinger Ave SM2 . . . . .58 D2
Abinger Cl Dorking RH5 . . .136 C3
  Wallington SM6 . . . . .60 E5
Abinger Common Cty
  Sch RH5 . . . . .134 D1
Abinger Common Rd
  RH5 . . . . .155 F7
Abinger Ct SM6 . . . . .60 E5
Abinger Dr RH1 . . . . .139 E7
Abinger Gdns TW7 . . . . .5 E4
Abinger Hammer
  Village Sch RH5 . . . . . . .133 F4
Abinger House 2 KT2 . . . . .18 B1
Abinger La RH5 . . . . .134 C2
Abinger Rd RH5 . . . . .156 C3
Abinger Way GU4 . . . . .110 B6
Aboyne Dr SW20 . . . . .39 A7
Aboyne Rd SW17 . . . . .20 D5
Abrahams Rd RH11 . . . . . .201 A1
Acacia Ave Brentford TW8 . . .6 B7
  Littleton TW17 . . . . .34 A4
  Sandhurst GU47 . . . . .45 D1
  Woking GU22 . . . . .89 D7
Acacia Cl Penge SE20 . . . . .43 A7
  Woodham KT15 . . . . .51 F1
Acacia Ct Bracknell RG12 . . .27 B6
  5 West Norwood SW16 . . . .22 A3
Acacia Dr Banstead KT17 . . .77 D5
  Cheam SM3 . . . . .40 A1
  Woodham KT15 . . . . .51 F1
Acacia Gdns BR4 . . . . .63 C8
Acacia Gr Dulwich SE21 . . . .22 D6
  Kingston u T KT3 . . . . .38 E6
Acacia House RH2 . . . . . . .118 A3
Acacia Mews UB7 . . . . .2 D8
Acacia Rd Beckenham BR3 . .43 F6
  Guildford GU1 . . . . .109 D1
  Hampton TW12 . . . . .16 A2
  Mitcham CR4 . . . . .41 B7
  South Norwood SW16 . . . . .41 E8
  Staines TW18 . . . . .13 B3
Academy Cl GU15 . . . . .65 E8
Academy Gdns CR0 . . . . . . .42 F1
Accommodation La UB7 . . . .2 C8
Accommodation Rd KT16 . .50 E6
Ace Par KT9 . . . . .56 E7
Acer Dr GU24 . . . . .67 F6
Acer Rd TN16 . . . . .83 D3
Acheulian Cl GU9 . . . . .146 C2
Achilles Pl GU21 . . . . .69 C2
Ackroyd Rd SE23 . . . . .23 E8
Acorn Cl
  East Grinstead RH19 . . . . .205 E8
  1 Hampton TW12 . . . . . . .16 B2
  Horley RH6 . . . . .161 C4
Acorn Dr RG40 . . . . .25 C7
Acorn Gdns SE19 . . . . .42 F8
Acorn Gr Harlington UB3 . . .3 F7
  Kingswood KT20 . . . . .97 F3
  Woking GU22 . . . . .89 E6
Acorn Keep GU9 . . . . .125 D8
Acorn Mews GU14 . . . . .85 A7
Acorn Rd GU17 . . . . .64 B5
Acorn Way SE23 . . . . .23 D5
Acorns RH13 . . . . .218 A4
Acorns Cty Fst Sch The
  Betchworth RH3 . . . . .116 D1
  Leigh RH2 . . . . .138 A3
Acorns The Crawley RH11 .201 B1
  21 Putney SW19 . . . . .19 D7
Acorns Way KT10 . . . . .55 C5
Acre La SM5 . . . . .60 A6
Acre Rd Kingston u T KT2 . . .37 E8
  Mitcham SW19 . . . . .20 D2
Acres Gdns KT20 . . . . .97 D8
Acres Platt GU6 . . . . .174 F4
Action Cl TW15 . . . . .34 C8
Acuba House SW18 . . . . . . .20 B7
Acuba Rd SW18 . . . . .20 B6
Adair Cl SE25 . . . . .43 B6
Adair Wlk GU24 . . . . .87 B6
Adams Cl KT5 . . . . .37 F3
Adams Croft GU24 . . . . .87 C3
Adams Ct 2 CR8 . . . . .80 A7
Adams House 3 SW17 . . . .21 C3
Adams Park Rd GU9 . . . . . .125 D3

Adams Rd BR3 . . . . .43 E4
Adams Way SE25, CR0 . . . . .43 A3
Adams Wlk 11 KT1 . . . . .37 E7
Adamson Ct 6 RH11 . . . . . .201 B1
Adamsrill Prim Sch SE26 . .23 E5
Adamsrill Rd SE23, SE26 . . .23 E4
Adare Wlk SW16, SW2 . . . . .21 F5
Addington Bsns Ctr CR9 . . .63 E1
Addington Court Golf
  Course CR0 . . . . .63 A2
Addington Ct 7 SW14 . . . . .7 D4
Addington Golf Course
  CR0, CR9 . . . . .62 E6
Addington Gr SE26 . . . . .23 E4
Addington High Sch CR0 . .82 E7
Addington Palace Golf
  Course CR0 . . . . .62 E5
Addington Palace (the
  Royal Sch of Church
  Music) CR9 . . . . .62 F4
Addington Rd
  Sanderstead CR2 . . . . .81 A8
  Selsdon CR2 . . . . .62 C1
  Thornton Heath CR0 . . . . . .42 A1
  West Wickham BR4, CR0 . . . .63 D6
  West Wickham BR4 . . . . . . .63 E8
Addington Village Rd CR0 .63 A5
Addiscombe Ave CR0 . . . . . .43 A2
Addiscombe Court Rd
  CR0, CR9 . . . . .61 E8
Addiscombe Rd
  Crowthorne RG45 . . . . .45 C4
  Croydon CR0, CR9 . . . . . . .61 E8
  South Croydon CR0 . . . . . . .61 E8
Addison Ave TW3 . . . . .5 C6
Addison Cl CR3 . . . . .100 D5
Addison Ct GU1 . . . . .130 F7
Addison Gdns KT5 . . . . .37 F5
Addison Rd Caterham CR3 100 D6
  Croydon SE25 . . . . .43 A5
  Farnborough GU16 . . . . . . .85 E8
  Guildford GU1 . . . . .130 F7
  Teddington TW11 . . . . .17 B2
  8 Woking GU21 . . . . .69 F2
Addison's Cl CR0 . . . . .62 F8
Addlestone House KT15 . . .52 B7
Addlestone Moor KT15 . . . .52 C8
Addlestone Pk KT15 . . . . . .52 B5
Addlestone Rd KT13, KT15 .52 D6
Addlestone Sta KT15 . . . . .52 D6
Adecroft Way KT8 . . . . .36 C6
Adela Ave KT3 . . . . .39 B5
Adelaide Cl Crawley RH11 181 D1
  Horsham RH12 . . . . .217 F4
Adelaide Ct 15 BR3 . . . . . . .24 A1
Adelaide Pl KT13 . . . . .53 D6
Adelaide Rd Ashford TW15 . .13 D3
  Heston TW5 . . . . .4 E6
  Kingston u T KT6 . . . . .37 E4
  Richmond TW9 . . . . .6 F3
  Teddington TW11 . . . . .16 F2
  Walton-on-T KT12 . . . . . . .54 B7
Adelina Mews SW12 . . . . . .21 D7
Adelphi Cl RH10 . . . . .202 D4
Adelphi Rd KT17 . . . . .76 D6
Adenmore Rd SE6 . . . . .24 A8
Adisham House 7 SE20 . . .23 C1
Adlers La RH5 . . . . .115 A4
Adlington Pl GU14 . . . . .85 E2
Admiral Ct SM5 . . . . .40 E1
Admiral Rd RH11 . . . . .201 A3
Admiral's Bridge La
  RH19 . . . . .205 C2
Admiral's Wlk The CR5 . . . .99 F7
Admirals Ct GU1 . . . . .110 B2
Admiralty Rd TW11 . . . . . . .16 F2
Admiralty Way GU15 . . . . . .64 F4
Adolf St SE6 . . . . .24 B4
Adrian Ct RH11 . . . . .201 B1
Advance Rd SE27 . . . . .22 C4
Adversane Ct RH11 . . . . . .217 D4
Aerodrome Way TW5 . . . . . .4 C8
Aerospace Bvd GU14 . . . . .105 A7
Agar Cl KT6 . . . . .56 F8
Agar House 6 KT1 . . . . .37 E6
Agate House
  New Malden KT4 . . . . .38 E1
  12 Penge SE26 . . . . .23 B3
Agate La RH12 . . . . .217 F5
Agates La KT21 . . . . .95 D8
Agincourt Pl SL5 . . . . .29 C6
Agnes Scott Ct 5 KT13 . . . .53 B7
Agnew Rd SE23 . . . . .23 D8
Agraria Rd GU2 . . . . .130 B7
Ailsa Ave TW1 . . . . .6 B2
Ailsa Cl RH11 . . . . .201 B3
Ailsa Rd TW1 . . . . .6 B2
Ainger Cl GU12 . . . . .105 D2
Ainsdale Way GU21 . . . . . . .69 A1
Ainsworth Rd CR0, CR9 . . . .61 B8
Aintree Cl SL3 . . . . .1 E6
Aintree House SE26 . . . . . . .23 B2
Aintree Rd RH10 . . . . .202 A4
Air Forces Meml TW20 . . . .11 D4
Airborne House 10 SM6 . . .60 B6
Airbourne Forces Mus
  GU11 . . . . .105 A5
Aircraft Espl GU14 . . . . .85 C1
Airedale Rd SW12 . . . . .20 F8
Airport Way Horley RH6 . . .182 B8
  Stanwell TW19 . . . . .2 A3
Airport Way Rdbt W RH6 181 E8
Aisne Rd GU16 . . . . .66 E1
Aitken Cl CR4 . . . . .40 F2
Aitken House GU27 . . . . . .208 C7
Aitken Rd SE6 . . . . .24 B6
Akabusi Cl CR0 . . . . .43 A3
Akehurst Cl RH10 . . . . .183 B3

Akehurst St SW15 . . . . .19 A8
Akerman Rd KT6 . . . . .37 C3
Alamein Rd GU11 . . . . .105 B3
Alan Hilton Ct KT16 . . . . . . .51 D6
Alan Rd SW19 . . . . .19 E3
Alan Turing Rd GU2 . . . . . .108 D1
Alanbrooke Cl GU21 . . . . . . .68 C1
Alanbrooke Rd GU11 . . . . .105 D6
Albain Cres TW15 . . . . .13 E6
Albans Cl SW16 . . . . .21 E5
Albany Cl Esher KT10 . . . . . .55 A2
  Mortlake SW14 . . . . .7 B3
Albany Cres KT10 . . . . .55 E4
Albany Ct Frimley GU16 . . . .65 C1
  Kingston u T KT2 . . . . .17 E2
  Oatlands Park KT13 . . . . . . .53 E8
  Richmond TW10 . . . . .17 B5
  3 Weybridge KT13 . . . . . . .53 B6
Albany Ho 6 TW8 . . . . .6 E8
Albany Mews
  Kingston u T KT2 . . . . .17 D2
  Sutton SM1 . . . . .59 B5
Albany Par 4 TW8 . . . . .6 E8
Albany Park Ind Est GU15 .65 C1
Albany Park Rd
  Kingston u T KT2 . . . . .17 D2
  Leatherhead KT22 . . . . .95 A8
Albany Pk Camberley GU15 .65 B5
  Frimley GU15 . . . . .65 C1
  Poyle SL3 . . . . .1 D7
Albany Pl Brentford TW8 . . . .6 E8
  Egham TW20 . . . . .12 B4
Albany Rd Brentford TW8 . . . .6 E8
  Crawley RH11 . . . . .201 C6
  Hersham KT12 . . . . .54 D6
  New Malden KT3 . . . . .38 D5
  Richmond TW10 . . . . .6 E2
  Wimbledon SW19 . . . . .20 B3
Albany Reach KT7 . . . . .36 F4
Albany Terr 5 TW10 . . . . . . .6 F2
Albanys The RH2 . . . . .118 A3
Albatross Gdns CR2 . . . . . . .81 D8
Albemarle SW19 . . . . .19 D6
Albemarle Ave TW2 . . . . . . .15 F7
Albemarle Gdns KT3 . . . . . .38 D5
Albemarle Lodge SE26 . . . .23 E3
Albemarle Pk BR3 . . . . .44 B8
Albemarle Rd BR2, BR3 . . . .44 C8
Albemarle Prim Sch
  SW19 . . . . .19 E6
Albermarle Prim Sch
  (Annexe) SW19 . . . . .19 E7
Albert Ave KT16 . . . . .33 A6
Albert Carr Gdns SW16 . . . .21 E3
Albert Crane Ct RH11 . . . .201 A8
Albert Dr Putney SW19 . . . . .19 E6
  Sheerwater GU21, KT14 . . .70 D5
Albert Gr SW20 . . . . .39 D8
Albert Rd Addlestone KT15 .52 D6
  Aldershot GU11 . . . . .105 B2
  Ashford TW15 . . . . .13 F3
  Ashstead KT21 . . . . .75 F1
  Bagshot GU19 . . . . .47 E1
  Bracknell RG42 . . . . .27 B8
  Camberley GU15 . . . . .65 C5
  Carshalton SM5 . . . . .59 D5
  Crowthorne RG45 . . . . .45 B5
  Croydon CR0, SE25 . . . . . . .43 B5
  Englefield Green TW20 . . . . .11 D2
  Epsom KT17 . . . . .76 F6
  Farnborough GU14 . . . . . . .85 C2
  Hampton TW12 . . . . .16 C3
  Horley RH6 . . . . .161 A3
  Hounslow TW3 . . . . .5 A3
  Kingston u T KT1 . . . . .37 F7
  Merstham RH1 . . . . .119 C6
  Mitcham CR4 . . . . .40 F6
  New Malden KT3 . . . . .38 F5
  Penge SE20 . . . . .23 D2
  Richmond TW10 . . . . .6 F2
  Sutton SM1 . . . . .59 D5
  Teddington TW11 . . . . .16 F2
  Twickenham TW1 . . . . .16 F7
  Warlingham CR6 . . . . .81 F2
  Wokingham RG40 . . . . .25 B5
Albert Rd N RH2 . . . . .117 F2
Albert Wlk RG45 . . . . .45 B5
Alberta Ave SM1 . . . . .58 F5
Alberta Dr RH6 . . . . .162 A3
Albertine Cl KT17 . . . . .77 B3
Albery Cl RH12 . . . . .217 B4
Albion Cl RH10 . . . . .202 D5
Albion Ct SM2 . . . . .59 D3
Albion Par GU21 . . . . .68 C2
Albion Pl SE25 . . . . .43 A6
Albion Rd Hounslow TW3 . . . .5 A3
  Kingston u T KT2 . . . . .38 C8
  Reigate RH2 . . . . .139 C8
  Sandhurst GU47 . . . . .64 B8
  Sutton SM2 . . . . .59 D3
  Twickenham TW2 . . . . .16 E7
Albion St CR0, CR9 . . . . . . .42 B1
Albion Villas Rd
  SE23, SE26 . . . . .23 C5
Albion Way RH12 . . . . .217 C2
Albury Ave East Ewell SM2 .58 C1
  Hounslow TW7 . . . . .5 F7
  Isleworth TW7 . . . . .5 F7
Albury Cl Hampton TW12 . . .16 B2
  Longcross KT16 . . . . .50 A7
Albury Ct 4 Croydon CR0 . . .61 C6
  Mitcham CR4 . . . . .40 D7
  Sutton SM1 . . . . .59 C6
Albury Keep RH6 . . . . .161 B4
Albury Lodge 10 SW2 . . . . .21 F8
Albury Pl RH1 . . . . .119 E6
Albury Rd Chessington KT9 .56 E5
  Guildford GU1 . . . . .131 A8

Albury Rd continued
  Hersham KT12 . . . . .53 F4
  Merstham RH1 . . . . .119 C6
Albury St SL5 . . . . .132 C4
Alcester Ct 4 SM6 . . . . .60 B6
Alcester Rd SM6 . . . . .60 B6
Alcock Cl SM6 . . . . .60 D3
Alcock Rd TW5 . . . . .4 D7
Alcocks Cl KT20 . . . . .97 E7
Alcocks La KT20 . . . . .97 E7
Alcorn Cl SM3 . . . . .59 A8
Alcot Cl RG45 . . . . .45 B4
Alden Ct CR0 . . . . .61 D7
Aldenham Terr RG12 . . . . . .27 C3
Aldenholme RH1 . . . . .53 E4
Alder Cl Ash Vale GU12 . . . .106 A7
  Crawley Down RH10 . . . . .204 B8
  Englefield Green TW20 . . . . .11 E3
Alder Croft CR5 . . . . .79 F3
Alder Ct 3 SW16 . . . . .22 A3
Alder Rd
  Headley Down GU35 . . . . .187 B6
  Mortlake SW14 . . . . .7 D4
Alderbrook Prim Sch
  SW12 . . . . .21 B8
Alderbrook Rd
  Balham SW12 . . . . .21 B8
  Cranleigh GU6 . . . . .174 C3
Aldergrove Gdns TW4 . . . . . .4 E5
Alderman Judge Mall 6
  KT1 . . . . .37 E7
Alderman Willey Cl RG41 . .25 B6
Aldermead TW3 . . . . .5 B3
Aldermoor Rd SE6 . . . . .23 F5
Alderney Ave TW5 . . . . .5 B7
Alders Ave RH19 . . . . .185 E3
Alders Rd RH2 . . . . .118 B3
Alders The Feltham TW13 . . .15 E4
  Heston TW5 . . . . .4 F8
  Streatham SW16 . . . . .21 C4
  West Byfleet KT14 . . . . .71 C7
  West Wickham BR4 . . . . . . .63 B8
Alders View Dr RH19 . . . . .185 E3
Aldersbrook Dr KT2 . . . . . . .17 F2
Aldersey Rd GU1 . . . . .109 F1
Aldersgrove KT8 . . . . .36 D4
Aldershot Military Mus
  GU11 . . . . .105 C2
Aldershot Rd Ash GU12 . . .105 F1
  Church Crookham GU13 . . .104 A6
  Fairlands GU3 . . . . .108 D5
  Guildford GU2, GU3 . . . . . .108 D5
  Pirbright GU24, GU3 . . . . . .87 F2
  Wood St V GU3 . . . . .107 E5
Aldershot Sta GU11 . . . . . .105 B1
Alderside Wlk TW20 . . . . . . .11 E3
Aldersmead Ave CR0 . . . . . .43 D3
Aldersmead Rd BR3 . . . . . . .23 E1
Alderstead La RH1 . . . . .99 D2
Alderton KT2 . . . . .38 B8
Alderton Ct KT8 . . . . .35 F5
Alderton Rd CR0 . . . . .43 A2
Alderwick Dr TW3 . . . . .5 D4
Alderwood Cl CR3 . . . . . . .100 E2
Aldingbourne Cl RH11 . . . .200 F7
Aldis Mews SW17 . . . . .20 E3
Aldis St SW17 . . . . .20 E3
Aldous House TW18 . . . . . . .12 E4
Aldren Rd SW17 . . . . .20 C5
Aldrich Cres CR0 . . . . .63 C2
Aldrich Gdns SM3 . . . . .58 F7
Aldrich Terr SW18 . . . . .20 C6
Aldridge Rise KT3 . . . . .38 E3
Aldrin Pl GU14 . . . . .84 D4
Aldrington Rd SW16 . . . . . . .21 C4
Aldro Sch GU8 . . . . .149 C7
Aldwick Cl GU14 . . . . .85 A6
Aldwick Rd CR0 . . . . .60 F6
Aldworth Cl RG12 . . . . .27 A5
Aldworth Gdns RG45 . . . . . .45 A5
Aldwych Cl RH10 . . . . .202 D4
Aldwyn Ct TW20 . . . . .11 B2
Alexa Ct SM2 . . . . .59 A4
Alexander Cl TW2 . . . . .16 F6
Alexander Ct
  Beckenham BR3 . . . . .44 D8
  14 Surbiton KT6 . . . . .37 D2
Alexander Evans Mews
  SE23 . . . . .23 D6
Alexander Godley Cl KT21 .95 F8
Alexander Rd Coulsdon CR5 79 B4
  Egham TW20 . . . . .12 C3
  Reigate RH2 . . . . .139 A6
Alexander Wlk RG12 . . . . . .27 B4
Alexanders Wlk CR3 . . . . .101 A1
Alexandra Ave
  Camberley GU15 . . . . .65 A5
  Sutton SM1 . . . . .59 A7
  Warlingham CR6 . . . . .81 F2
Alexandra Cl Ashford TW15 14 D1
  Staines TW18 . . . . .13 D2
  Walton-on-T KT12 . . . . . . .54 A8
Alexandra Cotts SE20 . . . . .23 D2
Alexandra Cres BR1 . . . . . . .24 F2
Alexandra Ct Ashford TW15 14 D2
  10 Crawley RH10 . . . . .201 D5
  1 Farnborough GU14 . . . . .85 C3
Alexandra Dr Surbiton KT5 . .38 A2
  West Norwood SE19 . . . . . .22 E2
Alexandra Gdns Chiswick W4 7 E7
  Hounslow TW3 . . . . .5 B5
  Knaphill GU21 . . . . .68 D1
  Wallington SM5 . . . . .60 A2
Alexandra Inf Sch
  Kingston u T KT2 . . . . .18 A1

Alexandra Inf Sch *continued*
Penge BR3 23 D1
Alexandra Jun & Inf Sch TW3 5 B5
Alexandra Jun Sch SE26 23 D2
Alexandra Lodge
12 Guildford GU1 130 F8
1 Weybridge KT13 53 B6
Alexandra Pl Croydon CR0 42 E1
Guildford GU1 130 F7
South Norwood SE25 42 D4
Alexandra Rd
Addlestone KT15 52 D6
Aldershot GU11 104 F2
Ash GU12 105 F1
Ashford TW15 14 E2
Biggin Hill TN16 103 B8
10 Brentford TW8 6 D8
Croydon CR0 42 E2
Englefield Green TW20 11 C2
Epsom KT17 76 F6
Farnborough GU14, GU11 85 C1
Hounslow TW3 5 B5
Kingston u T KT2 18 A1
Mitcham SW19 20 E1
Mortlake SW14 7 D4
Penge SE26 23 D2
Richmond TW9 6 F5
Thames Ditton KT7 36 F4
Twickenham TW1 6 C1
Warlingham CR6 81 F2
Wimbledon SW19 20 A3
Alexandra Sq SM4 40 A4
Alexandra Terr GU1 130 E8
Alexandra Wlk 8 SE19 22 E3
Alfold By-Pass Alfold GU6 193 F7
Alfold Crossways GU6 194 A5
Alfold Cotts GU6 193 F2
Alfold La GU6 194 A7
Alfold Rd Alfold GU8 193 B3
Cranleigh GU6 194 B7
Dunsfold GU8 193 B3
Alfonso Cl GU12 126 C8
Alford Cl GU4 110 A4
Alford Ct 5 SM2 59 B3
Alford Gn CR0 63 D4
Alfred Butt House SW17 20 F5
Alfred Cl RH10 202 E5
Alfred Hurley House SW17 20 C4
Alfred Mizen Prim Sch The CR4 41 D6
Alfred Rd Croydon SE25 43 A4
Farnham GU9 125 C1
Feltham TW13 15 C6
Kingston u T KT1 37 F6
Sutton SM1 59 C5
Alfreton Cl SW19 19 D5
Alfriston KT5 37 F3
Alfriston Ave CR0 41 E2
Alfriston Cl KT5 37 F3
Alfriston Rd GU16 86 C7
Algar Cl TW7 6 A4
Algar Rd TW7 6 A4
Algarve Rd SW18 20 B7
Alice Gough Memorial Homes RG12 27 B6
Alice Holt Forest Visitor Ctr GU10 166 C8
Alice Mews 8 TW11 16 F3
Alice Rd GU11 105 B2
Alice Ruston Pl GU22 89 C8
Alice Way TW3 5 B3
Alicia Ave RH10 202 C6
Alington Gr SM6 60 D2
Alison Cl Croydon CR0 43 D1
Farnborough GU14 84 F3
Woking GU21 69 E4
Alison Dr GU15 65 F5
Alison Way GU11 104 F2
Alison's Rd GU11 105 B4
All England Lawn Tennis & Croquet Club The SW19 19 E5
All Hallows Catholic Sch GU9 125 F7
All Saint's Prim Sch SE19 42 E8
All Saints' Benhilton C of E Prim Sch SM1 59 B7
All Saints C of E Prim Sch SW19 20 C1
All Saints Carshalton CE Sch SM5 60 A5
All Saints CE Inf Sch GU10 147 C3
All Saints Cl RG40 25 C7
All Saints Cres GU14 64 E1
All Saints Ct TW5 4 D6
All Saints Dr CR2 81 A7
All Saints Inf Sch KT22 95 A8
All Saints Rd
Lightwater GU18 48 C1
Merton SW19 20 C1
Sutton SM1 59 C7
All Souls' Rd SL5 29 A5
Allan Cl KT3 38 D4
Allbrook Cl TW11 16 E3
Allbrook House 5 SW15 19 A8
Allcard Cl RH12 217 D4
Allcot Cl Crawley RH11 200 E3
East Bedfont TW14 14 F7
Allcott House TW7 5 F4
Allden Ave GU11, GU12 126 D7
Allden Cotts GU7 150 B4
Allden Gdns GU12 126 D7
Alldens Hill GU5, GU8 151 D1
Alldens La GU8 151 B1
Allen Cl Streatham CR4 41 C8
Sunbury TW16 35 B8
Allen House Pk GU22 89 C7
Allen Rd
Great Bookham KT23 94 B1
Penge BR3 43 D7
Sunbury TW16 35 B7
Thornton Heath CR0 42 A1
Allen's Cl RH19 206 D6
Allenby Ave CR2 61 C2
Allenby Rd Biggin Hill TN16 83 E2
Forest Hill SE23 23 E5
Sandhurst GU15 65 A6
Allendale GU8 148 C3
Allendale Cl
Forest Hill SE26 23 D3
Sandhurst GU47 45 A2
Allenford House SW15 7 F1
Allenswood 12 SW19 19 E7
Allerford Ct SE6 24 B5
Allerford Rd SE6 24 B4
Allerton Ct SM3 58 D8
Allerton House 4 SW19 20 C1
Alleyn Cres SE21 22 D6
Alleyn Pk SE21 22 E5
Alleyn Rd SE21 22 E5
Allgood Cl SM4 39 D3
Alliance Ct TW15 14 C4
Allingham Ct GU7 150 F7
Allingham Gdns RH12 218 B5
Allingham Rd RH2 139 A6
Allington Ave TW17 34 E6
Allington Cl SW19 19 D3
Allington Ct CR0 43 C3
Allison Gr SE21 22 E7
Alloway Cl 4 GU21 69 B1
Allsmoor La RG12 27 F6
Allum Gr KT20 97 B6
Allwood Cl SE26 23 D4
Allyington Way RH10 202 D5
Allyn Cl TW18 12 F2
Alma Cl Aldershot GU12 105 D2
Knaphill GU21 68 E1
Alma Cres SM1 58 E5
Alma Ct CR3 100 C6
Alma Gdns GU16 86 E8
Alma Ho 7 TW8 6 E8
Alma La GU9 125 C7
Alma Pl Penge SE19 22 F1
Thornton Heath CR7 42 A4
Alma Rd Carshalton SM5 59 E5
Headley Down GU35 187 C5
Reigate RH2 118 B3
Thames Ditton KT10, KT7 36 E1
Alma Sq GU14 105 C8
Alma Terr SW18 20 D8
Alma Way GU9 125 D7
Almer Rd SW20 19 A1
Almners Rd Chertsey KT16 32 C2
Lyne KT16 32 B1
Almond Ave Carshalton SM5 59 F8
Woking GU22 89 D6
Almond Cl Charlton TW17 34 C7
Crawley RH11 201 A5
Englefield Green TW20 11 B2
Guildford GU1 109 D5
Almond Gr TW8 6 B7
Almond Rd KT19 76 D8
Almond Way CR4 41 D5
Almorah Rd TW5 4 D6
Alms Heath GU23 92 B6
Almsgate GU3 129 C2
Almshouse La KT9 56 D2
Almshouses Dorking RH4 136 B8
Mickleham RH5 115 C8
Sunbury TW16 34 F8
Alnwick Gr SM4 40 B5
Alpha Ct CR6 81 A1
Alpha Rd Chobham GU24 49 F1
Crawley RH11 201 C6
Croydon CR0 42 E1
Surbiton KT5 37 F3
Teddington TW12 16 D3
Woking GU22 70 C4
Alpha Way TW20 32 C8
Alphabet Gdns SM5 40 D3
Alphea Cl SW19 20 E1
Alphington Ave GU16 65 F1
Alphington Gn GU16 65 F1
Alpine Ave KT5 57 C8
Alpine Cl Farnborough GU14 84 D3
South Croydon CR0 61 E7
Alpine Rd Redhill RH1 119 A4
Walton-on-T KT12 35 A2
Alpine View SM1 59 E5
Alresford Rd GU2 130 A8
Alric Ave KT3 38 F6
Alsace Wlk GU15 65 B1
Alsford Cl GU18 66 F7
Alsom Ave KT19, KT4 58 A6
Alston Cl KT7 37 B2
Alston Rd SW17 20 D4
Alt Gr SW19 19 E1
Alterton Cl GU21 69 A2
Althorne Rd RH1 140 A7
Althorp Rd SW17 20 F7
Alton Cl TW7 5 F5
Alton Ct 19 Beckenham BR3 24 A1
Egham TW18 32 E8
Alton Gdns Beckenham BR3 24 A1
Twickenham TW2 16 D8
Alton House 1 RH1 119 A3
Alton Rd Croydon CR0, CR9 61 A7
Farnham GU10, GU9 145 D7
Richmond TW10, TW9 6 E3
Roehampton SW15 19 A7
Alton Ride GU17 64 C6
Altwood Prim Sch CR2 81 A6
Altyre Cl BR3 43 F4
Altyre Rd CR0, CR9 61 D8
Altyre Way BR3 43 F4
Alvernia Cl GU7 150 C2
Alvernia Lodge SM1 59 C8
Alverstoke Gdns GU11 104 E1
Alverston Gdns SE25 42 E4
Alverstone Ave SW18, SW19 20 A6
Alverstone Rd KT3 38 F5
Alvia Gdns SM1 59 C6
Alway Ave KT19 57 D5
Alwin Pl GU9 125 B7
Alwyn Cl CR0 63 B3
Alwyne Ct GU21 69 E3
Alwyne Rd SW19 19 F2
Alwyns Cl KT16 33 A3
Alwyns La KT16 33 A3
Amalgamated Dr TW8 6 B8
Amanda Ct TW15 13 F6
Ambassador RG12 26 F4
Ambassador Cl TW3 4 E5
Amber Ct Aldershot GU12 105 C2
Mitcham CR4 40 E5
Staines TW18 12 F3
Amber Hill GU15 66 B4
Ambercroft Way CR5 100 B8
Amberley Cl
Crawley RH10 202 C6
Horsham RH12 218 A6
Send Marsh GU23 90 F2
Amberley Ct SM2 59 C3
Amberley Dr KT15 70 F8
Amberley Gdns KT19 57 F6
Amberley Gr Croydon CR0 42 F2
Forest Hill SE26 23 B3
Amberley Grange GU11 125 F8
Amberley Rd
Horsham RH12 218 A6
Milford GU8 149 E2
Amberley Way Heston TW4 4 C2
Morden SM4 39 F2
Amberside Cl TW2 5 D1
Amberwood Dr GU15 65 F7
Amberwood Rise KT3 38 E3
Amblecote KT11 73 E7
Ambleside Catford BR1 24 D2
Godalming GU7 151 A5
13 Putney SW19 19 E7
Ambleside Ave
Beckenham BR3 43 E4
Streatham SW16 21 D4
Walton-on-T KT12 35 C1
Ambleside Cl
Crawley RH11 200 D5
Farnborough GU14 84 E3
Mytchett GU16 86 A2
Redhill RH1 140 B4
Ambleside Cres GU9 125 A6
Ambleside Cty Jun Sch KT12 35 C1
Ambleside Dr TW14 14 F7
Ambleside Gdns
Selsdon CR2 62 D1
Streatham SW16 21 D3
Sutton SM2 59 C4
Ambleside Rd GU18 67 B8
Ambleside Sch SM2 58 E2
Ambleside Way TW20 12 B1
Ambrey Way CR8, SM6 60 D2
Amen Cnr SW17 21 A2
Amen Corner Bsns Pk RG12 26 D7
Amenity Way SM4 39 C2
American Comm Sch
Esher KT11 54 C1
Virginia Water TW20 31 C7
American Magna Carta Meml TW20 11 D6
American Sch in Switzerland (English Branch) The TW20 32 C6
Amersham Rd CR0 42 D3
Amesbury Ave SW2 21 F6
Amesbury Cl KT4 39 C1
Amesbury Rd TW13 15 D6
Amesbury Sch GU26 188 E1
Amey Dr KT23 94 C3
Amhurst Gdns TW7 6 A5
Amis Ave Chessington KT19 57 B5
Woodham KT15 52 A1
Amis Rd GU21 88 E8
Amity Gr SW20 39 C8
Amlets La GU6 174 E5
Ampere Way CR0, CR9 41 F1
Amroth Cl SE23 23 B7
Amstel Way GU21 68 F1
Amundsen Rd RH12 217 D6
Amy Johnson Prim Sch SM6 60 E3
Amy Rd RH8 122 E6
Amyand Cotts 12 TW1 6 B1
Amyand Park Gdns 3 TW1 17 B8
Amyand Park Rd TW1 17 A8
Anarth Ct KT13 34 E1
Ancaster Cres KT3 39 A3
Ancaster Dr SL5 28 E8
Ancaster Rd BR3 43 D6
Anchor Cotts RH7 163 E8
Anchor Cres GU21 68 D2
Anchor Hill GU21 68 D2
Anchor Meadow GU14 84 F4
Anchorage Cl SW19 20 A3
Anderson Ave GU2 109 B5
Anderson Cl KT19 76 B7
Anderson Dr TW15 14 C4
Anderson House SW17 20 D3
Anderson Pl GU19 47 E4
Anderson Rd KT13 53 D7
Anderson's Pl TW3 5 B3
Andhurst Ct KT2 38 B8
Andon Ct BR3 43 E6
Andover Cl
East Bedfont TW14 14 F7
Epsom KT19 76 D8
Andover Ct TW19 13 D8
Andover Rd
Blackwater GU17 64 C6
Twickenham TW2 16 D7
Andover Way GU11, GU9 126 B7
Andreck Ct BR3 44 C7
Andrew Cl RG40 25 E5
Andrew Ct SE23 23 D6
Andrew Ewing Prim Sch TW5 4 F7
Andrew Reed House SW18 19 E8
Andrew's Cl KT17 76 F6
Andrewartha Rd GU14 85 E2
Andrewes House SM1 59 A6
Andrews Cl KT4 58 D8
Andrews Rd GU14 84 E5
Andromeda Cl RH11 200 E4
Anerley Ct SE20 23 B1
Anerley Gr SE19 22 F1
Anerley Hill SE19 22 F2
Anerley Park Rd SE20 23 B1
Anerley Pk SE20 23 B1
Anerley Prim Sch SE20 43 A8
Anerley Rd SE20, SE19 43 B8
Anerley Sch SE20 43 A8
Anerley Sta SE20 43 B8
Anerley Station Rd SE20 43 B8
Anerley Vale SE19 23 A1
Anfield Cl SW12 21 C8
Angas Ct 4 KT13 53 C5
Angel Ct GU3 129 A3
Angel Gate GU1 130 D8
Angel Hill SM1 59 B7
Angel Hill Dr SM1 59 B7
Angel Mews SW15 19 A8
Angel Rd KT7 37 A1
Angela Ct 2 SE23 23 C7
Angelfield TW3 5 B2
Angelica Gdns CR0 43 D1
Angelica Rd Bisley GU24 68 A4
Guildford GU2 109 A5
Angell Cl RH10 202 C5
Angers Cl GU15 66 C7
Anglers Reach KT6 37 D4
Angles Rd SW16 21 E4
Anglesea House KT1 37 D5
Anglesea Rd KT1 37 D5
Anglesey Ave GU14 84 F7
Anglesey Cl Ashford TW15 14 A5
Crawley RH11 201 C2
Anglesey Court Rd SM5 60 A4
Anglesey Gdns SM5 60 A4
Anglesey Rd GU12 105 D1
Angus Cl Chessington KT9 57 A5
Horsham RH12 217 D4
Angus House 12 SW12 21 D8
Anlaby Rd TW11 16 E3
Ann Parkes Ct TW5 4 D5
Annandale Dr GU10 146 D6
Annandale Rd Croydon CR0 62 A8
Guildford GU2 130 B7
Anne Armstrong Cl GU11 105 D5
Anne Boleyn's Wlk
Cheam SM2, SM3 58 E3
Kingston u T KT2 17 E3
Anne Way KT8 36 B5
Anne's Wlk CR3 100 E7
Annella Ct GU11 105 D8
Anners Cl TW20 32 C6
Annesley Dr CR0 62 F7
Annett Cl TW17 34 E5
Annett Rd KT12 35 A2
Annie Brookes Cl TW18 12 D5
Anningsley Pk KT16 51 C1
Annisdowne RH5 133 F1
Annsworthy Ave CR7, SE25 42 D6
Annsworthy Cres CR7 42 D7
Ansell Gr SM5 41 A1
Ansell Rd Dorking RH4 136 B8
Frimley GU16 65 E1
Upper Tooting SW17 20 F5
Anselm Cl CR0 61 F7
Ansford Rd BR1, SE6 24 D4
Ansley Cl CR2 81 B5
Anslie Wlk 8 SW12 21 B8
Anson Cl CR3, CR8 100 D7
Anstice Cl W4 7 E7
Anstie Grange Dr RH5 157 B5
Anstie La RH5 156 F4
Anstiebury Cl RH5 157 C3
Anston Ct 3 GU2 108 E1
Anthony Ct TW7 5 F4
Anthony Rd CR0, SE25 43 A3
Anthony West House RH3 137 B7
Antigua Wlk SE19 22 D3
Antlands La Burstow RH6 183 B6
Crawley RH6 182 E5
Antlands La E RH6 182 F5
Antlands La W RH6 182 E6
Anton Cres SM1 59 A7
Antrobus Cl SM1 58 F5
Anvil Cl SW16 21 C1
Anvil La KT11 73 A5
Anvil Rd TW16 35 A6
Anyards Rd KT11 73 B5
Anzio Cl GU11 105 A2
Apeldoorn Dr CR8, SM6 60 E2
Aperdele Rd KT22 75 A1
Aperfield Rd TN16 83 E2
Apers Ave GU22 89 F6
Apex Cl Beckenham BR3 44 B8
Oatlands Park KT13 53 D7
Apex Dr GU16 65 D1
Apley Rd RH2 139 A6
Aplin Way Hounslow TW7 5 E6
Lightwater GU18 48 A1
Apollo Pl GU21 89 A8
Apollo Rise GU14 84 D4
Apple Garth GU7 150 C7
Apple Gr KT9 56 E6
Apple Mkt KT1 37 D7
Apple Tree Cl KT23 94 C3
Apple Tree Way GU47 45 D1
Appleby Cl TW2 16 D6
Appleby Ct GU15 65 B6
Appleby Gdns TW14 14 F7
Appledore RG12 26 F3
Appledore Cl Hayes BR2 44 F4
Upper Tooting SW12, SW17 20 F6
Appledore Mews GU14 85 A7
Appledown Rise CR5 79 C4
Applefield RH10 201 E7
Applegarth Claygate KT10 55 F5
New Addington CR0 63 B3
Applegarth Ave GU2 108 D1
Applegarth Inf & Jun Sch CR0 63 B4
Applelands Cl GU10 146 A4
Appleton Gdns KT3 39 A3
Appleton Sq CR4 40 E8
Appletree Cl
Godalming GU7 150 F2
6 Penge SE20 43 B8
Appletree Ct GU4 110 D3
Appletree Pl 4 RG42 27 A8
Appletrees Pl GU22 89 C8
Appley Dr GU15 65 B6
Approach Rd Ashford TW15 14 C2
East Molesey KT8 36 A4
Farnham GU9 125 C1
Merton SW20 39 C7
Purley CR8 80 B7
Tatsfield CR6, TN16 103 B5
Approach The RH19 185 F6
April Cl Ashstead KT21 75 F1
Camberley GU15 65 C2
Feltham TW13 15 A5
Horsham RH12 217 C4
April Glen SE23 23 D5
Aprilwood Cl KT15 70 F8
Apsley Ct Crawley RH11 200 F4
Sutton SM2 59 C4
Apsley Rd Croydon SE25 43 B5
Kingston u T KT3 38 C6
Aquarius TW1 17 B7
Aquarius Ct RH11 200 E4
Aquila Cl KT21 95 E6
Arabella Dr SW15 7 E3
Aragon Ave Ewell KT17 58 B2
Thames Ditton KT7 36 F4
Aragon Cl Ashford TW16 14 F1
New Addington CR0 63 E1
Aragon Ct Bracknell RG12 27 C5
Knaphill GU21 68 D2
Aragon Rd Kingston u T KT2 17 E3
West Barnes SM4 39 E2
Aram Ct GU22 70 B4
Arbor Cl BR3 44 B7
Arbour Cl KT22 94 F4
Arbourfield Cl SW2 21 F7
Arbrook La KT10 55 D4
Arbury Terr SE26 23 B5
Arbutus Cl RH1 139 C7
Arbutus Rd RH1 139 C6
Arcade The 11 GU11 105 A2
Arch Rd KT12 54 D7
Archbishop Lanfranc Sch The CR0 41 E3
Archbishop Tenison's Sch CR0 61 F7
Archbishop's Pl 3 SW2 21 F8
Archdale Pl KT3 38 B6
Archdeacon Cambridge's Prim Sch (C of E) TW2 16 E6
Archer Cl KT2 17 E1
Archer Rd SE25 43 B5
Archers Ct RH10 201 D8
Archway Cl Wallington SM6 60 E7
Wimbledon SW19 20 B4
Archway Mews RH4 136 A8
Archway Pl RH4 136 A8
Archway St SW13, SW14 7 E4
Arcturus Rd RH11 200 E3
Arcus Rd BR1 24 E2
Arden 17 SW19 19 D7
Arden Cl Bracknell RG12 28 A7
Reigate RH2 139 B5
Arden Mead Cotts RH7 164 A8
Arden Rd RH10 201 F4
Ardenrun RH7 164 B8
Ardenrun Cotts RH7 164 A7
Ardent Cl SE25 42 E6
Ardesley Wood KT13 53 E6
Ardfern Ave SW16 42 A6
Ardfillan Rd SE6 24 D6
Ardgowan Rd SE6 24 E7
Ardingly RG12 27 A4
Ardingly Cl Crawley RH11 201 B8
South Croydon CR0 62 D7
Ardingly Ct KT18 76 D5
Ardleigh Gdns SM3 40 A2
Ardley Cl SE23, SE6 23 E5
Ardlui Rd SE27 22 C6

Ard–Ave 225

Ardmay Gdns KT6 .37 E4
Ardmore Ave GU2 .109 B3
Ardmore House GU2 .109 B3
Ardmore Way GU2 .109 B3
Ardoch Rd SE6 .24 D6
Ardrossan Ave GU15 .66 A5
Ardrossan Gdns KT4 .58 A7
Ardshiel Dr RH1 .139 E7
Ardwell Rd SW2 .21 E6
Arena L Ctr GU15 .65 C6
Arena La GU11 .104 E5
Arena The RG12 .27 A7
Arenal Dr RG45 .45 C3
Arethusa Way GU24 .67 F3
Arford Comm GU35 .187 A6
Argent Cl TW20 .12 C2
Argent Terr GU47 .64 E8
Argosy Gdns TW18 .12 F2
Argosy La TW19 .13 D8
Argus Wlk RH11 .201 A3
Argyle Ave
Isleworth TW2, TW3 .5 A1
Twickenham TW3 .5 A1
Argyle House SM2 .59 C4
Argyle Rd TW3 .5 B2
Argyle St GU24 .87 A6
Argyll Ct 15 SW2 .21 E8
Ariel Way TW4 .4 B4
Arkell Gr SW16 .22 B1
Arkendale RH19 .185 A4
Arkindale Rd SE6 .24 C5
Arklow Mews 3 KT6 .56 E8
Arkwright Dr RG42 .26 D7
Arkwright House 23 SW2 .21 E8
Arkwright Rd Poyle SL3 .1 E5
South Croydon CR2 .61 F2
Arlington Cl Bracknell RG42 27 A8
Sutton SM1 .59 A8
Twickenham TW1 .6 C1
Arlington Ct Reigate RH2 .118 A3
4 Twickenham TW1 .6 C1
Arlington Dr SM5 .59 F8
Arlington Lodge KT13 .53 B6
Arlington Rd Ashford TW15 .13 F3
Richmond TW10 .17 D6
Surbiton KT6 .37 D3
Teddington TW11 .16 F4
Twickenham TW1 .6 C1
Arlington Sq RG12 .27 A7
Arlington Terr GU11 .104 F2
Armadale Rd Feltham TW14 .4 A2
Woking GU21 .69 A2
Armeston KT3 .38 D2
Armfield Cl KT8 .35 F4
Armfield Cres CR4 .40 F7
Armitage Ct SL5 .29 C3
Armitage Dr GU16 .65 F1
Armstrong Cl KT12 .35 A3
Armstrong Mall GU14 .84 D4
Armstrong Rd
Englefield Green TW20 .11 C2
Feltham TW13 .15 E3
Armstrong Way GU14 .84 B1
Armytage Rd TW5 .4 D7
Arnal Cres SW18 .19 E8
Arncliffe RG12 .27 A4
Arndale Way TW20 .12 A3
Arne Cl RH11 .200 F3
Arne Gr RH6 .160 E5
Arnella Ct GU14 .105 D8
Arnewood Cl Oxshott KT22 .74 B5
Roehampton SW15 .19 A7
Arney's La CR4 .41 A3
Arnfield Cl RH11 .200 E5
Arngask Rd SE6 .24 D8
Arnhem Cl GU11 .105 B2
Arnhem Dr CR0 .82 D8
Arnison Rd KT8 .36 D5
Arnold Cres TW7 .5 D2
Arnold Dr KT9 .56 D4
Arnold Rd Mitcham SW17 .20 F1
Sheerwater GU21 .70 B4
Staines TW18 .13 C1
Arnulf St SE6 .24 B4
Arnull's Rd SW16 .22 B2
Arosa Rd 3 TW1 .6 D1
Arragon Gdns
Streatham SW16 .21 E1
West Wickham BR4 .63 B7
Arragon Rd
3 Twickenham TW1 .17 A7
Twickenham TW1 .17 A8
Wandsworth SW18 .20 A7
Arragon Wlk KT14 .71 F6
Arran Cl Crawley RH11 .201 B3
Wallington SM6 .60 C6
Arran Rd SE6 .24 C6
Arran Way KT10 .55 B8
Arrancourt RH12 .217 B2
Arras Ave SM4 .40 C4
Arrivals Rd RH6 .181 F8
Arrol Rd BR3 .43 D6
Arrow Ind Est GU14 .84 F2
Arrow Rd GU14 .84 F2
Artel Croft RH10 .202 A6
Arterberry Rd SW20, SW19 39 D8
Arthur Cl Bagshot GU19 .47 E1
Farnham GU9 .125 B1
Arthur Ct CR0 .61 D7
Arthur Rd Biggin Hill TN16 .83 C3
Crawley RH11 .200 E6
Farnham GU9 .125 C1
Horsham RH13 .217 D1
6 Kingston u T KT2 .18 A1
West Barnes KT3 .39 B4
Wimbledon SW19 .20 A5
Wokingham RG41 .25 A6
Arthur St GU11 .105 B2
Arthur's Bridge Rd GU21 .69 D2
Artillery Rd
1 Aldershot GU11 .105 B2
Farnborough GU11, GU14 .105 D8
7 Guildford GU1 .109 D1
Artillery Terr GU1 .109 D1
Artington Wlk GU2 .130 C6
Arun Way RH13 .217 E1
Arundale KT1 .37 D5
Arundel Ave Ewell KT17 .58 B1
Merton SM4 .39 F5
South Croydon CR2 .62 A1
Arundel Cl Crawley RH10 .202 C6
Croydon CR0, CR9 .61 B7
Hampton TW12 .16 B3
Arundel Ct BR2 .44 E7
Arundel House
Croydon CR0 .61 D5
Reigate RH2 .139 B5
Arundel Rd Belmont SM2 .58 F3
Dorking RH4 .136 A7
Frimley GU15 .66 C4
Hounslow TW4 .4 C4
Kingston u T KT1 .38 C7
Thornton Heath CR0 .42 D3
Arundell Pl 6 GU9 .125 B2
Arunside RH12 .217 A1
Arunside Cty Prim Sch RH12 .217 A2
Ascalon Ct 19 SW2 .21 F8
Aschurch Rd CR0 .42 F2
Ascot Ct GU11 .105 A1
Ascot Heath Inf Sch SL5 .8 E1
Ascot Heath Jun Sch SL5 .8 E1
Ascot House SE26 .23 B2
Ascot Mews SM6 .60 C2
Ascot Race Course SL5 .28 F6
Ascot Rd
East Bedfont TW14, TW15 .14 B6
Mitcham SW17 .21 A2
Ascot Sta SL5 .29 A5
Ascot Towers SL5 .28 F7
Ascot Wood SL5 .29 A6
Asford Gdns KT11 .73 D3
Ash Church Rd GU12 .106 B2
Ash Cl Ash GU12 .106 B3
Blackwater GU17 .64 C5
Box Hill KT20 .116 C4
Carshalton SM5 .59 F8
Crawley Down RH10 .204 C8
Kingston u T KT3 .38 D7
Lingfield RH7 .164 E5
Merstham RH1 .119 C5
Penge SE20 .43 C7
Pyrford GU22 .71 A4
Woking GU22 .89 E7
Ash Combe GU8 .191 A4
Ash Ct Ottershaw KT16 .51 C5
West Ewell KT19 .57 C6
2 West Norwood SW16 .22 A3
Ash Dr RH1 .140 B7
Ash Gr East Bedfont TW14 .14 E7
Guildford GU2 .109 A2
Heston TW5 .4 D7
Penge SE20 .43 C7
Staines TW18 .13 C2
West Wickham BR4 .44 C1
Ash Grange Cty Prim Sch GU12 .106 B2
Ash Green La E GU12 .127 C8
Ash Green La W
Ash GU12 .126 F8
Ash, Ash Green GU12 .127 C8
Ash Green Rd GU12 .106 C1
Ash Hill Rd GU12 .106 B3
Ash Keys RH10 .201 E5
Ash La GU8 .148 C2
Ash Lodge 2 TW16 .14 F1
Ash Lodge Cl GU12 .106 A1
Ash Lodge Dr GU12 .106 A1
Ash Manor Sch GU12 .126 F8
Ash Mews KT18 .76 E6
Ash Rd Aldershot GU12 .126 D8
Cheam SM3, SM4 .39 F1
Crawley RH10 .202 A8
Croydon CR0 .63 A8
Littleton TW17 .34 A5
Pirbright GU24, GU3 .88 A1
Woking GU22 .89 E7
Ash St GU12 .106 A1
Ash Sta GU12 .106 B2
Ash Tree Cl
Croydon BR3, CR0 .43 E3
Farnborough GU14 .84 C3
Grayswood GU27 .189 F1
1 Surbiton KT6 .37 E1
Ash Tree Way CR0 .43 E3
Ash Vale GU8 .191 A5
Ash Vale Sta GU12 .106 A7
Ashbourne RG12 .26 F3
Ashbourne Cl Ash GU12 .106 C3
Coulsdon CR5 .79 C1
Ashbourne Rd CR4, SW17 .21 A1
Ashbourne Terr 1 SW19 .20 A1
Ashbrook Rd SL4 .11 B8
Ashburnham Pk KT10 .55 C6
Ashburnham Rd
Crawley RH10 .202 A4
Richmond TW10 .17 B5
Ashburton Ave CR0 .43 B1
Ashburton Cl CR0 .43 A1
Ashburton Gdns CR0 .62 A8
Ashburton Jun & Inf Sch CR0 .43 B3
Ashburton Rd CR0, CR9 .62 A8
Ashburton Sch CR0 .43 B2
Ashbury Cres GU4 .110 C3
Ashbury Dr GU17 .65 A1
Ashbury Pl SW19 .20 C2
Ashby Ave KT19, KT9 .57 A4
Ashby Ct RH13 .217 E1
Ashby Grange 7 SM6 .60 C4
Ashby Way UB7 .3 A7
Ashby Wlk CR0 .42 C3
Ashcombe Ave KT6 .37 D2
Ashcombe Par GU22 .90 A7
Ashcombe Rd
Dorking RH4 .115 A1
Merstham RH1 .119 C8
Wallington SM5 .60 A4
Wimbledon SW19 .20 A3
Ashcombe Sch The RH4 .115 B1
Ashcombe Sq KT3 .38 C6
Ashcombe Terr KT20 .97 B7
Ashcroft GU4 .130 E2
Ashcroft Pk KT11 .73 E6
Ashcroft Rd KT9 .56 F7
Ashcroft Rise CR5 .79 E3
Ashdale KT23 .94 C1
Ashdale Cl Stanwell TW19 .13 E6
Twickenham TW2 .16 C8
Ashdale Way TW2 .16 B8
Ashdene Cl TW15 .14 C1
Ashdene Cres GU12 .106 A3
Ashdene House TW20 .11 C2
Ashdene Rd GU12 .106 A2
Ashdown Ave GU14 .85 E2
Ashdown Cl
Beckenham BR3 .44 B7
Bracknell RG12 .28 A7
Reigate RH2 .139 B5
Ashdown Dr RH10 .201 E3
Ashdown Gate RH19 .185 D2
Ashdown Gdns CR2 .81 B4
Ashdown Pl KT7 .37 A2
Ashdown Rd Ewell KT17 .77 A6
Forest Row RH18 .206 F2
Kingston u T KT1 .37 E7
Reigate RH2 .139 B5
Ashdown View RH19 .205 E7
Ashdown Way SW17 .21 A6
Ashen Gr SW19 .20 A6
Ashen Vale CR2 .62 D2
Ashenden Rd GU2 .108 F1
Ashfield Ave TW13 .15 B7
Ashfield Cl Beckenham BR3 .24 A1
Richmond TW10 .17 E7
Ashfields RH2 .118 B3
Ashford Ave TW15 .14 B2
Ashford C of E Fst & Mid Sch TW15 .14 B2
Ashford Cl TW15 .13 E4
Ashford Cres TW15 .13 E5
Ashford High Sch The TW15 .13 E5
Ashford Hospl TW15 .13 E6
Ashford Ind Est TW15 .14 C4
Ashford Manor Golf Club TW15 .13 F2
Ashford Park Cty Prim Sch TW15 .13 D4
Ashford Rd
Feltham TW13, TW15 .14 E4
Littleton TW15, TW17 .14 C1
Staines TW18 .33 D8
Ashford Sta TW15 .13 F5
Ashgrove Rd Ashford TW15 14 D3
Catford BR1 .24 D2
Ashlake Rd SW16 .21 E4
Ashlea Ct CR6 .81 A1
Ashleigh Ave TW20 .12 C1
Ashleigh Cl RH6 .160 F3
Ashleigh Ct SE26 .23 B2
Ashleigh Gdns SM1 .59 B8
Ashleigh House SW14 .7 E4
Ashleigh Point 8 SE26 .23 D5
Ashleigh Rd
Horsham RH12 .217 C4
Mortlake SW14 .7 E4
Penge SE20 .43 B6
Ashley Ave Epsom KT18 .76 D6
Morden SM4 .40 A4
Ashley Cl Frimley GU16 .86 A6
Little Bookham KT23 .93 F2
Oatlands Park KT12, KT13 .34 F1
Ashley Ct 5 Epsom KT18 .76 D6
Knaphill GU21 .68 F1
Ashley Ctr KT18 .76 D6
Ashley Dr Banstead SM7 .78 A5
Blackwater GU17 .64 C4
Hounslow TW7 .5 E8
Twickenham TW2 .16 B7
Walton-on-T KT12 .54 A7
Ashley Gdns
Richmond TW10 .17 D6
Shalford GU4 .130 F2
Ashley House GU7 .150 E8
Ashley Inf Sch KT12 .35 A1
Ashley La CR0 .61 B6
Ashley Park Ave KT12 .53 F8
Ashley Park Cres KT12 .35 A1
Ashley Park Rd KT12 .54 A7
Ashley Rd Epsom KT18 .76 E4
Farnborough GU14 .85 D4
Hampton TW12 .36 A8
Knaphill GU21 .68 F1
Richmond TW9 .6 E4
Thames Ditton KT7 .36 F3
Thornton Heath CR7 .41 F5
Walton-on-T KT12 .54 A8
Westcott RH4 .135 C6
Wimbledon SW19 .20 B2
Ashley Rise KT12 .54 A7
Ashley Way GU24 .67 D6
Ashling Rd CR0, CR9 .43 A1
Ashlyn's Pk KT11 .73 E6
Ashlyns Way KT9 .56 D4
Ashmead Rd TW14 .15 A7
Ashmere Ave BR3 .44 D7
Ashmere Cl SM3 .58 D5
Ashmill Ct CR0 .42 C3
Ashmore Ct TW5 .5 A8
Ashmore House RH11 .181 D1
Ashmore La
Biggin Hill BR2, TN16 .83 C8
Rusper RH12 .199 C6
Ashridge GU14 .84 F7
Ashridge Gn 3 RG42 .27 B8
Ashridge Rd RG40 .25 D8
Ashridge Way
Ashford TW16 .15 A2
Merton SM4, SW20 .39 F5
Ashstead La GU7 .150 C2
Ashstead Sta KT21 .75 E3
Ashtead Ct 15 SW19 .19 D7
Ashtead Hospl The KT21 .95 E8
Ashtead La GU7 .150 D2
Ashtead Woods Rd KT21 .75 C3
Ashton Cl Cheam SM1 .59 A6
Hersham KT12 .54 B4
Ashton Ct BR3 .43 F8
Ashton Gdns TW4 .4 F3
Ashton House SW15 .19 B8
Ashton Rd 2 GU21 .68 F2
Ashtree Ave CR4 .40 D7
Ashtree Ct TW15 .14 B3
Ashtrees GU6 .174 E1
Ashtrees The GU12 .106 B2
Ashurst 3 KT18 .76 D6
Ashurst Cl Horsham RH12 .218 A5
Kenley CR8 .80 D4
Penge SE20 .43 B8
Ashurst Dr Box Hill KT20 .116 B5
Crawley RH10 .202 D6
Littleton TW17 .33 E5
Ashurst Rd Ash Vale GU12 .105 F4
Tadworth KT20 .97 C6
Ashurst Wlk CR0 .62 B8
Ashurstwood Abbey RH19 .206 E6
Ashurstwood Cty Prim Sch RH19 .206 E6
Ashvale Rd SW17 .20 F3
Ashview Cl TW15 .13 E3
Ashview Gdns TW15 .13 E3
Ashville Way RG41 .25 A5
Ashway Ctr 5 KT2 .37 E8
Ashwell Ave GU15 .65 F6
Ashwell Ct TW15 .13 E6
Ashwood 5 Crawley RH11 201 D5
Warlingham CR6 .101 C7
Ashwood Gdns CR0 .63 C4
Ashwood Pk
6 Belmont SM2 .59 A3
Fetcham KT22 .94 C4
Woking GU22 .70 A1
Ashwood Rd
Englefield Green TW20 .11 B2
Woking GU22 .70 A1
Ashworth Pl GU2 .108 F1
Aslett St SW18 .20 C8
Asmar Cl CR5 .79 E4
Aspen Cl Guildford GU4 .110 D4
Staines TW18 .12 F5
Stoke D'Abernon KT11 .73 E3
Aspen Ct TW9 .7 A7
Aspen Gdns Ashford TW15 .14 C3
Mitcham CR4 .41 A4
Aspen House Sch SW2 .21 F8
Aspen Sq KT13 .53 D7
Aspen Vale CR3 .80 F1
Aspen Way Banstead KT17 .77 D5
Feltham TW13 .15 B5
Horsham RH12 .217 E4
Aspin Way GU17 .64 B5
Aspinall House SW12 .21 E7
Asprey Gr CR3 .101 A3
Asquith House SM7 .77 F4
Assembly Wlk SM5 .40 E2
Assher Rd KT12 .54 E7
Assheton-Bennett House KT6 .37 E4
Astleham Rd TW17 .33 E6
Astley House 3 SE27 .22 C4
Aston Cl KT21 .75 C1
Aston Ct RH11 .201 B1
Aston Gn TW5 .4 C5
Aston Rd Claygate KT10 .55 E5
Merton SW20 .39 C7
Aston Way KT18 .76 F3
Astonville St SW18 .20 A7
Astor Cl Addlestone KT15 .52 D6
Kingston u T KT2 .18 B2
Astoria Mansions 18 SW16 21 E5
Astoria Par SW16 .21 E5
Astra Bsns Ctr RH1 .161 A7
Astra Mead RG42 .8 B2
Atalanta Cl CR8 .61 A1
Atbara Ct TW11 .17 B2
Atbara Rd TW11 .17 B2
Atcham Rd TW3 .5 C3
Atfield Gr GU20 .48 D4
Atheldene Rd SW18 .20 C7
Athelney Prim Sch SE6 .24 A5
Athelney St SE6 .24 A5
Athelstan Cl RH10 .202 E6
Athelstan House KT1 .37 F5
Athelstan House Sch TW12 .36 A8
Athelstan Rd KT1 .37 F5
Athena Cl KT1 .37 F6
Atherfield House RH1 .139 C6
Atherfield Rd RH2 .139 C6
Atherley Way TW4 .15 F8
Atherton Cl Shalford GU4 .130 E3
Stanwell TW19 .2 D1
Atherton Dr SW19 .19 D4
Atherton House CR2 .61 E4
Athlone KT10 .55 E4
Athlone Rd SW2 .22 A8
Atholl House 11 RH1 .118 F1
Atkins Cl GU21 .69 A1
Atkins Dr BR4 .63 D8
Atkins Rd SW4, SW12 .21 D8
Atkinson Ct RH6 .161 B2
Atkinson Morley's Hospl SW20 .19 B1
Atkinson Rd RH10 .202 C4
Atlanta Ct CR7 .42 C6
Atrebatti Rd GU47 .45 C1
Attebrouche Ct RG12 .27 D2
Attfield Cl GU12 .105 F1
Attleborough Ct SE21 .23 B6
Attlee Cl CR7 .42 C4
Attlee House 5 RH11 .201 B2
Attwood Cl CR2 .81 B5
Atwater Cl SW2 .22 A7
Atwood KT23 .93 E3
Atwood Ave TW9 .7 A5
Atwood House SE21 .22 E5
Aubyn Hill SE27 .22 D4
Auchinleck Ct RH10 .204 B7
Auchinleck Way GU11 .104 E2
Auckland Cl
Crawley RH11 .181 D1
South Norwood SE19 .42 F8
Auckland Gdns SE19 .42 F8
Auckland Hill SE27 .22 C4
Auckland Rd
Caterham CR3 .100 E5
Kingston u T KT1 .37 F5
South Norwood SE19, SE25 .42 F8
Auckland Rise SE19 .42 E8
Audley Cl KT15 .52 B5
Audley Ct Surbiton KT5 .37 F3
Twickenham TW2 .16 D5
Audley Cty Prim Sch CR3 100 F6
Audley Dr CR2, CR6 .81 C4
Audley Firs KT12 .54 C6
Audley House KT15 .52 B5
Audley Pl SM2 .59 B3
Audley Rd TW10 .6 F2
Audley Way SL5 .28 D6
Audrey Cl BR3 .44 B3
Audric Cl KT2 .38 A8
Augur Cl TW18 .12 F3
August La GU5 .153 D7
Augusta Cl KT8 .35 F6
Augusta Rd TW2 .16 C6
Augustine Cl SL3 .1 E4
Augustus Cl TW8 .6 D7
Augustus Ct Hounslow TW3 .5 C3
8 Putney SW19 .19 E7
South Norwood SE19 .22 E1
Streatham SW16 .21 D6
Augustus Gdns GU15 .66 C5
Augustus Rd SW19 .19 E7
Aultone Way
Carshalton SM5 .59 F7
Sutton SM1 .59 C8
Aurelia Gdns CR7 .41 F3
Aurelia Rd CR0, CR7, CR9 .41 F3
Auriol Cl KT19 .57 E7
Auriol Cty Jun Sch KT19 .57 F6
Auriol Park Rd KT19, KT4 .57 E7
Aurum Cl RH6 .161 B2
Austen Cl RH19 .185 B1
Austen Rd
Farnborough GU14 .85 A6
Guildford GU1 .130 F8
Austin Cl Coulsdon CR8 .80 B1
Forest Hill SE23, SE6 .23 F8
Twickenham TW1 .6 C2
Austin House 19 KT6 .37 E4
Austin's Cotts 10 GU9 .125 B2
Austyn Gdns KT5 .38 B1
Autumn Cl SW19 .20 C2
Autumn Dr SM2 .59 B2
Avalon Cl SW20 .39 E7
Avarn Rd SW17 .20 F2
Avebury RG12 .27 A3
Avebury Cl RH12 .218 A7
Avebury Rd SW19 .39 F8
Aveley La GU10, GU9 .146 C7
Aveling Cl Crawley RH10 .202 C4
Purley CR8 .79 F6
Aven Cl GU6 .174 E2
Avening Rd SW18 .20 A8
Avening Terr SW18 .20 A8
Avenue C KT15 .52 E7
Avenue Cl Cranford TW5 .4 B6
Tadworth KT20 .97 B5
Avenue Cres TW5 .4 B7
Avenue Ct Penge SE20 .43 C8
Tadworth KT20 .97 B4
Avenue De Cagny GU24 .87 F5
Avenue Elmers KT6 .37 E4
Avenue Gdns Cranford TW5 .4 B7
Horley RH6 .161 C2
Mortlake SW14 .7 E4
South Norwood SE25 .43 A7
Teddington TW11 .16 F2
Avenue One KT15 .52 E6
Avenue Park Rd SE21, SE27 .22 B6
Avenue Prim Sch The SM2 .59 A1
Avenue Rd Banstead SM7 .78 B4
Belmont SM2 .59 A1

Avenue Rd *continued*
Caterham CR3 100 E5
Cobham KT11 73 D3
Cranleigh GU6 174 F1
Egham TW18 12 D3
Epsom KT18 76 D5
Farnborough GU14 85 D3
Feltham TW13 14 F5
Grayshott GU26 188 C3
Hampton TW12 36 B8
Hounslow TW7 5 F6
Kingston u T KT1 37 E6
Mitcham SW16 41 D7
New Malden KT3 38 E5
South Norwood, Annerley SE25 43 A7
South Norwood, Elmers End BR3, SE20 43 D8
Tatsfield TN16 103 E7
Teddington TW11 17 A2
Wallington SM6 60 C3
Wimbledon SW20 39 B7
Avenue S KT5 38 A2
Avenue Sucy GU15 65 B4
Avenue Terr KT3 38 C6
Avenue The
Aldershot GU11, GU12 126 C7
Beckenham BR3 44 C8
Belmont SM2 58 F2
Biggin Hill TN16 103 F5
Brockham RH3, RH5 116 A1
Camberley GU15 65 B5
Chobham GU24 50 A2
Claygate KT10 55 E5
Compton GU3, GU7 129 C1
Coulsdon CR5 79 D4
Cranford TW5 4 A6
Crowthorne RG45 45 B5
Dormansland RH19 186 B6
Egham TW20 12 B4
Ewhurst GU6 175 E6
Godalming GU7 150 F2
Grayshott GU26 188 D3
Hampton TW12 15 F2
Haslemere GU27 207 F7
Horley RH6 160 F2
Hounslow TW3 5 B2
Isleworth TW1 6 C2
Lightwater GU18 48 A1
4 New Malden KT4 39 A1
North Ascot SL5 8 F1
Oxshott KT10, KT22 74 F8
Richmond TW9 6 F5
Rowledge GU10 145 F3
South Croydon CR0 61 E7
South Nutfield RH1 140 E6
Staines TW18 33 B8
Stoneleigh KT17, SM3 58 C3
Sunbury TW16 35 B7
Surbiton KT5 37 F3
Tadworth KT20 97 B5
Twickenham TW1 6 B2
West Wickham BR4 44 E2
Whyteleafe CR3 101 A8
Woodham KT15 52 A1
Worcester Park KT4 57 F8
Worplesdon GU3 88 E1
Avenue Three KT15 52 E7
Avenue Two KT15 52 E6
Averil Gr SW16 22 B2
Avern Gdns KT8 36 B5
Avern Rd KT8 36 B5
Avery Ct SE20 23 B1
Aviary Rd GU22 71 A3
Aviary Way RH10 184 C1
Aviemore Cl BR3 43 F4
Aviemore Way BR3 43 E4
Avington Cl GU1 109 E1
Avington Gr SE20 23 C1
Avoca Rd SW17 21 A4
Avocet Cres GU47 64 E8
Avon Cl Addlestone KT15 52 A4
Ash GU12 105 F1
Farnborough GU14 84 E7
Sutton SM1 59 C6
Worcester Park KT4 58 A8
Avon Ct GU9 125 C1
Avon House 9 RH1 118 F2
Avon Rd Ashford TW16 14 F1
Farnham GU9 125 C1
Avon Wlk RH11 200 F5
Avondale GU12 105 F7
Avondale Ave
Hinchley Wood KT10 56 A7
New Malden KT4 38 F1
Staines TW18 12 F1
Avondale Cl Hersham KT12 54 C5
Horley RH6 161 A5
Avondale Ct SM2 59 C3
Avondale Gdns TW4 4 F2
Avondale High CR3 101 A6
Avondale House 6 SW14 7 D4
Avondale Rd
Aldershot GU11 126 B8
Ashford TW15, TW19 13 D5
Bromley BR1 24 F2
Catford BR1 24 F2
Mortlake SW14 7 D4
South Croydon CR2 61 C4
Wimbledon SW19 20 B3
Avonmore Ave GU1 109 F2
Avonwick Rd TW3 5 B5
Avro Way Byfleet KT13 52 E1
Wallington SM6 60 E3
Axbridge RG12 27 E4
Axes La RH1 140 D2
Axford House SW2 22 B7
Axwood KT18 76 C4
Aycliffe Ct KT1 38 A7
Ayebridges Ave TW20 12 C1
Ayjay Cl GU11 126 A7
Aylesbury Ct SM1 59 C7
Aylesford Ave BR3 43 E4
Aylesworth Spur SL4 11 B8
Aylett Rd Croydon SE25 43 B5
Isleworth TW7 5 E5
Ayling Ct GU9 125 F7
Ayling Hill GU11 104 F1
Ayling La GU11 125 F8
Aylward Rd Forest Hill SE23 23 D6
Merton SW20 39 F6
Aymer Cl TW18 32 E8
Aymer Dr TW18 32 E8
Aysgarth RG12 27 A3
Aysgarth Ct SM1 59 B7
Aysgarth Rd SE21 22 E8
Ayshe Court Dr RH13 217 E3
Azalea Ct GU22 89 D8
Azalea Dr GU27 207 F8
Azalea Way GU15 66 B6
Azelea Ct CR8 80 B8

B

Babbacombe Cl KT9 56 D5
Babbs Mead GU9 125 A1
Baber Dr TW14 4 C1
Babington Ct SW16 21 D3
Babington Rd SW16 21 D3
Babylon La KT20, RH2 118 B8
Bachelor's La GU23 92 A3
Back Gn KT12 54 C4
Back La Binstead GU10 166 B8
Brentford TW8 6 D8
Crawley RH10 203 D1
East Clandon GU4 111 D4
Elstead GU8 148 D4
Plaistow RH14 211 E2
Richmond TW10 17 C6
Back Rd TW11 16 E2
Bacon Cl GU47 64 D6
Bacon La GU10 167 C3
Badajos Rd GU11 104 F3
Baden Cl TW18 13 B1
Baden Dr RH6 160 E4
Baden Powell Cl KT6 56 F8
Baden Rd GU2 109 B3
Bader Cl CR8 80 D4
Bader Ct GU14 84 F8
Badger Cl Feltham TW13 15 B5
Guildford GU2 109 B4
Hounslow TW4 4 C4
Badger Ct GU10 146 A5
Badger Dr GU18 48 A1
Badger Way GU10 124 D8
Badgers Cl Ashford TW15 13 F3
Farncombe GU7 150 D8
Horsham RH12 217 F6
Woking GU21 69 C1
Badgers Copse
Frimley GU15 65 E4
Worcester Park KT4 57 F8
Badgers Cross GU8 149 E1
Badgers Ct 4 KT17 76 E6
Badgers Hill GU25 31 C4
Badgers Hollow GU7 150 D6
Badgers La CR6 101 C8
Badgers Lodge 5 KT17 76 E6
Badgers Way
Bracknell RG12 27 F7
East Grinstead RH19 185 F2
Loxwood RH14 213 A4
Badgers Wlk
Kingston u T KT3 38 E7
Purley CR8 79 C8
Whyteleafe CR3 80 F1
Badgers Wood CR3 100 D2
Badgerwood Dr GU16 65 D2
Badingham Dr KT22 94 E4
Badminton Rd SW12 21 A8
Badshot Lea Cty Inf Sch GU9 126 A6
Badshot Lea Rd GU11, GU9 126 A6
Badshot Pk GU9 126 A6
Bagden Hill KT23 114 D5
Bagot Cl KT21 75 F3
Bagshot Cty Inf Sch GU19 47 E2
Bagshot Gn GU19 47 E3
Bagshot Rd Ascot SL5 29 C2
Bracknell RG12 27 C4
Bracknell SL5 48 A8
Brookwood GU21, GU22, GU24, GU3 88 C5
Englefield Green TW20 11 C2
Knaphill GU21, GU22, GU24, GU3 88 C5
Pirbright GU21, GU22, GU24, GU3 88 C5
West End GU24 68 B8
Woking GU21, GU22, GU24, GU3 88 C5
Bagshot Sta GU19 47 E4
Bahram Rd KT19 57 D1
Baigents La GU20 48 D4
Bailes La Flexford GU3 107 D2
Normandy GU3 107 D3
Bailey Cl Frimley GU16 85 D8
Horsham RH12 217 F7
Bailey House 11 SE26 23 B3
Bailey Pl SE26 23 D2
Bailey Rd RH4 135 C6
Baileys Cl GU17 64 C4
Bailing Hill RH12 216 E7
Baillie Rd GU1 130 F8
Bain Ave GU15 65 B2
Bainbridge cl KT2 17 E3
Baines Cl CR0 61 D5
Bainton Mead GU21 69 A2
Baird Cl RH10 182 A1
Baird Dr GU3 108 B2
Baird Gdns SE19, SE21 22 E4
Baird Rd GU14 85 C6
Bakeham La TW20 11 D1
Bakehouse Barn Cl RH12 217 E7
Bakehouse Rd RH6 161 A5
Baker Cl RH10 201 D4
Baker La CR4 41 A7
Baker St KT13 53 B6
Baker's Cl RH7 164 E5
Baker's La RH7 164 E4
Bakers Ct SE25 42 E6
Bakers End SW20 39 E7
Bakers Gdns SM5 59 E8
Bakers Mead RH9 121 C6
Bakers Way RH5 178 C5
Bakery Mews KT6 38 A1
Bakewell Dr KT3 38 E7
Balaam House SM1 59 A6
Balaclava Rd KT6 37 C2
Balchins La RH4 135 B6
Balcombe Ct RH10 202 D7
Balcombe Gdns RH6 161 C2
Balcombe House 3 SW2 21 F7
Balcombe Rd Crawley, Tinsley Green RH10, RH6 182 D5
Crawley, Worth RH10 202 D5
Horley RH6 161 B2
Baldreys GU9 146 A8
Baldry Gdns SW16 21 F2
Baldwin Cl RH10 202 C3
Baldwin Cres GU4 110 C3
Baldwin House 15 SW2 22 A7
Baldwins Hill Cty Prim Sch RH19 185 D3
Balfont Cl CR2 81 A6
Balfour Ave GU22 89 F5
Balfour Cres RG12 27 B4
Balfour Gdns RH18 206 E1
Balfour Rd Croydon SE25 43 A5
Hounslow TW3 5 B4
Merton SW19 20 B1
Wallington SM5 59 F3
Weybridge KT13 53 A6
Balgowan Cl KT3 38 E5
Balgowan Prim Sch BR3 43 E7
Balgowan Rd BR3 43 F7
Balham Gr SW12 21 A8
Balham High Rd
Balham SW12, SW17 21 A7
Upper Tooting SW12 21 A7
Balham Hill SW12 21 B8
Balham New Rd SW12 21 B8
Balham Park Mansions SW12 20 F7
Balham Park Rd SW12, SW17 21 A7
Balham Sta SW12 21 B7
Balham Station Rd SW12 21 B7
Balintore Ct 8 GU47 64 D8
Ball and Wicket La GU9 125 C7
Ballands N The KT22 94 E5
Ballands' S The KT22 94 E4
Ballantyne Dr KT20 97 F6
Ballantyne Rd GU14 85 A6
Ballard Cl KT2 18 D1
Ballard Ct GU15 66 A8
Ballard Rd GU15 66 A8
Ballards Farm Rd CR2 62 A4
Ballards Gn KT20 97 E8
Ballards La RH8 123 C6
Ballards Rise CR2 62 A4
Ballards Way CR0, CR2 62 B4
Ballater Rd CR2 61 F5
Ballencrieff Rd SL5 29 F2
Ballfield Rd GU7 150 E6
Ballina St SE23 23 D8
Balliol Cl RH10 182 D1
Balliol Way GU47 45 E1
Balloch Rd SE6 24 D6
Ballsdown GU8 191 A3
Balmain Ct TW3 5 B6
Balmoral RH19 206 A8
Balmoral Ave BR3 43 E5
Balmoral Cres
East Molesey KT8 36 A6
Hale GU9 125 B6
Balmoral Ct
11 Belmont SM2 59 A3
6 Crawley RH11 201 B2
North Cheam KT4 58 B8
West Norwood SE27 22 C4
Balmoral Dr Frimley GU16 85 F8
Woking GU22 70 C3
Balmoral Gdns CR2 61 D1
Balmoral Grange TW18 33 B7
Balmoral Rd Ash GU12 106 B4
Kingston u T KT1 37 F5
North Cheam KT4 58 B8
Balmoral Way SM2 59 A1
Balquhain Cl KT21 75 D2
Baltic Cl SW19 20 D1
Balvernie Gr SW18 20 A8
Bamford Rd BR1 24 D3
Bampfylde Cl SM6 60 C7
Bampton Rd SE23 23 D5
Bampton Way GU21 69 A2
Banavie Gdns BR3 44 C8
Banbury RG12 27 E2
Banbury Cl GU16 86 A7
Banbury Ct 8 SM2 59 A3
Bancroft Cl TW15 14 A3
Bancroft Ct RH2 118 B1
Bancroft Rd
Crawley RH10 202 D5
Reigate RH2 118 B1
Band La 1 TW20 12 A3
Banders Rise GU1 110 C2
Bandon Hill Prim Sch SM6 60 D4
Bandon Rise SM6 60 D5
Banfor Ct SM6 60 C4
Bank Ave CR4 40 D7
Bank La Crawley RH10 201 D6
Kingston u T KT2 17 E1
Roehampton SW15 7 E2
Bank Mews SM1 59 C4
Bank Rd GU11 105 D5
Bank Willow TW10 17 B5
Bank's La KT11, KT24 93 B5
Bankfoot Rd BR1 24 E4
Bankhurst Rd SE4, SE6 23 F8
Banks House TW7 5 E5
Banks Rd RH10 202 C5
Banks Way GU1 109 F4
Bankside Heath End GU9 125 F7
South Croydon CR2 61 F4
Woking GU21 69 B1
Bankside Cl Biggin Hill TN16 83 C1
Carshalton SM5 59 E4
Elstead GU8 148 D3
Isleworth TW7 5 F3
Bankside Dr KT7 56 B8
Bankside Way 6 SE19 22 E2
Banning House 4 SW19 19 D7
Bannister Cl
Streatham SW2 22 A7
Witley GU8 170 F6
Bannister's Rd GU2 129 F7
Banstead Cty Inf Sch SM7 77 F4
Banstead Cty Jun Sch SM7 77 F4
Banstead Downs Golf Club SM2 78 A8
Banstead Rd Banstead SM7 77 D7
Belmont SM7 77 D7
Carshalton SM2, SM5 59 E3
Caterham CR3 100 D5
East Ewell KT17 77 D7
Purley CR8 80 A8
Sutton SM2, SM5 59 E3
Banstead Rd S SM2 59 D1
Banstead Sta SM7 77 F5
Banstead Way SM6 60 E5
Barbara Cl TW17 34 B4
Barber Cl RH10 202 C2
Barber Dr GU6 174 E4
Barberry Way GU17 64 F2
Barbon Cl GU15 66 D3
Barclay Cl KT23 94 B4
Barclay Rd CR0, CR9 61 D7
Barcombe Ave SW2 21 F6
Bardney Rd SM4 40 B5
Bardolph Ave CR0 62 F2
Bardolph Rd TW9 6 F4
Bardon Wlk GU21 69 B2
Bardsley Cl CR0 61 F7
Bardsley Dr GU9 146 A7
Barfield Ct 9 RH1 119 A3
Barfield Sch GU10 126 B3
Barfields RH1 120 C2
Barford La GU10 167 E1
Barfreston Way SE20 43 B8
Bargate Ct KT3 39 A2
Bargate Ct 1 GU2 108 E1
Bargate Rise GU7 150 C4
Barge Cl GU11 105 E5
Bargery Rd SE6 24 B7
Bargrove Cl 8 SE20 23 A1
Bargrove Cres SE6 23 F6
Barham Cl KT13 53 C6
Barham Rd
Croydon CR0, CR2 61 C5
Wimbledon SW20 19 A1
Barhatch La GU6 174 F6
Barhatch Rd GU6 174 F4
Baring Rd CR0, CR9 43 A1
Barker Gn RG12 27 B4
Barker House SE21 22 E5
Barker Rd KT16 32 F2
Barker Wlk SW16 21 D5
Barkham Rd RG41 25 A5
Barkhart Dr RG40 25 C7
Barkhart Gdns RG40 25 C7
Barkis Mead GU47 45 E2
Barley Cl RH10 201 D5
Barley Mow Cl GU21 68 D2
Barley Mow Ct RH3 116 C1
Barley Mow Hill GU35 187 A6
Barley Mow La GU21 68 D3
Barley Mow Rd TW20 11 C3
Barley Mow Way TW17 34 A5
Barleymead RH6 161 B4
Barlow Cl SM6 60 E3
Barlow Rd Crawley RH11 200 E3
Hampton TW12 16 A1
Barmeston Rd SE6 24 B6
Barmouth Rd CR0 62 D8
Barn Cl Ashford TW15 14 B3
Bracknell RG12 27 D7
Camberley GU15 65 E6
Epsom KT18 76 C4
Oxshott KT22 74 D4
Woodmansterne SM7 78 D4
Barn Cres CR8 80 D6
Barn Field SM7 78 B5
Barn Meadow La KT23 93 F3
Barn Rd KT15 52 B2
Barnard Cl Frimley GU16 85 F8
Sunbury TW16 15 B1
Wallington SM6 60 D3
Barnard Ct 1
Knaphill GU21 68 E1
Streatham SW16 21 F5
Barnard Gdns KT3 39 A5
Barnard Rd Chelsham CR6 102 B8
Mitcham CR4 41 A7
Barnards Pl CR2 61 B2
Barnato Cl KT14 71 E7
Barnby Rd GU21 68 D2
Barncroft GU9 125 C1
Barnes Bridge Sta SW13 7 E5
Barnes Cl GU14 85 D4
Barnes Ct CR7 42 C6
Barnes End KT3 39 A4
Barnes High St SW13 7 F5
Barnes Hospl SW14 7 E4
Barnes Rd Farncombe GU7 150 E8
Frimley GU16 85 E8
Barnes Wallis Dr KT13, KT14 71 E8
Barnett Cl Leatherhead KT22 95 B8
Wonersh GU5 152 C8
Barnett Ct RG12 27 C7
Barnett Gn RG12 27 B3
Barnett La Lightwater GU18 66 F7
Wonersh GU5 152 C7
Barnett Row GU4 109 D6
Barnett Wood Cty Inf Sch KT21 75 D2
Barnett Wood La
Ashstead KT21, KT22 75 D1
Leatherhead KT22 95 B8
Barnett's Shaw RH8 122 D8
Barnfield Cranleigh GU6 174 E3
New Malden KT3 38 E3
Barnfield Ave Croydon CR0 62 C8
Kingston u T KT2 17 E3
Mitcham CR4 41 B6
Barnfield Cl Coulsdon CR5 100 C8
Wandsworth SW17 20 C5
Barnfield Cotts RH7 165 A1
Barnfield Gdns KT2 17 E3
Barnfield Rd
Crawley RH10, RH11 201 E7
South Croydon CR2 61 E2
Tatsfield TN16 103 D6
Barnfield Way RH8 123 A2
Barnfield Wood Cl BR3 44 D3
Barnfield Wood Rd BR3 44 D3
Barnhill Ave BR2 44 F4
Barnlea Cl TW13 15 E6
Barnmead GU24 49 F1
Barnmead Rd BR3 43 E8
Barns The GU8 149 C8
Barnsbury Cl KT3 38 C5
Barnsbury Cres KT5 38 C1
Barnsbury Cty Inf & Jun Schs GU22 89 D6
Barnsbury La KT5 38 C1
Barnscroft SW20 39 B6
Barnsfold La RH12 213 E6
Barnsford Cres GU24 68 A6
Barnsley Cl GU12 86 B2
Barnsnap Cl RH12 217 D6
Barnway TW20 11 C3
Barnwood Cl
Crawley RH10 202 C7
Guildford GU3 108 E3
Barnwood Ct GU2, GU3 108 E3
Barnwood Cty Inf Sch GU2 108 E2
Barnwood Rd GU2, GU3 108 E3
Barnyard The KT20 97 A3
Baron Cl SM2 59 B1
Baron Ct CR4 40 E5
Baron Gr CR4 40 E5
Baron's Hurst KT18 76 C3
Baron's Way RH2 139 A5
Baron's Wlk CR0 43 E3
Barons Ct SM6 60 D7
Barons The TW1 6 B1
Barons Way TW20 12 D2
Baronsfield Rd TW1 6 B1
Barossa Rd GU15 65 D7
Barr Beacon SE23 23 C8
Barr's La GU21 68 D3
Barracane Dr RG45 45 B5
Barrack Path 8 GU21 68 F1
Barrack Rd
Aldershot GU11 105 A2
Guildford GU2 109 A4
Hounslow TW4 4 E3
Barrards Hall CR2 80 D8
Barrens Brae GU22 70 A1
Barrens Cl GU22 90 A8
Barrens Pk GU22 90 A8
Barrett Cres RG40 25 E6
Barrett Rd KT22, KT23 94 D3
Barrhill Rd SW2 21 E6
Barricane GU21 89 B8
Barrie Cl CR5 79 C3
Barrie Rd GU9 125 A7
Barrihurst La GU6 173 D2
Barringer Sq SW17 21 A4
Barrington Ct
Dorking RH4 136 A6
Staines TW18 12 F2
Barrington Lodge KT13 53 C5
Barrington Rd Cheam SM3 40 A1
Crawley RH10 201 D3
Dorking RH4 136 A6
Horsham RH13 217 E2
Purley CR8 79 C7
Barrington Wlk 8 SE19 22 E2
Barrow Ave SM5 59 F3

Barrow Ct SE6 .24 F7
Barrow Green Rd
Oxted RH8 .122 C6
Tandridge RH9 .122 C6
Barrow Hedges Cl SM5 .59 E3
Barrow Hedges Prim Sch SM5 .59 E3
Barrow Hedges Way SM2, SM5 .59 E3
Barrow Hill KT4 .57 E8
Barrow Hill Cl KT4 .57 E8
Barrow Hills Sch GU8 .170 E4
Barrow Rd Croydon CR0 .61 A5
Streatham SW16 .21 D2
Barrowsfield CR2 .81 A7
Barry Cl RH10 .201 E3
Barry Sq RG12 .27 D2
Barry Terr TW15 .13 F6
Bars The GU1 .130 D8
Barsons Cl SE20 .23 C1
Barston Rd SE27 .22 C5
Barstow Cres SW2 .21 F7
Bartholomew Cl GU27 .208 D8
Bartholomew Ct RH4 .136 A6
Bartholomew Way RH12 .218 A7
Bartlett St CR0, CR2 .61 D5
Barton Cl Addlestone KT15 .52 A4
Aldershot GU11 .104 E1
Shepperton TW17 .34 B3
Barton Cres RH19 .206 A8
Barton Ct BR2 .44 D6
Barton Gn KT3 .38 D7
Barton Pl GU1 .110 B4
Barton Rd GU5 .152 A7
Barton The KT11 .73 D7
Barton Wlk RH10 .202 B4
Bartons Way GU14 .84 D7
Barttelot Rd RH12 .217 D2
Barwell Bsns Pk KT9 .56 D2
Barwood Ave BR4 .44 B1
Basden Gr TW13 .16 A6
Basemoors RG12 .27 E7
Bashford Way RH10 .202 D8
Basil Gdns Croydon CR0 .43 D1
West Norwood SE27 .22 C3
Basildene Rd TW4, TW5 .4 D4
Basildon Cl SM2 .59 B2
Basildon Way RH11 .200 E2
Basing Cl KT7 .36 F2
Basing Dr GU11 .126 B7
Basing House SE6 .24 A4
Basing Rd SM7 .77 F4
Basing Way KT7 .36 F2
Basingfield Rd KT7 .36 F2
Basinghall Gdns SM2 .59 B2
Baskerville Rd SW18 .20 E8
Basset Cl KT15 .52 C1
Bassett Cl Frimley GU16 .85 E8
Sutton SM2 .59 B2
Bassett Gdns TW7 .5 C7
Bassett Rd Crawley RH10 .202 D3
Woking GU22 .70 C3
Bassetts Hill RH7 .165 A2
Bassingham Rd SW18 .20 C8
Bat and Ball La
Rowledge GU10 .146 A5
Wrecclesham GU10, GU9 .146 A6
Batavia Cl TW16 .35 C8
Batavia Rd TW16 .35 B8
Batcombe Mead RG12 .27 E2
Bateman Gr GU12 .126 F8
Batemans Ct RH10 .202 A3
Bates Cres Croydon CR0 .61 A5
Streatham SW16 .21 C1
Bates Wlk KT15 .52 C4
Bateson Way GU21 .70 C5
Bath Ct 3 SE26 .23 A5
Bath House Rd CR0, CR9 .41 E1
Bath Pas KT1 .37 D7
Bath Rd Camberley GU15 .65 D6
Cranford TW3, TW4, TW5 .4 E5
Harlington TW6, UB7, TW5 .3 D6
Harmondsworth TW6, UB7 .2 E6
Hounslow TW3, TW4, TW5 .4 E5
Mitcham CR4 .40 D6
Poyle SL3, UB7, TW6 .1 E6
Bathgate Rd SW19 .19 D5
Bathurst Ave SW19 .40 B8
Batsworth Rd CR4 .40 D6
Batt's Cnr GU10 .166 E7
Batten Ave GU21 .88 E3
Battenberg Wlk 10 SE19 .22 E3
Battersby Rd SE6 .24 D5
Battle Cl SW19 .20 C2
Battlebridge House RH1 .119 B5
Battlebridge La RH1 .119 B5
Batts Hill RH2 .118 E3
Batty's Barn Cl RG40 .25 D5
Baty House SW2 .21 F7
Baudwin Rd SE6 .24 E6
Bavant Rd SW16 .41 F7
Bawtree Cl SM2 .59 C1
Bax Cl GU6 .174 E2
Baxter Ave RH1 .118 F1
Baxter Cl RH10 .202 B4
Bay Cl RH6 .160 E6
Bay Dr RG12 .27 E7
Bay Rd RG12 .27 E8
Bay Tree Ave KT22 .95 A7
Bayards CR6 .81 C1
Baydon Ct BR2 .44 F6
Bayeux KT20 .97 D5
Bayfield Ave GU16 .65 E2
Bayfield Rd RH6 .160 E4
Bayford Cl GU17 .65 A1
Bayham Rd SM4 .40 C5
Bayhorne La RH6 .161 C1
Bayleaf Cl TW12 .16 D3
Baylis Wlk RH11 .201 B1
Bayliss Ct 2 GU1 .130 C8
Baynards Rd RH12 .195 A2
Bays Cl SE26 .23 C3
Baysfarm Ct TW6, UB7 .2 C6
Baywood Cl GU14 .84 C5
Bazalgette Cl KT3 .38 D4
Bazalgette Gdns KT3 .38 D4
Beach Gr TW13 .16 A6
Beachborough Rd BR1 .24 C4
Beachy Rd RH11 .201 A1
Beacon Cl Banstead SM7 .77 D3
Rowledge GU10 .146 A5
Beacon Ct Colnbrook SW3 .1 C7
Horsham RH13 .218 A4
Beacon Gr SM5 .60 A6
Beacon Hill
Dormansland RH7 .186 B8
Woking GU21 .89 C8
Beacon Hill Ct GU26 .188 D6
Beacon Hill Cty Prim Sch GU26 .188 C6
Beacon Hill Rd
Beacon Hill GU26 .188 D6
Crondall GU10 .124 E8
Beacon House 10 SE26 .23 B3
Beacon Rd TW19, TW6 .3 A1
Beacon Rdbt TW6 .3 A1
Beacon Sch The KT20 .77 E2
Beacon View Rd GU8 .148 C2
Beacon Way SM7 .77 E3
Beaconsfield Pl KT17 .76 E7
Beaconsfield Rd
Claygate KT10 .55 E3
Kingston u T KT3 .38 D7
Langley Vale KT18 .96 E8
Old Woking GU22 .89 F7
Surbiton KT5 .37 F2
Thornton Heath CR0 .42 D3
Twickenham TW1 .6 B1
Beaconshaw BR1 .24 E1
Beadle Ct CR4 .40 E6
Beadles La RH8 .122 D4
Beadlow Cl SM4 .40 D3
Beadman Pl SE27 .22 B4
Beadman St SE27 .22 B4
Beadnell Rd SE23 .23 D7
Beaford Gr SW20 .39 F6
Beagle Cl TW13 .15 B4
Beale Cl RG40 .25 B7
Beale Ct RH11 .201 A3
Beale's La KT13 .53 B7
Beales La GU10 .145 F7
Beales Rd KT23 .94 B1
Bealeswood La GU10 .166 F6
Beam Hollow GU9 .125 C7
Bean Oak Rd RG40 .25 F6
Bear La GU9 .125 C3
Bear Rd TW13 .15 D4
Beard Rd TW10 .17 F3
Beard's Hill TW12 .36 A8
Beard's Rd TW15, TW16 .14 E2
Beardell St SE19 .22 F2
Beards Hill Cl TW12 .36 A8
Beare Green Cotts RH5 .157 D2
Beare Green Ct RH5 .157 D4
Bearfield Rd KT2 .17 E1
Bears Den KT20 .97 F5
Bears Rail Pk SL4 .10 F8
Bearsden Way RH12 .216 D3
Bearwood Cl KT15 .52 A4
Bearwood Cotts GU10 .145 F7
Beasley's Ait La TW16, TW17 .34 F3
Beatrice Ave SW16 .41 F7
Beatrice Rd Oxted RH8 .122 E6
1 Richmond TW10 .6 F2
Beatrix Potter Prim Sch SW18 .20 C7
Beattie Cl
East Bedfont TW14 .14 F7
Little Bookham KT23 .93 F3
Beatty Ave GU1 .110 A2
Beauchamp Rd
East Molesey KT8 .36 C4
South Norwood CR7, SE25 .42 D8
Sutton SM1 .59 A6
Twickenham TW1 .17 A8
Beauclare Cl KT21 .95 D6
Beauclerc Cty Inf Sch TW16 .35 C6
Beauclere House SM2 .59 C3
Beauclerk Cl TW13 .15 B7
Beauclerk House 10 SW16 .21 E5
Beaufield Gate GU27 .208 D7
Beaufort Cl Putney SW19 .19 B8
Reigate RH2 .117 F2
Woking GU22 .70 C3
Beaufort Ct TW10 .17 C4
Beaufort Cty Prim Sch GU21 .68 F3
Beaufort Gdns Heston TW5 .4 E6
North Ascot SL5 .28 E8
South Norwood SW16 .21 F1
Beaufort House SW20 .39 D8
Beaufort Rd Farnham GU9 .125 C3
Kingston u T KT1, KT5, KT6 .37 E5
Reigate RH2 .117 F2
Richmond TW10 .17 C4
Twickenham TW1 .17 C8
Woking GU22 .70 C3
Beaufort Way KT17 .58 A3
Beauforts TW20 .11 C3
Beaufoy House 3 SE27 .22 B5
Beaufront Cl GU15 .66 A7
Beaufront Rd GU15 .66 B7
Beaulieu Ave SE26 .23 B4
Beaulieu Cl Bracknell RG12 .28 A6
Beaulieu Cl continued
Hounslow TW4 .4 F2
Mitcham CR4 .41 A8
4 Twickenham TW1 .6 D1
Beaulieu Gdns GU17 .64 C5
Beaumaris Par GU16 .85 F8
Beaumont Ave TW9 .6 F4
Beaumont Cl RH11 .200 E5
Beaumont Ct Ascot SL5 .28 F5
Mitcham CR4 .41 A7
Beaumont Dr TW15 .14 D3
Beaumont Gdns RG12 .27 E4
Beaumont Gr GU11 .104 E2
Beaumont House 1
Streatham SW2 .21 E7
Wimbledon SW19 .20 A5
Beaumont Jun Sch GU11 .104 F2
Beaumont Pl TW7 .5 F2
Beaumont Prim Sch CR8 .80 A5
Beaumont Rd Purley CR8 .80 A6
Putney SW15, SW19 .19 E8
South Norwood SE19 .22 C2
Beaumont Sq GU6 .174 F3
Beaumont Terr 1 SE13 .24 E8
Beaumonts RH1 .139 F1
Beaver Cl Hampton TW12 .36 B8
Horsham RH12 .217 F6
9 Penge SE20 .23 A1
Wokingham RG41 .25 B3
Beaver Water World TN16 .103 B5
Beavers Cl Farnham GU9 .125 A2
Guildford GU3 .108 E2
Beavers Comm Prim Sch TW4 .4 C4
Beavers Cres TW4 .4 D3
Beavers Hill GU9 .124 F2
Beavers La TW4 .4 C4
Beavers Rd GU9 .125 A2
Beck Ct BR3 .43 D6
Beck Gdns GU9 .125 A6
Beck Ind Est The GU12 .126 D8
Beck La BR3 .43 D6
Beck River Pk BR3 .44 A8
Beck Way BR3 .44 A6
Beckenham Bsns Ctr BR3 .23 E2
Beckenham Ct BR3 .44 A8
Beckenham Gr BR2 .44 D7
Beckenham Hill Rd BR3, SE6 .24 C3
Beckenham Hill Sta SE6 .24 C3
Beckenham Hospl BR3 .43 F7
Beckenham Junction Sta BR3 .44 A8
Beckenham La BR1, BR2 .44 F7
Beckenham Place Pk BR3 .24 B1
Beckenham Rd
Beckenham BR3 .43 E8
Penge BR3 .43 E8
West Wickham BR3, BR4 .44 C2
Beckenshaw Gdns SM7 .78 E4
Becket Cl Croydon SE25 .43 A3
2 Merton SW19 .40 B8
Becket Wood RH5 .158 C4
Beckett Ave CR8 .80 B4
Beckett Cl Streatham SW16 .21 D6
Wokingham RG40 .25 E6
Beckett La RH11 .181 D1
Beckett Way 11 RH19 .205 F8
Beckett Wlk BR3 .23 E2
Becketts Cl TW14 .4 B1
Becketts Pl KT1 .37 D8
Beckford Ave RG12 .27 B3
Beckford Rd CR0, SE25 .42 F3
Beckford Way RH10 .202 B2
Beckingham Rd GU2 .109 A2
Beckley Cotts KT23 .94 C1
Beckmead Sch BR3 .44 A1
Beckway Rd SW16 .41 D7
Beckworth Pl KT13 .53 E8
Beclands Rd SW17 .21 A2
Becmead Ave SW16 .21 D4
Becondale Rd SE19 .22 E3
Bedale Cl RH11 .201 C4
Beddington Cross CR0 .41 E2
Beddington Farm Rd
Croydon CR0 .60 F8
Wallington CR0, CR9 .41 E1
Beddington Gdns SM5, SM6 .60 A4
Beddington Gr SM6 .60 D5
Beddington Inf Sch SM6 .60 C6
Beddington La CR0 .60 E8
Beddington Manor SM2 .59 D4
Beddington Park Cotts SM6 .60 D7
Beddington Park Prim Sch CR0 .60 D7
Beddlestead La CR6 .103 A6
Bedelsford Sch KT1 .37 E6
Bedfont Cl
East Bedfont TW14 .3 C1
Mitcham CR4 .41 A7
Bedfont Ct TW19 .2 B4
Bedfont Green Cl TW14 .14 C7
Bedfont Ind Pk N TW15 .14 C5
Bedfont Inf Sch TW14 .3 E1
Bedfont Jun Sch TW14 .3 E1
Bedfont La TW14, TW13 .14 F8
Bedfont Rd
East Bedfont TW13, TW14 .14 D6
Feltham TW13, TW14 .14 D6
Stanwell TW19 .2 F1
Bedford Ave GU16 .85 F5
Bedford Cres GU16 .85 F5
Bedford Ct 6 Richmond TW9 .6 F3
South Norwood SE19 .42 F8
Bedford Hill Balham SW12 .21 B6
Bedford Hill continued
Streatham SW16 .21 B6
Upper Tooting SW12, SW16, SW17 .21 B6
Bedford House 3 GU1 .130 C8
Bedford La Frimley GU16 .85 F6
Sunningdale SL5 .30 B4
Bedford Pk CR0 .42 C1
Bedford Pl CR0 .42 D1
Bedford Rd Guildford GU1 .130 C8
Horsham RH13 .217 D1
North Cheam KT4 .58 C8
Twickenham TW2 .16 D5
Bedgebury Gdns SW19 .19 E6
Bedlow Way CR0 .60 F6
Bedser Cl CR7 .42 C6
Bedster Gdns KT8 .36 B6
Bedwardine Rd SE19 .22 E1
Beech Ave Brentford TW8 .6 B7
Camberley GU15 .65 D4
Effingham KT24 .113 D6
Farnham GU10 .146 C5
South Croydon CR2 .61 D1
Tatsfield TN16 .103 D8
Beech Cl Ashford TW15 .14 D3
Blindley Heath RH7 .163 E8
Byfleet KT14 .71 E7
Carshalton SM5 .59 F8
Chiddingfold GU8 .191 A4
Cobham KT11 .74 A8
Dorking RH4 .136 A8
Effingham KT24 .113 D7
Hersham KT12 .54 C6
Putney SW15 .19 A8
Stanwell TW19 .13 D8
Sunbury TW16 .35 D7
Wimbledon SW19 .19 C2
Beech Close Ct KT11 .73 F8
Beech Copse CR2 .61 E5
Beech Cres KT20 .116 C5
Beech Ct Beckenham BR3 .23 F1
4 Guildford GU1 .130 F8
Teddington TW11 .17 C2
4 West Norwood SW16 .22 A3
Beech Dr Blackwater GU17 .64 D4
Kingswood KT20 .97 F5
Reigate RH2 .118 D1
Send Marsh GU23 .91 A3
Beech Farm Rd CR6 .102 D8
Beech Fields RH19 .185 F3
Beech Gdns
Crawley Down RH10 .204 A8
Woking GU21 .69 E4
Beech Glen RG12 .27 B5
Beech Gr Addlestone KT15 .52 B6
Burgh Heath KT18 .77 B2
Caterham CR3 .100 E1
Great Bookham KT23 .114 A8
Guildford GU2 .108 F1
Kingston u T KT3 .38 D6
Mitcham CR4 .41 D5
Pirbright GU24 .87 C7
Pirbright GU24 .87 D7
Beech Hall KT16 .51 C3
Beech Hanger End GU26 .188 B3
Beech Hill
Bowlhead Green GU8 .189 F8
Headley Down GU35 .187 B5
Woking GU22 .89 D4
Beech Hill Rd
Headley Down GU35 .187 A5
Sunningdale SL5 .29 F3
Beech Holme RH10 .204 B8
Beech Holt KT22 .95 C5
Beech House Heston TW5 .4 E7
New Addington CR0 .63 B4
Beech House Rd CR0, CR9 .61 D7
Beech La Flexford GU3 .107 A1
Grayshott GU26 .188 B4
Guildford GU2 .130 C6
Beech Lodge TW18 .12 E3
Beech Rd Biggin Hill TN16 .83 C2
East Bedfont TW14 .14 E8
Epsom KT18 .76 F4
Farnborough GU14 .85 A7
Frimley GU16 .85 F6
Haslemere GU27 .208 D8
Horsham RH12 .218 B5
Merstham RH1 .99 C1
Oatlands Park KT13 .53 D6
Reigate RH2 .118 A4
Thornton Heath SW16 .41 F6
Beech Ride GU47 .45 B1
Beech Tree Cl RH10 .201 D7
Beech Tree Dr GU9 .126 A5
Beech Tree La TW18 .33 B7
Beech Tree Pl SM1 .59 B5
Beech Way Epsom KT17 .76 F4
Godalming GU7 .150 D3
Selsdon CR2 .81 D7
Twickenham TW13 .16 A5
Beech Wlk KT17 .77 A8
Beech Wood CR3 .100 F3
Beechcroft Ashstead KT21 .95 F8
Kingston u T KT2 .38 B8
Beechcroft Ave Kenley CR8 .80 D4
Kingston u T KT1, KT3 .38 C7
Beechcroft Cl Ascot SL5 .29 D5
Heston TW5 .4 E7
Streatham SW16 .21 F3
Beechcroft Ct RG12 .27 B6
Beechcroft Dr GU2 .129 D6
Beechcroft Lodge SM2 .59 C3
Beechcroft Manor KT13 .53 D7
Beechcroft Mansions SW16 .21 F3
Beechcroft Rd
Chessington KT9 .56 F7
Beechcroft Rd continued
Mortlake SW14 .7 C4
Upper Tooting SW17 .20 E6
Beechcroft Sch SW17 .20 E6
Beechdene KT20 .97 B5
Beechen Cliff Way TW7 .5 F5
Beechen La KT20 .97 F2
Beechen Pl SE23 .23 C6
Beeches Ave The SM5 .59 E3
Beeches Cl Kingswood KT20 .98 A4
Penge SE20 .43 C8
Beeches Cres RH10 .201 E4
Beeches Head RH19 .186 F5
Beeches La RH19 .206 D6
Beeches Rd Cheam SM3 .39 E1
Upper Tooting SW17 .20 F5
Beeches The Ash Vale GU12 .85 F1
Banstead SM7 .78 B3
Bramley GU5 .151 F6
Fetcham KT22 .94 E3
Hounslow TW3 .5 B6
Mitcham CR4 .40 E4
Staines TW18 .13 A3
Beeches Wlk SM2, SM5 .59 E2
Beeches Wood KT20 .98 A5
Beechey Cl RH10 .183 B3
Beechey Way RH10 .183 B3
Beechfield SM7 .78 B6
Beechfield Ct 7 CR0 .61 C6
Beechfield Rd SE6 .23 F7
Beeching Cl GU12 .106 B3
Beeching Way RH19 .185 E1
Beechland Cotts KT20 .117 F7
Beechlawn GU1 .130 F8
Beechmeads KT11 .73 D6
Beechmont Ave GU25 .31 D4
Beechmont Cl BR1 .24 E3
Beechmore Gdns SM3 .58 D8
Beechnut Dr GU17 .64 B6
Beechnut Ind Est 9 GU12 .105 B1
Beechnut Rd 8 GU12 .105 B1
Beecholme KT17 .77 E5
Beecholme Ave CR4 .41 B8
Beecholme Fst Sch CR4 .41 B8
Beechrow KT2 .17 E4
Beechside RH10 .201 E5
Beechtree Ave TW20 .11 B2
Beechvale 3 GU22 .69 F1
Beechway GU1 .110 B2
Beechwood Ave
Ashford TW16 .15 A2
Kingswood KT20 .98 A6
Oatlands Park KT13 .53 E6
Richmond TW9 .7 A6
Staines TW18 .13 B2
Thornton Heath CR7 .42 B5
Wallington CR5 .79 B4
Beechwood Cl
Knaphill GU21 .68 E2
Long Ditton KT6 .37 D2
North Ascot SL5 .8 F1
Oatlands Park KT13 .53 E6
Beechwood Ct
Carshalton SM5 .59 F6
Chiswick W4 .7 D8
Sutton SM1 .59 A5
Walton-on-T KT12 .54 A7
Beechwood Dr KT11 .74 A8
Beechwood Gdns CR3 .101 A5
Beechwood La CR6 .101 D8
Beechwood Manor KT13 .53 E6
Beechwood Pk KT22 .95 C5
Beechwood Rd
Caterham CR3 .101 A5
Knaphill GU21 .68 D2
South Croydon CR2 .61 E2
Wentworth GU25 .31 B1
Beechwood Villas RH1 .161 A7
Beechwoods Ct SE19 .22 F3
Beecot La KT12 .54 C8
Beeding Cl RH12 .218 A5
Beedingwood Dr RH12 .218 F6
Beedon Dr RG12 .26 E3
Beehive La RG12 .26 C7
Beehive Rd
Bracknell RG12, RG42 .26 D7
Staines TW18 .12 F3
Beehive Ring Rd RH6 .182 B4
Beehive Way RH2 .139 B5
Beeleigh Rd SM4 .40 B5
Beeston Way TW14 .4 C1
Beeton's Ave GU12 .106 A4
Beggar's Roost La SM1, SM2 .59 A4
Beggars La Chobham GU24 .68 C8
Gomshall RH5 .133 E4
Beggarshouse La RH6 .180 C8
Begonia Pl 1 TW12 .16 A2
Behenna Cl RH11 .200 E5
Beira St SW12 .21 B8
Belcroft Cl BR1 .24 F1
Beldam Bridge Rd GU24 .68 A6
Beldham Gdns KT8 .36 B6
Beldham Rd GU10, GU9 .145 F7
Belenoyd Ct SW16 .21 F5
Belfast Rd SE25 .43 B5
Belfield Rd KT19 .57 E3
Belfry The RH1 .118 F2
Belgrade Rd TW12 .36 B8
Belgrave Cl KT12 .54 B6
Belgrave Cres TW16 .35 B8
Belgrave Ct GU17 .64 D3
Belgrave Manor GU22 .89 E8
Belgrave Rd Barnes SW13 .7 F7

Belgrave Rd continued
Hounslow TW4 .4 F4
Mitcham CR4 .40 D6
South Norwood SE25 .42 F5
Sunbury TW16 .35 B8
Belgrave Wlk CR4 .40 D6
Belgravia Ct RH6 .161 B3
Belgravia Gdns BR1 .24 E2
Belgravia House 1 TW11 .17 C1
Belgravia Mews KT1 .37 D5
Bell Bridge Rd KT16 .32 F1
Bell Cl GU14 .85 C6
Bell Cnr KT16 .32 F2
Bell Cres CR5 .99 B6
Bell Ct KT5 .57 B8
Bell Ctr RH10 .181 F2
Bell Dr SW18 .19 E8
Bell Farm Jun Sch KT12 .54 C6
Bell Foundry La RG40 .25 C8
Bell Gn SE6 .23 F4
Bell Green La
BR3, SE26, SE6 .23 F4
Bell Hammer RH19 .205 E8
Bell House 15 SW2 .22 A8
Bell House Gdns RG41 .25 B6
Bell La Blackwater GU17 .64 C5
Fetcham KT22 .94 D4
Rowledge GU10 .145 E3
Twickenham TW1 .17 A7
Bell Lane Cl KT22 .94 D4
Bell Meadow
Dulwich SE19 .22 E4
Godstone RH9 .121 C3
Bell Pl GU19 .47 F3
Bell Rd East Molesey KT8 .36 D4
Hounslow TW3 .5 B3
Kingsley Green GU27 .208 B3
Warnham RH12 .217 A8
Bell St RH2 .139 B8
Bell Vale La
Haslemere GU27 .208 C4
Lurgashall GU27 .208 C4
Bell View BR3 .23 F1
Bell Weir Cl TW19 .12 B6
Bellamy House Heston TW5 .5 A8
Upper Tooting SW17 .20 D4
Bellamy Rd RH10 .202 C2
Bellamy St SW12 .21 B8
Belland Dr GU11 .104 E1
Bellasis Ave SW2 .21 E6
Belle Vue Cl
Aldershot GU12 .105 D2
Staines TW18 .33 A8
Belle Vue Ent Ctr GU12 .105 E2
Belle Vue Inf Sch GU12 .105 D2
Belle Vue Rd GU12 .105 D2
Bellever Hill GU15 .65 E5
Bellevue Pk CR7 .42 C5
Bellevue Rd
Kingston u T KT1 .37 E6
Upper Tooting SW17 .20 F7
Bellew Rd GU16 .86 B7
Bellew St SW17 .20 C5
Bellfield CR0 .62 F3
Bellfields Ct GU1 .109 C5
Bellfields Rd GU1 .109 D3
Bellingham Cl GU15 .66 C4
Bellingham Gn SE6 .24 A5
Bellingham Rd SE6 .24 C5
Bellingham Sta SE6 .24 B5
Bellingham Trad Est SE6 .24 B6
Bellmarsh Rd KT15 .52 B6
Bellmore Ct 5 CR0 .42 F1
Bello Cl SE24, SW2 .22 B7
Belloc Cl RH10 .202 C7
Belloc Ct RH13 .218 A3
Bells La SL3 .1 B4
Belltrees Gr 1 SW16 .22 A3
Bellwether La RH1 .162 B7
Belmont KT13 .53 C4
Belmont Ave
Guildford GU2 .108 F4
West Barnes KT3 .39 A5
Belmont Cl GU14 .84 F7
Belmont Mews GU15 .65 C3
Belmont Rd Beckenham BR3 43 F7
Belmont SM2 .59 A1
Camberley GU15 .65 C4
Crowthorne RG45 .45 B6
Croydon SE25 .43 B4
Leatherhead KT22 .95 A5
Reigate RH2 .139 C8
Twickenham TW2 .16 D6
Wallington SM6 .60 C5
Belmont Rise SM1, SM2 .58 F3
Belmont Sch RH5 .155 D6
Belmont Sta SM2 .59 B1
Belmore Ave GU22 .70 D3
Belsize Gdns SM1 .59 B6
Belstone Mews GU14 .85 A7
Beltane Dr SW19 .19 D5
Belthorn Cres SW12 .21 C8
Belton Rd GU15 .65 E5
Belvedere Ave SW19 .19 E3
Belvedere Cl Esher KT10 .55 B5
Guildford GU2 .109 B3
Teddington TW11 .16 E3
Weybridge KT13 .53 A5
Belvedere Ct
Blackwater GU17 .64 D3
Crawley RH10 .202 B7
8 Kingston u T KT2 .18 A1
Belvedere Dr SW19 .19 E3
Belvedere Gdns KT8 .36 A4
Belvedere Gr SW19 .19 E3
Belvedere Rd
Biggin Hill TN16 .83 F1
Farnborough GU14 .85 C2
Penge SE19 .22 F1
Belvedere Sq SW19 .19 E3
Belvoir Cl GU16 .65 F1
Belvoir Lodge SE22 .23 A8
Belvoir Rd SE22 .23 A8
Benbow La GU8 .193 C4
Benbrick Rd GU2 .130 A8
Benbury Cl BR1 .24 C3
Bence The TW20 .32 B6
Bench Field CR2 .61 F5
Benchfield Cl RH19 .186 B1
Bencombe Rd CR8 .80 A5
Bencroft Rd SW16 .21 C1
Bencurtis Pk BR4 .63 D8
Bendon Valley SW18 .20 B8
Benedict Dr TW14 .14 D8
Benedict Fst Sch CR4 .40 D6
Benedict Prim Sch CR4 .40 D6
Benedict Rd CR4 .40 D6
Benedict Wharf CR4 .40 E6
Benen-Stock Rd TW19 .2 A2
Benett Gdns SW16 .41 E7
Benfleet Cl Cobham KT11 .73 E7
Sutton SM1 .59 C7
Benham Cl Chessington KT9 56 C4
Coulsdon CR5, CR8 .80 B1
Benham Gdns TW3, TW4 .4 F2
Benhams Cl RH6 .161 A5
Benhams Dr RH6 .161 A5
Benhill Ave SM1 .59 C6
Benhill Rd SM1 .59 D6
Benhill Wood Rd SM1 .59 C6
Benhilton Gdns SM1 .59 B7
Benhurst Cl CR2 .62 D1
Benhurst Ct 13 Penge SE20 .43 B8
Streatham SW16 .22 A3
Benhurst Gdns CR2 .62 C1
Benhurst La SW16 .22 A3
Benin St SE13 .24 D8
Benjamin Ct TW15 .14 C1
Benjamin Rd RH10 .202 D4
Benner La GU24 .68 A7
Bennet Cl KT1 .37 C8
Bennett Cl Cobham KT11 .73 A6
Crawley RH10 .202 B2
Bennett Ct GU15 .65 C5
Bennett House 2 SW4 .21 D8
Bennett St W4 .7 E8
Bennett Way GU4 .111 B6
Bennetts Ave CR0 .62 E8
Bennetts Cl CR4, SW16 .41 B8
Bennetts Farm Pl KT23 .93 F2
Bennetts Rd RH13 .217 E1
Bennetts Way CR0 .62 F8
Bennetts Wood RH5 .178 C5
Bens Acre RH13 .218 A2
Bensbury Cl SW15 .19 C8
Bensham Cl CR7 .42 C5
Bensham Gr CR7 .42 C7
Bensham La CR0, CR7 .42 B3
Bensham Manor
Rd CR0, CR7 .42 C5
Bensham Manor Sch CR7 .42 C4
Bensington Ct TW14 .3 D1
Benson Cl TW3 .5 A3
Benson Prim Sch CR0 .62 E7
Benson Rd
Croydon CR0, CR9 .61 A7
Forest Hill SE23 .23 C7
Benson's La RH12 .199 C1
Bentall Sh Ctr The 10 KT2 .37 E7
Benthall Gdns CR8 .80 C2
Bentham Ave GU21 .70 C4
Bentley Cl SW19 .20 A5
Bentley Copse GU15 .66 B4
Bentley Dr KT13 .53 A2
Benton's La SE27 .22 C4
Benton's Rise SE27 .22 D3
Bentsbrook Cl RH5 .136 B3
Bentsbrook Cotts RH5 .136 B3
Bentsbrook Pk RH5 .136 B3
Bentsbrook Rd RH5 .136 B3
Benwell Ct TW16 .35 A8
Benwell Rd GU24 .88 A8
Benwick Ct SE20 .43 C8
Benwood Ct SM1 .59 C7
Beomonds KT16 .33 A2
Beomonds Row KT16 .33 A2
Berberis Cl GU1 .109 C3
Bere Rd RG12 .27 E3
Beresford Ave
Tolworth KT5 .38 C2
Twickenham TW1 .6 C1
Beresford Cl GU16 .85 F6
Beresford Ct 11 TW1 .6 C1
Beresford Gdns TW4 .4 F2
Beresford House SE21 .22 E5
Beresford Rd Belmont SM2 .58 F3
Dorking RH4 .136 B7
Kingston u T KT2 .37 F8
Kingston u T, Norbiton KT3 .38 C5
Bergenia Ct GU24 .67 E6
Berkeley Ave TW4 .4 A5
Berkeley Cl Crawley RH11 .200 E2
Stanwell TW19 .12 D6
Berkeley Cres GU16 .86 A8
Berkeley Ct Ashstead KT21 .75 F1
Oatlands Park KT13 .53 E8
16 Streatham SW2 .22 A7
Wallington SM6 .60 C6
Berkeley Dr
East Molesey KT8 .36 A6
Winkfield SL4 .9 B7
Berkeley Gdns
Claygate KT10 .56 A4
Berkeley Gdns continued
Pyrford KT14 .70 F5
Walton-on-T KT12 .34 F2
Berkeley House 11 TW8 .6 D8
Berkeley Pl Epsom KT18 .76 D4
Wimbledon SW19 .19 D2
Berkeley Prim Sch TW5 .4 D7
Berkeley Waye TW5 .4 D7
Berkeleys The KT22 .94 E3
Berkley Cl TW2 .16 E5
Berkley Ct Guildford GU1 .109 E1
7 Twickenham TW1 .17 A8
Berkley Mews TW16 .35 C6
Berkshire Cl CR3 .100 D5
Berkshire House SE6 .24 A4
Berkshire Rd GU15 .65 F8
Berkshire Sq CR4 .41 E5
Berkshire Way
Bracknell RG12 .26 D6
Mitcham CR4 .41 E5
Bernard Ct GU15 .65 B4
Bernard Gdns SW19 .19 F3
Bernard Rd SM5, SM6 .60 B6
Berne Rd CR7 .42 C4
Bernel Dr CR0 .62 F7
Bernersh Cl GU47 .45 C1
Berney House BR3 .43 E4
Berney Rd CR0 .42 D2
Berridge Rd SE19 .22 E3
Berrington Dr KT24 .92 F3
Berry Ct TW4 .4 F2
Berry La Pirbright GU3 .88 C2
West Norwood SE21, SE27 .22 D4
Woking GU22, GU3 .88 D4
Berry Meade KT21 .75 F2
Berry Wlk KT21 .95 F8
Berry's La KT14 .71 D8
Berrybank GU47 .64 E6
Berrycroft RG12 .27 D8
Berrylands Surbiton KT5 .37 F3
West Barnes SW20 .39 C5
Berrylands Ct 7 SM2 .59 B3
Berrylands Rd KT5 .37 F3
Berrylands Sta KT5 .38 B5
Berryman's La SE26 .23 D4
Berrymeade Wlk RH11 .200 E5
Berryscourt KT14 .71 D8
Berryscroft Ct TW18 .13 C1
Berryscroft Rd TW18 .13 C1
Berstead Wlk 1 RH11 .200 F3
Bert Rd CR7 .42 C4
Bertal Rd SW17 .20 D4
Bertie Rd SE26 .23 D2
Bertram Cotts SW19 .20 A1
Bertram House Sch SW17 21 A6
Bertram Rd KT2 .18 A1
Bertrand House 11 SW16 .21 E5
Berwyn Ave TW3 .5 B6
Berwyn Rd
Mortlake SW14, TW10 .7 B3
Streatham SE24 .22 B7
Beryl Harding House 3
SW19 .19 D1
Berystede KT2 .18 B1
Besley St SW16 .21 C2
Bessant Dr TW9 .7 B6
Bessborough Rd SW15 .19 A7
Bessborough Wks KT8 .35 F4
Beswick Gdns RG12 .27 F8
Beta Rd Chobham GU24 .49 F1
Farnborough GU14 .85 A5
Woking GU22 .70 B3
Beta Way TW20 .32 C8
Betchets Green Rd RH5 .157 C6
Betchley Cl RH19 .185 E3
Betchworth Cl SM1 .59 D5
Betchworth Sta RH3 .116 E3
Betchworth The RH4 .116 A1
Betchworth Way CR0 .63 C2
Betchworth Works RH6 .180 D6
Bethany Waye TW14 .14 E8
Bethel Cl GU9 .125 D6
Bethel La GU9 .125 D6
Bethersden Cl BR3 .23 F1
Bethesda Ct 8 SE20 .23 C1
Bethlem Royal Hospl The
BR3 .44 A2
Bethune Cl RH10 .202 D5
Bethune Rd RH13 .217 E1
Betjeman Cl CR5 .79 F2
Betley Ct KT12 .54 B7
Betony Cl CR0 .43 D1
Betts Cl BR3 .43 E7
Betts Way Crawley RH10 .181 D2
Long Ditton KT6 .37 B1
Penge SE20 .43 B8
Bettswood Ct 16 SE20 .43 B8
Betula Cl CR8 .80 D4
Between Streets KT11 .73 A5
Beulah Ave CR7 .42 C7
Beulah Cres CR7 .42 C7
Beulah Gr CR0 .42 C3
Beulah Hill SE19, SW16 .22 C1
Beulah Inf Sch CR7 .42 C6
Beulah Jun Sch CR7 .42 C6
Beulah Rd Merton SW19 .19 F1
South Norwood CR7 .42 C6
Sutton SM1 .59 A6
Beulah Wlk CR3 .101 E7
Bevan Ct Crawley RH11 .201 B1
Croydon CR0 .61 A5
Beverley Ave Hounslow TW4 .4 F3
Wimbledon SW20 .38 F8
Beverley Cl
Addlestone KT15 .52 D5
Ash GU12 .105 F1
Chessington KT9 .56 C6
East Ewell KT17 .77 C8
Beverley Cl continued
Frimley GU15 .66 D6
Oatlands Park KT13 .53 E8
Beverley Cotts SW15 .18 E5
Beverley Cres GU14 .84 F2
Beverley Ct Hounslow TW4 .4 F3
Kingston u T SW20 .38 F8
Beverley Gdns Barnes SW13 .7 F4
2 North Cheam KT4 .39 A1
Beverley House BR1 .24 D3
Beverley Hts RH2 .118 B3
Beverley Hyrst 7 CR0 .61 F8
Beverley La KT2 .18 E1
Beverley Lodge 6 TW10 .6 E2
Beverley Mansions TW4 .4 F3
Beverley Rd Barnes SW13 .7 F4
Kenley CR3 .80 F2
Mitcham CR4 .41 D5
New Malden KT3 .39 A5
North Cheam KT4 .58 C8
Penge SE20 .43 B7
Sunbury TW16 .34 F8
Teddington KT1 .37 C8
Beverley Sch KT3 .39 A4
Beverley Trad Est SM4 .39 D2
Beverley Way
Kingston u T KT3, SW20, KT2 .38 F8
Wimbledon KT3, SW20 .39 A6
Beverley Way (Kingston
By Pass) KT3, SW20 .39 A6
Beverley Way Kingston
Bypass KT3 .38 F8
Beverstone Rd CR7 .42 B5
Bevill Allen Cl SW17 .20 F3
Bevill Cl SE25 .43 A6
Bevin Sq SW17 .20 F5
Bevington Rd BR3 .44 B7
Bew Ct SE21 .23 A8
Bewbush Dr RH11 .200 F3
Bewbush Fst Sch RH11 .200 F3
Bewbush Manor RH11 .200 E2
Bewbush Mid Sch RH11 .200 F3
Bewlys Rd SE27 .22 B3
Bexhill Cl TW13 .15 E6
Bexhill Rd Forest Hill SE4 .23 F8
Mortlake SW14 .7 C4
Beynon Rd SM5 .59 F5
Bglws The CR3 .100 D4
Bicester Rd TW9 .7 B4
Bickersteth Rd SW17 .20 F2
Bickley Ct RH11 .201 A3
Bickley St SW17 .20 F3
Bicknell Rd GU16 .65 E2
Bickney Way KT22 .94 C5
Bicknoller Cl SM2 .59 B1
Bidborough Cl BR2 .44 F4
Biddulph Rd CR2 .61 C2
Bideford Cl
Farnborough GU14 .85 A7
Feltham TW13 .15 F5
Bideford Rd BR1 .24 F5
Bidhams Cres KT20 .97 C6
Bidmead Ct KT6 .56 E7
Bield The RH2 .139 A7
Bietigheim Way 2 GU15 .65 C6
Big Common La RH1 .120 B3
Biggin Ave CR4 .40 F8
Biggin Cl RH11 .201 C4
Biggin Hill SE19, SW16 .22 B1
Biggin Hill Airport TN16 .83 D5
Biggin Hill Bsns Pk TN16 .83 D4
Biggin Hill Cl KT2 .17 C3
Biggin Hill Jun & Inf Schs
TN16 .83 E3
Biggin Way
CR7, SE19, SW16 .22 C1
Bigginwood Rd SW16 .42 B8
Bignor Cl RH12 .218 A7
Bilberry Cl RH11 .201 B3
Bilbets RH12 .217 C3
Billesden Rd GU24 .87 D7
Billet Rd TW18, TW19 .13 A5
Billhurst Cotts RH7 .164 D4
Billingshurst Rd RH12 .216 D3
Billinton Dr RH10 .202 B5
Billockby Cl KT9 .56 F4
Billsley Ct SE25 .42 E5
Bilton Ind Est RG12 .26 E5
Binbury Row TW18 .12 E4
Binfield Rd
Bracknell, Dowlesgreen RG40 25 F7
Bracknell, Priestwood RG42 .27 A8
Byfleet KT14 .71 E7
South Croydon CR2 .61 F5
Wokingham RG40 .25 F7
Binfields GU9 .125 C3
Bingham Cnr CR0 .43 A1
Bingham Dr Knaphill GU21 .68 F1
Staines TW18 .13 D1
Bingham Rd CR0, CR9 .43 B1
Bingley Rd TW16 .15 A1
Binhams Lea GU8 .192 F5
Binhams Meadow GU8 .192 F5
Binley House SW15 .7 F1
Binney Ct RH10 .182 E1
Binscombe Cres GU7 .150 E8
Binscombe Jun Sch GU7 129 E1
Binscombe La GU7 .150 E7
Binstead Cl RH11 .201 B8
Binsted Dr GU17 .64 D5
Binton La GU10 .126 E3
Birch Ave Caterham CR3 .100 D3
Leatherhead KT22 .94 F8
Birch Circ GU7 .150 F8
Birch Cl Brentford TW8 .6 B7
Camberley GU15 .65 E8
Crawley Down RH10 .204 C8
Hounslow TW3 .5 D5
Birch Cl continued
New Haw KT15 .52 D2
Rowledge GU10 .146 A4
Send Marsh GU23 .90 F2
Teddington TW11 .17 A3
Woking GU21 .89 C8
Birch Ct Ashstead KT21 .75 D2
Sutton SM1 .59 C6
9 Wallington SM6 .60 B6
Birch Dr GU17 .64 D3
Birch Gn TW18 .13 A4
Birch Gr Bracknell RG12 .27 C5
Guildford GU1 .109 C4
Kingswood KT20 .97 F3
Lewisham SE12 .24 F8
Upper Halliford TW17 .34 E7
Woking GU22 .70 D4
Birch Hill CR0 .62 D5
Birch Hill Prim Sch RG12 .27 B1
Birch Hill Rd RG12 .27 B2
Birch La Purley CR8 .79 E8
West End GU24 .67 D7
Winkfield RG12, SL5 .28 B8
Birch Lea RH10 .182 A1
Birch Platt GU24 .67 D6
Birch Rd Farncombe GU7 .151 A8
Feltham TW13 .15 D3
Headley Down GU35 .187 B6
Windlesham GU20 .48 E4
Birch Side RG45 .45 A6
Birch Tree Ave BR4 .63 F6
Birch Tree View GU18 .48 A1
Birch Tree Way CR0 .62 B8
Birch Vale KT11 .74 A6
Birch Way Ash Vale GU12 .106 A7
Warlingham CR6 .81 E1
Birch Wlk CR4 .41 B8
Birchanger GU7 .150 E4
Birchanger Rd SE25 .43 A4
Birchcroft Cl CR3 .100 C2
Birchdale Cl KT14 .71 C8
Birchend Cl CR2 .61 D4
Birches Cl Epsom KT18 .76 E4
Mitcham CR4 .40 F6
Birches Ind Est RH19 .185 A3
Birches Rd RH12 .218 B5
Birches The
Beckenham BR2 .44 F5
Blackwater GU17 .64 B5
Crawley RH10 .202 A7
East Horsley KT24 .92 E1
Farnborough GU14 .84 D4
South Norwood SE25 .42 F7
Twickenham TW4 .15 F8
Woking GU22 .69 F1
Birchett Rd
Aldershot GU11 .105 A2
Farnborough GU14 .84 E6
Birchetts Cl 2 RG42 .27 B8
Birchfield Cl
Addlestone KT15 .52 B6
Coulsdon CR5 .79 F3
Birchfield Gr KT17 .58 C1
Birchfields GU15 .65 C4
Birchgrove KT11 .73 D5
Birchington Rd KT5 .37 F2
Birchlands GU47 .45 E2
Birchlands Ave SW12 .20 F8
Birchway RH1 .140 B7
Birchwood Ave
Beckenham BR3 .43 F5
Hackbridge SM5, SM6 .60 B7
Birchwood Cl
Crawley RH10 .202 C3
Horley RH6 .161 B4
Morden SM4 .40 B5
Birchwood Dr
Lightwater GU18 .48 C1
West Byfleet KT14 .71 A7
Birchwood Gr TW12 .16 A2
Birchwood La
Caterham CR3 .100 B2
Oxshott KT10, KT22 .55 E1
Birchwood Rd
Streatham SW17 .21 B3
West Byfleet KT14, KT15 .71 A7
Bird Mews RG40 .25 B6
Bird Wlk TW2 .15 F7
Bird-In-Hand Pas SE23 .23 C6
Birdham Cl RH11 .201 B8
Birdhaven GU10, GU9 .146 A6
Birdhurst CR3 .100 F7
Birdhurst Ave CR2 .61 D6
Birdhurst Ct SM6 .60 C3
Birdhurst Gdns CR2 .61 D6
Birdhurst Rd
Mitcham SW19 .20 E2
South Croydon CR2 .61 E5
Birdhurst Rise CR2 .61 E5
Birds Hill Dr KT22 .74 D6
Birds Hill Rd KT22 .74 D6
Birds Hill Rise KT22 .74 D6
Birdsgrove GU21 .68 B1
Birdswood Dr GU21 .88 E7
Birdwood Cl Selsdon CR2 .81 D8
Teddington TW11 .16 E4
Birdwood Rd GU15 .64 F6
Birdworld & Underwater
World GU10 .145 B3
Birkbeck Hill SE21 .22 B7
Birkbeck Pl
Sandhurst GU47 .45 E1
West Norwood SE21 .22 C6
Birkbeck Rd Penge BR3 .43 D7
Wimbledon SW19 .20 B2
Birkbeck Sta SE20 .43 C6
Birkdale RG12 .26 E2
Birkdale Ct SL5 .29 C4

Birkdale Dr RH11 . . . . . . .200 D5
Birkdale Gdns CR0 . . . . .62 D6
Birkenhead Ave KT2 . . . . . . .37 F8
Birkenholme Cl GU35 . . .187 C4
Birkhall Rd SE6 . . . . .24 D6
Birkheads Rd RH2 . . . . . . .118 A2
Birkwood Cl SW12 . . . . .21 D8
Birling House 4 SE20 . . . . .23 C1
Birnham Cl GU23 . . . . .91 A3
Birtley Rd GU5 . . . . .152 B4
Birtley Rise GU5 . . . . .152 A5
Biscoe Cl TW5 . . . . .5 A8
Bisenden Rd CR0 . . . . .61 E8
Bisham Cl Carshalton CR4 . .40 F1
 Crawley RH10 . . . . .202 D3
Bishams Ct CR3 . . . . .100 F3
Bishop Bell Sch RH10 . . .201 F3
Bishop Challoner Sch
 BR2 .44 D7
Bishop David Brown Sch
 GU21 . . . . .70 D6
Bishop Duppa's
 Almshouses 7 TW10 . . . . .6 E2
Bishop Duppas Pk TW17 . .34 E2
Bishop Fox Way KT8 . . . . . .35 F5
Bishop Gilpins Prim Sch
 SW19 . . . . .19 F3
Bishop Perrin (C of E) Sch
 TW2 . . . . .16 B7
Bishop Reindorp CE Sch
 GU1 . . . . .109 C4
Bishop Sumner Dr GU9 .125 C6
Bishop Thomas Grant
 Catholic Sec Sch SW16 . .21 F3
Bishop Wand C of E Sec
 Sch TW16 . . . . .34 F7
Bishop's Cl CR5 . . . . .80 A1
Bishop's Cotts RH3 . . . . . .116 B2
Bishop's Hall KT1 . . . . .37 D7
Bishop's La SL4 . . . . .8 B7
Bishop's Mead GU9 . . . . . .125 B2
Bishop's Pl SM1 . . . . .59 C5
Bishop's Rd CR0 . . . . .42 B2
Bishopdale RG12 . . . . .27 A5
Bishopric RH12 . . . . .217 B2
Bishopric Ct RH12 . . . . . . .217 B2
Bishops Cl SM1 . . . . .59 A7
Bishops Ct 1 Ashford TW16 14 F1
 Guildford GU2 . . . . .130 C7
Bishops Dr
 East Bedfont TW14 . . . . . . .3 D1
 Wokingham RG40 . . . . .25 C7
Bishops Gr Hampton TW12 .15 F4
 Windlesham GU20 . . . . .48 C4
Bishops Hill KT12 . . . . .35 A2
Bishops Park Rd SW16 . . . .41 E8
Bishops Rd GU9 . . . . .125 B2
Bishops Sq SM1 . . . . .174 F3
Bishops Way TW20 . . . . . . .12 D2
Bishops Wlk CR0, CR9 . . . . .62 E5
Bishops Wood GU8 . . . . . . .68 F2
Bishopscourt 6 CR0 . . . . . .61 F8
Bishopsford Rd SM4 . . . . . .40 D3
Bishopsgate Rd SL4, TW20 .11 B5
Bishopsmead Cl
 East Horsley KT24 . . . . . .112 E7
 Epsom KT19 . . . . .57 D1
Bishopsmead Ct KT19 . . . .57 E1
Bishopsmead Dr KT24 . . .112 F6
Bishopsmead Par KT24 . .112 F6
Bishopsthorpe Rd SE26 . . .23 D4
Bishopstone Wlk RH11 . .201 C1
Bisley C of E Prim Sch
 GU24 . . . . .68 A3
Bisley Cl KT4 . . . . .39 C1
Bisley House SW19 . . . . . . .19 D6
Bitmead Cl RH11 . . . . .200 E5
Bittams La KT15, KT16 . . . . .51 E6
Bittern Cl Crawley RH11 . .200 D5
 Sandhurst GU47 . . . . .64 D8
Bitterne Dr GU21 . . . . .69 A2
Bittoms The KT1 . . . . .37 D6
Black Dog Wlk RH10 . . . . .201 E8
Black Horse Way RH12 . . .217 C2
Black Lake Cl TW20 . . . . . . .32 A8
Black Pond La GU10 . . . . .146 C6
Black Prince Cl KT14 . . . . .71 F5
Blackberry Cl
 Guildford GU1 . . . . .109 B4
 Upper Halliford TW17 . . . . .34 E5
Blackberry Farm Cl TW5 . .4 E7
Blackberry La RH7 . . . . . . .185 E8
Blackberry Rd RH19, RH7 .185 D8
Blackbird Cl GU47 . . . . .64 D8
Blackborough Cl RH2 . . . .118 C1
Blackborough Rd RH2 . . .118 D1
Blackbridge Ct RH12 . . . . .217 B2
Blackbridge La RH12 . . . .217 A1
Blackbridge Rd GU22 . . . . .89 D7
Blackbrook Rd
 Dorking RH5 . . . . .136 E2
 South Holmwood RH5 . . . .157 E8
Blackburn The KT23 . . . . . .93 F3
Blackburn Trad Est SW19 . .2 F1
Blackburn Way GU7 . . . . . .151 A5
Blackbush Cl SM2 . . . . .59 B3
Blackcap Cl RH11 . . . . .201 C4
Blackcap Pl GU47 . . . . .64 E8
Blackdown Ave GU22 . . . . .70 E4
Blackdown Cl GU22 . . . . . . .70 D3
Blackdown Prim Sch
 GU16 . . . . .86 B8
Blackdown Rd GU16 . . . . . .86 C8
Blackett Cl TW18, TW20 . . . .32 F7
Blackett Rd RH10 . . . . .202 C5
Blackfold Rd RH10 . . . . . .202 A5
Blackford Cl CR2 . . . . .61 B2

Blackham House SW19 . . .19 E2
Blackheath RH10 . . . . .202 D8
Blackheath Gr GU5 . . . . . .152 B8
Blackheath La Albury GU5 152 B3
 Wonersh GU5 . . . . .152 C8
Blackheath Rd GU9 . . . . . .125 A7
Blackhills GU35 . . . . .187 C4
Blackhorse La Croydon CR0 43 A2
 Lower Kingswood
 KT20, RH2 . . . . .118 C7
Blackhorse Rd GU21, GU22 88 E6
Blacklands Cres RH18 . . .206 F3
Blacklands Meadow RH1 119 E2
Blacklands Rd SE6 . . . . .24 C4
Blackman Gdns GU11 . . . .126 B8
Blackman's La CR6 . . . . . . .82 F5
Blackmeadows RG12 . . . . .27 C3
Blackmoor Cl SL5 . . . . .28 D7
Blackmore Cres GU21 . . . . .70 C5
Blackmore House SE23 . . .23 F7
Blackmore's Gr TW11 . . . . .17 A2
Blackness La GU22 . . . . .89 E8
Blacknest Cotts GU8 . . . . .192 C3
Blacknest Gate Rd SL5 . . . .30 B6
Blacknest Rd GU25, SL5 . . .30 E6
Blackshaw Rd SW17 . . . . . .20 D3
Blacksmith Cl KT21 . . . . . . .95 F8
Blacksmith La GU4 . . . . . .131 D3
Blacksmith's La TW18 . . . . .33 C6
Blacksmiths Hill CR2 . . . . .81 B6
Blacksmiths La KT16 . . . . . .33 A2
Blackstone Cl
 Farnborough GU14 . . . . . . .84 D6
 Reigate RH1 . . . . .139 E8
Blackstone Hill RH1, RH2 .118 E1
Blackstone House SE21 . . .22 E5
Blackstroud La
 E GU18, GU24 . . . . .67 D8
Blackstroud La W GU18 . . .67 D8
Blackthorn Cl
 Crawley RH11 . . . . .181 C1
 Horsham RH13 . . . . .218 A2
 Reigate RH2 . . . . .139 C7
Blackthorn Cres GU14 . . . .84 F8
Blackthorn Dr GU18 . . . . . .67 B7
Blackthorn Rd
 Biggin Hill TN16 . . . . .83 E3
 Reigate RH2 . . . . .139 C7
Blackthorne Ave CR0 . . . . .43 C1
Blackthorne Cres SL3 . . . . .1 E5
Blackthorne Ind Pk SL3 . . .1 F5
Blackthorne Rd
 Great Bookham KT23 . . . . .94 C1
 Poyle SL3 . . . . .1 E4
Blackwater La RH10 . . . . .202 D6
Blackwater Sta GU17 . . . . .64 E4
Blackwater Way GU14 . . .126 D8
Blackwell Ave
 GU2 . . . . .108 D1
Blackwell Cty Prim Sch
 RH19 . . . . .185 E3
Blackwell Farm Rd RH19 185 F3
Blackwell Hollow RH19 . .185 F3
Blackwell Rd RH19 . . . . . .185 F2
Blackwood Cl KT14 . . . . . . .71 C7
Bladen Cl KT13 . . . . .53 E4
Blades Cl KT22 . . . . .95 D7
Bladon Cl GU1 . . . . .110 A2
Bladon Ct Beckenham BR2 .44 E7
 Streatham SW16 . . . . .21 E2
Blagdon Rd KT3 . . . . .38 F5
Blagdon Wlk TW11 . . . . . . .17 C2
Blair Ave KT10 . . . . .55 C8
Blair Ct Beckenham BR3 . . .44 B8
 Catford SE6 . . . . .24 F7
Blairderry Rd SW2 . . . . . . .21 E6
Blaise Cl GU14 . . . . .85 D3
Blake Cl Carshalton SM5 . . .40 E1
 Crawley RH10 . . . . .201 F2
 Crowthorne RG45 . . . . .45 C4
 Wokingham RG40 . . . . .25 E8
Blake House BR3 . . . . .24 B2
Blake Rd Croydon CR0 . . . . .61 E8
 Mitcham CR4 . . . . .40 E6
Blake's Gn BR4 . . . . .44 C1
Blake's La
 East Clandon GU4 . . . . . . .111 F3
 West Horsley GU4 . . . . . . .111 F3
Blakeden Dr KT10 . . . . .55 F4
Blakehall Rd SM5 . . . . .59 F4
Blakemore Rd
 Streatham SW16 . . . . .21 E5
 Thornton Heath CR7 . . . . . .41 F4
Blakeney Ave BR3 . . . . .43 F8
Blakeney Cl KT19 . . . . .76 D8
Blakeney Rd BR3 . . . . .43 F8
Blakes Ave KT3 . . . . .38 F3
Blakes La KT3 . . . . .38 F4
Blakes Terr KT3 . . . . .39 A4
Blakewood Cl TW13 . . . . . .15 C4
Blakewood Cl SE20 . . . . . . .23 B1
Blanchards Hill GU4 . . . . .109 E8
Blanchland Rd SM4 . . . . . .40 B4
Blanchman's Rd CR6 . . . . .81 E1
Blandfield Rd SW12 . . . . . .21 A8
Blandford Ave Penge BR3 . .43 E7
 Twickenham TW2 . . . . .16 B7
Blandford Cl
 Wallington CR0 . . . . .60 E7
 Woking GU22 . . . . .70 B2
Blandford Rd Penge BR3 . . .43 E7
 Teddington TW11 . . . . .16 E3
Blane's La SL5 . . . . .28 C3

Blanford Rd RH2 . . . . .139 C8
Blanks La
 Charlwood RH5, RH6 . . . .159 B2
 Cudworth RH5, RH6 . . . . .159 B2
Blashford St SE13 . . . . .24 D8
Blatchford Cl RH13 . . . . . .217 F3
Blatchford Ct KT12 . . . . . . .35 A1
Blatchford Rd RH13 . . . . . .217 F3
Blay's La TW20 . . . . .11 B2
Blean Gr SE20 . . . . .23 C1
Blegborough Rd SW16 . . . .21 C2
Blencarn Cl GU21 . . . . .68 F3
Blendworth
 Point 4 SW15 . . . . .19 B7
Blenheim 26 SW19 . . . . . . .19 D7
Blenheim Bsns Ctr CR4 . . .40 F7
Blenheim Cl
 Crawley RH10 . . . . .182 D1
 East Grinstead RH19 . . . . .186 A3
 Tongham GU10 . . . . .126 E3
 Wallington SM6 . . . . .60 C3
 West Barnes SW20 . . . . . . .39 C6
 West Byfleet KT14 . . . . . . .70 F6
Blenheim Cres Hale GU9 .125 A5
 South Croydon CR2 . . . . . . .61 C3
Blenheim Ct Egham TW18 . .12 C4
 Farnborough GU14 . . . . . . .85 D2
 Richmond TW9 . . . . .6 F4
 South Norwood SE19 . . . . .42 E8
 Sutton SM2 . . . . .59 C4
Blenheim Fields RH18 . . .206 E3
Blenheim Gdns
 Kingston u T KT2 . . . . .18 B1
 Sanderstead CR2 . . . . .81 A7
 Wallington SM6 . . . . .60 C3
 Woking GU22 . . . . .89 B8
Blenheim High Sch KT19 .57 D1
Blenheim House TW3 . . . . .5 A4
Blenheim Park Rd CR2 . . . .61 C2
Blenheim Pk GU11 . . . . . .105 C5
Blenheim Rd Epsom KT19 . .76 E8
 Farnborough GU14 . . . . . .217 D4
 Horsham RH12 . . . . .217 D4
 Penge SE20 . . . . .23 C1
 Sutton SM1 . . . . .59 B7
 West Barnes SW20 . . . . . . .39 C6
Blenheim Way TW7 . . . . . . .6 A6
Bleriot Rd TW5 . . . . .4 C7
Bletchingley Cl RH1 . . . . .119 C6
Bletchingley Golf Course
 RH1 . . . . .120 E3
Bletchingley Rd
 Bletchingley RH1, RH9 . . .121 B4
 Godstone RH1, RH9 . . . . . .121 B4
 Merstham RH1 . . . . .119 E6
 Nutfield RH1 . . . . .120 A2
 Nutfield, South
 Merstham RH1 . . . . .119 E6
Bletchingley Ct CR7 . . . . . .42 B5
Bletchmore Cl UB3 . . . . .3 D8
Blewburton Wlk RG12 . . . .27 E5
Blewfield GU7 . . . . .150 F2
Bligh Cl RH10 . . . . .201 F4
Bligh House 4 SE27 . . . . . .22 C4
Blighton La GU10 . . . . .126 E3
Blincoe Cl SW19 . . . . .19 D6
Blind Cnr SE25 . . . . .43 B5
Blindley Ct RH7 . . . . .163 E8
Blindley Rd RH10 . . . . .182 D1
Bloggs Way GU6 . . . . .174 D3
Blomfield Dale RG42 . . . . .26 D7
Blondell Ct UB7 . . . . .2 D8
Bloom Gr SE27 . . . . .22 B5
Bloomfield Cl GU21 . . . . . .68 E1
Bloomfield Rd KT1 . . . . . . .37 E6
Bloomhall Rd SE19 . . . . . . .22 D3
Bloomsbury Cl KT19 . . . . . .57 E1
Bloomsbury Ct Cranford TW5 4 B6
 Guildford GU1 . . . . .130 F7
Bloomsbury Way SW17 . . .64 D3
Bloor Cl RH12 . . . . .217 D7
Blossom Cl CR2 . . . . .61 F5
Blossom Waye TW5 . . . . . . .4 C1
Blount Ave RH19 . . . . .185 C1
Bloxham Cres TW12 . . . . . .35 F8
Bloxham Rd GU6 . . . . .175 A3
Bloxworth Cl
 9 Bracknell RG12 . . . . .27 F5
 Wallington SM6 . . . . .60 C7
Blue Anchor Alley 3 TW9 . .6 E3
Blue Ball La TW20 . . . . .11 F3
Blue Barn Way KT13 . . . . . .72 A8
Blue Cedars SM7 . . . . .77 D5
Blue Cedars Pl KT11 . . . . . .73 D7
Blue Coat Wlk RG12 . . . . . .27 D4
Blue Sch The TW7 . . . . .6 A4
Bluebell Cl Crawley RH11 .201 B3
 East Grinstead RH19 . . . . .185 B1
 Forest Hill SE19, SE26 . . . .22 F4
 Horsham RH12 . . . . .217 E5
 Wallington CR4 . . . . .41 B1
Bluebell Hill RG12 . . . . . . .27 E8
Bluebell Rise GU18 . . . . . . .67 B8
Blueberry Gdns CR5 . . . . . .79 F3
Bluefield Cl TW12 . . . . .16 A3
Bluegates Stoneleigh KT17 .58 A3
 Wimbledon SW19 . . . . .19 E3
Bluehouse Gdns RH8 . . . .123 A7
Bluehouse La RH8 . . . . . . .122 F7
Bluethroat GU47 . . . . .64 E8
Bluff Cove GU11 . . . . .105 C3
Blundel La Oxshott KT11 . . .74 B4
 Stoke D'Abernon KT11 . . . . .74 B4
Blundell Ave RH6 . . . . .160 F4
Blunden Rd GU14 . . . . .84 F5
Blunt Rd CR0 . . . . .61 D5

Blunts Ave UB7 . . . . .3 A7
Blunts Way RH12 . . . . .217 C3
Blyth Cl TW1 . . . . .5 E1
Blyth Rd BR1, BR2 . . . . .44 F8
Blythe Cl SE23 . . . . .23 F8
Blythe Hill SE23, SE6 . . . . .23 F8
Blythe Hill La SE23, SE6 . .23 F7
Blythe Vale SE23, SE6 . . . .23 F7
Blythwood Cl SL5 . . . . .28 E2
Blythwood Dr GU16 . . . . . .65 D2
Blythwood Pk BR1 . . . . . . .44 F8
Blytons The RH19 . . . . . . .185 B1
Boar Hill RH5 . . . . .135 L1
Board School Rd GU21 . . . .69 F3
Bocketts Farm Pk KT22 . . . .94 F2
Bockhampton Rd KT2 . . . . .17 F1
Boddicott Cl SW19 . . . . . . .19 E6
Bodens Ride SL5 . . . . .28 F1
Bodiam Cl RH10 . . . . .202 C6
Bodiam Rd SW16 . . . . .21 C1
Bodley Cl KT3 . . . . .38 E4
Bodley Manor Way SE24 . .22 A8
Bodley Rd KT3 . . . . .38 E4
Bodmin Gr SM4 . . . . .40 B4
Bodmin St SW18 . . . . .20 A7
Bodnant Gdns SW20 . . . . . .39 B6
Bog La RG12 . . . . .28 A5
Bognor Rd
 Beare Green RH5 . . . . .157 B2
 Ockley RH5 . . . . .157 B2
 Warnham RH12, RH5 . . . . .197 D4
Bois Hall Rd KT15 . . . . .52 D5
Bolderwood Way BR4 . . . . .63 B8
Bolding House La GU24 . . .67 F7
Boleyn Ave KT17 . . . . .58 B1
Boleyn Cl Crawley RH10 . .202 D3
 Staines TW18 . . . . .12 E3
Boleyn Ct East Molesey KT8 .36 D5
 11 Redhill RH1 . . . . .119 A2
Boleyn Dr KT8 . . . . .35 F5
Boleyn Gdns BR4 . . . . .63 B8
Boleyn Wlk KT22 . . . . .94 F7
Bolingbroke Gr SW11 . . . . .20 F8
Bolingbroke House BR3 . . .24 B8
Bolney Ct Crawley RH11 . .200 F3
 Kingston u T KT6 . . . . .37 C4
Bolsover Gr RH1 . . . . .119 C6
Bolstead Rd CR4 . . . . .41 B8
Bolters La SM7 . . . . .78 A4
Bolters Rd RH6 . . . . .161 A5
Bolters Rd S RH6 . . . . .160 F5
Bolton Cl Chessington KT9 .56 E4
 Penge SE20 . . . . .43 A7
Bolton Gdns Bromley BR1 . .24 F2
 Teddington TW11 . . . . .17 A2
Bolton Rd Chessington KT9 .56 E4
 Chiswick W4 . . . . .7 C7
 Crawley RH10 . . . . .202 C2
Bolton's La
 Harlington TW6, UB7 . . . . . .3 C7
 Pyrford GU22 . . . . .71 A3
Boltons Cl GU22 . . . . .71 A3
Bomer Cl UB7 . . . . .3 A7
Bonchurch Cl SM2 . . . . . . .59 B3
Bond Fst Sch CR4 . . . . .40 F7
Bond Gdns SM6 . . . . .60 C6
Bond Rd Mitcham CR4 . . . . .40 E7
 Surbiton KT6 . . . . .56 F8
 Warlingham CR6 . . . . .81 E1
Bond St TW20 . . . . .11 C3
Bond's La RH5 . . . . .136 B1
Bone Mill La RH9 . . . . .121 E1
Bonehurst Rd RH1, RH6 . .161 A7
Bones La RH6, RH7 . . . . . .163 B2
Bonner Hill Rd KT1 . . . . . . .38 A6
Bonners Ct GU22 . . . . .89 F5
Bonnetts La RH11, RH6 . . .181 A3
Bonnys Rd RH2 . . . . .138 D8
Bonser Rd TW1 . . . . .16 F6
Bonsey Cl GU22 . . . . .89 E6
Bonsey La GU22 . . . . .89 E6
Bonsey's La GU24, KT16 . . .50 C2
Bonsor Dr KT20 . . . . .97 E5
Bonus Pastor RC Sch BR1 24 E4
Bonville Rd BR1 . . . . .24 F3
Bookham Ct
 Little Bookham KT23 . . . . . .93 F4
 Mitcham CR4 . . . . .40 D6
Bookham Gr KT23 . . . . .94 B1
Bookham Ind Pk KT23 . . . .93 F4
Bookham Rd KT11 . . . . .93 D7
Bookham Sta KT23 . . . . . . .93 F4
Bookhurst Hill GU6 . . . . . .175 A4
Bookhurst Rd GU6 . . . . . .175 A4
Booth Dr TW18 . . . . .13 C2
Booth House 2 SW2 . . . . .22 A8
Booth Rd Crawley RH11 . .200 E3
 Croydon CR0, CR9 . . . . .61 B8
Boothby House 3 SW16 . .21 C3
Boothroyd House TW7 . . . . .5 F4
Borage Cl RH11 . . . . .201 A3
Border Chase RH10 . . . . .183 A2
Border Cres SE26 . . . . .23 B3
Border End GU27 . . . . .207 D6
Border Gate CR4 . . . . .40 F8
Border Gdns CR0 . . . . .63 B6
Border Rd Forest Hill SE26 .23 B3
 Haslemere GU27 . . . . .207 D6
Bordesley Rd SM4 . . . . . . .40 B5
Bordon Wlk 6 SW15 . . . . .19 A8
Boreen The GU35 . . . . .187 B5
Borelli Mews GU9 . . . . . . .125 C2
Borelli Yd GU9 . . . . .125 C2
Borers Arms Rd RH10 . . .183 C3
Borers Yard Ind Est
 RH10 . . . . .183 D2
Borland Rd TW11 . . . . .17 B1

Borough Grange CR2 . . . . .81 A7
Borough Hill CR0, CR9 . . . .61 B7
Borough Rd
 Farncombe GU7 . . . . .150 D5
 Godalming GU7 . . . . .150 D5
 Hounslow TW7 . . . . .5 F6
 7 Kingston u T KT2 . . . . . .18 A1
 Mitcham CR4 . . . . .40 E7
 Tatsfield TN16 . . . . .103 D6
Borough The
 Brockham RH3 . . . . .137 A8
 Farnham GU9 . . . . .125 B2
Borrowdale Cl
 Crawley RH11 . . . . .201 B4
 Sanderstead CR2 . . . . .80 F6
 Thorpe Lea TW20 . . . . .12 B1
Borrowdale Dr CR2 . . . . . . .80 F7
Borrowdale Gdns GU15 . . .66 D4
Bosbury Rd SE6 . . . . .24 C5
Boscombe Cl TW20 . . . . . . .32 B6
Boscombe Gdns SW16 . . . .21 E2
Boscombe House CR0 . . . .42 D1
Boscombe Rd
 Merton SW19 . . . . .40 B8
 Mitcham SW17 . . . . .21 A2
 North Cheam KT4 . . . . .39 D1
Bosham Rd RH10 . . . . .202 C3
Boshers Gdns TW20 . . . . . .11 F2
Bosman Dr GU20 . . . . .48 B6
Bostock House TW5 . . . . . . .5 A8
Boston Ct
 South Norwood SE25 . . . . .42 F5
 Sutton SM2 . . . . .59 C3
Boston Gdns W4 . . . . .7 E8
Boston Manor Rd TW8 . . . .6 C8
Boston Rd CR0 . . . . .42 A3
Boswell House 5 SW16 . . .21 C3
Boswell Rd Crawley RH10 .201 E3
 Thornton Heath CR7 . . . . . .42 C5
Boswood Ct TW4 . . . . .4 F4
Botany Hill GU10 . . . . .126 D1
Botery's Cross RH1 . . . . . .120 B2
Bothwell Rd CR0 . . . . .63 C1
Botsford Rd SW20 . . . . .39 E2
Boucher Cl TW11 . . . . .16 F3
Boughton Ave BR2 . . . . . . .44 F2
Boughton Hall Ave GU23 . .90 F3
Bouldish Farm Rd SL5 . . . .29 A5
Boulevard The
 Crawley RH10, RH11 . . . . .201 E6
 4 Upper Tooting SW17 . . .21 A6
Boullen Ct SM1 . . . . .59 C6
Boulogne Rd CR0 . . . . .42 C3
Boulters House RG12 . . . . .27 E5
Boulters
 Rd 2 GU11, GU12 . . . . . . .105 B2
Boulthurst Way RH8 . . . . .123 B3
Boundaries Mansions 4
 SW12 . . . . .21 A7
Boundaries Rd
 Balham SW12 . . . . .21 A7
 Feltham TW13 . . . . .15 C7
 Upper Tooting SW12, SW17 .21 A7
Boundary Bsns Ct CR4 . . . .40 D6
Boundary Bsns Ctr GU21 . .70 A4
Boundary Cl
 Crawley RH11 . . . . .201 E7
 Kingston u T KT1 . . . . .38 B6
 Penge SE20 . . . . .43 A7
Boundary Cotts GU4 . . . . .132 A4
Boundary House TW1 . . . . .6 B2
Boundary Rd
 Binstead GU10 . . . . .145 E2
 Crawley RH11 . . . . .201 E7
 Dockenfield GU10 . . . . . . .166 D2
 Farnborough GU14 . . . . . . .85 C2
 Frensham GU10 . . . . .145 E2
 Grayshott GU26 . . . . .188 D3
 Mitcham SW19 . . . . .20 D2
 Staines TW15 . . . . .13 C3
 Wallington SM5, SM6 . . . . .60 A3
 Woking GU21 . . . . .70 A4
Boundary Rd E KT15 . . . . . .52 B2
Boundary Rd N KT15 . . . . .52 B2
Boundary Rd W KT15 . . . . .52 B2
Boundary Way
 Addington CR0 . . . . .63 A5
 Woking GU21 . . . . .70 A4
Boundfield Rd SE6 . . . . . . .24 E6
Boundstone Cl GU10 . . . . .146 B5
Boundstone Rd GU10 . . . .146 A4
Bourbon House SE6 . . . . . .24 C4
Bourdon Rd SE20 . . . . .43 C7
Bourg-de-Peage Ave
 RH19 . . . . .186 A1
Bourke Hill CR5 . . . . .78 F1
Bourley La GU10 . . . . .104 A2
Bourley Rd
 Aldershot GU11 . . . . .104 C2
 Crondall GU10 . . . . .104 C2
Bourne Ave KT16 . . . . .33 A6
Bourne Cl Chilworth GU4 .131 B3
 West Byfleet KT14 . . . . . . .71 B6
Bourne Ct Aldershot GU11 126 A8
 Chiswick W4 . . . . .7 C8
 1 Purley CR8 . . . . .80 A8
Bourne Cty Inf Sch The
 GU10 . . . . .146 D6
Bourne Dene GU10 . . . . . .146 A5
Bourne Dr CR4 . . . . .40 D7
Bourne Firs GU10 . . . . . . .146 D5
Bourne Gr Ashstead KT21 . .95 D8
 Farnham GU10 . . . . .146 E7
Bourne Grove Cl GU10 . . .146 E7

Bourne Grove Dr GU10 ..146 E7
Bourne Hall Mus KT17 ...57 F2
Bourne House TW15 ......14 A3
Bourne Mill Ind Est GU9 .125 E3
Bourne Mill Rdbt
  GU10, GU9 ....125 E3
Bourne Park Cl CR8 .....80 E3
Bourne Rd Farncombe GU7 150 F7
  Merstham RH1 ....119 C5
  Wentworth GU25 ....31 D4
  Woodham KT15 ....52 B2
Bourne St CR0, CR9 ......61 B8
Bourne Vale RH4 ....44 F1
Bourne View CR8 ....80 E3
Bourne Way
  Addlestone KT15 ....52 C5
  Cheam SM1 ....58 F5
  Coney Hall BR2, BR4 ...63 F8
  West Ewell KT19 ....57 C6
  Woking GU22 ....89 D5
Bournefield Rd CR3 ......81 A1
Bournemouth Rd SW19 ...40 A8
Bourneside GU25 ....31 A2
Bourneside Gdns SE6 ....24 C3
Bourneside Rd KT15 .....52 D5
Bournevale Rd SW16 ....21 E4
Bourns Ct RH13 ....217 E3
Bournville Rd SE13, SE6 ..24 A8
Bousley Rise KT16 ....51 D4
Bouverie Gdns CR8 ......79 F5
Bouverie Rd CR5 ....79 A1
Boveney Rd SE23 ....23 D8
Boveney House RG12 .....27 C5
Bovey House 3 RH1 ....119 A3
Bovill Rd SE23 ....23 D8
Bovingdon Sq CR4 ....41 E5
Bowater Rd RH10 ....202 C3
Bowater Ridge KT13 .....53 D1
Bowden Cl TW14 ....14 E7
Bowden Rd SL5 ....29 D4
Bowen Dr SE19, SE21 ....22 E5
Bower Ct GU22 ....70 B3
Bower Hill Cl RH1 ......140 E6
Bower Hill La RH1 .....140 D7
Bower Rd GU10 ....146 A5
Bowerland La RH7 ......164 E7
Bowers Cl GU4 ....110 B5
Bowers Farm Dr GU4 ...110 B5
Bowers La GU4 ....110 A6
Bowers Pl RH10 ....204 B8
Bowes Cl RH13 ....217 E3
Bowes Rd Egham TW18 ...12 E2
  Walton-on-T KT12 ......54 B8
Bowie Cl SW4 ....21 D8
Bowland Dr RG12 ....27 E2
Bowley Cl SE19 ....22 F2
Bowley La SE19 ....22 F3
Bowlhead Green Rd GU8 170 B1
Bowling Green Cl SW19 ..19 B8
Bowling Green Ct GU16 ..85 E7
Bowling Green La RH12 .217 D3
Bowling Green Rd GU24 ..49 E2
Bowlings The GU15 ......65 C6
Bowman Ct RH10 ....201 D7
Bowman Mews SW18 .....19 F7
Bowman's Meadow SM6 ..60 B7
Bowmans Lea SE23 ......23 C8
Bowness 7 RH11 ......200 D5
Bowness Cres KT2, SW15 .18 E3
Bowness Dr TW4 ....4 E3
Bowness Rd SE6 ....24 B8
Bowring House GU7 .....150 F6
Bowsley Ct TW13 ....15 A6
Bowsprit The KT11 ......73 C4
Bowyer Cres RG40 ....25 C8
Bowyers Cl KT21 ....75 F1
Box Cl RH11 ....201 C1
Box Hill Ctry Pk RH4 ..115 D4
Box Hill Sch RH5 ......115 B8
Box La RH19 ....206 E6
Box Ridge Ave CR8 ......79 F7
Boxall Rd SE21 ....22 E8
Boxall Wlk RH13 ....217 D1
Boxall's Gr GU11 ......126 A8
Boxall's La GU11 ......126 B7
Boxford Cl CR2 ....81 D7
Boxford Ridge RG12 .....27 B6
Boxgrove Ave GU1 ......110 A3
Boxgrove Cty Prim Sch
  GU1 ....110 B2
Boxgrove La GU1 ....110 B2
Boxgrove Rd GU1 ......110 A2
Boxhill Rd RH4 ....115 E3
Boxhill Way RH3 ....137 B5
Boxhill & Westhumble Sta
  RH5 ....115 B4
Boxley Rd SM4, SW19 ....40 C5
Boxwood Way CR6 ....81 D2
Boyce House SW16 ....21 C3
Boyd Ct SL5 ....18 A1
Boyd Ct RG42 ....27 A8
Boyd Rd SW19 ....20 D2
Boyland Rd BR1 ....24 F3
Boyle Farm Rd KT7 ......37 A3
Brabazon Ave SM6 ....60 E3
Brabazon Rd TW5 ....4 D7
Braboeuf Manor (Coll of
  Law) GU2 ....130 C5
Brabon Rd GU2 ....109 F2
Brabourne Cl 7 SE19 ...22 E3
Brabourne Rise BR3 .....44 D4

Brabrook Ct SM6 ....60 B5
Bracebridge GU15 ....65 A5
Bracewood Gdns CR0 ....61 F7
Bracken Ave Balham SW12 .21 A8
  West Wickham CR0 ......63 B7
Bracken Bank SL5 ....28 C8
Bracken Cl Ashford TW16 .14 F2
  Copthorne RH10 ....183 B2
  Crawley RH10 ....201 E8
  Little Bookham KT23 ...93 F3
  Twickenham TW4 ....16 A8
  Wonersh GU5 ....152 B6
Bracken End TW7 ....5 D2
Bracken Gr RH11 ....218 B5
Bracken Hill Cl BR1 .....44 F8
Bracken Hill La BR1 .....44 F8
Bracken Path KT18 ......76 B6
Bracken Way
  Chobham GU24 ....49 F1
  Guildford GU3 ....108 D4
Brackendale GU1 ....38 B7
Brackendale Cl
  Frimley GU15 ....65 E3
  Hounslow TW5 ....5 B6
Brackendale Cl 2 BR3 ..24 A1
Brackendale Rd GU15 ....65 D4
Brackendene GU12 ......106 C3
Brackendene Cl GU21 ....70 A4
Brackenhale Comp Sch
  RG12 ....27 B5
Brackenhill KT11 ....74 B7
Brackenlea GU7 ....150 D7
Brackens BR3 ....24 A1
Brackens The RG45 ......45 A7
Brackenside RH6 ....161 B4
Brackenwood
  Frimley GU15 ....66 D5
  Sunbury TW16 ....35 A8
Brackenwood Rd GU21 ...88 D8
Bracklesham Cl GU14 ....85 A7
Brackley KT13 ....53 D5
Brackley Cl SM6 ....60 E3
Brackley Rd BR3 ....24 A1
Brackley Way
  Blackwater GU17 ....84 A5
  Farnborough GU14 .....84 C6
Bracklyn Ct N1 ....84 C6
Brackman Gdns KT9 .....56 B6
Bramall Gdns KT2 ....18 A1
Bramber Cl Crawley RH10 202 D4
  Horsham RH13 ....218 B5
Bramble Acres Cl SM2 ...59 A3
Bramble Bank GU16 .....86 A6

Bramble Banks SM5 .....60 A2
Bramble Cl
  Copthorne RH10 ....183 B3
  Croydon CR0 ....63 B6
  Guildford GU3 ....108 A7
  Redhill RH1 ....140 A7
  Upper Halliford TW17 ..34 D6
Bramble Hedge Farm
  (Ind Est) KT11 ....72 C5
Bramble La TW12 ....15 F2
Bramble Rise KT11 ......73 C5
Bramble Twitten RH19 ..186 A1
Bramble Wlk GU23 ....90 F3
Bramble Wlk KT18 ......76 B6
Brambledene Cl GU21 ....69 C1
Brambledown TW18 ......33 B8
Brambledown Cl BR2, BR4 44 E4
Brambledown Rd
  South Croydon CR2 .....61 E3
  Wallington SM6, SM6 ...60 B3
Bramblegate RG45 ....45 A6
Brambles Cl Ash GU12 ..106 B1
  Brentford TW7, TW8 .....6 B7
  Caterham CR3 ....100 E5
Brambles Pk GU5 ......151 F6
Brambles The
  Farncombe GU7 ....150 D7
  8 Wimbledon SW19 ....19 F3
Brambleton Ave GU9 .....146 B7
Brambletye Cty Jun Sch
  RH1 ....140 A7
Brambletye La RH18 ...206 D4
Brambletye Park Rd RH1 140 A7
Brambletye Rd RH10 ...202 A5
Brambletye Sch RH19 ..206 C5
Bramblewood RH2 ......119 B6
Bramblewood Cl SM5 ....40 E1
Brambling Cl RH13 ....218 A1
Brambling Rd RH13 ....218 A1
Bramcote GU15 ....66 C5
Bramcote Ave CR4 ......40 F5
Bramcote Ct CR4 ....40 F5
Bramerton Rd BR3 ......43 F6
Bramham Gdns KT9 ......56 B6
Bramley Ave Coulsdon CR5 .79 C4
  Sunbury TW17 ....34 E6
Bramley CE Inf Sch GU5 .152 A5
Bramley Cl Chertsey KT16 .33 B1
  Crawley RH10 ....201 F6
  Croydon CR2 ....61 C5
  Staines TW18 ....13 C2
  Twickenham TW2 ....5 C1
Bramley Ct Mitcham CR4 ..40 D7
  Redhill RH1 ....118 E3
  Wallington SM6 ....60 C5
Bramley Hill CR0, CR2 ...61 C6
Bramley Ho TW3 ....4 F3
Bramley House
  1 Kingston u T KT2 ...18 B1
  Redhill RH1 ....140 A8
  Roehampton SW15 ....7 F1
Bramley La GU17 ....64 B5
Bramley Park Ct GU5 ...151 F6
Bramley Rd
  Camberley GU15 ....65 B2
  Carshalton SM1 ....59 D5
  East Ewell SM2 ....58 D2
Bramley Way
  Ashtead KT21 ....75 F2
  Hounslow TW4 ....4 F2
  West Wickham BR4 ......63 B8
Bramley Wlk RH6 ....161 C3
Bramleyhyrst CR2 ....61 C5
Brampton Gdns KT12 ....54 C5
Brampton Rd CR0 ....42 F3
Bramshaw Rise KT3 ......38 E3
Bramshot La
  Blackwater GU17 ....84 A5
  Farnborough GU14 .....84 C6
Bramshott Ct 3 KT6 ....37 E3
Bramston Rd SW17 ......20 C5
Bramswell Rd GU7 .....150 F6
Bramwell Cl TW16 ....35 D7
Bramcaster La CR8 ......80 C8
Brancaster Rd SW16 ....21 E5
Brancker Cl SM6 ....60 E3
Brandon Cl Crawley RH10 202 D4
  Frimley GU15 ....66 D4
Brandon House BR3 .....24 B3
Brandon Rd SM1 ....59 B6
Brandreth Rd SW17 .....21 B6
Brandries The SM6 ......60 D7
Brands Rd SL3 ....1 B8
Brandsland RH2 ....139 B6
Brandy Way SM2 ....59 A3
Brangbourne Rd BR1 ....24 C3
Brangwyn Cres SW19 ....40 D7
Branksome Cl
  Camberley GU15 ....65 E6
  Walton-on-T KT12 ......35 D1
Branksome Hill Rd GU47 .64 E8
Branksome Park Rd GU15 .65 E6
Branksome Rd SW19 .....40 A8
Branksome Way KT3 .....38 D8
Bransby Rd KT9 ....56 E4
Branscombe Ct BR2 .....44 E4
Branstone Ct 9 TW9 .....6 F6
Branstone Rd TW9 ....6 F6
Brantridge Rd RH10 ...201 F4
Brantwood Ave TW7 ......6 A3
Brantwood Cl 1 KT14 ...71 A6
Brantwood Ct KT14 .....70 F6
Brantwood Dr KT14 .....70 F6
Brantwood Gdns KT14 ...71 A6
Brantwood Rd CR2 ......61 D2
Brassey Cl TW14 ....15 A7
Brassey Rd RH8 ....123 A6

Brasted Cl Belmont SM2 ..59 A1
  Forest Hill SE26 ....23 C4
Brasted Lodge 11 BR3 ..24 A1
Brathway Rd SW18 ......20 A8
Bratten Ct CR0 ....42 D3
Bravington Cl TW17 .....33 F4
Braxted Pk SW16 ....21 F2
Bray Cl RH10 ....202 D4
Bray Ct KT9 ....56 F5
Bray Gdns GU22 ....70 E3
Bray Rd Guildford GU2 ..130 B8
  Stoke D'Abernon KT11 ..73 B3
Braybourne Dr TW7 ......5 F7
Braybrooke Gdns SE19 ..22 E1
Braycourt Ave KT12 .....35 C2
Braye Cl GU47 ....45 C1
Braywick Ct 9 KT2 .....18 A1
Braywood Ave TW20 .....12 A2
Braziers La SL4, SL5 .....8 D4
Breakfield CR5 ....79 E3
Breakspeare SE21 ......22 F5
Breamore St SW15 ......19 A7
Breamwater Gdns TW10 .17 B5
Brecon Ct
  Farnborough GU14 .....84 D7
  Mitcham CR4 ....41 E6
  North Cheam KT4 ....58 C8
Brecon House SW18 .....20 A8
Bredhurst Cl SE20 ......23 C2
Bredinghurst SE22 .....23 A8
Bredon Rd CR0 ....42 F2
Bredune CR8 ....80 D4
Breech La KT20 ....97 A2
Breech The RT18, TW19 ..13 A5
Bremans Row SW18 .....20 C6
Bremer Rd TW18, TW19 ..13 A5
Bremner Ave RH6 ......160 F4
Brenchley Cl BR2 ....44 F3
Brenda Rd SW17 ....20 F6
Brende Gdns KT8 ....36 B5
Brendon Cl Esher KT10 ..55 C4
  Harlington UB7 ....3 C7
Brendon Dr KT10 ....55 C4
Brendon House SM2 .....59 C4
Brendon Rd GU14 ....84 D7
Brenley Cl CR4 ....41 A6
Brent House BR1 ....24 D3
Brent Knoll Spec Sch
  SE26 ....23 D5
Brent Lea TW8 ....6 C7
Brent Rd Brentford TW8 ..6 C8
  South Croydon CR2 .....62 B2
Brent Way TW8 ....6 D7
Brentford Bsns Ctr The ..6 C7
Brentford High St TW8 ...6 D8
Brentford House 7 TW4 .17 B8
Brentford Sch for Girls
  TW8 ....6 D8
Brentford Sta TW8 ......6 C8
Brentmoor GU24 ....67 D6
Brentside TW8 ....6 D7
Brentside Executive Ctr
  TW8 ....6 B8
Brentwaters Bsns Pk TW8 .6 C7
Brentwood Ct KT15 .....52 B6
Brereton House 4 SW2 ..22 A8
Breston Cross KT23 .....93 F1
Bret Harte Rd GU16 ....65 E1
Bretherton Ct CR2 .....61 E4
Bretlands Rd KT16 .....51 E8
Brett House 1 SW15 ....19 D8
Brett House Ct 2 SW15 .19 D8
Brettgrave KT19 ....57 C1
Brettingham Ct RH11 ..200 E3
Brew House La RH3 ....137 B5
Brewer Rd RH10 ....201 E4
Brewer St RH1 ....120 C4
Brewers Cl GU14 ....85 A5
Brewers La 11 TW9 ......6 D2
Brewery La KT14 ....71 E6
Brewery Mews Bsns Ctr
  TW7 ....6 A4
Brewery Rd GU21 ....69 E2
Brewhurst La RH14 ....213 A2
Breydon Wlk RH10 ....202 B4
Brian Ave CR2 ....80 E7
Briane Rd KT19 ....57 C1
Briar Ave Lightwater GU18 .67 A8
  South Norwood SW16 ...21 F1
Briar Banks SM5 ....60 A2
Briar Cl Crawley RH11 ..181 C1
  Hampton TW12 ....15 F3
  Isleworth TW7 ....5 F2
  West Byfleet KT14 .....71 C8
Briar Ct Cheam SM3 .....58 C6
  Hampton TW12 ....16 B3
Briar Gdns BR2 ....44 F1
Briar Gr CR2 ....81 A6
Briar Hill CR8 ....79 E8
Briar La Croydon CR0 ...63 B6
  Wallington SM5 ....60 A2
Briar Patch GU7 ......150 D6
Briar Rd Littleton TW17 ..34 A4
  Send GU23 ....90 B4
  Thornton Heath CR0 ....41 F6
  Twickenham TW2 ....16 E7
Briar Way GU4 ....110 B5
Briar Wlk KT14 ....71 A7
Briardale SW19 ....19 F7
Briarleas Ct GU14 .....105 D8
Briars Cl GU14 ....84 D3
Briars Cross RH8 ......123 D5
Briars Ct KT22 ....74 D5
Briars The Ash GU12 ...106 B1
  Stanwell TW19 ....2 A1
Briars Wood RH6 ......161 C4

Briarswood Cl RH10 ...202 D8
Briarwood Ct SE16 .....14 E5
Briarwood Ct 5 KT4 ....39 A1
Briarwood Rd
  Knaphill GU21 ....88 D8
  Stoneleigh KT17 ....58 A4
Briary Lodge BR3 ....44 C8
Briavels Ct KT18 ....76 E4
Brick Farm Cl TW9 ....7 B6
Brick Kiln La RH8 .....123 C6
Brickfield Ct TW9 ......3 D8
Brickfield La UB3 ....3 D8
Brickfield Rd
  Outwood RH1 ....162 C8
  South Norwood CR7, SW16 .42 B8
  Wimbledon SW19 ....20 B5
Brickhouse La RH7, RH9 .163 C4
Bricklands RH10 ......204 B7
Bricksbury Hill GU9 ...125 C7
Brickwood Cl SE26 .....23 B5
Brickwood Rd CR0 ......61 E8
Brickyard Copse RH5 ..177 C4
Brickyard La
  Crawley Down RH10 ...204 B8
  Wotton RH5 ....134 D2
Brideake Cl RH11 .....201 A3
Bridge Barn La GU21 ...69 D1
Bridge Cl Byfleet KT14 ..71 F7
  Lower Halliford KT12 ..34 F1
  Staines TW18 ....12 E4
  Teddington TW11 ....16 F4
  Woking GU21 ....69 C2
Bridge Cotts GU6 .....174 B3
Bridge Ct Cranleigh GU6 .174 B3
  Leatherhead KT22 ......95 A5
  2 Weybridge KT13 ....53 B6
  Woking GU21 ....69 D2
Bridge End GU15 ....65 B4
Bridge Gdns
  East Molesey KT8 ......36 D5
  Littleton TW15 ....14 C1
Bridge La GU25, KT16 ...31 F3
Bridge Mead GU24 ......87 F1
Bridge Mews
  Godalming GU7 ....150 E4
  Tongham GU10 ....126 F7
  Woking GU21 ....69 D2
Bridge Par CR8 ....80 A7
Bridge Pl CR0 ....42 E1
Bridge Rd Aldershot GU11 126 A8
  Ascot SL5 ....29 D4
  Bagshot GU19 ....47 E3
  Beckenham BR3 ....23 F1
  Camberley GU15 ....65 B3
  Chertsey KT16 ....33 B2
  Chessington KT9 ....56 E5
  Cobham KT11 ....73 B4
  Cranleigh GU6 ....174 E3
  East Molesey KT8 ......36 E5
  Epsom KT17 ....76 F7
  Farnborough GU14 .....84 F4
  Farncombe GU7 ....150 E5
  Haslemere GU27 ....208 C7
  Hounslow TW3 ....5 D4
  Isleworth TW3, TW7 .....5 D4
  Penge BR3 ....23 F1
  Rudgwick RH12 ....214 D7
  Sutton SM2 ....59 B4
  Twickenham TW1 ....6 B1
  Wallington SM6 ....60 C5
  Weybridge KT13 ....52 F6
Bridge Row CR0 ....42 D1
Bridge Sq GU9 ....125 C2
Bridge St Colnbrook SL3 ..1 D7
  Godalming GU7 ....150 E4
  Guildford GU1 ....130 C8
  Leatherhead KT22 ......95 A5
  Richmond TW10 ....10 D2
  Staines TW18 ....12 E4
  Walton-on-T KT12 ......34 F2
Bridge View
  Ascot SL5 ....30 B2
  Chipstead CR5 ....98 E8
  Twickenham TW2 ....16 C8
Bridge Way
  Chipstead CR5 ....98 E8
  Twickenham TW2 ....16 C8
Bridge Wks GU4 ....110 C4
Bridge Works GU15 .....65 B3
Bridgefield GU9 ....125 D2
Bridgefield Cl SM7 .....77 C4
Bridgefield Rd SM1, SM2 .59 A4
Bridgeham Cl KT13 .....53 A5
Bridgeham Way RH6 ...162 B2
Bridgehill Cl GU2 .....109 A3
Bridgelands RH10 .....183 A3
Bridgeman Rd TW11 ....17 A2
Bridgemead GU16 ....85 D8
Bridges Ct RH12 ......218 A5
Bridges La CR0 ....60 E6
Bridges Rd SW19 ....20 B1
Bridges Road Mews SW19 20 B2
Bridgetown Cl 5 SE19 ..22 E3
Bridgewater Rd KT13 ...53 D4
Bridgewood Cl SE20 ....23 B1
Bridgewood Rd
  North Cheam KT17, KT4 .58 A6
  Streatham SW16 ....21 D1
Bridgford St SW17, SW18 .20 C6
Bridle Cl Grayshott GU26 .188 A3
  Kingston u T KT1 ......37 D5
  Sunbury TW16 ....35 A6
  West Ewell KT19 ....57 D5
Bridle Ct GU11 ....104 E2
Bridle La
  Oxshott KT11, KT22 ....74 B4
  Twickenham TW1 ....6 B1
Bridle Path CR0 ....60 E7
Bridle Path The KT17 ...58 C1
Bridle Rd Addington CR0 .63 A6
  Croydon CR0 ....63 A7

Bridle Rd *continued*
Epsom KT17 ... 76 F6
Bridle Rd The CR8 ... 60 E1
Bridle Way Crawley RH10 ... 202 D7
Croydon CR0 ... 63 A6
Bridle Way The SM6 ... 60 C5
Bridlepath Way TW14 ... 14 E8
Bridleway Cl KT17 ... 58 C1
Bridlington Cl TN16 ... 103 B8
Bridport Rd CR7 ... 42 B6
Brier Lea KT20 ... 97 F1
Brier Rd KT20 ... 97 B8
Brierley CR0 ... 63 B4
Brierley Cl SE25 ... 43 A5
Brierley Rd SW12 ... 21 C6
Brierly Cl GU2 ... 109 A3
Briggs Cl CR4 ... 41 B8
Bright Hill GU1 ... 130 E7
Brightlands Rd RH2 ... 118 C3
Brightman Rd SW18 ... 20 D7
Brighton Cl KT15 ... 52 C5
Brighton Rd
Addlestone KT15 ... 52 C5
Aldershot GU11, GU12 ... 126 C8
Banstead SM2 ... 78 A7
Burgh Heath KT20, SM2, SM7 ... 77 F3
Coulsdon CR5, CR8 ... 79 D4
Crawley RH11 ... 201 D4
Croydon CR2, CR8 ... 61 C3
Godalming GU7 ... 151 A1
Hooley CR5, RH1 ... 99 B6
Horley RH6 ... 160 F2
Horsham RH13 ... 217 E1
Kingston u T KT6 ... 37 D3
Kingswood KT20 ... 97 E5
Lower Kingswood KT20 ... 117 F8
Purley CR8 ... 80 B8
Redhill RH1 ... 139 F8
Redhill RH1 ... 139 F8
Salfords RH1 ... 140 A2
South Croydon CR2 ... 61 C3
Sutton SM2 ... 59 B2
Brightside Ave TW18 ... 13 C1
Brightwell Cl CR0 ... 42 A1
Brightwell Cres SW17 ... 20 F3
Brightwells Rd GU9 ... 125 C2
Brigstock Rd Coulsdon CR5 ... 79 B3
Thornton Heath CR7 ... 42 B5
Brimshot La GU24 ... 49 E2
Brindle Cl GU11 ... 126 B7
Brindles The SM7 ... 77 F2
Brindley House 22 SW12 ... 21 E8
Brine Ct KT6 ... 37 D4
Brinkley Rd KT4 ... 58 B8
Brinkworth Pl SL4 ... 11 B8
Brinn's La GU17 ... 64 C5
Brinsworth Cl TW2 ... 16 D6
Brisbane Ave SW19 ... 40 B8
Brisbane Cl RH11 ... 181 D1
Briscoe Rd SW19 ... 20 D2
Brisson Cl KT10 ... 54 F4
Bristol Cl Crawley RH10 ... 182 D1
Stanwell TW19 ... 2 E1
Bristol Ct 10 TW19 ... 2 E1
Bristol Rd SM4 ... 40 C4
Bristow Cty Inf Sch GU15 ... 65 B2
Bristow Rd
Camberley GU15 ... 65 B3
Hounslow TW3 ... 5 C4
Wallington CR0 ... 60 E6
West Norwood SE19 ... 22 E3
Britannia Ind Est SL3 ... 1 E5
Britannia Rd KT5 ... 37 F2
Britannia Way TW19 ... 13 D8
British Home & Hospl for Incurables SE27 ... 22 B3
Briton Cl CR2 ... 80 E8
Briton Cres CR2 ... 80 E8
Briton Hill Rd CR2 ... 61 F1
Brittain Ct GU47 ... 64 C7
Brittain Rd KT12 ... 54 D5
Britten Cl Ash GU12 ... 106 B2
Crawley RH11 ... 200 F3
Horsham RH13 ... 218 B4
Brittens Cl GU2, GU3 ... 109 A6
Britton Cl SE6 ... 24 D8
Brixton Hill SW2 ... 21 E8
Brixton Hill Pl SW2 ... 21 E8
Broad Acres GU7 ... 150 E8
Broad Cl KT12 ... 54 E7
Broad Green Ave CR0 ... 42 B2
Broad Ha'penny GU10 ... 146 A5
Broad Highway KT11 ... 73 D5
Broad La Bracknell RG12 ... 27 D6
Hampton TW12 ... 16 A2
Parkgate RH2, RH5 ... 158 E6
Broad Oak TW16 ... 14 F2
Broad Oaks KT6 ... 57 B8
Broad Oaks Way BR2 ... 44 F4
Broad St Guildford GU3 ... 108 D3
Teddington TW11 ... 16 F2
West End GU24 ... 67 D6
Wokingham RG40 ... 25 C6
Wood St V GU3 ... 108 D3
Broad St Wlk RG40 ... 25 C6
Broad Wlk
Burgh Heath KT18 ... 97 D8
Caterham CR3 ... 100 F5
Cranleigh GU6 ... 174 F1
Crawley RH10 ... 201 D6
Frimley GU16 ... 65 E2
Heston TW5 ... 4 E6
Lower Kingswood CR5 ... 99 A4
Richmond TW9 ... 6 F7
Broadacre TW18 ... 13 A3
Broadacres GU3 ... 108 E2
Broadbridge Heath Rd RH12 ... 216 D4
Broadbridge La
Burstow RH6 ... 183 B8
Smallfield RH6 ... 162 A2
Broadbridge Ret Pk RH12 ... 216 E3
Broadcoombe CR2 ... 62 D3
Broadfield Barton 4 RH11 ... 201 B2
Broadfield Cl
Burgh Heath KT20 ... 97 C7
Croydon CR0 ... 60 F8
Broadfield Dr RH11 ... 201 B3
Broadfield East Cty Fst Sch RH11 ... 201 C2
Broadfield East Cty Mid Sch RH11 ... 201 C2
Broadfield North Cty Fst & Mid Sch RH11 ... 201 B2
Broadfield Pl RH11 ... 201 B2
Broadfield Rd Catford SE6 ... 24 E7
Peaslake GU5 ... 154 D8
Broadfields KT8 ... 36 E3
Broadford La GU24 ... 68 E7
Broadford Pk GU4 ... 130 D2
Broadford Rd GU4 ... 130 D2
Broadgates Rd SW18 ... 20 D7
Broadham Green Rd RH8 ... 122 D2
Broadham Pl RH8 ... 122 D4
Broadhurst Ashstead KT21 ... 75 E3
Farnborough GU14 ... 84 C5
Broadhurst Cl 8 TW10 ... 6 F2
Broadhurst Gdns RH2 ... 139 B6
Broadlands
Farnborough GU14 ... 85 E2
Feltham TW13 ... 16 A5
Frimley GU16 ... 85 F8
Horley RH6 ... 161 C4
Broadlands Ave
Shepperton TW17 ... 34 C3
Streatham SW16 ... 21 E6
Broadlands Cl SW16 ... 21 E6
Broadlands Ct
Bracknell RG42 ... 26 E8
Richmond TW9 ... 7 A7
Broadlands Dr
Sunningdale SL5 ... 29 D2
Warlingham CR6 ... 101 C8
Broadlands Mansions 2 SW16 ... 21 E6
Broadlands Way KT3 ... 38 F3
Broadley Gn GU20 ... 48 D4
Broadmead Ashstead KT21 ... 75 F2
Catford SE6 ... 24 A5
Farnborough GU14 ... 84 D3
Horley RH6 ... 161 C4
Merstham RH1 ... 119 C7
Broadmead Ave KT4 ... 39 A2
Broadmead Cl TW12 ... 16 A2
Broadmead Inf Sch CR0 ... 42 D2
Broadmead Jun Sch CR0 ... 42 D3
Broadmead Rd GU22, GU23 ... 90 B5
Broadmeads GU23 ... 90 B5
Broadmere Cty Prim Sch The GU21 ... 70 D6
Broadmoor Cott RH5 ... 156 A8
Broadmoor Cty Prim Sch RG45 ... 45 D4
Broadmoor Hospl RG45 ... 45 E5
Broadoaks Cres KT14 ... 71 B6
Broadview Est TW19 ... 14 A8
Broadview Rd SW16 ... 21 D1
Broadwater Cl
Hersham KT12 ... 54 A5
Sheerwater GU21 ... 70 D7
Wraysbury TW19 ... 11 E8
Broadwater House 1 KT13 ... 53 B7
Broadwater Inf Sch SW17 ... 20 E4
Broadwater Jun Sch SW17 ... 20 E4
Broadwater Rd SW17 ... 20 E4
Broadwater Rd N KT12 ... 54 A5
Broadwater Rd S KT12 ... 54 A5
Broadwater Rise GU1 ... 131 A8
Broadwater Sch GU7 ... 151 A8
Broadway Bracknell RG12 ... 27 C7
Knaphill GU21 ... 68 C1
Staines TW18 ... 13 B2
Tolworth KT6 ... 38 B1
Winkfield SL4 ... 9 B7
Broadway Ave
Thornton Heath CR0 ... 42 D4
Twickenham TW1 ... 6 B1
Broadway Cl CR2 ... 81 B5
Broadway Ct
Beckenham BR3 ... 44 C6
Wimbledon SW19 ... 19 F2
Broadway Gdns CR4 ... 40 E5
Broadway House GU21 ... 68 C1
Broadway Mkt SW17 ... 20 F4
Broadway Rd
Lightwater GU18 ... 48 C2
Windlesham GU18, GU20 ... 48 C2
Broadway The Cheam SM3 ... 58 E4
Crawley RH10 ... 201 D6
Laleham TW18 ... 33 C7
Mortlake SW13 ... 7 E5
Sandhurst GU47 ... 64 B8
Sutton SM1 ... 59 C6
Thames Ditton KT10 ... 36 E1
Tolworth KT6 ... 38 A1
Wallington SM6 ... 60 E6
Wimbledon SW19 ... 19 F2
Woking GU21 ... 69 F2
Woodham KT15 ... 52 A1
Broadwell Ct TW5 ... 4 D6
Broadwell Rd GU10 ... 145 F6
Broadwood Cl RH12 ... 218 A5
Broadwood Cotts RH5 ... 178 E6
Broadwood Rise RH11 ... 201 A2
Brock Rd RH11 ... 181 B1
Brock Way GU25 ... 31 C5
Brock's Cl GU7 ... 151 A5
Brockbridge House SW15 ... 7 F1
Brockenhurst KT8 ... 35 F3
Brockenhurst Ave KT4 ... 38 E1
Brockenhurst Cl GU21 ... 69 F5
Brockenhurst Rd
Aldershot GU11 ... 126 B8
Ascot SL5 ... 29 B3
Bracknell RG12 ... 28 A6
Croydon CR0 ... 43 B2
Brockenhurst Way SW16 ... 41 D7
Brockham Cl SW19 ... 19 F3
Brockham Cres CR0 ... 63 D3
Brockham Ct 6 SM2 ... 59 B3
Brockham Cty Sch RH3 ... 137 B7
Brockham Dr SW2 ... 21 F8
Brockham Hill Pk KT20 ... 116 C4
Brockham House 14 SW2 ... 21 F8
Brockham La RH3, RH4 ... 116 A1
Brockhamhurst Rd RH3 ... 137 B2
Brockholes Cross KT24 ... 113 A6
Brockhurst Cl RH12 ... 216 F1
Brockhurst Cotts GU6 ... 193 F4
Brockhurst Lodge GU9 ... 146 B7
Brocklebank Ct CR6 ... 81 A1
Brocklebank Rd SW18 ... 20 C8
Brocklesby Rd SE25 ... 43 B5
Brockley Combe KT13 ... 53 D6
Brockley Pk SE23 ... 23 E8
Brockley Rise SE23 ... 23 E8
Brockley View SE23 ... 23 E8
Brockman Rise BR1 ... 24 D4
Brocks Dr Cheam SM3 ... 58 E7
Fairlands GU3 ... 108 C5
Brockshot Cl 1 TW8 ... 6 D8
Brockton GU7 ... 150 E5
Brockway Cl GU1 ... 110 B2
Brockwell Park Gdns SE24 ... 22 B8
Brockworth KT2 ... 38 B8
Broderick House SE21 ... 22 E5
Brodie House 7 SM6 ... 60 B6
Brodie Rd GU1 ... 130 E8
Brodrick Gr KT23 ... 94 A1
Brodrick Rd SW17 ... 20 E6
Brograve Gdns BR3 ... 44 B7
Broke Ct GU4 ... 110 C4
Brokes Cres RH2 ... 118 A3
Brokes Rd RH2 ... 118 A3
Bromford Cl RH8 ... 123 A2
Bromleigh Ct SE21, SE22 ... 23 B6
Bromley Ave BR1 ... 24 E1
Bromley Cres BR2 ... 44 F6
Bromley Ct BR1 ... 24 F1
Bromley Gdns BR2 ... 44 F6
Bromley Gr BR2 ... 44 D7
Bromley Hill BR1 ... 24 E2
Bromley Pk BR1 ... 44 F8
Bromley Rd Beckenham BR3 ... 44 B8
Beckenham BR2, BR3 ... 44 D7
Catford SE6, BR1 ... 24 B5
Bromley Road Infs Sch BR3 ... 44 B8
Brompton Cl Hounslow TW4 ... 4 F2
Penge SE20 ... 43 A7
Bromwich House 3 TW10 ... 6 E1
Bronson Rd SW20 ... 39 E7
Bronte Ct 14 RH1 ... 119 A2
Brontes The RH19 ... 185 D1
Brook Ave GU9 ... 125 F7
Brook Cl Ash GU12 ... 106 B3
East Grinstead RH19 ... 186 B1
Epsom KT19 ... 57 E2
Sandhurst GU47 ... 45 E1
Stanwell TW19 ... 13 F8
West Barnes SW20 ... 39 B6
Wokingham RG41 ... 25 A8
Brook Ct Beckenham BR3 ... 43 F8
6 Brentford TW8 ... 6 D8
Cheam SM3 ... 58 C6
Mortlake SW14 ... 7 E4
Brook Dr Ashford TW16 ... 14 E2
Bracknell RG12 ... 27 E5
Brook Farm Rd KT11 ... 73 D4
Brook Gdns Barnes SW13 ... 7 F4
Farnborough GU14 ... 84 F2
Kingston u T KT2 ... 38 C8
Brook Gn Bracknell RG42 ... 26 F8
Chobham GU24 ... 49 F1
Brook Hill
Farley Green GU5 ... 153 D8
Oxted RH8 ... 122 C5
Brook House
Cranleigh GU6 ... 174 F4
Heath End GU9 ... 125 D6
4 Twickenham TW1 ... 17 A8
Brook La Chobham GU24 ... 68 D8
Farley Green GU5 ... 132 E1
Faygate RH12 ... 218 C8
Send GU23 ... 90 E5
Brook La Bns Ctr 4 TW8 ... 6 D8
Brook La N 3 TW8 ... 6 D8
Brook Mead KT19 ... 57 E4
Brook Meadow GU8 ... 191 C3
Brook Rd Bagshot GU19 ... 47 E2
Brook GU8 ... 190 D8
Camberley GU15 ... 65 B4
Chilworth GU4 ... 131 C3
Horsham RH12 ... 217 E6
Merstham RH1 ... 119 C7
Redhill RH1 ... 139 F8
Surbiton KT6 ... 56 E8
Thornton Heath CR7 ... 42 C5
Twickenham TW1 ... 6 A1
Brook Rd *continued*
Wormley GU8 ... 170 E1
Brook Rd S TW8 ... 6 D8
Brook St KT1 ... 37 E7
Brook Trad Est The GU12 ... 105 E2
Brook Valley RH5 ... 136 B1
Brook Way KT22 ... 75 A1
Brookdale Rd Catford SE6 ... 24 B8
2 Lewisham SE6 ... 24 B8
Brooke Ct 7 KT2 ... 17 D4
Brooke Forest GU3 ... 108 C5
Brookehowse Rd SE6 ... 24 B5
Brookers Cl KT21 ... 75 D2
Brookers Cnr RG45 ... 45 C5
Brookers House KT21 ... 75 D2
Brookers Row RG45 ... 45 C6
Brookfield Farncombe GU7 ... 151 A8
Woking GU21 ... 69 B3
Brookfield Ave SM1, SM5 ... 59 E7
Brookfield Cl
Ottershaw KT16 ... 51 D4
Redhill RH1 ... 140 A3
Brookfield Gdns KT10 ... 55 F4
Brookfield Rd GU12 ... 105 F3
Brookfields Ave CR4 ... 40 E4
Brookhill Cl RH10 ... 183 A3
Brookhill Rd RH10 ... 183 A3
Brookhouse Rd GU14 ... 84 F3
Brookhurst Rd KT15 ... 52 B4
Brooklands GU11 ... 104 E1
Brooklands Ave SW18 ... 20 B6
Brooklands Cl
Charlton TW16 ... 34 E8
Cobham KT11 ... 73 E4
Heath End GU9 ... 125 D7
Brooklands Coll KT13 ... 52 F4
Brooklands Ct
Kingston u T KT1 ... 37 D5
Mitcham CR4 ... 40 D7
New Haw KT15 ... 52 D1
Reigate RH2 ... 118 B3
Brooklands Ind Est KT13 ... 52 E1
Brooklands La KT13 ... 52 F4
Brooklands Mus KT13 ... 53 A2
Brooklands Rd
Crawley RH11 ... 201 C1
Heath End GU9 ... 125 E7
Thames Ditton KT7 ... 37 A1
Weybridge KT13 ... 53 B3
Weybridge KT13, KT14 ... 72 A8
Brooklands Sch RH2 ... 118 B3
Brooklands The TW7 ... 5 D6
Brooklands Way
East Grinstead RH19 ... 205 D8
Heath End GU9 ... 125 E7
Redhill RH1 ... 118 E3
Brookley Cl GU10 ... 126 C3
Brookleys GU24 ... 49 F1
Brooklyn SE20 ... 23 A1
Brooklyn Ave SE25 ... 43 B5
Brooklyn Cl Carshalton SM5 ... 59 E8
Woking GU22 ... 89 E8
Brooklyn Ct GU22 ... 89 E8
Brooklyn Gr SE25 ... 43 B5
Brooklyn Rd Croydon SE25 ... 43 B5
Woking GU22 ... 89 E8
Brookmead CR4 ... 41 C3
Brookmead Ct
Cranleigh GU6 ... 174 E2
Farnham GU9 ... 125 B1
Brookmead Rd CR0 ... 41 C3
Brooks Cl KT13 ... 53 A1
Brooks House 6 SW2 ... 22 A7
Brooks La W4 ... 7 A8
Brooks Rd W4 ... 7 A8
Brooksby Cl GU17 ... 64 B5
Brookscroft CR0 ... 62 E1
Brookside
Beare Green RH5 ... 157 F6
Chertsey KT16 ... 32 E2
Colnbrook SL3 ... 1 C7
Copthorne RH10 ... 183 A3
Cranleigh GU6 ... 174 E1
Cranleigh GU6 ... 174 E3
Crawley RH10 ... 201 F7
Guildford GU4 ... 109 D6
Hale GU9 ... 125 D6
Sandhurst GU47 ... 64 C8
South Godstone RH9 ... 142 D5
Wallington SM5 ... 60 A5
Wokingham RG41 ... 25 A7
Brookside Ave TW15 ... 13 D3
Brookside Cl TW13 ... 15 A5
Brookside Cres 1 KT4 ... 39 A1
Brookside Way CR0 ... 43 D3
Brookview RH10 ... 183 A3
Brookview Rd SW16, SW17 ... 21 C3
Brookwell La GU5 ... 152 B2
Brookwood RH6 ... 161 B4
Brookwood Ave SW13 ... 7 F5
Brookwood Cl BR2 ... 44 F5
Brookwood Cty Fst & Mid Sch GU24 ... 88 A7
Brookwood Hospl GU21 ... 68 C1
Brookwood House RH6 ... 161 B6
Brookwood Lye Rd GU21, GU22 ... 88 C7
Brookwood Rd
Farnborough GU14 ... 85 D4
Hounslow TW3 ... 5 B6
Wandsworth SW18 ... 20 A7
Brookwood Sta GU24 ... 88 A6
Broom Acres GU47 ... 45 B1
Broom Bank CR6 ... 102 C8
Broom Cl Blackwater GU17 ... 64 E4
Esher KT10 ... 55 B5
Teddington KT1, TW11 ... 17 D1
Broom Field GU18 ... 67 A7
Broom Gdns CR0 ... 63 A7
Broom Hall KT22 ... 74 D5
Broom La GU24 ... 49 E3
Broom Lock TW11 ... 17 C2
Broom Pk KT1 ... 17 D1
Broom Rd Croydon CR0 ... 63 A7
Richmond TW11 ... 17 C3
Teddington KT1, TW11 ... 17 C2
Broom Squires GU26 ... 188 F4
Broom Water TW11 ... 17 C3
Broom Water W TW11 ... 17 C3
Broom Way KT13 ... 53 E6
Broomcroft Cl GU22 ... 70 D3
Broomcroft Dr GU22 ... 70 D3
Broomdashers Rd RH10 ... 201 F7
Broome Cl RH12 ... 217 D5
Broome Ct 3 TW9 ... 7 A6
Broome Lodge TW18 ... 13 B3
Broome Rd TW12 ... 35 F8
Broome St KT18 ... 96 C1
Broomehall Rd
Coldharbour RH5 ... 156 D2
Ockley RH5 ... 177 E8
Broomers La GU6 ... 175 E5
Broomfield Elstead GU8 ... 148 E4
Guildford GU2 ... 108 E2
Staines TW18 ... 13 A2
Sunbury TW16 ... 35 A8
Broomfield Cl
Guildford GU3 ... 108 E3
Sunningdale SL5 ... 30 B2
Broomfield Cotts KT20 ... 97 E8
Broomfield Ct KT13 ... 53 B4
Broomfield Dr SL5 ... 30 B3
Broomfield La GU10 ... 146 A1
Broomfield Pk
Sunningdale SL5 ... 30 B2
Westcott RH4 ... 135 C6
Broomfield Rd
Beckenham BR3 ... 43 F6
Richmond TW9 ... 6 F6
Surbiton KT5 ... 37 F1
Teddington TW11 ... 17 C2
Woodham KT15 ... 71 B8
Broomfield Ride KT22 ... 74 D7
Broomfields KT10 ... 55 C5
Broomhall Bldgs SL5 ... 30 B2
Broomhall End GU21 ... 69 E3
Broomhall La
Sunningdale SL5 ... 30 A3
Woking GU21 ... 69 E3
Broomhall Rd
South Croydon CR2 ... 61 D2
Woking GU21 ... 69 E3
Broomhill GU10 ... 124 D8
Broomhill Rd GU14 ... 84 D5
Broomhurst Ct RH4 ... 136 B5
Broomlands La RH8 ... 123 E8
Broomleaf Cnr GU9 ... 125 D2
Broomleaf Rd GU9 ... 125 E2
Broomleigh Bsns Pk SE6 ... 23 F3
Broomloan La SM1 ... 59 A8
Broomsquires Rd GU19 ... 47 F2
Broomwood Cl CR0 ... 43 D4
Broomwood Way GU10 ... 146 C6
Broseley Gr SE26 ... 23 E3
Broster Gdns SE25 ... 42 F6
Brough Cl KT2 ... 17 D3
Brougham Pl GU9 ... 125 B7
Broughton Ave TW10 ... 17 C4
Broughton Mews GU16 ... 65 F1
Broughton Rd CR7 ... 42 A3
Brow The RH1 ... 140 A4
Browell House GU4 ... 110 D2
Browells La TW13 ... 15 B6
Brown Bear Ct TW13 ... 15 D4
Brown Cl SM6 ... 60 E3
Brown's Hill RH1 ... 141 D2
Brown's Rd KT5, KT6 ... 37 F2
Browne House 9 SE26 ... 23 B3
Browngraves Rd UB7 ... 3 C7
Brownhill Rd SE6 ... 24 C8
Browning Ave
Carshalton SM1 ... 59 E6
North Cheam KT4 ... 39 B1
Browning Cl
Crawley RH10 ... 202 C7
Frimley GU15 ... 66 C4
Hampton TW12 ... 15 F4
Browning Rd KT22 ... 94 D2
Browning Way TW5 ... 4 D6
Brownings The 1 RH19 ... 185 C1
Brownlow Rd Redhill RH1 ... 118 E1
South Croydon CR0 ... 61 F6
Brownrigg Cres RG12 ... 27 E8
Brownrigg Rd TW15 ... 14 A4
Browns La KT24 ... 113 D8
Browns Wlk GU10 ... 145 F5
Browns Wood RH19 ... 185 E4
Brownsover Rd GU14 ... 84 C4
Brox La
Addlestone KT15, KT16 ... 51 D2
Ottershaw KT15, KT16 ... 51 D2
Woodham KT15, KT16 ... 51 D2
Brox Rd KT16 ... 51 D4
Broxholm Rd SE27, SW16 ... 22 A5
Broxted Rd SE23, SE6 ... 23 F6
Bruce Ave TW17 ... 34 C3
Bruce Cl KT14 ... 71 E6
Bruce Dr CR2 ... 62 D2
Bruce Hall Mews SW17 ... 21 A4
Bruce Lawns SW17 ... 21 A4
Bruce Rd Mitcham CR4 ... 21 A1
South Norwood SE25 ... 42 D5
Brudenell Rd SW17 ... 21 A4

Brumana Cl KT13 . . . .**53** B4
Brumfield Rd KT19 . . . .**57** C5
Brunel Cl Cranford TW5 . . . . . .**4** B7
  South Norwood SE19 . . . . .**22** F2
Brunel Ct SW13 . . . .**7** F5
Brunel Ctr RH10 . . . .**181** F2
Brunel Dr RG45 . . . .**45** C8
Brunel House 25 SW2 . . . . .**21** E8
Brunel Pl RH10 . . . .**201** C5
Brunel Univ Coll Osterley
  Campus TW7 . . . .**5** F7
Brunel Univ Coll
  (Twickenham Campus)
  TW1 . . . .**6** B3
Brunel Univ (Runnymede
  Campus) TW20 . . . .**11** C5
Brunel Wlk 3 TW4 . . . .**16** A8
Brunner Ct TW16 . . . .**51** C5
Brunner House SE6 . . . .**24** C4
Brunswick RG12 . . . .**27** A2
Brunswick Cl
  Crawley RH10 . . . .**202** A4
  Thames Ditton KT7 . . . .**36** F1
  Twickenham TW2 . . . .**16** D5
  Walton-on-T KT12 . . . .**54** C8
Brunswick Ct
  Crawley RH10 . . . .**202** A4
  Kingston u T KT2 . . . .**17** D2
  2 Penge SE19 . . . .**23** A1
Brunswick Dr GU24 . . . .**87** D7
Brunswick Gr KT11 . . . .**73** C6
Brunswick Mews SW16 . . .**21** D2
Brunswick Pl SE19 . . . .**23** A1
Brunswick Rd
  Kingston u T KT2 . . . .**38** A8
  Pirbright, Alexander
   Barracks GU24 . . . .**87** C6
  Pirbright, Blackdown
   Barracks GU16, GU24 . . . . .**86** E6
  Sutton SM1 . . . .**59** B6
Bruntile Cl GU14 . . . .**85** D1
Brushwood Rd RH12 . . . . . .**218** B6
Bruton Rd SM4 . . . .**40** C5
Bruton Way RG12 . . . .**27** E2
Bryan Cl TW16 . . . .**15** A1
Bryanston Ave TW2 . . . .**16** B7
Bryanstone Ave GU2 . . . . .**109** A4
Bryanstone Cl GU2 . . . .**108** F4
Bryanstone Ct SM1 . . . .**59** C7
Bryanstone Gr GU2 . . . .**108** F5
Bryce Cl RH12 . . . .**218** A5
Bryce Gdns GU11 . . . .**126** C7
Bryden Cl SE26 . . . .**23** E3
Brympton Cl RH4 . . . .**136** A5
Bryn Rd GU10 . . . .**145** F7
Brynford Cl GU21 . . . .**69** E4
Bryony House RG42 . . . .**26** E8
Bryony Rd GU1 . . . .**110** B4
Bryony Way TW16 . . . .**15** A2
Buchan Country Park
  RH11 . . . .**200** E1
Buchan The GU15 . . . .**66** A8
Buchanan House
  Dulwich SE21 . . . .**22** E5
  Wandsworth SW18 . . . .**20** A8
Buchans Lawn RH11 . . . . . .**201** B2
Bucharest Rd SW18 . . . .**20** C8
Buckfast Rd SM4 . . . .**40** B5
Buckhurst Ave CR4, SM5 . . .**40** F1
Buckhurst Cl
  East Grinstead RH19 . . . . .**185** C3
  Redhill RH1 . . . .**118** F3
Buckhurst Cotts RH12 . . . .**214** D8
Buckhurst Gr RG40 . . . .**25** F5
Buckhurst Hill RG12 . . . . . .**27** F5
Buckhurst La SL5 . . . .**30** A6
Buckhurst Mead RH19 . . . .**185** C4
Buckhurst Rd Ascot SL5 . . .**29** F7
  Frimley GU16 . . . .**85** F6
Buckhurst Way RH19 . . . . .**185** C4
Buckingham Ave
  East Molesey KT8 . . . .**36** B4
  Feltham TW14 . . . .**4** B1
  South Norwood CR7 . . . . . .**42** A8
Buckingham Cl
  Guildford GU1 . . . .**109** F2
  Hampton TW12 . . . .**15** F3
Buckingham Ct
  Belmont SM2 . . . .**59** A2
  Crawley RH11 . . . .**201** B2
  Staines TW18 . . . .**13** A4
  Wokingham RG40 . . . .**25** C6
Buckingham Dr RH19 . . . . .**206** A8
Buckingham Gate RH6 . . . .**182** C7
Buckingham Gdns
  Hampton KT8 . . . .**36** B7
  South Norwood CR7 . . . . . .**42** A7
Buckingham La SE23 . . . . . .**23** E8
Buckingham Prim Sch
  TW12 . . . .**15** F3
Buckingham Rd
  Hampton TW12, TW13 . . . . .**15** F3
  Kingston u T KT1 . . . .**37** F5
  Mitcham CR4 . . . .**41** E4
  Richmond TW10 . . . .**17** D6
  South Holmwood RH5 . . . .**157** C6
Buckingham Way SM6 . . . . .**60** C2
Buckland Cl GU14 . . . .**85** C8
Buckland Cnr RH2 . . . .**117** D2
Buckland Ct RH3 . . . .**117** A2
Buckland Cty Jun & Inf
  Sch TW18 . . . .**13** C1
Buckland Inf Sch KT9 . . . . . .**56** F6
Buckland La RH3 . . . .**117** B5

Buckland Rd
  Chessington KT9 . . . .**56** F5
  East Ewell SM2 . . . .**58** D2
  Lower Kingswood KT20 . . . .**117** F7
  Reigate RH2 . . . .**117** D2
Buckland Way KT4 . . . .**39** C1
Buckland Wlk SM4 . . . .**40** C5
Bucklands Rd TW11 . . . .**17** C2
Bucklebury RG12 . . . .**27** A2
Buckleigh Ave SW20 . . . . . .**39** F6
Buckleigh Rd SW16 . . . .**21** E1
Buckleigh Way SE19 . . . . . .**22** F1
Bucklers' Way SM5 . . . .**59** F7
Buckles Way SM7 . . . .**77** E3
Buckley Pl RH10 . . . .**204** A8
Buckmans Rd RH11 . . . . . .**201** D6
Bucknills Cl KT18 . . . .**76** C5
Bucks Cl KT14 . . . .**71** B5
Buckswood Dr RH11 . . . . . .**201** A4
Buckthorn Cl RG40 . . . .**25** E7
Buddhapadipa Temple The
  SW19 . . . .**19** D4
Budebury Rd TW18 . . . .**13** A3
Budge La CR4 . . . .**40** F2
Budge's Cotts RG40 . . . .**25** E8
Budge's Gdns RG40 . . . .**25** E7
Budge's Rd RG40 . . . .**25** D7
Budgen Cl RH10 . . . .**182** D1
Budgen Dr RH1 . . . .**119** A3
Budham Way RG12 . . . .**27** B3
Buff Ave SM7 . . . .**78** B4
Buffbeards La GU27 . . . . . .**207** E6
Buffers Ct KT22 . . . .**95** A8
Bug Hill CR6 . . . .**101** D7
Bugkingham Way GU16 . . . . .**65** F1
Bulbrook Row RG12 . . . .**27** E7
Bulganak Rd CR7 . . . .**42** C5
Bulkeley Cl TW20 . . . .**11** C3
Bull Hill KT22 . . . .**95** A6
Bull La Bracknell RG42 . . . . . .**27** B8
  Woking GU4 . . . .**89** F1
Bullard Rd TW11 . . . .**16** F2
Bullbeggars La
  Godstone RH9 . . . .**121** C3
  Woking GU21 . . . .**69** B3
Bullbrook Dr RG12 . . . .**27** F8
Buller Ct GU14 . . . .**85** C1
Buller Rd CR7 . . . .**42** D6
Bullers Rd GU9 . . . .**125** E6
Bullfinch Cl Horley RH6 . . . .**160** E4
  Horsham RH12 . . . .**217** C7
  Sandhurst GU47 . . . .**64** E8
Bullfinch Ct 3 SE21 . . . .**22** D6
Bullfinch Rd CR2 . . . .**62** D1
Bullrush Cl CR0 . . . .**42** E3
Bulls Alley SW14 . . . .**7** D5
Bullswater Common Rd
  GU24, GU3 . . . .**88** A2
Bullswater La TW3 . . . .**5** A4
Bulstrode Ave TW3 . . . .**5** A4
Bulstrode Gdns TW3 . . . .**5** A4
Bulstrode Rd TW3 . . . .**5** A4
Bunbury Way KT17 . . . .**77** B4
Bunce Common Rd
  RH2, RH3 . . . .**137** E2
Bunce Dr CR3 . . . .**100** D4
Bunch La GU27 . . . .**208** B8
Bunch Way GU27 . . . .**208** A6
Bundy's Way TW18 . . . .**12** F2
Bungalow Rd SE25 . . . .**42** E5
Bungalows The SW16 . . . . . .**21** B1
Bunting Cl Horsham RH13 . .**217** F3
  Mitcham CR4 . . . .**40** F4
Buntings The GU9 . . . .**145** F8
Bunyan Cl RH11 . . . .**200** E3
Bunyard Dr GU21 . . . .**70** C5
Burbage Gn RG12 . . . .**27** F4
Burbage Rd SE21, SE24 . . . . .**22** D8
Burbeach Cl RH11 . . . .**201** B3
Burberry Cl KT3 . . . .**38** E7
Burbidge Rd TW17 . . . .**34** A5
Burchets Hollow GU5 . . . . .**154** D7
Burchetts Way TW4 . . . .**34** B3
Burcote 6 KT13 . . . .**53** D4
Burcote Rd SW18 . . . .**20** D8
Burcott Gdns KT15 . . . .**52** D4
Burcott Rd CR8 . . . .**80** A5
Burden Way GU2 . . . .**109** A5
Burdenshott Ave TW10 . . . . . .**7** B3
Burdenshott Rd
  Guildford GU4 . . . .**109** C8
  Woking GU22, GU3, GU4 . . .**89** A2
Burdett Ave SW20 . . . .**39** A8
Burdett Cl RH10 . . . .**202** D5
Burdett Rd Richmond TW9 . . .**6** F4
  Thornton Heath CR0 . . . . . .**42** D3
Burdock Cl Crawley RH11 . .**201** A2
  Croydon CR0 . . . .**43** D1
  Lightwater GU18 . . . .**67** B8
Burdon La SM2 . . . .**58** A2
Burdon Pk SM2 . . . .**58** F2
Burfield Cl SW17 . . . .**20** D4
Burfield Dr CR6 . . . .**101** C8
Burfield Rd SL4, TW19 . . . . . .**11** B8
Burford Rd RG40 . . . .**25** E5
Burford La KT17 . . . .**77** C8
Burford Lea GU8 . . . .**148** E4
Burford Rd Camberley GU15 **65** B4
  Forest Hill SE6 . . . .**23** F6
  Horsham RH13 . . . .**217** E2
  New Malden KT4 . . . .**39** A2
  Sutton SM1 . . . .**59** A8
Burford Way CR0 . . . .**63** C4
Burges Gn TW18 . . . .**13** A3
Burgess Cl TW13 . . . .**15** E4
Burgess Mews SW19 . . . . . .**20** B1
Burgess Rd SM1 . . . .**59** B6

Burgh Cl RH10 . . . .**182** D1
Burgh Heath Rd
  KT17, KT18 . . . .**76** F4
Burgh Mount SM7 . . . .**77** F4
Burgh Wood SM7 . . . .**77** F4
Burghead Cl GU47 . . . .**64** D7
Burghfield KT17 . . . .**76** F4
Burghill Rd SE26 . . . .**23** E4
Burghley Ave KT3 . . . .**38** D8
Burghley House SW19 . . . . .**19** E5
Burghley Pl CR4 . . . .**40** F5
Burghley Rd SW19 . . . .**19** E4
Burgoyne Rd Ashford TW16 .**14** F2
  Camberley GU15 . . . .**66** A6
  South Norwood SE25 . . . . .**42** F5
Burham Cl SE20 . . . .**23** C1
Burhill Cty Inf Sch KT12 . . . .**54** D4
Burhill Rd KT12 . . . .**54** C3
Buriton House 9 SW15 . . . .**19** B7
Burke Cl SW15 . . . .**7** E3
Burlands RH11 . . . .**181** A1
Burlea Cl KT12 . . . .**54** B5
Burleigh Cl
  Addlestone KT15 . . . .**52** B5
  Crawley Down RH10 . . . . .**204** B8
Burleigh Ct KT22 . . . .**95** A5
Burleigh Cty Inf Sch
  RH10 . . . .**204** B8
Burleigh Gdns
  Ashford TW15 . . . .**14** C3
  Woking GU21 . . . .**69** F2
Burleigh La
  Crawley Down RH10 . . . . .**204** C7
  North Ascot SL5 . . . .**28** E8
Burleigh Pk KT11 . . . .**73** E7
Burleigh Rd
  Addlestone KT15 . . . .**52** B5
  Cheam SM3, SM4 . . . .**39** E1
  Frimley GU16 . . . .**85** D8
  North Ascot SL5 . . . .**28** E8
Burleigh Way RH10 . . . .**204** B8
Burleigh Wlk SE6 . . . .**24** C7
Burley Cl Loxwood RH14 . . .**213** A4
  Mitcham SW16 . . . .**41** D7
Burley Orchard KT16 . . . . . .**33** A3
Burley Way GU17 . . . .**64** C6
Burleys Rd RH10 . . . .**202** C6
Burlingham Cl GU4 . . . .**110** D3
Burlington Cl TW9 . . . .**7** A6
Burlington Ct TW14 . . . .**14** D4
Burlington Ct 6
  Aldershot GU11 . . . .**105** A1
  Blackwater GU17 . . . .**64** D3
  Chiswick W4 . . . .**7** C7
Burlington Jun Sch KT3 . . . .**38** F5
Burlington La W4 . . . .**7** E8
Burlington Rd
  Hounslow TW7 . . . .**5** D6
  New Malden KT3 . . . .**38** F5
  South Norwood CR7 . . . . . .**42** D7
Burlsdon Way RG12 . . . .**27** E8
Burma Rd KT16 . . . .**49** F8
Burma Terr 11 SE19 . . . .**22** E3
Burmarsh Ct SE20 . . . .**43** C8
Burmester House SW17 . . . .**20** C5
Burmester Rd SW17 . . . .**20** C5
Burn Cl KT15 . . . .**52** D6
Burn Moor Chase RG12 . . . .**27** E2
Burnaby Cres W4 . . . .**7** C8
Burnaby Gdns W4 . . . .**7** B8
Burnbury Rd SW12 . . . .**21** C7
Burne-Jones Dr GU47 . . . . . .**64** D6
Burnell Ave TW10 . . . .**17** C3
Burnell House 19 SW2 . . . . .**22** A7
Burnell Rd SM1 . . . .**59** B6
Burnet Ave GU1, GU4 . . . . .**110** B4
Burnet Cl GU24 . . . .**67** E6
Burnet Gr KT19 . . . .**76** C6
Burney Ave KT5 . . . .**37** F4
Burney Cl KT23 . . . .**94** C2
Burney Ct 6 RH11 . . . .**201** A3
Burney House 4 SW16 . . . . .**21** C3
Burney Rd RH5 . . . .**115** A4
Burnham Cl GU21 . . . .**68** D1
Burnham Dr
  North Cheam KT4 . . . .**58** D8
  Reigate RH2 . . . .**118** A2
Burnham Gdns
  Cranford TW5 . . . .**4** B6
  Croydon CR0 . . . .**42** F2
Burnham Manor GU15 . . . . .**66** A8
Burnham Pl RH13 . . . .**217** D1
Burnham Rd Knaphill GU21 .**68** D1
  Morden SM4 . . . .**40** B5
Burnham St KT2 . . . .**38** A8
Burnham Way SE26 . . . .**23** F3
Burnhams Rd KT23 . . . .**93** E3
Burnhill Rd BR3 . . . .**44** A7
Burns Ave TW14 . . . .**4** A1
Burns Cl Farnborough GU14 .**84** F6
  Horsham RH12 . . . .**217** E7
  Mitcham SW17 . . . .**20** D2
Burns Ct SM6 . . . .**60** B3
Burns Dr SM7 . . . .**77** E5
Burns Rd RH10 . . . .**202** C8
Burns Way Crawley RH12 . .**200** C1
  East Grinstead RH19 . . . . .**185** C1
  Heston TW5 . . . .**4** D6
Burnsall Cl GU14 . . . .**85** B6
Burnside KT21 . . . .**75** F1
Burnside Cl TW1 . . . .**6** B2

Burntcommon La GU23 . . . .**91** A2
Burntwood Cl
  Caterham CR3 . . . .**101** A6
  Wandsworth SW18 . . . .**20** E7
Burntwood Ct SW17 . . . .**20** C5
Burntwood Grange Rd
  SW18 . . . .**20** E7
Burntwood La
  Caterham CR3 . . . .**101** A6
  Wandsworth SW17 . . . .**20** D6
Burntwood Sch SW17 . . . . . .**20** C5
Burntwood View SE19 . . . . .**22** F3
Burnwood Park Rd KT12 . . . .**54** B6
Burpham Court Farm
  Park GU4 . . . .**109** F7
Burpham La GU4 . . . .**110** A5
Burpham Prim Sch GU4 . . .**110** A5
Burr Hill La GU24 . . . .**49** F2
Burr Rd SW18 . . . .**20** A8
Burrell Cl CR0 . . . .**43** E3
Burrell Ct RH11 . . . .**200** F4
Burrell House 6 TW1 . . . . . .**17** B8
Burrell Rd GU16 . . . .**85** C8
Burrell Row BR3 . . . .**44** A7
Burrell The RH4 . . . .**135** C6
Burritt Rd KT1 . . . .**38** A7
Burrow Hill Gn GU24 . . . .**49** E2
Burrow Hill Sch GU16 . . . . . .**65** F1
Burrow Wlk SE21 . . . .**22** C8
Burrows Cross GU5 . . . . . .**133** C2
Burrows Hill Cl TW19, TW6 . . .**2** C3
Burrows La GU5 . . . .**133** C3
Burrwood Gdns GU12 . . . . .**106** A4
Burstead Cl KT11 . . . .**73** D7
Burston Gdns RH19 . . . . . .**185** D4
Burstow House RH6 . . . . . .**161** B6
Burstow Prim Sch RH6 . . . .**162** B3
Burstow Rd SW20 . . . .**39** E8
Burtenshaw Rd KT7 . . . .**37** A3
Burton Cl Chessington KT9 . .**56** D3
  Horley RH6 . . . .**161** A2
  Windlesham GU20 . . . .**48** D4
Burton Ct KT7 . . . .**37** A3
Burton Gdns TW5 . . . .**4** F6
Burton House SE26 . . . .**23** B3
Burton Rd KT2 . . . .**17** E1
Burton's Rd TW12 . . . .**16** C4
Burtons Ct RH12 . . . .**217** C2
Burtwell La SE21, SE27 . . . . .**22** D4
Burwash Rd RH10 . . . .**202** A5
Burway Cres KT16 . . . .**33** A5
Burwood Ave CR8 . . . .**80** B5
Burwood Cl Guildford GU1 . .**110** D2
  Hersham KT12 . . . .**54** C4
  Reigate RH2 . . . .**118** D1
  Tolworth KT6 . . . .**38** A1
Burwood Ct SE23 . . . .**23** C8
Burwood Park Rd KT12 . . . . .**53** F5
Burwood Rd
  Hersham KT12, KT13 . . . . . .**54** B4
  Hersham KT12 . . . .**54** D5
Bury Cl GU21 . . . .**69** D3
Bury Fields GU2 . . . .**130** C7
Bury Gr SM4 . . . .**40** B4
Bury La GU21 . . . .**69** C3
Bury St GU2 . . . .**130** C7
Burys Court Sch RH2 . . . . .**138** C3
Burys The GU7 . . . .**150** E5
Burywood Hill RH5 . . . .**177** E7
Busbridge CE Jun Sch
  GU7 . . . .**150** F2
Busbridge Cty Inf Sch
  GU7 . . . .**150** F2
Busbridge La GU7 . . . .**150** E3
Busby House SW16 . . . .**21** C4
Busch Cl TW7 . . . .**6** B6
Busch Cnr TW7 . . . .**6** B6
Busdens Cl GU8 . . . .**170** F8
Busdens La GU8 . . . .**170** F8
Busdens Way GU8 . . . .**170** F8
Bush Cl KT15 . . . .**52** C5
Bush Cottages 8 SW18 . . . .**20** A3
Bush La GU23 . . . .**90** D3
Bush Rd Littleton TW17 . . . . .**33** F4
  Richmond TW9 . . . .**6** F8
Bush Wlk RG40 . . . .**25** C6
Bushbury La RH3 . . . .**137** A5
Bushell Cl SW2 . . . .**21** F6
Bushell House 3 SE27 . . . . .**22** C4
Bushetts Gr RH1, RH2 . . . . .**119** B6
Bushey Cl CR3, CR8 . . . .**80** C3
Bushey Croft RH8 . . . .**122** C5
Bushey Ct SW20 . . . .**39** B7
Bushey Down SW12 . . . .**21** B6
Bushey Fst Sch KT3 . . . .**39** B6
Bushey La SM1 . . . .**59** A6
Bushey Mid Sch SW20 . . . . .**39** B6
Bushey Rd Croydon CR0 . . . . .**63** A8
  Merton SW20 . . . .**39** D7
  Sutton SM1 . . . .**59** A6
  Sutton SM1 . . . .**59** B6
  West Barnes SW20 . . . .**39** D7
Bushey Way BR3 . . . .**44** D4
Bushfield RH14 . . . .**211** F2
Bushfield Dr RH1 . . . .**140** A4
Bushnell Rd SW17 . . . .**21** B5
Bushwood Rd TW9 . . . .**7** A8
Bushy Ct KT1 . . . .**37** C8
Bushy Hill Dr GU1 . . . .**110** C3
Bushy Hill Jun Sch GU1 . . .**110** D2
Bushy Park Gdns TW12 . . . . .**16** B3
Bushy Park Rd TW11 . . . .**17** B1
Bushy Rd
  Fetcham KT22, KT23 . . . . . .**94** B5
  Teddington TW11 . . . .**16** F1
Bushy Shaw KT21 . . . .**75** C2

Business Ctr The RG41 . . . .**25** B4
Busk Cres GU14 . . . .**84** F3
Bute Ave TW10 . . . .**17** E6
Bute Ct SM6 . . . .**60** C5
Bute Gdns SM6 . . . .**60** C5
Bute Gdns W SM6 . . . .**60** C5
Bute Rd Thornton Heath CR0 .**42** A1
  Wallington SM6 . . . .**60** C6
Butler Rd Bagshot GU19 . . . .**47** F2
  Crowthorne RG45 . . . .**45** B6
Butlers Dene Rd CR3 . . . . .**102** A7
Butlers Hill KT24 . . . .**112** B5
Butlers Rd RH13 . . . .**218** B4
Butt Cl GU6 . . . .**174** E4
Butter Hill Dorking RH4 . . . .**136** A7
  Hackbridge SM5, SM6 . . . . .**60** A6
Buttercup Cl RG40 . . . .**26** A6
Buttercup Sq TW19 . . . .**13** D7
Butterfield Camberley GU15 .**65** B4
  East Grinstead RH19 . . . . .**185** B3
Butterfield Cl TW1 . . . .**5** F1
Butterfly Wlk CR6 . . . .**101** C7
Buttermer Cl GU10 . . . .**145** F7
Buttermere Cl
  East Bedfont TW14 . . . .**14** F7
  Farnborough GU14 . . . .**84** E4
  Horsham RH12 . . . .**218** B6
  West Barnes SM4 . . . .**39** D3
Buttermere Ct GU12 . . . . . .**105** F4
Buttermere Dr GU15 . . . .**66** D4
Buttermere Gdns
  Bracknell RG12 . . . .**27** C6
  Sanderstead CR8 . . . .**80** C5
Buttermere Way TW20 . . . . .**12** B1
Buttersteep
  Rise GU20, SL5 . . . .**28** C1
Butterworth Ct SW16 . . . . . .**21** E5
Butts Cl RH11 . . . .**201** B7
Butts Cotts Feltham TW13 . . .**15** F5
  4 Woking GU21 . . . .**69** A1
Butts Cres TW13 . . . .**16** A5
Butts House TW13 . . . .**16** A5
Butts Rd Catford BR1 . . . .**24** E3
  Woking GU21 . . . .**69** A2
Butts The TW8 . . . .**6** D8
Buxton Ave CR3 . . . .**100** E6
Buxton Cres SM3 . . . .**58** E6
Buxton Dr KT3 . . . .**38** D7
Buxton La CR3 . . . .**100** E6
Buxton Rd Ashford TW15 . . . .**13** D3
  Mortlake SW14 . . . .**7** E4
  Thornton Heath CR7 . . . . . .**42** B4
Byards Croft SW16 . . . .**41** D4
Byatt Wlk TW12 . . . .**15** E2
Bychurch End 9 TW11 . . . . .**16** F3
Bycroft St SE20 . . . .**23** D1
Bycroft Way RH10 . . . .**202** B8
Bye Ways TW2 . . . .**16** B5
Byerley Way RH10 . . . .**202** F7
Byers La RH9 . . . .**142** C1
Byeway The SW14 . . . .**7** C4
Byeways The KT5 . . . .**38** A4
Byfield Ct KT3 . . . .**39** A5
Byfield Rd TW7 . . . .**6** A4
Byfleet Cnr KT14 . . . .**71** F6
Byfleet Cty Prim Sch KT14 .**71** D6
Byfleet Ind Est KT14 . . . .**71** D8
Byfleet & New Haw Sta
  KT15 . . . .**52** D1
Byfleet Rd
  New Haw KT14, KT15 . . . . . .**52** D2
  Weybridge KT11, KT13, KT14 **72** C6
Byfleet Tech Ctr The KT14 .**71** D4
Byfleets La RH12 . . . .**216** D6
Byfrons The GU14 . . . .**85** D2
Bygrove CR0 . . . .**63** B3
Bygrove Rd SW19 . . . .**20** D2
Bygrove Rd SW19 . . . .**20** D2
Bylands GU22 . . . .**70** A1
Byne Rd Carshalton SM5 . . . .**59** E8
  Penge SE20, E26 . . . .**23** C3
Bynes Rd CR2 . . . .**61** D3
Byrd Rd RH11 . . . .**200** F3
Byrefield Rd GU2 . . . .**108** F4
Byrne Ct 1 CR8 . . . .**80** A7
Byrne Rd SW12 . . . .**21** B6
Byron Ave Carshalton SM1 . .**59** D6
  Coulsdon CR5 . . . .**79** F3
  Cranford TW4 . . . .**4** B5
  Frimley GU15 . . . .**66** B3
  West Barnes KT3 . . . .**39** A4
Byron Ave E SM1 . . . .**59** D6
Byron Cl Crawley RH10 . . . .**202** B7
  Forest Hill SE26 . . . .**23** E4
  Hampton TW12 . . . .**15** F4
  Horsham RH12 . . . .**217** E6
  Knaphill GU21 . . . .**68** E2
  Walton-on-T KT12 . . . .**35** E1
Byron Ct Dulwich SE21 . . . . .**23** A7
  1 Richmond TW10 . . . .**17** D4
  South Norwood CR7 . . . . . .**42** C7
Byron Dr RG45 . . . .**45** B3
Byron Gdns SM1 . . . .**59** D6
Byron Gr 2 RH19 . . . .**185** C1
Byron House BR3 . . . .**24** B2
Byron Inf Sch CR5 . . . .**79** F2
Byron Jun Sch CR5 . . . .**79** F2
Byron Pl KT22 . . . .**95** B5
Byron Rd Addlestone KT15 . . .**52** E6
  South Croydon CR2 . . . .**62** B1
Byton Rd SW17 . . . .**20** F7
Byttom Hill RH5 . . . .**115** C8
Byward Ave TW14 . . . .**4** C1
Byway The SM2 . . . .**59** D2
Byways The Ashstead KT21 . .**75** D1
  Worcester Park KT19 . . . . . .**57** F6
Bywood RG12 . . . .**27** A2
Bywood Ave CR0 . . . .**43** D3

Bywood Cl CR8 .... 80 B4
Bywood Terr CR0 .... 43 C3
Byworth Cl GU9 .... 124 F2
Byworth Rd GU9 .... 124 F2

C

Cabbell Pl KT15 .... 52 C6
Cabell Rd GU2 .... 108 E2
Cabin Moss RG12 .... 27 E2
Cable House Sch GU21 .... 69 E4
Cabrera Ave GU25 .... 31 D3
Cabrera Cl GU25 .... 31 D3
Cabrol Rd GU14 .... 85 A5
Caburn Ct RH11 .... 201 C4
Caburn Hts RH11 .... 201 C4
Cackstones The RH10 .... 202 D7
Cadbury Cl Ashford TW16 .... 14 E1
Isleworth TW7 .... 6 A6
Cadbury Rd TW16 .... 14 E2
Caddy Cl 4 TW20 .... 12 A3
Cadley Terr SE23 .... 23 C6
Cadmer Cl KT3 .... 38 E5
Cadnam Cl GU11 .... 126 C6
Cadnam Point 14 SW15 .... 19 B7
Cadogan Cl Beckenham BR3 .... 44 D7
Teddington TW11 .... 16 E3
Cadogan Ct SM2 .... 59 B4
Cadogan Ho 11 GU1 .... 130 F8
Cadogan Rd KT6 .... 37 D4
Cadogen Rd GU11 .... 105 D7
Caen Wood Rd KT21 .... 75 C1
Caenshill Rd KT13 .... 53 A3
Caenswood Hill KT13 .... 53 A1
Caenwood Cl KT13 .... 53 A4
Caerleon Cl GU26 .... 188 C6
Caernarvon GU16 .... 85 F8
Caernarvon Cl CR4 .... 41 E6
Caernarvon Ct 3 KT5 .... 37 F4
Caesar Ct GU11 .... 104 E2
Caesar's Camp Rd GU15 .... 66 A8
Caesar's Cl GU15 .... 66 A8
Caesar's Way TW17 .... 34 D3
Caesars Ct GU9 .... 125 C7
Caesars Wlk CR4 .... 40 F4
Caffins Cl RH10 .... 201 E8
Caillard Rd KT14 .... 71 E8
Cain Rd RG12, RG42 .... 26 E7
Cain's La TW14 .... 3 E2
Cairn Cl GU15 .... 66 B3
Cairndale Cl BR1 .... 24 F1
Cairngorm Pl GU14 .... 84 E7
Cairo New Rd CR0, CR9 .... 61 B8
Caister House 10 SW12 .... 21 B8
Caistor Mews SW12 .... 21 B8
Caistor Rd SW12 .... 21 B8
Caithness Dr KT18 .... 76 D5
Caithness Rd CR4 .... 21 B1
Calbourne Rd SW12 .... 21 A8
Caldbeck Ave KT4 .... 39 B1
Caldbeck House 7 RH11 .... 200 F3
Calder Rd SM4 .... 40 C4
Calder Way SL3 .... 1 E4
Calderdale Cl RH11 .... 201 B4
Caldwell Rd GU20 .... 48 D5
Caledon Pl GU1 .... 110 A4
Caledon Rd SM5, SM6 .... 60 A6
Caledonia Rd TW19 .... 13 E7
Caledonian House RH10 .... 201 D8
Caledonian Way RH6 .... 182 B8
Calfridus Way RG12 .... 27 F6
California Ct SM2 .... 59 B1
California Rd KT3 .... 38 C6
Callander Rd SE6 .... 24 C6
Calley Down Cres
CR0, CR9 .... 63 D1
Callis Farm Cl TW19 .... 2 E1
Callisto Ct RH11 .... 200 E3
Callow Field CR8 .... 80 A6
Callow Hill GU25, TW20 .... 31 C7
Calluna Ct GU22 .... 69 F1
Calluna Dr RH10 .... 183 A3
Calmont Rd BR1 .... 24 E2
Calonne Rd SW19 .... 19 D4
Calshot Rd TW6 .... 3 B5
Calshot Way Frimley GU16 .... 86 A7
Harlington TW6 .... 3 A5
Calthorpe Gdns SM1 .... 59 C7
Calton Gdns GU11 .... 126 C7
Calverley Cl BR3 .... 24 B2
Calverley Rd KT17 .... 58 A4
Calvert Cl GU12 .... 105 D1
Calvert Cres RH4 .... 115 B1
Calvert Ct 5 TW9 .... 6 F3
Calvert Rd Dorking RH4 .... 115 B2
Effingham KT24 .... 113 B7
Calvin Cl GU15 .... 66 B4
Calvin Wlk RH11 .... 200 E3
Camac Rd TW2 .... 16 D7
Camber Cl RH10 .... 202 C6
Camberley Ave SW20 .... 39 B7
Camberley Cl SM3 .... 58 D7
Camberley Ct 8 SM2 .... 59 B3
Camberley Cty Inf Sch
GU15 .... 65 C5
Camberley Heath Golf
Course GU15 .... 66 B5
Camberley Rd TW6 .... 3 A4
Camberley Sta GU15 .... 65 D5
Camberley Towers GU15 .... 65 D5
Cambisgate SW19 .... 19 E3
Camborne Cl TW6 .... 3 A4
Camborne Cres TW6 .... 3 A4
Camborne Rd Belmont SM2 .... 59 B3
Croydon CR0 .... 43 A2
Sutton SM2 .... 59 B3
Wandsworth SW18 .... 20 A8
Camborne Rd *continued*
West Barnes SM4 .... 39 D4
Camborne Rd S TW6 .... 3 A4
Camborne Way
Harmondsworth TW6 .... 3 A4
Heston TW5 .... 5 A6
Cambray Rd SW12 .... 21 C7
Cambria BR3 .... 44 B7
Cambria Cl TW3 .... 5 A3
Cambria Ct Feltham TW14 .... 15 B8
Staines TW18 .... 12 E4
Cambria Gdns TW19 .... 13 E8
Cambria House SE26 .... 23 A4
Cambrian Cl
Camberley GU15 .... 65 B5
West Norwood SE27 .... 22 B5
Cambrian Rd
Farnborough GU14 .... 84 D7
Richmond TW10 .... 6 F1
Cambridge Ave KT3, SW20 .... 38 F7
Cambridge Cl
Harmondsworth UB7 .... 2 D8
Hounslow TW4 .... 4 E3
Knaphill GU21 .... 68 F1
Wimbledon SW20 .... 39 B8
Cambridge Cotts TW9 .... 7 A8
Cambridge Cres TW11 .... 17 A3
Cambridge Ct SW20 .... 39 B8
Cambridge Gdns KT1 .... 38 A7
Cambridge Gr SE20 .... 43 B8
Cambridge Grove Rd
Kingston u T KT1 .... 38 A6
5 Kingston u T KT1 .... 38 A7
Cambridge House 2
TW11 .... 17 A3
Cambridge House Sch
SW20 .... 39 C8
Cambridge Meadows
GU9 .... 125 A1
Cambridge Park Ct TW1 .... 17 D8
Cambridge Pk TW1 .... 6 C1
Cambridge Pl GU9 .... 125 C2
Cambridge Rd
Aldershot GU11 .... 104 F2
Barnes SW13 .... 7 F5
Carshalton SM5 .... 59 E5
Crowthorne RG45 .... 45 C4
Croydon SE20, SE25 .... 43 B6
East Molesey KT8 .... 35 F5
Hampton TW12 .... 15 F1
Horsham RH13 .... 217 D2
Hounslow TW4 .... 4 E3
Kingston u T KT1 .... 38 A7
Littleton TW15, TW17 .... 14 C1
Mitcham CR4 .... 41 C6
New Malden KT3 .... 38 E5
Richmond TW9 .... 7 A7
Sandhurst GU47 .... 45 E1
Teddington TW11 .... 17 A3
Twickenham TW1 .... 6 D1
Walton-on-T KT12 .... 35 B3
Wimbledon SW20 .... 39 B8
Cambridge Rd E GU14 .... 85 D1
Cambridge Rd W GU14 .... 85 C1
Cambridge Sq GU15 .... 65 C6
Cambridge Wlk 3 GU15 .... 65 C6
Camden Ave TW13 .... 15 C7
Camden Gdns
South Norwood CR7 .... 42 B6
Sutton SM1 .... 59 B5
Camden Hill Rd SE19 .... 22 E2
Camden Jun Sch SM5 .... 59 F6
Camden Rd Carshalton SM5 .... 59 F6
Lingfield RH7 .... 164 D4
Sutton SM1 .... 59 B5
Camden Way CR7 .... 42 B6
Cameford Ct 20 SW12 .... 21 E8
Camel Cl KT2 .... 17 D3
Camellia Ct
21 Beckenham BR3 .... 24 A1
West End GU24 .... 67 F6
Camellia Pl TW2 .... 16 B8
Camelot Cl Biggin Hill TN16 .... 83 C3
Wimbledon SW19 .... 20 A4
Camelot Ct RH11 .... 200 E6
Camelsdale Cty Fst Sch
GU27 .... 207 F5
Camelsdale Rd
Kingsley Green GU27 .... 207 F5
Linchmere GU27 .... 207 F5
Cameron Cl GU6 .... 174 E1
Cameron Ct 3 SW19 .... 19 E7
Cameron House BR1 .... 44 F8
Cameron Lodge TW3 .... 5 C3
Cameron Rd
Farnborough GU11 .... 105 D7
Forest Hill SE6 .... 23 F6
Thornton Heath CR0 .... 42 B3
Cameron Sq CR4 .... 40 E8
Camgate Est TW19 .... 13 F8
Camilla Cl Ashford TW16 .... 14 F2
Great Bookham KT23 .... 94 B2
Camilla Dr RH5 .... 115 A5
Camille Cl SE25 .... 43 A6
Camlan Rd BR1 .... 24 F4
Camm Gdns
5 Kingston u T KT1 .... 37 F7
Thames Ditton KT7 .... 36 F2
Camomile Ave CR4 .... 40 F8
Camp End Rd KT11, KT13 .... 72 C8
Camp Farm Rd GU11 .... 105 D5
Camp Hill GU10, GU9 .... 147 C8
Camp Rd
Farnborough GU14 .... 105 C8
Wimbledon SW19 .... 19 C3
Woldingham CR3 .... 101 E6
Camp View SW19 .... 19 B3
Campbell Ave GU22 .... 89 F6
Campbell Cl
Aldershot GU11 .... 126 C7
Streatham SW16 .... 21 D4
Twickenham TW2 .... 16 D7
Campbell Cres RH19 .... 185 B1
Campbell Ct Dulwich SE21 .... 23 A7
Leatherhead KT22 .... 95 B5
Campbell House 6 SM6 .... 60 B6
Campbell Pl GU16 .... 65 F3
Campbell Rd
Aldershot GU11 .... 105 A3
Caterham CR3 .... 100 D6
Crawley RH10 .... 202 C5
Thornton Heath CR0 .... 42 B3
Twickenham TW2 .... 16 D6
Weybridge KT13 .... 53 A3
Campden Rd CR0, CR2 .... 61 E5
Campen Cl SW19 .... 19 E6
Camphill Ct KT14 .... 71 A7
Camphill Ind Est KT14 .... 71 B8
Camphill Rd KT14, KT15 .... 71 B7
Campion Cl
Blackwater GU17 .... 64 F3
South Croydon CR2 .... 61 E6
Campion Dr KT20 .... 97 B7
Campion House
Bracknell RG42 .... 26 E8
6 Redhill RH1 .... 119 A4
Campion House
(Seminary) TW7 .... 5 D6
Campion Rd
Horsham RH12 .... 217 E5
Hounslow TW7 .... 5 F6
Campion Way RG40 .... 25 E7
Camrose Ave TW13 .... 15 C4
Camrose Cl Croydon CR0 .... 43 E2
Morden SM4 .... 40 A5
Can Hatch KT20 .... 77 E1
Canada Ave RH1 .... 140 A5
Canada Dr RH1 .... 140 A5
Canada House RH1 .... 140 A5
Canada Rd Byfleet KT14 .... 71 D8
Cobham KT11 .... 73 C6
Frimley GU16 .... 86 E8
Canadian Ave SE6 .... 24 B7
Canal Cl GU11 .... 105 D5
Canal Cotts GU12 .... 106 A4
Canal Wlk Croydon CR0 .... 42 F3
Forest Hill SE26 .... 23 C3
Canberra Cl Crawley RH11 .... 181 D1
Horsham RH12 .... 217 F4
Canberra Pl RH12 .... 217 F5
Canberra Rd TW6 .... 3 A4
Canbury Ave KT2 .... 37 F8
Canbury Bsns Pk 3 KT2 .... 37 E8
Canbury Ct KT2 .... 17 E1
Canbury Mews SE26 .... 23 A5
Canbury Park Rd KT2 .... 37 F8
Candlerush Cl GU22 .... 70 B2
Candover Cl UB7 .... 2 D7
Candy Croft KT23 .... 94 B2
Cane Cl SM6 .... 60 E3
Canewdon Cl GU22 .... 89 E8
Canford Dr KT15 .... 52 B8
Canford Gdns KT3 .... 38 E3
Canham Rd SE25 .... 42 E6
Canmore Gdns SW16 .... 21 C1
Canning Rd
Aldershot GU12 .... 105 D2
Croydon CR0, CR9 .... 61 F8
Cannizaro Rd SW19 .... 19 D3
Cannon Cl Hampton TW12 .... 16 B2
Sandhurst GU47 .... 64 F8
West Barnes SW20 .... 39 C6
Cannon Cres GU24 .... 68 E8
Cannon Gr KT22 .... 94 E6
Cannon Hill RG12 .... 27 C3
Cannon Hill La
Merton KT3, SM4, SW20 .... 39 E5
West Barnes KT3,
SM4, SW20 .... 39 E5
Cannon House SE26 .... 23 B2
Cannon Side KT22 .... 94 E5
Cannon Way
East Molesey KT8 .... 36 B5
Fetcham KT22 .... 94 E6
Canon's Hill CR5, CR8 .... 80 A1
Canon's Wlk CR0 .... 62 D7
Canonbie Rd SE23 .... 23 C8
Canonbury Cotts RH12 .... 199 F6
Canons Cl RH2 .... 117 F2
Canons L Ctr The CR4 .... 40 F5
Canons La KT20 .... 97 F8
Canopus Way TW19 .... 13 E8
Cansiron La RH19 .... 206 F6
Cantelupe Rd RH19 .... 185 F1
Canter The RH10 .... 202 E7
Canterbury Cl BR3 .... 44 B8
Canterbury Ct
Ashford TW15 .... 13 F4
Dorking RH4 .... 136 A8
South Croydon CR2 .... 61 C3
Canterbury Gr SE27, SW16 .... 22 A4
Canterbury Mews KT22 .... 74 C6
Canterbury Rd Ash GU12 .... 106 A3
Crawley RH10 .... 201 E2
Farnborough GU14 .... 85 D2
Feltham TW13 .... 15 E6
Guildford GU2 .... 108 F3
Morden SM4 .... 40 C3
Thornton Heath CR0, CR7 .... 42 A2
Cantley Cres RG41 .... 25 A8
Cantley Gdns SE19 .... 42 F8
Canute Ct SW16 .... 22 A5
Canvey Cl RH11 .... 201 C3
Cape Copse RH12 .... 214 D7
Capel KT5 .... 37 F2
Capel Ave SM6 .... 60 F5
Capel CE (VA) Fst Sch
RH5 .... 178 D6
Capel Ct SE20 .... 43 C8
Capel La RH11 .... 200 F5
Capel Lodge
5 Richmond TW9 .... 6 F6
15 Streatham SW2 .... 21 F8
Capel Rd RH12 .... 199 A8
Capella House RH5 .... 178 C5
Capern Rd SW18 .... 20 C7
Capital Ind Est CR4 .... 40 F4
Capital Pk GU22 .... 90 B6
Caplan Est CR4 .... 41 C8
Capper Rd GU15 .... 65 A7
Capri Rd CR0 .... 42 F2
Capricorn Cl RH11 .... 200 E4
Capsey Rd RH11 .... 200 E6
Capstans Wharf 7 GU21 .... 68 F1
Capstone Rd BR1 .... 24 F4
Caradon Cl GU21 .... 69 B1
Caradon Ct 7 TW1 .... 6 C1
Caraway Cl RH11 .... 201 B2
Caraway Pl Guildford GU2 .... 109 A6
Hackbridge SM6 .... 60 B7
Carberry Rd 11 SE19 .... 22 E2
Carbery La SL5 .... 29 B6
Card Hill RH18 .... 206 F1
Cardamom Cl GU2 .... 109 A5
Cardigan Cl GU21 .... 68 F1
Cardigan Rd Richmond TW10 .... 6 E1
Wimbledon SW19 .... 20 C2
Cardinal Ave
Kingston u T KT2 .... 17 E2
West Barnes SM4 .... 39 E3
Cardinal Cl
West Barnes SM4 .... 39 E3
Worcester Park KT19, KT4 .... 58 A6
Cardinal Cres KT3 .... 38 C7
Cardinal Dr KT12 .... 35 D1
Cardinal Newman RC Sch
KT12 .... 54 D7
Cardinal Rd TW13 .... 15 B7
Cardinal Road Inf Sch
TW13 .... 15 B7
Cardinal's Wlk
Ashford TW16 .... 14 E2
Hampton TW12 .... 16 C1
Cardingham GU21 .... 69 B2
Cardington Sq TW4 .... 4 D3
Cardwell Cres SL5 .... 29 C4
Cardwells Keep GU2 .... 109 A4
Carew Cl CR5 .... 100 B8
Carew Ct SM2 .... 59 B2
Carew House SW16 .... 22 A5
Carew Manor Sch SM6 .... 60 D7
Carew Rd Ashford TW15 .... 14 C2
Mitcham CR4 .... 41 A7
Thornton Heath CR7 .... 42 B5
Wallington SM6 .... 60 C4
Carey House RH11 .... 201 C6
Carey Rd RG40 .... 25 C5
Carey's Copse RH6 .... 162 B3
Carey's Wood RH6 .... 162 B3
Carfax RH12 .... 217 C2
Carfax Ave GU10 .... 126 F8
Cargate Ave GU11 .... 105 A1
Cargate Gr GU11 .... 105 A1
Cargate Hill GU11 .... 104 F1
Cargate Terr GU11 .... 104 F1
Cargill Rd SW18 .... 20 C7
Cargo Forecourt Rd RH6 .... 181 D7
Cargo Rd RH6 .... 181 D7
Cargreen Rd SE25 .... 42 F5
Carholme Rd SE23 .... 23 F7
Carisbrook Ct 1 SW16 .... 21 F5
Carisbrooke GU16 .... 85 F8
Carisbrooke Ct SM2 .... 58 F3
Carisbrooke Rd CR4 .... 41 E5
Carleton Ave SM6 .... 60 D2
Carleton Cl KT10 .... 36 D1
Carlingford Gdns CR4 .... 21 A1
Carlingford Rd SM4 .... 39 D3
Carlinwark Dr GU15 .... 65 F7
Carlisle Cl KT2 .... 38 A8
Carlisle Inf Sch TW12 .... 16 B2
Carlisle Rd Cheam SM1 .... 58 F4
Hampton TW12 .... 16 B1
Rushmoor GU10 .... 168 C6
Carlisle Way SW17 .... 21 A3
Carlos St GU7 .... 150 E4
Carlton Ave Feltham TW14 .... 4 C1
South Croydon CR2 .... 61 E3
Carlton Cl Chessington KT9 .... 56 D4
Frimley GU15 .... 66 B3
Woking GU21 .... 70 A5
Carlton Cres SM3 .... 58 E6
Carlton Ct Horley RH6 .... 161 A5
12 Penge SE20 .... 43 B8
South Norwood SE19 .... 42 F8
Staines TW18 .... 13 A3
Carlton Gn RH1 .... 118 E4
Carlton House Cheam SM1 .... 58 F4
Hounslow TW4 .... 5 A1
Carlton Park Ave SW20 .... 39 D7
Carlton Rd Ashford TW16 .... 14 F1
Blindley Heath RH9 .... 142 C2
Headley Down GU35 .... 187 C5
Kingston u T KT3 .... 38 E7
Mortlake SW14 .... 7 C3
Redhill RH1 .... 118 E4
South Croydon CR2 .... 61 D3
Walton-on-T KT12 .... 35 B2
Woking GU21 .... 70 A5
Carlton Terr SE26 .... 23 C5
Carlton Tye RH6 .... 161 C3
Carlwell St SW17 .... 20 E3
Carlyle Cl KT8 .... 36 B7
Carlyle Ct RG45 .... 45 C5
Carlyle Rd Croydon CR0 .... 62 A8
Staines TW18 .... 13 A1
Carlyon Cl
Farnborough GU14 .... 85 C4
Mytchett GU16 .... 85 F4
Carlys Cl BR3 .... 43 D7
Carmalt Gdns KT12 .... 54 C5
Carman Wlk RH11 .... 201 B1
Carmarthen Cl GU14 .... 85 A7
Carmel Cl 9 GU22 .... 69 E1
Carmichael Ct SW13 .... 7 F5
Carmichael House 17
SE21 .... 22 E4
Carmichael Mews SW18 .... 20 D8
Carmichael Rd SE25 .... 43 A5
Carminia Rd SW17 .... 21 B6
Carnac St SE21, SE27 .... 22 D5
Carnation Dr RG42 .... 8 B2
Carnegie Cl KT6 .... 56 F8
Carnegie Pl SW19 .... 19 D5
Carnforth Cl KT19 .... 57 B4
Carnforth Rd SW16 .... 21 D1
Carnoustie RG12 .... 26 E2
Carole House 14 SE20 .... 43 B8
Carolina Rd CR7 .... 42 C8
Caroline Cl Hounslow TW7 .... 5 E7
South Croydon CR0 .... 61 E6
Streatham SW16 .... 21 F5
Caroline Ct Ashford TW15 .... 14 B2
Catford SE6 .... 24 D4
Crawley RH11 .... 201 D4
17 Surbiton KT6 .... 37 D2
Caroline Dr RG41 .... 25 A7
Caroline Pl UB3 .... 3 E7
Caroline Rd SW19 .... 19 F1
Carolyn Cl GU21 .... 88 F8
Carpenter Cl KT17 .... 57 F2
Carpenters Ct TW2 .... 16 E6
Carrick Cl TW7 .... 6 A4
Carrick Gate KT10 .... 55 C7
Carrington Ave TW3 .... 5 B2
Carrington Cl Croydon CR0 .... 43 E2
Redhill RH1 .... 118 F2
Carrington Lodge 3 TW10 .... 6 E2
Carrington Pl KT10 .... 55 C6
Carrington Rd TW10 .... 7 A3
Carrinton La GU12 .... 106 A8
Carroll Ave GU1 .... 110 B1
Carroll Cres SL5 .... 28 F5
Carrow Rd KT12 .... 54 D7
Carshalton Beeches Sta
SM5 .... 59 F4
Carshalton Coll SM5 .... 59 F7
Carshalton Gr SM1 .... 59 D5
Carshalton High Sch for
Boys SM5 .... 59 E8
Carshalton High Sch for
Girls SM5 .... 59 E7
Carshalton Lodge KT13 .... 53 E7
Carshalton Park Rd SM5 .... 59 F5
Carshalton Pl SM5 .... 60 A5
Carshalton Rd
Camberley GU15 .... 47 A1
Carshalton SM1, SM5 .... 59 D5
Mitcham CR4 .... 41 A4
Sutton SM1, SM5 .... 59 D5
Wallington SM7 .... 78 F6
Woodmansterne SM7 .... 78 F6
Carshalton Sta SM5 .... 59 F6
Carson Rd SE21 .... 22 D6
Carstairs Rd SE6 .... 24 C5
Carswell Rd SE6 .... 24 C8
Cartbridge Cl GU23 .... 90 B4
Carter Cl SM6 .... 60 D3
Carter Rd Crawley RH10 .... 202 D3
Mitcham SW19 .... 20 D2
Carter's Cotts RH1 .... 139 E7
Carter's Rd KT17 .... 76 F4
Carterdale Cotts RH5 .... 178 C5
Carters Cl KT4 .... 39 D1
Carters La GU22 .... 90 D7
Carters Wlk GU9 .... 125 D8
Cartersmead Cl RH6 .... 161 B4
Carthouse Cotts GU4 .... 110 C4
Carthouse La GU21 .... 68 E5
Cartmel Cl RH2 .... 118 E3
Cartmel Ct BR2 .... 44 E7
Cartmel Gdns SM4 .... 40 C4
Carwarden House Sch
GU15 .... 66 A3
Caryl House 6 SW19 .... 19 D7
Carylls Cotts RH12 .... 199 F1
Cascades CR0 .... 62 F1
Caselden Cl KT15 .... 52 C5
Casewick Rd SE27 .... 22 B4
Casher Rd RH10 .... 202 C3
Cassel Hospl The TW10 .... 17 D4
Cassilis Rd TW1 .... 6 B1
Cassino Cl GU11 .... 105 B2
Cassiobury Ave TW14 .... 14 F8
Cassland Rd CR7 .... 42 D5
Casslee Rd SE6 .... 23 F8
Cassocks Sq TW17 .... 34 D2
Castillon Rd SE6 .... 24 E6
Castlands Rd SE6 .... 23 F6
Castle Ave KT17 .... 58 B2
Castle Cl Beckenham BR2 .... 44 E6
Bletchingley RH1 .... 120 C2
Charlton TW16 .... 14 E1
Frimley GU15 .... 65 F4
Reigate RH2 .... 139 B5
Wimbledon SW19 .... 19 D5
Castle Ct Belmont SM2 .... 59 A4
Forest Hill SE26 .... 23 E4
Morden SM4 .... 40 D4

Castle Dr Horley RH6 . . . . .161 C2
Reigate RH2 . . . . .139 B4
Castle Gdns RH4 . . . . .115 F1
Castle Gn KT13 . . . . .53 E7
Castle Grove Rd GU24 . . . . . .68 C2
Castle Hill Farnham GU9 . .125 B3
Guildford GU1 . . . . .130 D7
Castle Hill Ave CR0 . . . . . . .63 C2
Castle Hill Prim Sch CR0 .63 C4
Castle Hill Rd TW20 . . . . . .11 C5
Castle House 10 SM2 . . . . . .59 A3
Castle Par KT17 . . . . .58 A3
Castle Rd Aldershot GU11 .104 E4
Broadbridge Heath RH12 . .216 D3
Camberley GU15 . . . . .65 F4
Epsom KT18 . . . . .76 B4
Isleworth TW7 . . . . .5 F5
Kingswood CR5 . . . . .98 E6
Oatlands Park KT13 . . . . . .53 E7
Woking GU21 . . . . .69 F5
Castle Sq Bletchingley RH1 120 C2
Guildford GU1 . . . . .130 D7
Castle St Bletchingley RH1 .120 C2
Farnham GU9 . . . . .125 B3
Guildford GU1 . . . . .130 D7
Kingston u T KT2 . . . . .37 E7
Castle The RH12 . . . . .217 C2
Castle View KT18 . . . . .76 B5
Castle View Rd KT13 . . . . . .53 B6
Castle Way Ewell KT17 . . . . .58 A2
Feltham TW13 . . . . .15 C4
Wimbledon SW19 . . . . . . .19 D5
Castle Wlk TW16 . . . . .35 C6
Castle Yd 17 TW10 . . . . .6 D2
Castlecombe Dr SW19 . . . . .19 D8
Castlecraig Ct GU47 . . . . . .64 D7
Castledine Rd SE20 . . . . . . .23 B1
Castlefield Rd RH2 . . . . . .118 A1
Castlegate TW9 . . . . .6 F4
Castlemaine Ave
Ewell KT17 . . . . .58 B2
South Croydon CR0, CR2 . . .61 F5
Castleman House SL5 . . . . .29 D4
Castleton Cl Banstead SM7 .78 A4
Croydon CR0 . . . . .43 E3
Castleton Ct KT5 . . . . .37 F4
Castleton Dr SM7 . . . . .78 A5
Castleton Rd CR4 . . . . .41 D5
Caswell Cl GU14 . . . . .84 F6
Catalina Rd TW6 . . . . .3 A4
Catalpa Cl GU1 . . . . .109 C3
Catena Rise GU18 . . . . .48 B3
Cater Gdns GU3 . . . . .108 F3
Caterfield La
Crowhurst RH7 . . . . .143 F3
Oxted RH7, RH8 . . . . .144 A5
Caterham By-Pass CR3 . .101 B4
Caterham Cl GU24 . . . . . . .87 E6
Caterham Dene Hospl
CR3 . . . . .100 F4
Caterham
Dr CR3, CR5, CR8 . . . . . . .100 C8
Caterham Sch CR3 . . . . . .100 C1
Caterham Sch Prep CR3 .100 F1
Caterham Sta CR3 . . . . . .101 A3
Caterways RH12 . . . . .217 A3
Catford Bridge Sta SE6 . . .24 A8
Catford Broadway SE6 . . . .24 B8
Catford Cty Sch SE6 . . . . .24 C5
Catford Cty Sch (Annexe)
BR1 . . . . .24 E4
Catford Hill SE6 . . . . .24 A7
Catford Rd SE6 . . . . .24 A8
Catford Sta SE6 . . . . .24 A8
Cathedral Cl GU2 . . . . . . .130 B8
Cathedral Hill Ind Est
GU2 . . . . .109 A2
Cathedral View GU2 . . . . .108 F1
Catherine Baird Ct 12
SW12 . . . . .21 B8
Catherine Cl KT14 . . . . .71 F1
Catherine Ct 3 SW19 . . . . .19 F3
Catherine Dr TW16 . . . . . . .14 F2
Catherine Drive TW9 . . . . . . .6 E3
Catherine Gdns TW3 . . . . . . .5 D4
Catherine Howard Ct 6
KT13 . . . . .53 B7
Catherine Rd KT6 . . . . .37 D4
Catherine Wheel Rd TW8 . .6 D7
Catherington Sch RH11 .181 D2
Cathill La RH5 . . . . .177 C3
Cathles Rd SW12 . . . . .21 C8
Catlin Cres TW17 . . . . .34 E4
Catlin Gdns RH9 . . . . .121 B5
Catling Cl SE23 . . . . .23 D5
Caton Cl BR2 . . . . .44 E7
Cator Cl CR0 . . . . .82 E8
Cator Cres CR0 . . . . .82 E8
Cator La BR3 . . . . .43 F8
Cator Park Girls Sch BR3 .23 E1
Cator Rd Penge SE20, SE26 .23 D2
Wallington SM5 . . . . .59 F5
Catteshall Hatch GU7 .151 A6
Catteshall La GU7 . . . . . . .150 F4
Catteshall Rd GU7 . . . . . . .151 A5
Catteshall Terr GU7 . . . . .151 A5
Catteshall Wks GU7 . . . . .151 A6
Causeway TW14, TW4 . . . . . .4 B3
Causeway Ct 1 GU21 . . . . . .68 F1
Causeway E TW20 . . . . .12 C4
Causeway The
Carshalton SM5 . . . . .60 A8
Claygate KT10 . . . . .55 F3
Egham TW18, TW20 . . . . . .12 C4
Horsham RH12 . . . . .217 C1

Causeway The continued
Sutton SM2 . . . . .59 C2
Teddington TW11 . . . . .16 F2
Wimbledon SW19 . . . . . . .19 C3
Cavalier Way RH19 . . . . . .205 F7
Cavalry Cres TW4 . . . . .4 D3
Cavalry Ct GU11 . . . . .104 E2
Cavans Rd GU11 . . . . .105 C6
Cave Rd TW10 . . . . .17 C4
Cavell Rd RH10 . . . . .202 C5
Cavendish Ave KT3 . . . . . . .39 B5
Cavendish Cl Ashford TW16 14 F2
Horsham RH12 . . . . .217 D7
Cavendish Ct Ashford TW16 14 F2
Blackwater GU17 . . . . .64 D3
Poyle SL3 . . . . .1 E6
Cavendish Dr KT10 . . . . . . .55 E5
Cavendish Gdns RH1 . . . . .119 A2
Cavendish House TW1 . . . . . .6 A1
Cavendish Jun & Inf Sch
W4 .7 E2
Cavendish Meads SL5 . . . . .29 D3
Cavendish Mews GU11 . . .105 A1
Cavendish Rd
Aldershot GU11 . . . . .105 A1
Ashford TW16 . . . . .14 F2
Balham SW12 . . . . .21 B8
Chiswick W4 . . . . .7 C6
Mitcham SW19 . . . . .20 E1
New Malden KT3 . . . . .38 F5
Redhill RH1 . . . . .119 A2
Sutton SM2 . . . . .59 C3
Thornton Heath CR0 . . . . . .42 B1
Weybridge KT13 . . . . .53 C3
Woking GU22 . . . . .89 D8
Cavendish Terr TW13 . . . . .15 A6
Cavendish Way BR4 . . . . . . .44 B1
Caverleigh Way KT4 . . . . . .39 B2
Caversham Ave SM3 . . . . . .58 E8
Caversham House 8 KT1 .37 E7
Caversham Rd KT1 . . . . . . .37 F7
Caves Farm Cl GU47 . . . . . .64 A8
Cawnpore St SE19 . . . . . . .22 E3
Cawsey Way GU21 . . . . .69 E2
Cawston Ct BR1 . . . . .24 F1
Caxton Ave KT15 . . . . .52 A4
Caxton Gdns GU2 . . . . . . .109 B2
Caxton House RH8 . . . . . . .123 F3
Caxton La RH8 . . . . .123 E4
Caxton Rd SW19 . . . . .20 C3
Caxton Rise RH1 . . . . .119 A2
Caxtons Ct GU1 . . . . .110 A3
Caygill Cl BR2 . . . . .44 F5
Cayley Ct SM6 . . . . .60 E3
Cearn Way CR5 . . . . .79 F4
Cecil Cl Ashford TW15 . . . . .14 C1
Chessington KT9 . . . . .56 D6
Cecil Ct 3 CR0 . . . . .61 F8
Cecil Lodge KT9 . . . . .56 D6
Cecil Mansions 2 SW17 . .21 A6
Cecil Pl CR4 . . . . .40 F4
Cecil Rd Ashford TW15 . . . .14 C2
Cheam SM1, SM2 . . . . .58 F4
Hounslow TW3 . . . . .5 C5
Merton SW19 . . . . .20 B1
Thornton Heath CR0 . . . . . .41 F3
Cedar Ave Blackwater GU17 64 D5
Cobham KT11 . . . . .73 C4
Twickenham TW2 . . . . .5 C1
Cedar Cl Aldershot GU12 .126 E8
Bagshot GU19 . . . . .47 E3
Crawley RH11 . . . . .181 C1
Dorking RH4 . . . . .136 B7
East Molesey KT8 . . . . .36 E5
Epsom KT17 . . . . .76 F5
Esher KT10 . . . . .54 F3
Horsham RH12 . . . . .217 C3
Kingston u T KT2 . . . . .18 D4
Laleham TW18 . . . . .33 C6
Reigate RH2 . . . . .139 C7
Wallington SM5 . . . . .60 C3
Warlingham CR6 . . . . .101 E4
West Norwood SE21 . . . . . .22 C6
Wokingham RG40 . . . . .25 C6
Cedar Ct 8 Brentford TW8 . .6 D8
Egham TW20 . . . . .12 A4
Haslemere GU27 . . . . .208 B6
Mortlake SW14 . . . . .7 C3
Ottershaw KT16 . . . . .51 C5
Sanderstead CR2 . . . . .81 A8
Stoneleigh KT17 . . . . .58 A3
Sutton SM2 . . . . .59 C3
Wimbledon SW19 . . . . . . .19 D5
Cedar Dr Fetcham KT22 . . . .94 E4
Sunningdale SL5 . . . . .30 A2
Cedar Gdns Sutton SM2 . . .59 C4
Woking GU21 . . . . .69 B1
Cedar Gr Bisley GU24 . . . . .68 A4
Weybridge KT13 . . . . .53 C6
Cedar Hill KT18 . . . . .76 C3
Cedar House
Charlton TW16 . . . . .14 F1
New Addington CR0 . . . . . .63 B4
Cedar Hts TW10 . . . . .17 E7
Cedar La GU16 . . . . .85 D8
Cedar Lodge
Crawley RH11 . . . . .201 D4
Milford GU8 . . . . .149 F2
Cedar Rd Cobham KT11 . . . .73 B5
Cranford TW5 . . . . .4 C5
Croydon CR0, CR9 . . . . . . .61 C8
East Bedfont TW14 . . . . . . .14 D7
East Molesey KT8 . . . . .36 E5
Farnborough GU14 . . . . . . .85 C3
Sutton SM2 . . . . .59 C4
Teddington TW11 . . . . .17 A3

Cedar Rd continued
Weybridge KT13 . . . . .53 A6
Woking GU22 . . . . .89 C7
Cedar Terr TW9 . . . . .6 E3
Cedar Tree Gr SE27 . . . . . . .22 B3
Cedar Way Charlton TW16 . .14 E1
Guildford GU1 . . . . .109 C4
Kenley CR8 . . . . .80 C3
Kingswood KT20 . . . . .97 E7
Cedarcroft Rd KT4 . . . . .56 F6
Cedars 2 Bracknell RG12 . .27 F5
Woodmansterne SM7 . . . . .78 F5
Cedars Ave CR4 . . . . .41 A6
Cedars Ct GU1 . . . . .110 A4
Cedars House 5 SW27 . . . .22 B3
Cedars Prim Sch The TW5 .4 A7
Cedars Rd Barnes SW13 . . . .7 F5
Beckenham BR3 . . . . .43 F7
Morden SM4 . . . . .40 A5
Teddington KT8 . . . . .37 C8
Wallington SM6 . . . . .60 E6
Cedars The
Ashstead KT21, KT22 . . . . .95 D6
Byfleet KT14 . . . . .71 F7
Guildford GU1 . . . . .110 A4
Milford GU8 . . . . .170 E8
Reigate RH2 . . . . .118 D1
Teddington TW11 . . . . .16 F2
Wallington SM6 . . . . .60 C6
Cedarville Gdns SW16 . . . .21 F2
Cedarways GU9 . . . . .146 B7
Celandine Cl
1 Crawley RH11 . . . . .201 B1
Crowthorne RG45 . . . . .45 C6
Celandine Rd KT12 . . . . . . .54 E6
Celia Cres TW15 . . . . .13 D2
Celia Ct 3 TW9 . . . . .6 F6
Celtic Ave BR2 . . . . .44 E6
Celtic Rd KT14 . . . . .71 F5
Cemetery La TW17 . . . . . . .34 B2
Cemetery Pales
Brookwood GU24 . . . . .88 A6
Pirbright GU24 . . . . .87 F5
Centaurs Bsns Pk TW7 . . . .6 A8
Central Ave
East Molesey KT8 . . . . .35 F4
Isleworth TW3, TW7 . . . . . . .5 C3
Wallington SM6 . . . . .60 E5
Central Ct KT15 . . . . .52 B6
Central Hill SE19, SE27 . . . .22 D2
Central La SL4 . . . . .9 B7
Central Par Feltham TW14 . .15 C8
Heston TW5 . . . . .5 A7
Kingston u T KT6 . . . . .37 E3
New Addington CR0, CR9 . .63 C1
Penge SE20 . . . . .23 D1
Central Pk Est TW4 . . . . .4 D3
Central Rd Morden SM4 . . . .40 B4
North Cheam KT4 . . . . .58 A8
Central Sq KT8 . . . . .35 F5
Central Terr BR3 . . . . .43 D6
Central Veterinary
Laboratory KT15 . . . . .52 B2
Central Way Feltham TW14 . .4 B2
Oxted RH8 . . . . .122 D8
Sutton SM5 . . . . .59 E3
Winkfield SL4 . . . . .9 B7
Central Wlk RG40 . . . . .25 C6
Centre The Feltham TW13 . .15 B6
Walton-on-T KT12 . . . . .34 F1
Centurion Cl 4 GU47 . . . . .64 D8
Centurion Ct SM6 . . . . .60 B8
Century Rd TW20 . . . . .12 C3
Century Way GU24 . . . . . . .87 D8
Cerne Rd SM4 . . . . .40 C3
Cerotus Pl KT16 . . . . .32 F2
Chadacre Rd KT17 . . . . . . .58 B5
Chadhurst Cl RH5 . . . . . . .136 D4
Chadwick Ave SW19 . . . . . .20 A2
Chadwick Cl
Crawley RH11 . . . . .201 B1
Teddington TW11 . . . . .16 E2
Chadworth Way KT10 . . . . .55 D5
Chaffers Mead KT21 . . . . . .75 F3
Chaffinch Ave CR0 . . . . . . .43 D3
Chaffinch Cl
Crawley RH11 . . . . .201 D8
Croydon CR0 . . . . .43 D3
Horsham RH12 . . . . .217 D7
Chaffinch Rd BR3 . . . . .43 E8
Chaffinch Way RH6 . . . . . .160 E4
Chagford St SW19 . . . . . . .20 E1
Chailey Cl
3 Crawley RH11 . . . . .201 A3
Heston TW5 . . . . .4 D6
Chailey Pl KT12 . . . . .54 E6
Chalcot Cl SM2 . . . . .59 A3
Chalcot Mews SW16 . . . . . .21 E5
Chalcott Gdns KT6 . . . . . . .37 C1
Chaldon Cl RH1 . . . . .139 E7
Chaldon Common Rd
CR3 . . . . .100 C2
Chaldon Rd Caterham CR3 100 D4
Crawley RH11 . . . . .201 C1
Chaldon Way CR5 . . . . .79 E1
Chale Wlk SM2 . . . . .59 B2
Chalet Ct CR7 . . . . .42 B4
Chalfont Dr GU14 . . . . .85 C2
Chalfont Rd SE25 . . . . .42 F6
Chalford Cl KT8 . . . . .36 A5
Chalford Ct SE21 . . . . .22 D7
Chalford Rd SE21 . . . . .22 D4
Chalgrove Ave SM4 . . . . . . .40 A4
Chalgrove Rd SM2 . . . . . . .59 D3
Chalice Cl SM6 . . . . .60 D4

Chalk La Ashstead KT21 . . . .96 A8
East Horsley KT24 . . . . . . .112 F4
Epsom KT18 . . . . .76 E3
Shackleford GU8 . . . . .149 D8
Chalk Paddock KT18 . . . . . .76 D4
Langley Vale KT18, KT21 . . .96 E8
Sutton SM1 . . . . .59 C5
Chalk Pit Rd Banstead SM7 78 D4
Chalk Rd Farncombe GU7 .150 E5
Ifold RH14 . . . . .212 C3
Chalkenden Cl SE20 . . . . . .23 B1
Chalkley Cl CR4 . . . . .41 A7
Chalkpit La Dorking RH4 . .136 A8
Oxted RH8 . . . . .122 D8
Woldingham CR3, RH8 . . .102 C1
Chalkpit Terr RH4 . . . . . . .115 A1
Chalkpit Wood RH8 . . . . . .122 D8
Chalky La KT9 . . . . .56 D1
Challen Ct RH12 . . . . .217 B3
Challenge Ct KT22 . . . . . . .95 B8
Challenge Rd TW15 . . . . . . .14 D5
Challice Way SW2 . . . . .21 F7
Challin St SE20 . . . . .43 C8
Challis Pl RG42 . . . . .26 E8
Challock Cl TN16 . . . . .83 C3
Challoner Ct BR2 . . . . .44 D7
Challoners Cl KT8 . . . . .36 D5
Chalmers Ct RH6 . . . . .180 E6
Chalmers Rd Ashford TW15 14 C3
Banstead SM7 . . . . .78 C4
Chalmers Rd E TW15 . . . . .14 C3
Chalmers Way TW14 . . . . . . .4 B2
Chalner House 21 SW2 . . . .22 A7
Chamber La GU10 . . . . . . .145 C7
Chamberlain Cres BR4 . . . .44 B2
Chamberlain Way KT6 . . . . .37 E2
Chamberlain Wlk TW13 . . .15 E4
Chambers House 3 SW16 21 C4
Chambers Rd GU12 . . . . . .106 B6
Chamomile Gdns GU14 . . .84 C5
Champion Cres SE26 . . . . . .23 E4
Champion Rd SE26 . . . . . . .23 E4
Champness Cl 9 SE27 . . . .22 D4
Champneys Cl SM2 . . . . . . .58 F3
Chancellor Gdns CR2 . . . . .61 B2
Chancellor Gr SE21 . . . . . . .22 C5
Chancery La BR3 . . . . .44 B7
Chanctonbury Chase
RH1 . . . . .119 A1
Chanctonbury Dr SL5 . . . . .29 C3
Chanctonbury Gdns SM2 . .59 B3
Chanctonbury Way RH11 201 C4
Chandler CE (VA) Jun
Sch GU8 . . . . .170 F5
Chandler Cl
Crawley RH10, RH11 . . . . .201 D4
Hampton TW12 . . . . .36 A8
Chandler Ct
2 Tolworth KT5 . . . . .38 B1
8 Wallington SM6 . . . . . . .60 B4
Chandlers KT20 . . . . .97 B6
Chandlers Cl TW14 . . . . . . .14 F8
Chandlers Field Sch KT8 .36 A4
Chandlers Rd GU12 . . . . . .106 B4
Chandlers Way 11 SE24 . . .22 A8
Chandon Lodge SM2 . . . . . .59 C3
Chandos Rd TW18 . . . . . . .114 C8
Channel Cl TW5 . . . . .5 A6
Channings GU21 . . . . .69 E4
Channon Ct 3 KT6 . . . . . . .37 E4
Chantlers Cl RH19 . . . . . . .185 C2
Chanton Dr SM2 . . . . .58 C1
Chantrey Cl KT21 . . . . .95 C8
Chantrey Rd RH10 . . . . . . .201 E3
Chantry Cl Farnham GU9 . .125 A2
Horley RH6 . . . . .160 F4
Chantry Cotts GU4 . . . . . . .131 B3
Chantry Ct GU16 . . . . .65 D1
Chantry Hurst KT18 . . . . . .76 D4
Chantry La GU5 . . . . .132 F4
Chantry Rd Bagshot GU19 . .47 D2
Chertsey KT16 . . . . .33 C2
Chessington KT9 . . . . .57 A5
Chilworth GU4 . . . . .131 B3
Chantry View Rd GU1 . . . .130 E6
Chantry Way CR4 . . . . .40 D6
Chantry Wood Nature
Trail GU1 . . . . .130 E5
Chantrys Ct GU9 . . . . .125 A2
Chantrys The GU9 . . . . . . .125 A1
5 Sandhurst GU47 . . . . . .64 D8
Tolworth KT6 . . . . .57 A7
Chapel Ave KT15 . . . . .52 B6
Chapel Cl Bracknell RG12 . .27 B4
Milford GU8 . . . . .149 F2
Chapel Ct RH4 . . . . .136 B7
Chapel Farm Park RH5 . . .115 A5
Chapel Fields GU7 . . . . . . .150 D7
Chapel Gn CR8 . . . . .80 A6
Chapel Gr Addlestone KT15 .52 B6
Burgh Heath KT18 . . . . . . .97 C8
Chapel Hill Dunsfold GU8 .192 F3
Effingham KT24 . . . . .113 D7
Chapel La
Ashurst Wood RH19 . . . . .206 D6
Bagshot GU19 . . . . .47 D2
Copthorne RH10 . . . . .183 F4
Farnborough GU14 . . . . . . .84 F8
Forest Row RH18 . . . . .206 F2
Great Bookham KT23 . . . .114 D5
Milford GU8 . . . . .149 F2
Pirbright GU24 . . . . .88 A4
Westcott RH4 . . . . .135 C6
Westhumble RH5 . . . . .115 C6
Chapel Lane Ind Est RH4 135 C6
Chapel Park Rd KT15 . . . . .52 B6
Chapel Rd Camberley GU15 .65 B5
Charlwood RH6 . . . . .180 F7
Hounslow TW3 . . . . .5 B4
Limpsfield RH8 . . . . .123 C5

Chapel Rd continued
Redhill RH1 . . . . .118 F1
Rowledge GU10 . . . . .145 E3
Smallfield RH6 . . . . .162 B4
Tadworth KT20 . . . . .97 D4
Twickenham TW1 . . . . .17 B8
Warlingham CR6 . . . . .81 D1
West Norwood SE27 . . . . . .22 B4
Chapel Sq Sandhurst GU15 .64 A4
Thorpe GU25 . . . . .31 E5
Chapel St
Farnborough GU14 . . . . . . .85 D6
Guildford GU1 . . . . .130 D7
6 Woking GU21 . . . . .69 F2
Chapel View CR2 . . . . .62 C3
Chapel Way KT18, KT20 . . . .77 F2
Chapelhouse Cl GU2 . . . . .108 E1
Chaplain's Hill RG45 . . . . . .45 D4
Chaplin Cres TW16 . . . . . . .14 E2
Chapman House 2 SE27 . .22 B5
Chapman Rd
Crawley RH10 . . . . .202 C2
Thornton Heath CR0 . . . . . .42 A1
Chapman's La
East Grinstead RH19 . . . . .185 B1
East Grinstead RH19 . . . . .185 D1
Chapter Way TW12 . . . . . . .16 A4
Chara Pl W4 . . . . .7 D8
Charcot House SW15 . . . . . .7 F8
Chargate Cl KT12 . . . . .54 A4
Charing Ct BR2 . . . . .44 E7
Charlbury Cl 7 RG12 . . . . .27 F5
Charlecombe Ct TW18 . . . .13 B3
Charlecote Cl GU14 . . . . . . .85 D3
Charlecote Gr SE26 . . . . . .23 B5
Charles Ct 5 TW11 . . . . . . .16 E3
Charles Darwin Sch TN16 .83 F3
Charles Dickens Ct SE25 . .43 A5
Charles Hill GU10 . . . . . . .147 E6
Charles Mills Ct SW16 . . . .21 E2
Charles Rd Merton SW19 . .40 A8
Staines TW18 . . . . .13 D2
Charles Sq RG12 . . . . .27 C7
Charles St Chertsey KT16 . .32 F1
Croydon CR9 . . . . .61 C7
Hounslow TW3 . . . . .4 F5
Mortlake SW13, SW14 . . . . .7 F5
Charles Staunton House
SE27 . . . . .22 D4
Charlesfield Rd RH6 . . . . . .160 F4
Charleston Cl TW13 . . . . . .15 A5
Charleston Ct RH10 . . . . . .202 B3
Charleville Cir SE19, SE26 .23 A3
Charlmont Rd SW17 . . . . . .20 F2
Charlock Cl RH11 . . . . .201 A2
Charlock Way GU1 . . . . . . .110 B4
Charlotte Cl GU9 . . . . .125 D8
Charlotte Ct RH11 . . . . . . .201 C6
Charlotte Gr RH6 . . . . .162 A4
Charlotte Mews 4 KT10 . . .55 B6
Charlotte Rd Barnes SW13 . .7 F6
Wallington SM6 . . . . .60 C4
Charlotte Sq 5 TW10 . . . . . .6 F2
Charlton Ave KT12 . . . . .54 B6
Charlton Ct GU47 . . . . .45 D1
Charlton Dr TN16 . . . . .83 D2
Charlton Gdns CR5 . . . . . . .79 C1
Charlton Ho 5 TW8 . . . . . . .6 E8
Charlton Kings KT13 . . . . . .53 E7
Charlton La TW17 . . . . .34 D5
Charlton Rd TW17 . . . . .34 C7
Charlwood CR0 . . . . .62 F2
Charlwood Cl KT23 . . . . . . .94 B3
Charlwood Cty Inf Sch
RH6 . . . . .180 F7
Charlwood Dr KT22 . . . . . . .74 D4
Charlwood House 1 SW2 .21 F7
Charlwood La RH5 . . . . . . .180 A5
Charlwood Rd
Crawley RH6, RH11 . . . . . .181 C4
Hookwood RH6, RH11 . . . .181 C8
Rusper RH11, RH6 . . . . . . .180 E2
Charlwood Sq CR4 . . . . . . .40 D6
Charlwood Wlk RH11 . . . . .181 B1
Charlwoods Bsns Ctr
RH19 . . . . .185 D2
Charlwoods Pl RH19 . . . . . .185 E3
Charlwoods Rd RH19 . . . . .185 E3
Charm Cl RH6 . . . . .160 E4
Charman Rd RH1 . . . . .118 E1
Charmans Cl RH12 . . . . . . .218 B5
Charminster Ave SW19 . . . .40 B7
Charminster Ct 3 KT6 . . . .37 D2
Charminster Rd KT4 . . . . . .39 D1
Charmouth Ct TW10 . . . . . . .6 F2
Charnwood SL5 . . . . .29 F3
Charnwood Ave SW19 . . . . .40 B7
Charnwood Cl KT3 . . . . . . .38 E5
Charnwood Rd SE25 . . . . . .42 D5
Charrington Rd 2
CR0, CR9 . . . . .61 C8
Charrington Way RH12 . . . .216 C3
Charsley Rd SE6 . . . . .24 B6
Chart Cl Bromley BR2 . . . . . .44 E8
Croydon CR0 . . . . .43 C3
Dorking RH5 . . . . .136 D5
Mitcham CR4 . . . . .40 F5
Chart Downs RH5 . . . . .136 D4
Chart Gdns RH5 . . . . .136 C4
Chart House Rd GU12 . . . .106 A7
Chart La Dorking RH4, RH5 136 C4
Reigate RH2 . . . . .139 C8
Chart La S RH5 . . . . .136 D5
Charta Rd TW20 . . . . .12 C2
Charta Rd E TW20 . . . . . . .12 C2
Charta Rd S TW20 . . . . . . .12 C2
Charta Rd W TW20 . . . . . . .12 C3
Charter Cres TW4 . . . . .4 C3

Charter Ct KT3 38 E6
Charter Rd KT1 38 B6
Charter Sq KT1 38 B7
Charterhouse GU7 150 C7
Charterhouse Cl RG12 27 E4
Charterhouse Rd GU7 150 D6
Charters Cl SE19 22 E3
Charters La SL5 29 D4
Charters Rd SL5 29 E2
Charters Sch SL5 29 D2
Charters Way SL5 29 F2
Chartfield Rd RH2 139 C8
Chartham Gr SE27 22 B5
Chartham Rd SE25 43 B6
Charts Cl GU6 174 E2
Chartway RH2 118 B1
Chartwell Frimley GU16 85 F6
25 Putney SW19 19 D7
Wrecclesham GU9 145 F6
Chartwell Cl 2 CR0 42 D1
Chartwell Court Grange RH4 136 B4
Chartwell Gdns
Cheam SM3 58 E6
Farnborough GU11 105 C7
Chartwell Lodge 5 BR3 24 A1
Chartwell Pl Cheam SM3 58 F6
Epsom KT18 76 E5
Chartwell Way 4 SE20 43 B8
Charwood SW16 22 A4
Charwood Rd RG40 25 F7
Chase Bridge Inf Sch TW2 5 E1
Chase Bridge Jun Sch TW2 5 E1
Chase Cotts GU26 188 C1
Chase Ct Isleworth TW7 6 A5
Merton SW20 39 E7
Chase End KT19 76 D7
Chase Gdns TW2 16 D8
Chase La GU27 208 E3
Chase Rd KT17, KT19 76 D7
Chase The Ashstead KT21 75 C1
Coulsdon CR5 79 D5
Crawley RH10 202 A5
Crowthorne RG45 45 A6
East Horsley KT24 92 F1
Farnborough GU14 85 D6
Guildford GU2 130 A8
Kingswood KT20 98 B6
Oxshott KT22 74 C4
Reigate RH2 139 D8
South Norwood SW16 22 A1
Sunbury TW16 35 B8
Wallington CR0, SM6 60 F5
Chasefield Cl GU1, GU4 110 A4
Chasefield Rd SW17 20 F4
Chaseley Ct KT13 34 E1
Chasemore Cl CR4 40 F2
Chasemore Gdns CR0 61 A5
Chaseside Ave SW20 39 E7
Chaseside Gdns KT16 33 B2
Chasewater Ct 5 GU11 105 A1
Chatelet Cl RH6 161 B4
Chatfield Cl GU14 85 C2
Chatfield Ct CR3 100 D5
Chatfield Dr GU4 110 C3
Chatfield Rd CR0 42 B1
Chatfields RH11 201 B4
Chatham Ave BR2 44 F2
Chatham Cl SM3 39 F2
Chatham Rd KT1, KT2 38 A7
Chathill RH8 143 B6
Chatley Heath Semaphore Tower KT11 72 D1
Chatsfield KT17 58 A1
Chatsworth Ave
Haslemere GU27 208 C8
Merton SW20 39 E7
Chatsworth Cl BR2, BR4 63 F8
Chatsworth Cres TW3, TW7 5 D4
Chatsworth Gdns KT3 38 F4
Chatsworth Gr GU9 125 B6
Chatsworth Hts GU15 66 B7
Chatsworth Inf Sch TW3 5 C3
Chatsworth Jun Sch TW3 5 C3
Chatsworth Lodge BR4 63 C8
Chatsworth Pl Mitcham CR4 40 F6
Oxshott KT22 74 D6
Teddington TW11 17 A4
Chatsworth Rd Cheam SM3 58 E6
Chiswick W4 7 C8
Croydon CR0, CR9 61 D7
Farnborough GU14 85 E3
Chatsworth Way SE27 22 C5
Chattern Hill TW15 14 B4
Chattern Rd TW15 14 C4
Chatterton Ct TW9 6 F5
Chatton Row GU24 68 A2
Chaucer Ave Cranford TW4 4 B5
3 East Grinstead RH19 185 C1
Richmond TW9 7 A5
Weybridge KT13 53 A3
Chaucer Cl Banstead SM7 77 E5
Wokingham RG40 25 F6
Chaucer Ct GU2 130 C7
Chaucer Gdns SM1 59 A7
Chaucer Gn CR0 43 C2
Chaucer Gr GU15 65 D5
Chaucer House Sutton SM1 59 A7
2 West Norwood SE27 22 C4
Chaucer Rd Ashford TW15 13 F4
Crawley RH10 202 C8
Crowthorne RG45 45 B4
Farnborough GU14 84 F6
Sutton SM1 59 A6
Chaucer Way KT15 52 A4
Chavey Down Rd RG42 8 B2
Chaworth Cl KT16 51 C4
Chaworth Rd KT16 51 C4
Chawridge La SL4 8 C7
Cheam Cl Bracknell RG12 27 D4
Burgh Heath KT20 97 B6
Cheam Common Inf Sch KT4 58 B8
Cheam Common Jun Sch KT4 58 B8
Cheam Common Rd KT4 58 C7
Cheam Court Flats SM3 58 E4
Cheam Fields Prim Sch SM3 58 E5
Cheam High Sch SM3 58 E6
Cheam Mansions SM3 58 E3
Cheam Park Farm Inf Sch SM3 58 E7
Cheam Park Farm Jun Sch SM3 58 E7
Cheam Park Way SM3 58 E4
Cheam Rd Belmont SM2 58 C1
Cheam SM1 59 A4
East Ewell KT17, SM2 58 C1
Ewell SM2 58 C1
Cheam Sta SM2 58 E3
Cheapside GU21 69 D5
Cheapside C of E Prim Sch SL5 29 E8
Cheapside Rd SL5 29 D7
Cheddar Rd TW6 3 A5
Cheeseman Cl
Hampton TW12 15 E2
Wokingham RG40 25 D7
Chelford Rd BR1, E6 24 D3
Chellows La RH7 143 F2
Chelmsford Cl SM2 59 A2
Chelsea Cl Hampton TW12 16 C3
New Malden KT4 39 A2
Chelsea Fields SW19 40 D8
Chelsea Gdns SM3 58 E6
Chelsfield Gdns SE26 23 C5
Chelsham Common Rd CR6 82 A3
Chelsham Court Rd CR6 82 E2
Chelsham Rd Croydon CR2 61 D4
Warlingham CR6 81 F2
Chelsham Terr CR6 81 F1
Cheltenham Ave 9 TW1 17 A8
Cheltenham Cl KT3 38 C6
Cheltenham Villas CR7 42 A3
Chelwood Cl
Crawley RH10 201 F4
Ewell KT17 76 F7
Chelwood Gdns TW9 7 A5
Cheney Ct SE23 23 D7
Cheniston Cl KT14 71 A6
Cheniston Ct SL5 30 A2
Chennells Way RH12 217 E5
Chennestone Cty Prim Sch TW16 35 B7
Chepstow Cl RH10 202 E6
Chepstow Rd CR0 61 F8
Chequer Grange RH18 206 E1
Chequer Rd RH19 185 F1
Chequer Tree Cl GU21 68 E3
Chequers Cl Horley RH6 161 A4
Walton on t H KT20 97 A2
Chequers Ct
7 Croydon CR0 42 F1
Horsham RH13 217 E2
Walton on t H KT20 97 A2
Chequers Dr RH6 161 A4
Chequers La KT20 97 A2
Chequers Pl RH4 136 B7
Cherbury Cl RG12 27 E5
Cherimoya Gdns KT8 36 B6
Cherington Way SL5 28 E7
Cheriton Ave BR2 44 F4
Cheriton Ct
South Norwood SE25 42 E4
Walton-on-T KT12 35 C1
Cheriton Sq SW17 21 A6
Cheriton Way GU17 64 D5
Cherkley Hill KT22, RH5 95 D1
Cherrimans Orch GU27 207 F6
Cherry Cl Banstead KT17 77 D5
Carshalton SM5 59 F8
Merton SM4 39 E5
7 Streatham SW2 22 A8
Cherry Cres TW8 6 B7
Cherry Ct RH13 217 D1
Cherry Green Cl RH1 140 B7
Cherry Hill Gdns CR0 60 F6
Cherry La RH11 181 C1
Cherry Lodge 7 GU12 105 B1
Cherry Orch Ashstead KT21 76 B1
Staines TW18 13 A3
Cherry Orchard Gdns
6 Croydon CR0 61 D8
East Molesey KT8 35 F6
Cherry Orchard Rd
Croydon CR0 42 E1
East Molesey KT8 36 A6
Cherry St GU21 69 E1
Cherry Tree Ave
Guildford GU2 108 F1
Haslemere GU27 207 F7
Staines TW18 13 B2
Cherry Tree Cl
Crawley RH10 202 D8
Farnborough GU14 84 C5
Farnham GU9 125 C3
Sandhurst GU47 45 D1
Cherry Tree Ct CR5 79 F1
Cherry Tree Dr
Bracknell RG12 27 D6
Streatham SW16 21 E5
Cherry Tree Gn CR2 81 B5
Cherry Tree La GU7 150 D8
Cherry Tree Rd
Milford GU8 149 E1
Rowledge GU10 145 E3
Cherry Tree Wlk
Beckenham BR3 43 F5
Coney Hall BR4 63 F6
Cherry Way Horton SL3 1 C4
Upper Halliford TW17 34 E5
West Ewell KT19 57 D4
Cherrydale Rd GU15 66 D5
Cherryhill Gr GU11 104 F1
Cherryhurst GU8 171 B1
Cherrywood Ave TW20 11 B1
Cherrywood Cl KT2 18 A1
Cherrywood Ct 1 TW11 17 A3
Cherrywood La SM4, SW20 39 E5
Cherrywood Rd GU14 85 B7
Chertsey Bridge Rd KT16, TW18 33 D2
Chertsey Bvd KT16 32 F1
Chertsey Cl CR8 80 B4
Chertsey Cres CR0 63 C1
Chertsey Ct SW14 7 B4
Chertsey Dr SM3 58 E8
Chertsey House TW13 16 A5
Chertsey La TW18 12 F2
Chertsey Rd
Addlestone KT15 52 B8
Ashford TW15 &TW16 TWTW16 14 D2
Burrowhill GU20, GU24 49 C6
Byfleet KT14 71 D8
Chertsey KT15 52 B8
Chobham GU24, KT16, GU21 50 D1
Feltham TW13 &TW16 TW16 14 E4
Feltham, Ashford Common TW13, TW16 14 D2
Lower Halliford TW17 34 A2
Shepperton TW17 33 F2
Twickenham TW2 16 D7
Windlesham GU20 48 E5
Woking GU21 69 F3
Chertsey St Guildford GU1 130 D8
Upper Tooting SW17 21 A3
Chertsey Sta KT16 32 F1
Chertsey Wlk KT16 33 A2
Chervil Cl TW13 15 A5
Cherwell Cl SL3 1 B8
Cherwell Ct Teddington KT1 17 D1
West Ewell KT19 57 C6
Cherwell Wlk RH11 200 F5
Cheselden Rd GU1 130 E8
Cheseman St SE26 23 B5
Chesfield Rd KT2 17 E1
Chesham Cl SM2 58 E1
Chesham Cres SE20 43 C8
Chesham Ct SW18 20 D8
Chesham Mews 14 GU1 130 F8
Chesham Rd
Guildford GU1 130 F8
Kingston u T KT1, KT2 38 A7
Penge SE20 43 C8
Cheshire Cl
Mitcham CR4, SW16 41 E6
Ottershaw KT16 51 D4
Cheshire Gdns KT9 56 D4
Cheshire House
Cheam SM4 40 B2
Ottershaw KT16 51 D4
Chesney Cres CR0 63 C3
Chessholme Ct TW16 14 E1
Chessholme Rd TW15 14 C2
Chessington Cl KT19 57 C4
Chessington Comm Coll KT9 56 D3
Chessington Hall Gdns KT9 56 D4
Chessington Hill Pk KT9 57 A5
Chessington North Sta KT9 56 E5
Chessington Par KT9 56 D5
Chessington Park KT9 57 A6
Chessington Rd Ewell KT19 57 D3
West Ewell KT19 57 D3
Chessington South Sta KT9 56 D3
Chessington Way BR4 63 B8
Chessington World of Adventures KT9 56 C1
Chester Ave Richmond TW10 6 F1
Twickenham TW2 15 F7
Chester Cl Ash GU12 106 B2
Ashford TW15 14 D3
Dorking RH4 115 C1
Guildford GU2 108 F3
1 Richmond TW10 6 F1
Sutton SM1 59 A8
Chester Gdns SM4 40 C3
Chester House KT1 38 B7
Chester Rd Ash GU12 106 B2
Effingham KT24 113 B7
Harlington TW6 3 A4
Hounslow TW4 4 B4
Wimbledon SW19, SW20 19 C2
Chester Way GU10 126 F6
Chesterblade La RG12 27 E2
Chesterfield Cl RH19 184 C4
Chesterfield Ct KT6 37 E4
Chesterfield Dr KT10 56 A8
ChesterfieldHouse 6 SW16 21 C3
Chesterfield Rd
Ashford TW15 13 E3
Chiswick W4 7 C8
West Ewell KT19 57 D3
Chesters RH6 160 E5
Chesters Rd GU15 66 B5
Chesters The KT3 38 E8
Chesterton Cl RH19 205 F7
Chesterton Ct RH13 218 A4
Chesterton Dr
Merstham RH1 119 E7
Stanwell TW19 13 F7
Chesterton Terr KT1 38 A7
Chestnut Ave
Aldershot GU12 126 E8
Camberley GU15 66 A6
Coney Hall BR4 63 E6
Farnham GU9 146 A8
Guildford GU2 130 C5
Hampton TW12 16 A1
Hampton, Hampton Court KT8 &KT11 36 F7
Haslemere GU27 208 C7
11 Mortlake SW14 7 D4
Tatsfield TN16 103 E5
Thames Ditton KT10 36 D1
Wentworth GU25 30 F5
Weybridge KT13 53 C3
Whiteley Village KT12 53 E2
Worcester Park KT19 57 E6
Chestnut Cl
Addlestone KT15 52 D5
Ashford, Chattern Hill TW15 14 B4
Ashford, Felthamhill TW16 14 F2
Blackwater GU17 64 E4
Carshalton SM5 40 F1
Catford SE6 24 C4
East Grinstead RH19 186 A1
Englefield Green TW20 11 C2
Grayshott GU26 188 C3
Harlington UB7 3 B7
Kingswood KT20 98 A4
Redhill RH1 140 B7
Send Marsh GU23 91 A3
West Norwood SE27, SW16 22 A4
Chestnut Copse RH8 123 B2
Chestnut Cres KT12 53 E2
Chestnut Ct
Aldershot GU12 105 D2
Beckenham BR3 24 A1
5 Croydon CR0 61 C6
Feltham TW13 15 D3
Horsham RH13 217 E2
Hounslow TW3 5 A4
Kingston u T KT3 38 E6
Chestnut Dr TW20 11 D2
Chestnut End GU35 187 A4
Chestnut Gdns RH12 217 C5
Chestnut Gr Balham SW12 21 A7
Isleworth TW7 6 A3
Kingston u T KT3 38 D6
Mitcham CR4 41 D5
South Croydon CR2 62 C3
Staines TW18 13 C2
Woking GU22 89 E7
Chestnut Grove Sch SW12 21 A7
Chestnut House SE27 22 C5
Chestnut La Chobham GU24 49 C4
Weybridge KT13 53 A6
Chestnut Manor Cl TW18 13 B3
Chestnut Mead RH1 118 E2
Chestnut Pl Ashtead Kt21 95 E8
Ewell KT17 77 A8
Chestnut Rd Ashford TW15 14 B4
Farnborough GU14 85 A5
Guildford GU1 109 D1
Horley RH6 161 B5
Kingston u T KT2 17 E1
Merton SW20 39 D7
Twickenham TW2 16 E6
West Norwood SE21, SE27 22 C5
Chestnut Way
Bramley GU5 152 A4
Feltham TW13 15 B5
Godalming GU7 150 F2
Chestnut Wlk
Crawley RH11 181 C1
Felcourt RH19 185 C8
Upper Halliford TW17 34 E5
Whiteley Village KT12 53 E2
Chestnuts The Horley RH6 161 A5
Penge BR3 43 D6
Walton-on-T KT12 54 A8
Cheston Ave CR0 43 F1
Chesworth Cl RH13 217 C1
Chesworth Cres RH13 217 C1
Chesworth Cty Jun Sch RH13 217 E3
Chesworth Gdns RH13 217 C1
Chesworth La RH12, RH13 217 C1
Cheswycks Sch GU16 86 B5
Chetwode Cl RG40 25 E6
Chetwode Dr KT20 77 D1
Chetwode Pl GU11 126 C7
Chetwode Rd
Burgh Heath KT20 97 C8
Upper Tooting SW17 20 F5
Chetwode Terr GU11 104 E1
Chetwood Rd RH11 200 D2
Chevening Cl RH11 201 C1
Chevening Rd SE19 22 D2
Chevington Villas RH1 120 F3
Cheviot Cl Banstead SM7 78 B4
Farnborough GU14 84 E7
Frimley GU15 66 C4
Harlington UB3 3 D7
Sutton SM2 59 D2
Cheviot Gdns SE27 22 B4
Cheviot Rd SE27 22 B3
Cheviot Wlk RH11 201 B6
Chevremont GU1 130 E8
Chewter Cl GU19 47 F3
Chewter La GU20 48 B6
Cheyham Gdns SM2 58 D1
Cheyham Way SM2 58 E1
Cheylesmore Dr GU16 66 D3
Cheyne Ave TW2 15 F7
Cheyne Ct Banstead SM7 78 B4
4 Wallington SM6 60 B4
Cheyne Hill KT5 37 F5
Cheyne Rd TW15 14 D2
Cheyne Way GU14 84 F8
Cheyne Wlk Croydon CR0 62 A8
Horley RH6 161 A1
Cheynell Wlk RH11 200 F4
Chichele Gdns CR0 61 E6
Chichele Rd RH8 122 E7
Chichester Cl
Crawley RH10 201 E2
Dorking RH4 115 B1
Hampton TW12 15 F2
Witley GU8 170 E5
Chichester Ct Ewell KT17 57 F2
Stanwell TW19 13 E7
Chichester Dr CR8 79 F7
Chichester Mews SE27 22 A4
Chichester Rd Ash GU12 106 A3
Dorking RH4 115 B2
South Croydon CR0 61 F7
Chichester Terr RH12 217 D2
Chichester Way TW14 15 C8
Chiddingfold Rd GU8 192 C3
Chiddingly Cl RH10 202 B5
Chiddingstone Cl SM2 59 A1
Chilberton Dr RH1 119 C5
Chilbolton TW20 11 E3
Chilbrook Rd KT11 73 A1
Chilchester Ct BR3 44 B6
Chilcombe House 7 SW15 19 A8
Chilcroft La GU27 208 B1
Chilcroft Rd GU27 207 F7
Chilcrofts Rd GU27 208 A1
Child Cl RG40 25 D8
Childebert Rd SW17 21 B6
Childerly KT1 38 A6
Childrens Trust (Tadworth Court) The KT20 97 D6
Childs Hall Cl KT23 93 F2
Childs Hall Dr KT23 93 F2
Childs Hall Rd KT23 93 F2
Childs La 10 SE19 22 E2
Chilham Cl GU16 85 F8
Chillerton Rd SW17 21 B3
Chillingford House SW17 20 C4
Chillingham Way GU15 65 C4
Chillingworth Gdns TW1 16 F5
Chilmans Dr KT23 94 B2
Chilmark Gdns
Merstham RH1 119 E6
New Malden KT3 39 A3
Chilmark Rd SW16 41 D8
Chilmead 1 RH1 118 F2
Chilmead La RH1 119 D3
Chilsey Green Rd KT16 32 E2
Chiltern GU22 89 C5
Chiltern Ave
Farnborough GU14 84 D4
Twickenham TW2 16 A7
Chiltern Cl Crawley RH11 201 B6
Farnborough GU14 84 D4
Haslemere GU27 208 B5
North Cheam KT4 58 C8
South Croydon CR0 61 E7
Chiltern Dr KT5 38 B4
Chiltern Gdns BR2 44 F5
Chiltern Rd Sandhurst GU47 45 A1
Sutton SM2 59 C1
Chilterns The SM2 59 B2
Chilthorne Cl SE6 23 F8
Chiltington Ct RH12 217 D4
Chilton Ct KT12 54 A6
Chilton Rd TW9 7 A4
Chiltons Cl SM7 78 B4
Chilworth CE Inf Sch GU4 131 D3
Chilworth Ct
8 Putney SW19 19 D7
13 Redhill RH1 118 F2
Chilworth Gdns SM1 59 C7
Chilworth Rd GU4, GU5 132 A4
Chilworth Sta GU4 131 E3
Chimneys Ct SW19 19 C1
Chinchilla Dr TW4 4 C5
Chine The GU10 145 F5
Chingford Ave GU14 85 D5
Chingley Cl BR1 24 E2
Chinthurst La
Shalford GU4, GU5 130 F2
Wonersh GU5 152 A7
Chinthurst Pk GU4 130 E1
Chinthurst Sch KT20 97 C4
Chippendale Cl GU17 64 E4
Chippendale Rd RH11 201 B1
Chippenham 4 KT1 37 F7
Chipstead Ave CR7 42 B5
Chipstead Cl Belmont SM2 59 B2
Coulsdon CR5 79 A3
Penge SE19 22 F1
Redhill RH1 140 A7
Chipstead Ct GU21 68 E2
Chipstead House 4 SW2 21 E7
Chipstead La CR5, KT20 98 B3
Chipstead Sta CR5 78 F1
Chipstead Valley Prim Sch CR5 79 A3
Chipstead Valley Rd
Chipstead CR5 79 B3
Coulsdon CR5 79 B3

Chipstead Way CR5, SM7 . .78 F3
Chirton Wlk GU21 . . . . . . .69 A1
Chisbury Cl RG12 . . . . .27 E3
Chisholm Rd Croydon CR0 . .61 E8
13 Richmond TW10 . . . . . . .6 F1
Chislehurst Rd TW10 . . . . .6 E2
Chislet Cl BR3 . . . . .24 A1
Chiswick Cl GU4 . . . . .60 F7
Chiswick Comm Sch W4 . . .7 B7
Chiswick House W4 . . . . . . .7 E7
Chiswick La S W4 . . . . .7 F8
Chiswick Mall W4 . . . . .7 F8
Chiswick Quay W4 . . . . . . .7 C6
Chiswick Sq W4 . . . . .7 E8
Chiswick Sta W4 . . . . .7 C7
Chiswick Staithe W4 . . . . . .7 C6
Chiswick Village W4 . . . . . .7 B8
Chithurst La RH6, RH7 . .162 F2
Chittenden Cotts
GU23, KT14 . . . . .71 E3
Chitterfield Gate UB7 . . . . .3 A7
Chitty's Wlk GU3 . . . . . .108 F5
Chive Ct GU14 . . . . .84 C4
Chivelston **27** SW19 . . . .19 D7
Chivenor Gr KT2 . . . . .17 D3
Chobham Cl KT16 . . . . . . .51 B4
Chobham Common
(Nature Reserve) KT16 . .49 F6
Chobham Gdns SW19 . . . .19 D6
Chobham Golf Course
GU21 . . . . .68 C5
Chobham La KT16, GU24 . .50 A8
Chobham Park La GU24 . . .50 B2
Chobham Rd
Chobham GU21 . . . . .69 E3
Frimley GU16 . . . . .66 A2
Knaphill GU21 . . . . .68 D3
Ottershaw KT16 . . . . .51 B4
1 Woking GU21 . . . . . . .69 F2
Woking, Horsell Common
GU21, GU24 . . . . .69 D5
Chobham St Lawrence
Cof E Prim Sch GU24 . . . .68 E8
Choir Gn GU21 . . . . .68 E2
Cholmeley Rd KT7 . . . . . . .37 B3
Cholmondeley Wlk TW9 . . .6 C2
Chrislaine Cl TW19 . . . . . . .2 D1
Chrismas Ave GU12 . . . .105 C1
Chrismas Pl GU12 . . . . . .105 C1
Christ Church C of E
Prim Sch Purley CR8 . . . .61 B1
Streatham SW2 . . . . .21 F7
Christ Church C of E Sch
KT16 . . . . .51 D4
Christ Church CE Inf Sch
KT3 . . . . .38 E6
Christ Church CE Jun Sch
KT3 . . . . .38 D6
Christ Church CE Prim
Sch KT5 . . . . .38 A3
Christ Church Mount
KT19 . . . . .76 B7
Christ Church Prim Sch
SE23 . . . . .23 D6
Christ Church Rd
Beckenham BR3 . . . . .44 A4
Epsom KT18 . . . . .76 A6
Surbiton KT5 . . . . .37 F3
Christ the King RC Fst Sch
TW19 . . . . .2 E1
Christ's Sch (East Side)
SW14 . . . . .7 D4
Christ's Sch (West Side)
TW10 . . . . .6 F2
Christabel Cl TW7 . . . . .5 E4
Christchurch Ave **4** TW11 17 A3
Christchurch C of E Fst
Sch GU25 . . . . .31 B6
Christchurch Cl SW19 . . . .20 D1
Christchurch Cotts GU25 . .31 B6
Christchurch Dr GU47 . . . .64 D6
Christchurch Gdns KT19 . .76 B8
Christchurch House **2**
SW2 . . . . .21 E7
Christchurch Hts **9** RH2 .118 F1
Christchurch Pk SM2 . . . . .59 C3
Christchurch Pl KT19 . . . . .76 B8
Christchurch Rd
Harlington TW6 . . . . .3 A4
Mitcham SW19 . . . . .20 D1
Mortlake SW14 . . . . .7 C2
Purley CR8 . . . . .80 B8
Streatham SW2 . . . . .21 F7
Virginia Water GU25 . . . . .31 C3
Christchurch Way **2** GU21 69 F2
Christian Fields SW16 . . . .22 A1
Lightwater GU18 . . . . .48 C1
Little Bookham KT23 . . . . .93 F3
Christie Dr SE25 . . . . .43 A4
Christie House BR4 . . . . . .44 B1
Christies RH19 . . . . .205 D8
Christine Cl GU12 . . . . . .105 F1
Christmas Hill GU4 . . . . .130 F2
Christmaspie Ave GU3 . .107 B1
Christopher Ct
Ashford TW15 . . . . .13 E4
6 Croydon CR0 . . . . . . .43 A1
Tadworth KT20 . . . . .97 C4
Christopher Rd RH19 . . .185 E1
Christy Rd TN16 . . . . .83 C4
Chrystie La KT23 . . . . .94 B1
Chuck's La KT20 . . . . .97 B3
Chudleigh Ct **4** GU14 . . .85 B4
Chudleigh Gdns SM1 . . . . .59 C7

Chudleigh Rd TW1, TW2 . .16 F8
Chulsa Rd SE26 . . . . .23 B3
Chumleigh Wlk KT5 . . . . .37 F5
Church Almshouses **8** TW9 6 F3
Church App Dulwich SE21 . .22 D5
Thorpe TW20 . . . . .32 C6
Church Ave Beckenham BR3 44 A8
Farnborough GU14 . . . . . .85 C3
Mortlake SW14 . . . . .7 D4
Church Circ GU14 . . . . . . .85 C1
Church Cl Addlestone KT15 .52 B6
6 Epsom KT17 . . . . .76 E6
Fetcham KT22 . . . . .94 D3
Grayswood GU27 . . . . . .189 F2
Hounslow TW4 . . . . .4 F5
Laleham TW18 . . . . .33 C6
Lower Kingswood KT20 . .117 F8
Milford GU8 . . . . .149 F1
Pirbright GU24 . . . . .87 F6
Woking GU21 . . . . .69 E3
Church Ct Forest Hill SE26 . .23 E3
Reigate RH2 . . . . .118 B1
Church Dr BR4 . . . . .63 E7
Church Farm La SM3 . . . . .58 E4
Church Field House KT11 .73 B5
Church Gdns Dorking RH4 136 B8
Leatherhead KT22 . . . . . .95 B7
Church Gn Elstead GU8 . .148 C3
Hersham KT12 . . . . .54 C4
Church Gr KT1 . . . . .37 C7
Church Hill
Aldershot GU11, GU12 . .126 C8
Camberley GU15 . . . . . . .65 E5
Caterham CR3 . . . . .100 F3
Merstham RH1 . . . . .99 B1
Nutfield RH1 . . . . .119 F2
Purley CR8 . . . . .60 E1
Shamley Green GU5 . . . .152 E4
Shere GU5 . . . . .133 A4
Tatsfield TN16 . . . . .103 D5
Wallington SM5 . . . . .59 F5
Wimbledon SW19 . . . . . . .19 F3
Woking GU21 . . . . .69 D3
Church Hill House Hospl
RG12 . . . . .27 A3
Church Hill Rd
Cheam SM1, SM3 . . . . . .58 E6
Kingston u T KT6 . . . . . . .37 E4
Ascot SL5 . . . . .29 D5
Ash GU12 . . . . .106 B2
Binstead GU10 . . . . .145 E3
Bisley GU21, GU24 . . . . . .68 A4
Bletchingley RH1 . . . . . .120 D3
Broadbridge Heath RH12 .216 D3
Brook GU8 . . . . .190 C8
Burgh Heath KT18, SM7 . .77 E2
Burstow RH6 . . . . .182 F7
Caterham CR3 . . . . .100 A3
Chelsham CR6 . . . . .82 C3
Chessington KT9 . . . . .56 F4
Copthorne RH10 . . . . . . .183 B3
Cranleigh GU6 . . . . .174 E3
Crawley RH10 . . . . .201 F6
Crondall GU10 . . . . .124 D8
East Grinstead RH19 . . . .185 F1
Farnborough GU14 . . . . . .84 E4
Godstone RH9 . . . . .121 D3
Grayshott GU26 . . . . . . .188 C3
Hambledon GU8 . . . . . . .171 D2
Haslemere GU27 . . . . . . .208 D7
Headley KT18 . . . . .96 D2
Hooley CR5 . . . . .99 B5
Merton SW19 . . . . .39 F8
Oxted RH8 . . . . .122 E6
Pirbright GU24 . . . . .87 D4
Send GU23 . . . . .90 C1
Shere GU5 . . . . .133 A4
Sunningdale SL5 . . . . .30 B4
Teddington TW11 . . . . . . .16 F3
Thames Ditton KT7 . . . . . .37 A3
Twickenham TW1 . . . . . . .17 A7
Upper Tooting SW17 . . . . .21 A3
Upper Tooting,
Furzedown SW17 . . . . . . .21 B4
Wallington SM6 . . . . .60 D7
Wallis Wood RH5 . . . . . .176 F1
Warlingham CR6 . . . . .81 D2
Weybridge KT13 . . . . .53 A6
Witley GU8 . . . . .170 E2
Wormley GU8 . . . . .170 E2
Worplesdon GU3 . . . . . .108 E8
Wrecclesham GU10 . . . . .145 F7
Church La E GU11 . . . . . .126 B8
Church La W GU11 . . . . .105 A1
Church Lane Ave CR5 . . . .99 B5
Church Lane Dr CR5 . . . . .99 B5
Church Meadow KT6 . . . . .56 C8
Church Mews KT15 . . . . . .52 C6
Church Par TW15 . . . . .13 F4
Church Pas GU9 . . . . . . .125 B2
Church Path
Aldershot GU14 . . . . .105 C8
Ash GU12 . . . . .106 A3
Croydon CR0, CR9 . . . . . .61 C8
Merton SW19 . . . . .40 A7
Mitcham CR4 . . . . .40 E6
7 Woking GU21 . . . . . .69 F2
Church Pl CR4 . . . . .40 E6
Church Rd Addlestone KT15 .52 B5
Church St W GU21 . . . . . . .69 E2
Church Stretton Rd TW3 . .5 C2
Church Terr **20** TW10 . . . .6 D2
Church Vale SE23 . . . . .23 D6
Church View GU12 . . . . . .106 A2
Church View Cl RH6 . . . . .160 F2
Church Villa TW16 . . . . . . .35 B6
Church Way Oxted RH8 . .122 F3
South Croydon CR2 . . . . . .81 A8

Church Rd *continued*
Bracknell RG12 . . . . .27 C7
Broadbridge Heath RH12 . .216 D3
Burstow RH6 . . . . .183 A7
Byfleet KT14 . . . . .71 E6
Caterham CR3 . . . . .100 F3
Cheam SM3 . . . . .58 E4
Claygate KT10 . . . . .55 F3
Copthorne RH10 . . . . . . .183 B3
Crawley, Lowfield
Heath RH11 . . . . .181 E5
Crawley, Worth RH10 . . . .202 E6
Croydon CR0, CR9 . . . . . .61 C7
Dunsfold GU8 . . . . .192 D5
East Molesey KT8 . . . . . . .36 D6
Egham TW20 . . . . .12 A3
Epsom KT17 . . . . .76 E6
Feltham TW13 . . . . .15 D3
Fetcham KT23 . . . . .94 A3
Frimley GU16 . . . . .65 D1
Guildford GU1 . . . . .130 D8
Haslemere GU27 . . . . . . .208 C7
Haslemere,
Shottermill GU27 . . . . . .207 F6
Heston TW5 . . . . .4 B8
Heston TW5 . . . . .5 A8
Horley RH6 . . . . .160 F2
Horley RH6 . . . . .161 A3
Horne RH6 . . . . .162 F5
Horsham RH12 . . . . .218 B5
Hounslow TW7 . . . . .5 E7
Kenley CR8 . . . . .80 C4
Kingston u T KT1 . . . . .37 F7
Leatherhead KT22 . . . . . . .95 B5
Lingfield RH7 . . . . .164 D4
Little Bookham KT23 . . . . .93 F4
Long Ditton KT6 . . . . .37 C1
Lower Halliford TW17 . . . . .34 B2
Milford GU8 . . . . .149 F1
Mitcham CR4, SW19 . . . . .40 D7
New Malden KT4 . . . . .38 E4
Purley CR8 . . . . .60 E1
Redhill RH1 . . . . .139 E7
Reigate RH2 . . . . .139 A7
Richmond TW10, TW9 . . . .6 E2
Richmond, Ham
Common TW10 . . . . .17 E4
Sandhurst GU15 . . . . .64 F7
Sandhurst, Owlsmoor GU47 . .45 E1
South Norwood SE19 . . . . .22 E1
Sunningdale SL5 . . . . .30 A3
Teddington TW11 . . . . . . .16 F3
Turners Hill RH10 . . . . . .204 A3
Wallington SM6 . . . . .60 D7
Warlingham CR6 . . . . .81 D2
West End GU24 . . . . .67 F7
West Ewell KT19 . . . . .57 D3
Whyteleafe CR3 . . . . .100 F8
Wimbledon SW19 . . . . . . .19 E4
Windlesham GU20 . . . . . . .48 C4
Winkfield SL4 . . . . .8 C5
Winkfield, Chavey Down SL5 . .28 B8
Woking, Horsell GU21 . . . .69 E4
Woking, St John's GU21 . . .89 A8
Woldingham CR3 . . . . . . .101 E4
Church Rd E
Crowthorne RG45 . . . . . . .45 B5
Farnborough GU14 . . . . . .85 D2
Church Rd W GU14 . . . . . .85 C1
Church Rise
Chessington KT9 . . . . .56 F4
Forest Hill SE23 . . . . .23 D6
Church Road Ind Est
RH11 . . . . .181 E5
Church Road Trad Est
RH11 . . . . .181 E5
Church Row GU23 . . . . . . .91 C6
Church Side Epsom KT18 . .76 B6
Gatton RH2 . . . . .118 F4
Church Sq TW17 . . . . .34 B2
Church St
Aldershot GU11 . . . . .104 F2
Betchworth RH3 . . . . .137 E8
Chiswick W4 . . . . .7 F8
Cobham KT11 . . . . .73 B4
Crawley RH11 . . . . .201 C6
Crowthorne RG45 . . . . . . .45 B4
Croydon CR0, CR9 . . . . . .61 C8
Dorking RH4 . . . . .136 A7
Effingham KT24 . . . . .113 D8
Epsom KT17, KT18 . . . . . .76 E6
Ewell KT17 . . . . .58 A2
Godalming GU7 . . . . .150 D4
Hampton TW12 . . . . .36 C8
Isleworth TW7 . . . . .6 B5
Kingston u T KT1 . . . . .37 D7
Leatherhead KT22 . . . . . . .95 B5
Old Woking GU22 . . . . . . .90 C6
Reigate RH2 . . . . .118 B1
Rudgwick RH12 . . . . .214 E8
Rudgwick, Cox Green RH12 .195 E1
Staines TW18 . . . . .12 E4
Sunbury TW16 . . . . .35 B6
Twickenham TW1 . . . . . . .17 A7
Walton-on-T KT12 . . . . . . .35 A2
Warnham RH12 . . . . .216 F8
Weybridge KT13 . . . . .53 A6
Church St E GU21 . . . . . . .69 F2

Church Wlk
Bletchingley RH1 . . . . . . .120 D2
Brentford TW8 . . . . .6 C8
Caterham CR3 . . . . .101 A3
Chertsey KT16 . . . . .33 A3
Crawley RH10 . . . . .201 D6
Horley RH6 . . . . .160 F2
Leatherhead KT22 . . . . . . .95 B5
Mitcham SW16 . . . . .41 C7
Reigate RH2 . . . . .118 C1
15 Richmond TW10 . . . . .6 D2
Thames Ditton KT7 . . . . . .36 F3
Walton-on-T KT12 . . . . . . .35 A1
West Barnes SW20 . . . . . .39 C6
Weybridge KT13 . . . . .53 B8
Churchcroft Cl SW12 . . . . .21 A8
Churchdown BR1 . . . . .24 E4
Churchfield Rd
Reigate RH2 . . . . .117 F2
Walton-on-T KT12 . . . . . . .35 A1
Weybridge KT13 . . . . .53 A6
Churchfields
East Molesey KT8 . . . . . . .36 A6
Guildford GU4 . . . . .110 A6
Witley GU8 . . . . .170 E4
Woking GU21 . . . . .69 E3
Churchfields Ave
Feltham TW13 . . . . .16 A5
Weybridge KT13 . . . . .53 B6
Churchfields Prim Sch
BR3 . . . . .43 D6
Churchfields Rd BR3 . . . . .43 E7
Churchill Ave
Aldershot GU12 . . . . .126 C8
Horsham RH12 . . . . .217 B3
Churchill Cl
East Bedfont TW14 . . . . . .14 F7
Farnborough GU14 . . . . . .85 B8
Fetcham KT22 . . . . .94 E4
Warlingham CR6 . . . . .81 D2
Churchill Cres GU14 . . . . .85 B8
Churchill Ct
Crawley RH10 . . . . .182 A1
Staines TW18 . . . . .13 C2
Churchill Dr KT13 . . . . . . .53 C6
Churchill House SM7 . . . . .77 F4
Churchill Rd
Guildford GU1 . . . . .130 F8
North Ascot SL5 . . . . .28 F7
Smallfield RH6 . . . . .162 B3
South Croydon CR2 . . . . . .61 C3
Churchill Way TW16 . . . . .15 A2
Churchley Rd SE26 . . . . . .23 B4
Churchley Villas SE26 . . . .23 B4
Churchmore Rd SW16 . . . .41 D8
Churchside Cl TN16 . . . . . .83 C2
Churchview Rd TW2 . . . . . .16 D6
Churston Cl **17** SW2 . . . .22 A7
Churston Dr SM4 . . . . .39 E4
Churt Rd Beacon Hill GU26 188 C8
Headley Down GU10, GU35 .187 C8
Churt Wynde GU26 . . . . .188 D7
Chuters Cl GU14 . . . . .71 F7
Chuters Gr KT17 . . . . .76 F7
Cibber Rd SE23 . . . . .23 D6
Cinder Path GU22 . . . . . . .89 C8
Cinderford Way BR1 . . . . .24 E4
Cinnamon Gdns GU2 . . . .109 A6
Cintra Ct SE19 . . . . .22 F2
Cintra Pk SE19 . . . . .22 F1
Circle Gdns Byfleet KT14 . .71 F6
Merton SW19 . . . . .40 A7
Circle Hill Rd RG45 . . . . . .45 C5
Circle Rd KT12 . . . . .53 E2
Circle The GU7 . . . . .150 F6
Cissbury Cl RH12 . . . . . . .218 A6
Cissbury Hill RH11 . . . . . .201 C4
Cissbury House **6** SE26 . .23 A5
City Bsns Ctr RH13 . . . . .217 D1
City of London
Freemen's Sch KT21 . . . .96 A8
City Prospect **8** SE19 . . .22 E2
City Wharf House KT7 . . . .37 B3
Clacket La TN16 . . . . .103 E2
Clairvale Rd SW16, SW17 . .21 B4
Clairville Ct **1** RH2 . . . .118 D1
Clairville Point **12** SE23 . .23 D5
Clammer Hill GU27 . . . . .189 F1
Clandon Ave TW20 . . . . . .12 C1
Clandon CE Inf Sch GU4 .111 A4
Clandon Cl KT17 . . . . .58 A4
Clandon Ct GU14 . . . . .85 D3
Clandon House **12** KT2 . . .18 B2
Clandon Mews RH4 . . . . .136 B4
Clandon Pk GU4 . . . . .111 A1
Clandon Rd Guildford GU1 130 E8
Send Marsh GU4, GU23 . . .91 A1
West Clandon GU4, GU23 . .111 A8
Clandon Regis Golf
Club GU4 . . . . .111 B4
Clandon Sta GU4 . . . . . . .111 B6
Clanfield House **12** SW15 . .19 A7
Clanfield Ride GU17 . . . . . .64 D5
Clapgate La RH13 . . . . . .215 C5
Clappers
Gate RH10, RH11 . . . . . .201 D7
Clappers La GU24 . . . . . . .68 D8
Clappers Meadow GU6 . .194 A3
Clare Av RG40 . . . . .25 C7
Clare Cl Crawley RH10 . . .182 C1
West Byfleet KT14 . . . . . . .71 A6
Clare Cotts RH1 . . . . .120 B3
Clare Cres RH1 . . . . .120 B3
Clare Ct Wimbledon SW19 . .19 E1
Woldingham CR3 . . . . . . .102 A4
Clare Gdns TW20 . . . . .12 A3
Clare Hill KT10 . . . . .55 B5

Clare Hill Golf Course
KT10 . . . . .55 B4
Clare Hill (No 1) KT10 . . . .55 B5
Clare Hill (No 2) KT10 . . . .55 B5
Clare House Prim Sch
BR3 . . . . .44 C7
Clare Lawn Ave SW14 . . . . .7 D2
Clare Mead GU10 . . . . . .145 F4
Clare Rd Hounslow TW4 . . . .4 F4
Stanwell TW19 . . . . .13 E8
Clare Wood KT22 . . . . . . .75 B1
Claredale GU22 . . . . .89 E8
Claredale Ct SM2 . . . . .59 C3
Clarefield Ct SL5 . . . . .30 A3
Claremont TW17 . . . . .34 B3
Claremont Ave
Camberley GU15 . . . . .65 F5
Esher KT10 . . . . .54 F4
Hersham KT12 . . . . .54 D6
Sunbury TW16 . . . . .35 B8
West Barnes KT3 . . . . .39 B4
Woking GU22 . . . . .89 E8
Claremont Cl
Hamsey Green CR2 . . . . . .81 B4
Hersham KT12 . . . . .54 D5
4 Streatham SW2 . . . . .21 F7
Claremont Ct RH4 . . . . . .136 B5
Claremont Dr Esher KT10 . .55 B4
Shepperton TW17 . . . . . . .34 B3
Claremont End KT10 . . . . .55 B4
Claremont Fan Court Sch
KT10 . . . . .55 A3
Claremont Gdns KT6 . . . . .37 E4
Claremont Gr W4 . . . . .7 E7
Claremont Hospl KT6 . . . .37 D3
Claremont Landscape Gdn
KT10 . . . . .54 F3
Claremont Park Rd KT10 . .55 B4
Claremont Rd
Claygate KT10 . . . . .55 E3
Croydon CR0 . . . . .43 A1
Egham TW18 . . . . .12 D3
Kingston u T KT6 . . . . . . .37 E4
Redhill RH1 . . . . .119 A4
Teddington TW11 . . . . . . .16 F4
Twickenham TW1 . . . . .6 C1
West Byfleet KT14 . . . . . . .71 A7
Claremont Terr KT7 . . . . . .37 B2
Claremount Cl KT18 . . . . . .77 C2
Claremount Gdns KT18 . . .77 D2
Clarence Ave
Kingston u T KT3 . . . . .38 D7
Streatham SW4 . . . . .21 D8
Clarence Cl
Aldershot KT12 . . . . .105 C2
Hersham KT12 . . . . .54 B6
Clarence Ct RH6 . . . . .161 D4
Clarence Dr
Camberley GU15 . . . . .66 B7
2 East Grinstead RH19 . .205 F7
Englefield Green TW20 . . . .11 C4
Clarence House KT12 . . . . .54 B5
Clarence La SW15 . . . . .7 F1
Clarence Rd
Biggin Hill TN16 . . . . .83 F1
Hersham KT12 . . . . .54 B6
Horsham RH13 . . . . .217 E1
Reigate RH1 . . . . .139 D6
Richmond TW9 . . . . .7 A6
Sutton SM1 . . . . .59 B5
Teddington TW11 . . . . . . .17 A2
Thornton Heath CR0 . . . . .42 D2
Wallington SM6 . . . . .60 B5
Wimbledon SW19 . . . . . . .20 B2
Clarence St Egham TW20 . .11 F2
Kingston u T KT1, KT2 . . . .37 E7
4 Richmond TW9 . . . . . . .7 A6
Staines TW18 . . . . .12 E4
Clarence Terr TW3 . . . . .5 B3
Clarence Way RH6 . . . . . .161 D4
Clarence Wlk RH1 . . . . . .139 D6
Clarendon Cres TW2 . . . . .16 D5
Clarendon Ct
Blackwater GU17 . . . . .64 D3
1 Richmond TW9 . . . . . . .7 A6
Clarendon Cty Prim Sch
TW15 . . . . .13 F4
Clarendon Gate KT16 . . . . .51 D4
Clarendon Gr CR4 . . . . . . .40 F6
Clarendon Rd
Ashford TW15 . . . . .13 F4
Croydon CR0, CR9 . . . . . .61 B8
Mitcham SW19 . . . . .20 E1
Redhill RH1 . . . . .118 F2
Wallington SM6 . . . . .60 C4
Clarendon Sch TW12 . . . . .16 B2
Clarens St SE6 . . . . .23 F6
Clares The CR3 . . . . .101 A3
Clareville Rd CR3 . . . . . . .101 A3
Clarewood Dr GU15 . . . . . .65 E6
Clarice Way SM6 . . . . .60 E2
Claridge Gdns RH7 . . . . .165 A2
Claridges Mead RH7 . . . .165 A2
Clark Pl GU6 . . . . .173 F2
Clark Rd RH11 . . . . .201 A1
Clark Way TW5 . . . . .4 D7
Clarke Cres GU15 . . . . . . .64 E7
Clarke's Ave KT4, SM3 . . . .58 D8
Clarks Hill GU10 . . . . .124 D1
Clarks La CR6, TN16 . . . .103 C4
Claudia Pl SW19 . . . . .19 E7
Claverdale Rd SW2 . . . . . .22 A8
Claverdon RG12 . . . . .27 A2
Clavering Cl TW1 . . . . .17 A4
Claverton KT21 . . . . .75 E2
Clay Ave CR4 . . . . .41 B7

Clay Hall La RH10 . . . . . . .183 C4
Clay La
Guildford, Burpham GU4 . .110 A5
Guildford, Jacobswell GU4 .109 E7
Headley KT18 . . . . .96 B3
Horne RH7 . . . . .163 D3
Nutfield RH1 . . . . .140 D7
South Nutfield RH1 . . . . . .140 D7
Wokingham RG40 . . . . .25 F5
Claycart Rd
Aldershot GU11 . . . . .104 D4
Aldershot GU11 . . . . .104 E3
Claydon Ct TW18 . . . . .13 A4
Claydon Dr CR0 . . . . .60 E6
Claydon Gdns GU17 . . . . . . .65 A1
Claydon Rd GU21 . . . . .69 A3
Clayford RH7 . . . . .165 B2
Claygate Cres CR0 . . . . .63 D4
Claygate La
Hinchley Wood KT10 . . . . . . .56 A8
Thames Ditton KT7 . . . . .37 A1
Claygate Lodge Cl KT10 . . . . .55 E3
Claygate Prim Sch KT10 . .55 E3
Claygate Rd RH4 . . . . .136 B5
Claygate Sta KT10 . . . . .55 E4
Clayhall House 3 RH2 . . . . .118 A2
Clayhall La RH2 . . . . .138 E6
Clayhanger GU1, GU4 . . . . .110 C3
Clayhill Cl Bracknell RG12 . . .28 A6
Leigh RH2 . . . . .138 A2
Clayhill Rd RH2 . . . . .137 F1
Claylands Ct SE19 . . . . .22 D3
Claymore Cl SM3, SM4 . . . . .40 C4
Claypole Dr TW5 . . . . .4 E6
Clayton Dr GU2 . . . . .108 F4
Clayton Gr RG12 . . . . .27 E8
Clayton Hill RH11 . . . . .201 C4
Clayton House KT7 . . . . .37 B1
Clayton Mead RH9 . . . . . . .121 B4
Clayton Rd
Chessington KT10, KT9 . . . . .56 D6
Ewell KT17 . . . . .76 E6
Farnborough GU14 . . . . .64 F1
Isleworth TW7 . . . . .5 E4
Clear Water Pl KT6 . . . . .37 C3
Cleardene RH4 . . . . .136 B7
Cleardown GU22 . . . . .70 B1
Clears Cotts RH2 . . . . .117 E3
Clears The RH2 . . . . .117 E3
Clearsprings GU18 . . . . .67 A8
Cleave Prior CR5 . . . . .98 E8
Cleave's Almshouses 1
KT2 . . . . .37 E7
Cleaveland Rd KT6 . . . . .37 D4
Cleaverholme Cl SE25 . . . . . .43 B3
Cleeve TW14 . . . . .14 E7
Cleeve Hill SE23 . . . . .23 B7
Cleeve House RG12 . . . . .27 E5
Cleeve Rd KT22 . . . . .95 A7
Cleeve The GU1 . . . . .110 A1
Cleeves Ct 6 RH1 . . . . .119 C4
Clement Cl CR8 . . . . .80 B3
Wimbledon SW19 . . . . .19 E3
Clement Rd Penge BR3 . . . . .43 D8
Wimbledon SW19 . . . . .19 E3
Clements Ct TW4 . . . . .4 D3
Clements House KT22 . . . . . .95 A8
Clements Mead KT22 . . . . . .95 A8
Clements Rd KT12 . . . . .54 B8
Clensham Ct SM3 . . . . .59 A8
Clensham La SM1 . . . . .59 A8
Clerics Wlk TW17 . . . . .34 D3
Clerks Croft RH1 . . . . .120 D2
Clevedon KT13 . . . . .53 D5
Clevedon Ct
Farnborough GU14 . . . . .85 D3
Frimley GU16 . . . . .86 A8
West Norwood SE21 . . . . . . .22 D5
Clevedon Gdns TW5 . . . . .4 B6
Clevedon Rd
Kingston u T KT1 . . . . .38 A7
Penge SE20 . . . . .43 D8
Twickenham TW1 . . . . .6 D1
Cleveland Ave
Hampton TW12 . . . . .15 F1
Merton SW20 . . . . .39 F7
Cleveland Cl KT12 . . . . .54 B7
Cleveland Dr TW18 . . . . .33 B8
Cleveland Gdns
Barnes SW13 . . . . .7 F5
Worcester Park KT4 . . . . . . .57 F8
Cleveland Pk TW19 . . . . .2 F1
Cleveland Rd Barnes SW13 . . .7 F5
Isleworth TW7 . . . . .6 A3
New Malden KT3 . . . . .38 E5
Worcester Park KT4 . . . . . . .57 E8
Cleveland Rise SM4 . . . . . . .39 D2
Cleves Ave KT17 . . . . .58 B2
Cleves Cl KT11 . . . . .73 B5
Cleves Cres CR0 . . . . .82 C8
Cleves Ct Epsom KT17 . . . . .76 F7
Kingston u T KT6 . . . . .37 E3
Knaphill GU21 . . . . .68 D2
Cleves Rd TW10 . . . . .17 C5
Cleves Sch KT13 . . . . .53 F6
Cleves Way Ashford TW16 . . .14 F2
Hampton TW12 . . . . .15 F1
Cleves Wood KT13 . . . . .53 E6
Clewborough Dr GU15 . . . . . .66 B6
Clewborough House Sch
GU15 . . . . .66 B6
Clews La GU24 . . . . .68 B3
Clifden Centre(Richmond
Adult & Community Coll)
TW1 . . . . .16 F7
Clifden House 7 TW8 . . . . . . .6 D8
Clifden Rd Brentford TW8 . . . .6 D8
Twickenham TW1 . . . . .16 F7

Cliff End CR8 . . . . .80 B7
Cliffe Rd Croydon CR2 . . . . . .61 D5
Cliffe Rise GU7 . . . . .150 C2
Cliffe Wlk 2 SM1 . . . . .59 C5
Clifford Ave
Mortlake SW14, TW10, TW9 . . .7 B4
Wallington SM6 . . . . .60 C6
Clifford Ct SW18 . . . . .20 D8
Clifford Gr TW15 . . . . .14 A4
Clifford House BR3 . . . . .24 B2
Clifford Manor Rd GU4 . .130 E5
Clifford Rd Croydon SE25 . . . .43 A5
Hounslow TW4 . . . . .4 D4
Richmond TW10 . . . . .17 D6
Clifton Av SM2 . . . . .78 B8
Clifton Ave TW13 . . . . .15 C4
Clifton Cl Caterham CR3 . .100 D4
Chertsey KT15 . . . . .52 B8
Rowledge GU10 . . . . .146 A4
8 Stanwell TW19 . . . . .2 E1
Clifton Gdns GU16 . . . . .85 F6
Clifton Hill Sch GU16 . .100 D4
Clifton Lodge (Brunel Univ
Coll Twickenham Campus)
TW1 . . . . .6 B2
Clifton Mews SE25 . . . . .42 E5
Clifton Par TW13 . . . . .15 C4
Clifton Park Ave SW20 . . . .39 C7
Clifton Pl SM7 . . . . .78 A4
Clifton Rd Coulsdon CR5 . . . .79 C4
Crawley RH10 . . . . .202 C5
Harlington TW6 . . . . .3 C1
Hounslow TW7 . . . . .5 E5
Kingston u T KT2 . . . . .37 F8
South Norwood SE25 . . . . . . .42 E5
Teddington TW11 . . . . .16 E4
Wallington SM6 . . . . .60 B5
Wimbledon SW19 . . . . .19 D2
Wokingham RG41 . . . . .25 A8
Clifton Terr RH4 . . . . .136 B6
Clifton Way GU21 . . . . .68 F2
Cliftons La RH2 . . . . .117 D2
Cliftonville RH4 . . . . .136 B6
Climping Rd RH11 . . . . .201 B8
Cline Rd GU1 . . . . .130 F7
Clinton Ave KT8 . . . . .36 C5
Clinton Cl GU21 . . . . .68 D1
Clinton Hill RH7 . . . . .186 A8
Clinton House
New Malden KT3 . . . . .38 D1
6 Surbiton KT6 . . . . .37 D2
Clinton Rd KT22 . . . . .95 C4
Clintons Gn RG42 . . . . .27 A8
Clippesby Cl KT9 . . . . .56 F4
Clipstone Rd TW3 . . . . .5 A4
Clive Ct Streatham SW16 . . . .21 D3
Tolworth KT6 . . . . .57 A8
Clive Gn RG12 . . . . .27 B4
Clive House 3 Croydon CR0 42 F1
Redhill RH1 . . . . .118 E3
Clive Rd Aldershot GU12 . . .105 D1
Esher KT10 . . . . .55 B6
Feltham TW14 . . . . .4 A1
Mitcham SW19 . . . . .20 E2
Teddington TW1 . . . . .17 A4
West Norwood SE21, SE27 . . .22 D5
Clive Way RH10 . . . . .202 C6
Cliveden Pl TW17 . . . . .34 C3
Cliveden Rd SW19 . . . . .39 F8
Clock Barn La GU8 . . . . . . .171 E6
Clock House Cl KT14 . . . . . . .71 F7
Clock House Cotts RH5 . . . .178 C2
Clock House Ct BR3 . . . . . . .43 E7
Clock House Mead KT11 . . . .74 B5
Clock House Rd BR3 . . . . . . .43 E7
Clock House Sta BR3 . . . .43 E8
Clock Tower Rd TW7 . . . . .5 F4
Clockhouse Cl SW19 . . . . . . .19 C6
Clockhouse Ct GU1 . . . . . . .109 C5
Clockhouse La
Ashford TW14, TW15 . . . . . .14 B5
Bramley GU5 . . . . .151 F7
East Bedfont TW14, TW15 . . .14 B5
Clockhouse La E TW20 . . . . .12 B1
Clockhouse La W TW20 . . . .12 A1
Clockhouse Rd GU14 . . . . . . .85 B4
Clodhouse Hill GU22 . . . . . . .88 D5
Cloister Cl TW11 . . . . .17 B3
Cloister Gdns SE25 . . . . .43 B3
Cloisters The Frimley GU16 . .65 D1
Old Woking GU22 . . . . .90 B6
Clone The 5 KT2 . . . . .18 B1
Clonmel
Rd TW11, TW12, TW2 . . . . .16 D4
Clonmore St SW18 . . . . .19 F7
Close The Beckenham BR3 . . .43 E5
Bracknell RG12 . . . . .27 C5
Brockham RH3 . . . . .137 B5
Cheam SM3 . . . . .39 F2
Croydon SE25 . . . . .43 A3
East Grinstead RH19 . . . . . .205 D6
Esher KT10 . . . . .55 B3
Farnham GU9 . . . . .125 D1
Frimley GU16 . . . . .85 C8
Godalming GU7 . . . . .150 F3
Horley RH6 . . . . .161 C1
Hounslow TW7 . . . . .5 E8
Ifold RH14 . . . . .212 D3
Kingston u T KT3 . . . . .38 C7
Lightwater GU18 . . . . .48 A1
Mitcham CR4 . . . . .40 F5
Mortlake TW9 . . . . .7 B4
North Ascot SL5 . . . . .28 D7
Purley CR8 . . . . .61 B1
Purley, Russell Hill CR8 . . . . .60 F1

Close The continued
Reigate RH2 . . . . .139 B8
Sandhurst GU47 . . . . .64 E8
Surbiton KT6 . . . . .37 E3
Virginia Water GU25 . . . . . . .31 D4
Wallington SM5 . . . . .59 E2
West Byfleet KT14 . . . . .71 A6
Wonersh GU5 . . . . .152 B7
Closeworth Rd GU14 . . . . . .105 E8
Cloudesdale Rd SW17 . . . . . .21 B6
Clouston Cl SM6 . . . . .60 E5
Clouston Rd GU14 . . . . .84 F5
Clovelly Ave CR6 . . . . .101 B8
Clovelly Dr GU26 . . . . .188 D7
Clovelly Pl GU26 . . . . .188 D7
Clovelly Rd
Beacon Hill GU26 . . . . .188 C7
Hounslow TW3 . . . . .5 B5
Clover Cl RG40 . . . . .25 E7
Clover Ct GU22 . . . . .89 D8
Clover Field RH12 . . . . .215 D4
Clover Hill CR5 . . . . .99 B6
Clover House TW3 . . . . .5 C6
Clover Lea GU7 . . . . .150 E8
Clover Rd GU2 . . . . .108 E2
Clover Way Carshalton CR4 . .41 A1
Smallfield RH6 . . . . .162 C3
Cloverfields RH6 . . . . .161 B4
Cloverlands RH10 . . . . .201 F8
Clovers Cotts RH12 . . . . . . .199 F1
Clovers End RH12 . . . . .218 A5
Clovers Way RH12 . . . . .218 D7
Clowders Rd SE6 . . . . .23 F5
Clowser Cl 4 SM1 . . . . .59 C5
Club La RG45 . . . . .45 D5
Club Row GU24 . . . . .87 D8
Clubhouse Rd GU11 . . . . . . .104 F5
Clump Ave KT20 . . . . .116 C4
Clumps Rd GU10 . . . . .146 B4
Clumps The TW15 . . . . .14 D4
Clyde Ave CR2 . . . . .81 B4
Clyde Cl RH1 . . . . .119 A2
Clyde Ct RH1 . . . . .119 A2
Clyde Rd Croydon CR0 . . . . .61 F8
Stanwell TW19 . . . . .13 E7
Sutton SM1 . . . . .59 A5
Wallington SM6 . . . . .60 C4
Clyde Terr SE23 . . . . .23 C6
Clyde Vale SE23 . . . . .23 C6
Clydesdale Cl TW7 . . . . .5 F4
Clydesdale Gdns TW10 . . . . . .7 B3
Clymping Dene TW14 . . . . . .15 B8
Clytha Ct SE27 . . . . .22 C4
Clyve Way TW18 . . . . .32 E8
Coach House Cl GU16 . . . . . .65 E3
Coach House La SW19 . . . . . .19 D5
Coach Rd Brockham RH3 . . .137 D4
Brockham, Pixham RH4 . . . .115 E1
Crawley, North
Terminal RH6 . . . . .181 F8
Crawley, South
Terminal RH6 . . . . .182 B7
North Ascot SL5 . . . . .8 E1
Ottershaw KT16 . . . . .51 C4
Coachlads Ave GU2 . . . . . . .108 F1
Coachmans Dr RH11 . . . . . .201 B8
Coalbrook Mansions
SW12 . . . . .21 B7
Coaldale Wlk SE21 . . . . .22 C8
Coast Hill RH4, RH5 . . . . . .134 F4
Coast Hill La RH4 . . . . .135 A5
Coates Wlk TW8 . . . . .6 E8
Coatham Pl GU6 . . . . .174 F3
Cob Cl RH10 . . . . .204 C8
Cob Wlk RH11 . . . . .201 A6
Cobb's Rd TW4 . . . . .4 F3
Cobbets Ridge GU10 . . . . . .147 C8
Cobbett Cl RH10 . . . . .202 C8
Cobbett Rd Guildford GU2 . .108 F2
Twickenham TW2 . . . . .16 A7
Cobbets Cl GU21 . . . . .69 B2
Cobbetts Farm GU24 . . . . . .68 A3
Cobbetts Hill KT13 . . . . .53 B3
Cobbetts Way GU10, GU9 . .145 F6
Cobbetts Wlk GU24 . . . . .68 A4
Cobbler's Wlk TW11 . . . . . . .16 F1
Cobblers RH12 . . . . .215 D4
Cobbles Cres RH10 . . . . . . .201 E7
Cobden La GU27 . . . . .208 D7
Cobden Mews SE26 . . . . .23 B3
Cobden Rd SE25 . . . . .43 A4
Cobham Ave KT3 . . . . .39 A4
Cobham Bus Mus KT11 . . .72 B2
Cobham Cl SM6 . . . . .60 E4
Cobham Ct CR4 . . . . .40 D7
Cobham Gate KT11 . . . . .73 B5
Cobham Park Rd KT11 . . . . .73 C2
Cobham Rd
Fetcham KT11, KT22, KT23 . .94 C6
Heston TW5 . . . . .4 C7
Kingston u T KT1, KT2 . . . . .38 A7
Cobham & Stoke
D'Abernon Sta KT11 . . . .73 E2
Cobham Way
Crawley RH10 . . . . .182 B4
East Horsley KT24 . . . . .92 E1
Cobnor Cl RH11 . . . . .200 F4
Cobs Way KT15 . . . . .52 C1
Coburg Cres SW2 . . . . .22 A7
Cochrane Ct KT23 . . . . .94 A2
Cochrane Pl GU20 . . . . .48 D1
Cochrane Rd SW19 . . . . .19 F1
Cock La KT22 . . . . .94 C5
Cock's La Newell Green SL4 . .8 A6
Winkfield RG42 . . . . .8 A6
Cock-A-Dobby GU47 . . . . . . .45 A1
Cocks Cres KT3 . . . . .38 F5
Cockshot Hill RH2 . . . . .139 B7

Cockshot Rd RH2 . . . . .139 C8
Codrington Ct GU21 . . . . . . .68 F1
Codrington Hill SE23, SE4 . .23 E8
Cody Cl Ash Vale GU12 . . . .105 F5
Wallington SM6 . . . . .60 D3
Cody Rd GU14 . . . . .84 F3
Coe Ave SE25 . . . . .43 A3
Coe Cl GU11 . . . . .105 A1
Cogman's La RH6 . . . . .162 D4
Cokenor Wood GU10 . . . . . .145 F6
Cokers La SE21 . . . . .22 D7
Colborne Way KT4 . . . . .58 C8
Colburn Ave CR3 . . . . .100 F3
Colburn Cres GU1 . . . . .110 A4
Colburn Way SM1 . . . . .59 D7
Colby Rd Dulwich SE19 . . . . .22 E3
Walton-on-T KT12 . . . . .35 A1
Colchester Vale RH18 . . . . .206 E2
Colchester Villas CR7 . . . . . .42 A3
Colcokes Rd SM7 . . . . .78 A3
Cold Harbour La GU12 . . . . .105 F1
Coldharbour Cl TW20 . . . . . .32 C6
Coldharbour La
Bletchingley RH1 . . . . .120 F1
Dorking RH4, RH5 . . . . .135 F3
Egham TW20 . . . . .32 D6
Purley CR8 . . . . .61 A1
Pyrford GU22 . . . . .70 F4
South Holmwood RH5 . . . . . .156 F6
West End GU24 . . . . .67 F8
Coldharbour Rd
Croydon CR0 . . . . .61 A5
Pyrford GU22, KT14 . . . . . . .70 F4
Coldharbour Sch 2 GU1 . .61 A5
Coldshott RH8 . . . . .123 A2
Cole Cl RH11 . . . . .201 B1
Cole Court Lodge 8 TW1 .17 A8
Cole Gdns TW5 . . . . .4 A7
Cole Park Gdns TW1 . . . . . . .6 A1
Cole Park View 2 TW1 . . . . .6 A1
Cole Rd TW1 . . . . .6 A1
Cole's La RH5 . . . . .178 B5
Colebrook KT16 . . . . .51 D4
Colebrook Cl SW19 . . . . .19 D8
Colebrook Rd SW16 . . . . . . .41 E8
Colebrook Rise BR2 . . . . . . .44 E7
Colebrook Pl KT16 . . . . .51 C3
Colebrooke Rd RH1 . . . . . . .118 E3
Coleford Bridge Rd
Farnborough GU14 . . . . .85 D4
Mytchett GU14, GU16 . . . . . .85 D4
Coleford Cl GU16 . . . . .85 D3
Coleford Paddocks GU16 . . .85 E4
Colekitchen La GU5 . . . . . . .133 D6
Coleman Cl SE25 . . . . .43 A7
Coleman Ct SW18 . . . . .20 A8
Coleman Rd GU12 . . . . .105 D1
Coleridge Ave
Crowthorne RG45 . . . . .45 C4
Mytchett RH12 . . . . .217 E6
Sutton SM1 . . . . .59 E6
Coleridge Cres SL3 . . . . .1 D7
Coleridge Ct 2 RH10 . . . . . .1 D7
Coleridge Rd Ashford TW15 .13 F4
Croydon CR0 . . . . .43 C2
Coles La RH5 . . . . .178 C5
Colesburg Rd BR3 . . . . .43 F7
Colescroft Hill CR8 . . . . .80 A4
Coleshill Rd TW11 . . . . .16 E2
Colesmead Rd RH1 . . . . . . .118 F4
Colet Rd RH11 . . . . .201 D3
Coleville Rd GU14 . . . . .84 F5
Coley Ave GU22 . . . . .70 A2
Colfe Rd SE23 . . . . .23 E7
Colgate Cl RH11 . . . . .201 B8
Colin Cl Coney Hall BR4 . . . .63 F7
Croydon CR0 . . . . .62 F7
Colin Ct SW16 . . . . .21 D6
Colin Rd CR3 . . . . .101 A4
Coliston Rd SW18 . . . . .20 A8
Coll of Liberal Arts SM1 . .59 B5
Coll of St Barnabas RH7 .185 F8
Coll of Tech Three
Bridges Outpost RH10 . .202 A7
Collamore Ave SW18 . . . . . .20 E7
Collards La GU27 . . . . .208 D6
College Ave Egham TW20 . . .12 B2
Epsom KT17 . . . . .76 F5
College Cl Addlestone KT15 .52 D7
Camberley GU15 . . . . .65 D7
East Grinstead RH19 . . . . . .185 F1
Lingfield RH7 . . . . .164 D4
Twickenham TW2 . . . . .16 D7
College Cres Redhill RH1 . .119 A4
Sandhurst GU47 . . . . .64 E8
College Ct SE20 . . . . .62 A8
College Fields Bsns Ctr
SW19 . . . . .40 E8
College Gdns Dulwich SE21 .22 E7
Farnham GU9 . . . . .125 B2
New Malden KT3 . . . . .38 F4
Upper Tooting SW17 . . . . . . .20 C6
College Gn SE19 . . . . .22 E1
College Hill
Godalming GU7 . . . . .150 C2
Haslemere GU27 . . . . .208 C6
College Hill Terr GU27 . . . .208 C6
College House GU8 . . . . . . .171 E5
College La
East Grinstead RH19 . . . . . .185 F1
Woking GU22 . . . . .89 C8
College Rd Ash GU12 . . . . .106 B3
Bracknell RG12 . . . . .27 D5
Crawley RH10 . . . . .201 E6
Croydon CR0, CR9 . . . . .61 D8

Cla–Col 237

College Rd continued
Dulwich SE19, SE21 . . . . . . .22 E6
Epsom KT17 . . . . .76 F5
Ewell KT17 . . . . .77 B5
Guildford GU1 . . . . .130 D8
Hounslow TW7 . . . . .5 F6
Mitcham SW19 . . . . .20 D2
Sandhurst GU47 . . . . .64 E8
Woking GU22 . . . . .70 B3
College Rdbt 1 KT1 . . . . . . .37 E6
College Ride Bagshot GU19 47 C2
Camberley GU15 . . . . .65 D7
College Town Inf Sch
GU47 . . . . .64 E8
College Town Jun Sch
GU47 . . . . .64 E8
College Way TW15 . . . . .13 F4
College Wlk KT1 . . . . .37 E6
Collendean La RH6 . . . . . . .159 F4
Collens Field GU24 . . . . .87 F4
Collette Ct SE25 . . . . .42 E4
Colley La RH2 . . . . .117 E3
Colley Manor Dr RH2 . . . . .117 D2
Colley Way RH2 . . . . .117 D2
Collier Cl Farnborough GU14 84 D5
West Ewell KT19 . . . . .57 B4
Collier Row RH10 . . . . .201 D4
Collier Way GU4 . . . . .110 D3
Collier's Wood Sta SW19 .20 D1
Colliers CR3 . . . . .101 A2
Colliers Cl GU21 . . . . .69 B2
Colliers Water La CR7 . . . . . .42 A4
Collingdon GU6 . . . . .174 F1
Collingsbourne KT15 . . . . . . .52 B6
Collingtree Rd SE26 . . . . . . .23 C4
Collingwood GU14 . . . . .85 E2
Collingwood Ave KT5 . . . . . .38 C1
Collingwood Cl
4 East Grinstead RH19 . . . .205 F7
Horley RH6 . . . . .161 B4
3 Penge SE20 . . . . .43 B8
Twickenham TW2, TW4 . . . . .16 A8
Collingwood Coll GU15 . . . . .66 A8
Collingwood Cres GU1 . . . . .110 B2
Collingwood Mount GU15 .66 A7
Collingwood Pl
Camberley GU15 . . . . .66 B8
Walton-on-T KT12 . . . . .54 B7
Collingwood Rd
Crawley RH10 . . . . .202 D5
Horsham RH12 . . . . .217 C4
Mitcham CR4 . . . . .40 E6
Sutton SM1 . . . . .59 A6
Collingwood Rise GU15 . . . . .66 A7
Collins Gdns GU12 . . . . . . .106 B2
Collins Rd RH11 . . . . .200 E4
Collis Prim Sch TW11 . . . . .17 B2
Collyer Ave CR0 . . . . .60 E6
Collyer Rd CR0 . . . . .60 E6
Collyer's Sixth Form Coll
RH12 . . . . .217 C4
Colman Cl KT18 . . . . .77 C2
Colman House RH1 . . . . . . .118 F3
Colman Way RH1 . . . . .118 F4
Colmans Hill GU5 . . . . .154 E7
Colmer Rd SW16 . . . . .21 E1
Coln Trad Est SL3 . . . . .1 F6
Colnbrook By-Pass
Brands Hill SL3, UB7 . . . . . . .1 D7
Colnbrook SL3, UB7 . . . . .1 D7
Harmondsworth UB7 . . . . .2 C7
Colnbrook C of E Comb
Sch SL3 . . . . .1 D7
Colnbrook for Poyle SL3 . . . .1 F6
Upper Tooting SW17 . . . . . . .20 D4
Colndale Rd SL3 . . . . .1 E5
Colne Bank SL3, TW19 . . . . . .1 C4
Colne Ct KT19 . . . . .57 C6
Colne Dr KT12 . . . . .54 D7
Colne House 2 RH1 . . . . . .118 F2
Colne Lodge KT12 . . . . .54 D7
Colne Rd TW1, TW2 . . . . . . .16 F7
Colne Reach TW19 . . . . .1 F2
Colne Way Ash GU12 . . . . . .106 A1
Wraysbury TW19 . . . . .12 B6
Colne Wlk RH11 . . . . .200 F5
Colnebridge Cl TW18 . . . . . .12 E3
Coloma Convent Girls Sch
CR9 . . . . .62 D7
Colonel's La KT16 . . . . .33 A3
Colonial Ave TW2 . . . . .5 C1
Colonial Rd TW14 . . . . .14 E8
Colonsay Rd RH11 . . . . .201 B3
Colony Gate GU16 . . . . .66 D2
Colson Rd CR0, CR9 . . . . . . .61 E8
Colson Way SW16 . . . . .21 C4
Colston Ave SM1, SM5 . . . . .59 F6
Colston Rd SW14 . . . . .7 C3
Colston Ct SM5 . . . . .59 F6
Coltash Rd RH10 . . . . .202 A5
Coltsfoot Dr
Guildford GU1, GU4 . . . . . .110 B4
Horsham RH12 . . . . .217 E5
Coltsfoot La RH8 . . . . .123 A2
Columbia Ave KT4 . . . . .38 F2
Columbia Ct KT3 . . . . .39 E8
Columbine Ave CR2 . . . . . . .61 B3
Columbus Dr GU14 . . . . .84 C4
Colville Gdns GU18 . . . . . . .67 C8
Colvin Cl SE26 . . . . .23 C3
Colvin Rd CR7 . . . . .42 A4
Colwood Gdns SW19 . . . . . .20 D1
Colworth Rd CR0 . . . . .43 A1
Colwyn Cl Crawley RH11 . .200 F4

Colwyn Cl continued
Streatham SW16 . . . .**21** C3
Colwyn Cres TW3 . . . .**5** C6
Colyton Cl GU21 . . . .**69** C1
Combe House SW14 . . . .**7** C5
Combe Hurst KT2 . . . . . .**18** C3
Combe La
Bramley GU5, GU8 . . . .**151** D2
Chiddingfold GU8 . . . .**191** A7
Farnborough GU14 . . . .**85** A6
Shere GU5, GU4 . . . .**133** B8
Whiteley Village KT12 . . . . . .**53** F2
Wormley GU8 . . . .**170** F1
Combe Martin Coll KT2 . . .**18** C3
Combe Rd GU7 . . . .**150** E8
Combe Rise GU10 . . . .**146** D5
Combe View GU8 . . . .**191** A5
Combemartin Rd SW18 . . .**19** E7
Combermere Rd SM4 . . . . .**40** B4
Comeragh Cl GU22 . . . .**89** A7
Comforts Farm Ave RH8 .**123** A3
Comfrey Cl
Farnborough GU14 . . . .**84** C5
Wokingham RG40 . . . .**25** E8
Commerce Rd TW8 . . . .**6** C7
Commerce Way CR0 . . . . . .**60** F8
Commercial Rd
Aldershot GU12 . . . .**126** C8
Guildford GU1 . . . .**130** D8
Staines TW18 . . . .**13** A2
Commercial Way GU21 . . . .**69** F2
Commodore Ct GU14 . . . .**105** B8
Common Cl GU21 . . . .**69** D5
Common House Rd GU8 .**192** F4
New Haw KT15 . . . .**52** C2
Common Rd Claygate KT10 .**56** A3
Redhill RH1 . . . .**139** F7
Common Side KT18 . . . .**76** A4
Common The GU6 . . . .**174** A3
Commonfield Rd SM7 . . . . .**78** B6
Commonfields GU24 . . . . . .**67** F6
Commonside KT22, KT23 . . .**94** A5
Commonside Cl SM2 . . . . . .**78** B8
Commonside E SW16 . . . . . .**21** E2
Commonside E CR4 . . . .**41** B6
Commonwealth Lodge
Sch CR8 . . . .**79** D7
Commonwealth Rd CR3 . .**101** A4
Community Cl TW5 . . . .**4** B6
Como Rd SE23 . . . .**23** E6
Compass Hill TW10 . . . .**6** D1
Compassion Cl RH11 . . . . .**200** E5
Compasses Mobile Home
Pk GU6 . . . .**193** F5
Compassion Cl RH11 . . . . .**200** E4
Comper Cl RH11 . . . .**200** E4
Comport Gn CR0 . . . .**82** E7
Compton Cl Bracknell RG12 .**26** E3
Esher KT10 . . . .**55** D5
Sandhurst GU47 . . . .**45** C1
Compton Cres
Chessington KT9 . . . .**56** E4
Chiswick W4 . . . .**7** C8
Compton Ct
7 Guildford GU1 . . . .**130** F8
Sutton SM1 . . . .**59** C6
9 West Norwood SE19 . . . .**22** E3
Compton Hts GU3 . . . .**129** D6
Compton Place Bsns Ctr
GU15 . . . .**65** A4
Compton Rd Croydon CR0 . .**43** B1
Wimbledon SW19 . . . .**19** F2
Compton Way GU10 . . . . . .**126** A3
Comptons Brow La RH13 .**218** A3
Comptons La RH12, RH13 .**217** F3
Comsaye Wlk RG12 . . . .**27** C4
Conal Ct SW16 . . . .**21** D3
Conaways Cl KT17 . . . .**58** A1
Concorde Bsns Pk TN16 . . .**83** D4
Concorde Cl TW3 . . . .**5** B5
Concorde House KT15 . . . . .**52** B6
Condor Ct GU2 . . . .**130** C2
Condor Rd TW18 . . . .**33** C6
Conduit La CR0 . . . .**62** A5
Conduit The RH1 . . . .**120** D6
Coney Acre SE21 . . . .**22** C7
Coney Cl RH11 . . . .**201** B8
Coney Croft RH12 . . . .**218** B5
Coney Hall Par BR4 . . . .**63** E7
Coney Hill Rd BR4 . . . .**63** E8
Coney Hill Sch BR2 . . . .**63** F7
Coneyberry RH2 . . . .**139** D5
Coneybury Cl RH11 . . . .**201** B8
Coneybury Cl CR6 . . . .**101** B8
Coneyhurst La GU6 . . . . . .**175** D7
Conford Dr GU4 . . . .**130** E2
Coniers Way GU1, GU4 . . . .**110** B4
Conifer Cl RH2 . . . .**118** A3
Conifer Cl 28 SW19 . . . .**19** D7
Conifer Dr GU15 . . . .**66** A6
Conifer Gdns
Streatham SW16 . . . .**21** F5
Sutton SM1 . . . .**59** B8
Conifer La TW20 . . . .**12** C3
Conifers KT13 . . . .**53** F6
Conifers Cl Horsham RH12 .**218** B6
Teddington TW11 . . . .**17** C1
Conifers The RG45 . . . .**45** A4
Coningsby RG12 . . . .**27** C5
Coningsby Ct CR4 . . . .**41** A7
Coningsby Rd CR2 . . . .**61** C2
Conisborough Cres SE6 . . .**24** C5
Conista Ct GU21 . . . .**68** F3
Coniston Cl Barnes SW13 . . .**7** F7

Coniston Cl continued
Chiswick W4 . . . .**7** C7
Crawley RH11 . . . .**200** D4
Farnborough GU14 . . . .**84** E3
Frimley GU16 . . . .**66** C3
Horsham RH12 . . . .**218** B6
West Barnes SM4 . . . .**39** D3
Coniston Ct
Beckenham BR3 . . . .**44** C8
Chessington KT9 . . . .**56** E7
Lightwater GU18 . . . .**48** B1
Penge SE26 . . . .**23** B2
3 Wallington SM6 . . . .**60** B6
Weybridge KT13 . . . .**53** B4
Coniston Dr GU9 . . . .**125** A6
Coniston Gdns SM2 . . . .**59** D4
Coniston Rd Catford BR1 . . .**24** E2
Coulsdon CR5 . . . .**79** C3
Croydon CR0 . . . .**43** A2
Old Woking GU22 . . . .**90** B7
Twickenham TW2 . . . .**5** B1
Coniston Way
Chessington KT9 . . . .**56** E7
Redhill RH2 . . . .**118** E2
Thorpe Lea TW20 . . . .**12** B1
Connaught Ave
Ashford TW15 . . . .**13** E4
Hounslow TW4 . . . .**4** E3
Mortlake SW14 . . . .**7** C3
Connaught Bsns Ctr
Mitcham CR4 . . . .**40** F4
Wallington CR9 . . . .**60** F4
Connaught Cl SM1 . . . .**59** D8
Connaught Cres GU24 . . . . .**87** F7
Connaught Gdns
Crawley RH10 . . . .**201** D8
Morden SM4 . . . .**40** C5
Connaught Rd
Aldershot GU12 . . . .**105** D2
Bagshot GU19 . . . .**47** C3
Brookwood GU24 . . . .**87** F7
Camberley GU15 . . . .**65** D5
Carshalton SM1 . . . .**59** D8
New Malden KT3 . . . .**38** E5
4 Richmond TW10 . . . .**6** F2
Teddington TW11, TW12 . . . .**16** D3
Connaught Sch The
GU12 . . . .**126** D2
Connell House 6 SM6 . . . . .**60** C4
Connington 2 KT1 . . . .**38** A7
Connop Way GU16 . . . .**65** F3
Conquest Rd KT15 . . . .**52** A5
Conrad Dr KT4 . . . .**39** D1
Consfield Ave KT3 . . . .**39** A4
Consort Dr GU15 . . . .**66** C7
Consort Mews TW7 . . . .**5** D2
Consort Way E RH6 . . . .**161** A3
Consort Way E RH6 . . . .**161** B2
Constable Gdns TW7 . . . .**5** D2
Constable Rd RH10 . . . .**201** F2
Constable Way GU47 . . . . . .**64** E6
Constable Wlk SE21 . . . .**22** E5
Constance Cres BR2 . . . .**44** F1
Constance Rd Sutton SM1 . .**59** C6
Thornton Heath CR0 . . . .**42** B2
Twickenham TW2 . . . .**16** B8
Constantine House SW2 . . .**22** B7
Constitution Hill GU22 . . . .**89** E8
Contley House Hotel RG40 **25** D4
Control Tower Rd
Crawley RH6 . . . .**181** D6
Harlington TW6 . . . .**3** B4
Convent Cl BR3 . . . .**24** C1
Convent Hill SE19 . . . .**22** C2
Convent of the Sacred
Heart Digby-Stuart Coll
SW15 . . . .**7** F2
Convent Rd TW15 . . . .**14** B3
Conway Dr Ashford TW15 . . .**14** C2
Farnborough GU14 . . . .**84** D4
Sutton SM2 . . . .**59** B4
Conway Gdns CR4 . . . .**41** E5
Conway House
Reigate RH2 . . . .**139** A4
6 Streatham SW2 . . . .**21** F7
Conway Rd Feltham TW13 . . .**15** D3
Harlington TW6 . . . .**3** B4
Twickenham TW4 . . . .**16** A8
Wimbledon SW20 . . . .**39** C8
Conway Wlk TW12 . . . .**15** F2
Conyer's Rd SW16 . . . .**21** D3
Conyers Cl KT12 . . . .**54** D5
Cook Rd Crawley RH10 . . . . .**201** F4
Horsham RH12 . . . .**217** D6
Cookes La SM3 . . . .**58** E4
Cookham Cl GU47 . . . .**45** C1
Cookham Rd RG12 . . . .**26** E7
Cooks Hill RH12 . . . .**214** A8
Cooks Mead RH12 . . . .**199** D7
Coolarne Rise GU15 . . . .**66** A6
Coolgardie Rd TW15 . . . .**14** C3
Coolham Ct RH11 . . . .**200** F6
Coolhurst La RH13 . . . .**218** A1
Coombe Ave CR0 . . . .**61** E6
Coombe Bank KT2, KT3 . . . .**38** E8
Coombe Cl Crawley RH11 .**181** D1
Frimley GU16 . . . .**85** D8
Hounslow TW3 . . . .**5** A3
Coombe Cotts RH3 . . . .**116** D4
Coombe Cres TW12 . . . .**15** E1
Coombe Ct Beckenham BR3 .**43** F8
Tadworth KT20 . . . .**97** C4
Coombe Dr KT15 . . . .**51** F4
Coombe End KT2 . . . .**18** D1
Coombe Gdns
New Malden KT3 . . . .**38** F5
Wimbledon SW20 . . . .**39** A8

Coombe Girls Sch KT3 . . . .**38** D7
Coombe Hill Glade KT2 . . .**18** E1
Coombe Hill Golf Course
KT2 . . . .**18** C1
Coombe Hill Inf Sch KT3 . .**38** D8
Coombe Hill Jun Sch KT3 .**38** D8
Coombe Hill Rd
East Grinstead RH19 . . . . . .**205** D6
Kingston u T KT2 . . . .**18** E1
Coombe House Chase
KT3 . . . .**38** D8
Coombe La
South Croydon CR0 . . . .**62** B5
Wimbledon SW20 . . . .**39** B7
Worplesdon GU3 . . . .**108** D3
Coombe La W KT2 . . . .**18** E1
Coombe Lane Flyover
SW20 . . . .**38** F8
Coombe Manor GU24 . . . . . .**68** B4
Coombe Neville KT2 . . . .**18** D1
Coombe Pine RG12 . . . .**27** D3
Coombe Pk KT2 . . . .**18** D3
Coombe Rd Croydon CR0 . . .**61** E6
Forest Hill SE26 . . . .**23** B4
Hampton TW12 . . . .**15** F2
Kingston u T KT3 . . . .**38** E6
Kingston u T, Norbiton KT2 . .**38** A8
South Croydon CR0, CR2 . . .**61** E6
Coombe Ridings KT2 . . . . . .**18** C3
Coombe Rise KT2 . . . .**38** C8
Coombe The RH3 . . . .**116** D4
Coombe Way KT14 . . . .**71** F7
Coombe Wlk SM1 . . . .**59** B7
Coombe Wood Golf
Course KT2 . . . .**18** C1
Coombe Wood Hill CR8 . . .**80** C6
Coombe Wood Rd KT2 . . . .**18** C3
Coombefield Cl KT3 . . . .**38** E4
Coombelands La KT15 . . . . .**52** A4
Coomber Way CR0, CR4 . . . .**41** D2
Coombes The GU5 . . . .**152** A5
Cooper Cl RH6 . . . .**162** A3
Cooper Cres SM5 . . . .**59** F7
Cooper Ct GU14 . . . .**85** C4
Cooper House
Hounslow TW4 . . . .**4** F4
7 West Norwood SW27 . . .**22** B3
Cooper Rd
Croydon CR0, CR9 . . . .**61** B6
Guildford GU1 . . . .**130** F8
Windlesham GU20 . . . .**48** D4
Cooper Row RH10 . . . .**201** D3
Cooper's Hill La TW20 . . . . .**11** D4
Cooper's Hill Rd
Nutfield RH1 . . . .**120** A1
South Nutfield RH1 . . . .**141** B5
Cooper's Terr GU9 . . . .**125** C3
Cooper's Yd SE19 . . . .**22** E2
Coopers Cl TW18 . . . .**12** E3
Coopers Hill Dr GU24 . . . . .**87** C7
Coopers Rise GU7 . . . .**150** C3
Cootes Ave RH12 . . . .**217** A3
Copeland House SW17 . . . .**20** D4
Copelands BR3 . . . .**23** F1
Copelands Cl GU15 . . . .**66** D4
Copeman Cl SE26 . . . .**23** C3
Copenhagen Way KT12 . . . .**54** B7
Copenhagen Wlk RG45 . . . .**45** B4
Copers Cope Rd BR3 . . . . . .**23** F1
Copleigh Dr KT20 . . . .**97** E7
Copley Cl Knaphill GU21 . . . .**88** E8
Redhill RH1 . . . .**118** E3
Copley Pk SW16 . . . .**21** F2
Copley Way KT20 . . . .**97** D7
Copnall Way RH12 . . . .**217** D2
Coppard Gdns KT9 . . . .**56** C4
Copped Hall Dr GU15 . . . . . .**66** C6
Copped Hall Way GU15 . . . .**66** C6
Coppedhall 1 SE21 . . . .**22** D6
Copper Beech Cl GU22 . . . .**89** B6
Copper Beeches TW7 . . . . . .**5** D6
Copper Cl SE19 . . . .**22** F1
Copper Mill Dr TW7 . . . .**5** F5
Copper Mill La SW17 . . . . . .**20** C4
Copperfield Ave GU47 . . . . .**45** E2
Copperfield Cl CR2, CR8 . . .**80** C8
Copperfield Cl KT22 . . . .**95** A6
Copperfield Pl RH12 . . . . . .**217** B4
Copperfield Rise KT15 . . . .**51** F4
Copperfields
Beckenham BR3 . . . .**44** C8
Fetcham KT22 . . . .**94** C5
Coppermill Rd TW19 . . . .**1** D3
Coppice Cl Guildford GU2 .**108** D2
Heath End GU9 . . . .**125** E6
West Barnes SM4 . . . .**39** C6
Coppice Dr TW19 . . . .**11** D8
Coppice La RH2 . . . .**117** F3
Coppice Pl GU8 . . . .**190** F8
Coppice Rd RH12 . . . .**218** A5
Coppice The Ashford TW15 .**14** B2
Crawley Down RH10 . . . . . .**204** B8
Coppice Wlk RH10 . . . .**202** A7
Copping Cl CR0 . . . .**61** E6
Coppins The CR0 . . . .**63** B4
Coppsfield KT8 . . . .**36** A6
Copse Ave Heath End GU9 .**125** E8
West Wickham BR4 . . . .**63** B7
Copse Cl Camberley GU15 . .**66** A6
Chilworth GU4 . . . .**131** C3
Crawley Down RH10 . . . . . .**204** B8
East Grinstead RH19 . . . . . .**186** A3
Horsham RH12 . . . .**217** F6
Copse Cres RH11 . . . .**201** C3
Copse Dr RG41 . . . .**25** A7
Copse Edge Cranleigh GU6 **174** F4
Elstead GU8 . . . .**148** C3

Copse Edge Ave KT17 . . . . .**76** F6
Copse End GU15 . . . .**66** A6
Copse Glade KT6 . . . .**37** D1
Copse Hill Purley CR8 . . . . . .**79** E6
Sutton SM2 . . . .**59** B3
Wimbledon SW20 . . . .**19** B1
Copse La RH6 . . . .**161** C4
Copse Rd Cobham KT11 . . . . .**73** B6
Knaphill GU21 . . . .**88** E3
Linchmere GU27 . . . .**207** D5
Reigate RH1 . . . .**139** D7
South Nutfield RH1 . . . .**140** F4
Copse Side GU7 . . . .**129** D1
Copse The Caterham CR3 .**101** A1
Farnborough GU14 . . . .**84** D3
Fetcham KT22, KT23 . . . .**94** B4
Rowledge GU10 . . . .**145** F4
South Nutfield RH1 . . . .**140** F4
Copse View CR2 . . . .**62** E2
Copse Way GU10 . . . .**145** F6
Copse Wood Ct RH1 . . . . . .**118** C3
Copsem La Esher KT10 . . . . .**55** C3
Oxshott KT22 . . . .**55** C1
Copsem Way KT10 . . . .**55** C4
Copsen Wood KT22 . . . .**74** C8
Copsleigh Ave RH1 . . . .**140** A3
Copsleigh Cl RH1 . . . .**140** A3
Copsleigh Way RH1 . . . .**140** A3
Copt Hill La KT20 . . . .**97** F7
Copthall Gdns TW1 . . . .**16** F7
Copthall Way KT15 . . . .**52** A1
Copthorne Ave SW12 . . . . . .**21** D8
Copthorne Bank
RH10, RH6 . . . .**183** C4
Copthorne CE
(Controlled) Sch RH10 .**183** B3
Copthorne Chase TW15 . . .**13** F4
Copthorne Cl TW17 . . . .**34** C3
Copthorne Common
Rd RH10 . . . .**183** C3
Copthorne Dr GU18 . . . .**48** B1
Copthorne Rd
Copthorne RH10 . . . .**182** F1
Crawley RH10 . . . .**202** B8
Domewood RH10, RH19 . . .**184** D4
Felbridge RH10, RH19 . . . . .**184** D1
Leatherhead KT22 . . . .**95** B7
Copthorne Rise CR8 . . . .**80** D6
Copthorne Sch Trust Ltd
RH10 . . . .**183** E3
Copthorne Way RH10 . . . . .**182** F2
Copyhold Rd RH19 . . . .**205** D8
Corban Rd TW3 . . . .**5** A4
Corbet Cl CR4, SM6 . . . .**60** A8
Corbet Rd KT17 . . . .**57** E1
Corbett Cl CR0 . . . .**82** D7
Corbett Dr GU18 . . . .**66** F7
Corbiere Ct SW19 . . . .**19** D2
Corby Cl RH11 . . . .**200** E3
Corby Dr TW20 . . . .**11** C2
Cordelia Croft RG42 . . . .**27** E8
Cordelia Gdns
Ash Vale GU12 . . . .**85** F1
Stanwell TW19 . . . .**13** E8
Cordelia Rd TW19 . . . .**13** E8
Corderoy Pl KT16 . . . .**32** F3
Cordrey Gdns CR5 . . . .**79** E4
Cordrey House KT15 . . . .**52** B8
Cordwalles Cty Jun Sch
GU15 . . . .**65** F8
Cordwalles Rd GU15 . . . .**65** F8
Corfe Cl KT21 . . . .**75** C1
Corfe Gdns GU16 . . . .**65** F1
Corfe Way GU14 . . . .**85** C1
Coriander Cl GU14 . . . .**84** C4
Coriander Cres GU2 . . . . . .**109** A6
Corium House RG42 . . . .**27** A2
Cork Tree House 3 SW27 . .**22** B3
Corkran Rd KT6 . . . .**37** E2
Corkscrew Hill BR4 . . . .**63** D7
Cormongers La RH1 . . . . . .**119** D2
Cormorant Cl SM1 . . . .**58** F7
Cormorant Ct 12 SE21 . . . . .**22** D6
Cormorant Pl GU47 . . . .**64** E7
Cornbunting Cl GU47 . . . . . .**64** D3
Cornelia Cl GU14 . . . .**84** D3
Corner Farm Cl KT20 . . . . . .**97** C5
Corner Fielde SW2 . . . .**21** F7
Cornerside TW15 . . . .**14** C1
Cornerstone Sch The
KT18 . . . .**76** C6
Corney Rd W4 . . . .**7** E8
Cornfield Rd RH2 . . . .**139** C8
Cornfields GU7 . . . .**151** A8
Cornflower La CR0 . . . .**43** D1
Cornford Gr SW12 . . . .**21** B6
Cornhill Cl KT15 . . . .**52** B8
Cornish Gr SE20 . . . .**43** B8
Cornwall Ave Byfleet KT14 . .**71** F5
Claygate KT10 . . . .**55** F3
Cornwall Cl GU15 . . . .**65** F7
Cornwall Gdns 6 RH19 . . .**205** F8
Cornwall Rd Belmont SM2 . .**59** A2
Thornton Heath CR0, CR9 . . .**61** B8
Twickenham TW1 . . . .**17** A7
Cornwall Way TW18 . . . .**12** E2
Cornwalls Cl CR3 . . . .**100** E3
Coronation Cotts GU8 . . . .**191** C5
Coronation Rd
Aldershot GU11 . . . .**126** B7
Ascot SL5 . . . .**29** A2
Bracknell SL5 . . . .**29** A2
East Grinstead RH19 . . . . . .**205** E7
Coronation Sq RG40 . . . .**25** D7
Coronet Cl RH10 . . . .**202** E7
Coronet The RH6 . . . .**161** C6
Corporation Ave TW4 . . . .**4** E3

Corpus Christi RC Prim
Sch KT3 . . . .**38** C6
Corrib Dr SM1 . . . .**59** E5
Corrie Gdns GU25 . . . .**31** C2
Corrie Rd Addlestone KT15 .**52** B5
Old Woking GU22 . . . .**90** C7
Corrigan Ave CR5 . . . .**79** A5
Corry Rd GU26 . . . .**188** C6
Corsair Cl TW19 . . . .**13** E8
Corsair Rd TW19 . . . .**13** E8
Corscombe Cl KT2 . . . .**18** C3
Corsehill St SW16 . . . .**21** C2
Corsham Way RG45 . . . .**45** B5
Corsletts Ave RH12 . . . .**216** D3
Corsten Hollow 4 RH1 . . . .**139** F8
Corunna Dr RH13 . . . .**217** F2
Cosdach Ave SM6 . . . .**60** D3
Cosedge Cres CR0, CR9 . . . .**61** B5
Cosford Rd GU8 . . . .**169** G4
Coteford St SW17 . . . .**21** A4
Cotelands CR0 . . . .**61** E7
Cotford Rd CR7 . . . .**42** C5
Cotherstone KT19 . . . .**57** D2
Cotherstone Rd SW2 . . . .**21** F7
Cotland Acres RH1 . . . .**139** D7
Cotsford Ave KT3 . . . .**38** D4
Cotswold Cl Crawley RH11 .**201** B6
Farnborough GU14 . . . .**84** E7
Hinchley Wood KT10 . . . .**55** F8
Kingston u T KT2 . . . .**18** C2
Staines TW18 . . . .**13** A3
Cotswold Ct RH13 . . . .**217** G2
Cotswold Rd
Hampton TW12 . . . .**16** A2
Sutton SM2 . . . .**59** B1
Cotswold St SE27 . . . .**22** B4
Cotswold Way KT4 . . . .**58** C8
Cottage Cl Horsham RH12 .**218** B6
Ottershaw KT16 . . . .**51** C4
Cottage Farm Way TW20 . .**32** C6
Cottage Gdns GU14 . . . .**84** F4
Cottage Gr KT6 . . . .**37** D3
Cottage Pl RH13 . . . .**183** E3
Cottage Rd KT19 . . . .**57** D3
Cottenham Dr SW20 . . . .**19** B1
Cottenham Par SW20 . . . . . .**39** B7
Cottenham Park Rd SW20 .**39** B8
Cottenham Pl SW20 . . . .**19** B1
Cottenhams RH7 . . . .**163** E8
Cotterill Rd KT6 . . . .**37** F1
Cottesbrooke Cl SL3 . . . .**1** D6
Cottesloe Cl GU24 . . . .**67** F3
Cottesmore RG12 . . . .**27** A2
Cottimore Ave KT12 . . . .**35** B2
Cottimore Cres KT12 . . . . . .**35** B2
Cottimore La
Walton-on-T KT12 . . . .**35** B2
Walton-on-T KT12 . . . .**35** D1
Cottimore Terr KT12 . . . .**35** B2
Cottingham Ave RH12 . . . . .**217** D7
Cottingham Rd SE20 . . . .**23** D1
Cottington Rd TW13 . . . .**15** D4
Cotton Hill BR1 . . . .**24** D4
Cotton House 18 SW12 . . . . .**21** E8
Cotton Row RH5 . . . .**176** C8
Cotton Wlk RH11 . . . .**201** A1
Cottongrass Cl CR0 . . . .**43** D1
Cottrell Flats GU14 . . . .**105** D8
Cotts Wood Dr GU4 . . . .**110** A6
Couchmore Ave KT10 . . . . . .**55** E8
Coulsdon C of E Prim Sch
CR5 . . . .**79** F1
Coulsdon Coll CR5 . . . .**100** A8
Coulsdon Court
Municipal Golf Course
CR5 . . . .**79** F3
Coulsdon Court Rd CR5 . . . .**79** F3
Coulsdon High Sch CR5 . .**100** B7
Coulsdon House 5 SW2 . . . .**21** E7
Coulsdon La CR5 . . . .**99** A8
Coulsdon Pl CR3 . . . .**100** D5
Coulsdon Rd
Caterham CR3, CR5 . . . .**100** B7
Coulsdon CR3, CR5 . . . .**100** B7
Coulsdon Rise CR5 . . . .**79** E3
Coulsdon South Sta CR5 . . .**79** D3
Coulthurst Ct SW16 . . . .**21** E1
Council Cotts
Charlwood RH6 . . . .**180** C6
Loxwood RH14 . . . .**213** A2
Plaistow RH14 . . . .**211** D3
West End GU24 . . . .**67** E6
Countisbury Gdns KT15 . . . .**52** B5
Countisbury House SE26 . . .**23** A5
Country Way TW13, TW16 . . .**15** C3
Countryways Experience
The GU6 . . . .**193** E2
County Mall RH10 . . . .**201** E5
County Oak Ind Est RH10 .**181** D3
County Oak La RH11 . . . . . .**181** D3
County Oak Ret Pk RH11 .**181** D2
County Oak Way
RH10, RH11 . . . .**181** D3
County Rd CR7 . . . .**42** B7
Courier House 17 SW2 . . . . .**22** A8
Courland Rd KT15 . . . .**52** B7
Course Rd SL5 . . . .**29** A6
Court Ave CR5 . . . .**100** A8
Court Bushes Rd CR3 . . . . .**101** B7
Court Cl
East Grinstead RH19 . . . . . .**185** F1
Twickenham TW13, TW2 . . . .**16** B5
Court Close Ave
TW13, TW2 . . . .**16** B5
Court Cres Chessington KT9 **56** D4
East Grinstead RH19 . . . . . .**185** F1
Court Downs Rd BR3 . . . .**44** B7
Court Dr Carshalton SM1 . . . .**59** E6

Court Dr *continued*
Croydon CR0 .60 F6
Court Farm Ave KT19 .57 D5
Court Farm Gdns KT19 .76 C8
Court Farm Ind Est TW19 .2 F1
Court Farm Rd CR6 .81 A2
Court Gdns GU15 .65 D5
Court Green Hts GU22 .89 C7
Court Haw SM7 .78 E4
Court Hill Sanderstead CR2 .80 E7
Woodmansterne CR5 .78 F2
Court House Mansions KT19 .76 D7
Court La Dulwich SE21 .22 F8
Epsom KT19 .76 C6
Court Lane Gdns SE21 .22 E8
Court Lodge Cty Inf Sch RH6 .160 F3
Court Lodge Rd RH6 .160 F3
Court Rd
10 Aldershot GU11 .105 A2
Banstead SM7 .78 A4
Caterham CR3 .100 E4
South Norwood SE25 .42 F6
Tyler's Green RH9 .121 C4
Court The
Dockenfield GU10 .166 D3
Guildford GU2 .130 C7
Warlingham CR6 .81 E1
Court Way TW1, TW2 .16 F8
Court Wood La CR0 .62 F1
Courtenay Ave SM2 .59 A2
Courtenay Dr BR3 .44 D7
Courtenay Mews GU21 .70 A3
Courtenay Rd
Heath End GU9 .125 E7
North Cheam KT4, SM3 .58 C7
Penge BR3, SE20 .23 D2
Woking GU21 .70 A3
Courtfield Rd TW15 .14 B2
Courtfield Rise BR4 .63 D7
Courthope Rd SW19 .19 E3
Courthope Villas SW19 .19 E1
Courtland Ave SW16 .21 F1
Courtlands Beckenham BR3 .44 B7
Richmond TW10 .7 A2
10 Sutton SM2 .59 B3
Walton-on-T KT12 .35 A2
Courtlands Ave Esher KT10 55 A4
Hampton TW12 .15 F2
Richmond TW9 .7 B5
West Wickham BR2 .44 F1
Courtlands Cl CR2 .62 A1
Courtlands Cres SM7 .78 A3
Courtlands Dr KT19 .57 F4
Courtlands Rd KT5 .38 A2
Courtleas KT11 .74 A6
Courtney Cl SE19 .22 E2
Courtney Cres SM5 .59 F2
Courtney Pl Cobham KT11 .73 F7
Croydon CR0 .61 A7
Courtney Rd
Croydon CR0, CR9 .61 A7
Harlington TW6 .3 A4
Mitcham SW19 .20 E1
Courts Hill Rd GU27 .208 B6
Courts Mount Rd GU27 .208 B6
Courts The SW16 .21 E1
Courtside SE23 .23 C5
Courtwood Prim Sch CR0 .62 F1
Courtyard The
Addlestone KT15 .52 C6
Cranleigh GU6 .153 E1
1 Crawley RH10 .201 D5
Crawley, Whitevane Hill RH13 .218 E4
East Grinstead RH19 .186 B1
Coutts Ave KT9 .56 E5
Coval Gdns SW14 .7 B3
Coval La SW14 .7 B3
Coval Rd SW14 .7 C3
Cove Cty Inf Sch GU14 .84 E6
Cove Cty Jun Sch GU14 .84 E5
Cove Manor Cty Inf Sch GU14 .84 E6
Cove Manor Cty Jun Sch GU14 .84 F6
Cove Rd GU14 .84 F4
Cove Sch GU14 .84 E5
Coveham Cres KT11 .73 A6
Coventry Rd SE25 .43 A5
Coverack Cl CR0 .43 E2
Coverdale Ct RH19 .185 C3
Coverdale Gdns CR0 .61 F7
Covert Cl RH10 .201 E7
Covert La RG12 .27 C5
Covert The Ascot SL5 .29 B2
Farnborough GU14 .84 E8
Coverton Rd SW17 .20 E3
Coverts Cl GU9 .125 E4
Coverts Rd KT10 .55 F3
Coves Farm Wood RG42 .26 D7
Covey Cl Farnborough GU14 .85 A8
Merton SW19 .40 B7
Covey The RH10 .202 E8
Covington Gdns SW16 .22 B1
Covington Way
South Norwood SW16 .22 A1
South Norwood SW16 .22 B1
Streatham SW16 .21 F2
Cow La GU7 .150 D4
Cowden St SE6 .24 A4
Cowdray Cl RH10 .202 C5
Cowdrey Rd SW19 .20 C3
Cowfold Cl RH11 .200 F3
Cowick Rd SW17 .20 F4
Cowleaze Rd KT2 .37 E8
Cowley Ave KT16 .32 F2
Cowley Cl CR2 .62 C2
Cowley Cres KT12 .54 C6
Cowley La KT16 .32 F2
Cowley Rd SW14 .7 E4
Coworth Cl SL5 .30 B4
Coworth Park Sch GU24 .49 B6
Coworth Rd SL5 .30 A4
Cowper Ave SM1 .59 D6
Cowper Cl KT16 .32 F3
Cowper Gdns SM6 .60 C4
Cowper Rd Richmond TW10 .17 F3
Wimbledon SW19 .20 C2
Cowshot Cres GU24 .87 D7
Cowslip La RH5 .115 B7
Cox Cnr RH5 .177 A7
Cox Green Rd
Cranleigh RH12 .195 C2
Ewhurst RH12 .195 C2
Cox House RH12 .217 B2
Cox La Chessington KT9 .56 F6
West Ewell KT19 .57 C5
Coxbridge GU9 .124 F1
Coxcomb Wlk RH11 .201 A4
Coxcombe La GU8 .191 B4
Coxdean KT18 .97 C8
Coxgreen GU47 .64 D6
Coxley Rise CR8 .80 C6
Coxs Ave TW17 .34 E6
Coxwell Rd SE19 .22 E1
Crab Hill BR3 .24 D1
Crab Hill La RH1 .140 F4
Crabbet Rd RH10 .202 B7
Crabtree Cl KT23 .94 C1
Crabtree Cnr TW20 .32 B8
Crabtree Dr KT22 .95 C2
Crabtree La Churt GU10 .168 A2
Great Bookham KT23 .94 C1
Headley KT22 .96 C1
Westhumble RH5 .115 A5
Crabtree Office Village TW20 .32 C8
Crabtree Rd
Camberley GU15 .65 B2
Crawley RH11 .201 C7
Thorpe TW20 .32 C7
Crabwood RH8 .122 E7
Craddocks Ave KT21 .75 F3
Craddocks Par KT21 .75 E2
Cradhurst Cl RH4 .135 C6
Craig Rd TW10 .17 C4
Craigans RH11 .201 A5
Craigen Ave CR0 .43 B1
Craigmore Tower GU22 .89 E8
Craignair Rd SW2 .22 A8
Craignish Ave SW16 .41 F7
Craigside Kingston u T KT2 .38 B8
Purley CR8 .79 F5
Craigwell Ave TW13 .15 A5
Craigwell Cl TW18 .32 E8
Crail Cl RG41 .25 A3
Crake Pl GU47 .64 D8
Crakell Rd RH2 .139 C8
Cramhurst La GU8 .170 E6
Cramond Ct TW14 .14 E7
Crampshaw La KT21 .95 F7
Crampton Rd SE20 .23 C2
Cranborne Ave KT6, KT9 .57 A7
Cranborne Wlk RH10 .201 F4
Cranbourne Cl
Horley RH6 .161 B5
Thornton Heath SW16 .41 E6
Cranbourne Cotts SL4 .9 B6
Cranbourne Sch SL5 .9 A4
Cranbrook Ct 9 TW8 .6 D8
Cranbrook Dr
Thames Ditton KT10 .36 C1
Twickenham TW2 .16 B7
Cranbrook House SE19 .42 D8
Cranbrook Rd Hounslow TW4 4 F3
South Norwood CR7 .42 C7
Wimbledon SW19 .19 E1
Cranbrook Terr GU6 .174 F3
Crane Ave TW7 .6 A2
Crane Ct Sandhurst GU47 .64 D8
West Ewell KT19 .57 C6
Crane House Catford BR1 .24 D3
Feltham TW13 .16 A5
Crane Inf Sch TW13 .15 F6
Crane Jun Sch TW13 .15 F6
Crane Lodge Rd TW5 .4 B8
Crane Mead Ct TW1 .16 F8
Crane Park Rd TW2 .16 B6
Crane Rd Stanwell TW19 .3 A1
Twickenham TW2 .16 E7
Crane Way TW2 .16 C8
Cranebrook TW2 .16 C6
Craneford Cl TW2 .16 F8
Craneford Way TW2 .16 F8
Cranes Dr KT5 .37 F5
Cranes Park Ave KT5, KT6 .37 F5
Cranes Park Cres KT5 .37 F5
Cranes Pk KT5, KT6 .37 E4
Craneswater TW6 .3 F7
Cranfield Ct 6 GU21 .68 F1
Cranfield Rd E SM5 .60 A2
Cranfield Rd W SM5 .60 A2
Cranford Ave TW19 .13 F8
Cranford Cl Purley CR8 .80 C6
Stanwell TW19 .13 E8
Wimbledon SW20 .19 B1
Cranford Comm Sch TW5 .4 B8
Cranford Ct SM1 .59 C6
Cranford Jun & Inf Schs TW4 .4 B5
Cranford La Cranford UB3 .4 A7
Harlington UB3 .3 E7
Hatton TW6 .3 F6
Hatton, Hatton Cross TW6 .3 F4
Cranford La *continued*
Heston TW5 .4 D7
Cranford Lodge SW19 .19 E6
Cranford Rise KT10 .55 C5
Cranleigh Cl Penge SE20 .43 B7
Sanderstead CR2 .81 A7
Cranleigh Ct
Farnborough GU14 .84 F4
Mitcham CR4 .40 D6
Richmond TW9 .7 A4
Cranleigh Cty Inf Sch GU6 .174 E3
Cranleigh Gdns
Kingston u T KT2 .17 F2
Sanderstead CR2 .81 A7
South Norwood SE25 .42 E6
Sutton SM1 .59 B8
Cranleigh House SW20 .39 B7
Cranleigh Mead GU6 .174 F2
Cranleigh Rd
Ewhurst GU6 .175 D4
Feltham TW13 .14 F4
Merton SW19 .40 A6
Thames Ditton KT10 .36 C1
Wonersh GU5 .152 C7
Cranleigh Sch GU6 .174 C5
Cranleigh Village Hospl GU6 .174 D3
Cranley Cl GU1 .110 A1
Cranley Gdns SM6 .60 C3
Cranley Pl GU21 .68 D1
Cranley Rd Guildford GU1 .109 F1
Hersham KT12 .53 F5
Cranmer Cl
Warlingham CR6 .81 E2
West Barnes SM4 .39 E3
Weybridge KT13 .53 A3
Cranmer Ct Hampton TW12 .16 B3
Kingston u T KT2 .17 D4
Cranmer Farm Cl CR4 .40 F5
Cranmer Gdns CR6 .81 E2
Cranmer Mid Sch CR4 .40 F5
Cranmer Rd
Croydon CR0, CR9 .61 C7
Hampton TW12 .16 B3
Kingston u T KT2 .17 E3
Mitcham CR4 .40 F5
Cranmer Terr SW17 .20 D3
Cranmer Wlk RH10 .202 C5
Cranmore Ave TW7 .5 C7
Cranmore Cl GU11 .104 E1
Cranmore Ct GU16 .85 F4
Cranmore Gdns GU11 .104 E1
Cranmore La
Aldershot GU11 .104 E1
West Horsley KT24 .112 C6
Cranmore Rd Catford BR1 .24 F5
Mytchett GU16 .86 A4
Cranmore Sch KT24 .112 C6
Cranston Cl
Hounslow TW3, TW4 .4 E5
Reigate RH2 .139 B8
Cranston Rd
East Grinstead RH19 .185 F2
Forest Hill SE23 .23 E6
Cranstoun Cl GU3 .108 F5
Crantock Rd SE6 .24 C6
Cranwell Ct CR0 .62 D8
Cranwell Gr
Lightwater GU18 .66 F8
Littleton TW17 .33 F5
Cranwell Rd TW6 .3 B5
Craster Rd SW2 .21 F8
Cravan Ave TW13 .15 A6
Craven Cl GU10 .146 C6
Craven Gdns SW19 .20 B3
Craven House
13 Farnham GU9 .125 B2
2 Mortlake SW14 .7 D4
Craven Rd Crawley RH10 .202 B5
Croydon CR0 .43 B1
Kingston u T KT2 .37 F8
Cravens The RH6 .162 A3
Crawford Cl TW7 .5 E5
Crawford Gdns
Camberley GU15 .65 B5
Horsham RH13 .217 E4
Crawfurd Way RH19 .185 F3
Crawley Ave
Crawley RH10 .182 C1
Crawley, Ifield RH10, RH11 .201 A6
Crawley Chase RG42 .8 B2
Crawley Coll
Crawley RH10 .201 E6
Crawley, Three Bridges RH10 .202 A6
Crawley Coll (West Green Annexe) RH11 .201 C7
Crawley Down CE (Controlled) Sch RH10 .204 B8
Crawley Down Rd
East Grinstead RH19 .184 F4
Felbridge RH19 .184 F4
Crawley Dr GU15 .65 F6
Crawley Hill GU15 .65 F5
Crawley Hospl RH11 .201 C6
Crawley La RH10 .202 C7
Crawley Leisure Pk RH11 .201 D7
Crawley Mus Ctr RH11 .201 C5
Crawley Rd Crawley RH12 .200 B1
Faygate RH12 .218 D7
Horsham RH12 .218 B5
Crawley Ridge GU15 .65 F6
Crawley Ridge Cty Inf Sch GU15 .65 F6
Crawley Ridge Cty Jun Sch GU15 .65 F7
Crawley Sta RH10 .201 E5
Crawley Wood Cl GU15 .65 F5
Crawshaw Rd KT16 .51 D4
Crawters Cl RH10 .201 F7
Cray Ave KT21 .75 F2
Crayke Hill KT9 .56 E3
Crayonne Cl TW16 .34 E8
Crealock St SW18 .20 B8
Creasys Dr RH11 .201 B1
Credenhill St SW16 .21 C2
Crediton Way KT10 .56 A5
Credon Cl GU14 .84 F5
Cree's Meadow GU20 .48 D3
Creek Rd KT8 .36 E5
Creek The TW16 .35 A4
Creeland Gr SE6 .23 F7
Cremorne Gdns KT19 .57 D2
Crerar Cl GU14 .84 D3
Crescent Ct KT6 .37 D4
Crescent Day Hospl CR0 .63 C1
Crescent Gdns SW19 .20 A5
Crescent Gr CR4 .40 E5
Crescent La GU12 .106 B5
Crescent Rd
Beckenham BR3 .44 B7
Bletchingley RH1 .120 C2
Caterham CR3 .101 A3
East Grinstead RH19 .185 D1
Kingston u T KT2 .18 B1
Reigate RH2 .139 A7
Shepperton TW17 .34 C4
Wimbledon SW20 .39 D8
Wokingham RG40 .25 C5
Crescent The
Ashford TW15 .13 F3
Barnes SW13 .7 F5
Beckenham BR3 .44 A8
Belmont SM2 .78 A8
Bracknell RG12 .27 C5
Carshalton SM1 .59 D5
Chertsey KT16 .33 A6
East Molesey KT8 .36 A5
Egham TW20 .11 F2
Epsom KT18 .76 A4
Farnborough GU14 .85 C3
Felcourt RH19 .185 C8
Guildford GU2 .109 A3
Harlington UB7 .3 D7
Heath End GU9 .125 D8
Horley RH6 .182 B8
Horsham RH12 .217 A2
Kingston u T KT6 .37 E4
Kingston u T, Norbiton KT3 .38 C7
Leatherhead KT22 .95 B5
Lower Halliford TW17 .34 F2
Reigate RH2 .118 B1
Thornton Heath CR0, SE25 .42 D3
West Wickham BR4 .44 E3
Weybridge KT13 .53 A7
Wimbledon SW19 .20 A5
Woldingham CR3 .102 A4
Crescent Way Horley RH6 .161 A1
South Norwood SW16 .22 A1
Crescent Wood Rd SE21, SE26 .23 A5
Cressage Ho 9 TW8 .6 E8
Cressall Cl KT22 .95 B7
Cressall Mead KT22 .95 B7
Cressingham Gr SM1 .59 C6
Cresswell Rd Croydon SE25 43 A5
Feltham TW13 .15 E4
Twickenham TW1 .6 D1
Crest Hill GU5 .133 E1
Crest Rd South Croydon CR2 .62 B3
West Wickham BR2 .44 F2
Crest The Surbiton KT5 .38 A4
10 West Norwood SW27 .22 B3
Cresta Dr KT15 .51 F1
Creston Ave GU21 .68 E3
Creston Way KT4 .39 D1
Crestwood Way TW4 .4 E2
Creswell GU21 .68 D2
Crewdson Rd RH6 .161 B3
Crewe's Ave CR6 .81 C3
Crewe's Cl CR6 .81 C2
Crewe's Farm La CR6 .81 E2
Crewe's La CR6 .81 D3
Crichton Ave SM6 .60 D6
Crichton Rd SM5 .59 F3
Cricket Cl GU26 .188 D6
Cricket Ct RH19 .185 E3
Cricket Field Gr RG45 .45 D4
Cricket Field Rd RH12 .217 B1
Cricket Gn
Hambledon GU8 .171 C1
Mitcham CR4 .40 F5
Cricket Green Sch CR4 .40 E6
Cricket Hill RH1 .140 F7
Cricket La Farnham GU10 .146 D6
Penge BR3 .23 E3
Cricket View KT13 .53 B5
Cricket Way KT13 .53 E8
Cricketers Cl
Chessington KT9 .56 D6
Ockley RH5 .177 C4
Cricketers La
Windlesham GU20 .48 D4
Winkfield RG42 .8 A3
Cricketers Wlk SE26 .23 C3
Cricklade Ave SW2 .21 F6
Crieff Ct 3 TW11, KT8 .17 C1
Criffel Ave SW2 .21 D7
Crimea Rd Aldershot GU11 105 B2
Frimley GU16 .86 D8
Crimp Hill
Englefield Green SL4, TW20 .11 A6
Old Windsor SL4, TW20 .11 A6
Cripley Rd GU14 .84 D6
Cripplecrutch Hill
Chiddingfold GU27 .209 F5
Fisherstreet GU27 .209 F5
Cripps House RH11 .201 B2
Crispen Rd TW13 .15 E4
Crispin Cl Ashstead KT21 .75 F1
Wallington SM6 .60 E8
Crispin Cres SM6 .60 D8
Critchmere Hill GU27 .207 E7
Critchmere La GU27 .207 E6
Critchmere Vale GU27 .207 E6
Critten La KT24, RH5 .113 D2
Crittenden Lodge BR4 .44 A1
Crocker Cl SL5 .28 F8
Crockers La RH7 .163 D4
Crockerton Rd SW17 .20 F6
Crockford Cl KT15 .52 C6
Crockford Park Rd KT15 .52 C5
Crockham Cl RH11 .201 C4
Crocknorth Rd KT24 .113 A2
Crocus Cl CR0 .43 D1
Croffets KT20 .97 D6
Croft Ave Dorking RH4 .115 B1
West Wickham BR4 .44 C1
Croft Cl Harlington UB7 .3 C7
Wokingham RG41 .25 A2
Croft Rd Aldershot GU11 .126 B8
Carshalton SM1 .59 E5
Godalming GU7 .150 E4
Merton SW19 .20 C1
South Norwood SW16 .22 A1
Witley GU8 .170 E5
Wokingham RG40 .25 A1
Woldingham CR3 .102 A5
Croft The Crawley RH11 .201 A6
Epsom KT17 .76 F5
Heston TW5 .4 E7
Croft Way Frimley GU16 .65 F2
Horsham RH12 .217 A3
Richmond TW10 .17 B5
Crofter's Cl GU47 .64 A8
Crofters Cl TW7 .5 D2
Crofters Mead CR0 .62 F2
Croftleigh Ave CR8 .80 B3
Crofton KT21 .75 E1
Crofton Ave Chiswick W4 .7 D7
Walton-on-T KT12 .54 C7
Crofton Cl Bracknell RG12 .27 E4
Ottershaw KT16 .51 C3
Crofton Terr TW9 .6 F3
Crofts Cl GU8 .191 B5
Crofts The TW17 .34 E5
Croftside The SE25 .43 A6
Croham Cl CR2 .61 E4
Croham Hurst Golf Course CR2 .62 A3
Croham Hurst Sch CR2 .61 F5
Croham Manor Rd CR2 .61 E4
Croham Mount CR2 .61 E3
Croham Park Ave CR0, CR2 61 F5
Croham Rd
Croydon CR0, CR2 .61 E5
South Croydon CR2 .61 E5
Croham Valley Rd CR2 .62 B3
Croindene Rd SW16 .41 E8
Cromer Ct SW16 .21 E5
Cromer Rd Croydon SE25 .43 B6
Harlington TW6 .3 A5
Mitcham SW17 .21 A2
Cromford Way KT3 .38 D8
Crompton Fields RH10 .181 E1
Crompton Way RH10 .181 E1
Cromwell Ave KT3 .38 F4
Cromwell Cl KT12 .35 B1
Cromwell Ct 15 KT2 .18 A1
Cromwell Gr CR3 .100 C6
Cromwell House CR0 .61 B7
Cromwell Pl
Cranleigh GU6 .174 F1
1 East Grinstead RH19 .205 F7
Mortlake SW14 .7 C4
Cromwell Rd Ascot SL5 .29 B4
Beckenham BR3 .43 E6
Camberley GU15 .65 D7
Caterham CR3 .100 C6
Feltham TW13 .15 B7
Hounslow TW3 .5 A3
Kingston u T KT2 .37 E8
Redhill RH1 .118 F1
Teddington TW11 .17 A2
Thornton Heath CR0 .42 D2
Wimbledon SW19 .20 B3
Worcester Park KT19, KT4 .57 E7
Cromwell St TW3 .5 A3
Cromwell Way GU14 .85 C7
Cromwell Wlk 1 RH1 .118 F1
Crondall Ct GU15 .65 B4
Crondall House SW15 .19 A7
Crondall La GU10, GU9 .124 D2
Crondall Rd GU10 .145 A6
Cronks Hill RH1, RH2 .139 D7
Cronks Hill Cl RH1 .139 D7
Cronks Hill Rd RH1 .139 D7
Crooksbury Rd
Farnham GU10 .126 C2
Tilford GU10 .147 D8
Crosby Cl TW13 .15 E4
Crosby Hill Dr GU15 .65 F7
Crosby Way GU9 .125 A1
Crosby Wlk SE24 .22 A8
Cross Deep TW1 .17 A6
Cross Deep Gdns TW1 .16 F6
Cross Farm Cty Inf Sch GU16 .85 E6
Cross Fell RG12 .27 A5

Cross Gates Cl RG12 . . . .**27** F6
Cross Gdns GU16 . . . .**85** F6
Cross Keys RH10 . . . .**201** D6
Cross La Burstow RH6 . . . . .**162** C1
  Frimley GU16 . . . .**85** F6
  Ottershaw KT16 . . . .**51** C4
Cross Lances Rd TW3 . . . .**5** B3
Cross Lanes GU1 . . . .**130** F8
Cross Oak La RH1, RH6 . . . .**161** C7
Cross Rd Ash GU12 . . . .**106** B3
  Belmont SM2 . . . .**59** A1
  Carshalton SM1 . . . .**59** D5
  Croydon CR0 . . . .**42** D1
  Feltham TW13 . . . .**15** E4
  Kingston u T KT2 . . . .**17** F1
  Merton SW19 . . . .**20** A1
  Oatlands Park KT13 . . . .**53** D7
  Purley CR8 . . . .**80** B6
  Tadworth KT20 . . . .**97** C5
  Wentworth SL5 . . . .**30** A1
Cross St
  6 Aldershot GU11 . . . .**105** A2
  Farnborough GU14 . . . . . .**105** C8
  Hampton TW12 . . . .**16** C3
  Mortlake SW13 . . . .**7** E4
  Wokingham RG40 . . . .**25** C6
Crossacres GU22 . . . .**70** E4
Crossfield Pl KT13 . . . .**53** B3
Crossland Rd Redhill RH1 . .**119** A1
  Thornton Heath CR7 . . . . . .**42** B3
Crosslands KT16 . . . .**51** E6
Crosslands Rd KT19 . . . .**57** D4
Crossley CI TN16 . . . .**83** D4
Crossman Ct RH11 . . . .**201** B1
Crossman Houses 19
  SW12 . . . .**21** E8
Crosspath RH10 . . . .**201** E7
Crossroads The KT24 . . . . . .**113** D7
Crosswater La GU10 . . . .**167** F4
Crossway Bracknell RG12 . . .**27** C7
  Crawley RH6 . . . .**181** F8
  Walton-on-T KT12 . . . .**54** B8
  West Barnes KT3, SW20 . . . .**39** C5
Crossways Aldershot GU12 . .**105** F1
  Charlton TW16 . . . .**14** F1
  Churt GU10 . . . .**167** C7
  Crawley RH10 . . . .**202** A7
  Effingham KT24 . . . .**113** D8
  Egham TW20 . . . .**12** D2
  South Croydon CR0, CR2 . . .**62** F3
  Sutton SM2 . . . .**59** D2
  Tatsfield TN16 . . . .**103** C7
Crossways CI TN16 . . . .**103** C7
Crossways CI RH10 . . . .**201** F7
Crossways Cotts
  Alfold Crossways GU6 . . . . .**194** A3
  Rudgwick RH12 . . . .**213** F6
Crossways Ct TN16 . . . .**103** C7
Crossways La RH2 . . . .**118** D7
Crossways Rd
  Beckenham BR3 . . . .**44** A5
  Grayshott GU26 . . . .**188** D3
  Mitcham CR4 . . . .**41** B6
Crossways The
  Abinger Hammer RH5 . . . . .**134** B3
  Coulsdon CR5 . . . .**100** A8
  Guildford GU2 . . . .**129** F7
  Heston TW5 . . . .**4** F7
  Lower Kingswood RH2 . . . . .**118** C7
  Merstham RH1 . . . .**119** C6
Crosswell CI TW17 . . . .**34** C7
Crouch CI BR3 . . . .**24** A7
Crouch La SL4 . . . .**9** A7
Crouch Oak La KT15 . . . .**52** C6
Crouchfield RH4 . . . .**136** C4
Crouchmans SE21, SE26 **23** A5
Crowberry Cl RH11 . . . .**201** A2
Crowborough CI CR6 . . . .**81** E1
Crowborough Dr CR6 . . . .**81** E1
Crowborough Rd SW17 . . . . .**21** A3
Crowhurst SE25 . . . .**43** A6
Crowhurst CI RH10 . . . .**202** E6
Crowhurst Keep RH10 . . . . .**202** E6
Crowhurst La
  Crowhurst RH7, RH8 . . . . . .**143** D4
  Tandridge RH7 . . . .**143** D5
Crowhurst Mead RH9 . . . . .**121** C5
Crowhurst Rd
  Crowhurst RH7 . . . .**164** D7
  Lingfield RH7 . . . .**164** D7
Crowhurst Village Rd
  RH7 . . . .**143** E2
Crowland Rd CR7 . . . .**42** D5
Crowland Wlk SM4 . . . .**40** C3
Crowley Ct CR0 . . . .**61** A5
Crowmarsh Gdns SE23 . . . . .**23** C8
Crown Arc KT1 . . . .**37** D7
Crown CI Colnbrook SW3 . . . . .**1** C7
  Walton-on-T KT12 . . . .**35** C2
Crown Cotts Bracknell SL5 .**28** C4
  Englefield Green TW20 . . . . .**11** A1
Crown Ct Godalming GU7 . .**150** E4
  4 Twickenham TW1 . . . .**17** B8
Crown Dale SE19, SE27 . . . . .**22** D2
Crown Dr GU9 . . . .**126** A5
Crown Hill Ct SL5 . . . .**29** B4
Crown Hts GU1 . . . .**130** E6
Crown La Farnham GU9 . . . .**126** A5
  Merton SM4, SW19 . . . .**40** A6
  South Norwood SE19, SW16 .**22** A3
  Wentworth GU25 . . . .**31** D3
Crown Lane Gdns SE27 . . . . .**22** A3
Crown Lane Prim Sch
  SE27 . . . .**22** B3
Crown Meadow SL3 . . . .**1** B7

Crown Par Morden SM4 . . . . .**40** A5
  South Norwood SE19 . . . . . .**22** B2
Crown Pas KT1 . . . .**37** D7
Crown Pl GU47 . . . .**45** E1
Crown Point SE19 . . . .**22** B2
Crown Rd Kingston u T KT3 . .**38** C8
  Morden SM4, SW19 . . . .**40** B5
  Sutton SM1 . . . .**59** B6
  Twickenham TW1 . . . .**6** B1
  Wentworth GU25 . . . .**31** C3
Crown Rise KT16 . . . .**32** F1
Crown Row RG12 . . . .**27** D3
Crown St TW20 . . . .**12** A4
Crown Terr TW9 . . . .**6** F3
Crown Wood Cty Prim
  Sch RG12 . . . .**27** E3
Crown Yard TW3 . . . .**5** C4
Crownbourne Ct SM1 . . . . . .**59** B6
Crownpits La GU7 . . . .**150** D3
Crowntree Cl TW7 . . . .**5** F8
Crowther Rd SE25 . . . .**43** A5
Crowthorne C of E Sch
  RG45 . . . .**45** C5
Crowthorne CI SW18 . . . .**19** F7
Crowthorne Lodge RG12 . . .**27** B5
Crowthorne Rd
  Bracknell RG40, RG12 . . . . . .**26** F2
  Bracknell,
  Easthampstead RG12 . . . . . .**27** A5
  Sandhurst GU47 . . . .**45** B2
Crowthorne Rd N RG12 . . . .**27** B6
Croxall House KT12 . . . .**35** C3
Croxden Wlk SM4 . . . .**40** C3
Croxted CI SE21 . . . .**22** C8
Croyde CI GU14 . . . .**85** A7
Croydon Airport Ind Est
  CR9 . . . .**60** F4
Croydon Coll CR9 . . . .**61** D8
Croydon Coll Annexe CR0 .**42** D1
Croydon Coll (Selhurst
  Tertiary Ctr) SE25 . . . .**42** D4
Croydon Flyover The
  CR0, CR9 . . . .**61** C7
Croydon General Hospl
  CR9 . . . .**42** C1
Croydon Gr CR0 . . . .**42** B1
Croydon High Sch CR0 . . . . .**62** C1
Croydon La Banstead SM7 . . .**78** D6
  Wallington SM7 . . . .**78** D6
Croydon La S SM7 . . . .**78** B5
Croydon Rd Beckenham BR3 **43** E6
  Caterham CR3 . . . .**101** A5
  Chelsham CR6 . . . .**102** D5
  Coney Hall BR2, BR4 . . . .**63** F7
  Croydon CR0 . . . .**60** D7
  Harlington TW6 . . . .**3** B4
  Mitcham CR0, CR9 . . . .**41** C4
  Penge SE20 . . . .**43** C8
  Reigate RH2 . . . .**118** C2
  Tatsfield TN16 . . . .**103** F3
  Titsey CR6 . . . .**102** D5
  Wallington CR0, SM5, SM6 . . .**60** D7
Croydon Rd Ind Est SE25 . . .**43** D5
Croydon Water Palace
  CR9 . . . .**61** A4
Croydonbarn La
  RH6, RH9 . . . .**163** B4
Croylands Dr KT6 . . . .**37** E2
Croysdale Ave TW16 . . . .**35** A6
Crozier Dr CR2 . . . .**62** B1
Cruikshank Lea GU47 . . . . . .**64** E6
Crunden Rd CR2 . . . .**61** D3
Crundwell Ct GU9 . . . .**125** D3
Crusader Gdns CR0 . . . .**61** E7
Crusoe Rd CR4 . . . .**20** F1
Crutchfield La Sidlow RH6 **160** B5
  Walton-on-T KT12 . . . .**54** B1
Crutchley Rd Catford SE6 . .**24** E6
  Wokingham RG40 . . . .**25** D7
Crystal Ct SE19 . . . .**22** F3
Crystal Palace National
  Sports Ctr SE19 . . . .**23** A2
Crystal Palace Par SE19 . . .**22** F3
Crystal Palace Park Rd
  SE19, SE26 . . . .**23** B3
Crystal Palace Sta SE19 . . .**23** A2
Crystal Palace Station Rd
  SE19 . . . .**23** A2
Crystal Terr SE19 . . . .**22** D2
Crystal View Ct BR1 . . . .**24** D4
Cubitt St CR0 . . . .**60** F5
Cubitt Way GU21 . . . .**68** D1
Cuckfield CI RH11 . . . .**200** D5
Cuckmere Cres RH11 . . . . . .**200** F5
Cuckoo La GU24 . . . .**67** D6
Cuckoo Vale GU24 . . . .**67** D6
Cuda's CI KT19 . . . .**57** F6
Cuddington Ave KT19, KT4 .**57** F7
Cuddington CI KT20 . . . .**97** D7
Cuddington Croft Cty Fst
  & Mid Sch SM2 . . . .**58** D2
Cuddington Cty Prim Sch
  KT4 . . . .**58** A6
Cuddington Glade KT19 . . . .**76** A7
Cuddington Golf Course
  SM2 . . . .**77** E7
Cuddington Park CI SM7 . . .**77** F6
Cuddington
  Way SM2, SM7 . . . .**77** D8
Cudham Dr CR0 . . . .**82** C8
Cudham Rd TN16 . . . .**103** E8
Cudham St SE6 . . . .**24** C8
Cudworth La RH5 . . . .**179** E8
Cuffs Hill RH10 . . . .**202** E2
Culham Ho RG12 . . . .**27** E5
Culham House RG12 . . . .**27** E5
Cull's Rd GU3 . . . .**107** B1
Cullens Mews **4** GU11 . . .**105** A1

Cullerne CI KT17 . . . .**57** F1
Cullesden Rd CR8 . . . .**80** B4
Culmer Hill GU8 . . . .**170** F2
Culmington Rd CR2 . . . .**61** C2
Culsac Rd **1** KT6 . . . .**56** E8
Culver Dr RH8 . . . .**122** E5
Culver Rd GU47 . . . .**45** D1
Culverden Ct **5** KT13 . . . . . .**53** D7
Culverden Rd SW12 . . . .**21** C6
Culverden Terr KT13 . . . .**53** D7
Culverhay KT21 . . . .**75** E3
Culverhouse Sch SW16 . . . . .**21** F5
Culverlands Cres GU12 . . . .**106** A3
Culverley Rd SE6 . . . .**24** C7
Culvers Ave SM5, CR4 . . . . . .**59** F8
Culvers House Prim Sch
  CR4 . . . .**41** A1
Culvers Retreat SM5 . . . .**59** F8
Culvers Way SM5 . . . .**59** F8
Culverstone CI BR2 . . . .**44** F4
Culworth House GU1 . . . . . .**130** E8
Cumber House SW18 . . . .**20** A7
Cumberland
  Ave GU2, GU3 . . . .**109** A6
Cumberland CI Epsom KT19 **57** E1
  2 Twickenham TW1 . . . .**6** B1
  6 Wimbledon SW20 . . . . . .**19** D1
Cumberland Ct **4** CR0 . . . . .**42** D1
Cumberland Dr
  Bracknell RG12 . . . .**27** E8
  Chessington KT9 . . . .**56** F7
  Hinchley Wood KT10 . . . .**55** F8
Cumberland House KT2 . . . . .**18** B1
Cumberland Lodge SL4 . . . . .**10** D4
Cumberland Pl Catford SE6 **24** C7
  Sunbury TW16 . . . .**35** A5
Cumberland Rd
  Ashford TW15 . . . .**13** D5
  Barnes SW13 . . . .**7** F6
  Beckenham BR2 . . . .**44** F6
  Croydon SE25 . . . .**43** B3
  Frimley GU15 . . . .**66** C4
  Richmond TW9 . . . .**7** A7
Cumberland St TW18 . . . . . .**12** D3
Cumberlands CR8 . . . .**80** D4
Cumberlow Ave SE25 . . . .**43** A6
Cumbernauld Gdns TW16 .**14** F3
Cumbernauld Wlk RH11 . . .**200** E2
Cumbrae Gdns KT6 . . . .**56** D8
Cumbria CI GU14 . . . .**85** E1
Cumnor Gdns KT17 . . . .**58** A4
Cumnor House Sch CR2 . . . .**61** B2
Cumnor Rd SM2 . . . .**59** C4
Cumnor Rise CR8 . . . .**80** C2
Cumnor Way RG12 . . . .**27** E5
Cunliffe CI KT18 . . . .**96** B3
Cunliffe Rd KT19 . . . .**57** F6
Cunliffe St SW16 . . . .**21** C2
Cunningham Ave GU1 . . . . .**110** B2
Cunningham CI BR4 . . . .**63** B8
Cunningham Rd SM7 . . . .**78** D4
Cunnington Rd GU14 . . . .**85** D2
Cunworth Ct RG12 . . . .**26** F3
Curfew Bell Rd KT16 . . . .**32** F2
Curl Way RG41 . . . .**25** A5
Curlew Cl CR2 . . . .**81** D8
Curlew Ct KT6 . . . .**57** A7
Curlew Gdns GU4 . . . .**110** D3
Curley Hill Rd GU18 . . . .**66** F7
Curling CI CR5 . . . .**100** A2
Curling Vale GU2 . . . .**130** A7
Curly Bridge CI GU14 . . . . . .**84** F8
Curnick's La SE27 . . . .**22** C4
Curran Ave SM6 . . . .**60** A7
Currie Hill CI SW19 . . . .**19** F4
Currie House **18** SW12 . . . . .**21** D8
Curteys Wlk RH11 . . . .**201** A3
Curtis CI GU15 . . . .**66** C7
Curtis Field Rd SW16 . . . .**22** A4
Curtis Gdns RH4 . . . .**136** A8
Curtis Rd Dorking RH4 . . . . .**136** A8
  Twickenham TW4 . . . .**15** F8
  West Ewell KT19 . . . .**57** C6
Curvan CI KT17 . . . .**57** F1
Curzon Ave RH12 . . . .**217** B3
Curzon CI KT13 . . . .**53** A6
Curzon Rd
  Thornton Heath CR7 . . . .**42** A3
  Weybridge KT13 . . . .**53** A5
Cusack CI TW1 . . . .**16** F4
Cuthbert Gdns SE25 . . . .**42** E6
Cuthbert Retreat Ash GU12 .**106** B6
  Thornton Heath CR0, CR9 . . .**61** B8
Cuttinglye La RH10 . . . .**184** A1
Cuttinglye Rd RH10 . . . .**184** C2
Cutts Rd GU11 . . . .**105** D7
Cyclamen CI **4** TW12 . . . . . .**16** A2
Cyclamen Way KT19 . . . .**57** C5
Cygnet Ave TW14 . . . .**15** D8
Cygnet CI GU21 . . . .**69** B3
Cygnets CI RH1 . . . .**119** A3
Cygnets The Feltham TW15 .**15** E4
  Staines TW18 . . . .**12** F3
Cypress Ave TW2 . . . .**16** C8
Cypress Ct Sutton SM1 . . . . .**59** A4
  7 West Norwood SW16 . . . . .**22** A4
Cypress Gr GU12 . . . .**105** F7
Cypress Hill Ct GU14 . . . .**64** F1
Cypress Inf Sch SE25 . . . . . .**42** E6
Cypress Jun Sch SE25 . . . . .**42** E6
Cypress Lodge SE25 . . . .**42** E6
Cypress Rd Guildford GU1 .**109** C4
  South Norwood SE25 . . . . . .**42** E6
Cypress Way
  Banstead KT17 . . . .**77** D5
  Blackwater GU17 . . . .**64** B5
  Grayshott GU26 . . . .**188** D2
Cypress Wlk TW20 . . . .**11** B2

Cyprus Rd GU16 . . . .**86** D8

D

D'abernon CI KT10 . . . .**55** A6
D'Abernon Dr KT11 . . . .**73** E3
D'arcy Rd SM3 . . . .**58** D6
Dacre CI CR0 . . . .**41** E2
Dacres Rd SE23 . . . .**23** D5
Daffodil CI Croydon CR0 . . . . .**43** D1
  7 Hampton TW12 . . . .**16** A2
Daffodil Dr GU24 . . . .**68** A3
Dafforne Rd SW17 . . . .**21** A5
Dagden Rd GU4 . . . .**130** E3
Dagley La GU4 . . . .**130** D3
Dagmar Rd
  4 Kingston u T KT2 . . . .**18** A1
  South Norwood SE25 . . . . . .**42** E4
Dagnall Pk CR0, SE25 . . . . . .**42** E4
Dagnall Rd SE25 . . . .**42** E4
Dagnan Rd SW12 . . . .**21** C8
Dahlia Gdns CR4 . . . .**41** D5
Dahomey Rd SW16 . . . .**21** C2
Daimler Way SM6 . . . .**60** E3
Dainford CI BR1 . . . .**24** D3
Dairy CI CR7 . . . .**42** C7
Dairyfields RH11 . . . .**201** A5
Dairymans Wlk GU4 . . . . . .**110** B6
Daisy CI CR0 . . . .**43** D1
Dakin CI RH10 . . . .**202** C2
Dakins The RH19 . . . .**205** E8
Dalcross RG12 . . . .**27** E3
Dalcross Rd TW4, TW5 . . . .**4** E5
Dale Ave TW4 . . . .**4** E4
Dale CI Addlestone KT15 . . . . .**52** B5
  Horsham RH12 . . . .**217** F5
  Sunningdale SL5 . . . .**30** A4
  Wrecclesham GU10 . . . .**145** F7
Dale Ct **3** KT2 . . . .**17** F1
Dale Gdns GU47 . . . .**64** A8
Dale Lodge Rd SL5 . . . .**30** A4
Dale Park Ave SM5 . . . .**59** F8
Dale Park Rd SE19 . . . .**42** D8
Dale Rd Ashford TW16 . . . .**14** F1
  Cheam SM1 . . . .**58** F6
  Forest Row RH18 . . . .**206** F1
  Purley CR8 . . . .**80** B7
  Walton-on-T KT12 . . . .**34** F2
Dale View
  Haslemere GU27 . . . .**207** F5
  Headley KT18 . . . .**96** B4
  Woking GU21 . . . .**69** B1
Dalebury Rd SW17 . . . .**20** F6
Dalegarth Gdns CR8 . . . .**80** D6
Daleham Rd TW20 . . . .**12** A2
Daleside Rd
  Streatham SW17 . . . .**21** B3
  West Ewell KT19 . . . .**57** D4
Dalewood Gdns
  Crawley RH10 . . . .**201** F8
  North Cheam KT4 . . . .**58** B8
Dalkeith Rd SE21 . . . .**22** C8
Dallas Rd Cheam SM3 . . . . . .**58** E4
  Forest Hill SE26 . . . .**23** B5
Dallaway Gdns RH19 . . . . . .**185** E1
Dalley Ct GU47 . . . .**64** D7
Dallington CI KT12 . . . .**54** C4
Dalmain Rd SE23 . . . .**23** D7
Dalmain Prim Sch SE23 . . .**23** E7
Dalmally Rd CR0 . . . .**43** A2
Dalmeny Ave SW16 . . . .**42** A7
Dalmeny Cres TW3 . . . .**5** D3
Dalmeny Rd
  North Cheam KT4 . . . .**58** B7
  Wallington SM5 . . . .**60** A3
Dalmore Ave KT10 . . . .**55** F4
Dalmore Rd SE21 . . . .**22** C6
Dalston CI GU15 . . . .**66** D3
Dalton Ave CR4 . . . .**40** E7
Dalton CI RH11 . . . .**201** B1
Dalton House **7** SW12 . . . . .**21** B8
Dalton St SE27 . . . .**22** B5
Damascene Wlk SE21 . . . . . .**22** C7
Damask Ct GU24 . . . .**67** E6
Damer House **9** SW10 . . . . . .**6** F1
Dampier Wlk RH11 . . . .**201** B1
Dan Bryant House **5**
  SW12 . . . .**21** C8
Danbrook Rd SW16 . . . .**41** E8
Danbury Mews SM5, SM6 . . .**60** B6
Dancer Rd TW9 . . . .**7** A4
Dane Ct GU22 . . . .**70** F4
Dane Rd Ashford TW15 . . . . . .**14** D2
  Merton SW19 . . . .**40** E8
  Warlingham CR6 . . . .**81** D2
Danebury CR0 . . . .**63** B4
Danebury Prim Sch SW15 .**18** F8
Danebury Wlk GU16 . . . .**85** F8
Daneby Rd SE6 . . . .**24** C5
Danecourt Gdns CR0 . . . .**61** F7
Danehurst TW8 . . . .**6** C7
Danehurst Ct TW20 . . . .**11** E2
Danehurst Cres RH13 . . . . .**217** F2
Danehurst Ct KT17 . . . .**76** F6
Danemore La RH9 . . . .**142** F7
Danes CI KT22 . . . .**74** C5
Danes Hill GU22 . . . .**70** B1
Danes Hill Jun Sch KT22 . . .**74** C6
Danes Hill Sch KT22 . . . .**74** D6
Danes Way KT22 . . . .**74** D5
Danesbury Rd TW13 . . . .**15** B7
Danescourt Cres SM1 . . . . . .**59** C8
Danesfield GU23 . . . .**90** F4
Danesfield CI KT12 . . . .**54** C8
Daneshill RH1 . . . .**118** E2
Daneshill CI RH1 . . . .**118** E2
Danesmead GU11 . . . .**74** A8

Danesrood GU1 . . . .**130** F8
Daneswood Ave SE6 . . . .**24** C5
Daneswood CI KT13 . . . .**53** C5
Danetree CI KT19 . . . .**57** C3
Danetree Rd KT19 . . . .**57** D3
Danetree Sch KT19 . . . .**57** C4
Daniel CI SW17, SW19 . . . . . .**20** E2
Daniel Ct **3** BR3 . . . .**24** A1
Daniel Way SM7 . . . .**78** B5
Daniell Way CR0, CR9 . . . .**41** F1
Daniels La CR6 . . . .**81** F4
Danley La GU27 . . . .**207** A3
Danses CI GU4 . . . .**110** D3
Danvers Way CR3 . . . .**100** C4
Dapdune Ct GU1 . . . .**109** C1
Dapdune Rd GU1 . . . .**109** D1
Daphne Ct KT4 . . . .**57** E8
Daphne St SW18 . . . .**20** C8
Darby CI CR3 . . . .**100** C5
Darby Cres TW16 . . . .**35** C7
Darby Gdns TW16 . . . .**35** C7
Darby Green La GU17 . . . . . .**64** B6
Darby Green Rd GU17 . . . . . .**64** B5
Darcy Ave SM6 . . . .**60** C6
Darcy CI CR5 . . . .**100** B8
Darcy PI KT21 . . . .**75** F2
Darcy Rd Ashtead KT21 . . . . .**75** F2
  Isleworth TW7 . . . .**6** A6
  Thornton Heath SW16 . . . . . .**41** E7
Darell Prim Sch TW9 . . . .**7** A4
Darell Rd TW9 . . . .**7** A4
Darent House BR1 . . . .**24** D3
Darenth Way RH6 . . . .**160** F6
Darfield Rd GU1 . . . .**110** A4
Dargate CI SE19 . . . .**22** F1
Dark La GU3 . . . .**128** B4
Darlaston Rd SW19 . . . .**19** E1
Darley CI Addlestone KT15 . . .**52** C5
  Croydon CR0 . . . .**43** E3
Darley Dene Ct KT15 . . . .**52** C6
Darley Dene Inf Sch KT15 .**52** C5
Darley Dr KT3 . . . .**38** D7
Darley Gdns SM4 . . . .**40** B3
Darleydale RH11 . . . .**201** C3
Darleydale CI GU47 . . . .**45** D2
Darlington Ct SE6 . . . .**24** F7
Darlington House **2** KT6 . .**37** D2
Darlington Rd SE27 . . . .**22** B5
Darmaine CI CR2 . . . .**61** C3
Darnley Pk KT13 . . . .**53** B7
Darracott CI GU15 . . . .**66** B8
Darrell Ct BR2 . . . .**44** E6
Dart CI SL3 . . . .**1** B8
Dart Ct RH19 . . . .**186** A3
Dart Rd GU14 . . . .**84** D6
Dartmouth Ave GU21 . . . .**70** D5
Dartmouth CI RG12 . . . .**27** E6
Dartmouth Gn GU21 . . . .**70** D5
Dartmouth House CR0 . . . . . .**42** B2
Dartmouth Path GU21 . . . . . .**70** D5
Dartmouth PI Chiswick W4 . . .**7** E8
  Forest Hill SE23 . . . .**23** C6
Dartmouth Rd SE23, SE26 .**23** C5
Dartnell Ave KT14 . . . .**71** C7
Dartnell CI KT14 . . . .**71** B7
Dartnell Cres KT14 . . . .**71** B7
Dartnell Ct KT14 . . . .**71** C7
Dartnell Park Rd KT14 . . . . . .**71** C8
Dartnell PI KT14 . . . .**71** B7
Dartnell Rd CR0 . . . .**42** F2
Darvel CI GU21 . . . .**69** A3
Darvills La GU9 . . . .**125** C2
Darwall Dr SL5 . . . .**28** D7
Darwin CI RH12 . . . .**217** F4
Darwin Gr GU11 . . . .**105** C3
Daryngton Dr GU1 . . . .**110** B1
Dashwood CI
  Bracknell RG12 . . . .**27** D8
  West Byfleet KT14 . . . .**71** C7
Dashwood Ct TW3 . . . .**5** C3
Dashwood House SE21 . . . . .**22** F5
Dassett Rd SE27 . . . .**22** B3
Datchet Rd Forest Hill SE6 . . .**23** F6
  Horton SL3 . . . .**1** A4
Daux Hill RH12 . . . .**217** B6
Davenant Rd CR0, CR9 . . . . . .**61** B6
Davenport CI TW11 . . . .**17** A2
Davenport Lodge TW5 . . . .**4** F7
Davenport Rd RG12 . . . .**27** E8
Daventry CI SL3 . . . .**1** F6
Daventry Ct RG42 . . . .**27** B8
David CI UB3 . . . .**3** E7
David House SE25 . . . .**43** A6
David Livingstone Prim
  Sch CR7 . . . .**42** C2
David Rd SL3 . . . .**1** F5
David's Rd SE23 . . . .**23** C7
Davidson Inf Sch CR0 . . . . . .**42** F2
Davidson Jun Sch CR0 . . . . .**42** F2
Davidson Lodge CR0 . . . .**42** E2
Davidson Rd CR0, SE25 . . . . .**42** F3
Davies CI Croydon CR0, SE25 **43** A3
  Farncombe GU7 . . . .**150** D7
Davies Walk TW7 . . . .**5** D6
Davis CI RH11 . . . .**201** A1
Davis Gdns GU47 . . . .**64** E7
Davis Rd Chessington KT9 . . .**57** A6
  Weybridge KT13 . . . .**52** F1
Davos CI GU22 . . . .**89** E8
Davy CI RG40 . . . .**25** C5
Dawell Dr TN16 . . . .**83** C2
Dawes Ave TW7 . . . .**6** A3
Dawes Ct KT10 . . . .**55** C6
Dawes Green Cotts RH2 .**138** A3
Dawley Ride SL3 . . . .**1** E6
Dawlish Ave SW18 . . . .**20** B6
Dawn CI TW4 . . . .**4** E4
Dawn Redwood CI SL3 . . . . . .**1** A4

Dawn Wlk BR2 . . . . .44 D7
Dawnay Cl SL5 . . . . .28 F8
Dawnay Gdns SW18 . . . . . .20 D6
Dawnay Rd Camberley GU15 65 B7
  Great Bookham KT23 . . . . . .94 C1
  Wandsworth SW17, SW18 . . .20 D6
Dawney Hill GU24 . . . . .87 F5
Dawneys Cl GU24 . . . . .87 F5
Dawsmere Cl GU15 . . . . . . .66 C5
Dawson Rd Byfleet KT14 . . . .71 E8
  Kingston u T KT1 . . . . .37 F6
Dax Ct TW14 . . . . .35 C6
Day Ct GU6 . . . . .173 F2
Day's Acre CR2 . . . . .61 F1
Daybrook Rd SW19 . . . . . . .40 B6
Daymerslea Ridge KT22 . . . .95 C6
Daysbrook Rd SW2 . . . . . . .21 F7
Dayseys Hill RH1 . . . . .162 A8
Dayspring GU2 . . . . .109 B5
Daytone House SW20 . . . . . .39 D8
De Broome Rd TW13 . . . . . .15 C7
De Burgh House SW19 . . . . .20 C1
De Burgh Pk SM7 . . . . .78 B4
De Frene Rd SE23, SE26 . . . .23 E5
De Havilland Dr KT13 . . . . .71 E8
De Havilland Rd Heston TW5 4 C7
  Wallington SM6 . . . . .60 E3
De Havilland Way TW19 . . . .2 E1
De La Warr Rd RH19 . . . . . .185 F1
De Lara Way GU21 . . . . .69 D1
De Montfort Par ■ SW16 . . .21 E5
De Montfort Rd SW16 . . . . .21 E6
De Ros Pl TW20 . . . . .12 A2
de Stafford Sch CR3 . . . .100 F6
De'arn Gdns CR4 . . . . .40 E6
De-Vitre Gn RG40 . . . . .25 F7
Deacon Cl Downside KT11 . . .93 B8
  Wallington SM6 . . . . .60 E2
  Wokingham RG40 . . . . .25 C8
Deacon Ct RH7 . . . . .164 C4
Deacon Field GU2 . . . . . . .109 A2
Deacon Rd KT2 . . . . .37 F8
Deacons Wlk TW12 . . . . . . .16 A4
Deadbrook La GU12 . . . . . .105 E3
Deal Rd SW17 . . . . .21 A2
Dean Cl GU22 . . . . .70 E3
Dean Ct Farncombe GU7 . . .150 D6
  ⑩ Kingston u T KT2 . . . . . . .18 A1
Dean Gr RG40 . . . . .25 C7
Dean La CR3, CR5, RH1 . . . .99 D3
Dean Par GU15 . . . . .65 F8
Dean Rd Croydon CR0 . . . . . .61 D6
  Farncombe GU7 . . . . .150 D6
  Hampton TW12 . . . . .16 A3
  Isleworth TW3 . . . . .5 B2
Dean Wlk KT23 . . . . .94 B1
Deanery Pl GU7 . . . . .150 D4
Deanery Rd GU7 . . . . .150 E6
Deanfield Gdns CR0 . . . . . . .61 D6
Deanhill Ct SW14 . . . . .7 B3
Deanhill Rd SW14 . . . . .7 B3
Deanoak La Leigh RH2 . . . .159 D8
  Sidlow RH2 . . . . .159 D8
Deans Cl Chiswick W4 . . . . . .7 B8
  South Croydon CR0 . . . . .61 F7
  Walton on t H KT20 . . . . . . .97 B3
Deans Ct GU20 . . . . .48 D4
Deans Gate Cl SE23 . . . . . .23 D5
Deans La Nutfield RH1 . . . .120 A2
  Walton on t H KT20 . . . . . . .97 B2
Deans Rd Merstham RH1 . . .119 C5
  Sutton SM1 . . . . .59 B7
Deans Wlk CR5 . . . . .80 A1
Deansfield CR3 . . . . .100 F2
Deansgate RG12 . . . . .27 B2
Dearmer House ⑥ SW2 . . . .22 A8
Debden Cl KT2 . . . . .17 D3
Deborah Cl TW7 . . . . .5 E6
Deburgh Rd SW19 . . . . .20 C1
Decon Pl CR3 . . . . .100 C4
Dedham House SE6 . . . . . . .24 C4
Dedisham Cl RH10 . . . . . . .202 A5
Dedswell Dr GU4 . . . . .111 A6
Dee Rd TW9 . . . . .6 F3
Dee Way KT19 . . . . .57 E1
Deedman Cl GU12 . . . . . . .106 A2
Deep Dene GU27 . . . . .207 E6
Deep Well Dr GU15 . . . . . . .65 E5
Deepcut Bridge Rd GU16 . . .86 C7
Deepdale Bracknell RG12 . . .27 A5
  Wimbledon SW19 . . . . .19 D4
Deepdale Ave BR2 . . . . .44 F5
Deepdene GU10 . . . . .146 D7
Deepdene Ave
  Dorking RH4, RH5 . . . . .136 C6
  South Croydon CR0 . . . . .61 F7
Deepdene Avenue
  Rd RH4 . . . . .115 C1
Deepdene Ct BR2 . . . . .44 E6
Deepdene Dr RH5 . . . . . . .136 C6
Deepdene Gdns
  Dorking RH4, RH5 . . . . .136 C8
  Streatham SW2 . . . . .21 F8
Deepdene Lodge ⑧ SW2 . . .21 F8
Deepdene Park Rd RH5 . . .136 D8
Deepdene Point SE26 . . . . .23 D5
Deepdene Vale RH4 . . . . . .115 C1
Deepdene Wood RH5 . . . . .136 D7
Deepfield Rd RG12 . . . . . . .27 D7
Deepfield Way CR5 . . . . . . .79 E3
Deepfields RH6 . . . . .160 F5
Deeprose Cl GU3 . . . . .109 B5
Deepwell Cl TW7 . . . . .6 A6
Deer Leap GU18 . . . . .67 A8
Deer Park Cl KT2 . . . . .18 B1
Deer Park Gdns CR4 . . . . . .40 D5
Deer Park Rd SW19 . . . . . . .40 C7
Deer Park Way BR4 . . . . . . .63 F8

Deer Rock Hill RG12 . . . . . .27 C3
Deer Rock Rd GU15 . . . . . .65 F8
Deerbarn Rd GU2 . . . . . . .109 B2
Deerbrook Rd SE24, SW2 . . .22 B7
Deerhurst KT2 . . . . .38 B8
Deerhurst Cl TW13 . . . . . . .15 B4
Deerhurst Rd SW16 . . . . . . .21 F3
Deerings Rd RH2 . . . . .118 C1
Deerleap GU35 . . . . .187 C4
Deerleap Rd RH4 . . . . .135 B6
Deers Farm GU23, KT14 . . . .71 E3
Deerswood Cl
  Caterham CR3 . . . . .101 A3
  Crawley RH11 . . . . .201 B7
Deerswood Ct RH11 . . . . . .201 A7
Deerswood Lower Sch
  RH11 . . . . .201 A8
Deerswood Upper Sch
  RH11 . . . . .201 A8
Deeside Rd SW17 . . . . .20 D5
Defiant Way SM6 . . . . .60 E3
Defoe Ave TW9 . . . . .7 A7
Defoe Cl SW17, SW19 . . . . .20 E1
Delabole Rd RH1 . . . . .119 E6
Delamare Cres CR0 . . . . . . .43 C3
Delamere Rd Reigate RH2 . .139 C5
  Wimbledon SW20 . . . . .39 D8
Delaporte Cl KT17 . . . . .76 E7
Delcombe Ave KT4 . . . . . . .39 C1
Delderfield KT21 . . . . .95 D6
Delfont St RH10 . . . . .202 D4
Delia St SW18 . . . . .20 B8
Dell Cl Fetcham KT22 . . . . . .94 E4
  Haslemere GU27 . . . . .208 A7
  Mickleham RH5 . . . . .115 C8
  Wallington SM6 . . . . .60 C6
Dell Close Cotts RH5 . . . . .115 C8
Dell Gr GU16 . . . . .65 F2
Dell House CR2 . . . . .61 C2
Dell La KT17 . . . . .58 A5
Dell Rd KT17 . . . . .58 A4
Dell The Brentford TW8 . . . . .6 C8
  Burgh Heath KT20 . . . . .97 C6
  East Grinstead RH19 . . . . . .186 B1
  Englefield Green SL4 . . . . . . .11 A5
  Feltham TW14 . . . . .15 B8
  Heath End GU9 . . . . .125 D7
  Horley RH6 . . . . .161 B4
  Reigate RH2 . . . . .118 A2
  Sidlow RH6 . . . . .160 C5
  South Norwood SE19 . . . . . .42 F8
  Woking GU21 . . . . .69 C1
Dell Wlk KT3 . . . . .38 E7
Dellbow Rd TW14 . . . . .4 B7
Dellfield Ct BR3 . . . . .44 C8
Delmey Cl CR0 . . . . .61 F7
Delphian Ct ⑤ SW16 . . . . . .22 A4
Delta Bglws RH6 . . . . .161 A1
Delta Cl Chobham GU24 . . . .49 F1
  Worcester Park KT4 . . . . . . .57 F7
Delta Dr RH6 . . . . .161 A1
Delta House RH6 . . . . .161 A1
Delta Rd Chobham GU24 . . . .49 F1
  Woking GU21 . . . . .69 A3
  Worcester Park KT19, KT4 . . .57 F7
Delta Way TW20 . . . . .32 C8
Delves KT20 . . . . .97 D6
Delville Cl GU14 . . . . .84 D3
Demesne Rd SM6 . . . . .60 E6
Dempster Cl KT6 . . . . .37 C1
Dempster House GU9 . . . . .125 D8
Den Cl BR2, BR3 . . . . .44 D6
Den Rd BR2 . . . . .44 D6
Denbigh Cl SM1 . . . . .58 F5
Denbigh Gdns TW10 . . . . . . .6 F1
Denbigh Rd
  Haslemere GU27 . . . . .208 D5
  Hounslow TW3 . . . . .5 B5
Denby Dene GU12 . . . . . . .106 B2
Denby Rd KT11 . . . . .73 C7
Denchers Plat RH11 . . . . . .181 D1
Dencliffe TW15 . . . . .14 A3
Dendy St SW12 . . . . .21 A7
Dene Ave TW3 . . . . .5 A3
Dene Cl ② Bracknell RG12 . .27 C8
  Farnham GU10 . . . . .146 A6
  Haslemere GU27 . . . . .208 C6
  Hayes BR2 . . . . .44 F1
  Horley RH6 . . . . .160 E5
  Worcester Park KT4 . . . . . . .57 F8
Dene Ct GU1 . . . . .110 B3
Dene Gdns KT7 . . . . .56 A8
Dene La GU10 . . . . .146 C6
Dene La W GU10 . . . . .146 E5
Dene Rd Ashstead KT21 . . . .95 F8
  Farnborough GU14 . . . . .84 F3
  Guildford GU1 . . . . .130 E8
Dene St RH4 . . . . .136 B7
Dene Street Gdns RH4 . . . .136 B7
Dene The
  Abinger Hammer RH5 . . . . .134 B3
  Belmont SM2 . . . . .77 B3
  East Molesey KT12, KT8 . . . .35 F4
  South Croydon CR0 . . . . .62 D6
Dene Tye RH10 . . . . .202 D7
Dene Wlk GU10 . . . . .146 C6
Denefield Dr CR8 . . . . .80 D4
Denehurst Gdns
  Mortlake TW10 . . . . .7 A3
  Twickenham TW2 . . . . .16 D8
Denehyrst Ct GU1 . . . . . . .130 E8
Denewood ⑧ KT17 . . . . . . .76 E6
Denfield RH4 . . . . .136 C5
Denham Cres CR4 . . . . .40 F5
Denham Ct SE26 . . . . .23 B5
Denham Rd GU2 . . . . .27 C3

Denham Rd Egham TW20 . . .12 A4
  Ewell KT17 . . . . .76 F7
  Feltham TW14 . . . . .15 C8
Denholm Gdns GU1, GU4 . .110 A4
Denison Rd Feltham, Lower
  Feltham TW13 . . . . .14 F4
  Mitcham SW19 . . . . .20 D2
Denleigh Gdns KT7 . . . . . . .36 E5
Denly Way GU20 . . . . .48 C1
Denman Dr Ashford TW15 . . .14 B2
  Claygate KT10 . . . . .56 A5
Denmans RH10 . . . . .202 D7
Denmark Ave SW19 . . . . . . .19 E1
Denmark Ct Morden SM4 . . .40 A4
  ② Weybridge KT13 . . . . .53 B7
Denmark Gdns SM5 . . . . . . .59 F7
Denmark Rd
  Carshalton SM5 . . . . .59 F7
  Croydon SE25 . . . . .43 B4
  Guildford GU1 . . . . .130 E8
  Kingston u T KT1 . . . . .37 E6
  Twickenham TW2 . . . . .16 D5
  Wimbledon SW19 . . . . .19 D2
Denmark Sq GU12 . . . . . . .105 E2
Denmark St
  Aldershot GU12 . . . . .105 E2
  Wokingham RG40 . . . . .25 C5
Denmead Ct RG12 . . . . .27 E3
Denmead House SW15 . . . . . .7 F1
Denmead Lower Sch
  TW12 . . . . .16 B1
Denmead Rd CR0 . . . . .42 B1
Denmead Upper Sch
  TW12 . . . . .16 B1
Denmore Ct SM6 . . . . .60 B5
Dennan Rd KT6 . . . . .37 F1
Denne Par RH12, RH13 . . . .217 C1
Denne Rd Crawley RH11 . . .201 D5
  Horsham RH12 . . . . .217 C1
Dennett Rd CR0 . . . . .42 A2
Denning Ave CR0 . . . . .61 A5
Denning Cl TW12 . . . . .15 F3
Denningtons The KT4 . . . . . .57 E8
Dennis Cl Ashford TW15 . . . .14 D1
  Redhill RH1 . . . . .118 E3
Dennis House SM1 . . . . .59 A6
Dennis Park Cres SW20 . . . .39 E8
Dennis Rd KT8 . . . . .36 C5
Dennis Reeve Cl CR4 . . . . . .40 F8
Dennis Way GU1 . . . . .109 E6
Dennistoun Cl GU15 . . . . . .65 D5
Densole Cl BR3 . . . . .43 E8
Denton Cl RH1 . . . . .140 A4
Denton Gr KT12 . . . . .54 E8
Denton Rd Twickenham TW1 . .6 D1
  Wokingham RG40 . . . . .25 C6
Denton Way Frimley GU16 . . .65 D2
  Woking GU21 . . . . .69 A2
Dents Gr KT20 . . . . .117 F7
Denvale Wlk GU21 . . . . .69 A1
Denwood SE23 . . . . .23 D5
Denzil Rd GU2 . . . . .130 B8
Departures Rd RH6 . . . . . . .181 F8
Depot Rd Crawley RH11 . . .181 D1
  Epsom KT17 . . . . .76 E6
  Horsham RH13 . . . . .217 E2
  Hounslow TW3, TW7 . . . . .5 D4
Derby Arms Rd KT18 . . . . . .76 F2
Derby Cl KT18 . . . . .97 B8
Derby Hill SE23 . . . . .23 C6
Derby Hill Cres SE23 . . . . . .23 C6
Derby Rd Cheam SM1, SM2 .58 F4
  Guildford GU2 . . . . .108 F1
  Haslemere GU27 . . . . .208 B7
  Hounslow TW3 . . . . .5 B3
  Merton SW19 . . . . .20 A1
  Mortlake SW14 . . . . .7 B3
  Surbiton KT5, KT6 . . . . .38 A1
  Thornton Heath CR0 . . . . . . .42 B1
Derby Stables Rd KT18 . . . .76 F2
Derek Ave Hackbridge SM6 . .60 B6
  West Ewell KT19 . . . . .57 B5
Derek Cl KT19 . . . . .57 B5
Derek Horn Ct GU15 . . . . . .65 B6
Deri Dene Cl ② TW19 . . . . . .2 E1
Dering Pl CR0 . . . . .61 C6
Dering Rd CR0, CR9 . . . . . . .61 C6
Derinton Rd SW17 . . . . .21 A4
Deronda Rd SE24, SW2 . . . .22 B7
Deroy Cl SM5 . . . . .59 F4
Deroy Ct SM5 . . . . .59 F4
Derrick Ave CR2 . . . . .61 C1
Derrick House ⑱ SW2 . . . . .22 A7
Derrick Rd BR3 . . . . .43 F5
Derry Cl GU12 . . . . .105 F5
Derry Rd Farnborough GU14 .84 F8
  Wallington CR0, SM6 . . . . . .60 E7
Derrydown GU22 . . . . .89 C6
Derwent Ave
  Ash Vale GU12 . . . . .105 F4
  Kingston u T SW15 . . . . .18 E4
Derwent Cl
  Addlestone KT15 . . . . .52 D5
  Claygate KT10 . . . . .55 F4
  Crawley RH11 . . . . .200 F5
  East Bedfont TW14 . . . . .14 D7
  Farnborough GU14 . . . . .84 E4
  Hale GU9 . . . . .125 A6
  Horsham RH12 . . . . .218 B6
Derwent Dr CR8 . . . . .80 E6
Derwent House
  Penge SE26 . . . . .43 B7
  Reigate RH2 . . . . .139 A7
Derwent Lodge KT4 . . . . . . .58 B8
Derwent Rd
  Lightwater GU18 . . . . .67 B8
  Penge SE20 . . . . .43 B7
  Thorpe Lea TW20 . . . . .12 B1

Derwent Rd continued
  Twickenham TW2 . . . . .5 B1
  West Barnes SW4 . . . . .39 D3
Derwent Wlk SM6 . . . . .60 B3
Desborough Cl TW17 . . . . . .34 A2
Desborough Ct SE25 . . . . . .43 B5
Desford Way TW15 . . . . . . .13 F6
Desmond Anderson Cty
  Fst Sch RH10 . . . . .201 E2
Desmond Anderson Cty
  Mid Sch RH10 . . . . .201 E2
Despard House SW2 . . . . . .22 A6
Detherick Ct TW3 . . . . .5 C3
Detillens La RH8 . . . . .123 A6
Detling Rd RH11 . . . . .201 C1
Dettingen Rd GU16 . . . . . . .86 E8
Devana End SM5 . . . . .59 F7
Devas Rd SW20 . . . . .39 C8
Devenish La GU20, SL5 . . . .29 C1
Devenish Rd
  Ascot GU20, SL5 . . . . .29 D2
  Sunningdale GU20, SL5 . . . .29 D2
Deverill Ct SE20 . . . . .43 C8
Devey Cl KT2 . . . . .18 D3
Devil's La TW20 . . . . .12 C2
Devitt Cl KT21 . . . . .76 A3
Devoil Cl GU4 . . . . .110 B5
Devoke Way KT12 . . . . .54 D8
Devon Ave TW2 . . . . .16 C7
Devon Bank GU2 . . . . .130 C6
Devon Cl Kenley CR8 . . . . . .80 E3
  Sandhurst GU47 . . . . .64 D7
Devon Cres RH1, RH2 . . . . .118 C1
Devon House
  Caterham CR3 . . . . .100 F3
  Knaphill GU21 . . . . .68 D2
  Penge SE20 . . . . .23 B1
Devon Rd Belmont SM2 . . . .58 E2
  Hersham KT12 . . . . .54 C6
  Merstham RH1 . . . . .119 C5
Devon Way Chessington KT9 56 C6
  West Ewell KT19 . . . . .57 B5
Devon Waye TW5 . . . . .4 F7
Devoncroft Gdns TW1 . . . . .17 A8
Devonshire Ave
  Sheerwater GU21 . . . . .70 D6
  Sutton SM2 . . . . .59 C3
Devonshire Ct
  Croydon CR0 . . . . .44 A1
  Feltham TW13 . . . . .15 B6
  ⑥ Richmond TW9 . . . . .6 F6
Devonshire Dr
  Camberley GU15 . . . . .65 F7
  Long Ditton KT6 . . . . .56 D8
Devonshire Gdns W4 . . . . . .7 C7
Devonshire House
  ⑭ Balham SW12 . . . . .21 B8
  Hounslow TW3 . . . . .5 C4
  Sutton SM2 . . . . .59 C3
Devonshire Pl GU11 . . . . . .104 F1
Devonshire Prim Sch SM2 59 C3
Devonshire Rd Chiswick W4 . .7 E8
  Feltham TW13 . . . . .15 E4
  Forest Hill SE23 . . . . .23 C8
  Hackbridge SM5, SM6 . . . . . .60 A6
  Horsham RH13 . . . . .217 D2
  Mitcham SW17, SW19 . . . . . .20 D2
  Sutton SM2 . . . . .59 C3
  Thornton Heath CR0 . . . . . . .42 D2
  Weybridge KT13 . . . . .53 A6
Devonshire St W4 . . . . .7 E8
Devonshire Way CR0, CR9 . .62 F8
Devonshires The KT18 . . . . .76 F5
Dewar Cl RH11 . . . . .200 E5
Dewar House SW17 . . . . . . .20 E3
Dewey St SW17 . . . . .20 F3
Dewlands RH9 . . . . .121 C4
Dewlands Cl GU6 . . . . .174 E3
Dewlands La GU6 . . . . .174 E3
Dewsbury Gdns KT4 . . . . . . .58 A7
Dexter Dr RH19 . . . . .205 E8
Diamedes Ave TW19 . . . . . .13 D7
Diamond Ct ❹ RH1 . . . . . .119 A2
Diamond Est SW17 . . . . . . .20 E5
Diamond Hill GU15 . . . . . . .65 E7
Diamond Ridge GU15 . . . . .65 E7
Diana Gdns KT6 . . . . .56 F7
Dianthus Cl KT16 . . . . .32 E2
Dianthus Ct GU22 . . . . .69 D1
Dianthus Pl RG42 . . . . .8 B2
Dibdin Cl SM1 . . . . .59 A7
Dibdin Rd SM1 . . . . .59 A8
Diceland Rd SM7 . . . . .77 E3
Dick Sheppard Sch SE24 . .22 A8
Dick Turpin Way TW14 . . . . . .3 F3
Dickens Cl
  East Grinstead RH19 . . . . . .185 C1
  Richmond TW10 . . . . .17 C6
Dickens Dr KT15 . . . . .51 F4
Dickens Rd RH10 . . . . .201 E3
Dickenson's La SE25 . . . . . .43 A3
Dickenson's Pl SE25 . . . . . .43 A3
Dickerage Hill KT3 . . . . .38 C6
Dickerage Rd KT1, KT2, KT3 38 C7
Dickins Way RH13 . . . . .217 F1
Dickinson Rd TW13 . . . . . . .15 D3
Digby Pl CR0 . . . . .61 F7
Digby Way KT14 . . . . .71 F7
Digdens Rise KT18 . . . . .76 C4
Dillon Gdns SW15 . . . . .19 B7
Dillwyn Cl SE26 . . . . .23 E4
Dilston Rd KT22 . . . . .95 A8
Dingle Rd TW15 . . . . .14 B3
Dingle The RH11 . . . . .201 B6
Dingley La SW16 . . . . .21 D6
Dingwall Ave CR0, CR9 . . . .61 C8

Dingwall Rd
  Croydon CR0, CR9 . . . . .61 D8
  Wallington SM5 . . . . .59 F2
  Wandsworth SW18 . . . . .20 C8
Dinsdale Cl GU22 . . . . .70 A1
Dinsdale Gdns SE25 . . . . . .42 E4
Dinsmore Rd SW12 . . . . . . .21 B8
Dinton Rd Kingston u T KT2 .18 A1
  Mitcham SW17, SW19 . . . . . .20 D2
Dione Wlk RH11 . . . . .200 E4
Dippenhall Rd GU10 . . . . . .124 C2
Dippenhall St GU10 . . . . . .124 A5
Dirdene Cl KT17 . . . . .76 F7
Dirdene Gdns KT17 . . . . . . .76 F7
Dirdene Gr KT17 . . . . .76 F7
Dirtham La KT24 . . . . .113 B6
Dirty La RH19 . . . . .206 E2
Discovery Pk RH10 . . . . . . .182 A2
Disraeli Ct SL3 . . . . .1 B8
Distillery Wlk ⑭ TW8 . . . . . .6 E8
Ditches La CR3, CR5 . . . . . .99 E6
Ditchling RG12 . . . . .27 A2
Ditchling Hill RH11 . . . . . . .201 C4
Ditton Cl KT7 . . . . .37 A2
Ditton Grange Cl KT6 . . . . . .37 D1
Ditton Grange Dr KT6 . . . . . .37 D1
Ditton Hill KT6 . . . . .56 D8
Ditton Hill Rd KT6 . . . . .37 C1
Ditton Lawn KT7 . . . . .37 A1
Ditton Pl ⑦ SE20 . . . . .43 B8
Ditton Rd KT6 . . . . .37 E1
Ditton Reach KT7 . . . . .37 B3
Dittoncroft Cl CR0 . . . . .61 E6
Dixon Dr KT13 . . . . .52 F1
Dixon Pl BR4 . . . . .44 B1
Dixon Rd SE25 . . . . .42 F6
Dobbins PI RH11 . . . . .200 E5
Doble Ct CR2 . . . . .81 A8
Dobson Rd RH11 . . . . .181 D1
Dock Rd TW8 . . . . .6 D7
Dockenfield St GU10 . . . . . .166 C1
Dockett Eddy La TW17 . . . . .33 F1
Dockett Moorings KT16 . . . .33 F1
Dockwell's Ind Est TW14 . . . .4 C2
Doctors Cl SE26 . . . . .23 C3
Doctors La CR3 . . . . .100 A3
Dodbrooke Rd SE27 . . . . . . .22 B5
Dodd's La GU24 . . . . .71 A5
Dodds Cres KT14 . . . . .71 B5
Dodds Pk RH3 . . . . .137 B7
Doel Cl SW19 . . . . .20 C1
Dogflud Way GU9 . . . . .125 C3
Doggett Rd Catford SE6 . . . .24 A8
  Lewisham SE6 . . . . .24 A8
Doghurst Ave UB7 . . . . .3 B7
Doghurst Dr UB7 . . . . .3 B7
Doghurst La CR5 . . . . .98 F7
Doland Ct SW17 . . . . .20 F2
Dolby Terr RH6 . . . . .180 E6
Dollis Cl RH10 . . . . .202 C5
Dollis Cl GU9 . . . . .125 D3
Dollis Dr GU9 . . . . .125 D3
Dolphin Cl
  Haslemere GU27 . . . . .207 E6
  Kingston u T KT6 . . . . .37 D4
Dolphin Ct Merton SW19 . . .20 A1
  Stanwell TW19 . . . . .13 A5
  ❷ Wallington SM6 . . . . .60 B4
Dolphin Ct N TW19 . . . . . . .13 A5
Dolphin Rd TW16 . . . . .34 E8
Dolphin Rd N TW16 . . . . . . .34 E8
Dolphin Rd S TW16 . . . . . . .34 E8
Dolphin Rd W TW16 . . . . . . .34 E8
Dolphin Sq W4 . . . . .7 E7
Dolphin St KT2 . . . . .37 E8
Doman Rd GU15 . . . . .65 A4
Dome Hill CR3 . . . . .120 E8
Dome Hill Peak CR3 . . . . . .100 E1
Dome Hill Pk SE26 . . . . . . .22 F4
Dome Way RH1 . . . . .118 F2
Dominion Rd CR0 . . . . .42 F2
Donald Lynch House CR4 . .40 F7
Donald Rd CR0, CR9 . . . . . . .41 F2
Donald Woods Gdns KT5 . .57 C8
Doncaster Wlk RH10 . . . . . .202 A4
Doncastle Rd RG12 . . . . . . .26 F6
Donkey La
  Abinger Common RH5 . . . . .155 D8
  Crawley RH6 . . . . .182 D7
Donnafields GU24 . . . . .68 A3
Donne Cl RH10 . . . . .202 B8
Donne Gdns GU22 . . . . .70 E4
Donne Pl CR4 . . . . .41 B5
Donnington Cl GU15 . . . . . .65 B4
Donnington Ct ❷ RH11 . . . .200 F3
Donnington Rd KT4 . . . . . . .58 A8
Donnybrook RG12 . . . . .27 A2
Donnybrook Rd SW16 . . . . . .21 D1
Donovan Cl KT19 . . . . .57 D1
Donyngs Place Recn Ctr
  RH1 . . . . .118 E2
Doods Brow Sch RH1 . . . . .119 F2
Doods Park Rd RH2 . . . . . .118 C1
Doods Pl RH2 . . . . .118 D2
Doods Rd RH2 . . . . .118 C2
Doods Way RH2 . . . . .118 D2
Doomsday Garden RH13 . . .218 A1
Doone Cl TW11 . . . . .17 A2
Dora Rd SW19 . . . . .20 A4
Dora's Green La GU10 . . . .124 C5
Doradus Ct ⑳ SW19 . . . . . .19 D7
Doral Way SM5 . . . . .59 F5
Doran Dr RH2 . . . . .118 D1
Doran Gdns RH2 . . . . .118 D1

Dorcas Ct GU15 . . . . **65** B3
Dorchester Ct
Reigate RH2 . . . .**118** C2
Staines TW18 . . . .**13** A4
5 Streatham SW16 . . . .**21** E6
Woking GU22 . . . .**70** A3
Dorchester Dr TW14 . . . .**3** E1
Dorchester Gr W4 . . . .**7** E8
Dorchester Mews
New Malden KT3 . . . .**38** D5
Twickenham TW1 . . . .**6** C1
Dorchester Prim Sch KT4 .**39** C1
Dorchester Rd Cheam SM4 .**40** C2
Morden CR4 . . . .**40** C2
North Cheam KT4 . . . .**39** C1
Weybridge KT13 . . . .**53** B7
Dore Gdns SM4 . . . .**40** B2
Doreen Cl GU14 . . . .**84** E7
Dorian Dr SL5 . . . .**29** E8
Doric Dr KT20 . . . .**97** F7
Dorien Rd SW20 . . . .**39** D7
Dorin Ct Pyrford GU22 . . . . .**70** E4
Warlingham CR6 . . . .**101** B7
Doris Rd TW15 . . . .**14** C2
Dorking Bsns Pk RH4 . . . .**136** A8
Dorking Cl KT14 . . . .**58** D8
Dorking (Deepdene) Sta
RH4 . . . .**115** C1
Dorking General Hospl
RH4 . . . .**136** B6
Dorking Mus RH4 . . . .**136** A7
Dorking Rd Chilworth GU4 .**131** E3
Epsom KT18 . . . .**76** B4
Great Bookham KT23 . . . . .**114** C8
Leatherhead KT22 . . . .**95** B3
Lower Kingswood KT20 . . . .**116** F7
Tadworth KT20 . . . .**97** C3
Walton on t H KT20 . . . .**97** C3
Warnham RH12, RH5 . . . . .**198** B4
Dorking Sta RH4 . . . .**115** C1
Dorking West Sta RH4 . . . .**136** A8
Dorlcote GU8 . . . .**170** E6
Dorlcote Rd SW18 . . . .**20** E8
Dorling Dr KT17 . . . .**76** F7
Dorly Cl TW17 . . . .**34** E4
Dorman's Cl RH7 . . . .**186** A8
Dormans Ave RH7 . . . .**165** A2
Dormans Gdns RH19 . . . . .**185** E6
Dormans High St RH7 . . . .**186** A8
Dormans Park Rd
Dormans Park RH19 . . . . . .**185** E6
East Grinstead RH19 . . . . . .**185** D3
Dormans Rd RH7 . . . .**165** A2
Dormans Sta RH7 . . . .**185** F8
Dormans Station Rd
Dormans Park RH7 . . . .**185** F7
Dormansland RH7 . . . .**185** F7
Dormansland Prim Sch
RH7 . . . .**186** A8
Dormer Cl RG45 . . . .**45** A5
Dormers Cl GU7 . . . .**150** D7
Dormy House The GU25 . . .**30** F3
Dorney Gr KT13 . . . .**53** B8
Dorney Way TW4 . . . .**4** E2
Dornford Gdns CR5 . . . . . .**100** C8
Dornton Rd
South Croydon CR2 . . . .**61** D5
Upper Tooting SW12, SW17 . .**21** C6
Dorrien Wlk SW16 . . . .**21** D6
Dorrington Ct SE25 . . . .**42** E7
Dorrit Cres GU3 . . . .**108** E3
Dorryn Ct SE26 . . . .**23** D3
Dorset Ave RH19 . . . .**185** D3
Dorset Ct Camberley GU15 . .**65** F8
Epsom KT17 . . . .**76** F7
Dorset Dr GU22 . . . .**70** B2
Dorset Gdns
East Grinstead RH19 . . . . . .**185** C3
Thornton Heath SW16 . . . . . .**41** F5
Dorset House 2 SE20 . . . . .**43** B8
Dorset Rd Ash GU12 . . . . . .**106** B5
Ashford TW15 . . . .**13** D5
Belmont SM2 . . . .**59** A1
Merton SW19 . . . .**40** A7
Mitcham CR4 . . . .**40** E7
Penge BR3 . . . .**43** D6
Dorset Sq KT19 . . . .**57** D1
Dorset Way Byfleet KT14 . . .**52** D7
Twickenham TW2 . . . .**16** D7
Dorset Waye TW5 . . . .**4** F7
Dorsten Sq RH11 . . . .**200** F3
Dorton Way GU23 . . . .**91** B6
Douai Cl GU14 . . . .**85** C4
Douai Gr TW12 . . . .**36** C8
Douglas Ave KT3 . . . .**39** B5
Douglas Cl Guildford GU4 .**109** D6
Wallington SM6 . . . .**60** E4
Douglas Ct CR3 . . . .**100** D5
Douglas Dr Croydon CR0 . . .**63** A7
Godalming GU7 . . . .**150** F5
Douglas Gr GU10 . . . .**146** C5
Douglas Gracey
House SW18 . . . .**19** E8
Douglas Houghton
House 11 RH1 . . . .**118** F2
Douglas House
Little Bookham KT23 . . . .**94** A3
Twickenham TW1 . . . .**6** B2
Douglas Mews SM7 . . . .**77** F3
Douglas Pl GU14 . . . .**85** A5
Douglas Rd
Addlestone KT15 . . . .**52** B7
Hounslow TW3 . . . .**5** B4
Kingston u T KT1 . . . .**38** B7

Douglas Rd continued
Reigate RH2 . . . .**118** B2
Stanwell TW19 . . . .**2** D1
Surbiton KT6 . . . .**37** F1
Thames Ditton KT10 . . . .**55** B8
Douglas Robinson Ct
SW16 . . . .**21** E1
Douglas Sq SM4 . . . .**40** A3
Doultons The TW18 . . . .**13** A2
Dounesforth Gdns SW18 . .**20** B7
Dove Cl Crawley RH11 . . . . .**201** D8
Selsdon CR2 . . . .**81** D8
Dove Ct TW19 . . . .**13** E8
Dovecote Cl KT13 . . . .**53** D7
Dovecote Gdns 8 SW14 . . . .**7** D4
Dovedale Cl Guildford GU1 .**110** A4
Sandhurst GU47 . . . .**45** D2
Dovedale Cres RH11 . . . . . .**201** B4
Dovedale Rise CR4 . . . .**20** F1
Dovehouse Gn 1 KT13 . . . . .**53** D6
Dover Ct GU6 . . . .**175** A3
Dover Gdns SM5 . . . .**59** F7
Dover House
7 Beckenham BR3 . . . .**24** A1
15 Penge SE20 . . . .**43** B8
Dover House Rd SW15 . . . . .**19** B8
Dover Rd SE19 . . . .**22** D2
Dover Terr TW9 . . . .**7** A5
Dovercourt Ave CR7 . . . .**42** A5
Dovercourt La SM1 . . . .**59** C7
Dovercourt Rd SE21, SE22 . .**22** E8
Doverfield Rd
Guildford GU4 . . . .**110** A4
Streatham SW2 . . . .**21** F8
Dovers Green Inf Sch
RH2 . . . .**139** C5
Dovers Green Rd RH2 . . . . .**139** B4
Doversmead GU21 . . . .**68** E3
Doveton Rd CR2 . . . .**61** D5
Dowanhill Rd SE6 . . . .**24** D7
Dowdeswell Cl SW15 . . . .**7** E3
Dowding Ct RG45 . . . .**45** C6
Dowding Rd TN16 . . . .**83** D4
Dowell House SE21 . . . .**22** F5
Dower Ave SM6 . . . .**60** B2
Dower House GU8 . . . .**170** F8
Dower Wlk RH11 . . . .**201** A5
Dowes House 13 SW16 . . . . .**21** E5
Dowlands Cl RH10, RH6 . . .**183** D7
Dowlans Cl KT23 . . . .**114** A8
Dowlans Rd KT23 . . . .**114** B8
Dowler Ct 2 KT2 . . . .**37** F8
Dowman Cl 2 SW19 . . . .**20** B1
Down Hall Rd KT2 . . . .**37** D8
Down La GU3 . . . .**129** B4
Down Lodge Ct KT18 . . . .**76** E5
Down Rd Guildford GU1 . . . .**110** B1
Teddington TW11 . . . .**17** B2
Down St KT8 . . . .**36** A4
Down Yhonda GU8 . . . .**148** C3
Downbury Prim Sch BR1 . .**24** E4
Downderry Rd BR1 . . . .**24** E4
Downe Cl RH6 . . . .**160** E5
Downe Golf Course BR6 . .**83** E7
Downe Rd CR4 . . . .**40** F7
Downer Meadow GU7 . . . . .**150** E8
Downes Cl TW1 . . . .**6** B1
Downfield 7 KT4 . . . .**39** A1
Downfield House RH1 . . . . . .**38** D1
Downham Enterprise Ctr
SE6 . . . .**24** F6
Downham La BR1 . . . .**24** D3
Downham Way BR1 . . . .**24** E4
Downhurst Rd GU6 . . . .**175** E6
Downing Ave GU2 . . . .**129** F8
Downing House 3 SW19 . . .**20** A1
Downing St GU9 . . . .**125** B2
Downland Cl
Burgh Heath KT18 . . . .**77** B1
Wallington CR5 . . . .**79** B5
Downland Ct RH11 . . . .**201** C4
Downland Dr RH11 . . . .**201** C3
Downlands Gdns KT18 . . . . .**77** B1
Downland Pl RH11 . . . .**201** C4
Downland Way KT18 . . . .**77** B1
Downlands Rd CR8 . . . .**79** F6
Downmill Rd RG12 . . . .**26** F7
Downs Ave KT18 . . . .**76** F4
Downs Bridge Rd
BR2, BR3 . . . .**44** D8
Downs Court Rd CR8 . . . . . .**80** B6
Downs Ct Purley CR8 . . . . . .**61** B1
2 Redhill RH1 . . . .**119** A4
10 Wimbledon SW19 . . . . . .**19** D1
Downs Est KT17 . . . .**77** C5
Downs Hill BR2, BR3 . . . .**44** D8
Downs Hill Rd KT18 . . . .**76** E5
Downs La KT22 . . . .**95** B3
Downs Rd
Ashtead KT18, KT21 . . . .**96** C7
Beckenham BR3 . . . .**44** B7
Coulsdon CR5 . . . .**79** D1
Epsom KT17, KT18 . . . .**76** E3
Mickleham RH5 . . . .**115** C7
Purley CR8 . . . .**80** B8
South Norwood CR7 . . . .**42** C8
Sutton SM2 . . . .**78** C8
Downs Side SM2 . . . .**77** F8
Downs The
Leatherhead KT22 . . . .**95** C2
Wimbledon SW19, SW20 . . . .**19** D1
Downs View Dorking RH4 .**115** B1
Hounslow TW7 . . . .**6** A6
Tadworth KT20 . . . .**97** B6
Downs View Lodge 9 KT6 .**37** E3
Downs View Rd KT23 . . . . .**114** C8
Downs Way Epsom KT18 . . . .**76** F3
Great Bookham KT23 . . . . . .**94** C1

Downs Way continued
Oxted RH8 . . . .**122** E8
Tadworth KT20 . . . .**97** B6
Downs Way Cty Inf Sch
RH8 . . . .**122** E8
Downs Wood KT18 . . . .**77** B2
Downsend Lodge Pre Prep
Sch KT22 . . . .**95** B6
Downsend Sch KT22 . . . .**95** D7
Downsend Sch (Epsom
Lodge) KT17 . . . .**76** F7
Downshire Way
Bracknell RG12, RG42 . . . . .**27** A7
Bracknell RG12 . . . .**27** B6
Downside
Beacon Hill GU26 . . . .**188** D7
Epsom KT18 . . . .**76** E5
Twickenham TW1 . . . .**16** F5
Downside Bridge Rd KT11 **73** B4
Downside Cl SW19 . . . .**20** C2
Downside Common Rd
KT11 . . . .**73** C1
Downside Ct RH1 . . . .**119** C6
Downside Orch GU22 . . . . . .**70** A2
Downside Rd
Downside KT11 . . . .**73** B2
Guildford GU4 . . . .**131** B8
Sutton SM2 . . . .**59** E4
Downsman Ct RH10 . . . . . .**201** D3
Downsview Ave GU22 . . . . . .**89** F6
Downsview Ct GU1 . . . .**109** C5
Downsview Gdns
Dorking RH4 . . . .**136** B6
South Norwood SE19 . . . .**22** C1
Downsview Prim Sch
SE19 . . . .**22** C1
Downsview Rd
Headley Down GU35 . . . . . .**187** C5
Horsham RH12 . . . .**218** B6
South Norwood CR7, SE19 . . .**22** C1
Downsway Guildford GU1 . .**110** A1
South Croydon CR2 . . . .**80** E8
Whyteleafe CR3 . . . .**80** F2
Downsway Cl KT20 . . . .**97** A6
Downsway The SM2 . . . .**59** C2
Downswood RH2 . . . .**118** D4
Downton Ave SW2 . . . .**21** F7
Downview Cl
Beacon Hill GU26 . . . .**188** D6
Downside KT11 . . . .**93** B8
Doyle Rd SE25 . . . .**43** A5
Dr Johnson Ave SW17 . . . . .**21** B5
Dragon La KT13 . . . .**53** A1
Dragoon Ct GU11 . . . .**104** E2
Drake Ave Caterham CR3 . .**100** C5
Mytchett GU16 . . . .**86** A1
Staines TW18 . . . .**12** F3
Drake Cl Bracknell RG12 . . . .**27** B4
Horsham RH12 . . . .**217** E6
Drake Ct Dulwich SE19 . . . . .**22** F3
Kingston u T KT5 . . . .**37** F5
Drake Rd Chessington KT9 . .**57** A5
Crawley RH10 . . . .**201** E3
Horley RH6 . . . .**160** E3
Mitcham CR4 . . . .**41** A3
Thornton Heath CR0, CR9 . . .**41** F4
Drake's Cl KT10 . . . .**55** A6
Drakefield Rd SW17 . . . .**21** A5
Drakes Ct SE23 . . . .**23** C7
Drakes Way GU22 . . . .**89** D5
Drakewood Rd SW16 . . . . . .**21** D1
Drax Ave SW20 . . . .**19** A1
Draxmont SW19 . . . .**19** E2
Dray Ct GU2 . . . .**130** B8
Draycot Rd KT6 . . . .**38** A1
Draycott RG12 . . . .**27** E4
Drayhorse Dr GU19 . . . .**47** E2
Draymans Way TW7 . . . .**5** F4
Drayton Cl Bracknell RG12 . . .**27** D7
Fetcham KT22 . . . .**94** E3
Hounslow TW4 . . . .**4** F2
Drayton Ct Tolworth KT5 . . . .**57** B8
West Byfleet KT14 . . . .**71** A6
Drayton Rd CR0, CR9 . . . . . .**61** B8
Dresden Way KT13 . . . .**53** C5
Drew House 12 SW16 . . . . . .**21** E5
Drew Pl CR3 . . . .**100** D4
Drewstead Rd SW16 . . . .**21** D6
Drift The
East Horsley KT11, KT24 . . . .**92** E3
Martyr's Green KT11, KT24 . . .**92** E3
Drift Way SL3 . . . .**1** C7
Driftway The Banstead SM7 **77** C4
Leatherhead KT22 . . . .**95** C4
Mitcham CR4 . . . .**41** A8
Driftway (Worple Road)
The KT22 . . . .**95** B4
Driftwood Dr CR8 . . . .**80** C2
Drill Hall Rd KT16 . . . .**33** A2
Drive Rd CR5 . . . .**99** F7
Drive Spur KT20 . . . .**98** B6
Drive The Artington GU3 . . .**130** B5
Ashford TW15 . . . .**14** D1
Banstead SM7 . . . .**77** E3
Beckenham BR3 . . . .**44** A8
Belmont SM2 . . . .**77** F7
Cobham KT11 . . . .**73** F5
Copthorne RH10 . . . .**183** C3
Coulsdon CR5, CR8 . . . .**79** E5
Cranleigh GU6 . . . .**174** F2
Farnham GU9 . . . .**146** B7
Feltham TW14 . . . .**15** C8
Fetcham KT22 . . . .**94** E5
Godalming GU7 . . . .**150** F2
Guildford GU2 . . . .**108** F1
Guildford GU3 . . . .**130** A2
Headley KT18, KT22 . . . .**96** A3
Horley RH6 . . . .**161** B1

Drive The continued
Hounslow TW3, TW7 . . . .**5** D5
Ifold RH14 . . . .**212** D2
Kingston u T KT2 . . . .**18** C1
Leatherhead KT22, KT18 . . . .**95** F4
Morden SM4 . . . .**40** D4
Shackleford GU7, GU8 . . . . .**149** E4
South Norwood CR7 . . . .**42** D5
Thames Ditton KT10 . . . .**36** C1
Thorpe GU25 . . . .**31** F4
Wallington CR8, SM6 . . . . . .**60** D1
West Ewell KT19 . . . .**57** F4
West Wickham BR4 . . . .**44** D2
Wimbledon SW19, SW20 . . . .**19** C1
Woking GU22 . . . .**89** B7
Wonersh GU5 . . . .**152** B6
Drivers Mead RH7 . . . .**164** D3
Drodges Cl GU5 . . . .**151** F8
Droitwich Cl Bracknell RG12 **27** E6
Forest Hill SE26 . . . .**23** A5
Drove Rd GU4 . . . .**132** A2
Drovers Ct 8 KT1 . . . .**37** E7
Drovers Rd CR2 . . . .**61** D5
Drovers Way Ash GU12 . . . .**106** C1
Bracknell RG12 . . . .**27** F6
Hale GU9 . . . .**125** A6
Druid's Cl KT21 . . . .**95** F7
Druids Way BR2 . . . .**44** D5
Drumaline Ridge KT4 . . . . . .**57** E8
Drummond Cl RG12 . . . .**27** F8
Drummond Ct 4 GU1 . . . . .**109** D1
Drummond Ctr CR9 . . . .**61** C8
Drummond Gdns KT19 . . . . .**76** B8
Drummond Rd
Crawley RH11 . . . .**200** E5
Croydon CR0, CR9 . . . .**61** C8
Guildford GU1 . . . .**109** D1
Drummonds Pl TW9 . . . .**6** E3
Drungewick La RH14 . . . . . .**213** D2
Drury Cl RH10 . . . .**202** D4
Drury Cres CR0, CR9 . . . . . .**61** A8
Dry Arch Rd SL5 . . . .**29** F3
Dryden RG12 . . . .**27** A2
Dryden Ct 11 TW10 . . . .**17** D4
Dryden Rd
Farnborough GU14 . . . .**84** F6
Wimbledon SW19 . . . .**20** C2
Drynham Pk KT13 . . . .**53** E7
Du Cane Ct SW12 . . . .**21** A7
Ducavel House SW2 . . . .**21** F7
Duck's Wlk TW1 . . . .**6** C2
Dudley Cl KT15 . . . .**52** C7
Dudley Dr SM4 . . . .**39** E2
Dudley Gr KT18 . . . .**76** C5
Dudley Rd Ashford TW15 . . . .**13** F4
East Bedfont TW14 . . . .**14** D7
Kingston u T KT1 . . . .**37** F6
Richmond TW9 . . . .**7** A5
Walton-on-T KT12 . . . .**35** A2
Wimbledon SW19 . . . .**20** A2
Dudset La TW5 . . . .**4** A6
Duffield Rd KT20 . . . .**97** B3
Duffins Orch KT16 . . . .**51** C3
Duke Cl RH10 . . . .**202** C2
Duke Of Cambridge Cl
TW2 . . . .**5** D1
Duke Of Cornwall Ave
GU15 . . . .**46** D1
Duke Of Edinburgh Rd
SM1 . . . .**59** D8
Duke of Kent Sch GU6 . . . .**154** D2
Duke St Richmond TW10, TW9 **6** D2
Sutton SM1 . . . .**59** D6
Woking GU21 . . . .**69** F2
Duke's Ave W4 . . . .**7** D8
Duke's Dr Farncombe GU7 .**150** B7
Newdigate RH5 . . . .**179** D6
Duke's Hill GU19 . . . .**47** E5
Duke's La
Old Windsor SL4, SL5 . . . . . .**10** B3
Winkfield SL5 . . . .**9** F1
Duke's Ride RG45 . . . .**45** B5
Dukes Ave Hounslow TW4 . . . .**4** E2
Kingston u T KT2, TW10 . . . . .**17** D4
New Malden KT3 . . . .**38** F6
Richmond KT2, TW10 . . . . . .**17** D4
Dukes Cl Ashford TW15 . . . . .**14** C4
Cranleigh GU6 . . . .**175** A2
Hale GU9 . . . .**125** A6
Hampton TW12 . . . .**15** F3
Dukes Covert GU19 . . . .**47** E6
Dukes Ct Addlestone KT15 . .**52** C6
Beckenham BR3 . . . .**43** E6
Dukes Green Ave TW14 . . . . .**4** A2
Dukes Hill CR3, CR6 . . . . . .**101** C7
Dukes Pk GU11 . . . .**105** D6
Dukes Rd KT12 . . . .**54** D5
Dukes Ride RH5 . . . .**136** D4
Dukes Way BR4 . . . .**63** E7
Dukes Wlk GU9 . . . .**125** A6
Dukes Wood RG45 . . . .**45** B5
Dukeshill Rd RG42 . . . .**27** B8
Dukesthorpe Rd SE26 . . . . . .**23** D4
Dulverton Ct 12 KT6 . . . .**37** E4
Dulverton Rd CR2 . . . .**62** C1
Dulwich and Sydenham
Hill Golf Course SE21 . . . .**22** F6
Dulwich Bsns Ctr SE23 . . . .**23** D7
Dulwich Coll
(Endowed) SE21 . . . .**22** E6
Dulwich Coll Picture
Gal SE21 . . . .**22** E6
Dulwich Coll Prep
Sch SE21 . . . .**22** E5
Dulwich Comm SE21 . . . .**22** E7
Dulwich Ct SE22 . . . .**23** B7
Dulwich Oaks The SE21 . . . .**22** F5
Dulwich Village SE21 . . . . . .**22** E8

Dulwich Wood Ave SE19 . .**22** E3
Dulwich Wood Pk
SE21, SE19 . . . .**22** E4
Dumbarton Ct 16 SW2 . . . . .**21** E8
Dumbleton Cl KT2 . . . .**38** B8
Dumphreys House 5
SW4 . . . .**21** D8
Dumville Dr RH9 . . . .**121** B4
Dunally Pk TW17 . . . .**34** E2
Dunbar Ave Beckenham BR3 **43** E5
Thornton Heath CR7, SW16 . .**42** A7
Dunbar Ct Carshalton SM1 . .**59** D5
Walton-on-T KT12 . . . .**35** C1
Dunbar Rd Frimley GU16 . . . .**85** F7
Kingston u T KT3 . . . .**38** C5
Dunbar St SE27 . . . .**22** C5
Dunboe Pl TW17 . . . .**34** C2
Dunbridge House SW15 . . . . .**7** F1
Duncan Dr Guildford GU1 . .**110** A2
Wokingham RG40 . . . .**25** E5
Duncan Gdns TW18 . . . .**13** A2
Duncan Rd
Burgh Heath KT20 . . . .**97** E8
Richmond TW9 . . . .**6** E3
Duncombe Ct TW18 . . . .**12** F1
Duncombe Hill SE23 . . . .**23** E8
Duncombe House 7
SW19 . . . .**19** D7
Duncombe Rd GU7 . . . .**150** D2
Duncroft Cl RH2 . . . .**117** F1
Dundaff Cl GU15 . . . .**66** A5
Dundas Cl RG12 . . . .**27** B5
Dundas Gdns KT8 . . . .**36** B6
Dundee Rd SE25 . . . .**43** B4
Dundela Gdns KT17, KT4 . . .**58** B6
Dundonald Prim Sch
SW19 . . . .**19** F1
Dundonald Rd SW19 . . . .**19** F1
Dundrey Cres RH1 . . . .**119** E6
Dundry House 8 SE26 . . . . . .**23** A5
Dunedin Dr CR3 . . . .**100** E2
Dunelm Gr SE27 . . . .**22** C5
Dunfee Way KT14 . . . .**71** E7
Dunfield Gdns SE6 . . . .**24** B3
Dunfield Rd SE6 . . . .**24** B3
Dungates La RH3 . . . .**117** A2
Dunheved Cl CR7 . . . .**42** A3
Dunheved Rd N CR7 . . . .**42** A3
Dunheved Rd S CR7 . . . .**42** A3
Dunheved Rd W CR7 . . . .**42** A3
Dunhill Point 12 SW15 . . . . .**19** B7
Dunkeld Rd SE25 . . . .**42** D5
Dunkirk St 12 SE27 . . . .**22** C4
Dunleary Cl TW4 . . . .**15** F8
Dunley Dr CR0 . . . .**63** C4
Dunlin Cl RH1 . . . .**139** F4
Dunlin Ct 11 SE21 . . . .**22** D6
Dunlin Rise GU4 . . . .**110** D3
Dunmail Dr CR2, CR8 . . . . . .**80** E6
Dunmore GU2 . . . .**108** D2
Dunmore Rd SW20 . . . .**39** D8
Dunmow Cl TW13 . . . .**15** E4
Dunnets GU21 . . . .**68** E2
Dunning's Rd RH19 . . . .**205** E7
Dunnings Mill L Complex
RH19 . . . .**205** E6
Dunnock Ct 10 SE21 . . . .**22** D6
Dunnymans Rd SM7 . . . .**77** F4
Dunoon Gdns SE23 . . . .**23** D8
Dunoon Rd SE23 . . . .**23** C8
Dunottar Cl RH1 . . . .**139** D7
Dunraven Ave RH1 . . . .**140** B2
Dunraven House 11 TW9 . . . .**6** F6
Dunraven Lower Sch
SW16 . . . .**21** F5
Dunraven Upper Sch
SW16 . . . .**21** F5
Dunsborough Cotts GU23 .**91** C7
Dunsbury Cl SM2 . . . .**59** B2
Dunsdon Ave GU2 . . . .**130** B8
Dunsfold CE Prim Sch
GU8 . . . .**192** F6
Dunsfold Cl RH11 . . . .**201** A5
Dunsfold Common Rd
GU8 . . . .**192** F6
Dunsfold Ct 9 SM2 . . . .**59** B3
Dunsfold House
10 Kingston u T KT2 . . . .**18** B2
7 Streatham SW2 . . . .**21** F8
Dunsfold Rd Alfold GU6 . . .**193** E3
Alfold Crossways GU6 . . . . .**193** E3
Bramley GU5, GU8 . . . .**173** C1
Dunsfold GU6, GU8 . . . . . .**193** B8
Plaistow GU8, RH14 . . . . . .**211** D4
Dunsfold Rise CR5 . . . .**79** D6
Dunsfold Way CR0 . . . .**63** C3
Dunsmore Rd KT12 . . . .**35** B3
Dunstable Rd
East Molesey KT8 . . . .**35** F5
Richmond TW10, TW9 . . . .**6** E3
Dunstall Pk GU14 . . . .**85** A7
Dunstall Rd SW19, SW20 . . .**19** C2
Dunstall Way KT8 . . . .**36** B6
Dunstan Ct TW18 . . . .**13** A4
Dunstan Rd CR5 . . . .**79** D2
Dunstan's Rd SE22 . . . .**23** A8
Dunster Ave SM4 . . . .**39** D1
Dunster House SE6 . . . .**24** B5
Dunton Cl KT6 . . . .**37** E1
Dunton Ct SE26 . . . .**23** B6
Dunton House 14 SW16 . . . .**21** E5
Duntshill Rd SW18 . . . .**20** B7
Dunvegan Cl KT8 . . . .**36** B5
Dunvegan House 12 RH1 . .**118** F1
Dupont Rd SW20 . . . .**39** D1
Duppas Ave CR0 . . . .**61** B6
Duppas Cl TW17 . . . .**34** D4
Duppas Ct CR0 . . . .**61** B7

Duppas Hill La CR0 61 B6
Duppas Hill Rd CR0 61 B6
Duppas Hill Terr CR0, CR9 61 B7
Duppas Jun Sch CR0 61 B5
Duppas Rd CR0, CR9 61 B7
Dura Den Cl BR3 24 B1
Durand Cl SM5 40 F1
Durban Rd Beckenham BR3 43 F7
West Norwood SE27 22 D4
Durbin Rd KT9 56 F6
Durfold Dr RH2 118 C1
Durfold Rd RH12 217 D7
Durfold Wood RH14 211 D5
Durfold Wood Woodlands Wlks GU8 211 C6
Durford Cres SW15 19 B7
Durham Ave BR2 44 F5
Durham Cl Crawley RH10 201 E2
Guildford GU2 108 F3
Wimbledon SW20 39 B7
Durham Ct
Leatherhead KT22 95 A5
Teddington TW11 16 E4
Durham Hill BR1 24 F4
Durham Rd Beckenham BR2 44 F6
Feltham TW14 15 C8
Sandhurst GU47 45 E2
Wimbledon SW20 39 B8
Durkins Rd RH19 185 D3
Durleston Park Dr KT23 94 C2
Durley Mead RG12 27 F4
Durlston Rd KT2 17 E2
Durnford House SE6 24 B5
Durning Rd SE19 22 D3
Durnsford Ave
SW18, SW19 20 A6
Durnsford Rd SW18, SW19 20 B5
Durnsford Way GU6 175 A2
Durrell Way TW17 34 D3
Durrington Ave SW20 19 C1
Durrington Park Rd SW20 39 C8
Dutch Barn Cl TW19 2 D1
Dutch Gdns KT2 18 B2
Dutchells Copse RH12 217 E7
Dutton House SW2 22 B7
Duval Pl GU19 47 E3
Duxford 10 KT1 38 A7
Duxhurst La RH2 160 B7
Dwelly La Haxted TN8 165 D8
Limpsfield TN8 144 D3
Dyehouse Rd GU8 169 C4
Dyer House TW12 36 B8
Dyer's Field RH6 162 B3
Dyers Almshouses RH10 201 D7
Dykes Ct 11 SW2 21 F7
Dykes Path GU22 70 C4
Dykes Way BR2 44 F6
Dymes Path SW19 19 D6
Dynevor Pl GU3 108 C5
Dynevor Rd TW10 6 E2
Dysart Ave KT2, TW10 17 C4
Dysart Sch KT2 17 D4
Dyson Ct RH4 136 A7
Dyson Wlk RH11 201 B1

E

Eady Cl RH13 217 F2
Eagle Cl Crowthorne RG45 45 A7
Wallington SM6 60 E4
Eagle Ct 9 SE21 22 D6
Eagle Hill SE19 22 D2
Eagle House Sch GU47 45 B2
Eagle Rd Farnborough GU14 85 B2
Guildford GU1 109 D1
Eagle Trad Est CR4 40 F3
Eagles Dr TN16 83 D1
Eagles Nest GU47 45 A1
Ealing Rd TW8 6 E8
Eardley Prim Sch SW16 21 C2
Eardley Rd SW16 21 C2
Earl Rd SW14 7 C3
Earle Gdns KT2 17 E1
Earles Meadow RH12 218 B6
Earleswood KT11 73 E7
Earleydene SL5 29 B1
Earls Gr GU15 65 E6
Earlsbrook Rd RH1 139 F7
Earlsfield Prim Sch SW18 20 C6
Earlsfield Rd SW18 20 C8
Earlsfield Sta SW18 20 C7
Earlsthorpe Rd SE26 23 D4
Earlswood RG12 27 B2
Earlswood Ave CR7 42 A4
Earlswood Cl RH13 218 A4
Earlswood Ct RH1 139 F7
Earlswood Cty Inf & Nurs Sch RH1 140 A8
Earlswood House 2 SW2 21 F7
Earlswood Rd RH1 139 F7
Earlswood Sta RH1 139 F7
Early Commons RH10 201 F7
Easby Cres SM4 40 B3
Easedale House TW7 5 F2
Eashing La
Godalming GU7, GU8 150 A3
Shackleford GU7, GU8 149 F3
Eashing Point 5 SW15 19 B7
Easington Pl GU1 130 F8
East Ave Heath End GU9 125 D6
Wallington CR0 60 F5
Whiteley Village KT12 53 F1
East Croydon Sta CR9 61 D8
East Dr Beckenham BR3 44 C4
Wallington SM5 59 F2
Wentworth GU25 31 B3
East Flexford La GU3 128 F6
East Gdns
Mitcham SW17, SW19 20 E2
Woking GU22 70 C2
East Gn GU17 64 C4
East Grinstead Rd RH7 164 D3
East Grinstead Sta RH19 185 D1
East Grinstead Town Mus RH19 185 F2
East Hill Biggin Hill TN16 83 B1
Dormans Park RH19 185 E6
Oxted RH8 122 F6
South Croydon CR2 61 E1
Woking GU22 70 C2
East Hill Ct RH8 122 E5
East Hill La RH10 183 D5
East Hill Rd RH8 122 E6
East La Kingston u T KT1 37 D6
West Horsley KT24 92 D2
East Meads GU2 130 A8
East Park La RH7 163 C1
East Pk RH10, RH11 201 D5
East Pl SE27 22 C4
East Ramp TW6 3 B6
East Rd East Bedfont TW14 14 D8
Kingston u T KT2 37 E8
Merton SW19 20 C2
Reigate RH2 117 F2
Weybridge KT13 53 D3
Wimbledon SW19 20 C2
East Resr (Nature Reserve) RH9 121 B5
East Ring GU10 127 A7
East Shalford La GU4 131 A3
East Sheen Ave SW14 7 D3
East Sheen Prim Sch SW14 7 E3
East St Brentford TW8 6 C7
Ewell KT17 76 E7
Farnham GU9 125 C3
Great Bookham KT23 94 B2
Horsham RH12 217 C1
Rusper RH12 199 E7
Turners Hill RH10, RH19 204 C4
East Station Rd GU12 105 B1
East Stratton Cl RG12 27 F4
East Surrey Coll RH1 119 A4
East Surrey Hospl RH1 118 E1
East Surrey Hospl The RH1 140 A5
East Surrey Mus CR3 101 A3
East View La GU6 174 C3
East Way CR0 62 E7
East Whipley La
Rowly GU5 173 F7
Shamley Green GU5 173 F8
East Wlk RH2 118 B1
Eastbank Rd TW12 16 C3
Eastbourne Gdns SW14 7 C4
Eastbourne Rd
Blindley Heath RH9 142 E4
Chiswick W4 7 C8
Felbridge RH7 184 E8
Feltham TW13 15 D6
Godstone RH9 121 D2
Mitcham SW17 21 A2
Newchapel RH7, RH9 163 F5
South Godstone RH9 142 E4
Eastbrook Cl GU21 70 A3
Eastbury Gr W4 7 E8
Eastbury La GU3 129 A3
Eastbury Rd KT2 17 E1
Eastchurch Rd TW6 3 E5
Eastchurch Road Rdbt TW6 3 E5
Eastcote Ave KT8 36 A4
Eastcroft Ct GU1 131 A8
Eastcroft Mews RH12 216 F1
Eastcroft Rd KT19 57 E3
Eastdean Ave KT18 76 B6
Easter Way RH9 142 F5
Eastern Ave KT16 33 A6
Eastern Ind Area RG12 27 D7
Eastern La RG45 45 F4
Eastern Perimeter Rd TW14 3 F5
Eastern Rd
Aldershot GU12 105 E2
Bracknell RG12 27 D7
Eastern View TN16 83 C2
Eastfield Rd RH1 140 C8
Eastfields GU8 170 F5
Eastfields High Sch CR4 41 B7
Eastfields Rd CR4 41 A7
Eastgate SM7 77 F5
Eastgate Gdns GU1 130 E8
Easthampstead Park Sch RG12 26 D3
Easthampstead Rd
Bracknell RG12 27 A7
Wokingham RG40 25 E4
Eastheath Ave RG41 25 A4
Eastheath Gdns RG41 25 B3
Eastlands Cl RH8 122 D8
Eastlands Cres SE21, SE22 22 F8
Eastlands Way RH8 122 D8
Eastleigh Cl SM2 59 B3
Eastleigh Rd TW6 3 F4
Eastleigh Way TW14 15 A7
Eastleigh Wlk 10 SW15 19 A8
Eastmead
Farnborough GU14 85 B3
Woking GU21 69 B2
Eastmearn Rd SE21, SE27 22 C6
Eastmont Rd KT10 55 F8
Eastney Rd CR0 42 B1
Eastnor Cl RH2 138 F6
Eastnor Rd RH2 139 A6
Easton House 4 SE27 22 B5
Eastry Ave BR2 44 F3
Eastway Crawley RH6 182 B7
Epsom KT19 76 D8
Eastway *continued*
Guildford GU2 108 F1
Merton SM4, SW20 39 E5
Wallington SM6 60 C6
Eastwell Cl BR3 23 E1
Eastwick Ct 2 SW19 19 D7
Eastwick Cty Inf Sch KT23 94 B3
Eastwick Cty Mid Sch KT23 94 B3
Eastwick Dr KT23 94 B4
Eastwick Park Ave KT23 94 B3
Eastwick Rd
Great Bookham KT23 94 B2
Hersham KT12 54 B5
Eastwood Crawley RH10 201 F6
3 Weybridge KT13 53 D4
Eastwood Lodge GU5 151 F7
Eastwood Rd GU5 151 F7
Eastwood St SW16 21 C2
Eastworth Rd KT15, KT16 33 A1
Eaton Ct Guildford GU1 110 A3
Sutton SM2 59 D4
Eaton Dr KT2 18 A1
Eaton Ho GU1 130 F7
Eaton Park Rd KT11 73 F5
Eaton Pk KT11 73 E5
Eaton Rd Camberley GU15 65 B4
Isleworth TW3, TW7 5 D3
Sutton SM2 59 D4
Eatonville Rd SW17 20 F6
Eatonville Villas SW17 20 F6
Ebba's Way KT18 76 B4
Ebbage Ct 5 GU22 69 E1
Ebbisham Ct KT18 76 C4
Ebbisham La KT20 97 A4
Ebbisham Rd Epsom KT18 76 B5
North Cheam KT4 58 C8
Ebenezer Wlk CR4 41 C8
Ebisham Cl RH4 136 A7
Ebor Cotts SW15 18 E5
Ebsworth St SE23 23 D8
Ecclesbourne Inf Sch CR7 42 C4
Ecclesbourne Jun Sch CR7 42 C4
Ecclesbourne Rd CR7 42 C4
Eccleshill Beckenham BR2 44 F5
Dorking RH5 136 C3
Echelford Cty Mid Sch TW15 14 B3
Echelforde Dr TW15 14 A4
Echo Barn La GU10 145 F5
Echo Pit Rd GU1, GU4 130 E6
Ecob Cl GU3 108 F5
Ecton Rd KT15 52 B6
Ector Rd SE6 24 E6
Eddeys Cl GU35 187 B6
Eddeys La GU35 187 B6
Eddington Hill RH11 201 B1
Eddington Rd RG12 26 E3
Eddisbury House 7 SE26 23 A5
Eddy Rd GU12 105 C1
Eddystone Wlk TW19 13 E8
Ede Cl TW4 4 F4
Ede Ct KT17 76 F7
Ede's Cotts KT21 95 D8
Eden Cl KT15 52 B1
Eden Grove Rd KT14 71 E6
Eden Park Ave BR3 44 A4
Eden Park Sch BR3 43 F4
Eden Park Sta BR3 44 A4
Eden Rd Crawley RH11 200 F4
Croydon CR0 61 D6
Penge BR3 43 E8
West Norwood SE27 22 B3
Eden St KT1, KT2 37 E7
Eden Vale
Dormans Park RH19 185 E5
East Grinstead RH19 185 E5
Eden Way Beckenham BR3 44 A3
Warlingham CR6 81 E1
Eden Wlk 5 KT1 37 E7
Edenbrook RH7 164 E4
Edencourt Rd SW16 21 B2
Edencroft GU5 151 F7
Edenfield Gdns KT4 57 F7
Edenham High Sch CR0 43 F2
Edenhurst Pl SM2 59 A4
Edenside Rd KT23 93 F3
Edensor Gdns W4 7 E7
Edensor Rd W4 7 E7
Edenvale Cl CR4 21 A1
Edenvale Rd CR4 21 A1
Ederline Ave SW16 42 A7
Edgar Cl RH10 202 E5
Edgar Ct KT3 38 E6
Edgar Rd
South Croydon CR2 61 D2
Tatsfield TN16 103 D6
Twickenham TW4 15 F8
Edgbarrow Rise GU47 45 A2
Edgbarrow Sch RG45 45 C3
Edgbarrowhill Star RG45 45 A3
Edgcumbe Park Dr RG45 45 A5
Edge Cl KT13 53 A3
Edge Hill SW19 19 D1
Edge Hill Ct SW19 19 D1
Edge Point Cl SE27 22 B3
Edgeborough Ct 6 GU1 130 F8
Edgeborough Sch GU10 146 C3
Edgecombe Cl KT2 18 D1
Edgecombe House SW19 19 E8
Edgecoombe CR2 62 D2
Edgecumbe Ct 2 CR0 43 A1
Edgedale Cl RG45 45 B5
Edgefield Cl
Cranleigh GU6 174 C4
Redhill RH1 140 A4
Edgehill Ct KT12 35 C1
Edgehill House 2 RH1 118 F1
Edgehill Rd Mitcham CR4 41 B8
Purley CR2, CR8 61 B1
Edgeley KT23 93 E3
Edgell Cl GU25 31 F6
Edgell Rd TW18 12 F3
Edgemoor Rd GU16 66 C3
Edgewood Cl RG45 45 A7
Edgewood Gn CR0 43 D1
Edgeworth Cl CR3 81 A1
Edgington Rd SW16 21 D2
Edinburgh Cl GU12 106 A5
Edinburgh Ct Catford SE6 24 F7
2 Kingston u T KT1 37 E6
West Barnes SM4 39 D4
Edinburgh Dr TW15, TW18 13 D2
Edinburgh Rd SM1 59 D8
Edinburgh Way RH19 205 F7
Edith Gdns KT5 38 B2
Edith Rd
Thornton Heath SE25 42 D4
Wimbledon SW19 20 B2
Edmonds Ct 4 RG12 27 C8
Edmund Rd CR4 40 E6
Edna Rd SW20 39 D7
Edrich Rd RH11 201 A1
Edridge House 9 SE27 22 B5
Edridge Rd CR0, CR9 61 D7
Edward Alleyn House SE21 22 E8
Edward Ave
Camberley GU15 65 A5
Morden CR4, SM4 40 D4
Edward Cl TW12 16 C3
Edward Ct TW18 13 C2
Edward II Ave KT14 71 F5
Edward Pauling House TW14 14 F8
Edward Pauling Prim Sch TW13 14 E6
Edward Pinner Ct 5 KT6 56 E8
Edward Rd Biggin Hill TN16 83 E1
Coulsdon CR5 79 D4
Croydon CR0 42 E2
Farnham GU9 146 C7
Hampton TW12 16 C3
Hatton TW14 3 E2
Penge SE20 23 D2
Windlesham GU20 48 D4
Edward St 2 GU11 105 A2
Edward Way TW15 13 F6
Edwards Cl KT4 58 D8
Edwin Cl KT24 92 D2
Edwin Rd
Twickenham TW1, TW2 16 E7
West Horsley KT24 92 D2
Edwin Stray House TW13 16 A5
Edwina Ct SM1 59 B6
Eelmoor Plain Rd GU11 104 D5
Eelmoor Rd
Aldershot GU11 104 D5
Farnborough GU14 84 F2
Eelmoor Road Trad Est GU14 85 A2
Effingham Cl SM2 59 B3
Effingham Common Rd KT24 93 C2
Effingham Ct
Mitcham SW19 20 E1
Woking GU22 89 E8
Effingham House 9 KT2 18 B2
Effingham House Golf Club KT24 113 D7
Effingham Junction Sta KT24 93 A4
Effingham La RH10 183 E4
Effingham Lodge 1 KT6 37 E4
Effingham Pl KT24 113 D8
Effingham Rd
Burstow RH10, RH6 183 D6
Domewood RH10, RH6 183 D6
Reigate RH2 139 B8
Thames Ditton KT6, KT7 37 C2
Thornton Heath CR0 41 F2
Effort St SW17 20 E3
Effra Ct SE19 22 E1
Effra Rd SW19 20 B2
Egbury House SW15 7 F1
Egerton Ct
5 Guildford GU2 108 E1
5 Richmond TW10 6 E2
Egerton House W4 7 C8
Egerton Pl KT13 53 C4
Egerton Rd Guildford GU2 129 F8
New Malden KT3 38 F5
Sandhurst GU15 64 F7
Sandhurst GU15 65 A7
South Norwood SE25 42 E6
Twickenham TW2 16 E8
Weybridge KT13 53 C4
Eggar's Ct GU12 105 B1
Eggar's Hill GU11 126 A8
Egham By-Pass TW20 12 A4
Egham Cl Cheam SM3 58 E8
Putney SW19 19 E6
Egham Cres SM3 58 D8
Egham Ct KT6 37 D4
Egham Hill Egham TW20 11 F3
Englefield Green TW20 11 D2
Egham Hill Rdbt TW20 11 F3
Egham Mus TW20 12 A3
Egham Sta TW20 12 A3
Egleston Rd SM4 40 B3
Egley Dr GU22 89 D5
Egley Rd GU22 89 D6
Eglinton Rd GU10 168 B7
Eglise Rd CR6 81 E2
Egmont Ave KT6 37 F1
Egmont Park Rd KT20 97 A2
Egmont Rd New Malden KT3 38 F5
Surbiton KT6 38 A1
Sutton SM2 59 C3
Walton-on-T KT12 35 B2
Egmont Way KT20 97 E8
Egremont Rd SE27 22 A5
Eight Acres GU26 188 C7
Eighteenth Rd CR4 41 E5
Eileen Rd SE25 42 D4
Eisenhower House KT8 37 C8
Eland Pl CR9 61 B7
Eland Rd Aldershot GU12 105 D1
Croydon CR0, CR9 61 B7
Elberon Ave CR0 41 C3
Elborough Rd SE25 43 A4
Elborough St SW18 20 A7
Elbow Meadow SL3 1 F6
Elcho Rd GU24 87 D8
Elder Cl GU1, GU4 110 A4
Elder Gdns 9 SE27 22 C4
Elder Oak Cl SE20 43 B8
Elder Rd Bisley GU24 68 A4
West Norwood SE27 22 C3
Elder Way RH5 136 C3
Elderberry Gr 10 SE27 22 C4
Eldergrove GU14 85 E2
Eldersley Cl RH1 118 F3
Eldersley Gdns RH1 118 F3
Elderslie Cl BR3 44 B3
Elderton Rd SE26 23 E4
Eldertree Pl CR4 41 C8
Eldertree Way CR4 41 C8
Elderwood SE27 22 C3
Eldon Ave Croydon CR0 62 C8
Heston TW5 5 A7
Eldon Ct KT13 53 C5
Eldon Dr GU10 146 D5
Eldon Pk SE25 43 B5
Eldon Rd CR3 100 D6
Eldrick Ct TW14 14 D7
Eldridge Cl TW14 15 A7
Eleanor Ave KT19 57 D1
Eleanor Ct GU1 130 D7
Eleanor Gr SW13, SW14 7 F4
Eleanor House 6 SW19 40 B8
Elfin Gr TW11 16 F3
Elfrida Cres SE6 24 A4
Elfrida Inf & Jun Sch SE6 24 A4
Elgar Ave Crowthorne RG45 45 B7
Thornton Heath SW16 41 E6
Tolworth KT5, KT6 38 B2
Elgar House Kenley CR8 80 C5
Twickenham TW2 5 D1
Elgar Way RH13 218 B4
Elger Way RH10 183 A4
Elgin Ave TW15 14 C2
Elgin Cl RH13 217 F3
Elgin Cres Caterham CR3 101 A5
Harlington TW6 3 E5
Elgin Ct 6 CR0 61 C6
Elgin Gdns GU1 110 A2
Elgin Rd Croydon CR0 61 F8
Sutton SM1 59 C7
Wallington SM6 60 C4
Weybridge KT13 53 B5
Elgin Way GU16 85 F8
Eliot Bank SE23, SE26 23 B6
Eliot Bank Prim Sch SE23 23 B6
Eliot Cl GU15 66 B7
Eliot Dr GU27 207 E6
Eliot House 10 TW10 6 F1
Elizabeth Ave
Bagshot GU19 47 F2
Staines TW18 13 D2
Elizabeth Cl Bracknell RG12 27 C5
Cheam SM1 58 F8
Farncombe GU7 150 E7
Elizabeth Cotts 5 TW9 7 A6
Elizabeth Cres RH19 185 F3
Elizabeth Ct Horley RH6 161 A3
Sunbury TW16 35 C6
Teddington TW11 16 E3
West Barnes SM4 39 E2
Whyteleafe CR3 80 F1
Elizabeth Gdns Ascot SL5 29 B4
Sunbury TW16 35 C6
Elizabeth Hart Ct KT13 52 F5
Elizabeth House CR3 101 A3
Elizabeth Rd
Farncombe GU7 150 E7
Wokingham RG40 25 D6
Elizabeth Way
Feltham TW13 15 C4
South Norwood SE19 22 D1
Elizabethan Cl TW19 13 D8
Elizabethan Way
Crawley RH10 202 C5
Stanwell TW19 13 D8
Elkins Gdns GU4 110 A4
Ellacombe House 1 SW2 22 A8
Elland Rd KT12 54 D8
Ellenborough Cl RG12 27 D8
Ellenbridge Way CR2 61 E2
Elleray Ct GU12 106 A5
Elleray Rd TW11 16 F2
Ellerdine Rd TW3 5 D3
Ellerker Gdns TW10 6 E1
Ellerman Ave TW2, TW4 15 F7
Ellerslie Ct 6 SM6 60 B4
Ellerton Rd Surbiton KT6 37 F1
Wandsworth SW17, SW18 20 D7
Wimbledon SW20 19 A1
Ellery Cl GU6 174 E1
Ellery Rd SE19 22 D1

Elles Ave GU1 . . . . .110 C1
Elles Cl GU14 . . . . .85 B3
Elles Rd GU14 . . . . .84 F2
Ellesfield Ave RG12 . . . . . .26 E5
Ellesmere Ave BR3 . . . . . . .44 B7
Ellesmere Ct Chiswick W4 . . .7 D8
Penge SE20 . . . . .43 B7
Weybridge KT12 . . . . .53 E4
Ellesmere Dr CR2 . . . . .81 B5
Ellesmere Pl KT12 . . . . .53 E5
Ellesmere Rd
Twickenham TW1 . . . . .6 C1
Weybridge KT13 . . . . .53 E4
Ellice Rd RH8 . . . . .122 F6
Ellies Mews TW15 . . . . .13 E6
Ellingham GU22 . . . . .89 E8
Ellingham Prim Sch KT9 . .56 D3
Ellingham Rd KT9 . . . . .56 D4
Ellington Rd Feltham TW13 . .14 F4
Hounslow TW3 . . . . .5 B5
Ellington Way KT18 . . . . . . .77 B2
Elliot Cl RH10 . . . . .202 C4
Elliot Park GU12 . . . . .105 E2
Elliot Rise SL5 . . . . .28 D7
Elliott Ct GU21 . . . . .70 A3
Elliott Gdns TW17 . . . . .34 A5
Elliott Rd CR7 . . . . .42 B5
Ellis Ave GU2 . . . . .129 F7
Ellis Cl CR5 . . . . .99 F7
Ellis Farm Cl GU22 . . . . . . .89 D5
Ellis Rd Coulsdon CR5 . . . . .99 F7
Crowthorne RG45 . . . . . . .45 B6
Mitcham CR4 . . . . .40 F3
Ellisfield Dr SW15 . . . . .19 A8
Ellison Rd Barnes SW13 . . . . .7 F5
Streatham SW16 . . . . .21 E1
Ellison Way
Tongham GU10 . . . . .126 F7
Wokingham RG40 . . . . . . .25 B6
Ellman Rd RH11 . . . . .200 F4
Ellora Rd SW16 . . . . .21 D3
Ellson Cl RH10 . . . . .202 C4
Ellswood Ct [18] KT6 . . . . . .37 D2
Elm Bank Gdns SW13 . . . . . .7 E5
Elm Bank Mansions SW13 . .7 E5
Elm Bridge La GU22 . . . . . .90 A8
Elm Cl Box Hill KT20 . . . . .116 C5
Carshalton SM5 . . . . .40 F1
Leatherhead KT22 . . . . . . .95 B5
Send Marsh GU23 . . . . . . .91 A3
South Croydon CR2 . . . . . .61 E4
Stanwell TW19 . . . . .13 D7
Tolworth KT5 . . . . .38 C2
Twickenham TW13, TW2 . . .16 B6
Warlingham CR6 . . . . .81 D2
West Barnes SW20 . . . . . .39 C5
Woking GU21 . . . . .69 D4
Elm Cotts RH5 . . . . .115 C8
Elm Court Sch SE27 . . . . . .22 C6
Elm Cres Heath End GU9 . .125 D7
Kingston u T KT2 . . . . . . .37 E8
Elm Ct Catford SE6 . . . . . . .24 B7
[5] Charlton TW16 . . . . . .14 F1
Knaphill GU21 . . . . .68 D2
Mitcham CR4 . . . . .40 F7
Sandhurst GU47 . . . . .45 E2
Elm Dr Chobham GU24 . . . . .49 F1
East Grinstead RH19 . . . . .186 A1
Leatherhead KT22 . . . . . . .95 B4
Sunbury TW16 . . . . .35 C7
Winkfield SL4 . . . . .9 B7
Elm Gdns Burgh Heath KT18 .97 C8
Claygate KT10 . . . . .55 F4
Mitcham CR4 . . . . .41 D5
Elm Gr Bisley GU24 . . . . . . .68 A3
Caterham CR3 . . . . .100 E5
Cranleigh GU6 . . . . .174 A3
Epsom KT18 . . . . .76 C5
Heath End GU9 . . . . .125 D7
Horsham RH13 . . . . .217 E1
Kingston u T KT2 . . . . . . .37 E8
Sutton SM1 . . . . .59 B6
Wimbledon SW19 . . . . . . .19 E1
Elm Grove Par SM6 . . . . . . .60 A7
Elm Grove Rd
Cobham KT11 . . . . .73 D3
Farnborough GU14 . . . . . .85 B4
Elm Hill Bglws GU3 . . . . . .106 E3
Elm House [2] KT2 . . . . . . .17 F1
Elm La Ash GU10 . . . . .126 F8
Forest Hill SE6 . . . . .23 F6
Ockham GU23 . . . . .92 A4
Elm Park Rd SE25 . . . . .42 F6
Elm Pk Streatham SW2 . . . . .21 F8
Sunningdale GU20, SL5 . . .29 E1
Elm Pl GU11 . . . . .126 C8
Elm Rd Beckenham BR3 . . . . .43 F7
Carshalton CR4, SM6 . . . . .41 A1
Chessington KT9 . . . . .56 E6
Claygate KT10 . . . . .55 F4
East Bedfont TW14 . . . . . . .14 D8
Farncombe GU7 . . . . .150 D4
Heath End GU9 . . . . .125 D7
Kingston u T KT2 . . . . . . .37 F8
Kingston u T KT3 . . . . . . .38 D6
Leatherhead KT22 . . . . . . .95 B5
Mortlake SW14 . . . . .7 C3
Purley CR8 . . . . .80 B6
Redhill RH1 . . . . .118 E1
South Norwood CR7 . . . . . .42 D5
Stoneleigh KT17 . . . . .57 F4
Warlingham CR6 . . . . .81 D2
Woking GU21 . . . . .69 D1
Woking, Horsell GU21 . . . .69 F4
Elm Rd W SM4 . . . . .39 F2

Elm Tree Ave KT10 . . . . .36 E2
Elm Tree Cl
Addlestone KT16 . . . . .51 E8
Ashford TW15 . . . . .14 B3
Elm View GU12 . . . . .106 B3
Elm Way North Cheam KT4 . .58 C7
West Ewell KT19 . . . . .57 D5
Elm Wlk SW20 . . . . .39 D5
Elm Wood Prim Sch SE27 .22 D5
Elmbank Ave
Englefield Green TW20 . . . .11 B2
Guildford GU2 . . . . .130 A8
Elmbourne Rd SW17 . . . . . .21 B5
Elmbridge Ave KT5 . . . . . . .38 C3
Elmbridge Cotts GU6 . . . . .174 B3
Elmbridge La GU22 . . . . . . .89 F8
Elmbridge Rd GU6 . . . . . . .173 F2
Elmbrook Cl TW16 . . . . .35 B8
Elmbrook Rd SM1 . . . . .58 F6
Elmcourt Rd SE21, SE27 . . . .22 B6
Elmcroft
Little Bookham KT23 . . . . .94 A3
[12] Woking GU21 . . . . . . .69 E1
Elmcroft Cl Chessington KT9 56 E7
Feltham TW14 . . . . .3 F1
Frimley GU16 . . . . .85 F7
Elmcroft Dr Ashford TW15 . .14 A3
Chessington KT9 . . . . .56 E7
Elmdene KT5 . . . . .38 C1
Elmdene Cl BR3 . . . . .43 F4
Elmdon Rd Hatton TW6 . . . . .3 F4
Hounslow TW5 . . . . .4 E5
Elmer Cotts KT22 . . . . .95 A4
Elmer Gdns TW7 . . . . .5 D4
Elmer Mews KT22 . . . . .95 A5
Elmer Rd SE6 . . . . .24 C8
Elmer's Dr TW11 . . . . .17 B2
Elmers End Rd
Beckenham BR3 . . . . .43 D5
Penge BR3, SE20 . . . . . . .43 C6
Elmers End Sta BR3 . . . . . .43 D5
Elmers Rd
Croydon CR0, SE25 . . . . . .43 A2
Ockley RH5 . . . . .177 C4
Elmerside Rd BR3 . . . . .43 E5
Elmfield KT23 . . . . .94 A4
Elmfield Ave Mitcham CR4 . .41 A8
Teddington TW11 . . . . . . .16 F3
Elmfield House GU4 . . . . . .110 C3
Elmfield Mansions [5]
SW17 . . . . .21 A6
Elmfield Rd SW17 . . . . .21 B6
Elmfield Way CR2 . . . . .61 F2
Elmgate Ave TW13 . . . . .15 C5
Elmgrove Cl GU21 . . . . .88 D8
Elmgrove Rd Croydon CR0 . .43 B2
Weybridge KT13 . . . . .53 A7
Elmhurst Ave CR4 . . . . .21 A1
Elmhurst Ballet Sch GU15 65 D5
Elmhurst Ct Croydon CR0 . .61 D5
Guildford GU1 . . . . .130 F8
Elmhurst Dr RH4 . . . . .136 B5
Elmhurst Lodge SM2 . . . . . .59 C3
Elmhurst Sch for Boys
CR2 . . . . .61 D5
Elmore Rd CR5 . . . . .99 A6
Elmpark Gdns CR2 . . . . . . .62 C1
Elms Cotts CR4 . . . . .40 F7
Elms Ct SW19 . . . . .20 B1
Elms Rd Aldershot GU11 . . .105 A2
Wokingham RG40 . . . . . . .25 B5
Elms The Ash GU10 . . . . . .126 F8
Ashford TW15 . . . . .14 A3
Claygate KT10 . . . . .55 F3
Croydon CR0 . . . . .42 C1
Mortlake SW13 . . . . .7 F4
Elmscott Rd BR1 . . . . .24 F3
Elmshorn KT17 . . . . .77 C3
Elmside Guildford GU2 . . . .130 A8
Milford GU8 . . . . .149 F1
New Addington CR0 . . . . . .63 B4
Elmsleigh Ct SM1 . . . . .59 B7
Elmsleigh Ctr The TW18 . .12 F4
Elmsleigh House TW2 . . . . .16 D6
Elmsleigh Rd
Farnborough GU14 . . . . . .84 F4
Staines TW18 . . . . .12 F3
Twickenham TW2 . . . . . . .16 D6
Elmslie Cl KT18 . . . . .76 C5
Elmstead RH19 . . . . .205 E8
Elmstead Cl KT19 . . . . .57 E5
Elmstead Gdns KT4 . . . . . . .58 A7
Elmstead Rd KT14 . . . . .71 A5
Elmsway TW15 . . . . .14 A3
Elmswood KT23 . . . . .93 F3
Elmsworth Ave TW3 . . . . .5 B5
Elmtree Cl KT14 . . . . .71 E6
Elmtree Rd TW11 . . . . .16 E3
Elmwood Ave TW13 . . . . . . .15 A5
Elmwood Cl Ashstead KT21 75 D2
Hackbridge SM6 . . . . .60 B8
Stoneleigh KT17 . . . . .58 A3
Elmwood Ct KT21 . . . . .75 D2
Elmwood Dr KT17 . . . . .58 A3
Elmwood Inf Sch CR0 . . . . .42 B3
Elmwood Jun Sch CR0 . . . .42 B2
Elmwood Rd Chiswick W4 . . .7 C8
Knaphill GU21 . . . . .88 D8
Mitcham CR4 . . . . .40 F6
Redhill RH1 . . . . .119 B5
Thornton Heath CR0 . . . . .42 B2
Elmworth Gr SE21 . . . . .22 D6
Elphinstone Cl SW16 . . . . . .21 E2
Elsdon Rd GU21 . . . . .69 A1
Elsenham St SW18, SW19 . .19 F6
Elsenwood Cres GU15 . . . . .66 A6
Elsenwood Dr GU15 . . . . . . .66 A7
Elsinore Ave TW19 . . . . .13 E8

Elsinore Rd SE23 . . . . .23 E7
Elsinore Way TW9 . . . . .7 B4
Elsley Cl GU16 . . . . .85 F6
Elsrick Ave SM4 . . . . .40 A4
Elstan Way CR0 . . . . .43 E2
Elstead Ct SM4 . . . . .39 E1
Elstead Gn GU8 . . . . .148 D4
Elstead House [12] SW2 . . . .21 F8
Elstead Rd Milford GU8 . . . .149 C3
Seale GU10 . . . . .127 B3
Shackleford GU7, GU8 . . . .149 E6
The Sands GU10 . . . . . . .127 A2
Elsted Cl RH11 . . . . .201 B8
Elston Pl GU12 . . . . .126 C8
Elston Rd GU11, GU12 . . . .126 C8
Elstree Hill BR1 . . . . .24 E1
Elsworth Cl TW14 . . . . .14 E7
Elsworthy KT7 . . . . .36 E3
Elthorne Ct TW13 . . . . .15 C7
Elton Rd Kingston u T KT2 . .38 A8
Purley CR8 . . . . .79 C7
Elveden Cl GU22 . . . . .71 B2
Elveden Ct RH12 . . . . .95 C6
Elveden Rd KT11 . . . . .73 C8
Elvington Gn BR2 . . . . .44 F4
Elvino Rd SE26 . . . . .23 E3
Elwell Cl TW20 . . . . .12 A2
Elwill Way BR3 . . . . .44 D5
Ely Cl Crawley RH10 . . . . . .201 F2
Frimley GU16 . . . . .86 A7
Kingston u T SW20 . . . . . .38 F7
Ely Ct KT1 . . . . .38 A6
Ely House [7] RH1 . . . . . . .118 F1
Ely Rd Hatton TW6 . . . . .3 F3
Hounslow TW4 . . . . .4 C4
Thornton Heath CR0 . . . . .42 D4
Elystan Cl SM6 . . . . .60 C2
Embankment The
Twickenham TW1 . . . . . . .17 A7
Wraysbury TW19 . . . . .11 C7
Embassy Ct
Kingston u T KT6 . . . . . . .37 D4
[7] Wallington SM6 . . . . . .60 B4
Embassy Gdns BR3 . . . . . . .43 F8
Ember Cl KT15 . . . . .52 D5
Ember Ctr KT12 . . . . .54 E8
Ember Farm Ave KT8 . . . . . .36 D3
Ember Farm Way KT8 . . . . . .36 D3
Ember Gdns KT10, KT8 . . . .36 E2
Ember House BR1 . . . . .24 D3
Ember La KT10, KT8 . . . . . .36 D2
Embercourt
Rd KT10, KT7, KT8 . . . . . .36 E3
Emberwood RH11 . . . . .201 D8
Embleton Rd GU35 . . . . . . .187 B6
Embleton Wlk TW12 . . . . . . .15 F3
Emerton Rd KT22 . . . . .94 C6
Emery Down Cl RG12 . . . . . .28 A6
Emley Rd KT15 . . . . .52 B6
Emlyn La KT22 . . . . .95 A5
Emlyn Rd Horley RH6 . . . . .160 E4
Redhill RH1 . . . . .140 A7
Emmanuel Cl GU2 . . . . . . .109 B8
Emmanuel House SE21 . . . .22 D5
Emmanuel Rd SW12 . . . . . .21 D7
Emmbrook Rd RG41 . . . . . . .25 A8
Emmbrook Sch The RG41 25 A8
Emmeline Ct KT12 . . . . .35 C2
Emmetts Cl GU21 . . . . .69 D2
Empire Villas RH1 . . . . . . .161 B7
Empress Ave GU14 . . . . .85 B5
Emsworth Cl RH10 . . . . . . .202 C3
Emsworth St SW2 . . . . .21 F6
Ena Rd SW16 . . . . .41 E6
Endale Cl SM5 . . . . .59 F8
Endeavour Way
Wallington CR0 . . . . .41 E2
Wimbledon SW19 . . . . . . .20 B4
Enderley House SE19 . . . . . .42 F8
Enderley Rd KT5 . . . . .38 B2
Endlesham Ct [3] SW12 . . . .21 A8
Endlesham Rd SW12 . . . . . .21 A8
Endsleigh Cl CR2 . . . . .62 C1
Endsleigh Gdns
Hersham KT12 . . . . .54 C5
Kingston u T KT6 . . . . . . .37 C3
Endsleigh Mansions [4]
SW16 . . . . .21 E5
Endsleigh Rd RH1 . . . . . . .119 C6
Endway KT5 . . . . .38 B2
Enfield Rd Ash GU12 . . . . .106 B5
Crawley RH11 . . . . .201 C2
Harlington TW6 . . . . .3 E5
Enfield Road Rdbt TW6 . . . . .3 E5
Engadine Cl CR0 . . . . .61 F7
Engadine St SW18 . . . . .20 A7
Engalee RH19 . . . . .185 C2
Englefield RH12 . . . . .216 F2
Englefield Cl
Englefield Green TW20 . . . .11 C2
Thornton Heath CR0 . . . . .42 C3
Englefield Green Cty Inf
Sch TW20 . . . . .11 C3
Englefield Rd GU21 . . . . . . .68 D2
Engleheart Dr TW14 . . . . .3 F1
Engleheart Rd SE6 . . . . .24 C8
Englehurst TW20 . . . . .11 C2
Englemere Pk SL5 . . . . .28 D5
Englemere Pond Nature
Trail SL5 . . . . .28 C6
Englesfield GU15 . . . . .66 D5
Engliff La GU22 . . . . .71 A3
Enid Wood House RG12 . . . .27 C7
Enmore Ave SE25 . . . . .43 A4
Enmore Gdns SW14 . . . . .7 D2
Enmore Rd SE25 . . . . .43 A4
Ennerdale RG12 . . . . .27 A5
Ennerdale Cl Cheam SM1 . . .58 F6
Crawley RH11 . . . . .201 B4

Ennerdale Cl continued
East Bedfont TW14 . . . . . . .14 F7
Ennerdale Gr GU9 . . . . . . .125 A6
Ennerdale Rd TW9 . . . . .6 F5
Ennismore Ave GU1 . . . . . .109 F1
Ennismore Gdns KT7 . . . . . .36 E3
Ennor Ct SM4 . . . . .58 C6
Ensham Sch SW17 . . . . .20 F3
Ensham Sec Sch (Annexe)
SW17 . . . . .20 E4
Ensign Cl Purley CR8 . . . . . .61 A1
Stanwell TW19 . . . . .13 D7
Ensign Way TW19 . . . . .13 D7
Enterdent Cotts RH9 . . . . .121 D2
Enterdent Rd RH9 . . . . . . .121 D2
Enterprise Cl CR0 . . . . .42 A1
Enterprise Est GU1 . . . . . .109 E5
Enterprise House KT12 . . . . .35 B2
Enterprise Way TW11 . . . . . .16 F2
Envis Way GU3 . . . . .108 C4
Eothen Cl CR3 . . . . .101 A3
Epping Way RG12 . . . . .27 F5
Epping Wlk RH10 . . . . .201 F4
Epsom Cl GU15 . . . . .65 C8
Epsom Coll KT17 . . . . .77 A5
Epsom Cty Prim Sch KT19 .76 E8
Epsom Downs Cty Inf Sch
KT20 . . . . .96 D8
Epsom Downs Metro Ctr
KT20 . . . . .97 B7
Epsom Downs Sta KT17 . . . .77 B4
Epsom & Ewell High Sch
KT19 . . . . .57 C5
Epsom General Hospl
KT18 . . . . .76 C4
Epsom La N KT18, KT20 . . . .97 B7
Epsom La S KT20 . . . . .97 C5
Epsom Pl GU6 . . . . .174 F3
Epsom Rd
Ashtead KT18, KT21 . . . . .76 A2
Cheam SM4 . . . . .39 F2
Crawley RH10 . . . . .202 A4
Croydon CR0 . . . . .61 A6
East Clandon GU4 . . . . . .111 D3
Ewell KT17 . . . . .76 F8
Guildford GU4 . . . . .110 F2
Guildford GU1 . . . . .130 F8
Guildford, Merrow
GU1, GU4 . . . . .110 C1
Leatherhead KT22 . . . . . . .95 C6
Morden SM4 . . . . .39 F2
West Clandon GU4 . . . . . .111 D3
West Horsley GU4, KT24 . .112 C6
Epsom Sq TW6 . . . . .3 F5
Epsom Sta KT18 . . . . .76 D6
Epworth Rd TW7, TW8 . . . . . .6 B7
Eresby Dr BR3 . . . . .44 A1
Erica Cl GU24 . . . . .67 E6
Erica Ct GU22 . . . . .69 D1
Erica Dr RG40 . . . . .25 D5
Erica Gdns CR0 . . . . .63 B7
Erica Way Copthorne RH10 183 A2
Horsham RH12 . . . . .217 D5
Eridge Cl RH10 . . . . .202 C6
Erin Cl BR1 . . . . .24 E1
Erindale Ct BR3 . . . . .44 A8
Eriswell Cres KT12 . . . . .53 F4
Eriswell Rd KT12 . . . . .53 F5
Erkenwald Cl KT16 . . . . . . .32 E3
Ermine Cl TW4 . . . . .4 C5
Ermyn Cl KT21 . . . . .95 D6
Ermyn Way KT21, KT22 . . . .95 D6
Erncroft Way TW1 . . . . .5 F1
Ernest Ave SE27 . . . . .22 B4
Ernest Bevin Sch SW17 . . . .20 E6
Ernest Cotts KT17 . . . . .57 F3
Ernest Gdns W4 . . . . .7 B8
Ernest Gr BR3 . . . . .43 F4
Ernest Rd KT1 . . . . .38 B7
Ernest Sq KT1 . . . . .38 B7
Ernle Rd SW20 . . . . .19 C1
Erridge Rd SW19 . . . . .40 A7
Errol Gdns KT3 . . . . .39 A5
Erskine Cl Carshalton SM1 . .59 E7
Crawley RH11 . . . . .200 E2
Erskine Rd SM1, SM5 . . . . . .59 D7
Esam Way SE27, SW16 . . . . .22 A3
Escombe Dr GU2, GU3 . . . .109 B6
Escot Rd TW16 . . . . .14 E1
Escott Pl KT16 . . . . .51 D4
Esher Ave Cheam SM3 . . . . . .58 D7
Walton-on-T KT12 . . . . . . .35 A1
Esher Church Sch KT10 . . . .55 C5
Esher Cl KT10 . . . . .55 B5
Esher Coll KT7 . . . . .36 E2
Esher Cres TW6 . . . . .3 F5
Esher Gdns SW19 . . . . .19 D6
Esher Gn KT10 . . . . .55 B6
Esher Green Dr KT10 . . . . . .55 B7
Esher Mews CR4 . . . . .40 F6
Esher Park Ave KT10 . . . . . .55 C5
Esher Place Ave KT10 . . . . .55 B6
Esher Rd
Camberley GU15 . . . . .47 A1
East Molesey KT8 . . . . . . .36 D4
Hersham KT10, KT12 . . . . .54 E6
Esher Sta KT10 . . . . .55 D8

Essendene Lodge Sch
CR3 . . . . .100 E4
Essendene Rd CR3 . . . . . . .100 E5
Essex Ave TW7 . . . . .5 E4
Essex Cl Addlestone KT15 . . .52 C6
Frimley GU16 . . . . .86 A7
West Barnes SM4 . . . . . . .39 D2
Essex Ct Barnes SW13 . . . . . .7 F5
South Norwood SE19 . . . . .22 D2
Essex Dr GU6 . . . . .173 F2
Essex Gr SE19 . . . . .22 D2
Essex House [5] CR0 . . . . . .61 D8
Essex Tower [5] SE20 . . . . . .43 B8
Estcots Cty Prim Sch
RH19 . . . . .186 A1
Estcots Dr RH19 . . . . .186 A1
Estcourt Rd CR0, SE25 . . . . .43 B3
Estella Ave KT3, SW20 . . . . .39 B5
Estoria Cl SW2 . . . . .22 A8
Estreham Rd SW16 . . . . .21 D2
Estridge Cl TW3 . . . . .5 A3
Eswyn Rd SW17 . . . . .20 F3
Ethel Rd TW15 . . . . .13 E3
Ethelbert Rd SW20 . . . . .39 D8
Ethelbert St SW12 . . . . .21 B7
Ethelworth Ct [4] SW2 . . . . .22 A7
Etherley Hill RH5 . . . . .177 A7
Etherow St SE22 . . . . .23 A8
Etherstone Gn SW16 . . . . . .22 A4
Etherstone Rd SW16 . . . . . .22 A4
Eton Ave Heston TW5 . . . . . . .5 A8
New Malden KT3 . . . . .38 D5
Eton Cl SW18 . . . . .20 B8
Eton Ct TW18 . . . . .12 F3
Eton Pl GU9 . . . . .125 B7
Eton Rd UB3 . . . . .3 F7
Eton St TW10 . . . . .6 E2
Ettrick Ct GU14 . . . . .105 B8
Etwell Pl KT5 . . . . .37 F3
Eureka Rd KT1 . . . . .38 A7
Europa Park Rd GU1 . . . . .109 C2
Eurythmy Sch RH19 . . . . . .205 E6
Eustace Cres RG40 . . . . . . .25 D8
Eustace Rd GU4 . . . . .110 D3
Euston Rd CR0 . . . . .42 A1
Evans Cl RH10 . . . . .202 D5
Evans Gr TW13 . . . . .16 A6
Evans Rd SE6 . . . . .24 E6
Eve Rd Isleworth TW7 . . . . . . .6 A3
Sheerwater GU21 . . . . . . .70 B4
Evedon RG12 . . . . .27 B2
Evelina Rd SE20 . . . . .23 D1
Eveline Rd CR4 . . . . .40 F8
Evelyn Ave GU11 . . . . .126 B8
Evelyn Cl Twickenham TW2 . .16 B8
Woking GU22 . . . . .89 D3
Evelyn Cotts
Abinger Common RH5 . . . .155 D8
South Godstone RH9 . . . .142 E6
Evelyn Cres TW16 . . . . .34 F8
Evelyn Ct CR0 . . . . .42 A2
Tyler's Green RH9 . . . . . .121 C5
Evelyn Gdns Richmond TW9 . .6 E3
Richmond, Ham TW10 . . . .17 C5
Evelyn Rd Richmond TW9 . . . .6 E4
Richmond, Ham TW10 . . . .17 C5
Wimbledon SW19 . . . . . . .20 B2
Evelyn Terr TW9 . . . . .6 E4
Evelyn Way
Stoke D'Abernon KT11 . . . .73 F3
Sunbury TW16 . . . . .34 F8
Wallington SM6 . . . . .60 D6
Evelyn Woods Rd GU11 . . . .105 C7
Evendon's Cl RG41 . . . . .25 A3
Evendon's La RG41 . . . . . . .25 A3
Evening Hill BR3 . . . . .24 C1
Evenlode Way GU47 . . . . . . .64 D8
Everard La CR3 . . . . .101 B5
Everest Ct
South Norwood SE19 . . . . .42 E8
Woking GU21 . . . . .68 E3
Everest Rd Camberley GU15 65 D8
Crowthorne RG45 . . . . . . .45 B6
Stanwell TW19 . . . . .13 E8
Everglade TN16 . . . . .83 D1
Everglades BR2 . . . . .44 E6
Evergreen Ct TW19 . . . . .13 D8
Evergreen Rd GU16 . . . . . . .66 A3
Evergreen Way TW19 . . . . . .13 D8
Evergreens The GU8 . . . . . .171 B1
Everlands Cl [6] GU22 . . . . . .69 E1
Eversfield Ct [2] RH2 . . . . .118 C1
Eversfield Rd
Horsham RH13 . . . . .217 E1
Reigate RH2 . . . . .118 B1
Richmond TW9 . . . . .6 F5
Eversley Cres TW7 . . . . .5 D6
Eversley Pk SW19 . . . . .19 B3
Eversley Rd
Kingston u T KT5 . . . . . . .37 F4
South Norwood SE19 . . . . .22 D1
Eversley Way Croydon CR0 . .63 A7
Thorpe TW20 . . . . .32 C7
Everton Rd CR0 . . . . .43 A1
Evesham Cl Belmont SM2 . . .59 A3
Reigate RH2 . . . . .117 F2
Evesham Gn SM4 . . . . .40 B3
Evesham Rd
Morden SM4 . . . . .40 B3
Reigate RH2 . . . . .117 F2
Evesham Rd N RH3 . . . . . . .117 F2
Evesham Wlk GU47 . . . . . . .45 D1
Ewart Rd SE23 . . . . .23 D8
Ewelands RH6 . . . . .161 C4
Ewell By-Pass KT17 . . . . . . .58 A2
Ewell Castle Sch KT17 . . . . .58 A2
Ewell Court Ave KT19 . . . . . .57 E5
Ewell Downs Rd KT17 . . . . . .58 B1
Ewell East Sta KT17 . . . . . . .58 B1

Ewell Grove Cty Inf Sch
 KT17 . . . . .57 F1
Ewell House KT17 . . . . .57 F1
Ewell House Gr KT17 . . . . . .57 F1
Ewell Park Gdns KT17 . . . . .58 A3
Ewell Park Way KT17 . . . . . .58 A3
Ewell Rd Cheam SM2, SM3 . .58 D4
 Surbiton KT5, KT6 . . . . .37 F2
 Thames Ditton KT6, KT7 . . . .37 B2
 Tolworth KT6 . . . . .38 B1
Ewell West Sta KT19 . . . . . .57 E2
Ewelme Rd SE23 . . . . .23 C7
Ewen Cres SW2 . . . . .22 A8
Ewhurst Ave CR2 . . . . .61 C2
Ewhurst C of E Fst Sch
 GU6 . . . . .175 E5
Ewhurst Cl Crawley RH11 . . .201 C6
 East Ewell SM2 . . . . .58 C2
Ewhurst Ct CR4 . . . . .40 D6
Ewhurst Rd Cranleigh GU6 .174 E3
 Crawley RH11 . . . . .201 C7
Ewhurst GU5, GU6 . . . . . . .154 E3
Ewins Cl GU12 . . . . .106 A2
Ewood La
 Beare Green RH5 . . . . .157 F6
 Parkgate RH5 . . . . .158 C6
Ewshot Hill Cross GU10 .124 D7
Exbury Rd SE6 . . . . .24 A6
Excalibur Cl RH11 . . . . . . .200 E5
Excelsior Cl KT1 . . . . .38 A7
Exchange Rd Ascot SL5 . . . .29 C4
 Crawley RH10 . . . . .201 E6
Exchange The 6 CR8 . . . . .80 A8
Exeforde Ave TW15 . . . . . . .14 A4
Exeter Cl RH10 . . . . .201 E2
Exeter Ct Kingston u T KT6 . .37 E4
 Mitcham SW19 . . . . .20 E1
Exeter House TW15 . . . . . . .16 A6
Exeter Rd Ash GU12 . . . . . .106 A3
 Croydon CR0 . . . . .42 F2
 Feltham TW13 . . . . .15 F5
 Harlington TW6 . . . . .3 E4
Exeter Way TW6 . . . . .3 E5
Explorer Ave TW19 . . . . . . .13 E7
Eyebright Cl CR0 . . . . .43 D1
Eyhurst Cl KT20 . . . . .97 F3
Eyhurst Spur KT20 . . . . .97 F3
Eyles Cl RH12 . . . . .217 B4
Eylewood Rd SE27 . . . . .22 C3
Eynella Rd SE21 . . . . .22 F8
Eyston Dr KT13 . . . . .53 A1

F

Fabyc House TW9 . . . . .7 A7
Factory Cotts GU10 . . . . . .124 D2
Factory La CR0, CR9 . . . . . .61 B8
Fagg's Rd Feltham TW14 . . . . .4 A2
 Hatton TW14 . . . . .4 A2
Fair Green Ct 1 CR4 . . . . .40 F6
Fair La CR5, RH2 . . . . .98 D1
Fair Oak Cl KT22 . . . . .74 D7
Fair St TW3 . . . . .5 C4
Fair View RH12 . . . . .217 A3
 Kingston u T KT3 . . . . .38 E6
Fairacres Hounslow TW7 . . . .5 D6
 Kingston u T KT3 . . . . .38 E6
Fairacres Burgh Heath KT20 97 C4
 Cobham KT11 . . . . .73 F7
 New Addington CR0 . . . . . . .62 F2
Fairbairn Cl CR8 . . . . .80 A6
Fairbourne KT11 . . . . .73 D6
Fairbourne Cl GU21 . . . . . . .69 A1
Fairbourne La CR3 . . . . . . .100 C4
Fairbourne Way GU2 . . . . .109 A4
Fairbriar Ct 9 RH11 . . . . . .76 E6
Fairchildes Ave CR0 . . . . . .82 D7
Fairchildes Cotts CR9 . .82 F6
Fairchildes Prim Sch CR9 .82 E7
Faircroft SE26 . . . . .23 C4
Fairdene CR5 . . . . .98 F6
Fairdene Rd CR5 . . . . .79 D2
Fairfax RG42 . . . . .27 A8
Fairfax Ave Ewell KT17 . . . . .58 B2
 Redhill RH1 . . . . .118 F2
Fairfax Cl KT12 . . . . .35 B1
Fairfax Mews GU14 . . . . . . .85 D2
Fairfax Rd
 Farnborough GU14 . . . . .85 C7
 Old Woking GU22 . . . . .90 B7
 Teddington TW11 . . . . .17 B1
Fairfield App TW19 . . . . . . .11 B7
Fairfield Ave Horley RH6 . . .161 A1
 Staines TW18 . . . . .12 F4
 Twickenham TW2 . . . . .16 B7
Fairfield Cl
 Great Bookham KT23 . . . . . .94 B1
 Mitcham SW19 . . . . .20 E1
 West Ewell KT19 . . . . .57 E5
Fairfield Ct RH4 . . . . .115 B1
Fairfield Dr Dorking RH4 . . .136 B8
 Frimley GU16 . . . . .65 E3
Fairfield E KT1 . . . . .37 E7
Fairfield Ind Est KT1 . . . . . .37 F6
Fairfield La GU24 . . . . .68 A7
Fairfield N KT1, KT2 . . . . . . .37 E7
Fairfield Path CR0, CR9 . . . .61 D7
Fairfield Pk KT11 . . . . .73 D5
Fairfield Pl KT1 . . . . .37 E6
Fairfield Rd
 Beckenham BR3 . . . . .44 A7
 East Grinstead RH19 . . . . .205 F8
 Kingston u T KT1 . . . . .37 E7
 Leatherhead KT22 . . . . .95 B6
 South Croydon CR0, CR9 . . .61 E7
Fairfield Rise GU2 . . . . . . .108 F2

Fairfield S KT1 . . . . .37 F7
Fairfield The GU9 . . . . . . .125 C2
Fairfield W KT1 . . . . .37 E7
Fairfield Way Coulsdon CR5 79 D5
 West Ewell KT19 . . . . .57 E5
Fairfield Wlk KT22 . . . . .95 B6
Fairfields SE6 . . . . .24 B8
Fairfields Rd TW3 . . . . .5 C4
Fairford SE6 . . . . .24 A7
Fairford Ave CR0 . . . . .43 D4
Fairford Cl Croydon CR0 . . . .43 D4
 Pyrford KT14 . . . . .70 F5
 Reigate RH2 . . . . .118 C3
Fairford Ct SM2 . . . . .59 B3
Fairford Gdns KT4 . . . . .57 F7
Fairgreen Rd CR7 . . . . .42 B4
Fairhaven TW20 . . . . .11 F3
Fairhaven Ave CR0 . . . . . . .43 D3
Fairhaven Ct Croydon CR2 . .61 C5
 1 Egham TW20 . . . . .11 F3
Fairhaven Rd RH1 . . . . . . .119 A5
Fairholme
 East Bedfont TW14 . . . . . . .14 E8
 2 New Malden KT3 . . . . . .38 E5
Fairholme Cres CR3 . . . . . .75 C2
Fairholme Gdns GU9 . . . . .125 C1
Fairholme Jun & Inf Schs
 TW14 . . . . .14 D7
Fairholme Rd
 Ashford TW15 . . . . .13 F3
 Cheam SM1 . . . . .58 F4
 Thornton Heath CR0 . . . . . .42 A2
Fairings The KT12 . . . . .54 B6
Fairlands Ave
 Little Bookham KT23 . . . . . .93 F3
 Weybridge KT13 . . . . .53 E5
Fairlands GU3 . . . . .108 C5
 Sutton SM1 . . . . .59 A8
 Thornton Heath CR7 . . . . . .42 A4
Fairlands Ct GU3 . . . . .108 C5
Fairlands Rd GU3 . . . . .108 D5
Fairlawn
 Little Bookham KT23 . . . . . .93 F3
 Weybridge KT13 . . . . .53 E5
Fairlawn Cl Claygate KT10 . .55 F4
 Feltham TW13 . . . . .15 F4
 Kingston u T KT2 . . . . .18 C2
Fairlawn Cres RH19 . . . . . .185 B2
Fairlawn Dr
 East Grinstead RH19 . . . . .185 B2
 Redhill RH1 . . . . .139 E7
 Reigate RH1 . . . . .139 E7
Fairlawn Gr SM7 . . . . .78 D6
Fairlawn Pk Forest Hill SE26 23 E3
 Woking GU21 . . . . .69 E4
Fairlawn Prim Sch SE23 .23 C8
Fairlawn Prim Sch
 Annexe SE23 . . . . .23 C7
Fairlawn Rd Merton SW19 . .19 F1
 Sutton SM2, SM5 . . . . .78 C8
Fairlawnes SM6 . . . . .60 B5
Fairlawns Addlestone KT15 .52 B5
 Guildford GU1 . . . . .110 C1
 Horley RH6 . . . . .161 B2
 Sunbury TW16 . . . . .35 A6
 Twickenham TW1 . . . . .6 C1
 Woodham KT15 . . . . .70 F8
Fairlawns Cl TW18 . . . . . . .13 B2
Fairleas BR3 . . . . .44 B7
Fairlie Gdns SE23 . . . . .23 C8
Fairlight TW12 . . . . .16 B3
Fairlight Cl KT4 . . . . .58 C6
Fairlight Rd SW17 . . . . .20 D4
Fairline Ct BR3 . . . . .44 C7
Fairlop Wlk GU6 . . . . .173 F2
Fairmead Tolworth KT5, KT6 38 B1
 Woking GU21 . . . . .69 C1
Fairmead Cl Heston TW5 . . . .4 D7
 Kingston u T KT3 . . . . .38 D6
 Sandhurst GU47 . . . . .64 E7
Fairmead Rd CR0 . . . . .42 A2
Fairmeads KT11 . . . . .73 F6
Fairmile Ave Cobham KT11 . .73 F6
 Streatham SW16 . . . . .21 D3
Fairmile Hts KT11 . . . . .74 A6
Fairmile La KT11 . . . . .73 E5
Fairmile Park Copse KT11 .73 F6
Fairmile Park Rd KT11 . . . .73 F6
Fairoak Cl CR8 . . . . .80 B4
Fairoak La
 Chessington KT9, KT22, KT10 75 B8
 Oxshott KT10, KT22, KT9 . . .74 E8
Fairoaks Airport GU24 . . . .50 E1
Fairoaks Ct KT15 . . . . .52 B5
Fairs Rd KT22 . . . . .95 A8
Fairstone Ct RH6 . . . . .161 B4
Fairview KT17 . . . . .77 E8
Fairview Ave GU22 . . . . . . .69 F1
Fairview Cl Forest Hill SE26 .23 E3
 Woking GU22 . . . . .69 F1
Fairview Cotts GU25 . . . . . .31 D3
Fairview Ct Ashford TW15 . . .14 A3
 Kingston u T KT2 . . . . .38 B8
 Staines TW18 . . . . .13 A2
Fairview Dr TW17 . . . . .33 F4
Fairview Gdns GU9 . . . . . .125 D6
Fairview House 17 SW2 . . .21 F8
Fairview Pl SW2 . . . . .21 F8
Fairview Rd Ash GU12 . . . .106 B3
 Carshalton SM1, SM5 . . . . .59 E5
 Ewell KT17 . . . . .76 F8
 Headley Down GU35 . . . . . .187 C5
 Thornton Heath SW16 . . . . .41 F8
 Wokingham RG40 . . . . .25 C5
Fairview Terr 187 A6
Fairwater Dr KT15 . . . . .52 D2
Fairwater House TW11 . . . .17 A4
Fairway Chertsey KT16 . . . . .33 B1
 Copthorne RH10 . . . . .183 B2
 Crawley RH11 . . . . .200 D4

Fairway continued
 Guildford GU1 . . . . .110 D1
 Sutton SM5 . . . . .78 C8
 West Barnes SW20 . . . . . . .39 C6
Fairway Cl
 Copthorne RH10 . . . . .183 A2
 Croydon BR3, CR0 . . . . . . .43 E4
 Hounslow TW4 4
 West Ewell KT19 . . . . .57 C6
 Woking GU23 . . . . .89 B7
Fairway Cty Inf Sch RH10 183 B3
Fairway Est TW4 . . . . .4 C2
Fairway Gdns BR3 . . . . .44 D3
Fairway Hts GU15 . . . . .66 B6
Fairway The
 East Molesey KT8 . . . . .36 B6
 Frimley GU15 . . . . .66 A3
 Godalming GU7 . . . . .150 F2
 Heath End GU9 . . . . .125 D7
 Kingston u T KT3 . . . . .38 D8
 Leatherhead KT22 . . . . .75 A1
 Pirbright GU22, GU24 . . . . .88 C3
 Weybridge KT13 . . . . .72 A8
Fairways Ashford TW15 . . . .14 B2
 Beacon Hill GU26 . . . . .188 B6
 Kenley CR8 . . . . .80 C2
 Teddington TW11 . . . . .17 D1
Fairways The RH1 . . . . .139 D6
Fairwell La KT24 . . . . .112 F7
Fairwyn Rd SE26 . . . . .23 E4
Fakenham Way GU47 . . . . . .45 D2
Falaise TW20 . . . . .11 F3
Falaise Cl GU11 . . . . .105 B3
Falcon Cl Chiswick W4 . . . . . .7 C8
 Crawley RH11 . . . . .201 D8
 Lightwater GU18 . . . . .66 F8
Falcon Ct Frimley GU16 . . . .65 D1
 Sheerwater GU21 . . . . .70 C6
 8 West Norwood SE21 . . . .22 D6
Falcon Dr TW19 . . . . .2 E1
Falcon Rd Guildford GU1 . . .109 D1
 Hampton TW12 . . . . .15 F1
Falcon Way Feltham TW14 . . .4 B2
 Sunbury TW16 . . . . .34 E7
Falcon Wood KT22 . . . . . . .94 F8
Falconhurst 4
 Kingston u T KT6 . . . . .37 E4
 Oxshott KT22 . . . . .74 D4
Falconry Ct KT1 . . . . .37 E6
Falcons Cl TN16 . . . . .83 D2
Falconwood
 East Horsley KT24 . . . . .92 F3
 Englefield Green TW20 . . . . .11 E3
Falconwood Rd CR0 . . . . . .63 A3
Falcourt Cl SM1 . . . . .59 B5
Falkland Ct GU14 . . . . .105 E8
Falkland Gr RH4 . . . . .136 A6
Falkland House SE6 . . . . . .24 C4
Falkland Park Ave SE25 . .42 E7
Falkland Rd RH4 . . . . .136 A6
Falklands Dr RH13 . . . . . . .218 B4
Falkner Rd GU9 . . . . .125 B2
Fallow Deer Cl RH13 . . . . .218 B4
Fallowfield Way RH6 . . . . . .161 B4
Fallsbrook Rd SW16 . . . . . .21 C2
Falmer Cl RH11 . . . . .201 D4
Falmouth Cl GU15 . . . . .66 A4
Falmouth Rd KT12 . . . . .54 C6
Falstone GU21 . . . . .69 B1
Fambridge Cl SE26 . . . . . . .23 F4
Famet Ave CR8 . . . . .80 C6
Famet Cl CR8 . . . . .80 C6
Famet Gdns CR8 . . . . .80 C5
Famet Wlk CR8 . . . . .80 C6
Fanchford Rd RH2 . . . . . . .117 C1
Fanes Cl RG42 . . . . .26 E8
Fanfare The GU22 . . . . .70 C4
Fanshawe Rd TW10 . . . . . . .17 C4
Faraday Ave RH19 . . . . . . .205 F6
Faraday Ct RH10 . . . . .181 F2
Faraday Ctr The RH10 . . . .181 F1
Faraday House
 2 Balham SW12 . . . . .21 B8
 5 Hampton TW12 . . . . .15 F1
Faraday Rd Crawley RH10 .181 F2
 East Molesey KT8 . . . . .36 A5
 Farnborough GU14 . . . . . . .85 C6
 Wimbledon SW19 . . . . .20 B2
Faraday Way CR0, CR9 . . . .41 F1
Farcrosse Cl GU47 . . . . .64 C8
Fareham House 18 SW15 .19 A7
Fareham Rd TW14 . . . . .15 C8
Farewell Pl CR4 . . . . .40 E8
Farhalls Cres RH12 . . . . . .217 F6
Faringdon Cl GU47 . . . . . . .45 C1
Faringdon Dr RG12 . . . . . . .27 D4
Farington Acres KT13 . . . . .53 D7
Faris Barn Dr KT15 . . . . . . .70 F8
Faris La KT15 . . . . .70 F8
Farleigh Ave BR2 . . . . .44 F2
Farleigh Court Rd CR6 . . . . .82 B5
Farleigh Ct Croydon CR2 . . .61 C5
 2 Guildford GU1 . . . . .108 E1
Farleigh Cty Prim
 Sch CR6 . . . . .81 E2
Farleigh Dean Cres CR0 . . .82 B8
Farleigh House 7 KT2 . . . .18 B2
Farleigh Rd
 Warlingham CR6 . . . . .81 E2
 Woodham KT15 . . . . .71 A8
Farleton Cl KT13 . . . . .53 D4
Farley Copse RG42 . . . . . . .26 E8
Farley Croft BR2 . . . . .44 E7
Farley Ct GU14 . . . . .85 C7
Farley Heath Rd GU5 . . . . .153 C6
Farley House SE26 . . . . . . .23 B5
Farley Moor RG42 . . . . .26 D8

Farley Pk RH8 . . . . .122 D5
Farley Pl SE25 . . . . .43 A5
Farley Rd Lewisham SE6 . . . .24 C8
 South Croydon CR2 . . . . . . .62 B2
Farleycroft 1 CR0 . . . . .43 A1
Farlington Pl SW15 . . . . . . .19 B8
Farlington Sch RH12 . . . . .216 B6
Farlton Rd SW18 . . . . .20 B8
Farm App RH9 . . . . .163 C5
Farm Ave Horsham RH12 . . .217 B3
 Streatham SW16 . . . . .21 E4
Farm Cl Ascot SL5 . . . . .29 C4
 Bracknell RG42 . . . . .26 F8
 Byfleet KT14 . . . . .71 F7
 Chertsey KT16 . . . . .32 A3
 Coney Hall BR4 . . . . .63 F7
 Crawley RH10 . . . . .202 A7
 Crowthorne RG45 . . . . .45 C7
 East Grinstead RH19 . . . . .206 B8
 East Horsley KT24 . . . . . . .112 F4
 Egham TW18 . . . . .12 E3
 Fairlands GU3 . . . . .108 C6
 Fetcham KT22 . . . . .94 E3
 Guildford GU1 . . . . .109 D4
 Lower Halliford TW17 . . . . . .34 A2
 Loxwood RH14 . . . . .213 A3
 Sutton SM2 . . . . .59 D3
 Wallington SM6 . . . . .60 C1
 Warnham RH12 . . . . .216 F1
Farm Dr Croydon CR0 . . . . . .62 F8
 Purley CR8 . . . . .79 D8
Farm Fields CR2 . . . . .80 F8
Farm La Addlestone KT15 . . .52 A3
 Ashstead KT21, KT18 . . . . . .76 B2
 Croydon CR0 . . . . .62 F8
 East Horsley KT24 . . . . . . .112 F4
 Purley CR8 . . . . .60 C1
 Send GU23 . . . . .90 C3
 Wallington CR8 . . . . .60 C1
Farm Rd Aldershot GU12 . . .105 E3
 Frimley GU16 . . . . .65 F2
 Morden SM4 . . . . .40 B4
 Old Woking GU22 . . . . .90 B7
 Staines TW18 . . . . .13 B2
 Sutton SM2 . . . . .59 D3
 Thames Ditton KT10 . . . . . .55 B8
 Twickenham TW4 . . . . .15 C7
Farm View KT20 . . . . .117 E8
Farm Way North Cheam KT4 58 C7
 Stanwell TW19 . . . . .1 F1
Farm Wlk GU12 . . . . .127 C8
Farmdale Rd SM2, SM5 . . . .59 E3
Farmer's Rd TW18 . . . . .12 E3
Farmfield Dr BR6 . . . . .181 B8
Farmfield Hospl RH6 . . . . .160 B1
Farmfield Rd RH11 . . . . . . .24 E3
Farmhouse Cl GU22 . . . . . .70 D4
Farmhouse Rd SW16 . . . . . .21 C1
Farmington Ave SM1 . . . . . .59 D7
Farmleigh Cl RH10 . . . . . . .202 C8
Farmleigh Gr KT12 . . . . . . .53 F5
Farmstead Rd SE6 . . . . .24 B4
Farmview KT11 . . . . .73 D3
Farnaby Rd BR1, BR2 . . . . . .44 E8
Farnan Rd SW16 . . . . .21 C3
Farnborough Ave CR2 . . . . .62 E3
Farnborough Bsns Ctr
 GU14 . . . . .84 F2
Farnborough Coll of Tech
 GU14 . . . . .85 C2
Farnborough Cres
 Coney Hall BR2 . . . . .44 F1
 South Croydon CR2 . . . . . . .62 E2
Farnborough Gate Ret Pk
 GU14 . . . . .85 C5
Farnborough Grange Cty
 Jun Sch GU14 . . . . .85 A7
Farnborough Grange Inf
 Sch GU14 . . . . .85 A8
Farnborough Hill Sch
 GU14 . . . . .85 C5
FarnboroughHouse 1
 SW15 . . . . .19 A7
Farnborough Ind Est
 GU14 . . . . .85 A4
Farnborough North Sta
 GU14 . . . . .85 D6
Farnborough Rd
 Aldershot GU11 . . . . .104 E3
 Farnborough GU14 . . . . . . .85 C5
 Heath End GU11, GU9 . . . .125 D7
Farnborough (Sixth
 Form) Coll GU14 . . . . . . .85 B6
Farnborough St GU14 . . . . .85 D6
Farnborough Sta GU14 . . . .85 B5
Farncombe C of E Inf Sch
 GU7 . . . . .150 E7
Farncombe Hill GU7 . . . . .150 E7
Farncombe St GU7 . . . . . .150 E7
Farncombe Sta GU7 . . . . .150 F7
Farnell Mews RH13 . . . . . . .53 B7
Farnell Rd Isleworth TW7 . . . .5 D4
 Stanwell TW19 . . . . .2 A6
Farnell's Almshouses TW7 .5 F5
Farnham Bsns Ctr GU9 . . .125 C3
Farnham Bsns Pk GU9 . . .125 B1
Farnham By-Pass
 GU10, GU9 . . . . .125 C1
Farnham Castle GU9 . . . . .125 B3
Farnham Cl RG12 . . . . .27 D7
Farnham Coll GU9 . . . . . . .125 C1
Farnham Com Hospl
 GU9 . . . . .125 E4
Farnham Ct SM3 . . . . .58 E4
Farnham Gdns SW20 . . . . . .39 B7
Farnham La GU27 . . . . . . .208 A7

Ewe-Fel 245

Farnham Park Cl GU9 . . . .125 B6
Farnham Park Dr GU9 . . . .125 B6
Farnham Rd
 Elstead GU10, GU8 . . . . . .148 C4
 Guildford, Guildford Park
 GU1, GU2, GU3 . . . . .130 B7
 Guildford, Onslow Village
 GU2, GU3 . . . . .129 E6
Farnham Rd Hospl GU2 . .130 B7
Farnham Sta GU9 . . . . . . .125 C2
Farnham Trad Est GU9 . . .125 F4
Farnhurst La GU6, GU8 . . .193 F4
Farningham RG12 . . . . .27 E3
Farningham Cres CR3 . . . .101 A4
Farningham Ct SW16 . . . . . .21 D1
Farningham Rd CR3 . . . . . .101 A4
Farnley GU21 . . . . .68 F2
Farnley Rd CR7, SE25 . . . . .42 D5
Farnsworth House 8
 SW27 . . . . .22 B3
Farquhar Rd Dulwich SE19 .22 F3
 Wimbledon SW19 . . . . .20 A5
Farquharson Rd CR0 . . . . . .42 C1
Farrell Cl GU15 . . . . .65 C3
Farren Rd SE23 . . . . .23 E6
Farrer's Pl CR0 . . . . .62 D6
Farriers KT18 . . . . .96 C5
Farriers Cl KT17 . . . . .76 E7
Farriers Ct Belmont SM2 . . . .58 E3
 Wimbledon SW19 . . . . .19 E1
Farriers Rd KT17 . . . . .76 E8
Farriers The GU5 . . . . .152 A5
Farthingfield House GU9 .125 C3
Farthings GU21 . . . . .68 E3
Farthings The 1 KT2 . . . . .38 A8
Farwig La BR1 . . . . .44 F8
Fassett Rd KT1 . . . . .37 E5
Fauconberg Ct W4 . . . . .7 C8
Fauconberg Rd W4 . . . . .7 C8
Faulkner Pl GU19 . . . . .47 E4
Faulkner's Cl KT12 . . . . . . .54 C5
Faversham Rd
 Beckenham BR3 . . . . .43 F7
 Forest Hill SE6 . . . . .23 F7
 Morden SM4 . . . . .40 B3
 Sandhurst GU47 . . . . .45 D1
Fawcett Cl SW16 . . . . .22 A4
Fawcett Rd CR0, CR9 . . . . .61 C7
Fawcus Cl KT10 . . . . .55 F4
Fawler Mead RG12 . . . . . . .27 F5
Fawley Cl GU6 . . . . .174 F2
Fawns Manor Cl TW14 . . . . .14 C7
Fawns Manor Rd TW14 . . . .14 D7
Fawsley Cl SL3 . . . . .1 E7
Fay Rd RH12 . . . . .217 C5
Faygate Bsns Ctr RH12 . .199 F1
Faygate Cl
 Blindley Heath RH9 . . . . . . .142 E1
 Rusper RH12 . . . . .199 F4
Faygate Rd SW2 . . . . .21 F6
Faygate Sta RH12 . . . . . . .199 F5
Fayland Ave SW16 . . . . .21 C3
Fearn Cl KT24 . . . . .112 E6
Fearnley Cres TW12 . . . . . .15 F2
Feathers La TW19 . . . . .12 A6
Featherbed La CR0 . . . . . . .63 A1
Feathers RH7 . . . . .142 D1
Featherstone Ave SE23 . . . .23 C6
Fee Farm Rd KT10 . . . . .55 F3
Felbridge Ave RH10 . . . . . .202 D7
Felbridge Cl
 East Grinstead RH19 . . . . .185 C3
 Frimley GU16 . . . . .65 F1
 Streatham SW16 . . . . .22 A4
 Sutton SM2 . . . . .59 B2
Felbridge Ct
 East Grinstead RH19 . . . . .185 A4
 Harlington UB3 . . . . .3 D8
Felbridge Ctr The RH19 . .185 A3
Felbridge Cty Prim Sch
 RH19 . . . . .184 F4
Felbridge Rd RH19 . . . . . . .184 D3
Felcot Rd RH19 . . . . .184 C4
Felcote House RH2 . . . . . .138 F7
Felcott Cl KT12 . . . . .54 C7
Felcott Rd KT12 . . . . .54 C7
Felcourt Cotts RH19 . . . . .185 C8
Felcourt La RH19 . . . . .164 C1
Felcourt Rd
 Dormans Park RH19, RH7 . .185 C7
 Felcourt RH19, RH7 . . . . . .185 C7
Felday Glade RH5 . . . . .155 B5
Felday Houses RH5 . . . . . .155 C2
Felday Rd RH5 . . . . .133 F3
Felix Dr GU4 . . . . .111 A7
Felix La TW17 . . . . .34 F3
Felix Rd KT12 . . . . .35 A3
Fell Rd CR0, CR9 . . . . .61 C7
Felland Way RH2 . . . . .139 D5
Fellbrook TW10 . . . . .17 B5
Fellow Gn GU24 . . . . .67 F6
Fellow Green Rd GU24 . . . .67 F6
Fellowes Ct UB3 . . . . .3 D8
Fellowes Rd SM1, SM5 . . . .59 E8
Fellows Rd GU14 . . . . .85 D1
Felmingham Rd SE20 . . . . . .43 C7
Felnex Trad Est SM6 . . . . . .60 A8
Felsberg Rd SW2 . . . . .21 E8
Felside Ct KT13 . . . . .53 A5
Felstead Rd KT19 . . . . .76 D8
Feltham Arena TW14 . . . . . .15 A8
Feltham Ave KT8 . . . . .36 E5

Feltham Corporate Ctr
TW13 . . . . .15 B5
Feltham Hill Jun & Inf Schs
TW13 . . . . .14 F5
Feltham Hill Rd
Ashford TW15 . . . . .14 C2
Feltham TW13 . . . . .15 B4
Feltham Rd Ashford TW15 .14 C4
Mitcham CR4 . . . . .41 A7
Redhill RH1 . . . . .139 F4
Feltham Sch The TW13 . .15 C6
Feltham Sta TW13 . . . . . .15 B7
Feltham Wlk RH1 . . . . .139 F4
Felthambrook Ind Ctr
TW13 . . . . .15 B5
Felthambrook Ind Est
TW13 . . . . .15 B5
Felthambrook Way TW13 .15 B3
Feltonfleet SchTrust Ltd
KT11 . . . . .72 E6
Felwater Ct RH19 . . . . .185 A3
Fenby Cl RH13 . . . . . . .218 C4
Fenchurch Rd RH10 . . .202 B4
Fencote RG12 . . . . .27 D3
Fendall Rd KT19 . . . . . . .57 C5
Fender House RH12 . . .217 B2
Fengates Rd RH1 . . . . . .118 E1
Fenhurst Cl RH12 . . . . .216 F1
Fenn's Way GU1 . . . . . . .69 E4
Fennel Cl Croydon CR0 . . .43 D1
Farnborough GU14 . . . . .84 B4
Guildford GU1 . . . . . . .110 B4
Fennel Cres RH11 . . . . .201 B2
Fennells Mead KT17 . . . .57 F2
Fenner House KT12 . . . . .54 A6
Fenning Ct CR4 . . . . . . .40 E5
Fenns La GU24 . . . . .67 G5
Fenns Yd GU1 . . . . .125 B2
Fennscombe Ct GU24 . . .67 F6
Fenstanton Prim Sch SW2 22 A7
Fenton Ave TW18 . . . . . .13 C3
Fenton Cl RH1 . . . . .119 A1
Fenton House TW5 . . . . . .5 A8
Fenton Rd RH1 . . . . . . .119 A1
Fentum Rd GU2 . . . . . . .109 A3
Fenwick Cl GU21 . . . . . . .69 B1
Ferguson Ave KT5 . . . . . .37 F4
Ferguson Cl BR2, BR3 . . . .44 D6
Fermandy La RH10 . . . .184 A1
Fermor Rd SE23 . . . . . . .23 E7
Fern Ave CR4 . . . . .41 D5
Fern Cl Crowthorne RG45 . .45 A7
Frimley GU16 . . . . .66 C3
Warlingham CR6 . . . . . .81 E1
Fern Cotts RH5 . . . . . . .133 E4
Fern Gr TW14 . . . . .15 B8
Fern Lodge ⏃ SW16 . . . . .22 A3
Fern Rd GU7 . . . . .150 F6
Fern Towers CR3 . . . . . .101 A2
Fern Way RH12 . . . . . .217 D5
Fern Wlk TW15 . . . . .13 D3
Fernbank Ave KT12 . . . . .35 E2
Fernbank Cres SL5 . . . . .28 D8
Fernbank Pl SL5 . . . . . . .28 D7
Fernbank Rd
Addlestone KT15 . . . . . .52 A5
North Ascot SL5 . . . . . . .28 D8
Fernbrae Cl GU10 . . . . .146 B3
Ferndale GU3 . . . . .108 C3
Ferndale Ave
Addlestone KT16 . . . . . .51 E7
Hounslow TW4 . . . . .4 E4
Ferndale Rd Ashford TW15 .13 E3
Banstead SM7 . . . . .77 F4
Croydon SE25 . . . . .43 B4
Woking GU21 . . . . .69 C5
Fernden La GU27 . . . . .208 C2
Fernden Rise GU7 . . . . .150 E7
Ferndown Crawley RH10 .182 D2
Horley RH6 . . . . .161 A5
⏃ Kingston u T KT6 . . . .37 E4
Ferndown Cl
Guildford GU1 . . . . . . .131 A8
Sutton SM2 . . . . .59 D4
Ferndown Gdns
Cobham KT11 . . . . .73 C6
Farnborough GU14 . . . . .84 E4
Fernery The TW18 . . . . . .12 E3
Ferney Ct KT14 . . . . .71 D8
Ferney Meade Way TW7 . .6 A5
Ferney Rd KT14 . . . . .71 D7
Fernfell Golf & Ctry
Club GU6 . . . . .174 F6
Fernham Rd CR7 . . . . . . .42 C6
Fernhill KT22 . . . . .74 D5
Fernhill Cl
Crawley Down RH10 . . .184 B1
Farnborough GU17 . . . . .64 F1
Hale GU9 . . . . .125 B6
Woking GU22 . . . . .89 D7
Fernhill Ct KT2 . . . . .17 D3
Fernhill Cty Prim
Sch GU14 . . . . .64 F1
Fernhill Dr GU9 . . . . . .125 B6
Fernhill Gdns KT2 . . . . . .17 E3
Fernhill La
Farnborough GU17 . . . . .64 F1
Hale GU9 . . . . .125 B6
Woking GU22 . . . . .89 C7
Fernhill Pk GU22 . . . . . .89 D7
Fernhill Rd
Blackwater GU14, GU17 . .64 E2
Crawley RH6 . . . . .182 D7
Farnborough, Hawley
GU14, GU17 . . . . .64 E2

Fernhill Rd continued
Farnborough, West Heath
GU14, GU17 . . . . .84 E6
Fernhill Sch GU14 . . . . . .64 F1
Fernhill Wlk GU17 . . . . . .64 F1
Fernhurst Cl RH11 . . . . .201 B8
Fernhurst Rd Ashford TW15 14 C4
Croydon CR0 . . . . .43 B1
Ferniehurst GU15 . . . . . .65 F4
Fernihough Cl KT13 . . . . .72 A8
Fernlands Cl KT16 . . . . . .51 E7
Fernlea KT23 . . . . .94 B3
Fernlea Rd Balham SW12 . .21 B7
Mitcham CR4 . . . . .41 A8
Fernleigh Cl Croydon CR0 . .61 A6
Walton-on-T KT12 . . . . . .54 B7
Fernleigh Rise GU16 . . . .86 C7
Fernley House GU7 . . . .150 E8
Ferns Cl CR2 . . . . .62 B1
Ferns Mead GU9 . . . . . .125 B1
Ferns The GU9 . . . . .125 C7
Fernside Ave TW13 . . . . .15 B4
Fernside Rd SW12 . . . . . .21 A8
Fernthorpe Rd SW16 . . . .21 C2
Fernwood
New Addington CR0, CR2 . .62 E2
Putney SW19 . . . . .19 F7
Fernwood Ave SW16 . . . .21 D4
Feroners Cl RH10 . . . . .202 A4
Ferrard Cl SL5 . . . . .28 D8
Ferrers Ave SM6 . . . . . . .60 D6
Ferrers Rd SW16 . . . . . . .21 D3
Ferriby Ct RG12 . . . . .27 C7
Ferring Cl RH11 . . . . . . .201 B8
Ferrings SE21 . . . . .22 E5
Ferris Ave CR0 . . . . .62 F7
Ferroners Ct RH10 . . . . .202 A4
Ferry Ave TW18 . . . . .12 E1
Ferry La Barnes SW13 . . . . .7 F8
Brentford TW8 . . . . .6 E8
Chertsey KT16 . . . . .33 A3
Guildford GU2, GU3 . . . .130 C5
Laleham TW18 . . . . .33 C6
Lower Halliford TW17 . . . .34 A1
Richmond TW9 . . . . .6 F8
Wraysbury TW19 . . . . . . .1 A1
Ferry Rd East Molesey KT8 . .36 A6
Richmond TW10 . . . . . . .17 B3
Thames Ditton KT7 . . . . .37 B3
Twickenham TW1 . . . . . .17 B7
Ferry Sq ⏃ TW8 . . . . .6 E8
Ferry Wks TW17 . . . . . . .34 A1
Ferrymoor TW10 . . . . . . .17 B5
Fetcham Common
La KT22 . . . . .94 B6
Fetcham Park Dr KT22 . . .94 E4
Fetcham Village Cty Inf
Sch KT22 . . . . .94 D5
Fettes Rd GU6 . . . . .175 A3
Fiddicroft Ave SM7 . . . . .78 C5
Field Cl Chessington KT9 . .56 C5
Cranford TW4 . . . . .4 B6
East Molesey KT8 . . . . . .36 B4
Guildford GU4 . . . . .110 D3
Hamsey Green CR2 . . . . .81 B5
Harlington UB7 . . . . .3 C7
Field Ct Oxted RH8 . . . . .122 E8
Wimbledon SW19 . . . . . .20 A5
Field End Coulsdon CR5 . . .79 D5
Farnham GU9 . . . . .125 F4
West End GU24 . . . . .67 F6
Field House Cl SL5 . . . . . .29 A1
Field La Brentford TW8 . . . .6 C7
Farncombe GU7 . . . . . .150 F7
Frimley GU16 . . . . .65 E1
Teddington TW11 . . . . . .17 A3
Field Pk RG12 . . . . .27 D8
Field Pl KT3 . . . . .38 F3
Field Rd Farnborough GU14 .64 F1
Feltham TW14 . . . . .4 B1
Field Stores App GU11 . .105 C3
Field View Egham TW20 . . .12 C3
Feltham TW13 . . . . .14 D5
Field Way Aldershot GU12 .105 E3
New Addington CR0 . . . . .63 B4
Send Marsh GU23 . . . . . .90 F2
Tongham GU10 . . . . . . .126 D7
Field Wlk RH6 . . . . .162 C4
Fieldcommon La KT12 . . .35 F1
Fielden Pl RG12 . . . . .27 D7
Fieldend Horsham RH12 . .218 B5
Teddington TW11 . . . . . .16 F4
Fieldend Rd SW16 . . . . . .41 C8
Fieldhouse Rd SW12 . . . .21 C7
Fieldhouse Villas SM7 . . .78 E4
Fieldhurst Cl KT15 . . . . . .52 B5
Fielding Ave TW2 . . . . . .16 C5
Fielding Gdns RG45 . . . . .45 B4
Fielding House W4 . . . . . .7 E8
Fielding Rd GU47 . . . . . . .64 E6
Fieldings The
Forest Hill SE23 . . . . . . .23 C7
Horley RH6 . . . . .161 C4
Woking GU21 . . . . .68 F3
Fieldsend Rd SM3 . . . . . .58 E5
Fieldside Rd BR1 . . . . . . .24 D3
Fieldview Horley RH6 . . .161 B4
Wandsworth SW17, SW18 .20 D7
Fieldway GU27 . . . . .208 C2
Fife Rd Kingston u T KT2 . .37 E7
Mortlake SW14 . . . . .7 C2
Fife Way KT23 . . . . .94 A2
Fifehead Cl TW15 . . . . . .13 E2
Fifield La GU10 . . . . . . .146 C2
Fifield Path SE23 . . . . . . .23 D5
Fifth Cross Rd TW2 . . . . .16 D6

Figge's Rd CR4 . . . . .21 A1
Filbert Cres RH11 . . . . .201 A6
Filby Rd KT9 . . . . .56 F4
Filey Cl Biggin Hill TN16 .103 B8
Crawley RH11 . . . . .200 F4
Sutton SM2 . . . . .59 C3
Filmer Ct GU7 . . . . .150 E5
Filmer Gr GU7 . . . . .150 E5
Finborough Rd SW17 . . . .20 F2
Finch Ave SE27 . . . . .22 D4
Finch Cl GU21 . . . . .68 C2
Finch Dr TW14 . . . . .15 D8
Finch Rd ⏃ GU1 . . . . . . .109 D1
Finch's Cross RH8 . . . . .144 A8
Finchampstead Rd
RG41, RG40 . . . . .25 B3
Finchdean House SW15 . .18 F8
Finches Rise GU1 . . . . . .110 C3
Findhorn Cl GU47 . . . . . .64 D7
Findings The GU14 . . . . . .84 E8
Findlay Dr GU3 . . . . .108 F5
Findon Ct KT15 . . . . .51 F5
Findon Rd RH11 . . . . . . .201 B8
Findon Way RH12 . . . . . .216 D3
Finlay Gdns KT15 . . . . . .52 C6
Finlays Cl KT9 . . . . .57 A5
Finmere RG12 . . . . .27 C2
Finnart Cl KT13 . . . . .53 C6
Finney Dr GU20 . . . . .48 D4
Finney La TW7 . . . . .6 A6
Finsbury Cl RH11 . . . . . .201 C2
Finstock Gn RG12 . . . . . . .27 F5
Finton House Sch SW17 . .20 F6
Fintry Pl GU14 . . . . .84 E7
Fintry Wlk GU14 . . . . . . .84 E7
Finucane Ct TW9 . . . . . . .6 F4
Fiona Cl KT23 . . . . .94 A3
Fir Acre Rd GU12 . . . . . .106 A6
Fir Cl KT12 . . . . .35 A2
Fir Dr GU17 . . . . .64 D3
Fir Gr KT3 . . . . .38 F3
Fir Grange Ave KT13 . . . .53 B5
Fir Rd Cheam SM3 . . . . . .39 F1
Feltham TW13 . . . . .15 C3
Fir Tree Alley ⏃ GU11 . . .105 A2
Fir Tree Ave GU27 . . . . .207 D6
Fir Tree Cl Ascot SL5 . . . .29 A2
Banstead KT17 . . . . .77 C4
Crawley RH11 . . . . .181 B1
Esher KT10 . . . . .55 C5
Leatherhead KT22 . . . . . .95 C4
Streatham SW16 . . . . . . .21 C3
Worcester Park KT19 . . . .57 F6
Fir Tree Gdns CR0 . . . . . .63 A6
Fir Tree Gr SM5 . . . . .59 F3
Fir Tree Rd
Banstead KT17, SM7 . . . .77 D5
Guildford GU1 . . . . .109 D4
Hounslow TW4 . . . . .4 E3
Leatherhead KT22 . . . . . .95 C4
Fir Tree Wlk RH2 . . . . . .118 D1
Fir Wlk KT17, SM3 . . . . . .58 D4
Firbank Cotts RH6 . . . . .183 C7
Firbank Dr GU21 . . . . . . .89 B8
Firbank La GU21 . . . . . . .89 B8
Firbank Pl TW20 . . . . . . .11 B2
Firbank Way RH19 . . . . .185 D1
Fircroft Cl GU22 . . . . . . .69 F1
Fircroft Ct ⏃ GU22 . . . . .69 F1
Fircroft Prim Sch SW17 . .20 F5
Fircroft Rd Chessington KT9 56 F6
Upper Tooting SW17 . . . .20 F5
Firdene KT5 . . . . .38 C1
Fire Bell Alley KT6 . . . . . .37 E3
Fire Station Cotts CR8 . . .79 F6
Fire Station Flats ⏃ KT17 .76 E6
Fire Station Rd GU11 . . .105 B3
Fireball Hill SL5 . . . . . . .29 D2
Firefly Cl SM6 . . . . .60 E3
Firfield Rd
Addlestone KT15 . . . . . .52 A6
Farnham GU9 . . . . .146 A7
Firfields KT13 . . . . .53 B4
Firgrove GU21 . . . . .89 B8
Firgrove Ct
⏃ Farnborough GU14 . . . .85 B4
Farnham GU9 . . . . .125 C1
Firgrove Hill GU9 . . . . . .125 C1
Firgrove Par ⏃ GU14 . . . .85 B4
Firgrove Rd ⏃ GU14 . . . . .85 B4
Firhill Rd SE6 . . . . .24 A5
Firlands Bracknell RG12 . . .27 C4
Horley RH6 . . . . .161 B4
Weybridge KT13 . . . . . . .53 E4
Firlands Ave GU15 . . . . . .65 D5
Firle Cl RH10 . . . . .201 E8
Firmston House ⏃ SW14 . .7 D4
Firs Ave Bramley GU5 . . .152 A5
Mortlake SW14 . . . . .7 C3
Firs Cl Claygate KT10 . . . . .55 E4
Dorking RH4 . . . . .136 A5
Farnborough GU14 . . . . .85 C2
Forest Hill SE23 . . . . . . .23 E8
Mitcham CR4 . . . . .41 B8
Firs Dr TW5 . . . . .4 B7
Firs La GU5 . . . . .152 D4
Firs Rd CR8 . . . . .80 B4
Firs The Artington GU3 . . .130 B5
Bisley GU24 . . . . .68 A3
⏃ Bracknell RG12 . . . . . .27 F5
Caterham CR3 . . . . .100 D5
Claygate KT10 . . . . .55 E4
⏃ Forest Hill SE26 . . . . . .23 B3
Forest Hill SE26 . . . . . . .23 C3
Sutton SM2 . . . . .59 B3
Wimbledon SW20 . . . . . .19 A1
Firsby Ave CR0 . . . . .43 D1
Firsdene Cl KT16 . . . . . . .51 D4

First Ave East Molesey KT8 .36 A5
Mortlake SW14 . . . . .7 C4
Walton-on-T KT12 . . . . . .35 B3
West Ewell KT19 . . . . . . .57 E2
Woodham KT15 . . . . .52 B2
First Cl KT8 . . . . .36 C6
First Cross Rd TW2 . . . . .16 E6
First Quarter Bsns Pk
KT19 . . . . .76 E3
Firstway SW20 . . . . .39 C7
Firsway GU2 . . . . .109 A2
Firswood Ave KT19 . . . . .57 F5
Firtree Ave CR4 . . . . .41 A7
Firtree Ct BR2 . . . . .44 F6
Firway GU26 . . . . .187 E5
Firwood Cl GU21 . . . . . . .88 E8
Firwood Cl GU15 . . . . . . .65 C5
Firwood Dr GU15 . . . . . . .65 C5
Firwood Rd GU25 . . . . . .30 E3
Fisher Cl Crawley RH10 . .201 E4
Croydon CR0 . . . . .42 F1
Hersham KT12 . . . . .54 B6
Fisher La Chiddingfold GU8 210 F2
Dunsfold GU8 . . . . .211 B7
Fisher Rowe Cl GU5 . . . .152 A6
Fisherdene KT10 . . . . . . .56 A3
Fisherman Cl TW10 . . . . .17 C4
Fishermen's Cl GU11 . . .105 E5
Fishers Ct Horsham RH12 .217 C4
⏃ Teddington TW11 . . . . .16 F3
Fishers Wood SL5 . . . . . .30 C1
Fishponds Cl RG41 . . . . . .25 A4
Fishponds Est RG41 . . . . .25 A4
Fishponds Rd
Upper Tooting SW17 . . . .20 F4
Wokingham RG41 . . . . . .25 A4
Fiske Ct ⏃ Merton SW19 . .20 C1
Sutton SM2 . . . . .59 C3
Fitch Ct CR4 . . . . .41 A7
Fitchet Cl RH11 . . . . . . .201 B8
Fitz Wygram Cl TW12 . . . .16 C3
Fitzalan Rd Claygate KT10 . .55 E3
Horsham RH12, RH13 . . .218 A4
Fitzgeorge Ave KT2, KT3 . .38 D8
Fitzgerald Ave SW14 . . . . .7 E4
Fitzgerald Rd Mortlake SW14 7 D4
Thames Ditton KT7 . . . . .37 B3
Fitzherbert House ⏃ TW10 .6 F1
Fitzjames Ave CR0 . . . . . .62 A8
Fitzjohn Cl GU4 . . . . . . .110 C4
Fitzrobert Pl TW20 . . . . . .12 A3
Fitzroy Cres W4 . . . . .7 D7
Fitzroy Gdns SE19 . . . . . .22 E1
Fitzwilliam Ave TW9 . . . . .6 F5
Fitzwilliam House TW9 . . . .6 D3
Fitzwilliam Hts SE23 . . . .23 C6
Five Acres RH10 . . . . . . .201 E8
Five Oaks Cl GU21 . . . . . .88 E8
Five Oaks Rd Broadbridge
Heath RH12, RH13 . . . . .216 B2
Slinfold RH12, RH13 . . . .216 B2
Fiveacre Cl CR7 . . . . .42 A3
Flag Cl CR0 . . . . .43 D1
Flambard Way GU7 . . . . .150 D4
Flamborough Cl TN16 . . .103 B8
Flamsteed Hts RH11 . . . .201 B1
Flanchford House ⏃
RH2 . . . . .118 A2
Flanchford Rd Leigh RH2 .138 D5
Reigate RH2 . . . . .138 D5
Reigate RH2 . . . . .138 D5
Flanders Cotts GU5 . . . .152 A6
Flanders Cres SW17, SW19 20 F2
Flanders Ct TW20 . . . . . .12 C3
Flatford House SE6 . . . . .24 C4
Flats The GU17 . . . . .64 C4
Flaxley Rd SM4 . . . . .40 B4
Flaxmore Ct CR7 . . . . . . .42 D7
Fleece Rd KT6 . . . . .37 C1
Fleet Cl KT8 . . . . .35 F4
Fleet Rd Aldershot GU11 .104 D6
Blackwater GU17 . . . . . .84 A4
Church Crookham
GU13, GU14 . . . . .104 C4
Farnborough GU14 . . . . .84 C4
Fleet Terr SE6 . . . . .24 C8
Fleetside KT8 . . . . .36 A4
Fleetway TW20 . . . . .32 C6
Fleetwood Cl
Chessington KT9 . . . . . .56 D3
South Croydon CR0 . . . . .61 F7
Tadworth KT20 . . . . .97 D7
Fleetwood Ct ⏃
Stanwell TW19 . . . . .2 E1
⏃ West Byfleet KT14 . . . .71 A6
Fleetwood Rd KT3 . . . . . .38 B6
Fleetwood Sq KT3 . . . . . .38 B6
Fleming Cl GU14 . . . . . . .85 D6
Fleming Ct CR0 . . . . .60 F5
Fleming Mead CR4, SW19 .20 F1
Fleming Way
Crawley RH10, RH11 . . .181 F2
Isleworth TW7 . . . . .5 F3
Flemish Fields KT16 . . . . .33 A2
Fletcher Cl Crawley RH10 .201 E4
Ottershaw KT15, KT16 . . .51 E4
Fletcher Gdns RG42 . . . . .26 D8
Fletcher Rd KT16 . . . . . . .51 D4
Fletchers Cl RH13 . . . . .217 E1
Fleur Gates ⏃ SW19 . . . .19 D8
Flexford Gr RG12 . . . . . . .26 E3
Flexford Rd GU3 . . . . . . .107 C1
Flexlands Sch GU24 . . . . .68 F8
Flimwell Cl BR1 . . . . .24 E3
Flint Cl Banstead SM7 . . . .78 B5
Crawley RH10 . . . . .202 B1
Great Bookham KT23 . . . .94 C1
Redhill RH1 . . . . .118 F2

Flint Hill RH4, RH5 . . . . .136 B5
Flint Hill Cl RH4 . . . . . . .136 B4
Flintgrove RG12 . . . . .27 D8
Flintlock Cl TW19 . . . . . . .2 A3
Flitwick Grange GU8 . . . .149 F1
Flock Mill Pl SW18 . . . . . .20 B7
Flood La ⏃ TW1 . . . . .17 A7
Flora Gdns CR0 . . . . .82 C8
Floral Cl KT21 . . . . .75 C1
Floral House KT16 . . . . . .32 F1
Florence Ave Morden SM4 .40 C4
Woodham KT15 . . . . .71 A8
Florence Cl KT12 . . . . . . .35 B2
Florence Cotts
Kingston u T SW15 . . . . .18 E5
Winkfield SL4 . . . . .8 C7
Florence Ct SW19 . . . . . . .19 E3
Florence Gdns
Chiswick W4 . . . . .7 C8
Staines TW18 . . . . .13 B1
Florence House ⏃ KT2 . . .17 F1
Florence Rd Feltham TW13 .15 B7
⏃ Kingston u T KT2 . . . . .17 F1
Penge BR3 . . . . .43 E7
Sandhurst GU47 . . . . . . .64 E7
South Croydon CR2 . . . . .61 D2
Walton-on-T KT12 . . . . . .35 B2
Wimbledon SW19 . . . . . .20 B2
Florence Terr SW15 . . . . .18 E5
Florence Way SW12 . . . . .20 F7
Florian Ave SM1 . . . . .59 D6
Florida Ct Beckenham BR2 . .44 F5
Staines TW18 . . . . .13 A3
Florida Rd Shalford GU4 . .130 E3
South Norwood CR7 . . . . .42 B8
Florys Ct ⏃ SW19 . . . . . .19 E7
Flower Cres KT16 . . . . . . .51 C4
Flower La
Tyler's Green RH9 . . . . .121 D6
Woldingham RH9 . . . . . .121 D6
Flower Wlk GU2 . . . . . . .130 C6
Flowersmead SW17 . . . . .21 A6
Floyd's La GU22 . . . . .71 A3
Foden Rd GU11 . . . . .105 A1
Foley Mews KT10 . . . . . . .55 E4
Foley Rd Biggin Hill TN16 . .83 D1
Claygate KT10 . . . . .55 E3
Folly Hill Farnham GU9 . .125 B6
Hale GU9 . . . . .125 A5
Folly Hill Cty Inf Sch
GU9 . . . . .125 A6
Folly La RH5 . . . . .157 B7
Folly La N GU9 . . . . .125 B6
Folly La S GU9 . . . . .125 A6
Follyfield Rd SM7 . . . . . . .78 A5
Fontaine Ct BR3 . . . . .43 F8
Fontaine Rd SW16 . . . . . .21 C6
Fontenoy Rd SW12, SW17 .21 C6
Fonthill Cl SE20 . . . . .43 A7
Fonthill Ct SE23 . . . . .23 C8
Fontley Way SW15 . . . . . .19 A8
Fontmell Cl TW15 . . . . . . .14 A3
Fontmell Pk TW15 . . . . . .14 A3
Fontwell Rd RH10 . . . . . .202 A4
Forbes Chase GU47 . . . . .64 D7
Forbes Cl RH10 . . . . .202 B4
Forbes Ct SE19 . . . . .22 E3
Forburys GU9 . . . . .146 B8
Ford Cl Ashford TW15 . . . .13 E2
Littleton TW17 . . . . .34 A4
Thornton Heath CR7 . . . .42 B4
Ford La GU10, GU9 . . . . . .146 B6
Ford Manor Cotts RH7 . . .165 B2
Ford Manor Rd RH7 . . . . .165 B2
Ford Rd Ashford TW15 . . . .13 F4
Bisley GU24 . . . . .67 F4
Chertsey KT16 . . . . .33 B1
Chobham GU24 . . . . .49 C1
Old Woking GU22 . . . . . .90 B4
Fordbridge Ct TW15 . . . . .13 E4
Fordbridge Rd
Ashford TW15 . . . . .13 F3
Sunbury TW16 . . . . .35 A5
Upper Halliford TW16, TW17 .34 F3
Fordel Rd SE6 . . . . .24 D7
Fordingbridge Cl
Chertsey KT16 . . . . .33 B1
Horsham RH12 . . . . .217 C1
Fordington House SE26 . .23 B5
Fordmill Rd SE6 . . . . .24 A6
Fordwater Rd KT15, KT16 . .33 C1
Fordwater Trad Est KT16 .33 C1
Fordwells Dr RG12 . . . . . .27 F5
Fordyce House ⏃ SW16 . . .21 C4
Foreman Pk GU12 . . . . . .106 B2
Foreman Rd GU12 . . . . . .106 B1
Forest Cl Bracknell SL5 . . .28 C6
Crawley Down RH10 . . . .204 B8
East Horsley KT24 . . . . . .92 F2
Horsham RH12 . . . . .218 A4
Woking GU22 . . . . .70 D4
Forest Cres KT21 . . . . . . .76 A3
Forest Croft SE23 . . . . . . .23 B6
Forest Dene Ct SM2 . . . . .59 C4
Forest Dr Charlton TW16 . .14 F1
Farnham GU10 . . . . .146 C4
Kingswood KT20 . . . . . . .98 A6
Forest End Rd GU47 . . . . .64 A8
Forest Glade GU10 . . . . .145 D3
Forest Gn RG12 . . . . .27 D7
Forest Hill Bsns Ctr SE23 .23 C6
Forest Hill Rd SE23 . . . . .23 B5
Forest Hill Ind Est SE23 . .23 C6
Forest Hill Sch SE23 . . . . .23 C8
Forest Hill Sec Sch SE23 . .23 C6
Forest Hill Sta SE23 . . . . .23 C6
Forest Hills GU15 . . . . . . .65 B4
Forest La KT24 . . . . .92 F3

Forest Lodge 2
East Grinstead RH19 ....**205** F8
Forest Hill SE23 ....**23** C5
Forest Oaks RH13 ....**218** B4
Forest Rd Cheam SM3, SM4 .**40** A2
Crawley RH12 ....**218** D5
Crowthorne RG45 ....**45** C5
East Horsley KT24 ....**92** F2
Feltham TW13 ....**15** C6
North Ascot RG42 ....**8** D2
Richmond TW9 ....**7** A7
Windsor SL4 ....**9** E7
Winkfield RG42, SL5 ....**8** D2
Woking GU22 ....**70** D4
Forest Ridge BR3 ....**44** A6
Forest Row Bsns Pk
RH18 ....**206** F4
Forest Row C of E Inf
Sch RH18 ....**206** F2
Forest Sch The RH13 ...**217** F1
Forest Side KT4 ....**38** F1
Forest View RH10 ......**202** A3
Forest View Rd RH19 ...**205** E6
Forest Wlk KT21 ....**76** A3
Forest Wlk GU6 ....**173** F2
Forestdale GU26 ....**188** E3
Forestdale Ctr The CR0 ..**62** F3
Forestdale Prim Sch CR0 .**62** F2
Forester Rd RH10 ....**201** E4
Foresters Cl Knaphill GU21 .**68** F1
Wallington SM6 ....**60** D3
Foresters Dr CR8, SM6 ....**60** D3
Foresters Prim Sch SM6 ..**60** D4
Foresters Sq RG12 ....**27** E6
Foresters Way RG45 .....**45** E8
Forestfield Crawley RH10 .**202** B3
Horsham RH13 ....**218** A4
Forestholme Cl SE23 .....**23** C6
Forge Ave CR5 ....**100** B7
Forge Cl
Broadbridge Heath RH12 .**216** D4
Farnham GU9 ....**125** D3
Forge Dr KT10 ....**56** A3
Forge End GU21 ....**69** E2
Forge La
Broadbridge Heath RH12 .**216** D4
Cheam SM2, SM3 ....**58** E3
Crawley RH10 ....**202** A7
Farnborough GU11 ....**105** A6
Feltham TW13 ....**15** E3
Sunbury TW16 ....**35** A6
Forge Lane Inf Sch TW13 .**15** E3
Forge Lane Jun Sch TW13 .**15** E3
Forge Rd Crawley RH10 ..**202** A7
Headley GU35 ....**166** A1
Forge Steading SM7 ......**78** B4
Forge The Harlington UB3 ..**3** D8
Warnham RH12 ....**216** E7
Forge Wood RH10 ....**182** D3
Forge Wood Ind Est
RH10 ....**182** B2
Forgefield TN16 ....**83** D3
Forman Ct TW1 ....**16** F7
Forrest Gdns SW16 ......**41** F6
Forrester Path SE26 .....**23** C4
Forster House SE6 ....**24** D5
Forster Park Sch SE6 ....**24** E6
Forster Rd Beckenham BR3 .**43** E6
Streatham SW2 ....**21** E8
Thornton Heath CR0 ......**42** C2
Forsyte Cres SE19 ....**42** E8
Forsyte Ct KT2 ....**38** B8
Forsyth Path GU21 ......**70** D6
Forsyth Rd GU21 ....**70** C5
Forsythe Shades BR3 .....**44** C8
Forsythia Pl GU1 ....**109** C3
Fort La RH2 ....**118** B5
Fort Narrien GU15 ....**64** F7
Fort Rd Box Hill KT20 ....**116** B4
Guildford GU1 ....**130** E6
Fortescue Ave TW2 ....**16** C5
Fortescue Rd
Mitcham SW19 ....**20** D1
Weybridge KT13 ....**52** F6
Forth Cl GU14 ....**84** D6
Fortrose Cl GU47 ....**64** D7
Fortrose Gdns SW12, SW2 .**21** E7
Fortune Dr GU6 ....**174** E1
Fortyfoot Rd KT22 ....**95** C6
Forum The KT8 ....**36** B5
Forval Cl CR4 ....**40** F4
Foss Ave CR0, CR9 ....**61** A5
Foss Rd SW17 ....**20** D4
Fosse Way KT14 ....**70** F6
Fosseway RG45 ....**45** A5
Fossewood Dr GU15 ......**65** D7
Fosterdown RH9 ....**121** B6
Fosters Gr GU20 ....**48** B6
Fosters La GU21 ....**68** C2
Foulser Rd SW17 ....**21** A5
Foulsham Rd CR7 ....**42** D6
Foundation Units GU1 ...**109** F5
Founders Gdns SE19 ......**22** C1
Foundry Ct RH13 ....**217** E4
Foundry Ct KT16 ....**33** A2
Foundry La
Haslemere GU27 ....**208** A6
Horsham RH12, RH13 ....**217** E3
Horton SL3 ....**1** B4
Foundry Mews KT16 ......**33** A2
Fountain Ct
New Malden KT3 ....**38** C5
Penge SE26 ....**23** C5
Fountain Dr Dulwich SE19 ..**22** F4
Wallington SM6 ....**59** F2
Fountain Rd Redhill RH1 ..**139** E7
South Norwood CR7 ....**42** C7
Upper Tooting SW17 ......**20** D4

Fountains Ave TW13 ......**15** F5
Fountains Cl
Crawley RH11 ....**201** A4
Feltham TW13 ....**15** F5
Fountains Garth RG12 .....**27** A6
Four Acres Cobham KT11 ..**73** E6
Guildford GU1, GU4 ......**110** C3
Four Seasons Cres SM3 ....**58** F8
Four Square Ct TW4 ....**5** A1
Four Wents KT11 ....**73** C5
Fourth Cross Rd TW2 ......**16** D6
Fourth Dr CR5 ....**79** D3
Fowler Cl Crawley RH11 ...**181** B1
Weybridge KT13 ....**53** D5
Woking GU22 ....**70** D4
Fowler Rd
Farnborough GU14 ....**84** F3
Mitcham CR4 ....**41** A7
Fowler's Rd GU11 ....**105** D6
Fowlers La RG42 ....**27** B8
Fowlers Mead GU24 ....**49** E2
Fowlerscroft GU3 ....**129** B2
Fox Cl Crawley RH11 .....**181** B1
Weybridge KT13 ....**53** D5
Woking GU22 ....**70** D4
Fox Covert Fetcham KT22 ..**94** D3
Lightwater GU18 ....**67** A8
Fox Covert Cl SL5 ....**29** C4
Fox Dene GU7 ....**150** C2
Fox Gr KT12 ....**35** B2
Fox Heath GU14 ....**84** C3
Fox Hill SE19 ....**22** F1
Fox Hill Gdns SE19 ....**22** F1
Fox Hill Prim Sch RG12 ...**27** B4
Fox Hills La GU12 ....**106** C3
Fox Hills Rd KT16 ....**51** B5
Fox La KT23 ....**93** F3
Fox La N KT16 ....**32** F1
Fox La S KT16 ....**32** F1
Fox Rd Bracknell RG12 ....**27** C5
Farnham GU9 ....**146** C7
Haslemere GU27 ....**207** E6
Fox Way GU10 ....**124** D8
Fox Yd GU9 ....**125** B2
Foxacre CR3 ....**100** E5
Foxborough Hill GU5 .....**151** D6
Foxborough Hill Rd
GU5 ....**151** D6
Foxbourne Rd SW17 ....**21** A6
Foxbridge La RH14 ......**212** C1
Foxburrows Ave GU2 .....**108** F2
Foxcombe CR0 ....**63** B4
Foxcombe Rd 6 SW15 .....**19** A7
Foxdown Cl GU15 ....**65** C5
Foxearth Cl TN16 ....**83** E1
Foxearth Rd CR2 ....**62** C2
Foxearth Spur CR2 ....**62** C2
Foxenden Rd GU1 ....**109** E1
Foxes Dale BR2 ....**44** D6
Foxes Path GU4 ....**89** F1
Foxglove Ave
Beckenham BR3 ....**24** B1
Horsham RH12 ....**217** E6
Foxglove Cl TW19 ....**13** D7
Foxglove Gdns
Guildford GU4 ....**110** C3
Purley CR8 ....**79** F8
Foxglove La KT9 ....**57** A6
Foxglove Way CR4 ....**41** B1
Foxglove Wlk RH11 ......**201** B3
Foxgrove Dr GU21 ....**70** A4
Foxgrove Rd BR3 ....**24** C1
Foxheath RG12 ....**27** E4
Foxhill Cres GU15 ....**66** B8
Foxhills GU21 ....**69** C2
Foxhills Cl KT16 ....**51** C4
Foxholes Rudgwick RH12 ..**214** D8
Weybridge KT13 ....**53** D5
Foxhurst Rd GU12 ....**106** A4
Foxlake Rd KT14 ....**71** F7
Foxleigh Chase RH12 ....**217** F5
Foxley Cl Blackwater GU17 .**64** E4
Redhill RH1 ....**140** A4
Foxley Ct SM2 ....**59** C3
Foxley Gdns CR8 ....**80** B6
Foxley Hall CR8 ....**80** A6
Foxley Hill Rd CR8 ....**80** A7
Foxley La CR8 ....**60** E1
Foxley Rd Purley CR8 .....**80** B5
Thornton Heath CR7 ......**42** B5
Foxoak Hill KT12, KT13 ...**53** E1
Foxon Cl CR3 ....**100** E6
Foxon La CR3 ....**100** E6
Foxon Lane Gdns CR3 ....**100** E6
Foxtail House TW3 ....**5** C6
Foxton KT1 ....**38** A6
Foxwarren KT10 ....**55** F2
Foxwood Cl TW13 ....**15** B5
Frailey Cl GU22 ....**70** B3
Frailey Hill GU22 ....**70** B3
Framfield Cl RH11 ....**201** A8
Framfield Rd CR4 ....**21** A1
Frampton Cl SM2 ....**59** A3
Frampton Rd TW4 ....**4** E2
France Hill Dr GU15 ......**65** C3
France Hill Sch GU15 .....**65** C2
Frances Ct SE25 ....**42** F4
Franche Court Rd SW17 ...**20** C5
Francis Ave TW13 ....**15** F4
Francis Barber Cl SW16 ...**21** F4
Francis Chichester Cl SL5 .**29** B4
Francis Cl Littleton TW17 ..**34** A1
West Ewell KT19 ....**57** D6
Francis Cnr KT24 ....**133** B8
Francis Ct Guildford GU2 ..**109** B3
Kingston u T KT5 ....**37** E5
Francis Edwards Way
RH11 ....**200** E2
Francis Gr SW19 ....**19** F2

Francis Rd Caterham CR3 .**100** D5
Hounslow TW4 ....**4** D5
Thornton Heath CR0 ......**42** B2
Wallington SM6 ....**60** C4
Francis Way GU15 ....**66** C4
Franciscan Prim Sch
SW17 ....**21** A3
Franciscan Rd SW17 ......**21** A4
Frangate KT24 ....**112** E8
Frank Dixon Cl SE21 ......**22** E7
Frank Dixon Way SE21 ....**22** E7
Frank Towell Ct TW14 .....**15** A7
Frankland House 4 SW12 .**21** B8
Franklands Dr KT15 ....**51** F8
West Norwood SE27 ....**22** B5
Franklin Cl Kingston u T KT1 .**38** A6
West Norwood SE27 ....**22** B5
Franklin Cres CR4 ....**41** C5
Franklin Ct 2 GU2 ......**108** F1
Franklin House BR2 ....**44** F4
Franklin Ind Est SE20 .....**43** C8
Franklin Rd Crawley RH10 **202** C5
Penge SE20 ....**43** C8
Walton-on-T KT12 ....**35** A3
Franklin Way CR0, CR9 ....**41** F2
Franklyn Rd
Godalming GU7 ....**150** B3
Walton-on-T KT12 ....**35** B3
Franks Ave KT3 ....**38** C5
Franks House TW7 ....**6** B3
Franks Rd GU2 ....**109** A3
Franksfield GU5 ....**154** E7
Fransfield Gr SE26 ....**23** B5
Frant Cl SE20 ....**23** C1
Frant Rd CR0, CR7 ....**42** B4
Franthorne Way SE6 ......**24** B5
Fraser Gdns RH4 ....**136** A8
Fraser Mead GU47 ....**64** E6
Fraser Rd RG42 ....**27** B8
Frederick Cl SM1 ....**58** F5
Frederick Gdns SM1 ....**58** F5
Frederick Rd SM1 ....**58** F5
Frederick Sanger Rd
GU2 ....**129** D8
Frederick St GU11 ....**105** A2
Free Prae Rd KT16 ....**33** A1
Freeborn Way RG12 ....**27** E7
Freedown La SM2 ....**78** C6
Freehold Ind Ctr TW4 ......**4** C2
Freelands Ave CR2 ....**62** D2
Freelands Rd KT11 ....**73** B5
Freeman Cl TW17 ....**34** E5
Freeman Dr KT8 ....**35** F5
Freeman House 13 SW2 ....**21** E8
Freeman Rd
Morden CR4, SM4 ....**40** D4
Warnham RH12 ....**216** F8
Freemantle Rd GU19 ......**47** F4
Freemantles Sch (Specl
Sch) KT16 ....**32** E2
Freemason's Rd CR0 ......**42** E1
Freesia Dr GU24 ....**68** A3
Freethorpe Cl SE19 ....**42** E8
French Gdns
Blackwater GU17 ....**64** D4
Cobham KT11 ....**73** C5
French La GU8 ....**169** E3
French St TW16 ....**35** C7
Frenchaye KT15 ....**52** C5
Frenches Ct 4 RH1 ......**119** A3
Frenches Rd RH1 ....**119** B4
Frenches The RH1 ....**119** A3
Frenchlands Hatch KT24 .**112** E8
Frensham RG12 ....**27** D3
Frensham C of E Fst Sch
GU10 ....**167** D7
Frensham Ct CR4 ....**40** D7
Frensham Ctry Pk GU10 .**167** E5
Frensham Dr
New Addington CR0 ....**63** C3
Roehampton SW15 ....**19** A6
Frensham Heights Rd
GU10 ....**146** A2
Frensham Heights Sch
GU10 ....**146** A2
Frensham House 7 KT6 ...**37** E4
Frensham La GU35, GU10 .**166** F2
Frensham Rd
Crowthorne RG45 ....**45** B7
Farnham GU10, GU9 .....**146** D6
Purley CR8 ....**80** B5
Frensham Vale GU10 .....**146** C4
Frensham Way KT17 ....**77** C3
Fresham House RH2 ......**118** A1
Freshborough Ct 1 GU1 .**130** F8
Freshfield SE26 ....**117** E8
Freshfield Bank RH18 ....**206** E2
Freshfield Cl RH10 ......**202** A5
Freshfields CR0 ....**43** F1
Freshford St SW17, SW18 ..**20** C5
Freshmount Gdns KT19 ...**76** B8
Freshwater Cl SW17 ....**21** A2
Freshwater Rd SW17 ......**21** A2
Freshwood Cl BR3 ....**44** B8
Freshwood Way SM6 ......**60** C2
Frewin Rd SW18 ....**20** D7
Friar Mews SE27 ....**22** B5
Friar's Gate GU2 ....**130** A7
Friars Ave SW15 ....**18** F5
Friars Croft GU4 ....**110** C4
Friars Ct Farnham GU9 ...**125** D7
5 Wallington SM6 ....**60** B6
Friars Keep RG12 ....**27** B5
Friars La TW9 ....**.6** D2
Friars Orch KT22 ....**94** D6
Friars Rd GU25 ....**31** D5
Friars Rise GU22 ....**70** A1
Friars Rookery RH10 ....**201** F6

Friars Stile Pl 9 TW10 ....**6** E1
Friars Stile Rd TW10 ....**6** E1
Friars Way KT16 ....**33** A3
Friars Wood CR0 ....**62** E2
Friary Bridge GU1 ....**130** C7
Friary Ct GU21 ....**68** F1
Friary Ho 4 GU1 ....**130** C8
Friary Pas GU1 ....**130** C7
Friary Rd Ascot SL5 ....**29** B3
Wraysbury TW19 ....**11** C8
Friary St GU1 ....**130** C7
Friary The 5 GU1 ....**130** C8
Friary Way RH10 ....**201** E5
Friday Rd CR4 ....**20** F1
Friday St Faygate RH12 ..**198** E6
Ockley RH5 ....**177** E4
Rusper RH12 ....**198** E6
Warnham RH12 ....**216** E7
Friday Street Rd RH5 ....**155** E8
Friend Ave GU12 ....**105** D1
Friends Cl RH11 ....**181** D1
Friends' Rd CR0, CR9 .....**61** D7
Friends Rd CR8 ....**80** B7
Friendship Way RG12 .....**27** B6
Friern Rd SE22 ....**23** A8
Frimley Ave SM6 ....**60** F5
Frimley Bsns Pk GU16 ....**85** B8
Frimley CE Jun Sch GU16 .**85** E7
Frimley Cl
New Addington CR0 ....**63** C3
Putney SW19 ....**19** E6
Frimley Cres CR0 ....**63** C3
Frimley Gdns CR4 ....**40** E6
Frimley Green Rd GU16 ...**85** E7
Frimley Grove Gdns GU16 **65** E1
Frimley Hall Dr GU15 .....**65** F6
Frimley High St GU16 ....**85** D8
Frimley House CR4 ....**40** E6
Frimley Park Hospl GU16 .**65** D2
Frimley Rd Ash Vale GU12 **106** A8
Camberley GU15 ....**65** B3
Chessington KT9 ....**56** E5
Frimley GU15, GU16 ......**65** C1
Frinton Rd SW17 ....**21** A2
Friston Wlk RH11 ....**201** A7
Frith End Rd GU34, GU35 .**166** A6
Frith Hill Rd
Farncombe GU7 ....**150** D6
Frimley GU16 ....**66** B1
Frith Knowle KT12 ....**54** B5
Frith Pk RH19 ....**185** E3
Frith Rd CR0, CR9 ....**61** C8
Fritham Cl KT3 ....**38** E3
Friths Dr RH2 ....**118** B4
Frithwald Rd KT16 ....**32** F1
Frobisher RG12 ....**27** C2
Frobisher Cl CR8 ....**80** C2
Frobisher Cres TW19 ......**13** E8
Frobisher Ct Belmont SM2 .**58** F3
Forest Hill SE23 ....**23** B6
Frobisher Gdns
Guildford GU1 ....**110** A2
Stanwell TW19 ....**13** E8
Frodsham Way GU47 ......**45** E2
Frog Grove La GU3 ......**107** F4
Frog Hall RG40 ....**25** E5
Frog La Bracknell RG12 ....**27** A6
Woking GU4 ....**89** E2
Froggetts La RH5 ....**176** C1
Frogmore Cl SM3 ....**58** E7
Frogmore Comm Coll
GU46 ....**64** A5
Frogmore Ct GU12 ....**64** C4
Frogmore Cty Infs Sch
GU17 ....**64** B5
Frogmore Cty Jun Sch
GU17 ....**64** B5
Frogmore Gdns SM3 ....**58** E6
Frogmore Gr GU17 ....**64** C4
Frogmore Park Dr GU17 ..**64** C4
Frogmore Rd GU17 ....**64** C4
Frome Cl GU14 ....**84** D6
Fromondes Rd SM3 ....**58** E5
Fromow Gdns GU20 ....**48** D4
Froxfield Down 6 RG12 ...**27** F4
Fruen Rd TW14 ....**14** F8
Fry Cl RH11 ....**201** B1
Fry's Cross GU8 ....**193** A2
Fryern Wood CR3 ....**100** C3
Frylands Ct CR0 ....**82** C8
Fryston Ave Croydon CR0 ..**62** A8
Wallington CR5 ....**79** B5
Fuchsia Way GU4 ....**67** G6
Fuel Farm Rd RH6 ....**181** D6
Fulbourn 4 KT1 ....**38** A7
Fulbourne Cl RH1 ....**118** C1
Fulford Rd Caterham CR3 .**100** D6
West Ewell KT19 ....**57** D3
Fulham Cl RH11 ....**201** B2
Fullbrook Ave KT15 ....**71** A8
Fullbrook Cty Sec Sch
KT15 ....**71** A8
Fullbrooks Ave KT4 ....**38** F1
Fuller Wood CR0 ....**63** A6
Fuller's Ave KT6 ....**56** F8
Fullers Ave KT6 ....**56** F8
Fullers Farm Rd KT24 ...**112** B1
Fullers Rd Binstead GU10 .**145** D3
Rowledge GU10 ....**145** D3
Fullers Way N KT6 ....**56** F6
Fullers Way S KT6 ....**56** F7
Fullers Wood La RH1 ....**119** C5
Fullerton Cl KT14 ....**71** F5
Fullerton Ct TW11 ....**16** F3
Fullerton Dr KT14 ....**71** F5
Fullerton Rd Byfleet KT14 .**71** F5
Croydon CR0 ....**42** F2
Sutton SM5 ....**59** E2

Fullerton Way KT14 ....**71** E5
Fullmer Way KT15 ....**51** F1
Fulmar Cl 1 RH11 ....**200** D5
Fulmar Ct 5 SE21 ....**22** D6
Fulmar Dr RH19 ....**186** B3
Fulmer Cl TW12 ....**15** E3
Fulstone Cl TW4 ....**4** F3
Fulvens GU5 ....**133** E1
Fulwell Golf Course TW12 **16** C4
Fulwell Park Ave TW2 .....**16** C6
Fulwell Rd TW11, TW12 ....**16** D4
Fulwell Sta TW11 ....**16** D4
Fulwood Gdns TW1 ....**.6** A1
Fulwood Wlk SW19 ....**19** E7
Furlong Cl CR4 ....**41** B1
Furlong Rd RH4 ....**135** C6
Furlong Way RH6 ....**181** F8
Furlough The GU22 ....**70** A2
Furmage St SW18 ....**20** B8
Furnace Dr RH10 ....**201** F4
Furnace Farm Rd RH10 ..**202** A4
Furnace Par RH10 ....**202** A4
Furnace Pl RH10 ....**202** A4
Furnace Rd RH10 ....**184** C3
Furneaux Ave SE27 ....**22** B3
Furness Rd SM4 ....**40** B3
Furness Ct GU6 ....**173** F2
Furnival Cl GU25 ....**31** D3
Furrows Pl CR3 ....**100** F4
Furrows The KT12 ....**54** C8
Furse Cl GU15 ....**66** C4
Further Green Rd SE6 .....**24** E7
Furtherfield GU6 ....**174** E4
Furtherfield Cl CR0 ....**42** A3
Furze Cl Ash Vale GU12 ..**106** A7
Redhill RH1 ....**118** C3
Furze Ct CR0 ....**62** A8
Furze Field KT22 ....**74** E6
Furze Gr KT20 ....**97** F6
Furze Hill Kingswood KT20 .**97** F6
Purley CR8 ....**79** F8
Furze Hill Cres RG45 ......**45** C4
Furze Hill Rd GU35 ......**187** C4
Furze La
East Grinstead RH19 .....**185** B4
Farncombe GU7, GU3 ....**150** F8
Purley CR8 ....**79** F8
Furze Rd Addlestone KT15 ..**51** F4
Rudgwick RH12 ....**214** D8
South Norwood CR7 ......**42** C6
Furze Vale Rd GU35 ......**187** B4
Furzebank SL5 ....**29** D5
Furzedown Dr TW20 ....**11** E2
Furzedown Dr SW17 ....**21** B3
Furzedown Prim Sch
SW17 ....**21** A2
Furzedown Rd
Streatham SW17 ....**21** B3
Sutton SM2 ....**78** C8
Furzefield RH11 ....**201** C2
Furzefield Chase RH19 ...**185** E6
Furzefield Cres RH2 .....**139** C7
Furzefield Cty Prim Sch
RH1 ....**119** D7
Furzefield Rd
East Grinstead RH19 .....**185** D4
Horsham RH12 ....**218** B5
Reigate RH2 ....**139** C7
Furzehill RH1 ....**118** E2
Furzeland House 2 KT3 ...**38** E2
Furzemoors RG12 ....**27** B4
Furzen La
Ellen's Green RH12, RH5 .**196** B4
Wallis Wood RH12, RH5 ..**196** B4
Furzewood TW16 ....**35** A8
Fyfield Cl
Beckenham BR2, BR3 .....**44** D5
Blackwater GU17 ....**64** D5

G

Gable Ct Forest Hill SE26 ..**23** B4
9 Redhill RH1 ....**119** A2
Gable End GU14 ....**85** B4
Gable Lodge BR4 ....**44** C1
Gables Ave TW15 ....**13** F3
Gables Cl Ash Vale GU12 .**106** A5
Farnborough GU14 ....**85** A4
Old Woking GU22 ....**89** F7
Gables Ct GU22 ....**89** F7
Gables The Banstead SM7 ..**77** F2
Copthorne RH10 ....**183** B3
Elstead GU8 ....**148** C3
Horsham RH12 ....**217** D4
Oxshott KT22 ....**74** C7
Weybridge KT13 ....**53** C5
Gabriel Cl TW13 ....**15** D4
Gabriel Dr GU15 ....**66** B4
Gabriel Rd RH10 ....**202** C2
Gabriel St SE23 ....**23** E8
Gadbridge La GU6 ....**175** E4
Gadbrook Rd RH3 ....**137** D4
Gaffney Cl GU11 ....**105** D7
Gage Cl RH10 ....**184** C1
Gage Ridge RH18 ....**206** E2
Gainsborough RG12 ....**27** C3
Gainsborough Cl
Beckenham BR3 ....**24** A1
Camberley GU15 ....**65** F7
Farnborough GU14 ....**85** D2
Thames Ditton KT10 ......**36** E1
Gainsborough Ct
Dulwich SE21 ....**22** E6

Gainsborough Ct continued
Walton-on-T KT12 . . . . .54 A6
Gainsborough Dr
North Ascot SL5 . . . . .28 D7
Sanderstead CR2 . . . . .81 A6
Gainsborough Gdns TW7 . .5 D2
Gainsborough Mews SE26 23 B5
Gainsborough Rd
Crawley RH10 . . . . .201 F3
Epsom KT19 . . . . .57 C1
New Malden KT3 . . . . .38 D2
Richmond TW9 . . . . .6 F4
Gaist Ave CR3 . . . . .101 B5
Galahad Ho RH1 . . . . .119 A2
Galahad Rd RH11 . . . . . . .200 E6
Galba Ct 1 TW8 . . . . .6 D7
Gale Cl Hampton TW12 . . .15 E2
Mitcham CR4 . . . . .40 D6
Gale Cres SM7 . . . . .78 A2
Gale Dr GU18 . . . . .48 A1
Gales Dr RH10 . . . . .201 F6
Gales Pl RH10 . . . . .201 F6
Galgate Cl 4 SW19 . . . . . .19 E7
Gallery Rd Dulwich SE21 . . .22 D7
Pirbright GU24 . . . . .87 D8
Galleymead Rd SL3 . . . . . . .1 F6
Gallop The
South Croydon CR2 . . . . .62 B3
Sutton SM2 . . . . .59 D2
Gallwey Rd GU11 . . . . .105 C3
Galpin's Rd CR4, CR7 . . . . .41 F5
Galsworthy Rd
Chertsey KT16 . . . . .33 A2
Kingston u T KT2 . . . . .38 B8
Galton Rd SL5 . . . . .29 F3
Galvani Way CR0, CR9 . . . .41 F1
Galvins Rd GU4 . . . . .109 A4
Gambles La GU23 . . . . .91 C2
Gambole Rd SW17 . . . . . . .20 E4
Gander Green Cres TW12 .36 A8
Gander Green La
KT4, SM1, SM3 . . . . .58 F7
Gangers Hill CR3, RH9 . . . .121 F7
Ganghill GU1 . . . . .110 A3
Gannet Ct 4 SE21 . . . . .22 D6
Ganymede Ct RH11 . . . . . . .200 E3
Gap Rd SW19 . . . . .20 B3
Gapemouth Rd GU16, GU24 86 E5
Garbetts Way GU10 . . . . . .126 F6
Garbrand Wlk KT17 . . . . . . .57 F2
Garden Ave CR4 . . . . .21 B1
Garden Cl Addlestone KT15 .52 D6
Ashford TW15 . . . . .14 C2
Banstead SM7 . . . . .78 A4
East Grinstead RH19 . . . . . .205 F7
Farnborough GU14 . . . . .84 E3
Hampton TW12 . . . . .15 F3
Leatherhead KT22 . . . . .95 C3
Putney SW15 . . . . .19 B8
Shamley Green GU5 . . . . . . .152 D4
Wallington SM6 . . . . .60 E5
Garden Ct 5 Belmont SM2 .59 A3
4 Richmond TW9 . . . . .6 F6
South Croydon CR0 . . . . .61 F7
Garden Flats SW16 . . . . . . .21 E5
Garden House La RH19 . . .205 F7
Garden La SW2 . . . . .21 F7
Garden Pl RH10 . . . . .217 C4
Garden Rd Mortlake TW9 . . .7 A4
Penge SE20 . . . . .43 C8
Walton-on-T KT12 . . . . .35 B2
Garden The KT24 . . . . .113 D7
Garden Wlk Beckenham BR3 43 F8
Crawley RH11 . . . . .201 C6
Hooley CR5 . . . . .99 B4
Horsham RH12 . . . . .217 C4
Garden Wood Rd RH19 . . .205 C8
Gardener's Hill Rd GU10 .146 B4
Gardener's Wlk KT23 . . . . .94 B1
Gardeners Cl RH12 . . . . . .216 E8
Gardeners Ct RH13 . . . . . .217 D1
Gardeners Gn RH12 . . . . . .199 C6
Gardeners Rd CR0 . . . . .42 B1
Gardenfields KT20 . . . . . . .97 E8
Gardenia Ct 1 BR3 . . . . . . .24 A1
Gardenia Dr GU24 . . . . .67 F6
Gardens The
Beckenham BR3 . . . . .44 D7
Esher KT10 . . . . .55 A6
Hatton TW14 . . . . .3 D1
Pirbright GU24 . . . . .87 F5
Tongham GU10 . . . . .126 F7
Gardner House TW13 . . . . .15 F6
Gardner Ind Est SE26 . . . .23 F3
Gardner La RH10 . . . . .204 A8
Gardner Pl TW14 . . . . .4 B1
Gardner Rd GU1 . . . . .109 D1
Garendon Gdns SM4 . . . . . .40 B2
Garendon Rd SM4 . . . . .40 B2
Gareth Cl KT4 . . . . .58 D8
Gareth Ct SW16 . . . . .21 D5
Garfield Prim Sch SW19 . .20 C2
Garfield Rd
Addlestone KT15 . . . . .52 C6
Camberley GU15 . . . . .65 C5
2 Twickenham TW1 . . . . . . .17 A7
Wimbledon SW19 . . . . .20 C2
Garibaldi Rd RH1 . . . . .139 F8
Garland Rd RH19 . . . . .185 D2
Garland Way CR3 . . . . .100 D5
Garlands Rd
Leatherhead KT22 . . . . .95 C6
Redhill RH1 . . . . .118 F1
Garlichill Rd KT17, KT18 . . .77 B2

Garlies Rd SE23 . . . . .23 E5
Garnet House KT4 . . . . . . .38 D1
Garnet Rd CR7 . . . . .42 D5
Garrad's Rd SW16 . . . . . . .21 D4
Garrard Rd SM7 . . . . .78 A3
Garrat La SW17, SW18 . . . .20 C5
Garratt Cl CR0 . . . . .60 E6
Garratt La SW17, SW18 . . . .20 C5
Garratt Park Sec Sch
SW18 . . . . .20 C5
Garratt Terr SW17 . . . . . . .20 E4
Garratts La SM7 . . . . .78 A4
Garrett Cl RH10 . . . . .202 C4
Garraway House SE21 . . . . .22 F5
Garrett Ct RH10 . . . . .202 C4
Garrick Cl Hersham KT12 . . .54 B6
1 Richmond TW9 . . . . .6 D2
Staines TW18 . . . . .13 A1
Garrick Cres CR0 . . . . .61 E8
Garrick Gdns KT8 . . . . .36 A6
Garrick House Chiswick W4 .7 E8
2 Kingston u T KT1 . . . . . . .37 E5
7 Streatham SW16 . . . . . . .21 C3
Garrick Rd TW9 . . . . .7 A5
Garrick Way GU16 . . . . . . .85 E7
Garrick Wlk RH10 . . . . . . .201 E3
Garrick's Ait KT8 . . . . .36 C7
Garrison Cl TW4 . . . . .4 F2
Garrison La KT9 . . . . .56 E3
Garrones The RH10 . . . . . .202 E7
Garside Cl TW12 . . . . .16 B2
Garson La TW19 . . . . .11 D8
Garson Rd KT10 . . . . .54 F4
Garson's La SL4 . . . . .8 A7
Garston Gdns CR8 . . . . . . .80 D4
Garston La CR8 . . . . .80 D4
Garstons The KT23 . . . . . . .94 A2
Garswood RG12 . . . . .27 D3
Garth Cl Farnham GU9 . . . .146 A2
Kingston u T KT2 . . . . .17 F3
West Barnes SM4 . . . . .39 D2
Garth Ct W4 . . . . .7 D8
Garth High Sch SM4 . . . . .40 D3
Garth Hill Sch RG12 . . . . . .27 C8
Garth Rd Chiswick W4 . . . . . .7 D8
Kingston u T KT2 . . . . .17 F3
West Barnes SM4 . . . . .39 D2
Garth The Ash GU10, GU12 105 F1
Cobham KT11 . . . . .73 E6
Farnborough GU14 . . . . .85 D4
Hampton TW12 . . . . .16 B2
Garthorne Rd SE23 . . . . . . .23 D8
Garthside TW10 . . . . .17 E3
Gartmoor Gdns SW19 . . . . .19 F7
Garton Cl RH11 . . . . .200 E5
Garvens SE19 . . . . .22 E3
Gascoigne Rd
New Addington CR0 . . . . .63 C2
Weybridge KT13 . . . . .53 B7
Gasden Copse GU8 . . . . . .170 D5
Gasden Dr GU8 . . . . .170 D6
Gasden La GU8 . . . . .170 D6
Gaskyns Cl RH12 . . . . .214 D7
Gassiot Rd SW17 . . . . .20 F4
Gassiot Way SM1 . . . . .59 D7
Gasson Wood Rd RH11 . . .200 E4
Gaston Bell Cl TW9 . . . . . . .6 F4
Gaston Bridge Rd
Shepperton TW17 . . . . .34 D3
Upper Halliford TW17 . . . . . .34 E4
Gaston Rd CR4 . . . . .41 A6
Gaston Way TW17 . . . . .34 D4
Gatcombe Ct BR3 . . . . .24 A1
Gate Ct 4 KT13 . . . . .53 B7
Gate House 4 KT6 . . . . . . .37 E1
Gate St GU5 . . . . .173 D7
Gateford Dr RH12 . . . . . . .217 F6
Gatehouse Cl KT2 . . . . .18 C1
Gates Cl RH10 . . . . .202 C2
Gates Green Rd BR4 . . . . . .63 F7
Gatesden Rd KT22 . . . . . . .94 C4
Gateside Rd SW17 . . . . . . .20 F5
Gatestone Ct 9 SE19 . . . . .22 E2
Gatestone Rd SE19 . . . . . . .22 E2
Gateway The GU21 . . . . . . .70 C5
Gateways Guildford GU1 . .131 B8
Kingston u T KT6 . . . . .37 E4
Gateways Ct SM6 . . . . .60 B5
Gateways The 6 D3
Gatfield Gr TW13 . . . . .16 A6
Gatfield House TW13 . . . . .16 A6
Gatley Ave KT19 . . . . .57 B5
Gatley Dr GU1 . . . . .109 F4
Gatton Bottom
Gatton RH2, RH1 . . . . .118 E7
Lower Kingswood RH1, RH2 119 B8
Merstham RH1, RH2 . . . . . .119 B8
Gatton Cl Reigate RH2 . . . .118 C4
Sutton SM2 . . . . .59 B2
Gatton Park Ct RH1 . . . . . .118 E4
Gatton Park Rd RH1, RH2 118 E4
Gatton Point RH1 . . . . .119 A5
Gatton Rd Reigate RH2 . . . .118 C4
Upper Tooting SW17 . . . . . . .20 E4
Gatwick Airport Sta RH6 .182 B7
GatwickAirport-London
RH6 . . . . .181 F7
Gatwick Gate RH11 . . . . . .181 E5
Gatwick Metro Ctr RH6 . . .161 B4
Gatwick Park Hospl RH6 .160 E2
Gatwick Rd
Crawley RH10, RH6 . . . . . . .182 A3
Wandsworth SW18 . . . . .19 F8
Gatwick Way RH6 . . . . . . .181 F8
Gatwick Zoo RH6 . . . . .180 D6
Gauntlet Cres CR3, CR8 . . .100 D7
Gauntlett Rd SM1 . . . . .59 D5
Gavell Rd KT11 . . . . .73 A6
Gaveston Cl KT14 . . . . .71 F6

Gaveston Rd KT22 . . . . .95 A7
Gavina Cl SM4 . . . . .40 E4
Gayfere Rd KT17 . . . . .58 A5
Gayhouse La RH1 . . . . .162 E8
Gayler Cl RH1 . . . . .120 F2
Gaynesford Rd
Forest Hill SE23 . . . . .23 D6
Wallington SM5 . . . . .59 F3
Gaysland Cotts RH7 . . . . . .143 A2
Gayton Cl KT21 . . . . .75 E1
Gayton Ct New Malden KT3 .38 F4
Reigate RH2 . . . . .118 A2
Gaywood Cl SW2 . . . . .22 A7
Gaywood Rd KT21 . . . . .75 F1
Geary Cl RH6 . . . . .162 B1
Gedge Ct CR4 . . . . .40 E5
Geffers Ride SL5 . . . . .28 E7
Gemini Cl RH11 . . . . .200 E4
Gemma Ct BR3 . . . . .43 F7
Genesis Bsns Pk GU21 . . . .70 C4
Geneva Cl TW17 . . . . .34 E7
Geneva Rd Kingston u T KT1 37 E5
Thornton Heath CR7 . . . . . . .42 C4
Genoa Rd SE20 . . . . .43 C8
Gentles La GU30, GU35 . . .187 A4
Genyn Rd GU2 . . . . .130 B8
George Abbot Sch GU1 . .110 A3
George Denyer Cl GU27 . .208 C7
George Eliot Cl GU8 . . . . .170 F5
George Gdns GU11 . . . . . .126 C2
George Groves Rd SE20 . . .43 A8
George Horley Pl RH5 . . . .158 B1
George House 8 SE26 . . . . .23 B3
George Pinion Ct RH12 . . .217 B3
George Rd Farncombe GU7 150 F7
Guildford GU1 . . . . .109 D1
Kingston u T KT2 . . . . .18 C1
Milford GU8 . . . . .149 F2
New Malden KT3 . . . . .38 F4
George Sq SW19 . . . . .40 A6
George St
Croydon CR0, CR9 . . . . .61 D8
Hounslow TW3, TW5 . . . . .4 F5
Pirbright GU24 . . . . .87 A6
Richmond TW10 . . . . .6 D2
Staines TW18 . . . . .13 B4
George Wyver Cl SW18 . . .19 E8
George's Rd TN16 . . . . . . .103 D7
Georgeham Rd GU47 . . . . . .45 D7
Georgelands GU23 . . . . .91 B6
Georges Terr CR3 . . . . .100 D5
Georgetown Ct 4 SE19 . . .22 E3
Georgia Rd
Kingston u T KT3 . . . . .38 C5
South Norwood CR7 . . . . . . .42 B8
Georgian Cl
Camberley GU15 . . . . .65 E7
Crawley RH10 . . . . .202 D5
Staines TW18 . . . . .13 B4
Georgian Ct CR0, CR9 . . . . .42 D1
Georgina Ct 5 TW1 . . . . . . .6 C1
Gerald Ct RH13 . . . . .217 E2
Geraldine Rd W4 . . . . .7 A8
Gerard Ave TW4 . . . . .16 A8
Gerard Rd SW13 . . . . .7 F6
Germander Dr GU24 . . . . . .68 A4
Gerrards Mead SM7 . . . . . .77 F3
Ghent St SE6 . . . . .24 A6
Ghyll Cres RH13 . . . . .217 F1
Gibb's Acre GU24 . . . . .87 F4
Gibbet La GU15 . . . . .66 A7
Gibbon Rd KT2 . . . . .17 F1
Gibbons Cl Crawley RH10 .202 C4
Sandhurst GU47 . . . . .64 C8
Gibbs Ave SE19 . . . . .22 D3
Gibbs Brook La
Crowhurst RH7, RH8 . . . . . .143 D7
Oxted RH7, RH8 . . . . .143 D7
Gibbs Cl SE19 . . . . .22 D3
Gibbs House
6 Balham SW12 . . . . .21 B8
Bromley BR1 . . . . .44 F8
Gibbs Sq SE19 . . . . .22 D3
Giblets La RH12 . . . . .217 F3
Giblets Way RH12 . . . . . . .217 E7
Gibraltar Cres KT19 . . . . . .57 E1
Gibson Cl Chessington KT9 .56 C5
Isleworth TW7 . . . . .5 D4
Gibson Ct KT10 . . . . .55 F7
Gibson House SM1 . . . . . . .59 A6
Gibson Pl TW19 . . . . .2 C1
Gibson Rd SM1 . . . . .59 B5
Gibson's Hill
South Norwood SW16 . . . . . .22 A1
South Norwood SW16 . . . . . .22 A2
Gidd Hill CR5 . . . . .79 A3
Giffard Dr GU14 . . . . .84 F5
Giffard Way GU2 . . . . .109 A4
Giffards Cl RH19 . . . . .185 F1
Giffards Meadow GU9 . . . .125 E1
Giggs Hill Rd KT7 . . . . .37 A2
Giggshill Gdns KT7 . . . . . . .37 A1
Gilbert Cl 1 SW19 . . . . . . .40 B8
Gilbert Rd Frimley GU15 . . .65 C1
Merton SW19 . . . . .20 C1
Gilbert Scott Jun & Inf
Sch CR2 . . . . .62 E3
Gilbert St TW3 . . . . .5 C4
Gilbey Rd SW17 . . . . .20 E4
Gilders Rd KT9 . . . . .56 F4
Giles Coppice SE19 . . . . . . .22 F4
Giles Travers Cl TW20 . . . .32 C6
Gilesmead KT18 . . . . .76 E5
Gilham La RH18 . . . . .206 E2
Gilham's Ave SM7 . . . . .77 E7
Gill Ave GU2 . . . . .129 E8

Gillett Ct RH13 . . . . .218 B4
Gillett House RH13 . . . . . .218 B4
Gillett Rd CR7 . . . . .42 D5
Gillette Cnr TW7 . . . . .6 A7
Gillham's La GU27 . . . . . . .207 A5
Gilliam Gr CR8 . . . . .61 A1
Gillian Ave GU11, GU12 . . .126 C8
Gillian Cl GU12 . . . . .126 D8
Gillian Park Rd SM3 . . . . . .39 F1
Gilliat Dr GU4 . . . . .110 D3
Gilligan Cl RH12 . . . . .217 B2
Gilmais KT23 . . . . .94 C2
Gilmore Cres TW15 . . . . . . .14 A2
Gilpin Ave SW14 . . . . .7 D3
Gilpin Cl CR4 . . . . .40 E7
Gilpin Cres TW2 . . . . .16 B8
Gilpin Way UB3 . . . . .3 D7
Gilsland Rd CR7 . . . . .42 D5
Gilton Rd SE6 . . . . .24 E5
Gimcrack Hill KT22 . . . . . . .95 B5
Gingers Cl GU6 . . . . .174 F2
Ginhams Rd RH11 . . . . . . .201 B6
Gipsy Hill SE19, SE27 . . . . .22 E3
Wokingham RG40 . . . . .25 C4
Gipsy Hill Sta SE19 . . . . . .22 E3
Gipsy La Bracknell RG12 . . .27 D7
Wokingham RG40 . . . . .25 C4
Gipsy Rd SE21, SE27 . . . . . .22 D4
Gipsy Road Gdns SE27 . . . .22 D4
Girdwood Rd SW18, SW19 .19 E8
Girling Way TW14 . . . . .4 A4
Girton Cl GU47 . . . . .45 E1
Girton Gdns CR0 . . . . .63 A7
Girton Rd SE26 . . . . .23 D3
Gittens Cl BR1 . . . . .24 F4
Giunevere Ho RH1 . . . . . . .119 A2
Glade Cl KT6 . . . . .56 D8
Glade Gdns CR0 . . . . .43 E2
Glade House SL5 . . . . .29 D4
Glade Spur KT20 . . . . .98 B6
Glade The Ascot SL5 . . . . . .29 C4
Belmont SM2 . . . . .58 E2
Binstead GU10 . . . . .145 B1
Coulsdon CR5, CR8 . . . . . . .100 A8
Crawley RH10 . . . . .202 A4
Croydon CR0 . . . . .43 D3
Fetcham KT22 . . . . .94 B5
Heath End GU9 . . . . .125 D7
Horsham RH13 . . . . .218 A5
Kingswood KT20 . . . . .98 B6
Mytchett GU16 . . . . .86 A2
Sheerwater KT14 . . . . .70 E6
Staines TW18 . . . . .13 B2
Stoneleigh KT17 . . . . .58 A4
West Wickham BR4 . . . . .63 B7
Glades The RH19 . . . . .186 B1
Gladeside CR0 . . . . .43 D3
Gladeside Ct CR6 . . . . .101 B7
Gladiator St SE23 . . . . .23 E8
Gladiator Way
GU11, GU14 . . . . .105 A8
Gladioli Cl 6 TW12 . . . . . . .16 A2
Gladsmuir Cl KT12 . . . . . . .54 C8
Gladstone Ave Feltham TW14 4 B1
Twickenham TW2 . . . . .16 D8
Gladstone Ct 5 SW19 . . . . .20 A1
Gladstone Gdns TW3 . . . . . .5 C6
Gladstone Mews 3 SE20 . .23 C1
Gladstone Pl KT8 . . . . .36 E4
Gladstone Rd
Ashstead KT21 . . . . .75 D1
Croydon CR0 . . . . .42 D2
Horsham RH12 . . . . .217 D3
Kingston u T KT1 . . . . .38 A6
Merton SW19 . . . . .20 A1
Surbiton KT6 . . . . .56 E8
Glamis Cl GU16 . . . . .85 F7
Glamis Ho 10 RH2 . . . . . . .118 F1
Glamorgan Cl CR4, SW16 . .41 E6
Glamorgan Rd KT1 . . . . . . .17 C1
Glanfield Rd BR3 . . . . .43 F5
Glanty The TW20 . . . . .12 B4
Glanville House 4 SW12 . .21 C8
Glanville Wlk 8 RH11 . . . .201 A3
Glasbrook Ave TW2 . . . . . . .15 F7
Glasford St SW17 . . . . .20 F2
Glasmill La BR2 . . . . .44 F7
Glassonby Wlk GU15 . . . . . .66 C5
Glastonbury Prim Sch
SM4 . . . . .40 B2
Glastonbury Rd Cheam CR4 40 A2
Morden SM4 . . . . .40 A2
Glayshers Hill GU35 . . . . . .187 B6
Glazebrook Cl SE21 . . . . . . .22 D6
Glazebrook Rd TW11 . . . . . .16 F1
Glaziers La GU3 . . . . .107 C2
Gleave Cl RH19 . . . . .186 A2
Glebe Ave CR4 . . . . .40 E7
Glebe Cl Crawley RH10 . . . .201 E7
Great Bookham KT23 . . . . . .94 A1
Lightwater GU18 . . . . .48 C1
Sanderstead CR2 . . . . .80 E8
Glebe Cotts Feltham TW13 .16 A5
West Clandon GU4 . . . . .111 B3
Glebe Ct Guildford GU1 . . .109 F1
Mitcham CR4 . . . . .40 E6
Glebe Gdns Byfleet KT14 . . .71 E5
New Malden KT3 . . . . .38 E2
Glebe House TW13 . . . . . . .16 A5
Glebe Hyrst CR2 . . . . .80 F7
Glebe La
Abinger Common RH5 . . . . .155 D8
Rushmoor GU10 . . . . .168 C5
Glebe Path CR4 . . . . .40 E6
Glebe Rd Ashstead KT21 . . .75 D1
Belmont SM2 . . . . .58 E2
Cranleigh GU6 . . . . .174 E4
Dorking RH4 . . . . .135 F7
Egham TW20 . . . . .12 C2

Glebe Rd continued
Farnborough GU14 . . . . .84 F5
Merstham CR5 . . . . .99 B3
Staines TW18 . . . . .13 B3
Wallington SM5 . . . . .59 F4
Warlingham CR6 . . . . .81 D2
Glebe Sch BR4 . . . . .63 D8
Glebe Side TW1 . . . . .5 F1
Glebe Sq CR4 . . . . .40 E6
Glebe The Blackwater GU17 .64 E4
Copthorne RH10 . . . . .183 B3
Ewhurst GU6 . . . . .175 E6
Felbridge RH19 . . . . .185 A4
Horley RH6 . . . . .160 F3
Leigh RH2 . . . . .138 A2
New Malden KT4 . . . . .38 F1
Streatham SW16 . . . . .21 D4
Glebe Way Coney Hall BR4 .63 E7
Feltham TW13 . . . . .16 A5
Sanderstead CR2 . . . . .80 F8
West Wickham BR4 . . . . .63 D8
Glebeland Ctr RH4 . . . . . . .136 A7
Glebeland Gdns TW17 . . . . .34 C3
Glebeland Rd GU15 . . . . . . .64 E6
Glebelands Claygate KT10 . .55 F2
Crawley Down RH10 . . . . . . .204 A7
East Molesey KT8 . . . . .36 B5
Loxwood RH14 . . . . .212 F4
Glebelands Rd
East Bedfont TW14 . . . . .15 A8
Wokingham RG40 . . . . .25 C7
Glebelands Sch GU6 . . . . .174 D3
Glebewood RG12 . . . . .27 C4
Gledhow Wood KT20 . . . . . .98 B5
Gleeson Mews KT15 . . . . . .52 C6
Glen Albyn Rd SW19 . . . . . .19 D6
Glen Ave TW15 . . . . .14 A4
Glen Cl Beacon Hill GU26 . .188 C6
Kingswood KT20 . . . . .97 E4
Littleton TW17 . . . . .34 A5
Glen Court Flats GU26 . . .188 C6
Glen Ct Addlestone KT15 . . .51 F5
Bromley BR1 . . . . .24 F1
10 Penge SE20 . . . . .43 B8
Staines TW18 . . . . .12 F1
Glen Dale Mews BR3 . . . . . .44 B8
Glen Gdns CR0, CR9 . . . . . .61 A6
Glen Innes GU47 . . . . .45 E1
Glen Rd Beacon Hill GU26 . .188 C6
Chessington KT9 . . . . .56 F7
Grayshott GU26 . . . . .188 C3
Glen Road End SM6 . . . . . . .60 B2
Glen The Addlestone KT15 . .51 F5
Ascot SL5 . . . . .29 D5
Beckenham BR2 . . . . .44 E7
Croydon CR0 . . . . .62 D7
Redhill RH1 . . . . .139 F8
Glen Vue RH19 . . . . .185 E1
Glen Wlk TW7 . . . . .5 D2
Glena Mount SM1 . . . . .59 C6
Glenalmond House TW15 . .13 E5
Glenavon Cl KT10 . . . . .56 A4
Glenavon Ct KT4 . . . . .58 B8
Glenbow Rd BR1 . . . . .24 E3
Glenbuck Ct 6 KT6 . . . . . . .37 E3
Glenbuck Rd KT6 . . . . .37 E3
Glenburnie Rd SW17 . . . . . .20 F5
Glencairn Rd SW16 . . . . . . .21 E1
Glencoe Cl GU16 . . . . .86 A8
Glencoe Rd KT13 . . . . .53 A7
Glendale Cl
Horsham RH12 . . . . .218 A6
Woking GU21 . . . . .69 C1
Glendale Dr GU4 . . . . .110 C5
Glendale Rise CR8 . . . . .80 B4
Glendene Ave KT24 . . . . . . .92 E1
Glendon House 9 RH10 . . .201 D5
Glendower Gdns 10 SW14 . .7 D4
Glendower Rd SW14 . . . . . . .7 D4
Glendyne Cl RH19 . . . . . . .206 A8
Glendyne Way RH19 . . . . . .206 A8
Gleneagle Lodge BR3 . . . . .44 A8
Gleneagle Mews SW16 . . . .21 D3
Gleneagle Rd SW16 . . . . . . .21 D3
Gleneagles Cl TW19 . . . . . . .2 D1
Gleneagles Ct
Crawley RH10, RH11 . . . . . .201 D5
3 Teddington TW11 . . . . . . .17 A3
Gleneagles Dr GU14 . . . . . .84 C3
Gleneagles House RG12 . . .26 E3
Gleneldon Mews SW16 . . . .21 E4
Gleneldon Rd SW16 . . . . . . .21 E4
Glenfarg Rd SE6 . . . . .24 D7
Glenfield Cl RH3 . . . . .137 B5
Glenfield Cotts RH6 . . . . . .180 C5
Glenfield House RG12 . . . . .27 C5
Glenfield Rd Ashford TW15 .14 C2
Banstead SM7 . . . . .78 B4
Brockham RH3 . . . . .137 B6
Streatham SW12 . . . . .21 C7
Glenhaven Dr TW19 . . . . . . .2 A2
Glenheadon Cl KT22 . . . . . .95 D4
Glenheadon Rise KT22 . . . .95 D4
Glenhurst BR3 . . . . .44 C8
Glenhurst Cl GU17 . . . . .64 E4
Glenhurst Ct SE19 . . . . .22 F3
Glenhurst Rd TW8 . . . . .6 C7
Glenhurst Rise SE19 . . . . . .22 D1
Glenister Park Rd SW16 . . .21 D1
Glenlea GU26 . . . . .188 E1
Glenlion Ct 2 KT13 . . . . . . .53 D7
Glenmill TW12 . . . . .15 F3
Glenmore Cl KT15 . . . . .52 B6
Glenmore House 6 TW10 . . .6 E1
Glenmore Rd GU16 . . . . . . .86 A2
Glenn Ave CR8 . . . . .80 B8

Glennie Ct SE21 . . . . .23 A7
Glennie Rd SE27, SW16 . . . . .22 A5
Glentanner Way SW17 . . . . . .20 D5
Glenthorne Ave CR0, CR9 . .43 C1
Glenthorne Cl SM3 . . . . .40 A1
Glenthorne Gdns SM3 . . . . . .40 A1
Glenthorne High Sch SM3 40 A1
Glenthorne Rd KT1 . . . . .37 F5
Glenthorne Rd SM4 . . . . .39 D4
Glenview Cl RH10 . . . . .201 F8
Glenville Gdns GU26 . . . . . .188 F4
Glenville Mews SW18 . . . . . . .20 A8
Glenville Rd KT2 . . . . .38 A8
Glenwood Bracknell RG12 . .27 D5
Dorking RH5 . . . . .136 C5
Virginia Water GU25 . . . . . .31 C8
Glenwood Rd
Forest Hill SE6 . . . . .24 A7
Hounslow TW3 . . . . .5 D4
Stoneleigh KT17 . . . . .58 A4
Glenwood Way CR0 . . . . .43 D3
Globe Farm La GU17 . . . . . .64 B5
Glorney Mead GU9 . . . . . . .126 A6
Glory Mead RH4, RH5 . . .136 C4
Glossop Rd CR2 . . . . .61 D2
Gloster Cl GU12 . . . . .105 F5
Gloster Ct GU21 . . . . .69 F3
Gloster Rd New Malden KT3 38 E5
Old Woking GU22 . . . . .90 A7
Gloucester Cl
East Grinstead RH19 . . . .206 A8
Frimley GU16 . . . . .85 E6
Thames Ditton KT7 . . . . . . .37 A1
Gloucester Cres TW18 . . . . .13 D2
Gloucester Ct Richmond TW9 7 A7
8 Surbiton KT6 . . . . .37 D2
Gloucester Dr TW18, TW19 12 D5
Gloucester Gdns
Bagshot GU19 . . . . .47 E3
Sutton SM1 . . . . .59 B8
Gloucester Lodge 5 CR0 . .61 F7
Gloucester Rd
Aldershot GU11 . . . . .126 C7
Bagshot GU19 . . . . .47 E3
Crawley RH10 . . . . .201 E2
Croydon CR0 . . . . .42 E2
Feltham TW13 . . . . .15 C7
Guildford GU2 . . . . .108 F3
Hampton TW12 . . . . .16 B1
Hounslow TW4 . . . . .4 E3
Kingston u T KT1, KT2 . . . .38 B7
Redhill RH1 . . . . .118 F2
Richmond TW9 . . . . .7 A7
Teddington TW11 . . . . .16 E3
Thornton Heath CR0 . . . . . .42 E2
Twickenham TW2 . . . . .16 C7
Glover's Rd
Charlwood RH6 . . . . .180 D7
Reigate RH2 . . . . .139 B8
Glovers Field GU27 . . . . . .207 F6
Gloxinia Wlk TW12 . . . . .16 A2
Glyn ADT Tech Sch KT17 57 F8
Glyn Cl Ewell KT17 . . . . .58 A1
South Norwood SE19, SE25 .42 E8
Glyn Ct SE27 . . . . .22 A5
Glyn Rd KT4, SM3 . . . . .58 D8
Glyndale Grange SM2 . . . . .59 B4
Glynde Pl RH12 . . . . .217 B2
Glynswood Frimley GU15 . . .65 F3
Rowledge GU10 . . . . .146 A4
Glynwood Ct SE23 . . . . .23 C6
Goat Rd CR4 . . . . .40 F7
Goat Wharf TW8 . . . . .6 E8
Goaters Rd SL5 . . . . .28 C7
Goatsfield Rd TN16 . . . . . .103 C7
Godalming Ave SM6 . . . . . . .60 F5
Godalming Bsns Ctr GU7 150 F4
Godalming Coll GU7 . . . . .150 D2
Godalming Cty Mid Sch
GU7 . . . . .150 F5
Godalming Rd
Dunsfold GU8 . . . . .193 A8
Hascombe GU8 . . . . .172 E3
Godalming Sta GU7 . . . . . .150 D4
Goddard Cl Crawley RH10 .202 B3
Littleton TW17 . . . . .33 F6
Goddard House SW19 . . . . .19 D6
Goddard Rd BR3 . . . . .43 E5
Goddards La GU15 . . . . .65 B3
Godfrey Ave TW2 . . . . .16 D8
Godfrey Way TW4 . . . . .15 F8
Godley Rd Byfleet KT14 . . . . .71 F6
Wandsworth SW18 . . . . . . .20 D7
Godolphin Cl SM2 . . . . .77 F8
Godolphin House 4 SW2 .22 A7
Godolphin Rd KT13 . . . . . . .53 D4
Godric Cres CR0 . . . . .63 D1
Godson Rd CR0, CR9 . . . . . .61 A7
Godstone Farm RH9 . . . . . .121 C3
Godstone Fst Sch RH9 . .121 B3
Godstone Green Rd RH9 .121 B4
Godstone Hill
Tyler's Green RH9 . . . . . . .121 C5
Woldingham CR3, RH9 . . .121 C4
Godstone House 1 KT2 . .18 B2
Godstone Mount 3 CR8 . .80 B7
Godstone Rd
Bletchingley RH1 . . . . . . .120 F2
Caterham CR3 . . . . .101 A3
Kenley CR3, CR8 . . . . .80 D4
Lingfield RH7 . . . . .164 C4
Oxted RH8, RH9 . . . . .122 C5
Purley CR8 . . . . .80 D4
Sutton SM1 . . . . .59 C6
Twickenham TW1 . . . . .6 B1
Whyteleafe CR3 . . . . .80 D4
Godstone Sta RH9 . . . . . . .142 E5

Godwin Cl KT19 . . . . .57 C4
Goffs Cl RH11 . . . . .201 C5
Goffs La RH11 . . . . .201 B6
Goffs Park Rd RH11 . . . . . .201 C4
Goffs Rd TW15 . . . . .14 D2
Gogmore Farm Cl KT16 . . .32 F2
Gogmore La KT16 . . . . .33 A2
Goidel Cl SM6 . . . . .60 D6
Gold Cup La SL5 . . . . .28 D8
Goldcliff Cl SM4 . . . . .40 A4
Goldcrest Cl RH6 . . . . .160 E4
Goldcrest Way
New Addington CR0 . . . . . .63 D3
Wallington CR8 . . . . .60 D1
Golden Ct 10 TW9 . . . . .6 D2
Golden Mews SE20 . . . . . . .43 C8
Golden Orb Wood RG42 . .26 D8
Goldfinch Cl
Crawley RH11 . . . . .201 D8
Horsham RH12 . . . . .217 C7
Goldfinch Gdns GU4 . . . . .110 D2
Goldfinch Rd CR0, CR2 . . . .62 E1
Goldfort Wlk GU21 . . . . .68 D1
Goldhill GU10 . . . . .146 C6
Golding Cl Chessington KT9 .56 C4
Crawley RH10 . . . . .202 C5
Goldings The GU21 . . . . .68 F3
Goldney Rd GU15 . . . . .66 C4
Goldrings Rd KT22 . . . . .74 C6
Goldsmith Way RG45 . . . . . .45 B4
Goldsmiths Cl GU21 . . . . . . .69 C1
Goldstone Farm View
KT23 . . . . .114 A8
Goldsworth Orch 6 GU21 .69 A1
Goldsworth Park Ctr
GU21 . . . . .69 A2
Goldsworth Park Trad Est
GU21 . . . . .69 B3
Goldsworth Prim Sch
GU21 . . . . .69 A1
Goldsworth Rd GU21 . . . . .69 D2
Goldsworth Road Ind Est
GU21 . . . . .69 D2
Goldwell Rd CR7 . . . . .41 F5
Gole Rd GU24 . . . . .87 D6
Golf Cl Pyrford GU22 . . . . . . .70 E5
South Norwood SW16 . . . . .42 A8
Golf Club Dr KT2 . . . . .18 D1
Golf Club Rd
Weybridge KT13 . . . . .53 C1
Woking GU22 . . . . .89 B7
Golf Dr GU15 . . . . .65 F4
Golf Links Ave GU26 . . . . .188 A6
Golf Rd CR8 . . . . .80 D1
Golf Side Belmont SM2 . . . .77 E8
Twickenham TW2 . . . . .16 D5
Golf Side Cl KT3 . . . . .38 E7
Goliath Cl SM6 . . . . .60 E3
Gomer Gdns TW11 . . . . .17 A2
Gomer Pl TW11 . . . . .17 A2
Gomshall Ave SM6 . . . . .60 E5
Gomshall Gdns CR8 . . . . . . .80 E4
Gomshall La GU5 . . . . .133 D4
Gomshall Rd KT17, SM2 . . .58 C1
Gomshall Sta GU5 . . . . . . .133 E4
Gong Hill Dr GU10 . . . . . . .146 D4
Gong Hill Frensham Rd
GU10 . . . . .146 D4
Gonston Cl SW19 . . . . .19 E6
Gonville Prim Sch CR7 . .41 F4
Gonville Rd CR7 . . . . .41 F4
Good Shepherd RC Prim
Sch Catford BR1 . . . . .24 F4
New Addington CR0 . . . . . .63 B3
Goodbehere House 7
SE27 . . . . .22 C4
Goodchild Rd RG40 . . . . . . .25 D6
Goodden Cres GU14 . . . . . .84 F3
Goodenough Rd SW19 . . . . .19 F1
Goodenough Way CR5 . . . . .99 F7
Goodhart Way BR4 . . . . .44 E3
Goodhew Rd CR0, SE25 . . . .43 A3
Gooding Cl KT3 . . . . .38 C4
Goodland House 1 KT3 . .38 E2
Goodman Cres SW2 . . . . . . .21 D6
Goodman Pl TW18 . . . . .12 F4
Goodson House SM4 . . . . . .40 C2
Goodways Dr RG12 . . . . . . .27 D7
Goodwin Cl Crawley RH11 .200 F3
Mitcham CR4 . . . . .40 D6
Goodwin Gdns CR0, CR2 . .61 B4
Goodwin Rd CR0 . . . . .61 B5
Goodwins Cl RH19 . . . . . . .185 D3
Goodwood Cl
Camberley GU15 . . . . .65 C5
Crawley RH10 . . . . .202 A3
Morden SM4 . . . . .40 A5
Goodwood House SE26 . . .23 B2
Goodwood Par BR3 . . . . . . .43 E5
Goodwood Pl GU14 . . . . . . .85 E3
Goodwood Rd RH1 . . . . . . .118 F3
Goodwyns Pl RH4 . . . . .136 B5
Goodwyns Rd RH4 . . . . . . .136 C4
Goose Gn GU5 . . . . .133 C4
Goose Green Cl RH12 . . . .217 D5
Goose La GU22 . . . . .89 B5
Goose Rye Rd Woking GU3 .89 A2
Worplesdon GU3 . . . . .88 E1
Goossens Cl 1 SM1 . . . . . .59 C5
Gordon Ave
Camberley GU15 . . . . .65 C5
Isleworth TW1 . . . . .6 B2
Mortlake SW14 . . . . .7 E3
South Croydon CR2, CR8 . .61 C1
Gordon Cl
Addlestone KT16 . . . . .51 E7
Staines TW18 . . . . .13 B2

Gordon Cres
Camberley GU15 . . . . .65 C4
Croydon CR0 . . . . .42 F1
Gordon Dr
Addlestone KT16 . . . . .51 E7
Shepperton TW17 . . . . . . .34 D2
Gordon Rd
Aldershot GU11 . . . . .105 A1
Ashford TW15 . . . . .13 E5
Beckenham BR3 . . . . .43 F6
Camberley GU15 . . . . .65 C5
Caterham CR3 . . . . .100 D6
Chiswick W4 . . . . .7 B8
Claygate KT10 . . . . .55 E3
Crowthorne RG45 . . . . .45 D3
Farnborough GU14 . . . . . .105 D8
Horsham RH12 . . . . .217 D4
Hounslow TW3 . . . . .5 C3
Kingston u T KT2 . . . . .37 F8
Redhill RH1 . . . . .119 A4
Richmond TW9 . . . . .6 F5
Shepperton TW17 . . . . . . .34 D3
Surbiton KT5 . . . . .37 F2
Wallington SM5 . . . . .59 F4
Gordon's Sch GU24 . . . . .67 E7
Gordondale Rd
SW18, SW19 . . . . .20 A6
Gordons Way RH8 . . . . . . .122 D7
Gore Rd SW20 . . . . .39 C7
Goring Rd TW18 . . . . .12 E3
Goring's Mead RH13 . . . . .217 D1
Gorling Cl RH11 . . . . .200 E5
Gorrick Sq RG41 . . . . .25 B3
Gorringe Park Ave
CR4, SW17 . . . . .21 A1
Gorringe Park Mid Sch
CR4 . . . . .41 A8
Gorringes Brook RH12 . . .217 D6
Gorse Bank GU18 . . . . .67 A8
Gorse Cl Burgh Heath KT20 .97 B7
Copthorne RH10 . . . . .183 B2
Crawley RH11 . . . . .201 B1
Wrecclesham GU10 . . . . .146 B6
Gorse Cotts GU27 . . . . . . .207 C8
Gorse Ct GU4 . . . . .110 C3
Gorse Dr RH6 . . . . .162 C3
Gorse End RH12 . . . . .217 D5
Gorse Hill La GU25 . . . . . . .31 D5
Gorse Hill Rd GU25 . . . . . . .31 D5
Gorse La Chobham GU24 . . .49 E3
Wrecclesham GU10 . . . . .146 B6
Gorse Pl RG42 . . . . .8 B1
Gorse Rd Croydon CR0 . . . . .63 A7
Frimley GU16 . . . . .65 E2
Gorse Rise SW17 . . . . .21 A3
Gorselands GU9 . . . . .125 C7
Gorselands Cl Ash GU12 .106 A5
Headley Down GU35 . . . . .187 C4
West Byfleet KT14 . . . . .71 C8
Gorsewood Rd GU21 . . . . . .88 E7
Gort Cl GU11 . . . . .105 C7
Gosberton Rd SW12 . . . . . . .21 A7
Gosbury Hill KT9 . . . . .56 E6
Gosden Cl Crawley RH10 . .202 A5
Shalford GU5 . . . . .151 E4
Gosden Comm GU5 . . . . . .151 F7
Gosden Cotts GU5 . . . . . . .151 F7
Gosden Hill Rd GU4 . . . . . .110 C5
Gosden House Sch GU5 .151 E8
Gosden Rd GU24 . . . . .67 F6
Gosfield Rd KT19 . . . . .76 D7
Gosnell Cl GU16 . . . . .66 D3
Gosport House 9 SW15 . . .19 A7
Gossops Dr RH11 . . . . .201 A5
Gossops Green Cty Fst
Sch RH11 . . . . .201 A5
Gossops Green Cty Mid
Sch RH11 . . . . .201 A5
Gossops Green La RH11 .201 A5
Gossops Par RH11 . . . . . . .200 F5
Gostling Rd TW2 . . . . .16 A7
Goston Gdns CR7 . . . . .42 A6
Gostrode La GU8 . . . . .210 A6
Gothic Ct Harlington UB3 . . .3 D8
Sandhurst GU47 . . . . .64 B7
Gothic Rd TW2 . . . . .16 D6
Goudhurst Cl RH10 . . . . . .202 E6
Goudhurst House 10
SE20 . . . . .23 C1
Goudhurst Keep RH10 . . .202 E6
Goudhurst Rd BR1 . . . . .24 F3
Gough House 4 KT1 . . . . . .37 E7
Gough's La RG12 . . . . .27 D8
Gough's Meadow GU47 . . .64 B7
Gould Ct Dulwich SE19 . . . .22 E3
Guildford GU4 . . . . .110 D3
Gould Rd East Bedfont TW14 14 E8
Twickenham TW2 . . . . .16 E7
Goulding Gdns CR7 . . . . . . .42 C7
Government House Rd
GU11, GU14 . . . . .105 B7
Government Rd
Aldershot GU11 . . . . .105 E4
Farnborough GU11 . . . . . .105 E4
Governor's Rd GU15 . . . . . .64 F6
Govett Ave TW17 . . . . .34 C4
Govett Gr GU47 . . . . .20 D5
Gower Pk GU47 . . . . .64 D7
Gower Rd Horley RH6 . . . . .160 E3
Hounslow TW5 . . . . .5 F8
Weybridge KT13 . . . . .53 D4
Gower The TW20 . . . . .32 C6
Gowland Pl BR3 . . . . .43 F7
Graburn Way KT8 . . . . .36 D6
Grace Bennett Cl GU14 . . .85 A3
Grace Bsns Ctr CR4 . . . . .40 F3
Grace House SE26 . . . . .23 B3
Grace Path SE26 . . . . .23 C4

Grace Rd Crawley RH11 . . .201 A1
Thornton Heath CR0 . . . . . .42 C3
Grace Reynolds Wlk 4
GU15 . . . . .65 C6
Gracedale Rd SW16, SW17 .20 F3
Gracefield Gdns SW16 . . . .21 E5
Gracious Pond Rd GU24 . .50 B4
Gradient The SE26 . . . . .23 A4
Graemesdyke Ave SW14 . . .7 B3
Graffham Cl RH11 . . . . .201 B8
Grafton Cl Twickenham TW4 .15 F7
West Byfleet KT14 . . . . .70 F6
Worcester Park KT4 . . . . . .57 D7
Grafton Ct 14 TW7 . . . . .5 F4
Grafton Park Rd KT4 . . . . . .57 E8
Grafton Rd Kingston u T KT3 38 E6
Thornton Heath CR0 . . . . . .42 A1
Worcester Park KT4, KT19 .57 E7
Grafton Way KT8 . . . . .35 F5
Graham Ave CR4 . . . . .41 A8
Graham Cl CR0 . . . . .63 A8
Graham Gdns KT6 . . . . .37 E1
Graham House
5 Balham SW12 . . . . .21 B8
Little Bookham KT23 . . . . . .94 A3
Redhill RH1 . . . . .118 A3
Graham Rd Hampton TW12 .16 A4
Merton SW19 . . . . .19 F1
Mitcham CR4 . . . . .41 A8
Purley CR8 . . . . .80 A6
Windlesham GU20 . . . . .48 C4
Grainford Ct RG40 . . . . .25 C5
Grainger Rd TW7 . . . . .5 F5
Grampian Cl UB3 . . . . .3 D7
Grampian Rd GU47 . . . . . . .45 A4
Granada St SW17 . . . . .20 F3
Granard Rd SW11, SW12 . . .20 F8
Granary Cl RH6 . . . . .161 A5
Granary Way RH12 . . . . . . .217 A1
Grand Ave Camberley GU15 .65 C6
Tolworth KT5 . . . . .38 B5
Grand Avenue Prim Sch
KT5 .38 C3
Grand Avenue Prim Sch
(Upper Sch) KT5 . . . . .38 C3
Grand Dr KT3, SM4, SW20 .39 C5
Grand Par Crawley RH10 . .201 D6
Mortlake SW14 . . . . .7 C3
Tolworth KT6 . . . . .38 A1
Grand Stand Rd
KT17, KT18 . . . . .77 A2
Grand View Ave TN16 . . . . .83 C3
Granden Rd SW16 . . . . .41 E7
Grandfield Ct W4 . . . . .7 D8
Grandis Cotts GU23 . . . . . . .91 B5
Grandison Rd KT4 . . . . .58 C7
Grange Ave
Crowthorne RG45 . . . . .45 B6
South Norwood SE25 . . . . .42 E7
Twickenham TW2 . . . . .16 E6
Grange Cl Ashstead KT22 . . .95 D7
Bletchingley RH1 . . . . .120 D2
Crawley RH10 . . . . .202 A4
East Molesey KT8 . . . . .36 B5
Godalming GU7 . . . . .151 A5
Guildford GU2 . . . . .109 B5
Heston TW5 . . . . .4 F8
Merstham RH1, RH2 . . . . .119 B7
Grange Cres RH10 . . . . . . .204 B7
Grange Ct Egham TW20 . . . .11 F3
Hackbridge SM6 . . . . .60 B7
Littleton TW17 . . . . .34 A5
Merstham RH2 . . . . .119 B7
South Godstone RH9 . . . .142 E5
Staines TW18 . . . . .13 A3
Sutton SM2 . . . . .59 B3
Walton-on-T KT12 . . . . .54 A8
Grange Cty Inf Sch The
KT15 . . . . .52 A1
Grange Dr Merstham RH1 .119 B7
Woking GU21 . . . . .69 E4
Grange End RH6 . . . . .162 A3
Grange Farm Rd GU12 . . .106 A3
Grange Gdns
Banstead SM7 . . . . .78 B6
South Norwood SE25 . . . . .42 E7
Grange Hill SE25 . . . . .42 E7
Grange La SE21 . . . . .22 F6
Grange Lodge SW19 . . . . . .19 D2
Grange Mansions KT17 . . .57 F3
Grange Meadow SM7 . . . . .78 B6
Grange Mills SW12 . . . . . .21 C7
Grange Park Pl SW20 . . . . .19 B1
Grange Park Rd CR7 . . . . . .42 D6
Grange Pk Cranleigh GU6 .174 F3
Woking GU21 . . . . .69 F5
Grange Pl TW18 . . . . .33 C7
Grange Rd Ash GU12 . . . . .106 B1
Ashstead KT21, KT22 . . . . .95 D7
Belmont SM2 . . . . .59 A3
Bracknell RG12 . . . . .27 C8
Camberley GU15 . . . . .65 E5
Caterham CR3 . . . . .101 A2
Chessington KT9 . . . . .56 E6
Crawley Down RH10 . . . . .204 A7
East Molesey KT8 . . . . .36 B5
Egham TW20 . . . . .11 F3
Farnborough GU14 . . . . . . .85 B7
Guildford GU2, GU3 . . . . .109 B5
Hersham KT12 . . . . .54 E6
Kingston u T KT1 . . . . .37 E6
Rushmoor GU10 . . . . .168 C7
South Croydon CR2 . . . . . .61 C2
South Norwood SE19, SE25 .42 D7
Sutton SM2 . . . . .59 A3
Tongham GU10 . . . . .126 E6
Woking GU21 . . . . .69 E4
Woodham KT15 . . . . .52 B1

Grange Specl Sch The
GU11 . . . . .126 B8
Grange The Chobham GU24 .49 E1
Croydon CR0 . . . . .62 F8
Frensham GU10 . . . . .167 D7
Horley RH6 . . . . .161 A6
New Malden KT3 . . . . .39 A4
Walton-on-T KT12 . . . . .54 B8
Wimbledon SW19 . . . . .19 D2
Worcester Park KT19 . . . . .57 D6
Grange Vale SM2 . . . . .59 B3
Grangecliffe Gdns SE25 . . .42 E7
Grangefields Rd GU4 . . . .109 D6
Grangemill Rd SE6 . . . . .24 A6
Grangemill Way SE6 . . . . . .24 A6
Grangemount KT22 . . . . . . .95 D7
Grangeway RH6 . . . . .162 A3
Grangewood La BR3 . . . . . .23 F2
Gransden Cl GU6 . . . . .175 E5
Granston Way RH10 . . . . . .204 C8
Grant Cl TW17 . . . . .34 B3
Grant Pl 2 CR0 . . . . .42 F1
Grant Rd Crowthorne RG45 .45 C4
Croydon CR0 . . . . .42 F1
Grant Way TW7, TW8 . . . . . . .6 A8
Grant Wlk SL5 . . . . .29 E1
Grantchester 3 KT1 . . . . . .38 A7
Grantham Cl GU47 . . . . .45 E1
Grantham House TW16 . . . .14 E1
Grantham Rd W4 . . . . .7 E7
Grantley Ave GU5 . . . . .152 B6
Grantley Cl GU4 . . . . .130 E2
Grantley House SW19 . . . . .19 D7
Grantley Rd
Cranford TW4, TW5 . . . . . . .4 C5
Guildford GU2 . . . . .109 A2
Granton Rd SW16 . . . . .41 C8
Grants Cotts KT10 . . . . .55 D8
Grants La TN8, RH8 . . . . . .144 C6
Grantwood Cl RH1 . . . . . . .140 B4
Granville Ave
Feltham TW13 . . . . .15 A6
Hounslow TW3, TW4 . . . . . .5 A2
Granville Cl Byfleet KT14 . . .71 F6
South Croydon CR0 . . . . . .61 E8
Weybridge KT13 . . . . .53 C4
Granville Gdns SW16 . . . . .21 F1
Granville Rd
Limpsfield RH8 . . . . .123 A7
Merton SW19 . . . . .20 A1
Wandsworth SW18 . . . . . . .19 F8
Weybridge KT13 . . . . .53 C4
Woking GU22 . . . . .89 F7
Granwood Ct 5 TW7 . . . . . . .5 E6
Grasmere Ave
Kingston u T SW15 . . . . . . .18 E4
Merton SW19 . . . . .40 A6
Twickenham TW3 . . . . .5 B1
Grasmere Cl
East Bedfont TW14 . . . . . . .14 E7
Guildford GU1 . . . . .110 B2
Thorpe Lea TW20 . . . . .12 B1
Grasmere Ct SE26 . . . . .23 A3
Grasmere Gdns RH12 . . . .218 B6
Grasmere Rd Bromley BR1 .24 F1
Croydon SE25 . . . . .43 B4
Farnborough GU14 . . . . . . .84 E4
Hale GU9 . . . . .125 A6
Lightwater GU18 . . . . .48 B1
Purley CR8 . . . . .80 B8
Streatham SW16 . . . . .21 F3
Grasmere Way KT14 . . . . . .71 F7
Grassfield Cl CR5 . . . . .99 C8
Grasslands RH6 . . . . .162 A3
Grassmere RH6 . . . . .161 C4
Grassmount
Forest Hill SE23 . . . . .23 B6
Wallington CR8 . . . . .60 C1
Grassway SM6 . . . . .60 C6
Grately House 10 SW15 . . .19 B7
Grattons Dr RH10 . . . . .182 C1
Grattons The RH13 . . . . . . .215 E3
Gravel Hill
Leatherhead RH4 . . . . .95 B6
South Croydon CR0, CR2 . .62 E4
Gravel Hill Rd GU10 . . . . . .145 A3
Gravel Pits GU5 . . . . .133 C4
Gravel Pits La GU5 . . . . . .133 C4
Gravel Rd
Farnborough GU14 . . . . . .105 D8
Hale GU9 . . . . .125 B7
Twickenham TW2 . . . . .16 E7
Graveley 7 KT1 . . . . .38 A7
Gravelly Hill CR3 . . . . .120 F7
Gravenel Gdns SW17 . . . . .20 E3
Graveney Gr SE20 . . . . .23 C1
Graveney Rd
Crawley RH10 . . . . .202 C5
Upper Tooting SW17 . . . . . .20 E4
Graveney Sch SW17 . . . .21 B3
Gravetts La GU3 . . . . .108 C3
Gravetye Cl RH10 . . . . .202 A4
Gray Ct 8 KT2 . . . . .17 D4
Gray Pl KT16 . . . . .51 D4
Gray's La KT21 . . . . .95 F8
Grayham Cres KT3 . . . . .38 D5
Grayham Rd KT3 . . . . .38 D5
Graylands GU21 . . . . .69 E3
Graylands Cl GU21 . . . . .69 E3
Graylands Ct 5 GU1 . . . . .130 E8
Grays Cl GU27 . . . . .208 E8
Grays La TW15 . . . . .14 B4
Grays Rd GU7 . . . . .150 F7
Grays Wood RH6 . . . . .161 C4
Grayscroft Rd SW16 . . . . . .21 D1

Grayshot Dr GU17 . . . . .64 C5
Grayshott Prim Sch
GU26 . . . . .188 D3
Grayshott Rd GU26, GU35 .187 C5
Grayswood CE (VA) Fst
Sch GU27 . . . . .189 F2
Grayswood Dr GU16 . . . . . .86 A2
Grayswood Gdns SW20 . . . .39 B7
Grayswood Pl GU27 . . . . . .208 E8
Grayswood Point 14 SW15 .19 A7
Grayswood Rd
Grayswood GU27 . . . . .189 F1
Haslemere GU27 . . . . .189 F1
Grazely Ct SE19 . . . . .22 E3
Great Austins GU9 . . . . . . .146 D8
Great Bookham Cty Mid
Sch KT23 . . . . .94 B2
Great Brownings SE21 . . . . .22 F4
Great Chertsey Rd
Chiswick SW14, W4 . . . . .7 D6
Feltham TW13, TW2 . . . . . . .16 A5
Great Elshams SM7 . . . . . . .78 A3
Great George St GU7 . . . . .150 E4
Great Goodwin Dr GU1 . . .110 B3
Great Hollands Inf Sch
RG12 . . . . .26 F4
Great Hollands Jun Sch
RG12 . . . . .26 F4
Great Hollands Rd RG12 . . .26 F3
Great Hollands Sq RG12 . . .26 F3
Great House Ct 4 RH19 . . .205 F4
Great Oaks Pk GU4 . . . . . .110 C5
Great Quarry GU1 . . . . . . .130 D6
Great South-West Rd
East Bedfont TW14, TW6,
TW4, TW5 . . . . .3 D2
Feltham TW6, TW14 . . . . . . .3 D2
Hatton TW6, TW14 . . . . .3 D2
Hounslow TW5 . . . . .4 B4
Great Tattenhams KT18 . . .77 C1
Great West Rd
Brentford TW8 . . . . .6 B8
Cranford TW5 . . . . .4 F6
Heston TW5 . . . . .4 F6
Hounslow TW5, TW7 . . . . . . .5 C6
Great West Road Cedars La
W4 . . . . .7 C8
Great West Road Chiswick
W4 . . . . .7 F8
Great West Road
Ellesmere Rd W4 . . . . .7 D8
Great West Road Hogarth
La W4 . . . . .7 E8
Great West Trad Est TW8 . .6 B8
Great Woodcote Dr CR8 . . .60 D1
Great Woodcote Pk
CR8, SM6 . . . . .60 E1
Greatfield Cl GU14 . . . . . . .85 B8
Greatfield Rd GU14 . . . . . . .85 B8
Greatford Dr GU1 . . . . . . .110 D1
Greatham Rd RH10 . . . . . .202 C3
Greatham Wlk 8 SW15 . . .19 A7
Greathed Manor RH7 . . . . .165 C1
Greathurst End KT23 . . . . . .93 F3
Greatlake Ct RH6 . . . . .161 B4
Greatstone House 13 SE20 .23 C1
Greatwood Cl KT16 . . . . . . .51 C2
Greaves Pl SW17 . . . . .20 E4
Grebe Cres RH13 . . . . .218 A1
Grebe Terr 4 KT1 . . . . .37 E6
Grecian Cres SE19, SW16 . .22 E2
Green Acre GU11 . . . . .104 F1
Green Acres CR0 . . . . .61 F7
Green Bsns Ctr The TW20 .12 C4
Green Cl Beckenham BR2 . . .44 E6
Carshalton SM5 . . . . .59 F8
Feltham TW13 . . . . .15 E3
Green Court Ave CR0 . . . . .62 B8
Green Court Gdns CR0 . . . .62 B8
Green Croft RG40 . . . . .25 E8
Green Cross La GU10 . . . .168 A1
Green Ct TW16 . . . . .14 F2
Green Curve SM7 . . . . .77 F4
Green Dene
East Horsley KT24 . . . . . . .112 E3
West Horsley KT24 . . . . . . .112 E3
Green Dr Send Marsh GU23 .90 F4
Wokingham RG40 . . . . .25 E4
Green Dragon Jun & Inf
Sch TW8 . . . . .6 E8
Green End KT9 . . . . .56 E6
Green Farm Rd GU19 . . . . .47 F3
Green Finch Cl RG45 . . . . . .45 A6
Green Hedges 8 TW1 . . . . . .6 C1
Green Hedges Ave RH19 .185 D2
Green Hedges Cl RH19 . . .185 D2
Green Hill BR6 . . . . .83 F7
Green Hill Cl GU15 . . . . .66 C6
Green Hill Rd GU15 . . . . . . .66 C6
Green House The 5 SW19 .19 E7
Green La
Addlestone KT15, KT16 . . . . .51 E7
Alfold Crossways GU6 . . . . .193 F4
Ascot SL5 . . . . .29 E8
Ashford TW16 . . . . .14 F2
Ashstead KT22 . . . . .95 D6
Ashstead, Lower
Ashstead KT21 . . . . .75 D1
Bagshot GU19 . . . . .47 F2
Blackwater GU17 . . . . .64 B4
Blackwater, Hawley GU17 . .64 B4
Burstow RH6 . . . . .182 F6
Byfleet KT14 . . . . .71 F7
Caterham CR3 . . . . .100 C5
Cheam SM4 . . . . .40 B3

Green La continued
Chertsey KT15, KT16 . . . . . .51 E7
Chessington KT9 . . . . .56 E7
Chobham GU24 . . . . .49 F1
Churt GU10 . . . . .168 A1
Cobham KT11 . . . . .73 E7
Copthorne RH10 . . . . .183 F4
Crawley, Northgate RH10 . .201 E8
Crawley, Worth RH10 . . . . .202 D6
Cudworth RH5 . . . . .179 D8
Dockenfield GU10 . . . . .166 E6
East Molesey KT8 . . . . .36 B4
Egham TW20 . . . . .12 B3
Egham TW18 . . . . .32 E8
Farncombe GU7, GU3 . . . . .150 E8
Farnham GU9 . . . . .146 A7
Farnham, Weybourne GU9 .125 F5
Faygate RH12 . . . . .198 F4
Feltham TW13 . . . . .15 E3
Guildford GU1 . . . . .110 B1
Heath End GU9 . . . . .125 F5
Hersham KT12 . . . . .54 B5
Hounslow TW4 . . . . .4 C3
Kingsley Green GU27 . . . . .208 B4
Leatherhead KT22 . . . . .95 D6
Leigh RH2 . . . . .158 E8
Lingfield RH7 . . . . .164 C4
Lower Kingswood KT20 . . . . .97 F1
Milford GU8 . . . . .170 E8
Morden SM4 . . . . .40 B3
New Malden KT3 . . . . .38 C4
North Cheam KT4 . . . . .39 A1
Penge SE20 . . . . .23 D1
Purley GU9 . . . . .60 D1
Redhill RH1 . . . . .118 E3
Redhill, Whitebushes RH1 . .140 A4
Reigate RH2 . . . . .117 F1
Sandhurst GU47 . . . . .64 C7
Shamley Green GU5 . . . . . .153 A7
Shepperton TW17 . . . . .34 C4
South Norwood CR7, SW16 .42 B8
South Nutfield RH1 . . . . . . .140 F1
Streatham SW16 . . . . .21 F1
Tilford GU10 . . . . .147 E6
West Clandon GU4 . . . . . . .111 B8
West Horsley GU23, KT24 . . .92 B3
Wood St V GU3 . . . . .108 A3
Green La E GU3 . . . . .128 B8
Green La W GU3 . . . . .127 E8
Green Lane Ave KT12 . . . . .54 C5
Green Lane Cl
Addlestone KT16 . . . . .51 E8
Byfleet KT14 . . . . .71 F7
Camberley GU15 . . . . .65 C7
Green Lane Cotts GU10 . .167 F1
Green Lane Cty Inf Sch
GU7 . . . . .129 E1
Green Lane Gdns CR7 . . . . .42 C7
Green Lane Prim Sch KT4 .39 B2
Green Lanes KT19 . . . . .57 E2
Green Leaf Ave SM6 . . . . . .60 D6
Green Leas Ashford TW16 . .14 F2
Kingston u T KT1 . . . . .37 E6
Green Leas Cl TW16 . . . . . .14 F2
Green Man La TW14 . . . . . . .4 A3
Green Mead KT10 . . . . .54 F4
Green Pk TW18 . . . . .12 E5
Green Rd KT16, TW20 . . . . .32 B5
Green Sch for Girls The
TW7 . . . . .6 A6
Green St TW16 . . . . .35 A8
Green The Bracknell RG12 . .27 B5
Broadbridge Heath RH12 . .216 D4
Burgh Heath KT20 . . . . .97 E8
Carshalton SM6 . . . . .60 A8
Chiddingfold GU8 . . . . .191 C3
Claygate KT10 . . . . .55 F4
Copthorne RH10 . . . . .183 B3
Crawley RH11 . . . . .201 C7
Ewell KT17 . . . . .77 A7
Ewhurst GU6 . . . . .175 E4
Farnham GU9 . . . . .126 A6
Feltham TW13 . . . . .15 B6
Fetcham KT22 . . . . .94 D3
Frimley GU16 . . . . .85 F6
Hale GU9 . . . . .125 C6
Heston TW5 . . . . .5 A8
Kingston u T KT3 . . . . .38 C7
Merton SM4 . . . . .39 E5
New Addington CR0 . . . . . . .62 F2
Richmond TW9 . . . . .6 D2
Staines TW18 . . . . .13 D3
Sutton SM1 . . . . .59 B7
The Sands GU10 . . . . .126 E1
Twickenham TW2 . . . . .16 E6
Tyler's Green RH9 . . . . .121 C4
Warlingham CR6 . . . . .81 D1
Whiteley Village KT12 . . . . . .53 E1
Wimbledon SW19 . . . . .19 D3
Woldingham CR3 . . . . .102 A4
Green View
Chessington KT9 . . . . .56 F3
Godstone RH9 . . . . .121 B4
Green Way
Aldershot GU12 . . . . .105 E3
Redhill RH1 . . . . .118 E3
Sunbury TW16 . . . . .14 F2
Green Wlk Crawley RH10 . .201 E8
Hampton TW12 . . . . .15 F2
Green Wood SL5 . . . . .28 C8
Green Wrythe Cres SM5 . . .40 E1
Green Wrythe La
SM4, SM5 . . . . .40 E2
Green Wrythe Prim Sch
SM5 .40 D3
Green's School La GU14 . . .85 A4
Greenacre Knaphill GU21 . . .68 C2
Whyteleafe CR3 . . . . .101 B7

Greenacre Ct TW20 . . . . . . .11 C2
Greenacre Pl SM6 . . . . .60 B8
Greenacre Sch for Girls
SM7 .78 B6
Greenacres Crawley RH10 .202 A5
Farnham GU10 . . . . .126 C2
Great Bookham KT23 . . . . . .94 A3
Horsham RH12 . . . . .217 C4
Oxted RH8 . . . . .122 E8
Greenaway Terr TW19 . . . . .13 E7
Greenbank Way GU15 . . . . .65 D2
Greenbush La GU6 . . . . . . .174 F1
Greencroft
2 Farnborough GU14 . . . . .85 B4
Guildford GU1 . . . . .110 B1
Greencroft Rd TW5 . . . . .4 F6
Greene Fielde End TW18 . .13 D1
Greenfield Ave KT5 . . . . . . .38 B3
Greenfield House 28
SW19 . . . . .19 D7
Greenfield Link CR5 . . . . . .79 E4
Greenfield Rd
Farnham GU9, GU10 . . . . . .146 A7
Slinfold RH13 . . . . .215 D3
Wrecclesham GU9 . . . . .145 F7
Greenfield Sch GU22 . . . . . .89 E8
Greenfield Way RG45 . . . . . .45 A4
Greenfields Cl Horley RH6 .160 E5
Horsham RH12 . . . . .218 A6
Greenfields Pl RH5 . . . . . .157 D4
Greenfields Rd
Horley RH6 . . . . .160 F5
Horsham RH12 . . . . .218 A5
Greenfields Sch
East Grinstead RH19 . . . . . .205 D6
Forest Row RH18 . . . . .206 C1
Greenfields Way RH12 . . . .218 A6
Greenfinch Way RH12 . . . .217 D7
Greenford Rd SM1 . . . . .59 B6
Greenham House TW7 . . . . . .5 B4
Greenham Wlk GU21 . . . . . .69 C1
Greenham Wood RG12 . . . .27 C3
Greenhanger GU10 . . . . . . .188 A8
Greenhayes Ave SM7 . . . . .78 A4
Greenhayes Cl RH2 . . . . . .118 C1
Greenhayes Gdns SM7 . . . .78 A4
Greenhayes Sch BR4 . . . . . .63 C8
Greenheys Pl GU22 . . . . . . .69 F1
Greenhill SM1 . . . . .59 C8
Greenhill Ave CR3 . . . . .101 B6
Greenhill Cl
Godalming GU7 . . . . .150 D3
Wrecclesham GU9 . . . . .146 A7
Greenhill Gdns GU4 . . . . . .110 C3
Greenhill La CR6 . . . . .81 F2
Greenhill Rd GU9 . . . . .146 D8
Greenhill Way
Farnham GU9 . . . . .146 A7
Wrecclesham GU9 . . . . .146 A7
Greenhills GU9 . . . . .146 E8
Greenholme GU15 . . . . .66 D5
Greenhow RG12 . . . . .27 A6
Greenhurst La RH8 . . . . . . .123 A3
Greenhurst Rd SE27 . . . . . .22 A3
Greenlake Terr TW18 . . . . . .13 A1
Greenlands Rd
Camberley GU15 . . . . .65 B1
Staines TW18 . . . . .13 A4
Weybridge KT13 . . . . .53 C7
Greenlaw Gdns KT3 . . . . . . .38 F2
Greenlea Pk SW19 . . . . .40 E8
Greenleaf Cl 5 SW2 . . . . . . .22 A8
Greenleas GU16 . . . . .65 E2
Greenleaves Ct TW15 . . . . .14 B2
Greenmead KT3 . . . . .43 A4
Greenmeads GU22 . . . . .89 E5
Greeno Cres TW17 . . . . .34 A4
Greenoak Rise TN16 . . . . . .83 C1
Greenoak Way SW19 . . . . . .19 D4
Greenock Rd SW16 . . . . . . .41 D8
Greensand Cl RH1 . . . . .119 D7
Greensand Rd RH1 . . . . . . .119 A2
Greenside Cl Catford SE6 . .24 D6
Guildford GU4 . . . . .110 C3
Greenside Cotts GU23 . . . . .91 C6
Greenside Rd CR0 . . . . .42 A2
Greenside Wlk TN16 . . . . . .83 B1
Greensleeves Manor SM2 .59 B4
Greenstede Ave RH19 . . . .185 F2
Greenvale Prim Sch CR2 . . .81 D8
Greenvale Rd GU21 . . . . . . .68 C1
Greenvale Spec Sch SE23 .23 E5
Greenview Ave CR0 . . . . . . .43 E3
Greenview Ct TW15 . . . . . . .13 F4
Greenway
Great Bookham KT23 . . . . . .94 B4
Horsham RH12 . . . . .217 B3
Tatsfield TN16 . . . . .103 C7
Wallington SM6 . . . . .60 C6
West Barnes SW20 . . . . .39 C5
Greenway Cl KT14 . . . . .71 A6
Greenway Dr TW18 . . . . . . .33 D8
Greenway Gdns CR0 . . . . . .62 F7
Greenway Jun Sch RH12 .217 B3
Greenway The Epsom KT18 .76 A5
Hounslow TW4 . . . . .4 F1
Oxted RH8 . . . . .123 B2
Greenways
Beckenham BR3 . . . . .44 A7
Egham TW20 . . . . .11 E3
Forest Hill SE26 . . . . .23 C4
Hinchley Wood KT10 . . . . . . .55 E6
Sandhurst GU47 . . . . .45 B1
Walton on t H KT20 . . . . .97 B2
Greenways Dr SL5 . . . . .29 C1
Greenways The 1 TW1 . . . . .6 A1
Greenways Wlk RH11 . . . . .201 C1
Greenwich Cl RH11 . . . . . .201 C5

Greenwood
4 Bracknell RG12 . . . . .27 F5
8 Putney SW19 . . . . .19 D8
Greenwood Cl
Hinchley Wood KT7 . . . . .37 A1
Merton SM4 . . . . .39 E5
Woodham KT15 . . . . .70 F8
Greenwood Ct 2 RH11 . . .201 B1
Greenwood Dr RH1 . . . . . . .140 A4
Greenwood Gdns CR3 . . . .101 A2
Greenwood La TW12 . . . . . .16 B3
Greenwood Pk KT2 . . . . . . .18 E1
Greenwood Prim Sch CR4 41 D6
Greenwood Rd
Crowthorne RG45 . . . . .45 B6
Hinchley Wood KT7 . . . . .56 A8
Isleworth TW7 . . . . .5 F4
Knaphill GU21 . . . . .88 E7
Mitcham CR4 . . . . .41 D6
Pirbright GU24 . . . . .87 C7
Thornton Heath CR0, CR9 . .42 C2
Greenwood The GU1 . . . . .110 A1
Gregan Ct GU11 . . . . .104 F1
Gregory Cl Crawley RH10 .202 C2
Woking GU21 . . . . .69 C2
Gregory Ct CR8 . . . . .80 B6
Gregsons RH12 . . . . .216 E8
Grena Gdns TW9 . . . . .6 F3
Grena Rd TW10, TW9 . . . . . . .6 F3
Grenaby Ave CR0 . . . . .42 D2
Grenaby Rd CR0 . . . . .42 D2
Grenadier Rd GU12 . . . . . .106 B4
Grenadiers Way GU14 . . . . .84 C3
Grendon Cl RH6 . . . . .160 F5
Grenehurst Pk RH5 . . . . . .178 B4
Grenfell Cl RG45 . . . . .45 C6
Grenfell Rd CR4, SW17 . . . . .20 F2
Grennell Cl SM1 . . . . .59 D8
Grennell Rd SM1 . . . . .59 C8
Grenside Rd KT13 . . . . .53 B7
Grenville Cl Cobham KT11 . .73 E6
Tolworth KT5 . . . . .38 C1
Grenville Ct SE19 . . . . .22 F3
Grenville Gdns GU16 . . . . . .85 E6
Grenville Mews TW12 . . . . .16 B3
Grenville Rd
New Addington CR0 . . . . . . .63 C2
Shackleford GU8 . . . . .149 D7
Gresham Ave CR6 . . . . .81 E1
Gresham Cl RH8 . . . . .122 F7
Gresham Ct
Farnborough GU14 . . . . . . .105 C8
Hounslow TW3 . . . . .5 C6
Staines TW18 . . . . .13 A3
Gresham House
2 Teddington TW11 . . . . . .16 F3
3 Thames Ditton KT7 . . . . . .37 A2
Gresham Ind Est GU12 . . .105 E2
Gresham Prim Sch CR2 . . . .81 A8
Hampton TW12 . . . . .16 A2
Hounslow TW3, TW5 . . . . . . .5 C6
Limpsfield RH8 . . . . .122 F6
Penge BR3 . . . . .43 E7
Staines TW18 . . . . .13 A3
Gresham Way
Frimley GU16 . . . . .85 E6
Wimbledon SW19 . . . . .20 A5
Gresham Way Est SW19 . . .20 B5
Gresham Wlk RH10 . . . . . .201 E3
Gressenhall Rd SW18 . . . . .19 F8
Greta Bank KT24 . . . . .92 C1
Greville Ave CR2 . . . . .62 D1
Greville Cl Ashstead KT21 . .95 E8
Guildford GU2 . . . . .108 E1
Twickenham TW1 . . . . .17 B8
Greville Ct Ashstead KT21 . .75 E1
Fetcham KT23 . . . . .94 C2
Greville Cty Prim Sch The
KT21 .75 F2
Greville Park Ave KT21 . . . .75 E1
Greville Park Rd KT21 . . . . .75 E1
Greville Rd TW10 . . . . .6 F1
Grey Alders KT17 . . . . .77 C5
Grey Court Sch TW10 . . . . .17 C5
Greycot Rd BR3 . . . . .24 A3
Greyfields Cl CR8 . . . . .80 B6
Greyfriars 16 SE26 . . . . .23 A5
Greyfriars Dr Ascot SL5 . . . .29 B3
Bisley GU24 . . . . .68 A4
Greyfriars Rd GU23 . . . . . . .91 A3
Greyhound Cl GU12 . . . . . .105 F1
Greyhound La SW16 . . . . . .21 D2
Greyhound Rd SM1 . . . . . . .59 C5
Greyhound Slip RH10 . . . . .202 D7
Greyhound Terr SW16 . . . . .41 C8
Greylees GU7 . . . . .150 E5
Greys Ct GU11 . . . . .104 F1
Greystead Pk GU10 . . . . . .145 E5
Greystead Rd SE23 . . . . . . .23 C8
Greystoke Ct RG45 . . . . . . .45 A4
Greystone Cl CR2 . . . . .81 C8
Greystones Cl RH1 . . . . . . .139 D7
Greystones Dr RH2 . . . . . . .118 C3
Greyswood St SW16 . . . . . .21 B2
Greythorne Rd GU21 . . . . . .69 A1
Greywaters GU5 . . . . .152 A6
Grice Ave TN16 . . . . .83 C6
Grier Cl RH11 . . . . .200 E5
Grierson House SW16 . . . . .21 C5
Grierson Rd SE23 . . . . .23 D8
Grieve Cl GU10 . . . . .126 D2
Griffin Cl Ashstead KT21 . . .95 E8
8 Brentford TW8 . . . . .6 B8
Great Bookham KT23 . . . . . .94 B1
Griffin Ctr KT1 . . . . .37 D7
Griffin Ctr The TW14 . . . . . . .4 B1
Griffin Pk (Brentford FC)
TW8 . . . . .6 D8

Griffin Way
Great Bookham KT23 . . . . . .94 B1
Sunbury TW16 . . . . .35 A4
Griffiths Cl KT4 . . . . .58 B8
Griffiths Rd SW19 . . . . .20 B1
Griffon Cl GU14 . . . . .84 C3
Griggs Meadow GU8 . . . . .192 F7
Grimwade Ave CR0 . . . . . . .62 A7
Grimwood Rd TW1 . . . . .16 F8
Grindall Cl CR0 . . . . .61 B6
Grindley Gdns CR0 . . . . . . .42 F3
Grindstone Cres GU21 . . . .68 B3
Grindstone Handle Cnr
GU21 . . . . .68 C3
Grinstead La RH19 . . . . . . .205 E1
Grisedale Cl
Crawley RH11 . . . . .201 C4
Sanderstead CR8 . . . . .80 E5
Grisedale Gdns CR8 . . . . . .80 E5
Grizedale Terr SE23 . . . . . . .23 B6
Grobars Ave GU21 . . . . .69 C4
Groom Cres SW18 . . . . .20 D8
Groombridge Cl KT12 . . . . .54 B5
Groombridge House SE20 23 D4
Groombridge Way RH12 . .216 F1
Groomfield Cl SW17 . . . . . .21 A4
Grooms The RH10 . . . . .202 D8
Grosslea SM4 . . . . .40 B4
Grosvenor Ave
Mortlake SW14 . . . . .7 A4
Richmond TW10 . . . . .6 E2
Wallington SM5, SM6 . . . . . .60 A4
Grosvenor Ct
Blackwater GU17 . . . . .64 D3
Guildford GU4 . . . . .110 A3
Morden SM4 . . . . .40 A5
Penge SE19 . . . . .22 F2
Richmond TW10 . . . . .6 F1
1 Sutton SM2 . . . . .59 C4
Teddington TW11 . . . . .17 A2
Wimbledon SW19 . . . . .19 E2
Grosvenor Gdns
Kingston u T KT2 . . . . .17 D2
Mortlake SW14 . . . . .7 E4
Wallington SM6 . . . . .60 C3
Grosvenor Hill SW19 . . . . . .19 E2
Grosvenor Ho 8 GU1 . . . . .130 F8
Grosvenor Pl 1
Oatlands Park KT13 . . . . . . .53 D7
9 Woking GU21 . . . . .69 F2
Grosvenor Rd
Aldershot GU11 . . . . .105 A1
Brentford TW8 . . . . .6 D8
Croydon SE25 . . . . .43 A5
East Grinstead RH19 . . . . . .185 D1
Godalming GU7 . . . . .150 E3
Hounslow TW3, TW4 . . . . . . .4 F4
Langley Vale KT18, KT21 . . . .96 E8
Richmond TW10 . . . . .6 E2
Staines TW18 . . . . .13 A1
Twickenham TW1 . . . . .17 A7
Wallington SM6 . . . . .60 B5
West End GU24 . . . . .68 D6
West Wickham BR4 . . . . .63 B8
Groton Rd SW18 . . . . .20 B6
Grotto Rd Twickenham TW1 .16 F6
Weybridge KT13 . . . . .53 B7
Grove Ave Epsom KT17 . . . .76 E6
Sutton SM1, SM2 . . . . .59 A4
Twickenham TW1 . . . . .16 F7
Grove Cl Cranleigh GU6 . . .174 F1
Forest Hill SE23 . . . . .23 E7
8 Kingston u T KT1 . . . . . . .37 F5
Old Windsor SL4 . . . . .11 B8
Grove Cnr KT23 . . . . .94 B1
Grove Cres Feltham TW13 . .15 E4
Kingston u T KT1 . . . . .37 E6
Walton-on-T KT12 . . . . .35 B2
Grove Cross Rd GU16 . . . . .65 D1
Grove Ct East Molesey KT8 .36 D4
Egham TW20 . . . . .12 A3
Forest Hill SE26 . . . . .23 E4
Hounslow TW3 . . . . .5 A3
8 Kingston u T KT1 . . . . . . .37 E6
Kingston u T KT3 . . . . .38 E6
Penge SE20 . . . . .23 B1
Grove Cty Prim Sch The
GU16 . . . . .65 E2
Grove End GU19 . . . . .47 F5
Grove End La KT10 . . . . .36 D1
Grove End Rd GU9 . . . . . . .146 B8
Grove Farm Ct CR4 . . . . . . .40 F4
Grove Gdns TW11 . . . . .17 A4
Grove Heath La GU23 . . . . .91 D4
Grove Heath N GU23 . . . . . .91 B5
Grove Heath Rd GU23 . . . . .91 B4
Grove House
7 Epsom KT17 . . . . .76 E6
Old Windsor SL4 . . . . .11 C8
6 Redhill RH1 . . . . .118 F1
Walton-on-T KT12 . . . . .35 B2
Grove House Froebel Ed
Inst SW15 . . . . .7 F1
Grove House Prim Sch
SE27 .22 B6
Grove Jun & Inf Sch W4 . . .7 C8
Grove La Kingston u T KT1 . .37 E5
Wallington CR5 . . . . .79 B5
Winkfield RG42 . . . . .8 B4
Grove Park Bridge W4 . . . . .7 C7
Grove Park Gdns W4 . . . . . .7 C7
Grove Park Rd W4 . . . . .7 B7
Grove Park Terr W4 . . . . .7 B8
Grove Pl KT13 . . . . .53 C7
Grove Prep Sch The
GU26 . . . . .188 D1
Grove Rd Ash GU12 . . . . . .106 A3
Ashstead KT21 . . . . .95 F8

Grove Rd *continued*
Barnes SW13 . . . . .7 F5
Beacon Hill GU26 . . . . . . .188 C6
Camberley GU15 . . . . .65 F5
Cheam SM2 . . . . .59 A4
Chertsey KT16 . . . . .32 F3
Cranleigh GU6 . . . . .174 F1
East Molesey KT8 . . . . .36 D5
Epsom KT17, KT18 . . . . . . .76 E6
Godalming 150 C3
Guildford GU1 . . . . .110 C1
Horley RH6 . . . . .160 F4
Hounslow TW3 . . . . .5 A3
Hounslow TW7 . . . . .5 E6
Kingston u T KT6 . . . . .37 D4
Lingfield RH7 . . . . .164 E5
Merton SW19 . . . . .20 C1
Mitcham CR4 . . . . .41 B7
Richmond TW10 . . . . .6 F1
🟥 Richmond TW10 . . . . .6 F2
Shepperton TW17 . . . . .34 C3
Sutton SM2 . . . . .59 A4
Tatsfield TN16 . . . . .103 C7
Thornton Heath CR7 . . . . . .42 A5
Twickenham TW2 . . . . .16 D5
Woking GU21 . . . . .69 F3
Grove Rd Prim Sch TW3 . .5 A3
Grove Shaw KT20 . . . . . .97 E3
Grove Terr TW11 . . . . . . .17 A4
Grove The Addlestone KT15 .52 B5
Aldershot GU11 . . . . .105 A1
Biggin Hill TN16 . . . . .83 C1
Caterham CR3 . . . . .100 C6
Coulsdon CR5 . . . . .79 D5
Crawley RH11 . . . . .201 C6
Egham TW20 . . . . .12 A3
Epsom KT17 . . . . .76 E6
Farnborough GU14 . . . . .85 D1
Frimley GU16 . . . . .65 D1
Horley RH6 . . . . .161 B2
Hounslow TW7 . . . . .5 E6
North Ascot SL5 . . . . .28 C8
Teddington TW11 . . . . .17 A4
🟥 Twickenham TW1 . . . . . . .6 B1
Walton-on-T KT12 . . . . .35 B2
West Wickham BR4 . . . . .63 C7
Woking GU21 . . . . .69 F3
Grove Way KT10 . . . . . . .36 C1
Grove Wood Hill CR5 . . . .79 D5
Grovebarns TW18 . . . . . .13 A2
Grovebell Ind Est GU9 . .145 F7
Grovefields Ave GU16 . . . .65 D1
Grovehill Ct BR1 . . . . .24 F2
Grovehill Rd RH1 . . . . . . .118 F1
Groveland Ave SW16 . . . . .21 F1
Groveland Rd BR3 . . . . . . .43 F6
Groveland Way KT3 . . . . . .38 D4
Grovelands
East Molesey KT8 . . . . .36 A5
Farnham GU10 . . . . .146 F2
Horley RH6 . . . . .161 B2
Kingston u T KT1 . . . . .37 D5
Grovelands Rd CR8 . . . . . .79 F7
Grovelands Sch KT12 . . . .35 B3
Groveley Rd TW13, TW16 . .14 F3
Groveside KT23 . . . . .114 A8
Groveside Cl
Carshalton SM5 . . . . .59 E8
Great Bookham KT23 . . . . .114 A8
Grovestile Waye TW14 . . .14 D8
Grovewood 🟥 TW9 . . . . . . .7 A4
Grovewood Ct 🟥 TW7 . . . . .5 E6
Grub St RH8 . . . . .123 C6
Guardian Ct SL8 . . . . . . .148 C3
Guards Ct SL5 . . . . .30 B2
Guerdon Pl RG12 . . . . . . .27 D2
Guernsey Cl
Crawley RH11 . . . . .201 A2
Guildford GU4 . . . . .110 A6
Heston TW5 . . . . .5 A7
Guernsey Farm Dr GU21 . .69 D4
Guernsey Gr SE24 . . . . . . .22 C8
Guildables La RH8, TN8 . .144 E7
Guildcroft GU1 . . . . .110 A1
Guildersfield Rd SW16 . . . .21 E1
Guildford Ave TW13 . . . . . .15 A6
Guildford Business Park
Rd GU2 . . . . .109 B2
Guildford Castle GU1 . . . .130 D7
Guildford Cath GU2 . . . . .109 B1
Guildford Coll
Markenfield House
GU1 . . . . .109 D1
Guildford Cty Sch GU2 . .130 B7
Guildford & Godalming
By-Pass Rd
Compton GU3 . . . . .129 E6
Guildford GU2 . . . . .129 E6
Shackleford GU7 . . . . .149 F6
Guildford Golf Club GU1 .110 C1
Guildford High Sch for
Girls GU1 . . . . .109 A1
Guildford Ind Est GU2 . . .109 A2
Guildford Lodge Dr KT24 112 F6
Guildford Mus GU1 . . . . . .130 D7
Guildford Park Ave GU2 . .130 B8
Guildford Park Rd GU2 . . .130 C8
Guildford Rd
Abinger Hammer RH5 . . . . .134 C3
Addlestone KT16 . . . . .51 C6
Aldershot GU11, GU12 . . . .126 D7
Ash GU2, GU3 . . . . .106 D3
Bagshot GU19 . . . . .47 E3
Bisley GU24 . . . . .67 F7
Broadbridge Heath RH12 . .216 B6
Chertsey KT16 . . . . .32 F1
Cranleigh GU6 . . . . .174 F4
Farncombe GU7 . . . . .151 B7

Guildford Rd *continued*
Farnham GU10, GU9 . . . . . .125 F4
Farnham, Runfold GU10 . . .126 B4
Fetcham KT22 . . . . .94 F3
Frimley GU16 . . . . .85 F6
Great Bookham KT23 . . . . . .94 A1
Horsham RH12 . . . . .217 A2
Lightwater GU18, GU19 . . . .48 B1
Mytchett GU16 . . . . .86 B5
Normandy GU3 . . . . .107 B4
Ottershaw KT16 . . . . .51 C5
Pirbright GU3 . . . . .88 C2
Rowhook RH12, RH13 . . . . .215 C7
Rowly GU6 . . . . .174 B6
Rudgwick RH12 . . . . .214 C6
Shamley Green GU5 . . . . . .153 A1
Slinfold RH12, RH13 . . . . . .215 C1
Thornton Heath CR0 . . . . . .42 D3
West End GU24 . . . . .67 F7
West End, Castle Green
GU21, GU24 . . . . .68 D6
Westcott RH4 . . . . .135 C6
Windlesham GU19 . . . . .47 F2
Woking GU22, GU4 . . . . . . .89 E8
Woking, Westfield
GU22, GU4 . . . . .89 D4
Wotton RH5 . . . . .134 C3
Guildford Rd E GU14 . . . . .85 C1
Guildford Rd W GU14 . . . . .85 C1
Guildford Road Trad Est
GU9 . . . . .125 D3
Guildford Sch of Acting
GU2 . . . . .130 D7
Guildford St Chertsey KT16 .33 A2
Staines TW18 . . . . .13 A2
Guildford Sta GU1 . . . . . .130 C8
Guildford Way SM6 . . . . . .60 E5
Guildown Ave GU2 . . . . . .130 B6
Guildown Rd GU2 . . . . . . .130 C6
Guileshill La GU23 . . . . . .91 F5
Guilford Ave KT5 . . . . .37 F4
Guillemont Fields GU14 . .84 D5
Guillemont Jun Sch GU14 84 D7
Guillemot Path 🟥 RH11 . .200 D5
Guinevere Rd RH11 . . . . . .200 E6
Guinness Ct Crawley RH11 201 C2
🟥 Knaphill GU21 . . . . .68 F1
🟥 South Croydon CR0 . . . . .61 F8
Gull Cl SM6 . . . . .60 E3
Gulliver Ct CR0 . . . . .61 B3
Gumbrells Cl GU3 . . . . . . .108 C5
Gumley Gdns 🟥 SW14 . . . . .6 A4
Gumley House Convent
Sch for Girls TW7 . . . . . . .6 A4
Gun Hill GU11 . . . . .105 B3
Gun Pit Rd RH7 . . . . .164 D4
Gunnell Cl SE25 . . . . .43 A3
Gunners Rd SW18 . . . . .20 D6
Gunning Cl RH11 . . . . .201 A3
Gunters Mead KT22 . . . . . .74 C8
Gunton Rd SW17 . . . . .21 A2
Gurdon's La GU8 . . . . .170 F2
Gurney Cres CR0 . . . . .41 F1
Gurney Rd SM5 . . . . .60 A6
Gurney's Cl 🟥 RH1 . . . . . .139 F8
Guy Rd CR0, SM6 . . . . .60 D7
Gwydor Rd BR3 . . . . .43 D6
Gwydyr Rd BR2 . . . . .44 F6
Gwynne Ave CR0 . . . . .43 D2
Gwynne Gdns RH19 . . . . .185 C2
Gwynne House 🟥 SW2 . . . .21 F7
Gwynne Rd CR3 . . . . .100 D4
Gwynne Vaughan Ave
GU2 . . . . .109 B5

H
H Jones Cres GU11 . . . . . .105 C3
Habershon Dr GU16 . . . . . .66 D2
Haccombe Rd SW19 . . . . . .20 C2
Hackbridge Inf Sch SM6 . .41 A1
Hackbridge Jun Sch SM5 .41 A1
Hackbridge Park Gdns
SM5 . . . . .59 F8
Hackbridge Rd SM5, SM6 . .60 A8
Hackbridge Sta SM6 . . . . .60 B8
Hackenden Cl RH19 . . . . .185 E3
Hackenden La RH19 . . . . .185 E3
Hacketts La GU22 . . . . .70 F4
Hackhurst La RH5 . . . . . . .133 F4
Hackington Cres BR3 . . . . .24 A2
Haddenham Ct SW17 . . . . .20 D4
Haddington Rd BR1 . . . . . .24 D4
Haddon Cl New Malden KT3 .38 F4
Oatlands Park KT13 . . . . . . .53 D6
Haddon Rd SM1 . . . . .59 B6
Hadfield Rd TW19 . . . . .2 D1
Hadleigh Cl SW20 . . . . .39 F7
Hadleigh Dr SM2 . . . . .59 B2
Hadleigh Gdns GU16 . . . . .85 E6
Hadley Cl SL3 . . . . .1 E6
Hadley Pl KT13 . . . . .53 A3
Hadley Rd CR4 . . . . .41 D5
Hadley Wood Rise CR8 . . . .80 B5
Hadleys GU10 . . . . .145 E3
Hadlow Pl SE19 . . . . .23 A1
Hadmans Cl RH12 . . . . . . .217 C1
Hadrian Ct Stanwell TW19 . .13 E8
Wallington SM6 . . . . .60 E3
Hadrian Ct 🟥 SM2 . . . . . . .59 B3
Hadrian Way
Stanwell TW19 . . . . .13 D8
Stanwell TW19 . . . . .13 E8
Hadrians GU9 . . . . .125 E4
Hafton Rd SE6 . . . . .24 E6

Haggard Rd TW1 . . . . .17 B8
Haig Pl SM4 . . . . .40 A3
Haig Rd Aldershot GU12 . .105 C1
Biggin Hill TN16 . . . . .83 E2
Sandhurst GU47 . . . . .64 F6
Haigh Cres RH1 . . . . .140 B7
Hailes Cl SW19 . . . . .20 C2
Hailes Rd SW17 . . . . .37 D2
Hailey Pl GU6 . . . . .174 F4
Hailsham Ave SW2 . . . . . . .21 F6
Hailsham Cl
Sandhurst GU47 . . . . .45 D1
Surbiton KT6 . . . . .37 D2
Hailsham Rd SW17 . . . . . . .21 A2
Haines Ct KT13 . . . . .53 D5
Haines Wlk SM4 . . . . .40 B2
Haining Gdns GU16 . . . . . .86 A3
Hainthorpe Rd SE27 . . . . .22 B4
Halcyon Ct SW16 . . . . .33 B7
Haldane Pl SW18 . . . . .20 B7
Hale Cty Prim Sch GU9 . .125 B7
Hale End RG12 . . . . .27 F5
Hale Ends GU22 . . . . .89 B6
Hale House Cl GU10 . . . . .167 F1
Hale House La GU10 . . . . .168 B2
Hale Pit Rd KT23 . . . . .94 C1
Hale Pl GU9 . . . . .125 E5
Hale Rd Farnham GU9 . . . .125 D4
Hale GU9 . . . . .125 D4
Hale Rdbt GU9 . . . . .125 E5
Hale Reeds GU9 . . . . .125 E6
Hale St TW18 . . . . .12 F4
Hale Way SW18 . . . . .85 D8
Halebourne La GU24 . . . . .49 A2
Hales Ct 🟥 SW11 . . . . .17 A3
Hales Field GU27 . . . . . . .208 C6
Hales House 🟥 SW12 . . . . .21 B8
Hales Oak GU3 . . . . .94 C1
Halesowen Rd SM4 . . . . . .40 B2
Haleswood KT11 . . . . .73 C6
Halewood RG12 . . . . .26 F3
Half Acre TW8 . . . . .6 D8
Half Acre Mews TW8 . . . . . .6 D8
Half Moon Hill GU27 . . . .208 C6
Half Moon St GU19 . . . . . . .47 E3
Half Way Cotts GU10 . . . .124 C3
Halford Rd TW10 . . . . .6 E2
Halfpenny Cl GU4 . . . . . . .131 D3
Halfpenny Cross KT11 . . . .73 A2
Halfpenny Ct SL5 . . . . .30 B2
Halfpenny La
Guildford GU4 . . . . .131 C5
Sunningdale SL5 . . . . .30 A2
Halfway La GU7 . . . . .150 B4
Haliburton Rd TW1, TW7 . . .6 A3
Halifax Cl Crawley RH10 . .182 E1
Farnborough GU14 . . . . .84 F3
Halifax St SE26 . . . . .23 B5
Halimote Rd GU11 . . . . . .105 A1
Haling Down Pas CR8 . . . .61 C1
Haling Gr CR2 . . . . .61 C3
Haling Manor High Sch
CR2 . . . . .61 B3
Haling Manor High Sch
(Pampisford Wing) CR2 . .61 B2
Haling Park Gdns CR2 . . . .61 B4
Haling Park Rd CR2 . . . . . .61 C4
Haling Rd CR2 . . . . .61 D4
Hall Cl Camberley GU15 . . . .65 E6
Farncombe GU7 . . . . .150 E7
Hall Ct TW11 . . . . .16 F3
Hall Dene Cl GU1 . . . . . . .110 C2
Hall Dr SE26 . . . . .23 C3
Hall Farm Dr TW2 . . . . . . .16 D8
Hall Grove (Sch) GU19 . . .48 A5
Hall Hill RH8 . . . . .122 D4
Hall La UB3 . . . . .3 D7
Hall Pl GU21 . . . . .70 A3
Hall Place Dr KT13 . . . . . . .53 E5
Hall Rd Bramley GU5 . . . . .151 F6
Isleworth TW7 . . . . .5 D2
Wallington SM6 . . . . .60 B2
Hall Sch Wimbledon
SW15 . . . . .19 A5
Hall Way CR8 . . . . .80 B6
Hallam Rd GU7 . . . . .150 F5
Halland Cl RH10 . . . . .202 A7
Hallane House SE27 . . . . . .22 C3
Halley Cl RH11 . . . . .201 B1
Halley Dr SL5 . . . . .28 C7
Halley's App GU21 . . . . . . .69 A1
Halley's Ct 🟥 GU21 . . . . . .69 A1
Halley's Wlk KT15 . . . . . . .52 C3
Hallgrove Bottom GU19 . . .47 F5
Halliards The KT12 . . . . . . .35 A3
Halliford Cl TW17 . . . . .34 E5
Halliford Rd
Sunbury TW16 . . . . .35 A5
Upper Halliford TW16, TW17 .34 F5
Halliford Sch TW17 . . . . . .34 C2
Hallington Cl GU21 . . . . . .69 B2
Hallmark Cl GU47 . . . . .64 E8
Hallmead Rd SM1 . . . . .59 B7
Hallowell Ave CR0 . . . . . . .60 E6
Hallowell Cl CR4 . . . . .41 A6
Hallowfield Way CR4 . . . . .40 E6
Halls Farm Cl GU21 . . . . . .68 D2
Hallsland RH10 . . . . .204 C8
Hallsland Way RH8 . . . . . .122 F3
Halnaker Wlk 🟥 RH11 . . . .200 D5
Halsford Croft RH19 . . . . .185 B3
Halsford Gn RH19 . . . . . . .185 B3
Halsford La RH19 . . . . .185 B3
Halsford Park Cty Prim
Sch RH19 . . . . .185 C2
Halsford Park Rd RH19 . . .185 C2
Halters End GU26 . . . . . . .188 A3
Ham Cl TW10 . . . . .17 C5
Ham Comm TW10 . . . . .17 D5

Ham Farm Rd KT2, TW10 . .17 E4
Ham Gate Ave
Richmond TW10 . . . . .17 E4
Richmond, Richmond
Park TW10 . . . . .18 A4
Ham House TW10 . . . . .17 D3
Ham La Elstead GU8 . . . . .148 E4
Englefield Green TW20 . . . . .11 B4
Ham Ridings TW10 . . . . . . .17 F3
Ham St TW10 . . . . .17 C5
Ham The TW8 . . . . .6 C7
Ham View CR0 . . . . .43 E3
Hamble Ave GU17 . . . . .64 D5
Hamble Cl GU21 . . . . .69 A2
Hamble Ct KT1 . . . . .17 D1
Hamble Wlk GU21 . . . . .69 A2
Hambleden Ct RG12 . . . . . .27 E5
Hambledon Ct 🟥 SM6 . . . .60 B4
Hambledon Gdns SE25 . . . .42 F6
Hambledon Hill KT18 . . . . .76 C3
Hambledon House 🟥 KT2 .18 B2
Hambledon Inf Sch GU8 .171 D2
Hambledon Pk GU8 . . . . . .171 B1
Hambledon Pl
Dulwich SE21 . . . . .22 F7
Little Bookham KT23 . . . . . .94 A4
Hambledon Rd
Caterham CR3 . . . . .100 D4
Godalming GU8, GU7 . . . . .171 D5
Hambledon GU8, GU7 . . . .171 D5
Hydestile GU8, GU7 . . . . . .171 D5
Wandsworth SW18 . . . . .19 F8
Hambledon Vale KT18 . . . .76 C3
Hambleton Cl Frimley GU16 66 B3
North Cheam KT4 . . . . .58 C8
Hambleton Ct RH11 . . . . . .201 C4
Hambleton Hill RH11 . . . . .201 C4
Hambridge Way SW2 . . . . .22 A8
Hambro Rd SW16 . . . . .21 D3
Hambrook Rd SE25 . . . . . . .43 B6
Hamers House 🟥 SW2 . . . .22 A8
Hamesmoor Rd GU16 . . . . .85 F4
Hamesmoor Way GU16 . . . .85 F4
Hamfield Cl RH8 . . . . .122 C6
Hamilton Ave Cheam SM3 . .58 E8
Cobham KT11 . . . . .73 A6
Pyrford GU22 . . . . .70 E3
Tolworth KT6, SM3 . . . . . . .57 A8
Hamilton Cl TW13 . . . . . . .14 F3
Hamilton Cl Chertsey KT16 .32 F1
Epsom KT19 . . . . .76 C7
Guildford GU2 . . . . .109 A6
Purley CR8 . . . . .80 B7
Hamilton Cres TW3 . . . . . . .5 B2
Hamilton Ct Catford SE6 . . .24 F7
Cobham KT11 . . . . .73 A6
Croydon CR0 . . . . .43 A1
Farnborough GU17 . . . . .64 E1
Great Bookham KT23 . . . . . .94 B2
Hamilton Dr
Guildford GU2 . . . . .109 A6
Sunningdale SL5 . . . . .29 E2
Hamilton House
Chiswick W4 . . . . .7 E8
🟥 Richmond TW9 . . . . .6 E3
Hamilton Mews KT13 . . . . .53 A6
Hamilton Par TW13 . . . . . . .15 A4
Hamilton Pl
Guildford GU2 . . . . .109 A6
Kingswood KT20 . . . . .97 F4
Sunbury TW16 . . . . .15 A1
Hamilton Rd Brentford TW8 .6 D8
Feltham TW13 . . . . .14 F4
Horsham RH12 . . . . .217 B3
Merton SW19 . . . . .20 B1
South Norwood CR7 . . . . . . .42 D6
Twickenham TW2 . . . . .16 E7
West Norwood SE27 . . . . . . .22 D4
Hamilton Road Ind Est
SE27 . . . . .22 D4
Hamilton Road Mews 🟥
SW19 . . . . .20 B1
Hamilton Way SM6 . . . . . . .60 D2
Hamlash Cotts GU10 . . . .146 C1
Hamlash La GU10 . . . . . . .146 C1
Hamlet Rd SE19 . . . . .23 A1
Hamlet St RG42 . . . . .27 E8
Hamlyn Gdns SE19 . . . . . . .22 E1
Hamm Court Est KT13 . . . . .52 F8
Hamm Moor La KT15 . . . . .52 E6
Hammelton Rd BR1 . . . . . . .44 F8
Hammer Hill GU27 . . . . . . .207 C6
Hammer La
Grayshott GU10, GU26 . . . .187 E6
Haslemere GU27, GU30 . . .207 E6
Haslemere GU26 . . . . .207 C8
Linchmere GU27 . . . . .207 C5
Hammer Vale GU27 . . . . . .207 B6
Hammer Yd RH10 . . . . .201 D5
Hammerfield Dr RH5 . . . . .133 F3
Hammerpond Rd RH13 . . .217 F1
Hammersley Rd GU11 . . . .105 C7
Hammerwood
Copse GU27 . . . . .207 D5
Hammerwood Rd RH19 . . .206 E6
Hammond Ave CR4 . . . . . . .41 B7
Hammond Cl
Hampton TW12 . . . . .36 A8
Woking GU21 . . . . .69 C4
Hammond Cty Jun Sch
GU18 . . . . .48 A1
Hammond Rd GU21 . . . . . . .69 C4
Hammond Way GU18 . . . . . .48 B1
Hamond Cl CR2 . . . . .61 B2
Hampden Ave BR3 . . . . .43 E7
Hampden Rd RH10 . . . . . . .182 E1

Hampden Rd
Beckenham BR3 . . . . .43 E7
Kingston u T KT1 . . . . .38 A6
Hamper's La RH13 . . . . . . .218 A2
Hampers Ct RH13 . . . . .217 D2
Hampshire Cl GU12 . . . . . .126 D7
Hampshire Ct
Addlestone KT15 . . . . .52 C5
Barnes SW13 . . . . .7 F5
Hampshire Rd GU15 . . . . . .65 F8
Hampstead La RH4 . . . . . .135 F6
Hampstead Rd RH4 . . . . . .136 A6
Hampton Cl SW20 . . . . .19 C1
Hampton Court Ave KT8 . .36 E3
Hampton Court Cres KT8 .36 D6
Hampton Court Palace
KT8 . . . . .36 F6
Hampton Court Par KT8 . .36 E6
Hampton Court Rd
KT1, KT8 . . . . .37 B6
Hampton Court Sta KT8 . .36 E6
Hampton Court Way
KT10, KT7, KT8 . . . . .36 E3
Hampton Farm Ind Est
TW13 . . . . .15 E5
Hampton Gr KT17 . . . . .76 F8
Hampton Hill Bsns Pk
TW12 . . . . .16 C3
Hampton Hill Jun Mix Sch
TW12 . . . . .16 C3
Hampton Inf Sch TW12 . . .16 A1
Hampton Jun Sch TW12 . .36 A8
Hampton La TW13 . . . . .15 E4
Hampton Lodge RH6 . . . . .161 A2
Hampton Rd Hale GU9 . . . .125 B6
North Cheam KT4 . . . . .58 B8
Redhill RH1 . . . . .139 F4
Teddington TW11, TW12 . . .16 E3
Thornton Heath CR0 . . . . . .42 C6
Twickenham TW2 . . . . .16 D5
Hampton Rd E TW13 . . . . .15 F5
Hampton Rd W TW13 . . . . .15 E5
Hampton Road Ind Pk
CR0 . . . . .42 C3
Hampton Sch TW12 . . . . . .16 A3
Hampton Sta TW12 . . . . . .36 A8
Hampton Wick Inf Sch
KT1 . . . . .17 D1
Hampton Wick Sta KT1 . . .37 D1
Hamsey Green Cty Inf Sch
CR6 . . . . .81 B3
Hamsey Green Cty Jun Sch
CR6 . . . . .81 B3
Hamsey Green Gdns CR6 . .81 C3
Hamsey Way CR2 . . . . .81 B4
Hanbury Dr TN16 . . . . .83 B6
Hanbury Path GU21 . . . . . .70 D5
Hanbury Rd RH11 . . . . . . .200 E5
Hanbury Way GU15 . . . . . . .65 C3
Hancock Rd SE19 . . . . .22 D2
Hancocks Mount SL5 . . . . .29 D3
Hancombe Rd GU47 . . . . . .45 A1
Handcroft Rd CR0 . . . . .42 B1
Handel House TW2 . . . . .5 D1
Handside Cl KT4 . . . . .39 D1
Handsworth
House 🟥 RH10 . . . . .201 D5
Hanford Cl SW18 . . . . .20 A7
Hanger Hill KT13 . . . . .53 B5
Hanley Pl BR3 . . . . .24 A1
Hannah Cl BR3 . . . . .44 C6
Hannah Ct SW19 . . . . .19 C1
Hannah Peschar Gall &
Gdn RH5 . . . . .177 A2
Hannay Wlk SW16 . . . . . . .21 D6
Hannen Rd SE27 . . . . .22 B5
Hannibal Rd TW19 . . . . . . .13 E8
Hannibal Way CR0 . . . . . . .60 F4
Hanning Lodge TW3 . . . . . . .5 C7
Hanover Ave TW13 . . . . . . .15 A6
Hanover Cl Cheam SM3 . . . .58 F6
Crawley RH10 . . . . .201 F3
Englefield Green TW20 . . . . .11 B2
Frimley GU16 . . . . .65 E1
Merstham RH1 . . . . .119 C7
Richmond TW9 . . . . .7 A7
Hanover Ct Dorking RH4 . . .135 F7
Horsham RH13 . . . . .217 F3
🟥 Penge SE19 . . . . .23 A1
Woking GU22 . . . . .89 E8
Hanover Gdns
Bracknell RG12 . . . . .26 F2
Farnborough GU14 . . . . .84 C4
Hanover House KT6 . . . . . . .38 A1
Hanover Rd SW19 . . . . .20 C1
Hanover St CR0, CR9 . . . . . .61 B7
Hanover Terr TW7 . . . . .6 A6
Hanover Wlk KT13 . . . . .53 E7
Hansler Gr KT8 . . . . .36 D5
Hanson Cl Balham SW12 . . .21 B8
Beckenham BR3 . . . . .24 B2
Camberley GU15 . . . . .66 B7
Guildford GU1 . . . . .109 F4
Mortlake SW14 . . . . .7 C4
Hanworth Cl RG12 . . . . . . .27 A2
Hanworth La KT16 . . . . .32 F1
Hanworth Rd
Bracknell RG12 . . . . .27 A2
Feltham TW13 . . . . .15 B7
Hampton TW12 . . . . .16 B3
Hounslow TW3, TW4 . . . . . . .5 B2
Redhill RH1 . . . . .139 F4
Sunbury TW16 . . . . .15 A1
Twickenham TW4 . . . . .15 F8

Hanworth Terr TW3 .....5 B3
Hanworth Trad Est
Chertsey KT16 .....32 F1
Feltham TW13 .....15 E5
Harberson Rd SW12 .....21 B7
Harbin House 5 SW2 .....22 A7
Harbledown Rd CR2 .....81 A8
Harborough Rd SW16 .....21 F4
Harbour Cl GU14 .....85 A8
Harbourfield Rd SM7 .....78 B4
Harbridge Ave SW15 .....19 A8
Harbury Rd SM5 .....59 E3
Harcourt Ave SM6 .....60 B6
Harcourt Cl Egham TW20 ..12 C2
Isleworth TW7 .....6 A4
Harcourt Field SM6 .....60 B6
Harcourt Lodge 2 SM6 ...60 B6
Harcourt Rd Bracknell RG12 27 B4
Camberley GU15 .....65 B5
Merton SW19 .....20 A1
Thornton Heath CR7 .....42 A3
Wallington SM6 .....60 B6
Harcourt Way RH9 .....142 E6
Hardcastle Cl SE25 .....43 A3
Hardcourts Cl BR4 .....63 B7
Hardel Rise SW2 .....22 B7
Hardel Wlk SE24, SW2 .....22 A8
Hardell Cl TW20 .....12 A3
Hardham Cl RH11 .....201 A8
Harding Cl Kingston u T KT2 .37 F8
South Croydon CR0 .....61 F7
Harding Ct SE25 .....42 F7
Harding House SM6 .....60 C2
Harding Pl SE23 .....23 E8
Harding Rd KT18 .....96 E8
Hardings La SE20 .....23 D2
Hardman Rd KT2 .....37 E7
Hardwell Way RG12 .....27 E5
Hardwick Cl KT22 .....74 C4
Hardwick La KT16 .....32 D1
Hardwick Rd RH1 .....139 D7
Hardwicke Ave TW5 .....5 A6
Hardwicke Rd
Reigate RH2 .....118 A2
Richmond TW10 .....17 C4
Hardy Cl Crawley RH10 ...202 C7
Dorking RH5 .....136 B3
Horley RH6 .....160 E3
Horsham RH12 .....217 B4
Hardy Gn RG45 .....45 B4
Hardy Rd SW19 .....20 B1
Hardys Cl KT8 .....36 E5
Hare Hill KT15 .....51 F4
Hare Hill Cl GU22 .....71 A4
Hare La Claygate KT10 .....55 E4
Crawley RH11 .....201 B8
Farncombe GU7 .....150 F6
Horne RH7 .....163 D5
Harebell Hill KT11 .....73 E5
Harecroft
Dorking RH4, RH5 .....136 C4
Fetcham KT23 .....94 C3
Haredon Cl SE23 .....23 D8
Harefield KT10 .....55 E7
Harefield Ave SM2 .....58 E2
Harefield Rd SW16 .....21 F1
Harelands Cl GU21 .....69 C2
Harelands La GU21 .....69 C2
Harendon KT20 .....97 D6
Hares Bank CR0 .....63 D1
Harestone Dr CR3 .....100 F2
Harestone Hill CR3 .....100 F2
Harestone La CR3 .....100 E2
Harestone Valley Rd CR3 .100 F2
Harewood Cl
Crawley RH10 .....182 A1
Reigate RH2 .....118 C4
Harewood Gdns CR2 .....81 C4
Harewood Rd
Guildford GU4 .....110 C4
Hounslow TW7 .....5 F6
Mitcham SW19 .....20 E2
South Croydon CR2 .....61 E4
Harfield Rd TW16 .....35 D7
Harkness Cl KT17 .....77 C3
Harland Ave CR0 .....62 A7
Harland Fst Sch CR4 .....40 D7
Harlech Ct 1 SE23 .....23 C7
Harlech Gdns TW5 .....4 C7
Harlech Rd GU17 .....64 D4
Harlequin Ave TW8 .....6 A8
Harlequin Cl TW7 .....5 E2
Harlequin Rd TW11 .....17 B1
Harlington Cl UB7 .....3 C7
Harlington Cnr UB3 .....3 D6
Harlington Rd
E TW13, TW14 .....15 C7
Harlington Rd W TW14 .....4 B1
Harlow Ct 4 RH2 .....118 D1
Harman Pl CR8 .....80 B8
Harmans Dr RH19 .....186 B1
Harmans Mead RH19 .....186 B1
Harmans Water Cty Inf
Sch RG12 .....27 E4
Harmans Water Cty Jun
Sch RG12 .....27 E4
Harmans Water Rd RG12 .27 D4
Harmar Cl RG40 .....25 E6
Harmes Way GU14 .....105 D7
Harmondsworth La UB7 ....2 E8
Harmondsworth Prim Sch
UB7 .....2 D8
Harmony Cl Crawley RH11 200 E4
Wallington SM6 .....60 E2
Harms Gr GU4 .....110 C4
Harold Rd Carshalton SM1 ..59 D6
Crawley RH10 .....202 E5
South Norwood SE19 .....22 D1
Haroldslea RH6 .....161 E2
Haroldslea Cl RH6 .....161 C1
Haroldslea Dr RH6 .....161 D1
Harpenden Rd SE27, SW16 .22 B6
Harper Dr RH10 .....202 C2
Harper's Rd GU12 .....106 C2
Harpesford Ave GU25 .....31 C4
Harps Oak La RH1, RH2 ...99 A2
Harpurs KT20 .....97 D5
Harrier Cl GU6 .....174 E4
Harrier Ct RH10 .....182 D1
Harriet Gdns CR0 .....62 A8
Harriet Tubman Cl SW2 ..22 A8
Harrington Cl Leigh RH2 ..138 A2
Wallington CR0 .....60 E8
Harrington Ct 7 CR0 .....61 D8
Harrington Rd SE25 .....43 B5
Harriotts Cl KT22 .....95 C7
Harriotts La KT21, KT22 ...95 C8
Harris City Tech Coll SE19 .42 F8
Harris Cl Crawley RH11 ...201 B3
Hounslow TW5 .....5 A6
Harris Lodge SE6 .....24 C7
Harris Way TW16 .....34 E8
Harrison Cl RH2 .....139 B8
Harrison Ct TW17 .....34 B4
Harrison's Rise CR0, CR9 ..61 B7
Harrodian Sch SW13 .....7 F7
Harrogate Ct 2 SE26 .....23 A5
Harrow Bottom Rd GU25 ..31 F3
Harrow Cl Chertsey KT15 ...52 B8
Chessington KT9 .....56 D3
Dorking RH4 .....136 A6
Harrow Gate Gdns RH4 ..136 A5
Harrow Gdns CR6 .....81 F3
Harrow La GU7 .....150 E7
Harrow Lodge SM2 .....59 D4
Harrow Rd Ashford TW15 ..14 A6
Carshalton SM1, SM2, SM5 ..59 E4
Warlingham CR6 .....81 F3
Harrow Rd E RH4 .....136 B6
Harrow Rd W RH4 .....136 A6
Harrow Way TW17 .....34 C7
Harrowdene GU6 .....174 E4
Harrowdene Ct SW19 .....19 E3
Harrowdene Gdns TW11 ..17 A1
Harrowlands Pk RH4 .....136 B6
Harrowsley Ct RH6 .....161 B4
Hart Cl Bletchingley RH1 ...120 E2
1 Bracknell RG42 .....27 B8
Farnborough GU14 .....84 E8
Hart Dene Cl GU19 .....47 E3
Hart Dyke Cl RG41 .....25 B2
Hart Gdns RH4 .....136 B8
Hart House SW2 .....22 A7
Hart Rd Byfleet KT14 .....71 E6
Dorking RH4 .....136 B8
Hart The GU9 .....125 B2
Hart's La RH9 .....142 D7
Harte Rd TW3 .....4 F5
Hartfield Cres SW19 .....19 F1
Hartfield Gr SE20 .....43 C8
Hartfield Rd
Chessington KT9 .....56 D5
Forest Row RH18 .....206 F2
Merton SW19 .....20 A1
Hartford Rd KT19 .....57 B4
Hartford Rise GU15 .....65 D6
Hartham Cl TW7 .....6 A6
Hartham Rd TW7 .....6 A6
Harting Ct RH11 .....200 F3
Hartington Ct W4 .....7 B7
Hartington Pl RH2 .....118 A3
Hartington Rd Chiswick W4 ..7 C6
Twickenham TW1 .....6 B1
Hartland Cl KT15 .....52 C2
Hartland Pl GU14 .....85 A7
Hartland Rd
Addlestone KT15 .....52 A3
Cheam SM4 .....40 B2
Hampton TW12 .....16 B4
Isleworth TW7 .....6 A4
Hartland Way Croydon CR0 .62 E8
Morden SM4 .....39 F2
Hartlands The TW5 .....4 B8
Hartley Cl GU17 .....64 B5
Hartley Down CR5, CR8 ....79 F5
Hartley Farm CR8 .....79 F4
Hartley Hill CR8 .....79 F4
Hartley Old Rd CR8 .....79 F5
Hartley Rd CR0 .....42 C2
Hartley Way CR5, CR8 .....79 F4
Harts Gdns GU2 .....109 B4
Harts Leap Cl GU47 .....45 B1
Harts Leap Rd GU47 .....64 A8
Harts Yd 14 GU9 .....125 B2
Hartscroft CR0 .....62 E2
Hartsgrove GU8 .....191 B5
Hartshill GU2 .....108 D2
Hartshill Wlk GU21 .....69 B3
Hartspiece Rd RH1 .....140 B7
Hartswood RH5 .....136 D4
Hartswood Ave RH2 .....139 A5
Hartswood House 10 SW2 .21 E7
Harvard Hill W4 .....7 B8
Harvard Rd Hounslow TW7 ...5 E6
Sandhurst GU47 .....45 E1
Harvest Bank Rd BR4 .....63 F7
Harvest Ct Beckenham BR3 .24 A1
Littleton TW17 .....34 A5
Harvest Hill
East Grinstead RH19 .....205 E8
Godalming GU7 .....150 D4
Harvest La KT7 .....37 A3
Harvest Rd Crawley RH10 .202 C4
Harvest Rd *continued*
Englefield Green TW20 .....11 D2
Feltham TW13 .....15 A5
Harvest Ride
RG12, RG42, SL5 .....28 A8
Harvester Rd KT19 .....57 D1
Harvesters RH12 .....217 D5
Harvesters Cl TW7 .....5 D2
Harvestside RH6 .....161 C4
Harvey Cl RH11 .....201 A1
Harvey Dr TW12 .....36 A8
Harvey Lodge GU1 .....130 E8
Harvey Rd
Farnborough GU14 .....84 C5
Guildford GU1 .....130 E8
Twickenham TW4 .....15 F8
Walton-on-T KT12 .....35 A2
Harwarden Cl RH10 .....204 C8
Harwood Ave CR4 .....40 E6
Harwood Gdns SL4 .....11 B8
Harwood Pk RH1 .....161 A8
Harwood Rd RH12, RH13 .218 A3
Harwoods Cl 3 RH19 .....205 F7
Harwoods La RH19 .....205 F7
Hascombe Ct RH11 .....201 A5
Hascombe House 11 SW15 19 B7
Haseley End SE23 .....23 C8
Haseltine Prim Sch SE6 ...23 F4
Haseltine Rd SE26 .....23 F4
Haslam Ave SM3, SM4 .....39 E1
Hasle Dr GU27 .....208 B6
Haslemere Ave
Cranford TW5 .....4 C5
Mitcham CR4, SW19 .....40 D7
Wimbledon SW18 .....20 B6
Haslemere Cl Frimley GU16 66 C3
Hampton TW12 .....15 F3
Wallington SM6 .....60 E5
Haslemere & District
Hospl GU27 .....208 D7
Haslemere Educational
Mus GU27 .....208 D7
Haslemere Fst Sch CR4 ...40 D7
Haslemere & Heathrow Est
The TW4 .....4 B4
Haslemere Ind Est
Feltham TW14 .....4 A2
Wimbledon SW18 .....20 B6
Haslemere Prep Sch
GU27 .....208 D5
Haslemere Rd Brook GU8 .170 C5
Kingsley Green GU27 .....208 B1
Thornton Heath CR7 .....42 B4
Witley GU8 .....170 C5
Haslemere Sta GU27 .....208 B6
Haslett Ave E RH10 .....202 A6
Haslett Ave W
RH10, RH11 .....201 D5
Haslett Rd TW17 .....34 E7
Hassall Ct GU22 .....90 A6
Hassocks Cl SE23, SE26 .....23 B5
Hassocks Ct 3 RH11 .....200 F3
Hassocks Rd SW16 .....41 D8
Haste Hill GU27 .....208 D5
Hastings Cl GU16 .....86 A7
Hastings Dr KT6 .....37 C3
Hastings Pl 1 CR0 .....42 F1
Hastings Rd Crawley RH10 202 C6
Croydon CR0 .....42 F1
Hatch Cl Addlestone KT15 ..52 B7
Alfold Crossways GU6 .....194 A3
Hatch End
Forest Row RH18 .....206 F2
Windlesham GU20 .....48 C4
Hatch Gdns KT20 .....97 D7
Hatch Hill GU27 .....208 B1
Hatch La
Harmondsworth TW6, UB7 ...2 D7
Kingsley Green GU27 .....208 B2
Ockham GU23 .....72 B1
Ockham GU23 .....92 B7
South Nutfield RH1 .....140 F3
Wormley GU8 .....190 D8
Hatch Pl TW10 .....17 F3
Hatch Rd SW16 .....41 E7
Hatch Ride RG45 .....45 B7
Hatch Ride Cty Prim Sch
RG45 .....45 B7
Hatches The Farnham GU9 145 F8
Frimley GU16 .....85 F6
Hatchet La SL4, SL5 .....9 B5
Hatchett Rd TW14 .....14 C7
Hatchetts Dr GU27 .....207 D7
Hatchford Park Sch KT11 .72 E1
Hatchgate RH6 .....160 F2
Hatchgate Copse RG12 .....26 E3
Hatchlands RH12 .....218 A7
Hatchlands Pk GU4 .....111 F5
Hatchlands Rd RH1 .....118 E1
Hatfield Cl Belmont SM2 .....59 B2
Mitcham CR4 .....40 D5
West Byfleet KT14 .....71 B7
Hatfield Gdns GU14 .....85 E3
Hatfield House 16 KT6 .....37 E4
Hatfield Mead SM4 .....40 A4
Hatfield Prim Sch SM4 .....39 E3
Hatfield Rd KT21 .....95 F8
Hatfield Wlk RH11 .....200 E2
Hathaway Ct 10 RH1 .....119 A2
Hathaway Rd CR0 .....42 B2
Hatherleigh Cl
Chessington KT9 .....56 D5
Morden SM4 .....40 A5
Hatherleigh House SM4 ..40 A5
Hatherley Rd TW9 .....6 F6
Hatherop Rd TW12 .....15 F1
Hathersham Cl RH6 .....162 A4
Hathersham La RH1, RH6 .161 F6
Hathersley House 3 SW2 .22 A8
Hatherwood KT21 .....95 E6
Hatton Cross Rdbt TW6 ....3 F4
Hatton Cross Sta TW6 .....3 F3
Hatton Gdns CR4 .....40 F4
Hatton Gn TW14 .....4 A3
Hatton Hill GU20 .....48 C5
Hatton Rd
East Bedfont TW14 .....14 D8
Hatton TW14, TW6 .....3 E2
Thornton Heath CR0 .....42 A1
Havana Rd SW18, SW19 ...20 A6
Havelock Cotts GU22 .....89 D5
Havelock Hall 8 CR0 .....42 F1
Havelock House
4 Croydon CR0 .....42 F1
Farnborough GU14 .....105 C8
Forest Hill SE23 .....23 C7
Havelock Rd Croydon CR0 ..61 F8
Wimbledon SW19 .....20 C3
Wokingham RG41 .....25 A6
Havelock St RG41 .....25 A6
Havelock Wlk SE23 .....23 C6
Haven Cl SW19 .....19 D5
Haven Ct BR3 .....44 C7
Haven Gdns RH10 .....184 B1
Haven Rd Ashford TW15 ....14 B5
Rudgwick RH12, RH14 .....214 D3
Haven The Ashford TW16 ...15 A1
Richmond TW9 .....7 A4
Haven Way GU9 .....125 D4
Havenbury Est RH4 .....136 A8
Havenbury Ind Est RH4 ..135 F8
Havengate RH12 .....217 F5
Haverfield Gdns TW9 .....7 A7
Haverhill Rd SW12 .....21 C7
Havers Ave KT12 .....54 D5
Haversham Cl
Crawley RH10 .....201 F6
Twickenham TW1 .....6 D1
Haversham Dr RG12 .....27 B3
Haversham House RH6 ..161 B5
Havisham Pl SW16 .....22 B1
Hawarden Gr SE24 .....22 C8
Hawarden Rd CR3 .....100 C6
Hawes Down Schs BR4 ...44 D1
Hawes La BR4 .....63 E8
Hawes Rd KT20 .....97 D7
Haweswater House TW1 ...5 F2
Hawk La RG12 .....27 D5
Hawk's Hill KT22 .....94 F4
Hawke Rd SE19 .....22 E2
Hawkedale Fst Sch TW16 .34 F6
Hawker Cl SM6 .....60 E3
Hawker Ct 14 KT2 .....18 A1
Hawker Rd GU12 .....105 F5
Hawkes Cl RG41 .....25 A7
Hawkes Leap GU20 .....48 B6
Hawkes Rd CR4 .....40 F8
Hawkesbourne Rd RH12 .217 F5
Hawkesfield Rd SE23, SE6 .23 F6
Hawkesley Cl TW1 .....17 A4
Hawkesmoor Rd RH11 ...200 E4
Hawkesmoore Dr RH5 ...157 C4
Hawkesworth Dr GU19 .....47 E1
Hawkewood Rd TW16 .....35 A6
Hawkfield Ct TW7 .....5 E5
Hawkhirst Rd CR8 .....80 E3
Hawkhurst KT11 .....74 A5
Hawkhurst Gdns KT9 .....56 E6
Hawkhurst Rd SW16 .....41 D8
Hawkhurst Way
New Malden KT3 .....38 D4
West Wickham BR4 .....63 B8
Hawkhurst Wlk RH10 .....202 B4
Hawkins Cl RG12 .....28 A7
Hawkins Rd Crawley RH10 201 E4
Teddington TW11 .....17 B2
Hawkins Way Catford SE6 ..24 A3
Wokingham RG40 .....25 E6
Hawkley Gdns SE27 .....22 B6
Hawkridge RH12 .....195 E1
Hawkridge Ct RG12 .....27 E6
Hawks Hill Cl KT22 .....94 F4
Hawks Rd KT1 .....37 F7
Hawksbrook La BR3 .....44 C3
Hawkshead Cl BR1 .....24 E1
Hawkshill Cl KT10 .....55 A4
Hawkshill Way KT10 .....55 A4
Hawksview KT11 .....73 F6
Hawksway TW18 .....12 F5
Hawkswell Cl GU21 .....68 F2
Hawkswell Wlk GU21 .....68 F3
Hawkswood Ave GU16 .....65 F2
Hawkswood House RG42 ..26 E8
Hawkwood Dell KT23 .....94 A1
Hawkwood Rise KT23 .....94 A1
Hawley Cl TW12 .....15 F2
Hawley Ct GU14 .....84 E8
Hawley Cty Prim Sch
GU17 .....64 E3
Hawley Garden Cotts
GU17 .....64 D4
Hawley Gn GU17 .....64 E3
Hawley La GU14 .....85 B8
Hawley Lodge GU14 .....64 F2
Hawley Place Sch GU17 ...64 E1
Hawley Rd GU14, GU17 .....64 F3
Hawley Way TW15 .....14 B3
Hawmead RH10 .....204 C8
Haworth Rd RH10 .....202 C5
Hawth (Arts Ctr) The
RH10 .....201 F5
Hawth Ave RH10 .....201 F4
Hawth Cl RH10 .....201 E4
Hawthorn Ave CR7 .....42 B8
Hawthorn Cl Banstead SM7 .77 E5
Bracknell RG42 .....27 A8
Hawthorn Cl *continued*
Cranford TW5 .....4 B7
Crawley RH11 .....181 C1
Hampton TW12 .....16 A3
Horsham RH12 .....217 C4
Redhill RH1 .....140 A4
Woking GU22 .....89 E7
Hawthorn Cres
Selsdon CR2 .....81 C8
Upper Tooting SW17 .....21 A3
Hawthorn Ct Richmond TW9 .7 B6
8 West Norwood SW16 .....22 A3
Hawthorn Dr BR4 .....63 E6
Hawthorn Gr SE20 .....43 B8
Hawthorn Hatch TW8 .....6 B7
Hawthorn La
Newell Green SL4 .....8 A7
Rowledge GU10 .....145 F3
Hawthorn Rd Brentford TW8 .6 B7
Carshalton SM1, SM2, SM5 ..59 E4
Frimley GU16 .....65 F2
Godalming GU7 .....150 B2
Send Marsh GU23 .....91 A3
Wallington SM5, SM6 .....60 B3
Woking GU22 .....89 D7
Hawthorn Way Bisley GU24 68 A3
Redhill RH1 .....140 B8
Upper Halliford TW17 .....34 D5
Woodham KT15 .....52 C1
Hawthorndene Cl BR2 .....63 F8
Hawthorndene Rd BR2 ....63 F8
Hawthorne Ave
Biggin Hill TN16 .....83 D4
Mitcham CR4 .....40 D7
Wallington SM5 .....60 A3
Winkfield SL4 .....9 B6
Hawthorne Cl
Aldershot GU12 .....126 E7
Sutton SM1 .....59 C8
Hawthorne Cotts RH6 ...183 C7
Hawthorne Cres GU17 ....64 E4
Hawthorne Ct TW19 .....13 D8
Hawthorne Dr SL4 .....9 B7
Hawthorne Pl KT17 .....76 E7
Hawthorne Rd TW20 .....12 C4
Hawthorne Way
Guildford GU4 .....110 B5
Stanwell TW19 .....13 D8
Winkfield SL4 .....9 B7
Hawthorns Sch (Pendell
Court) The RH1 .....120 B4
Hawthorns The
Belmont SM2 .....59 A4
Ewell KT17 .....58 A3
Oxted RH8 .....123 A2
Poyle SL3 .....1 F6
Haxted Mill Mus TN8 .....165 D8
Haxted Rd
Haxted RH7, TN8 .....165 C7
Lingfield RH7, TN8 .....165 C7
Haybarn Dr RH12 .....217 E7
Haycroft Cl CR8 .....80 B1
Haycroft Rd KT6 .....56 E7
Hayden Ct KT15 .....71 B8
Haydn Ave CR8 .....80 A4
Haydon House 2 TW11 ...17 C1
Haydon Park Rd SW19 ....20 B3
Haydon Pl GU1 .....130 D8
Haydon's Rd Merton SW19 .20 C2
Wimbledon SW19 .....20 C2
Haydons Road Sta SW19 ..20 C3
Hayes Barton GU22 .....70 D3
Hayes Chase BR4 .....44 E3
Hayes Cres SM3 .....58 D6
Hayes Ct Streatham SW12 ..21 E7
Wimbledon SW19 .....19 E2
Hayes Hill BR2 .....44 E1
Hayes Hill Rd BR2 .....44 F1
Hayes La
Beckenham BR2, BR3 .....44 D5
Kenley CR8, CR3 .....80 B3
Purley CR8 .....80 B3
Slinfold RH13 .....215 D2
Hayes Mead Rd BR2 .....44 E1
Hayes Prim Sch The CR8 ..80 B3
Hayes Sta BR2 .....44 F1
Hayes The KT18 .....96 E8
Hayes Way BR3 .....44 D5
Hayes Wlk RH6 .....162 A4
Hayesend House SW17 ...20 C4
Hayesford Park Dr BR2 ...44 F4
Hayfields RH6 .....161 C4
Haygarth Pl SW19 .....19 D3
Haygreen Cl KT2 .....18 B2
Haylett Gdns KT1 .....37 D5
Hayling Ave TW13 .....15 A5
Hayling Ct Cheam SM3 .....58 C6
Crawley RH11 .....201 C3
Haymeads Dr KT10 .....55 C4
Haymer Gdns KT4 .....58 A7
Hayne Rd BR3 .....43 F8
Haynes La SE19 .....22 E2
Haynt Wlk SW20 .....39 E6
Hays Bridge Bsns Ctr
RH9 .....163 C6
Hays Bridge Houses RH9 163 B7
Hays Wlk SM2 .....58 D1
Haysleigh Gdns SE20 .....43 A7
Haysleigh House SE20 ....43 B7
Haywain The RH8 .....122 D5
Hayward Cl SW19 .....40 B8
Hayward Rd KT7 .....36 F2
Haywardens RH7 .....164 D5
Haywards RH10 .....182 D1
Haywood RG12 .....27 C2
Hazel Ave
Farnborough GU14 .....84 F3
Guildford GU1 .....109 C5

Hazel Bank Ewhurst GU6 175 E5
South Norwood SE25 42 E7
Tolworth KT5 38 C1
Hazel Cl Brentford TW8 6 B7
Crawley RH11 181 C1
Crawley Down RH10 204 C8
Croydon CR0 43 D1
Englefield Green TW20 11 B2
Mitcham CR4 41 D5
Reigate RH2 139 C7
Twickenham TW2 16 C8
Hazel Ct Guildford GU1 109 D5
Warlingham CR6 81 E1
9 West Norwood SW16 22 A3
Hazel Dr GU23 90 F2
Hazel Gr Forest Hill SE26 23 D4
Haslemere GU26 188 E2
Staines TW18 13 C2
Hazel Mead KT17 58 A1
Hazel Par KT22 94 C5
Hazel Rd Ash GU12 127 C8
Mytchett GU16 86 A2
Reigate RH2 139 C7
Hazel Way Chipstead CR5 78 F1
Crawley Down RH10 204 C8
Fetcham KT22 94 C4
Hazel Wlk RH5 136 C4
Hazelbank Ct KT16 33 C1
Hazelbank Rd Catford SE6 24 E6
Chertsey KT16 33 C2
Hazelbury Cl SW19 40 A7
Hazeldene KT15 52 C5
Hazeldene Ct CR8 80 D4
Hazelhurst Beckenham BR3 44 D8
Horley RH6 161 C4
Hazelhurst Cl GU4 110 B6
Hazelhurst Cres RH12 216 F1
Hazelhurst Ct SE6 24 C3
Hazelhurst Dr RH10 202 E6
Hazelhurst Rd SW17 20 D4
Hazelhurst Sch SW20 39 D8
Hazell Hill RG12 27 C6
Hazell Rd GU9 124 F1
Hazelmere Cl Hatton TW14 3 E1
Leatherhead KT22 95 B8
Hazelmere Ct 10 SW2 21 F7
Hazelwick Ave RH10 202 B8
Hazelwick Mill La RH10 202 A8
Hazelwick Rd RH10 202 A7
Hazelwick Sch RH10 202 A8
Hazelwood RH11 201 A5
Hazelwood Ave SM4 40 B5
Hazelwood Cl RH10 203 F8
Hazelwood Cotts
Cranleigh GU6 194 D4
Godalming GU7 150 D4
Hazelwood Ct KT6 37 E3
Hazelwood Gr CR2 81 B6
Hazelwood House BR2 44 E6
Hazelwood La CR5 98 F8
Hazelwood Lodge BR4 44 C2
Hazelwood Rd
Knaphill GU21 68 E1
Oxted RH8 123 B3
Hazelwood Sch RH8 123 A4
Hazledean Rd CR0, CR9 61 D8
Hazleden Cross RH19 205 B6
Hazledene Rd W4 7 C8
Hazlemere Gdns KT4 39 A1
Hazlewood GU8 148 E4
Hazlitt Cl TW13 15 E4
Hazon Way KT19 76 C7
Headcorn Pl CR7 41 F5
Headcorn Rd Bromley BR1 24 F3
Thornton Heath CR7 41 F5
Headington Cl RG40 25 D8
Headington Dr RG40 25 D8
Headington Rd SW18 20 C6
Headlam Rd SW4 21 D8
Headland Way RH7 164 D4
Headley Ave CR0, SM6 60 F5
Headley Cl
Chessington KT19 57 A4
Crawley RH10 182 D1
Headley Common
Rd KT18, KT20 116 D7
Headley Ct SE26 23 C3
Headley Dr
Burgh Heath KT18 97 B8
New Addington CR0 63 C3
Headley Gr
Burgh Heath KT20 97 C7
Headley KT20 116 D7
Headley Heath App KT20 116 B4
Headley Hill Rd GU35 187 A5
Headley Rd Ashstead KT18 96 C6
Grayshott GU26 188 C3
Headley KT18 96 A4
Hindhead GU26 188 C3
Langley Vale KT21 96 C8
Leatherhead KT18, KT22 95 E4
Mickleham RH5 115 E7
Headon Ct GU9 125 D1
Headway Cl TW10 17 C4
Headway The KT17 57 F2
Hearn Vale GU35 187 A7
Hearn Wlk RG12 27 E8
Hearne Rd W4 7 A8
Hearnville Prim Sch SW12 21 A7
Hearnville Rd SW12 21 A7
Hearsey Gdns GU17 64 C6
Heath Bsns Ctr The TW3 5 C3
Heath Cl Banstead SM7 78 B5
Beacon Hill GU26 188 C7
Broadbridge Heath RH12 216 E3
Harlington UB3 3 D7
Heath End GU9 125 C7
Stanwell TW19 2 C1
Heath Cl *continued*
Virginia Water GU25 31 D5
Wokingham RG41 25 B4
Heath Cnr GU15 66 A3
Heath Cotts GU26 188 C6
Heath Ct RH12 216 E3
Heath Dr Brookwood GU24 88 A7
Send GU23 90 B5
Sutton SM2 59 C2
Walton on t H KT18 97 A2
West Barnes SW20 39 C5
Heath End Sch GU9 125 E6
Heath Gdns TW1 16 F6
Heath Gr Ashford TW16 14 F1
Penge SE20 23 C1
Heath Hill
Dockenfield GU10 166 E3
Dorking RH4 136 B7
Heath Hill Rd N RG45 45 B5
Heath Hill Rd S RG45 45 B4
Heath House
Thornton Heath CR7 42 A4
Weybridge KT13 53 A6
Heath La Albury GU5 132 E2
Crondall GU10 124 B7
Godalming GU7, GU8 151 A2
Heath End GU9 125 C7
Heath Mead SW19 19 D5
Heath Mill La GU3 88 C2
Heath Rd Bagshot GU19 47 E3
Caterham CR3 100 D3
Isleworth TW3, TW7 5 C3
Linchmere GU27 207 D5
Oxshott KT22 74 C7
South Norwood CR7 42 C6
Twickenham TW1 16 F7
Weybridge KT13 53 A5
Woking GU21 69 F4
Heath Ridge Gn KT11 74 A6
Heath Rise Camberley GU15 65 D5
Hayes BR2 44 F3
Virginia Water GU25 31 D5
Westcott RH4 135 C5
Heath The CR3 100 C3
Heath View KT24 92 F2
Heath Way RH12 217 D5
Heathacre SL3 1 E6
Heatham Pk TW2 16 F8
Heathbridge KT13 53 A4
Heathcote KT20 97 D5
Heathcote Cl GU12 106 A3
Heathcote Dr RH19 185 C2
Heathcote Rd Ash GU12 106 B3
Camberley GU15 65 D5
Epsom KT18 76 E6
Twickenham TW1 6 B2
Heathcroft Ave TW16 14 F1
Heathdale Ave TW4 4 E4
Heathdene KT20 77 E1
Heathdene Rd
Streatham SW16 21 F1
Wallington SM5, SM6 60 B3
Heathdown Rd GU22 70 D4
Heathedge SE23, SE26 23 B6
Heather Cl Aldershot GU11 104 E1
Ash GU12 106 B5
Copthorne RH10 183 B2
Guildford GU2 109 B3
Hampton TW12 35 F8
Horsham RH12 217 D5
Isleworth TW7 5 D2
Kingswood KT20 97 E5
Lewisham SE13 24 D7
Woking GU21 69 C4
Woodham KT15 52 B1
Wrecclesham GU9 145 F6
Heather Cotts GU12 106 A8
Heather Ct
10 Aldershot GU11 105 A1
Hindhead GU26 188 F4
Heather Dr SL5 30 B2
Heather Gdns Belmont SM2 59 A4
Farnborough GU14 84 E2
Heather Mead GU16 65 F2
Heather Mead Ct GU16 65 F2
Heather Pl 4 KT10 55 B6
Heather Ridge Arc GU15 66 C4
Heather Ridge Cty Inf Sch
GU15 66 D4
Heather Way
Chobham GU24 49 E3
Hindhead GU26 188 F4
South Croydon CR2 62 D2
Heather Wlk
Crawley RH11 201 B3
Pirbright GU24 87 D7
Smallfield RH6 162 C3
Twickenham TW4 16 A8
Whiteley Village KT12 53 F1
Heatherdale Cl KT2 18 B1
Heatherdale Rd GU15 65 D4
Heatherdeane KT24 92 D2
Heatherdene Cl CR4 40 E5
Heatherdene Mansions 2
TW1 6 D1
Heatherlands
Ashford TW16 15 A2
Horley RH6 161 B4
Heatherley Cl GU15 65 B5
Heatherley Rd GU15 65 B5
Heathermount RG12 27 E5
Heathermount Dr RG45 45 A6
Heathermount Sch SL5 29 D3
Heathers Land RH4 136 C4
Heathers The TW19 13 F8
Heatherset Cl KT10 55 C5
Heatherset Gdns SW16 21 F1
Heatherside Dr GU25 31 A3
Heatherside Rd KT19 57 D3
Heathervale Rd KT15 52 B1
Heatherway
Crowthorne RG45 45 A5
Felbridge RH19 184 F7
Heatherwood Hospl SL5 28 E6
Heathfield Cobham KT11 74 A5
Crawley RH10 202 D8
Reigate RH2 138 D8
Heathfield Ave Ascot SL5 29 E4
Wandsworth SW18 20 D8
Heathfield Cl
Godalming GU7 150 E2
Woking GU22 70 A1
Heathfield Ct Ashford TW15 13 E5
Penge SE20 23 C1
Wandsworth SW18 20 D8
Heathfield Dr
Mitcham SW19 20 E1
Redhill RH1 139 E4
Heathfield Gdns CR0 61 D6
Heathfield Inf Sch TW2 16 A7
Heathfield Jun Sch TW2 16 A7
Heathfield N TW1, TW2 16 F8
Heathfield Rd Bromley BR1 24 F1
Croydon CR0 61 D6
Hersham KT12 54 E6
Wandsworth SW18 20 D8
Woking GU22 70 A1
Heathfield S TW1, TW2 16 F8
Heathfield Sch SL5 28 B7
Heathfield Sq SW18 20 D8
Heathfield Vale CR2 62 E2
Heathhurst Rd CR2 61 E2
Heathland Sch The TW4 4 F1
Heathland St GU11 105 A2
Heathlands Tadworth KT20 97 D5
Upper Tooting SW12 21 B6
Weybridge KT13 53 C5
Heathlands Cl
Sunbury TW16 35 A7
Twickenham TW1 16 F7
Woking GU21 69 E5
Heathlands Country Mkt
RG40 25 E1
Heathlands Ct
Hounslow TW4 4 E2
Mitcham CR4 41 A6
Heathlands Rd RG40 25 E2
Heathlands Sch SW19 19 C5
Heathlands Way TW4 4 E2
Heathmere Prim Sch
SW15 19 A7
Heathmoors RG12 27 C4
Heathpark Dr GU20 48 E4
Heathrise GU23 91 B4
Heathrow GU5 133 C4
Heathrow Airport London
TW6 3 A5
Heathrow Bvd UB7 2 F7
Heathrow Causeway Est
TW4 4 B4
Heathrow Central Sta TW6 3 B4
Heathrow Cl TW6 2 B6
Heathrow International
Trad Est TW4 4 B4
Heathrow Sch UB7 2 F8
Heathrow Terminal 4 Sta
TW6 3 C1
Heathshot 8 TW10 6 E1
Heathside
Hinchley Wood KT10 55 E7
Twickenham TW4 15 F8
Weybridge KT13 53 B5
Heathside Cl KT10 55 E7
Heathside Cres GU22 69 F2
Heathside Ct KT20 97 C4
Heathside Gdns GU22 70 A2
Heathside La GU26 188 D6
Heathside Park Rd GU22 70 A1
Heathside Pk GU15 66 C7
Heathside Rd GU22 69 F1
Heathside Sch KT13 52 F4
Heathvale Bridge
Rd GU12 106 A6
Heathview Ct SW19 19 D6
Heathview Gdns SW15 19 C8
Heathview Rd
Thornton Heath CR7 42 A5
Witley GU8 170 E7
Heathway Camberley GU15 65 D5
Caterham CR3 100 D2
Croydon CR0 62 F7
East Horsley KT24 93 A3
North Ascot SL5 28 E8
Heathway Cl GU15 65 D5
Heathwood KT20 97 C4
Heathwood Ct
Hounslow TW3 5 B3
Streatham SW12 21 C7
Heathwood Point 7 SE26 23 D5
Heathyfields Rd GU9 125 A6
Heaton Rd CR4 21 A1
Heavers Farm Prim Sch
SE25 42 F4
Hebdon Rd SW17 20 F5
Heddon Cl TW7 6 A3
Heddon Wlk 1 GU14 85 A7
Hedge Cnr KT20 97 C4
Hedge Croft Cotts GU23 91 B6
Hedge Wlk SE6 24 B4
Hedgecourt Pl RH19 184 E4
Hedgehog La GU27 208 B5
Hedgerley Ct GU21 69 C2
Hedgeside RH11 201 C1
Hedgeway GU2 130 A7
Hedingham Cl RH6 161 C4
Hedley Rd TW4 16 A8
Heelas Rd RG41 25 A5
Heenan Cl GU16 85 E7
Heighton Gdns CR0 61 B5
Heights Cl Banstead SM7 77 E3
Wimbledon SW20 19 B1
Heights The BR3 24 C1
Helder Gr SE12 24 F8
Helder St CR2 61 D4
Heldmann Cl TW7 5 D3
Helen Ave TW14 15 B8
Helen Cl KT8 36 B5
Helen Ct GU14 85 B4
Helena Cl SM6 60 E3
Helford Wlk 3 GU21 69 A1
Helgiford Gdns TW16 14 E1
Helicon House RH11 201 C5
Helix Ho TW7 6 B5
Helksham Cl GU47 45 D1
Helme Cl SW19 19 F3
Helmsdale Bracknell RG12 27 E4
3 Woking GU21 69 B1
Helmsdale Rd SW16 21 D1
Helston Cl GU16 86 A7
Helvellyn Cl TW20 12 C1
Helvetia St SE6 23 F6
Hemingford Rd SM3 58 C6
Hemlock Cl KT20 97 E4
Hemming Cl 7 TW12 36 A8
Hempshaw Ave SM7 78 F3
Hemsby Rd KT9 56 F4
Hemsby Wlk RH10 202 B4
Henage Cnr GU24 49 E2
Henbane Ct 2 RH11 201 B2
Henbit Cl KT20 97 B8
Henchley Dene GU4 110 D4
Henderson Ave GU2 109 B5
Henderson Hospl SM2 59 B2
Henderson Rd
Biggin Hill TN16 83 C7
Crawley RH11 201 B1
Thornton Heath CR0 42 D3
Wandsworth SW18 20 E8
Henderson Way RH12 216 F1
Hendfield Ct 5 SM6 60 B4
Hendham Rd SW17 20 F6
Hendon Terr TW15 14 D2
Hendon Way TW19 2 D1
Hendrick Ave SW12 20 F8
Heneage Cres CR0 63 C1
Henfield Rd SW19, SW20 39 F8
Henfold Cotts RH5 158 A2
Henfold Dr RH5 157 E3
Henfold La RH5 157 F5
Hengelo Gdns CR4 40 D5
Hengist Cl RH12 217 A1
Hengist Way BR2, BR3 44 E5
Hengrave Rd SE23 23 D8
Hengrove Cres TW15 13 D5
Henhurst Cross La RH5 157 A2
Henley Ave SM3 58 E7
Henley Bank GU2 130 A7
Henley Cl Crawley RH10 202 D3
Farnborough GU14 84 E8
Hounslow TW7 5 F6
Henley Ct Mitcham CR4 41 A6
Old Woking GU22 90 A7
Henley Dr Frimley GU16 85 E7
Kingston u T KT2 18 F1
Henley Gate GU24, GU3 107 C8
Henley Lodge SE25 42 F5
Henley Way TW13 15 D3
Henley Wood CR6 82 A2
Hennel Cl SE23 23 C5
Hennessy Ct GU21 70 C6
Henry Cavendish Prim Sch
SW12 21 C7
Henry Doulton Dr SW17 21 B4
Henry Hatch Ct SM2 59 C3
Henry Peters Dr TW11 16 E3
Henry Tyndale Sch GU14 85 D6
Hensford Gdns SE26 23 B4
Henshaw Cl RH11 200 F4
Henslow Way GU21 70 D5
Henson Rd RH10 202 B7
Hensworth Rd TW15 13 D3
Henty Cl RH11 200 E3
Hepburn Gdns BR2 44 F1
Hepple Cl TW7 6 B5
Hepplewhite Cl RH11 201 B1
Hepworth Croft GU47 64 E6
Hepworth Ct SM3 40 A1
Hepworth Rd SW16 21 E1
Hepworth Way KT12 34 F1
Heracles Cl SM6 60 E3
Herald Ct 5 GU12 105 B1
Herald Gdns SM6 60 B7
Herbert Cl RG12 27 B4
Herbert Cres GU21 68 E1
Herbert Gdns W4 7 B8
Herbert Rd Kingston u T KT1 37 F6
Merton SW19 19 F1
Herbs End GU14 84 C5
Hereford Cl Crawley RH10 201 E2
Epsom KT18 76 D6
Guildford GU2 108 F3
Staines TW18 33 B8
Hereford Copse GU22 89 B8
Hereford Ct 6 CR0 42 F1
Hereford Gdns TW2 16 C7
Hereford Ho 9 GU11 105 A1
Hereford La GU9 125 B7
Hereford Rd TW13 15 C7
Hereford Way KT9 56 D5
Hereward Ave CR8 61 A1
Hereward Rd SW17 20 F4
Heriot Rd KT16 33 A2
Heritage Ct 2 TW20 12 A3
Heritage House 22 SW19 19 D7
Heritage Lawn RH6 161 C4
Herlwyn Gdns SW17 20 F4
Herm Cl Crawley RH11 201 A2
Hounslow TW7 5 C7
Hermes House BR3 43 E8
Hermes Way SM6 60 D3
Hermitage Cl
Claygate KT10 56 A4
Farnborough GU14 85 D1
Frimley GU16 65 F1
Littleton TW17 34 A5
Hermitage Ct TW18 12 F3
Hermitage Cty Jun Sch
The GU21 88 E8
Hermitage Dr SL5 28 E7
Hermitage Gdns SE19 22 C1
Hermitage La Croydon CR0 43 A3
East Grinstead RH19 205 F8
Streatham SW16 21 F1
Hermitage Par SL5 29 A6
Hermitage Rd
East Grinstead RH19 185 D3
Kenley CR8 80 C3
Knaphill GU21 88 D8
South Norwood SE19 22 D2
Hermitage The Barnes SW13 7 F6
Feltham TW13 14 F5
Forest Hill SE23 23 C7
Kingston u T KT1 37 D5
Richmond TW10 6 E2
Hermitage Woods Cres
GU21 88 E7
Hermits Rd RH10 201 F7
Hermonger La RH12 195 F2
Herndon Cl TW20 12 A4
Herne Rd KT6 56 E8
Heron Cl Cheam SM1 58 F5
Crawley RH11 201 C8
Guildford GU2 109 B4
Mytchett GU16 85 F4
North Ascot SL5 28 D8
Heron Ct Dorking RH4 136 A8
5 Kingston u T KT1 37 E6
Stanwell TW19 13 E7
6 West Norwood SE21 22 D6
Heron Dale KT15 52 D5
Heron House KT1 37 C8
Heron Pl RH19 205 F8
Heron Rd Croydon CR0 61 E8
Isleworth TW1 6 B3
Heron Shaw GU6 174 E1
Heron Sq 25 TW10 6 D2
Heron Way RH13 218 A1
Heron Way Cty Prim Sch
RH13 218 A1
Heron Wlk GU21 70 C5
Heron Wood Rd GU12 126 D7
Heron's Way RG40 25 E7
Herondale Bracknell RG12 27 C2
Haslemere GU27 207 E6
Selsdon CR2 62 D2
Herondale Ave SW18 20 E7
Heronfield TW20 11 C2
Heronry The KT12 54 A4
Herons Cl RH10 184 B5
Herons Croft KT13 53 D4
Herons L Ctr The GU27 207 F6
Herons Lea RH10 184 A4
Herons Pl TW7 6 B4
Herons Way GU24 87 D6
Herons Wood Ct RH6 161 B4
Heronscourt GU18 67 C8
Herontye Dr RH19 206 A8
Herrett St GU12 126 D8
Herretts Gdns GU12 105 D1
Herrick Cl Crawley RH10 202 C8
Frimley GU16 66 C3
Herrick Ct 4 TW10 17 D4
Herrings La GU20 48 D4
Herschel Wlk 9 RH11 201 B1
Herschell Rd SE23 23 E8
Hersham Cl SW15 19 A8
Hersham Gdns KT12 54 C6
Hersham Rd Hersham KT12 54 D6
Walton-on-T KT12 54 B7
Hersham Sta KT12 54 E7
Hersham Trad Est KT12 54 E8
Hershell Ct SW14 7 B3
Hertford Ave SW14 7 E3
Hertford Lodge 10 SW19 19 E7
Hertford Sq CR4 41 E5
Hertford Way CR4 41 E5
Hesiers Hill CR6 82 E2
Hesiers Rd CR6 82 F3
Hesketh Cl GU6 174 E3
Heslop Ct 2 SW12 21 A7
Heslop Rd SW12 20 F7
Hessle Gr KT17 76 F8
Hester Terr TW9 7 A4
Hesterman Way CR0, CR9 41 F1
Heston Ave TW5 4 E7
Heston Comm Sch TW5 5 A7
Heston Grange TW5 4 F8
Heston Grange La TW5 4 F8
Heston Ind Mall TW5 4 F7
Heston Inf Sch TW5 5 A7
Heston Jun Sch TW5 5 A7
Heston Phoenix
Distribution Pk TW5 4 C8
Heston Rd Heston TW5 5 A7
Redhill RH1 139 F4
Heston Wlk RH1 139 F4
Hetherington Rd TW17 34 C7
Hethersett Cl RH2 118 C4
Hetley Gdns 1 SE19 22 F1

Heverfield Ct CR4 . . . .**20** F1
Hevers Ave RH6 . . . .**161** A4
Hewers Way KT20 . . . .**97** C7
Hewitt Cl CR0 . . . .**63** A7
Hewitts Ind Est GU6 . . . . .**174** B3
Hewlett Pl GU19 . . . .**47** F3
Hewshott La GU30 . . . . . .**207** A5
Hexal Rd SE6 . . . .**24** E5
Hexham Cl Crawley RH10 . .**202** E6
Sandhurst GU47 . . . .**45** D2
Hexham Gdns TW7 . . . .**6** A7
Hexham Rd Cheam SM4 . . .**40** B1
West Norwood SE27 . . . .**22** C6
Hextalls La RH1 . . . .**120** E6
Heybridge Ave SW16 . . . . . .**21** F2
Heydon Ct BR4 . . . .**63** E8
Heyford Ave SW20 . . . .**39** F6
Heyford Rd CR4 . . . .**40** E7
Heymede KT22 . . . .**95** C4
Heythorp St SW18 . . . .**19** F6
Heythorpe Cl GU21 . . . .**68** F2
Heyward Ct SM2 . . . .**59** A4
Heywod Dr GU19 . . . .**47** D3
Hibernia Gdns TW3 . . . .**5** A2
Hibernia Rd TW3 . . . .**5** A3
Hickey's Almshouses 🔲
TW9 . . . .**6** F3
Hickling Wlk RH10 . . . . . .**202** B4
Hickmans Cl RH9 . . . .**121** C4
Hicks La GU17 . . . .**64** B5
Hidaburn Ct 🔲 SW16 . . . . .**21** C4
Hidcote Gdns SW20 . . . . . .**39** B6
Hidcote House SM2 . . . .**59** C3
Hidecote Cl GU22 . . . .**70** B3
Higgins Wlk TW12 . . . .**15** E2
Higgs La GU19 . . . .**47** D3
High Ashton 🔟🔲 KT2 . . . . .**18** B1
High Ashurst (Outdoor Ctr)
RH5 . . . .**116** A7
High Barn Rd KT24, RH5 . .**113** E3
High Beech Bracknell RG12 . .**27** F5
South Croydon CR2 . . . .**61** E3
High Beeches
Banstead KT17, SM7 . . . .**77** D5
Frimley GU16 . . . .**65** D2
High Beeches Cl CR8 . . . . . .**60** D1
High Broom Cres BR4 . . . . . .**44** B2
High Cedar Dr SW20 . . . . . .**19** B1
High Close Sch RG40 . . . . .**25** C7
High Down Rd SM2 . . . .**78** B8
High Dr
Kingston u T KT2, KT3 . . . . . .**38** C7
Oxshott KT22 . . . .**74** D5
Woldingham CR3 . . . .**102** A5
High Fields SL5 . . . .**29** F4
High Foleys KT10 . . . .**56** B3
High Gables BR2 . . . .**44** E7
High Garth KT10 . . . .**55** C4
High Hill Rd Chelsham CR6 . .**82** C5
Fickleshole CR6 . . . .**82** C5
High La Haslemere GU27 . .**208** C8
Warlingham CR3, CR6 . . . . .**101** F8
High Level Dr SE26 . . . .**23** A4
High Limes 🔲 SE19 . . . .**22** E2
High Loxley Rd GU8 . . . . . .**193** B7
High Mead BR4 . . . .**63** E8
High Meadow Cl RH4 . . . . .**136** B6
High Meadow Pl RH16 . . . . .**32** E7
High Oaks RH11 . . . .**201** B4
High Par The SW16 . . . .**21** E5
High Park Ave
East Horsley KT24 . . . .**92** F1
Richmond TW9 . . . .**7** A6
High Park Rd
Farnham GU9 . . . .**125** C3
Richmond TW9 . . . .**7** A6
High Path SW19 . . . .**40** C8
High Path Rd GU1 . . . .**110** C1
High Pewley GU1 . . . .**130** E7
High Pine Cl KT13 . . . .**53** C5
High Pines CR6 . . . .**101** C8
High Pitfold GU26 . . . .**188** D1
High Rd Byfleet KT14 . . . . . .**71** E6
Chipstead CR5, RH2 . . . .**98** F4
Kingswood CR5, RH2 . . . .**98** F4
Lower Kingswood CR5, RH2 . .**98** F4
High Ridge GU7 . . . .**150** D2
High St Addlestone KT15 . . .**52** B6
Aldershot GU11 . . . .**105** A2
Aldershot GU11, GU12 . . . . .**105** B1
Ascot SL5 . . . .**29** A4
Ascot, Sunninghill SL5 . . . . . .**29** D4
Bagshot GU19 . . . .**47** E3
Banstead SM7 . . . .**78** B4
Beckenham BR3 . . . .**44** A7
Bletchingley RH1 . . . .**120** D2
Bracknell RG12 . . . .**27** B7
Bracknell RG12 . . . .**27** C7
Bramley GU5 . . . .**151** F6
Brentford TW8 . . . .**6** E8
Brentford, Brentford End TW8 . .**6** D7
Camberley GU15 . . . .**65** D6
Carshalton SM5 . . . .**60** A6
Caterham CR3 . . . .**100** E4
Cheam SM1, KT17 . . . .**58** E4
Chobham GU24 . . . .**68** E8
Claygate KT10 . . . .**55** F4
Cobham KT11 . . . .**73** B4
Colnbrook SL3 . . . .**1** C7
Cranford TW5 . . . .**4** B7
Cranleigh GU6 . . . .**174** D3
Crawley RH10 . . . .**201** D6
Crowthorne RG45 . . . .**45** C5
Croydon CR0, CR9 . . . .**61** C7

High St continued
Croydon, Woodside SE25 . . . .**43** A5
Dorking RH4 . . . .**136** B8
East Grinstead RH19 . . . . . .**205** F8
East Molesey KT8 . . . .**36** A5
🔲 Egham TW20 . . . .**11** F3
Esher KT17, KT18 . . . .**76** D6
Esher KT17 . . . .**55** B6
Ewell KT17 . . . .**58** A2
Feltham TW13 . . . .**15** A6
Godalming GU7 . . . .**150** D4
Godstone RH9 . . . .**121** C4
Great Bookham KT23 . . . .**94** B2
Guildford GU1, GU2 . . . .**130** D7
Hampton TW12 . . . .**16** C2
Harlington UB3 . . . .**3** D8
Harmondsworth UB7 . . . .**2** D8
Haslemere GU27 . . . .**208** D7
Heston TW5 . . . .**4** B7
Horley RH6 . . . .**161** B3
Hounslow TW3 . . . .**5** B4
Kingston u T KT1 . . . .**37** D6
Knaphill GU21 . . . .**68** C2
Limpsfield RH8 . . . .**123** B7
Lingfield RH7 . . . .**164** D4
Merstham RH1 . . . .**119** B7
New Malden KT3 . . . .**38** E5
Nutfield RH1 . . . .**119** F2
Old Woking GU22 . . . .**90** B6
Oxshott KT22 . . . .**74** D5
Oxted RH8 . . . .**122** D5
Penge SE19, SE20, BR3 . . . .**23** C1
Purley CR8 . . . .**80** A8
Redhill RH1 . . . .**118** F2
Reigate RH2 . . . .**118** A1
Ripley GU23 . . . .**91** C6
Rowledge GU10 . . . .**145** A4
Rusper RH12 . . . .**199** D7
Sandhurst GU47 . . . .**64** A8
Sandhurst, Little
Sandhurst GU47 . . . .**45** A1
Shepperton TW17 . . . .**34** C3
South Norwood CR7, SE25 . . .**42** D5
South
Norwood,Woodside SE25 . . . .**43** A6
Staines TW18 . . . .**12** F4
Stanwell TW19 . . . .**2** D1
Sunningdale SL5 . . . .**30** A4
Sutton SM1, SM2 . . . .**59** B5
Sutton SM1 . . . .**59** B6
Tadworth KT20 . . . .**97** C4
Teddington TW11 . . . .**17** A3
Teddington, Hampton
Hill TW12 . . . .**16** C2
Teddington, Hampton
Wick KT1 . . . .**37** D8
Thames Ditton KT7 . . . .**37** A3
Twickenham TW2 . . . .**16** C8
Tyler's Green RH9 . . . .**121** C4
Walton-on-T KT12 . . . .**35** A1
West End GU24 . . . .**67** F7
West Wickham BR4 . . . .**44** B1
Weybridge KT13 . . . .**53** A6
Wimbledon SW19 . . . .**19** D3
Woking GU21 . . . .**69** F2
Woking, Horsell GU21 . . . . . .**69** C3
High St Mews SW19 . . . .**19** E3
High Standing CR3 . . . .**100** C2
**High Street Collier's
Wood** SW17, SW19 . . . .**20** D2
High Street Gn GU8 . . . . . .**191** F2
**High Street
Harlington** TW6 . . . .**3** D7
High The SW16 . . . .**21** E5
High Thicket Rd GU10 . . . .**166** D5
High Tree Cl KT15 . . . .**52** A5
High Trees Croydon CR0 . . . .**43** E1
Streatham SW2 . . . .**22** A7
High Trees Cl CR3 . . . .**100** F5
High Trees Ct
Caterham CR3 . . . .**100** F4
Sidlow RH6 . . . .**160** A4
High Trees Rd RH2 . . . .**139** D8
High View Belmont SM2 . . . .**77** F8
Gomshall GU5 . . . .**133** C4
🔳 Penge SE19 . . . .**22** F1
High View Ave CR0, SM6 . . . .**60** F5
High View Cl
Farnborough GU14 . . . .**85** A4
South Norwood SE19, SE25 . . .**42** F7
High View Lodge 🔳
GU1 . . . .**105** A2
High View Prim Sch SM6 . .**60** E7
High View Rd
Farnborough GU14 . . . .**85** A4
Guildford GU2 . . . .**129** E6
Lightwater GU18 . . . .**66** F8
South Norwood SE19 . . . .**22** D2
Highacre RH4 . . . .**136** B4
Highams Hill RH11 . . . . . .**200** F5
Highams La GU20, GU24 . . . .**49** A5
Highbarrow Rd CR0 . . . .**43** A1
Highbirch Cl RH12 . . . . . .**218** B5
Highbury Ave CR7 . . . .**42** B7
Highbury Cl
New Malden KT3 . . . .**38** C4
West Wickham BR4 . . . .**63** B8
Highbury Cres GU15 . . . . . .**66** A8
Highbury Gr GU27 . . . .**208** C8
Highbury Rd SW19 . . . .**19** E3
Highclere Ascot SL5 . . . .**29** D4
Guildford GU1 . . . .**110** A4
Highclere Cl
Bracknell RG12 . . . .**27** E7
Kenley CR8 . . . .**80** C4
Highclere Ct GU21 . . . .**68** C2

Highclere Dr GU15 . . . .**66** A7
Highclere Gdns GU21 . . . . .**68** D2
Highclere Rd
Aldershot GU12 . . . .**126** D8
Kingston u T KT3 . . . .**38** D6
Knaphill GU21 . . . .**68** C2
Highclere St SE26 . . . .**23** E4
Highcliffe BR3 . . . .**44** B8
Highcliffe Dr SW15 . . . .**7** F1
Highcotts La GU4, GU23 . . . .**91** A1
Highcroft
Beacon Hill GU26 . . . .**188** D6
Milford GU8 . . . .**170** F8
Purley CR8 . . . .**79** F5
Shamley Green GU5 . . . .**152** E4
🔲 Surbiton KT5 . . . .**37** F4
Highcroft Ct KT23 . . . .**94** A4
Highcroft Dr RH12 . . . .**195** E1
Highcross Way 🔲 SW15 . . . .**19** A7
Highdaun Dr SW16 . . . .**41** F5
Highdene 🔳 GU22 . . . .**69** F1
Highdown KT4 . . . .**57** F8
Highdown Ct RH10 . . . .**202** B3
Highdown Way RH12 . . . . .**217** F6
Higher Alham RG12 . . . .**27** E2
Higher Dr
Belmont KT17, SM7 . . . .**77** D6
East Horsley KT24 . . . .**112** E8
Purley CR8 . . . .**80** A6
Higher Gn KT17 . . . .**77** A6
Highercombe Rd GU27 . . . .**208** E8
Highfield Bracknell RG12 . . .**26** F3
Feltham TW14 . . . .**15** A7
Shalford GU4 . . . .**130** F1
Woodmansterne SM7 . . . .**78** E2
Highfield Ave GU11 . . . . . .**126** A8
Highfield Cl
Aldershot GU11 . . . .**126** B8
Englefield Green TW20 . . . . . .**11** C2
Farnborough GU14 . . . .**84** F4
Farnham GU9 . . . .**146** B7
Long Ditton KT6 . . . .**37** C1
Oxshott KT22 . . . .**74** D8
Wokingham RG40 . . . .**25** B6
Highfield Cres GU26 . . . . . .**188** F4
Highfield Ct
Englefield Green TW20 . . . . . .**11** D2
Mitcham CR4 . . . .**40** E7
Highfield Dr
Beckenham BR2 . . . .**44** F5
West Ewell KT19 . . . .**57** F4
West Wickham BR4 . . . .**63** C7
Highfield Gdns GU11 . . . . .**126** B8
Highfield Hill SE19 . . . .**22** E1
Highfield Inf Sch BR2 . . . . .**44** E5
Highfield Jun Sch BR2 . . . . .**44** E5
Highfield La
Puttenham GU3 . . . .**128** A3
Thursley GU8 . . . .**169** B2
Highfield Path GU14 . . . . . .**84** F4
Highfield Rd
Biggin Hill TN16 . . . .**83** C3
Carshalton SM1 . . . .**59** E5
Caterham CR3 . . . .**101** A5
Chertsey KT16 . . . .**33** A1
East Grinstead RH19 . . . . . .**185** D3
Farnborough GU14 . . . .**84** F4
Feltham TW13 . . . .**15** A7
Hounslow TW7 . . . .**5** F6
Purley CR8 . . . .**61** A1
Tolworth KT5 . . . .**38** C2
Upper Halliford TW16 . . . .**34** F4
Walton-on-T KT12 . . . .**35** A1
West Byfleet KT14 . . . .**71** A6
Highfield Sch SW18 . . . .**20** E8
Highfields Ashstead KT21 . . .**95** D8
East Horsley KT24 . . . .**112** F7
Fetcham KT22 . . . .**94** D3
Forest Row RH18 . . . .**206** F2
Sutton SM1 . . . .**59** A8
Highgate Ct Crawley RH11 .**201** C2
Farnborough GU14 . . . .**85** C5
Highgate House 🔳 SE26 . . .**23** A5
Highgate La GU14 . . . .**85** C5
Highgate Rd RH18 . . . .**206** F1
Highgate Wlk SE23 . . . .**23** C6
Highgrove 🔲 GU14 . . . .**85** B7
Highgrove Ct BR3 . . . .**24** A1
Highgrove House GU4 . . . .**110** C3
Highland Cotts SM6 . . . .**60** C6
Highland Croft BR3 . . . .**24** B2
Highland Lodge 🔲 SE19 . . . .**22** F1
Highland Pk TW13 . . . .**14** F4
Highland Rd
Aldershot GU12 . . . .**105** D2
Beare Green RH5 . . . .**157** D3
Bromley BR1, BR2 . . . .**44** F8
Camberley GU15 . . . .**65** E8
Purley CR8 . . . .**80** A5
West Norwood SE19 . . . .**22** E2
Highland View GU6 . . . . . .**174** C7
Highlands Ave
Horsham RH13 . . . .**217** E2
Leatherhead KT22 . . . .**95** C5
Highlands Cl
Farnham GU9 . . . .**146** B7
Hounslow TW3 . . . .**5** B6
Leatherhead KT22 . . . .**95** B5
Highlands Cres
Horsham RH13 . . . .**217** E2
Highlands Ct SE19 . . . .**22** E2
Highlands Heath SW15 . . . . .**19** C8
Highlands Pk KT22 . . . .**95** D4
Highlands Rd
Heath End GU9 . . . .**125** C7
Horsham RH13 . . . .**217** F2
Leatherhead KT22 . . . .**95** C5
Reigate RH2 . . . .**118** D2

Highlands The KT24 . . . .**92** E2
Highmead GU7 . . . .**150** F6
Highpoint KT13 . . . .**53** A5
Highridge Cl KT18 . . . .**76** E5
Highridge Ct KT18 . . . .**76** E5
Highview CR3 . . . .**100** E2
Highview Cres GU15 . . . .**46** F1
Highview Ct
🔲 Putney SW19 . . . .**19** E7
🔲 Reigate RH2 . . . .**118** D1
Highview High Sch SM6 . . . .**60** D7
Highway RG45 . . . .**45** A5
Highway The SM2 . . . .**59** C2
Highwayman's Ridge
GU20 . . . .**48** B6
Highwold CR5 . . . .**79** A1
Highwood Cl CR8 . . . .**80** C2
Highwoods Caterham CR3 .**100** E2
Leatherhead KT22 . . . .**95** C6
Hilary Ave CR4 . . . .**41** A6
Hilary Dr RG45 . . . .**45** B6
Hilbert Rd SM3 . . . .**58** D7
Hilborough Cl SW19 . . . .**20** C1
Hildenborough Gdns BR1 . .**24** F2
Hildenborough House BR3 . .**23** F1
Hildenlea Pl BR2 . . . .**44** E7
Hildenley Cl RH1 . . . .**119** D7
Hildens The RH4 . . . .**135** C5
Hilder Gdns GU14 . . . .**85** D3
Hilders La TN8 . . . .**144** F4
Hilders The KT21 . . . .**76** B2
Hilditch House 🔳 TW10 . . . . .**6** F1
Hildreth St SW12 . . . .**21** B7
Hildreth Street Mews
SW12 . . . .**21** B7
Hilgay GU1 . . . .**109** F1
Hilgay Cl GU1 . . . .**109** F1
Hilgay Ct GU1 . . . .**109** F1
Hill Cl Purley CR8 . . . .**80** C6
Woking GU21 . . . .**69** D3
Wonersh GU5 . . . .**152** B6
Hill Copse View RG12 . . . . .**27** E8
Hill Cres Kingston u T KT5 . .**37** F4
North Cheam KT4 . . . .**58** C8
Hill Crest
Dormans Park RH19 . . . . . .**185** E6
Elstead GU8 . . . .**148** D4
Hill Crest Dr GU10 . . . .**145** F4
Hill Ct Farncombe GU7 . . . .**150** E6
Haslemere GU27 . . . .**208** B6
🔳 Kingston u T KT2 . . . .**18** B1
🔲 Kingston u T KT6 . . . .**37** E4
Hill Dr SW16 . . . .**41** F6
Hill Field Rd TW12 . . . .**35** F8
Hill Gr TW13 . . . .**15** F8
Hill House Cl RH10 . . . .**204** A5
Hill House Dr
Hampton TW12 . . . .**36** A8
Reigate RH2 . . . .**139** B7
Weybridge KT13 . . . .**72** A8
Hill House Rd SW16 . . . .**21** F3
Hill La KT20 . . . .**97** E6
Hill Manor RH12 . . . .**217** A2
Hill Mead RH12 . . . .**217** B3
Hill Park Dr KT22 . . . .**94** F8
Hill Rd Beacon Hill GU26 . .**188** C6
Carshalton SM5 . . . .**59** E4
Fetcham KT23 . . . .**94** B5
Grayshott GU26 . . . .**188** C3
Haslemere GU27 . . . .**208** C6
Heath End GU9 . . . .**125** D7
Mitcham CR4 . . . .**21** B1
Purley CR8 . . . .**79** F7
Sutton SM1 . . . .**59** B5
Hill Rise Dorking RH4 . . . . .**115** A1
Forest Hill SE23 . . . .**23** B7
Hinchley Wood KT10 . . . .**56** B8
Richmond TW10 . . . .**6** D2
Hill St TW10 . . . .**6** D2
Hill The CR3 . . . .**100** F3
Hill Top SM3, SM4 . . . .**39** F2
Hill View CR4 . . . .**41** E5
Hill View Cl Purley CR8 . . . . .**80** B8
Tadworth KT20 . . . .**97** C6
Hill View Cres GU2 . . . .**108** F3
Hill View Ct 🔳 GU22 . . . .**69** E1
Hill View Rd Claygate KT10 . .**56** A3
Farnham GU9 . . . .**124** F2
Twickenham TW1 . . . .**6** A1
Woking GU22 . . . .**69** F1
Hillacre CR3 . . . .**100** E2
Hillard Ct SM6 . . . .**60** D4
Hillars Heath Rd CR5 . . . . . .**79** E4
Hillary Cl
East Grinstead RH19 . . . . . .**186** A3
Farnham GU9 . . . .**146** B7
Hillary Cres KT12 . . . .**35** C1
Hillary Ct TW19 . . . .**13** E7
Hillary House 🔟 RH1 . . . . . .**118** F2
Hillary Rd GU9 . . . .**146** B7
Hillbarn CR2 . . . .**80** E8
Hillberry RG12 . . . .**27** C2
Hillbrook Gdns KT13 . . . . . .**53** A3
Hillbrook Prim Sch &
Hillcroft Sch Annexe
SW17 . . . .**21** A4
Hillbrook Rd SW17 . . . .**21** A4
Hillbrook Rise GU9 . . . .**125** B6
Hillbrow New Malden KT3 . . .**38** F6
🔳 Reigate RH2 . . . .**118** C1
🔳 Richmond TW10 . . . .**6** E1
Hillbrow Cl GU3 . . . .**108** B2
Hillbrow Cotts RH9 . . . . . .**121** C3
Hillbrow Ct RH9 . . . .**121** C3
Hillbrow Rd Catford BR1 . . . .**24** E2
Esher KT10 . . . .**55** B5
Hillbury Cl CR6 . . . .**81** C1
Hillbury Gdns CR6 . . . .**81** C1

Hillbury Rd
Upper Tooting SW17 . . . .**21** B5
Warlingham CR3, CR6 . . . . . .**81** B1
Hillcote Ave SW16 . . . .**22** A1
Hillcrest Heath End GU9 . . .**125** D8
Weybridge KT13 . . . .**53** B6
Hillcrest Ave KT16 . . . .**51** E6
Hillcrest Cl Beckenham BR3 . .**43** F3
Crawley RH10 . . . .**202** D6
Epsom KT18 . . . .**76** F4
Forest Hill SE26 . . . .**23** A4
Hillcrest Ct Sutton SM2 . . . . .**59** D4
Weybridge KT13 . . . .**53** B6
Hillcrest Gdns KT10 . . . .**55** F7
Hillcrest House GU4 . . . . . .**110** C3
Hillcrest Par CR5 . . . .**79** B5
Hillcrest Rd
Biggin Hill TN16 . . . .**83** D3
Camberley GU15 . . . .**66** B7
Guildford GU2 . . . .**108** F2
Kenley CR3 . . . .**80** F2
Wallington CR8 . . . .**60** F1
Hillcrest View BR3 . . . .**43** F3
Hillcroft CR5, CR8 . . . .**79** D6
Hillcroft Coll KT6 . . . .**37** E3
Hillcroft Cty Prim Sch
Caterham CR3 . . . .**100** E4
Whyteleafe CR3 . . . .**100** F6
Hillcroome Rd SM2 . . . .**59** D5
Hillcross Ave Merton SM4 . . .**39** E4
West Barnes SM4 . . . .**39** E4
Hillcross Mid Sch SM4 . . . . .**39** F5
Hilldale Rd SM1 . . . .**58** F6
Hilldeane Rd CR8 . . . .**61** A1
Hilldown Ct SW16 . . . .**21** E1
Hilldown Rd
Streatham SW16 . . . .**21** F1
West Wickham BR2 . . . .**44** F1
Hilley Field La KT22 . . . .**94** C6
Hillfield Ave SM4 . . . .**40** D3
Hillfield Cl Guildford GU1 . .**110** C3
Redhill RH1 . . . .**119** A1
Hillfield Rd RH1 . . . .**119** A1
Hillford Pl RH1 . . . .**140** A3
Hillgarth GU26 . . . .**188** D5
Hillgate Pl SW12 . . . .**21** B8
Hillhouse La RH12 . . . .**194** F1
Hillhurst Gdns CR3 . . . . . .**100** E7
Hillier Gdns CR0 . . . .**61** A5
Hillier House GU2 . . . .**130** A7
Hillier Lodge TW12 . . . .**16** D3
Hillier Mews GU1 . . . .**110** A1
Hillier Pl KT9 . . . .**56** C4
Hillier Rd GU1 . . . .**110** A1
Hillier's La CR0, SM6 . . . . . .**60** E7
Hillingdale Biggin Hill TN16 . .**83** F1
Crawley RH11 . . . .**201** C1
Hillingdon Ave TW19 . . . . . .**13** E7
Hillmead RH11 . . . .**200** F6
Hillmont Rd KT10 . . . .**55** E7
Hillmore Gr SE26 . . . .**23** E3
Hillmount 🔳 GU22 . . . .**69** E1
Hillrise Brands Hill SL3 . . . . . .**1** A8
Walton-on-T KT12 . . . .**34** F2
Hills Farm La RH12 . . . . . .**216** F1
Hills Pl RH12 . . . .**217** A2
Hillsborough Ct GU14 . . . . .**84** E8
Hillsborough Pk GU15 . . . . .**66** C5
Hillside Ascot SL5 . . . .**29** C4
Banstead SM7 . . . .**77** E4
Crawley Down RH10 . . . .**204** B8
Forest Row RH18 . . . .**206** E3
Horsham RH12 . . . .**217** A2
Sandhurst GU15 . . . .**64** F7
Wentworth GU25 . . . .**31** C3
Wimbledon SW19 . . . .**19** D2
Woking GU22 . . . .**89** D7
Hillside Ave CR8 . . . .**80** B8
Hillside Cl Banstead SM7 . . .**77** E3
Brockham RH3 . . . .**137** A8
Crawley RH10 . . . .**201** B4
East Grinstead RH19 . . . . . .**185** E3
Headley Down GU35 . . . .**187** A6
Knaphill GU21 . . . .**68** D2
Merton SM4 . . . .**39** E5
Hillside Cres GU16 . . . .**85** F7
Hillside Ct Guildford GU1 . .**130** E8
🔳 Kingston u T KT2 . . . .**18** B1
Hillside Gdns
Addlestone KT15 . . . .**51** F5
Brockham RH3, RH5 . . . . . .**116** A1
Streatham SW2 . . . .**22** A6
Wallington SM6 . . . .**60** C3
Hillside La Coney Hall BR2 . . .**63** F8
Heath End GU9 . . . .**125** D8
Hillside Pk SL5 . . . .**29** F1
Hillside Rd
Aldershot GU11 . . . .**126** A8
Ash GU12 . . . .**106** B3
Ashtead KT21 . . . .**75** F2
Beckenham BR2 . . . .**44** F6
Belmont SM2 . . . .**58** F3
Coulsdon CR5 . . . .**79** F1
Croydon CR0 . . . .**61** B6
East Ewell KT17 . . . .**58** C1
Farnham GU10 . . . .**146** C3
Heath End GU9 . . . .**125** D7
Kingston u T KT5 . . . .**38** A4
Linchmere GU27 . . . .**207** F5
Streatham SW2 . . . .**22** A6
Tatsfield TN16 . . . .**103** E8
Warlingham CR3, CR6 . . . . . .**81** A1
Whyteleafe CR3, CR6 . . . . . .**81** A1
Hillside Way GU7 . . . .**150** D7
Hillsmead Way CR2 . . . .**81** B6
Hillspur Cl GU2 . . . .**108** F2
Hillspur Rd GU2 . . . .**108** F2
Hilltop Cl Ascot SL5 . . . .**29** C4

Hilltop Cl continued
Guildford GU3 . . . . .108 F5
Leatherhead KT22 . . . . .95 C4
Hilltop Ct SE19 . . . . .42 D8
Hilltop La CR3, RH1 . . . . . .100 A1
Hilltop Rd Kenley CR3 . . . . .80 F2
Reigate RH2 . . . . .139 B7
Hilltop Rise KT23 . . . . .94 C1
Hilltop Wlk Whyteleafe CR3 . .80 F2
Wimbledon SW20 . . . . .19 B1
Hillview Ct SE19 . . . . .22 E4
Hillview Dr RH1 . . . . .140 A8
Hillview Rd SM1 . . . . .59 D7
Hillworth BR3 . . . . .44 B7
Hillworth Rd SW2 . . . . .22 A8
Hilly Mead SW19 . . . . .19 E1
Hillybarn Rd RH11 . . . . . . .180 C1
Hilsea Point 7 SW15 . . . . . .19 B7
Hilton Ct RH6 . . . . .161 C4
Himley Rd SW17 . . . . .20 F2
Hinchcliffe Cl SM6 . . . . .60 F3
Hinchley Cl KT10 . . . . .55 F7
Hinchley Dr KT10 . . . . .55 F7
Hinchley Way KT10 . . . . . . .56 A7
Hinchley Wood Prim Sch
KT10 . . . . .56 A8
Hinchley Wood Sch KT10 . .56 A8
Hinchley Wood Sta KT10 . . .55 F7
Hindell Cl GU14 . . . . .85 A8
Hindhead Cl RH11 . . . . .201 C4
Hindhead Point 6 SW15 . . .19 B7
Hindhead Rd GU26, GU27 . .188 F2
Hindhead Way SM6 . . . . . . .60 E5
Hindsley's Pl SE23 . . . . .23 C6
Hinkler Cl SM6 . . . . .60 E3
Hinstock Cl GU14 . . . . .85 A3
Hinton Ave TW4 . . . . .4 D3
Hinton Cl RG45 . . . . .45 B7
Hinton Dr RG45 . . . . .45 B7
Hinton Rd SM6 . . . . .60 C4
Hipley Ct GU1 . . . . .131 A8
Hipley St GU22 . . . . .90 B7
Hitchcock Cl TW17 . . . . .33 F6
Hitchings Way RH2 . . . . . . .139 A5
Hither Green Hospl SE13 . .24 D8
Hither Green La SE13 . . . . . .24 C8
Hitherbury Cl GU2 . . . . .130 C6
Hitherfield Prim Sch SW2 . .22 A6
Hitherfield Rd SW16, SW27 .22 A6
Hitherhooks Hill RG42 . . . . .26 E8
Hithermoor Rd TW19 . . . . . . .2 A2
Hitherwood GU6 . . . . .174 E2
Hitherwood Cl RH2 . . . . . . .118 E3
Hitherwood Ct SE21 . . . . . . .22 F4
Hitherwood Dr SE19, SE21 . .22 F4
Hoadly Rd SW16 . . . . .21 D6
Hobart Gdns CR7 . . . . .42 D6
Hobart Pl 14 TW10 . . . . .6 F1
Hobart Rd KT4 . . . . .58 B7
Hobbs Cl KT14 . . . . .71 B6
Hobbs Ind Est RH7 . . . . . . .184 D7
Hobbs Rd Crawley RH10 . . .201 A2
5 West Norwood SE27 . . . .22 C4
Hobill Wlk KT5 . . . . .37 F3
Hocken Mead RH10 . . . . . . .202 D8
Hockering Gdns GU22 . . . . . .70 B1
Hockering Rd GU22 . . . . .70 B1
Hockford Cl GU3 . . . . .88 B1
Hodge La SL5 . . . . .9 A3
Hodges Cl GU19 . . . . .47 E1
Hodgkin Cl RH10 . . . . .202 C6
Hodgson Gdns GU1, GU4 . .110 A4
Hoe Bridge Sch GU22 . . . . . .90 C8
Hoe Cotts GU5 . . . . .154 E8
Hoe La Hascombe GU8 . . . . .172 D4
Peaslake GU5, RH5 . . . . . .154 F8
Hoebridge Golf Ctr GU22 . . .90 C8
Hoebrook Glade GU22 . . . . . .89 E6
Hogarth Ave TW15 . . . . .14 C2
Hogarth Bsns Pk W4 . . . . . . .7 E8
Hogarth Cl GU47 . . . . .64 E6
Hogarth Cres
Mitcham CR4, SW19 . . . . . .40 D8
Thornton Heath CR0 . . . . . .42 C2
Hogarth Ct Dulwich SE19 . . . .22 F4
Heston TW5 . . . . .4 E7
Hogarth Gdns TW5 . . . . .5 A7
Hogarth House 6 SE27 . . . . .22 C4
Hogarth La W4 . . . . .7 E8
Hogarth Rd RH10 . . . . .201 F3
Hogarth Roundabout W4 . . . .7 E8
Hogarth Way TW12 . . . . .36 C8
Hoghatch La GU9 . . . . .125 A6
Hogoak La SL4 . . . . .8 A8
Hogscross La CR5 . . . . .98 F5
Hogshill La KT11 . . . . .73 C5
Hogspudding La RH5 . . . . . .158 C1
Hogtrough La
Nutfield RH1 . . . . .140 D8
Oxted RH8 . . . . .122 B6
Hogwood Rd RH14 . . . . .212 C3
Holbeach Mews SW12 . . . . . .21 B7
Holbeach Prim Sch SE6 . . . .24 B8
Holbeach Rd SE6 . . . . .24 B8
Holbeck RG12 . . . . .26 F3
Holbein Rd RH10 . . . . .202 C6
Holberry House 5 SE21 . . . . .22 E4
Holborn Way CR4 . . . . .40 F7
Holbreck Pl GU22 . . . . .69 F1
Holbrook Cl GU9 . . . . .125 F8
Holbrook Cty Prim Sch
RH12 . . . . .217 E7
Holbrook House 5 SW2 . . . . .21 F7
Holbrook Meadow TW20 . . . .12 C2

Holbrook School La
RH12 . . . . .217 E7
Holbrook Way GU11 . . . . . . .126 E7
Holcon Ct RH1 . . . . .119 A4
Holder Rd Aldershot GU12 . .105 E1
Crawley RH10 . . . . .202 B3
Holderness Way SE27 . . . . . .22 B3
Holderness Rd
Isleworth TW7 . . . . .6 A6
6 Upper Tooting SW17 . . . .21 A6
Holdfast La GU27 . . . . .208 F7
Holdsworth House 5
SW2 . . . . .22 A8
Hole Hill RH4 . . . . .135 B7
Holford Rd GU1 . . . . .110 C1
Holland Ave Belmont SM2 . . .59 A4
Wimbledon SW20 . . . . .38 F8
Holland Cl Coney Hall BR2 . . .63 F6
Farnham GU9 . . . . .146 E8
Redhill RH1 . . . . .118 F1
Holland Cres RH8 . . . . .123 A2
Holland Cty Jun Sch
RH8 . . . . .123 A1
Holland Dr SE23 . . . . .23 E5
Holland Gdns TW20 . . . . . . .32 F5
Holland La RH8 . . . . .123 A2
Holland Pines RG12 . . . . . . .26 F2
Holland Rd Croydon SE25 . . .43 A4
Oxted RH8 . . . . .123 A1
Holland Way BR2 . . . . .63 F6
Hollands Field RH13 . . . . . .216 E4
Hollands The
Feltham TW13 . . . . .15 D4
New Malden KT4 . . . . .38 F1
Hollands Way
East Grinstead RH19 . . . . .186 A4
Warnham RH12 . . . . .216 F8
Holles Cl TW12 . . . . .16 A3
Hollies Ave KT14 . . . . .70 F6
Hollies Cl
South Norwood SW16 . . . . .22 A2
Twickenham TW1 . . . . .16 F6
Hollies Ct KT15 . . . . .52 C5
Hollies Way 2 SW12 . . . . . . .21 A8
Hollin Ct RH10, RH11 . . . . . .181 E1
Hollingbourne Cres
RH11 . . . . .201 C1
Hollingsworth Rd CR0, CR2 62 B4
Hollington Cres KT3 . . . . . . .39 A3
Hollingworth Cl KT8 . . . . . . .35 F5
Hollingworth Ct 7 KT6 . . . . .37 D2
Hollis Wood Dr GU2 . . . . . .145 E5
Hollman Gdns SW16 . . . . . . .22 B2
Hollow Cl GU2 . . . . .130 B8
Hollow La
Dormansland RH19, RH7 . .186 D6
Virginia Water GU25 . . . . . .31 C6
Wotton RH5 . . . . .134 D2
Hollow The Crawley RH10 . .200 F5
Shackleford GU7 . . . . .149 F4
Holloway Dr GU25 . . . . .31 E5
Holloway Hill
Godalming GU7 . . . . .150 D4
Lyne KT16 . . . . .51 D8
Holloway La UB7 . . . . .2 E8
Holloway St TW3 . . . . .5 B4
Holly Acre GU2 . . . . .89 C4
Holly Ave Frimley GU16 . . . . .66 B3
Walton-on-T KT12 . . . . .35 D1
Woodham KT15 . . . . .52 A1
Holly Bank Rd GU22 . . . . . . .89 C8
Holly Bush Ind Pk GU12 . . .105 E5
Holly Bush La
Farnborough GU11 . . . . . . .105 E6
Hampton TW12 . . . . .15 F1
Holly Cl Aldershot GU12 . . . .105 C2
Crawley RH10 . . . . .202 A8
Englefield Green TW20 . . . . .11 B2
Farnborough GU14 . . . . .85 A4
Feltham TW13 . . . . .15 E3
Headley Down GU35 . . . . . .187 C5
Horsham RH12 . . . . .218 B5
Longcross KT16 . . . . .50 A7
Woking GU21 . . . . .89 B8
Holly Cott KT7 . . . . .37 A1
Holly Cres BR3 . . . . .43 F4
Holly Ct 9 Belmont SM2 . . . .59 A3
Leatherhead KT22 . . . . .95 A5
Holly Gn KT13 . . . . .53 D6
Holly Grove Cl TW3 . . . . .4 F3
Holly Hedge Cl GU16 . . . . . . .65 E2
Holly Hedge Rd
Cobham KT11 . . . . .73 B5
Frimley GU16 . . . . .65 E2
Holly Hill Dr SM7 . . . . .78 A3
Holly Hock GU4 . . . . .68 A4
Holly Hough KT20 . . . . .116 B5
Holly House
Bracknell RG12 . . . . .27 B3
Brentford TW8 . . . . .6 C8
Holly La Banstead SM7 . . . . .78 C5
Godalming GU7 . . . . .150 C4
Woodmansterne SM7 . . . . . .78 C2
Worplesdon GU3 . . . . .108 D7
Holly La E SM7 . . . . .78 B3
Holly La W SM7 . . . . .78 B2
Holly Lea GU4 . . . . .109 D7
Holly Lodge Mid Sch
GU12 . . . . .105 E5
Holly Rd Aldershot GU12 . . .105 D1
Farnborough GU14 . . . . .85 A4
Hampton TW12 . . . . .16 C2
Hounslow TW3 . . . . .5 B3
Reigate RH2 . . . . .139 B7
Twickenham TW1 . . . . .17 A7
Holly Ridge GU24 . . . . .67 F6
Holly Spring Cty Inf Sch
RG12 . . . . .27 E7

Holly Spring Cty Jun Sch
RG12 . . . . .27 E7
Holly Spring La RG12 . . . . . .27 D8
Holly Tree Rd CR3 . . . . .100 E5
Holly Way Blackwater GU17 .64 D4
Mitcham CR4 . . . . .41 D6
Holly Wlk SL4 . . . . .9 A4
Hollybank GU24 . . . . .67 F6
Hollybank Cl TW12 . . . . .16 A3
Hollybank Rd KT14 . . . . .71 A5
Hollybush Rd
Crawley RH10 . . . . .201 E8
Kingston u T KT2 . . . . .17 E2
Hollybush Ride GU19, GU20 47 A5
Hollycombe TW20 . . . . .11 D4
Hollycroft Cl
Harmondsworth UB7 . . . . . . .3 A8
South Croydon CR2 . . . . . . .61 E5
Hollycroft Gdns UB7 . . . . .3 A8
Hollydene RH1 . . . . .44 F8
Hollyfield Rd KT5 . . . . .37 F2
Hollyfield Sch KT6 . . . . .37 E4
Hollymead SM5 . . . . .59 F7
Hollymead Rd CR5 . . . . .79 A1
Hollymoak Rd CR5 . . . . .79 A1
Hollymoor La GU19 . . . . .57 D1
Hollymount Prim Sch
SW20 . . . . .39 C8
Hollyridge GU27 . . . . .208 B6
Hollytree Cl SW19 . . . . .19 D7
Hollytree Gdns GU16 . . . . . . .85 D8
Hollywoods CR0 . . . . .62 F2
Holm Cl KT15 . . . . .70 E7
Holm Ct Dorking RH4 . . . . . .136 B4
Farncombe GU7 . . . . .150 D7
Holman Ct KT17 . . . . .58 A2
Holman Rd KT19 . . . . .57 C5
Holmbank Dr TW17 . . . . .34 E5
Holmbrook Cl GU14 . . . . .84 C4
Holmbrook Gdns GU14 . . . . .84 C4
Holmbury Ave RG45 . . . . . . .45 A7
Holmbury Cl RH11 . . . . .201 C4
Holmbury Ct Mitcham SW19 20 E1
Upper Tooting SW17 . . . . . .20 F5
Holmbury Dr RH5 . . . . .136 C4
Holmbury Gr CR0 . . . . .62 F3
Holmbury Hill Rd RH5 . . . . .155 B3
Holmbury Rd RH5 . . . . .155 D1
Holmbush Cl RH12 . . . . .217 D6
Holmcroft Crawley RH10 . . .201 E5
Walton on t H KT20 . . . . . . .97 B2
Holmdene Cl BR3 . . . . .44 C7
Holme Chase KT13 . . . . .53 C4
Holme Cl RG45 . . . . .45 A4
Holmes Cl Ascot SL5 . . . . . . .29 C3
Woking GU23 . . . . .89 F6
Wokingham RG41 . . . . .25 A4
Holmes Cres RG41 . . . . .25 A4
Holmes Rd Merton SW19 . . . .20 C1
Twickenham TW1 . . . . .16 F6
Holmesdale KT3 . . . . .53 D4
Holmesdale Ave SW14 . . . . . .7 B3
Holmesdale Cl
Guildford GU1 . . . . .110 B2
South Norwood SE25 . . . . . .42 F6
Holmesdale Rd
Dorking RH5 . . . . .136 C3
Reigate RH2 . . . . .118 B2
Richmond TW9 . . . . .6 F6
South Norwood SE25 . . . . . .42 E5
South Nutfield RH1 . . . . . . .140 F7
Teddington TW11 . . . . .17 C2
Thornton Heath CR0 . . . . . .42 A4
Holmethorpe Ave RH1 . . . . .119 B4
Holmethorpe Ind Est
RH1 . . . . .119 B4
Holmewood Cl RG41 . . . . . . .25 A2
Holmewood Gdns SW2 . . . . .21 F8
Holmewood Rd
South Norwood SE25 . . . . . .42 E6
Streatham SW2 . . . . .21 F8
Holmgrove House CR8 . . . . .80 A7
Holming End RH12 . . . . .218 B5
Holmoaks House BR3 . . . . . .44 C7
Holmsdale Cty Inf Sch
RH2 . . . . .118 B3
Holmshaw Cl SE26, SE6 . . . .23 E4
Holmsley Cl KT3 . . . . .38 F2
Holmsley House SW15 . . . . . .18 F8
Holmwood 4 KT5 . . . . .37 F3
Holmwood Ave CR2 . . . . .80 F6
Holmwood Cl
Addlestone KT15 . . . . .52 A5
Cheam SM2 . . . . .58 D3
East Horsley KT24 . . . . .112 E6
Holmwood Gdns SM6 . . . . . .60 B4
Holmwood Rd
Chessington KT9 . . . . .56 E5
East Ewell SM2, SM2 . . . . . .58 C2
Holmwood Sta RH5 . . . . . . .157 C4
Holmwood View Rd RH5 .136 B1
Holne Chase SM4 . . . . .40 A4
Holroyd Rd KT10 . . . . .55 F2
Holstein Ave KT13 . . . . .53 A6
Holsworthy Way KT9 . . . . . . .56 C5
Holt Cl GU1 . . . . .85 C7
Holt La RG41 . . . . .25 B7
Holt Pound La GU10 . . . . . . .145 C5
Holt Sch The RG41 . . . . .25 B7
Holt The Morden SM4 . . . . . .40 A5
Wallington SM6 . . . . .60 C6
Holt Wood CR6 . . . . .82 A3
Holton Heath 8 RG12 . . . . . . .27 F5
Holtwood Rd KT22 . . . . .74 C6
Holtye Ave RH19 . . . . .186 A3
Holtye Rd RH19 . . . . .186 B3
Holtye Wlk RH10 . . . . .202 A4

Holy Cross Catholic Prim
Sch SE6 . . . . .24 C7
Holy Cross Hospl GU27 . .207 F7
Holy Cross RC Convent
Sch KT3 . . . . .38 E4
Holy Cross RC Prep Sch
KT2 . . . . .18 C1
Holy Family RC Prim Sch
The SW15 . . . . .52 A5
Holy Ghost RC Prim Sch
SW12 . . . . .21 A8
Holy Trinity C of E Inf Sch
SW17 . . . . .20 F6
Holy Trinity C of E Prim
Sch Forest Hill SE23 . . . . . .23 C6
Streatham SW2 . . . . .21 F8
West End GU24 . . . . .68 A7
Wimbledon SW19 . . . . .20 B2
Holy Trinity CE Aided Sch
SL5 . . . . .30 A3
Holy Trinity CE Jun Sch
TW10 . . . . .7 A3
Holy Trinity CE Sch The
RH11 . . . . .201 A4
Holy Trinity Church of
England Jun Sch SM6 . . .60 C6
Holybourne Ave SW15 . . . . . .19 A8
Holyhead Ct KT1 . . . . .37 D5
Holyhook Cl RG45 . . . . .45 A6
Holyoake Ave GU21 . . . . .69 C2
Holyoake Cres GU21 . . . . . . .69 C2
Holyrood RH19 . . . . .206 A8
Holyrood Pl RH11 . . . . .201 B2
Holywell Cl
Farnborough GU14 . . . . .85 A7
Stanwell TW19 . . . . .13 E7
Holywell Way TW19 . . . . .13 E7
Homan House 6 SW4 . . . . . .21 D8
Hombrook Dr RG42 . . . . .26 E8
Hombrook House RG42 . . . . .26 E8
Home Cl Carshalton SM5 . . . .59 F8
Crawley RH10 . . . . .202 C8
Fetcham KT22 . . . . .94 D6
Home Ct KT6 . . . . .37 D2
Home Farm Cl
Betchworth RH3 . . . . .137 D8
Burgh Heath KT18 . . . . .77 D2
Esher KT10 . . . . .55 B4
Farnborough GU14 . . . . .85 D6
Ottershaw KT16 . . . . .51 A3
Thames Ditton KT7 . . . . .36 F2
Upper Halliford TW17 . . . . . .34 E5
Home Farm Cotts GU8 . .149 C5
Home Farm Gdns KT12 . . . . .54 C8
Home Farm Rd GU7 . . . . . . .150 F2
Home Meadow SM7 . . . . .78 A3
Home Park Cl GU5 . . . . .151 F6
Home Park Rd SW19 . . . . . . .19 F4
Home Park Wlk KT1 . . . . . . .37 D5
Home Pk RH8 . . . . .123 A4
Homebeech House 7
GU22 . . . . .69 E1
Homecoppice House 1
BR1 . . . . .24 F1
Homecourt TW14 . . . . .15 A7
Homecroft Rd SE26 . . . . .23 C3
Homefield Morden SM4 . . . . .40 A5
Thursley GU8 . . . . .169 C3
Homefield Cl Horley RH6 . . .161 B4
Leatherhead KT22 . . . . .95 C6
Woodham KT15 . . . . .70 E7
Homefield Gdns
Burgh Heath KT20 . . . . .97 C7
Mitcham CR4, SW19 . . . . . .40 D7
Homefield Pk SM1, SM2 . . . . .59 B4
Homefield Prep Sch SM1 .59 A5
Homefield Rd
Coulsdon CR3, CR5 . . . . . .100 B7
Walton-on-T KT12 . . . . .35 E2
Warlingham CR6 . . . . .101 C8
Wimbledon SW19 . . . . .19 E3
Homegreen House GU27 208 A6
Homeland Dr SM2 . . . . .59 B2
Homelands KT22 . . . . .95 C6
Homelands Dr SE19 . . . . .22 E1
Homelea GU14 . . . . .85 B8
Homeleigh Cres GU12 . . . . .106 A8
Homeleigh Ct 8 SW16 . . . . . .21 E5
Homemead SW12 . . . . .21 B6
Homemead Rd CR0 . . . . .41 C3
Homepark House GU9 . . . . .125 C2
Homer Rd CR0 . . . . .43 D3
Homersham Rd KT1 . . . . . . .38 B7
Homesdale Rd CR3 . . . . .100 D4
Homestall GU2 . . . . .108 D2
Homestall Rd RH19 . . . . . . .206 E8
Homestead GU6 . . . . .174 A4
Homestead Gdns KT10 . . . . .55 E5
Homestead Rd
Caterham CR3 . . . . .100 D4
Staines TW18 . . . . .13 B2
Homestead Way CR0 . . . . . . .82 D7
Homesteads The BR3 . . . . . .24 B2
Homewalk House SE26 . . . . .23 C4
Homewater House 1
KT17 . . . . .76 E6
Homewaters Ave TW16 . . . . .34 F8
Homewood GU6 . . . . .175 A3
Homewood Cl TW12 . . . . .15 F2
Homewood Gdns SE25 . . . . .42 E4
Homewoods 2 SW12 . . . . . . .21 C8
Homeworth House 8
GU22 . . . . .69 E1
Homildon House 10 SE26 . .23 A5
Homington Ct KT2 . . . . .17 F1
Homstead The RH6 . . . . . . .162 B1

Hone Hill GU47 . . . . .64 B8
Hones Yard Bsns Pk
GU9 . . . . .125 D2
Honey Hill RG40 . . . . .26 A1
Honeybrook
Rd SL3, SW4 . . . . .21 C8
Honeycrock La RH1 . . . . . . .140 B2
Honeyhill Rd RG42 . . . . .27 A8
Honeypot La TN8 . . . . .144 D4
Honeypots Rd GU22 . . . . . . .89 D5
Honeysuckle Bottom
KT24 . . . . .112 E2
Honeysuckle Cl
Crowthorne RG45 . . . . .45 A7
Horley RH6 . . . . .161 C4
Honeysuckle Gdns CR0 . . . . .43 D1
Honeysuckle La
Crawley RH11 . . . . .181 C1
Dorking RH5 . . . . .136 C4
Headley Down GU35 . . . . . .187 B5
Honeysuckle Wlk RH12 . .218 A5
Honeywood La
Ockley RH5 . . . . .196 F5
Rowhook RH5 . . . . .196 F5
Honeywood Rd
Horsham RH13 . . . . .218 A4
Isleworth TW7 . . . . .6 A3
Honeywood Wlk SM5 . . . . . . .59 F6
Honister Hts CR8 . . . . .80 E5
Honister Wlk GU15 . . . . .66 D4
Honley Rd SE6 . . . . .24 B8
Honnor Rd TW18 . . . . .13 D1
Honor Oak Rd SE23 . . . . .23 C8
Hood Ave SW14 . . . . .7 C2
Hood Cl CR0, CR9 . . . . .42 B1
Hood Rd SW20 . . . . .18 F1
Hook Heath Ave GU22 . . . . . .89 C8
Hook Heath Gdns GU22 . . . . .88 F6
Hook Heath Rd GU22 . . . . . . .89 B6
Hook Hill CR2 . . . . .61 E1
Hook Hill La GU22 . . . . .89 C6
Hook Hill Pk GU22 . . . . .89 B6
Hook House 9 SW27 . . . . . . .22 B3
Hook La Gomshall GU5 . . . .133 C2
Puttenham GU3 . . . . .128 D3
West End GU24 . . . . .67 C6
Hook Mill La GU18 . . . . .48 D2
Hook Rd Chessington KT6 . . .56 E7
Epsom KT19, KT17 . . . . . . .57 C2
Ewell KT19 . . . . .76 D8
Surbiton KT6, KT9 . . . . .56 E7
Hook Rise N Surbiton KT6 . . .57 B8
Tolworth KT6, KT9 . . . . .57 B8
Hook Rise S KT6, KT9 . . . . . .57 B8
Hook Rise South KT6 . . . . . . .56 E7
Hook Underpass KT6 . . . . . . .56 E7
Hooke Rd KT24 . . . . .92 F2
Hookfield KT18, KT19 . . . . . . .76 C6
Hookfield Mews KT19 . . . . . .76 C6
Hookhouse Rd GU8 . . . . . . .192 D6
Hookley Cl GU8 . . . . .148 E3
Hookley La GU8 . . . . .148 E3
Hookstile La GU9 . . . . .125 C1
Hookstone La GU24 . . . . .67 F8
Hookwood Bglws RH8 . . . . .123 B6
Hookwood Cnr RH8 . . . . . . .123 B7
Hookwood Cotts KT18 . . . . . .96 C3
Hooley La RH1 . . . . .139 F8
Hoover House SE6 . . . . .24 C4
Hope Ave RG12 . . . . .27 E2
Hope Cl SM1 . . . . .59 C5
Hope Ct RH11 . . . . .201 B1
Hope Fountain GU15 . . . . . . .65 F4
Hope Grant's Rd GU11 . . .105 A4
Hope La GU9 . . . . .125 B6
Hope Pk BR1 . . . . .24 F1
Hope St GU8 . . . . .148 C4
Hopeman Cl GU47 . . . . .64 D7
Hopes Cl TW5 . . . . .5 A8
Hopfield GU21 . . . . .69 E3
Hopfield Ave KT14 . . . . .71 E6
Hophurst Cl RH10 . . . . .204 B8
Hophurst Dr RH10 . . . . .204 B8
Hophurst Hill RH10, RH19 184 D2
Hophurst La RH10 . . . . .184 B1
Hopkins Ct RH11 . . . . .201 B1
Hoppety The KT20 . . . . .97 D5
Hoppingwood Ave KT3 . . . . . .38 E6
Hopton Gdns KT3 . . . . .39 A3
Hopton Rd SW16 . . . . .21 E3
Hopwood Cl SW17 . . . . .20 C5
Horace Rd KT1 . . . . .37 F6
Horatio Ave RG42 . . . . .27 E8
Horatius Way CR0 . . . . .60 F4
Hordern House RH12 . . . . . .217 A1
Horewood Rd RG12 . . . . .27 B3
Horley Cty Inf Sch RH6 . .161 A3
Horley Lodge La RH1 . . . . . .161 A8
Horley Rd Crawley RH6 . . . .181 B7
Hookwood RH6 . . . . .181 B7
Redhill RH1 . . . . .139 F5
Horley Row RH6 . . . . .161 A4
Horley Sta RH6 . . . . .161 B2
Hormer Cl GU47 . . . . .45 D1
Horn Rd GU14 . . . . .84 E5
Hornbeam Cl
Farnborough GU14 . . . . .84 C5
Horsham RH13 . . . . .217 F1
Sandhurst GU47 . . . . .45 D1
Hornbeam Cres TW8 . . . . .6 B7
Hornbeam Rd
Guildford GU1 . . . . .109 C3
Reigate RH2 . . . . .139 C6
Hornbeam Terr SM5 . . . . . . .40 E1
Hornbeam Wlk KT12 . . . . . . .53 F2

Hornby Ave RG12 ....27 D2
Hornchurch Cl KT2 .....17 D3
Hornchurch Hill CR3 ...80 F1
Horndean Cl
　Crawley RH10 ....182 D2
　3 Roehampton SW15 ..19 A7
Horndean Rd RG12 .....27 F3
Horne Rd TW17 ....34 A5
Hornecourt Hill RH6 ..162 F7
Horner La CR4 ....40 D7
Hornhatch GU4 ....131 B3
Hornhatch Cl GU4 ....131 B3
Hornhatch La GU4 ....131 B2
Horniman Dr SE23 .....23 C8
Horniman Grange 7 SE23 23 C7
Horniman Mus & Gdns
　SE23 ....23 B7
Horniman Prim Sch SE23 23 B7
Hornshill La RH12 ....213 F7
Horsa Cl SM6 ....60 E3
Horse Fair KT1 ....37 D7
Horse Gate Ride SL5 ...29 A3
Horse Hill RH6 ....160 B4
Horsebrass Dr GU19 ...47 E2
Horsecroft SM7 ....77 F2
Horsell Birch Woking GU21 69 A4
　Woking 69 B4
Horsell C of E Sch GU21 .69 C3
Horsell Common Rd GU21 69 C5
Horsell Ct KT16 ....33 B2
Horsell Moor GU21 .....69 D3
Horsell Park Cl GU21 ..69 D3
Horsell Pk GU21 ....69 E3
Horsell Rise GU21 .....69 E4
Horsell Rise Cl GU21 ..69 D4
Horsell Vale GU21 .....69 E3
Horsell Village Cty Inf Sch
　GU21 ....69 D4
Horsell Way GU21 .....69 C3
Horseshoe Bend GU26 188 B3
Horseshoe Cl
　Camberley GU15 ......65 F8
　Crawley RH10 ....202 D7
Horseshoe Cres GU15 ..65 F8
Horseshoe La
　Ash Vale GU12 ......106 A7
　Cranleigh GU6 ......174 D4
Horseshoe La E GU1 ..110 C2
Horseshoe La W GU1 ..110 B1
Horseshoe Ridge KT13 .72 C8
Horseshoe The
　Banstead SM7 ....77 F4
　Coulsdon CR5, CR8 ....79 D6
　Godalming GU7 ......150 C4
Horsham Bsns Pk RH12 198 C4
Horsham Hospl RH12 ..217 C1
Horsham Mus RH12 ....217 C1
Horsham Rd Alfold GU6 193 F8
　Beare Green RH5 ....157 C4
　Beare Green, Holmwood
　Cnr RH5 ....157 C6
　Bramley GU5, GU4 ....151 E7
　Bramley, Palmers Cross
　GU5, GU6 ....173 D5
　Capel RH5 ....178 D8
　Capel RH5 ....178 D8
　Cranleigh GU6 ......174 E1
　Cranleigh GU6, RH12 .194 C1
　Crawley RH11 ....201 B4
　Crawley, Palmers Cross
　GU5, GU6 ....173 D5
　Dorking RH4 ....136 A6
　Dorking, Mid
　Holmwood RH5 ......136 B2
　East Bedfont TW14 .....3 C1
　Ellen's Green GU6 ...176 B1
　Ewhurst GU6 ....175 F3
　Holmbury St M GU5,
　RH5, GU6 ....155 C5
　Rowhook RH5, RH12 ..196 D5
　Rusper RH12 ....199 B5
　Sandhurst GU47 ......45 D1
　Shalford GU4 ....130 E3
　South Holmwood RH5 .157 C6
　Wallis Wood RH12, RH5 196 D5
　Wallis Wood, Mayes Green
　RH5, GU6 ....176 E4
Horsham Sta RH13 ....217 D2
Horsley Cl KT19 ....76 D6
Horsley Dr Kingston u T KT2 17 D3
　New Addington CR0 ....63 C3
Horsley Rd KT11, KT24 .93 B7
Horsley Sta KT24 ......92 C2
Horsneile La RG42 .....27 B8
Horton Country Park
　KT19 ....57 A3
Horton Hill KT19 ......76 C8
Horton Hospl KT19 ....76 B8
Horton La KT19, KT18 ..57 B2
Horton Park Children's
　Farm KT19 ....57 A1
Horton Rd Colnbrook SL3 .1 A6
　Horton SL3 ....1 A6
　Poyle SL3, TW19 ......1 E4
　Stanwell TW19 ....2 A2
Horton Trad Est SL3 ....1 C4
Horton Way CR0 ....43 D4
Horvath Cl KT13 ....53 D6
Hosack Rd SW12, SW17 .21 A6
Hoskins Pl RH19 ......186 A4
Hoskins Place Ind Est
　GU15 ....65 B3
Hoskins Rd RH8 ......122 E6
Hospital Bridge Rd TW2 16 B7
Hospital Hill GU11 ...105 A3

Hospital of the Holy
Trinity (Almshouses)
　CR9 ....61 C8
Hospital Rd
　Aldershot GU11 .....105 B3
　Hounslow TW3 ....5 A4
Hospital Way SE13 .....24 D7
Hotham Cl KT8 ....36 A6
Hotham Rd SW19 ......20 C1
Houblon Rd TW10 ....6 E2
Houghton Cl TW12 .....15 E2
Houghton Rd RH10 ...202 C3
Houlder Cres GU19 ....61 B4
Houlton Cl GU19 ......47 F2
Hound House Rd GU5 .154 A5
Hounslow Ave TW3 ......5 B3
Hounslow Bsns Pk TW3 .5 B3
Hounslow Central Sta TW3 5 B4
Hounslow East Sta TW3 .5 C5
Hounslow Ed Ctr (Specl
　Sch) The TW4 ....4 E4
Hounslow Gdns TW3 ....5 B2
Hounslow Heath Jun & Inf
　Schs TW4 ....4 E4
Hounslow Manor Sch TW4 .5 C4
Hounslow Sta TW3 ......5 B2
Hounslow Town Prim Sch
　TW3 ....5 D4
Hounslow West Sta TW3 .4 E5
Houseman Rd GU14 ....84 F6
Houston Ct 3 CR0 .....42 E1
Houston Rd SE23, SE6 ..23 E5
Houstoun Ct TW5 ....4 F7
Hove Gdns SM1 ....40 B1
Hovenden House 6 SE21 22 E4
How La CR5 ....79 A1
Howard Ave KT17 ......58 A1
Howard Cl Ashford TW16 14 F2
　Ashstead KT21 ....75 F1
　Hampton TW12 ....16 C2
　Leatherhead KT22 .....95 C4
　Walton on t H KT20 ...97 A2
　West Horsley KT24 ....92 D2
Howard Cole Way GU11 104 E2
Howard Ct Beckenham BR3 .44 C7
　Effingham KT24 .....113 D8
　Reigate RH2 ....118 B2
Howard Dr GU14 ....84 B4
Howard Gdns GU1 ....110 A2
Howard House Penge SE20 43 C8
　Reigate RH2 ....118 B2
Howard of Effingham Sch
　KT24 ....113 E8
Howard Prim Sch CR0 ..61 D5
Howard Rd Coulsdon CR5 .79 D5
　Crawley RH11 ....200 D2
　Croydon SE25 ....43 A3
　Dorking RH4 ....136 A7
　Dorking, North
　Holmwood RH5 ......136 C3
　East Horsley KT24 ....93 A4
　Great Bookham KT23 114 C8
　Horsham RH13 ......218 A4
　Isleworth TW7 ....5 F4
　New Malden KT3 ......38 F5
　Penge SE20 ....43 C8
　Reigate RH2 ....139 B8
　Surbiton KT5 ....37 F3
　Wokingham RG40 .....25 C5
Howard Ridge GU4 ....110 A5
Howard St KT7 ....37 B3
Howards Cl GU22 ......90 A7
Howards Crest Cl BR3 ..44 C7
Howards La KT15 ......51 F3
Howards Rd GU22 ......89 F7
Howberry Rd CR7 ......42 D7
Howden Ct SE25 ....42 F7
Howden Rd SE25 ....42 F7
Howe Dr CR3 ....100 D5
Howell Hill Cl KT17 ...77 C8
Howell Hill Gr KT17 ...58 C1
Howgate Rd SW14 ......7 D4
Howitts Cl KT10 ....55 A5
Howland House 9 SW16 21 E5
Howley Rd CR0, CR9 ...61 C7
Howmic Ct 1 TW1 ......6 C1
Howorth Ct RG12 ......27 E5
Howson Terr TW10 ......6 E1
Hoylake Cl RH11 .....200 D5
Hoylake Gdns CR4 .....41 C6
Hoyle Hill RH5 ....157 D1
Hoyle Rd SW17 ....20 E3
Harmondsworth Moor
　Ctry Pk UB7 ....2 B7
Hubbard Dr KT9 ....56 C4
Hubbard Rd SE27 ......22 C4
Hubberholme RG12 ....27 A6
Huddleston Cres RH1 ..119 D7
Hudson Ct Guildford GU2 108 F1
　4 Merton SW19 ......40 B8
Hudson Rd Crawley RH10 201 E4
　Harlington UB7 ....3 D8
Hudsons KT20 ....97 D6
Huggins Pl SW2 ....21 F7
Hugh Herland KT1 .....37 E6
Hughenden Rd KT4 .....39 A2
Hughes Ct CR0 ....42 A1
Hughes Rd Ashford TW15 14 C2
　Wokingham RG40 .....25 E7
Hughes Wlk CR0 ....42 C2
Hullbrook La GU5 ....152 D4
Hullmead GU5 ....152 E4
Hulton Cl KT22 ....95 C4
Hulverston Cl SM2 .....59 B2

Humber Way GU47 .....64 D8
Humbolt Cl GU2 .....108 F1
Hummer Rd TW20 ......12 A4
Humphrey Cl KT22 .....94 C5
Humphries Yd RG12 ....27 C5
Hungerford Cl GU47 ...64 C8
Hungerford Sq 3 KT13 .53 D6
Hungry Hill La GU23 ...91 D3
Hunstanton Cl
　Colnbrook SW3 ....1 C7
　Crawley RH11 ....200 D5
Hunston Rd SM4 ....40 B1
Hunter Cl SW12 ....21 A7
Hunter House RH10 ...201 D3
Hunter Rd
　Crawley RH10, RH11 .201 D4
　Farnborough GU14 ....84 F3
　Guildford GU1 ......130 E8
　South Norwood CR7 ...42 D6
　Wimbledon SW20 .....39 C8
Hunters Chase RH9 ...142 F6
Hunters Cl RH13 ......76 C6
Hunters Ct 5 TW9 ......6 D2
Hunters Meadow SE19 .22 E4
Hunters Rd KT9 ....56 E6
Hunters The BR3 ......44 C8
Hunters Way CR0 ......61 E6
Huntersfield Cl RH2 ..118 B4
Hunting Cl KT10 ....55 A6
Hunting Gate Dr KT9 ..56 E3
Hunting Gate Mews
　Sutton SM1 ....59 B7
　Twickenham TW2 .....16 E7
Huntingdon Cl CR4, SW16 41 E5
Huntingdon Ct SW14 ....7 C4
Huntingdon Gdns
　Chiswick W4 ....7 C7
　North Cheam KT4 .....58 C7
Huntingdon Rd
　Redhill RH1 ....118 F1
　Woking GU21 ....68 F2
Huntingfield CR0 ......62 F2
Huntingfield Way TW20 12 D2
Huntingford Cl GU26 .188 C7
Huntley House 7 SE21 .22 E4
Huntley Way SW20 .....39 A7
Huntly Rd SE25 ....42 E5
Hunts Cl GU2 ....108 D2
Hunts Hill Rd GU3 ...107 A4
Hunts Slip Rd SE21 ....22 E6
Huntsgreen Ct RG12 ...27 E7
Huntsman Cl
　Fetcham KT22 ....94 D3
　Warlingham CR6 .....101 C8
Huntsmans Cl CR3 ...100 C6
Huntsmans Meadow SL5 28 F8
Huntsmoor Rd KT19 ...57 D5
Huntspill St SW17 .....20 C5
Huntsworth Ct SE6 ....24 A7
Hurland La GU30, GU35 187 A3
Hurlands Bsns Ctr GU9 125 F4
Hurlands Cl GU10, GU9 125 F4
Hurlands La GU8 ......192 F2
Hurlands Pl GU9 .....125 F4
Hurley Cl KT12 ....54 B8
Hurley Ct RG12 ....27 E5
Hurley Gdns GU4 .....110 A4
Hurlstone Rd SE25 .....42 E4
Hurn Court Rd TW5 .....4 D5
Hurn Ct TW5 ....4 D5
Hurnford Cl CR2 ....61 E1
Huron Rd SW17 ....21 A5
Hursley Ct 11 KT6 .....37 D2
Hurst Ave RH12 ......217 D3
Hurst Cl Chessington KT9 57 A5
　Crawley RH11 ....200 F4
　Hayes BR2 ....44 F1
　Headley KT18 ....96 C3
　Woking GU22 ....89 C7
Hurst Croft GU1 .....130 E6
Hurst Ct Beckenham BR3 .24 A1
　Horsham RH12 ......217 D3
　South Norwood SE25 ..42 F5
Hurst Dr KT20 ....97 A1
Hurst Farm Cl GU8 ...149 F2
Hurst Farm Rd RH19 ..205 D7
Hurst Gr KT12 ....34 F1
Hurst Green Cl RH8 ..123 A4
Hurst Green Cty Prim Sch
　RH8 ....123 A3
Hurst Green Rd RH8 ..122 F3
Hurst Green Sta RH8 ..122 F3
Hurst Hill Cotts GU5 ..152 B4
Hurst House 7 SE26 ...23 B3
Hurst La East Molesey KT8 36 C6
　Headley KT18 ....96 C4
　Thorpe TW20 ....32 A7
Hurst Lodge 4 KT13 ...53 D4
Hurst Lodge Sch SL5 ..29 F2
Hurst Park Cty Prim Sch
　KT8 ....36 A6
Hurst Rd Aldershot GU11 105 C4
　Croydon CR0 ....61 D5
　East Molesey KT8, KT12 36 B6
　Epsom KT19 ....76 D8
　Farnborough GU14 ....85 B8
　Horley RH6 ....160 E4
　Horsham RH12 ......217 D3
　Walton-on-T KT8&KT12 35 D5
Hurst View Rd CR2 .....61 E3
Hurst Way Pyrford GU22 70 E5
　South Croydon CR2 ....61 E5
Hurstbourne KT10 .....55 F4
Hurstbourne House SW15 7 F1
Hurstbourne Priors CR2 61 E4

Hurstbourne Rd SE23 ..23 E7
Hurstcourt Rd SM1 ....59 B8
Hurstdene Ave Hayes BR2 44 F1
　Staines TW18 ....13 B2
Hurstfield Rd KT8 .....36 A6
Hurstlands RH8 ......123 A3
Hurstleigh Cl RH1 ....118 F3
Hurstleigh Dr RH1 ...118 F3
Hurstmere Cl GU26 ...188 B3
Hurstview Grange CR0 ..61 B3
Hurstwood SL5 ....29 A3
Hurtmore Chase GU7 .150 B7
Hurtmore Rd
　Farncombe GU7 .....150 B7
　Shackleford GU7 ....150 B7
Hurtwood House Sch
　(International Sixth
　Form Coll) RH5 .....155 A2
Hurwood Rd KT12 ......35 F2
Hussar Cl GU11 ......104 E2
Hussars Cl TW4 ....4 E4
Hutchingson's Rd CR0 ..82 C8
Hutchins House 8 SW4 .21 D8
Hutchins Way RH6 ....160 F5
Hutsons Cl RG40 ......25 C3
Hutton Cl GU20 ....48 D3
Hutton Rd GU12 ......106 A6
Huxley Cl GU7 ....150 D7
Huxley Rd GU2 ....129 D8
Hyacinth Cl 3 TW12 ...16 A2
Hyacinth Rd SW15 .....19 A7
Hyde Cl TW16 ....14 E2
Hyde Ct TW4 ....4 F2
Hyde Dr RH11 ....200 E5
Hyde Farm Sch SW12 ..21 D7
Hyde Heath Ct RH10 ..202 D8
Hyde La
　Beacon Hill GU10, GU8 168 E1
　Thursley GU8 ....169 A2
Hyde Rd Richmond TW10 ..6 F2
　Sanderstead CR2, CR8 ..80 E6
Hyde Terr TW15, TW16 ..14 E2
Hyde Wlk SM4 ....40 A2
Hydestile Cotts GU8 ..171 D5
Hydethorpe Rd SW12 ..21 C7
Hydons The GU8 .....171 E5
Hylands Cl Crawley RH10 202 A5
　Epsom KT18 ....76 C4
Hylands Mews KT18 ....76 C4
Hylands Rd KT18 ......76 C4
Hylton Lodge KT12 ....54 C5
Hyndewood 14 SE23 ...23 D5
Hyon Ct RH11 ....200 E4
Hyperion Ct RH11 ....200 E4
Hyperion House 1 SW2 21 F7
Hyperion Pl KT19 ......57 D2
Hyperion Wlk RH6 ...161 B1
Hyrstdene CR0 ....61 B6
Hythe Cl RG12 ....27 E4
Hythe End Rd TW19 ....12 A5
Hythe Field Ave TW20 .12 D2
Hythe Park Rd TW20 ...12 D2
Hythe Rd Egham TW18 .12 D2
　South Norwood CR7, SE25 42 D7
Hythe Sch The TW18 ...12 D3
Hythe The TW18 ......12 E3

I

Ian Ct SE23 ....23 C6
Iberian Ave CR0, SM6 ..60 E6
Iberian Way GU15 .....66 B6
Ibis La W4 ....7 C6
Ibotson Ct SL3 ....1 E6
Ibsley Gdns SW15 .....19 A7
Ibstock Place Sch SW15 7 E1
Icehouse Wood RH8 ..122 F4
Icklesham House 9
　RH11 ....200 F3
Icklingham Gate KT11 ..73 C7
Icklingham Rd KT11 ...73 D6
Iden Cl BR2 ....44 E6
Idlecombe Rd SW17 ...21 A2
Idmiston Rd
　New Malden KT4 ......38 F2
　West Norwood SE21, SE27 22 C6
Idmiston Sq KT4 ....38 F2
Ifield Ave RH11 ......201 C7
Ifield Cl RH1 ....139 E7
Ifield Com Sch RH11 .201 A7
Ifield Cty Mid Sch RH11 201 A6
Ifield Fst Sch RH11 ...201 A8
Ifield Gn RH11 ......181 A1
Ifield Rd Charlwood RH6 180 E5
　Crawley RH11 ....201 C6
　Crawley, West Green RH11 201 C6
Ifield St RH11 ....200 F8
Ifield Sta RH11 ......201 A6
Ifield Wood RH11 ....180 E1
Ifold Bridge La RH14 .212 D4
Ifold Rd RH1 ....140 A7
Ifoldhurst RH14 .....212 C2
Ightham House BR3 ....23 F1
Ikona Ct KT13 ....53 C5
Ildersly Gr SE21 ......22 D6
Ilex Cl
　Englefield Green TW20 11 B1
　Sunbury TW16 ....35 C7
Ilex House KT15 ....52 A1
Ilex Way SW16 ....22 A3
Ilford Ct GU6 ....173 F2
Ilfracombe Rd BR1 ....24 F5
Ilkley St SE19 ....22 D2
Illingworth Cl CR4 ....40 D6
Illingworth Gr RG12 ...27 F8
Imber Cl KT7 ....36 F3
Imber Court Trad Est KT8 36 D3
Imber Cross KT7 ......36 F3

Imber Gr KT10 ....36 D2
Imber Park Rd KT10 ...36 D1
Imberhorne La RH19 ..185 B2
Imberhorne Lower Sch
　RH19 ....185 D3
Imberhorne Sch RH19 185 B3
Imberhorne Way RH19 185 B3
Imjin Cl GU11 ....105 B3
Immanuel & St Andrew C
　of E Prim Sch SW16 ..21 E2
Impact Ct SE20 ....43 B7
Imperial Gdns CR4 ....41 B6
Imperial House GU25 ..31 E4
Imperial Rd TW14 .....14 E8
Imperial Way CR0, CR9 61 A4
Impington 8 KT1 ......38 A7
Imran Ct KT12 ....126 C8
Ince Rd KT12 ....53 E4
Inchmery Rd SE6 ......24 C7
Inchwood Bracknell RG12 27 C1
　Croydon BR4, CR0 ....63 B6
Independent Bsns Pk The
　RH19 ....185 A3
Ingatestone Rd SE25 ..43 B5
Ingham Cl CR2 ....62 D2
Ingham Rd CR2 ....62 D2
Ingle Dell GU15 ....65 D4
Ingle House SW12 .....21 D7
Ingleboro Dr CR8 ......80 D6
Ingleby Way SM6 ......60 D3
Inglehurst KT15 ....52 B1
Inglemere Ct CR4, SW17 20 F1
Inglemere Rd
　Forest Hill SE23 ......23 D5
　Mitcham CR4, SW17 ..20 F1
Ingleside SL3 ....1 F6
Ingleside Cl BR3 ......24 A1
Ingleton RG12 ....27 A6
Ingleton Rd SM5 ......59 E2
Inglewood Addlestone KT16 51 F7
　New Addington CR0 ...62 E2
　Woking GU21 ....69 B1
Inglewood Ave GU15 ..66 D5
Inglewood Ct 2 BR1 ...24 F1
Inglis Rd CR0 ....42 F1
Ingram Cl RH12 ......217 A2
Ingram High Sch for Boys
　CR7 ....42 C8
Ingram House KT8 .....37 C8
Ingram Rd CR7 ....42 C8
Ingrams Almshouses TW7 .6 C4
Ingrams Cl KT12 ......54 C5
Ingrebourne House BR1 24 D3
Inholms La RH5 ......136 C3
Inkerman Rd GU21 ....68 E1
Inkerman Way GU21 ...68 E1
Inman Rd SW18 ....20 C8
Inner Park Rd SW19 ...19 D6
Inner Ring E TW6 ....3 B4
Inner Ring W TW6 ......3 A4
Innes Cl SW20 ....39 E7
Innes Gdns SW15 ......19 B8
Innes Lodge SE23 .....23 D5
Innes Rd RH12 ......217 F4
Innes Yd CR0, CR9 ....61 C7
Innings La RG12 ......27 E8
Innisfail Gdns GU11 ..125 F8
Inst of Oceanographic
　Sciences GU8 ....170 F1
Institute Rd
　Aldershot GU12 .....105 D1
　Westcott RH4 ....135 C6
Instone Cl SM6 ....60 E3
Instow Gdns GU14 .....85 A7
Inval Hill GU27 ......208 C8
Inveresk Gdns KT4 ....58 A7
Inverness Ct SL6 ......31 C4
Inverness Rd Hounslow TW3 5 A3
　North Cheam KT4 .....39 D1
Inverness Way GU47 ..64 D7
Invicta Cl TW14 ....14 F7
Invicta Ct KT9 ....56 F5
Invincible Rd GU14 ....85 A3
Inwood Cl CR0 ....62 E8
Inwood Ct 1 KT12 .....54 C8
Inwood Rd TW3 ....5 C3
Iona Cl Crawley RH11 .200 E5
　Forest Hill SE13, SE4, SE6 24 A8
Ipsley Lodge GU10 ...126 E5
Ipswich Rd SW17 ......21 A2
Irene Rd KT11 ....74 B5
Ireton Ave KT13 ....53 F8
Iris Cl Croydon CR0 ...43 D1
　Surbiton KT6 ....37 F2
Iris Rd Bisley GU24 ....68 A4
　West Ewell KT19 ......57 B5
Iron La GU5 ....151 D5
Irons Bottom Rd RH2 .159 F8
Irvine Ct CR7 ....42 A3
Irvine Dr GU14 ....84 E8
Irvine Pl GU25 ....31 E4
Irving Wlk RH10 .....201 E3
Irwin Dr RH12 ....217 A2
Irwin Rd GU2 ....130 A7
Isabel Cotts KT18 .....76 B5
Isabella Ct 8 TW10 .....6 F1
Isbells Dr RH2 ....139 B7
Isham Rd SW16 ....41 E7
Isis Ct W4 ....7 B7
Isis St SW18 ....20 C6
Isis Way GU47 ....64 D8
Island Cl TW18 ....12 E4
Island Cotts The KT11 .73 B1
Island Farm Ave KT8 ..35 F4
Island Farm Rd KT8 ...36 A4
Island House SW19 ....40 C5

Island Rd CR4, SW19 20 F1
Islay Gdns TW4 4 D2
Isleworth Bsns Complex TW7 5 F5
Isleworth Sta TW7 5 F5
Isleworth & Syon Sch for Boys TW7 5 E7
Isleworth Town Sch TW7 6 A5
Itchingwood Common Rd RH8 123 E2
Ivanhoe Cl RH11 181 D1
Ivanhoe House 11 SW12 21 B8
Ivanhoe Rd TW4 4 D4
Iveagh Cl RH11 201 C1
Iveagh Ct Beckenham BR3 44 B6
Bracknell RG12 27 C4
Iveagh Rd GU2 130 B7
Ively Rd GU14 84 D1
Ively Rdbt GU14 84 E2
Iverna Gdns TW14 3 D2
Ivers Way CR0 63 B3
Ivestor Terr SE23 23 C8
Ivor Cl GU1 131 A8
Ivory Ct TW13 15 A7
Ivory Wlk RH11 200 E3
Ivy Cl TW16 35 C7
Ivy Dene La RH19 206 D6
Ivy Dr GU18 67 A7
Ivy Gdns CR4 41 D6
Ivy House CR0 43 D1
Ivy La Farnham GU9 125 B2
Hounslow TW4 4 F3
Woking GU22 70 B1
Ivy Mill Cl RH9 121 B3
Ivy Mill La
Bletchingley RH1, RH9 121 B3
Godstone RH1, RH9 121 B3
Ivy Rd Aldershot GU12 105 E2
Hounslow TW3 5 B3
Tolworth KT6 38 A1
Upper Tooting SW17 20 E3
Ivybank GU7 150 E6
Ivybridge Cl 3 TW1 17 A8
Ivybridge Jun & Inf Sch TW1 5 F1
Ivychurch Cl SE20 23 C1
Ivydale Rd SM5 59 F8
Ivyday Gr SW16 21 F5
Ivydene
East Molesey KT12, KT8 35 F4
Knaphill GU21 68 B1
Ivydene Cl Redhill RH1 140 B4
Sutton SM1 59 C6
Ivymount Rd SE27 22 A5

J

Jackass La RH9 121 F4
Jackdaw Cl RH11 201 C8
Jackdaw La RH12 217 E6
Jackman's La GU21 89 B8
Jackson Cl Bracknell RG12 27 B4
Crawley GU6 173 F2
Epsom KT18 76 D5
Jackson's Pl CR0 42 E1
Jackson's Way CR0 63 B7
Jacob Cl RG42 26 D7
Jacob Rd GU15 65 A7
Jacobean Cl RH10 202 C5
Jacobs Well Rd GU4 109 D6
Jaggard Way SW12 20 F8
Jail La TN16 83 E3
Jamaica Rd CR7 42 B3
James Boswell 1 SW16 22 A4
James Dixon Prim Sch SE20 23 B1
James Est CR4 40 F7
James Rd Camberley GU15 65 B2
Shalford GU3 130 C1
James St TW3 5 D4
James Watt Way RH10 182 A4
James Way GU15 65 B2
Jameston RG12 27 C1
Jamieson House TW4 15 F8
Jamnagar Cl TW18 12 F2
Janoway Hill GU21 89 C8
Japonica Cl GU21 69 C1
Japonica Ct GU12 105 F1
Jarrett Cl SW2 22 B7
Jarrow Cl SM4 40 B4
Jarvis Rd CR2 61 D4
Jasmin Rd KT19 57 B5
Jasmine Cl Redhill RH1 140 A4
Woking GU21 68 F3
Jasmine Ct Horsham RH12 217 C2
11 Wallington SM6 60 B4
Jasmine Gdns CR0 63 B7
Jasmine Gr SE20 43 B8
Jasmine Way KT7 36 E5
Jason Cl Redhill RH1 139 E4
Weybridge KT13 53 C5
Jasons Dr GU4 110 C4
Jasper House KT4 38 D1
Jasper Rd Dulwich SE19 22 F2
West Norwood SE19 22 F2
Javelin Ct RH10 182 D1
Jawahar Bagh SW16 22 B2
Jay Ave KT15 52 E7
Jay's La Fisherstreet GU27 209 C3
Lurgashall GU27 209 C3
Jays Nest Cl GU17 64 D4
Jayson Ct 7 CR0 43 A1
Jeal Oakwood Ct KT18 76 E5
Jean House SW17 20 E3
Jean Humbert House 2 SE27 22 D4
Jeans Ct 10 RH11 201 B1
Jeddere Cotts RH7 165 A2
Jeffries Pas GU1 130 D8
Jeffries Rd KT24 112 C5
Jeffs Cl TW12 16 B2
Jeffs Rd SM1 58 F6
Jefton Ct SM6 60 C4
Jemmett Cl KT2 38 B8
Jengar Cl SM1 59 B6
Jenkins' Hill London Rd GU19 47 D2
Jenkins Pl GU11 105 D8
Jenner Dr GU24 68 A6
Jenner Rd Crawley RH10 181 F3
Guildford GU1 130 E8
Jennett Rd CR0, CR9 61 A7
Jennifer Rd BR1 24 F5
Jennings Cl KT15 52 C2
Jenny La RH7 164 C4
Jenson Way SE19 22 F1
Jeppo's La CR4 40 F5
Jerome Cnr GU47 45 E2
Jersey Cl Addlestone KT16 51 F7
Guildford GU4 110 B6
Jersey Rd Crawley RH11 201 A2
Hounslow TW5, TW7 5 D7
Mitcham SW17 21 B2
Jerviston Gdns SW16 22 A2
Jesmond Cl CR4 41 B6
Jesmond Rd CR0 42 F2
Jessamy Rd KT13 53 B8
Jesses La GU5 154 C8
Jessie's Hollow GU5 133 C1
Jessiman Terr TW17 34 A4
Jessops Way CR0, CR4 41 C3
Jeston House 10 SE27 22 B5
Jevington RG12 27 C1
Jewell House 3 SW12 21 C8
Jewels Hill Biggin Hill TN16 83 A6
West Wickham CR6 83 A6
Jews Wlk SE26 23 B4
Jeypore Rd SW18 20 C8
Jig's La S RG42 27 E8
Jillian Cl TW12 16 A1
Jobson's La
Fisherstreet GU27 209 D2
Lurgashall GU27 209 D1
Jocelyn Rd TW9 6 E4
Jock's La RG42 26 E8
Jockey Mead RH12 217 A1
Jodrell Cl TW7 6 A6
Joe Hunte Ct 2 SW27 22 B3
John Austin Cl KT2 37 F8
John Baird Ct SE26 23 D4
John Baird House 14 SE20 23 C1
John Barter House TW3 4 F5
John Busch Sch TW7 6 B6
John Cl GU11, GU9 125 E8
John Cobb Rd KT13 53 A3
John Dee House 3 SW14 7 D4
John Fisher Sch The CR8 60 E1
John Gale Ct KT17 57 F2
John Kaye Ct TW17 34 A4
John Kirk House 5 SW16 21 E5
John Nightingale Sch KT8 35 F6
John Nike Way RG12 26 C7
John Paul II RC Sec Sch SW19 19 D8
John Pounds House RH11 201 D4
John Ruskin Sixth Form Coll CR2 62 E3
John Russell Cl GU2 109 A4
John St Croydon SE25 43 A5
Hounslow TW3, TW5 4 E5
John Wesley Ct 5 TW1 17 A7
John Wiskar Dr GU6 174 D2
John's Rd TN16 103 D7
John's Terr CR0 42 E1
Johns La SM4 40 C4
Johns Wlk CR3 101 A8
Johnsdale RH8 122 F6
Johnson Rd Heston TW5 4 C7
Thornton Heath CR0 42 D2
Johnson Wlk RH10 201 E3
Johnson's Cl SM5 59 F7
Johnsons Dr TW12 36 C8
Johnston Gr GU2 109 A5
Johnston Wlk GU2 109 A5
Joinville Pl KT15 52 D6
Jolesfield RH11 200 F3
Jolliffe Rd RH1 99 C1
Jones Cnr SL5 28 E8
Jones Wlk 6 TW10 6 F1
Jonquil Gdns 5 TW12 16 A2
Jonson Cl CR4 41 B6
Jordan Cl CR2 80 F8
Jordans Cl Crawley RH11 201 D8
Guildford GU1 110 A2
Redhill RH1 140 A4
Stanwell TW19 13 C8
Jordans Cres RH11 181 D1
Jordans The RH19 205 E8
Josef Perrin House 1 SE27 22 D4
Joseph Hood Fst Sch SW20 39 E6
Joseph Locke Way KT10 55 A8
Joseph's Rd GU1 109 D2
Josephine Ave KT20 117 F8
Josephine Cl KT20 117 F8
Jubilee Ave North Ascot SL5 28 E8
Twickenham TW2 16 C7
Wokingham RG41 25 B7
Jubilee Cl
Farnborough GU14 84 D4
North Ascot SL5 28 E8
Stanwell TW19 13 C8
Teddington KT1 37 C8
Jubilee Cres KT15 52 D5
Jubilee Ct Bracknell RG12 27 C6
Hounslow TW3 5 B4
Staines TW18 13 A4
Thornton Heath CR7 42 A5
Jubilee Dr GU12 106 A6
Jubilee Hall Rd GU14 85 C4
Jubilee House 5 TW12 36 A8
Jubilee La
Grayshott GU26 188 C3
Rowledge GU10 146 A5
Jubilee Rd Aldershot GU11 126 B7
Cheam SM3 58 D3
Mytchett GU16 86 A2
Rudgwick RH12 214 D8
Jubilee Terr
Brockham RH3 137 C5
Dorking RH4 136 B8
Jubilee Villas KT10 36 E1
Jubilee Way
Chessington KT4, KT9 57 B7
East Bedfont TW14 15 A7
Merton SW19 40 B8
Tolworth KT4, KT9 57 B7
Jubilee Wks SW19 40 C7
Jubilee Wlk RH10 202 A6
Judge Wlk KT10 55 E4
Judge's Terr RH19 205 E8
Julian Cl GU21 69 C1
Julian Hill KT13 53 B3
Julian House SE21 22 E4
Julian Taylor Path SE23 23 B6
Julians Prim Sch SW16 22 A4
Julien Rd CR5 79 D4
Juliet Gdns RG42 27 F8
Julius Ct TW8 6 E7
Julius Hill RG42 27 F8
Jumps Rd GU10 168 B3
Junction Pl GU27 207 F6
Junction Rd Ashford TW15 14 D3
Croydon CR2 61 D5
Dorking RH4 136 A7
Lightwater GU18 48 B1
June Cl CR5 79 B5
June La RH1 140 B2
Junewood Cl KT15 70 F8
Juniper RG12 27 C1
Juniper Cl Biggin Hill TN16 83 E2
Chessington KT9 56 F5
Guildford GU1 109 C6
Reigate RH2 139 C7
Juniper Ct Belmont SM2 59 A4
Hounslow TW3 5 B3
Juniper Dr GU24 68 A4
Juniper Gdns Ashford TW16 14 F2
Mitcham CR4 41 C8
Juniper Hall (Field Study Ctr) RH5 115 C6
Juniper Pl GU4 130 D2
Juniper Rd Crawley RH11 181 C1
Farnborough GU14 84 C5
Reigate RH2 139 C7
Juniper Terr GU4 130 D2
Juniper Wlk RH3 137 C7
Jura Cl RH11 201 B3
Justin Cl TW8 6 D7
Jutland Gdns CR5 99 F7
Jutland Pl TW20 12 C3
Jutland Rd SE6 24 C8
Juxon Cl RH11 200 F4

K

Kaithwood House RH12 218 B5
Kangley Bridge Ctr SE26 23 F3
Kangley Bridge Rd
Forest Hill SE26 23 F3
Penge SE26 23 F3
Karen Ct BR1 44 F8
Kashmir Cl KT15 52 D2
Katharine Rd 1 TW1 17 A7
Katharine St CR0, CR9 61 C7
Katherine Cl KT15 52 A4
Katherine Ct SE23 23 C7
Kathleen Moore Ct BR4 63 C8
Kay Ave KT15 52 E7
Kay Cres GU35 187 B6
Kaye Ct GU1 109 C5
Kaye Don Way KT13 53 A1
Kayemoor Rd SM2 59 E4
Kaynes Pk SL5 28 E8
Keable Rd GU10 145 E7
Kearton Cl CR8 80 C2
Keates Gn RG42 27 B8
Keats Ave RH1 119 B3
Keats Cl Horsham RH12 217 F7
Mitcham SW17, SW19 20 D2
Keats House BR3 24 B2
Keats Pl RH19 185 D1
Keats Way Crowthorne RG45 45 B6
Croydon CR0 43 C3
Keble Cl Crawley RH10 182 D1
New Malden KT4 38 F1
Keble St SW17 20 C4
Keble Way GU47 45 E2
Kedeston Ct SM3 40 B1
Keedonwood Rd
Bromley BR1 24 F3
Catford BR1 24 F3
Keeley Rd CR0, CR9 61 C8
Keeling House 2 TW11 16 E3
Keen's Rd CR0 61 C6
Keens Cl SW16 21 D3
Keens La GU2, GU3 108 F5
Keens Park Rd GU3 108 F5
Keep Hatch Cty Inf Sch RG40 25 D7
Keep Hatch Cty Jun Sch RG40 25 D7
Keep The Catford SE6 24 B7
Kingston u T KT2 17 F1
Keepers Cl GU4 110 D4
Keepers Combe RG12 27 C3
Keepers Mews TW11 17 C2
Keepers Terr GU25 31 B4
Keepers Wlk GU25 31 D4
Keephatch Rd RG40 25 E7
Keevil Dr SW19 19 E8
Keir Hardie House 7 RH11 201 B1
Keith Lucas Rd GU14 84 F2
Keith Park Cres TN16 83 C3
Keldholme RG12 27 A6
Kelling Gdns CR0 42 B2
Kellino St SW17 20 F4
Kelly Cl TW17 34 E7
Kelmscott 5 SE23 23 D5
Kelsey Cl RH6 160 F3
Kelsey Gate BR3 44 B7
Kelsey La BR3 44 A6
Kelsey Park Ave BR3 44 B7
Kelsey Park Rd BR3 44 A7
Kelsey Park Sch BR3 44 A6
Kelsey Sq BR3 44 A7
Kelsey Way BR3 44 A6
Kelso Cl RH10 202 E7
Kelso Ct SE20 23 B1
Kelso Rd SM5 40 C2
Kelvedon Ave KT12 53 F3
Kelvedon Cl KT2 18 A2
Kelvin Ave KT22 94 F8
Kelvin Bsns Ctr RH10 181 F2
Kelvin Cl KT19 57 A4
Kelvin Ct Chiswick W4 7 C7
Isleworth TW7 5 E5
8 Penge SE20 43 B8
8 Twickenham TW1 6 B1
Kelvin Dr TW1 6 B1
Kelvin Gdns CR0 41 E2
Kelvin Gr Chessington KT6 56 E7
Forest Hill SE26 23 B5
Kelvin Grove Prim Sch
Forest Hill SE26 23 B5
Forest Hill SE23 23 E7
Kelvin La RH10 181 F2
Kelvin Way RH10 181 F2
Kelvinbrook KT8 36 B6
Kelvington Cl CR0 43 E2
Kelyway House 20 SW2 22 A8
Kemble Cl KT13 53 D6
Kemble Cotts KT15 52 A6
Kemble Rd
Croydon CR0, CR9 61 B7
Forest Hill SE23 23 D7
Kembleside Rd TN16 83 C1
Kemerton Rd
Beckenham BR3 44 B7
Croydon CR0 42 F2
Kemishford GU22 89 A4
Kemnal Pk GU27 208 D7
Kemp Ct GU19 47 F2
Kemp Gdns CR0 42 C3
Kempshott Rd
Horsham RH12 217 B4
Streatham SW16 21 E1
Kempston House SM2 59 B2
Kempton Ave TW16 35 B8
Kempton Ct
Farnborough GU14 84 F2
Sunbury TW16 35 B8
Kempton Park Race Course TW16 15 C1
Kempton Park Sta TW16 15 B1
Kempton Wlk CR0 43 E3
Kemsing Cl Coney Hall BR2 63 F8
Thornton Heath CR7 42 C5
Kemsley Rd TN16 103 D8
Kendal Cl
East Bedfont TW14 14 F7
Farnborough GU14 84 E4
Redhill RH2 118 D2
Kendal Ct 7 CR0 42 E1
Kendal Gdns SM1 59 C8
Kendal Gr GU15 66 D4
Kendal House
5 Croydon CR0 42 E1
Penge SE20 43 B7
Kendale Cl RH10 202 C2
Kendale Rd BR1 24 E3
Kendall Ave Penge BR3 43 E7
South Croydon CR2 61 D2
Kendall Ave S CR2 61 D1
Kendall Ct 4 SE19 22 F1
Kendall House SE12 24 F8
Kendall Rd Isleworth TW7 6 A5
Penge BR3 43 E7
Kendor Ave KT19 76 C8
Kendra Hall Rd CR2 61 B3
Kendrey Gdns TW2 16 E8
Kendrick Cl RG40 25 C5
Kenilford Rd SW12 21 B8
Kenilworth Ave
Bracknell RG12 27 D8
Oxshott KT11 74 B5
Wimbledon SW19 20 A4
Kenilworth Cl
Banstead SM7 78 B3
Crawley RH11 201 B2
Kenilworth Ct TW2 16 E6
Kenilworth Dr KT12 54 D7
Kenilworth Gdns TW18 13 C3
Kenilworth Rd
Ashford TW15, TW19 13 D5
Farnborough GU14 84 C5
Penge SE20 43 D8
Kenilworth Rd *continued*
Stoneleigh KT17 58 A5
Kenilworth Terr 3 SM2 59 A3
Kenley Cl CR3 100 E7
Kenley Gdns CR7 42 B5
Kenley House 5 CR0 43 A1
Kenley La CR8 80 D3
Kenley Prim Sch CR3 80 E3
Kenley Rd
Headley Down GU35 187 C5
Kingston u T KT1, KT3 38 B7
Merton SW19 40 A6
Twickenham TW1 6 B1
Kenley Sta CR8 80 C5
Kenley Wlk SM3 58 D6
Kenlor Rd SW17 20 D3
Kenmara Cl RH10 182 A1
Kenmara Ct RH10 182 A2
Kenmare Dr CR4 20 F1
Kenmare Rd CR7 42 A3
Kenmore Cl Frimley GU16 85 D8
Richmond TW9 7 A7
Kenmore Rd CR8 80 B5
Kennard Ct RH18 206 E3
Kennedy Ave RH19 185 D3
Kennedy Cl CR4 41 A7
Kennedy Ct TW15 14 C3
Kennedy Rd RH13 217 D1
Kennel Ave SL5 28 F8
Kennel Cl
Fetcham KT22, KT23 94 C3
North Ascot SL5 8 F2
Kennel Gn SL5 28 E8
Kennel La Fetcham KT22 94 C4
Frensham GU10 146 C2
Hookwood RH6 160 D2
Windlesham GU20 48 C5
Kennel Ride SL5 8 F1
Kennel Wood SL5 28 F8
Kennel Wood Cres CR0 82 D8
Kennels La GU14 84 C2
Kennet Cl Ash GU12 106 A1
Crawley RH11 200 F5
Farnborough GU14 84 E6
Kennet House 6 RH1 118 F2
Kennet Rd TW7 5 F4
Kennet Sq CR4 40 E8
Kenneth Rd SM7 78 D4
Kennoldes SE21 22 D6
Kenrick Sq RH1 120 E1
Kensington Ave CR7 42 A8
Kensington Avenue Inf Sch CR7 42 A8
Kensington Avenue Jun Sch CR7 42 A8
Kensington Rd RH11 201 C2
Kensington Terr CR2 61 D3
Kent Cl Mitcham CR4, SW16 41 E5
Staines TW18 13 D2
Kent Dr TW11 16 E3
Kent Gate Way
Addington CR0 63 B5
New Addington CR0, CR2 62 F4
Kent Hatch Rd
Limpsfield RH8, TN8 123 D4
The Chart RH8, TN8 123 D4
Kent House La BR3 23 E3
Kent House Rd
Forest Hill SE26, BR3 23 E2
Penge SE26, BR3 23 E2
Kent House Sta BR3 43 E8
Kent House Station App BR3 43 D8
Kent Lodge 9 SW19 19 D7
Kent Rd East Molesey KT8 36 C5
Kingston u T KT1 37 D6
Richmond TW9 7 A7
West Wickham BR4 44 B1
Windlesham GU20 48 D5
Woking GU22 70 C3
Kent Tower SE20 23 B1
Kent Way KT6 56 F8
Kentigern Dr RG45 45 E5
Kenton Ave TW16 35 E7
Kenton Cl Bracknell RG12 27 D7
Frimley GU16 65 F1
Kenton Ct SE26 23 E4
Kenton Way GU21 68 F2
Kentwyns Rise RH1 140 F8
Kenwood Cl UB7 3 A8
Kenwood Dr
Beckenham BR3 44 C6
Hersham KT12 54 B5
Kenwood Pk KT13 53 D4
Kenwood Ridge CR8 80 B2
Kenworth Gr GU18 48 A1
Kenwyn Rd SW20 39 C8
Kenya Ct RH6 160 F4
Kenyngton Dr TW16 15 A3
Kenyngton Manor Prim Sch TW16 15 A2
Kenyons KT24 112 B7
Keogh Barracks GU16 86 B1
Keogh Cl GU12 86 B2
Keppel Rd RH4 115 B1
Keppel Spur SL4 11 B8
Kepple Pl GU19 47 F3
Kerria Way GU24 67 F6
Kerrill Ave CR5 100 A8
Kerrsland Cotts GU7 149 F7
Kerry Terr GU21 70 B3
Kersey Dr CR2 81 D7
Kershaw House 7 SE27 22 B5
Keston Ave
Coulsdon CR5, CR8 100 B8

Keston Ave continued
Woodham KT15 . . . .**71** A8
Keston Avenue Jun &
Inf Schs CR5 . . . .**100** A8
Keston Rd CR7 . . . .**42** A3
Kestrel Ave TW18 . . . .**12** F5
Kestrel Cl Crawley RH11 . .**201** C8
Crondall GU10 . . . .**124** D7
Guildford GU4 . . . .**110** D3
Horsham RH12 . . . .**217** E5
Kingston u T KT2 . . . .**17** D4
Kestrel House GU9 . . . . . .**146** A8
Kestrel Way CR0 . . . .**63** D2
Keswick Ave
Kingston u T KT2, SW15 . . .**18** E3
Merton SW19 . . . .**40** A7
Upper Halliford TW17 . . . . .**34** E6
Keswick Cl Crawley RH11 .**200** D4
Frimley GU15 . . . .**66** D4
Sutton SM1 . . . .**59** C6
Keswick Dr GU18 . . . .**67** B8
Keswick Rd
Fetcham KT22, KT23 . . . . . .**94** C2
Thorpe Lea TW20 . . . .**12** B1
Twickenham TW2 . . . .**5** C1
West Wickham BR4 . . . .**63** E8
Witley GU8 . . . .**170** D6
Kettering Ct CR7 . . . .**42** C5
Kettering St SW16 . . . . . .**21** C2
Kettlewell Cl GU21 . . . .**69** E4
Kettlewell Dr GU21 . . . .**69** E5
Kettlewell Hill GU21 . . . . . .**69** E4
Ketton Gn RH1 . . . .**119** D7
Kevan Dr GU23 . . . .**90** E2
Kevin Cl TW4 . . . .**4** D5
Kew Bridge Rd TW8 . . . .**6** F8
Kew Cres SM3 . . . .**58** F7
Kew Foot Rd TW9 . . . .**6** E4
Kew Gardens Rd TW9 . . . . . .**7** A6
Kew Gardens Sta TW9 . . . . . .**7** A6
Kew Gn TW9 . . . .**6** F8
Kew Lodge ❿ TW9 . . . .**6** F6
Kew Observatory TW9 . . . . .**6** C4
Kew Palace TW9 . . . .**6** E7
Kew Rd TW9, W4 . . . .**6** F5
Kew Ret Pk TW9 . . . .**7** B6
Key Cross GU10 . . . .**147** D5
Keymer Cl TN16 . . . .**83** D3
Keymer Rd Crawley RH11 . .**201** D4
Streatham SW2 . . . .**21** F6
Keynsham Rd SM4 . . . .**40** B1
Keynsham Way GU47 . . . . . .**45** D2
Keynsham Wlk SM4 . . . .**40** B1
Keysham Ave TW5 . . . .**4** A6
Keywood Dr TW16 . . . .**15** A2
Khama Rd SW17 . . . .**20** E4
Khartoum Rd
Upper Tooting SW17 . . . .**20** D4
Witley GU8 . . . .**170** E6
Kibble Gn RG12 . . . .**27** C3
Kidborough Down KT23 . . .**114** A8
Kidborough Rd RH11 . . . . .**200** F4
Kidbrooke Park
(Mia Hall Sch)
RH18 . . . .**206** D1
Kidbrooke Rise RH18 . . . . .**206** E2
Kidmans Cl RH12 . . . .**217** F5
Kidworth Cl RH6 . . . .**160** F5
Kielder Wlk GU15 . . . .**66** C4
Kier Pk SL5 . . . .**29** C6
Kilberry Cl TW7 . . . .**5** D6
Kilcorral Cl KT17 . . . .**77** A5
Kildare Rd SE6 . . . .**24** D7
Killasser Ct KT20 . . . .**97** C4
Killearn Rd SE6 . . . .**24** D7
Killester Gdns KT17, KT4 . .**58** B6
Killick House SM1 . . . .**59** B6
Killicks GU6 . . . .**174** F4
Killieser Ave SW2 . . . .**21** E6
Killigrew House TW16 . . . . .**14** E1
Killinghurst La
GU27,GU8 . . . .**209** D8
Killross Rd TW14 . . . .**14** D7
Kilmarnock Pk RG12 . . . . .**118** B2
Kilmartin Ave SW16 . . . .**42** A6
Kilmartin Gdns GU16 . . . . . .**65** F1
Kilmington Cl RG12 . . . .**27** E2
Kilmiston Ave TW17 . . . .**34** C3
Kilmiston House TW17 . . . . .**34** C3
Kilmore Dr GU15 . . . .**66** B4
Kilmorey Gdns TW1 . . . .**6** B3
Kilmorey Rd TW1 . . . .**6** B3
Kilmorie Prim Sch SE23 . . .**23** E6
Kilmorie Rd SE23 . . . .**23** E6
Kilmuir Cl GU47 . . . .**64** D7
Kiln Cl UB3 . . . .**3** D8
Kiln Copse GU6 . . . .**174** E4
Kiln Fields GU27 . . . .**208** D8
Kiln La Bracknell RG12 . . . . .**27** A7
Brockham RH3 . . . .**116** C1
Ewell KT17 . . . .**76** E8
Farnham GU10, GU9 . . . . . .**146** C6
Horley RH6 . . . .**161** A5
Ripley GU23 . . . .**91** B3
Sunningdale SL5 . . . .**30** A4
Kiln Meadows GU3 . . . .**108** C5
Kiln Mews SW17 . . . .**20** D3
Kiln Rd RH10 . . . .**204** B7
Kiln Way Aldershot GU11 . .**126** B7
Grayshott GU26 . . . .**187** E5
Kiln Wlk RH1 . . . .**140** A4
Kilnfield Rd RH12 . . . .**214** D8
Kilnmead RH10, RH11 . . . . .**201** E7
Kilnmead Cl RH10 . . . .**201** E7
Kilnside KT10 . . . .**56** A3

Kilnwood La
Crawley RH12 . . . .**200** B3
Faygate RH12 . . . .**199** F3
Kilrue La KT12 . . . .**53** F6
Kilrush Terr GU21 . . . .**70** A3
Kilsha Rd KT12 . . . .**35** C3
Kimber Ct GU4 . . . .**110** D3
Kimber Cl The SW18 . . . . . .**20** A8
Kimber Rd SW18 . . . .**20** B8
Kimberley RG12 . . . .**27** C1
Kimberley Cl RH6 . . . .**160** E3
Kimberley Pl ❺ CR8 . . . .**80** A8
Kimberley Rd
Crawley RH10 . . . .**202** B7
Penge BR3 . . . .**43** D7
Thornton Heath CR0, CR7 . . .**42** B3
Kimberley Ride KT11 . . . . . .**74** B6
Kimberley Wlk KT12 . . . .**35** B2
Kimbers La GU9 . . . .**125** D3
Kimble Rd Mitcham SW17 . .**20** D3
Mitcham SW17 . . . .**20** D3
Kimbolton Cl SE12 . . . .**24** F8
Kimmeridge RG12 . . . .**27** E3
Kimpton Bsns Ctr SM3 . . . .**58** F8
Kimpton House SW15 . . . . .**19** A8
Kimpton Ind Est SM3 . . . . . .**58** F8
Kimpton Rd SM3 . . . .**58** F8
Kinburn Dr TW20 . . . .**11** C3
Kindell House ❹ SW14 . . . . .**7** D4
Kindersley Cl RH19 . . . .**186** B3
Kinfauns Rd SW2 . . . .**22** A6
King Acre Ct TW18 . . . .**12** E5
King Alfred Ave SE6 . . . .**24** A4
King Athelstan Prim Sch
KT1 . . . .**37** F6
King Charles Cres KT5 . . . .**37** F2
King Charles' Rd KT5, KT6 .**37** F3
King Charles Wlk ❻ SW19 **19** E7
King Edward Dr KT6 . . . .**56** E7
King Edward's Gr TW11 . . . .**17** C2
King Edward's Sch GU8 . . .**170** F1
King Edwards Rd SL5 . . . . . .**28** E8
King Edwards Rise SL5 . . . .**28** E8
King Garth Mews SE23 . . . .**23** C6
King Gdns CR0 . . . .**61** B5
King George Ave
East Grinstead RH19 . . . . . .**185** C3
Walton-on-T KT12 . . . .**35** D1
King George Cl TW16 . . . . . .**14** E3
King George Sq TW10 . . . . . .**6** F1
King George V1 Ave TN16 .**83** D3
King George VI Ave CR4 . . . .**40** F5
King George's Cotts GU8 .**192** B6
King George's Dr KT15 . . . .**52** A1
King George's Lodge
GU2 . . . .**109** A4
King George's Trad Est
KT9 . . . .**57** A7
King Henry's Dr
New Addington CR0 . . . .**82** E8
West Wickham CR0 . . . .**82** E8
King Henry's Rd KT1, KT3 . .**38** B6
King St Chertsey KT16 . . . . .**33** A1
East Grinstead RH19 . . . . . .**185** E1
Richmond TW10, TW9 . . . . . .**6** D2
Twickenham TW1 . . . .**17** A7
King Street Par ❻ TW1 . . . .**17** A7
King William IV Gdns
SE20 . . . .**23** C2
King's Ave Ashford TW16 . . .**14** F2
Hounslow TW3, TW5 . . . .**5** B6
King's Cl Staines TW18 . . . . .**13** D1
Thames Ditton KT7 . . . .**37** A2
King's Coll Sch SW19 . . . . .**19** D2
King's Court Prim Sch
SL4 . . . .**11** B8
King's Ct
Aldershot GU10, GU12 . . . .**126** E8
Beckenham BR3 . . . .**44** B6
Wimbledon SW19 . . . .**20** A2
King's Dr KT7 . . . .**37** B2
King's Head La KT14 . . . .**71** D3
King's House Jun Sch
TW10 . . . .**6** F2
King's House Sch TW10 . . . .**6** F2
King's Keep GU47 . . . .**45** B1
King's La SM1, SM2 . . . .**59** D5
King's Paddock TW12 . . . . .**36** C8
King's Pas TW12 . . . .**37** D8
King's Rd Aldershot GU11 . .**104** F1
Ascot SL5 . . . .**29** C4
Cranleigh GU6 . . . .**174** F2
Crowthorne RG45 . . . .**45** C5
Croydon SE25 . . . .**43** A6
Egham TW20 . . . .**12** A4
Farncombe GU7 . . . .**150** F6
Haslemere GU27 . . . .**208** A6
Horsham RH12, RH13 . . . . .**217** E3
Kingston u T KT2 . . . .**18** E1
Long Ditton KT6 . . . .**37** C1
Mortlake SW14 . . . .**7** D4
Teddington TW11, TW12 . . . .**16** D3
Twickenham TW1 . . . .**6** B1
Wimbledon SW19 . . . .**20** A2
King's Ride Bracknell SL5 . . .**28** D5
Camberley GU15 . . . .**65** B4
King's Shade Wlk ❶ KT18 .**76** D6
King's Terr ❽ TW7 . . . .**6** A4
King's Way GU24 . . . .**87** D8
King's Wlk GU15 . . . .**64** F6
Kingcup Cl CR0 . . . .**43** D1
Kingcup Dr GU24 . . . .**68** A4
Kingfield Cl GU22 . . . .**89** F7
Kingfield Dr GU22 . . . .**89** F7
Kingfield Gdns GU22 . . . . . .**89** F7
Kingfield Rd GU22 . . . .**89** F7
Kingfield Sch GU22 . . . .**90** A7

Kingfisher Cl
Crawley RH10 . . . .**182** A1
Farnborough GU14 . . . .**84** D6
Hersham KT12 . . . .**54** E5
Putney SW19 . . . .**19** E6
Kingfisher Ct Cheam SM1 . .**58** F5
Dorking RH4 . . . .**136** A8
East Molesey KT8 . . . .**36** E5
Isleworth TW7 . . . .**5** B2
Sheerwater GU21 . . . .**70** C5
Kingfisher Dr
Guildford GU4 . . . .**110** C3
Redhill RH1 . . . .**119** A3
Staines TW18 . . . .**12** F4
Teddington TW11 . . . .**17** B4
Kingfisher Gdns CR2 . . . . . .**62** D1
Kingfisher Lodge TW11 . . . .**17** A4
Kingfisher Rise RH19 . . . . .**205** F8
Kingfisher Sports Ctr The
KT1 . . . .**37** E7
Kingfisher Way
Beckenham CR0 . . . .**43** D4
Horsham RH12 . . . .**217** C5
Kingfisher Wlk GU12 . . . . .**105** F2
Kingham Cl SW18 . . . .**20** C8
Kings Ave Ash GU10, GU12 .**126** F8
Bromley BR1 . . . .**24** F2
Byfleet KT14 . . . .**71** D7
New Malden KT3 . . . .**38** F4
Redhill RH1 . . . .**139** E7
Streatham SW12, SW4 . . . . .**21** D8
Wallington SM5 . . . .**59** F3
Kings Chase KT8 . . . .**36** C6
Kings Cl KT12 . . . .**35** B1
Kings Copse ❾ RH19 . . . . .**205** F8
Kings Cres GU5 . . . .**65** C8
Kings Cross La RH1 . . . . . .**140** E5
Kings Ct Horsham RH13 . . .**217** E3
❶❻ Kingston u T KT2 . . . . . .**18** A1
❶❶ Roehampton SW15 . . . . .**19** A8
Tadworth KT20 . . . .**97** C5
❸ Wallington SM6 . . . .**60** B4
Kings Dr KT5 . . . .**38** A3
Kings Dr The KT12 . . . .**53** F2
Kings Farm Ave TW10 . . . . . .**7** A3
Kings Gate GU7 . . . .**150** F6
Kings Hall Rd BR3 . . . .**43** E8
Kings Keep KT6 . . . .**37** E5
Kings La
Englefield Green TW20 . . . . .**11** A2
Windlesham GU20 . . . .**48** E5
Wrecclesham GU10 . . . .**145** F6
Kings' Manor Sch GU2 . . . .**108** E1
Kings Mead
Smallfield RH6 . . . .**162** B3
South Nutfield RH1 . . . .**140** E7
Kings Mead Pk KT10 . . . . . .**55** B3
Kings Mill La
Salfords RH1 . . . .**140** D5
South Nutfield RH1 . . . .**140** D5
Kings Rd Belmont SM2 . . . . .**59** A4
Biggin Hill TN16 . . . .**83** C2
Feltham TW13 . . . .**15** C7
Horley RH6 . . . .**161** A3
Mitcham CR4 . . . .**41** A6
Richmond TW10, TW9 . . . . . .**6** F2
Shalford GU4 . . . .**130** E2
Walton-on-T KT12 . . . .**35** B1
West End GU24 . . . .**68** A6
Woking GU21 . . . .**70** A3
Wonersh GU5 . . . .**152** B8
Woodham KT15 . . . .**71** B8
Kings Ride Gate TW10 . . . . . .**7** A3
Kings Way CR0 . . . .**60** F5
Kings Wlk CR2 . . . .**81** B5
Kings's Rd ❷ GU1 . . . .**109** D1
Kingsbridge House ❶❶
SE20 . . . .**43** B8
Kingsbridge Rd
Walton-on-T KT12 . . . .**35** B2
West Barnes SM4 . . . .**39** D2
Kingsbrook KT22 . . . .**75** A1
Kingsbury Cres TW18 . . . . .**12** D4
Kingsbury Dr SL4 . . . .**11** B8
Kingsclear Pk GU15 . . . .**65** D4
Kingsclere Cl SW15 . . . .**19** A8
Kingscliffe Gdns SW19 . . . .**19** F7
Kingscote Hill RH11 . . . . . .**201** B4
Kingscote Rd
Croydon CR0, CR9 . . . .**43** B2
Kingston u T KT3 . . . .**38** D6
Kingscote Sta RH19 . . . . . .**204** F4
Kingscourt Rd SW16 . . . . . .**21** E5
Kingscroft Cty Inf Sch
TW18 . . . .**13** A3
Kingscroft Cty Jun Sch
TW18 . . . .**13** A2
Kingscroft La RG42 . . . .**8** A6
Kingscroft Rd
Leatherhead KT22 . . . .**95** B7
Woodmansterne SM7 . . . . . .**78** E4
Kingsdale Rd SE20 . . . .**23** D1
Kingsdale Sch SE21 . . . .**22** E5
Kingsdene KT20 . . . .**97** B5
Kingsdown ❶ SW19 . . . .**19** D1
Kingsdown Ave CR2, CR8 . . .**61** C2
Kingsdown Rd Cheam SM3 .**58** E5
Ewell KT17 . . . .**77** A6
Kingsdowne Rd KT6 . . . .**37** F2
Kingsfield GU5 . . . .**153** F7
Kingsfield Bsns Pk RH1 . .**140** A8
Kingsfold Cl RH11 . . . .**198** B5
Kingsford Ave SM6 . . . .**60** E3
Kingsgate Bsns Ctr KT2 . . .**37** E8
Kingsgate Rd KT2 . . . .**37** E8
Kingshill Ave KT4 . . . .**39** B2
Kingslake ❷ GU21 . . . .**68** E1
Kingsland RH5 . . . .**158** A1

Kingsland Ct RH10 . . . .**202** A6
Kingslea Horsham RH13 . . .**217** E3
Leatherhead KT22 . . . .**95** A7
Kingslee Ct SM2 . . . .**59** B3
Kingsleigh Pl CR4 . . . .**40** F6
Kingsleigh Wlk BR2 . . . .**44** F5
Kingsley Ave Banstead SM7 **78** A4
Camberley GU15 . . . .**65** D3
Carshalton SM1 . . . .**59** D6
Englefield Green TW20 . . . . .**11** B2
Hounslow TW3 . . . .**5** C5
Kingsley Cl
Crowthorne RG45 . . . .**45** B3
Horley RH6 . . . .**160** F5
Kingsley Ct Dr KT4 . . . .**57** F8
Worcester Park KT4 . . . .**57** F8
Kingsley Gr RH2 . . . .**139** B5
Kingsley House ❽ KT6 . . . . .**37** E4
Kingsley Inf Sch CR9 . . . . . .**42** A1
Kingsley Jun Sch CR9 . . . . .**42** A1
Kingsley Rd Crawley RH11 .**201** A3
Farnborough GU14 . . . .**84** F5
Horley RH6 . . . .**160** F5
Hounslow TW3 . . . .**5** C5
Thornton Heath CR0 . . . .**42** A1
Wimbledon SW19 . . . .**20** B3
Kingslyn Cres SE19 . . . .**42** E8
Kingsmead Biggin Hill TN16 .**83** D3
Cranleigh GU6 . . . .**174** E3
Farnborough GU14 . . . .**85** B4
Frimley GU16 . . . .**85** E7
Richmond TW10 . . . .**6** F1
Woking GU21 . . . .**70** A3
Kingsmead Ave
Mitcham CR4 . . . .**41** C6
North Cheam KT4 . . . .**58** B7
Sunbury TW16 . . . .**35** C7
Tolworth KT6 . . . .**57** A8
Kingsmead Cl
Horsham RH12 . . . .**218** B6
Teddington TW11 . . . .**17** B2
West Ewell KT19 . . . .**57** D3
Kingsmead Ct BR1 . . . .**24** F1
Kingsmead Lodge SM2 . . . .**59** D4
Kingsmead Pl RH12 . . . .**216** C3
Kingsmead Sh Ctr GU14 . . .**85** B3
Kingsmere SE6 . . . .**24** B7
Kingsmere Rd
Bracknell RG42 . . . .**26** F8
Putney SW19 . . . .**19** D6
Kingsnympton Pk KT2 . . . . .**18** B2
Kingsridge SW19 . . . .**19** E6
Kingsthorpe Rd SE26 . . . . . .**23** D4
Kingston Ave Cheam SM3 . .**58** E7
East Horsley KT24 . . . .**92** E1
Feltham TW14 . . . .**3** F1
Leatherhead KT22 . . . .**95** B6
Kingston Bsns Ctr KT9 . . . .**56** F7
Kingston By - Pass KT6 . . . .**57** B8
Kingston By-Pass
KT6, KT7, KT9 . . . .**56** C7
Kingston Cl TW11 . . . .**17** B2
Kingston Coll of F Ed KT1 **37** E6
Kingston Coll of F Ed
(M V Annex) KT2 . . . .**37** E8
Kingston Cres
Beckenham BR3 . . . .**43** F8
Staines TW15 . . . .**13** D2
Kingston Gdns CR0 . . . .**60** E7
Kingston Gram Sch KT2 . . .**37** F7
Kingston Hall Rd KT1 . . . . . .**37** D6
Kingston Hill KT2 . . . .**18** C2
Kingston Hill Pl KT2, TW10 **18** C4
Kingston Hospl KT2 . . . .**38** B8
Kingston House Gdns
KT22 . . . .**95** B6
Kingston La
Teddington TW11 . . . .**17** B2
West Horsley KT24 . . . .**112** A8
Kingston Lodge ❶ KT3 . . . .**38** E5
Kingston Mus KT1 . . . .**37** E7
Kingston Poly (Gipsy Hill
Ctr) KT2 . . . .**18** D3
Kingston Rd
Ashford TW15, TW17 . . . . . .**13** F2
Ashtead KT22, KT9 . . . .**75** A3
Camberley GU15 . . . .**47** A1
Ewell KT17, KT19, KT4,
KT5, KT6 . . . .**57** D6
Kingston u T KT1, KT3 . . . . .**38** C5
Leatherhead KT22 . . . .**75** A1
Merton SW19, SW20 . . . .**39** E7
New Malden KT3 . . . .**38** C5
Putney SW15, SW19 . . . .**19** B7
Roehampton SW15, SW19 . .**19** B7
Staines TW15, TW18 . . . . . .**13** B2
Teddington TW11 . . . .**17** B2
Tolworth KT17, KT19, KT4,
KT5, KT6 . . . .**57** D6
Worcester Park KT17, KT19,
KT4, KT5, KT6 . . . .**57** D6
Kingston Rise KT15 . . . .**52** A1
Kingston Sq SE19 . . . .**22** D3
Kingston Sta KT2 . . . .**37** E8
Kingston Univ
Kingston u T KT2 . . . .**18** D3
Kingston u T KT1 . . . .**37** E6
Kingston Univ Annex KT1 .**37** F7
Kingston Univ
Roehampton Vale Ctr
SW15 . . . .**18** F5
Kingston Vale SW15 . . . .**18** E5

Kingstons Ind Est GU12 . .**105** E2
Kingsway Aldershot GU11 . .**104** E1
Blackwater GU17 . . . .**64** E5
Coney Hall BR4 . . . .**63** F7
Mortlake SW14, TW9 . . . .**7** B4
Stanwell TW19 . . . .**13** E7
West Barnes KT3 . . . .**39** C4
Woking GU21 . . . .**69** D1
Kingsway Ave Selsdon CR2 .**62** D1
Woking GU21 . . . .**69** D1
Kingsway Bsns Pk GU21 . . .**70** C5
Kingsway Bsns Pk The
TW12 . . . .**35** F8
Kingsway Rd SM3 . . . .**58** E3
Kingsway Terr KT13 . . . .**53** A2
Kingsway The KT17 . . . .**57** F1
Kingswear House SE23 . . . .**23** C6
Kingswick Cl SL5 . . . .**29** D5
Kingswick Dr SL5 . . . .**29** D5
Kingswood Ave
Beckenham BR2, BR3 . . . . .**44** E5
Hampton TW12 . . . .**16** B2
Hamsey Green CR2 . . . .**81** C4
Hounslow TW3, TW5 . . . .**4** F5
Thornton Heath CR7 . . . .**42** A4
Kingswood Cl
Englefield Green TW20 . . . . .**11** B4
Guildford GU1 . . . .**110** C2
New Malden KT3 . . . .**38** F3
Surbiton KT6 . . . .**37** E2
Weybridge KT13 . . . .**53** B3
Kingswood Ct
❻ Richmond TW10 . . . .**6** F2
Woking GU21 . . . .**69** E3
Kingswood Cty Prim Sch
KT20 . . . .**117** F7
Kingswood Dr
Belmont SM2 . . . .**59** B2
Carshalton SM5 . . . .**40** F1
Dulwich SE19, SE21 . . . .**22** F4
Sutton SM2 . . . .**59** B2
Kingswood Firs GU26 . . . . .**188** C2
Kingswood Golf Course
KT20 . . . .**98** A3
Kingswood Hall of
Residence TW20 . . . .**11** D4
Kingswood House ❸ KT2 . .**18** B2
Kingswood House Sch
KT18 . . . .**76** C6
Kingswood La CR6 . . . .**81** C4
Kingswood Pk GU15 . . . .**97** C6
Kingswood Prim Sch
SE27 . . . .**22** D3
Kingswood Rd
Beckenham BR2 . . . .**44** E6
Merton SW19 . . . .**39** F8
Penge SE20 . . . .**23** C2
Streatham SW2 . . . .**21** E8
Tadworth KT20 . . . .**97** F6
Kingswood Rise TW20 . . . . .**11** D4
Kingswood Sta KT20 . . . .**97** F6
Kingswood Way
Hamsey Green CR2 . . . .**81** C6
Selsdon CR2 . . . .**81** D7
Wallington SM6 . . . .**60** E5
Kingsworth Cl BR3 . . . .**43** E4
Kingsworthy Cl KT1 . . . .**37** F6
Kinloss Rd SM5 . . . .**40** C2
Kinnaird Ave Bromley BR1 . .**24** F2
Chiswick W4 . . . .**7** C7
Kinnaird Cl BR1 . . . .**24** F2
Kinnear Ct SW20 . . . .**39** D8
Kinnersley Wlk RH2 . . . . . .**139** B4
Kinnibrugh Dr RH7 . . . .**165** A1
Kinross Ave Ascot SL5 . . . . .**28** F4
Worcester Park KT4 . . . .**58** A8
Kinross Cl TW16 . . . .**14** F3
Kinross Ct SL5 . . . .**28** F4
Kinross Dr TW16 . . . .**14** F3
Kinsey House SE21 . . . .**22** E4
Kintyre Cl SW16 . . . .**41** F6
Kintyre Ct ❶❼ SW2 . . . .**21** E8
Kinver Rd SE26 . . . .**23** C4
Kipings KT20 . . . .**97** D5
Kipling Cl RH10 . . . .**202** C8
Kipling Ct RH13 . . . .**218** A4
Kipling Dr SW17 . . . .**20** D2
Kipling Way RH19 . . . .**185** C1
Kirby Cl KT19 . . . .**57** F5
Kirby Rd GU21 . . . .**69** D2
Kirby Way KT12 . . . .**35** C3
Kirdford Cl RH11 . . . .**201** A8
Kirk Rise SM1 . . . .**59** B7
Kirkby Cl GU16 . . . .**65** E1
Kirkdale SE26 . . . .**23** B5
Kirkfield GU2 . . . .**109** A4
Kirkgate The ❷ KT17 . . . . . .**76** E6
Kirkham Cl GU47 . . . .**45** D2
Kirkland Ave GU21 . . . .**68** F3
Kirkleas Rd KT6 . . . .**37** E1
Kirklees Rd CR7 . . . .**42** A4
Kirkley Rd SW19 . . . .**40** A8
Kirkly Cl CR2 . . . .**61** E2
Kirkstall Gdns SW2 . . . .**21** E7
Kirkstall Rd SW2 . . . .**21** E7
Kirksted Rd SM4 . . . .**40** B1
Kirkstone Cl GU15 . . . .**66** D4
Kirkstone Way BR1 . . . .**24** E1
Kirrane Cl KT3 . . . .**38** F4
Kirriemuir Gdns GU12 . . . .**106** D3
Kirtley Rd SE26 . . . .**23** E4
Kitchener Rd
Farnborough GU11 . . . .**105** D6
South Norwood CR7 . . . .**42** D6
Kitchenride Cnr KT16 . . . . . .**51** A6
Kites Cl RH11 . . . .**201** C6
Kithurst Cl RH11 . . . .**201** D4
Kitley Gdns SE19 . . . .**42** F8
Kitsmead RH10 . . . .**183** C4

Kitsmead La KT16 . . . . . .50 D8
Kittiwake Cl
Crawley RH11 . . . . .200 D4
Selsdon CR0, CR2 . . . . . .62 E1
Kittiwake Pl SM1 . . . . . . .58 F5
Klondyke Villas GU27 . . . .190 A1
Knaggs House 1 GU11 . . .16 E3
Knapdale SE23 . . . . .23 B6
Knapp Rd TW15 . . . . .13 F4
Knapton Mews SW17 . . . . .21 A2
Knaresborough Dr SW18 . .20 B7
Kneller Gdns TW7 . . . . .5 D1
Kneller Rd New Malden KT3 .5 D1
Twickenham TW2 . . . . . . .5 D1
Knepp Cl RH10 . . . . .202 C6
Knight's Hill SE19, SE27 . .22 B4
Knight's Hill Sq SE27 . . . .22 B4
Knight's Pk KT1 . . . . .37 E6
Knighton Cl Crawley RH10 182 D2
Croydon CR2 . . . . .61 B2
Knighton Park Rd SE26 . . .23 D3
Knighton Rd RH1 . . . . . .140 A7
Knightons La GU8 . . . . . .193 A2
Knights Cl TW20 . . . . . . .12 D2
Knights Ct Kingston u T KT1 .37 E6
Penge BR3 . . . . .43 E8
Knights Pl RH1 . . . . .119 A2
Knights Rd GU15 . . . . . . .125 E7
Knights Way GU15 . . . . . .66 C4
Knightsbridge Cres TW18 .13 B2
Knightsbridge Ho 10 GU1 130 F8
Knightsbridge Ho GU15 . . .65 E7
Knightswood
Bracknell RG12 . . . . . . .27 B1
Woking GU21 . . . . .68 F1
Knightwood Cl RH2 . . . . .139 A7
Knightwood Cres KT3 . . . .38 E3
Knipp Hill KT11 . . . . .73 F6
Knob Hill RH12 . . . . .198 A1
Knobfield RH5 . . . . .154 F8
Knockhundred La GU26 . .207 C8
Knole Cl Crawley RH10 . . .202 D7
Croydon CR0 . . . . .43 C3
Knole Gr RH19 . . . . .185 C3
Knoll Ct SE19 . . . . .22 F3
Knoll Park Rd KT16 . . . . .32 F1
Knoll Quarry GU7 . . . . . .150 E6
Knoll Rd Camberley GU15 . .65 D6
Dorking RH4 . . . . .136 A5
Farncombe GU7 . . . . . . .150 E6
Knoll The Beckenham BR3 .44 B8
Cobham KT11 . . . . .74 A6
Leatherhead KT22 . . . . . .95 C6
Knoll Wood GU7 . . . . . . .150 D6
Knollmead KT4, KT5 . . . . .38 C1
Knollmead Prim Sch KT4 .57 C8
Knolls Cl KT4 . . . . .58 B7
Knolls The KT17 . . . . .77 C3
Knolly's Cl SE27, SW16 . . .22 A5
Knolly's Rd SE27, SW16 . . .22 A5
Knollys Rd GU11 . . . . . . .104 F3
Knott Park House KT22 . . .74 C4
Knowl Hill GU22 . . . . .70 B1
Knowl Hill Sch The GU24 . .87 E5
Knowle Cl RH10 . . . . . . .183 C3
Knowle Dr RH10 . . . . . . .183 B3
Knowle Gdns KT14 . . . . . .70 F6
Knowle Gn TW18 . . . . . . .13 A3
Knowle Gr GU25 . . . . . . .31 C2
Knowle Grove Cl GU25 . . .31 C2
Knowle Hill GU25 . . . . . . .31 C2
Knowle La GU6, RH12 . . . .194 D4
Knowle Lodge CR3 . . . . .101 A4
Knowle Park Ave TW18 . . .13 B3
Knowle Pk KT11 . . . . .73 E4
Knowle Rd TW2 . . . . .16 E7
Knowlton Gn BR2 . . . . . . .44 F4
Knox Rd GU2 . . . . .109 B6
Kohat Cl SW19 . . . . .104 F2
Kohat Rd SW19 . . . . .20 B3
Kohima Cl GU11 . . . . . . .105 B3
Koonowla Cl TN16 . . . . . .83 D4
Kooringa CR6 . . . . .101 B8
Korda Cl TW17 . . . . .33 F6
Kreisel Wlk TW9 . . . . .6 F8
Kristina Ct SM2 . . . . .59 A4
Krooner Rd GU15 . . . . . . .65 B3
Kuala Gdns SW16 . . . . . . .41 F8
Kyle Cl RG12 . . . . .27 B5
Kynaston Ave CR7 . . . . . . .42 C4
Kynaston Cres CR0, CR7 . .42 C4
Kynaston Ct CR3 . . . . . . .100 E2
Kynaston House 7 SW2 . . .21 F7
Kynaston Rd CR0, CR7 . . . .42 C4
Kynersley Cl SM5 . . . . . . .59 F7

L

La Retraite RC Girls Sch
SW12 . . . . .21 C4
Laburnam Ct 12 SW16 . . . .22 A3
Laburnum Ave SM1 . . . . . .59 E7
Laburnum Cl 2
Aldershot GU11 . . . . . . .105 A1
Guildford GU1 . . . . .109 C4
Laburnum Cres TW16 . . . .35 B8
Laburnum Ct CR4 . . . . . . .41 A7
Laburnum Gdns CR0 . . . . .43 D1
Laburnum Gr Brands Hill SL3 .1 B8
Hounslow TW3 . . . . .4 F3
Kingston u T KT3 . . . . . .38 D7

Laburnum Pas 1 GU11 . .105 A1
Laburnum Pl TW20 . . . . . .11 B2
Laburnum Rd
Aldershot GU11 . . . . . . .105 A2
Chertsey KT16 . . . . .33 A1
Epsom KT18 . . . . .76 E6
Heath End GU9 . . . . . . .125 E7
Merton SW19 . . . . .20 C1
Mitcham CR4 . . . . .41 A7
Woking GU22 . . . . .89 D7
Laburnum Way TW19 . . . .13 F7
Laburnums The GU17 . . . .64 B5
Lacey Ave CR5 . . . . .100 A4
Lacey Cl TW20 . . . . .12 C1
Lacey Dr Coulsdon CR5 . .100 B7
Hampton TW12 . . . . .35 F8
Lackford Rd CR5 . . . . .78 F1
Lacock Cl SW19 . . . . .20 C2
Lacy Gn CR5 . . . . .100 A2
Ladas Rd SE27 . . . . .22 C3
Ladbroke Cotts 2 RH1 . .119 A2
Ladbroke Ct 7 RH1 . . . .119 A3
Ladbroke Gr RH1 . . . . . .119 A2
Ladbroke Hurst RH7 . . . .165 A1
Ladbroke Rd Epsom KT18 . .76 D5
Horley RH6 . . . . .161 B5
Redhill RH1 . . . . .119 A3
Ladbrook Rd SE25 . . . . . . .42 D5
Ladderstile Ride
Kingston u T KT2 . . . . . .18 C3
Richmond KT2, TW10 . . .18 B3
Ladlands SE22 . . . . .23 A8
Lady Booth Rd 1 KT1 . . .37 E7
Lady Eleanor Holles Sch
The (Jun Girls) TW12 . . . .16 B3
Lady Eleanor Holles Sch
The (Senior Girls) TW12 .16 B3
Lady Hay KT4 . . . . .57 F8
Lady Margaret Rd
Crawley RH11 . . . . .201 A7
Sunningdale SL5 . . . . . . .29 F2
Lady Margaret Wlk RH11 201 A7
Ladybank RG12 . . . . .27 B1
Ladycross GU8 . . . . .170 E8
Ladycross Mews GU8 . . .170 E8
Ladyegate Cl RH5 . . . . . .136 D8
Ladyegate Rd RH5 . . . . .136 D8
Ladygate Dr GU26 . . . . . .188 A3
Ladygrove CR2 . . . . .62 D2
Ladygrove Dr GU4 . . . . . .110 B6
Ladymead GU1 . . . . .109 C2
Ladymead Cl RH10 . . . . .202 C3
Ladymead Retail Ctr GU1 109 C2
Ladythorpe Cl KT15 . . . . .52 B6
Ladywood Ave GU14 . . . . .84 C4
Ladywood Rd KT6 . . . . . . .57 A8
Laffan's Rd GU11 . . . . . .104 E6
Lafone Ave TW13 . . . . . . .15 C6
Lafone House 11 SW2 . . .21 E8
Lagham Pk RH9 . . . . .142 E6
Lagham Rd RH9 . . . . . . .142 F5
Laglands Cl RH2 . . . . . . .118 C3
Laings Ave CR4 . . . . .40 F7
Laings Cnr CR4 . . . . .40 F8
Lainlock Pl TW3 . . . . .5 B6
Lainson St SW18 . . . . . . .20 A8
Laird Ct GU19 . . . . .47 E1
Lairdale Cl SE21 . . . . .22 C8
Laird Way SE21 . . . . .21 B7
Lake Cl Byfleet KT14 . . . . .71 D7
6 Wimbledon SW19 . . . .19 F3
Lake Cotts GU8 . . . . .169 F4
Lake End Way RG45 . . . . . .45 A4
Lake Gdns Hackbridge SM6 .60 B7
Richmond TW10 . . . . . . .17 B6
Lake House 4 SW27 . . . . .22 B3
Lake La Dockenfield GU10 .166 E6
Horley RH1, RH6 . . . . . .161 C6
Lake Rd Croydon CR0 . . . .62 F8
Frimley GU16 . . . . .86 B6
Ockley RH5 . . . . .177 D6
Virginia Water GU25 . . . .31 B5
Wimbledon SW19 . . . . . .19 F3
Lake Side The GU17 . . . . .64 C4
Lake View RH5 . . . . .136 C4
Lake View Rd
Copthorne RH19 . . . . . .184 C4
Domewood RH19 . . . . . .184 C4
Dormans Park RH19 . . . .185 F5
Dormansland RH19 . . . .185 F5
Lakehall Gdns CR7 . . . . . .42 B4
Lakehall Rd CR7 . . . . .42 B4
Lakehurst Rd KT19 . . . . . .57 E5
Lakeland Dr GU16 . . . . . . .65 E1
Lakeman Ct CR7 . . . . .42 C7
Lakers Lea RH14 . . . . . . .212 F1
Lakers Rise SM7 . . . . .78 E3
Lakes Cl GU4 . . . . .131 B3
Lakeside Beckenham BR3 . .44 B6
3 Bracknell RG42 . . . . . .27 C8
Hackbridge SM6 . . . . . . .60 B6
Horsham RH12 . . . . . . .217 C5
10 Kingston u T KT2 . . . .18 B1
Oatlands Park KT13 . . . . .53 E8
Redhill RH1 . . . . .119 A3
West Ewell KT19 . . . . . . .57 D3
Lakeside Cl Ash Vale GU12 105 F4
Knaphill GU21 . . . . .88 E8
South Norwood SE25 . . . .43 A7
Lakeside Cty Prim Sch
GU16 . . . . .65 F1
Lakeside Dr KT10 . . . . . . .55 C4
Lakeside Est SL3 . . . . .2 A8
Lakeside Gdns GU14 . . . . .84 D1
Lakeside Grange KT13 . . . .53 C7
Lakeside Rd
Ash Vale GU11, GU12 . . .105 F4

Lakeside Rd continued
Colnbrook SL3 . . . . .1 F7
Farnborough GU14 . . . . .105 A2
Lakeview Rd SE27 . . . . . . .22 B3
Laleham C of E Prim Sch
TW18 . . . . .33 C7
Laleham Ct GU21 . . . . . . .69 E3
Laleham Lea Prep Sch
CR8 . . . . .60 E1
Laleham Rd Catford SE6 . . .24 C8
Lewisham SE6 . . . . .24 C8
Littleton TW17 . . . . .34 B3
Shepperton TW17 . . . . . .34 B3
Staines TW18 . . . . .12 F2
Lamb's Bsns Pk RH9 . . . .142 C5
Lamberhurst Rd SE27 . . . .22 A4
Lamberhurst Wlk RH10 . .202 A5
Lambert Ave TW9 . . . . .7 B4
Lambert Cl TN16 . . . . .83 D3
Lambert Cotts RH1 . . . . .120 E2
Lambert Cres GU17 . . . . . .64 C4
Lambert Rd SM7 . . . . .78 B5
Lambert's Pl CR0 . . . . .42 D1
Lambert's Rd KT6 . . . . . . .37 F4
Lambeth Cl RH11 . . . . . . .201 A2
Lambeth Inst Strand Ctr
SW2 . . . . .21 F8
Lambeth Prospect SE19 . .22 D2
Lambeth Rd CR0 . . . . .42 B1
Lambly Hill GU25 . . . . . . .31 D6
Lamborne Cl GU47 . . . . . .45 A1
Lambourn Cl RH19 . . . . .185 E3
Lambourne Ave SW19 . . . .19 F4
Lambourne Cl RH10 . . . . .201 A4
Lambourne Cres GU21 . . .70 D6
Lambourne Dr
Bagshot GU19 . . . . .47 D2
Cobham KT11 . . . . .73 D4
Lambourne Gr
Bracknell RG12 . . . . .27 E7
Kingston u T KT1 . . . . . .38 D7
Lambourne Way GU10 . . .126 F7
Lambs Cres RH12 . . . . . .217 F5
Lambs Farm Cl RH12 . . . .218 A5
Lambs Farm Rd RH12 . . .218 A6
Lambs Green Rd RH12 . . .199 F6
Lambyn Croft RH6 . . . . . .161 C4
Lamerock Rd BR1 . . . . . . .24 F4
Lammas Ave CR4 . . . . . . .41 A7
Lammas Cl GU1 . . . . .151 A6
Lammas Ct
Farncombe GU7 . . . . . . .150 E5
Stanwell TW19 . . . . .12 D5
Lammas Dr TW18 . . . . . . .12 D4
Lammas Gate GU7 . . . . . .150 F6
Lammas Gn SE26 . . . . . . .23 B5
Lammas Hill KT10 . . . . . . .55 A5
Lammas La KT10 . . . . .55 A6
Lammas Rd
Godalming GU7 . . . . . . .151 A5
Richmond TW10 . . . . . . .17 C4
Lammermoor Rd SW12 . . .21 B8
Lampard La GU10 . . . . . .167 E2
Lampeter Cl 4 GU22 . . . .69 E1
Lampton Ave TW5 . . . . .5 B6
Lampton Ct TW5 . . . . .5 B6
Lampton House Cl SW19 . .19 D4
Lampton Park Rd TW3 . . . . .5 B5
Lampton Rd TW3, TW5 . . . .5 B5
Lampton Sch TW5 . . . . .5 A6
Lanain Ct SE12 . . . . .24 F8
Lanark Cl Frimley GU16 . . .65 E2
Horsham RH13 . . . . .217 E2
Lancaster Ave
Farnham GU9 . . . . .146 D8
Mitcham CR4 . . . . .41 E4
West Norwood SE21, SE27 .22 C6
Wimbledon SW19 . . . . . .19 D3
Lancaster Cl
Ash Vale GU12 . . . . .105 F5
Beckenham BR2 . . . . . . .44 F5
Crawley RH10 . . . . .182 D1
Englefield Green TW20 . . .11 D3
Kingston u T KT2 . . . . . .17 D3
Stanwell TW19 . . . . .2 E1
Woking GU21 . . . . .70 A3
Lancaster Cotts 1 TW10 . .6 E1
Lancaster Ct
1 Banstead SM7 . . . . . . .77 F5
1 Belmont SM2 . . . . .59 A3
Epsom KT19 . . . . .57 D1
Stanwell TW19 . . . . .13 E7
Walton-on-T KT12 . . . . . .35 B2
Lancaster Dr
Camberley GU15 . . . . . . .65 D6
East Grinstead RH19 . . . .186 A3
Lancaster Gdns
Kingston u T KT2 . . . . . .17 D3
Wimbledon SW19 . . . . . .19 E3
Lancaster House
Bracknell RG12 . . . . .27 B4
Wandsworth SW18 . . . . . .20 B8
Lancaster Mews 2 TW10 . .6 E1
Lancaster Pk TW10 . . . . . .6 E1
Lancaster Pl Hounslow TW5 .4 D5
Twickenham TW1 . . . . . . .17 A8
Wimbledon SW19 . . . . . .19 D3
Lancaster Rd
South Norwood SE25 . . . .43 A6
Wimbledon SW19 . . . . . .19 E3
Lancaster Way GU14 . . . . .85 C7
Lancelot Cl RH11 . . . . . . .200 E4
Lancelot Ho RH1 . . . . . . .119 A2
Lancer Ct GU11 . . . . .104 E2
Lanchester Dr RG45 . . . . .45 C7
Lancing Cl RH11 . . . . . . .201 A4
Lancing Ct RH12 . . . . . . .218 A4

Lancing Rd Feltham TW13 . .14 F6
Thornton Heath CR0 . . . . .41 F2
Landen Ct RG40 . . . . .25 B4
Landen Pk RH6 . . . . .160 E5
Landgrove Rd SW19 . . . . .20 A3
Landon Way TW15 . . . . . .14 B2
Landscape Rd CR6 . . . . . .101 B8
Landsdowne Cl KT5 . . . . . .57 B8
Landseer Cl Mitcham SW19 40 D8
Sandhurst GU47 . . . . . . .64 C6
Landseer Rd
Cheam SM1, SM2 . . . . . .59 A4
New Malden KT3 . . . . . . .38 D2
Lane Cl KT15 . . . . .52 B5
Lane Ct SW11 . . . . .20 F8
Lane End Epsom KT18 . . . .76 B5
Hambledon GU8 . . . . . . .191 B8
Lane End Dr GU21 . . . . . .68 C2
Lane House RH13 . . . . . . .217 D2
Lane The Chertsey KT16 . . .33 A6
Ifold RH14 . . . . .212 C4
Thorpe GU25 . . . . .31 E6
Thursley GU8 . . . . .169 C4
Lanercost Cl SW2 . . . . . . .22 A6
Lanercost Rd
Crawley RH11 . . . . .201 C5
Streatham SW2 . . . . .22 A6
Lanesborough Prep Sch
GU1 . . . . .109 F1
Lang Cl KT23 . . . . .94 B3
Langaller La KT23 . . . . . . .94 B6
Langborough Rd RG40 . . .25 C5
Langbourne Prim Sch
SE21 . . . . .22 E5
Langbourne Way KT10 . . . .56 A4
Langcroft Cl SM5 . . . . .59 F7
Langdale Ave CR4 . . . . . . .40 F6
Langdale Cl
Farnborough GU14 . . . . .84 E4
Mortlake SW14 . . . . .7 B3
Woking GU21 . . . . .69 C3
Langdale Dr SL5 . . . . .28 E7
Langdale Rd
Crawley RH11 . . . . .200 D4
Thornton Heath CR7 . . . . .42 A5
Langdon Cl GU15 . . . . . . .66 C4
Langdon Pl SW14 . . . . .7 C4
Langdon Rd SM4 . . . . .40 C4
Langdon Wlk SM4 . . . . . . .40 C4
Langham Ct GU7 . . . . . . .150 F4
Langham Ct Farnham GU9 146 C2
12 Twickenham TW1 . . . . .6 C1
Wimbledon SW20 . . . . . .39 C7
Langham Dene CR8 . . . . . .80 B4
Langham Gdns TW10 . . . . .17 C4
Langham House CI TW10 . .17 D4
Langham Pk GU7 . . . . . . .150 F4
Langham Pl Chiswick W4 . . .7 E8
Egham TW20 . . . . .11 F3
Langham Rd
Teddington TW11 . . . . . .17 B2
Wimbledon SW20 . . . . . .39 C8
Langholm Cl SW12 . . . . . .21 D8
Langhorn Dr TW2 . . . . . . .16 E8
Langhurst Cl RH12 . . . . . .198 E4
Langhurst La RH12 . . . . .200 A8
Langhurstwood Rd RH12 198 D3
Langland Gdns CR0 . . . . . .62 F8
Langlands Rise KT19 . . . . .76 C6
Langley Ave
North Cheam KT4, SM3 . . .58 D8
Surbiton KT6 . . . . .37 E1
Langley Cl Guildford GU1 .109 D2
Langley Vale KT18 . . . . . .96 C8
Langley Cres UB3 . . . . .3 F7
Langley Ct RH2 . . . . .118 B2
Langley Dr
Aldershot GU11 . . . . . . .126 A8
Camberley GU15 . . . . . . .65 D6
Crawley RH11 . . . . .201 D8
Langley Gr KT3 . . . . .38 E7
Langley Green Cty Fst
Sch RH11 . . . . .181 D1
Langley Green Cty Mid
Sch RH11 . . . . .201 C8
Langley La RH11 . . . . . . .201 A8
Langley Oaks Ave CR2 . . . .62 A1
Langley Par RH11 . . . . . . .181 C1
Langley Park Golf Course
BR3 . . . . .44 C2
Langley Park Rd
SM1, SM2 . . . . .59 C3
Langley Park Sch for Boys
BR3 . . . . .44 B3
Langley Park Sch for Girls
BR3 . . . . .44 C3
Langley Pl RH11 . . . . .181 C1
Langley Rd Beckenham BR3 .43 E5
Isleworth TW7 . . . . .5 F5
Merton SW19 . . . . .40 A8
Selsdon CR2 . . . . .62 D2
Staines TW18 . . . . .12 F2
Surbiton KT6 . . . . .37 E2
Langley Vale Rd
KT18, KT21 . . . . .76 E1
Langley Way BR4 . . . . .44 E2
Langley Wlk
Crawley RH11 . . . . .181 B1
Woking GU22 . . . . .89 E8
Langmans Way GU21 . . . . .68 E3
Langmead St SE27 . . . . . .22 C4
Langport Ct KT12 . . . . . . .35 C1
Langridge Dr RH19 . . . . .205 E8
Langridge House RH12 . .217 B2
Langridge Mews TW12 . . .15 F2
Langroyd Rd SW17 . . . . . .20 F6
Langshott RH6 . . . . .161 C4
Langshott Cl KT15 . . . . . . .70 F8

Langshott Cty Inf Sch
RH6 . . . . .161 C3
Langshott La RH6 . . . . . .161 C4
Langsmead RH7 . . . . .163 E8
Langstone Rd RH10 . . . . .202 C3
Langthorne Ct SE6 . . . . . .24 C4
Langton Ave KT17 . . . . . . .76 F8
Langton Cl Addlestone KT15 52 B7
Woking GU21 . . . . .68 F2
Langton Dr GU35 . . . . . . .187 A7
Langton House 5 SW16 . . .21 C4
Langton Pl SW18 . . . . .20 A7
Langton Rd KT8 . . . . .36 C5
Langton Rise SE22, SE23 . .23 B8
Langton Way Egham TW20 .12 C2
South Croydon CR0 . . . . .61 E6
Langwood Chase TW11 . . .17 C2
Lanherne House 5 SW19 .19 D1
Lanigan Dr TW3 . . . . .5 B2
Lankton Cl BR3 . . . . .44 C8
Lansbury Ave TW14 . . . . . .4 B1
Lansbury Rd RH11 . . . . . .201 B1
Lansdell Rd CR4 . . . . .41 A7
Lansdown GU1 . . . . .110 A1
Lansdown Cl
Horsham RH12 . . . . .218 B6
Knaphill GU21 . . . . .88 F8
Walton-on-T KT12 . . . . . .35 C1
Lansdowne Cl
Twickenham TW1 . . . . . . .16 F7
Wimbledon SW20 . . . . . .19 D1
Lansdowne Copse 1 KT4 .58 A8
Lansdowne Ct Purley CR8 . .61 B1
2 Worcester Park KT4 . . . .58 A8
Lansdowne Hill SE27 . . . . .22 B5
Lansdowne Pl SE19 . . . . . .22 F1
Lansdowne Rd
Aldershot GU11 . . . . . . .105 A1
Croydon CR0 . . . . .42 D1
Frimley GU16 . . . . .86 A8
Hounslow TW3 . . . . .5 B4
Purley CR8 . . . . .80 A7
Staines TW18 . . . . .13 B1
West Ewell KT19 . . . . . . .57 D3
Wimbledon SW19, SW20 . .19 C1
Lansdowne Wood Cl 11
SE27 . . . . .22 B5
Lanswood Ct KT4 . . . . . . .58 A8
Lantern Cl SW20 . . . . .39 D8
Lanyon Cl RH12 . . . . .218 A6
Lanyon Mews RH12 . . . . .218 A6
Lapse Wood Wlk SE22 . . . .23 B7
Lapwing Cl Horsham RH13 217 F3
Selsdon CR0, CR2 . . . . . .62 E1
Lapwing Ct KT6 . . . . .57 A7
Lapwing Gr GU4 . . . . .110 D3
Lara Cl KT9 . . . . .56 E3
Larbert Rd SW16 . . . . . . .21 C1
Larby Pl KT17 . . . . .57 E1
Larch Ave Ascot SL5 . . . . .29 C4
Guildford GU1 . . . . .109 C4
Wokingham RG41 . . . . . .25 A7
Larch Cl Camberley GU15 . .65 E8
Kingswood KT20 . . . . . . .98 C6
Reigate RH1 . . . . .139 C7
Upper Tooting SW12 . . . .21 B6
Warlingham CR6 . . . . . . .101 E8
Larch Cres KT19 . . . . .57 B4
Larch End RH12 . . . . .217 B4
Larch Rd GU35 . . . . .187 B6
Larch Tree Way CR0 . . . . . .63 A7
Larch Way GU14 . . . . .84 C3
Larches Ave SW14 . . . . . . .7 D3
Larches The
Horsham RH12 . . . . .218 C6
Woking GU21 . . . . .69 E3
Larches Way
Blackwater GU17 . . . . . . .64 B5
Crawley Down RH10 . . . .204 C8
Larchvale Ct 4 SM2 . . . . .59 B3
Larchwood 5 RG12 . . . . .27 F5
Larchwood Cl SM7 . . . . . .77 E4
Larchwood Dr TW20 . . . . .11 B2
Larchwood Glade GU15 . . .66 A7
Larchwood Rd GU21 . . . . .88 D8
Larcombe Ct CR0 . . . . .61 F6
Larges Bridge Dr RG12 . . .27 D6
Larges La RG12 . . . . .27 C7
Largewood Ave KT6 . . . . . .57 A8
Lark Ave TW18 . . . . .12 F5
Lark Rise Crawley RH11 . .201 C8
East Horsley KT24 . . . . .112 E4
Larkbere Rd SE26 . . . . . . .23 E4
Larkfield Cobham KT11 . . .73 A6
Ewhurst GU6 . . . . .175 E4
Larkfield Cl Coney Hall BR2 .63 F8
Farnham GU9 . . . . .124 F2
Larkfield Ct RH6 . . . . . . .162 A3
Larkfield Rd Farnham GU9 124 F2
Richmond TW9 . . . . .6 E3
Larkhall Cl KT12 . . . . .54 C4
Larkham Cl TW13 . . . . . . .14 E5
Larkin Cl CR5 . . . . .79 F2
Larkins Rd RH6 . . . . .181 D2
Larks Way GU21 . . . . .68 C3
Larksfield
Englefield Green TW20 . . .11 C1
Horley RH6 . . . . .161 B4
Larkspur Cl GU11 . . . . . .126 A7
Larkspur Ct SM6 . . . . .60 B3
Larkspur Way
Dorking RH5 . . . . .136 D4
West Ewell KT19 . . . . . . .57 C5
Larkswood Cl GU47 . . . . . .45 A1
Larkswood Dr RG45 . . . . .45 B5

Lascombe La GU3 ....128 B4
Lashmere Copthorne RH10 183 D3
Cranleigh GU6 ....174 B3
Laski Ct RH11 ....201 B1
Lasswade Ct KT16 ....32 F2
Lasswade Rd KT16 ....32 F2
Lastingham Ct TW18 ......13 A2
Latchmere Cl KT2, TW10 ...17 F2
Latchmere Jun & Inf Schs
KT2 ....17 F2
Latchmere La
Kingston u T KT2, TW10 ..17 F3
Richmond KT2, TW10 .....17 F3
Latchmere Rd KT2 ....17 F2
Latchwood La GU10 .....146 D5
Lateward Rd TW8 ....6 D8
Latham Ave GU16 ....65 E2
Latham Cl Biggin Hill TN16 .83 C3
5 Twickenham TW1 .....17 A8
Latham Rd TW1 ....16 F8
Latham's Way CR0 ....60 F8
Lathwood House **6** SE26 .23 B3
Latimer RG12 ....27 B1
Latimer Cl Crawley RH11 ..181 D1
North Cheam KT4 ....58 B6
Woking GU21 ....70 B3
Latimer House GU7 .....150 E3
Latimer Rd
Croydon CR0, CR9 ....61 B7
Godalming GU7 ....150 E4
Teddington TW11 ....16 F3
Wimbledon SW19 ....20 B2
Wokingham RG41 ....25 B5
Latton Cl Esher KT10 ......55 B6
Walton-on-T KT12 ....35 E2
Latymer Cl KT13 ....53 C6
Laud Dr RH10 ....202 D5
Laud Rd CR0, CR9 ....61 C7
Laud Way RG40 ....25 E6
Lauder Cl GU16 ....65 E2
Lauderdale La GU4 ....84 D3
Lauderdale Dr TW10 ......17 D5
Lauderdale House TW18 ..12 F3
Laughton Rd RH12 ....217 F5
Launceston Ct CR7 ....42 A3
Laundry La GU47 ....64 E5
Laundry Rd GU1 ....130 C8
Laundry Way RH5 ....178 C5
Lauradale RG12 ....27 A5
Laurel Ave
Englefield Green TW20 ...11 B3
Twickenham TW1 ....16 F7
Laurel Cl Camberley GU15 .65 D4
Crawley RH10 ....202 A3
Farnborough GU14 ....84 C3
Poyle SL3 ....1 E1
Upper Tooting SW17 .....20 E3
Laurel Cres Croydon CR0 ..63 A7
Sheerwater GU21 ....70 D6
Laurel St SE25 ....42 E4
Laurel Dene RH19 ......185 F1
Laurel Dr RH8 ....122 F4
Laurel Gdns
Aldershot GU11 ....126 A7
Hounslow TW4 ....4 C3
Woodham KT15 ....52 B1
Laurel Gr Forest Hill SE26 .23 C4
Penge SE20 ....23 C1
Rowledge GU10 ....145 A5
Wrecclesham GU10 .....146 A5
Laurel House SM4 ....40 B4
Laurel Manor SM2 ....59 C3
Laurel Rd Teddington TW12 .16 D3
Wimbledon SW20 ....39 B8
Laurel Wlk RH13 ....217 F1
Laureldene GU3 ....107 B1
Laurels The Banstead SM7 ..77 F2
Cobham KT11 ....73 E4
Crawley RH10 ....182 A1
Heath End GU9 ....125 F7
6 Oatlands Park KT13 ...53 D7
Laurier Rd CR0 ....42 F2
Lauriston Cl GU21 ....68 D2
Lauriston Rd SW19 ....19 D2
Lauser Rd TW19 ....13 C8
Laustan Cl GU1 ....110 C2
Lavant Cl RH11 ....200 F5
Lavender Ave Mitcham CR4 .40 F8
North Cheam SM4, SM3 ..58 C7
Lavender Cl
Caterham CR3 ....100 C2
Coulsdon CR5 ....99 C8
Redhill RH1 ....140 B4
Wallington SM5 ....60 B6
Lavender Ct KT8 ....36 B6
Lavender Gr CR4 ....40 E8
Lavender La GU10 ......145 F4
Lavender Park Rd KT14 ...71 A6
Lavender Pk SL5 ....28 C6
Lavender Rd
Carshalton SM1 ....59 D6
Thornton Heath CR0 ......41 F3
Wallington SM5 ....60 A6
West Ewell KT19 ....57 B4
Woking GU22 ....70 B3
Lavender Vale SM6 ....60 D4
Lavender Way CR0 ....43 D3
Lavengro Rd SE27 ....22 C6
Laverock Sch RH8 ......122 E7
Laverstoke Gdns SW15 ..19 A8
Lavington Cl RH11 .....201 A4
Lavington Rd CR0 ....60 F7
Lavinia Ct BR1 ....24 E1
Lawbrook La
Gomshall GU5 ....154 C7

Lawbrook La continued
Peaslake GU5 ....154 C7
Lawday Link GU9 ....125 A7
Lawday Pl GU9 ....125 A7
Lawday Place La GU9 ....125 A7
Lawdon Gdns CR0 ....61 A6
Lawford Cl SM6 ....60 E2
Lawford Gdns CR8 ....80 C3
Lawford Rd W4 ....7 C7
Lawford's Hill Cl GU3 ....88 C3
Lawford's Hill Rd GU3 ...88 C3
Lawman Ct **2** TW9 ......6 F6
Lawn Cl KT3 ....38 E7
Lawn Cres TW9 ....7 A5
Lawn Rd Beckenham BR3 ..23 F1
Guildford GU2 ....130 C6
Lawns Rd RH12 ....195 A3
Lawns The Belmont SM2 ..58 E3
Farnborough GU14 ....84 E3
Milford GU8 ....149 F1
North Ascot SL5 ....28 D6
Purley CR8 ....61 B1
South Norwood SE19 ....42 D8
1 Wimbledon SW19 .....19 F3
Lawnsmead Cotts GU5 ..152 B7
Lawnwood Ct GU7 ......151 A5
Lawrence Ave KT3 ....38 E2
Lawrence Cl
Guildford GU4 ....110 B6
Wokingham RG40 ....25 D6
Lawrence Cres GU20 .....48 D4
Lawrence Est TW4 ....4 C3
Lawrence Gr RG42 ....26 D8
Lawrence La RH3 ....117 B3
Lawrence Lodge GU15 ...65 D7
Lawrence Rd
Hampton TW12 ....15 F1
Hounslow TW4 ....4 C3
Richmond TW10 ....17 C4
South Norwood SE25 ....42 F5
Lawrence Way GU15 ......64 F4
Lawrence Weaver Cl SM4 .40 A3
Lawrie Park Ave SE26 ....23 B3
Lawrie Park Cres SE26 ...23 B3
Lawrie Park Gdns SE26 ..23 B3
Lawrie Park Rd
Forest Hill SE19, SE26 ...23 C3
Penge SE19, SE26 ....23 C3
Laws Cl RH11 ....200 E5
Laws Terr GU11 ....105 C3
Lawson Cl SW19 ....19 D5
Lawson Ct **18** KT6 ....37 D2
Lawson Way SL5 ....30 B3
Lawson-Hunt Ind Pk
RH12 ....216 C4
Laxton Cl CR7 ....42 C5
Laxton Gdns RH1 ....119 D7
Layard Rd CR7 ....42 D7
Layburn Cres SL3 ....1 B8
Layhams Rd
Coney Hall BR2, BR4, CR6 .63 F5
West Wickham BR4 ....63 F1
Layton Cres CR0 ....61 B5
Layton Ct KT13 ....53 B6
Layton Pl TW9 ....7 A6
Layton Rd TW3 ....5 B3
Layton's La TW16 ....34 F7
Le Chateau CR0 ....61 D7
Le Marchant Rd
GU15, GU16 ....65 F3
Le May Cl RH6 ....161 A4
Le Personne Rd CR3 ....100 D5
Lea Cl Ash GU12 ....106 A1
Crawley RH11 ....200 F5
Farnham GU9 ....126 A6
Lea Croft RG45 ....45 B6
Lea Ct GU9 ....125 F7
Lea Rd Beckenham BR3 ...44 A7
Camberley GU15 ....65 B2
Lea The TW20 ....12 C1
Lea Way GU12 ....105 F3
Leach Gr KT22 ....95 C5
Leachcroft Ave SW12 .....20 F8
Leachcroft Cl Kenley CR8 ..80 C3
Staines TW18 ....13 B4
Leaf Cl KT7, KT8 ....36 E4
Leaf Gr SE27, SW16 ......22 A3
Leafield Cl
South Norwood SW16 ....22 B2
Woking GU21 ....69 B1
Leafield Copse RG12 .....27 F5
Leafield Rd
Merton SW19, SW20 .....39 F6
Sutton SM1 ....59 A8
Leafy Way CR0 ....61 F8
Leamington Ave SM4 .....39 F5
Leamington Cl TW3 ....5 C2
Leamington Ct **4** SE26 ..23 A5
Leander Ct **5** KT6 ....37 D2
Leander Rd **4**
Streatham SW2 ....21 F8
Thornton Heath CR7 ......41 F5
Leapale La GU1 ....130 D8
Leapale Rd GU1 ....130 D8
Leas Cl KT9 ....56 F3
Leas La GU1 ....81 D1
Leas Rd Guildford GU1 ...130 C8
Warlingham CR6 ....81 D1
Leather Cl CR4 ....41 A7
Leatherhead By-Pass
Rd KT22 ....95 D5
Leatherhead General
Hospl KT22 ....95 C5
Leatherhead Golf Club
KT22 ....75 A3

Leatherhead Ind Est KT22 .95 A6
Leatherhead Mus of
Local History KT22 ......95 B5
Leatherhead Rd
Ashstead KT21, KT22 ....95 E7
Chessington KT9 ....75 C6
Fetcham KT22, KT23 .....94 C2
Great Bookham KT22, KT23 .94 A3
Oxshott KT22 ....74 D4
Leatherhead Sta KT22 ...95 A6
Leaveland Cl BR3 ....44 A5
Leaves Gn RG12 ....27 D3
Leaves Green Cres BR2 ..83 C8
Leaves Green Rd BR2 ....83 D8
Leavesden Rd KT13 ......53 B5
Leazes Ave CR3 ....100 A4
Lebanon Ave TW13 ....15 D3
Lebanon Cl **11** TW1 .....17 B8
Lebanon Dr KT11 ....74 A6
Lebanon Gdns TN16 .....83 D2
Lebanon Pk TW1 ....17 B8
Lebanon Rd CR0 ....42 E1
Lechford Rd RH6 ....161 A1
Leckford Rd SW18 ....20 C7
Leckhampton Pl SW2 ....22 A8
Leconfield Ave SW13, SW15 .7 F4
Ledbury Pl CR0 ....61 C6
Ledbury Rd
Croydon CR0, CR9 ....61 D6
Reigate RH2 ....118 A3
Ledger Cl GU1 ....110 B3
Ledger Dr KT15 ....51 F4
Ledgers Rd CR6 ....82 B1
Ledrington Rd SE19 ......23 A2
Lee Ct GU11 ....126 C8
Lee Hollow GU5 ....133 C1
Lee Rd Aldershot GU11 ..104 C2
Merton SW19 ....40 B8
Lee St RH6 ....160 E4
Leech La KT18, KT22 .....96 C1
Leechcroft Rd SM6 ......60 A7
Leechpool La RH12, RH13 218 A4
Leechpool Lane Cty Prim
Sch RH13 ....218 A4
Leechpool & Owlbeech
Nature Reserve RH13 ..218 C4
Leeds Ct Carshalton SM5 .59 F7
Catford SE6 ....24 B5
Leegate Cl GU21 ....69 B3
Leehurst GU8 ....149 F1
Lees The CR0 ....62 F8
Leeson House **8** TW1 ....17 B8
Leeward Gdns SW19 .....19 F2
Leewood Way KT24 .....113 D8
Legge Cres GU11 ....104 E1
Legion Ct SM4 ....40 A3
Legrace Ave TW4, TW5 ....4 C5
Legsheath La RH19 .....205 D1
Leicester RG12 ....27 E2
Leicester Ave CR4 ....41 E5
Leicester Cl KT4 ....58 C6
Leicester House **2** KT7 ..37 A2
Leicester Rd CR0 ....42 E2
Leigh Cl Addlestone KT15 ..51 F3
New Malden KT3 ....38 C5
Leigh Cres CR0 ....63 C3
Leigh Ct CR0 ....82 E8
Leigh Hill Rd KT11 ....73 D5
Leigh House **4** KT2 ......18 B2
Leigh La GU9 ....146 E8
Leigh Orchard Cl SW16 ..21 F5
Leigh Pl KT11 ....73 C5
Leigh Place La RH9 .....121 E3
Leigh Place Rd RH2 ....138 A3
Leigh Rd Betchworth RH3 .137 C2
Cobham KT11 ....73 B5
Isleworth TW3 ....5 D3
Leigham Ave SW16 ......21 E5
Leigham Court Rd
SE27, SW16, SW21 .....22 A4
Leigham Dr TW7 ....5 E7
Leigham Hall **3** SW16 ..21 E5
Leigham Hall Par **2** SW16 21 E5
Leigham Vale
SE27, SW16, SW2 ......22 A6
Leighlands RH10 ....202 C8
Leighton Gdns
Sanderstead CR2 ....81 B6
Thornton Heath CR0 .....42 B1
Leighton House **7** KT6 ...37 E3
Leighton St CR0 ....42 B1
Leighton Way KT18 ......76 D5
Leinster Ave SW14 ....7 C3
Leisure La KT14 ....71 B7
Leith Cl RG45 ....45 A7
Leith Gr RH5 ....157 D4
Leith Hill Rd
Abinger Common RH5 ...155 F5
Wotton RH5 ....156 A4
Leith Hill Tower RH5 ....156 B3
Leith House Reigate RH2 .139 A6
16 Streatham SW2 ....21 F8
Leith Lea RH5 ....157 D4
Leith Rd Beare Green RH5 .157 D4
Ewell KT17 ....76 E7
Leith Towers **11** SM2 ....59 B3
Leith Vale Cotts RH5 ....177 A2
Leith View RH5 ....136 C3
Leith View Rd RH12 ....218 A5
Lelithcote Gdns SW16 ...21 F4
Leithcote Path SW16 ....21 F5
Lela Ave TW4, TW5 ....4 C5
Lemington Gr RG12 ......27 B2
Lemmington Way RH12 ..218 A7
Lemon's Farm Rd RH5 ...155 F4
Lendore Rd GU16 ....85 D8
Lenelby Rd KT6 ....38 A1

Leney Cl RG40 ....25 D8
Lenham Rd
South Norwood CR7 .....42 D7
Sutton SM1 ....59 C5
Lennard Ave BR4 ....63 E8
Lennard Cl BR4 ....63 E8
Lennard Rd
Penge BR3, SE20, SE26 ..23 E2
Thornton Heath CR0 .....42 C1
Lennox Ct **13** RH1 ......119 A2
Lennox Gdns CR0 ....61 B6
Lenten Cl GU5 ....133 D1
Lenton Rise TW9 ....6 E4
Leo Ct **4** TW8 ....6 D7
Leof Cres SE6 ....24 B3
Leominster Rd SM4 ......40 C4
Leominster Wlk SM4 ....40 C4
Leonard Ave SM4 ....40 C4
Leonard Cl GU16 ....85 D8
Leonard Rd CR4, SW16 ..41 C8
Leonardslee Ct RH10 ...202 B3
Leopold Ave
Farnborough GU14 ......85 B5
Wimbledon SW19 ....19 F3
Leopold Rd Crawley RH11 .201 C6
Wimbledon SW19 ....19 F4
Leopold Terr SW19 ......20 A3
Leppington RG12 ....27 B2
Leret Way KT22 ....95 B6
Lesbourne Rd RH2 .....139 B8
Lescombe Ct SE23 ....23 E5
Lescombe Rd SE23, SE6 ..23 E5
Lesley Ct **8** SM6 ....60 B6
Leslie Gdns SM2 ....59 A3
Leslie Gr CR0 ....42 E1
Leslie Park Rd CR0 ......42 E1
Leslie Rd Chobham GU24 ..49 E1
Dorking RH4 ....115 D1
Lessing St SE23 ....23 E8
Lessingham Ave SW17 ...21 A4
Lessness Rd SM4 ....40 C4
Lestor Ct TW7 ....5 F4
Letchworth Ave TW14 ...14 F8
Letchworth Cl RH11 ....200 E3
Letchworth St SW17 .....20 F4
Letcombe Sq RG12 ......27 E5
Levana Cl SW19 ....19 E7
Levehurst House SE27 ...22 C3
Levendale Rd SE23, SE6 ..23 F6
Leveret Cl CR0 ....82 D8
Leveret La RH11 ....201 B8
Leverkusen Rd RG12 .....27 B6
Levern Dr GU9 ....125 C6
Leverson St SW16 ....21 C2
Levett House **1** SW16 ...21 C2
Levett Rd KT22 ....95 B7
Levylsdene GU1 ....110 D1
Lewes Cl RH10 ....202 C6
Lewes Ct **3** CR4 ....40 F6
Lewes House RH2 ......139 B5
Lewes Rd
Ashurst Wood RH19 ....206 C6
East Grinstead RH19 ...206 C6
Forest Row RH18 ....206 F2
Lewesdon Cl **13** SW19 ..19 D7
Lewin Ct SW16 ....21 E2
Lewin Rd Mortlake SW14 ..7 D4
Streatham SW16 ....21 D2
Lewins Rd KT18 ....76 B5
Lewis Cl KT15 ....52 C6
Lewis Rd Mitcham CR4 ...40 E7
18 Richmond TW10 ......6 D2
Sutton SM1 ....59 B6
Lewis Sports & L Ctr SE19 42 F8
Lewisham Cl RH11 .....201 C2
Lewisham Way GU47 .....45 D2
Lexden Rd CR4 ....41 D5
Lexington Ct CR8 ....80 C8
Lexton Gdns SW12 ......21 D7
Ley Rd GU14 ....85 A8
Leybourne Pk TW9 ....7 A6
Leybourne Ave KT14 .....71 F6
Leybourne Cl Byfleet KT14 .71 F6
Crawley RH11 ....201 C1
Leyburn Gdns CR0 ......61 E8
Leycester Cl GU20 ....48 B6
Leyfield KT4 ....38 F1
Leylands La TW19 ....2 A2
Leylands Rd
Abinger Common RH5 ...155 F5
Wotton RH5 ....156 A6
Leys Rd KT22 ....74 D7
Leys The KT22 ....54 E6
Leyside RG45 ....45 A5
Leyton Rd SW19 ....20 C1
Liberty Ave SW19 ....40 D8
Liberty Hall Rd KT15 ....52 A6
Liberty La KT15 ....52 B5
Liberty Mid Sch CR4 ....40 E7
Liberty Rise KT15 ....52 A4
Licensed Victuallers Sch
SL5 ....28 C6
Lichfield Ct
Kingston u T KT6 ....37 E4
Richmond TW9 ....6 E3
Lichfield Gdns TW10, TW9 ..6 E2
Lichfield Rd Hounslow TW4 ..4 C4
Richmond TW9 ....6 F6
Lichfield Terr **1** TW9 ....6 E2
Lichfield Way CR2 ....62 D2
Lichfields RG12 ....27 E7
Lickfolds Rd GU10 .....145 E3
Liddel Way SL5 ....28 E5
Liddell Ct **3** CR8 ....80 A7
Liddington Hall Dr GU3 .108 E4
Liddington Hall Est GU3 108 E4
Liddington New Rd GU3 .108 E4

Lidiard Rd SW18 ....20 C6
Lido Rd GU1 ....109 D2
Lidsey Cl RH10 ....202 C6
Lidstone Cl GU21 ....69 B2
Lightwater Ctry Pk GU18 .47 F1
Lightwater Meadow GU18 .67 B8
Lightwater Rd GU18 .....67 C8
Lightwater Village Cty Inf
Sch GU18 ....48 A1
Lightwood RG12 ....27 D3
Lilac Ave GU22 ....89 D7
Lilac Cl GU1 ....109 C5
Lilac Gdns CR0 ....63 A7
Lilian Rd CR4, SW16 .....41 C8
Lilian Rolfe House **5**
SE27 ....22 D4
Lilleshall Rd SM4 ....40 D3
Lilley Dr KT20 ....98 B5
Lillie Rd TN16 ....83 D1
Lilliput Childrens Ctr
KT4 ....54 C5
Lily Hill Dr RG12 ....27 E7
Lily Hill Rd RG12 ....27 E7
Lilyfields Chase GU6 ...175 E4
Lime Ave Camberley GU15 .66 A6
Horsham RH12 ....218 A4
Winkfield SL4 ....9 F5
Lime Cl Carshalton SM5 ..59 F8
Copthorne RH10 ....183 B3
Crawley RH11 ....181 C1
Reigate RH2 ....139 B6
West Clandon GU4 .....111 B7
Lime Cres TW16 ....35 C7
Lime Ct CR4 ....40 D7
Lime Gr Addlestone KT15 .52 A6
Guildford GU1 ....109 B5
Kingston u T KT3 ....38 E6
Twickenham TW1 ....6 A1
Warlingham CR6 ....81 E1
West Clandon GU4 .....111 B7
Woking GU22 ....89 E6
Lime Lodge **3** TW16 ....14 F1
Lime Meadow Ave CR2 ...81 B6
Lime St GU11 ....104 F2
Lime St Rdbt GU11 ....104 F2
Lime Tree Ave KT10, KT7 .36 E1
Lime Tree Cl KT23 ....94 A3
Lime Tree Ct KT21 ....75 E1
Lime Tree Gr CR0 ....62 F7
Lime Tree Rd TW5 ....5 B6
Lime Tree Wlk
Coney Hall BR4 ....63 F6
Thorpe GU25 ....31 E5
Lime Wlk RG12 ....27 C5
Limebush Cl KT15 ....52 C2
Limecroft Cl KT19 ....57 D3
Limecroft Rd GU21 ......68 B2
Limekiln Pl SE19 ....22 E1
Limerick Cl Bracknell RG42 .27 A8
Streatham SW12 ....21 C8
Limerick Ct **11** SW12 ....21 C8
Limerick House GU22 ....70 A1
Limes Ave Barnes SW13 ...7 F7
Carshalton SM5 ....40 F1
Croydon CR0, CR9 ....61 A7
Horley RH6 ....161 B1
Penge SE20 ....23 B1
Limes Ct TW15 ....14 A3
Limes Ct BR3 ....44 B7
Limes Field Rd SW14 .....7 E4
Limes Rd Beckenham BR3 ..44 B7
Egham TW20 ....11 F3
Farnborough GU14 ......84 C5
Thornton Heath CR0 .....42 D2
Weybridge KT13 ....53 A6
Limes The Belmont SM2 ..59 A4
Dormans Park RH19 ....185 A5
East Molesey KT8 ....36 B5
Woking GU21 ....70 A3
Woking, Horsell GU21 ...69 D4
Limetree Cl SW2 ....21 F7
Limetree Pl CR4 ....41 B8
Limetree Wlk **2** SW17 ..21 A3
Limeway Terr RH4 .....115 A1
Limewood Cl GU21 ......88 D7
Limpsfield Ave
Putney SW19 ....19 D6
Thornton Heath CR7 ....41 F4
Limpsfield CE Inf Sch
RH8 ....123 C6
Limpsfield Chart Golf
Club RH8 ....123 C6
Limpsfield Grange Sch
RH8 ....123 A8
Limpsfield Rd
Chelsham CR6 ....102 B8
Hamsey Green CR2, CR6 ..81 C3
Sanderstead CR2, CR6 ...81 C3
Warlingham CR2, CR6 ...81 C3
Linacre Dr
Cranleigh GU6, RH12 ...195 C4
Ewhurst GU6, RH12 ....195 C4
Lince La RH4 ....135 D6
Linchmere Pl RH11 ....201 A7
Linchmere Rd
Lewisham SE12 ....24 F8
Linchmere SE27 ....207 C4
Linchmere, Hammer GU27 207 D5
Lincoln Ave
Twickenham TW2 ....16 C6
Wimbledon SW19 ....19 D5
Lincoln Cl Ash Vale GU12 105 F5
Crawley RH10 ....201 E3
Croydon SE25 ....43 B3
Frimley GU15 ....66 B4
Horley RH6 ....161 A2
Lincoln Ct TW12 ....15 F3
Lincoln Dr GU22 ....70 D3

Lincoln Lodge BR3 ....44 B7
Lincoln Rd Croydon SE25 ...43 B6
Dorking RH4 ....115 C1
Feltham TW13 ....15 F5
Guildford GU2 ....108 F3
Kingston u T KT3 ....38 C6
Mitcham CR4 ....41 E4
North Cheam KT4 ....39 B1
Lincoln Terr 4 SM2 ....59 A3
Lincoln Way TW16 ....34 E8
Lincoln Wlk KT19 ....57 D1
Lincolns Mead RH7 .....164 C3
Lincombe Rd BR1 ....24 F5
Lind Rd SM1 ....59 C5
Linda Ct KT9 ....56 D6
Lindale SW19 ....19 E6
Lindale Cl GU25 ....30 F5
Lindbergh Rd SM6 ....60 E3
Linden 3 RG12 ....27 F4
Linden Ave Coulsdon CR5 ..79 B3
East Grinstead RH19 ......185 C2
Hounslow TW3 ....5 B2
Thornton Heath CR7 ....42 B5
Linden Bridge Sch KT4 ...57 E7
Linden Cl Crawley RH10 ..202 A3
Horsham RH12 ....217 E4
Tadworth KT20 ....97 D7
Thames Ditton KT7 ....37 A2
Woodham KT15 ....71 A8
Linden Cres KT1 ....37 F7
Linden Ct Beckenham BR3 ..44 B6
Camberley GU15 ....65 F7
Englefield Green TW20 .....11 B2
Leatherhead KT22 ....95 B6
Penge SE20 ....23 B1
Linden Dr CR3 ....100 C3
Linden Gdns KT22 ....95 C6
Linden Gr Kingston u T KT3 .38 E6
Penge SE20 ....23 C2
Teddington TW11 ....16 F3
Walton-on-T KT12 ....53 F8
Warlingham CR6 ....81 E1
Linden Lea RH4 ....136 C5
Linden Leas BR4 ....63 D8
Linden Lodge Sch SW19 ..19 E7
Linden Pit Path KT22 .....95 B6
Linden Pl Ewell KT17 ......76 E7
Mitcham CR4 ....40 E5
Staines TW18 ....13 A4
Linden Rd Guildford GU1 ..109 D1
Hampton TW12 ....36 A8
Headley Down GU35 ......187 C5
Leatherhead KT22 ....95 B6
Weybridge KT13 ....53 C2
Linden Way
Send Marsh GU23 ....90 F3
Shepperton TW17 ....34 C4
Wallington CR8 ....60 C1
Woking GU22 ....89 F6
Lindenhill Rd RG42 ....26 F8
Lindens Cl KT24 ....113 E7
Lindens The Chiswick W4 ...7 D6
Copthorne RH10 ....183 B3
Farnham GU9 ....125 D1
New Addington CR0 ....63 C4
Lindfield Gdns GU1 ......109 F2
Lindfield Rd CR0 ....42 F3
Lindgren Wlk RH11 ......201 B1
Lindisfarne Rd SW20 ......19 A1
Lindley Ct Teddington KT1 ..37 C8
West Byfleet KT14 ....71 B7
Lindley Pl TW9 ....7 A6
Lindley Rd
Tyler's Green RH9 ....121 C5
Walton-on-T KT12 ....54 D7
Lindon Bennett Sch TW13 15 D3
Lindores Rd SM5 ....40 C1
Lindsay Cl Chessington KT9 .56 E3
Epsom KT18 ....76 C6
Stanwell TW19 ....2 D2
Lindsay Dr TW17 ....34 D3
Lindsay Rd Hampton TW12 .16 B4
North Cheam KT4 ....58 B8
Woodham KT15 ....71 B8
Lindsey Cl CR4, SW16 .....41 E5
Lindsey Gdns TW14 ....14 D8
Lindum Dene GU11 ......105 A1
Lindum Rd TW11 ....17 C1
Lindums The BR3 ....23 F2
Lindway SE27 ....22 B3
Linersh Dr GU5 ....152 A6
Linersh Wood GU5 ......152 A6
Linersh Wood Cl GU5 ...152 B5
Lines Rd GU11 ....105 D7
Linfield Cl KT12 ....54 B5
Linford Ct CR4 ....40 E8
Ling Cres GU35 ....187 B6
Ling Dr GU18 ....66 F7
Ling's Coppice SE21 ......22 D6
Lingfield Ave KT1, KT5 .....37 F5
Lingfield Common Rd
RH7 ....164 C6
Lingfield Ct SW19 ....19 D2
Lingfield Dr RH10 ....202 E7
Lingfield Gdns CR5 ......100 B8
Lingfield Hospital Sch
RH7 ....165 A4
Lingfield House SE26 .....23 B2
Lingfield Park Race
Course RH7 ....164 E2
Lingfield Prim Sch RH7 .164 D4
Lingfield Rd
Dormans Park RH19 ......185 D3
East Grinstead RH19 ......185 D3
Edenbridge TN8 ....165 F8
Haxted TN8 ....165 F8
North Cheam KT4 ....58 C7
Wimbledon SW19 ....19 D2
Lingfield Sta RH7 ....164 E4
Lingwell Rd SW17 ....20 E5
Lingwood RG12 ....27 C3
Lingwood Gdns TW7 ......5 E7
Link La SM6 ....60 E4
Link Prim Day Sch The
CR0 ....60 E6
Link Rd Addlestone KT15 ...52 E6
Carshalton CR4, SM6 ......41 A1
East Bedfont TW14 ....14 F8
Link Sec Day Sch The CR0 60 F6
Link The Crawley RH11 ...201 D6
Teddington TW11 ....16 F2
Link Way Richmond TW10 ...17 B6
Staines TW18 ....13 B2
Link's Rd KT17 ....77 A5
Linkfield KT8 ....36 B6
Linkfield Cnr RH1 ....118 E2
Linkfield Gdns RH1 ......118 E1
Linkfield La RH1 ....118 F3
Linkfield Rd TW7 ....5 F5
Linkfield St RH1 ....118 E1
Linklater's Cotts GU14 ....84 B6
Links Ave SM4 ....40 A5
Links Brow KT22 ....94 E4
Links Cl Ashstead KT21 ....75 C2
Ewhurst GU6 ....175 E6
Links Gdns SW16 ....22 A1
Links Green Way KT11 ....74 A5
Links Pl KT21 ....75 D2
Links Prim Sch SW17 .....21 A2
Links Rd Ashford TW15 ....13 E3
Ashstead KT21 ....75 C2
Bramley GU5 ....151 E7
Mitcham SW16, SW17 ......21 A2
West Wickham BR4 ....44 C1
Links The North Ascot SL5 ..28 E7
Walton-on-T KT12 ....54 A8
Links View Ave RH3, RH5 .116 A1
Links View Rd Croydon CR0 63 A7
Hampton TW12 ....16 C4
Links Way Beckenham BR3 .44 A3
Effingham KT24 ....113 E7
Farnborough GU14 ....84 C3
Mitcham SW17 ....21 A2
Linkscroft Ave TW15 ......14 B2
Linkside KT3 ....38 E7
Linkside E GU26 ....188 C7
Linkside N GU26 ....188 B7
Linkside S GU26 ....188 C6
Linkside W GU26 ....188 B6
Linkway Camberley GU15 ...65 C4
Crawley RH6 ....182 C7
Crowthorne RG45 ....45 A5
Guildford GU2 ....108 F2
West Barnes SW20 ....39 B5
West Barnes KT3, SW20 ....39 B6
Woking GU22 ....70 C2
Linkway The SM2 ....59 C2
Linley Ct 1 Dulwich SE21 ...22 E4
Sutton SM1 ....59 C6
Linnell Rd RH1 ....140 B8
Linnet Cl CR2 ....62 D1
Linnet Gr GU4 ....110 D3
Linnet Mews SW12 ....21 A8
Linsford Bsns Pk GU16 ....85 F3
Linsford La GU16 ....85 F3
Linslade Cl TW4 ....4 E2
Linstead Rd GU14 ....84 E8
Linstead Way SW18, SW19 .19 E8
Linton Cl CR4, SM5 ....40 F2
Linton Glade CR0 ....62 E1
Linton Gr SE27 ....22 C3
Linton's La KT17 ....76 E7
Lintott Ct TW19 ....2 D1
Lintott Gdns RH13 ....217 E3
Lion and Lamb Way 7
GU9 ....125 B2
Lion and Lamb Yd 5
GU9 ....125 B2
Lion Ave TW1 ....16 F7
Lion Cl Haslemere GU27 ...207 F7
Littleton TW17 ....33 E6
Lion Ctr The TW13 ....15 E5
Lion Gate Gdns TW9 ....6 F4
Lion Gn GU27 ....207 F6
Lion Green Rd CR5 ....79 D3
Lion La Haslemere GU27 ..207 F7
Turners Hill RH10 ....204 A4
Lion Mead GU27 ....207 F6
Lion Park Ave KT9 ....57 A6
Lion Rd Thornton Heath CR0 42 C4
Twickenham TW1, TW2 .....16 F7
Lion Ret Pk GU22 ....70 B3
Lion Way TW8 ....6 D7
Lion Wharf Rd TW7 ....6 B4
Liphook Cres SE23 ....23 C8
Liphook Rd
Haslemere GU27 ....207 F6
Linchmere GU27 ....207 B4
Lipsham Cl SM7 ....78 D6
Lisbon Ave TW2 ....16 C6
Liscombe RG12 ....27 B2
Liscombe House RG12 .....27 B2
Liskeard Dr 2 GU14 ......85 A6
Lisle Cl SW17 ....21 B4
Lismore 9 SW19 ....19 F3
Lismore Cl TW7 ....6 A5
Lismore Cres RH11 ......201 B3
Lismore Rd CR2 ....61 E4
Lissoms Rd CR5 ....79 A1
Lister Ave RH19 ....205 F6
Lister Cl SW19 ....40 E8
Lister Ct 1 CR8 ....80 B7
Litchfield Ave SM4 ....39 F2
Litchfield Rd SM1 ....59 C6
Litchfield Way GU2 ......129 F7
Lithgow's Rd TW14, TW6 ....3 F3
Little Acre BR3 ....44 A6
Little Austins Rd GU9 ...146 D8
Little Birch Cl KT15 ......52 D2
Little Bookham St KT23 ...93 F2
Little Bornes SE21 ....22 E4
Little Borough RH3 .....137 A8
Little Brownings SE23 .....23 B6
Little Browns La TN8 ....144 F4
Little Collins RH1 ....162 B7
Little Common La RH1 ..120 C3
Little Comptons RH13 ...217 F2
Little Crabtree RH11 .....201 C7
Little Cranmore La KT24 .112 C6
Little Ct BR4 ....63 E8
Little Dimocks SW12 ......21 B6
Little Elms UB3 ....3 D7
Little Ferry Rd TW1 ....17 B7
Little Gn GU8 ....148 D4
Little Grebe RH12 ....217 C5
Little Green La
Addlestone KT16 ....51 E7
Wrecclesham GU9 ....146 A6
Little Halliards KT12 ......35 A3
Little Hatch RH12 ....217 F5
Little Haven La RH12 ....217 F5
Little Heath La KT11 ......74 A5
Little Heath Rd GU24 .....49 E2
Little Hide GU1 ....110 B3
Little Kiln GU7 ....150 E8
Little King St RH19 ......185 E1
Little London Shere GU5 ..132 F2
Witley GU8 ....170 E5
Little Lullenden RH7 .....164 E5
Little Manor Gdns GU6 ..174 E2
Little Mead GU21 ....68 F3
Little Mead Ind Est GU6 .174 B3
Little Moor GU47 ....45 C1
Little Moreton Cl KT14 ....71 B7
Little Orch Woking GU21 ...70 A5
Woodham KT15 ....71 A8
Little Orchard Way GU4 .130 E1
Little Orchards KT18 ......76 E5
Little Paddock GU15 ......66 A8
Little Park Dr TW13 ......15 E6
Little Park Enterprises
RH6 ....180 E3
Little Platt GU2 ....108 D2
Little Queens Rd TW11 ....16 F2
Little Ringdale RG12 ......27 E5
Little Roke Ave CR8 ....80 B5
Little Roke Rd CR8 ....80 C5
Little St GU2 ....109 B5
Little St Leonards SW14 ....7 C4
Little Sutton La SL3 ....1 B8
Little Tangley Flats GU5 .131 C1
Little Thatch GU7 ....150 F6
Little Thurbans Cl GU9 ..146 A6
Little Tumners Ct GU7 ...150 E6
Little Warren Cl GU4 ....131 B7
Little Wellington St 9
GU11 ....105 A2
Little Wildwood GU6 ....174 F1
Little Woodcote La
CR8, SM5, SM6 ....79 B8
Littlebourne 2 SE13 ......24 E8
Littlebrook Cl CR0 ....43 D3
Littlecote Cl SW19 ....19 E8
Littlecroft Rd 2 TW20 .....11 F3
Littledale Cl RG12 ....27 E6
Littlefield Cl Ash GU12 ..106 A1
Fairlands GU3 ....108 D5
9 Kingston u T KT1 ....37 E7
Littlefield Cotts GU3 ....108 B6
Littlefield Ct UB7 ....2 D7
Littlefield Gdns GU12 ...106 A1
Littlefield Way GU3 .....108 D5
Littleford La GU4, GU5 ..152 F7
Littlehaven Cty Inf Sch
RH12 ....217 F5
Littleheath Rd CR2 ....62 B2
Littlemead KT10 ....55 D6
Littlers Cl SW19 ....40 D8
Littlestone Cl BR3 ....24 A2
Littleton C of E Fst Sch
TW17 ....34 A6
Littleton Cross GU3 .....130 A4
Littleton House 4 RH2 ...118 A2
Littleton La Artington GU3 130 A3
Littleton TW17, TW18 ......33 E4
Reigate RH2 ....138 E7
Littleton Rd TW15, TW17 ..14 C1
Littleton St SW18 ....20 C6
Littlewick Cotts GU21 ....68 F4
Littlewick Rd GU21 ....68 E3
Littlewood GU6 ....174 F3
Littlewood House CR2 ....81 B5
Littleworth Ave KT10 .....55 D5
Littleworth Common Rd
KT10 ....55 D7
Littleworth La KT10 ....55 D6
Littleworth Pl KT10 ....55 D6
Littleworth Rd
Hinchley Wood KT10 ......55 E6
Puttenham GU10, GU8 ...148 C8
The Sands GU10 ....126 F1
Liverpool Rd
Kingston u T KT2 ....18 A1
South Norwood CR7 ....42 C6
Livesey Cl KT1 ....37 F6
Livingstone Ct TW19 ......13 E7
Livingstone Rd
Caterham CR3 ....100 D5
Crawley RH10 ....201 E4
Horsham RH13 ....217 D1
Hounslow TW3 ....5 C3
South Norwood CR7 ....42 D7
Llanaway Cl GU7 ....150 F6
Llanaway House GU7 ....150 F6
Llanaway Rd GU7 ....150 F6
Llangar Gr RG45 ....45 A5
Llanthony Rd SM4 ....40 D4
Llanvair Cl SL5 ....29 A3
Llanvair Dr SL5 ....28 F3
Llewellyn Ct SE20 ....43 C8
Lloyd Ave
Thornton Heath SW16 ......41 E8
Wallington CR5 ....79 B5
Lloyd Ct 6 SE27 ....22 B5
Lloyd House BR3 ....24 B2
Lloyd Park Ave CR0 ....61 F6
Lloyd Rd KT4, SM3 ....58 D7
Lloyds Ct RH10 ....181 E1
Lloyds Way BR3 ....43 F4
Lobelia Rd GU24 ....68 A4
Lochinvar St SW12 ....21 B8
Lochinver RG12 ....27 B2
Lock Cl GU21, KT15 ....70 E7
Lock La GU22, GU23, KT14 ..71 C3
Lock Rd Farnborough GU11 105 D5
Guildford GU1 ....109 D4
Richmond TW10 ....17 C4
Lock's La CR4 ....41 A7
Locke King Rd KT13 ......53 A3
Locke Way GU21 ....69 F2
Locke-King Cl KT13 ......53 A3
Lockesley Sq KT6 ....37 D3
Lockfield Cotts GU21 .....69 A1
Lockfield Dr GU21 ....68 F2
Lockhart Rd KT11 ....73 C6
Lockhurstahatch La GU5 ..153 E6
Locks Meadow RH7 ......165 A1
Locks Ride SL5 ....8 C2
Locksley Dr GU21 ....68 F2
Locksmeade Rd TW10 .....17 C4
Lockswood GU24 ....88 B7
Lockton Chase SL5 ....28 D6
Lockton House RG40 .....25 C6
Lockwood Cl
Farnborough GU14 ....84 E8
Forest Hill SE26 ....23 D4
Horsham RH12 ....218 A5
Lockwood Ct RH10 ......201 F8
Lockwood Path GU21 .....70 E6
Lockwood Way KT9 ....57 A5
Lodden Lodge SM2 ....59 C3
Loddon Cl GU15 ....66 A6
Loddon Rd GU14 ....84 D6
Loddon Way GU12 ......106 A1
Loder Cl GU21 ....70 D6
Lodge Ave CR0, CR9 ......61 A7
Lodge Cl Brentford TW7 .....6 B6
Carshalton CR4 ....41 A1
Crawley RH11 ....201 C6
Dorking RH5 ....136 C3
E Ewell KT17 ....58 C1
East Grinstead RH19 ......185 D1
Englefield Green TW20 .....11 D3
Fetcham KT22 ....94 D5
Stoke D'Abernon KT11 .....73 F3
Lodge Gdns BR3 ....43 F4
Lodge Hill CR8 ....80 A4
Lodge Hill Cl GU10 ......146 D6
Lodge Hill Rd GU10 .....146 E7
Lodge La Beckenham BR3 ..44 B5
New Addington CR0, R9 .....63 B3
Salfords RH1 ....139 F1
South Croydon CR0 ....63 A4
South Holmwood RH5 .....157 F8
Lodge Pl SM1 ....59 B5
Lodge Rd Fetcham KT22 ...94 D5
Sutton SM1 ....59 B5
Thornton Heath CR0 ....42 B2
Wallington SM6 ....60 B5
Lodge Sch CR8 ....79 D8
Lodge Way Ashford TW15 ..13 E6
Charlton TW17 ....34 C7
Lodgebottom Rd
KT22, RH5 ....116 A8
Lodsworth GU14 ....84 D3
Lofthouse Pl KT9 ....56 C4
Logan Cl TW4 ....4 F4
Logmore La RH4 ....135 D3
Lois Dr TW17 ....34 B4
Lollesworth La KT24 ....112 C8
Loman Rd GU16 ....86 A4
Lomas Cl CR0 ....63 C3
Lombard Bsns Pk
Merton SW19 ....40 B7
Thornton Heath CR9 ....41 F2
Lombard Rd SW19 ....40 B7
Lombard St GU8 ....149 B7
Lombardy Cl GU21 ....68 F2
Lomond Gdns CR2 ....62 E3
Loncin Mead Ave KT15 ...52 C2
London Butterfly House
TW8 ....6 B6
London Cross KT24 ......112 F4
London Fields House
RH11 ....201 C2
London Inst The SW17 ....21 B3
London La Bromley BR1 ....24 F1
Shere GU5 ....133 A5
London Rd Ascot SL5 ......29 D5
Ashford TW15, TW18,
TW19, TW14 ....13 D5
Bagshot GU15, GU19 ....47 C1
Blackwater GU15, GU17 ....64 E4
Bracknell RG42 ....26 B7
Bracknell RG12, SL5 ....28 C6
Bracknell, Binfield
RG12, RG42 ....26 C7
Brands Hill SL3 ....1 B8
Brentford TW7, TW8 ....6 B6
Bromley BR1 ....24 F1
Camberley GU15 ....65 C6
Caterham CR3 ....100 D4
London Rd *continued*
Cheam KT17 ....58 C6
Crawley RH10 ....181 E3
Dorking RH4 ....115 C3
East Grinstead RH19 ......185 C3
Englefield Green TW20 .....11 C1
Ewell KT17 ....58 C6
Forest Hill SE22, SE23 ......23 C7
Forest Row RH18 ....206 E4
Guildford GU1 ....109 F1
Guildford, Burpham
GU1, GU4 ....110 B4
Hackbridge SM6, CR4 ......60 B7
Hindhead GU26 ....188 F4
Horsham RH12 ....217 C2
Hounslow TW3, TW7, TW1,
TW8 ....5 D5
Isleworth TW7, TW8 ....6 B6
Kingston u T KT1, KT2 ......37 F7
Mitcham CR4, SW17 ....40 F6
Morden SM4 ....40 A5
North Cheam KT4, SM3, SM4 .58 C6
Redhill RH1 ....119 A3
Reigate RH2 ....118 A2
Send Marsh GU23 ....90 E1
Stoneleigh KT17, KT4, SM3 ..58 C6
Sunningdale, Blacknest SL5 ..30 B6
Sunningdale, Shrubs Hill SL5 .30 C4
Thornton Heath CR0,
CR7, SW16 ....42 A3
Twickenham TW1 ....17 A7
Virginia Water GU25 ....31 B7
Wentworth SL5, GU25 ......30 C4
Westhumble RH4 ....115 C3
Windlesham GU19, GU20 ....48 C7
Wokingham RG42, RG12 ....26 C7
London Rd N RH1 ....99 B2
London Rd S
Merstham RH1 ....119 B6
Redhill RH1 ....119 B6
London Road Sta GU1 ...109 E1
London St KT16 ....33 A2
Lone Oak RH6 ....162 B1
Loneacre GU20 ....48 E4
Lonesome La
Reigate RH1, RH2 ....139 D3
Salfords RH1, RH2 ....139 D3
Lonesome Prim Sch CR4 ..41 B7
Lonesome Way CR4 ....41 C8
Long Acre RH10 ....204 A8
Long Beech Dr GU14 .....84 C3
Long Bridge GU9 ....125 C2
Long Cl RH10 ....202 D6
Long Copse Cl KT23 ......94 B4
Long Ditton Cty Inf Sch
KT6 ....37 C1
Long Dyke GU1 ....110 B3
Long Garden Mews 3
GU9 ....125 B2
Long Garden Way GU9 ..125 B2
Long Garden Wlk 4 GU9 125 B2
Long Garden Wlk E 2
GU9 ....125 B2
Long Garden Wlk W 1
GU9 ....125 B2
Long Gore GU7 ....150 E8
Long Grove Rd KT19 ......57 B1
Long Hill The Sands GU10 .126 E1
Woldingham CR3 ....101 F6
Long Hill Rd RG12, SL5 ....28 A7
Long Houses GU24 ....87 D3
Long La Croydon CR0 .....43 C3
Stanwell TW15, TW19 ......13 F7
Long Lodge Dr KT12 ......54 C7
Long Meadow Cl BR3, BR4 44 C2
Long Mickle GU47 ....45 B1
Long Rd The GU10 ......146 A2
Long Reach Ockham GU23 ..92 B3
West Horsley KT24 ....92 B3
Long Shaw KT22 ....95 A7
Long Wlk Burgh Heath KT18 97 D8
Kingston u T KT3 ....38 C6
Long Wlk The SL4 ....10 D7
Long's Way RG40 ....25 E7
Longacre GU12 ....106 A2
Longacre Pl SM5 ....60 A4
Longacre Sch GU5 ....152 D4
Longbourne Gn GU7 .....150 E8
Longbourne Way KT16 ....32 F3
Longboyds KT11 ....73 B4
Longbridge Gate RH6 ...181 E8
Longbridge Rd
Crawley RH6 ....181 F8
Horley RH6 ....160 F1
Longbridge Rdbt RH6 ...160 E2
Longbridge Wlk RH6 ....160 F1
Longchamp Cl RH6 ......161 C3
Longcroft Ave SM7 ....78 C5
Longcross Rd KT16, GU24 ..50 C7
Longcross Sta GU25 ....30 F1
Longdene Rd GU27 ......208 B6
Longdown Cl GU10 ......146 C6
Longdown La N KT17 ......77 A6
Longdown La S KT17, KT18 77 A4
Longdown Lodge GU47 ....64 B8
Longdown Rd Catford SE6 .24 A4
Ewell KT17 ....77 A6
Farnham GU10 ....146 C5
Guildford GU4 ....131 B6
Sandhurst GU47 ....45 B1
Longfellow Cl RH12 .....217 E7
Longfellow Rd KT4 ....39 B1
Longfield BR1 ....44 F8
Longfield Ave CR4, SM6 ...41 A1
Longfield Cl GU14 ....85 B8

Longfield Cres
Burgh Heath KT20 . . . .**97** C7
Forest Hill SE23, SE26 . . . . . .**23** C5
Longfield Dr Mitcham SW19 **40** E8
Mortlake SW14 . . . .**7** B2
Longfield Rd Ash GU12 . .**106** A2
Dorking RH4 . . . .**135** F6
Horsham RH12 . . . .**217** A1
Longfield St SW18 . . . .**20** A8
Longford Ave Feltham TW14 . .**3** F1
Stanwell TW19 . . . .**13** E2
Longford Cl
Camberley GU15 . . . .**65** D4
Hampton TW12 . . . .**16** A4
Longford Ct KT19 . . . .**57** C6
Longford Gdns SM1 . . . .**59** C8
Longford House
Catford BR1 . . . .**24** D3
Hampton TW12 . . . .**16** A4
Longford Ind Est TW12 . . .**16** B2
Longford Rd TW2 . . . .**16** B7
Longford Rdbt TW6, UB7 . .**2** B6
Longford Sch TW14 . . . .**14** F8
Longford Way TW19 . . . .**13** E7
Longford Wlk 9 SW2 . . . . . .**22** A8
Longheath Dr KT23 . . . .**93** E3
Longheath Gdns CR0 . . . . . .**43** C4
Longhedge House SE26 . . . .**23** A4
Longhill Rd SE6 . . . .**24** D5
Longhope Dr GU10 . . . . . .**146** A6
Longhurst Rd
Crawley RH11 . . . .**201** A1
Croydon CR0 . . . .**43** B3
East Horsley KT24 . . . .**112** E6
Longlands Ave CR5 . . . .**79** A5
Longlands Ct CR4 . . . .**41** A8
Longlands Way GU15 . . . . . .**66** D5
Longleat Sq GU14 . . . .**85** E3
Longleat Way TW14 . . . . . .**14** D8
Longley Rd Farnham GU9 .**125** D1
Thornton Heath CR0 . . . .**42** B2
Upper Tooting SW17 . . . .**20** F2
Longmead GU1 . . . .**110** C1
Longmead Bsns Ctr KT19 .**76** D8
Longmead Cl CR3 . . . .**100** E5
Longmead House SW17 . . . .**22** C3
Longmead Rd Epsom KT19 .**57** E1
Thames Ditton KT7 . . . .**36** F2
Upper Tooting SW17 . . . .**20** F3
Longmeadow
Frimley GU15, GU16 . . . .**65** F3
Little Bookham KT23 . . . .**93** F2
Longmere Gdns KT20 . . . . . .**97** C8
Longmere Rd RH10 . . . . . .**201** D8
Longmoors RG42 . . . .**26** E8
Longmore Rd KT12 . . . .**54** E6
Longpoles Rd GU6 . . . . . .**174** F2
Longridge Gr GU22 . . . .**70** E5
Longs Cl GU22 . . . .**71** A3
Longs Ct 2 TW9 . . . .**6** F3
Longsdon Way CR3 . . . .**101** A3
Longshot Ind Est RG12 . . . .**26** E7
Longshot La RG12 . . . .**26** E7
Longside Cl TW20 . . . .**32** C8
Longstaff Cres SW18 . . . . . .**20** A8
Longstaff Rd SW18 . . . .**20** A8
Longstone Rd SW17 . . . .**21** B3
Longthornton Rd SW16 . . . .**41** D7
Longton Ave SE26 . . . .**23** A4
Longton Gr SE26 . . . .**23** B4
Longwater Rd RG12 . . . .**27** C3
Longwood Dr SW15 . . . .**19** B8
Longwood Rd CR8 . . . .**80** D3
Longwood View RH10 . . . .**202** A3
Longyard House RH6 . . . . .**161** B5
Lonsdale Gdns CR7, SW16 .**41** F5
Lonsdale Mews 4 TW9 . . . .**7** A4
Lonsdale Rd Barnes SW13 . .**7** F7
Croydon SE25 . . . .**43** B5
Dorking RH4 . . . .**136** B8
Weybridge KT13 . . . .**53** A3
Look Out Discovery Ctr
The RG12 . . . .**27** D1
Loop Rd Epsom KT18 . . . .**76** C3
Old Woking GU22 . . . .**89** F7
Loppets Rd RH10 . . . .**201** F3
Loraine Gdns KT21 . . . .**75** E2
Loraine House 1 SM5 . . . . .**60** B6
Loraine Rd W4 . . . .**7** B8
Lord Chancellor Wlk KT2 .**38** C8
Lord Knyvett Cl TW19 . . . . . .**2** D1
Lordell Pl SW19 . . . .**19** C2
Lords Cl Feltham TW13 . . . . .**15** E6
West Norwood SE21 . . . .**22** C6
Lordsbury Field SM6 . . . .**60** C1
Lordsgrove Cl KT20 . . . .**97** B2
Lordshill Rd GU5 . . . .**152** C5
Lordship La SE21, SE22 . . . .**23** A8
Loretto Cl GU6 . . . .**175** A3
Lorian Dr RH2 . . . .**118** C2
Loriners RH10 . . . .**201** D3
Loring Rd TW7 . . . .**5** F5
Lorne Ave CR0 . . . .**43** D2
Lorne Gdns Croydon CR0 . .**43** D2
Knaphill GU21 . . . .**88** D8
Lorne Rd 2 TW10 . . . .**6** F2
Lorne The KT23 . . . .**94** A1
Lorraine Cty Inf Sch GU15 **65** A8
Lorraine Ct BR3 . . . .**44** C8
Lorraine Rd GU15 . . . .**65** B8
Lory Ridge GU19 . . . .**47** E4
Loseberry Rd KT10 . . . .**55** D5
Loseley Ho GU3 . . . .**129** E3
Loseley Rd GU7 . . . .**150** E8
Lothian Rd GU24 . . . .**87** A6

Lothian Wood KT20 . . . .**97** B5
Lotus Rd TN16 . . . .**83** F1
Loubet St SW17 . . . .**20** F2
Loudwater Cl TW16 . . . .**35** A5
Loudwater Rd TW16 . . . .**35** A5
Loughborough RG12 . . . .**27** E3
Louis Fields GU3 . . . .**108** C5
Louisa Ct TW2 . . . .**16** E6
Louisa House SW15 . . . .**7** F3
Louise Margaret
Maternity Hospl GU11 . .**105** B3
Louise Margaret Rd
GU11 . . . .**105** C3
Louisville Rd SW17 . . . .**21** A5
Lovat Wlk TW5 . . . .**4** E7
Lovatt Ct SW12 . . . .**21** B7
Love La Cheam SM3 . . . .**58** E4
Croydon SE25 . . . .**43** B6
Godstone RH9 . . . .**121** C3
Long Ditton KT6 . . . .**56** D8
Mitcham CR4 . . . .**40** E6
Morden SM4 . . . .**40** B2
Sutton SM1 . . . .**40** B2
Walton on t H KT20 . . . .**97** A1
Loveday House 2 SW2 . . . .**22** A7
Lovedean Ct RG12 . . . .**27** E3
Lovekyn Cl KT2 . . . .**37** F7
Lovel La SL5 . . . .**9** B3
Lovelace Cl KT24 . . . .**93** A4
Lovelace Dr GU22 . . . .**70** F3
Lovelace Gdns
Hersham KT12 . . . .**54** C5
Surbiton KT6 . . . .**37** D2
Lovelace Prim Sch KT9 . . .**56** C5
Lovelace Rd Bracknell RG12 **26** E5
Surbiton KT6 . . . .**37** D2
West Norwood SE21 . . . .**22** C7
Lovelands La
Lower Kingswood KT20 . . . .**118** B8
West End GU24 . . . .**68** C6
Loveletts RH11 . . . .**201** A5
Lovell House 4 SW19 . . . . . .**40** C8
Lovell Rd TW10 . . . .**17** C5
Lovells Cl GU18 . . . .**48** B1
Lovelock Cl CR8 . . . .**80** C2
Lovers La GU10 . . . .**167** C2
Lovett House 9 GU9 . . . . . .**125** B2
Lovett Dr SM5 . . . .**40** D2
Lovett Rd TW20 . . . .**12** C4
Low Cross Wood La SE21 .**22** F5
Low La GU9 . . . .**126** B6
Lowbury RG12 . . . .**27** E5
Lowburys RH4 . . . .**136** B4
Lowdells Cl RH19 . . . .**185** C4
Lowdells Dr RH19 . . . .**185** C4
Lowdells La RH19 . . . .**185** C3
Lower Addiscombe Rd
CR0 . . . .**42** E1
Lower Barn Cl RH12 . . . . . .**217** F5
Lower Barn Rd CR8 . . . .**80** D6
Lower Breache Rd GU6 . .**176** B4
Lower Bridge Rd RH1 . . . .**118** F1
Lower Broadmoor Rd
RG45 . . . .**45** D4
Lower Charles St GU15 . . . .**65** C6
Lower Church La 18 GU9 .**125** B2
Lower Church St CR0, CR9 .**61** B8
Lower Coombe St
CR0, CR9 . . . .**61** C6
Lower Court Rd KT19 . . . .**76** C8
Lower Ct KT19 . . . .**76** B8
Lower Dene RH19 . . . .**186** A1
Lower Downs Rd SW20 . . . .**39** D8
Lower Dunnymans 4 SM7 **77** F5
Lower Eashing GU7 . . . . . .**149** F4
Lower Edgeborough Rd
GU1 . . . .**130** F8
Lower Farm Rd KT23, KT24 **93** C3
Lower Farnham Rd
GU11, GU12 . . . .**126** C7
Lower Forecourt RH6 . . . .**182** B7
Lower George St 18 TW10 . .**6** D2
Lower Gn KT12 . . . .**54** D5
Lower Gn W CR4 . . . .**40** E6
Lower Green Rd
Esher KT10 . . . .**55** C8
Thames Ditton KT10 . . . .**55** C8
Lower Grove Rd TW10 . . . . . .**6** F2
Lower Guildford Rd GU21 **68** D1
Lower Ham La GU8 . . . .**148** E4
Lower Ham Rd KT2 . . . .**17** D2
Lower Hampton
Rd TW12, TW16 . . . .**35** D7
Lower Hanger GU27 . . . . . .**207** C6
Lower Hill Rd KT19 . . . .**76** B7
Lower House Rd GU8 . . . . .**169** F2
Lower Manor Rd
Farncombe GU7 . . . .**150** F6
Milford GU8 . . . .**149** E1
Lower Marsh La KT1, KT5 . .**38** A5
Lower Mere RH19 . . . .**205** F8
Lower Mill Field GU19 . . . . .**47** D2
Lower Morden La SM4 . . . . .**39** E3
Lower Mortlake Rd TW9 . . . .**6** F4
Lower Moushill La GU8 . .**149** D1
Lower Nelson St 4 GU11 **105** A2
Lower Northfield 5 SM7 . . .**77** F5
Lower Park Rd CR5 . . . .**78** E1
Lower Peryers KT24 . . . . . .**112** F2
Lower Pillory Down SM5 . . .**79** B7
Lower Rd Effingham KT24 .**113** D8
Fetcham KT22, KT23, KT24 . .**94** C3
Forest Row RH18 . . . .**206** F3
Grayswood GU27 . . . .**189** F2
Great Bookham KT22,
KT23, KT24 . . . .**94** C3
Purley CR8 . . . .**80** B6

Lower Rd *continued*
Reigate RH1 . . . .**139** D7
Sutton SM1 . . . .**59** C6
Lower Richmond Rd
SW14, TW9 . . . .**7** B4
Lower Sandfields GU23 . . .**90** D3
Lower Sawleywood 2
SM7 . . . .**77** F5
Lower Shott GU23 . . . .**94** B1
Lower South St GU7 . . . . . .**150** D4
Lower South View GU9 . . . .**125** C3
Lower Sq RH18 . . . .**206** E3
Lower St Haslemere GU27 .**208** C6
Shere GU5 . . . .**133** A4
Lower Sunbury Rd TW12 . .**36** A7
Lower Sydenham Sta SE6 .**23** F3
Lower Tanbridge Way
RH12 . . . .**217** B2
Lower Teddington Rd
KT1 . . . .**37** D8
Lower Village Rd SL5 . . . . . .**29** C4
Lower Weybourne La
Farnham GU9 . . . .**126** A6
Heath End GU9 . . . .**125** F6
Lower Wood Rd KT10 . . . . . .**56** B4
Lowestoft Wlk RH10 . . . . . .**202** B4
Loweswater Wlk GU15 . . . . .**66** D4
Lowfield Cl GU18 . . . .**67** A8
Lowfield Heath Rd
Charlwood RH6 . . . .**180** F5
Crawley RH6 . . . .**180** F5
Lowfield Rd RH13 . . . .**215** D3
Lowfield Way RH11 . . . .**181** E5
Lowicks Rd GU10 . . . .**168** C6
Lowlands Rd
Blackwater GU17 . . . .**64** C4
Stanwell TW19 . . . .**2** D2
Lowndes Bldgs GU9 . . . . . .**125** B3
Lowood Ct SE19 . . . .**22** F3
Lowry Cl GU47 . . . .**64** D6
Lowry Cres CR4 . . . .**40** E7
Lowther Hill SE23 . . . .**23** E8
Lowther Rd Barnes SW13 . . .**7** F6
Kingston u T KT2 . . . .**37** F8
Lowthorpe 5 GU21 . . . .**69** A1
Loxford Ct GU6 . . . .**173** F2
Loxford Rd CR3 . . . .**100** F2
Loxford Way CR3 . . . .**100** F2
Loxley Cl SE26 . . . .**23** D3
Loxley Rd Hampton TW12 . .**15** F4
Wandsworth SW18 . . . .**20** D7
Loxton Rd SE23 . . . .**23** E7
Loxwood Cl TW14 . . . .**14** E7
Loxwood Cty Prim Sch
RH14 . . . .**213** A4
Loxwood Rd Alfold GU6 . .**193** F2
Alfold Crossways GU6 . . . . .**193** F2
Ifold RH14 . . . .**212** A2
Loxwood RH12, RH14 . . . . .**213** D4
Loxwood, Alfold Bars
GU6, RH14 . . . .**212** F8
Plaistow RH14 . . . .**212** A2
Rudgwick RH12 . . . .**214** A6
Loxwood Wlk RH11 . . . .**201** A8
Lucan Dr TW18 . . . .**13** D1
Lucas Cl RH19 . . . .**186** A1
Lucas Ct SE26 . . . .**23** E3
Lucas Field GU27 . . . .**207** E6
Lucas Green GU24 . . . .**67** D4
Lucas Green Rd GU24 . . . . .**67** E5
Lucas Rd Penge SE20 . . . . . .**23** C2
Warnham RH12 . . . .**216** F8
Lucerne Cl GU22 . . . .**89** E8
Lucerne Ct 8 BR3 . . . .**24** A1
Lucerne Dr RH10 . . . .**202** D4
Lucerne Rd CR7 . . . .**42** C5
Lucie Ave TW15 . . . .**14** B2
Lucien Rd
Upper Tooting SW17 . . . .**21** A4
Wimbledon SW18 . . . .**20** B6
Lucille House SE26 . . . .**23** C4
Luckley Oakfield Sch
RG40 . . . .**25** B3
Luckley Path RG40 . . . .**25** C6
Luckley Rd RG41 . . . .**25** B3
Luckley Wood RG41 . . . .**25** B3
Lucraft House 12 SW2 . . . . .**21** E8
Luddington Ave
GU25, TW20 . . . .**31** F7
Ludford Cl CR0 . . . .**61** B6
Ludgrove Sch RG40 . . . .**25** D3
Ludlow RG12 . . . .**27** B2
Ludlow Cl GU16 . . . .**86** A7
Ludlow Rd Feltham TW13 . . .**15** A4
Guildford GU2 . . . .**130** B8
Ludovick Wlk SW15 . . . .**7** F3
Ludshott Gr GU35 . . . .**187** B5
Luke Rd GU11 . . . .**125** E8
Luke Rd E GU11 . . . .**125** F8
Lullarook Cl TN16 . . . .**83** C3
Lullington Rd SE20 . . . .**23** A1
Lulworth Ave TW5, TW7 . . . . .**5** C7
Lulworth Cl Crawley RH11 **201** B3
Farnborough GU14 . . . .**85** A7
Lulworth Cres CR4 . . . .**40** E7
Lumley Ct RH6 . . . .**161** A4
Lumley Gdns SM3 . . . .**58** E5
Lumley House KT3 . . . .**38** D1
Lumley Rd Cheam SM1, SM3 **58** E5
Horley RH6 . . . .**161** A3
Luna Rd CR7 . . . .**42** C6
Lunar Cl TN16 . . . .**83** D3
Lundy Cl RH11 . . . .**201** C4
Lunghurst Rd CR3 . . . .**102** A5
Lunham Rd SE19 . . . .**22** E2
Lupin Cl Bagshot GU19 . . . . .**47** C1
Croydon CR0 . . . .**43** D1
Streatham SW2 . . . .**22** B6

Lupin Ride RG45 . . . .**45** B7
Lupus Ct SE19 . . . .**42** D8
Luscombe Ct BR2 . . . .**44** E7
Lushington Dr KT11 . . . .**73** B5
Lushington House KT12 . . . .**35** C3
Lushington Rd SE6 . . . .**24** B3
Lusted Hall La
Biggin Hill TN16 . . . .**103** C7
Tatsfield TN16 . . . .**103** C7
Lusteds Cl RH4 . . . .**136** C4
Lutea House SM2 . . . .**59** C3
Luther Rd TW11 . . . .**16** F3
Lutwyche Rd SE23, SE6 . . . .**23** F6
Lutyens Cl RH11 . . . .**200** E4
Luxford Cl RH12 . . . .**217** F5
Luxford's La
Ashurst Wood RH19 . . . . . .**206** B6
Forest Row RH19 . . . .**206** B6
Lyall Ave SE21 . . . .**22** F4
Lyall Pl GU9 . . . .**125** B7
Lycett House 10 SW2 . . . . . .**21** E8
Lych Way GU21 . . . .**69** D3
Lyconby Gdns CR0 . . . .**43** E2
Lydbury RG12 . . . .**27** F6
Lydden Gr SW18 . . . .**20** B8
Lydden Rd SW18 . . . .**20** B8
Lydele Cl GU21 . . . .**69** F4
Lydford Cl
2 Farnborough GU14 . . . . . .**85** A7
Frimley GU16 . . . .**86** A7
Lydhurst Ave SW2 . . . .**21** F6
Lydney RG12 . . . .**27** B2
Lydney Cl SW19 . . . .**19** E6
Lydon House RH11 . . . .**181** D1
Lye Copse Ave GU14 . . . .**85** B8
Lye The KT20 . . . .**97** C5
Lye View Cotts GU21 . . . . . .**89** A8
Lyefield La GU6, RH5 . . . . . .**176** C5
Lyfield KT11, KT22 . . . .**74** B5
Lyford Rd SW18 . . . .**20** E7
Lyham Rd SW2 . . . .**21** E8
Lyle Cl CR4 . . . .**41** A2
Lymbourne Cl SM2 . . . .**59** A1
Lymden Gdns RH2 . . . .**139** B7
Lyme Regis Rd SM7 . . . .**77** F2
Lymer Ave SE19 . . . .**22** F3
Lymescote Gdns SM1 . . . . . .**59** A8
Lyminge Gdns SW17, SW18 **20** E7
Lymington Cl SW16 . . . .**41** D7
Lymington Ct SM1 . . . .**59** C7
Lymington Gdns KT19 . . . . . .**57** F5
Lyn Ct GU1 . . . .**131** A8
Lynchen Cl TW5 . . . .**4** B6
Lynchford La GU11, GU14 .**105** D8
Lynchford Rd GU14 . . . .**105** D8
Lyncroft Gdns Ewell KT17 . .**57** F2
Isleworth TW3 . . . .**5** C2
Lyndale Ct 3 RH1 . . . .**119** A4
Lyndale Rd RH1 . . . .**119** A4
Lynde House KT12 . . . .**35** C3
Lynden Gate SW15 . . . .**19** B8
Lynden Hurst CR0 . . . .**61** F8
Lyndhurst Ave
Aldershot GU11 . . . .**126** C6
Blackwater GU17 . . . .**64** C6
Mitcham SW16 . . . .**41** D7
Sunbury TW16 . . . .**35** A6
Tolworth KT5 . . . .**38** B1
Twickenham TW2, TW4 . . . . . .**16** A7
Lyndhurst Cl
Bracknell RG12 . . . .**28** A6
Crawley RH11 . . . .**201** D5
South Croydon CR0 . . . .**61** F7
Woking GU21 . . . .**69** D4
Lyndhurst Ct 7 SM2 . . . . . .**59** A3
Lyndhurst Dr KT3 . . . .**38** F2
Lyndhurst Farm Cl RH19 .**184** D4
Lyndhurst House 2 SW15 .**19** A8
Lyndhurst Rd Ascot SL5 . . .**29** A5
Coulsdon CR5 . . . .**79** A3
Reigate RH2 . . . .**139** A6
Thornton Heath CR7 . . . .**42** A5
Lyndhurst Sch GU15 . . . . . .**65** B5
Lyndhurst Way
Addlestone KT16 . . . .**51** E8
Belmont SM2 . . . .**59** A2
Lyndon Ave SM6 . . . .**60** A7
Lyndon Yd SW17 . . . .**20** B4
Lyndsey Cl GU14 . . . .**84** B4
Lyne Cl GU25 . . . .**31** F3
Lyne Crossing
Rd KT16, TW20 . . . .**32** B3
Lyne Ct GU25 . . . .**31** F2
Lyne La
Chertsey KT16, TW20 . . . .**32** A3
Lyne KT16 . . . .**32** A2
Lyne & Longcross Inf Sch
KT16 . . . .**51** B8
Lyne Place Manor GU25 . .**31** F2
Lyne Rd GU25 . . . .**31** E3
Lynegrove Ave TW15 . . . .**14** C3
Lyneham Rd RG45 . . . .**45** B5
Lynfield Ct SE23 . . . .**23** D8
Lynmouth Ave SM4 . . . .**39** D2
Lynmouth Gdns TW5 . . . .**4** D6
Lynn Cl TW15 . . . .**14** D3
Lynn Ct Streatham SW16 . . . .**21** D3
Whyteleafe CR3 . . . .**80** F1
Lynn Rd SW12 . . . .**21** B8
Lynn Way GU14 . . . .**84** F7
Lynn Wlk RH2 . . . .**139** B6
Lynne Cl CR2 . . . .**81** C8
Lynne Ct Forest Hill SE23 . . .**23** E8
18 Guildford GU1 . . . .**130** F8
South Croydon CR2 . . . .**61** E6
Wimbledon SW20 . . . .**39** B8
Lynne Wlk KT10 . . . .**55** C5

Lynscott Way CR2 . . . .**61** B2
Lynsted Ct BR3 . . . .**43** E7
Lynton KT7 . . . .**37** A2
Lynton Cl Chessington KT9 . .**56** E6
East Grinstead RH19 . . . . . .**186** A2
Farnham GU9 . . . .**146** A7
Isleworth TW7 . . . .**5** F3
Lynton Ct SM2 . . . .**59** C4
Lynton Park Ave RH19 . . . .**186** A2
Lynton Rd New Malden KT3 .**38** D4
Thornton Heath CR0, CR7 . . .**42** A3
Lynton Prep Sch KT17 . . . . .**76** F8
Lynwick St Rudgwick RH12 **214** C8
Rudgwick RH12 . . . .**214** C8
Rudgwick, Cox Green RH12 **195** D1
Lynwood GU2 . . . .**—**
Lynwood Ave Egham TW20 .**11** E2
Epsom KT17 . . . .**76** F5
Wallington CR5 . . . .**79** B4
Lynwood Chase 1 RG12 . . .**27** A8
Lynwood Cl GU21 . . . .**70** D6
Lynwood Cres SL5 . . . .**29** E3
Lynwood Ct RH12 . . . .**217** C3
Lynwood Dr Mytchett GU16 **86** A3
North Cheam KT4 . . . .**58** A8
Lynwood Flats SL5 . . . .**29** E4
Lynwood Gdns CR0 . . . .**60** F6
Lynwood Rd Epsom KT17 . . .**76** F5
Redhill RH1 . . . .**119** A3
Thames Ditton KT7 . . . .**36** F1
Upper Tooting SW17 . . . .**20** F4
Lynx Hill KT24 . . . .**112** F8
Lyon Cl RH10 . . . .**202** C2
Lyon Ct RH13 . . . .**217** C3
Lyon Rd Crowthorne RG45 . .**45** C6
Merton SW19 . . . .**40** C8
Walton-on-T KT12 . . . .**54** E8
Lyon Way GU16 . . . .**65** C1
Lyon Way Ind Est GU16 . . . .**65** C1
Lyons Cl RH13 . . . .**215** D3
Lyons Ct RH4 . . . .**136** B7
Lyons Dr GU2 . . . .**109** A4
Lyons Rd RH13 . . . .**215** E3
Lyonsdene KT20 . . . .**117** F8
Lyric Cl RH10 . . . .**202** D4
Lyric Mews SE26 . . . .**23** D4
Lyric Rd SW13 . . . .**7** F6
Lysander Rd CR0 . . . .**60** F4
Lysias Rd SW12 . . . .**21** B8
Lysons Ave GU11 . . . .**105** E4
Lysons Rd GU11 . . . .**105** A1
Lyster Mews KT11 . . . .**73** C6
Lytchet Minster Cl 4
RG12 . . . .**27** F4
Lytchgate Cl CR2 . . . .**61** E3
Lytcott Dr KT8 . . . .**35** F6
Lytham RG12 . . . .**26** E3
Lytham Ct SL5 . . . .**29** C4
Lytton Dr RH10 . . . .**202** D7
Lytton Gdns SM6 . . . .**60** D6
Lytton House 3 TW12 . . . . .**16** B2
Lytton Rd GU22 . . . .**70** B3
Lyveden Rd SW17, SW19 . . .**20** F2
Lywood Cl KT20 . . . .**97** C5

M

Mabbotts KT20 . . . .**97** C5
Mabel St GU21 . . . .**69** D2
Maberley Cres SE19 . . . .**23** A1
Maberley Ct SE19 . . . .**23** A1
Maberley Rd Penge SE19 . . .**23** A1
Penge, Elmers End BR3 . . . . .**43** D6
Macadam Ave RG45 . . . .**45** C7
MacArthur House 4 SW2 . .**21** E8
Macaulay Ave KT10 . . . .**55** E8
Macaulay Ct CR3 . . . .**100** E6
Macaulay Rd CR3 . . . .**100** E6
Macbeth Ct RG42 . . . .**27** E8
Macclesfield Rd CR0, SE25 **43** C4
Macdonald Ct TW3 . . . .**5** C3
Macdonald Rd
Heath End GU9 . . . .**125** D2
Lightwater GU18 . . . .**67** A8
Macfarlane La TW7 . . . .**6** A8
MacGregor House SW12 . . .**21** D7
Mackenzie Rd BR3 . . . .**43** D7
Mackie House SW2 . . . .**22** A8
Mackie Rd 18 SW2 . . . .**22** A8
Mackies Hill GU5 . . . .**154** D7
Macklin House SE23 . . . .**23** B6
Mackrells RH1 . . . .**139** C6
Macleod Rd RH13 . . . .**217** F1
Macmillan House SM7 . . . . .**77** F4
Macphail Cl RG40 . . . .**25** E8
Maddison Cl TW11 . . . .**16** F2
Maddox La KT23 . . . .**93** E3
Maddox Pk KT23 . . . .**93** E4
Madehurst Ct RH11 . . . .**200** F3
Madeira Ave Bromley BR1 . .**24** E1
Horsham RH12 . . . .**217** C3
Madeira Cl KT14 . . . .**71** A6
Madeira Cres KT14 . . . .**70** F6
Madeira Rd Mitcham CR4 . . .**40** F5
Streatham SW16 . . . .**21** E3
West Byfleet KT14 . . . .**71** A6
Madeira Wlk RH1, RH2 . . . .**118** D2
Madeline Rd SE20 . . . .**23** A1
Madgehole La GU5 . . . .**153** B3
Madingley RG12 . . . .**27** B1
Madingley Ct TW1 . . . .**6** C2
Madison Gdns BR2 . . . .**44** F6
Madox Brown End GU47 . . .**64** E6
Madrid Rd GU2 . . . .**130** B8
Maesmaur Rd TN16 . . . .**103** D6
Mafeking Ave TW8 . . . .**6** E8
Mafeking Rd TW19 . . . .**12** B6

Magazine Cotts GU4 . . .131 C3
Magazine Pl KT22 . . . . . . .95 B5
Magazine Rd CR3 . . . . . .100 B5
Magdala Rd Isleworth TW7 . .6 A4
South Croydon CR2 . . . . . .61 D3
Magdalen Cl KT14 . . . . . .71 E5
Magdalen Cres KT14 . . . . .71 E5
Magdalen Rd SE25 . . . . . .43 A4
Magdalen Rd SW18 . . . . . .20 D7
Magdalene Cl RH10 . . . . .182 C1
Magdalene Rd
Littleton TW17 . . . . .33 F6
Sandhurst GU47 . . . . .45 F2
Magellan Terr RH10 . . . . .182 A2
Magna Carta La TW19 . . . .11 E7
Magna Carta Sec Sch
TW20 . . . . .12 D2
Magna Rd TW20 . . . . .11 B2
Magnolia Cl
Kingston u T KT2 . . . . . . .18 B2
Sandhurst GU47 . . . . .45 D1
Magnolia Ct
3 Belmont SM2 . . . . . . .59 B3
Horley RH6 . . . . .161 A3
Penge SE26 . . . . .23 C3
Richmond TW9 . . . . .7 B6
Wallington SM6 . . . . .60 B5
Magnolia Dr TN16 . . . . . . .83 E3
Magnolia Rd W4 . . . . .7 B8
Magnolia Way
Dorking RH5 . . . . .136 D4
West Ewell KT19 . . . . . . .57 C5
Magnolia Wharf W4 . . . . . .7 B8
Magpie Cl Coulsdon CR5 . . .79 C1
Crondall GU10 . . . . .124 C8
Magpie Wlk RH10 . . . . . . .201 F8
Maguire Dr Frimley GU16 . .66 C3
Richmond TW10 . . . . .17 C4
Mahonia Cl GU24 . . . . . . .67 F6
Maida Rd GU11 . . . . .105 B4
Maiden La RH11 . . . . . . .201 C8
Maiden's Gn SL4 . . . . .8 B6
Maidenbower Cty Fst Sch
RH10 . . . . .202 C4
Maidenbower Dr RH10 . . .202 C4
Maidenbower La RH10 . . .202 C4
Maidenbower Pl RH10 . . .202 C4
Maidenbower Sq RH10 . . .202 C4
Maidenshaw Rd KT19 . . . .76 D7
Maids of Honour Row **4**
TW9 . . . . .6 D2
Maidstone Cres GU24 . . . .87 D6
Main Dr RG12, SL5 . . . . . .28 B8
Main Rd TN16 . . . . .83 C5
Main St Chertsey KT15 . . . .52 E7
Feltham TW13 . . . . .15 D3
Mainprize Rd RG12 . . . . . .27 E7
Mainstone Cl GU16 . . . . . .86 C7
Mainstone Rd GU24 . . . . . .67 F3
Mainwaring Ct CR4 . . . . . .41 A7
Mais House SE26 . . . . .23 B6
Maise Webster Cl TW19 . .13 D8
Maisonettes The SM1 . . . . .58 F5
Maitland Cl Hounslow TW4 . .4 F4
Walton-on-T KT12 . . . . . . .54 E8
West Byfleet KT14 . . . . . .71 A6
Maitland Rd
Farnborough GU14 . . . . . .105 B8
Penge SE26 . . . . .23 D2
Maitlands Cl GU10 . . . . . .126 F6
Maizecroft RH6 . . . . .161 C4
Majestic Way CR4 . . . . . . .40 F7
Major's Farm Rd SL3 . . . . .1 A8
Major's Hill RH10 . . . . . . .203 C5
Malacca Farm GU4 . . . . . .111 B7
Malan Cl TN16 . . . . .83 E2
Malcolm Cl SE20 . . . . .23 C1
Malcolm Dr KT6 . . . . .37 E1
Malcolm Gdns RH6 . . . . . .160 D1
Malcolm Prim Sch SE20 . . .23 C1
Malcolm Rd Coulsdon CR5 . .79 D4
Croydon CR0, SE25 . . . . . .43 A3
Penge SE20 . . . . .23 C1
Wimbledon SW19 . . . . . . .19 E2
Malden Ave SE25 . . . . .43 B6
Malden Ct KT3 . . . . .39 B6
Malden Golf Course KT3 . .38 F7
Malden Green Ave KT4 . . . .39 A1
Malden Hill KT3 . . . . .38 F6
Malden Hill Gdns KT3 . . . .38 F6
Malden Manor Prim Sch
KT3 . . . . .38 E2
Malden Manor Sta KT3 . . .38 E2
Malden Parochial CE
Prim Sch KT3 . . . . .38 E1
Malden Pk KT3 . . . . .38 F3
Malden Rd Cheam KT4, SM3 .58 C8
New Malden KT3, KT4 . . . .38 F2
Malden Way KT3 . . . . .39 A5
Malden Way (Kingston
By Pass) KT3, KT5 . . . . . .38 E4
Maldon Cl SM6 . . . . .60 C5
Maldon Rd SM6 . . . . .60 B5
Malet Cl TW20 . . . . .12 D2
Maley Ave SE27 . . . . .22 B6
Malham Cl RH10 . . . . .202 C3
Malham Fell RG12 . . . . . . .27 A5
Malham Rd SE23 . . . . .23 D7
Malham Road Ind Est
SE23 . . . . .23 D7
Mall The Brentford TW8 . . . .6 D8
Croydon CR9 . . . . .61 C8
6 Guildford GU1 . . . . . .130 C8
Hersham KT12 . . . . .54 D5
Kingston u T KT6 . . . . .37 D4
Mortlake SW14 . . . . .7 C2
Mall The (Prep Sch) TW2 . .16 D5
Mallard Cl Aldershot GU12 .105 F2

Mallard Cl continued
Haslemere GU27 . . . . . . .207 E6
Horley RH6 . . . . .161 A5
Horsham RH12 . . . . .217 C5
Redhill RH1 . . . . .119 A4
Twickenham TW4 . . . . . . .16 A8
Mallard Ct Dorking RH4 . .136 A8
6 Richmond TW10 . . . . . .6 D1
Mallard Pl
East Grinstead RH19 . . . .205 E6
Twickenham TW1 . . . . . . .17 A5
Mallard Rd CR2 . . . . .62 D1
Mallard Way SM6 . . . . . . .60 C2
Mallard Wlk BR3, CR0 . . . .43 D4
Mallard's Reach KT13 . . . .53 D8
Mallards The Frimley GU16 .65 F2
Laleham TW18 . . . . .33 B7
Mallards Way GU18 . . . . . .67 A8
Mallards Cres GU4 . . . . . .110 C4
Malling Cl CR0 . . . . .43 C3
Malling Gdns SM4 . . . . . . .40 C3
Malling House **9** BR3 . . .24 A1
Malling Way SM4 . . . . .44 F2
Mallinson Rd SM6 . . . . . . .60 D7
Mallow Cl Burgh Heath KT20 .97 B8
Croydon CR0 . . . . .43 D1
Horsham RH12 . . . . .217 E6
Malloy Ct GU21 . . . . .70 A3
Malmains Cl BR3 . . . . .44 D5
Malmains Way BR3 . . . . . .44 D5
Malmesbury Fst Sch **5** SM4 .40 C2
Malmesbury Mid Sch SM4 .40 C3
Malmesbury Rd SM4 . . . . .40 C3
Malmstone Ave RH1 . . . . .119 D6
Malt Hill TW20 . . . . .11 B3
Malt House SL4 . . . . .11 B8
Malt House Cl SL4 . . . . . . .11 B8
Malta Rd GU16 . . . . .86 E8
Maltby Rd KT9 . . . . .57 A4
Malthouse Ct GU4 . . . . . . .130 E4
Malthouse Dr TW13 . . . . . .15 D3
Malthouse La
Pirbright GU24, GU3 . . . . .88 C2
West End GU24 . . . . .67 F7
Malthouse Mead GU8 . . . .170 F5
Malthouse
Rd RH10, RH11 . . . . .201 D4
Malthouses The Bylfeet KT14 .71 F6
Oxted RH8 . . . . .122 F4
Staines TW18 . . . . .12 E4
Malthouse La GU8 . . . . . .171 C1
Malton House SE25 . . . . . .42 E5
Malus Cl KT15 . . . . .51 F3
Malus Dr KT15 . . . . .51 F3
Malvern Cl Mitcham CR4 . . .41 C6
Ottershaw KT16 . . . . .51 C4
Penge SE20 . . . . .43 A7
Surbiton KT6 . . . . .37 E1
Malvern Ct Belmont SM2 . .59 A3
Brands Hill SL3 . . . . .1 A8
Epsom KT18 . . . . .76 D5
3 Surbiton KT6 . . . . . . .37 E1
Malvern Dr TW13 . . . . .15 D3
Malvern Rd Crawley RH11 .201 C5
Farnborough GU14 . . . . . . .84 D7
Hampton TW12 . . . . .16 A1
Harlington UB3 . . . . .3 E7
Surbiton KT6 . . . . .37 E1
Thornton Heath CR7 . . . . .42 A5
Malyons The TW17 . . . . . . .34 D3
Manatee Pl SM6 . . . . .60 D7
Manby Lodge Cty Inf Sch
KT13 . . . . .53 C5
Manchester Rd CR7 . . . . . .42 C6
Mandeville Cl
Guildford GU2 . . . . .109 A4
Merton SW19 . . . . .39 E8
Mandeville Ct TW20 . . . . .12 A4
Mandeville Dr KT6 . . . . . . .37 D1
Mandeville Rd
Isleworth TW7 . . . . .6 A5
Littleton TW17 . . . . .34 A4
Mandora Rd GU11 . . . . . . .105 B4
Mandrake Rd SW17 . . . . . .20 F5
Manfield Cty Fst Sch
GU12 . . . . .106 B2
Manfield Pk GU6 . . . . .174 B8
Manfield Rd GU12 . . . . . .106 A2
Mangles Ct **1** GU1 . . . . .130 C8
Mangles Rd GU1 . . . . .109 D3
Manley Bridge Rd
Rowledge GU10 . . . . .145 E4
Wrecclesham GU10 . . . . . .145 E4
Mann's Cl TW7 . . . . .5 F2
Mannamead RH18 . . . . . . .96 E8
Mannamead Cl KT18 . . . . .96 E8
Manning Cl RH19 . . . . . . .185 D2
Manning Pl TW10 . . . . .6 F1
Mannings Cl RH10 . . . . . .182 D1
Manningtree Cl SW19 . . . .19 E7
Manoel Rd TW2 . . . . .16 C6
Manor Ave Caterham CR3 .100 E3
Hounslow TW4 . . . . .4 D5
Manor Chase KT13 . . . . . .53 B5
Manor Cl
East Horsley KT24 . . . . . .112 F7
Haslemere GU27 . . . . . . .207 F6
Horley RH6 . . . . .160 F3
New Malden KT4 . . . . . . .38 E1
Pyrford GU22 . . . . .70 F3
South Godstone RH9 . . . .142 F5
Tongham GU10 . . . . .126 F7
Warlingham CR6 . . . . .81 C2
Manor Cotts GU21 . . . . . . .68 E5

Manor Cres Byfleet KT14 . . .71 F6
Guildford GU2 . . . . .109 B3
Haslemere GU27 . . . . . . .207 F6
Pirbright GU24 . . . . .87 D7
Surbiton KT5 . . . . .38 A3
Manor Ct Horsham RH12 . .218 A5
Kingston u T KT2 . . . . . . .38 A8
Streatham SW16 . . . . .21 E5
Twickenham TW2 . . . . . . .16 C6
Weybridge KT13 . . . . .53 B6
Manor Dr Feltham TW13 . . .15 D3
Hinchley Wood KT10 . . . . .56 A7
Horley RH6 . . . . .160 F3
Sunbury TW16 . . . . .35 A7
Surbiton KT5 . . . . .38 A3
West Ewell KT19 . . . . .57 E4
Woodham KT15 . . . . .52 A1
Manor Dr N KT3, KT4 . . . . .38 D2
Manor Dr The KT4 . . . . . . .38 E1
Manor Farm Ave TW17 . . .34 B3
Manor Farm Bsns Ctr
GU10 . . . . .126 F5
Manor Farm Cl GU12 . . . .105 F1
Manor Farm Ct TW20 . . . .12 A3
Manor Farm La TW20 . . . .12 A3
Manor Farm Rd CR7, SW16 .42 A7
Manor Fields
Horsham RH12, RH13 . . . .218 A4
Milford GU8 . . . . .149 E2
Seale GU10 . . . . .127 B4
Manor Fst Sch The KT14 . .71 E5
Manor Gdns
Effingham KT24 . . . . .113 D7
Farncombe GU7 . . . . .150 E7
Farnham GU10 . . . . .146 D5
Guildford GU2 . . . . .109 B3
Hampton TW12 . . . . .16 C1
Merton SW20, SW20 . . . . .39 F7
Richmond TW10, TW9 . . . . .6 F3
South Croydon CR2 . . . . . .61 F4
Sunbury TW16 . . . . .35 A7
Manor Gn GU8 . . . . .149 E2
Manor Gr Beckenham BR3 . .44 B7
Richmond TW9 . . . . .7 A4
Manor Green Rd KT19 . . . .76 C7
Manor Hill SM7 . . . . .78 F4
Manor House SM6 . . . . . . .60 B5
Manor House Ct KT18 . . . .76 C6
Manor House Dr SL5 . . . . . .9 A1
Manor House Flats GU10 .126 F6
Manor House Sch KT23 . . .113 E8
Manor House The GU15 . . .65 D6
Manor House Way TW7 . . . .6 B6
Manor La Feltham TW13 . . .15 A6
Harlington UB3 . . . . .3 D8
Lewisham SE12 . . . . .24 F8
Lower Kingswood KT20 . . .118 A6
Shamley Green GU5 . . . . .152 E3
Sunbury TW16 . . . . .35 B7
Sutton SM1 . . . . .59 C5
Manor Lea GU27 . . . . .207 E6
Manor Lea Cl GU8 . . . . . .149 E2
Manor Lea Rd GU8 . . . . . .149 E2
Manor Leaze TW20 . . . . . .12 B3
Manor Lodge GU2 . . . . . . .109 B3
Manor Mount SE23 . . . . . .23 C7
Manor Park Cl BR4 . . . . . .44 B1
Manor Park Ctr (Coll of
Tech) GU11 . . . . .105 B1
Manor Park Ind Est
GU12 . . . . .105 C1
Manor Park Prim Sch
SM1 . . . . .59 C5
Manor Park Rd Sutton SM1 .59 C5
West Wickham BR4 . . . . . .44 B1
Manor Pk Richmond TW9 . . .6 F3
Staines TW18 . . . . .12 D1
Manor Pl
East Bedfont TW14 . . . . . .15 A7
Great Bookham KT23 . . . . .94 A1
Mitcham CR4 . . . . .41 C6
Staines TW18 . . . . .13 B3
Sutton SM1 . . . . .59 B6
Manor Rd
Aldershot GU11, GU12 . . .126 A8
Ash GU10, GU12 . . . . . . .126 F8
Ashford TW15 . . . . .14 A3
Beckenham BR3 . . . . .44 B7
Belmont SM2 . . . . .58 F2
Croydon SE25 . . . . .43 A6
East Grinstead RH19 . . . .185 C1
East Molesey KT8 . . . . . . .36 D5
Farnborough GU14 . . . . . . .85 D3
Farnham GU9 . . . . .125 E4
Guildford GU2 . . . . .109 B3
Horsham RH12 . . . . .218 A5
Merstham RH1 . . . . .119 C6
Merton SW20 . . . . .39 F7
Mitcham CR4, SW16 . . . . .41 C6
Reigate RH2 . . . . .117 F3
Richmond TW10, TW9 . . . . .6 F3
Send Marsh GU23 . . . . . . .90 F4
Tatsfield TN16 . . . . .103 E7
Teddington TW11 . . . . . . .17 B3
Twickenham TW2 . . . . . . .16 D6
Wallington SM5, SM6 . . . .60 B5
Walton-on-T KT12 . . . . . . .34 F2
West Wickham BR4 . . . . . .63 B8
Woking GU21 . . . . .69 C3
Wokingham RG41 . . . . . . .25 A2
Manor Rd N
Hackbridge SM5, SM6 . . . .60 B6
Hinchley Wood KT7 . . . . . .56 A8
Manor Rd S KT10 . . . . . . .55 E6
Manor Royal RH10, RH11 .181 E1
Manor Royal Ind Est
RH10 . . . . .181 D1
Manor The GU8 . . . . .149 F1

Manor Way Bagshot GU19 . .47 F3
Beckenham BR3 . . . . .44 A6
Egham TW20 . . . . .11 F2
Guildford GU2 . . . . .129 F6
Mitcham CR4, SW16 . . . . .41 C6
New Malden KT4 . . . . . . .38 F1
Old Woking GU22 . . . . . . .90 B6
Oxshott KT22 . . . . .74 C3
Purley CR8 . . . . .79 E7
South Croydon CR2 . . . . . .61 F4
Woodmansterne SM7 . . . . .78 F3
Manor Way The SM6 . . . . .60 B6
Manor Wlk
1 Aldershot GU12 . . . .105 B1
Weybridge KT13 . . . . .53 B5
Manor Wood Rd CR8 . . . . .79 E6
Manordene Cl KT7 . . . . . . .37 A1
Manorcrofts Rd TW20 . . . .12 A2
Manorcroft Sch TW20 . . . .12 A2
Manorfields RH11 . . . . . . .200 D2
Manorgate Rd KT2 . . . . . . .38 A8
Manorhouse La KT23 . . . .113 E8
Mansard Beeches SW17 . . .21 A3
Mansard Manor SM2 . . . . .59 C3
Manse Cl UB3 . . . . .3 D8
Mansel Cl GU2 . . . . .109 B6
Mansel Rd SW19 . . . . .19 F2
Mansell Way CR3 . . . . . . .100 D5
Mansfield Cl SL5 . . . . .28 D7
Mansfield Cres RG12 . . . . .27 B3
Mansfield Dr RH1 . . . . . . .119 D6
Mansfield Pl SL5 . . . . .28 D8
Mansfield Rd
Chessington KT9 . . . . .56 D5
South Croydon CR2 . . . . . .61 D4
Wokingham RG41 . . . . . . .25 A5
Manship Rd CR4 . . . . .41 A8
Manston Cl SE20 . . . . .43 C8
Manston Dr RG12 . . . . . . .27 C3
Manston Gr KT2 . . . . .17 D3
Manston Rd GU4 . . . . .110 A5
Mantilla Rd SW17 . . . . . . .21 A4
Mantlet Cl SW16 . . . . .21 C1
Manville Ct GU4 . . . . .130 E1
Manville Gdns SW17 . . . . .21 B5
Manville Rd SW17 . . . . . . .21 B5
Many Gates SW12 . . . . . . .21 B6
Manygate La TW17 . . . . . .34 C3
Maori Rd GU1 . . . . .130 F8
Mapel Ct **3** RG12 . . . . . .27 F5
Maple Cl Ash Vale GU12 . .106 A7
Blackwater GU17 . . . . .64 C5
Crawley RH11 . . . . .181 C1
Hampton TW12 . . . . .15 F2
Horsham RH12 . . . . .218 A5
Mitcham CR4 . . . . .41 E8
Whyteleafe CR3 . . . . .80 F2
Maple Ct Catford SE6 . . . . .24 B7
2 Croydon CR0 . . . . . . .61 C6
Englefield Green TW20 . . .11 B2
Kingston u T KT3 . . . . .38 D6
11 West Norwood SW16 . .22 A3
Woking GU21 . . . . .69 C3
Maple Dr Crowthorne RG45 .45 C7
East Grinstead RH19 . . . .186 A1
Lightwater GU18 . . . . .66 F8
Maple Gdns TW15, TW19 . .13 E6
Maple Gr Brentford TW8 . . . .6 B7
Guildford GU1 . . . . .109 D3
Woking GU22 . . . . .89 C6
Maple Gr Bsns Ctr TW4 . . .4 C3
Maple Ho **3** GU14 . . . . .118 F1
Maple House **2** KT6 . . . .37 E4
Maple Ind Est TW13 . . . . .15 A5
Maple Inf Sch KT6 . . . . . . .37 D4
Maple Leaf Ct
Biggin Hill TN16 . . . . .83 D3
Farnborough GU14 . . . . . . .84 F3
Maple Mews SW16 . . . . . .21 F3
Maple Pl KT17 . . . . .77 D5
Maple Rd Ashstead KT21 . .95 D8
Kingston u T KT6 . . . . .37 D4
Penge SE20 . . . . .43 C8
Redhill RH1 . . . . .139 F5
Send Marsh GU23 . . . . . . .91 A3
Whyteleafe CR3 . . . . .80 F2
Maple Way Feltham TW13 . .15 B5
Headley Down GU35 . . . . .187 B6
Hooley CR5 . . . . .99 B6
Maple Wlk Aldershot GU12 126 D8
Sutton SM2 . . . . .59 B1
Mapledale Ave CR0 . . . . . .62 B7
Mapledrakes Cl GU6 . . . . .175 E5
Mapledrakes Rd GU6 . . . .175 E5
Maplehatch Cl GU7 . . . . . .150 E2
Maplehurst Beckenham BR2 44 E7
Fetcham KT22 . . . . .94 D4
Maplehurst Cl KT1 . . . . . . .37 E5
Mapleleaf Cl CR2 . . . . .81 D8
Maples The Banstead SM7 . .78 B5
Ottershaw KT16 . . . . .51 C4
4 Teddington KT8 . . . . . .17 C1
Maplestead Rd SW2 . . . . . .21 F8
Maplethorpe Rd CR7 . . . . .42 B5
Marble Hill TW1 . . . . .17 C8
Marble Hill Cl TW1 . . . . . . .17 B8
Marble Hill Gdns TW1 . . . .17 B8
Marbles Way KT20 . . . . . . .97 D8
March Rd
6 Twickenham TW1 . . . .17 A8
Weybridge KT13 . . . . .53 A5
Marcheria Cl RG12 . . . . . . .27 B3
Marches Rd RH12 . . . . . . .197 E4
Marchmont House **10**
. . . . .21 C3
Marchmont Rd
Richmond TW10 . . . . .6 F2
Wallington SM6 . . . . .60 C3

Marchside Cl TW5 . . . . .4 D6
Marcus Ct Brentford TW8 . . .6 E7
Woking GU22 . . . . .69 E1
Marcuse Rd CR3 . . . . .100 D4
Mardale GU15 . . . . .66 C4
Mardell Rd CR0 . . . . .43 D4
Marden Ave BR2 . . . . .44 F3
Marden Cres CR0 . . . . .41 F3
Marden Lodge Cty Prim
Sch CR3 . . . . .101 B6
Marden Rd CR0 . . . . .41 F3
Mardens The RH11 . . . . . .201 B7
Mare Hill GU8 . . . . .170 E5
Mare Hill Cotts GU8 . . . . .170 D4
Mare La GU8 . . . . .170 D4
Mares Field House GU4 . . .110 D2
Mareschal Rd GU2 . . . . . .130 C7
Maresfield CR0 . . . . .61 E7
Mareth Cl GU11 . . . . .105 B2
Marfleet Cl SM5 . . . . .59 E8
Margaret Cl TW18 . . . . . . .13 D2
Margaret Lockwood Cl
KT5 . . . . .37 F5
Margaret Rd GU1 . . . . . . .130 C8
Margaret Roper RC Prim
Sch CR8 . . . . .61 A1
Margaret Way CR8 . . . . . .100 B8
Margery Gr KT20 . . . . .117 E6
Margery La KT20, RH2 . . .118 A6
Margin Dr SW19 . . . . .19 D4
Marham Gdns
Morden SM4 . . . . .40 C3
Wandsworth SW17, SW18 . .20 E7
Maria Theresa Cl KT3 . . . .38 D7
Marian Cl SM1 . . . . .59 B5
Marian Rd CR4, SW16 . . . .41 C8
Marian Vian Prim Sch
BR3 . . . . .43 E4
Mariette Way SM6 . . . . . . .60 E2
Marigold Cl RG45 . . . . .45 A6
Marigold Ct GU1 . . . . .109 E4
Marigold Dr GU24 . . . . . . .68 A4
Marigold Way CR0 . . . . . . .43 D1
Marina Ave KT3 . . . . .39 B4
Marina Cl KT16 . . . . .33 C1
Marina Way TW11 . . . . . . .17 D1
Mariner Gdns TW10 . . . . . .17 C5
Mariners Dr
Farnborough GU14 . . . . . . .85 C6
Normandy GU3 . . . . .107 A3
Marion Ave TW17 . . . . . . .34 B4
Marion Ct SW17 . . . . .20 E3
Marion Rd Crawley RH10 . .202 B3
Thornton Heath CR0 . . . . .42 D4
Marist RC Prim Sch KT4 . .70 F6
Marius Mansions **3** SW17 21 A6
Marius Rd SW17 . . . . .21 A6
Marjoram Cl
Farnborough GU14 . . . . . . .84 B4
Guildford GU2 . . . . .109 A5
Marjorie Fosters Way
GU24 . . . . .87 D8
Marjory Kinnon Sch TW14 . .3 D2
Mark Oak La KT22 . . . . . . .94 A6
Mark St RH2 . . . . .118 B2
Mark Way GU7 . . . . .150 B8
Markedge La CR5, RH2 . . . .98 F2
Markenfield Rd GU1 . . . . .109 D1
Markenhorn GU7 . . . . .150 D6
Market Par Croydon SE25 . .43 A5
Feltham TW13 . . . . .15 E6
Market Pl Brentford TW8 . . . .6 C7
Kingston u T KT1 . . . . .37 D7
Wokingham RG40 . . . . . . .25 C5
Market Rd TW9 . . . . .7 A4
Market Sq Horsham RH12 .217 D1
Reigate RH2 . . . . .118 A1
Staines TW18 . . . . .12 E4
Market St Bracknell RG12 . .27 B7
Guildford GU1 . . . . .130 D8
Market The SM1, SM4, SM5 .40 C4
Marketfield Rd **14** RH2 . .118 F1
Marketfield Way RH1 . . . . .119 A1
Markfield CR0 . . . . .81 F8
Markfield Rd CR3 . . . . . . .101 B2
Markham Ct GU15 . . . . . . .65 D6
Markham House **21** SE21 . .22 E4
Markham Mews RG40 . . . .25 C6
Markham Rd RH5 . . . . . . .178 C5
Markhole Cl TW12 . . . . . . .15 F1
Marks Rd Warlingham CR6 . .81 E1
Wokingham RG41 . . . . . . .25 A5
Marksbury Ave TW9 . . . . . .7 A4
Markville Gdns CR3 . . . . . .101 A2
Markway The TW16 . . . . . .35 C7
Markwell Cl SE26 . . . . .23 B4
Markwick La GU8 . . . . . . .172 C2
Marlang Ct BR3 . . . . .44 D8
Marlborogh Rd TW7, TW8 . .6 B7
Marlborough **11** SW19 . . .19 D7
Marlborough Cl
Crawley RH11 . . . . .201 C2
Hersham KT12 . . . . .54 D7
Horsham RH12 . . . . .217 D5
Mitcham SW19 . . . . .20 E2
Marlborough Ct
Dorking RH4 . . . . .136 B7
Wallington SM6 . . . . .60 C3
Wokingham RG40 . . . . . . .25 D7
Marlborough Cty Inf Sch
GU11 . . . . .105 C2
Marlborough Dr KT13 . . . . .53 C7
Marlborough Gdns KT6 . . .37 D2
Marlborough House
SW19 . . . . .19 D5

Marlborough Jun & Inf Sch
TW7 . . . . .6 A6
Marlborough Rd
Ashford TW15 . . . . .13 E3
Dorking RH4 . . . . . .136 B7
Feltham TW13 . . . . .15 D6
Hampton TW12 . . . .16 A2
Mitcham SW19 . . . . .20 E2
Richmond TW10 . . . .6 F1
South Croydon CR2 . . . . .61 C3
Sutton SM1 . . . . . .59 A8
Woking GU21 . . . . .70 A3
Marlborough Rise GU15 .65 E6
Marlborough Trad Est TW9 .7 B6
Marlborough View GU14 .84 C5
Marld The KT21 . . . . .75 F1
Marler Rd SE23 . . . .23 F7
Marles La RH14 . . . .214 C1
Marley Cl KT15 . . . .51 F4
Marley Combe Rd GU27 .207 F4
Marley Croft TW18 . . . .12 E5
Marley Hanger GU27 .208 A3
Marley La GU27 . . . . .207 E4
Marlfield Ct KT3 . . . . .38 F2
Marlin Cl TW16 . . . . .14 E2
Marling Ct TW12 . . . . .15 F2
Marlingdene Cl TW12 . . .16 A2
Marlings Cl CR3 . . . . .80 C2
Marlins Cl 3 SM1 . . . .59 C5
Marlow SE20 . . . . . .43 B6
Marlow Cres TW1 . . . .5 F1
Marlow Ct RH10 . . . . .201 D7
Marlow Dr SM3 . . . . . .58 E7
Marlow House TW11 . . . .17 A4
Marlow Rd SE20, SE25 . . .43 B7
Marlowe Ct Dulwich SE19 .22 F3
6 Kingston u T KT2 . . . .17 D4
Marlowe House KT1 . . . .37 D5
Marlowe Lodge CR0 . . . .62 E8
Marlowe Sq CR4 . . . . .41 C5
Marlowe Way CR0 . . . .60 E8
Marlpit Ave CR5 . . . . .79 E2
Marlpit Cl RH19 . . . . .185 E4
Marlpit La CR5 . . . . .79 E2
Marlyns Cl GU4 . . . . .110 A4
Marlyns Dr GU1, GU4 . . .110 A4
Marmion House 13 SW12 .21 B8
Marmot Rd TW4 . . . . .4 D4
Marncrest Ct KT12 . . . .54 B5
Marnell Way TW4 . . . .4 D4
Marneys Cl KT18 . . . . .76 A4
Marnfield Cres SW2 . . . .21 F7
Maroons Way SE6 . . . . .24 A3
Marqueen Towers SW16 .21 F1
Marquis Ct 1 KT1 . . . .37 E5
Married Quarters CR3 . . .100 C5
Marriott Ct TW14 . . . . .3 D1
Marriott House SE6 . . . .24 C4
Marriott Lodge KT15 . . .52 C6
Marrowbrook Cl GU14 . . .85 A4
Marrowbrook La GU14 . . .85 A3
Marrowells KT13 . . . . .53 F7
Marryat Pl SW19 . . . . .19 E4
Marryat Rd SW19 . . . .19 E3
Marsh Ave Epsom KT19 . . .57 E1
Mitcham CR4 . . . . .41 A7
Marsh Ct Crawley RH11 .201 B1
3 Merton SW19 . . . . .40 C8
Marsh Farm Rd TW2 . . .16 F7
Marsh La KT15 . . . . . .52 B6
Marshall Cl
Farnborough GU14 . . . . . .84 F7
Frimley GU16 . . . . . .66 D2
Hounslow TW4 . . . . . .4 F2
Sanderstead CR2 . . . .81 A6
Marshall House 3 KT3 . .38 E5
Marshall Par GU21 . . . .70 A4
Marshall Pl KT15 . . . . .52 C2
Marshall Rd Crawley RH10 202 C4
Farncombe GU7 . . . . .150 E6
Sandhurst GU47 . . . . .64 D6
Marshall's Rd SM1 . . . .59 B6
Marshalls GU9 . . . . . .146 B8
Marshalls Cl KT19 . . . .76 C6
Marsham Ct 19 SW19 . . .19 D7
Marshfields C of E Fst Sch
KT16 . . . . .51 E4
Marshwood Rd GU18 . . .67 D8
Marston KT19 . . . . . .76 C8
Marston Ave KT9 . . . . .56 E4
Marston Ct KT12 . . . . .35 C1
Marston Dr
Farnborough GU14 . . . . . .85 B7
Warlingham CR6 . . . . .81 E1
Marston House RH1 . . .118 F2
Marston Rd Farnham GU9 .124 F2
Richmond TW11 . . . . .17 B3
Woking GU21 . . . . . .69 B2
Marston Way
North Ascot SL5 . . . . .28 E7
South Norwood SE19 . . .22 C1
Martel Cl GU15 . . . . .66 C7
Martell Rd SE21 . . . . .22 C5
Martens Pl GU7 . . . . .150 E6
Martin Cl Crawley RH11 .201 D8
Selsdon CR2 . . . . . .62 D1
Warlingham CR6 . . . . .81 B3
Martin Cres CR0 . . . .42 A1
Martin Ct SW19 . . . .20 A1
Martin Gr SM4, SW19 . . .40 A6
Martin House 5 KT3 . . .38 E5
Martin Rd GU2 . . . . .109 A3
Martin Way Frimley GU16 .65 E2

Martin Way *continued*
Merton SW19, SW20, SM4 .39 E6
Woking GU21 . . . . . .69 A1
Martin's Heron Sta RG12 .27 F5
Martin's Rd BR2 . . . . .44 F7
Martindale SW14 . . . . .7 C2
Martindale Ave GU15 . . .66 C4
Martindale Cl GU4 . . .110 D3
Martindale Rd
Balham SW12 . . . . . .21 B8
Hounslow TW4 . . . . . .4 E4
Woking GU21 . . . . . .69 A1
Martineau Cl KT10 . . . .55 D6
Martineau Dr RH4 . . .136 B5
Martingale Cl TW16 . . .35 A5
Martingale Ct GU11 . . .104 E2
Martingales Cl TW10 . . .17 D5
Martins Cl Blackwater GU17 64 D4
Guildford GU1 . . . . . .110 C2
West Wickham BR4 . . . .63 D8
Martins Dr RG41 . . . . .25 B7
Martins La RG12 . . . . .27 E6
Martins The
Crawley Down RH10 . . . .204 C8
Forest Hill SE26 . . . . .23 B3
Martins Wood GU8 . . .170 E7
Martinsyde GU22 . . . . .70 C2
Martlet Cnr RH12 . . . .214 D7
Martlets Cl RH12 . . . .217 C5
Martlets The RH10 . . .201 E6
Marton Cl SE6 . . . . . .24 A5
Marts The RH12 . . . . .214 D7
Martyn Rd GU1 . . . . .130 D8
Martyns Pl RH19 . . . .206 A8
Martyr Rd GU1 . . . . .130 D8
Martyrs Ave GU11 . . . .181 D1
Martyrs La GU21 . . . . .70 B7
Marvell Cl RH10 . . . . .202 C8
Marwell Cl BR4 . . . . .63 F8
Mary Adelaide Cl SW15 .18 E5
Mary Rd GU1 . . . . . .130 C8
Mary Rose Cl TW12 . . .36 A8
Mary Vale GU7 . . . . . .150 D2
Mary's Terr TW1 . . . . .17 A8
Marygold House TW3 . . .5 C6
Maryhill Cl CR8 . . . . .80 C2
Maryland Cl KT1 . . . . .38 B7
Maryland Rd CR7 . . . .42 B8
Maryland Way TW16 . . .35 A7
Marymount International
Sch KT2 . . . . .18 C1
Masefield Ct 16 KT6 . . .37 D2
Masefield Gdns RG45 . . .45 B3
Masefield Rd
Crawley RH11 . . . . . .200 E3
Hampton TW13 . . . . .15 F4
Masefield Way TW19 . . .13 F7
Maskall Cl SW2 . . . . .22 A7
Maskani Wlk SW16 . . .21 C1
Maskell Rd SW17 . . . .20 C5
Maskell Way GU14 . . .84 D3
Mason Cl
East Grinstead RH19 . . .185 E2
Hampton TW12 . . . . .35 F8
Wimbledon SW20 . . . .39 D8
Mason Ct 3 SE19 . . . .22 E2
Mason Rd Crawley RH10 .201 E4
Farnborough GU14 . . . .84 E6
Mason Way GU11 . . .126 B7
Mason's Ave CR0, CR9 . . .61 C7
Mason's Bridge Rd
Redhill RH1 . . . . . . .140 C3
Salfords RH1 . . . . . .140 C3
Mason's Pl CR4 . . . . .40 F8
Masonic Hall RH12 . . .16 C3
Masons Paddock RH4 . .115 A1
Massetts Rd RH6 . . . .161 A2
Massingberd Way SW17 .21 B4
Master Cl RH8 . . . . . .122 E6
Mastin House SW18 . . .20 A7
Maswell Park Cres TW3 .5 C2
Maswell Park Rd TW3 . . .5 C1
Matham Rd KT8 . . . . .36 D4
Mathew Terr GU11 . . .105 C2
Mathews Cl GU14 . . .105 E8
Mathias Cl KT18 . . . . .76 C6
Mathon Ct GU1 . . . . .109 F1
Matilda Cl SE19 . . . . .22 D1
Matlock Cres SM3 . . . .58 E6
Matlock Gdns SM1, SM3 .58 E6
Matlock Pl SM1, SM3 . . .58 E6
Matlock Rd CR3 . . . . .100 E6
Matlock Way KT3 . . . .38 D8
Matthew Arnold Cl
Cobham KT11 . . . . . .73 A5
Staines TW18 . . . . . .13 C2
Matthew Arnold Sch The
TW18 . . . . .13 C2
Matthew Ct CR4 . . . .41 D4
Matthew Rd GU9 . . .125 E8
Matthew's Gdns RH2 . . .82 D8
Matthew's St RH2 . . .139 A5
Matthews Cl SL5 . . . .29 D5
Matthews Dr RH10 . . .202 C1
Matthews La TW18 . . .12 F4
Matthews Rd GU15 . . .65 C8
Matthewsgreen Rd RG41 ..25 A8
Matthey Pl RH10 . . .182 D1
Matthias Ct 12 TW10 . . .6 E1
Maultway Cl GU15 . . . .66 B8
Maultway Cres GU15 . . .66 B8
Maultway N GU15 . . . .47 B1
Maultway The
Camberley GU15, GU16 .66 D6
Frimley GU15, GU16 . . .66 D6
Maunsell Pk RH10 . . .202 B6
Maurice Ave CR3 . . . .100 D5
Maurice Ct 3 TW8 . . . .6 D7

Mavery Ct BR1 . . . . .24 F1
Mavins Rd GU9 . . . .146 D8
Mavis Ave KT19 . . . . .57 E5
Mavis Cl KT19 . . . . . .57 E5
Mawbey Rd KT16 . . . .51 D4
Mawson Cl SW20 . . . .39 E7
Mawson La W4 . . . . . .7 F8
Maxine Cl GU47 . . . . .45 B1
Maxton Wlk RH11 . . .201 B2
Maxwell Cl CR0 . . . . .41 E1
Maxwell Ct SE21 . . . . .23 A7
Maxwell Dr KT14 . . . .71 C8
Maxwell Rd TW15 . . .14 C2
Maxwell Way RH10 . . .182 A1
May Cl Chessington KT9 .56 F4
Godalming GU7 . . . . .150 B2
2 Sandhurst GU47 . . . .64 D8
May Cotts CR5 . . . . . .98 B2
May Cres GU12 . . . . .105 E1
May Ct 2 SW19 . . . . .40 C8
May Rd TW2 . . . . . . .16 E7
May's Hill Rd BR2 . . . .44 E6
Maybelle Cl RH5 . . . .157 D3
Mayberry Pl KT5 . . . .37 F2
Maybourne Cl SE26 . . .23 B3
Maybourne Grange CR0 .61 E8
Maybourne Rise GU22 ..89 D3
Maybury Bsns Ctr
Woking GU22 . . . . . .70 A2
Maybury Cl
Burgh Heath KT20 . . . .97 E8
Frimley GU16 . . . . . .85 D8
Maybury Ct GU22 . . . .70 B2
Maybury Cty Inf Sch
GU21 . . . . .70 A3
Maybury Hill GU21, GU22 .70 B2
Maybury Rd GU21 . . . .70 B2
Maybury Rough GU22 . . .70 B2
Maybury St SW17 . . . .20 E3
Maycross Ave SM4 . . .40 A5
Mayday Hospl CR7 . . .42 B3
Mayday Rd CR0, CR7 . . .42 B3
Maydwell Ave RH13 . .215 C2
Mayefield Rd CR7 . . . .41 F4
Mayell Cl KT22 . . . . .95 C4
Mayes Cl CR6 . . . . . .81 D1
Mayes La RH12 . . . . .197 F3
Mayfair Ave
New Malden KT4 . . . . .39 A1
Twickenham TW2 . . . . .16 C8
Mayfair Cl Beckenham BR3 .44 B8
Surbiton KT6 . . . . . .37 E1
Mayfair Ct Beckenham BR3 .44 B8
4 South Croydon CR0 . . .61 F8
Mayfield Crawley RH10 .202 D6
Dormansland RH7 . . . .165 A1
Hersham KT12 . . . . .54 C6
Rowledge GU10 . . . . .145 F3
Mayfield Ave KT15 . . .52 C1
Mayfield Cl Ashford TW15 .14 B2
Farnham GU9 . . . . . .126 B6
Hersham KT12 . . . . .54 A6
Hinchley Wood KT7 . . .37 B1
Penge SE20 . . . . . . .43 B8
Redhill RH1 . . . . . . .140 A3
Weybridge KT15 . . . . .52 C1
Mayfield Cres CR7 . . .41 F5
Mayfield Ct Redhill RH1 .139 F4
Sutton SM2 . . . . . . .59 D4
Mayfield Cty Inf Sch GU14 85 B6
Mayfield Cty Jun Sch
GU14 . . . . .85 A6
Mayfield Gdns Egham TW18 12 F2
Walton-on-T KT12 . . . .54 A6
Mayfield Gr KT23 . . .114 A2
Mayfield Rd
Camberley GU15 . . . . .65 B1
Farnborough GU14 . . .84 F7
Hersham KT12 . . . . .54 A6
Merton SW19 . . . . . .39 F8
South Croydon CR2 . . .61 D2
Sutton SM2 . . . . . . .59 D4
Weybridge KT13 . . . . .52 F5
Mayflower Cl RH10 . . .202 D5
Mayford Cl Balham SW12 .20 F8
Penge BR3 . . . . . . .43 D6
Woking GU22 . . . . . .89 D5
Mayford Rd SW12 . . . .21 A8
Mayhurst Ave GU22 . . .70 C3
Mayhurst Cl GU22 . . . .70 C3
Mayhurst Cres GU22 . . .70 C3
Maynard Ct TW18 . . . .13 A4
Maynooth Gdns CR4 . . .40 F2
Mayo Rd
Thornton Heath CR0 . . .42 D4
Walton-on-T KT12 . . . .35 A2
Mayow Rd SE23, SE26 . . .23 D4
Maypole Rd
Ashurst Wood RH19 . . .206 E6
East Grinstead RH19 . . .185 D2
Mayroyd Ave KT6 . . . .57 A8
Mays Cl KT13 . . . . . .52 F1
Mays Cnr GU23 . . . . .90 D3
Mays Gr GU23 . . . . . .90 D4
Mays Rd
Teddington TW11, TW12 .16 D3
Wokingham RG40 . . . .25 E6
Maysfield Rd GU23 . . .90 D4
Maytree Cl GU1 . . . . .109 C5
Maytree Ct CR4 . . . . .41 A6
Maytree Wlk SW2 . . . .22 A6
Maytrees GU21 . . . . .68 C2
Maywater Cl CR2 . . . .80 D8
Maywood Cl BR3 . . . .24 B1
Maywood Dr GU15 . . .66 C6
Maze Rd TW9 . . . . . .7 A7
McAlmont Ridge GU7 .150 D7

McCarthy Rd TW13 . . .15 D3
McCormick House 9 SW2 22 A7
McDonald House 1 KT2 .17 F1
Mcdonald's Almshouses
GU9 . . . . .125 A1
McDonough Cl KT9 . . .56 E6
McDougall Ct TW9 . . . .7 A5
McGechie Ho RH19 . .185 D3
McIndoe Rd RH19 . . .185 D3
McIntosh Cl SM6 . . . .60 E3
McIver Cl RH19 . . . .184 F4
McKay Rd GU11 . . . .105 C3
McKay Rd SW20 . . . .19 C2
Mckay Trad Est SL3 . . .1 E5
McKinlay Ct BR3 . . . .43 F7
Mcleod Cl SE21 . . . . .23 A7
McLeod House SE23 . . .23 C6
McMillan Ct SE6 . . . .24 F7
McNaughton Cl GU14 ..84 D3
McRae La CR4 . . . . . .40 F2
Meachen Ct RG40 . . . .25 C6
Mead Ave RH1 . . . . .140 A1
Mead Cl Cranleigh GU6 .174 E2
Egham TW20 . . . . . .12 B2
Redhill RH1 . . . . . . .119 F4
Mead Cres Carshalton SM1 .59 E6
Little Bookham KT23 . . .94 A2
Mead Ct Egham TW20 . . .12 C2
Woking GU21 . . . . . .68 E3
Mead Cty Inf Sch The
KT19 . . . . .57 F6
Mead Dr CR5 . . . . . .79 E3
Mead End KT21 . . . . .75 F3
Mead La Chertsey KT16 ..33 C1
Farnham GU9 . . . . . .125 B2
Mead Path SW17 . . . .20 C2
Mead Pl CR0 . . . . . .42 C1
Mead Rd Caterham CR3 .100 F4
Cranleigh GU6 . . . . .174 E2
Crawley RH10 . . . . . .201 F7
Hersham KT12 . . . . .54 E6
Hindhead GU26 . . . . .188 F4
Richmond TW10 . . . . .17 C6
Mead The Ashstead KT21 ..95 E8
Beckenham BR3 . . . . .44 C8
Dorking RH4 . . . . . .136 C4
Farnborough GU14 . . .85 B3
Wallington SM6 . . . . .60 D4
West Wickham BR4 . . .44 E7
Mead Way Coulsdon CR5 .79 F1
Croydon CR0 . . . . . .62 E8
Guildford GU4 . . . . .110 C6
Hayes BR2, BR4 . . . . .44 F3
Meadcroft House 4 KT3 .38 E2
Meade Cl W4 . . . . . .7 A8
Meade Ct Bagshot GU19 ..47 F3
Walton on t H KT20 . . .97 A3
Meades Cl RH7 . . . .165 B1
Meades The RH7 . . .165 A1
Meadfoot Rd SW16 . . .41 C8
Meadhurst Pk TW16 . . .14 E2
Meadhurst Rd KT16 . . .33 B1
Meadhurst Sports Club
TW16 . . . . .14 F3
Meadlands Dr TW10 . . .17 D6
Meadlands Prim Sch
TW10 . . . . .17 C4
Meadow App RH10 . .183 A3
Meadow Ave CR0 . . . .43 D7
Meadow Bank
East Horsley KT24 . . .112 E8
Farnham GU9 . . . . .125 B1
Meadow Bglws GU4 . .131 B3
Meadow Brook Ind Ctr
RH10 . . . . .182 A1
Meadow Cl Ash Vale GU12 .85 F1
Blackwater GU17 . . . .64 D4
Catford SE6 . . . . . . .24 A3
Copthorne RH10 . . . .183 A3
Farncombe GU7 . . . .150 E7
Hersham KT12 . . . . .54 F6
Hinchley Wood KT10 . . .55 F7
Horsham RH12 . . . . .218 A5
Milford GU8 . . . . . . .150 A1
Purley CR8 . . . . . . .79 D6
Richmond TW10 . . . . .17 C7
Sutton SM1 . . . . . . .59 C8
Twickenham TW4 . . . . .16 A8
West Barnes SW20 . . .39 C5
Meadow Cotts GU24 . . .67 F7
Meadow Croft Cl RH6 .182 C8
Meadow Ct Epsom KT18 .76 C6
Farnborough GU14 . . .84 F4
Staines TW18 . . . . . .12 E5
Meadow Dr GU23 . . . .90 F4
Meadow Farm La RH12 .217 F7
Meadow Gdns TW18 . . .12 D3
Meadow Hill
Coulsdon CR5, CR8 . . .79 C6
New Malden KT3 . . . . .38 E3
Purley CR5, CR8 . . . . .79 C6
Meadow House GU4 . .110 D2
Meadow La KT22 . . . .94 C5
Meadow Pl W4 . . . . . .7 E7
Meadow Rd Ashford TW15 .14 D3
Ashstead KT21 . . . . .75 D2
Bromley BR2 . . . . . .44 E7
Carshalton SM1 . . . . .59 E5
Claygate KT10 . . . . .55 E4
Feltham TW13 . . . . .15 E6
Guildford GU4 . . . . .110 A5
Merton SW19 . . . . . .20 C1
Wentworth GU25 . . . .30 E4
Wokingham RG41 . . . .25 A5
Meadow Rise Coulsdon CR5 79 D6
Knaphill GU21 . . . . .68 C2
Meadow Stile CR0, CR9 .61 C7

Meadow The RH10 . . .183 A3
Meadow Vale GU27 . .208 A6
Meadow Vale Prim Sch
RG42 . . . . .26 F8
Meadow View RH6 . . .162 C3
Meadow View Rd CR7 ..42 B4
Meadow Way
Addlestone KT15 . . . . .52 B6
Aldershot GU12 . . . . .105 F3
Blackwater GU17 . . . .64 C5
Bracknell RG42 . . . . .27 A8
Burgh Heath KT20 . . .77 E2
Chessington KT9 . . . .56 E5
Great Bookham KT23 ..94 B4
Reigate RH2 . . . . . .139 B5
Rowledge GU10 . . . .145 F3
West End GU24 . . . . .67 F6
West Horsley KT24 . . .92 D2
Wokingham RG41 . . . .25 A5
Meadow Waye TW5 . . . .4 E7
Meadow Wlk
Hackbridge SM6 . . . . .60 B7
Walton on t H KT20 . . .97 B3
West Ewell KT17, KT19 ..57 F3
Wokingham RG41 . . . .25 A6
Meadowbank KT5 . . . .37 F3
Meadowbank Gdns
TW4, TW5 . . . . .4 B6
Meadowbank Rd GU18 ..48 C1
Meadowbrook RH8 . . .122 D6
Meadowbrook Cl SL3 . . .1 F6
Meadowbrook Rd RH4 .136 A2
Meadowcroft Cl
Crawley RH11 . . . . . .200 F5
East Grinstead RH19 . . .185 C2
Meadowcroft Cty Fst Sch
KT16 . . . . .51 F7
Meadowfield Cl KT3 . . .39 C5
Meadowlands
Cobham KT11 . . . . . .73 A6
Crawley RH11 . . . . . .201 C6
Oxted RH8 . . . . . . .123 A4
West Clandon GU4 . . .111 B5
Meadowlea Cl UB7 . . . .2 D8
Meadows End TW16 . . .35 A8
Meadows Leigh Cl KT13 .53 C7
Meadows The Ash GU12 .106 B2
Churt GU10 . . . . . . .167 F1
Guildford GU2 . . . . .130 C6
Sandhurst GU47 . . . .64 C5
Warlingham CR6 . . . .81 E2
Meadowside
Great Bookham KT23 ..94 A4
Horley RH6 . . . . . . .161 B4
Twickenham TW1 . . . .17 D7
Walton-on-T KT12 . . .54 C8
Meadowside Rd SM2 . . .58 E2
Meadowview SW19 . . . .1 F2
Meadowview Rd
Catford SE6 . . . . . . .24 A3
Reigate RH2 . . . . . .118 F4
West Ewell KT19 . . . .57 E2
Meadow GU7 . . . . . .150 F6
Meadow Lock GU7 . . .151 F2
Meads Cty Prim Sch The
RH19 . . . . .205 E7
Meads Rd GU1 . . . . .110 B1
Meads The Cheam SM3 .58 E7
East Grinstead RH19 . . .205 E7
Haslemere GU27 . . . .207 F6
Weybridge KT13 . . . . .53 D4
Meadside 4 Epsom KT18 .76 D6
7 Woking GU21 . . . . .69 F1
Meadside Cl BR3 . . . .43 E8
Meadsview Ct 3 GU14 ..85 B4
Meadvale RH12 . . . . .216 F2
Meadvale Rd CR0 . . . .43 A3
Meadway Ashford TW15 .14 A4
Beckenham BR3 . . . . .44 C8
Effingham KT24 . . . .113 E2
Epsom KT19 . . . . . .76 C7
Esher KT10 . . . . . . .55 B2
Frimley GU16 . . . . . .65 F2
Haslemere GU27 . . . .207 F6
Oxshott KT22 . . . . . .74 E5
Staines TW18 . . . . . .13 A1
Tolworth KT5 . . . . . .38 C1
Twickenham TW2 . . . .16 D7
Warlingham CR6 . . . .81 C3
West Barnes SW20 . . .39 C5
Meadway Cl TW18 . . . .13 A1
Meadway Dr
New Haw KT15 . . . . .52 C2
Woking GU21 . . . . . .69 D4
Meadway The RH6 . . .161 B4
Meaford Way SE20 . . .23 B1
Meare Cl KT20 . . . . . .97 D4
Meath Green Ave RH6 .160 F5
Meath Green Cty Jun Sch
RH6 . . . . .160 F5
Meath Green La
Horley RH1, RH6 . . . .160 F5
Salfords RH1, RH6 . . .160 E6
Meath Sch KT16 . . . .51 D3
Medawar Rd GU2 . . .129 D8
Medcroft Gdns SW14 . . .7 C3
Mede Cl TW19 . . . . . .11 D7
Mede Ct TW18 . . . . . .12 E5
Mede Field KT22 . . . .94 D3
Medfield St SW15 . . . .19 B8
Medhurst Cl GU24 . . .49 F2
Medina Ave KT10 . . . .55 E7
Medlake Rd TW20 . . . .12 C2
Medland Cl CR4 . . . . .41 A1
Medlar Cl Crawley RH11 .181 C1
Guildford GU1 . . . . .109 C3
Medlar Dr GU17 . . . . .64 F3
Medora Rd SW2 . . . . .21 F8

Medway RH10 . . . . .204 A5
Medway Cl CRO 43 C3
Medway Ct Horsham RH12 218 B5
  South Norwood SE25 . . . .42 E4
Medway Dr
  East Grinstead RH19 . . . .205 D6
  Farnborough GU14 . . . . . .84 E7
Medwyn Wlk RH11 . . . . . .200 F5
Melbourne Cl Penge SE20 .23 A1
Melbourne Ct Penge SE20 .23 A1
  Twickenham TW2 . . . . . . .16 D7
Melbourne Mews SE6 . . .24 C8
Melbourne Rd
  Merton SW19 . . . . .40 A8
  Teddington TW11 . . . . . . .17 C2
  Wallington SM6 . . . . .60 C5
Melbourne Way RH12 . . .217 B5
  Claygate KT10 . . . . .56 B4
  West Byfleet KT14 . . . . . .71 A5
Melbury Gdns SW20 . . . .39 B8
Melbury House TW2 . . . . .16 D6
Meldone KT3 . . . . .38 D1
Meldone Cl KT5 . . . . .38 B3
Meldrum Cl RH8 . . . . . . .123 A3
Melfield Gdns SE6 . . . . . .24 C3
Melfont Ave CR7 . . . . . . .42 B6
Melford Cl KT9 . . . . .56 F5
Melford Ct Dulwich SE22 .23 A8
  Sutton SM2 . . . . .59 C3
Melford Rd SE21, SE22 . . .23 A7
Melfort Rd CR7, SW16 . . .42 B6
Meliot Rd SE6 . . . . .24 D6
Melksham Cl RH13 . . . . .217 E1
Meller Cl SM6 . . . . .60 E7
Mellison Rd SW17 . . . . . .20 E3
Mellor Cl KT12 . . . . .35 F2
Mellor Ct 2 SW19 . . . . . .20 C1
Mellor House SE21 . . . . . .22 E4
Mellow Cl SM7 . . . . .78 C5
Mellows Rd SM6 . . . . . . .60 D5
Melody Rd TN16 . . . . . . .83 C1
Melrose RG12 . . . . .27 B1
Melrose Ave
  Farnborough GU14 . . . . . .84 C5
  Mitcham CR4 . . . . .21 B1
  Thornton Heath SW16 . . . .42 A6
  Twickenham TW2 . . . . . . .16 B8
  Wimbledon SW19 . . . . . . .20 A5
Melrose Gdns
  Hersham KT12 . . . . .54 C5
  Kingston u T KT3 . . . . . . .38 D6
Melrose Rd Barnes SW13 . .7 F5
  Biggin Hill TN16 . . . . .83 C1
  Coulsdon CR5 . . . . .79 B4
  Merton SW19 . . . . .40 A8
  Weybridge KT13 . . . . .53 A5
Melrose Sch CR4 . . . . . . .40 E6
Melrose Tudor SM6 . . . . .60 E5
Melsa Rd SM4 . . . . .40 C3
Melton Ct 8 Croydon CR0 .61 F8
  2 Twickenham TW1 . . . . .17 B8
Melton Fields KT19 . . . . .57 D2
Melton Pl KT19 . . . . .57 D2
Melton Rd RH1 . . . . .119 C5
Melville Ave Frimley GU16 .65 F1
  South Croydon CR0, CR2 . .61 F5
  Wimbledon SW20 . . . . . . .19 A1
Melvin Ct 11 TW9 . . . . . . .7 A6
Melvin Rd SE20 . . . . .43 C8
Melvinshaw KT22 . . . . . . .95 C6
Membury Cl GU16 . . . . . .86 A7
Membury Wlk RG12 . . . . .27 F5
Memorial Cl TW5 . . . . .4 F8
Memory Cotts KT20 . . . . .97 E8
Mendip Cl Forest Hill SE26 .23 C4
  Harlington UB3 . . . . .3 D7
  North Cheam KT4 . . . . . . .58 C8
Mendip Rd Bracknell RG12 .27 E4
  Farnborough GU14 . . . . . .84 E7
Mendip Wlk RH11 . . . . . .201 B6
Menin Way GU9 . . . . . . .125 D1
Menlo Gdns SE19 . . . . . .22 D1
Meon Cl Farnborough GU14 .84 D6
  Tadworth KT20 . . . . .97 B5
Meon Ct TW7 . . . . .5 E5
Meopham Rd CR4, SW16 . .41 C8
Merantum Way
  Merton SW19 . . . . .40 C8
  Mitcham SW19 . . . . .40 C8
Mercer Cl Crawley RH10 .202 C3
  Thames Ditton KT7 . . . . . .36 F2
Mercer Rd RH12 . . . . . . .217 C8
Merchiston Rd SE6 . . . . . .24 D6
Mercia Wlk 5 GU21 . . . . .69 F2
Mercury Cl RH11 . . . . . . .200 E3
Mercury Ctr TW14 . . . . . . .4 B2
Mere Cl SW15, SW19 . . . .19 D8
Mere End CR0 . . . . .43 D2
Mere Rd Oatlands Park KT13 53 D7
  Shepperton TW17 . . . . . . .34 B3
  Tadworth KT20 . . . . .97 B4
  Walton on t H KT20 . . . . . .97 B4
Merebank RH5 . . . . .157 D4
Merebank La CR0, SM6 . . .60 F5
Merefield Gdns KT20 . . . .97 D8
Meretune Ct SM4 . . . . . . .39 F6
Merevale Cres SM4 . . . . . .40 C3
Mereway Industry TW2 . . .16 E7
Mereway Rd TW2 . . . . . . .16 E7
Mereworth Cl BR2 . . . . . . .44 F4
Mereworth Dr RH10 . . . . .202 D8
Meridian Ct Catford SE6 . .24 F7
  Croydon CR0 . . . . .61 A6
  Sunningdale SL5 . . . . .29 B1

Meridian Gr RH6 . . . . . . .161 C4
Meridian Way RH19 . . . . .185 F3
Merland Cl KT20 . . . . .97 C7
Merland Gn KT20 . . . . . . .97 C7
Merland Rise KT18, KT20 . .97 C8
Merland Rise Cty Prim
  Sch KT20 . . . . .97 C8
Merle Common Rd RH8 .144 A3
Merlewood RG12 . . . . . . .27 D4
Merlewood Cl CR3 . . . . . .100 C3
Merlin Cl Brands Hill SL3 . . .1 D8
  Crawley RH11 . . . . .200 E6
  Mitcham CR4 . . . . .40 E6
  South Croydon CR0 . . . . . .61 B8
Merlin Clove RG42 . . . . . . .8 B2
Merlin Ct Beckenham BR2 . .44 F5
  Frimley GU16 . . . . .65 D1
  Sheerwater GU21 . . . . . . .70 C5
Merlin Ctr RH11 . . . . . . .181 C1
Merlin Gr BR3 . . . . .44 A4
Merlin Way
  East Grinstead RH19 . . . .186 A3
  Farnborough GU14 . . . . . .84 D3
Merling Cl KT9 . . . . .56 D5
Merlins Cl GU9 . . . . .125 C1
Merrick House RH2 . . . . .118 C4
Merricks St SW14 . . . . . . .7 B3
Merrilands Rd KT4 . . . . . .39 C1
Merrilyn Cl KT10 . . . . .56 A4
Merrist Wood Coll
  (Agricultural) GU3 . . . . .108 C7
Merritt Gdns KT9 . . . . . . .56 C4
Merrivale Gdns GU21 . . . .69 C2
Merrow Bsns Ctr GU4 . . .110 D4
Merrow CE Fst Sch GU4 . .110 D3
Merrow Chase GU1 . . . . .110 D1
Merrow Common
  Rd GU4 . . . . .110 D4
Merrow Copse GU1 . . . . .110 B2
Merrow Croft GU1 . . . . . .110 C2
Merrow Ct Guildford GU1 .110 D1
  Mitcham CR4 . . . . .40 D7
Merrow La GU4 . . . . .110 D5
Merrow Rd SM2 . . . . .58 D2
Merrow St GU1, GU4 . . . .110 D2
Merrow Way CR0 . . . . . . .63 C4
Merrowdene GU5 . . . . . . .110 B3
Merrow Pk
  Frimley GU15 . . . . .65 F4
  Reigate RH2 . . . . .118 B3
Merryacres GU8 . . . . . . .170 E6
Merryhill Rd RH12 . . . . . .217 A3
Merryhill Rd RG42 . . . . . .27 B8
Merryhills TN16 . . . . .83 D3
Merryhills La RH14 . . . . .213 A5
Merrylands KT16 . . . . . . .51 E7
Merrylands Ct KT23 . . . . .93 F4
Merrylands Farm KT23 . . .94 A3
Merrylands Rd KT23 . . . . .93 F3
Merryman Dr RG45 . . . . . .45 A7
Merrymeet SM7 . . . . .78 F5
Merryweather Ct 1 KT3 . .38 E4
Merrywood GU22 . . . . . . .95 C6
Merrywood Gr KT20 . . . .117 C5
Merrywood Pk
  Frimley GU15 . . . . .65 F4
Merrywood Cl GU21 . . . .105 F1
  South Norwood CR7 . . . . . .42 D7
Mersham Rd CR7 . . . . . . .42 D7
Merstham Cty Prim Sch
  RH1 . . . . .119 C6
Merstham Rd RH1 . . . . . .120 A5
Merstham Sta RH1 . . . . .119 C7
Merton Abbey Prim Sch
  SW19 . . . . .40 B8
Merton Cl GU47 . . . . .45 F2
Merton Gdns KT20 . . . . . .97 D8
Merton Hall Gdns SW20 . .39 E8
Merton Hall
  Rd SW19, SW20 . . . . . . .39 E8
Merton High St SW19 . . . .20 C1
Merton House SW18 . . . . .20 A7
Merton Ind Pk SW19 . . . . .40 C8
Merton Mansions SW20 . .39 D7
Merton Park Fst Sch
  SW19 . . . . .40 A7
Merton Park Par SW19 . . .39 E8
Merton Park Sta SW19 . . .40 A8
Merton Pl 9 SW19 . . . . . .20 C1
Merton Rd Croydon SE25 . .43 A4
  Merton SW19 . . . . .20 B1
  Wandsworth SW18 . . . . . .20 A7
Merton Road Ind Est
  SW18 . . . . .20 A8
Merton Tech Coll SW19 . .39 F4
Merton Tech Coll (Annexe)
  SW19 . . . . .40 A8
Merton Way
  East Molesey KT8 . . . . . . .36 C6
  Leatherhead KT22 . . . . . . .95 A8
Merton Wlk KT22 . . . . . . .75 A1
Mervyn Rd TW17 . . . . . . .34 C2
Metana Ho RH10 . . . . . .182 A3
Metcalf Rd TW15 . . . . . . .14 B3
Metcalf Way RH11 . . . . . .181 D2
Metcalfe Wlk TW13 . . . . . .15 E4
Meteor Way SM6 . . . . . . .60 E3
Meteorological Off (HQ)
  RG12 . . . . .27 D7
Metro Bsns Ctr The SE26 .23 F3
Metro Ctr SM4 . . . . .39 D2
Metro Ind Ctr TW7 . . . . . . .5 E5
Meudon Ave GU14 . . . . . .85 B3
Meudon Ct KT6 . . . . .37 D4
Meville Ct GU2 . . . . .130 C6
Mews Ct RH19 . . . . .205 F6
Mews The Banstead SM7 . .78 B4
  Broadbridge Heath RH12 .216 D4
  Dunsfold GU8 . . . . .192 F5

Mews The continued
  16 Farnham GU9 . . . . . . .125 B2
  Guildford GU1 . . . . .130 C8
Mewsend TN16 . . . . .83 D1
Meyer House 1 SW12 . . .21 B8
Meyrick Cl GU21 . . . . . . .68 E3
Mezel Hill Cotts SL4 . . . . .10 C3
Miall Wlk SE26 . . . . .23 E4
Michael Cres RH6 . . . . . .161 A1
Michael Fields RH18 . . . .206 E2
Michael Rd SE25 . . . . . . .42 E6
Michaelmas Cl SW20 . . . .39 C6
Michaelson
  House 4 SE21 . . . . .22 E4
Michel's Row 2 TW9 . . . . .6 E3
Micheldever Way RG12 . . .27 F4
Michelet Cl GU18 . . . . . . .48 B1
Michelham Gdns
  Burgh Heath KT20 . . . . . . .97 C7
  Twickenham TW1 . . . . . . .16 F5
Michell Cl RH12 . . . . .217 A2
Michels Almshouses 11
  TW10 . . . . .6 E2
Michelsdale Dr 3 TW9 . . . .6 E3
Mickle Hill GU47 . . . . .45 A1
Mickfield Prep Sch
  RH2 . . . . .118 A2
Mickleham Dr KT22, RH5 . .95 C1
Mickleham Gdns SM3 . . . .58 E4
Mickleham Hall RH5 . . . . .115 C7
Mickleham Way CR0 . . . . .63 D3
Mid Holmwood La RH5 . . .136 B1
Mid St Nutfield RH1 . . . . .119 F1
  South Nutfield RH1 . . . . .140 F7
Middle Ave GU9 . . . . . . .146 D8
Middle Bourne La GU10 .146 C7
Middle Church La 12
  GU9 . . . . .125 B2
Middle Cl Coulsdon CR5 . .100 A7
  Ewell KT17 . . . . .76 E7
  Frimley GU15 . . . . .66 C6
Middle Farm Cl KT24 . . . .113 D8
Middle Farm Pl KT24 . . . .113 D8
Middle Gn TW18 . . . . .13 D1
Middle Gordon Rd GU15 . .65 D5
Middle Green Cl 3 KT5 . . .37 F3
Middle Hill
  Aldershot GU11 . . . . .105 A3
  Englefield Green TW20 . . . .11 D3
  Frensham GU10 . . . . .146 C1
Middle La Ewell KT17 . . . .76 E7
  Teddington TW11 . . . . . . .16 F2
Middle Mill KT5 . . . . .37 F6
Middle Old Pk GU9 . . . . .124 F4
Middle Rd
  Leatherhead KT22 . . . . . . .95 B6
  Mitcham SW16 . . . . .41 D7
Middle Row 1 RH19 . . . . .205 F8
Middle St Brockham RH3 .137 C5
  Croydon CR0, CR9 . . . . . .61 C7
  Horsham RH12 . . . . .217 C2
  Shere GU5 . . . . .133 A4
Middle Way SW16 . . . . . .41 D7
Middlefield Farnham GU9 .146 A7
  Horley RH6 . . . . .161 C4
Middlefields CR0 . . . . .62 E2
Middlemarch GU6 . . . . . .170 E5
Middlemead Cl KT23 . . . . .94 A2
Middlemead Rd KT23 . . . .93 F2
Middlemoor Rd GU16 . . . .85 E8
Middlesex Ct KT15 . . . . . .52 C6
Middlesex House 6 SE20 .23 C1
Middlesex Rd CR4 . . . . . .41 E4
Middleton Gdns GU14 . . . .84 E6
Middleton Rd
  Camberley GU15 . . . . .65 F7
  Carshalton CR4, SM5 . . . .40 D2
  Downside KT11 . . . . .93 C8
  Epsom KT19 . . . . .57 D1
  Horsham RH12 . . . . .217 A2
  Morden SM4 . . . . .40 D2
Middleton Way RH11 . . . .200 E5
Midgarth Cl KT22 . . . . . . .74 D6
Midgley Rd RH10 . . . . . . .201 F8
Midholm Rd CR0 . . . . .62 E8
Midhope Cl GU22 . . . . . . .89 E8
Midhope Gdns GU22 . . . . .89 E8
Midhope Rd GU22 . . . . . . .89 E8
Midhurst SE26 . . . . .23 C2
Midhurst Ave CR0 . . . . . . .42 A2
Midhurst Cl RH11 . . . . . . .201 A7
Midhurst Rd GU27 . . . . . .208 B5
Midleton Cl GU8 . . . . . . .149 F2
Midleton Industrial
  Estate Rd GU2 . . . . . . .109 B2
Midleton Rd
  Guildford GU2 . . . . .109 A2
  Guildford GU2 . . . . .109 B2
  Kingston u T KT3 . . . . . . .38 C7
Midmoor Rd
  Streatham SW12 . . . . .21 C7
  Wimbledon SW19 . . . . . . .39 E8
Midsummer Ave TW4 . . . . .4 F3
Midsummer Wlk GU21 . . .69 D3
Midway Cheam SM3, SM4 . .39 F2
  Walton-on-T KT12 . . . . . . .54 B8
Midway Ave
  Chertsey KT16 . . . . .33 A6
  Chertsey KT16 . . . . .33 B6
  Thorpe TW20 . . . . .32 B6
Midway Cl TW19 . . . . .13 B5
Miena Way KT21 . . . . .75 D2
Mike Hawthorn Dr GU9 . .125 C3
Milbanke Ct RG12 . . . . . . .26 F7
Milbanke Way RG12 . . . . .26 F7
Milborne Rd RH10 . . . . . .202 C2
Milborough Cres SE12 . . .24 E8
Milbourne La KT10 . . . . . .55 C5

Milbourne Lodge Jun Sch
  KT10 . . . . .55 C4
Milbourne Lodge Sch
  KT10 . . . . .55 C4
Milbrook KT10 . . . . .55 C4
Milburn Wlk KT18 . . . . . . .76 E4
Milburn House SW20 . . . .39 B7
Milden Cl GU16 . . . . .86 A6
Milden Gdns GU16 . . . . . .85 F6
Mile Path GU22 . . . . .89 B7
Mile Rd
  Carshalton CR4, SM6 . . . .41 A1
  Wallington CR0, CR4,
  CR9, SM6 . . . . .41 C1
Miles Ct CR9 . . . . .61 B8
Miles La Cobham KT11 . . .73 E6
  South Godstone RH9 . . . .142 F1
  Tandridge RH8, RH9 . . . . .143 A7
Miles Pl GU18 . . . . .66 F7
Miles Rd Ash GU12 . . . . .106 B3
  Epsom KT19 . . . . .76 D7
  Mitcham CR4 . . . . .40 E6
Miles's Hill
  Holmbury St M RH5 . . . . .155 D5
  Peaslake RH5 . . . . .155 C3
Milestone Cl Ripley GU23 .91 B5
  Sutton SM2 . . . . .59 D3
Milestone Rd SE19 . . . . . .22 F2
Milford By Pass Rd GU8 .149 D2
Milford Gdns CR0 . . . . . . .43 D4
Milford Gr SM1 . . . . .59 C6
Milford Heath Rd GU8 . . .170 E8
Milford Hospl GU7 . . . . . .171 C8
Milford Lodge GU8 . . . . .170 E8
Milford Rd GU8 . . . . .148 E4
Milford Sta GU8 . . . . . . .171 A7
Milking La
  Biggin Hill, Downe BR6 . . . .83 E7
  Biggin Hill, Leaves Green BR2 83 D8
Mill Bay La RH12 . . . . . . .217 B1
Mill Cl Bagshot GU19 . . . .47 D3
  Carshalton SM5 . . . . .60 A8
  East Grinstead RH19 . . . .205 E7
  Great Bookham KT23 . . . . .94 A3
  Haslemere GU27 . . . . . . .207 C6
  Horley RH6 . . . . .160 E4
  Wokingham RG41 . . . . . . .25 A7
Mill Copse Rd GU27 . . . .208 B4
Mill Cotts
  East Grinstead RH19 . . . .205 E7
  Rudgwick RH12 . . . . .214 D5
Mill Farm Ave TW16 . . . . .14 E1
Mill Farm Cres TW4 . . . . .15 E2
Mill Farm Rd RH13 . . . . .218 A4
Mill Field GU19 . . . . .47 D3
Mill Gdns SE26 . . . . .23 B5
Mill Gn CR4 . . . . .41 A2
Mill Green Bsns Pk CR4 . .41 A2
Mill Green Rd CR4 . . . . . .41 A2
Mill Hill RH3 . . . . .137 B8
Mill Hill La RH3 . . . . .116 B1
Mill House La KT16 . . . . . .32 B5
Mill La Ascot SL5 . . . . . . .30 A7
  Bracknell RG12 . . . . .26 F5
  Bramley GU5 . . . . .151 F6
  Byfleet KT14 . . . . .71 F6
  Carshalton SM5 . . . . .60 A7
  Chiddingfold GU8 . . . . . . .191 B3
  Chilworth GU4, GU5 . . . . .131 F4
  Copthorne RH10 . . . . . . .183 E3
  Crawley RH11 . . . . .201 A8
  Croydon CR0 . . . . .61 A7
  Dorking RH4 . . . . .136 B8
  Dunsfold GU8 . . . . .192 F4
  Ewell KT17 . . . . .57 F2
  Felbridge RH19 . . . . .184 E5
  Felcourt RH7 . . . . .164 F2
  Fetcham KT22 . . . . .95 A5
  Forest Green RH5 . . . . . .176 D7
  Frensham GU10 . . . . .167 B7
  Godalming GU7 . . . . .150 D4
  Guildford GU1 . . . . .130 D7
  Hookwood RH6 . . . . .160 D3
  Horton SL3 . . . . .1 C4
  Kingsley Green GU27 . . . .208 C3
  Merstham RH1 . . . . .119 D4
  Ockham GU23 . . . . .91 D8
  Oxted RH8 . . . . .122 F2
  Parkgate RH5 . . . . .158 D5
  Pirbright GU24 . . . . .87 E3
  Shalford GU3 . . . . .130 C1
  The Chart RH8 . . . . .123 F4
  Thorpe TW16, TW20 . . . . .32 C5
  Witley GU8 . . . . .170 F5
Mill Lane Trad Est CR0 . . .60 F7
Mill Mead TW18 . . . . .12 F4
Mill Pl KT1 . . . . .37 F6
Mill Plat Isleworth TW7 . . . .6 A5
  Isleworth TW7 . . . . .6 B4
Mill Plat Ave TW7 . . . . .6 A5
Mill Pond Rd GU20 . . . . . .48 B6
Mill Rd Cobham KT11 . . . .73 C4
  Crawley RH10 . . . . .202 B7
  Epsom KT17 . . . . .76 F7
  Ewell KT17 . . . . .76 F7
  Kingswood KT20 . . . . .97 D4
  Merton SW19 . . . . .20 C1
  South Holmwood RH5 . . . .157 D7
  Thames Ditton KT10 . . . . .55 A8
  Twickenham TW2 . . . . . . .16 C6
  Wokingham RG40 . . . . . . .25 D6
Mill Ride SL5 . . . . .28 C8
Mill Shaw RH8 . . . . .122 F3
Mill St Colnbrook SL3 . . . . .1 D7
  Kingston u T KT1 . . . . . . .37 E6
  Redhill RH1 . . . . .139 F8
Mill Stream GU9 . . . . . . .125 E6
Mill Vale BR2 . . . . .44 F7

Mill View Cl KT17 . . . . . . .57 F3
Mill View Gdns CR0 . . . . .62 D7
Mill Way
  East Grinstead RH19 . . . .205 E7
  Feltham TW14 . . . . .4 B2
  Headley KT18 . . . . .96 A2
Millais RH13 . . . . .218 A3
Millais Cl RH11 . . . . .200 F2
Millais Ct RH13 . . . . .218 A4
Millais Rd KT3 . . . . .38 E2
Millais Sch RH13 . . . . . . .217 F2
Millais Sch Lower Sch
  RH13 . . . . .217 F2
Millais Way KT19 . . . . . . .57 C6
Millan Cl KT15 . . . . .52 B1
Milland House 1 SW15 . . .19 A7
Millbank SM6 . . . . .60 D5
Millbourne Rd TW13 . . . . .15 E4
Millbrook Guildford GU1 . .130 D7
  Oatlands Park KT13 . . . . . .53 E6
Millbrook Way SL3 . . . . . . .1 E5
Millcombe Cl 5 GU21 . . . .69 B1
Millcroft House SE6 . . . . .24 B4
Miller House 9 SW2 . . . . .21 F7
Miller Rd Guildford GU4 . .110 C4
  Mitcham SW19 . . . . .20 C1
  Thornton Heath CR0 . . . . .42 A1
Miller's Ct TW20 . . . . .12 C3
Miller's La RH1 . . . . .162 C7
Millers Cl TW18 . . . . .13 B3
Millers Copse
  Langley Vale KT18 . . . . . . .96 D8
  Outwood RH1 . . . . .162 B7
Millers Gate RH12 . . . . . .217 D5
Millers Mead Ct SW19 . . .20 D1
Millfarm Bsns Pk TW4 . . .15 E8
Millfield Charlton TW16 . . .34 C8
  Kingston u T KT1 . . . . . . .37 F6
Millfield La KT20 . . . . .98 A2
Millfield Rd TW4 . . . . .15 F2
Millford GU21 . . . . .69 B2
Millford Cty Inf Sch GU8 .149 F1
Millgate Ct GU9 . . . . . . .125 D3
Millhedge Cl KT11 . . . . . .73 E3
Millholme Wlk GU15 . . . . .66 C4
Millhouse Pl SE27 . . . . . .22 B4
Millins Cl GU47 . . . . .45 E1
Millmead Byfleet KT14 . . .71 F7
  Guildford GU2 . . . . .130 C7
  Wokingham RG41 . . . . . . .25 A7
Millmead Terr GU2 . . . . .130 C7
Millpond Cotts GU8 . . . . .172 D4
Millpond Ct KT15 . . . . . . .52 E5
Mills Ho RG12 . . . . .105 D3
Mills Spur SL4 . . . . .11 B8
Mills's Rd KT12 . . . . .54 C5
Millside SM5 . . . . .59 F8
Millside Ct KT23 . . . . .94 A2
Millside Pl TW7 . . . . .6 B5
Millstream The GU27 . . . .207 E6
Millthorpe Rd RH12 . . . . .217 F4
Millview Cl RH2 . . . . .118 D3
Millway RH2 . . . . .118 D1
Millwood RH10 . . . . .204 D5
Millwood Rd TW3, TW7 . . . .5 C2
Milman Cl RG12 . . . . .28 A3
Milne Cl RH11 . . . . .200 E3
Milne Pk E CR0 . . . . .82 D8
Milne Pk W CR0 . . . . .82 D8
Milner App CR3 . . . . .101 A6
Milner Cl CR3 . . . . .101 A5
Milner Dr Cobham KT11 . .73 F7
  Twickenham TW2 . . . . . . .16 D8
Milner Rd Caterham CR3 .101 A6
  Kingston u T KT1 . . . . . . .37 D6
  Merton SW19 . . . . .40 B8
  Morden CR4, SM4 . . . . . .40 D4
  South Norwood CR7 . . . . . .42 D6
Milnthorpe Rd W4 . . . . . . .7 D8
Milnwood Rd RH12 . . . . .217 C3
Milstead Cl KT20 . . . . . . .97 B5
Milton Ave Carshalton SM1 .59 E6
  Croydon CR0 . . . . .42 D2
  Westcott RH4 . . . . .135 D6
Milton Cl Bracknell RG12 . .27 B3
  Carshalton SM1 . . . . .59 F6
  Horton SL3 . . . . .1 A4
Milton Cres RH19 . . . . . .205 C8
Milton Ct Kingston u T KT2 .17 E4
  Twickenham TW2 . . . . . . .16 E5
  Wokingham RG40 . . . . . . .25 B7
Milton Dr Littleton TW17 . .33 E5
  Wokingham RG40 . . . . . . .25 B7
Milton Gdns Epsom KT18 . .76 E5
  Stanwell TW19 . . . . .13 F7
  Wokingham RG40 . . . . . . .25 B6
Milton Grange GU12 . . . .106 A5
Milton House
  12 Beckenham BR3 . . . . . .24 A1
  5 Kingston u T KT2 . . . . .18 B2
  Sutton SM1 . . . . .59 A7
Milton Lodge TW1 . . . . . .16 F7
Milton Mount RH10 . . . . .182 D1
Milton Mount Ave RH10 .202 D8
Milton Mount Cty Fst &
  Mid Sch RH10 . . . . .202 C8
Milton Rd Addlestone KT15 .52 A4
  Caterham CR3 . . . . .100 D6
  Crawley RH10 . . . . .202 C2
  Croydon CR0 . . . . .42 D2
  Egham TW20 . . . . .11 D3
  Hampton TW12 . . . . .36 B8
  Horsham RH12 . . . . .217 C3
  Mitcham CR4 . . . . .21 A1

Milton Rd *continued*
Mortlake SW14 . . . . .7 D4
Sutton SM1 . . . . .59 A6
Wallington SM6 . . . . .60 D4
Walton-on-T KT12 . . . . .54 D7
Wimbledon SW19 . . . . .20 C2
Wokingham RG40, RG41 . . . . .25 B6
Milton St RH4 . . . . .135 D6
Milton Way KT23 . . . . .94 C2
Miltoncourt La RH4 . . . . .135 E7
Miltons Cres GU7 . . . . .150 B2
Milverton House SE23 . . . .23 E5
Milward Gdns RG12 . . . . . . .26 C7
Mina Rd SW19 . . . . .40 A8
Minard Rd SE6 . . . . .24 E7
Minchin Cl KT22 . . . . .95 A5
Mincing La GU24 . . . . .49 F2
Minden Rd Cheam SM3 . . . . .58 F8
Penge SE20 . . . . .43 B8
Mindleheim Ave RH19 . . . . .186 B2
Minehead Rd SW16 . . . . .21 F3
Minehurst Rd GU16 . . . . .85 F4
Minerva Cl TW19 . . . . .2 A2
Minerva Rd KT1 . . . . .37 F7
Minimax Cl TW14 . . . . .4 A1
Mink Ct TW4 . . . . .4 C5
Minley Cl GU14 . . . . .84 E4
Minley Rd Blackwater GU17 .84 A7
Farnborough GU14 . . . . .84 D5
Minniedale KT5 . . . . .37 F4
Minorca Ave GU16 . . . . .66 E2
Minorca Rd Frimley GU16 . . .66 E1
Weybridge KT13 . . . . .53 A6
Minshull Pl 24 BR3 . . . . .24 A1
Minstead Cl RG12 . . . . .27 F6
Minstead Gdns SW15 . . . . . .18 F8
Minstead Way KT3 . . . . .38 E3
Minster Ave SM1 . . . . .59 A8
Minster Ct Camberley GU15 .65 D7
Camberley, York Town GU15 . .64 F4
Minster Dr CR0 . . . . .61 E6
Minster Gdns KT8 . . . . .35 F5
Minster Rd GU7 . . . . .150 D1
Minsterley Ave
TW16, TW17 . . . . .34 E5
Minstrel Gdns KT5 . . . . .37 F5
Mint Gdns RH4 . . . . .136 A8
Mint La KT20 . . . . .118 A6
Mint Rd
Wallington SM5, SM6 . . . . . . .60 B6
Woodmansterne SM7 . . . . . . .78 C3
Mint St GU7 . . . . .150 D4
Mint The GU7 . . . . .150 D4
Mint Wlk Croydon CR0, CR9 .61 C7
Knaphill GU21 . . . . .68 E2
Warlingham CR6 . . . . .81 D2
Miranda Wlk RH11 . . . . .200 E4
Mirfield Ct SE20 . . . . .43 A7
Misbrooks Green
Rd RH5 . . . . .178 E8
Missenden Cl TW14 . . . . .14 F7
Missenden Gdns SM4 . . . . .40 C3
Mission Sq 13 TW8 . . . . .6 E8
Mistletoe Cl CR0 . . . . .43 D1
Mistley Ct 6 KT18 . . . . .76 D6
Misty's Field KT12 . . . . .35 C1
Mitcham Garden Village
CR4 . . . . .41 A8
Mitcham Ind Est CR4 . . . . . . .41 A8
Mitcham Junc CR4 . . . . .41 A4
Mitcham La SW16 . . . . .21 C3
Mitcham Pk CR4 . . . . .40 F5
Mitcham Rd
Camberley GU15 . . . . .47 A1
Thornton Heath CR0, CR9 . . . .41 F3
Upper Tooting SW17 . . . . .20 F3
Mitcham Sta CR4 . . . . .40 E5
Mitchell Gdns RH13 . . . . . . .215 E3
Mitchell's Row GU4 . . . . . . .130 E2
Mitchells Cl GU4 . . . . .130 E3
Mitchells Cotts GU4 . . . . . .131 E1
Mitchells Rd RH10 . . . . .201 F6
Mitchley Ave CR2, CR8 . . . . .80 D6
Mitchley Gr CR2 . . . . .81 A6
Mitchley Hill CR2 . . . . .80 F6
Mitchley View CR2 . . . . .81 A6
Mitford Wlk 11 RH11 . . . . . .201 A3
Mitre Cl Shepperton TW17 . .34 D3
Sutton SM2 . . . . .59 D3
Mixbury Gr KT13 . . . . .53 D4
Mixnams La KT16 . . . . .33 A6
Mizen Cl KT11 . . . . .73 D5
Mizen Way KT11 . . . . .73 D4
Moat Ct Ashstead KT21 . . . . .75 E2
Ottershaw KT16 . . . . .51 C4
Moat Rd RH19 . . . . .185 E2
Moat Side TW13 . . . . .15 C4
Moat The KT3 . . . . .38 E8
Moat Wlk RH10 . . . . .202 C7
Moats La RH1 . . . . .140 F3
Moberly Rd SW4 . . . . .21 D8
Model Cotts SW14 . . . . .7 C4
Moffat Ct
Upper Tooting SW17 . . . . .20 E4
Wimbledon SW19 . . . . .20 A3
Moffat Rd
South Norwood CR7 . . . . .42 D7
Upper Tooting SW17 . . . . .20 F4
Moffatts Cl GU47 . . . . .64 A8
Mogador Cotts KT20 . . . . . .117 D7
Mogador Rd KT20 . . . . .117 E7
Mogden La TW7 . . . . .5 F2
Moir Cl CR2 . . . . .62 A2
Moira Ct SW17 . . . . .21 A6

Mole Abbey Gdns KT8 . . . .36 B6
Mole Bsns Pk KT22 . . . . .95 A6
Mole Cl Crawley RH11 . . . . .201 B8
Farnborough GU14 . . . . .84 D6
Mole Ct KT19 . . . . .57 C6
Mole House KT12 . . . . .54 E5
Mole Rd Fetcham KT22 . . . . .94 D6
Hersham KT12 . . . . .54 D5
Mole St RH5 . . . . .177 B5
Mole Valley Pl KT21 . . . . . . .95 D8
Molember Ct KT7 . . . . .36 E5
Molember Rd KT8 . . . . .36 E4
Moles Cl RG40 . . . . .25 D5
Moles Hill KT10 . . . . .74 D8
Molesey Ave KT12, KT8 . . . .35 F4
Molesey Cl KT12 . . . . .54 E6
Molesey Dr SM3 . . . . .58 E7
Molesey Hospl KT8 . . . . .36 A4
Molesey Park Ave KT8 . . . . .36 B4
Molesey Park Cl KT8 . . . . . .36 C4
Molesey Park Rd KT8 . . . . . .36 C4
Molesey Rd
East Molesey KT12 . . . . .35 E2
Hersham KT12 . . . . .54 D5
Molesham Cl KT8 . . . . .36 B6
Molesham Way KT8 . . . . .36 B6
Molesley Rd Hersham KT12 .54 E8
Walton-on-T KT12 . . . . .54 E8
Molesworth Rd KT11 . . . . . . .73 A6
Moliner Ct 4 BR3 . . . . .24 A1
Molins Ct 5 RH11 . . . . .201 A3
Mollie Davis Ct SE19 . . . . . .22 F2
Mollison Dr SM6 . . . . .60 E3
Molly Huggins Cl SW12 . . . .21 C8
Molly Millar's La RG41 . . . . .25 A4
Molly Millar Bridge RG41 . . .25 B4
Molyneux Dr SW17 . . . . .21 B4
Molyneux Rd
Farncombe GU7 . . . . .150 F7
Weybridge KT13 . . . . .53 A5
Windlesham GU20 . . . . .48 D4
Monahan Ave CR8 . . . . .79 F8
Monarch Cl Coney Hall BR4 .63 F6
Crawley RH11 . . . . .201 A3
East Bedfont TW14 . . . . .14 E8
Monarch Mews
SE27, SW16 . . . . .22 A3
Monarch Par CR4 . . . . .40 F7
Monaveen Gdns KT8 . . . . . . .36 B6
Monby Lodge Inf Sch
KT13 .53 C5
Mondial Way UB7 . . . . .3 C7
Money Ave CR3 . . . . .100 E5
Money Rd CR3 . . . . .100 D5
Monivea Rd BR3 . . . . .23 F1
Monk's Wlk
Farnham GU10, GU9 . . . . . . .146 F8
Reigate RH2 . . . . .118 B1
Monkleigh Rd SM4, SW20 . .39 E5
Monks Ave KT8 . . . . .35 F4
Monks Cl Ascot SL5 . . . . . . .29 B3
Farnborough GU14 . . . . .85 C4
Monks Cres
Addlestone KT15 . . . . .52 B5
Walton-on-T KT12 . . . . .35 B1
Monks Ct RH2 . . . . .118 B1
Monks Dr SL5 . . . . .29 B3
Monks Gn KT22 . . . . .94 D6
Monks La
Limpsfield RH8, TN8 . . . . . . .144 E6
Rowhook RH5 . . . . .196 F5
Monks Orchard Rd
Beckenham BR3, CR0 . . . . . . .44 A1
Croydon BR3, CR0 . . . . .44 A1
Monks Orchard Sch CR0 . . . .43 D4
Monks Rd Banstead SM7 . . .78 A3
Virginia Water GU25 . . . . .31 D5
Monks Way Beckenham BR3 .44 A3
Harmondsworth UB7 . . . . .2 A3
Staines TW18 . . . . .13 D1
Monks' Well GU10 . . . . .147 C5
Monks Wlk SL5 . . . . .29 B3
Monksdene Gdns SM1 . . . . .59 B7
Monksfield RH10 . . . . .201 F7
Monkshanger GU9 . . . . .125 E2
Monkshood Cl RG40 . . . . . . .25 E7
Monkswell La CR5 . . . . .98 B2
Monkton La GU9 . . . . .125 E5
Monkton Pk GU9 . . . . .125 F4
Monmouth Ave KT1 . . . . .17 C1
Monmouth Cl CR4, SW16 . . .41 E5
Mono La TW13 . . . . .15 B6
Monro Dr GU2 . . . . .109 B4
Monroe Dr SW14 . . . . .7 B2
Mons Cl GU11 . . . . .105 E7
Mons Wlk TW20 . . . . .12 C3
Monsell Gdns TW18 . . . . . . .12 E3
Monson Rd RH1 . . . . .118 F4
Montacute Cl GU14 . . . . .85 D4
Montacute Rd
Forest Hill SE23, SE6 . . . . . . .23 F8
Morden SM4 . . . . .40 D3
New Addington CR0 . . . . .63 C2
Montagu Gdns SM6 . . . . . . .60 C6
Montague Ave CR2 . . . . .80 E7
Montague Cl
Camberley GU15 . . . . .65 B5
Lightwater GU18 . . . . .48 A1
Walton-on-T KT12 . . . . .35 A2
Wokingham RG40 . . . . .25 E7
Montague Dr CR3 . . . . .100 C5
Montague House (Coll &
Liby) RG40 . . . . .25 C6
Montague Rd Hounslow TW3 .5 B4
Merton SW19 . . . . .20 B1
Richmond TW10 . . . . .6 E1
Thornton Heath CR0 . . . . .42 B1
Montana Cl CR2 . . . . .61 D1

Montana Gdns
Beckenham SE6 . . . . .23 F3
5 Sutton SM1 . . . . .59 C5
Montana Rd
Upper Tooting SW17 . . . . .21 A5
Wimbledon SW20 . . . . .39 C8
Montem Rd Forest Hill SE23 23 F8
New Malden KT3 . . . . .38 E5
Montford Rd TW16 . . . . .35 A5
Montfort Pl SW19 . . . . .19 D7
Montfort Rise RH1 . . . . .139 F1
Montgomerie Dr GU2 . . . . .109 A6
Montgomery Ave KT10 . . . . .55 E8
Montgomery Cl
Mitcham CR4 . . . . .41 E5
Sandhurst GU47 . . . . .64 B8
Montgomery Ct
Chiswick W4 . . . . .7 C8
Leatherhead KT22 . . . . .95 C7
Montgomery House 5
SW14 . . . . .7 D4
Montgomery Rd
Farnborough GU14 . . . . .84 F3
2 Woking GU22 . . . . .69 E1
Montpelier Ct BR2 . . . . .44 F5
Montpelier Rd
Purley CR2, CR8 . . . . .61 B1
South Croydon CR2, CR8 . . . .61 B1
Sutton SM1 . . . . .59 C6
Montpelier Row TW1 . . . . . .17 C3
Montrave Rd SE20 . . . . .23 C1
Montrell Rd SW2 . . . . .21 E7
Montreux Ct RH11 . . . . .201 B6
Montrose Ave TW2 . . . . .16 B8
Montrose Cl Ashford TW15 . .14 C3
Frimley GU16 . . . . .65 E2
Montrose Gdns
Mitcham CR4 . . . . .40 F7
Oxshott KT22 . . . . .74 D7
Sutton SM1 . . . . .59 B8
Montrose Rd TW14 . . . . .3 D1
Montrose Way SE23 . . . . . . .23 D7
Montrose Wlk KT13 . . . . .53 B7
Montrouge Cres KT17 . . . . . .77 C3
Montserrat Cl SE19 . . . . .22 D3
Monument Bridge Ind Est
E GU21 . . . . .70 B4
Monument Bridge
Ind Est W GU21 . . . . .70 A4
Monument Hill KT13 . . . . . . .53 B6
Monument Hill Cty Prim
Sch GU22 . . . . .70 C4
Monument Rd
Sheerwater GU21 . . . . .70 B4
Weybridge KT13 . . . . .53 B7
Monument Way E GU21 . . . .70 B4
Monument Way W GU21 . . . .70 A4
Moon Ct KT22 . . . . .94 D6
Moon's La RH19, RH7, TN8 186 E8
Moons Hill GU10 . . . . .146 C2
Moons La RH13 . . . . .217 E1
Moor Cl GU47 . . . . .45 E1
Moor House Sch RH8 . . . . . .122 F3
Moor La Chessington KT9 . . .56 E5
Harmondsworth UB7 . . . . .2 C8
Lingfield RH7, TN8 . . . . .165 A4
Staines TW18 . . . . .12 D6
Stanwell TW19 . . . . .12 D6
Woking GU22 . . . . .89 F5
Moor Lane Jun Sch KT9 . . . . .56 E5
Moor Mead Rd TW1 . . . . .6 A1
Moor Park Cres RH11 . . . . .200 D5
Moor Park Gdns KT2 . . . . . . .18 E1
Moor Park House RG12 . . . .26 E3
Moor Park La GU10, GU9 . .126 A2
Moor Park Way GU9 . . . . . .125 F2
Moor Pl
East Grinstead RH19 . . . . . . .185 D2
Windlesham GU20 . . . . .48 B5
Moor Rd Farnborough GU14 .85 A8
Frimley GU16 . . . . .85 F8
Linchmere GU27 . . . . .207 C5
Moorcroft RH9 . . . . .121 C3
Moorcroft Cl RH11 . . . . .201 B7
Moorcroft Rd SW16 . . . . . . .21 E5
Moordale Ave RG42 . . . . . . .26 E8
Moore Cl Addlestone KT15 . .52 B5
Ash GU10 . . . . .126 F8
Mitcham CR4 . . . . .41 B7
Mortlake SW14 . . . . .7 C4
Wallington SM6 . . . . .60 E3
Moore Ct RH12 . . . . .217 A1
Moore Grove Cres TW20 . . .11 F1
Moore House 1 SE27 . . . . . .22 C4
Moore Rd Pirbright GU24 . . .87 B6
South Norwood SE19 . . . . . . .22 C2
Moore Way SM2 . . . . .59 A2
Moore's Rd RH4, RH5 . . . . .136 B8
Mooreland Rd BR1 . . . . .24 F1
Moores Gn RG40 . . . . .25 E8
Moorfield GU27 . . . . .207 F5
Moorfield Rd
Chessington KT9 . . . . .56 E5
Guildford GU1 . . . . .109 E5
Moorfields Cl TW18 . . . . .32 E8
Moorfields Rd 6 SW16 . . . . .21 C4
Moorhayes Dr TW18 . . . . . . .33 C6
Moorhead Rd RH12 . . . . . . .218 B5
Moorholme GU22 . . . . .89 B8
Moorhouse Rd RH8 . . . . . . .123 F5
Moorhurst La RH5 . . . . .157 B4
Moorings The
East Grinstead RH19 . . . . . . .185 A3
Hindhead GU26 . . . . .188 B3
Moorland Cl
Crawley RH10 . . . . .202 C3
Twickenham TW4 . . . . .16 A8

Moorland Rd UB7 . . . . .2 C8
Moorlands KT12 . . . . .54 A7
Moorlands Cl GU26 . . . . . . .188 E4
Moorlands Pl GU15 . . . . .65 B5
Moorlands Rd GU15 . . . . . . .65 B4
Moorlands The GU22 . . . . . . .89 F6
Moormead Dr KT19 . . . . .57 E5
Moormede Cres TW18 . . . . . .12 F4
Moors La GU8 . . . . .148 C3
Moors The GU10 . . . . .126 F7
Moorside Cl GU14 . . . . .65 A1
Moorside Rd BR1 . . . . .24 F4
Moorsom Way CR5 . . . . .79 D2
Moray Ave GU47 . . . . .64 D7
Moray House 11 KT6 . . . . . . .37 E4
Mordaunt Dr RG45 . . . . .45 B3
Morden Cl Bracknell RG12 . .27 F5
Burgh Heath KT20 . . . . .97 D7
Morden Court Par SM4 . . . . .40 A5
Morden Ct SM4 . . . . .40 B5
Morden Farm Mid Sch
SM4 . . . . .39 E2
Morden Fst Sch SM4 . . . . . . .40 A4
Morden Gdns CR4 . . . . .40 D5
Morden Hall Park SW19 . . . .40 C6
Morden Hall
Rd SM4, SW19 . . . . .40 A5
Morden House SM4 . . . . .40 A5
Morden Park Sch Sports
Ctr SM4 . . . . .39 F4
Morden Rd Merton SW19 . . .40 B7
Mitcham CR4, SM4, SW19 . . .40 D5
Morden Road Sta SW19 . . . .40 B7
Morden South Sta SM4 . . . .40 A4
Morden Sta SW19 . . . . .40 B6
Morden Way SM4 . . . . .40 A2
Mordred Rd SE6 . . . . .24 E6
More Circ GU7 . . . . .150 E7
More Cl CR8 . . . . .80 A8
More House Sch GU10 . . . . .146 C2
More La KT10 . . . . .55 B7
More Rd GU7 . . . . .150 E7
Morecambe Cl RH11 . . . . . .200 F4
Morecote Cl GU4 . . . . .130 E2
Moreland Ave SL3 . . . . .1 C7
Moreland Cl SL3 . . . . .1 C7
Morella Cl GU25 . . . . .31 D5
Morella Rd SW11, SW12 . . . .20 F8
Moremead Rd SE6 . . . . .24 A4
Morena St SE6 . . . . .24 B8
Moresby Ave KT5 . . . . .38 B2
Moreton Ave TW7 . . . . .5 E6
Moreton Cl GU10 . . . . .167 E1
Moreton Green Fst Sch
SM4 . . . . .40 D4
Moreton House SW17 . . . . . .20 D4
Moreton Rd
North Cheam KT4 . . . . .58 B8
South Croydon CR2 . . . . .61 D5
Morgan Ct TW15 . . . . .14 B3
Moring Rd SW17 . . . . .21 A4
Morkyns Wlk SE21 . . . . .22 E5
Morland Ave CR0 . . . . .42 E1
Morland Cl Hampton TW12 . .15 F3
Mitcham CR4 . . . . .40 E6
Morland Rd
Aldershot GU11 . . . . .126 C6
Croydon CR0 . . . . .42 F2
Penge SE20 . . . . .23 D2
Sutton SM1 . . . . .59 C5
Morland's Rd GU11 . . . . . . .105 D5
Morley Ct Beckenham BR3 . .44 D8
Beckenham BR2 . . . . .44 F5
Sunningdale SL5 . . . . .29 F3
Morley House SW2 . . . . .21 C8
Morley Rd Cheam SM3 . . . . .39 F1
Farnham GU9 . . . . .125 D1
South Croydon CR2 . . . . .61 F1
Twickenham TW1 . . . . .6 D1
Morningside Rd KT4 . . . . . . .58 C8
Mornington Cl TN16 . . . . . . .83 D2
Mornington Cres TW5 . . . . . . .4 B6
Mornington Rd TW15 . . . . . .14 C3
Mornington Wlk TW10 . . . . .17 C4
Morrell Ave
Horsham RH12 . . . . .217 F6
Horsham RH12 . . . . .218 A6
Morris Cl BR3, CR0 . . . . .43 E4
Morris Gdns SW18 . . . . .20 A8
Morris Rd
Farnborough GU14 . . . . .105 D8
Isleworth TW7 . . . . .5 F4
South Nutfield RH1 . . . . .140 E7
Morrish Rd SW2 . . . . .21 E8
Morrison Ct 5 RH11 . . . . . .201 B1
Morrison House SW2 . . . . . .22 A7
Morriss Ct 3 RH2 . . . . .118 F1
Morston Cl KT20 . . . . .97 B7
Mortaine Rd TW15 . . . . .13 D5
Mortimer Cl SW16 . . . . .21 D6
Mortimer Cres KT4 . . . . .57 D7
Mortimer Lodge 11 SW19 . .19 E7
Mortimer Rd
Biggin Hill TN16 . . . . .83 C7
Capel RH5 . . . . .178 D6
Mitcham CR4 . . . . .40 F8
Mortimer Sch SW16 . . . . .21 D6
Mortlake Cl CR0 . . . . .60 E7
Mortlake Dr CR4 . . . . .40 E8
Mortlake High St SW14 . . . . .7 D4
Mortlake Rd SW14, TW9 . . . . .7 A6
Mortlake Sta SW14 . . . . .7 C4

Morton KT20 . . . . .97 E8
Morton Cl Frimley GU16 . . . .85 F7
Woking GU22 . . . . .89 D4
Morton Gdns SM6 . . . . .60 C5
Morton House SE27 . . . . .22 D3

Morton Rd
East Grinstead RH19 . . . . . . .205 E7
Morden CR4, SM4 . . . . .40 C4
Woking GU21 . . . . .89 D4
Morval Cl GU14 . . . . .84 E4
Morven Rd SW17 . . . . .20 F5
Moselle Cl GU14 . . . . .84 D5
Moselle Rd TN16 . . . . .83 F1
Mosford Cl RH6 . . . . .160 F5
Mospey Cres KT17 . . . . .76 F4
Moss Gdns CR2 . . . . .62 D3
Moss La GU7 . . . . .150 D4
Moss Lane Cty Inf Sch
GU7 .150 D4
Mossfield KT11 . . . . .73 A6
Mosslea Rd Kenley CR3 . . . .80 F2
Penge SE20 . . . . .23 C2
Mossville Gdns SM4, SW20 .39 F5
Mostyn Rd SW19 . . . . .39 F7
Mostyn Terr RH1 . . . . .140 A8
Motspur Park Sta KT3 . . . . . .39 B4
Motspur Pk KT3 . . . . .39 A3
Motts Hill La
Tadworth KT20 . . . . .97 A4
Walton on t H KT20 . . . . .97 A4
Mouchotte Cl TN16 . . . . .83 C7
Moulton Ave TW3, TW5 . . . . . .4 F5
Mount Adon Pk SE21, SE22 .23 A8
Mount Angelus Rd SW15 . . .18 F8
Mount Ararat Rd TW10 . . . . . .6 E2
Mount Arlington BR2 . . . . . . .44 E7
Mount Ash Rd SE26 . . . . . . .23 B5
Mount Ave CR3 . . . . .100 C3
Mount Cl Crawley RH10 . . . .202 D7
Ewhurst GU6 . . . . .175 E5
Fetcham KT22 . . . . .94 F4
Kenley CR8 . . . . .80 D3
Wallington SM5 . . . . .60 A2
Woking GU22 . . . . .89 C6
Mount Cl The GU25 . . . . .31 D3
Mount Ct Guildford GU1 . . . .130 C7
6 Kingston u T KT2 . . . . .18 B1
West Wickham BR4 . . . . .63 E8
Mount Dr The RH2 . . . . .118 D3
Mount Ephraim La SW16 . . .21 D5
Mount Ephraim Rd SW16 . . .21 D5
Mount Felix KT12 . . . . .34 F2
Mount Gdns SE26 . . . . .23 B5
Mount Hermon Cl GU22 . . . .69 E1
Mount Hermon Rd GU22 . . . .69 E1
Mount La Bracknell RG12 . . .27 C7
Turners Hill RH10 . . . . .204 A4
Mount Lee TW20 . . . . .11 F3
Mount Nod Rd SW2, SW16 . .21 F5
Mount Park Ave CR2 . . . . . . .61 B2
Mount Pk SM5 . . . . .60 A2
Mount Pl GU1 . . . . .130 C7
Mount Pleasant
Biggin Hill TN16 . . . . .83 D2
Bracknell RG12 . . . . .27 C6
Effingham KT24 . . . . .113 E7
Ewell KT17 . . . . .57 F1
Farnham GU9 . . . . .125 A1
Guildford GU2 . . . . .130 C7
Sandhurst GU47 . . . . .45 A1
West Horsley KT24 . . . . .112 B6
West Norwood SE27 . . . . .22 C4
Weybridge KT13 . . . . .53 A7
Wokingham RG41 . . . . .25 A6
Mount Pleasant Cl GU18 . . .48 A1
Mount Pleasant Rd
Aldershot GU12 . . . . .105 C4
Caterham CR3 . . . . .101 A4
Kingston u T KT3 . . . . .38 C6
Lingfield RH7 . . . . .164 C4
Mount Prim Sch The KT3 . . . .38 C6
Mount Rd Chessington KT9 . .56 F5
Chobham GU24 . . . . .69 B7
Cranleigh GU6 . . . . .174 E2
Feltham TW13 . . . . .15 E5
Kingston u T KT3 . . . . .38 D6
Mitcham CR4 . . . . .40 E7
South Norwood SE19 . . . . . . .22 D2
Wimbledon SW18, SW19 . . . .20 B6
Woking GU22 . . . . .89 C6
Mount Rise Forest Hill SE23 23 C6
Reigate RH2 . . . . .139 D7
Mount St RH4 . . . . .136 A7
Mount The Cranleigh GU6 . .174 E2
Esher KT10 . . . . .55 A4
Ewell KT17 . . . . .57 F1
Ewhurst GU6 . . . . .175 E5
Fetcham KT22 . . . . .94 E4
Grayswood GU27 . . . . .189 F1
Guildford GU2 . . . . .130 C7
Headley Down GU35 . . . . . . .187 A6
Lower Kingswood KT20 . . . . . .97 F1
New Malden KT3 . . . . .38 F6
North Cheam KT4 . . . . .58 B6
Oatlands Park KT13 . . . . .53 E8
Rusper RH11, RH12 . . . . . . .180 B1
Rusper RH12 . . . . .200 B8
Wallington CR5 . . . . .79 B5
Warlingham CR6 . . . . .101 A8
Wentworth GU25 . . . . .31 D3
Woking GU21, GU22 . . . . .69 D1
Mount View GU11 . . . . .105 A1
Mount View Rd KT10 . . . . . . .56 B3
Mount Villas SE27 . . . . .22 B5
Mount Way SM5 . . . . .60 A2
Mountacre Cl SE26 . . . . .23 A4
Mountbatten Cl
Crawley RH11 . . . . .201 C1
6 West Norwood SE27 . . . . . .22 C5
Mountbatten Ct 15 GU11 . . .105 A2
Mountbatten Gdns BR3 . . . .43 E5
Mountbatten Rise GU47 . . . .45 A1
Mountcombe Cl KT6 . . . . . . .37 E2

Mountearl Gdns
　SW16, SW2 ....21 F5
Mountfield Cl SE6 .....24 D8
Mounthurst Rd BR2 ....44 F2
Mounts Hill SL4, SL5 ....9 C3
Mountsfield Cl TW19 ...2 A2
Mountside Caterham CR3 .100 F3
　Guildford GU2 ....130 C7
Mountview 5 SW16 .....21 F5
Mountview Cl RH1 ......139 E7
Mountview Dr RH1 ......139 E7
Mountwood KT8 ....36 B6
Mountwood Cl CR2 .....62 B1
Moushill La GU8 ......170 E8
Mowat Ct KT4 ....57 F8
Mowbray Ave KT14 ......71 E6
Mowbray Cres TW20 ....12 A3
Mowbray Ct SE19 ......42 E8
Mowbray Dr RH11 ......200 F4
Mowbray Gdns RH4 ....115 B3
Mowbray Rd
　Richmond TW10 ....17 C5
　South Norwood SE19 ...42 F8
Mower Pl GU6 ....174 E4
Moyne C 3 GU21 ....68 F1
Moyne Rd RH11 ....201 C2
Moyser Rd SW16, SW17 .21 B3
Muchelney Rd SM4 .....40 C3
Muckhatch La TW20 ....32 B7
Mudie House 8 SW2 ....21 E8
Muggeridge's Hill
　Capel RH12, RH5 .....198 E8
　Rusper RH12, RH5 ....198 E8
Muirdown Ave SW14 .....7 D3
Muirfield Cl RH11 .....200 D5
Muirfield House RG12 ..26 E3
Muirfield Rd GU21 ......69 A1
Muirkirk Rd SE6 ....24 C7
Mulberries The GU9 ...125 F4
Mulberry Ave TW19 .....13 E7
Mulberry Cl Ash GU12 .106 A4
　Crowthorne RG45 ......45 C4
　Horsham RH12 ....217 C5
　1 Sandhurst GU47 .....64 D8
　Streatham SW16 ....21 C4
　Weybridge KT13 ....53 B7
　Woking GU21 ....69 C5
Mulberry Cres TW8 .....6 C7
Mulberry Ct Ashstead KT21 75 D1
　1 Bracknell RG12 ......27 F4
　Guildford GU4 ....110 D3
　4 Surbiton KT6 ....37 D2
　Twickenham TW1 ....16 F5
　Wokingham RG40 ....25 C6
Mulberry La CR0 ....42 F1
Mulberry Mews 2 SM6 ..60 C4
Mulberry Rd RH1 ......181 B1
Mulberry Trees TW17 ...34 D2
Mulgrave Chambers SM2 .59 B4
Mulgrave Manor SM2 ...59 B4
Mulgrave Rd Belmont SM2 .59 A4
　Croydon CR0, CR9 .....61 D7
　Frimley GU16 ....65 F2
　Sutton SM2 ....59 A4
Mulgrave Way GU21 .....68 E1
Mulholland Cl CR4 .....41 B7
Mullards Cl CR4 ....40 F1
Mullein Wlk RH11 .....201 A2
Mullens Rd TW20 ......12 C3
Mullins Path SW14 ......7 D4
Mulroy Dr GU15 ....66 A6
Multon Rd SW18 ....20 D8
Muncaster Cl TW15 ....14 A4
Muncaster Rd TW15 ....14 B3
Muncies Mews SE6 .....24 C6
Munday's Boro GU3 ...128 A4
Munday's Boro Rd GU3 .128 A4
Munnings Dr GU47 .....64 C6
Munnings Gdns TW7 ....5 D2
Munro Way GU14 ......105 D8
Munroe House RH2 ....139 A4
Munslow Gdns SM1 .....59 D6
Munstead Ct SM2 ......59 C3
Munstead Heath Rd
　Bramley GU5, GU7, GU8 .151 C2
　Godalming GU5, GU7, GU8 .151 C3
Munstead Pk GU8 .....151 C2
Munstead View GU3 ...130 C4
Munstead View Rd GU5 .151 D5
Munster Ave TW4 ....4 E2
Munster Ct TW11 ......17 C2
Munster Rd TW11 ......17 C2
Murdoch Cl TW18 ......13 A3
Murdoch Rd RG40 ......25 D5
Murfett Cl SW19 ....19 E6
Murray Ave TW3 ....5 B2
Murray Ct Ascot SL5 ...29 C3
　Crawley RH11 ....201 A1
　Horsham RH13 ....218 B4
Murray Gn GU21 ....70 C5
Murray House KT16 ....51 D4
Murray Rd
　Farnborough GU14 .....84 F3
　Ottershaw KT15, KT16 ...51 D5
　Richmond TW10 ....17 C6
　Wimbledon SW19 ......19 D2
　Wokingham RG41 ......25 A6
Murray's La KT14 ......71 E5
Murray's Rd GU11 ....105 D5
Murrell Rd GU12 ......106 A3
Murrell Hill La RG42 ...26 C8
Murrells La GU15 ......65 B3
Murrells Wlk KT23 .....94 A3
Murreys The KT21 .....75 D1
Muschamp Inf Sch SM5 .59 E8
Muschamp Jun Sch SM5 .59 E8

Muschamp Rd SM1, SM5 .59 E8
Museum Hill GU27 ....208 D6
Museum of Richmond
　TW10 ....6 D2
Musgrave Ave RH19 ...205 E8
Musgrave Rd TW7 ....5 F6
Mushroom Castle La RG42 .8 B2
Musical Museum The TW8 .6 E8
Musquash Way TW4 .....4 C5
Mustard Mill Rd TW18 .12 F4
Mutton Hill RH7 ......186 B7
Mutton Oaks RG12 .....26 D8
Muybridge Rd KT3 .....38 C7
Mychell House 8 SW19 .20 C1
Mychett Cty Fst Sch GU16 .85 F4
Mychett Heath GU16 ...86 A3
Myers Way GU16 ....66 D2
Mylis Cl SE26 ....23 B4
Mylne Sq RG40 ....25 D6
Mylor Cl GU21 ....69 E5
Mynn's Cl KT18 ....76 B5
Mynterne Ct 16 SW19 ..19 D7
Myrna Cl SW19 ....20 E1
Myrtle Ave TW14 ....3 E2
Myrtle Cl Lightwater GU18 .67 B8
　Poyle SL3 ....1 E6
Myrtle Dr GU17 ....64 D5
Myrtle Gr KT3 ....38 C7
Myrtle Rd Croydon CR0 .63 A7
　Dorking RH4 ....136 A8
　Hampton TW12 ....16 C2
　Hounslow TW3 ....5 C5
　Sutton SM1 ....59 C5
Mytchett Lake Rd GU16 .86 A1
Mytchett Place Rd
　Mytchett GU12, GU16 ...86 C1
　Normandy GU12, GU16, GU24 .86 C1
Mytchett Rd GU12, GU16 .85 F3
Myton Rd SE21 ....22 D5

N

Naafi Rdbt GU11 ......105 B2
Nadine Ct SM6 ....60 C2
Nailsworth Cres RH1 ..119 D6
Nairn Cl GU16 ....65 E2
Nairn Ct 3 Wallington SM6 .60 C4
　Wimbledon SW19 ......20 B2
Naldrett Cl RH11 .....217 F4
Naldretts La RH12 ....214 D5
Nallhead Rd TW13 .....15 C3
Namba Roy Cl SW16 ...21 F4
Namton Dr CR7, SW16 .41 F5
Napier Cl Crowthorne RG45 .45 D5
　Farnborough GU11 ....105 E2
Napier Ct Caterham CR3 .100 E5
　10 Croydon CR0 ....61 F8
　1 Surbiton KT6 ....37 D2
　Woking GU21 ....69 E3
Napier Dr GU15 ....66 A8
Napier Gdns GU1 .....110 B3
Napier Lodge TW15 ....14 D2
Napier Rd Ashford TW15 .14 D1
　Crowthorne RG45 ......45 C4
　Croydon SE25 ....43 B5
　Harmondsworth TW6 ...2 D6
　Isleworth TW7 ....6 A3
　South Croydon CR2 ...61 D3
Napier Way RH10 .....182 A1
Napier Wlk TW15 ......14 D1
Napoleon Ave GU14 ....85 B6
Napoleon Rd TW1 ......17 B8
Napper Cl SL5 ....28 D7
Napper Pl GU6 ....174 E1
Narrow La CR6 ....101 B8
Naseby RG12 ....27 B1
Naseby Cl TW7 ....5 E6
Naseby Rd SE19 ....22 D2
Nash Cl Farnborough GU14 .84 F4
　Sutton SM1 ....59 D7
Nash Dr 6 RH1 ....119 A3
Nash Gdns North Ascot SL5 .28 E7
　Redhill RH1 ....118 F3
Nash Rd RH10 ....201 C3
Nassau Rd SW13 ....7 F6
Nasturtium Dr GU24 ...68 A4
Natal Rd
　South Norwood CR7 ...42 D6
　Streatham SW16 ....21 D2
Natalie Cl TW14 ....14 D8
Natalie Mews TW2 .....16 D5
National Physical
　Laboratory TW11 .....16 E2
National Wks TW1 ......4 F4
Nayland House SE6 ....24 C4
Neale Cl RH19 ....185 B3
Neath Gdns SM4 ......40 C3
Neb La RH8 ....122 D4
Needles Bank RH9 ....121 B4
Needles Cl RH12 .....217 B1
Neelem Ct GU14 ......85 C1
Neil Cl TW15 ....14 C3
Neil Wates Cres 18 SW2 .22 A7
Nelgarde Rd Catford SE6 .24 A8
　Lewisham SE6 ....24 A8
Nell Ball RH14 ....211 E2
Nell Gwynn Ave TW17 ..34 D3
Nell Gwynne Ave SL5 ..29 D5
Nell Gwynne Cl SL5 ...29 D5
Nello James Gdns SE27 .22 D4
Nelson Cl Aldershot GU12 .105 D1
　Biggin Hill TN16 ......83 E2
　Bracknell RG12 ....27 B1
　Crawley RH10 ....202 C5
　East Bedfont TW14 ....14 F7
　Heath End GU9 ....125 D8
　Thornton Heath CR0 ...42 B1

Nelson Cl *continued*
　Walton-on-T KT12 ......35 B1
Nelson Ct Carshalton SM5 .59 F7
　Chertsey KT16 ....33 A1
Nelson Gdns
　Guildford GU1 ....110 A2
　Twickenham TW3, TW4 ..5 A1
Nelson Grove Rd SW19 .40 C8
Nelson Ho 19 GU11 ...105 A2
Nelson Hospl SM4 ......39 F7
Nelson Prim Sch TW2 ...5 B1
Nelson Rd Ashford TW15 .13 E3
　Caterham CR3 ....100 D4
　Harmondsworth TW6 ...2 F6
　Heath End GU9 ....125 D8
　Horsham RH12 ....217 C3
　Merton SW19 ....20 C1
　New Malden KT3 ....38 D4
　Twickenham TW2, TW4 .16 B8
Nelson St 3 GU11 ....105 A2
Nelson Trad Est SW19 .40 B8
Nelson Way GU15 ......64 F4
Nene Gdns TW13 ....15 F6
Nene Rd TW6, UB7 ......3 B6
Nepean St 4 SW15 .....19 A8
Neptune Cl RH11 .....200 E4
Neptune Rd TW6 ....3 C6
Nesbit Ct RH11 ......200 E3
Nesbitt Sq SE19 ......22 E1
NESCOT Epsom's Coll of
　FE & HE KT17 ....77 A8
Nether Mount GU2 ....130 B7
Netheravon Rd S W4 ....7 F8
Netherby Pk KT13 .....53 E5
Netherby Rd SE23 .....23 C8
Nethercote Ave GU21 ..68 F2
Netherfield Rd SW17 ..21 A5
Netherlands The CR5 ..99 C8
Netherleigh Pk RH1 ..140 E6
Nethern Court Rd CR3 .102 A4
Netherne La CR5 ......99 C5
Netherton RG12 ....27 A5
Netherton Rd TW1 ......6 B2
Netherwood 11 RH11 ..201 B4
Netherwood Ct GU7 ..150 E5
Netley Cl Cheam SM3 ..58 D5
　New Addington CR0 ...63 C3
Netley Dr KT12 ....35 F2
Netley Gdns SM4 ......40 C2
Netley Rd Brentford TW8 ..6 E8
　Morden SM4 ....40 C2
Netley Rd (W) TW6 .....3 A4
Netley St GU11 ....105 C8
Nettlecombe RG12 .....27 D3
Nettlecombe Cl SM2 ...59 B2
Nettlefold Pl SE27 ....22 B5
Nettles Terr 3 GU1 ...109 D1
Nettleton Rd TW6 ....3 B6
Nettlewood Rd SW16 ..21 D1
Neuchatel Rd SE6 .....23 F6
Nevada Cl
　Farnborough GU14 ....84 D3
　Kingston u T KT3 .....38 C5
Nevelle Cl RG42 ....26 D8
Nevile Cl RH11 ....201 A3
Neville Ave KT3 ....38 D8
Neville Cl Banstead SM7 .78 B5
　Esher KT10 ....54 F4
　Hounslow TW3 ....5 B5
Neville Ct 10 SW12 ....21 C8
Neville Duke Rd GU14 ..84 F8
Neville Rd Croydon CR0 .42 C2
　Kingston u T KT1 .....38 A7
　Richmond TW10 ....17 C6
Neville Wlk SM5 ......40 E2
Nevis Rd SW17 ....21 A6
New Barn La Kenley CR3 .80 E3
　Wallis Wood RH5 .....177 A3
New Barns Ave CR4 ...41 E5
New Belmont House 4
　SE23 ....23 C7
New Berry La KT12 .....54 D5
New Chapel Sq TW13 ..15 B7
New Church Ct 3 SE19 .23 A1
New Cl Feltham TW13 ..15 E3
　Mitcham SW19 ....40 C6
New Colebrooke Ct SM5 .60 A3
New Cotts
　Betchworth RH3 ......116 D4
　Sidlow RH2 ....138 F1
　Turners Hill RH10 ....204 A4
New Cross Rd GU2 ...109 B3
New Cswy RH2 ....139 C6
New Ct KT15 ....52 C7
New Dawn Cl GU4 ....84 D3
New Epsom & Ewell
　Cottage Hospl The KT19 .75 E8
New Farthingdale RH7 .186 B8
New Forest Cotts GU22 .89 F7
New Forest Ride RG12 ..27 F4
New Green Pl SE19 ....22 E2
New Haw Jun Sch KT15 .52 A1
New Haw Rd KT15 .....52 C4
New Heston Rd TW5 ....4 F7
New House Farm La GU3 108 A2
New House La RH1 ....161 E8
New Inn La GU4 ......110 B4
New Kelvin Ave TW11 ..16 E2
New La GU22, GU4 .....89 F3
New Life Sch RH19 ...185 D3
New Lodge Dr RH8 ...122 F7
New Malden Sta KT3 ..38 E6
New Meadow SL5 ......28 D8
New Mile Rd SL5 ......29 C7
New Moorhead Dr RH12 .218 C6
New North Rd RH2 ...138 F6

New Par TW15 ....13 F4
New Park Ct 26 SW2 ...21 E8
New Park Par 14 SW2 ..21 E8
New Park Rd Ashford TW15 14 C3
　Cranleigh GU6 ....174 F2
　Streatham SW2 ....21 E8
　Streatham, Streatham Hill
　SW12, SW2 ....21 E7
New Pl CR0 ....63 A4
New Place Gdns RH7 ..164 E4
New Pond Rd
　Artington GU3 ....129 E1
　Compton GU3 ....129 E1
New Poplars The GU12 .106 A1
New Rd Albury GU5 ...132 D3
　Bagshot GU19 ....47 F3
　Blackwater GU17 ......64 E4
　Bracknell RG12 ....27 D7
　Brentford TW8 ....6 D8
　Carshalton CR4 ....41 A1
　Chilworth GU4 ....131 B3
　Crowthorne RG45 ......45 C5
　East Bedfont TW14 .....3 D1
　East Clandon GU4 ...111 E4
　East Molesey KT8 .....36 A6
　Egham TW18 ....12 C4
　Esher KT10 ....55 C6
　Feltham TW13 ....15 B7
　Feltham TW13 ....15 E3
　Forest Green RH5 ....176 E6
　Gomshall GU5 ....133 C4
　Harlington TW6, UB7 ...3 C4
　Hounslow TW3 ....5 B3
　Hydestile GU8 ....171 F5
　Kingston u T KT2 ......18 A1
　Limpsfield RH8 ......123 B5
　Linchmere GU27 .....207 F5
　Littleton TW17 ....34 B6
　Milford GU8 ....170 E8
　North Ascot SL5 ....8 F1
　Oxshott KT10, KT22 ....74 F8
　Richmond TW10 ....17 C4
　Sandhurst GU47 ......64 A8
　Smallfield RH6 ......162 B3
　Tadworth KT20 ....97 C4
　Tandridge RH8, RH9 ..143 A7
　Tongham GU10 ....126 F6
　Weybridge KT13 ....53 C5
　Windlesham GU19, GU20 .48 A4
　Wonersh GU5 ....152 B8
　Wormley GU8 ....191 A8
New Rd Units TW3 ......5 B3
New Residences KT1 ...51 C7
New Scotland Hill Cty
　Prim Sch GU47 ....45 A2
New Sq TW14 ....14 C4
New St Crawley RH10 ..202 A7
　Horsham RH13 ....217 D2
　Staines TW18 ....13 A4
New Town RH10 ....183 B3
New Victoria Hospl The
　KT3 ....38 E8
New Way GU7 ....150 C4
New Wickham La TW20 .12 B1
New Wokingham Rd RG45 45 A4
New Woodlands Sch BR1 .24 E4
New Zealand Ave KT12 .34 F1
Newall Rd TW6 ....3 C6
Newark Cl Guildford GU4 .110 B4
　Ripley GU23 ....91 A6
Newark Ct KT12 ....35 C1
Newark La
　Ripley GU22, GU23 ....91 A6
　Woking GU22 ....90 F8
Newark Rd Crawley RH10 .201 F8
　South Croydon CR2 ...61 D4
　Windlesham GU20 .....48 B6
Newbolt Ave SM3 ......58 D5
Newborough Gn KT3 ..38 D5
Newborough House
　SW19 ....20 D1
Newbridge Cl RH12 ...216 C3
Newbridge Ct
　Cranleigh GU6 ....174 B3
　Upper Tooting SW17 ..20 C4
Newbridge Point 3 SE23 .23 D5
Newbury Gdns KT19 ...57 F6
Newbury Rd TW6 ....2 F6
Newchapel Rd
　Lingfield RH7 ....164 B3
　Newchapel RH7 ......163 F2
Newcome Gdns SW16 ..21 E4
Newcome Pl GU12 ....126 D7
Newcome Rd GU9 ....125 D6
Newdigate Endowed CE
　Inf Sch RH5 ....158 B1
Newdigate House 6 KT2 .18 B2
Newdigate Rd
　Beare Green RH5 ....157 E2
　Rusper RH12 ....199 C8
Newenham Rd KT23 ...94 A1
Newent Cl SM5 ....40 F1
Newfield Ave GU14 ....84 E6
Newfield Cl TW12 .....36 A8
Newfield Rd GU12 ....106 A4
Newfoundland Rd GU16 .86 D8
Newgate CR0 ....42 C1
Newgate Ct TW13 .....15 C5
Newhache RH7 ....165 A1
Newhall Gdns KT12 ...54 C8
Newhaven Cres TW15 ..14 D2
Newhaven Rd SE25 ....42 D4
Newhouse 5 KT3 ......38 E2
Newhouse Cl KT3 .....38 E2
Newhouse Wlk SM4 ...40 C2
Newland House Sch TW1 .16 F4
Newland House Sch
　Annex TW1 ....16 F4

Newlands Ave
　Thames Ditton KT7 ....36 E1
　Woking GU22 ....89 F6
Newlands Cl Hersham KT12 54 E6
　Horley RH6 ....160 F5
Newlands Cnr GU4 ...132 A7
Newlands Cres RH19 .185 D2
Newlands Croft SE20 ..23 D3
Newlands Ct
　Addlestone KT15 ......52 B5
　Caterham CR3 ....100 C6
　Streatham SW16 ......21 E3
Newlands Dr Ash GU12 .106 B4
　Poyle SL3 ....1 E4
Newlands Estate GU8 ..170 F5
Newlands Flats GU1 ..109 F2
Newlands Pk
　Copthorne RH10 .....183 E3
　Forest Hill SE20, SE26 .23 D3
　Penge SE26 ....23 D3
Newlands Pl RH18 ....206 F3
Newlands Rd
　Camberley GU15 ......65 B1
　Crawley RH11 ....201 C5
　Horsham RH12 ....217 C4
　Thornton Heath SW16 .41 E7
Newlands The GU6 ....60 D3
Newlands Way KT9 ....56 C5
Newlands Wood CR0 ..62 F2
Newman Cl RH10 .....202 C4
Newman Rd CR0 ....41 F1
Newmans Cl GU27 ...125 A7
Newmans Ct GU9 .....125 A7
Newmarket Rd RH10 ..202 A4
Newminster Rd SM4 ...40 C3
Newnham Cl CR7 ......42 C7
Newnham Ct SE6 .....24 C7
Newport Jun Sch GU12 .105 D1
Newport Rd
　Aldershot GU12 .....105 D1
　Harmondsworth TW6 ...3 A6
Newquay Rd SE6 ......24 C6
Newry Rd TW1 ....6 A2
Newsham Rd 1 GU21 ..68 F2
Newstead Cl GU7 ....150 E2
Newstead Hall RH6 ...161 D1
Newstead House CR3 .101 B1
Newstead Rd SE12 ....24 F8
Newstead Rise CR3 ..101 B1
Newstead Way SW19 ..19 E4
Newstead Wlk SM4, SM5 .40 C2
Newton Ave RH19 ....205 F6
Newton Rd Crawley RH10 .181 F2
　Farnborough GU14 ....85 D6
　Isleworth TW7 ....5 F5
　Merton SW19 ....19 E1
　Purley CR8 ....79 C7
Newton Way GU10 ....126 F7
Newton Wood Rd KT21 .75 F3
Newtown Ct RH13 ....217 D3
Newtown Rd GU47 ....64 B8
Nicholas Gdns GU22 ..70 F3
Nicholas House SE26 ..23 B2
Nicholas Lodge KT10 ..55 A8
Nicholas Rd CR0 ......60 E6
Nicholass Ct 2 CR8 ...80 B7
Nicholes Rd TW3 ......5 A3
Nichols Cl KT9 ....56 C4
Nicholsfield RH14 ....212 F4
Nicholson Rd CR0 .....42 F1
Nicholson Wlk 3 TW20 .12 A3
Nicol Cl 6 TW1 ....6 B1
Nicola Ct CR2 ....61 C4
Nicosia Rd SW18 ......20 E8
Niederwald Rd SE26 ..23 E4
Nightingale Ave KT24 .92 D2
Nightingale Cl
　Carshalton SM5 ....60 A8
　Chiswick W4 ....7 C8
　Cobham KT11 ....73 D8
　Crawley RH11 ....201 C8
　East Grinstead RH19 .205 D7
　Farnborough GU14 ....84 C6
Nightingale Cres
　Bracknell RG12 ....27 D4
　West Horsley KT24 ....92 C2
Nightingale Ct
　2 Knaphill GU21 ......68 F1
　Penge SE19 ....22 F2
　8 Redhill RH1 ....119 A2
Nightingale Dr
　Mytchett GU16 ....86 A3
　West Ewell KT19 ......57 B4
Nightingale Gdns GU47 .64 B8
Nightingale La
　Balham SW11, SW12 ..20 F8
　Richmond TW10 ......17 E8
Nightingale Rd Ash GU12 .106 C3
　Carshalton SM5 ....60 A8
　East Horsley KT24 ....92 F2
　East Molesey KT8 .....36 B4
　Esher KT10 ....54 F4
　Farncombe GU7 .....150 E6
　Guildford GU1 ....109 E1
　Hampton TW12 ....16 A2
　Horsham RH12 ....217 D3
　Selsdon CR2 ....62 D1
　Walton-on-T KT12 .....35 B2
Nightingale Sq SW12 ..21 A8
Nightingale Way RH1 .120 E2
Nightingales GU14 ....111 E1
Nightingales The TW19 .13 F7
Nightjar Cl GU10 .....124 D8
Nimbus Rd KT19 ......57 D1
Nimrod Ct RH10 .....182 D1
Nimrod Rd SW16, SW17 .21 B3

Nine Elms Cl TW14 14 F7
Nine Mile Ride
Bracknell RG12, RG40 26 F1
Crowthorne RG12, RG40 26 F1
Nineacres Way CR5 79 E3
Ninehams Cl CR3 100 D7
Ninehams Gdns CR3 100 D7
Ninehams Rd
Caterham CR3 100 D6
Tatsfield TN16 103 D6
Nineteenth Rd CR4 41 E5
Ninfield Ct RH11 200 F2
Niton Rd TW9 7 A4
Niven Cl RH10 202 D5
Nobel Dr TW6 3 E7
Noble Cnr TW5 5 A6
Noble Ct CR4 40 D7
Noble St KT12 54 C7
Nobles Way TW20 11 E2
Noel Ct TW4 4 F4
Noel Terr SE23 23 C6
Noke Dr RH1 119 A2
Nonsuch Court Ave KT17 58 B1
Nonsuch Ct SM3 58 E4
Nonsuch High Sch for Girls SM3 58 D3
Nonsuch Ind Est KT17 76 E8
Nonsuch Prim Sch KT17 58 B5
Nonsuch Wlk SM2 58 D1
Noons Corner Rd RH5 156 A8
Norbiton Ave KT1, KT2 38 A7
Norbiton Common Rd KT1, KT3 38 B6
Norbiton Hall KT2 37 F7
Norbiton Sta KT1 38 A8
Norbury Ave Isleworth TW3 5 D3
South Norwood CR7, SW16 42 B7
Norbury Cl SW16 42 B8
Norbury Court Rd SW16 41 E7
Norbury Cres SW16 42 A7
Norbury Cross SW16 41 E6
Norbury Hill SW16 22 B1
Norbury Manor Girls High Sch CR7 42 A8
Norbury Rd Reigate RH2 117 F1
South Norwood CR7 42 C6
Norbury Rise SW16 41 E6
Norbury Sta SW16 41 F8
Norbury Trad Est SW16 41 F7
Norbury Way KT23 94 C2
Norcroft Gdns SE22 23 A8
Norcutt Rd TW2 16 E7
Norfolk Ave CR2 62 A1
Norfolk Cl Crawley RH11 200 E2
Horley RH6 161 A2
5 Twickenham TW1 6 B1
Norfolk Cotts RH1 140 E7
Norfolk Ct Dorking RH5 136 D3
Horsham RH12 218 B5
Surbiton KT5 37 F3
Norfolk Farm Cl GU22 70 D3
Norfolk Farm Rd GU22 70 D3
Norfolk House
2 Croydon CR0 61 D8
11 Merton SW19 20 C1
Penge SE20 43 C8
Norfolk House Rd SW16 21 E5
Norfolk La RH5 136 B1
Norfolk Rd Claygate KT10 55 E5
Dorking RH4 136 A7
Feltham TW13 15 C7
Horsham RH12, RH13 217 D2
Mitcham SW19 20 E2
South Holmwood RH5 157 C6
South Norwood CR7 42 C6
Norfolk Terr RH12, RH13 217 D2
Norgrove St SW12 21 A8
Norheads La
Biggin Hill TN16 83 B2
Chelsham TN16 83 B2
Norhyrst Ave SE25 42 F6
Nork Gdns SM7 77 E5
Nork Rise SM7 77 D3
Nork Way KT17, SM7 77 D4
Norlands La
Egham TW18, TW20 32 E7
Thorpe TW18, TW20 32 E7
Norley Vale SW15 19 A7
Norman Ave Ewell KT17 76 F7
Feltham TW13 15 F6
South Croydon CR2, CR8 61 C1
Twickenham TW1 17 C8
Norman Colyer Ct KT19 57 D1
Norman Cres TW5 4 D7
Norman Ct Farnham GU9 125 C1
9 Hampton TW12 36 A8
Streatham SW16 22 A3
Norman House
Feltham TW13 15 F6
Lower Halliford TW17 34 A2
Reigate RH2 138 F6
Norman Keep RG42 27 F8
Norman Rd Ashford TW15 14 D2
Merton SW19 20 C1
Sutton SM1 59 A5
Thornton Heath CR7 42 B4
Norman's Rd RH1, RH6 162 C5
Normandy RH12 217 C1
Normandy Cl
Crawley RH10 202 C4
7 East Grinstead RH19 205 F8
Forest Hill SE26 23 E5
Frimley GU16 86 E8
Normandy Gdns RH12 217 C1
Normandy Wlk TW20 12 C3
Normanhurst TW15 14 A3
Normanhurst Cl RH10 201 F6
Normanhurst Dr TW1 6 B2
Normanhurst Rd
Streatham SW2 21 F6
Walton-on-T KT12 54 D8
Normans La TN8 165 E7
Normansfield Ave
KT1, KT8 17 C1
Normansfield Hospl KT8 17 C1
Normanton RH2 117 D2
Normanton Ave
SW18, SW19 20 A6
Normanton Rd CR2 61 E4
Normanton St SE23 23 D6
Normington Cl SW16 22 A3
Norrels Dr KT24 92 F1
Norrels Ride KT24 92 F2
Norreys Ave RG40 25 D7
Norris Hill Rd GU13, GU14 104 A8
Norris Rd TW18 12 F4
Norstead Pl SW15 19 A6
North Acre SM7 77 F3
North Ash RH12 217 C4
North Ave Heath End GU9 125 D7
8 Richmond TW9 7 A6
Wallington SM5 60 A3
Whiteley Village KT12 53 E2
North Camp Sta GU12 105 F8
North Cl Ash GU12 105 E1
Crawley RH10 201 F7
Dorking RH5 136 C3
East Bedfont TW14 3 D1
Farnborough GU14 85 A8
Merton SM4 39 E5
North Comm KT13 53 C6
North Crofts SE21 23 B7
North Dene TW5 5 B6
North Down CR2 80 E7
North Downs Cres CR0 63 B1
North Downs Golf Course CR3 102 A2
North Downs Rd CR0 63 C1
North Dr Beckenham BR3 44 B5
Hounslow TW3, TW7 5 C5
Pirbright GU24 87 C6
Streatham SW16 21 C4
Wentworth GU25 30 E4
North End CR0, CR9 61 C8
North End La SL5 30 B2
North Farm Rd GU14 84 F8
North Farnborough Cty Inf Sch GU14 85 D5
North Feltham Trad Est TW14 4 B3
North Gate Rd GU14 85 C2
North Gdns SW19 20 D1
North Gn RG12 27 D8
North Gr KT16 32 F3
North Hatton Rd TW6 3 D6
North Heath Cl RH12 217 D5
North Heath Cty Prim Sch RH12 217 D5
North Heath Est RH12 217 D6
North Heath La RH12 217 E6
North Holmes Cl RH12 218 B5
North Hyde La TW5 4 F8
North La
Aldershot GU11, GU12 105 D2
Teddington TW11 16 F2
North Lodge Dr SL5 28 C7
North Mead Crawley RH10 201 E8
Redhill RH1 118 F4
North Minden House GU16 86 D7
North Moors GU1 109 E6
North Munstead La GU8 151 A1
North Par Chessington KT9 56 F5
Horsham RH12 217 C3
North Park La RH9 121 A5
North Pl Mitcham SW19 20 F1
Teddington TW11 16 F2
North Pole La BR2 63 F4
North Rd Ash Vale GU12 105 F4
Brentford TW8 6 E8
Crawley RH10 202 A7
East Bedfont TW14 3 D1
Guildford GU2 109 B4
Hersham KT12 54 C5
Heston TW5 4 C8
Kingston u T KT6 37 D3
Mitcham SW17, SW19 20 C2
Reigate RH2 138 F6
Richmond TW9 7 A5
West Wickham BR4 44 B1
Wimbledon SW17, SW19 20 C2
Winkfield SL5 28 B8
Woking GU21 70 A3
North Sheen Sta TW10 7 A3
North Side GU10 126 F7
North St Carshalton SM5 59 F6
Dorking RH4 136 A7
Egham TW20 11 F2
Farncombe GU7 150 E7
Guildford GU1 130 D8
Horsham RH12, RH13 217 D3
Isleworth TW7 6 A4
Leatherhead KT22 95 A6
Redhill RH1 118 F2
Turners Hill RH10 204 A4
Winkfield SL4 9 A6
North Station App RH1 140 F7
North Terminal App RH6 181 F8
North View SW19 19 C3
North View Cres KT18 77 C2
North Weald La KT2 17 D3
North Weylands Ind Est KT12 54 E8
North Wlk CR0 63 C5
North Worple Way SW14 7 D4
Northampton Cl RG12 27 E6
Northampton Rd CR0, CR9 62 A8
Northanger Rd SW16 21 E2
Northborough Rd SW16 41 E7
Northbourne GU7 150 F8
Northbrook Coll of Design & Tech RH12 217 C4
Northbrook Copse RG12 27 F3
Northbrook Rd
Aldershot GU11 126 B8
Thornton Heath CR0 42 D4
Northcliffe Cl KT4 57 E7
Northcote KT15 52 D6
Northcote Ave
Isleworth TW7 6 A2
Tolworth KT5 38 B2
Northcote Cl KT24 92 C2
Northcote Cres KT24 92 C2
Northcote La GU5 152 E6
Northcote Pk KT22 74 C4
Northcote Rd
Ash Vale GU12 106 A7
Farnborough GU14 84 F6
Isleworth TW1, TW7 6 A2
Kingston u T KT3 38 D6
Thornton Heath CR0 42 D3
West Horsley KT24 92 C2
Northcott RG12 27 A1
Northcroft Cl TW20 11 B3
Northcroft Gdns TW20 11 B3
Northcroft Rd
Englefield Green TW20 11 B3
West Ewell KT19 57 E3
Northcroft Villas TW20 11 B3
Northdown Cl RH12 217 F4
Northdown Ct RH9 121 C5
Northdown La GU1 130 E6
Northdown Rd
Belmont SM2 59 A1
Woldingham CR3 102 A2
Northdown Terr RH19 185 D3
Northdowns GU6 174 E1
Northend Ct KT23 94 C1
Northern Perimeter Rd
Harlington TW6 3 E6
Hatton TW6 3 E6
Northern Perimeter Road (W) TW6 2 D6
Northernhay Wlk SM4 39 E5
Northey Ave Belmont SM2 58 E1
East Ewell SM2 58 E1
Northfield Lightwater GU18 67 B8
Shalford GU4 130 E1
Witley GU8 170 F4
Northfield Cl GU12 105 D1
Northfield Cres SM3 58 E6
Northfield Ct TW18 33 B8
Northfield Pl KT13 53 B3
Northfield Rd Cobham KT11 73 B6
Heston TW5 4 D7
Staines TW18 33 B8
Northfields KT21 95 E8
Northgate Ave RH10 201 F7
Northgate Cty Fst Sch RH10 201 E7
Northgate Cty Mid Sch RH10 201 E7
Northgate Dr GU15 66 A7
Northgate Pl RH10 201 E7
Northgate Rd
Crawley RH10, RH11 201 D6
Crawley, North Terminal RH6 181 F8
Northington Cl RG12 27 F3
Northlands Bglws RH5 158 B1
Northlands Rd
Faygate RH12 198 F2
Horsham RH12 217 E7
Warnham RH12 197 D2
Northmead GU14 85 B4
Northmead GM Jun Sch GU2 109 B4
Northmoor 4 SE23 23 D5
Northolt Rd TW6 2 E6
Northover BR1 24 F5
Northrop Rd TW6 3 E6
Northspur Rd SM1 59 A7
Northstead Rd SW2 22 A6
Northumberland Ave TW7 6 A7
Northumberland Cl TW19 2 E1
Northumberland Cres TW14 3 E1
Northumberland Gdns
Hounslow TW7 6 A7
Mitcham CR4 41 D4
Northumberland Pl 26 TW10 6 D2
Northway Crawley RH6 181 F8
Farncombe GU7 150 B7
Guildford GU2 109 A3
Merton SM4, SW20 39 E5
Wallington SM6 60 C6
Northway Rd CR0 42 F2
Northwood Ave
Knaphill GU21 68 D1
Purley CR8 80 B6
Northwood Pk RH10 182 A2
Northwood Rd
Forest Hill SE23 23 F7
Harmondsworth TW6 2 D6
South Norwood CR7 42 C7
Wallington SM5 60 A4
Northwood Way 1 SE19 22 E2
Norton Ave KT5 38 B2
Norton Cl GU3 88 D1
Norton Ct BR3 43 F8
Norton Gdns SW16 41 E7
Norton House 4 KT3 38 E5
Norton Pk SL5 29 C4
Norton Rd Frimley GU15 66 C4
Wokingham RG40 25 C5
Norwegian Sch SW19 19 C1
Norwich Ave GU15 65 E3
Norwich Rd Crawley RH10 202 B5
South Norwood CR7 42 C6
Norwood Cl
Effingham KT24 113 E7
Twickenham TW2 16 D6
Norwood Cres TW6 3 C6
Norwood Farm La KT11 73 B8
Norwood Heights Sh Ctr SE19 22 E2
Norwood High St SE27 22 C4
Norwood Hill RH6 159 D3
Norwood Hospl SE19 22 D2
Norwood Junction Sta SE25 43 A5
Norwood Park Rd SE27 22 C3
Norwood Rd
Effingham KT24 113 E7
Streatham SE24, SE27 22 B7
West Norwood SE24, SE27 22 B7
Norwood Sch
West Norwood SE27 22 C3
West Norwood SE27 22 C4
Norwoodhill Rd RH6 159 F2
Noseby Ct KT12 54 C8
Notley End TW20 11 C1
Notre Dame Jun Sch RH7 164 F3
Notre Dame Sch RH7 164 F3
Notson Rd SE25 43 B5
Nottingham Cl GU21 68 F1
Nottingham Ct 5 GU21 68 F1
Nottingham Rd
Croydon CR2 61 C5
Isleworth TW7 5 F5
Upper Tooting SW17 20 F7
Nova Mews SM4 39 E2
Nova Rd CR0 42 C2
Nower Lodge Sch RH4 136 A6
Nower Rd RH4 136 A6
Nowhurst La RH12 216 A5
Noyna Rd SW17 20 F5
Nuffield Ct TW5 4 F7
Nuffield Dr GU47 45 E1
Nuffield Hospl GU2 108 E1
Nugee Ct RG45 45 B5
Nugent Ct Guildford GU2 109 B4
Streatham SW16 21 C4
Nugent Rd Guildford GU2 129 D8
South Norwood SE25 42 F6
Numa Ct TW8 6 D7
Nunappleton Way RH8 123 A3
Nuneaton RG12 27 E3
Nuneham SW16 21 D4
Nuns Wlk GU25 31 D4
Nuptown La SL4 8 A8
Nursery Ave CR0 62 D8
Nursery Cl Capel RH5 178 C5
Croydon CR0 62 D8
Ewell KT17 57 E1
Feltham TW14 15 B8
Frimley GU16 85 F7
Walton on t H KT20 97 B2
Woking GU21 69 C3
Woodham KT15 51 F1
Nursery Cotts GU21 88 F8
Nursery Gdns
Chilworth GU4 131 B3
Hounslow TW4 4 F2
Staines TW18 13 B1
Sunbury TW16 34 F7
Nursery Hill GU5 152 D5
Nursery La Hookwood RH6 160 D2
North Ascot SL5 28 E8
Nursery Rd
Farncombe GU7 150 F7
Knaphill GU21 68 D2
Merton SW19 40 B7
Mitcham CR4 40 E6
South Norwood CR7, SE25 42 D5
Sunbury TW16 34 F7
Sutton SM1 59 C6
Walton on t H KT20 97 B2
Wimbledon SW19 19 E1
Nurserylands RH11 201 A6
Nutborn House SW19 19 D2
Nutbourne GU9 125 E7
Nutbourne Cotts GU8 191 E7
Nutbourne Ct TW18 12 F1
Nutcombe La Dorking RH4 135 F7
Haslemere GU26, GU27 188 E1
Nutcroft Gr KT22 94 E6
Nutfield Church Prim Sch RH1 140 F8
Nutfield Cl SM5 59 E7
Nutfield Ct Camberley GU15 65 D7
Nutfield RH1 119 F2
Nutfield Marsh Rd RH1 119 E4
Nutfield Rd Coulsdon CR5 79 A3
Merstham RH1 119 C5
Nutfield RH1 119 C1
Redhill RH1 119 C1
Thornton Heath CR7 42 B5
Nutfield Sta RH1 140 E7
Nuthatch Cl GU10 124 D7
Nuthatch Gdns RH2 139 C5
Nuthatch Way RH12 217 D7
Nuthurst RG12 27 E4
Nuthurst Ave
Cranleigh GU6 174 E3
Streatham SW2 21 F6
Nuthurst Cl RH11 201 A7
Nutley RG12 27 A1
Nutley Ct RH2 118 A1
Nutley La RH2 117 F2
Nutmeg Ct GU14 84 C5
Nutshell La GU9 125 C6
Nutty La TW17 34 C6
Nutwell St SW17 20 E3
Nutwood GU7 150 D6
Nutwood Ave RH3 137 C8
Nutwood Cl RH3 137 C8
Nyefield Pk KT20 97 A1
Nylands Ave TW9 7 A5
Nymans Cl RH12 218 A7
Nymans Ct RH10 202 B3
Nymans Gdns SW20 39 B6
Nyon Gr SE23, SE6 23 F6

O

O'Connor Rd GU11 105 E7
Oak Ave Croydon CR0 63 B8
Egham TW20 12 D1
Hampton TW12, TW13 15 E2
Heston TW5 4 E7
Sandhurst GU47 45 D1
Oak Bank CR0 63 C4
Oak Cl Box Hill KT20 116 B5
Chiddingfold GU8 191 A4
Copthorne RH10 183 A3
Farncombe GU7 150 E8
Oak Cnr RH5 157 C4
Oak Cottage Cl Catford SE6 24 F7
Wood St V GU3 108 C2
Oak Cotts GU27 207 E6
Oak Croft RH19 206 A8
Oak Ct Crawley RH10 181 D2
Farnham GU9 125 B1
Oak Dell RH10 202 C7
Oak Dr KT20 116 B5
Oak End RH5 157 C3
Oak End Way KT15 70 F7
Oak Farm Cl GU17 64 C5
Oak Farm Com Sch GU14 84 F6
Oak Gdns CR0 63 A8
Oak Glade KT19 76 A7
Oak Gr Cranleigh GU6 174 F1
Loxwood RH14 213 A4
Sunbury TW16 15 B1
West Wickham BR4 44 C1
Oak Grange Rd GU4 111 B6
Oak Grove Cres GU15 64 F6
Oak Grove Rd SE20 43 C7
Oak Hill Epsom KT18 76 D3
Guildford GU4 110 C6
Surbiton KT6 37 E2
Wood St V GU3 108 B3
Oak Hill Cres KT6 37 E2
Oak Hill Gr KT6 37 E3
Oak Hill Rd KT6 37 E3
Oak House SE20 43 B7
Oak La
Broadbridge Heath RH12 216 E3
Englefield Green TW20 11 C5
Isleworth TW7 5 E3
Twickenham TW1 17 A8
Woking GU22 70 B3
Oak Leaf Cl KT19 76 C7
Oak Lodge
4 Charlton TW16 14 F1
Crowthorne RG45 45 C5
Oak Lodge Cl KT12 54 C5
Oak Lodge Dr
Salfords RH1 140 A1
West Wickham BR4 44 B2
Oak Lodge Prim Sch BR4 44 B2
Oak Lodge Sch SW12 21 A8
Oak Mead GU7 150 E8
Oak Park Gdns SW19 19 D7
Oak Pk KT14 70 E6
Oak Rd Caterham CR3 100 E5
Cobham KT11 73 E4
Crawley RH11 201 C5
Farnborough GU14 85 C3
Kingston u T KT3 38 D7
Leatherhead KT22 95 A8
Reigate RH2 118 B2
Oak Ridge RH4 136 B4
Oak Row CR4 41 C7
Oak Tree Cl
Aldershot GU12 126 E8
Ash Vale GU12 85 F1
Guildford, Burpham GU4 110 C6
Guildford, Jacobswell GU4 109 C6
Knaphill GU21 68 B1
Wentworth GU25 31 D3
Oak Tree Dr
Englefield Green TW20 11 C3
Guildford GU1 109 C5
Oak Tree La GU27 207 D6
Oak Tree Rd Knaphill GU21 68 B1
Milford GU8 149 F1
Oak Tree View GU9 125 E6
Oak Tree Way RH13 217 F4
Oak Way Ashstead KT21 76 A3
Crawley RH10 201 E8
Croydon CR0 43 D3
East Bedfont TW14 14 E7
Reigate RH2 139 D8
Oak Wlk RH12 199 F1
Oak's Rd GU21 69 E2
Oakapple Cl Crawley RH11 201 B1
Hamsey Green CR2 81 B5
Oakbank Fetcham KT22 94 D4
Woking GU22 89 E8
Oakbank Ave KT12 35 F2
Oakbrook BR3 44 B7
Oakcombe Cl KT3 38 E8

Oakcroft Bsns Ctr KT9 56 F6
Oakcroft Cl KT14 70 F5
Oakcroft House 3 KT3 38 E2
Oakcroft Rd
Chessington KT9 56 F6
Pyrford KT14 70 F5
Oakcroft Villas KT9 56 F6
Oakdale Beckenham BR3 44 C7
Bracknell RG12 27 D3
Oakdale Rd Epsom KT19 57 D2
Streatham SW16 21 E3
Weybridge KT13 53 A7
Oakdale Way CR4 41 A2
Oakdene Chobham GU24 49 F1
Kingswood KT20 97 E7
Sunningdale SL5 29 F3
1 West Norwood SE19 22 E3
Oakdene Ave KT7 37 A1
Oakdene Cl Brockham RH3 137 C7
Great Bookham KT23 114 C8
Oakdene Ct KT12 54 B7
Oakdene Dr KT5 38 C1
Oakdene Lodge SE20 23 B1
Oakdene Mews SM3 39 F1
Oakdene Par KT11 73 B5
Oakdene Rd
Brockham RH3 137 C7
Cobham KT11 73 B5
Godalming GU7 150 D3
Little Bookham KT23 93 F3
Redhill RH1 118 F1
Shalford GU3 130 C1
Oaken Coppice KT21 96 A8
Oaken Copse GU15 66 C7
Oaken Copse Cres GU14 85 B7
Oaken Dr KT10 55 F4
Oaken La KT10 55 E5
Oakengates RG12 27 A1
Oakenshaw Cl KT6 37 E2
Oakfield Plaistow RH14 211 E2
Woking GU21 68 A5
Oakfield Cl New Malden KT3 38 F4
Weybridge KT13 53 C6
Oakfield Ct Croydon CR2 61 C4
Wokingham RG41 25 A5
Oakfield Cty Jun Sch
KT22 94 D4
Oakfield Dr RH2 118 B3
Oakfield Gdns
Beckenham BR3 44 A4
Carshalton SM5 40 F1
3 Dulwich SE19 22 E3
Oakfield Glade KT13 53 C6
Oakfield Rd Ashford TW15 14 B3
Ashstead KT21 75 E1
Blackwater GU17 64 F3
Cobham KT11 73 B5
Penge SE20 23 B1
Thornton Heath CR0 42 C1
Wimbledon SW19 19 D5
Oakfield Sch Dulwich SE21 22 D7
Pyrford GU22 70 F4
Oakfield Way RH19 185 F3
Oakfields Camberley GU15 65 B5
Crawley RH10 202 D7
Guildford GU3 108 F3
Wallis Wood RH5 196 D8
Walton-on-T KT12 35 A1
West Byfleet KT14 71 B5
Oakhall Ct TW16 14 F3
Oakhall Dr TW16 14 F3
Oakham Cl SE6 23 F6
Oakham Dr BR2 44 F5
Oakhaven RH10, RH11 201 D4
Oakhill KT10 56 A4
Oakhill Cl KT21 75 C1
Oakhill Ct 6 Surbiton KT6 37 E3
Wimbledon SW19 19 D1
Oakhill Gdns KT13 53 E8
Oakhill Lodge CR8 80 A6
Oakhill Rd Addlestone KT15 51 F4
Ashstead KT21 75 C1
Beckenham BR3 44 C7
Headley Down GU35 187 B5
Horsham RH13 217 E2
Reigate RH2 139 B8
Sutton SM1 59 C7
Thornton Heath SW16 41 F8
Oakhurst Chobham GU24 49 E2
Grayshott GU26 188 D3
Oakhurst Cl 4 TW11 16 E3
Oakhurst Gdns RH19 185 C2
Oakhurst Grange Sch
CR3 100 D1
Oakhurst La RH14 212 E7
Oakhurst Rd KT19 57 D4
Oakhurst Rise SM5 59 E1
Oakington 6 KT1 38 A7
Oakington Dr TW16 35 C7
Oakland Ave GU9 125 E7
Oakland Way KT19 57 E4
Oaklands Croydon CR0 61 B5
Fetcham KT22 94 D3
Haslemere GU27 208 C7
Horley RH6 161 C3
Horsham RH13 217 E2
Purley CR8 80 C5
South Godstone RH9 142 E5
Twickenham TW2 16 C8
Oaklands Ave Hounslow TW7 5 F8
Thames Ditton KT10 36 D1
Thornton Heath CR7 42 A5
West Wickham BR4 63 B7
Oaklands Cl
Chessington KT9 56 C6
North Ascot SL5 8 F1
Shalford GU4 130 E1
Oaklands Ct KT15 52 B7
Oaklands Cty Jun Sch
RG45 45 A6
Oaklands Dr North Ascot SL5 8 F1
Redhill RH1 140 B7
Wokingham RG41 25 A5
Oaklands Gdns CR8 80 C5
Oaklands Inf Sch
Biggin Hill TN16 83 C3
Crowthorne RG45 45 A6
Oaklands La
Biggin Hill TN16 83 C5
Crowthorne RG45 45 B7
Oaklands Pk RG41 25 A4
Oaklands Rd Bromley BR1 24 E1
Mortlake SW14 7 D4
Oaklands Sch TW3 5 D4
Oaklands Way
Tadworth KT20 97 C5
Wallington SM6 60 D3
Oaklawn Rd Ashstead KT22 74 E2
Leatherhead KT22 74 E2
Oaklea GU12 106 A5
Oaklea Ct CR2 61 D2
Oakleigh Epsom KT18 76 E5
Lightwater GU18 67 C8
Oakleigh Ave KT6 57 B8
Oakleigh Ct Oxted RH8 122 E6
Penge SE20 23 B1
Oakleigh Rd RH12 217 F4
Oakleigh Way Mitcham CR4 41 B8
1 Tolworth KT6 38 B1
Oakley Ave CR0 60 E6
Oakley Cl Addlestone KT15 52 D6
East Grinstead RH19 206 B7
Hounslow TW7 5 D6
Oakley Cotts RH19 206 C7
Oakley Ct Carshalton CR4 41 A2
15 Redhill RH1 119 A2
Oakley Dell GU4 110 C3
Oakley Gdns SM7 78 B4
Oakley House GU7 150 E8
Oakley Rd Camberley GU15 65 B4
Croydon SE25 43 B4
Whyteleafe CR6 81 A1
Oakman House 29 SW19 19 D7
Oakmead Gn KT18 76 C4
Oakmead Pl CR4 40 E8
Oakmead Rd
Upper Tooting SW12 21 B7
Wallington CR0 41 D3
Oakridge GU24 67 F6
Oakridge La BR1 24 D3
Oakridge Rd BR1 24 E4
Oaks Ave Feltham TW13 15 E6
North Cheam KT4 58 B6
West Norwood SE19, SE27 22 E3
Oaks Cl Horsham RH12 218 B6
Leatherhead KT22 95 A6
Oaks Ct KT22 95 A6
Oaks La South Croydon CR0 62 C7
South Holmwood RH5 157 B8
Oaks Rd Purley CR8 80 B5
Reigate RH2 118 D2
South Croydon CR0 62 C6
Stanwell TW19 2 D1
Oaks Sports Ctr SM5 78 F8
Oaks The Bracknell RG12 27 D7
Dorking RH4 136 B4
East Grinstead RH19 206 B8
Epsom KT18 76 F5
Farnborough GU14 84 D3
Staines TW18 12 F4
West Byfleet KT14 71 A5
Wimbledon SW19 19 E2
Oaks Track SM5, SM6 60 B1
Oaks Way
Burgh Heath KT18 97 B8
Long Ditton KT6 37 D1
Purley CR8 80 C5
Wallington SM5 59 F3
Oaksford Ave SE26 23 B5
Oakshade Rd Catford BR1 24 D4
Oxshott KT22 74 C5
Oakshaw RH8 122 D8
Oakshaw Rd SW18 20 B8
Oakside Ct RH6 161 C4
Oakside La RH6 161 C4
Oaktree Way GU47 45 A1
Oaktrees Ash GU12 105 F1
Hale GU9 125 B6
Oakview RG40 25 B4
Oakview Gr CR0 43 E1
Oakview Rd SE6 24 B3
Oakway Aldershot GU12 126 E8
Beckenham BR2 44 D7
Knaphill GU21 88 E8
West Barnes SW20 39 C5
Oakway Dr GU16 65 E1
Oakwood Guildford GU2 109 A6
Wallington SM6 60 B2
Oakwood Ave
Beckenham BR2, BR3 44 C7
Mitcham CR4 40 D7
Purley CR8 80 C7
Oakwood Cl
East Horsley KT24 112 E8
Redhill RH1 119 A1
South Nutfield RH1 140 F7
Oakwood Ct
Beckenham BR3 44 C7
Bisley GU24 68 A3
Oakwood Dr
East Horsley KT24 112 E8
West Norwood SE19 22 E2
Oakwood Gdns
Knaphill GU21 68 B1
Sutton SM1 59 A8
Oakwood Ind Pk RH10 182 A2
Oakwood Independent Sch
CR8 80 B6
Oakwood Pk RH18 206 F2
Oakwood Pl CR0 42 A3
Oakwood Rd
Bletchingley RH1 120 A6
Bracknell RG12 27 E7
Horley RH6 161 B4
Knaphill GU21 88 E8
Thornton Heath CR0, CR7 42 A3
Thorpe GU25 31 C4
Wimbledon SW20 39 A8
Windlesham GU20 48 E4
Oakwood Rise CR3 100 E2
Oakwood Sch RH6 161 C3
Oareborough RG12 27 E4
Oast House Cl TW19 11 E8
Oast House Cres GU9 125 D6
Oast House La GU9 125 D6
Oast La GU11 126 B7
Oast Rd RH8 122 F4
Oates Cl BR2 44 D6
Oates Wlk RH10 201 F3
Oatfield Rd KT20 97 B6
Oatlands Crawley RH11 201 A5
Horley RH6 161 C4
Oatlands Ave
Oatlands Park KT13 53 E6
Weybridge KT13 53 E6
Oatlands Chase KT12, KT13 53 E7
Oatlands Cl KT13 53 D6
Oatlands Ct 3 SW19 19 D7
Oatlands Cty Inf Sch KT13 53 D6
Oatlands Dr
Oatlands Park KT13, KT12 53 D7
Weybridge KT13, KT12 53 D7
Oatlands Gn KT13 53 D7
Oatlands Mere KT13 53 D7
Oatlands Rd KT20 97 E8
Oban Rd SE25 42 D5
Obelisk Way GU15 65 C6
Oberon Way
Crawley RH11 200 E3
Littleton TW17 33 E6
Oberursel Way GU11 104 F2
Observatory Rd SW14 7 C3
Observatory Wlk 4 RH1 118 F1
Occam Rd GU2 129 D8
Ockenden Cl GU22 69 F1
Ockenden Gdns GU22 69 F1
Ockenden Rd GU22 69 F1
Ockfields GU8 149 F1
Ockford Ct GU7 150 D4
Ockford Dr GU7 150 C3
Ockford Rd GU7 150 D4
Ockford Ridge GU7 150 B2
Ockham Dr KT24 92 D3
Ockham La Downside KT11 92 D7
Martyr's Green GU23 92 D7
Ockham GU23 92 D7
Ockham Rd N
Ockham GU23 92 C3
West Horsley KT24 92 C3
Ockham Rd S KT24 112 E7
Ockley Ct GU4 110 B6
Ockley House 8 KT2 18 B2
Ockley Rd Ewhurst GU6 175 F6
Forest Green GU6, RH5 176 C7
Ockley RH5 177 B7
Streatham SW16 21 E5
Thornton Heath CR0, CR9 41 F2
Wotton GU6, RH5 176 C7
Ockley Sta RH5 178 A5
Ockleys Mead RH9 121 C5
Octagon Rd KT12 53 E1
Octavia RG12 27 A1
Octavia Cl CR4 40 E4
Octavia Rd TW7 5 F4
Octavia Way TW18 13 A2
October Ct BR2 44 F6
Odard Rd KT8 36 A5
Odette House 6 SE27 22 D4
Odiham Rd
Crondall GU9, GU10 124 D7
Heath End GU10, GU9 124 D7
Ogden House TW13 15 E4
Okeburn Rd SW17 21 A3
Okehurst Rd RH14 214 C1
Okingham Cl GU47 45 D1
Olaf Palme House TW13 15 B5
Old Acre KT14 71 A5
Old Ave
Sheerwater GU21, KT14 70 E6
Weybridge KT13 53 C3
Old Avenue Cl KT14 70 E6
Old Barn Cl SM2 58 E3
Old Barn Dr RH5 178 D6
Old Barn La Churt GU10 168 B1
Kenley CR3 80 F3
Old Barn Rd KT18 76 C2
Old Barn View GU7 150 C2
Old Bisley Rd GU16 66 C3
Old Bracknell Cl RG12 27 B6
Old Bracknell La E RG12 27 B6
Old Bracknell La W RG12 27 B6
Old Brickfield Rd GU11 126 B7
Old Bridge St KT1 37 D7
Old Brighton Rd S RH11 181 E5
Old Bromley Rd BR1 24 D3
Old Charlton Rd TW17 34 C4
Old Chertsey Rd GU24 50 C1
Old Chestnut Ave KT10 55 B4
Old Church La GU9 146 D7
Old Church Path KT10 55 B6
Old Claygate La KT10 56 A5
Old Common Rd KT11 73 B7
Old Compton La GU9 125 F2
Old Control Rd RH6 181 D6
Old Convent The RH19 185 E2
Old Cote Dr TW5 5 A8
Old Cotts GU3 130 C2
Old Court Rd GU2 130 A8
Old Crawley Rd RH12 218 C7
Old Cross Tree Way
GU12 127 C8
Old Ct KT21 95 E8
Old Dean Rd GU15 65 D7
Old Deer Park Gdns TW9 6 E4
Old Denne Gdns RH12 217 C1
Old Devonshire Rd SW12 21 B8
Old Dock Cl TW9 7 A8
Old Elstead Rd GU8 149 E2
Old Esher Cl KT12 54 D5
Old Esher Rd KT12 54 E5
Old Farleigh Rd
Chelsham CR0, CR2, CR6 81 E6
Selsdon CR0, CR6, CR22 81 E6
Old Farm Cl TW4 4 F3
Old Farm Pl GU12 105 F5
Old Farm Rd
Guildford GU1 109 D4
Hampton TW12 15 F2
Old Farmhouse Dr KT22 74 D4
Old Farnham La
Bentley GU10 124 A1
Farnham GU9 146 C8
Old Ford House CR0 60 E7
Old Forge Cres TW17 34 B3
Old Fox Cl CR3 100 B6
Old Frensham Rd
Farnham GU10 146 E4
Frensham GU10 146 E4
Old Green La GU15 65 C7
Old Guildford Rd
Mytchett GU12, GU16 86 C4
Warnham RH12 216 E4
Old Haslemere Rd GU27 208 C5
Old Heath Way GU9 125 C7
Old Hill GU22 89 D7
Old Horsham Rd RH11 201 B4
Old Hospital Cl
SW12, SW17 20 F7
Old House Cl Ewell KT17 57 F1
Wimbledon SW19 19 E3
Old House Gdns 9 TW1 6 C1
Old Kiln GU9 125 A2
Old Kiln Cl GU10 167 F2
Old Kiln Court Yd 15 GU9 125 B2
Old Kiln La Brockham RH3 137 C8
Churt GU10 167 F2
Old Kingston Rd KT4 57 C7
Old La Aldershot GU11 126 A7
Aldershot, North
Town GU12 105 E3
Dockenfield GU10 166 F4
East Horsley KT11 93 A5
Martyr's Green KT11 92 E7
Ockham GU23, KT11 72 B1
Oxted RH8 122 F5
Tatsfield TN16 103 D6
Old Lands Hill RG12 27 D8
Old Lane Gdns KT11 93 A5
Old Lodge Cl GU7 150 B3
Old Lodge La CR8 80 A3
Old Lodge Pl 7 TW1 6 B1
Old London Rd
Epsom KT17, KT18 77 A2
Mickleham RH5 115 C8
Old Malden La KT4 57 E8
Old Malt Way GU21 69 D2
Old Manor Cl RH11 201 A8
Old Manor Dr TW7 5 C1
Old Manor Gdns GU4 131 C3
Old Martyrs RH11 181 D1
Old Merrow St GU4 110 D3
Old Mill La RH1 119 B7
Old Mill Pl GU27 207 F7
Old Millmeads RH12 217 C5
Old Museum Ct GU27 208 D6
Old Nursery Pl TW15 14 B3
Old Oak Ave CR5 98 E8
Old Orch Byfleet KT14 71 F7
Sunbury TW16 35 C7
Old Orchard The GU9 146 A8
Old Palace La TW9 6 C2
Old Palace Rd
Croydon CR0, CR9 61 C7
Guildford GU2 130 A8
Weybridge KT13 53 B7
Old Palace Sch CR9 61 B7
Old Palace Terr 8 TW9 6 D2
Old Palace Yd 2 TW9 6 D2
Old Park Cl GU9 125 A6
Old Park La Farnham GU9 125 A4
Hale GU9 124 F6
Old Park Mews TW5 4 F7
Old Parvis Rd KT14 71 C7
Old Pasture Rd GU16, GU15 65 F3
Old Pharmacy Ct RG45 45 C4
Old Pond Cl GU15 65 C1
Old Portsmouth Rd
Artington GU2, GU3, GU7 130 C3
Frimley GU15 66 A5
Shalford GU2, GU3, GU7 130 C3
Thursley GU8 169 D4
Old Pottery Cl RH2 139 B7
Old Quarry The GU27 207 F4
Old Rd Addlestone KT15 51 F3
Buckland RH3 116 F1
East Grinstead RH19 185 F1
Old Rectory Cl
Bramley GU5 151 F6
Walton on t H KT20 97 A3
Old Rectory Dr GU12 106 B2
Old Rectory Gdns
Farnborough GU14 85 D4
Old Rectory Gdns *continued*
Godalming GU7 150 F2
Old Rectory La KT24 92 E1
Old Redstone Dr RH1 140 A8
Old Reigate Rd
Brockham RH3 116 C1
Dorking RH4 115 F2
Old Sawmill La RG45 45 C6
Old School Cl Ash GU12 106 A3
Merton SW19 40 A7
Penge BR3 43 E7
Old School Ct
Leatherhead KT22 95 B5
Wraysbury TW19 11 E8
Old School La
Brockham RH3 137 A7
Newdigate RH5 158 B1
Old School Mews KT13 53 D6
Old School Pl
Lingfield RH7 164 D4
Woking GU22 89 F6
Old School Sq KT7 36 F3
Old Schools La KT17 57 F2
Old St Mary's KT24 112 B6
Old Station App KT22 95 A6
Old Station Cl RH10 204 B7
Old Station Rd GU7 150 E6
Old Station Way GU7 150 E5
Old Surrey Mews
The RH9 121 C5
Old Swan Yd SM5 59 F6
Old Town CR0, CR9 61 B7
Old Town Mews GU9 125 A2
Old Tye Ave TN16 83 E3
Old Westhall Cl CR6 101 C8
Old Wickhurst La RH12 216 D2
Old Woking Rd
Old Woking GU22 90 C8
Pyrford GU22, KT14 70 D3
West Byfleet KT14 71 A6
Woking GU22 90 C8
Old Wokingham Rd
Bracknell RG45 45 C7
Crowthorne RG45 45 C7
Oldacre GU24 67 F7
Oldbury RG12 26 F6
Oldbury Cl Frimley GU16 85 F8
Horsham RH12 218 A7
Oldbury Rd KT16 32 E2
Olde Farm Dr GU17 64 B5
Olden La CR8 80 A7
Oldfield Gdns KT21 95 D8
Oldfield House SW16 21 B4
Oldfield House Sch TW12 35 F8
Oldfield Rd Hampton TW12 35 F8
Horley RH6 160 F1
Wimbledon SW19 19 E2
Oldfields Rd SM1, SM3 59 A8
Oldfields Trad Est SM1 59 A7
Oldfieldwood GU22 70 B2
Oldham House 10 SE21 22 E4
Oldhouse La Bisley GU24 68 A5
West End GU24 68 A5
Windlesham GU18 48 C2
Olding House 6 SW12 21 C8
Oldridge Rd SW12 21 B8
Oldstead RG12 27 D4
Oldstead Rd BR1 24 D4
Oldwood Chase GU14 84 C3
Oleander Cl RG45 45 A7
Olive Rd 3 SW19 20 C1
Oliver Ave SE25 42 F6
Oliver Cl Addlestone KT15 52 B6
Brentford W4 7 B8
Oliver Ct TW7 5 F4
Oliver Gr SE25 42 F5
Oliver Rd Ascot SL5 29 B5
Horsham RH12 217 A1
Kingston u T KT3 38 C7
Sutton SM1 59 D6
Olivier Rd RH10 202 D5
Ollerton RG12 27 A1
Olley Cl SM6 60 E4
Olveston Wlk SM4, SM5 40 D3
Olyffe Dr BR3 44 C8
Omega Rd GU21 70 A3
Omega Way TW20 32 C8
One Tree Cnr GU1 131 B8
One Tree Hill Rd GU4 131 B7
Ongar Cl KT15 51 F4
Ongar Hill KT15 52 A4
Ongar Pl KT15 52 A4
Ongar Place Inf Sch KT15 52 A4
Ongar Rd KT15 52 A5
Onslow Ave Belmont SM2 77 F8
Richmond TW10 6 E2
Onslow Avenue Mansions
TW10 6 E2
Onslow Cl
Thames Ditton KT7 36 E1
Woking GU22 70 A2
Onslow Cres GU22 70 A2
Onslow Cty Inf Sch GU2 129 F7
Onslow Dr SL5 9 A1
Onslow Gdns
Sanderstead CR2 81 A7
Thames Ditton KT7 36 E1
Wallington SM6 60 C3
Onslow House 1 KT2 37 F8
Onslow Lodge TW18 12 F1
Onslow Mews KT16 33 A3
Onslow Rd Guildford GU1 109 D1
Hersham KT12 54 A5
New Malden KT3 39 A5
Richmond TW10 6 E1

Onslow Rd continued
Sunningdale SL5 . . . . .30 B2
Thornton Heath CR0 . . . . .42 A1
Onslow St GU1 . . . . .130 C8
Onslow Way Pyrford GU22 . .70 F4
Thames Ditton KT7 . . . . .36 E1
Ontario Rd RH6 . . . . .162 A2
Onyx House KT4 . . . . .38 D1
Opal House KT4 . . . . .38 D1
Openview SW17, SW18 . . . . .20 D6
Opladen Way RG12 . . . . .27 E4
Opossum Dr TW4 . . . . .4 C4
Opus Park GU4 . . . . .109 D6
Oracle Ctr RG12 . . . . .27 C7
Orangery The TW10 . . . . . . .17 C6
Orchard Ave Ashford TW15 .14 C2
Carshalton CR4 . . . . .41 A1
Croydon CR0 . . . . .43 E1
Hatton TW14 . . . . .3 D2
Heston TW5 . . . . .4 E7
Hinchley Wood KT7 . . . . .56 A8
Kingston u T KT3 . . . . .38 E6
Woodham KT15 . . . . .70 F8
Orchard Bsns Ctr SE26 . . . . .23 F3
Orchard Bsns Ctr The
RH1 . . . . .161 A8
Orchard Cl Ash Vale GU12 .106 A5
Ashford TW15 . . . . .14 C2
Ashstead KT21 . . . . .95 D7
Banstead SM7 . . . . .78 B5
East Horsley KT24 . . . . .92 F3
Farnborough GU17 . . . . .64 F1
Farnham GU9 . . . . .126 A6
Fetcham KT22 . . . . .94 D5
Flexford GU3 . . . . .107 B1
Guildford GU1 . . . . .110 B1
Horley RH6 . . . . .160 F4
Leatherhead KT22 . . . . .94 F8
Walton-on-T KT12 . . . . .35 B2
West Barnes SW20 . . . . .39 C5
West End GU24 . . . . .67 D6
West Ewell KT19 . . . . .57 B4
Woking GU21 . . . . .70 B3
Wokingham RG40 . . . . .25 D6
Orchard Cotts
Charlwood RH6 . . . . .180 F7
Lingfield RH7 . . . . .165 B3
Orchard Ct Barnes SW13 . . . .7 F4
Bracknell RG12 . . . . .27 C7
Croydon BR3 . . . . .44 A1
Harmondsworth UB7 . . . . .2 C7
Hounslow TW7 . . . . .5 D2
Wallington SM6 . . . . .60 B5
Walton-on-T KT12 . . . . .34 F1
Orchard Cty Fst Sch The
KT8 . . . . .36 D5
Orchard Dene KT14 . . . . . . .71 A6
Orchard Dr Sunbury TW17 . .34 E6
Woking GU21 . . . . .69 F4
Orchard End
Caterham CR3 . . . . .100 E5
Fetcham KT22 . . . . .94 C3
Oatlands Park KT13 . . . . .53 E8
Rowledge GU10 . . . . .145 F3
Orchard Gate
Sandhurst GU47 . . . . .64 B8
Thames Ditton KT10 . . . . .36 D1
Orchard Gdns
Aldershot GU11 . . . . .126 C8
Chessington KT9 . . . . .56 E6
Cranleigh GU6 . . . . .174 F2
Effingham KT24 . . . . .113 E7
Epsom KT18 . . . . .76 C4
Sutton SM1 . . . . .59 A5
Orchard Gr Croydon CR0 . . .43 E2
Penge SE20 . . . . .23 A1
Orchard Hill
Rudgwick RH12 . . . . .214 C0
Windlesham GU20 . . . . .48 D3
Orchard House
Guildford GU4 . . . . .110 D2
Tongham GU10 . . . . .126 F7
Orchard House Cheyne
Ctr (Hospl) BR4 . . . . .63 C7
Orchard Jun & Inf Sch The
TW3 . . . . .5 A3
Orchard La
Thames Ditton KT8 . . . . .36 D3
Wimbledon SW20 . . . . .39 B8
Orchard Lea Cl GU22 . . . . . .70 E4
Orchard Mains GU22 . . . . . . .89 C8
Orchard Pl RG40 . . . . .25 C6
Orchard Rd Brentford TW8 . . .6 C8
Chessington KT9 . . . . .56 E6
Dorking RH4 . . . . .136 B6
Farnborough GU14 . . . . .85 A4
Farnham GU9 . . . . .126 A6
Guildford, Burpham GU4 . . . .110 B5
Guildford, Onslow
Village GU2 . . . . .129 F7
Hampton TW12 . . . . .15 F1
Hamsey Green CR2 . . . . .81 B5
Horsham RH13 . . . . .217 E2
Hounslow TW4 . . . . .5 A2
Kingston u T KT1 . . . . .37 E6
Mortlake TW9 . . . . .7 A4
Reigate RH2 . . . . .118 B1
Shalford GU4 . . . . .130 E3
Shere GU5 . . . . .133 A4
Smallfield RH6 . . . . .162 C3
Sunbury TW16 . . . . .15 B1
Sutton SM1 . . . . .59 A6
Twickenham TW1 . . . . .6 B2
Orchard Rise Croydon CR0 .43 F1
Kingston u T KT2 . . . . .38 C8

Orchard Rise continued
Mortlake TW10 . . . . .7 B3
Orchard School Sports Ctr
SE20 . . . . .43 A8
Orchard St
Crawley RH10, RH11 . . . . . . .201 D6
Thames Ditton KT7 . . . . .37 B2
Orchard The Banstead SM7 .78 A4
Dorking RH5 . . . . .136 C3
Ewell KT17 . . . . .57 F1
Ewell KT17, KT19 . . . . .57 F3
Haslemere GU27 . . . . .207 F5
Hounslow TW3 . . . . .5 C5
Lightwater GU18 . . . . .67 B8
Thorpe GU25 . . . . .31 E4
Weybridge KT13 . . . . .53 B6
Woking GU22 . . . . .89 E5
Orchard Way
Addlestone KT15 . . . . .52 B4
Aldershot GU11, GU12 . . . . .126 C8
Ashford TW15 . . . . .13 F6
Beckenham BR3, CR0 . . . . . . .43 E3
Camberley GU15 . . . . .65 B2
Carshalton SM1 . . . . .59 D6
Croydon BR3, CR0 . . . . .43 E3
Dorking RH4 . . . . .136 B6
East Grinstead RH19 . . . . . . .185 E1
Esher KT10 . . . . .55 C4
Flexford GU3 . . . . .107 B1
Lower Kingswood KT20 . . . . . .97 F1
Oxted RH8 . . . . .123 A2
Reigate RH2 . . . . .139 B6
Send GU23 . . . . .90 C2
Orchard Way Prim Sch
CR0 . . . . .43 E2
Orchardfield Rd GU7 . . . . . .150 F7
Orchardleigh KT22 . . . . .95 B5
Orchards Cl KT14 . . . . .71 A5
Orchards The
Ashford TW15 . . . . .14 D3
4 Crawley RH11 . . . . .200 D5
Horsham RH12 . . . . .217 F5
Orchid Dr GU24 . . . . .68 A4
Orchid Mead SM7 . . . . .78 B5
Orde Cl RH10 . . . . .182 D1
Ordnance Cl TW13 . . . . .15 A6
Ordnance Rd GU11 . . . . . . .105 C3
Ordnance Rdbt GU11 . . . . . .105 B2
Oregano Way GU2 . . . . .109 A6
Oregon Cl KT3 . . . . .38 C5
Orestan La KT24 . . . . .113 C8
Orford Ct Wallington SM6 . . .60 C5
West Norwood SE27 . . . . .22 B6
Orford Gdns TW1 . . . . .16 F6
Orford Rd SE6 . . . . .24 B5
Oriel Cl Crawley RH10 . . . . .182 C1
Mitcham CR4 . . . . .41 D6
Oriel Ct 6 CR0 . . . . .42 D1
Oriel Hill GU15 . . . . .65 D4
Oriel Jun & Inf Sch TW13 .15 E5
Oriental Cl GU22 . . . . .70 A2
Oriental Rd Ascot SL5 . . . . . .29 D5
Woking GU22 . . . . .70 A3
Orion RG12 . . . . .27 A1
Orion Ct RH11 . . . . .200 D4
Orion Ctr The CR0 . . . . .60 E8
Orlando Gdns KT19 . . . . .57 D1
Orlean Ct KT12 . . . . .54 C8
Orleans Cl KT10 . . . . .55 D8
Orleans Ct 10 TW1 . . . . .17 B8
Orleans Inf Sch TW1 . . . . . .17 B8
Orleans Park Sec Sch
TW1 . . . . .17 B8
Orleans Rd
South Norwood SE19 . . . . . . .22 D2
10 Twickenham TW1 . . . . . . .17 C8
Orltons La RH12 . . . . .179 F2
Ormanton Rd SE26 . . . . .23 A4
Orme Rd KT1, KT3 . . . . .38 B7
Ormeley Rd SW12 . . . . .21 B7
Ormerod Gdns CR4 . . . . .41 A8
Ormesby Wlk RH10 . . . . . . .202 B4
Ormond Ave
Hampton TW12 . . . . .36 B8
22 Richmond TW10 . . . . .6 D2
Ormond Cres TW12 . . . . .36 B8
Ormond Dr TW12 . . . . .16 B1
Ormond Rd TW10 . . . . .6 D2
Ormonde Ave KT19 . . . . .57 D1
Ormonde Lodge (West
London Ins of Higher
Education) TW1 . . . . .6 B2
Ormonde Rd
Farncombe GU7 . . . . .150 E6
Mortlake SW14 . . . . .7 C4
Woking GU21 . . . . .69 C3
Wokingham RG41 . . . . .25 A5
Ormsby SM2 . . . . .59 B3
Ormside Way RH1 . . . . .119 B4
Ormuz Cotts RH7 . . . . .164 C4
Orpin Rd RH1 . . . . .119 C5
Orpwood Cl TW12 . . . . .15 F2
Orwell Cl GU14 . . . . .84 E6
Orwell Gdns RH2 . . . . .139 B7
Orwell House 7 RH1 . . . . . .118 F2
Osborn La SE23 . . . . .23 E8
Osborn Rd GU9 . . . . .125 D4
Osborne Ave TW19 . . . . .13 F7
Osborne Cl Beckenham BR3 .43 E5
Feltham TW13 . . . . .15 A4
Frimley GU16 . . . . .85 F8
Osborne Ct Crawley RH11 . .201 B2
Farnborough GU14 . . . . .105 C8
10 Surbiton KT6 . . . . .37 E3
Osborne Dr GU18 . . . . .67 A8
Osborne Gdns CR7 . . . . .42 C7
Osborne Pl SM1 . . . . .59 D5
Osborne Rd Egham TW20 . . .11 F2

Osborne Rd continued
Farnborough GU14 . . . . .105 C8
Hounslow TW3, TW4 . . . . .4 F4
Kingston u T KT2 . . . . .17 E1
Redhill RH1 . . . . .119 A4
South Norwood CR7 . . . . .42 C7
Walton-on-T KT12 . . . . .35 A1
Wokingham RG40 . . . . .25 C6
Osbourne Terr 1 SW17 . . . . .21 A3
Osier Pl TW20 . . . . .12 C2
Osier Way
Banstead KT17, SM7 . . . . .77 E5
Mitcham CR4 . . . . .40 F4
Oslac Rd SE6 . . . . .24 B3
Oslo Ct SW19 . . . . .20 D1
Osman's Cl RG42 . . . . .8 B1
Osmond Gdns SM6 . . . . .60 C5
Osmund Cl RH10 . . . . .202 E6
Osmunda Bank RH19 . . . . . .185 E6
Osnaburgh Hill GU15 . . . . . .65 B5
Osney Cl RH11 . . . . .201 C5
Osney Wlk SM4, SM5 . . . . . . .40 D3
Osprey Cl Cheam SM1 . . . . . .58 F5
Fetcham KT22 . . . . .94 B3
Osprey Gdns CR0, CR2 . . . . .62 E1
Ospringe Cl 9 SE20 . . . . . . .23 C1
Ostade Rd SW2 . . . . .21 F8
Osterley Ave TW7 . . . . .5 D7
Osterley Cl RG40 . . . . .25 F5
Osterley Cres TW7 . . . . .5 F6
Osterley Ct TW7 . . . . .5 D6
Osterley Lodge 1 TW7 . . . . . .5 E6
Osterley Rd TW7 . . . . .5 E6
Osterley Sta TW7 . . . . .5 D7
Osterly Gdns CR7 . . . . .42 C7
Oswald Cl KT22 . . . . .94 C5
Oswald Rd KT22 . . . . .94 C5
Osward CR0 . . . . .62 F1
Osward Rd SW12, SW17 . . . .20 F7
Otford Cl SE20 . . . . .43 C8
Othello Gr RG42 . . . . .27 E8
Otho Ct 5 TW8 . . . . .6 D7
Otter Cl Crowthorne RG45 . . .45 A7
Ottershaw KT16 . . . . .51 B4
Otter Mdw KT22 . . . . .94 F8
Otterbourne Pl RH19 . . . . . .185 B1
Otterbourne Rd 1
CR0, CR9 . . . . .61 C8
Otterburn Gdns TW7 . . . . .6 A7
Otterburn St SW17 . . . . .20 F2
Otterden St SE6 . . . . .24 A4
Ottermead La KT16 . . . . .51 C4
Ottershaw House CR4 . . . . . .40 D7
Ottershaw Pk KT16 . . . . .51 A3
Ottways Ave KT21 . . . . .95 D8
Ottways La KT21, KT22 . . . . .95 D8
Otway Cl RH11 . . . . .200 F4
Oulton Wlk RH10 . . . . .202 B4
Our Lady of the Rosary
RC Sch TW18 . . . . .13 A2
Our Lady Queen of
Heaven RC Prim Sch
SW19 .19 D8
Our Lady Queen Of
Heaven RC Sch RH11 . . . . .201 B8
Our Lady & St Philip Neri
Prim Sch SE23 . . . . .23 E4
Our Lady & St Philip Neri
RC Sch Forest Hill SE23 . . . .23 D5
Forest Hill SE26 . . . . .23 E4
Our Lady's Prep Sch RG45 .45 B5
Our Ladys RC First Sch
KT16 . . . . .33 A1
Ouseley Rd
Upper Tooting SW12 . . . . .20 F7
Wraysbury TW19 . . . . .11 D8
Outdowns KT24 . . . . .113 B5
Outram Pl KT13 . . . . .53 C5
Outram Rd CR0 . . . . .42 E1
Outwood House 6 SW2 . . . .21 F8
Outwood La
Bletchingley RH1 . . . . .141 D7
Chipstead CR5, KT20 . . . . . . .98 C6
Kingswood CR5, KT20 . . . . . . .98 C6
Outwood RH1 . . . . .141 D1
Oval Prim Sch CR0 . . . . .42 E1
Oval Rd CR0 . . . . .42 E1
Oval The Banstead SM7 . . . .78 A5
Farncombe GU7 . . . . .150 F7
Guildford GU2 . . . . .130 A8
Wood St V GU3 . . . . .108 B2
Overbrae BR3 . . . . .24 A3
Overbrook Godalming GU7 .150 F3
West Horsley KT24 . . . . .112 B6
Overbury Ave BR3 . . . . .44 C6
Overbury Cres CR0 . . . . .63 C1
Overbury Ct BR3 . . . . .44 C6
Overdale Ashstead KT21 . . . .75 E3
Bletchingley RH1 . . . . .120 C2
Dorking RH5 . . . . .136 D8
Overdale Ave KT3 . . . . .38 D7
Overdale Rise GU16 . . . . .65 E3
Overdene Dr RH11 . . . . .201 A6
Overdown Rd SE6 . . . . .24 B4
Overford Cl GU6 . . . . .174 E2
Overford Dr GU6 . . . . .174 E2
Overhill CR6 . . . . .101 C8
Overhill Rd
Dulwich SE21, SE22 . . . . .23 A8
Wallington CR8 . . . . .61 A1
Overhill Way BR3 . . . . .44 D4
Overlord Cl GU15 . . . . .65 C8
Overstand Ct RH11 . . . . .201 A4
Overstone Gdns CR0 . . . . . . .43 F2
Overthorpe Cl GU21 . . . . .70 B4
Overton House SW15 . . . . . . .18 F8

Overton Rd SM2 . . . . .59 A3
Overton Shaw RH19 . . . . . . .185 E4
Overton's Yd CR0, CR9 . . . . . .61 C8
Oveton Way KT23 . . . . .94 B1
Ovett Cl SE19 . . . . .22 E2
Ovington Ct GU21 . . . . .68 F3
Owen Cl CR0 . . . . .42 D3
Owen House Feltham TW14 .15 A8
6 Twickenham TW1 . . . . .17 B8
Owen Pl KT22 . . . . .95 B5
Owen Rd Farncombe GU7 . .150 F6
Windlesham GU20 . . . . .48 D5
Owen Wlk 7 SE20 . . . . .23 A1
Owens Way SE23 . . . . .23 E8
Owl Cl CR2 . . . . .62 D1
Owlbeech Ct RH13 . . . . .218 B4
Owlbeech Pl RH13 . . . . .218 B4
Owlbeech Way RH13 . . . . . .218 B4
Owletts RH10 . . . . .202 D7
Owlscastle Cl RH12 . . . . . . .217 D5
Owlsmoor Cty Prim Sch
GU47 .45 E1
Owlsmoor Rd GU47 . . . . .45 D1
Ownstead Gdns CR2 . . . . . . .80 F8
Ownsted Hill CR0 . . . . .63 D1
Oxdowne Cl KT11 . . . . .74 B5
Oxenden Rd GU10 . . . . .126 A6
Oxenden Rd GU10, GU12 . .126 A6
Oxenhope RG12 . . . . .27 A5
Oxford Ave Harlington TW6 . . .3 F7
Merton SW20 . . . . .39 E7
Oxford Cl
Littleton TW15, TW17 . . . . . . .14 C1
Mitcham CR4 . . . . .41 C6
Oxford Cres KT3 . . . . .38 D3
Oxford Ct Epsom KT18 . . . . . .76 E5
17 Kingston u T KT6 . . . . .37 E4
Oxford Gdns W4 . . . . .7 A8
Oxford Rd
Carshalton SM2, SM5 . . . . . . .59 E5
Crawley RH10 . . . . .201 F2
Farnborough GU14 . . . . .85 C1
Guildford GU1 . . . . .130 D7
Horsham RH13 . . . . .217 C2
Redhill RH1 . . . . .118 E2
South Norwood SE19 . . . . . . .22 D2
Teddington TW11, TW12 . . . . .16 D3
Wallington SM6 . . . . .60 C5
Wokingham RG41 . . . . .25 A6
Oxford Terr GU1 . . . . .130 D7
Oxford Way TW13 . . . . .15 D4
Oxleigh Cl KT3 . . . . .38 E4
Oxlip Cl CR0 . . . . .43 D1
Oxshott Cl KT Ashstead KT22 .74 F3
Leatherhead KT22 . . . . .75 A4
Oxshott Rise KT11 . . . . .73 E5
Oxshott Sta KT22 . . . . .74 C6
Oxshott Way KT11 . . . . .73 E4
Oxted Cl CR4 . . . . .40 D6
Oxted Cty Sch RH8 . . . . .122 F7
Oxted Gn GU8 . . . . .170 E2
Oxted Hospl RH8 . . . . .122 D7
Oxted Rd Tandridge RH9 . . .121 D4
Tyler's Green RH9 . . . . .121 D4
Oxted Sta RH8 . . . . .122 E6
Oxtoby Way SW16 . . . . .41 D8
Oyster La KT14 . . . . .71 E7

P

Pacific Cl TW14 . . . . .14 F7
Packer Cl RH19 . . . . .186 A3
Packham Ct KT4 . . . . .58 C7
Packway GU9 . . . . .146 E2
Padbrook RH8 . . . . .123 A6
Padbury Cl TW14 . . . . .14 D7
Padbury Oaks UB7 . . . . .2 B6
Paddock
Beare Green RH5 . . . . .157 D4
Camberley GU15 . . . . .66 A6
Cobham KT11 . . . . .73 C5
Forest Hill SE26 . . . . .23 D4
Hambledon GU8 . . . . .171 C1
Lingfield RH7 . . . . .164 C4
New Malden KT4 . . . . .38 E1
Oxted RH8 . . . . .122 F4
Paddock Ct SW20 . . . . .39 C5
Paddock Gdns
East Grinstead RH19 . . . . . . .205 E7
South Norwood SE19 . . . . . . .22 E2
Paddock Gr RH5 . . . . .157 D4
Paddock House GU4 . . . . . . .110 D2
Paddock Sch SW15 . . . . .7 F3
Paddock The
Addington SE4 . . . . .63 A4
Bracknell RG12 . . . . .27 C6
Cranleigh GU6 . . . . .174 D3
Crawley RH10 . . . . .202 F6
Crowthorne RG45 . . . . .45 A6
Ewhurst GU6 . . . . .175 E4
Godalming GU7 . . . . .150 F3
Grayshott GU26 . . . . .188 A4
Guildford GU1 . . . . .110 D2
Haslemere GU27 . . . . .208 A8
Westcott RH4 . . . . .135 C6
Paddock Way
Grayswood GU27 . . . . .190 A2
Oxted RH8 . . . . .122 F4
Sheerwater GU21 . . . . .70 B5
Paddock Wlk CR6 . . . . .101 B8
Paddockhurst Rd
Crawley RH11 . . . . .201 A5
Crawley RH10 . . . . .203 C2
Paddocks Cl KT21 . . . . .75 E1
Paddocks Mead GU21 . . . . . .68 F3
Paddocks Rd GU4 . . . . .110 A5

Paddocks The
Flexford GU3 . . . . .107 C1
Great Bookham KT23 . . . . . . .94 B1
Oatlands Park KT13 . . . . .53 E7
Woodham KT15 . . . . .52 B1
Paddocks Way
Ashstead KT21 . . . . .75 E1
Chertsey KT16 . . . . .33 B1
Padstow Wlk
Crawley RH11 . . . . .200 F4
East Bedfont TW14 . . . . .14 F7
Padua Rd SE20 . . . . .43 C8
Padwick Rd RH13 . . . . .218 A2
Page Cl TW12 . . . . .15 E2
Page Cres CR0 . . . . .61 B5
Page Croft KT15 . . . . .52 B8
Page Ct RH13 . . . . .217 D1
Page Rd TW14 . . . . .3 D1
Page's Croft RG40 . . . . .25 D5
Page's Yd W4 . . . . .7 E8
Pageant Wlk CR0 . . . . .61 E7
Pagehurst Rd CR0 . . . . .43 B2
Paget Ave SM1 . . . . .59 D7
Paget Cl Camberley GU15 . . .66 B7
Hampton TW12 . . . . .16 D4
Paget La TW7 . . . . .5 E4
Paget Pl Kingston u T KT2 . . .18 C2
Thames Ditton KT7 . . . . .36 F1
Pagewood Cl RH10 . . . . .202 D4
Pagoda Ave TW9 . . . . .6 F4
Paice Gn RG40 . . . . .25 D7
Pain's Cl CR4 . . . . .41 B7
Paines Hill RH8 . . . . .123 C4
Paisley Rd SM5 . . . . .40 D3
Pakenham Cl SW12 . . . . .21 A7
Pakenham Rd RG12 . . . . .27 D2
Palace Ct
South Norwood CR7 . . . . .42 D5
Streatham SW2 . . . . .22 A6
Woking GU21 . . . . .70 A3
Palace Dr KT13 . . . . .53 B7
Palace Gn CR0 . . . . .62 F3
Palace Gr SE19 . . . . .22 F1
Palace Rd East Molesey KT8 .36 D6
Kingston u T KT1 . . . . .37 D5
Penge SE19 . . . . .22 F1
Streatham SE27, SW16, SW2 .22 A6
Woodham KT15 . . . . .52 B2
Palace Sq SE19 . . . . .22 F1
Palace View CR0 . . . . .62 F6
Palestine Gr SW19 . . . . .40 D8
Palewell Common Dr SW14 .7 D2
Palewell Pk SW14 . . . . .7 D3
Palgrave House 4 TW2 . . . . .16 C8
Pallingham Dr RH10 . . . . . . .202 C3
Palm Ct BR3 . . . . .43 F6
Palm Gr GU1 . . . . .109 C5
Palmer Ave KT4, SM3 . . . . . . .58 C6
Palmer C of E Jun Sch
The RG40 . . . . .25 D7
Palmer Cl Crowthorne RG45 .45 A8
Heston TW5 . . . . .5 A6
Horley RH6 . . . . .160 F5
Redhill RH1 . . . . .140 A8
West Wickham BR4 . . . . .63 D8
Palmer Cres
Kingston u T KT1 . . . . .37 E6
Ottershaw KT16 . . . . .51 D4
Palmer Rd RH10 . . . . .202 C3
Palmer School Rd RG40 . . . .25 C6
Palmer's Lodge GU2 . . . . . . .130 B8
Palmers Gr KT8 . . . . .36 A5
Palmers Rd Mortlake SW14 . .7 F4
Thornton Heath SW16 . . . . . . .41 F7
Palmersfield Rd SM7 . . . . . . .78 B5
Palmerston Cl
Farnborough GU14 . . . . .84 D3
Woking GU21 . . . . .70 A5
Palmerston Ct 9 KT6 . . . . . . .37 D2
Palmerston Gr 4 SW19 . . . . .20 A1
Palmerston House SM7 . . . . .77 F4
Palmerston Rd
Carshalton SM5 . . . . .60 B4
Hounslow TW3 . . . . .5 C6
Merton SW19 . . . . .20 A1
Mortlake SW14 . . . . .7 C3
Sutton SM1 . . . . .59 C5
Thornton Heath CR0 . . . . .42 D4
Twickenham TW2 . . . . .5 E1
Pampisford Rd
Croydon CR2, CR8 . . . . .61 B2
Purley CR2, CR8 . . . . .61 B2
Pams Way KT19 . . . . .57 D5
Pan's Gdns GU15 . . . . .65 F4
Pandora Ct 4 KT6 . . . . .37 E3
Pangbourne Ct SW17 . . . . . . .20 C4
Pankhurst Cl TW7 . . . . .5 F4
Pankhurst Ct 11 RH11 . . . . .201 B1
Pankhurst Dr RG12 . . . . .27 D4
Pankhurst Rd KT12 . . . . .35 C2
Panmuir Rd SW20 . . . . .39 B8
Panmure Rd SE26 . . . . .23 B5
Pannell Cl RH19 . . . . .185 D1
Pannells GU10 . . . . .146 D5
Pannells Cl KT16 . . . . .32 F1
Pannells Ct GU1 . . . . .130 D8
Pantile Rd KT13 . . . . .53 D6
Pantiles Cl GU21 . . . . .69 B1
Paper Mews RH4 . . . . .136 B8
Papercourt La GU23 . . . . .90 F6
Papplewick Sch SL5 . . . . .29 A2
Papworth Way SW2 . . . . .22 A8
Parade Cl GU23 . . . . .90 C4
Parade Mews SE27, SW2 . . . .22 B6
Parade The Ash GU12 . . . . . .106 A4
Ashford TW16 . . . . .14 F1
Burgh Heath KT20 . . . . .97 E8
Claygate KT10 . . . . .55 E4

Parade The *continued*
Coulsdon CR5 . . . . .80 A1
Epsom KT18 . . . . .76 D6
2 Kingston u T KT2 . . . . .37 E7
Wallington CR0 . . . . .60 F5
Wentworth GU25 . . . . .31 D3
Paradise Rd TW10 . . . . . . .6 E2
Paragon Gr KT5 . . . . .37 F3
Parbury Rise KT9 . . . . . . .56 E4
Parchmore Rd CR7 . . . . . .42 C6
Parchmore Way CR7 . . . . .42 B7
Pares CI GU21 . . . . .69 D3
Parfew Ct SE22 . . . . .23 B6
Parfitts CI GU9 . . . . .125 A2
Parfour Dr CR8 . . . . .80 C3
Parham Rd RH11 . . . . . . .200 F7
Parish Church C of E Inf
& Jun Schs CR9 . . . . .61 B7
Parish CI Ash GU12 . . . . .106 B1
Hale GU9 . . . . .125 A6
Parish Ct KT6 . . . . .37 E3
Parish House 6 RH11 . . . .201 D5
Parish La SE20, SE26 . . . .23 D1
Parish Rd GU14 . . . . .105 B8
Park Ave Bromley BR1 . . . .24 F2
Camberley GU15 . . . . .65 D4
Caterham CR3 . . . . .100 D3
Egham TW20 . . . . .12 C1
Isleworth TW3 . . . . .5 B1
Mitcham CR4 . . . . .21 B1
Mortlake SW14 . . . . .7 D3
Peper Harow GU8 . . . . . . .149 C5
Salfords RH1 . . . . .139 F1
Staines TW18 . . . . .13 A2
Upper Halliford TW17 . . . . .34 E6
Wallington SM5 . . . . .60 A4
West Wickham BR4 . . . . . .63 C8
Wokingham RG40 . . . . . . .25 B6
Park Ave E KT17 . . . . . . .58 A4
Park Ave W KT17 . . . . . . .58 A4
Park Avenue Mews CR4 . . .21 B1
Park Barn Dr GU2, GU3 . .108 E2
Park Barn E GU2 . . . . . . .108 F2
Park Chase
Godalming GU7 . . . . .150 E2
Guildford GU1 . . . . .109 E1
Park CI Binstead GU10 . . .145 A2
Brockham RH3 . . . . .137 B4
Esher KT10 . . . . .55 A4
Fetcham KT22 . . . . .94 D3
Grayswood GU27 . . . . . . .190 A1
Hampton TW12 . . . . .36 C8
Isleworth TW3, TW7 . . . . . .5 C2
Kingston u T KT2 . . . . .38 A8
Oatlands Park KT13 . . . . . .53 F8
Wallington SM5 . . . . .59 F4
Woodham KT15 . . . . .52 C1
Park Close Cotts TW20 . . .10 F3
Park Copse RH5 . . . . . . .136 D7
Park Corner Dr KT24 . . . .112 E7
Park Cotts 10 TW1 . . . . . . .6 B1
Twickenham TW2 . . . . .16 D7
Park Cres Sunningdale SL5 .29 F3
Twickenham TW2 . . . . .16 D7
Park Ct Beckenham BR3 . . .44 B6
Farnham GU9 . . . . .125 D3
New Malden KT3 . . . . .38 D5
Teddington KT1 . . . . .37 C8
Upper Tooting SW12 . . . . . .21 A7
Wallington SM6 . . . . .60 E5
West Norwood SE21 . . . . . .22 D5
Woking GU22 . . . . .69 F1
Park Dr Bramley GU5 . . . .151 F6
Cranleigh GU6 . . . . .174 F3
Mortlake SW14 . . . . .7 D3
Sunningdale SL5 . . . . .29 F3
Weybridge KT13 . . . . .53 B5
Woking GU22 . . . . .69 F1
Park End BR1 . . . . .44 F8
Park Farm CI RH12 . . . . .217 D7
Park Farm Ind Est GU15 . .65 C1
Park Farm Rd
Horsham RH12 . . . . .217 D7
Kingston u T KT2 . . . . .17 E1
Park Gate Cotts GU6 . . . .174 C3
Park Gate Ct
Teddington TW12 . . . . .16 C3
11 Woking GU22 . . . . .69 E1
Park Gdns KT2 . . . . .17 F3
Park Gn KT23 . . . . .94 A3
Park Hall Rd Dulwich SE21 .22 D5
Reigate RH2 . . . . .118 A3
West Norwood SE21 . . . . . .22 D5
Park Hall Road Trad Est
SE21 . . . . .22 D5
Park Hill Forest Hill SE23 . .23 C7
Richmond TW10 . . . . .6 F1
Wallington SM5 . . . . .59 F4
Park Hill CI SM5 . . . . . . .59 E5
Park Hill Ct
South Croydon CR0 . . . . . .61 E8
Upper Tooting SW17 . . . . . .20 F5
Park Hill Inf Sch CR0 . . . .61 E7
Park Hill Jun Sch CR0 . . . .61 E7
Park Hill Rd
Beckenham BR2 . . . . .44 F8
Ewell KT17 . . . . .76 F8
South Croydon CR0, CR2 . . .61 E7
Wallington SM6 . . . . .60 B3
Park Hill Rise CR0 . . . . . .61 F7
Park Hill Sch KT2 . . . . . . .18 A1
Park Ho 8 GU11 . . . . . . .105 A1
Park Horsley KT24 . . . . . .113 A6
Park House Penge SE26 . . .23 A3
Reigate RH2 . . . . .138 F7
Park House Cotts GU6 . . .174 F3
Park House Dr RH2 . . . . .138 F7
Park House Gdns TW1 . . . .6 C2

Park House Mid Sch
SW19 . . . . .19 F4
Park La Ashstead KT21 . . . .96 A8
Ashurst Wood RH19 . . . . .206 D6
Brook GU8 . . . . .190 A8
Camberley GU15 . . . . .65 C5
Cheam SM3 . . . . .58 E4
Cranford TW5 . . . . .4 A7
Croydon CR0, CR9 . . . . . . .61 D7
Guildford GU4 . . . . .110 D3
Hooley CR5 . . . . .99 D6
Horton SL3 . . . . .1 A4
Lingfield RH7 . . . . .164 F5
Ockley RH5 . . . . .177 F7
Reigate RH2 . . . . .138 E8
Teddington TW11 . . . . .16 F2
Wallington SM5, SM6 . . . . .60 A5
Winkfield SL4 . . . . .9 B7
Park La E RH2 . . . . .139 A7
Park Lawn CR7 . . . . .42 C7
Park Lawn Rd KT13 . . . . . .53 C6
Park Ley Rd CR3 . . . . . . .101 D6
Park Mansions SE26 . . . . .23 C5
Park Mead Cty Inf Sch
GU6 . . . . .175 A3
Park Mead Jun Sch GU6 175 A3
Park Mews 19 F8
Horsham RH12 . . . . .217 C1
4 Woking GU22 . . . . .69 F1
Park Prim Sch GU11 . . . .126 C7
Park Rd Albury GU5 . . . . .132 E2
Aldershot GU11 . . . . .126 B8
Ashford TW15 . . . . .14 B3
Ashstead KT21 . . . . .75 A1
Banstead SM7 . . . . .78 C3
Beckenham BR3 . . . . .23 F1
Bracknell RG12 . . . . .27 D8
Burstow RH6 . . . . .162 C1
Camberley GU15 . . . . .65 C4
Caterham CR3 . . . . .100 E4
Cheam SM3 . . . . .58 E4
Chiswick W4 . . . . .7 D8
Crowhurst RH7 . . . . .143 E2
Dormans Park RH19 . . . . .185 F6
East Grinstead RH19 . . . . .185 D1
East Molesey KT8 . . . . . . .36 C5
Egham TW20 . . . . .12 A4
Esher KT10 . . . . .55 B6
Farnborough GU11, GU14 . .105 E8
Farnham GU9 . . . . .125 D4
Faygate RH12 . . . . .199 F1
Feltham TW13 . . . . .15 D4
Fickleshole CR6 . . . . .82 E5
Forest Row RH18 . . . . . . .206 F2
Godalming GU7 . . . . .150 E2
Guildford GU1 . . . . .109 D1
Hackbridge SM6 . . . . .60 B8
Hampton TW12 . . . . .16 C3
Haslemere GU27 . . . . . . .208 C5
Isleworth TW3, TW7 . . . . . .5 C2
Isleworth TW7 . . . . .6 B5
Kenley CR8 . . . . .80 C4
Kingston u T KT2, TW10 . . .18 A1
Limpsfield RH8 . . . . .122 F7
Lower Halliford TW17 . . . . .34 A1
Mitcham SW19 . . . . .20 E2
New Malden KT3 . . . . .38 D5
Redhill RH1 . . . . .118 F3
Richmond TW10 . . . . .6 F1
Sandhurst GU47 . . . . .64 C8
Slinfold RH13 . . . . .215 D3
South Norwood SE25 . . . . .42 E5
Stanwell TW19 . . . . .2 C1
Sunbury TW16 . . . . .15 B1
Surbiton KT5 . . . . .37 C8
Teddington TW11 . . . . .16 F2
Teddington, Hampton
Wick KT1 . . . . .37 C8
Twickenham TW1 . . . . .6 C1
Wallington SM6 . . . . .60 B5
Woking GU22 . . . . .70 A2
Wokingham RG40 . . . . . . .25 B6
Woodmansterne CR5,
KT20, SM7 . . . . .78 C3
Park Rise Forest Hill SE23 . .23 E7
Horsham RH12 . . . . .217 B4
Leatherhead KT22 . . . . . . .95 B6
Park Rise Ct KT22 . . . . . . .95 B6
Park Rise Rd SE23 . . . . . .23 E7
Park Road House 3 KT2 . .18 A1
Park Row GU9 . . . . .125 B3
Park Sch The GU22 . . . . . .70 A2
Park Sheen SW14 . . . . .7 B3
Park Side KT15 . . . . .52 C1
Park Sq 1 KT10 . . . . .55 B6
Park St Bagshot GU19 . . . .47 E3
Camberley GU15 . . . . .65 C5
Croydon CR0, CR9 . . . . . . .61 C8
Guildford GU1, GU2 . . . . .130 C7
Horsham RH12 . . . . .217 D2
Poyle SL3 . . . . .1 D6
Slinfold RH13 . . . . .215 C3
Teddington TW11 . . . . .16 E2
Park Terr Carshalton SM5 . .59 E7
New Malden KT4 . . . . .39 A1
Park Terr E RH13 . . . . . . .217 D1
Park Terr W RH13 . . . . . .217 D1
Park The Forest Hill SE23 . .23 C7
Great Bookham KT23 . . . . .94 A3
Wallington SM5 . . . . .59 F5
Park View Addlestone KT15 .52 C5
Bagshot GU19 . . . . .47 D3
Crawley RH11 . . . . .201 C6
Great Bookham KT23 . . . . .94 A2
Horley RH6 . . . . .161 A3
Morden CR4 . . . . .40 D4

Park View *continued*
New Malden KT3 . . . . .38 F6
Purley CR8 . . . . .80 B8
Tandridge RH8 . . . . .143 B5
Park View Ct GU22 . . . . . .89 F8
Park View Rd
Salfords RH1 . . . . .140 A1
Woldingham CR3 . . . . .101 F5
Park Way Crawley RH10 . .202 C7
East Molesey KT8 . . . . . . .36 B6
Feltham TW14 . . . . .15 B8
Great Bookham KT23 . . . . .94 A4
Horsham RH12 . . . . .217 C2
Park Wood CI SM7 . . . . . .77 D4
Park Wood Rd SM7 . . . . . .77 D4
Park Wood View SM7 . . . . .77 D4
Park Works Rd RH1 . . . . .119 E2
Parkcroft Rd SE12 . . . . . . .24 F8
Parkdale Cres KT4 . . . . . .57 D7
Parke Rd TW16 . . . . .35 A5
Parker CI RH10 . . . . .202 D5
Parker Ct SW19 . . . . .19 E1
Parker Rd CR0, CR9 . . . . .61 C6
Parker's CI KT21 . . . . .95 E8
Parker's Hill KT21 . . . . . . .95 F8
Parker's La Ashstead KT21 .95 F8
Winkfield RG42 . . . . .8 B5
Parkers Ct GU19 . . . . .47 E3
Parkfield Godalming GU7 . .150 F2
Horsham RH11 . . . . .217 C3
3 Hounslow TW7 . . . . .5 E4
Parkfield Ave
Feltham TW13 . . . . .15 A5
Mortlake SW14 . . . . .7 E3
Parkfield CI RH11 . . . . . . .200 F6
Parkfield Cres TW13 . . . . .15 A5
Parkfield Par TW13 . . . . . .15 A5
Parkfield Rd TW13 . . . . . .15 A5
Parkfields Croydon CR0 . . .43 F1
Oxshott KT22 . . . . .74 D8
Parkfields Ave SW20 . . . . .39 B7
Parkfields CI SM5 . . . . . . .60 A6
Parkfields Rd TW10 . . . . . .17 F3
Parkgate CI KT2 . . . . .18 B2
Parkgate Gdns SW14 . . . . .7 D2
Parkgate Rd
Newdigate RH5 . . . . .158 C3
Parkgate RH5 . . . . .158 C3
Reigate RH2 . . . . .139 B8
Wallington SM5, SM6 . . . . .60 B5
Parkham Ct BR2 . . . . .44 F7
Parkhill CI GU17 . . . . .64 D4
Parkhill Rd GU17 . . . . . . .64 D4
Parkhurst KT19 . . . . .57 C1
Parkhurst Cotts GU10 . . . .187 F8
Parkhurst Fields GU10 . . . .167 F1
Parkhurst Gr RH6 . . . . . . .160 F4
Parkhurst Rd
Carshalton SM1 . . . . .59 D6
Guildford GU2 . . . . .109 B2
Horley RH6 . . . . .160 E4
Parkin House SE20 . . . . . .23 D1
Parkland Dr RG12 . . . . . . .27 E8
Parkland Gdns 12 SW19 . . .19 D7
Parkland Gr Ashford TW15 .14 A4
Heath End GU9 . . . . .125 F8
Hounslow TW7 . . . . .5 F6
Parkland Rd TW15 . . . . . . .14 A4
Parklands Addlestone KT15 .52 C5
Dorking RH5 . . . . .136 B3
Great Bookham KT23 . . . . .94 A4
Kingston u T KT5 . . . . .37 F4
Oxted RH8 . . . . .122 E4
Redhill RH1 . . . . .119 A3
Parklands CI SW14 . . . . . . .7 C2
Parklands Ct TW5 . . . . .4 D5
Parklands PI GU1 . . . . . . .110 B1
Parklands Rd SW16, SW17 .21 B3
Parklands Way KT4 . . . . . .57 E8
Parklawn Ave Epsom KT18 .76 B6
Horley RH6 . . . . .160 F5
Parkleigh Ct SW19 . . . . . .40 B7
Parkleigh Rd SW19 . . . . . .40 B7
Parkleys
Kingston u T KT2, TW10 . . .17 D4
Richmond KT2, TW10 . . . . .17 D4
Parkpale La RH3 . . . . . . .137 A4
Parkshot TW9 . . . . .6 E3
Parkside Beckenham BR3 . .44 B7
Cheam SM3 . . . . .58 E4
Crawley RH10 . . . . .201 E6
East Grinstead RH19 . . . . .185 C1
Hale GU9 . . . . .125 C6
Teddington TW12 . . . . .16 C3
Wimbledon SW19 . . . . .19 D4
Parkside Ave SW19 . . . . . .19 D3
Parkside Cres KT5 . . . . . .38 C3
Parkside Ct KT13 . . . . .53 A6
Parkside Gdns
Coulsdon CR5 . . . . .79 B2
Wimbledon SW19 . . . . .19 D4
Parkside Hospl SW19 . . . . .19 D5
Parkside Mews RH12 . . . . .217 D2
Parkside PI KT24 . . . . .92 F2
Parkside Prep Sch KT11 . .74 A1
Parkside Rd Hounslow TW3 . .5 B2
Sunningdale SL5 . . . . .30 A4
Parkstone Dr GU15 . . . . . .65 C4
Parkthorne Rd SW12 . . . . .21 D8
Parkview Lodge BR3 . . . . .44 B6
Parkview Rd CR0, CR9 . . . .43 A1
Parkview Vale GU4 . . . . . .110 C3
Parkway Camberley GU15 . .65 C3
Crowthorne RG45 . . . . . . .45 A5
Dorking RH4 . . . . .136 A8

Parkway *continued*
Guildford GU1 . . . . .109 E2
Horley RH6 . . . . .161 A3
New Addington CR0, CR9 . . .63 C1
Oatlands Park KT13 . . . . . .53 D6
West Barnes SM4, SW20 . . .39 D5
Parkway Sch The TW5 . . . . .4 A7
Parkway The TW5 . . . . .4 B7
Parkway Trad Est TW5 . . . . .4 C8
Parkwood BR3 . . . . .24 A1
Parkwood Ave KT10 . . . . . .36 C1
Parkwood Gr TW16 . . . . . .35 A6
Parkwood Rd
Biggin Hill TN16 . . . . .103 F6
Hounslow TW7 . . . . .5 F6
Nutfield RH1 . . . . .119 E2
Wimbledon SW19 . . . . .19 F3
Parley Dr GU21 . . . . .69 C1
Parliament Mews SW14 . . . .7 C5
Parliamentary Rd GU24 . . .87 A6
Parnall House 11 SE19 . . . .22 E4
Parnell CI RH10 . . . . .202 D4
Parnham Ave GU18 . . . . . .67 D8
Parr Ave KT17 . . . . .58 B2
Parr CI KT22 . . . . .94 F7
Parr Ct SW13 . . . . .15 C4
Parr's PI TW12 . . . . .16 A1
Parris Croft RH4 . . . . .136 C4
Parrs CI CR2 . . . . .61 D2
Parry CI Horsham RH13 . . .218 C4
Stoneleigh KT17 . . . . .58 A3
Parry Dr KT13 . . . . .53 A1
Parry Rd SE25 . . . . .42 E6
Parsley Gdns CR0 . . . . . . .43 D1
Parson's Mead CR0 . . . . . .42 B1
Parson's Mead Sch KT21 . .95 E8
Parson's Pightle CR5 . . . . .100 A7
Parsonage Bsns Pk RH12 217 E4
Parsonage CI
Warlingham CR6 . . . . .81 F3
Westcott RH4 . . . . .135 C5
Parsonage Farm Cty Inf
Sch GU14 . . . . .84 C5
Parsonage La RH4 . . . . . .135 C6
Parsonage Rd
Cranleigh GU6 . . . . .174 D3
Englefield Green TW20 . . . .11 D3
Horsham RH12, RH13 . . . .217 E4
Parsonage Sq RH4 . . . . . .136 A7
Parsonage Way
Frimley GU16 . . . . .65 E1
Horsham RH12 . . . . .217 E4
Parsons CI
Haslemere GU27 . . . . . . .208 C8
Horley RH6 . . . . .160 E4
Parsons Field GU47 . . . . . .64 B8
Parsons Gn GU27 . . . . . . .208 C8
Parsons Green Ct GU1 . . .109 D3
Parsons House 21 SW12 . . .21 B8
Parsons La GU26 . . . . . . .188 D6
Parsons Mead KT8 . . . . . .36 C6
Parsonsfield CI SM7 . . . . .77 D4
Parsonsfield Rd SM7 . . . . .77 D4
Parthia CI KT20 . . . . .97 B8
Partridge CI
Crondall GU10 . . . . .124 D8
Frimley GU16 . . . . .65 E1
Partridge Knoll CR8 . . . . . .80 B6
Partridge La
Newdigate RH5 . . . . .179 F3
Parkgate RH5 . . . . .158 C2
Partridge Mead SM7 . . . . .77 C4
Partridge Rd 8 TW12 . . . . .16 A2
Partridge Way GU4 . . . . . .110 D3
Parvis Rd Byfleet KT14 . . . .71 D7
West Byfleet KT14 . . . . . . .71 D7
Paschal Rd GU15 . . . . . . .65 F8
Passfields SE6 . . . . .24 C5
Passingham House TW5 . . . .5 A8
Pastens Rd RH8 . . . . .123 C4
Pasture Rd SE6 . . . . .24 F7
Pasture The RH10 . . . . . .202 C6
Pasture Wood Rd RH5 . . . .155 D6
Patching CI RH11 . . . . . . .200 F7
Patchings RH13 . . . . .217 F3
Paterson CI GU16 . . . . . . .66 C3
Pates Manor Dr TW14 . . . .14 D8
Path Link RH10 . . . . .201 E7
Path The SW19 . . . . .40 B8
Pathfield GU8 . . . . .191 B4
Pathfield CI
Chiddingfold GU8 . . . . . . .191 B4
Rudgwick RH12 . . . . .214 D7
Pathfield Rd
Rudgwick RH12 . . . . .214 D7
Streatham SW16 . . . . .21 D2
Pathfields GU5 . . . . .133 A4
Pathfields CI GU27 . . . . . .208 D7
Pathfinders The GU14 . . . .84 C3
Pathway The GU23 . . . . . . .90 F2
Patmore La KT12 . . . . .53 F4
Patricia Gdns SM2 . . . . . . .78 A8
Patrington CI RH11 . . . . . .201 A3
Patten Ash Dr RG40 . . . . . .25 E7
Patten Rd SW18 . . . . .20 E8
Pattenden Rd SE23, SE6 . .23 F7
Patterdale CI Catford BR1 . .24 E2
Crawley RH11 . . . . .201 C4
Patterson Ct SE19 . . . . . . .22 F2
Patterson Rd SE19 . . . . . . .22 F2
Paul CI GU11 . . . . .125 E8
Paul Gdns CR0 . . . . .61 F8
Paul Vanson Ct KT12 . . . . .54 D4
Paul's PI KT21 . . . . .96 B8
Pauline Cres TW2 . . . . . . .16 C7
Pauls Mead RH7 . . . . .164 E5
Paved Ct 9 TW9 . . . . .6 D2
Pavement The 11 SE27 . . . .22 C4

Pavilion Gdns TW18 . . . . . .13 B1
Pavilion Rd GU11 . . . . . . .104 E1
Pavilion Way RH19 . . . . . .205 E8
Pavilions End The GU15 . . .65 D3
Paviors GU9 . . . . .125 C3
Pawley CI GU10 . . . . .126 F7
Pawleyne CI SE20 . . . . . . .23 C1
Pawson's Rd CR0 . . . . .42 C4
Pax CI RH11 . . . . .200 E4
Paxton CI Richmond TW9 . . . .6 F5
Walton-on-T KT12 . . . . . . .35 C2
Paxton Ct Forest Hill SE26 . .23 E4
Mitcham CR4 . . . . .40 F7
Paxton Gdns GU21 . . . . . .70 E7
Paxton PI SE27 . . . . .22 E4
Paxton Prim Sch SE19 . . . .22 E2
Paxton Rd SE23 . . . . .23 E5
Payley Dr RG40 . . . . .25 E8
Payne CI RH10 . . . . .202 D8
Paynesfield Ave SW14 . . . . .7 D4
Paynesfield Rd
Tatsfield TN16 . . . . .103 D7
Tatsfield TN16 . . . . .103 D8
Peabody Est SE24 . . . . . . .22 C8
Peabody Hill SE21 . . . . . . .22 C7
Peabody Rd GU11, GU14 . .105 C8
Peacemaker CI RH11 . . . . .200 E4
Peach St RG40 . . . . .25 C6
Peach Tree CI GU14 . . . . . .85 A7
Peaches CI SM2 . . . . .58 E3
Peacock Ave TW14 . . . . . .14 D7
Peacock Cotts RG12 . . . . .26 C5
Peacock Gdns CR0, CR2 . .62 E1
Peacock La RG12 . . . . . . .26 A6
Peacock Wlk 9 RH11 . . . . .201 A3
Peacocks Sh Ctr The
GU21 . . . . .69 E2
Peak Hill SE26 . . . . .23 C4
Peak Hill Ave SE26 . . . . . .23 C4
Peak Hill Gdns SE26 . . . . .23 C4
Peak Rd GU2 . . . . .109 A4
Peak The SE26 . . . . .23 C5
Peakfield GU10 . . . . .167 C7
Peaks Hill CR8 . . . . .60 E1
Peaks Hill Rise CR8 . . . . . .60 F1
Peall Rd CR0 . . . . .41 F3
Pear Ave TW17 . . . . .34 E6
Pear Tree CI
Addlestone KT15 . . . . .52 A5
Mitcham CR4 . . . . .40 E7
Pear Tree Ct GU15 . . . . . . .66 B8
Pear Tree Hill RH1 . . . . . .161 A8
Pear Tree La GU10 . . . . . .145 F3
Pear Tree Rd
Addlestone KT15 . . . . .52 A5
Ashford TW15 . . . . .14 C3
Pearce CI CR4 . . . . .41 A7
Pearce House 7 SW1 . . . . .21 B8
Pearcefield Ave 5 SE23 . . .23 C7
Pearfield Rd SE23 . . . . . . .23 E5
Pearl Ct GU21 . . . . .68 E3
Pearmain CI TW17 . . . . . . .34 B4
Pears Rd TW3 . . . . .5 C4
Pearson Ct SM4 . . . . .40 B4
Pearson Rd RH10 . . . . . . .202 C6
Peartree Ave SW17 . . . . . .20 C5
Peartree CI CR2 . . . . .81 B5
Peary CI RH12 . . . . .217 D6
Peaslake La GU5 . . . . .154 D6
Peaslake Sch GU5 . . . . . .154 D6
Peat Comm GU8 . . . . .148 C2
Peatmore Ave GU22 . . . . . .71 A3
Peatmore CI GU22 . . . . . . .71 A3
Peatmore Dr GU24 . . . . . . .87 C6
Pebble CI KT20 . . . . .116 E6
Pebble Hill KT24 . . . . .112 C2
Pebble Hill Cotts RH8 . . . .123 B6
Pebble La KT18, KT21 . . . . .96 A5
Pebblehill Rd
Betchworth KT20, RH3 . . . .116 E5
Box Hill KT20, RH3 . . . . . .116 E5
Pebworth Ct 8 RH1 . . . . . .119 A3
Pebworth Lodge SE25 . . . .42 F5
Peckarmans Wood
SE21, SE26 . . . . .23 A5
Peek Cres SW19 . . . . .19 D3
Peeks Brook La
Crawley RH6 . . . . .182 E7
Horley RH6 . . . . .161 F2
Peel Ave GU14 . . . . .86 A7
Peel Ct GU14 . . . . .105 C8
Peel Ctr The RG12 . . . . . . .27 B7
Pegasus Ave GU12 . . . . . .105 E2
Pegasus CI GU27 . . . . . . .207 D5
Pegasus Ct Crawley RH11 .200 E4
Farnborough GU14 . . . . . .85 E1
Kingston u T KT1 . . . . .37 D6
Pegasus Rd
Croydon CR0, CR9 . . . . . . .61 A4
Farnborough GU14 . . . . . .84 F7
Pegasus Way RH19 . . . . . .186 B3
Pegg Rd TW5 . . . . .4 D7
Peggotty PI GU47 . . . . .45 E2
Pegler Way RH11 . . . . . . .201 D6
Pegwell CI RH11 . . . . .200 F4
Peket CI TW18 . . . . .32 E3
Peldon Ct TW10 . . . . .6 F2
Pelham Cts Bsns Ctr RH11 201 B2
Pelham Dr RH11 . . . . .201 A2
Pelham House CR3 . . . . . .100 F3
Pelham PI RH11 . . . . .201 B2

Pelham Prim Sch SW19 . . 20 A1
Pelham Rd Merton SW19 . . 20 A1
Penge BR3, SE20 . . . . 43 C7
Pelham Way KT23 . . . . 94 C1
Pelhams Cl KT10 . . . . 55 A6
Pelhams Wlk KT10 . . . . 55 A6
Pelinore Rd SE6 . . . . 24 E6
Pelling Hill SL4 . . . . 11 B7
Pelton Ave SM2 . . . . 59 B1
Pelton Ct CR2 . . . . 61 C4
Pemberley Chase KT19 . . . 57 B5
Pemberley Cl KT19 . . . . . . 57 B5
Pemberton House SE26 . . . 23 A4
Pemberton Pl KT10 . . . . . . 55 C7
Pemberton Rd KT8 . . . . 36 C5
Pembley Gn RH10 . . . . 183 E3
Pembridge Ave TW4 . . . . . . 15 F7
Pembroke RG12 . . . . 27 A1
Pembroke Ave
Hersham KT12 . . . . 54 D6
Surbiton KT5 . . . . 38 B4
Pembroke
Broadway GU15 . . . . 65 C5
Pembroke Cl Ascot SL5 . . . . 29 D4
Banstead SM7 . . . . 78 B2
Pembroke Ct GU22 . . . . 70 B3
Pembroke Gdns GU22 . . . . 70 A1
Pembroke Mews SL5 . . . . . 29 D4
Pembroke Pl TW7 . . . . 5 E5
Pembroke Rd
Crawley RH10 . . . . 182 C1
Mitcham CR4 . . . . 41 A7
South Norwood SE25 . . . . . . 42 E5
Woking GU22 . . . . 70 A2
Pembroke Villas TW9 . . . . . . 6 D3
Pembrook Lodge 2 SW16 . 21 F5
Pembury Ave
New Malden KT4 . . . . 39 A2
North Cheam KT4 . . . . 39 A2
Pembury Cl Hayes BR2 . . . . 44 F2
Wallington CR5 . . . . 79 A5
Pembury Ct UB3 . . . . 3 D8
Pembury Pl GU12 . . . . 105 C1
Pembury Rd SE25 . . . . 43 A5
Pemdevon Rd CR0 . . . . 42 A2
Penarth Ct SM2 . . . . 59 C3
Penates KT10 . . . . 55 D6
Penberth Rd SE6 . . . . 24 C7
Penceat Ct SE20 . . . . 43 C7
Pendarves Rd SW20 . . . . . . 39 C8
Pendell Ave UB3 . . . . 3 F7
Pendell Rd RH1 . . . . 120 B4
Pendennis Cl KT14 . . . . 71 A5
Pendennis Rd SW16 . . . . . . 21 E4
Penderel Rd TW3 . . . . 5 A2
Penderry Rise SE6 . . . . 24 D6
Pendine Pl RG12 . . . . 27 B4
Pendle House 13 SE26 . . . . 23 A5
Pendle Rd SW16 . . . . 21 B3
Pendlebury RG12 . . . . 27 A2
Pendleton Cl RH1 . . . . 139 F7
Pendleton Rd RH1 . . . . . . 139 E6
Pendragon Rd BR1 . . . . 24 F5
Pendragon Way GU15 . . . . 66 D3
Penerley Rd SE6 . . . . 24 B7
Penfold Cl CR0, CR9 . . . . . . 61 A7
Penfold Croft GU9 . . . . . . 125 F4
Penfold Ct CR4 . . . . 41 A7
Penfold Rd RH10 . . . . 202 B7
Penge East Sta SE20 . . . . . 23 C2
Penge La SE20 . . . . 23 D1
Penge Rd SE20, SE25 . . . . . 43 A6
Penge West Sta SE20 . . . . . 23 B2
Pengilly Rd GU9 . . . . 125 B1
Penhurst GU21 . . . . 69 F5
Peninsula Cl GU15 . . . . 66 B7
Peninsular Cl TW14 . . . . 3 E1
Penistone Rd SW16 . . . . . . 21 E1
Penn Cl RH11 . . . . 181 D1
Pennards The TW16 . . . . . . 35 C6
Pennefather's Rd GU11 . . 104 F3
Penner Cl SW19 . . . . 19 E6
Penners Gdns KT6 . . . . 37 E2
Pennine Cl RH11 . . . . 201 B6
Pennine Way
Farnborough GU14 . . . . 84 E7
Harlington UB7 . . . . 3 D7
Pennings Ave GU2, GU3 . . 108 F3
Pennington Cl 10 SE27 . . . . 22 D4
Pennington Dr KT13 . . . . . . 53 E7
Pennington Lodge 18 KT5 . 37 E4
Penns Wood GU14 . . . . 85 D1
Penny Dr GU3 . . . . 108 B2
Penny La TW17 . . . . 34 E2
Penny Mews SW12 . . . . 21 B8
Penny Royal SM6 . . . . 60 D4
Pennycroft CR0 . . . . 62 E2
Pennyfield KT11 . . . . 73 A6
Pennymead Dr KT24 . . . . . 112 F8
Pennymead Rise KT24 . . . . 112 F8
Pennypot La GU24 . . . . 68 C7
Penrhyn Cl GU11 . . . . 105 B1
Penrhyn Cres SW14 . . . . 7 C3
Penrhyn Gdns KT1 . . . . 37 D5
Penrhyn Rd KT1 . . . . 37 E6
Penrith Cl Beckenham BR3 . 44 B8
Redhill RH2 . . . . 118 E2
Penrith Pl SE27 . . . . 22 B6
Penrith Rd New Malden KT3 38 D5
South Norwood CR7 . . . . . . 42 C7
Penrith St SW16 . . . . 21 C2
Penrose Ct TW20 . . . . 11 C2
Penrose Rd KT22 . . . . 94 C5
Penryn Dr GU35 . . . . 187 C5
Penryn House 5 RH1 . . . . 119 A3
Pensfold La RH12, RH13 . . 214 E5
Pensford Ave TW9 . . . . 7 A5
Pensford Cl RG45 . . . . 45 B7
Penshurst Cl RH10 . . . . . . 202 D7
Penshurst Gn BR2 . . . . 44 F4
Penshurst Rd CR7 . . . . 42 B4
Penshurst Rise GU16 . . . . . 85 F8
Penshurst Way SM2 . . . . . . 59 A3
Penshurst Wlk BR2 . . . . 44 F4
Pentelow Gdns TW14 . . . . . . 4 A1
Penthorpe Sch RH12 . . . . 214 C7
Pentland Ave TW17 . . . . . . 34 A4
Pentland Pl GU14 . . . . 84 E7
Pentlands BR3 . . . . 44 C8
Pentlands Cl CR4 . . . . 41 B6
Pentney Rd
Streatham SW12 . . . . 21 C7
Wimbledon SW19, SW20 . . . 39 E8
Penton Ave TW18 . . . . 32 F8
Penton Ct TW18 . . . . 12 F2
Penton Hall TW18 . . . . 33 A8
Penton Hall Dr TW18 . . . . . 33 A8
Penton Hook Marina
Chertsey KT16 . . . . 33 A6
Egham TW18 . . . . 32 F7
Penton Hook Rd TW18 . . . 33 A8
Penton House SM2 . . . . 59 C3
Penton Rd TW18 . . . . 12 F1
Pentreath Ave GU2 . . . . . . 129 F8
Penwerris Ave TW5, TW7 . . . 5 C7
Penwerris Ct TW7 . . . . 5 C7
Penwith Dr GU27 . . . . 207 E5
Penwith Rd SW18 . . . . 20 B6
Penwith Wlk GU22 . . . . 89 D8
Penwood End GU22 . . . . . . 89 B6
Penwood Gdns RG12 . . . . . 26 D3
Penwood House SW15 . . . . . 7 F1
Penwortham Prim Sch
SW17 . . . . 21 B2
Penwortham Rd
South Croydon CR2 . . . . . . 61 D1
Streatham SW16 . . . . 21 C2
Peper Harow La GU8 . . . . 149 C6
Peperham House GU27 . . 208 C7
Peperham Rd GU27 . . . . . 208 C8
Peperharow Rd GU7 . . . . 150 C6
Peppard Rd RH10 . . . . 202 D3
Pepper Cl CR3 . . . . 100 E2
Pepperbox La GU5 . . . . . . 173 E4
Peppermint Cl CR0 . . . . 41 E2
Pepys Cl Ashstead KT21 . . . . 76 A2
Brands Hill SL3 . . . . 1 B8
Pepys Rd SW20 . . . . 39 C8
Perak Ct KT5 . . . . 38 C2
Percheron Cl TW7 . . . . 5 F4
Percheron Dr GU21 . . . . . . 88 C8
Percival Rd Feltham TW13 . . 14 F6
Mortlake SW14 . . . . 7 C3
Percival Way KT19 . . . . 57 D6
Percy Ave TW15 . . . . 14 A3
Percy Bilton Ct TW5 . . . . 5 B6
Percy Bryant Rd TW16 . . . . 14 E1
Percy Ct 1 KT5 . . . . 37 F3
Percy Gdns
3 Isleworth TW7 . . . . 6 A4
New Malden KT4 . . . . 38 E1
Percy House 4 SW16 . . . . . 21 C4
Percy Rd Carshalton CR4 . . . 41 A2
Croydon SE25 . . . . 43 A4
Guildford GU2 . . . . 109 B3
Hampton TW12 . . . . 16 A1
Horsham RH12 . . . . 217 B3
Isleworth TW7 . . . . 6 A3
Penge SE20 . . . . 43 D8
Twickenham TW2 . . . . 16 C7
Percy Way TW2 . . . . 16 C7
Peregrine Cl
Bracknell RG12 . . . . 27 B4
Cranleigh GU6 . . . . 174 E4
Peregrine Gdns CR0 . . . . . . 62 E8
Peregrine Rd TW16 . . . . . . 34 F7
Peregrine Way
SW19, SW20 . . . . 19 C1
Performing Arts & Tech
Sch SE25 . . . . 42 D3
Perifield SE21 . . . . 22 C7
Perimeter Rd E RH6 . . . . . 182 B6
Perimeter Rd N RH6 . . . . . 181 D7
Perimeter Rd S RH6 . . . . . 181 E5
Perkins Ct TW15 . . . . 13 F3
Perkins Way RG41 . . . . 25 A5
Perkstead Ct 7 RH11 . . . . 201 A3
Perleybrooke La GU21 . . . . 69 A2
Perowne St GU11 . . . . 104 F2
Perram Wks GU4 . . . . 110 C4
Perran Rd SE24, SW2 . . . . . 22 B6
Perran Wlk 16 TW8 . . . . 6 E8
Perrin Cl TW15 . . . . 13 F3
Perrin Ct GU21 . . . . 70 B4
Perring Ave GU14 . . . . 84 F8
Perrior Rd GU7 . . . . 150 E7
Perry Ave RH19 . . . . 185 E3
Perry Cl GU7 . . . . 151 B5
Perry Hill SE23, SE6 . . . . . . 23 F5
Perry House 2 SW2 . . . . . . 21 E8
Perry How KT4 . . . . 38 F1
Perry Oaks RG12 . . . . 27 E7
Perry Oaks Dr TW6, UB7 . . . 2 C5
Perry Rise SE23, SE6 . . . . . 23 E5
Perry Vale SE23 . . . . 23 D6
Perry Way Bracknell RG12 . . 27 E7
Farnham GU9 . . . . 125 B7
Lightwater GU18 . . . . 66 F7
Perryfield House 7
RH10 . . . . 201 D5
Perryfield Rd RH11 . . . . . . 201 D5
Perryfield Way TW10 . . . . . 17 B6
Perrylands RH6 . . . . 180 F7
Perrylands La RH6 . . . . . . 162 A2
Perrymount Prim Sch
SE23 . . . . 23 D6
Perryn Ct 2 TW1 . . . . 17 A8
Perrywood Bsns Pk RH1 . 140 B1
Persant Rd SE6 . . . . 24 E6
Perseverance Cotts GU23 . 91 C6
Persfield Mews KT17 . . . . . 57 F1
Persfield Rd KT17 . . . . 58 A1
Pershore Gr SM5 . . . . 40 D3
Perth Cl Crawley RH11 . . . 181 D1
Wimbledon SW20 . . . . 39 A7
Perth Rd BR3 . . . . 44 C7
Perth Way RH12 . . . . 217 F4
Perystreete SE23 . . . . 23 C6
Petauel Rd TW11 . . . . 16 E3
Petavel Rd TW11 . . . . 16 E2
Peter Ave RH8 . . . . 122 D6
Peter Kennedy Ct CR0 . . . . 43 F3
Peter's Path SE26 . . . . 23 B4
Peterborough Rd
Carshalton CR4, SM4, SM5 . . 40 E3
Crawley RH10 . . . . 201 E2
Guildford GU2 . . . . 108 F3
Peterhouse Cl GU47 . . . . . . 45 F2
Peterhouse Par RH10 . . . . 182 C1
Peterlee Wlk RH11 . . . . . . 200 E2
Petersfield Ave
TW15, TW18 . . . . 13 C2
Petersfield Cres CR5 . . . . . 79 E4
Petersfield Rd TW18 . . . . . 13 C3
Petersfield Rise SW15 . . . . 19 B7
Petersham Ave KT14 . . . . . . 71 E7
Petersham Cl Byfleet KT14 . 71 E7
Cheam SM1 . . . . 59 A5
Richmond TW10 . . . . 17 D6
Petersham Rd TW10 . . . . . . 17 E7
Peterstow Cl SW19 . . . . 19 E6
Peterwood Pk CR9 . . . . 60 F8
Peterwood Way CR0 . . . . . . 60 F8
Petrel Ct 7 SE21 . . . . 22 D6
Petridge Rd RH1 . . . . 139 F4
Petters Rd KT21 . . . . 75 F3
Petts La TW17 . . . . 34 A5
Petworth Cl Coulsdon CR5 . . 99 C8
Frimley GU16 . . . . 85 F8
Petworth Ct Crawley RH11 200 F3
Haslemere GU27 . . . . 208 D6
Petworth Dr RH12 . . . . 217 F7
Petworth Gdns SW20 . . . . . 39 B6
Petworth Rd
Chiddingfold GU8 . . . . 191 C4
Chiddingfold,
Ansteadbrook GU27 . . . . . 209 B6
Witley GU8 . . . . 170 F5
Wormley GU8 . . . . 171 A1
Pevensey Cl
Crawley RH10 . . . . 202 C5
Hounslow TW7 . . . . 5 C7
Pevensey Ct SW16 . . . . 22 A5
Pevensey House RH2 . . . . 139 B5
Pevensey Rd Feltham TW13 . 15 E7
Upper Tooting SW17 . . . . . . 20 D4
Pevensey Way GU16 . . . . . 86 A8
Peverel Rd RH11 . . . . 200 E5
Peveril Dr TW11 . . . . 16 D3
Pewley Bank GU1 . . . . 130 E7
Pewley Down Inf Sch
GU1 . . . . 130 E7
Pewley Hill GU1 . . . . 130 E7
Pewley Point GU1 . . . . 130 E7
Pewley Way GU1 . . . . 130 F7
Pewsey Vale RG12 . . . . 27 F4
Peyton's Cotts RH1 . . . . . 119 F3
Pharaoh Cl CR4 . . . . 40 F2
Pheasant Cl CR8 . . . . 80 B6
Philanthropic Rd RH1 . . . 140 B8
Philip Gdns CR0 . . . . 62 F8
Philip Rd TW18 . . . . 13 D2
Philip Southcote Sch
KT15 . . . . 52 C8
Philips House GU26 . . . . . 188 B3
Phillips Cl Ash GU10 . . . . . 126 E8
Crawley RH10 . . . . 202 C2
Godalming GU7 . . . . 150 D2
Phillips Cotts GU7 . . . . . . 150 B4
Phillips Hatch GU5 . . . . . 152 C8
Philpot La GU24 . . . . 69 C7
Phipp's Bridge Rd
CR4, SW19 . . . . 40 D6
Phoenix Bsns Pk RG12 . . . . 26 C7
Phoenix Cl BR4 . . . . 63 E8
Phoenix Coll SM4 . . . . 40 C4
Phoenix Ct
13 Aldershot GU11 . . . . . . 105 A2
Croydon SE25 . . . . 43 A4
Guildford GU1 . . . . 130 D7
Phoenix La RH19 . . . . 206 E6
Phoenix Pl TW18 . . . . 13 A3
Phoenix Rd SE20 . . . . 23 C2
Phoenix Way TW5 . . . . 4 D8
Phyllis Ave KT3 . . . . 39 B4
Phyllis House CR0 . . . . 61 B6
Piccards The GU2 . . . . . . 130 C5
Pickering RG12 . . . . 27 A5
Pickering Gdns SE25 . . . . . 42 F3
Picket Post Cl RG12 . . . . . . 27 F6
Pickets St SW12 . . . . 21 B8
Picketts Hill GU35 . . . . . . 166 C1
Picketts La RH1 . . . . 161 C8
Pickford St GU11 . . . . 105 B2
Pickhurst Gn BR2 . . . . 44 F2
Pickhurst Inf Sch BR2 . . . . 44 F3
Pickhurst Jun Sch BR2 . . . . 44 F3
Pickhurst La BR2, BR3, BR4 44 E2
Pickhurst Mead BR2 . . . . . 44 F2
Pickhurst Pk BR2 . . . . 44 F4
Pickhurst Rd GU8 . . . . 191 D2
Pickhurst Rise BR4 . . . . 44 D1
Pickins Piece SL3 . . . . 1 A5
Pickwick Cl TW4 . . . . 4 E2
Pickwick Rd SE21 . . . . 22 E8
Picquets Way KT20, SM7 . . . 77 F2
Picton Cl GU15 . . . . 66 B7
Picton House 1 SW4 . . . . . 21 E8
Pier Rd TW14 . . . . 4 B2
Pierrefondes Ave GU14 . . . 85 B5
Pierrepoint SE25 . . . . 42 E6
Pierson House 12 SE19 . . . . 22 E4
Pigbush La RH14 . . . . 213 A7
Pigeon La TW12 . . . . 16 A4
Pigeonhouse La
Lower Kingswood CR5 . . . . . 98 C3
Winkfield SL4, SL5 . . . . 8 E4
Piggott Ct RH13 . . . . 217 E1
Pigott Ct RG40 . . . . 25 D6
Pigott Rd RG40 . . . . 25 E8
Pike Cl GU11 . . . . 105 C2
Pikes Hill KT17 . . . . 76 E6
Pikes La RH7 . . . . 143 E2
Pikethorne SE23 . . . . 23 D6
Pilgrim Cl SM4 . . . . 40 B2
Pilgrim Hill SE27 . . . . 22 C4
Pilgrim House GU1 . . . . . . 130 D7
Pilgrim's Way CR2 . . . . 61 F5
Pilgrims Cl Farnham GU9 . 146 A8
Shere GU5 . . . . 133 A4
Westhumble RH5 . . . . 115 B4
Pilgrims La Caterham CR3 . 100 B1
Tatsfield RH8 . . . . 103 D3
Titsey RH8 . . . . 103 D3
Pilgrims Pl RH2 . . . . 118 A3
Pilgrims View GU12 . . . . . 127 C8
Pilgrims Way GU24 . . . . 68 A3
Pilgrims' Way
Guildford GU4 . . . . 130 E5
Reigate RH2 . . . . 118 A3
Pilgrims Way Shere GU5 . 133 A4
Westhumble RH5 . . . . 115 B4
Pilgrims Way Cotts RH3 . 116 C2
Pilgrims Way Cty Prim
Sch The GU9 . . . . 146 B8
Pilsden Cl SW19 . . . . 19 D7
Pilton Est The CR9 . . . . 61 B8
Pimms Cl GU4 . . . . 110 A5
Pinckards GU8 . . . . 191 B5
Pincott La KT24 . . . . 112 B6
Pincott Rd SW19 . . . . 40 C8
Pine Ave Camberley GU15 . . 65 D3
West Wickham BR4 . . . . 44 B1
Pine Bank GU26 . . . . 188 E4
Pine Cl Ash Vale GU12 . . . . 106 A6
Crawley RH11 . . . . 181 C1
Kenley CR8 . . . . 80 D2
Penge SE20 . . . . 43 C8
Sandhurst GU15 . . . . 64 E7
Woking GU21 . . . . 69 C3
Woodham KT15 . . . . 71 B8
Pine Coombe CR0 . . . . 62 D6
Pine Cres SM5 . . . . 78 D8
Pine Croft Rd RG41 . . . . . . 25 A2
Pine Ct Bracknell RG12 . . . . 27 E5
2 Weybridge KT13 . . . . 53 C5
Pine Dean KT23 . . . . 94 B2
Pine Dr GU17 . . . . 64 E3
Pine Gdns Horley RH6 . . . . 161 A2
Surbiton KT5 . . . . 38 A3
Pine Gr
East Grinstead RH19 . . . . . 185 B3
Farnham GU10 . . . . 146 E6
Weybridge KT13 . . . . 53 C5
Wimbledon SW19 . . . . 19 F3
Windlesham GU20 . . . . 48 D4
Pine Grove Mews 3 KT13 . 53 C5
Pine Hill KT18 . . . . 76 D4
Pine Mount Rd GU15 . . . . . 65 D4
Pine Pl KT17 . . . . 77 D5
Pine Rd GU22 . . . . 89 C7
Pine Ridge SM5 . . . . 60 A2
Pine Ridge Cty Inf Sch
GU15 . . . . 47 A1
Pine Ridge Dr GU10 . . . . . 146 C5
Pine Ridge Golf Ctr GU16 . 66 D2
Pine Shaw RH10 . . . . 202 D7
Pine Tree Cl TW5 . . . . 4 B6
Pine Tree Hill GU22 . . . . . . 70 D3
Pine Trees Bsns Pk TW18 . 12 E3
Pine View GU35 . . . . 187 C6
Pine View Cl
Chilworth GU4 . . . . 131 F3
Farnham GU9 . . . . 126 A5
Haslemere GU27 . . . . 208 C8
Pine Way TW20 . . . . 11 B2
Pine Way Cl RH19 . . . . 205 E7
Pine Wlk Caterham CR3 . . . 100 F5
Cobham KT11 . . . . 73 D5
East Horsley KT24 . . . . 112 F7
Great Bookham KT23 . . . . . 94 B2
Surbiton KT5 . . . . 38 A3
Sutton SM5 . . . . 59 D1
Woodmansterne CR5, SM7 . . 78 F2
Pine Wood TW16 . . . . 35 A8
Pineacre Ct GU22 . . . . 70 B2
Pinecote Dr SL5 . . . . 29 F2
Pinefields KT15 . . . . 52 B6
Pinefields Cl RG45 . . . . 45 B4
Pinehill Rd RG45 . . . . 45 C3
Pinehill Rise GU47 . . . . 64 C8
Pinehurst Ascot SL5 . . . . . . 29 D4
Horsham RH12 . . . . 217 C4
8 Woking GU22 . . . . 69 F1
Pinehurst Ave GU14 . . . . . . 85 B2
Pinehurst Cl KT20 . . . . 98 A5
Pinehurst Cotts GU14 . . . . . 85 B2
Pinel Cl GU25 . . . . 31 E5
Pines Ct 14 SW19 . . . . 19 D7
Pines Cty Inf Sch RG12 . . . 27 A2
Pines Cty Jun Sch RG12 . . 27 A2
Pines The Camberley GU15 . . 65 F7
Dorking RH4 . . . . 136 B6
Guildford GU3 . . . . 108 E3
Horsham RH12 . . . . 218 C5
Purley CR8 . . . . 80 C6
South Norwood SE19, SW16 . 22 B2
Sunbury TW16 . . . . 35 A6
Pinetrees Cl RH10 . . . . . . 183 B3
Pinewood Ave
Crowthorne RG45 . . . . 45 C6
Woodham KT15 . . . . 52 C1
Pinewood Cl
Broadbridge Heath RH12 . . 216 D3
South Croydon CR0 . . . . 62 E7
Woking GU21 . . . . 70 A4
Pinewood Cres GU14 . . . . . 84 C5
Pinewood Ct
Addlestone KT15 . . . . 52 D6
Woking GU21 . . . . 70 A3
Pinewood Dr TW18 . . . . 13 A3
Pinewood Gdns GU19 . . . . 47 C3
Pinewood Gr KT15 . . . . 52 B1
Pinewood Inf Sch GU14 . . 84 D7
Pinewood Mews TW19 . . . . . 2 D1
Pinewood Pk
Farnborough GU14 . . . . 84 C7
Woodham KT15 . . . . 71 B8
Pinewood Pl KT19 . . . . 57 D6
Pinewood Rd
Feltham TW13 . . . . 15 B5
Normandy GU12 . . . . 106 D3
Wentworth GU25 . . . . 31 A5
Pinfold Rd SW16 . . . . 21 E4
Pinglestone Cl TW6, UB7 . . . 2 E7
Pinkcoat Cl TW13 . . . . 15 B5
Pinkerton Pl SW16 . . . . 21 D4
Pinkhurst La RH13 . . . . . . 216 A2
Pioneers Ind Pk CR9 . . . . . 41 E1
Piper Rd KT1 . . . . 38 A6
Piper's End GU25 . . . . 31 D6
Pipers Cl KT11 . . . . 73 D3
Pipers End RH13 . . . . 215 E3
Pipers Gdns CR0 . . . . 43 E2
Pipers Patch 1 GU14 . . . . . 85 B4
Pipewell Rd SM5 . . . . 40 E3
Pippbrook Gdns RH4 . . . . 136 B8
Pippin Cl CR0 . . . . 43 F1
Pippins Ct TW15 . . . . 14 B2
Piquet Rd BR3, SE20 . . . . . . 43 C7
Pirbright Cres CR0 . . . . 63 C4
Pirbright Cty Prim Sch
GU24 . . . . 87 E5
Pirbright House 11 KT2 . . . 18 B2
Pirbright Rd
Farnborough GU14 . . . . 85 C3
Normandy GU3 . . . . 107 B6
Wandsworth SW18 . . . . 20 A7
Pirbright Terr GU24 . . . . . . 87 F4
Pirles Pl RH12 . . . . 217 C2
Pisley La RH5 . . . . 177 A4
Pit Farm Rd GU1 . . . . 110 A1
Pit Wood Gn KT20 . . . . 97 C7
Pitcairn Rd CR4 . . . . 20 F1
Pitchfont La CR6, RH8 . . . 102 F2
Pitfold Ave GU27 . . . . 207 D6
Pitfold Cl GU27 . . . . 207 E6
Pitlake CR0, CR9 . . . . 61 B8
Pitland St RH5 . . . . 155 C5
Pitson Cl KT15 . . . . 52 D6
Pitt Cres SW19 . . . . 20 B4
Pitt Pl KT17 . . . . 76 E5
Pitt Rd Epsom KT17 . . . . . . 76 E5
Thornton Heath CR0, CR7 . . 42 C4
Pitt Way GU14 . . . . 84 F5
Pitts Rd GU11 . . . . 105 B4
Pittville Gdns SE25 . . . . 43 A6
Pixfield Ct BR2 . . . . 44 F7
Pixham Firs RH4 . . . . 115 C2
Pixham La RH4 . . . . 115 C2
Pixholme Ct RH4 . . . . 115 C2
Pixholme Gr RH4 . . . . 115 C1
Pixton Way CR0, CR2 . . . . . 62 E2
Place Ct GU11 . . . . 126 C7
Place Farm Rd RH1 . . . . . 120 D4
Placehouse La CR5 . . . . 80 A1
Plaistow Cty Inf Sch
RH14 . . . . 211 F3
Plaistow Rd
Chiddingfold GU8 . . . . 210 D6
Dunsfold GU8 . . . . 192 D2
Ifold RH14 . . . . 212 D1
Loxwood RH14 . . . . 212 D1
Plaistow St RH7 . . . . 164 D4
Plane St SE26 . . . . 23 B5
Plane Tree Cres TW13 . . . . 15 B5
Plane Tree Wlk 4 SE19 . . . 22 E2
Planes The KT16 . . . . 33 C2
Plantagenet Cl KT19 . . . . . . 57 D6
Plantagenet Pk RG42 . . . . . 27 F8
Plantain Cres RH11 . . . . . 201 A2
Plantation La CR6 . . . . 101 E8
Plantation Row GU15 . . . . 65 B5
Plassy Rd SE6 . . . . 24 B8
Plat The RH12 . . . . 217 A3
Platt Meadow GU4 . . . . . . 110 D3
Platt The RH7 . . . . 186 A8
Platt's Eyot TW12 . . . . 36 A7
Plaws Hill GU5 . . . . 154 D6
Playden Ct 4 RH11 . . . . . . 201 A3
Playgreen Way SE6 . . . . . . 24 A4
Playground Cl BR3 . . . . 43 D7
Pleasant Gr CR0 . . . . 62 F7
Pleasant Pl KT12 . . . . 54 D4
Pleasure Pit Rd KT21 . . . . . 76 B1
Plesman Way SM6 . . . . 60 E2
Plevna Rd TW12 . . . . 36 B8

Pleydell Ave SE19 . . . . .22 F1
Plough Cl RH11 . . . . .200 F8
Plough Ind Est KT22 . . . . . .95 A7
Plough La Downside KT11 . .73 A2
Ewhurst GU6 . . . . .176 A5
Horsham RH12 . . . . .217 E5
Purley CR0, CR8, SM6 . . . . .60 F1
Wallington, Bandonhill
CR0, SM6 . . . . .60 E5
Wallington, Russell Hill SM6 .60 F2
Wimbledon SW17, SW19 . . . .20 C4
Wokingham RG40 . . . . .25 F6
Plough Lane Cl CR0, SM6 . .60 E5
Plough Rd
Dormansland RH7 . . . . . . .165 A2
Smallfield RH6 . . . . .162 C3
West Ewell KT19 . . . . .57 D3
Ploughlands RG42 . . . . .26 F8
Ploughmans End TW7 . . . . .5 D2
Plover Cl Crawley RH11 . . .201 C8
Staines TW18 . . . . .12 F5
Plovers Rd RH13 . . . . .217 F3
Plovers Rise GU24 . . . . .87 E7
Plowman House SW19 . . . .19 D6
Plummer La CR4 . . . . .40 F7
Plummer Rd SW4 . . . . .21 D8
Plumpton Way SM5 . . . . . .59 E7
Plumtree Cl SM6 . . . . .60 D3
Pocket Cl RG12 . . . . .26 D7
Pockford Rd GU8 . . . . .191 D4
Pocklington Ct SW15 . . . . .19 A7
Point (L Ctr) The RG12 . . . .27 B7
Point Royal RG12 . . . . .27 B4
Pointers Hill RH4 . . . . . . .135 C5
Pointers Rd KT11 . . . . .72 E2
Pointers The KT21 . . . . .95 E7
Polden Cl GU14 . . . . .84 E7
Polecroft La SE6 . . . . .23 F6
Poles La RH11, RH6 . . . . . .181 C3
Polesden Gdns SW20 . . . . . .39 B7
Polesden La Ripley GU23 . . .91 A6
Send Marsh GU23 . . . . .90 F5
Polesden Lacey KT23 . . . .114 B5
Polesden Rd KT23 . . . . . . .114 B6
Polesden View KT23 . . . . .114 B8
Polesteeple Hill TN16 . . . . .83 D2
Police Station Rd KT12 . . . .54 C4
Pollard Gr GU15 . . . . .66 C4
Pollard House KT4 . . . . .58 C6
Pollard Rd Morden SM4 . . . .40 D4
Woking GU22 . . . . .70 B3
Pollardrow Ave RG42 . . . . .26 F8
Pollards RH11 . . . . .201 A5
Pollards Cres SW16 . . . . . .41 E6
Pollards Dr RH13 . . . . .217 F2
Pollards Hill E SW16 . . . . .41 F6
Pollards Hill N SW16 . . . . .41 F6
Pollards Hill S SW16 . . . . .41 F6
Pollards Hill W SW16 . . . . .41 F6
Pollards Oak Cres RH8 . . .123 A3
Pollards Oak Rd RH8 . . . .123 A3
Pollards Wood Hill RH8 . .123 B5
Pollards Wood Rd
Limpsfield RH8 . . . . .123 B4
Thornton Heath SW16 . . . . .41 E6
Polsted La GU3 . . . . .129 C3
Polsted Rd SE6 . . . . .23 F8
Poltimore Rd GU2 . . . . . . .130 B7
Polworth Rd SW16 . . . . .21 E3
Polyanthus Way RG45 . . . .45 B8
Pond Cl Hersham KT12 . . . . .54 A4
Loxwood RH14 . . . . .212 F4
Pond Copse La RH14 . . . .212 F5
Pond Cottage La BR3, BR4 .44 A1
Pond Cotts SE21 . . . . .22 E7
Pond Farm Cl KT20 . . . . . . .97 B3
Pond Head La
Forest Green RH5 . . . . . . .176 E5
Wallis Wood RH5 . . . . .176 D3
Pond Hill Gdns SM3 . . . . . .58 E4
Pond House GU4 . . . . .110 D2
Pond La Frensham GU10 . . .167 C5
Peaslake GU5 . . . . .154 D7
Pond Meadow GU2 . . . . . .108 E2
Pond Meadow Sch GU2 .108 E2
Pond Moor Rd RG12 . . . . . .27 B4
Pond Piece KT22 . . . . .74 B6
Pond Rd Egham TW20 . . . . .12 C2
Headley Down GU35 . . . . .187 B4
Woking GU22 . . . . .89 B7
Pond Way
East Grinstead RH19 . . . . .186 B1
Teddington TW11 . . . . .17 C2
Pond Wood Rd RH10 . . . . .202 A8
Pondfield House SE27 . . . .22 C3
Pondfield Rd
Farncombe GU7 . . . . .150 F7
Kenley CR8 . . . . .80 B3
Rudgwick RH12 . . . . .214 D8
West Wickham BR2 . . . . . . .44 E1
Ponds La GU5 . . . . .153 F8
Ponds The KT13 . . . . .53 E4
Pondside Cl UB3 . . . . .3 D7
Pondtail Cl RH12 . . . . .217 D6
Pondtail Dr RH12 . . . . .217 D7
Pondtail Rd RH12 . . . . . . .217 D6
Ponsonby Rd SW15 . . . . . . .19 B8
Pontefract Rd BR1 . . . . . . .24 F3
Ponton House SW2 . . . . . . .22 A7
Pony Chase KT11 . . . . .73 F6
Pook Hill GU8 . . . . .190 F3
Pool Cl BR3 . . . . .24 A3
Pool Ct SE6 . . . . .24 A6
Pool End Cl TW17 . . . . .34 A4
Pool Rd Aldershot GU11 . . .126 C7
East Molesey KT12, KT8 . . . .35 F4
Poole Court Rd TW5 . . . . . . .4 E5
Poole Ct TW5 . . . . .4 E5
Poole Rd West Ewell KT19 . .57 D4
Woking GU21 . . . . .69 E1
Pooley Ave TW20 . . . . .12 B3
Pooley Green Cl TW20 . . . .12 C3
Pooley Green Rd TW20 . . . .12 C3
Pope Cl East Bedfont TW14 .14 F7
Mitcham SW17, SW19 . . . . .20 D2
Pope Ct 10 KT2 . . . . .17 D4
Pope's Ave TW2 . . . . .16 E6
Pope's Gr TW1, TW2 . . . . . .16 F6
Popes Cl SL3 . . . . .1 C7
Popes Gr CR0 . . . . .62 F7
Popes La RH8 . . . . .143 F8
Popes Mead GU27 . . . . . .208 C7
Popeswood Rd RG42 . . . . .26 D8
Popham Cl Bracknell RG12 .27 F4
Feltham TW13 . . . . .15 F5
Popham Gdns TW9 . . . . .7 B4
Poplar Ave
Leatherhead KT22 . . . . .95 C5
Mitcham CR4 . . . . .40 F8
Windlesham GU20 . . . . .48 B6
Poplar Cl Crawley RH11 . . .181 C1
Mytchett GU16 . . . . .86 A3
Poyle SL3 . . . . .1 E6
Poplar Cotts GU3 . . . . . . .108 E4
Poplar Cres KT19 . . . . .57 C4
Poplar Ct
4 Streatham SW16 . . . . . . .21 F5
13 Twickenham TW1 . . . . . . .6 C1
Wimbledon SW19 . . . . .20 A3
Poplar Dr KT17, SM7 . . . . . .77 D5
Poplar Farm Cl KT19 . . . . .57 C4
Poplar Fst Sch SW19 . . . . .40 A6
Poplar Gdns KT3 . . . . .38 D7
Poplar Gr Kingston u T KT3 .38 D6
Woking GU22 . . . . .89 E8
Poplar La BR3 . . . . .44 B4
Poplar Rd Ashford TW15 . . .14 C3
Cheam SM3 . . . . .39 F1
Leatherhead KT22 . . . . .95 C5
Merton SW19 . . . . .40 A7
Shalford GU4 . . . . .130 E2
Poplar Rd S SM4, SW19 . . .40 A6
Poplar Way TW13 . . . . .15 B5
Poplar Wlk Caterham CR3 .100 E4
Croydon CR0 . . . . .42 C1
Heath End GU9 . . . . .125 D7
Poplars Cl GU14 . . . . .84 C5
Poplars The Ascot SL5 . . . . .29 A4
Horsham RH13 . . . . .217 E3
Poppy La CR0, CR9 . . . . . . .43 C1
Poppy Pl RG40 . . . . .25 B6
Poppyhills Rd GU15 . . . . . .65 F8
Porchester SL5 . . . . .29 A5
Porchester Mead BR3 . . . . .24 B2
Porchester Rd KT1 . . . . .38 B7
Porchfield Cl SM2 . . . . .59 B1
Porlock House 5 SE26 . . . .23 A5
Porridge Pot Alley GU2 . .130 C7
Port Way GU24 . . . . .68 A3
Portal Cl SE27 . . . . .22 A5
Porteridges RH4 . . . . .136 C4
Portesbery Hill Dr GU15 . . .65 E6
Portesbery Rd GU15 . . . . . .65 E6
Portesbery Sch GU15 . . . . .65 D6
Porthcawe Rd SE26 . . . . . . .23 F4
Portia Gr RG42 . . . . .27 E8
Portland Ave KT3 . . . . .38 F2
Portland Cotts CR0 . . . . . . .41 D2
Portland Cres TW13, TW15 .14 D4
Portland Dr RH1 . . . . .119 D6
Portland House
5 East Grinstead RH19 . . . .205 F8
Merstham RH1 . . . . .119 D6
20 Streatham SW2 . . . . .22 A7
Portland House
Mews KT18 . . . . .76 D5
Portland Pl Croydon SE25 . .43 A5
Ewell KT17 . . . . .76 E7
Portland Rd Ashford TW15 . .13 E5
Croydon SE25 . . . . .43 B4
Dorking RH4 . . . . .136 A8
East Grinstead RH19 . . . . .205 F8
Kingston u T KT1 . . . . .37 F6
Mitcham CR4 . . . . .40 E7
Portland Terr TW9 . . . . .6 D3
Portley La CR3 . . . . .100 E6
Portley Wood Rd CR3 . . . .101 A7
Portman Ave SW14 . . . . .7 D4
Portman Cl 5 RG42 . . . . . . .27 A8
Portman Rd KT1 . . . . .37 F7
Portmore Park Rd KT13 . . . .53 A7
Portmore Quays KT13 . . . . .52 F6
Portmore Way KT13 . . . . . . .53 A7
Portnall Dr GU25 . . . . .30 F4
Portnall Rd GU25 . . . . .30 F4
Portnall Rise GU25 . . . . . . .30 F3
Portnalls Cl CR5 . . . . .79 B3
Portnalls Rd CR5 . . . . .79 B2
Portnalls Rise CR5 . . . . . . .79 C3
Portobello
House 6 SW27 . . . . .22 B3
Porton Ct KT6 . . . . .37 C3
Portsea House 3 SW15 . . . .19 B7
Portsmouth Ave KT7 . . . . . .37 A2
Portsmouth Rd
Camberley GU15 . . . . .66 A7
Cobham KT10, KT11 . . . . . . .73 C7
Downside KT11 . . . . .72 F6
Esher KT10 . . . . .55 A4
Esher KT10 . . . . .55 D7
Godalming GU7, GU8 . . . . .150 B2
Guildford GU2 . . . . .130 C6
Haslemere GU26 . . . . .188 E2
Hinchley Wood KT10, KT7 . . .55 E8
Hindhead GU26 . . . . .188 E2
Kingston u T KT1, KT6 . . . . .37 C3
Portsmouth Rd *continued*
Milford GU8 . . . . .149 E1
Ockham GU23 . . . . .91 D7
Putney SW15 . . . . .19 C8
Ripley GU23 . . . . .91 B4
Send Marsh GU23 . . . . .91 B4
Thames Ditton KT6, KT7 . . . .37 C3
Thursley GU8 . . . . .169 D3
Wisley GU23, KT11 . . . . . . .72 C3
Witley GU8 . . . . .170 B6
Portswood Pl SW15 . . . . . . .7 F1
Portugal Gdns TW2 . . . . . .16 C6
Portugal Rd GU21 . . . . .69 F3
Portway KT17 . . . . .58 A2
Portway Cres KT17 . . . . . . .58 A2
Post House La KT23 . . . . . . .94 A2
Post La TW2 . . . . .16 D7
Postford Mill Cotts GU4 .131 F5
Postmill Cl CR0, CR9 . . . . . .62 D7
Potley Hill Cty Prim Sch
GU46 . . . . .64 A5
Potley Hill Rd GU46 . . . . . .64 A5
Potter Cl CR4 . . . . .41 B7
Potter's La SW16 . . . . .21 D2
Potterhill Ct TW11 . . . . . . .17 B1
Potteries La GU16 . . . . .85 F4
Potteries The
Farnborough GU14 . . . . .84 D6
Ottershaw KT16 . . . . .51 E4
Potterne Cl 5
SW15, SW19 . . . . .19 D8
Potters Cl Croydon CR0 . . . .43 E1
Milford GU8 . . . . .149 F2
Potters Cres GU12 . . . . . .106 B2
Potters Croft RH13 . . . . . .217 E2
Potters Gate GU9 . . . . . . .125 A2
Potters Gate CE Prim Sch
GU9 . . . . .125 A2
Potters Gr KT3 . . . . .38 C5
Potters La GU23 . . . . .90 B2
Potters Way RH2 . . . . .139 C5
Pottersfield RH10 . . . . . . .201 D7
Pottery Ct GU10 . . . . .145 F6
Pottery La GU10 . . . . .145 F6
Pottery Rd TW8 . . . . .6 E8
Poulett Gdns TW1 . . . . .17 A7
Poullett House SW2 . . . . . .22 B7
Poulton Ave SM1, SM5 . . . .59 D7
Pound Cl Godalming GU7 . .150 E4
Long Ditton KT6 . . . . .37 C1
Loxwood RH14 . . . . .212 F5
Pound Cres KT22 . . . . .94 D6
Pound Ct Ashstead KT21 . . .75 F1
Wood St V GU3 . . . . .108 B2
Pound Farm La GU12 . . . .106 D1
Pound Field GU1 . . . . .109 D1
Pound Hill GU3 . . . . .108 B2
Pound Hill Cty Fst & Mid
Schs RH10 . . . . .202 C7
Pound Hill Par RH10 . . . . .202 C7
Pound Hill Pl RH10 . . . . . .202 C6
Pound La Epsom KT19 . . . . .76 D8
Godalming GU7 . . . . .150 E4
Windlesham GU20 . . . . .48 C4
Wood St V GU3 . . . . .108 B2
Pound Pl GU4 . . . . .130 F3
Pound Place Cl GU4 . . . . .130 F3
Pound Rd Aldershot GU12 .105 C1
Banstead SM7 . . . . .78 A2
Chertsey KT16 . . . . .33 B2
Pound St SM5 . . . . .59 F5
Poundfield Gdns GU22 . . . .90 C7
Poundfield La RH14 . . . . .212 B3
Povey Cross Rd RH6 . . . . .160 E1
Powder Mill La TW2, TW4 .16 A7
Powderham Ct GU21 . . . . . .68 D1
Powell Cl Chessington KT9 .56 D5
Guildford GU2 . . . . .129 F7
Horley RH6 . . . . .160 E4
Wallington SM6 . . . . .60 E3
Powell Corderoy Prim Sch
RH4 . . . . .135 F6
Powell Ct CR0 . . . . .61 C6
Powell's Wlk W4 . . . . .7 F8
Powells Cl RH4 . . . . .136 C4
Powers Ct TW1 . . . . .17 D8
Pownall Gdns TW3 . . . . .5 B3
Pownall Rd TW3 . . . . .5 B3
Poyle 14 Trad Est SL3 . . . . .1 E4
Poyle Cty Fst Sch SL3 . . . . .1 F6
Poyle Gdns RG12 . . . . .27 D8
Poyle House GU4 . . . . . . .110 D2
Poyle New Cotts SL3 . . . . . . .1 F5
Poyle Rd Guildford GU1 . . .130 E7
Poyle SL3 . . . . .1 E5
Tongham GU10 . . . . .127 B7
Poyle Tech Ctr The SL3 . . . .1 E5
Poynders Gdns SW12 . . . . .21 C8
Poynders Rd SW12, SW4 . .21 D8
Poynes Rd RH6 . . . . .160 E5
Poynings Rd RH11 . . . . . .200 E5
Prairie Cl KT15 . . . . .52 B7
Prairie Rd KT15 . . . . .52 B7
Pratts Cnr GU8 . . . . .193 A8
Pratts La KT12 . . . . .54 D6
Precinct The
Cranleigh GU6 . . . . .174 E4
East Molesey KT8 . . . . .36 B6
Egham TW20 . . . . .12 A3
Precincts The SM4 . . . . . . .40 A3
Prendergast House 7
SW4 . . . . .21 D8
Prentice Cl GU14 . . . . .85 B8
Prentice Ct 2 SW19 . . . . . . .19 F3
Prentis Rd SW16 . . . . .21 D4
Presburg Rd KT3 . . . . .38 E4
Presbury Ct GU21 . . . . .69 A1
Prescott RG12 . . . . .26 F2
Prescott Rd SL3 . . . . .1 E5
Presentation Mews SW2 . . .21 F7
Prestbury Cres SM7 . . . . . .78 F3
Preston Cl TW2 . . . . .16 E5
Preston Ct KT12 . . . . .35 C1
Preston Dr KT19 . . . . .57 F4
Preston Gr KT21 . . . . .75 C2
Preston La KT20 . . . . .97 C7
Preston Pl TW10 . . . . .6 E2
Preston Rd Littleton TW17 . .34 A4
South Norwood SE19 . . . . . .22 B2
Wimbledon SW20 . . . . .18 F1
Prestwick Cl RH11 . . . . . .200 D5
Prestwick La
Chiddingfold GU8 . . . . . . .190 C3
Grayswood GU8 . . . . .190 C3
Prestwood Cl RH11 . . . . . .181 B1
Prestwood Gdns CR0 . . . . .42 C2
Prestwood La
RH11, RH12, RH6 . . . . . . .180 C3
Pretoria Rd Chertsey KT16 . .32 F1
Streatham SW16 . . . . .21 C3
Pretty La CR5 . . . . .99 C6
Prey Heath Cl GU22 . . . . . .89 C3
Prey Heath Rd GU22 . . . . . .89 B3
Preymead Ind Est GU9 . . .126 B7
Price Cl SW17 . . . . .20 F5
Price Rd CR0 . . . . .61 B5
Price Way TW12 . . . . .15 E2
Prices La RH2 . . . . .139 B6
Prickley Wood BR2 . . . . . . .44 F1
Priddy's Yd 4 CR9 . . . . . . .61 C8
Prides Crossing SL5 . . . . . .9 A1
Pridham Rd CR7 . . . . .42 D5
Priest Ave RG40 . . . . .25 F5
Priest Croft Cl RH11 . . . . .201 A6
Priest Hill Englefield Green
TW19, TW20 . . . . .11 C6
Limpsfield RH8 . . . . .123 B6
Priest Hill Sch Sports Ctr
KT17 . . . . .77 B8
Priest La GU24 . . . . .67 C5
Priestfield Rd SE23 . . . . . .23 E5
Priestley Gdns GU22 . . . . . .90 A7
Priestley Rd
Guildford GU2 . . . . .129 D8
Mitcham CR4 . . . . .41 A7
Priestley Way RH10 . . . . .182 A3
Priests Bridge SW14, SW15 .7 E4
Priestwood Ave RG42 . . . . .26 F8
Priestwood Court Rd
RG42 . . . . .27 A8
Priestwood Sq 1 RG42 . . .27 A8
Prim Sch of Our Lady
Immaculate KT6 . . . . .38 B1
Primrose Ave RH6 . . . . . . .161 B1
Primrose Cl Carshalton CR4 41 B1
Catford SE6 . . . . .24 C3
Crawley RH11 . . . . .201 B3
Primrose Copse RH12 . . .217 E7
Primrose Ct
New Malden KT4 . . . . .39 A2
11 Streatham SW12 . . . . . . .21 D8
Primrose Dr GU24 . . . . .68 A4
Primrose Gdns GU14 . . . . . .84 E3
Primrose House 1 TW9 . . . .6 F6
Primrose La CR0 . . . . .43 D1
Primrose Rd KT12 . . . . .54 C5
Primrose Ridge GU7 . . . .150 B2
Primrose Way
Bramley GU5 . . . . .151 D5
Sandhurst GU47 . . . . .45 B1
Primrose Wlk
Bracknell RG12 . . . . .27 C4
Ewell KT17 . . . . .57 F3
Prince Albert Dr SL5 . . . . .28 D4
Prince Albert Sq RH1 . . . .140 A4
Prince Andrew Way SL5 . . .28 D7
Prince Charles Cres GU14 85 C8
Prince Charles Way SM6 . .60 B7
Prince Consort Dr SL5 . . . .28 D5
Prince Consort's Dr
Old Windsor SL4 . . . . .10 A6
Winkfield SL4 . . . . .9 F4
Prince Dr GU47 . . . . .45 A1
Prince George's Ave
SW20 . . . . .39 C7
Prince Georges Rd SW19 .40 D8
Prince Of Wales' Rd SM1 .59 D8
Prince Of Wales Rd RH1 .141 A2
Prince of Wales Wlk 1
GU15 . . . . .65 C6
Prince Rd SE25 . . . . .42 E4
Prince Regent Rd TW3 . . . . .5 C4
Prince William Ct TW15 . . .13 F3
Prince's Ave
Farnborough GU11 . . . . . . .105 C5
Farncombe GU7 . . . . .150 C7
Prince's Cl TW11, TW12 . . .16 D4
Prince's Dr KT22 . . . . .74 E7
Prince's Rd Mortlake SW14 . .7 D4
Redhill RH1 . . . . .139 F7
Teddington TW11, TW12 . . .16 D4
Weybridge KT13 . . . . .53 C5
Wimbledon SW19 . . . . .20 A2
Prince's St TW10, TW9 . . . . .6 E2
Princes Ave
Hamsey Green CR2 . . . . . . .81 B4
Tolworth KT6 . . . . .57 A8
Wallington SM5 . . . . .59 F2
Princes Cl Bagshot GU19 . . .47 E1
Hamsey Green CR2 . . . . . . .81 B4
Princes Ct New Malden KT3 .38 F6
Weybridge KT13 . . . . .53 B5
Princes Gdns GU3 . . . . . . .108 E8
Princes Mead GU14 . . . . . . .85 B4
Princes Mews TW3 . . . . .5 A3
Princes Rd Ashford TW15 . .13 F3
Princes Rd *continued*
Egham TW20 . . . . .11 F2
Feltham TW13 . . . . .14 F5
Kingston u T KT2 . . . . .18 A1
Penge SE20 . . . . .23 D2
Richmond TW10 . . . . .6 F2
Richmond, Kew TW9 . . . . . . .6 F6
Princes St SM1 . . . . .59 D6
Princes Way
Aldershot GU11 . . . . .105 A2
Coney Hall BR4 . . . . .63 F7
Croydon CR0 . . . . .60 F5
Putney SW15, SW19 . . . . . . .19 E7
Princess Anne Rd RH12 .214 D6
Princess Ct
Aldershot GU14 . . . . .105 C8
9 Wimbledon SW19 . . . . . . .19 D1
Princess Gdns GU22 . . . . . .70 B3
Princess House 1 RH1 . . .119 A2
Princess Margaret Rd
RH12 . . . . .214 D7
Princess Mary's Rd KT15 .52 C6
Princess Rd Crawley RH11 201 C6
Thornton Heath CR0 . . . . . . .42 C3
Woking GU22 . . . . .70 C3
Princess Sq RG12 . . . . .27 B7
Princess Way
Camberley GU15 . . . . .65 C5
Redhill RH1 . . . . .119 A2
Princethorpe Rd SE26 . . . .23 D4
Princeton Mews 3 KT2 . . .38 A8
Pringle Gdns Purley CR8 . . .60 F1
Streatham SW16 . . . . .21 C4
Prins Willem-Alexander
Sch GU22 . . . . .70 C2
Prior Ave SM2, SM5 . . . . . .59 E3
Prior Croft Cl GU15 . . . . . .66 A4
Prior End GU15 . . . . .66 A5
Prior Heath Cty Inf Sch
GU15 . . . . .66 A5
Prior Rd GU15 . . . . .66 A5
Prior's La GU17 . . . . .64 A5
Prioress Rd SE27 . . . . .22 B5
Priors Cl GU14 . . . . .85 B8
Priors Croft GU22 . . . . .90 A7
Priors Ct Ash GU12 . . . . . .105 E1
Woking GU21 . . . . .69 A1
Priors Field Sch GU7 . . . .129 A1
Priors Hatch La GU7 . . . .128 F1
Priors Lodge 4 TW10 . . . . . .6 E1
Priors Mead KT23 . . . . .94 C2
Priors The KT21 . . . . .95 D8
Priors Wlk RH10 . . . . .201 F6
Priors Wood GU27 . . . . . .207 F6
Priorsfield Rd GU7 . . . . . .129 A1
Priorswood GU3 . . . . .128 F2
Priory Ave SM3 . . . . .58 D6
Priory C of E Mid Sch
SW19 . . . . .20 B3
Priory Cl Beckenham BR3 . . .43 E6
Dorking RH4 . . . . .136 A5
Hampton TW12 . . . . .35 F8
Horley RH6 . . . . .160 F4
3 Merton SW19 . . . . .40 B8
Sheerwater GU21 . . . . .70 D6
Sunbury TW16 . . . . .15 A1
Sunningdale SL5 . . . . .30 A2
Walton-on-T KT12 . . . . .54 A7
Priory Cres Cheam SM3 . . . .58 D6
South Norwood SE19 . . . . . .22 C1
Priory Ct Camberley GU15 . .64 F5
Cheam SM3 . . . . .58 E6
Cheam SM1 . . . . .58 F5
Egham TW20 . . . . .12 C2
Hounslow TW3 . . . . .5 B4
Roehampton SW15 . . . . .7 F3
Priory Dr RH2 . . . . .139 A7
Priory Gdns Hampton TW12 .35 F8
Mortlake SW13 . . . . .7 F4
South Norwood SE25 . . . . . .42 F5
Priory Gn TW18 . . . . .13 B3
Priory Hospl The SW15 . . . . .7 F3
Priory House Sch SE6 . . . .24 B7
Priory La East Molesey KT8 .36 B5
Frensham GU10 . . . . .167 E8
Roehampton SW15 . . . . .7 F2
Priory Lodge BR4 . . . . .63 E7
Priory Mews TW18 . . . . . . .13 B3
Priory Pl KT12 . . . . .54 A7
Priory Rd Cheam SM3 . . . . .58 D6
Chessington KT9 . . . . .56 E7
Forest Row RH18 . . . . . . .206 D2
Hampton TW12 . . . . .16 A1
Isleworth TW3 . . . . .5 C2
Mitcham SW19 . . . . .20 D1
Reigate RH2 . . . . .139 A6
Richmond TW9 . . . . .7 A7
Sunningdale SL5 . . . . .30 A2
Thornton Heath CR0 . . . . . . .42 A2
Winkfield SL5 . . . . .28 B7
Priory Sch SE25 . . . . .42 F5
Priory Sch The SM7 . . . . . .78 A4
Priory St GU14 . . . . .85 D4
Priory The Croydon CR0 . . .61 A7
Godstone RH9 . . . . .121 B3
21 Kingston u T KT6 . . . . . .37 E4
Priory Way UB7 . . . . .2 E8
Priory Wlk RG12 . . . . .27 F5
Priscilla House 8 TW16 . . .14 F1
Probyn Rd SW2 . . . . .22 B6
Proctor Cl Crawley RH10 . .202 C4
Mitcham CR4 . . . . .41 A8
Proctor Gdns KT23 . . . . . . .94 B2
Proctors Cl TW14 . . . . .15 A7
Proctors Rd RG40 . . . . .25 F6

Profumo Rd KT12 ....54 D5
Progress Bsns Pk CR9 ....60 F8
Progress Way CR0 ....60 F8
Promenade Approach Rd
W4 ....7 E7
Promenade De Verdun
CR8 ....79 D8
Promenade The W4 ....7 E6
Prospect Ave GU14 ....85 B6
Prospect Cl Forest Hill SE26 23 B4
Hounslow TW5 ....4 F6
Prospect Cotts RG42 .....26 D8
Prospect Cres TW2 ....5 C1
Prospect La TW20 ....11 A3
Prospect Pl Crawley RH11 201 C6
Ewell KT17 ....76 E6
Staines TW18 ....12 F3
Wimbledon SW20 ....19 B1
Prospect Rd Ash GU12 ...106 A5
Farnborough GU14 ....85 A5
Rowledge GU10 ....145 E3
Thames Ditton KT6 ....37 C3
Prossers KT20 ....97 D6
Providence House GU19 ..47 E3
Providence La UB3 ....3 D7
Providence Pl Ewell KT17 ..76 E7
Farnham GU9 ....125 C2
Provincial Terr SE20 ......23 D1
Prune Hill TW20 ....11 E1
Prunus Cl GU24 ....67 E6
Public Record Office TW9 ..7 B7
Puckridge Hill Rd GU11 .104 E6
Puckshill GU21 ....68 D2
Puckshott Way GU27 ....208 D8
Puddenhole Cotts RH4 ..116 A2
Pudding La RH6 ....180 E7
Puffin Cl BR3, CR0 ....43 D4
Puffin Rd RH11 ....200 D5
Pulborough Rd SW18 ......19 F8
Pulborough Way TW4 .....4 C3
Pullman Ct SW2 ....21 F7
Pullman La GU7 ....150 C2
Pullmans Pl TW18 ....13 A3
Pump Alley 8 TW8 ....6 D7
Pump La SL5 ....29 E8
Pump Pail N CR0, CR9 ....61 C7
Pump Pail S CR0, CR9 .....61 C7
Pumping Station Rd W4 ...7 E8
Punch Copse Rd RH10 ...201 F7
Punchbowl La RH4, RH5 .136 D6
Punnetts Ct RH11 ....200 F2
Purbeck Ave KT3 ....38 F3
Purbeck Cl RH1 ....119 D7
Purbeck Ct 4 GU2 ....108 E1
Purbeck Dr GU21 ....69 F5
Purberry Gr KT17 ....57 F1
Purberry Shot KT17 ....57 F1
Purbrook Ct RG12 ....27 E3
Purbrook House 2 SW15 ..19 B7
Purcell House TW2 ....5 D1
Purcell Rd Crawley RH11 ..200 F3
Crowthorne RG45 ....45 B7
Purcell's Cl KT21 ....75 F1
Purdey Ct 3 KT4 ....39 A1
Purley Bury Ave CR8 ....80 C8
Purley Bury Cl CR8 ....80 C8
Purley Cl RH10 ....202 D3
Purley Ct CR8 ....61 B1
Purley & District War
Memorial Hospl CR8 .....80 A8
Purley Downs Rd CR2 .....80 E8
Purley Hill CR8 ....80 B7
Purley Knoll CR8 ....80 A8
Purley Oaks Prim Sch
CR2 ....61 D3
Purley Oaks Rd CR2 ....61 D1
Purley Oaks Sta CR2 ....61 D2
Purley Par 2 CR8 ....80 A8
Purley Park Rd CR8 ....61 B1
Purley Rd Purley CR8 ....80 A8
South Croydon CR2 ....61 D3
Purley Rise CR8 ....79 F7
Purley Sta CR8 ....80 A7
Purley Vale CR8 ....80 B6
Purley View Terr CR2 ......61 D3
Purley Way
Croydon CR0, CR9 ....61 A4
Frimley GU16 ....85 E8
Purley CR8 ....80 A8
Thornton Heath CR0, CR9 ...41 F1
Purmerend Cl GU14 ....84 C5
Pursers Hollow GU5 .....154 D8
Pursers La GU5 ....154 D8
Purslane RG40 ....25 D5
Purton Rd RH12 ....217 B4
Putney Heath SW15 ....19 B8
Putney Hill SW15 ....19 D8
Puttenham Common
Nature Trails GU3 ......148 E8
Puttenham Heath Rd
Puttenham GU3 ....128 E3
Wanborough GU3 ....128 E3
Puttenham Hill GU3 ....128 C5
Puttenham La GU3, GU8 ..128 C1
Puttenham Rd GU10 ....127 C4
Puttenham Sch CE (VA)
GU3 ....128 C4
Puttock Cl GU27 ....207 D5
Pye Cl CR3 ....100 D4
Pyecombe Ct 4 RH11 .....200 F3
Pyegrove Chase RG12 .....27 E2
Pyestock Cres GU14 ....84 C4
Pylbrook Rd SM1 ....59 B7
Pyle Hill GU22, GU4 ....89 D3
Pymers Mead Dulwich SE21 22 D7
Pymers Mead *continued*
West Norwood SE21 ....22 C7
Pyne Rd KT6 ....38 A1
Pyrcroft Grange Prim Sch
KT16 ....32 E3
Pyrcroft La KT13 ....53 B5
Pyrcroft Rd KT16 ....32 E2
Pyrford Common Rd GU22 70 E2
Pyrford Cty Prim Sch
GU22 ....71 A3
Pyrford Heath GU22 ....70 F3
Pyrford Rd
Pyrford GU22, KT14 ....71 A4
West Byfleet GU22, KT14 ...71 A4
Woking GU22, KT14 ....71 A4
Pyrford Woods Cl GU22 ...70 F4
Pyrford Woods Rd GU22 ..70 F4
Pyrland Rd TW10 ....6 F1
Pyrmont Gr SE27 ....22 B5
Pyrmont Rd W4 ....7 A8
Pytchley Cres SE19 ....22 C2

Q

Quadrangle Lodge SW19 .20 A2
Quadrangle The GU2 ....130 A8
Quadrant Ct RG12 ....27 E6
Quadrant Rd Richmond TW9 .6 D3
Thornton Heath CR7 ....42 B5
Quadrant The
Ash Vale GU12 ....106 A4
Merton SW20 ....39 E8
Richmond TW9 ....6 E3
Sutton SM2 ....59 C4
Quail Cl RH12 ....217 D7
Quail Gdns CR0 ....62 E1
Quakers Way GU3 ....108 C5
Qualitas RG12 ....26 F1
Quality St RH1 ....119 B7
Quantock Cl
Crawley RH11 ....201 B6
Harlington UB3 ....3 D7
Quantock Dr KT4 ....58 C8
Quarr Rd SM5 ....40 E3
Quarry Bank GU18 ....67 A8
Quarry Cl Horsham RH12 ..217 F6
Oxted RH8 ....122 E5
Quarry Gdns KT22 ....95 C5
Quarry Hill GU7 ....150 B3
Quarry Hill Pk RH2 ....118 C4
Quarry Park Rd SM1 ....58 F4
Quarry Rd Oxted RH8 ....122 E5
Shackleford GU7 ....150 A7
Woldingham RH9 ....121 C7
Quarry Rise Cheam SM1 ....58 F4
East Grinstead RH19 ....186 A3
Quarry St GU1 ....130 D7
Quarry The RH3 ....116 D3
Quarter Mile Rd GU7 .....150 E2
Quarterbrass Farm Rd
RH12 ....217 D7
Quartermaine Ave GU22 ..89 F5
Quarters Rd GU14 ....85 C2
Quay West TW11 ....17 B3
Quebec Cl RH6 ....162 A3
Quebec Gdns GU17 ....64 D4
Queen Adelaide Ct SE20 ..23 C2
Queen Adelaide Rd SE20 .23 C1
Queen Alexandra's Ct 5
SW19 ....19 F3
Queen Anne Ave BR2 ....44 F6
Queen Anne Dr KT10 ....55 E3
Queen Anne's Cl SL4 ....10 B5
Queen Anne's Gdns
Leatherhead KT22 ....95 B6
Mitcham CR4 ....40 F6
Queen Anne's Terr KT22 ..95 B6
Queen Annes Cl TW2 ....16 D5
Queen Annes Ct KT22 ....95 B6
Queen Annes Gate GU9 ..125 D7
Queen Eleanor's C of E
Jun Sch GU2 ....130 A8
Queen Eleanor's Rd GU2 129 F8
Queen Elizabeth Dr GU11 104 F2
Queen Elizabeth Gdns
SM4 ....40 A5
Queen Elizabeth Hospl
SM7 ....78 C1
Queen Elizabeth II
Jubilee Sch The RH13 ..217 F1
Queen Elizabeth Rd
Camberley GU15 ....46 D1
Kingston u T KT2 ....37 F7
Rudgwick RH12 ....214 D7
Queen Elizabeth Way
GU22 ....90 A8
Queen Elizabeth's Dr CR0 63 D1
Queen Elizabeth's Gdns
CR0 ....63 D1
Queen Elizabeth's
Training Coll KT22 ....74 D2
Queen Elizabeth's Wlk
SM6 ....60 D6
Queen Mary Ave
Camberley GU15 ....65 A5
West Barnes SM4, SW20 ......39 D4
Queen Mary Cl
Tolworth KT9 ....57 A8
Woking GU22 ....70 C3
Queen Mary Rd
Charlton TW17 ....34 C7
South Norwood SE19 ....22 B2
Queen Mary's Ave SM5 .....59 F3
Queen Mary's Dr KT15 ......52 A1
Queen St Aldershot GU12 .105 D2
Chertsey KT16 ....33 A1
Croydon CR0, CR9 ....61 C6
Godalming GU7 ....150 E4
Queen St *continued*
Gomshall GU5 ....133 C4
Horsham RH13 ....217 D1
Queen Victoria Cross
Roads GU15 ....65 A6
Queen Victoria Ct GU14 ...85 B5
Queen Victoria Hospl The
RH19 ....185 F3
Queen Victoria Way GU24 .87 D8
Queen's Ave
Aldershot GU11 ....105 B5
Farnborough GU11 ....105 B5
Queen's C of E Jun Mix
Sch The TW9 ....7 A7
Queen's C of E Jun Sch The
TW9 ....7 A7
Queen's Cl
Farnborough GU14 ....105 B8
North Ascot SL5 ....28 E8
Wallington SM6 ....60 B5
Queen's Ct
Beckenham BR3 ....44 A8
Croydon CR2 ....61 C5
Farnborough GU14 ....105 C8
1 Kingston u T KT2 ....18 A1
3 Richmond TW10 ....6 F1
Staines TW18 ....13 D2
Thornton Heath CR7 ....42 A4
Queen's Dr
Farncombe GU7 ....150 C7
Guildford GU2 ....109 A4
Thames Ditton KT7 ....37 A3
Queen's Gate Rd GU14 ....105 B8
Queen's Gdns TW5 ....4 E6
Queen's Hospl CR0 ....42 C3
Queen's House TW11 ....16 F2
Queen's Mead GU8 ....191 B4
Queen's Mead Rd BR2 ....44 F7
Queen's Park Rd CR3 ....100 E4
Queen's Pl Ascot SL5 ....29 A6
Morden SM4 ....40 A5
Queen's Rd Ascot SL5 ....29 D4
Beckenham BR3 ....43 E7
East Grinstead RH19 ....185 E1
Egham TW20 ....11 F2
Feltham TW13, TW14 ....15 B7
Guildford GU1 ....109 D1
Hampton TW12 ....16 B4
Horley RH6 ....161 A3
Hounslow TW3 ....5 B4
Kingston u T KT2 ....18 A1
Knaphill GU21 ....68 D1
Mitcham CR4 ....40 D6
Mortlake SW14 ....7 D4
New Malden KT3 ....38 F4
Richmond TW10 ....6 F1
Richmond, Richmond Park
KT2, TW10 ....18 A3
Teddington TW11 ....16 F2
Thames Ditton KT7 ....36 F4
Thornton Heath CR0 ....42 C3
Wallington SM6 ....60 B5
Wimbledon SW19 ....20 A2
Queen's Rdbt GU11 ....105 B7
Queen's Rise TW10 ....6 F1
Queen's Terr TW7 ....6 A3
Queen's Way GU24 ....87 D8
Queendale Ct GU21 ....68 F3
Queenhill Rd CR2 ....62 B1
Queenhythe Rd GU4 ....109 D7
Queens Acre SM2, SM3 ....58 E3
Queens Ave Byfleet KT14 ......71 D7
Feltham TW13 ....15 C4
Queens Cl Bisley GU24 ....68 A3
Walton on t H KT20 ....97 A3
Queens Court Ride KT11 .....73 A6
Queens Cres TW10 ....6 F2
Queens Ct 3 Redhill RH1 ....119 A2
Weybridge KT13 ....53 E4
Queens Dr Oxshott KT22 ....74 C8
Surbiton KT5 ....38 A3
Queens Gate RH6 ....182 A8
Queens Hill Rise SL5 ....29 C6
Queens Keep
Camberley GU15 ....65 D5
10 Twickenham TW1 ....6 C1
Queens La GU9 ....125 B7
Queens Park Gdns TW13 ......14 F5
Queens Pine RG12 ....27 E3
Queens Pl KT12, KT13 ....53 E5
Queens Rd Aldershot GU11 104 F2
Belmont SM2 ....78 A8
Bisley GU24 ....67 F1
Camberley GU15 ....65 B4
Farnborough GU14 ....105 D8
Hale GU9 ....125 C6
Hersham KT12 ....54 A6
Morden SM4 ....40 A5
Twickenham TW1 ....17 A7
Weybridge KT13 ....53 C5
Queens Reach KT8 ....36 E5
Queens Sq RH10 ....201 D6
Queens Way Croydon CR0 ....60 F5
Feltham TW13 ....15 C4
Queens Wlk TW15 ....13 D4
Queensberry House 6
TW9 ....6 D2
Queensbridge Pk TW7 ....5 E2
Queensbury Ct CR7 ....42 C7
Queensbury Pl GU17 ....64 C3
Queensfield Ct SM3 ....58 C6
Queensgate KT11 ....73 D7
Queenshill Lodge SL5 ....29 B6
Queensland Ave SW19 ....40 B8
Queensmead GU14 ....85 B3
Queensmead Ave KT17 ....58 B1
Queensmere Cl SW19 ....19 D6
Queensmere Rd SW19 ....19 D6
Queensmere
(Southlands Coll) SW19 .19 D6
Queensthorpe Rd SE26 ....23 D4
Queensville Rd SW12, SW4 21 D8
Queensway Coney Hall BR4 .63 F6
Cranleigh GU6 ....174 F2
Crawley RH10 ....201 E6
East Grinstead RH19 ....185 E1
Frimley GU16 ....86 A7
Hersham KT12 ....54 B5
Horsham RH13 ....217 C1
Redhill RH1 ....118 F2
Sunbury TW16 ....35 B7
Queensway N KT12 ....54 D6
Queensway S KT12 ....54 C5
Queenswood Ave
Hampton TW12 ....16 B2
Hounslow TW3, TW5 ....4 F5
Thornton Heath CR7 ....42 A4
Wallington CR0, SM6 ....60 D6
Queenswood Ct 11 SE27 ......22 D4
Queenswood Rd
Forest Hill SE23 ....23 E5
Knaphill GU21 ....88 D8
Quennel House 7 SW12 ......21 C8
Quennell Cl KT21 ....95 F8
Quennells Hill GU10 ....145 E6
Quentin Way GU25 ....31 B5
Quicks Rd SW19 ....20 B1
Quiet Cl KT15 ....52 A6
Quillot The KT12 ....53 F5
Quince Cl SL5 ....29 D5
Quince Dr GU24 ....68 B4
Quincy Rd TW20 ....12 A3
Quinneys GU14 ....85 D1
Quintilis RG12 ....26 F1
Quintin Ave SW20 ....39 F8
Quintin Ct W4 ....7 C7
Quintock House 2 TW9 ....7 A6
Quinton Cl Beckenham BR3 .44 C6
Hackbridge SM6 ....60 B6
Heston TW5 ....4 B7
Quinton Rd KT7 ....37 A1
Quinton St SW18 ....20 C6
Quintrell Cl GU21 ....69 B2

R

Rabbit La KT12 ....54 B3
Rabies Heath Rd
Bletchingley RH1 ....120 F2
Godstone RH1, RH9 ....121 B1
Raby Rd KT3 ....38 D5
Raccoon Way TW4 ....4 C5
Racecourse Rd
Crawley RH6 ....181 F8
Dormansland RH7 ....165 A2
Lingfield RH7 ....164 F3
Racecourse Way RH6 ....181 F8
Rachel Ct SM2 ....59 D3
Rackfield GU27 ....207 D7
Rackham Cl RH11 ....201 D4
Rackham Mews SW16 ....21 C2
Racks Ct GU1 ....130 D7
Rackstraw Rd GU47 ....45 D2
Racquets Court Hill GU7 .150 C6
Rad La Peaslake GU5 ....133 D1
Peaslake RH5 ....133 E1
Radbourne Rd SW12 ....21 D7
Radcliff Mews TW12 ....16 C3
Radcliffe Cl GU16 ....86 A7
Radcliffe Gdns SM5 ....59 E3
Radcliffe Rd CR0 ....61 F7
Radcliffe Way RG42 ....26 E8
Radcot Point 2 SE23 ....23 D5
Radford Cl GU9 ....125 E5
Radford Rd RH10, RH6 ......182 C4
Radius Pk TW6 ....3 F3
Radlet Ave SE23 ....23 B6
Radley Cl TW14 ....14 F7
Radley Ct BR1 ....24 C4
Radley Lodge 30 SW19 ....19 D7
Radnor Cl CR4 ....41 E5
Radnor Ct
6 Forest Hill SE23 ....23 D5
Redhill RH1 ....118 E1
Radnor Gdns TW1 ....16 F6
Radnor La
Abinger Common RH5 ....155 B7
Ewhurst RH5 ....155 A2
Radnor Rd Bracknell RG12 ..27 F6
Peaslake GU5, GU6 ....154 E4
Twickenham TW1 ....16 F6
Weybridge KT13 ....53 A7
Radnor Wlk CR0 ....43 E3
Radolphs KT20 ....97 D5
Radstock Way RH1 ....119 E7
Radstone Ct 1 GU22 ....69 F1
Rae Rd GU14 ....85 B1
Raebarn Ct 6 SW16 ....21 E5
Raeburn Ave Surbiton KT3 ..38 B3
Tolworth KT5, KT6 ....38 B3
Raeburn Cl KT1 ....17 D1
Raeburn Ct GU21 ....89 A8
Raeburn Way GU47 ....64 D6
RAF Staff Coll RG12 ....27 D5
Rag Hill TN16 ....103 E6
Rag Hill Cl TN16 ....103 E6
Rag Hill Rd TN16 ....103 E6
Raglan Cl Aldershot GU12 .105 C1
Frimley GU16 ....86 A8
Hounslow TW4 ....4 F2
Reigate RH2 ....118 D3
Raglan Ct CR0, CR2 ....61 B5
Raglan Prec The CR3 ....100 E5
Raglan Rd Knaphill GU21 .....68 E1
Reigate RH2 ....118 C3
Raglans House RH2 ....118 B4
Ragwort Ct 1 SE26 ....23 B3
Raikes La RH5 ....134 B2
Railey Rd RH10 ....201 E7
Railshead Rd TW1, TW7 ....6 B3
Railton Rd GU2 ....109 B5
Railway App Chertsey KT16 .32 F1
East Grinstead RH19 ....185 E1
10 Twickenham TW1 ....17 A8
Wallington SM6 ....60 B5
Railway Cotts CR8 ....79 F6
Railway Rd TW11 ....16 F4
Railway Side SW13, SW14 ....7 E4
Railway Terr Egham TW18 ...12 D3
Feltham TW13, TW14 ....15 A7
Rainbow Ct GU21 ....68 E3
Rainbow Ctr The KT17 ....76 E7
Rake La Milford GU8 ....171 A7
Witley GU8 ....170 F7
Rakers Ridge RH12 ....217 D5
Raleigh Ave SM6 ....60 D6
Raleigh Ct Beckenham BR3 ..44 B8
Crawley RH10 ....182 A3
Dulwich SE19 ....22 F3
Staines TW18 ....13 A4
Wallington SM6 ....60 B4
Raleigh Dr Esher KT10 ....55 D5
Smallfield RH6 ....162 A3
Tolworth KT5 ....38 C1
Raleigh Gdns CR4 ....40 F6
Raleigh House 1 KT7 ....37 A2
Raleigh Rd
Feltham TW13, TW14 ....14 F6
Penge SE20 ....23 D1
Richmond TW9 ....6 F4
Raleigh Sch The KT24 ....92 C2
Raleigh Way Feltham TW13 .15 C3
Frimley GU16 ....65 F3
Raleigh Wlk RH10 ....201 E4
Ralliwood Rd KT21 ....96 A8
Ralph Perring Ct BR3 ....44 A5
Ralphs Ride RG12 ....27 E6
Rama Cl SW16 ....21 E1
Rambler Cl SW16 ....21 C4
Ramblers Way 12 RH11 ....201 B1
Rame Cl SW17 ....21 A3
Ramillis Cl GU11 ....105 E7
Ramin Ct GU1 ....109 C4
Ramornie Cl KT12 ....54 F6
Rams La GU8 ....193 B3
Ramsay Rd GU20 ....48 E5
Ramsbury Cl RG12 ....26 E3
Ramsdale Rd SW17 ....21 A3
Ramsdean House 1 SW15 19 B7
Ramsden Rd Balham SW12 .21 A8
Godalming GU7 ....150 D3
Ramsey Cl Camberley GU15 .66 B8
Horley RH6 ....160 F3
Horsham RH12 ....217 D5
Ramsey Ct
18 Crawley RH11 ....201 B1
Croydon CR9 ....61 B8
Ramsey House SW19 ....40 B8
Ramsey Pl CR3 ....100 C5
Ramsey Rd CR7 ....41 F3
Ramslade Rd RG12 ....27 D5
Rances La RG40 ....25 E5
Randal Cres RH2 ....139 A7
Randall Schofield Ct
RH10 ....202 A7
Randalls Cotts KT11 ....73 B7
Randalls Cres KT22 ....95 A7
Randalls Park Ave KT22 ......95 A7
Randalls Park Dr KT22 ....95 A6
Randalls Rd KT22 ....94 E7
Randalls Way KT22 ....95 A7
Randell Cl GU17 ....64 E1
Randisbourne Gdns SE6 ....24 B5
Randle Rd TW10 ....17 C4
Randlesdown Rd SE6 ....24 B5
Randmore Ct 6 BR3 ....24 A1
Randolph Cl
Kingston u T KT2 ....18 C3
Knaphill GU21 ....68 E2
Oxshott KT11 ....74 A4
Randolph Dr GU14 ....84 C3
Randolph Rd KT17 ....76 F5
Ranelagh Cotts RH6 ....162 B2
Ranelagh Cres SL5 ....28 D8
Ranelagh Dr
Bracknell RG12 ....27 C6
Isleworth TW1 ....6 B2
Ranelagh Gdns W4 ....7 C7
Ranelagh Pl KT3 ....38 E4
Ranelagh Rd RH1 ....118 E1
Ranelagh Sch RG12 ....27 C6
Ranfurly Rd SM1 ....59 A8
Range Ride GU15 ....64 F7
Range The GU5 ....152 A4
Range View GU47 ....64 E8
Range Villas TW17 ....33 E2
Range Way TW17 ....34 A2
Rangefield Prim Sch BR1 .24 E3
Rangefield Rd Bromley BR1 24 F3
Catford BR1 ....24 F3
Rankine Cl GU9 ....126 A6
Ranmere St SW12 ....21 B7
Ranmore Ave CR0 ....61 F7
Ranmore Cl RH1 ....119 A4
Ranmore Common Rd
RH5 ....114 D2
Ranmore Ct
Kingston u T KT6 ....37 D4
Wimbledon SW20 ....39 D8
Ranmore Pl KT13 ....53 C5
Ranmore Rd Dorking RH4 .136 A8
East Ewell SM2 ....58 D2
Wotton RH4, RH5 ....114 E1

tann House 🏠 SW14 . . . . . .7 D4
tannoch Ct 🔟 KT6 . . . . . .37 E4
tansford House 🔟 SE21 . . . .22 E4
tansome Cl RH11 . . . . . . .200 E3
tanyard Cl KT9 . . . . .56 F7
tapallo Ct GU14 . . . . .85 C4
taphel Dr KT7 . . . . .37 A2
tapley Cl GU15 . . . . .65 F8
tapley Gn RG12 . . . . .27 C3
tapley's Rd GU24 . . . . . . .87 A2
tapsley La GU21 . . . . .68 B1
tastell Ave SW12 . . . . . . .21 D7
tatcliffe Rd GU14 . . . . . . .85 A8
tathbone House
  Crawley RH11 . . . . .201 B1
  🟦 Wimbledon SW19 . . . . .19 D1
tathern Prim Sch SE21 . . . .23 F7
tathern Rd SE23, SE6 . . . . .23 F7
tathgar Cl RH1 . . . . .140 A4
tathlin Rd RH11 . . . . . . .201 B3
taven Cl RH12 . . . . .217 E6
taven La RH11 . . . . .201 C8
tavendale Rd TW16 . . . . . .34 F7
tavendene Ct 🔟 RH10 . . . .201 D5
tavenfield Rd SW17 . . . . . .20 F5
tavens Cl Bromley BR2 . . . .44 F7
  Redhill RH1 . . . . .118 F2
tavens Wold CR8 . . . . .80 C4
tavensbourne 🔟 TW1 . . . . . .6 C1
tavensbourne Ave
  Bromley BR2, BR3 . . . . . .44 E8
  Catford BR2 . . . . .24 D1
  Stanwell TW19 . . . . .13 E7
tavensbourne Ct SE6 . . . . .23 D4
tavensbourne House BR1 24 D3
tavensbourne Park
  Cres SE6 . . . . .23 F8
tavensbourne Pk SE4, SE6 24 A8
tavensbourne Rd
  Forest Hill SE23 . . . . . . .23 F7
  Twickenham TW1 . . . . .6 C1
tavensbourne Sta BR3 . . . .24 D1
tavensbury Ave SM4 . . . . .40 C4
tavensbury Ct CR4 . . . . . .40 D5
tavensbury Gr CR4 . . . . . .40 D5
tavensbury La CR4 . . . . . .40 D5
tavensbury Rd SW18 . . . . .20 B6
tavensbury Terr SW18 . . . .20 B6
tavenscar Lodge 🔟 SW19 19 D1
tavenscar Rd Catford BR1 . .24 E4
  Surbiton KT6 . . . . .56 F8
tavenscote Cty Jun Sch
  GU16 . . . . .66 A3
tavenscourt TW16 . . . . . . .34 F8
tavenscroft Cl GU12 . . . . .106 C3
tavenscroft Ct RH12 . . . . .217 C3
tavenscroft Rd Penge BR3 .43 D7
  Weybridge KT13 . . . . .72 C8
tavensdale Gdns SE19 . . . .22 D1
tavensdale Rd Ascot SL5 . .29 A4
  Hounslow TW4 . . . . .4 E4
tavensfield TW20 . . . . . . .11 C2
tavensfield Gdns KT19 . . . .57 E6
tavenshead Cl CR2 . . . . . .81 C8
tavenside KT6 . . . . .37 D4
tavenslea Rd SW11, SW12 .20 F8
tavensmead Rd BR2 . . . . .24 D1
tavensroost SE19 . . . . . . .42 D8
tavenstone Jun & Inf Schs
  SW12 . . . . .21 A6
tavenstone Rd GU15 . . . . .66 D5
tavenstone St SW12 . . . . . .21 A7
tavensview Ct KT6 . . . . . . .37 D4
tavenswood Ave
  Tolworth KT6 . . . . .57 A8
  West Wickham BR4 . . . . . .44 C1
tavenswood Cl KT11 . . . . .73 D4
tavenswood Cres BR4 . . . . .44 C1
tavenswood Ct GU21 . . . . .69 F1
tavenswood Dr GU15 . . . . .66 A5
tavenswood Gdns TW7 . . . . .5 E6
tavenswood Rd
  Balham SW12 . . . . .21 B8
  Croydon CR0, CR9 . . . . . .61 B7
tawlins Ct CR2 . . . . .62 F3
tawlinson Rd GU15 . . . . . .64 F6
tawnsley Ave CR4 . . . . . . .40 E4
taworth Cl RH10 . . . . . . .202 C4
tay Cl Chessington KT9 . . . .56 C4
  Lingfield RH7 . . . . .164 C5
tay Cnr RH7 . . . . .164 B6
tay La Blindley Heath RH7 .163 F7
  Lingfield RH7 . . . . .164 B6
  Tandridge RH7 . . . . .164 B6
tay Rd KT8 . . . . .36 B4
taybell Ct TW7 . . . . .5 F5
tayford Ave SE12 . . . . . . .24 F8
tayleigh Ave TW11 . . . . . .16 E2
tayleigh Ct 🟦 KT1 . . . . . .37 F7
tayleigh Rd SW19 . . . . . . .39 F8
tayleigh Rise CR2 . . . . . . .61 E4
taymead Ave CR7 . . . . . . .42 A4
taymead Cl KT22 . . . . . . .94 F5
taymead Way KT22 . . . . . .94 F5
taymer Wlk RH6 . . . . . . .161 C4
taymond Cl
  Forest Hill SE26 . . . . . . .23 C3
  Poyle SL3 . . . . .1 E6
taymond Cres GU2 . . . . . .129 F8
taymond Rd
  Beckenham BR3 . . . . .43 E6
  Wimbledon SW19 . . . . . . .19 E2
taymond Way KT10 . . . . . .56 A4
taynald House 🔟 SW16 . . .21 E5
tayners Cl SL3 . . . . .1 A4
taynes Park High Sch
  KT3 . . . . .39 B6

Raynes Park Sta SW20 . . . .39 C7
Raynesfield SW20 . . . . . . .39 C6
Rays Rd BR4 . . . . .44 C2
Raywood Cl UB7 . . . . .3 C7
Read Rd KT21 . . . . .75 D2
Readens The SM7 . . . . . . .78 F3
Reading Arch Rd RH1 . . . .118 F1
Reading Rd
  Blackwater GU17 . . . . . . .64 B4
  Farnborough GU14 . . . . . .85 D1
  Sutton SM1 . . . . .59 C5
  Wokingham RG41 . . . . . . .25 A7
  Yateley GU17 . . . . .64 B4
Readman Ct 🟦 SM2 . . . . . .59 C4
Reads Rest La KT20 . . . . . .98 A7
Reapers Cl RH12 . . . . . . .217 D5
Reapers Way TW7 . . . . .5 D2
Rebecca Ct BR3 . . . . .44 A8
Recovery St SW17 . . . . . . .20 E3
Recreation Cl GU14 . . . . . .64 F1
Recreation Rd Bromley BR2 44 F7
  Forest Hill SE26 . . . . . . .23 D4
  Guildford GU1 . . . . .109 D1
  Rowledge GU10 . . . . . . .145 E3
Recreation Way CR4, SW16 41 E6
Rectory Cl Ashstead KT21 . .95 F8
  Bracknell RG12 . . . . .27 C5
  Byfleet KT14 . . . . .71 E6
  Ewhurst GU6 . . . . .175 E5
  Godalming GU7 . . . . . . .150 F2
  Guildford GU4 . . . . .110 D3
  Littleton TW17 . . . . .34 A6
  Long Ditton KT6 . . . . . . .37 C1
  Ockley RH5 . . . . .177 C3
  West Barnes SW20 . . . . . .39 C6
  Wokingham RG40 . . . . . . .25 C6
Rectory Ct Cranford TW5 . . . .4 C5
  Feltham TW13 . . . . .15 C4
  Sanderstead CR2 . . . . . . .80 F7
  Wallington SM6 . . . . .60 C6
Rectory Gdns BR3 . . . . . . .44 A8
Rectory Gn BR3 . . . . .43 F8
Rectory Gr
  Croydon CR0, CR9 . . . . . .61 B8
  Hampton TW12, TW13 . . . .15 F4
Rectory La Ashtead KT21 . . .95 F8
  Bracknell RG12 . . . . .27 B5
  Buckland RH3 . . . . .116 F3
  Byfleet KT14 . . . . .71 E6
  Charlwood RH6 . . . . . . .180 D7
  Crawley RH11 . . . . .200 F8
  Great Bookham KT23 . . . .113 F8
  Long Ditton KT6 . . . . . . .37 C1
  Shere GU5 . . . . .133 A4
  Streatham SW17 . . . . . . .21 A3
  Titsey TN16 . . . . .103 E4
  Wallington SM6 . . . . .60 C6
  Windlesham GU20 . . . . . .48 C4
  Woodmansterne CR5, SM7 .78 F3
Rectory Orch SW19 . . . . . .19 E4
Rectory Pk CR2 . . . . .80 F7
Rectory Rd Beckenham BR3 44 A8
  Cranford TW5 . . . . .4 C5
  Farnborough GU14 . . . . . .85 D4
  Lower Kingswood CR5 . . . .98 D2
  Sutton SM1 . . . . .59 B7
  Wokingham RG40 . . . . . . .25 C6
Rectory Row RG12 . . . . . . .27 B5
Rectory Sch SW12 . . . . . . .16 A3
Red Admiral St RH12 . . . .217 E5
Red Deer Cl RH13 . . . . . .218 B4
Red Gables Dr CR2 . . . . . .61 D1
Red House La
  Elstead GU8 . . . . .148 C2
  Walton-on-T KT12 . . . . . .54 A8
Red House Rd CR0, CR9 . . .41 D3
Red La Claygate KT10 . . . . .56 A4
  Headley Down GU35 . . . . .187 B7
  Limpsfield RH8 . . . . .144 B7
  South Holmwood RH5, RH3 .136 F1
Red Lion Bsns Ctr KT6 . . . .56 F7
Red Lion La Chobham GU24 49 E2
  Farnham GU9 . . . . .125 B1
Red Lion Rd Chobham GU24 49 E2
  Surbiton KT6 . . . . .57 A8
Red Lion St TW10 . . . . .6 D2
Red Lodge BR4 . . . . .44 C2
Red Lodge Rd BR3, BR4 . . .44 D2
Red Rd GU18, GU24, GU15 . .67 C7
Red River Ct RH12 . . . . . .217 B5
Redan Cl RH10 . . . . .105 C2
Redan Hill Est GU11 . . . . .105 C2
Redan Rd GU12 . . . . .105 C2
Redbarn Cl CR8 . . . . .80 B8
Redberry Gr CR8 . . . . .23 C5
Redcar House SE26 . . . . . .23 B2
Redcliffe Missionary
  Training Coll W4 . . . . .7 B7
Redclose Ave SM4 . . . . . . .40 A4
Redclyffe Terr 🟦 SM2 . . . . .59 A3
Redcote RH4 . . . . .115 D1
Redcourt Pyrford GU22 . . . .70 E4
  Woking GU22 . . . . .70 D4
Redcrest Gdns GU15 . . . . .65 F5
Redcroft Wlk GU6 . . . . . .174 E2
Redding Way GU21 . . . . . .68 C1
Reddington Cl CR2 . . . . . .61 D2
Redditch RG12 . . . . .27 D2
Redditch Cl RH11 . . . . . . .200 E2
Reddons Rd BR3 . . . . .23 E1
Reddown Rd CR5 . . . . . . .79 D2
Rede Ct KT13 . . . . .53 B7
Redehall Prep Sch RH6 . . .162 B7
Redehall Rd Burstow RH6 .183 C8
  Smallfield RH6 . . . . .162 B2
Redesdale Gdns TW7 . . . . . .6 A7
Redfern Ave TW2, TW4 . . . .16 A4
Redfern Rd SE6 . . . . .24 C8

Redford Ave
  Horsham RH12 . . . . .217 B4
  Thornton Heath CR7 . . . . .41 F5
  Wallington, Clock House CR5 .79 B4
  Wallington, Roundshaw SM6 .60 E4
Redford Cl TW13 . . . . .14 F6
Redgarth Ct RH19 . . . . . .185 B3
Redgrave Ct SE5 . . . . .42 F3
Redgrave Dr RH10 . . . . . .202 D5
Redgrove Ct GU12 . . . . . .105 F2
Redhall Ct CR3 . . . . .100 D4
Redhearne Fields GU10 . . .167 E2
Redhill Cl 🟦 SW2 . . . . . . .22 A6
Redhill Coll RH1 . . . . . . .140 B8
Redhill Distribution Ctr
  RH1 . . . . .161 A8
Redhill Rd KT11 . . . . .72 B5
Redhill Sta RH1 . . . . .119 A2
Redhouse Rd TN16 . . . . . .103 C6
Redkiln Cl RH13 . . . . .217 F4
Redkiln Way RH12, RH13 . .217 F4
Redlake La RG40 . . . . .25 F2
Redland Gdns KT8 . . . . . . .35 F5
Redlands Coulsdon CR5 . . .79 E3
Redlands CE Inf Sch The
  RH4 . . . . .136 B4
Redlands Cotts RH5 . . . . .136 B1
Redlands Ct BR1 . . . . .24 C1
Redlands Cty Jun Sch The
  RH4 . . . . .136 B4
Redlands La
  Crondall GU10 . . . . .124 B7
  Dorking RH5 . . . . .136 A1
Redlands The BR3 . . . . . . .44 B7
Redlands Way 🟦 SW2 . . . .21 F8
Redlane Cotts RH8 . . . . . .123 B2
Redleaves Ave TW15 . . . . .14 B2
Redlees Cl TW7 . . . . .6 A3
Redlin Ct RH1 . . . . .118 F3
Redmayne GU15 . . . . .66 C4
Redmayne Cl BR3 . . . . . . .44 B8
Redmore Rd SW18 . . . . . . .20 A8
Redroofs Cl BR3 . . . . .44 B8
Redruth House SM2 . . . . . .59 B3
Redshank Ct 🟦 RH11 . . . .200 D5
Redstart Cl CR0, CR9 . . . . .63 D1
Redstone Hill RH1 . . . . . .119 A1
Redstone Hollow RH1 . . . .140 A8
Redstone Manor RH1 . . . .119 A1
Redstone Pk RH1 . . . . . . .119 B1
Redstone Rd RH1 . . . . . . .140 A8
Redvers Buller Rd GU11 . .105 D7
Redvers Ct CR6 . . . . .81 C1
Redvers Rd Bracknell RG12 .27 B4
  Warlingham CR6 . . . . .81 D1
Redway Cotts GU21 . . . . . .88 F8
Redway Dr TW2 . . . . .16 C8
Redwing Ave GU7 . . . . . . .150 E8
Redwing Cl Horsham RH13 217 F3
  Selsdon CR2 . . . . .81 D8
Redwing Gdns KT14 . . . . . .71 B7
Redwing Rise GU4 . . . . . . .110 D3
Redwood TW20 . . . . .32 E2
Redwood Cl Crawley RH10 .201 E8
  Kenley CR8 . . . . .80 C5
Redwood Ct 🔟 KT6 . . . . . .37 D2
Redwood Dr Frimley GU15 . .66 D4
  Sunningdale SL5 . . . . .30 B3
Redwood Est TW5 . . . . .4 B8
Redwood Gr GU4 . . . . . . .131 C3
Redwood Manor GU27 . . . .208 C7
Redwood Mount RH2 . . . . .118 A4
Redwood Wlk KT6 . . . . . . .37 D1
Redwoods Addlestone KT15 .52 A4
  Roehampton SW15 . . . . . .19 A7
Reed Cl GU11 . . . . .105 D5
Reed Place Bsns Park
  TW17 . . . . .33 F1
Reed's Hill RG12 . . . . .27 B4
Reed's Sch KT11 . . . . .74 A7
Reedham Dr CR8 . . . . .80 A6
Reedham Park Ave CR8 . . . .80 A3
Reedham Sta CR8 . . . . . . .79 F6
Reedings RH11 . . . . .200 D4
Reeds The
  Frensham GU10 . . . . . . .146 E2
  Tilford GU10 . . . . .147 A3
Reedsfield Cl TW15 . . . . . .14 B5
Reedsfield Rd TW15 . . . . . .14 B4
Rees Gdns CR0 . . . . .42 F3
Reeve Ct GU2 . . . . .109 A5
Reeve Rd RH2 . . . . .139 C5
Reeves Cnr CR0, CR9 . . . . .61 B8
Reeves Rd GU11 . . . . . . .105 C1
Reeves Way RG41 . . . . . . .25 A4
Regal Cres SM6 . . . . .60 B7
Regal Ct 🟦 Guildford GU1 .109 D1
  🟦 Mitcham CR4 . . . . .40 F6
Regal Dr RH19 . . . . .205 F8
Regalfield Cl GU2 . . . . . . .109 A5
Regan Cl GU2 . . . . .109 B6
Regency Cl TW12 . . . . .15 F3
Regency Ct 🟦 Penge SE19 .23 A1
  🟦 Surbiton KT5 . . . . .37 F4
  Sutton SM1 . . . . .59 B6
Regency Dr KT14 . . . . .70 F6
Regency Gdns KT12 . . . . . .35 D1
Regency Lodge KT13 . . . . .53 E7
Regency Mews
  Beckenham BR3 . . . . .44 C8
  Isleworth TW7 . . . . .5 E2
Regency Wlk Croydon CR0 . .43 F3
  🟦 Richmond TW10 . . . . . . .6 E1
Regent Cl Cranford TW5 . . . .4 B6
  New Haw KT15 . . . . .52 D2
Regent Cres RH1 . . . . .118 F3
Regent Ct Bagshot GU19 . . .47 F3

Regent Ct continued
  Guildford GU2 . . . . .109 B3
Regent Lodge 🟦 SW2 . . . . .21 F7
Regent Pk KT22 . . . . .75 A1
Regent Pl Croydon CR0 . . . .42 F1
  Wimbledon SW19 . . . . . . .20 C3
Regent Rd KT5 . . . . .38 A4
Regent St W4 . . . . .7 A8
Regent Way KT16 . . . . .66 A1
Regents Cl Crawley RH11 . .201 C2
  South Croydon CR2 . . . . . .61 E4
  Whyteleafe CR3 . . . . .80 F1
Regents Ct
  🟦 Beckenham BR3 . . . . . .24 A1
  Bromley BR1 . . . . .24 F1
  Weybridge KT13 . . . . .53 B4
Regents Pl
  🟦 Kingston u T KT2 . . . . .37 E8
  Sandhurst GU47 . . . . .64 C8
Regents Wlk SL5 . . . . .29 C2
Regiment Cl GU14 . . . . . . .84 C3
Regina Coeli RC Prim Sch
  CR2 . . . . .61 B3
Regina Rd SE25 . . . . .43 A6
Reginald Ct BR3 . . . . .44 A8
Regis Ct East Bedfont TW14 . .3 D1
  Mitcham SW19 . . . . .40 E8
Regnolruf Ct KT12 . . . . . . .35 A2
Reid Ave CR3 . . . . .100 D6
Reid Ct SW14 . . . . .7 C5
Reidonhill Cotts GU21 . . . .68 B1
Reigate Ave SM3, SM4 . . . .40 B1
Reigate Cl RH10 . . . . .182 D1
Reigate Coll RH2 . . . . . . .118 B1
Reigate Day Hospl RH2 . . .139 A7
Reigate Gram Sch RH1 . . .118 C1
Reigate Heath Cotts RH2 117 C1
Reigate Hill RH2 . . . . .118 B4
Reigate Hill Cl RH2 . . . . . .118 B4
Reigate Parish Church
  Inf Sch RH2 . . . . .118 A1
Reigate Priory Cty Prim
  Sch RH2 . . . . .118 A1
Reigate Rd Banstead KT17 .77 C4
  Betchworth RH3, RH4,
    RH2, RH5 . . . . .116 D2
  Brockham RH3, RH4, RH2
    , RH5 . . . . .116 D2
  Burgh Heath KT18 . . . . . .77 C4
  Catford BR1 . . . . .24 F5
  Dorking RH4 . . . . .115 E1
  Ewell KT17 . . . . .77 C4
  Hookwood RH6 . . . . .160 C4
  Leatherhead KT22 . . . . . .95 D4
  Reigate RH2 . . . . .118 C1
  Sidlow RH2, RH6 . . . . . .160 C4
Reigate Sch RH2 . . . . .139 C6
Reigate Sch of Art &
  Design RH2 . . . . .118 D1
Reigate St Mary's Prep
  Sch RH2 . . . . .118 B1
Reigate Sta RH2 . . . . .118 A2
Reigate Way SM6 . . . . .60 E5
Reindorp Cl GU2 . . . . . . .130 A8
Relko Ct RH19 . . . . .76 D8
Relko Gdns SM1 . . . . .59 D5
Rembrandt Ct KT19 . . . . . .57 F4
Rembrandt Way KT12 . . . . .54 B8
Rendle Cl CR0, SE25 . . . . .43 A4
Renfree Way TW17 . . . . . . .34 A2
Renfrew Ct TW5 . . . . .4 E5
Renfrew Rd Hounslow TW5 . .4 E5
  Kingston u T KT2 . . . . . . .18 C1
Renmans The KT21 . . . . . .75 F3
Renmuir St SW17 . . . . . . .20 F2
Rennie Cl TW15 . . . . .13 D5
Rennie Terr RH1 . . . . .140 A8
Renown Cl CR0 . . . . .42 B1
Renshaw House 🟦 SW27 . .22 B3
Replingham Rd SW18 . . . . .20 A7
Repton Cl SM1, SM5 . . . . . .59 E5
Repton Ct BR3 . . . . .44 B8
Restmor Way SM5, SM6 . . .60 A8
Restormel Cl TW3 . . . . .5 A2
Restwell Ave GU6 . . . . . . .174 B6
Retreat Rd TW9 . . . . .6 D2
Retreat The
  Englefield Green TW20 . . .11 C3
  Mortlake SW14 . . . . .7 E4
  North Cheam KT4 . . . . . . .58 B8
  South Norwood CR7 . . . . .42 D5
  Surbiton KT5 . . . . .37 F3
Revell Cl KT22 . . . . .94 B5
Revell Dr KT22 . . . . .94 B5
Revell Rd Cheam SM1 . . . . .58 F4
  Kingston u T KT1 . . . . . . .38 B8
Revelstoke Ave GU14 . . . . .85 B6
Revelstoke Rd SW18, SW19 20 A6
Revesby Cl GU24 . . . . .67 D6
Revesby Rd SM5 . . . . .40 E3
Rewley Rd SM4 . . . . .40 D3
Rex Ave TW15 . . . . .14 A3
Rex House TW13 . . . . .15 E5
Reynard Cl RH12 . . . . . . .218 B5
Reynard Dr SE19 . . . . .22 F1
Reynolds Ave KT9 . . . . . . .56 E3
Reynolds Cl
  Carshalton SM4, SM5 . . . .40 F1
  Mitcham CR4, SW19 . . . . .40 D8
Reynolds Pl Crawley RH11 201 C7
  🟦 Richmond TW10 . . . . . . .6 F1
Reynolds Rd
  Crawley RH11 . . . . .201 C7
  New Malden KT3 . . . . . . .38 D2
Reynolds Way CR0 . . . . . . .61 E6
Rheingold Way SM6 . . . . . .60 E2
Rhine Banks GU14 . . . . . . .84 D5

Rhodes Cl TW20 . . . . .12 B3
Rhodes Ct TW20 . . . . .12 C3
Rhodes Way RH10 . . . . . . .201 F3
Rhodes-Moorhouse Ct
  SM4 . . . . .40 A3
Rhododendron Cl SL5 . . . . .8 E1
Rhododendron Rd GU16 . . .86 B8
Rhododendron Ride
  SL4, TW20 . . . . .10 F3
Rhododendron Wlk SL5 . . . .8 E1
Rhodrons Ave KT9 . . . . . . .56 E5
Rialto Rd CR4 . . . . .41 A7
Ribble Pl GU14 . . . . .84 E7
Ribblesdale RH4 . . . . .136 B5
Ribblesdale Rd SW16 . . . . .21 B3
Ricardo Rd GU5 . . . . .151 F5
Ricards Lodge High Sch
  SW19 . . . . .19 F3
Ricards Rd SW19 . . . . .19 F3
Rice's Cnr GU4 . . . . .131 A2
Rices Hill RH19 . . . . .185 E1
Richard Atkins Prim Sch
  SW2 . . . . .21 E8
Richard Challoner Sch
  KT3 . . . . .38 D2
Richard Thornton House
  SW19 . . . . .40 A7
Richards Cl Ash GU12 . . . .106 A5
  Harlington UB3 . . . . .3 D8
Richards Ct BR3 . . . . .43 D8
Richards Field KT19 . . . . . .57 D2
Richards Rd KT11 . . . . . . .74 B5
Richardson Ct 🟦 RH11 . . .201 B1
Richardson House TW7 . . . .5 F4
Richardson's Lawn Cotts
  SL4 . . . . .10 B5
Richbell Cl KT21 . . . . .75 D1
Richens Cl TW3 . . . . .5 D5
Richfield Ct BR3 . . . . .43 F8
Richland Ave CR5 . . . . .79 A5
Richlands Ave KT17 . . . . . .58 A6
Richmond Adult Coll TW9 9 D3
Richmond Athletic Gd TW9 6 D3
Richmond Ave
  Feltham TW14 . . . . .3 E1
  Merton SW20 . . . . .39 E8
Richmond Bridge TW1 . . . . .6 D1
Richmond Bridge
  Mansions 🟦 TW1 . . . . . . .6 D1
Richmond Cl
  Biggin Hill TN16 . . . . . . .103 B8
  Epsom KT18 . . . . .76 E5
  Farnborough GU14 . . . . . .84 D3
  Fetcham KT23 . . . . .94 C3
  Frimley GU16 . . . . .65 F1
Richmond Coll TW10 . . . . .17 E8
Richmond Cres TW18 . . . . .12 F3
Richmond Ct
  🟦 Kingston u T KT2 . . . . .18 A1
  Mitcham CR4 . . . . .40 D6
  Wimbledon SW20 . . . . . . .39 B7
Richmond Dr TW17 . . . . . .34 D3
Richmond Gn CR0 . . . . . . .60 E7
Richmond Hill TW10 . . . . . .6 E1
Richmond Hill Ct 🟦 TW10 . .6 E1
Richmond House
  🟦 Forest Hill SE26 . . . . . .23 A5
  Sandhurst GU47 . . . . .64 E7
Richmond House
  (Annexe of Rectory Sch)
  TW12 . . . . .15 F3
Richmond Mansions 🟦
  TW1 . . . . .6 D1
Richmond Park Rd
  Kingston u T KT2 . . . . . . .17 E1
  Mortlake SW14 . . . . .7 D3
Richmond Rd Coulsdon CR5 79 B4
  Farncombe GU7 . . . . . . .150 E6
  Horsham RH12 . . . . .217 D4
  Isleworth TW7 . . . . .6 A4
  Kingston u T KT2 . . . . . . .17 E2
  Sandhurst GU47 . . . . .64 E8
  Staines TW18 . . . . .12 F3
  Thornton Heath CR7 . . . . .42 B5
  Twickenham TW1 . . . . . . .17 B8
  Wallington CR0 . . . . .60 E7
  Wimbledon SW20 . . . . . . .39 B8
Richmond Sq RH19 . . . . . .185 D2
Richmond Sta TW9 . . . . . . .6 E3
Richmond Upon Thames
  Coll TW2 . . . . .16 E8
Richmond Way
  East Grinstead RH19 . . . .205 F8
  Fetcham KT23 . . . . .94 C3
Richmondwood SL5 . . . . . .30 B1
Rickard Cl SW2 . . . . .22 A7
Rickards Cl KT6 . . . . .56 E8
Ricketts Hill Rd TN16 . . . .103 E7
Rickfield RH11 . . . . .201 A5
Rickford Hill GU3 . . . . .88 D1
Rickman Cl RG12 . . . . .27 C3
Rickman Cres KT15 . . . . . .52 B7
Rickman Ct KT15 . . . . .52 B7
Rickman Hill CR5 . . . . .79 B2
Rickman Hill Rd CR5 . . . . .79 B2
Rickman's La RH14 . . . . . .211 F2
Ricksons La KT24 . . . . . . .112 B8
Rickwood RH6 . . . . .161 B4
Rickyard GU2 . . . . .108 D1
Riddens The RH12 . . . . . . .214 A6
Riddings The CR3 . . . . . . .100 F2
Riddlesdown Ave CR8 . . . . .80 C7
Riddlesdown High Sch
  CR2 . . . . .80 E5
Riddlesdown Rd CR3, CR8 .80 D5

Riddlesdown Sta CR8 . . . . .80 C6
Ride La GU5 . . . . .153 D7
Ride The RH14 . . . . .212 C2
Ride Way GU5, GU6 . . . . . .154 C1
Riders Way RH9 . . . . .121 C4
Rideway Cl GU15 . . . . .65 B4
Ridge Cl Brockham RH3 . . .137 B5
Woking GU22 . . . . .89 B6
Ridge Ct CR6 . . . . .81 A1
Ridge Gn RH1 . . . . .140 E6
Ridge Green Cl RH1 . . . . . .140 E6
Ridge House ☑ KT2 . . . . . . .18 B1
Ridge Langley CR2 . . . . . . .62 A2
Ridge Moor Cl GU26 . . . . .188 E5
Ridge Mount Rd SL5 . . . . . .30 A1
Ridge Pk CR8, SM6 . . . . . . .60 D1
Ridge Prim Sch SM3 . . . . . .39 E3
Ridge Rd Cheam SM3, SM4 . .39 F1
Mitcham CR4 . . . . .21 B1
Ridge The Coulsdon CR5 . . .79 E5
Epsom RH4 . . . . .94 D3
Fetcham KT22 . . . . .94 D3
Limpsfield CR3, CR6 . . . . .102 D2
Surbiton KT5 . . . . .38 A4
Twickenham TW2 . . . . .16 D8
Wallington CR8 . . . . .60 D1
Woking GU22 . . . . .70 B2
Woldingham CR3 . . . . .102 D2
Ridge Way Feltham TW13 . . .15 E5
Thorpe GU25 . . . . .31 E4
Ridge Way The CR2 . . . . . . .61 E1
Ridgedale RH10 . . . . .204 B8
Ridgegate Cl RH4 . . . . . . .118 D3
Ridgehurst Dr RH12 . . . . .216 F1
Ridgelands KT22 . . . . .94 D3
Ridgemead Rd TW20 . . . . . .11 B5
Ridgemount Guildford GU2 130 B8
Oatlands Park KT13 . . . . . .53 E8
Ridgemount Ave
Coulsdon CR5 . . . . .79 B2
Croydon CR0 . . . . .62 D8
Ridgemount Cl SE20 . . . . . .23 B1
Ridgemount Est GU16 . . . . .86 C7
Ridgemount Way RH1 . . . . .139 D7
Ridges The GU3 . . . . .130 C4
Ridgeside RH10 . . . . .201 F6
Ridgeway
East Grinstead RH19 . . . . .205 E7
Epsom KT19 . . . . .76 C7
Pyrford GU22 . . . . .71 A4
☑ Richmond TW10 . . . . .6 E1
Walton-on-T KT12 . . . . . . .34 F1
Wimbledon SW19, SW20 . . . .19 D2
Woking GU21 . . . . .69 D4
Ridgeway Cl
Cranleigh GU6 . . . . .175 A3
Dorking RH4 . . . . .136 A5
Lightwater GU18 . . . . .67 A8
Oxshott KT22 . . . . .74 C5
Woking GU21 . . . . .69 D4
Ridgeway Ct RH1 . . . . . . .118 F1
Ridgeway Dr RH4 . . . . . . .136 A4
Ridgeway Gdns GU21 . . . . . .69 D4
Ridgeway Prim Sch CR2 . . . .61 E1
Ridgeway Rd Dorking RH4 136 A4
Hounslow TW7 . . . . .5 E6
Redhill RH1 . . . . .118 F1
Ridgeway Rd N TW7 . . . . . . .5 E7
Ridgeway Sch The GU9 . . .146 C7
Ridgeway The
Bracknell RG12 . . . . .27 C6
Brookwood GU24 . . . . .88 A7
Cranleigh GU6 . . . . .174 F3
Croydon CR0 . . . . .60 F7
Fetcham KT22 . . . . .94 D3
Guildford GU1 . . . . .131 A8
Horley RH6 . . . . .161 A1
Horsham RH12 . . . . .217 B4
Lightwater GU18 . . . . .48 B1
Oxshott KT22 . . . . .74 C5
Ridgewell Cl SE26 . . . . . . .23 F4
Ridgewood Ctr (Hospl)
GU16 . . . . .66 C3
Ridgley Rd GU8 . . . . .191 B4
Ridgway Ct SW19 . . . . .19 D2
Ridgway Gdns SW19 . . . . . .19 D1
Ridgway Hill Rd GU9 . . . . .146 C8
Ridgway Pl SW19 . . . . .19 E2
Ridgway Rd Farnham GU9 .146 C8
Pyrford GU22 . . . . .70 F4
Ridgway The SM2 . . . . .59 D4
Riding Hill CR2 . . . . .81 A6
Riding The Cranleigh GU6 .174 E4
Sheerwater GU21 . . . . .70 B5
Ridings The
Addlestone KT15 . . . . .51 E4
Ashtead KT21 . . . . .75 D2
Biggin Hill TN16 . . . . .83 E2
Cobham KT11 . . . . .74 A7
Crawley RH10 . . . . .202 D7
East Horsley KT24 . . . . . . .92 F2
Epsom KT18 . . . . .76 F4
Ewell KT17 . . . . .57 F2
Frimley GU16 . . . . .66 B3
Kingswood KT20 . . . . .97 F7
Redhill RH2 . . . . .118 D3
Send Marsh GU23 . . . . .91 A4
Sunbury TW16 . . . . .35 A8
Surbiton KT5 . . . . .38 A4
Ridlands Gr RH8 . . . . .123 E5
Ridlands La RH8 . . . . .123 E5
Ridlands Rise RH8 . . . . . . .123 E4
Ridley Cl SW16 . . . . .21 E2
Ridley Rd Bromley BR2 . . . .44 F6
Merton SW19 . . . . .20 B1

Ridley Rd continued
Warlingham CR6 . . . . .81 D1
Ridsdale Rd Penge SE20 . . . .43 B8
Woking GU21 . . . . .69 B2
Riesco Dr CR0 . . . . .62 C4
Rifle Way GU14 . . . . .84 C3
Rigby Cl CR0, CR9 . . . . . . .61 A7
Rigg House ☑ SW4 . . . . . . .21 E8
Rikkyo Sch in England
The RH14 . . . . .213 D8
Riley House ☑ SW4 . . . . . . .21 D8
Rill Wlk RH19 . . . . .186 B1
Rillside RH10 . . . . .202 A3
Rimbault Cl GU11 . . . . . . .105 E7
Rinaldo Rd SW12 . . . . .21 B8
Ring Rd N RH6 . . . . .182 C8
Ring Rd S RH6 . . . . .182 C7
Ring The RG12 . . . . .27 C7
Ringley Ave RH6 . . . . .161 A2
Ringley Oak RH12 . . . . . . .217 F4
Ringley Park Ave RH2 . . . .139 D8
Ringley Park Rd RH2 . . . . .118 C1
Ringley Rd RH12 . . . . .217 E4
Ringmead Bracknell, Great
Hollands RG12 . . . . .26 C4
Bracknell, Hanworth RG12 . .27 B2
Ringmore Dr GU4 . . . . . . .110 C4
Ringmore Rd KT12 . . . . . . .54 C7
Ringmore Rise SE23 . . . . . .23 B8
Ringstead Rd
Carshalton SM1 . . . . .59 D5
Lewisham SE6 . . . . .24 B8
Ringwold Cl BR3 . . . . .23 E1
Ringwood RG12 . . . . .26 F2
Ringwood Ave Redhill RH1 118 F4
Thornton Heath CR0, CR9 . .41 E2
Ringwood Cl Ascot SL5 . . . .29 B5
Crawley RH10 . . . . .201 E4
Ringwood Gdns SW15 . . . . .19 A7
Ringwood Lodge ☑ RH1 .119 A4
Ringwood Rd
Blackwater GU17 . . . . .64 C6
Farnborough GU14 . . . . . . .85 C7
Thornton Heath CR0, CR9 . .41 E2
Ringwood Way TW12 . . . . . .16 A4
Ripley Ave TW20 . . . . .11 B2
Ripley By-Pass
Ockham GU23 . . . . .91 C4
Ripley GU23 . . . . .91 C4
Ripley C of E Inf Sch GU23 91 B6
Ripley Cl CR0 . . . . .63 C4
Ripley Court Sch Rose La
GU23 . . . . .91 C6
Ripley Ct CR4 . . . . .40 D7
Ripley Gdns Mortlake SW14 . .7 D4
Sutton SM1 . . . . .59 C6
Ripley House
☑ Kingston u T KT2 . . . . . .18 B2
Mortlake SW14 . . . . .7 E4
☑ Penge SE26 . . . . .23 B3
Ripley La RH9 Ripley GU23 . .91 F3
West Horsley KT24, GU23 . .112 A7
Ripley Rd
East Clandon GU4 . . . . . . .111 D6
Hampton TW12 . . . . .16 A1
Ripley GU23, GU4 . . . . . . .111 D7
Riplington Ct SW15 . . . . . . .19 B8
Ripon Cl Frimley GU15 . . . .66 D3
Guildford GU2 . . . . .108 F3
Ripon Gdns KT9 . . . . .56 D5
Ripon Rd GU14 . . . . .84 A7
Ripplesmere RG12 . . . . .27 D4
Ripplesmere Cl GU47 . . . . . .64 B8
Ripston Rd TW15 . . . . .14 D3
Risborough Dr KT4 . . . . . . .39 A2
Rise Rd SL5 . . . . .29 F3
Rise The Crawley RH10 . . . .202 D6
Crowthorne RG45 . . . . .45 A5
East Grinstead RH19 . . . . .205 F8
East Horsley KT24 . . . . . . .92 E1
Ewell KT17 . . . . .57 F1
South Croydon CR2 . . . . . .62 C2
Tadworth KT20 . . . . .97 C6
Wokingham RG41 . . . . .25 A7
Ritchie Cl RH10 . . . . .202 C2
Ritchie Rd CR0 . . . . .43 B3
Ritherdon Rd SW17 . . . . . . .21 B6
River Ave KT7 . . . . .37 A2
River Bank KT7 . . . . .36 F4
River Crane Way TW13 . . . . .15 F6
River Ct Kingston u T KT6 . .37 D4
Sheerwater GU21 . . . . .70 C5
River Gdns Carshalton SM5 .60 A7
Feltham TW14 . . . . .4 B2
River Gdns Bsns Ctr TW14 . .4 B3
River Grove Pk BR3 . . . . . . .43 F8
River Hill KT11 . . . . .73 B4
River House
Forest Hill SE26 . . . . .23 B5
Mortlake SW13 . . . . .7 E5
River Island Cl KT22 . . . . . .94 D7
River La Cobham KT11 . . . . .73 E3
Farnham GU10, GU9 . . . . .145 E7
Fetcham KT22 . . . . .94 D6
Leatherhead KT22 . . . . . . .94 E7
Richmond TW10 . . . . .17 D7
Wrecclesham GU10, GU9 . .145 E7
River Mead Crawley RH10 .181 A1
Horsham RH12 . . . . .217 B1
River Meads Ave
TW13, TW2 . . . . .16 B5
River Mount KT12 . . . . .34 F2
River Mount Gdns GU2 . . . .130 C6
River Park Ave TW18 . . . . . .12 D4
River Pk RH18 . . . . .32 F8
River Reach TW11 . . . . .17 C3
River View SE16 . . . . .52 C5
River View Gdns TW1 . . . . . .16 F6

River Way
Twickenham TW13, TW2 . . . .16 B6
West Ewell KT19 . . . . .57 E5
River Wlk KT12 . . . . .35 A3
Riverbank East Molesey KT8 36 E5
Staines TW18 . . . . .12 F2
Riverbank Way TW8 . . . . . . .6 C8
Riverdale Dorking RH4 . . . .115 C3
Wrecclesham GU10 . . . . . .145 E7
Riverdale Dr
Wandsworth SW18 . . . . . . .20 B7
Woking GU22 . . . . .89 F6
Riverdale Gdns TW1 . . . . . . .6 C2
Riverdale Rd Feltham TW13 .15 F4
Twickenham TW1 . . . . .6 C1
Riverdene Ind Est KT12 . . . .54 D5
Riverfield Rd TW18 . . . . . . .12 F2
Riverhead Dr SM2 . . . . .59 B1
Riverholme Dr KT19 . . . . . .57 E2
Rivermead Byfleet KT14 . . . .71 F6
East Molesey KT8 . . . . .36 C6
Kingston u T KT6 . . . . .37 D4
Rivermead Cl
New Haw KT15 . . . . .52 C3
Richmond TW11 . . . . .17 B3
Rivermead House TW16 . . . .35 C6
Rivermead Rd GU15 . . . . . . .65 B2
Rivernook Cl KT12 . . . . . . .35 C4
Rivers Cl GU14 . . . . .85 E1
Riversdale Prim Sch
SW18 . . . . .20 A7
Riversdale Rd KT7 . . . . .37 A3
Riversdell Cl KT16 . . . . . . .32 F2
Riverside Catford SE6 . . . . .23 F4
Dorking RH4 . . . . .115 D1
Egham TW20 . . . . .12 A5
Forest Row RH18 . . . . . . .206 E3
Guildford GU1 . . . . .109 D3
Horley RH6 . . . . .161 A1
Horsham RH12 . . . . .217 A2
Oatlands Park TW17 . . . . . .34 E2
Sunbury TW16 . . . . .35 D7
Twickenham TW1 . . . . .17 B7
Wraysbury TW19 . . . . .11 C8
Riverside Ave
East Molesey KT8 . . . . .36 D4
Lightwater GU18 . . . . .67 C8
Riverside Bsns Ctr
Guildford GU1 . . . . .109 C1
Wandsworth SW18 . . . . . . .20 B7
Riverside Bsns Pk
Farnham GU9 . . . . .125 D3
Merton SW19 . . . . .40 C8
Riverside Cl
Brookwood GU24 . . . . .87 F7
Farnborough GU14 . . . . . . .84 F5
Hackbridge SM6 . . . . .60 B7
Kingston u T KT1 . . . . .37 D5
Staines TW18 . . . . .32 F8
Riverside Ct Dorking RH4 .115 D1
Farnham GU9 . . . . .125 D3
Teddington KT1 . . . . .37 D5
Riverside Dr Bramley GU5 152 A7
Chiswick W4 . . . . .7 E6
Egham TW18 . . . . .12 E3
Esher KT10 . . . . .55 A6
Mitcham CR4 . . . . .40 E4
Richmond TW10 . . . . .17 B5
Staines TW18 . . . . .32 F8
Riverside Gdns
Cobham KT11 . . . . .73 A6
Old Woking GU22 . . . . .90 B6
Riverside House TW9 . . . . . .40 C5
Riverside Ind Pk GU9 . . . . .125 C3
Riverside L Ctr W4 . . . . .7 E6
Riverside Pk GU9 . . . . . . .125 D3
Riverside Pl TW19 . . . . .2 D1
Riverside Rd Hersham KT12 54 E6
Staines TW18 . . . . .12 F1
Stanwell TW19 . . . . .2 C1
Wandsworth SW17, SW19 . .20 C5
Riverside The KT8 . . . . .36 D6
Riverside Way GU15 . . . . . . .65 A3
Riverside Wlk Isleworth TW7 .5 E4
West Wickham BR4 . . . . . . .44 B1
Riverstone Ct KT2 . . . . .37 F8
Riverview GU14 . . . . .34 D2
Riverview Cty Fst Sch
KT19 . . . . .57 D6
Riverview Gr W4 . . . . .7 B8
Riverview Pk SE6 . . . . .24 A6
Riverview Rd Chiswick W4 . . .7 B8
West Ewell KT19 . . . . .57 D6
Riverway TW18 . . . . .33 B8
Riverway Est GU3 . . . . . . .151 C8
Riverwood Cl GU1 . . . . . . .109 C3
Rivey Cl KT14 . . . . .70 F5
Road House Est GU22 . . . . .90 A7
Roakes Ave KT15 . . . . .52 B8
Robert C KT12 . . . . .54 B5
Robert Gerard House ☑
SE27 . . . . .22 D4
Robert May Cty Fst Sch
The RH10 . . . . .201 F4
Robert St CR0, CR9 . . . . . .61 C7
Robert Way
Horsham RH12 . . . . .217 F7
Mytchett GU16 . . . . .85 F3
Roberts Cl Cheam SM3 . . . . .58 D3
Stanwell TW19 . . . . .2 C1
Roberts Ct SE20 . . . . .43 C8
Roberts House ☑ SE27 . . . . .22 B5
Roberts Rd
Aldershot GU12 . . . . .105 D1
Sandhurst GU15 . . . . .65 A6
Roberts Way TW20 . . . . . . .11 C1

Robertsbridge Rd SM5 . . . .40 D2
Robertson Ct ☑ GU21 . . . . .68 E1
Robertson House SW17 . . . .20 E3
Robertson Way GU12 . . . . .105 F1
Robey Dr RG12 . . . . .27 D2
Robin Cl Addlestone KT15 . .52 D5
Ash Vale GU12 . . . . .106 A3
Crawley RH10 . . . . .201 C8
East Grinstead RH19 . . . . .185 F2
Hampton TW12 . . . . .15 E3
Robin Ct SM6 . . . . .60 C4
Robin Gdns RH1 . . . . .119 A3
Robin Gr TW8 . . . . .6 C8
Robin Hill GU7 . . . . .150 D7
Robin Hill Dr GU15 . . . . . . .66 A3
Robin Hood Cl
Farnborough GU14 . . . . . . .85 A7
Knaphill GU21 . . . . .68 F1
Woking GU4 . . . . .89 F3
Robin Hood Cres GU21 . . . .68 E2
Robin Hood Ct SM1 . . . . . . .59 B5
Robin Hood Inf Sch SM1 .59 A5
Robin Hood Jun Sch SM1 .59 B5
Robin Hood La
Kingston u T SW15 . . . . . . .18 E4
Sutton SM1 . . . . .59 B5
Warnham RH12 . . . . .216 F5
Woking GU4 . . . . .89 F3
Robin Hood Prim Sch
SW15 . . . . .18 E3
Robin Hood Rd
Knaphill GU21 . . . . .68 F1
Knaphill GU21 . . . . .68 F1
Robin Hood Rdbt SW15 . . . .18 E5
Robin Hood Way
(Kingston By Pass)
KT2, SW15, SW20 . . . . . . .18 E3
Robin Hood Works GU21 . .68 E2
Robin La GU47 . . . . .45 C1
Robin Way Guildford GU2 .109 B5
Staines TW18 . . . . .12 F5
Robin's Bow GU15 . . . . .65 B4
Robin's Ct BR3 . . . . .44 D7
Robinhood Cl CR4 . . . . .41 C6
Robinhood La CR4 . . . . .41 C6
Robins Ct TW10 . . . . .6 E1
Robins Dale GU21 . . . . .68 C2
Robinson Ct ☑ TW9 . . . . . . .6 F3
Robinson Rd
Crawley RH11 . . . . .201 D5
Mitcham SW19 . . . . .20 E2
Robinsway KT12 . . . . .54 C6
Robinswood Ct RH12 . . . . .217 F4
Robinwood Pl SW15 . . . . . .18 D4
Robson Rd SE21, SE27 . . . .22 C5
Roby Dr RG12 . . . . .27 D2
Rochdale ☑ SE19 . . . . .22 E2
Roche Rd SW16 . . . . .41 F8
Roche Wlk SM4, SM5 . . . . .40 D3
Rochelle Ct BR3 . . . . .24 B1
Rochester Ave TW13 . . . . . .14 F6
Rochester Cl SW16 . . . . . . .21 E1
Rochester Ct SE25 . . . . . . .43 A7
Rochester Gdns
Caterham CR3 . . . . .100 C5
South Croydon CR0 . . . . . .61 E7
Rochester Par TW13 . . . . . .15 A5
Rochester Rd
Carshalton SM5 . . . . .59 F6
Egham TW20 . . . . .12 D2
Rochester Wlk RH2 . . . . . .139 B5
Rochford Way CR0 . . . . . . .41 E3
Rock Ave ☑ SW14 . . . . .7 D4
Rock Gdns GU11 . . . . .104 F1
Rock Hill SE19 . . . . .22 F1
Rock La GU10 . . . . .146 A5
Rockbourne Rd SE23 . . . . . .23 D7
Rockdale Dr GU26 . . . . . . .188 D3
Rockery The GU14 . . . . .84 E3
Rockfield Cl RH8 . . . . .122 F4
Rockfield Rd RH8 . . . . .122 F5
Rockfield Way ☑ GU47 . . . . .64 D8
Rockhampton Cl ☑ SE27 . . .22 A4
Rockhampton Rd
South Croydon CR2 . . . . . .61 E4
West Norwood SE27, SW16 . .22 A4
Rockingham Cl SW15 . . . . . .7 F3
Rockingham Ct ☑ BR3 . . . . .24 A1
Rockmount Jun Mix &
Inf Lower Schs SE19 . . . .22 D2
Rockmount Jun Mix &
Inf Upper Schs SE19 . . . .22 D2
Rockmount Rd SE19 . . . . . .22 D2
Rocks The RH19 . . . . .206 D6
Rockshaw Rd
Caterham RH1 . . . . .119 E8
Merstham RH1 . . . . .119 E8
Rockwell Gdns SE19 . . . . . .22 E4
Rocky La RH1, RH2 . . . . . .119 A6
Rocombe Cres SE23 . . . . . .23 C8
Rodborough Sch GU8 . . . .170 F7
Rodd Est TW17 . . . . .34 D4
Roden Gdns CR0, SE25 . . . .42 E3
Rodgate La GU27 . . . . .209 E5
Rodgers House ☑ SW4 . . . .21 D8
Roding Cl GU6 . . . . .173 F2
Rodmel Ct GU14 . . . . .85 E1
Rodmill La SW2 . . . . .21 E8
Rodney Cl New Malden KT3 .38 E4
Thornton Heath CR0 . . . . . .42 D6
Walton-on-T KT12 . . . . . . .35 C1
Rodney Gn ☑ KT12 . . . . . . .54 C8
Rodney Pl SW19 . . . . .40 C8
Rodney Rd Mitcham CR4 . . .40 E6
New Malden KT3 . . . . .38 E4
Twickenham TW4 . . . . .16 A8
Walton-on-T KT12 . . . . . . .54 C8
Rodney Way
Guildford GU1 . . . . .110 A2

Rodney Way continued
Poyle SL3 . . . . .1 E?
Rodona Rd KT13 . . . . .72 C?
Rodway Rd SW15 . . . . .19 A?
Rodwell Cl Addlestone KT15 52 C?
Walton-on-T KT12 . . . . . . .54 B?
Roe Way SM6 . . . . .60 E?
Roebuck Cl Ashtead KT21 . .95 E?
Feltham TW13 . . . . .15 E?
Horsham RH13 . . . . .218 B?
Reigate RH2 . . . . .118 A?
Roebuck Ct ☑ KT3 . . . . . . .38 E?
Roebuck Rd KT9 . . . . .57 A?
Roedean Cres SW15 . . . . . . .7 E?
Roedeer Copse GU27 . . . . .207 E?
Roehampton CE Prim Sch
SW15 . . . . .19 A?
Roehampton Club Golf
Course SW15 . . . . .19 A?
Roehampton Gate SW15 . . . .7 E?
Roehampton Gate Cty
Prim Sch SW15 . . . . .7 E?
Roehampton High St
SW15 . . . . .19 A?
Roehampton La
Putney SW15, SW19 . . . . . .19 A?
Roehampton SW15, SW19 . .19 A?
Roehampton Vale SW15 . . .18 F?
Roffes La CR3 . . . . .100 D?
Roffey Cl Horley RH6 . . . . .160 F?
Purley CR8 . . . . .80 B?
Roffey Cnr RH12 . . . . .218 B?
Roffey's Cl RH10 . . . . .183 A?
Roffords GU21 . . . . .69 B?
Roger Simmons Ct KT23 . .94 A?
Rogers Cl Caterham CR3 . . .101 D?
Coulsdon CR5, CR8 . . . . . . .80 B?
Rogers La CR6 . . . . .81 F?
Rogers Mead RH9 . . . . . . .121 B?
Rogers Rd SW17 . . . . .20 E?
Rogosa Rd GU24 . . . . .67 E?
Rojack Rd SE23 . . . . .23 D?
Roke Cl Purley CR8 . . . . . . .80 C?
Witley GU8 . . . . .170 E?
Roke La GU8 . . . . .170 E?
Roke Lane Cotts GU8 . . . . .170 F?
Roke Lodge Rd CR8 . . . . . . .80 B?
Roke Prim Sch Purley CR8 .80 B?
Purley CR8 . . . . .80 C?
Roke Rd CR8 . . . . .80 C?
Rokeby Cl RG12 . . . . .27 D?
Rokeby Ct GU21 . . . . .68 F?
Rokeby House ☑ SW12 . . . .21 B?
Rokeby Pl SW20 . . . . .19 B?
Rokeby Sch KT2 . . . . .18 C?
Rokell House BR3 . . . . .24 B?
Rokers La GU8 . . . . .149 D?
Roland Ct SE19 . . . . .42 F?
Roland Way KT4 . . . . .57 F?
Rollesby Rd KT19, KT9 . . . .57 A?
Rolleston Rd CR2 . . . . .61 D?
Rollit Cres TW3 . . . . .5 A?
Roma Read Cl SW15 . . . . . .19 B?
Roman Cl TW14 . . . . .4 C?
Roman Ind Est CR0 . . . . . . .42 E?
Roman Rd RH4 . . . . .136 B?
Roman Rise SE19 . . . . .22 D?
Roman Way Croydon CR9 . . .61 B?
Farnham GU9 . . . . .125 C?
Thornton Heath CR9 . . . . . .61 B?
Winkfield RG42 . . . . .27 F?
Romana Ct TW18 . . . . .13 A?
Romanby Ct ☑ RH1 . . . . . .139 F?
Romanfield Rd SW2 . . . . . . .21 F?
Romanhurst Ave BR2 . . . . . .44 E?
Romanhurst Gdns
BR2, BR3 . . . . .44 E?
Romans Bsns Pk GU9 . . . .125 D?
Romans Ind Pk GU9 . . . . .125 D?
Romans Way GU22 . . . . . . .71 A?
Romany Gdns SM3 . . . . . . .40 A?
Romany Prospect SE19 . . . .22 D?
Romayne Cl GU14 . . . . .85 A?
Romberg Rd SW17 . . . . .21 A?
Romeo Hill RG42 . . . . .27 F?
Romeyn Rd SW16 . . . . .21 F?
Romley Ct GU9 . . . . .125 D?
Rommany Ct SE27 . . . . .22 D?
Rommany Rd SE27 . . . . . . .22 D?
Romney Cl Ashford TW15 . .14 C?
Chessington KT9 . . . . .56 E?
Romney House RG12 . . . . . .27 E?
Romney Rd KT3 . . . . .38 D?
Romola Rd SE24, SW2 . . . . .22 B?
Romsey Cl Aldershot GU11 126 C?
Blackwater GU17 . . . . .64 C?
Romulus Ct ☑ TW8 . . . . . . .6 D?
Rona Cl RH11 . . . . .201 B?
Ronald Cl BR3 . . . . .43 F?
Ronald Ross Prim Sch
SW19 . . . . .19 E?
Ronelean Rd KT6 . . . . .56 F?
Ronneby Cl KT13 . . . . .53 E?
Ronson Way KT22 . . . . .95 A?
Ronver Rd SE12 . . . . .24 F?
Rook La CR3 . . . . .100 B?
Rook Way RH12 . . . . .217 F?
Rookeries Cl TW13 . . . . . . .15 C?
Rookery Cl KT22 . . . . .94 E?
Rookery Dr RH4 . . . . .135 A?
Rookery Hill Ashtead KT21 76 A?
Outwood RH1, RH6 . . . . . .162 B?
Rookery Rd TW18 . . . . .13 B?
Rookery The RH4 . . . . .135 A?
Rookery Way KT20 . . . . . . .117 F?
Rookley Cl SM2 . . . . .59 B?
Rooks Hill GU5 . . . . .152 C?

Rooksmead Rd TW16 . . . . .35 A7
Rookstone Rd SW17 . . . . . .20 F3
Rookwood Ave
 Sandhurst GU47 . . . . .45 E2
 Wallington SM6 . . . . .60 D6
 West Barnes KT3 . . . . .39 A5
Rookwood Cl RH1 . . . . . . .119 B6
Rookwood Ct GU2 . . . . . . .130 C6
Rookwood Pk RH12 . . . . . .216 F3
Roothill La RH3 . . . . .137 A3
Roper House 18 SE19, SE21 22 E4
Roper Way CR4 . . . . .41 A7
Ropers Wlk 13 SE24 . . . . . .22 A8
Rorkes Drift GU16 . . . . . . .86 A4
Rosa Ave TW15 . . . . .14 A4
Rosalind Franklin Cl GU2 129 E8
Rosamond St SE26 . . . . . . .23 B5
Rosamund Cl CR2 . . . . .61 D6
Rosamund Rd RH10 . . . . . .202 B3
Rosary Cl TW3, TW5 . . . . . . .4 E5
Rosary Gdns TW15 . . . . . . .14 B4
Rosary RC Inf Sch TW5 . . . .5 A8
Rosary RC Jun Sch TW5 . . .5 A8
Rose Ave Mitcham CR4 . . . .40 F8
 Morden SM4 . . . . .40 C4
Rose Bank Cotts GU22 . . . .89 E5
Rose Bushes KT17 . . . . . . .77 C3
Rose Cotts
 Enton Green GU8 . . . . . . .171 A2
 Esher KT10 . . . . .55 D5
Rose Ct 10 Wimbledon SW19 19 F3
 Wokingham RG40 . . . . .25 C6
Rose End KT4 . . . . .39 D1
Rose Gdns
 Farnborough GU14 . . . . . . .84 E3
 Feltham TW13 . . . . .15 A6
 Stanwell TW19 . . . . .13 D8
Rose Hill Dorking RH4 . . . .136 B7
 Sutton SM1, SM4 . . . . .40 B1
Rose Hill Pk W SM1 . . . . . .59 C8
Rose La GU23 . . . . .91 D5
Rose St RG40 . . . . .25 C6
Rose View KT15 . . . . .52 C5
Rose Wlk Purley CR8 . . . . . .79 D8
 Surbiton KT5 . . . . .38 B4
 West Wickham BR4 . . . . . .63 D8
Rose Wood GU22 . . . . .90 A8
Roseacre RH8 . . . . .123 A1
Roseacre Cl TW17 . . . . . . .34 A4
Roseacre Gdns GU4 . . . . .131 F3
Rosebank Epsom KT18 . . . .76 C5
 Penge SE20 . . . . .23 B1
Rosebank Cl TW11 . . . . . . .17 A2
Rosebay RG40 . . . . .25 E8
Roseberry Ave RH18, KT21 . .96 E8
 Kingston u T KT3 . . . . .38 F6
 South Norwood CR7 . . . . .42 C7
Rosebery Cl SM4 . . . . .39 D3
Rosebery Cres GU22 . . . . . .89 F7
Rosebery Gdns SM1 . . . . . .59 B6
Rosebery Rd
 Cheam SM1, SM2 . . . . .58 F4
 Isleworth TW3, TW7 . . . . . . .5 C2
 Kingston u T KT1 . . . . .38 B7
Rosebery Sch KT18 . . . . . .76 C5
Rosebery Sq KT1 . . . . .38 B7
Rosebine Ave TW2 . . . . . . .16 D8
Rosebriar Cl GU22 . . . . . . .71 A3
Rosebriars Caterham CR3 .100 E2
 Esher KT10 . . . . .55 C5
Rosebury Dr GU24 . . . . . . .68 A4
Rosecourt Rd CR0 . . . . . . .41 F3
Rosecroft Cl TN16 . . . . . . .83 F1
Rosecroft Gdns TW2 . . . . .16 D7
Rosedale Aldershot GU12 .105 C2
 Ashstead KT21 . . . . .75 C1
 Caterham CR3 . . . . .100 E4
Rosedale Cl RH11 . . . . . . .201 A4
Rosedale Gdns RG12 . . . . .27 A4
Rosedale Rd
 North Cheam KT17 . . . . . . .58 A5
 Richmond TW9 . . . . .6 E3
 Stoneleigh KT17 . . . . .58 A5
Rosedene Ave Morden SM4 40 A4
 Streatham SW16 . . . . .21 F5
 Thornton Heath CR0 . . . . .41 C4
Rosedene La GU47 . . . . . . .64 D7
Rosefield Cl SM5 . . . . .59 E5
Rosefield Gdns KT16 . . . . .51 D4
Rosefield Rd TW18 . . . . . . .13 A4
Roseheath Rd TW4 . . . . .4 F2
Rosehill Claygate KT10 . . . .56 A4
 Hampton TW12 . . . . .36 A8
Rosehill Ave
 Carshalton SM1, SM5 . . . . .40 C1
 Woking GU21 . . . . .69 C3
Rosehill Farm Meadow
 SM7 . . . . .78 B4
Rosehill Gdns SM1 . . . . . . .59 C8
Rosehill Rd TN16 . . . . .83 C2
Roseleigh Cl 3 TW1 . . . . . .6 D1
Rosemary Ave
 Ash Vale GU12 . . . . .106 A8
 East Molesey KT8 . . . . .36 A5
 Hounslow TW4 . . . . .4 D5
Rosemary Cl
 Farnborough GU14 . . . . . . .84 D4
 Oxted RH8 . . . . .123 A4
Rosemary Cotts SW19 . . . .19 C1
Rosemary Cres GU2 . . . . .109 A5
Rosemary Ct
 Haslemere GU27 . . . . .208 C4
 Horley RH6 . . . . .160 E4
Rosemary Gdns
 Blackwater GU17 . . . . .64 D5
 Chessington KT9 . . . . .56 E6
 Mortlake SW14 . . . . .7 C4

Rosemary La Alfold GU6 . .212 E8
 Blackwater GU17 . . . . .64 D5
 Charlwood RH6 . . . . .180 E7
 Horley RH6 . . . . .161 B3
 Mortlake SW14 . . . . .7 C4
 Rowledge GU10 . . . . .145 E4
 Thorpe TW20 . . . . .32 B6
Rosemead KT16 . . . . .33 B2
Rosemead Ave
 Feltham TW13 . . . . .14 F6
 Mitcham CR4, SW16 . . . . . .41 C7
Rosemead Cl RH1 . . . . . . .139 C7
Rosemead Rd SE27 . . . . . .22 C6
Rosemont Rd
 Kingston u T KT3 . . . . .38 C6
 Richmond TW10 . . . . .6 E1
Rosemount 5 SM6 . . . . . . .60 C4
Rosemount Ave KT14 . . . . .71 A6
Rosemount Par KT14 . . . . .71 A6
Rosemount Point SE23 23 D5
Rosendale Infs Sch SE21 . .22 C8
Rosendale Jun Sch SE21 . .22 C8
Rosendale Rd
 Streatham SE21, SE24 . . . .22 C7
 West Norwood SE21, SE24 .22 C7
Roseneath Ct CR3 . . . . . . .101 A3
Roseneath Dr GU8 . . . . . . .191 B4
Rosery The CR0 . . . . .43 D3
Roses Cotts RH4 . . . . .136 A7
Rosethorn Cl SW12 . . . . . .21 D8
Rosetrees GU1 . . . . .131 A8
Rosetta Ct SE19 . . . . .22 E1
Roseville Ave TW3, TW4 . . .5 A2
Rosevine Rd SW20 . . . . . . .39 C8
Rosewarne Cl GU21 . . . . . .69 A1
Rosewell Cl SE20 . . . . .23 B1
Rosewood Ct KT2 . . . . .18 A1
Rosewood Dr TW17 . . . . . .33 F4
Rosewood Gr SM1 . . . . . . .59 C8
Rosewood Way GU24 . . . . .67 E6
Rosina Ct SW17 . . . . .20 E3
Roskeen Ct SW19 . . . . .19 C1
Roslan Ct RH6 . . . . .161 B2
Roslyn Cl CR4 . . . . .40 D7
Ross Cl RH10 . . . . .201 F3
Ross Cts Croydon CR2 . . . .61 C4
 4 Putney SW15 . . . . .19 D8
Ross House TW2 . . . . .16 B6
Ross Par SM6 . . . . .60 B4
Ross Rd Cobham KT11 . . . .73 C4
 South Norwood SE25 . . . . .42 E6
 Twickenham TW2 . . . . .16 C7
 Wallington SM6 . . . . .60 C5
Rossal Ct SE20 . . . . .23 B1
Rossdale SM1 . . . . .59 E5
Rossendon Ct 1 SM6 . . . . .60 C4
Rossett Cl RG12 . . . . .27 B5
Rossetti Gdns CR5 . . . . . . .79 F1
Rossignol Gdns SM5 . . . . .60 A8
Rossindel Rd TW3 . . . . .5 A2
Rossiter Lodge GU1 . . . . .131 A8
Rossiter Rd SW12 . . . . .21 B7
Rosslea GU20 . . . . .48 A6
Rosslyn Ave Feltham TW14 . .4 A1
 Mortlake SW13, SW14 . . . . .7 B3
Rosslyn Cl Ashford TW16 . .14 E2
 Coney Hall BR4 . . . . .63 F7
Rosslyn House 8 TW9 . . . . .6 F6
Rosslyn Pk KT13 . . . . .53 D6
Rosslyn Rd TW1 . . . . .6 C1
Rossmore Cl RH10 . . . . . .182 D2
Rossmore Gdns GU11 . . . .104 F1
Rosswood Gdns SM6 . . . . .60 C4
Rostella Rd SW17 . . . . .20 D4
Rothbury Gdns TW7 . . . . . . .6 A7
Rothbury Wlk GU15 . . . . . .66 C4
Rother Cl GU47 . . . . .64 C8
Rother Cres RH11 . . . . . . .200 F5
Rother House 4 RH1 . . . . .118 F2
Rother Rd GU14 . . . . .84 E7
Rotherfield Ave RG41 . . . . .25 A7
Rotherfield Rd SM5 . . . . . .60 A5
Rotherhill Ave SW16 . . . . .21 D2
Rothermere Rd CR0 . . . . . .60 F5
Rothervale RH6 . . . . .160 F5
Rotherwick Ct GU14 . . . . .105 A8
Rotherwood Cl
 SW19, SW20 . . . . .39 E8
Rothes Rd RH4 . . . . .136 B8
Rothesay Ave Merton SW20 39 E7
 Mortlake SW14, SW14 . . . . .7 B3
Rothesay Rd SE25 . . . . . . .42 E5
Rothschild St SE27 . . . . . .22 C4
Rothwell House
 Crowthorne RG45 . . . . . . .45 C4
 Heston TW5 . . . . .5 A8
Rotunda Est The GU11 . . .105 B2
Rougemont Ave SM4 . . . . .40 A3
Rough Field RH19 . . . . . . .185 D4
Rough Rd GU22 . . . . .88 C5
Rough Rew RH4 . . . . .136 B4
Rough Way RH12 . . . . .217 F5
Roughets La RH1 . . . . . . .120 E6
Roughlands GU22 . . . . .70 E4
Rounce La GU24 . . . . .67 D6
Round Gr CR0 . . . . .43 D2
Round Hill SE23 . . . . .23 C5
Round Oak Rd KT13 . . . . . .52 F6
Roundabout Cotts RH12 .214 C5
Roundacre SW19 . . . . .19 D6
Roundals La GU8 . . . . .191 E8
Roundell House 14
 SE19, SE21 . . . . .22 E4
Roundhay Cl SE23 . . . . . . .23 D6
Roundhill GU22 . . . . .90 B8
Roundhill Dr GU22 . . . . . . .70 B1

Roundhill Way
 Guildford GU2 . . . . .108 F1
 Oxshott KT11 . . . . .74 B7
Roundshaw Ctr SM6 . . . . . .60 E3
Roundtable Rd BR1 . . . . . .24 F5
Roundthorn Way GU21 . . . .68 F3
Roundway Biggin Hill TN16 .83 D4
 Egham TW20 . . . . .12 C3
 Frimley GU15 . . . . .66 C6
Roundway Cl GU15 . . . . . . .66 C6
Roundway Ct RH10 . . . . . .201 D8
Roundway The KT10 . . . . . .55 F4
Roundwood View SM7 . . . .77 D4
Roundwood Way SM7 . . . .77 D4
Roupell House 7 KT2 . . . . .17 F1
Roupell Rd SW2 . . . . .21 F7
Rouse Gdns SE21 . . . . .22 E4
Routh Ct TW14 . . . . .14 D7
Routh Rd SW18 . . . . .20 E8
Row Hill KT15 . . . . .51 F4
Row La GU5 . . . . .153 E5
Row The RH7 . . . . .164 D4
Row Town KT15 . . . . .51 F3
Rowallan Ct SE6 . . . . .24 F7
Rowan 2 RG12 . . . . .27 F4
Rowan Ave TW20 . . . . .12 C3
Rowan Chase GU10 . . . . .146 A5
Rowan Cl Camberley GU15 .65 F8
 Crawley RH10 . . . . .201 F6
 Guildford GU1 . . . . .109 C4
 Horsham RH12 . . . . .218 B5
 Kingston u T KT3 . . . . .38 E7
 Mitcham SW16 . . . . .41 C8
 Reigate RH2 . . . . .139 C7
Rowan Cres SW16 . . . . . . .41 C8
Rowan Ct Forest Hill SE26 .23 C4
 11 Kingston u T KT2 . . . . . .18 A1
 Wimbledon SW20 . . . . .39 B7
Rowan Dr RG45 . . . . .45 C6
Rowan Gdns CR0 . . . . .61 F7
Rowan Gn KT13 . . . . .53 D6
Rowan Gr CR5 . . . . .99 B6
Rowan High Sch SW16 . . .41 C7
Rowan Mead KT20 . . . . . . .97 B8
Rowan Prep Sch KT10 . . . .55 F3
Rowan Rd Brentford TW8 . . .6 B7
 Mitcham SW16 . . . . .41 C7
Rowan Way RH12 . . . . . . .218 C5
Rowans Cl GU14 . . . . .64 E1
Rowans The Ashford TW16 .14 F3
 Grayshott GU26 . . . . .188 D2
 3 Woking GU22 . . . . .69 E1
Rowanside Cl GU35 . . . . .187 C4
Rowbarns Way KT24 . . . . .112 F5
Rowbury GU7 . . . . .151 A7
Rowcroft Cl GU12 . . . . . . .106 A6
Rowden Rd Penge BR3 . . . .43 F8
 West Ewell KT19 . . . . .57 C6
Rowdown Cres CR0 . . . . . .63 E2
Rowdown Inf & Jun Schs
 CR0 . . . . .63 D1
Rowe La GU24 . . . . .88 A3
Rowena House RH10 . . . . .181 D1
Rowfant Bsns Ctr RH10 . .203 E6
Rowfant Cl RH10 . . . . .202 E6
Rowfant Rd SW12, SW17 . .21 A6
Rowhill Ave GU11 . . . . . . .125 F8
Rowhill Cres GU11 . . . . . .125 F8
Rowhill Nature Trail
 GU9 . . . . .125 D8
Rowhills GU9 . . . . .125 D8
Rowhills Cl GU9 . . . . .125 F7
Rowhook Hill RH12 . . . . . .215 F8
Rowhook Rd
 Rowhook RH12 . . . . .196 E1
 Slinfold RH12 . . . . .216 A8
Rowhurst Ave KT15 . . . . . .52 B4
Rowland Cl RH10 . . . . .183 E5
Rowland Gr SE26 . . . . .23 B5
Rowland Hill Almshouses
 TW15 . . . . .14 A3
Rowland Rd GU6 . . . . .174 D3
Rowland Way
 Littleton TW15 . . . . .14 D1
 Merton SW19 . . . . .40 B8
Rowlands Rd RH12 . . . . . .218 A6
Rowledge CE (VC) Prim
 Sch GU10 . . . . .145 E3
Rowley Cl Bracknell RG12 . .27 E6
 Pyrford GU22 . . . . .71 B3
Rowley Ct CR3 . . . . .100 C5
Rowlls Rd KT1 . . . . .37 F6
Rowly Dr GU6 . . . . .174 A6
Rowly Edge GU6 . . . . .174 A6
Rowntree Rd TW2 . . . . . . .16 E7
Rowplatt La RH19 . . . . . . .184 E4
Roxborough Ave TW7 . . . . .5 F7
Roxburgh Cl GU15 . . . . . . .66 C4
Roxburgh Rd SE27 . . . . . . .22 B3
Roxeth Ct TW15 . . . . .14 A3
Roxford Cl TW17 . . . . .34 E4
Roxton Gdns CR0 . . . . .63 A5
Roy Gr TW12 . . . . .16 B2
Royal Alexandra & Albert
 Sch The RH2 . . . . .118 E6
Royal Ascot Golf Club SL5 29 B7
Royal Ave KT4 . . . . .57 E8
Royal Botanic Gardens
 TW9 . . . . .6 E6
Royal Cir SE27 . . . . .22 B5
Royal Cl KT4 . . . . .57 E8
Royal Ct 9 KT2 . . . . .18 B1
Royal Dr RT18 . . . . .97 B8
Royal Grammar Sch GU1 130 D4
Royal Holloway Univ of
 London TW20 . . . . .11 D2
Royal Horticultural
 Society Cotts KT14 .71 E3

Royal Horticultural
 Society's Garden GU23 . .71 E1
Royal Hosp SW19 . . . . .19 E8
Royal Hospl TW9 . . . . .6 E4
Royal Kent CE Prim Sch
 The KT22 . . . . .74 C5
Royal Logistic Corps Mus
 GU16 . . . . .86 D8
Royal Marsden Hospl
 (Surrey Branch) The
 SM2 . . . . .59 C1
Royal Mews KT8 . . . . .36 E6
Royal Mid-Surrey Golf
 Club TW9 . . . . .6 C6
Royal Military Acad GU15 .64 F6
Royal Military Acad Hospl
 GU15 . . . . .65 A8
Royal Military Sch of
 Music (Kneller Hall) TW2 .5 D1
Royal Oak Ctr The CR2 . . .61 C1
Royal Oak House RH10 . .204 B7
Royal Oak Rd GU21 . . . . . .69 D1
Royal Orchard Cl SW18 . . .19 E8
Royal Rd TW11 . . . . .16 D3
Royal Russell Sch
 (Ballards) CR9 . . . . .62 B5
Royal Sch for the Blind
 KT22 . . . . .95 C5
Royal Sch of Church
 Music RH5 . . . . .115 B4
Royal Sch The GU27 . . . . .189 A2
Royal School SL4 . . . . .10 C4
Royal Surrey County
 Hospl GU2 . . . . .108 E1
Royal Victoria Gdns SL5 .29 A4
Royal Way The GU16 . . . . .86 D7
Royal Wimbledon Golf
 Course SW19 . . . . .19 B2
Royal Wlk SM6 . . . . .60 B7
Royale Cl GU11 . . . . .126 C8
Royals The GU1 . . . . .130 E8
Royce Rd RH10 . . . . .182 A3
Roycroft Cl SW2 . . . . .22 A7
Roydon Ct KT12 . . . . .54 A6
Roydon Lodge KT15 . . . . . .52 D7
Roymount Ct TW2 . . . . . . .16 E5
Royston Ave Byfleet KT14 . .71 E7
 Carshalton SM1 . . . . .59 D7
 Wallington SM6 . . . . .60 D6
Royston Cl Cranford TW5 . . .4 B6
 Crawley RH10 . . . . .182 A2
 Walton-on-T KT12 . . . . . . .35 A1
Royston Ct
 Hinchley Wood KT10 . . . . .55 F8
 3 Richmond TW9 . . . . .6 F6
 Tolworth KT5 . . . . .57 A8
Royston Prim Sch SE20 . .43 B8
Royston Rd Byfleet KT14 . .71 E7
 Penge BR3, SE20 . . . . .43 B8
 Richmond TW10 . . . . .6 E2
Roystons The KT5 . . . . . . .38 B4
Rozeldene GU26 . . . . .188 E3
Rubens St SE6 . . . . .23 F6
Rubus Cl GU24 . . . . .67 E6
Ruckmans La RH5 . . . . . . .197 B7
Rudd Hall Rise GU15 . . . . .65 E4
Ruden Way KT17 . . . . .77 B4
Rudge Rise KT15 . . . . .51 F5
Rudgwick Cty Prim Sch
 RH12 . . . . .214 D7
Rudgwick Rd RH11 . . . . . .200 F7
Rudloe Rd SW12 . . . . .21 C8
Rudolph Ct SE22 . . . . .23 B8
Rudsworth Cl SL3 . . . . .1 D7
Ruffets Cl CR2 . . . . .62 B3
Ruffetts The CR2 . . . . .62 B3
Ruffetts Way KT20 . . . . . . .77 E1
Rufus Bsns Ctr SW18 . . . .20 B6
Rufwood RH10 . . . . .204 A8
Rugby Cl GU47 . . . . .45 E1
Rugby La SM2 . . . . .58 D2
Rugby Rd TW1, TW2, TW7 . . .5 E1
Ruggles-Brise Rd TW15 . . .13 D3
Ruislip St SW17 . . . . .20 F4
Rumsey Cl TW12 . . . . .15 F2
Runcorn Cl RH11 . . . . .200 E2
Runes Cl CR4 . . . . .40 E5
Runnemede Rd TW20 . . . .12 A4
Running Horse Yd 12 TW8 . .6 E8
Runnymeade Ctr The
 KT15 . . . . .52 B8
Runnymede SW19 . . . . . . .40 D8
Runnymede Cl TW2 . . . . . .16 B8
Runnymede Cotts SW19 . .12 D7
Runnymede Cres SW16 . . .41 E8
Runnymede Ct
 Egham TW20 . . . . .12 A4
 Farnborough GU14 . . . . . . .85 A7
 1 Wallington SM6 . . . . .60 B4
Runnymede Gdns TW2 . . .16 B8
Runnymede Hospl The
 KT16 . . . . .51 D7
Runnymede Rd TW2 . . . . . .5 B1
Runshooke Ct 11 RH11 . . .201 A3
Runtley Wood La GU4 . . . .89 F2
Runwick La GU10 . . . . . . .124 C8
Rupert Ct KT8 . . . . .36 A5
Rupert Rd GU2 . . . . .130 C8
Rural Life Centre GU10 . .146 F3
Rural Way Mitcham SW16 . .41 A1
 Redhill RH1 . . . . .119 A1
Ruscoe Dr GU22 . . . . .70 A2
Ruscoe House 12 SW27 . . .22 B3
Ruscombe Way TW14 . . . . .14 F8
Rush Croft GU7 . . . . .151 A8
Rush The SW20 . . . . .39 F8
Rusham Park Ave TW20 . . .12 A2
Rusham Rd Balham SW12 . .20 F8

Rusham Rd continued
 Egham TW20 . . . . .11 F2
Rushams Rd RH12 . . . . . .217 B3
Rushbury Ct 6 TW12 . . . . .36 A8
Rushden Cl SE19 . . . . .22 D1
Rushden Way GU9 . . . . . . .125 D7
Rushdene Wlk TN16 . . . . . .83 D2
Rushen Wlk SM5 . . . . .40 D1
Rushett Cl KT7 . . . . .37 B1
Rushett Dr RH4 . . . . .136 C4
Rushett La KT9 . . . . .75 D7
Rushett Rd KT7 . . . . .37 B2
Rushetts Pl RH11 . . . . . . .181 C1
Rushetts Rd Crawley RH11 181 B1
 Reigate RH2 . . . . .139 C5
Rushey Cl KT3 . . . . .38 D5
Rushey Gn SE6 . . . . .24 B8
Rushey Green Prim Sch
 SE6 . . . . .24 B7
Rushfords RH7 . . . . .164 E5
Rushmead TW10 . . . . .17 B5
Rushmead Cl CR0 . . . . .61 F6
Rushmere Ct KT4 . . . . .58 A8
Rushmere House 2 SW15 .19 A7
Rushmere Pl
 Englefield Green TW20 . . . .11 E3
 Wimbledon SW19 . . . . .19 D3
Rushmon Gdns KT12 . . . . .54 B7
Rushmon Pl SM3 . . . . .58 E4
Rushmoor Cl GU2 . . . . . . .108 F5
Rushmoor Ct GU14 . . . . . .105 C8
Rushmoor Independant
 Sch GU14 . . . . .85 C1
Rushmoor Rd GU11 . . . . .104 E4
Rusholme Gr SE19 . . . . . . .22 E3
Rushton Ave RH9 . . . . .142 D5
Rushworth Rd RH2 . . . . . .118 B2
Rushy House RG12 . . . . . . .27 E5
Rushy Meadow La SM5 . . .59 E7
Rushy Meadow Prim Sch
 SM5 . . . . .59 E7
Ruskin Ave Feltham TW14 . . .3 F1
 Richmond TW9 . . . . .7 A7
Ruskin Cl RH10 . . . . .182 C1
Ruskin Dr KT4 . . . . .58 C8
Ruskin Par CR0 . . . . .61 G5
Ruskin Rd Croydon CR0, CR9 61 B8
 Isleworth TW7 . . . . .5 F4
 Staines TW18 . . . . .12 F2
 Wallington SM5 . . . . .60 A5
Ruskin Way SW19 . . . . . . .40 D8
Rusper Cl CR5 . . . . .79 D3
Rusper Cty Prim Sch
 RH12 . . . . .199 C7
Rusper Rd Capel RH5 . . . .178 D2
 Crawley RH11 . . . . .200 E6
 Faygate RH12 . . . . .199 A1
 Horsham RH12 . . . . .217 E6
 Lambs Green RH11 . . . . . .200 D7
 Newdigate RH2, RH5 . . . . .179 C4
 Rusper RH11, RH12 . . . . . .200 D7
Ruspers Keep RH11 . . . . .200 F7
Russ Hill RH5, RH6 . . . . . .180 C5
Russel Cl Beckenham BR3 . .44 C6
 Bracknell RG12 . . . . .27 D3
Russell Cl
 Walton on t H KT20 . . . . . . .97 A2
 Woking GU21 . . . . .69 C4
Russell Ct Blackwater GU17 64 D5
 Bromley BR1 . . . . .24 F1
 Guildford GU1 . . . . .109 C4
 Hindhead GU26 . . . . .188 F4
 Leatherhead KT22 . . . . .95 B5
 Streatham SW16 . . . . .21 D4
 Surbiton KT6 . . . . .37 E2
 Wallington SM6 . . . . .60 C5
Russell Dr TW19 . . . . .2 D1
Russell Gdns
 Harmondsworth UB7 . . . . . .3 A8
 Richmond TW10 . . . . .17 C6
Russell Green Cl CR8 . . . . .61 A1
Russell Hill CR8 . . . . .60 F1
Russell Hill Par 4 CR8 . . . .80 A8
Russell Hill Pl CR8 . . . . . . .80 A8
Russell Hill Rd CR8 . . . . . .80 A8
Russell Kerr Cl W4 . . . . .7 C7
Russell Par 3 CR8 . . . . . . .80 A8
Russell Prim Sch The
 TW10 . . . . .17 D7
Russell Rd
 Lower Halliford TW17 . . . . .34 C2
 Merton SW19 . . . . .20 A1
 Mitcham CR4 . . . . .40 E6
 Twickenham TW1, TW2 . . . . .5 F1
 Walton-on-T KT12 . . . . . . .35 A3
 Woking GU21 . . . . .69 C4
Russell Sch The TW10 . . .17 D6
 Sutton SM1 . . . . .59 B5
Russell Way Crawley RH10 202 A3
 Sutton SM1 . . . . .59 B5
Russell Wlk 4 TW10 . . . . . . .6 F1
Russells KT20 . . . . .97 D5
Russells Cres RH6 . . . . . . .161 A2
Russet Ave TW16, TW17 . . .34 E6
Russet Cl Hersham KT12 . . .54 E7
 Horley RH6 . . . . .161 C3
 Stanwell TW19 . . . . .1 F1
 Tongham GU10 . . . . .126 E7
Russet Dr CR0 . . . . .43 E1
Russet Gdns GU15 . . . . . . .65 D3
Russet Glade GU11 . . . . . .125 E8
Russet Ho TW3 . . . . .4 F3
Russet Way RH5 . . . . .136 D4
Russets Ct CR3 . . . . .101 A2
Russetts Cl GU21 . . . . .69 F4

Russington Rd TW17 . . . .34 D3
Russley Gn RG40 . . . . .25 A1
Rusthall Cl CR0 . . . . .43 C3
Rustic Ave SW16 . . . . .21 B1
Rustington Wlk SM4 . . . . .39 F2
Ruston Ave KT5 . . . . .38 B2
Ruston Cl RH10 . . . . .202 D3
Ruston Way SL5 . . . . .28 E7
Rutford Rd SW16 . . . . .21 E3
Ruth Cl GU14 . . . . .84 C5
Ruthen Cl KT18 . . . . .76 B5
Rutherford Cl SM2 . . . . . . .59 D4
Rutherford Way RH10 . . . .182 A3
Rutherwick Cl RH6 . . . . . .160 F3
Rutherwick Rise CR5 . . . . . .79 E3
Rutherwyk Rd KT16 . . . . . .32 E2
Rutherwyke Cl KT17 . . . . . .58 A4
Rutland Cl Aldershot GU11 105 A3
  Ashtead KT21 . . . . .75 E2
  Epsom KT18 . . . . .57 D1
  Mitcham SW19 . . . . .20 E1
  Mortlake SW14 . . . . .7 C4
  Redhill RH1 . . . . .118 F2
Rutland Dr Morden SM4 . . .40 A2
  Richmond TW10 . . . . .17 E7
Rutland Gate BR2 . . . . .44 F5
Rutland Gdns CR0 . . . . . . .61 E6
Rutland Lodge SE6 . . . . . . .23 F6
Rutland Pk SE6 . . . . .23 F6
Rutland Rd Mitcham SW19 .20 E1
  Twickenham TW2 . . . . .16 D6
Rutland Terr GU11 . . . . . .105 A3
Rutland Wlk SE6 . . . . .23 F6
Rutlish Sch (Boys) SW20 . .39 F7
Rutson Rd KT14 . . . . .71 F5
Rutter Gdns CR4, SW19 . . .40 D5
Rutton Hill Rd GU8 . . . . . .189 E8
Ruxbury Ct TW15 . . . . .13 E5
Ruxbury Rd KT16 . . . . .32 D3
Ruxley Cl KT19 . . . . .57 B5
Ruxley Cres KT10 . . . . .56 B3
Ruxley Ct KT19 . . . . .57 C5
Ruxley La KT19 . . . . .57 C5
Ruxley Mews KT19 . . . . . . .57 B5
Ruxley Ridge KT10 . . . . . . .56 A3
Ryan Cl SW16 . . . . .21 E1
Ryan Dr TW8 . . . . .6 A8
Ryan Mount GU47 . . . . . . .64 A8
Rycott Path SE22 . . . . .23 A8
Rydal Cl Crawley RH11 . . .200 D4
  Farnborough GU14 . . . . . . .84 D3
  Frimley GU15 . . . . .66 D5
  Sanderstead CR8 . . . . .80 D6
Rydal Dr BR4 . . . . .63 E8
Rydal Gdns
  Kingston u T SW15 . . . . . . .18 E3
  Twickenham TW2, TW3 . . . . .5 B1
Rydal Pl GU18 . . . . .67 B8
Rydal Rd SW16 . . . . .21 D4
Rydal Way TW20 . . . . .12 B1
Ryde Cl GU23 . . . . .91 C6
Ryde Ct GU12 . . . . .105 C1
Ryde Heron GU21 . . . . .68 E2
Ryde Lands GU6 . . . . .174 F4
Ryde Pl TW1 . . . . .6 D1
Ryde The TW18 . . . . .33 B8
Ryde Vale Rd SW12 . . . . . .21 C6
Ryde's Hill Cres GU2 . . . .108 F5
Ryde's Hill Rd GU2, GU3 .108 F4
Rydens Ave KT12 . . . . .54 C8
Rydens Cl KT12 . . . . .54 C8
Rydens Gr KT12 . . . . .54 D6
Rydens Pk KT12 . . . . .54 C8
Rydens Rd KT12 . . . . .54 C8
Rydens Sch KT12 . . . . .54 C6
Rydens Way GU22 . . . . . . .90 A7
Ryder House ☑ SW19 . . . . .40 B8
Ryders Way RH12 . . . . . . .217 F7
Rydes Ave GU2 . . . . .108 F4
Rydes Hill Prep Sch GU2 .108 F3
Rydon Mews SW19 . . . . . . .19 C1
Rydon's La CR3, CR5 . . . .100 C7
Rydon's Wood Cl
  CR3, CR5 . . . . .100 C7
Rye Ash RH10 . . . . .202 A7
Rye Brook Rd KT22 . . . . . . .75 A1
Rye Cl Farnborough GU14 . .84 E7
  Guildford GU2 . . . . .108 E3
Rye Ct BR3 . . . . .43 F8
Rye Gr GU20, GU24 . . . . . .48 F2
Ryebridge Cl KT22 . . . . . . .95 A7
Ryebrook Bsns Pk KT22 . . .95 A7
Ryecotes Mead SE21 . . . . .22 E7
Ryecroft Dr RH12 . . . . . . .217 A3
Ryecroft Gdns GU17 . . . . . .64 E4
Ryecroft Rd SW16 . . . . . . .22 A2
Ryedale Ct ☑ KT17 . . . . . . .36 A8
Ryefield Path ☑ SW15 . . . .19 A7
Ryefield Rd SE19 . . . . .22 C2
Ryehill Ct KT3 . . . . .38 F2
Ryelands Crawley RH11 . . .201 A5
  Horley RH6 . . . . .161 C4
Ryelands Cl CR3 . . . . .100 E6
Ryelands Ct KT22 . . . . .75 A1
Ryelands Inf Sch SE25 . . . .43 B4
Ryelands Pl KT13 . . . . .53 E7
Ryemead La RG42, SL4 . . . . .8 C5
Ryersh La RH5 . . . . .178 C8
Ryfold Rd SW19 . . . . .20 A5
Ryland Cl TW13 . . . . .14 F4
Ryland House ☑ SW16 . . . .21 C3
Rylandes Rd CR2 . . . . .62 B1

Ryle Rd GU9 . . . . .146 B8
Rylton House KT12 . . . . . . .35 A1
Rymer Rd CR0 . . . . .42 E2
Rythe Ct KT7 . . . . .37 A2
Rythe House BR1 . . . . .24 D3
Rythe Rd KT10 . . . . .55 E5
Rythe The KT22 . . . . .55 C1

S

Sabah Ct TW15 . . . . .14 A3
Sable Cl TW4 . . . . .4 C4
Sable Ct ☑ KT3 . . . . .38 E4
Sabre Ct GU11 . . . . .104 C3
Sachel Court Rd
  GU6, GU8 . . . . .193 D3
Sackville Cl RH19 . . . . . . .185 C3
Sackville Cotts RH1 . . . . . .120 D1
Sackville Ct ☑ RH19 . . . . .205 F8
Sackville Gdns RH19 . . . . .185 C3
Sackville House ⑯ SW16 . .21 E5
Sackville La RH19 . . . . . . .185 C3
Sackville Rd SM2 . . . . .59 A3
Sackville Sch RH19 . . . . . .186 A1
Sacred Heart Catholic
  Prim Sch KT3 . . . . .39 A5
Sacred Heart Coll SL5 . . . .30 C3
Sacred Heart RC Prim Sch
  TW11 . . . . .17 B1
Saddleback Rd GU15 . . . . .65 E8
Saddlebrook Pk TW16 . . . .14 E1
Saddler Row RH10 . . . . . .201 D3
Saddlers Cl GU1 . . . . .110 D2
Saddlers Mews KT1 . . . . . .37 C8
Saddlers Scarp GU26 . . . .188 A4
Saddlers Way KT18 . . . . . . .96 D8
Saddlewood GU15 . . . . . . .65 C4
Sadler Cl CR4 . . . . .40 F7
Sadlers Ride KT8 . . . . .36 C7
Saffron Cl RH11 . . . . .201 A3
Saffron Ct GU14 . . . . .84 C4
Saffron Platt GU2 . . . . . . .109 A5
Saffron Rd RG12 . . . . .27 B5
Saffron Way KT6 . . . . .37 D1
Sailors La GU8 . . . . .169 A2
Sainfoin Rd SW17 . . . . .21 A6
Sainsbury Ctr The KT16 . . .33 A2
Sainsbury Rd SE19 . . . . . . .22 E3
Saint Hill Manor RH19 . . .205 C4
Saint Hill Rd RH19 . . . . . .205 C5
Saints Cl SE27 . . . . .22 B4
SS Peter & Paul's RC
  Prim Sch CR4 . . . . .40 F5
St Agatha's Dr KT2 . . . . . . .17 F2
St Agatha's Gr CR4, SM5 . .40 F1
St Agatha's RC Prim Sch
  KT2 . . . . .17 F1
St Agatha's RC Sch KT2 . . .17 F1
St Agnes Rd RH19 . . . . . . .185 E2
St Aidan's RC Prim Sch
  CR5 . . . . .79 C3
St Alban's Gdns TW11 . . . .17 A3
St Alban's Gr SM5 . . . . . . .40 E2
St Alban's RC Prim Sch
  KT8 . . . . .36 C4
St Alban's Rd RH2 . . . . . . .118 A3
St Alban's Rdbt GU14 . . . .105 C7
St Albans Ave
  Feltham TW13 . . . . .15 D3
  Weybridge KT13 . . . . .53 A7
St Albans House ☑ SW16 . .22 A4
St Albans Rd Cheam SM1 . .58 F6
  Kingston u T KT2 . . . . .17 E2
St Amunds Cl SE6 . . . . . . .24 A4
St Andrew's C of E Fst
  & Mid Sch RH10 . . . . . . .202 A4
St Andrew's CE Inf Sch
  GU9 . . . . .125 B2
St Andrew's Cl
  ☑ Hounslow TW7 . . . . .5 E6
  Reigate RH2 . . . . .139 B8
  Upper Halliford TW17 . . . . .34 D5
  Wraysbury TW19 . . . . .11 E8
St Andrew's Ct SW18 . . . . .20 C6
St Andrew's High Sch CR0 .61 B6
St Andrew's RC Sch KT22 .95 D7
St Andrew's RC Sch The
  Grange KT22 . . . . .95 D7
St Andrew's Rd
  Coulsdon CR5 . . . . .79 B4
  ☑ Croydon CR0, CR9 . . . . .61 C6
  Kingston u T KT6 . . . . .37 D3
St Andrew's Sch GU21 . . . .69 D3
St Andrew's Sch Cobham
  KT11 . . . . .73 C6
St Andrew's Sq KT6 . . . . . .37 D3
St Andrew's & St Mark's
  Sch KT6 . . . . .37 D4
St Andrew's Way KT16 . . . .85 F7
St Andrew's Wlk KT11 . . . .73 B4
St Andrews Bracknell RG12 .26 C3
  Cranleigh GU6 . . . . .174 B4
St Andrews Cl GU21 . . . . . .69 C2
St Andrews Ct Ascot SL5 . .29 C4
  Chiswick W4 . . . . .7 C6
St Andrews Gdns KT11 . . . .73 C6
St Andrews RC Prim Sch
  SW16 . . . . .21 E3
St Andrews Rd
  Carshalton SM5 . . . . .59 E7
  Crawley RH11 . . . . .200 D5
St Andrews Way RH8 . . . .123 F4
St Ann's Cl KT16 . . . . .32 F3
St Ann's Heath Cty Mid
  Sch GU25 . . . . .31 E4
St Ann's Hill SW18 . . . . . . .20 C8

St Ann's Hill Rd KT16 . . . .32 D3
St Ann's Rd KT16 . . . . .32 F3
St Ann's Sch SM4 . . . . .40 B4
St Ann's Way CR2 . . . . .61 B4
St Anne's Ave TW19 . . . . . .13 D8
St Anne's Dr RH1 . . . . . . .119 A2
St Anne's Prim Sch TW19 .13 E8
St Anne's RC Prim Sch
  Banstead SM7 . . . . .78 A3
  Chertsey KT16 . . . . .33 A1
St Anne's Rd
  Crawley RH10 . . . . .182 C2
  Godalming GU7 . . . . .151 A5
St Annes Glade GU19 . . . . .47 D3
St Annes Mount ☑ RH1 . .119 A2
St Annes Rise RH1 . . . . . .119 A2
St Annes Way ⑥ RH1 . . . .119 A2
St Anns Rd SW13 . . . . .7 F6
St Anselm's Ct SW16 . . . . .21 E3
St Anselm's RC Prim Sch
  SW17 . . . . .21 A5
St Anthony's Ct
  ⑦ Balham SW12 . . . . .21 A8
  Upper Tooting SW17 . . . . . .21 A6
St Anthony's Hospl KT4 . . .39 D1
St Anthony's Way TW14 . . . .3 F3
St Anthonys Cl
  Bracknell RG42 . . . . .27 A8
  Upper Tooting SW17 . . . . . .20 E6
St Antony's RC Prim Sch
  SE26 . . . . .43 B8
St Arvans Cl CR0 . . . . .61 E7
St Aubin Cl RH11 . . . . . . .200 F2
St Aubyn's Ave
  Hounslow TW3, TW4 . . . . . .5 A2
  Wimbledon SW19 . . . . .19 F3
St Aubyn's Ct SW19 . . . . . .19 E2
St Aubyn's Rd SE19 . . . . . .22 F2
St Augustine's Ave
  Croydon CR2 . . . . .61 C3
  South Croydon CR2 . . . . . .61 C3
St Augustine's Cl GU12 . .105 D1
St Augustines Ct BR3 . . . . .43 E7
St Augustines's RC Prim
  Sch SE6 . . . . .24 C3
St Austins GU26 . . . . .188 D3
St Barnabas Cl BR3 . . . . . .44 C7
St Barnabas Rd RH10 . . . .202 C7
St Barnabas' Gdns KT8 . . .36 A4
St Barnabas Rd
  Mitcham CR4 . . . . .21 A1
  Sutton SM1 . . . . .59 D5
St Bartholomew CE
  Prim Sch GU27 . . . . .208 C7
St Bartholomew's Cl
  SE26 . . . . .23 C4
St Bartholomew's
  Ct GU1 . . . . .130 F7
St Bartholomew's Prim
  Sch SE26 . . . . .23 C4
St Bede's C of E Mid Sch
  GU23 . . . . .90 D3
St Bede's RC Inf Sch
  SW12 . . . . .21 D7
St Bede's Sch RH2 . . . . . .118 E4
St Benedict's Cl
  Aldershot GU11 . . . . .105 A1
  Upper Tooting SW17 . . . . . .21 A3
St Benet's Gr SM4, SM5 . . .40 C2
St Benets Ct SW17 . . . . . . .20 E6
St Bernadette RC Jun
  Mix Sch SW12 . . . . .21 C8
St Bernadette RC Prim
  Sch GU14 . . . . .85 A5
St Bernards CR0 . . . . .61 E7
St Bernards Cl ⑧ SE27 . . .22 D4
St Boniface Catholic
  Prim Sch SW17 . . . . .20 F3
St Brelades Cl RH4 . . . . . .136 A5
St Brelades Rd RH11 . . . .200 F2
St Catherine's Convent
  Girls Prep & Senior Schs
  TW1 . . . . .17 A6
St Catherine's Cross
  RH1 . . . . .120 E2
St Catherine's Dr GU2 . . .130 B5
St Catherine's Hill GU2 . .130 C5
St Catherine's Jun Sch
  GU5 . . . . .151 F6
St Catherine's Pk GU1 . . .130 F7
St Catherine's RC Mid Sch
  SW20 . . . . .39 C4
St Catherine's Sch GU15 . .65 C4
St Catherine's Senior Sch
  GU5 . . . . .151 F6
St Catherines
  Weybridge KT13 . . . . .53 B7
  Woking GU22 . . . . .89 C8
St Catherines Bletchingley
  Village Cty Prim Sch
  RH1 . . . . .120 E2
St Catherines Cl SW17 . . . .20 E6
St Catherines Ct TW13 . . . .15 A7
St Catherines Rd
  Crawley RH10 . . . . .182 D1
  Frimley GU16 . . . . .86 A8
St Cecilia's RC Prim Sch
  SM3 . . . . .58 D8
St Chad's RC Prim Sch
  SE25 . . . . .42 E4
St Chads Cl KT6 . . . . .37 C2
St Charles Borromeo RC
  Prim Sch KT13 . . . . .53 A7
St Charles Pl KT13 . . . . . . .53 A5
St Christopher's RH7 . . . .164 D4
St Christopher's

St Christopher's Ct ☑
  KT12 . . . . .54 C8
St Christopher's Gn
  GU27 . . . . .208 A6
St Christopher's Hospice
  SE26 . . . . .23 C3
St Christopher's Mews
  SM6 . . . . .60 C5
St Christopher's Rd ☑
  Farnborough GU14 . . . . . . .85 A3
  Haslemere GU27 . . . . . . .208 A6
St Christopher's Sch BR3 .44 C7
St Christopher's Sch
  Trust Ltd KT18 . . . . .76 C5
St Christophers Cl RH12 .217 D4
St Christophers Day
  Hospl RH12 . . . . .217 D3
St Christophers Gdns
  North Ascot SL5 . . . . .28 D8
  Thornton Heath CR7 . . . . .42 A6
St Christophers Pl ❶
  GU14 . . . . .85 A3
St Clair Cl Oxted RH8 . . . .122 D5
  Reigate RH2 . . . . .118 C1
St Clair Dr KT4 . . . . .58 B6
St Clair's Rd CR0 . . . . .61 E8
St Claire Cotts RH7 . . . . . .165 B1
St Clare Bsns Pk SW12 . . .21 C7
St Clement Cl RH11 . . . . .200 F2
St Clements Ct GU14 . . . . .85 B7
St Clements RC Prim Sch
  KT17 . . . . .57 F2
St Cloud Rd SE27 . . . . .22 D4
St Crispin's Sch RG40 . . . .25 E6
St Crispins Way KT16 . . . . .51 C2
St Cross Rd Farnham GU9 .125 C3
  Frimley GU16 . . . . .86 B7
St Cuthbert Mayne RC
  Prim Sch GU6 . . . . .174 E3
St Cuthbert's Cl TW20 . . . .11 D2
St Cuthbert's RC Prim Sch
  TW20 . . . . .11 C1
St Cyprian's Sch SW17 . . . .20 F4
St David's CR5 . . . . .79 F2
St David's Cl
  Farnborough GU14 . . . . . . .84 F8
  Heath End GU9 . . . . .125 E7
  Reigate RH2 . . . . .118 C2
  West Wickham BR3, BR4 . . .44 B2
St David's Coll BR4 . . . . . .44 B2
St David's Jun Sch TW15 . .13 F5
St Davids Cl ❹ GU12 . . . .105 B1
St Davids Dr TW20 . . . . . . .11 C1
St Denis Rd SE27 . . . . .22 D4
St Deny's Cl GU21 . . . . . . .68 D1
St Dominic's Sch GU8 . . .171 C1
St Dunstan's C of E Prim
  Sch SM3 . . . . .58 E3
St Dunstan's Coll SE6 . . . .24 A7
St Dunstan's Hill SM1, SM3 58 E5
St Dunstan's La BR3 . . . . . .44 C4
St Dunstan's RC Prim Sch
  GU22 . . . . .70 A2
St Dunstan's Rd
  Cranford TW5 . . . . .4 B5
  Cranford TW5 . . . . .4 C5
  Feltham TW13 . . . . .14 F5
  South Norwood SE25 . . . . .42 F5
St Ebba's Hospl KT19 . . . .57 C2
St Edith Cl KT18 . . . . .76 C5
St Edmund Cl RH11 . . . . .181 D1
St Edmund's Catholic
  Prim Sch TW2 . . . . .16 B8
St Edmund's La TW2 . . . . .16 B8
St Edmund's RC Prim Sch
  GU7 . . . . .150 F2
St Edmunds Cl SW17 . . . . .20 E6
St Edmunds Sch GU26 . . .188 D3
St Edward's Cl RH19 . . . . .185 C1
St Edwards Cl CR0 . . . . . . .82 D8
St Elizabeth Dr KT18 . . . . .76 C5
St Elizabeth's RC Prim
  Sch TW10 . . . . .6 F1
St Elphege's RC Prim
  Sch SM6 . . . . .60 E4
St Faith's Rd SE24 . . . . . . .22 B7
St Fillans GU22 . . . . .70 B3
St Fillans Rd SE6 . . . . .24 C8
St Francis Gdns RH10 . . . .183 C4
St Francis of Assisi RC
  Sch RH10 . . . . .201 D4
St Francis RC Prim
  Sch CR3 . . . . .100 F6
St Francis RC Sch SL5 . . . .29 A3
St Francis Wlk RH11 . . . . .200 E4
St George's Ave KT13 . . . . .53 C4
St George's Bsns Ctr KT13 53 A2
St George's Cl
  Farnham GU9 . . . . .126 B6
  Weybridge KT13 . . . . .53 C5
St George's Coll KT15 . . . .52 D7
St George's Gdns
  Epsom KT17 . . . . .76 F5
  Horsham RH12 . . . . .217 E4
  Tolworth KT6 . . . . .57 B8
St George's Gr SW17 . . . . .20 D5
St George's Hill Artisan
  Golf Club KT13 . . . . .53 C2
St George's Hill Golf
  Course KT13 . . . . .72 B8
St George's Hospl SW17 . .20 D1
St George's Ind Est KT2 . .17 D1
St George's La SL5 . . . . . . .29 B5
St George's Lodge KT13 . .53 D5
St George's Rd
  ⑥ Aldershot GU11, GU12 .105 B1
  Beckenham BR3 . . . . .44 B8
  Camberley GU15 . . . . .65 D6

St George's Rd continued
  Farnham GU9 . . . . .125 C3
  Feltham TW13 . . . . .15 D7
  Isleworth TW1 . . . . .6 B1
  ☑ Kingston u T KT2 . . . . .18 A1
  Mitcham CR4 . . . . .41 B6
  Richmond TW9 . . . . .6 F3
  South Nutfield RH1 . . . . .140 E1
  Wallington SM6 . . . . .60 B5
  Weybridge KT13 . . . . .53 D4
  Wimbledon SW19 . . . . .19 F2
St George's Rd E GU12 . .105 B1
St George's Sch SL5 . . . . .29 B6
St George's Sq KT3 . . . . . .38 E6
St George's Wlk CR0, CR9 .61 C7
St Georges Cl RH6 . . . . . .161 B3
St Georges Coll Jun Sch
  KT15 . . . . .52 D7
St Georges Cotts RH7 . . . .143 E6
St Georges Ct
  Addlestone KT15 . . . . .52 C6
  Crawley RH10 . . . . .201 D8
  East Grinstead RH19 . . . .185 C3
  Penge SE20 . . . . .43 B8
St Georges Ind Est GU15 .65 B3
St Georges Rd
  Addlestone KT15 . . . . .52 C6
  Farnham GU10 . . . . .126 B4
St Georges Yd ⑰ GU9 . . .125 B2
St German's Rd SE23 . . . . .23 E7
St Giles C of E Inf Sch
  KT21 . . . . .75 F1
St Giles' Sch CR2 . . . . .61 B4
St Gothard Rd SE21, SE27 .22 D4
St Gregory's RC Inf Sch
  GU15 . . . . .65 B6
St Helen's Cres SW16 . . . .41 F8
St Helen's Rd SW16 . . . . . .41 F8
St Helena Terr ㉓ TW9 . . . .6 D2
St Helens KT7 . . . . .36 F2
St Helens Cres GU47 . . . . .64 B8
St Helier Ave SM4 . . . . .40 C3
St Helier Cl Crawley RH11 201 A2
  Wokingham RG41 . . . . .25 B3
St Helier Hospl SM5 . . . . . .40 C1
St Helier Sta SM5 . . . . .40 A4
St Heliers Ave TW3, TW4 . . .5 A2
St Hilary's Prep Sch GU7 150 D3
St Hilda's Ave TW15 . . . . . .13 E3
St Hilda's Cl
  Crawley RH10 . . . . .182 C1
  Horley RH6 . . . . .161 B3
  Knaphill GU21 . . . . .68 D2
St Hildas Cl SW17 . . . . . . .20 E6
St Hugh of Lincoln RC
  Primary Sch GU21 . . . . . . .88 D2
St Hugh's Cl RH10 . . . . . .182 C1
St Hugh's Rd SE20 . . . . . . .23 B1
St Hughes Cl SW17 . . . . . .20 E6
St Ignatius RC Fst & Mid
  Sch TW16 . . . . .35 A8
St Ives RH10 . . . . .202 C7
St Ives Sch GU27 . . . . . . .208 E8
St James Ave KT17 . . . . . . .77 A8
St James' Ave GU9 . . . . . .125 D2
St James Ave SM1 . . . . .59 A6
St James C of E Prim Sch
  KT13 . . . . .53 C2
St James CE Prim Sch
  GU8 . . . . .148 C3
St James Cl KT18 . . . . .76 E5
St James' Cl KT3 . . . . .38 F4
St James Cl GU21 . . . . .69 A1
St James Ct Ashtead KT21 75 D2
  Farnham GU9 . . . . .125 C3
St James' Ct ☑ KT1 . . . . . .37 E6
St James Ct CR0 . . . . .42 B2
St James Mews KT13 . . . . .53 B6
St James Rd SM5 . . . . .59 E4
St James' Rd
  Kingston u T KT6 . . . . .37 D3
  Mitcham CR4 . . . . .21 A1
  Purley CR8 . . . . .80 C6
St James Rd SM1, SM2 . . .59 A5
St James' Terr GU9 . . . . . .125 C3
St James The Great RC
  (Aided) Sch CR7 . . . . .42 B7
St James Wlk RH11 . . . . . .201 C2
St James's Ave
  Beckenham BR3 . . . . .43 E6
  Hampton TW12 . . . . .16 C3
St James's Cl SW17 . . . . . .20 F6
St James's Cotts ⑭ TW10 . .6 D2
St James's Dr
  Balham SW12, SW17 . . . . .20 F8
  Upper Tooting SW17 . . . . . .20 F7
St James's Lodge ❹ CR0 . .42 E1
St James's Pk CR0 . . . . . . .42 C2
St James's Pl GU6 . . . . . . .174 C3
St James's Rd Croydon CR0 42 D2
  East Grinstead RH19 . . . .185 D1
  Hampton TW12 . . . . .16 B3
  Kingston u T KT1 . . . . .37 D7
  Thornton Heath CR0 . . . . .42 D2
St James's Sch TW2 . . . . . .16 E5
St James' Terr ❸ SW12 . . .21 A7
St Joan Cl RH11 . . . . .181 D1
St John Baptist C of E
  Prim Sch BR1 . . . . .24 C4
St John Cl RH13 . . . . .217 E1
St John Fisher RC Prim
  Sch SW20 . . . . .39 D4
St John Rigby RC Coll
  BR4 . . . . .63 D6
St John The Baptist Sch
  GU22 . . . . .90 A8
St John the Baptist C of E
  Jun Sch KT1 . . . . .17 D1

t John's RH5 . . . . .136 C3
t John's Ave KT22 . . . . . .95 B6
t John's Beamont Prep
Sch TW20 . . . . .11 B6
t John's Beamont Sch
TW19 . . . . .11 B6
t John's C of E Fst Sch
GU10 . . . . .167 E1
t John's C of E Prim Sch
SE20 . . . . .23 C1
t John's CE Jun Sch
CR3 . . . . .101 B2
t John's CE Prim Sch
KT1 . . . . .37 E6
t John's CE (VA) Inf Sch
CR3 . . . . .101 A2
t John's Cl
East Grinstead RH19 . . . .185 E2
Guildford GU2 . . . . .130 A8
Leatherhead KT22 . . . . . . .95 C7
t John's Cotts 2 SE20 . . .23 C1
t John's Court KT1 . . . . . .37 E5
t John's Cres RH12 . . . . .216 C3
t John's Ct
Brookwood GU24 . . . . . . .87 F7
Farnborough GU14 . . . . . .84 D5
Isleworth TW7 . . . . .5 F5
t John's Cty Prim Sch
GU21 . . . . .68 E1
t John's Dr SW18 . . . . . . .20 B7
t John's Gr Barnes SW13 . .7 F5
1 Richmond TW9 . . . . .6 E3
t John's Hill CR8 . . . . . . .80 A2
t John's Hill
Rd GU21, GU22 . . . . .89 B8
t John's Hospl TW1 . . . . .17 A8
t John's Lye GU21 . . . . . .88 F8
t John's Lye (Festival
Path) GU21 . . . . .88 F8
t John's Meadow RH7 . . .163 E6
t John's RC Sch RH12 . . .217 A1
t John's Rd
Carshalton SM5 . . . . .59 E7
Crawley RH11 . . . . .201 C6
Croydon CR0, CR9 . . . . . . .61 B7
East Grinstead RH19 . . . .185 E2
East Molesey KT8 . . . . . . .36 D5
Farnborough GU14 . . . . . .84 E5
Farnham GU9 . . . . .146 B8
Feltham TW13 . . . . .15 F4
Guildford GU2 . . . . .130 A8
Isleworth TW7 . . . . .5 F5
Leatherhead KT22 . . . . . . .95 C6
North Ascot SL5 . . . . .8 F1
Penge SE20 . . . . .23 C2
Redhill RH1 . . . . .139 F7
Richmond TW9 . . . . .6 E3
Sandhurst GU47 . . . . .64 C7
Sutton SM1 . . . . .59 B8
Teddington KT1 . . . . .37 C7
Westcott RH4 . . . . .135 C6
Wimbledon SW19 . . . . . . .19 E2
Woking GU21 . . . . .69 B2
St John's Rise GU21 . . . . .89 B8
St John's Sch KT22 . . . . . .95 B6
St John's (Shirley) C of E
Prim Sch CR0 . . . . .62 D7
St John's St GU7 . . . . . . .150 F6
St John's Terrace Rd
RH1 . . . . .139 F7
St Johns Ave KT17 . . . . . .77 A7
South Godstone RH9 . . . .142 F5
Woking GU21 . . . . .89 A8
St Johns Cty Prim Sch
RH1 . . . . .139 E7
St Johns Dr KT12 . . . . . . .35 C1
St Johns Gr GU21 . . . . . .146 B8
St Johns Mews GU21 . . . .89 A8
St Johns Rd KT3 . . . . .38 C6
St Johns Rd SG45 . . . . . . .45 B4
St Johns Way KT16 . . . . . .33 A1
St Joseph's Convent
Prep Sch KT8 . . . . .36 C4
St Joseph's RC Coll SW16 22 B2
St Joseph's RC Inf Sch
SE19 . . . . .22 C2
St Joseph's RC Jun Sch
SE19 . . . . .22 C2
St Joseph's RC Prim Sch
Bracknell RG12 . . . . .27 D7
Dorking RH4 . . . . .136 A7
Epsom KT18 . . . . .76 C5
Kingston u T KT1 . . . . . . .37 F7
Redhill RH1 . . . . .118 E2
St Joseph's RC Sch GU2 .108 F3
St Joseph's
Rd GU11, GU12 . . . . . . .105 A1
St Joseph's Sch GU6 . . . .174 F6
St Josephs RC Prim Sch
GU11 . . . . .126 A8
St Jude's C of E Sch
TW20 . . . . .11 C2
St Jude's Cl TW20 . . . . . .11 C3
St Jude's Cotts TW20 . . . .11 C3
St Jude's Rd TW20 . . . . . .11 C3
St Julian's Cl SE27, SW16 .22 A4
St Julian's Farm Rd
SE27, SW16 . . . . .22 B4
St Katharines Rd CR3 . . .101 A2
St Kitts Terr SE19 . . . . . . .22 E3
St Lawrence C of E Mid
Sch KT8 . . . . .36 D5
St Lawrence Ct GU24 . . . .68 E8
St Lawrence Cty Prim
Sch KT24 . . . . .113 D8
St Lawrence RC Sch TW13 15 B6
St Lawrence Way CR3 . . .100 D4

St Lawrences Way RH2 . .118 A1
St Leonard's Gdns TW5 . . .4 E6
St Leonard's Rd
Claygate KT10 . . . . .55 F4
Croydon CR0, CR9 . . . . . . .61 B7
Kingston u T KT6 . . . . . . .37 D4
Thames Ditton KT7 . . . . . .37 A2
Windsor SL4 . . . . .9 D8
St Leonard's Sq KT6 . . . . .37 D4
St Leonard's Wlk SW16 . . .21 F1
St Leonards C of E Prim
Sch SW16 . . . . .21 D3
St Leonards Ct SW16 . . . . .7 C4
St Leonards Cty Inf Sch
RH13 . . . . .217 E2
St Leonards Dr RH10 . . . .202 A4
St Leonards Pk RH19 . . . .185 E1
St Leonards Rd
Burgh Heath KT18 . . . . . .97 C8
Horsham RH13 . . . . .218 A1
Mortlake SW14 . . . . .7 C4
St Louis Rd SE27 . . . . . . .22 D4
St Luke's C of E Prim Sch
Kingston u T KT2 . . . . . . .37 F8
Richmond TW9 . . . . .7 A6
West Norwood SE27 . . . . .22 C3
St Luke's Cl SE25 . . . . . . .43 B3
St Luke's Hospl GU1 . . . .130 F7
St Luke's Rd CR3 . . . . . . .80 F1
St Luke's Sq 9 GU16 . . . .130 F8
St Lukes Ct GU21 . . . . . . .70 C5
St Margaret Clitherow RC
Prim Sch RG12 . . . . .26 F2
St Margaret's GU1 . . . . . .109 F1
St Margaret's Ave
Cheam SM3 . . . . .58 E7
Dormans Park RH19 . . . . .185 F6
St Margaret's CE Sch
RH11 . . . . .201 B7
St Margaret's Ct 9 TW1 . . .6 B1
St Margaret's Dr TW1 . . . . .6 B2
St Margaret's Gr TW1 . . . . .6 A1
St Margaret's Rd
East Grinstead RH19 . . . .185 F3
Hooley CR5 . . . . .99 B6
Isleworth TW1 . . . . .6 B2
Twickenham TW1 . . . . .6 B2
St Margaret's Sta TW1 . . . .6 B1
St Margarets Bsns Ctr 11
TW1 . . . . .6 B1
St Margarets Ct RH12 . . .216 F7
St Margarets Dr KT18 . . . .76 C5
St Mark's C of E Prim Sch
Croydon SE25 . . . . .43 A5
Farnborough GU14 . . . . . .105 D8
St Mark's Catholic Sch
TW3 . . . . .5 A4
St Mark's CE Prim Sch
BR2 . . . . .44 F6
St Mark's CE (VA) Prim
Sch GU7 . . . . .150 B3
St Mark's Fst Sch CR4 . . . .40 F7
St Mark's Hill KT6 . . . . . . .37 E3
St Mark's La RH12 . . . . . .217 E6
St Mark's Pl SW19 . . . . . .19 F2
St Mark's Rd
Bracknell RG42 . . . . .26 C8
Croydon SE25 . . . . .43 A5
Teddington TW11 . . . . . . .17 B1
St Marks Cl GU14 . . . . . . .85 C1
St Marks Pl GU9 . . . . . . .125 B2
St Marks Rd KT18, KT20 . . .77 C1
St Martha's GU5 . . . . . . .154 E8
St Martha's Ave GU22 . . . .89 F6
St Martha's Ct GU4 . . . . .131 B3
St Martin's Ave KT18 . . . . .76 E5
St Martin's C of E Inf Sch
KT18 . . . . .76 D4
St Martin's C of E Jun Sch
KT18 . . . . .76 D4
St Martin's C of E Prim
Sch RH4 . . . . .136 A8
St Martin's C of E Sch
(Pixham) RH4 . . . . .115 C1
St Martin's Cl KT17 . . . . . .76 E6
St Martin's Ct
Staines TW15 . . . . .13 C3
West Norwood SE27 . . . . .22 B6
St Martin's Way SW17 . . . .20 C5
St Martin-in-the-Fields
High Sch SW2 . . . . .22 A7
St Martins Cl KT24 . . . . . .112 E6
St Martins Ct KT24 . . . . . .112 E6
St Louis Dr KT12 . . . . . . .54 C7
St Martins Mews RH4 . . .136 B7
St Mary Ave SM6 . . . . . . .60 B7
St Mary Magdalene C of E
Sec Sch TW10 . . . . .7 A2
St Mary's 4 KT13 . . . . . . .53 D7
St Mary's Ave
Beckenham BR2 . . . . .44 E6
Stanwell TW19 . . . . .13 D8
Teddington TW11 . . . . . . .16 F2
St Mary's C of E Inf Sch
KT22 . . . . .95 C5
St Mary's C of E Prim Sch
Chessington KT9 . . . . .56 F4
Long Ditton KT7 . . . . . . .37 D1
Winkfield RG42 . . . . .8 B3
St Mary's C of E Sch
TW19 . . . . .13 E8
St Mary's CE (Aided)
Sch RH19 . . . . .185 D2
St Mary's CE controlled
Inf Sch GU8 . . . . .149 E6
St Mary's CE JunSch RH8122 E7

St Mary's CE Prim Sch
KT14 . . . . .71 E6
St Mary's Church Sch
TW1 . . . . .17 A8
St Mary's Cl
Chessington KT9 . . . . .56 F3
Ewell KT17 . . . . .57 F2
Fetcham KT22 . . . . .94 D4
Oxted RH8 . . . . .122 E6
Stanwell TW19 . . . . .13 D8
Sunbury TW16 . . . . .35 A5
St Mary's Cottage Hospl
TW12 . . . . .35 F8
St Mary's Cres
Hounslow TW7 . . . . .5 E7
Stanwell TW19 . . . . .13 D8
St Mary's Ct
Kingston u T KT3 . . . . . . .38 E6
Wallington SM6 . . . . .60 C6
St Mary's Dr
Crawley RH10 . . . . .202 B8
East Bedfont TW14 . . . . . .14 C8
St Mary's Gdns
Bagshot GU19 . . . . .47 E3
Horsham RH12 . . . . .217 C1
St Mary's Gn TN16 . . . . . .83 C1
St Mary's Gr
Biggin Hill TN16 . . . . .83 C1
Chiswick W4 . . . . .7 B8
Richmond TW10, TW9 . . . . .6 F3
St Mary's High Sch CR0 . . .42 C1
St Mary's Hill SL5 . . . . . . .29 C4
St Mary's House RH12 . . .217 C1
St Mary's Mt CR3 . . . . . . .100 F3
St Mary's Pl GU9 . . . . . . .125 C3
St Mary's RC Inf Sch CR0 .42 D1
St Mary's RC Jun Sch
Carshalton SM5 . . . . .59 F5
Croydon CR0 . . . . .42 D1
St Mary's RC Prim Sch
Beckenham BR3 . . . . .24 C1
Chiswick W4 . . . . .7 B8
Isleworth TW7 . . . . .6 A4
Merton SW19 . . . . .20 A1
St Mary's RC Sch TW7 . . . .6 A4
St Mary's RC Sch Ascot SL5 .29 B2
Horsham RH12 . . . . .217 C1
St Mary's & St Peter's
Prim Sch TW11 . . . . .16 F3
St Mary's Univ Coll TW1 . .16 F5
St Marys CE (VA) Prim
Sch GU8 . . . . .191 C4
St Marys Cl GU47 . . . . . . .64 C8
St Marys La SL4 . . . . .8 D5
St Marys Rd KT22 . . . . . . .95 B4
St Marys Wlk RH1 . . . . . .120 D2
St Matthew's Ave KT6 . . . .37 F1
St Matthew's C of E
Prim Sch RH1 . . . . .118 F3
St Matthew's CE Fst Sch
SW20 . . . . .39 A8
St Matthew's CE Prim Sch
KT6 . . . . .37 E2
St Matthew's Ct TW15 . . . .14 A3
St Matthew's Rd RH1 . . . .118 F2
St Matthews (C of E) Sch
KT11 . . . . .73 B1
St Merryn Ct BR3 . . . . . . .24 A1
St Michael's Ave GU3 . . . .108 C6
St Michael's C of E Prim
Sch RG12 . . . . .27 A4
St Michael's CE (VA)
Fst Sch RH5 . . . . .115 C8
St Michael's Cl KT12 . . . . .54 C8
St Michael's Prim Sch
Forest Hill SE26 . . . . .23 E4
Wandsworth SW18 . . . . . .19 F8
St Michael's RC Prim Sch
TW15 . . . . .14 A3
St Michael's Rd
Aldershot GU11, GU12 . . . .105 B1
Croydon CR0 . . . . .42 C1
Farnborough GU14 . . . . . .85 B6
Sheerwater GU21 . . . . . . .70 D5
Wallington SM6 . . . . .60 C4
St Michael's & St Martin's
RC Prim Sch TW4 . . . . . . .4 F4
St Michaels C of E Inf
Sch GU11 . . . . .126 B8
St Michaels C of E Jun
Sch GU11 . . . . .126 C8
St Michaels Cl KT4 . . . . . .57 F8
St Michaels Cotts RG45 . . .45 C8
St Michaels Ct 1 KT13 . . . .53 C5
St Michaels Rd
Ashford TW15 . . . . .14 A3
Camberley GU15 . . . . .65 B5
Caterham CR3 . . . . .100 D5
East Grinstead RH19 . . . .185 C4
St Micheal's C of E Sch
SL5 . . . . .29 D4
St Mildred's Rd GU1 . . . . .109 C2
St Mildreds Rd SE12, SE6 . .24 B4

St Monica's Rd KT20 . . . . .97 F6
St Nazaire Cl TW20 . . . . . .12 C3
St Nicholas Ave KT23 . . . .94 B7
St Nicholas C of E Prim
Sch Cranleigh GU6 . . . . .174 D3
Shepperton TW17 . . . . . . .34 B3
St Nicholas Ct RH10 . . . . .202 C7
St Nicholas Ctr SM1 . . . . .59 B5
St Nicholas Dr TW17 . . . . .34 A2
St Nicholas Glebe SW17 . .21 A2
St Nicholas Hill KT22 . . . .95 B5
St Nicholas Rd Sutton SM1 .59 B5
Thames Ditton KT7 . . . . . .36 F3
St Nicholas Sch
Croydon CR9 . . . . .61 A6
Purley CR8 . . . . .80 A6
St Nicholas Specl Sch
RH1 . . . . .119 D6
St Nicholas Way SM1 . . . .59 B5
St Nicolas Ave GU6 . . . . .174 E3
St Nicolas CE Inf Sch
GU2 . . . . .130 C7
St Nicolas Cl GU6 . . . . . .174 E3
St Normans Way KT17 . . . .58 A1
St Olave's Cl TW18 . . . . . .12 F1
St Olave's Wlk SW16 . . . . .41 D7
St Omer Rd GU1 . . . . . . .131 A8
St Omer Ridge GU1 . . . . .131 A8
St Osmund's RC Prim Sch
SW13 . . . . .7 F6
St Oswald's Rd SW16 . . . .42 B8
St Patrick's RC Prim Sch
GU14 . . . . .85 D4
St Paul's C of E Jun Sch
KT2 . . . . .18 A1
St Paul's C of E Jun Sch
RG41 . . . . .25 A4
St Paul's Catholic Sch
TW16 . . . . .35 A8
St Paul's CE Inf Sch
GU10 . . . . .127 A7
St Paul's CE Prim Sch
Addlestone KT15 . . . . .52 A6
Chessington KT9 . . . . .56 E6
St Paul's CE (VA) Prim
Sch RH4 . . . . .136 B6
St Paul's Cl
Addlestone KT15 . . . . .52 A5
Ashford TW15 . . . . .14 C3
Carshalton SM5 . . . . .40 E1
Chessington KT9 . . . . .56 D6
Hounslow TW3, TW4 . . . . . .4 E5
St Paul's Ct TW4 . . . . .4 E5
St Paul's Gate RG41 . . . . .25 A6
St Paul's Rd Brentford TW8 . .6 D8
Egham TW18 . . . . .12 D2
South Norwood CR7 . . . . . .42 C6
St Paul's Rd E RH4, RH5 . .136 B7
St Paul's Rd W RH4 . . . . .136 B6
St Pauls C of E Prim Sch
TW8 . . . . .6 D8
St Pauls' CE Fst Sch
GU10 . . . . .126 F6
St Pauls Cl GU10 . . . . . . .126 F7
St Pauls Rd Richmond TW9 . .6 F4
Woking GU21 . . . . .70 B2
St Peter & St Paul CE
Inf Sch CR3 . . . . .100 A2
St Peter's CE Jun Sch
GU14 . . . . .85 C4
St Peter's Cl
Old Woking GU22 . . . . . . .90 C7
Staines TW18 . . . . .12 F2
St Peter's Gdns
West Norwood SE27 . . . . .22 A5
Wrecclesham GU10 . . . . . .145 F6
St Peter's Hospl SE1 . . . . .51 D7
St Peter's Prim Sch CR2 . .61 E4
St Peter's RC (Aided) Sch
RH19 . . . . .185 C1
St Peter's RC Comp Sch
GU1 . . . . .110 C2
St Peter's RC Prim Sch
KT22 . . . . .95 C7
St Peter's Rd
Crawley RH11 . . . . .201 C6
Croydon CR0, CR2 . . . . . . .61 D6
East Molesey KT8 . . . . . . .36 A5
Isleworth TW1 . . . . .6 B2
Old Woking GU22 . . . . . . .90 B7
St Peter's St CR0, CR2 . . . .61 D5
St Peter's Way
Addlestone KT15 . . . . .51 F6
Addlestone KT15, KT16 . . . .51 F7
Chertsey KT16 . . . . .52 B8
Frimley GU16 . . . . .85 F7
St Peters CE Inf Sch RH8 122 A2
St Peters CE Prim Sch
GU9 . . . . .146 A7
St Peters Cl SW17 . . . . . . .20 E6
St Peters Ct KT8 . . . . .36 A5
St Peters Mead GU22 . . . .90 B2
St Peters Pk GU11, GU9 . . .125 E8
St Peters Rd KT1 . . . . .38 A7
St Peters Way UB3 . . . . . . .3 D8
St Philip's Ave KT4 . . . . . .58 B8
St Philip's Rd KT6 . . . . . . .37 D3
St Philips Sch KT9 . . . . . . .56 F6
St Philomena's Sch SM5 . .59 E5
St Pier's La RH7, TN8 . . . .165 B5
St Pinnock Ave KT16 . . . . .33 A8
St Polycarp's RC Prim
Sch GU9 . . . . .125 D1
St Richard's with St
Andrew's CE Prim Sch
TW10 . . . . .17 B5

St Richards Ct TW10 . . . . .17 B5
St Robert Southwell RC
Sch RH11 . . . . .218 A6
St Sampson Rd RH11 . . . .200 F2
St Saviour's Coll SE27 . . . .22 D4
St Saviour's Pl GU1 . . . . .109 C1
St Saviour's Rd CR0 . . . . .42 C3
St Stephen's C of E Jun
Sch TW1 . . . . .6 B1
St Stephen's CE Prim Sch
RH9 . . . . .142 F6
St Stephen's Cl RH12 . . . .207 F6
St Stephen's Cres CR7 . . . .42 A6
St Stephen's Gdns GU1 . . .6 C1
St Stephen's Rd TW3, TW4 . .5 A2
St Stephens Ave KT21 . . . .75 E3
St Stephens Cl GU27 . . . . .208 C7
St Stephens Ct RH19 . . . .142 E5
St Swithun's Cl RH19 . . . .185 F1
St Teresa's Prep Sch
(Grove House) KT24 . . . .113 D7
St Teresa's RC Prim Sch
SM4 . . . . .40 D3
St Theresa Cl KT18 . . . . . .76 C5
St Theresa's RC Prim Sch
RG40 . . . . .25 D5
St Theresa's RC Sch TW14 . .3 F3
St Thomas' Cl KT6 . . . . . .37 F1
St Thomas Cl GU21 . . . . . .69 C2
St Thomas More RC
KT8 . . . . .36 C4
St Thomas of Canterbury
RC Mid Sch CR4 . . . . . . .41 A6
St Thomas of
Canterbury RC Sch
GU1 . . . . .110 B1
St Thomas' Rd W4 . . . . . . .7 C8
St Thomas Wlk SL3 . . . . . .1 D7
St Thomas's Dr GU4 . . . . .111 E4
St Thomas's Mews GU1 . .130 F7
St Vincent Cl
Crawley RH10 . . . . .202 D5
West Norwood SE27 . . . . .22 B3
St Vincent Rd
Twickenham TW2 . . . . .5 C1
Walton-on-T KT12 . . . . . . .54 B7
St Wilfrid's RC Sch RH11 201 B5
St William of York RC
Prim Sch SE23 . . . . .23 E7
St Winifred's RC Prim Sch
SE12 . . . . .24 F8
St Winifred's Rd
Biggin Hill TN16 . . . . .83 F1
Teddington TW11 . . . . . . .17 B2
St Winifreds CR8 . . . . .80 C4
Salamanca Pk GU11 . . . . .104 F3
Salamander Cl KT2 . . . . . .17 C3
Salamander Quay KT1 . . . .37 D8
Salbrook Rd RH1 . . . . . . .140 A1
Salcombe Dr SM4 . . . . . . .39 D1
Salcombe House SE23 . . . .23 C6
Salcombe Rd TW15 . . . . . .13 E5
Salcot Cres CR0 . . . . .63 C1
Salcott Rd CR0 . . . . .60 F6
Sale Garden Cotts RG40 . .25 C5
Salehurst Rd RH10 . . . . . .202 C6
Salem Pl CR0, CR9 . . . . . .61 C7
Salerno Cl GU11 . . . . . . .105 A2
Sales Ct 7 GU11 . . . . . . .105 A1
Salesian Catholic Comp
Sch KT16 . . . . .51 E8
Salesian Coll GU14 . . . . . .85 D1
Salesian Sch KT16 . . . . . .33 A1
Salesian View GU14 . . . . .105 E8
Salford Rd SW12, SW2 . . . .21 D7
Salfords Cty Prim Sch
RH1 . . . . .140 A3
Salfords Sta RH1 . . . . . . .140 B1
Salfords Way RH1 . . . . . . .140 A3
Salisbury Ave SM1, SM2 . . .58 F4
Salisbury Cl
Wokingham RG41 . . . . . . .25 A2
Worcester Park KT4 . . . . . .57 F7
Salisbury Gdns SW19 . . . .19 E1
Salisbury Gr GU16 . . . . . . .86 A3
Salisbury House SW19 . . . .19 D5
Salisbury Pl KT14 . . . . . . .71 C8
Salisbury Rd Ash GU12 . . .106 A3
Banstead SM7 . . . . .78 B5
Blackwater GU17 . . . . . . .64 C5
Crawley RH10 . . . . .201 C4
Croydon CR0, SE25 . . . . . .43 A3
Farnborough GU14 . . . . . .85 C3
Feltham TW13 . . . . .15 C7
Harlington TW6 . . . . .3 C1
Hounslow TW4 . . . . .4 C4
Kingston u T KT3 . . . . . . .38 C6
Richmond TW9 . . . . .6 E3
Tyler's Green RH9 . . . . . .121 C4
Wallington SM5 . . . . .59 F4
Wimbledon SW19 . . . . . . .19 E1
Woking GU22 . . . . .89 E8
Worcester Park KT19, KT4 . .57 E2
Salisbury Terr GU16 . . . . . .86 A3
Salix Cl TW16 . . . . .15 B1
Salliesfield TW2 . . . . .5 C1
Salmons La CR3 . . . . .100 F7
Salmons La W CR3 . . . . . .100 F7
Salmons Rd
Chessington KT9 . . . . .56 E4
Effingham KT24 . . . . .113 C6
Salt Box Rd
Guildford GU3, GU4 . . . . .109 A6
Worplesdon GU3, GU4 . . . .109 B6
Salt La GU8 . . . . .171 E5

Saltash Cl SM1 . . . . .58 F6
Saltbox Hill TN16 . . . . . . .83 B6
Saltdean Cl RH10 . . . . . .201 D3
Salter House 🖪 SW16 . . . . .21 C4
Salter's Hill SE19, SE27 . . .22 D3
Salterford Rd SW17 . . . . . .21 A2
Salterns Rd SW16 . . . . . .202 C3
Saltire Gdns 🖪 RG42 . . . . .27 A8
Saltram Rd GU14 . . . . . . .85 E2
Salvador SW17 . . . . .20 F3
Salvation Pl KT22 . . . . . . .95 A3
Salvington Rd RH11 . . . . .200 F3
Salwey Cl RG12 . . . . .27 B3
Samaritan Cl RH11 . . . . . .200 E4
Samarkand Cl GU15 . . . . . .66 B4
Sambrook Mews SE6 . . . . .24 B7
Samos Rd SE20 . . . . .43 B7
Samphire Cl RH11 . . . . . .201 A3
Sampleoak La
  Chilworth GU4 . . . . .131 E2
  Wonersh GU4 . . . . .131 E2
Sampson Bsns Pk GU15 . .65 B3
Sampson Ct SW17 . . . . . . .34 C4
Sampson Rd RG42 . . . . . . .26 D8
Sampson's
  Almshouses GU9 . . . . . .125 A1
Samuel Cody Sch The
  GU14 . . . . .105 B7
Samuel Ct BR3 . . . . .44 B6
Samuel Johnson Cl SW16 .21 F4
San Carlos App GU11 . . . .105 C2
San Feliu Ct RH19 . . . . . .186 B2
Sanctuary Rd TW19, TW6 . .3 A1
Sanctuary The SM4 . . . . . .40 A3
Sand Hill GU14 . . . . .85 B7
Sand Hill Ct GU14 . . . . . . .85 B7
Sandal Rd KT3 . . . . .38 E5
Sandalwood GU2 . . . . . . .130 B8
Sandalwood Ave KT16 . . . .51 E7
Sandalwood Rd TW13 . . . .15 B5
Sandbourne Ave SW19 . . . .40 B7
Sandcross Cty Sch RH2 . .138 F6
Sandcross La RH2 . . . . . .139 A5
Sanders Cl TW12 . . . . . . .16 C3
Sanders House SW16 . . . . .21 E4
Sandersfield Rd SM7 . . . . .78 B4
Sanderstead Cl SW12 . . . . .21 C8
Sanderstead Court Ave
  CR2 . . . . .81 A6
Sanderstead Ct CR2 . . . . . .81 A7
Sanderstead Hill CR2 . . . . .80 F8
Sanderstead Hts CR2 . . . . .81 A8
Sanderstead Rd CR2 . . . . . .61 D2
Sanderstead Sta CR2 . . . . .61 D2
Sandes Pl KT22 . . . . .75 A1
Sandfield Cty Prim Sch
  GU1 . . . . .130 D8
Sandfield Gdns CR7 . . . . . .42 B6
Sandfield Pl CR7 . . . . .42 C6
Sandfield Terr GU1 . . . . . .130 D8
Sandfields GU23 . . . . .90 D3
Sandford Ct GU11 . . . . . . .104 F1
Sandford Down RG12 . . . . .27 F4
Sandford Rd
  Aldershot GU11 . . . . . . .104 F1
  Heath End GU9 . . . . . . .125 B7
Sandgate House 🖪 BR3 . . . .24 A1
Sandgate La SW17, SW18 . .20 E7
Sandhawes Hill RH19 . . . .186 A4
Sandheath Rd GU26 . . . . .188 C7
Sandhill La RH10 . . . . . . .204 B4
Sandhills CR0, SM6 . . . . . .60 D6
Sandhills Ct GU25 . . . . . . .31 E4
Sandhills La GU25, TW20 . .31 F4
Sandhills Meadow TW17 . .34 C2
Sandhills Rd RH2 . . . . . . .139 A7
Sandhurst Ave KT5 . . . . . .38 B2
Sandhurst Ct CR2 . . . . . . .61 C2
Sandhurst La GU17 . . . . . .64 B6
Sandhurst Prim Sch SE6 . .24 E7
Sandhurst Rd Catford BR1 .24 D7
  Crowthorne RG45 . . . . . .45 B3
  Wokingham RG40 . . . . . .25 A1
Sandhurst Sch GU47 . . . . .45 D1
Sandhurst Sta GU47 . . . . .64 A8
Sandhurst Way CR2 . . . . . .61 E3
Sandiford House CR3 . . . .100 E3
Sandiford Rd SM3 . . . . . . .58 F8
Sandiland Cres BR2 . . . . . .63 F8
Sandilands CR0 . . . . .62 A7
Sandlands Gr KT20 . . . . . .97 A4
Sandlands Rd KT20 . . . . . .97 A3
Sandon Cl KT10 . . . . .36 D1
Sandon House 🖪 SW2 . . . . .21 E8
Sandown Ave KT10 . . . . . .55 C5
Sandown Cl
  Blackwater GU17 . . . . . . .64 D5
  Cranford TW5 . . . . .4 A6
Sandown Cres GU11 . . . . .126 B7
Sandown Ct 🖪 SM2 . . . . . . .59 B3
Sandown Dr Frimley GU16 . .65 E2
  Wallington SM5 . . . . .60 A2
Sandown Gate KT10 . . . . . .55 D7
Sandown House 23 B2
Sandown Ind Pk KT10 . . . . .55 A8
Sandown Lodge KT18 . . . . .76 D5
Sandown Park KT10 . . . . . .55 C8
Sandown Rd Coulsdon CR5 .79 A3
  Croydon SE25 . . . . .43 B4
  Esher KT10 . . . . .55 C6
Sandpiper Cl RH11 . . . . . .200 D4
Sandpiper Rd Cheam SM1 . .58 F6
  Selsdon CR2 . . . . .81 D8
Sandpit Hall Rd GU24 . . . . .69 A7

Sandpit Heath GU3 . . . . . .108 D5
Sandpit Rd Catford BR1 . . . .24 E3
  Redhill RH1 . . . . .139 F8
Sandpits Rd
  Richmond TW10 . . . . . . .17 D6
  South Croydon CR0 . . . . .62 D6
Sandra Cl TW3 . . . . .5 B2
Sandra House KT8 . . . . . . .36 D4
Sandringham Ave SW20 . . .39 E7
Sandringham Cl
  East Grinstead RH19 . . . .206 A8
  Farnborough GU14 . . . . .105 B8
  🖪 Putney SW19 . . . . .19 D7
  Pyrford GU22 . . . . .71 A3
Sandringham Ct
  Beckenham BR3 . . . . . . .44 C8
  Belmont SM2 . . . . .59 A2
Sandringham Cty Inf Sch
  GU16 . . . . .85 F7
Sandringham Dr TW15 . . . .13 D4
Sandringham Gdns TW5 . . .4 A6
Sandringham Pk KT11 . . . .74 A7
Sandringham Rd
  Crawley RH11 . . . . .201 B2
  North Cheam KT4 . . . . . .58 A7
  Stanwell TW19, TW6 . . . . .2 E2
  Thornton Heath CR0 . . . . .42 C4
Sandringham Way GU16 . . .85 F7
Sandrock GU27 . . . . .208 C6
Sandrock Hill Rd
  Rowledge GU10 . . . . . . .146 A5
  Wrecclesham GU10 . . . . .146 A5
Sandrock Pl CR0 . . . . .62 D6
Sandrock Rd RH4 . . . . . . .135 B5
Sandroyd Way KT11 . . . . . .74 A6
Sands Cl GU10 . . . . .126 D2
Sands Ct Farnham GU10 . .126 D2
  The Sands GU10 . . . . . .126 D2
Sandstone 🖪 TW9 . . . . .7 A7
Sandways 🖪 TW9 . . . . .7 A6
Sandy Cl GU22 . . . . .70 C2
Sandy Croft KT17 . . . . .58 C1
Sandy Cross GU10 . . . . . .126 F4
Sandy Ct KT11 . . . . .73 F6
Sandy Dr Cobham KT11 . . . .74 A8
  East Bedfont TW14 . . . . . .14 E7
Sandy Hill Rd
  Heath End GU9 . . . . . . .125 B7
  Wallington SM6 . . . . .60 C2
Sandy Holt KT11 . . . . .73 F6
Sandy La Albury GU5 . . . . .132 D2
  Artington GU2, GU3 . . . . .130 B5
  Belmont SM2 . . . . .58 E2
  Betchworth RH3 . . . . . . .116 E1
  Bletchingley RH1 . . . . . .120 C3
  Bracknell RG12 . . . . .27 C8
  Camberley GU15 . . . . . . .65 E6
  Chobham GU24 . . . . .49 E2
  Cobham KT11, KT22 . . . . .74 B7
  Crawley Down RH10 . . . .204 A8
  East Grinstead RH19 . . . .185 F1
  Farnborough GU14 . . . . . .84 D7
  Farncombe GU7 . . . . . . .150 D6
  Grayswood GU27 . . . . . .189 E1
  Haslemere GU26, GU27 . .207 C7
  Haslemere, Nutcombe GU26 188 F2
  Kingswood KT20 . . . . . . .98 A4
  Limpsfield RH8 . . . . .123 B7
  Mitcham CR4 . . . . .41 A8
  Normandy GU3 . . . . .107 D4
  North Ascot SL5 . . . . . . .28 C8
  Nutfield RH1 . . . . .119 E1
  Oxted RH8 . . . . .122 C6
  Pyrford GU22 . . . . .71 A3
  Reigate RH2 . . . . .138 B8
  Richmond TW10 . . . . . . .17 D6
  Rushmoor GU10 . . . . . . .168 B5
  Sandhurst GU47 . . . . .45 A2
  Send GU23 . . . . .90 C4
  Shere GU5 . . . . .133 A3
  South Nutfield RH1 . . . . .119 E1
  Sunningdale SL5 . . . . . . .30 A4
  Teddington KT8, TW11 . . . .17 B1
  Thorpe GU25 . . . . .31 E5
  Walton-on-T KT12 . . . . . . .35 C3
  Woking GU22 . . . . .70 C2
Sandy La N SM6 . . . . .60 D5
Sandy La S SM6 . . . . .60 C3
Sandy Lane Jun Sch RG12 27 C8
Sandy Rd KT15 . . . . .52 A4
Sandy Ride SL5 . . . . .29 E5
Sandy Way Cobham KT11 . .74 A7
  Croydon CR0 . . . . .62 F7
  Walton-on-T KT12 . . . . . . .34 C1
  Woking GU22 . . . . .70 C2
Sandycombe Rd
  East Bedfont TW14 . . . . . .15 A7
  Richmond TW9 . . . . .7 A5
Sandycoombe Rd TW1 . . . . .6 C1
Sanger Ave KT9 . . . . .56 F6
Sanger Dr GU23 . . . . .90 C4
Sangers Cty Jun Sch
  RH6 . . . . .160 F3
Sangers Dr RH6 . . . . .160 F3
Sangley Rd Catford SE6 . . . .24 C7
  South Norwood SE25 . . . . .42 E5
Santina Cl GU9 . . . . .125 D8
Sanway Cl GU14 . . . . .71 E5
Sanway Rd KT14 . . . . .71 E5
Sapho Ct GU21 . . . . .68 A3
Sapte Cl GU6 . . . . .175 A3
Saracen Cl CR0 . . . . .42 D3
Sarah House SW15 . . . . . . .7 F3
Sarah Way GU14 . . . . .85 B4
Sardeson House 🖪 SW27 . . .22 B3
Sarel Way RH6 . . . . .161 B5
Sargent Cl RH10 . . . . .201 F2
Sarjant Path SW19 . . . . . . .19 D6

Sark Cl Crawley RH11 . . . .201 A2
  Heston TW5 . . . . .5 A7
Sarsby Dr TW19 . . . . .12 A6
Sarsen Ave TW3 . . . . .5 A5
Sarsfeld Rd SW12, SW17 . .20 F7
Sarum RG12 . . . . .26 F1
Sarum Cres RG40 . . . . . . .25 D7
Sarum Gn KT13 . . . . .53 E7
Satellite Bsns Village The
  RH10 . . . . .181 E2
Satis Ct KT17 . . . . .76 F8
Saturn Cl RH11 . . . . .200 E4
Saturn Croft RG42 . . . . . . .8 B2
Saunders Cl RH10 . . . . . .202 B7
Saunders Copse GU22 . . . .89 B6
Saunders House 🖪 SW2 . . .22 A7
Saunders La GU22 . . . . . . .89 B5
Saundersfield House SM7 .78 B5
Saunton Ave UB3 . . . . .3 F7
Saunton Gdns 🖪 GU14 . . . .85 A6
Savernake Way RG42 . . . . .27 F4
Savernake Wlk RH10 . . . .201 F3
Savile Cl New Malden KT3 . .38 E4
  Thames Ditton KT7 . . . . . .37 A1
Savile Gdns CR0 . . . . .61 F8
Savill Gardens The SW20 . .10 E2
Savill Gdns SW20 . . . . . . .39 A6
Saville Cres TW15 . . . . . . .14 D2
Saville Gdns GU15 . . . . . . .66 B5
Saville Rd TW1 . . . . .16 F7
Saville Row BR2 . . . . .44 F1
Savin Lodge SM2 . . . . .59 C3
Savona Ct 🖪 SW19 . . . . . . .19 D1
Savona Ct SW20 . . . . .39 D8
Savoy Gr GU17 . . . . .64 D3
Sawkins Cl SW19 . . . . . . .19 E6
Sawtry Cl SM5 . . . . .40 E1
Sawyer House 🖪 SE21 . . . .22 E4
Sawyer's Hill TW10 . . . . . .17 F8
Saxby Rd SW2 . . . . .21 E8
Saxby's La RH7 . . . . .164 D5
Saxley RH6 . . . . .161 C4
Saxon Ave TW13 . . . . .15 F6
Saxon Bsns Ctr SW19 . . . .40 C8
Saxon Cl KT6 . . . . .37 D3
Saxon Cres RH12 . . . . . . .217 B4
Saxon Croft GU9 . . . . .125 C1
Saxon Cty Jun Sch TW17 . .34 A4
Saxon Dr RG42 . . . . .27 E8
Saxon House Feltham TW13 15 F6
  Reigate RH2 . . . . .138 F6
Saxon Rd Ashford TW15 . . .14 D2
  Bromley BR1 . . . . .24 F1
  Crawley RH10 . . . . .202 E5
  Thornton Heath CR0, SE25 .42 D4
  Walton-on-T KT12 . . . . . . .54 D7
Saxon Way
  Harmondsworth UB7 . . . . .2 C8
  Reigate RH2 . . . . .117 F2
Saxonbury Ave TW16 . . . . .35 B7
Saxonbury Cl CR4 . . . . . . .40 D6
Saxonbury Gdns KT6 . . . . .37 C1
Saxonfield Cl SW2 . . . . . . .21 F8
Saxons KT20 . . . . .97 D6
Sayer Ct 🖪 GU21 . . . . .68 E1
Sayer's Wlk TW10 . . . . . . .17 F8
Sayers Cl Fetcham KT22 . . .94 C4
  Frimley GU16 . . . . .85 E7
Sayers The 🖪 RH19 . . . . . .185 C1
Sayes Court Farm Dr KT15 52 B5
Sayes Court Jun Sch KT15 52 B5
Sayes Ct KT15 . . . . .52 C5
Scaitcliffe Sch SW20 . . . . .11 A5
Scallows Cl RH10 . . . . . . .202 A7
Scallows Rd RH10 . . . . . .202 A7
Scampton Rd TW6 . . . . . . .2 F1
Scania Wlk RG42 . . . . .8 B2
Scarborough Cl
  Belmont SM2 . . . . .77 F8
  Biggin Hill TN16 . . . . . . .83 C1
Scarborough Rd TW6 . . . . .3 C1
Scarbrook Rd CR0, CR9 . . .61 C7
Scarlet Oaks GU15 . . . . . . .65 E3
Scarlet Rd SE6 . . . . .24 E5
Scarlett Cl GU21 . . . . .68 E1
Scarlett's Rd GU11 . . . . . .105 A3
Scarlette Manor Wlk 🔟
  SE24 . . . . .22 A8
Scarth Rd SW13 . . . . .7 F4
Scawen Cl SM5 . . . . .60 A6
Schaffer Ho RH10 . . . . . .202 C4
Schiller International
  Univ BR4 . . . . .63 D6
Scholars Ct RH10 . . . . . . .204 A8
Scholars Rd SW12 . . . . . . .21 C7
Scholars Wlk GU2 . . . . . . .130 B8
School Cl Bisley GU24 . . . . .68 A4
  Guildford GU1 . . . . .109 D3
  Horsham RH12 . . . . .218 A6
School Cotts GU22 . . . . . . .89 C5
School Hill
  Crowthorne RG45 . . . . . .45 D4
  Merstham RH1 . . . . .119 C7
  Sandhurst GU47 . . . . .45 A1
  Seale GU10 . . . . .127 B4
  Warnham RH12 . . . . .216 F8
  Wrecclesham GU10 . . . . .145 F6
School House La TW11 . . . .17 C1
School Houses GU8 . . . . . .172 E4
School La Addlestone KT15 . .52 A6
  Ashurst Wood RH19 . . . .206 E6
  Bagshot GU19 . . . . .47 E2
  Chiddingfold GU8 . . . . . .191 C4
  Crondall GU10 . . . . .124 D8
  East Clandon GU4 . . . . . .111 A4
  Egham TW20 . . . . .12 A3
  Farnham GU10 . . . . .146 D6
  Fetcham KT22 . . . . .94 D5

School La continued
  Forest Row RH18 . . . . . .206 F2
  Lower Halliford TW17 . . . . .34 B2
  Mickleham RH5 . . . . .115 C8
  Ockham GU23 . . . . .92 B5
  Pirbright GU24 . . . . .87 E5
  Puttenham GU3 . . . . . . .128 C4
  Shackleford GU8 . . . . . . .149 E6
  Surbiton KT6 . . . . .38 A1
  Teddington KT1 . . . . .37 C8
  Walton on t H KT20 . . . . . .97 A3
  West Horsley KT24 . . . . .112 B6
  Westcott RH4 . . . . .135 D6
  Windlesham GU20 . . . . . .48 D4
School Pas 🖪 KT1 . . . . . . .37 F7
School Rd Ascot SL5 . . . . . .29 D4
  Ashford TW15 . . . . .14 B2
  East Molesey KT8 . . . . . .36 D5
  Binstead GU10 . . . . .145 E3
  Grayshott GU26 . . . . . . .188 B4
  Hampton TW12 . . . . .16 C2
  Harmondsworth UB7 . . . . .2 D8
  Hascombe GU8 . . . . . . .172 E4
  Hounslow TW3 . . . . .5 C4
  Linchmere GU27 . . . . . . .207 F5
  Teddington KT1 . . . . .37 C8
  Windlesham GU20 . . . . . .48 D4
School Road Ave TW12 . . . .16 C2
School Wlk TW16 . . . . .35 A6
Schroder Ct TW20 . . . . . . .11 B3
Scillonian Rd GU2 . . . . . . .130 B7
Scilly Isles KT10 . . . . .55 E8
Scizdons Climb GU7 . . . . .150 F4
Scoles Cres SW2 . . . . .22 A7
Scoresdale SE19 . . . . .42 E8
Scory Cl RH11 . . . . .201 A3
Scotia Rd 🖪 SW2 . . . . .22 A8
Scotland Bridge Rd KT15 . .71 A8
Scotland Cl GU12 . . . . . . .106 A5
Scotland Farm Rd GU12 . .106 A5
Scotland Hill
  Sandhurst GU47 . . . . .45 A1
  Sandhurst GU47 . . . . .64 A8
Scotland La GU27 . . . . . . .208 C5
Scotlands Cl GU27 . . . . . .208 B5
Scotlands Dr GU27 . . . . . .208 C5
Scots Cl TW19 . . . . .13 D7
Scotsdale Cl SM2 . . . . .58 E3
Scotshall La CR6 . . . . .82 C4
Scott Cl Guildford GU2 . . . .109 A3
  Thornton Heath SW16 . . . .41 F8
  West Ewell KT19 . . . . . . .57 C5
Scott Farm Cl KT7 . . . . . . .37 B1
Scott Gdns TW5 . . . . .4 D7
Scott House SW10 . . . . . . .17 C6
Scott Rd RH10 . . . . .201 F3
Scott Terr RG12 . . . . .27 E8
Scott Trimmer Way TW3 . . .4 E5
Scott's Ave Ashford TW16 . .14 E1
  Beckenham BR2 . . . . . . .44 D7
Scott's Cl GU14 . . . . .85 B7
Scott's Grove Cl GU24 . . . .68 C6
Scott's Grove Rd GU24 . . . .68 C6
Scott's Hill RH1, RH6 . . . .162 D5
Scott's La BR2, BR3 . . . . . .44 D7
Scott's Way TW16 . . . . . . .14 E1
Scott-Broadwood CE
  Inf Sch The Capel RH5 . .178 D4
  Ockley RH5 . . . . .177 D4
Scotts Dr TW12 . . . . .16 B1
Scotts Farm Rd KT19 . . . . .57 C4
Scrooby St 🖪 SE6 . . . . .24 B8
Scrutton Cl SW12 . . . . . . .21 D8
Scylla Cres TW6&TW14 . . . .14 B8
Scylla Pl GU21 . . . . .89 A8
Scylla Rd TW14, TW6 . . . . . .3 B1
Seabrook Dr BR4 . . . . .63 E8
Seaford Rd Crawley RH11 . .201 A2
  Stanwell TW19, TW6 . . . . .2 D6
  Wokingham RG40 . . . . . .25 D6
Seaforth Ave KT3 . . . . .39 B5
Seaforth Gdns KT19 . . . . . .57 F5
Seaforth Lodge SW13 . . . . .7 F5
Sealand Rd TW6 . . . . .3 A1
Seale La GU10, GU3 . . . . .126 E4
Seale Rd Elstead GU8 . . . .148 B7
  The Sands GU8 . . . . . . .148 B7
Seaman's Gn RH5 . . . . . .178 D8
Searchwood Rd CR6 . . . . . .81 B1
Searle Ct CR4 . . . . .40 E8
Searle Hill RH2 . . . . .139 A7
Searle's View RH12 . . . . . .217 F5
Seath House 🖪 SE26 . . . . .23 B3
Seaton Cl Putney SW15 . . . .19 B8
  Twickenham TW2 . . . . . . .5 D1
Seaton Dr TW15 . . . . .13 E6
Seaton Rd Camberley GU15 .65 B5
  Mitcham CR4 . . . . .40 E7
  Twickenham TW2 . . . . . . .5 C1
Sebastopol Rd 🖪 GU11 . . .105 B2
  Walton-on-T KT12 . . . . . . .35 B3
  Woodham KT15 . . . . .52 B2
Second Ave Mortlake SW14 . .7 E4
  Walton-on-T KT12 . . . . . . .35 B3
  Woodham KT15 . . . . .52 B2
Second Cl KT8 . . . . .36 C5
Second Cross Rd TW2 . . . .16 E6
Seddon Ct RH11 . . . . .201 B1
Seddon Rd SM4 . . . . .40 D4
Sedgefield Cl RH10 . . . . . .202 C6
Sedgehill Cl RH10 . . . . . .202 C6
Sedgehill Sch SE6 . . . . . . .24 B3
Sedgemoor GU14 . . . . .85 D7
Sedgeway SE6 . . . . .24 F7
Sedgewick Cl RH10 . . . . .202 C6
Sedgewick House SW19 . . .19 D6
Sedgewood Cl BR2 . . . . . . .44 F2
Sedley Ct SE26 . . . . .23 B6

Seebys Oak GU47 . . . . . . .64 E4
Seeley Dr SE21 . . . . .22 E4
Seely Rd SW17 . . . . .21 A2
Seething Wells Halls Of
  Residence KT6 . . . . .37 C3
Seething Wells La KT6 . . . .37 C3
Sefton Cl GU24 . . . . .67 F6
Sefton Ct TW5 . . . . .5 B6
Sefton Ho 🔟 GU11 . . . . . .105 A3
Sefton Lodge 🖪 TW1 . . . . . .6 C1
Sefton Rd Croydon CR0 . . . .43 A3
  Epsom KT19 . . . . .57 D1
Segal Cl SE23 . . . . .23 E8
Segrave Cl KT13 . . . . .53 A3
Segsbury Gr RG12 . . . . . . .27 F5
Sekhon Terr TW13 . . . . . . .16 A5
Selborne Ave GU11 . . . . . .126 C6
Selborne Cl GU17 . . . . . . .64 C6
Selborne Gdns GU9 . . . . .146 A5
Selborne Rd
  Kingston u T KT3 . . . . . . .38 E7
  South Croydon CR0 . . . . .61 F7
Selbourne Ave KT15 . . . . . .52 B2
Selbourne Cl
  Crawley RH10 . . . . .182 D2
  Woodham KT15 . . . . .52 B1
Selbourne Rd GU1 . . . . . .110 A8
Selbourne Sq RH9 . . . . . .121 C5
Selby Cl KT9 . . . . .56 E3
Selby Ct TW2 . . . . .16 C7
Selby Gn SM5 . . . . .40 E2
Selby Rd Ashford TW15 . . . .14 C2
  Carshalton SM5 . . . . .40 E2
  Penge SE20 . . . . .43 A7
Selby Wlk 🖪 GU21 . . . . . . .69 B1
Selbys RH7 . . . . .164 E5
Selcroft Rd CR8 . . . . .80 B7
Selham Cl RH11 . . . . .201 A4
  Woking GU21 . . . . .69 F4
Selhurst New Ct SE25 . . . . .42 E4
Selhurst New Rd SE25 . . . .42 E3
Selhurst Park SE25 . . . . . .42 E5
Selhurst Pl CR0, SE25 . . . .42 E3
Selhurst Rd
  South Norwood CR0, SE25 . .42 E4
  Thornton Heath CR0, SE25 .42 E4
Selhurst Sta SE25 . . . . . . .42 E4
Selkirk Rd Twickenham TW2 16 C7
  Upper Tooting SW17 . . . . .20 C4
Sellar's Hill GU7 . . . . .150 D7
Sellincourt Inf Sch SW17 . .20 E2
Sellincourt Jun Sch SW17 20 E2
Sellincourt Rd SW17 . . . . . .20 E2
Sellindge Cl BR3 . . . . .23 F1
Selsdon Ave CR2 . . . . .61 D4
Selsdon Cl KT6 . . . . .37 E4
Selsdon Cres CR2 . . . . . . .62 C1
Selsdon High Sch CR2 . . . .62 D3
Selsdon Park Golf Course
  CR2 . . . . .81 B4
Selsdon Park Rd
  New Addington CR0, CR2 . . .62 C2
  Selsdon CR0, CR2 . . . . . .62 C2
  South Croydon CR0, CR2 . .62 C2
Selsdon Prim Sch CR2 . . . .62 C2
Selsdon Rd Croydon CR2 . . .61 D4
  West Norwood SE27 . . . . .22 B4
  Woodham KT15 . . . . .71 A8
Selsdon Road Ind Est CR2 61 C4
Selsey Cl 🖪 RH11 . . . . . . .201 B2
Selsey Rd RH11 . . . . .201 A4
Selsfield Rd
  Turners Hill RH10, RH19 . .204 A2
  West Hoathly RH19 . . . . .204 B1
Seltops Cl GU6 . . . . .174 F2
Selwood Cl TW19 . . . . .2 C1
Selwood Gdns TW19 . . . . . .2 C1
Selwood Rd Cheam SM3 . . .39 F1
  Chessington KT9 . . . . . . .56 D6
  Croydon CR0 . . . . .43 B1
  Old Woking GU22 . . . . . . .90 B7
Selworthy Rd SE23, SE6 . . .23 F5
Selwyn Ave TW9 . . . . .6 F4
Selwyn Cl Crawley RH10 . .182 C1
  Hounslow TW4 . . . . .4 E3
Selwyn Ct 🖪 TW10 . . . . . . .6 F2
Selwyn Rd KT3 . . . . .38 D4
Semaphore Rd GU1 . . . . . .130 E7
Semley Rd SW16 . . . . .41 E7
Semper Cl GU21 . . . . .68 E2
Send Barns La Send GU23 . .90 E2
  Send Marsh GU23 . . . . . .90 E2
Send C of E Fst Sch GU23 .90 E3
Send Cl GU23 . . . . .90 C4
Send Hill GU23 . . . . .90 C3
Send Marsh Rd Send GU23 .90 E4
  Send Marsh GU23 . . . . . .90 E4
Send Rd GU23 . . . . .90 C4
Seneca Rd CR4 . . . . .42 C5
Senga Rd CR4 . . . . .41 A1
Senhouse Rd SM3 . . . . . . .58 D7
Sequoia Pk RH11 . . . . . . .201 D4
Serpentine Gn RH1 . . . . . .119 D6
Serrin Way RH12 . . . . . . .217 D4
Service Rd Crawley, North
  Terminal RH6 . . . . .181 F8
  Crawley, South
  Terminal RH6 . . . . .182 B7
Servite House
  Beckenham BR3 . . . . . . .43 F8
  Dorking RH4 . . . . .136 A5
  Knaphill GU21 . . . . .68 D2
Servius Ct 🖪 TW8 . . . . .6 D7
Setley Way RG12 . . . . .27 F6
Seven Acres SM5 . . . . .59 E8
Seven Arches App KT13 . . .53 A3
Seven Hills Cl KT12, KT13 . .53 E2

Seven Hills Rd KT12, KT13 .53 E3
Seven Hills Rd (South)
 KT11 . . . . .72 E6
Sevenoaks CI SM2 . . . . . . .59 B1
Severn CI GU47 . . . . .64 C8
Severn Cres SL3 . . . . .1 B8
Severn Dr
 Hinchley Wood KT10 . . . . .56 A8
 Walton-on-T KT12 . . . . . . .54 D8
Severn Rd Crawley RH10 . .202 C5
 Farnborough GU14 . . . . . . .84 E6
Seward Rd BR3 . . . . .43 D7
Sewell Ave RG41 . . . . .25 A8
Sewer's Farm Rd RH5 . . . .155 E4
Sewill RH6 . . . . .180 F7
Seychelle Ct BR3 . . . . .24 B1
Seymour Ave
 Caterham CR3 . . . . .100 C4
 Ewell KT17 . . . . .58 B2
 West Barnes SM4 . . . . . . .39 C3
Seymour CI KT8 . . . . .36 C4
Seymour Dr GU15 . . . . .66 B7
Seymour Gdns
 Feltham TW13 . . . . .15 C4
 Kingston u T KT5 . . . . . . .37 F4
 Twickenham TW1 . . . . . . .17 B8
Seymour Mews KT17 . . . . .58 A1
Seymour PI Croydon SE25 . .43 B5
Woking GU23 . . . . .89 B7
Seymour Rd Carshalton CR4 41 C4
 Crawley RH11 . . . . .201 B2
 East Molesey KT8 . . . . . . .36 C4
 Godalming GU7 . . . . .150 B3
 Hampton TW12 . . . . .16 C3
 Headley Down GU35 . . . .187 C4
 Teddington KT1 . . . . .37 D8
 Wallington SM5 . . . . .60 A5
 Wandsworth SW18 . . . . . .19 F8
 Wimbledon SW19 . . . . . . .19 D5
Seymour Terr SE20 . . . . . . .43 B8
Seymour Villas SE20 . . . . .43 A8
Seymour Way TW16 . . . . . .14 E1
Shabden Cotts CR5 . . . . . . .98 F6
Shabden Park CR5 . . . . .98 E5
Shabden Park Hospl CR5 .98 E5
Shackleford Rd
 Old Woking GU22 . . . . . . .90 A7
 Shackleford GU8 . . . . . . .149 E6
Shacklegate La TW11 . . . . .16 E4
Shackleton CI SE23 . . . . . . .23 B6
Shackleton Ct
 2 Dulwich SE21 . . . . .22 D6
 6 Stanwell TW19 . . . . .2 E1
Shackleton Rd RH10 . . . . .201 D3
Shackstead La GU7 . . . . . .150 D3
Shackster La GU7 . . . . . . .150 C3
Shadbolt CI KT4 . . . . .57 F8
Shady Nook GU9 . . . . .125 B6
Shadyhanger GU7 . . . . . . .150 E6
Shaef Way TW11 . . . . .17 A1
Shaftesbury Ave TW14 . . . . .4 A1
Shaftesbury CI RG12 . . . . . .27 D4
Shaftesbury Cres TW18 . . .13 D1
Shaftesbury Ct
 Farnborough GU14 . . . . .105 C8
 Wokingham RG40 . . . . . . .25 D7
Shaftesbury House SE25 . . .43 A3
Shaftesbury Mount GU17 .64 D3
Shaftesbury Rd
 Beckenham BR3 . . . . .43 F7
 Bisley GU24 . . . . .67 F3
 Carshalton SM5 . . . . .40 E2
 Crawley RH10 . . . . .202 D4
 Richmond TW9 . . . . .6 E4
 Woking GU22 . . . . .70 B2
Shaftesbury Way TW2 . . . .16 D5
Shafteswood Ct SW17 . . . . .20 F5
Shagbrook RH2 . . . . .117 C2
Shakespeare Ave TW14 . . . .4 A1
Shakespeare Gdns GU14 .84 D5
Shakespeare Rd KT15 . . . . .52 D6
Shakespeare Way
 Feltham TW13 . . . . .15 C4
 Winkfield RG42 . . . . .27 E8
Shalbourne Rise GU15 . . . .65 D5
Shalden House SW15 . . . . . .7 F1
Shalden Rd GU12 . . . . . . .126 D8
Shaldon Dr SM4 . . . . .39 E4
Shaldon Way KT12 . . . . . . .54 C7
Shale Gn RH1 . . . . .119 D6
Shalesbrook La RH18 . . . .206 F1
Shalford Cty Inf Sch GU4 130 E3
Shalford La GU4 . . . . .130 E4
Shalford Mill GU4 . . . . . . .130 D5
Shalford Rd GU1, GU4 . . .130 D5
Shalford Sta GU4 . . . . . . .130 E3
Shalston Villas KT5, KT6 . .37 F3
Shalstone Rd SW14, TW9 . . .7 B4
Shambles The GU1 . . . . . .130 C7
Shamrock CI Fetcham KT22 94 D6
 Frimley GU16 . . . . .85 D8
Shamrock House SE26 . . . .23 A4
Shamrock Rd CR0 . . . . .41 F3
Shandys CI RH12 . . . . .217 A1
Shanklin Ct GU12 . . . . . . .105 C1
Shannon Commercial Ctr
 KT3 . . . . .39 A5
Shannon Corner KT3 . . . . . .39 A5
Shannon Ct CR0 . . . . .42 C1
Shannon Way BR3 . . . . .24 B2
Shap Cres SM5 . . . . .40 F1
Sharon CI Crawley RH10 . .202 A4
 Epsom KT19 . . . . .76 C6
 Great Bookham KT23 . . . . .94 A3
 Long Ditton KT6 . . . . .37 C1
Sharonelle Ct RG40 . . . . . .25 B6
Sharpthorne CI RH11 . . . .200 E5
Shaw CI Ewell KT17 . . . . . .76 F8

Shaw CI continued
 Ottershaw KT16 . . . . .51 C4
 Sanderstead CR2 . . . . . . .80 F7
Shaw Cres CR2 . . . . .80 F7
Shaw Ct CR3 . . . . .100 D6
Shaw Dr KT12 . . . . .35 C2
Shaw Path BR1 . . . . .24 F5
Shaw Pk RG45 . . . . .45 B3
Shaw Rd Catford BR1 . . . . .24 F5
 Tatsfield TN16 . . . . .103 C7
Shaw Way SM6 . . . . .60 E3
Shawfield Cty Fst Sch
 GU12 . . . . .106 A3
Shawfield La GU12 . . . . . .105 F2
Shawfield Rd GU12 . . . . . .106 A3
Shawford Ct 9 SW15 . . . . . .19 A8
Shawford Rd KT19 . . . . . . .57 D4
Shawley Cres KT18 . . . . . . .77 D1
Shawley Cty Prim Sch
 KT18 . . . . .77 C1
Shawley Way KT18 . . . . . . .77 C1
Shaws Rd RH10 . . . . .201 F7
Shaxton Cres CR0 . . . . .63 C2
Shearing Dr SM4 . . . . .40 C2
Shears Ct TW16 . . . . .14 E1
Shearwater Ct 6 RH11 . . .200 D5
Shearwater Rd SM1 . . . . . .58 F5
Sheath La KT22 . . . . .74 C6
Sheen Common Dr
 SW14, TW10 . . . . .7 A2
Sheen Court Rd TW10 . . . . .7 A3
Sheen Gate Gdns SW14 . . . .7 C3
Sheen La SW14 . . . . .7 C3
Sheen Mount Jun Mix &
 Inf Sch SW14 . . . . .7 B2
Sheen Pk TW10, TW9 . . . . . .6 E3
Sheen Rd TW10, TW9 . . . . . .6 E3
Sheen Way SM6 . . . . .60 F5
Sheen Wood SW14 . . . . .7 C2
Sheendale Rd TW9 . . . . .6 F3
Sheenewood SE26 . . . . .23 B4
Sheep Leas GU24 . . . . . . .112 E2
Sheep Walk Mews SW19 . .19 E2
Sheep Wlk
 Langley Vale KT18 . . . . . . .96 D6
 Reigate RH2 . . . . .117 E4
Sheepbarn La CR6 . . . . .82 F7
Sheepcote CI TW5 . . . . .4 A7
Sheepfold Rd GU2 . . . . . . .108 F4
Sheephouse GU9 . . . . .146 C8
Sheephouse Gn RH5 . . . . .134 E3
Sheephouse La RH5 . . . . . .135 A2
Sheephouse Way KT3 . . . . .38 E2
Sheeplands Ave GU1 . . . . .110 C3
Sheeps Ditch CI TW18 . . . .13 A1
Sheepwalk Littleton TW17 . .34 A3
 Shepperton TW17 . . . . . . .33 F3
Sheepwalk La GU5 . . . . . .113 A1
Sheerwater Ave KT15 . . . . .70 F7
Sheerwater Bsns Ctr
 GU21 . . . . .70 C4
Sheerwater Cotts KT14 . . .70 F6
Sheerwater Rd KT14, KT15 .70 F6
Sheet Street Rd
 Old Windsor SL4 . . . . . . .10 A7
 Windsor SL4 . . . . .10 A7
Sheet's Heath La GU24 . . . .88 A7
Sheffield CI Crawley RH10 202 B4
 Farnborough GU14 . . . . . .84 F4
Sheffield Rd TW14, TW6 . . . .3 C2
Sheffield Way TW14, TW6 . .3 D2
Shefford Cres RG40 . . . . . .25 D8
Shelburne House 9 SW16 21 C3
Sheldon CI Crawley RH10 .202 D5
 Penge SE20 . . . . .43 B8
 Reigate RH2 . . . . .139 B8
Sheldon Ct 3 GU1 . . . . . .130 F8
Sheldon House TW11 . . . . .17 A2
Sheldon St CR0, CR9 . . . . .61 C7
Sheldrick CI CR4 . . . . .40 D7
Shelford 9 KT1 . . . . .38 A7
Shelford Rise SE19 . . . . . . .22 F1
Shelley Ave RG12 . . . . .27 E2
Shelley Ct Camberley GU15 .65 C5
 9 Kingston u T KT2 . . . . . .17 D4
 West Barnes KT3 . . . . .39 A4
Shelley Rd
 East Grinstead RH19 . . . .185 D1
 Horsham RH12 . . . . .217 B3
Shelley Way SW17 . . . . . . .20 D2
Shellwood Dr RH5 . . . . . . .136 C3
Shellwood Rd RH2, RH3 . .137 D1
Shelly CI SM7 . . . . .77 E4
Shelly Cty Prim Sch
 RH12 . . . . .216 E3
Shellys Ct RH13 . . . . .218 A3
Shelson Ave TW13 . . . . . . .14 F4
Shelton Ave CR6 . . . . .81 C2
Shelton CI Guildford GU2 .109 A6
 Warlingham CR6 . . . . .81 C2
Shelton Rd SW19 . . . . .40 A8
Shelvers Gn KT20 . . . . .97 C6
Shelvers Hill KT20 . . . . . . .97 B6
Shelvers Spur KT20 . . . . . .97 C6
Shelvers Way KT20 . . . . . . .97 D6
Shene Sec Sch SW14 . . . . . .7 C3
Shenley Rd TW5 . . . . .4 E6
Shenstone House SW16 . . .21 C3
Shenstone Pk SL5 . . . . .29 E5
Shepherd CI RH10 . . . . . . .201 E3
Shepherd's Hill
 Guildford GU2 . . . . .109 A3
 Haslemere GU27 . . . . . . .208 C6

Shepherd's Hill continued
 Merstham RH1 . . . . .99 C1
Shepherd's Hill Bglws
 GU27 . . . . .208 C6
Shepherd's La GU2 . . . . . .108 F4
Shepherd's Way GU4 . . . .130 E4
Shepherds Chase GU19 . . .47 E2
Shepherds CI TW17 . . . . . .34 B3
Shepherds Hill RG12 . . . . . .27 C8
Shepherds La GU20 . . . . . . .49 A6
Shepherds Way
 Horsham RH12 . . . . .218 A5
 South Croydon CR2 . . . . . .62 D3
 Tilford GU10 . . . . .147 D4
Shepherds' Wlk
 KT18 . . . . .96 B7
Shepherds Wlk GU14 . . . . .84 E7
Shepherdsgrove La RH19 186 F5
Shepley CI SM5 . . . . .60 A7
Shepley Ct SW16 . . . . .21 C4
Shepley Dr SL5 . . . . .30 D3
Shepley End SL5 . . . . .30 D4
Sheppard CI KT6 . . . . .37 E5
Sheppard House 8 SW2 . .22 A7
Shepperton Bsns Park
 TW17 . . . . .34 C4
Shepperton Court Dr
 TW17 . . . . .34 B3
Shepperton Ct TW17 . . . . .34 B3
Shepperton Rd
 TW17, TW18 . . . . .33 D5
Shepperton Sta TW17 . . . .34 C4
Shepperton Studios TW17 33 F6
Sheppey CI RH11 . . . . .201 B3
Sheraton CI GU17 . . . . .64 E4
Sheraton Dr KT19 . . . . .76 C6
Sheraton The 2 KT6 . . . . . .37 E4
Sheraton Wlk 13 RH11 . . .201 B1
Sherborne CI
 Burgh Heath KT18 . . . . . . .77 C2
 Poyle SL3 . . . . .1 E6
Sherborne Cres SM5 . . . . . .40 E2
Sherborne Ct
 Guildford GU2 . . . . .130 C7
 Penge SE20 . . . . .43 C7
Sherborne Rd Cheam SM3 .40 E4
 Chessington KT9 . . . . .56 E5
 East Bedfont TW14 . . . . . .14 D7
 Farnborough GU14 . . . . . .85 D1
Sherbourne GU5 . . . . .132 D5
Sherbourne Ct 2 TW12 . . .36 A8
Sherbourne Dr SL5 . . . . . . .30 A4
Sherbourne Gdns TW17 . .34 E2
Shere Ave KT17, SM2 . . . . .58 C1
Shere CE Inf Sch GU5 . . . .133 A4
Shere CI Chessington KT9 . .56 D5
 Dorking RH5 . . . . .136 C3
Shere Ct GU5 . . . . .133 B2
Shere La GU5 . . . . .133 A4
Shere Rd Albury GU4, GU5 .132 C6
 Ewhurst GU6 . . . . .175 D7
 Shere GU5 . . . . .133 B3
 West Clandon GU4, KT24 .111 B1
 West Horsley KT24 . . . . . .112 C4
Sherfield Gdns SW15 . . . . . .7 F1
Sheridan CI
 Aldershot GU11 . . . . .126 A8
 East Grinstead RH19 . . . .185 C1
Sheridan Ct TW4 . . . . .4 E2
Sheridan Dr RH2 . . . . .118 B3
Sheridan PI Hampton TW12 .36 C8
 Mortlake SW13 . . . . .7 F4
Sheridan Rd Frimley GU16 .85 D8
 Merton SW19 . . . . .39 F8
 Richmond TW10 . . . . .17 C5
Sheridan Way BR3 . . . . .43 F8
Sheridans Rd KT23 . . . . . . .94 C1
Sheringdale Prim Sch
 SW18 . . . . .19 F7
Sheringham Ave TW2 . . . . .16 A7
Sheringham Rd SE20 . . . . .43 C6
Sherland Rd TW1 . . . . .16 F7
Shermanbury Ct RH12 . . .217 B2
Sherringham Ave TW13 . . .15 A5
Sherrydon GU6 . . . . .174 F4
Sherwin Cres GU14 . . . . . .85 C7
Sherwood CI
 Bracknell RG12 . . . . .28 A7
 Fetcham KT22 . . . . .94 C4
Sherwood Cres RH2 . . . . .139 B5
Sherwood Ct SM4 . . . . .44 B1
Sherwood Park Rd
 Mitcham CR4 . . . . .41 D5
 Sutton SM1 . . . . .59 A5
Sherwood Park Sch SM6 .60 D7
Sherwood Park Rd CR4 . . .41 C5
Sherwood Rd Coulsdon CR5 79 C3
 Croydon CR0, CR9 . . . . . . .43 B1
 Hampton TW12 . . . . .16 C3
 Knaphill GU21 . . . . .68 E2
 Merton SW19 . . . . .19 F1
Sherwood Way BR4 . . . . . . .63 C8
Sherwood Wlk RH10 . . . . .201 F5
Shetland CI Crawley RH10 .202 E7
 Guildford GU4 . . . . .110 B6
Shewens Rd KT13 . . . . .53 D6
Shey Copse GU22 . . . . .70 C2
Shield Dr TW8 . . . . .6 A8
Shield Rd TW15 . . . . .14 D4
Shifford Path SE23 . . . . . . .23 D5
Shilburn Way GU21 . . . . . . .69 A1
Shildon CI GU15 . . . . .66 D3
Shillinglee Park Golf
 Course GU8 . . . . .210 D6
Shillinglee Rd RH14 . . . . .211 B4
Shimmings The GU1 . . . . .110 A2

Shinners CI SE25 . . . . .43 A4
Shinwell Wlk 3 RH11 . . . .201 B1
Ship Alley GU14 . . . . .85 C6
Ship Field CI TN16 . . . . . .103 C6
Ship La Farnborough GU14 .85 C6
 Mortlake SW14 . . . . .7 C5
Ship St RH19 . . . . .205 E8
Ship Yd KT13 . . . . .53 B7
Shipka Rd SW12 . . . . .21 B7
Shiplake Ct SW17 . . . . .20 D4
Shipley Bridge La RH10 .183 A3
Shipley Ct SE20 . . . . .43 A7
Shipley Rd RH11 . . . . .201 B4
Shipleybridge La
 RH10, RH6 . . . . .182 F4
Shipman Par SE23 . . . . . . .23 E6
Shipman Rd SE23 . . . . .23 D6
Shirburn CI SE23 . . . . .23 C8
Shire CI GU19 . . . . .47 E2
Shire Ct Aldershot GU11 . .104 E2
 Ewell KT17 . . . . .57 F3
Shire Horse Way TW7 . . . . . .5 F4
Shire Par RH10 . . . . .202 D7
Shire PI RH10 . . . . .202 D7
Shires CI KT21 . . . . .95 D8
Shires House KT14 . . . . . . .71 E6
Shires The TW10 . . . . .17 E4
Shirley Ave Belmont SM2 . .58 F1
 Carshalton SM5 . . . . .59 E6
 Coulsdon CR5, CR8 . . . . .100 B8
 Croydon CR0, CR9 . . . . . .43 C1
 Redhill RH1 . . . . .139 F4
Shirley Church Rd
 Addington CR0 . . . . .62 E7
 Croydon CR0 . . . . .62 D7
Shirley CI Crawley RH11 . .200 A1
 Isleworth TW3 . . . . .5 C2
Shirley Cres BR3 . . . . .43 E5
Shirley Ct Guildford GU1 . .130 D8
 Thornton Heath SW16 . . . .41 F6
Shirley Dr TW3 . . . . .5 C2
Shirley High Sch CR0 . . . . .62 D7
Shirley Hills Rd CR0 . . . . . .62 D5
Shirley Hts SM6 . . . . .60 C2
Shirley Hyrst KT13 . . . . . . .53 D4
Shirley Lodge SE26 . . . . . . .23 E4
Shirley Oaks Hospl CR0 . . .43 C2
Shirley Oaks Rd CR0, CR9 .62 D8
Shirley Park Golf Course
 CR0 . . . . .62 C7
Shirley Park Rd CR0 . . . . . .43 C1
 Wallington SM6 . . . . .60 C2
Shirley PI GU21 . . . . .68 C2
Shirley Rd
 Croydon CR0, CR9 . . . . . . .43 B1
Shirley Way CR0 . . . . .62 F7
Shoe La GU11 . . . . .105 A6
Sholto Rd TW6 . . . . .3 A2
Shop CI TW10 . . . . .17 D5
Shophouse La GU5 . . . . . .153 E7
Shord Hill CR8 . . . . .80 D3
Shore CI Feltham TW14 . . . .15 A8
 Hampton TW12 . . . . .15 E3
Shore Gr TW13 . . . . .16 A6
Shore's Rd GU21 . . . . .69 F5
Shoreham CI CR0 . . . . .43 C3
Shoreham Rd RH10 . . . . . .202 C3
Shoreham Rd (E) TW6 . . . . .2 E2
Shoreham Rd (W) TW6 . . . . .2 E2
Shorndean St SE6 . . . . .24 C7
Short CI RH11 . . . . .201 D8
Short Dale Rd GU11 . . . . . .126 C6
Short Gallop RH10 . . . . . . .202 D7
Short La Limpsfield RH8 . .123 B3
 Stanwell TW15, TW19 . . . .13 F7
Short Rd Chiswick W4 . . . . . .7 E8
 Stanwell TW19 . . . . .2 E1
Short St GU11 . . . . .105 A2
Short Way TW2 . . . . .16 C8
Shortacres RH1 . . . . .119 F2
Shortcroft Rd KT17 . . . . . . .57 F3
Shortfield Rd GU10 . . . . . .146 C1
Shortheath Crest GU9 . . . .145 F6
Shortheath Rd
 Farnham GU9, GU10 . . . .146 A7
 Wrecclesham GU9, GU10 .146 A7
Shortlands UB3 . . . . .3 D8
Shortlands Gdns BR1, BR2 .44 E7
Shortlands Gr BR2 . . . . . . .44 D6
Shortlands Rd
 Beckenham BR2, BR3 . . . .44 E6
 Kingston u T KT2 . . . . . . .17 F1
Shortlands Sta BR2 . . . . . .44 E7
Shorts Rd SM5 . . . . .59 E5
Shortsfield CI RH12 . . . . . .217 C5
Shortwood Ave TW18 . . . . .13 B5
Shortwood Cty Inf Sch
 TW18 . . . . .13 B5
Shotfield SM6 . . . . .60 B4
Shott CI SM1 . . . . .59 C5
Shottermill RH12 . . . . .218 A7
Shottermill Cty Fst Sch
 GU27 . . . . .207 F7
Shottermill Cty Jun Sch
 GU27 . . . . .207 F7
Shottermill Rd GU27 . . . . .207 E5
Shottfield Ave SW14 . . . . . . .7 E3
Shovelstrode La RH19 . . . .206 D8
Shrewsbury Ave SW14 . . . . .7 D3
Shrewsbury CI KT6 . . . . . . .56 E8
Shrewsbury House Sch
 KT6 . . . . .56 D8
Shrewsbury Rd
 Beckenham BR3 . . . . .43 E6
 Carshalton SM5 . . . . .40 E2
 Harlington TW14, TW6 . . . .3 D1

Shrewsbury Rd continued
 Redhill RH1 . . . . .118 E1
Shrewsbury Wlk 7 TW7 . . . .6 A4
Shrewton Rd SW17 . . . . . . .20 F1
Shrivenham CI 3 GU47 . . .64 D8
Shroffold Rd BR1 . . . . .24 E4
Shropshire CI CR4 . . . . .41 E5
Shrubbery Rd SW16 . . . . . .21 E4
Shrubbery The
 Farnborough GU14 . . . . . .84 D3
 2 Surbiton KT6 . . . . .37 E1
Shrubbs Hill GU24 . . . . .49 C2
Shrubbs Hill La SL5 . . . . . . .30 C3
Shrubbs La GU10 . . . . .145 F4
Shrubland Ct SM7 . . . . .77 F3
Shrubland Gr KT4 . . . . .58 C7
Shrubland Rd SM7 . . . . . . .78 A3
Shute End RG40, 41 . . . . . .25 B6
Sibthorp Rd CR4 . . . . .40 F7
Sibton Rd SM5 . . . . .40 E2
Sickle Mill GU27 . . . . .207 F6
Sickle Rd GU27 . . . . .208 A3
Sidbury CI SL5 . . . . .30 A4
Siddeley Dr TW4 . . . . .4 E5
Siddons Rd
 Croydon CR0, CR9 . . . . . . .61 B7
 Forest Hill SE23 . . . . .23 E6
Sidings The
 Aldershot GU11 . . . . .105 C3
 Rudgwick RH12 . . . . .214 D7
 Staines TW18 . . . . .13 B4
Sidlaws Rd GU14 . . . . .84 D6
Sidmouth Ave TW7 . . . . .5 E5
Sidney Gdns TW8 . . . . .6 D8
Sidney Rd Croydon SE25 . . .43 A4
 Penge BR3 . . . . .43 E7
 Staines TW18 . . . . .13 A4
 Twickenham TW1 . . . . . . .6 B1
 Walton-on-T KT12 . . . . . . .35 B1
Signal Ct RH7 . . . . .164 E5
Sigrist Sq 4 KT2 . . . . .37 E8
Silbury Ave CR4 . . . . .40 E8
Silbury House 9 SE26 . . . .23 A5
Silchester Ct CR7 . . . . .42 A5
Silchester Dr RH11 . . . . . .201 B4
Silkham Rd RH8 . . . . .122 E8
Silkin Wlk 8 RH11 . . . . . .201 B1
Silkmore La
 West Horsley KT24 . . . . . . .92 A2
 West Horsley KT24 . . . . . .112 A2
Silo CI GU7 . . . . .150 F8
Silo Dr GU7 . . . . .150 F8
Silo Rd GU7 . . . . .150 F8
Silver Birch CI KT15 . . . . . .70 E7
Silver Birches Way GU8 . .148 E3
Silver Blades Ice Rink
 SW16 . . . . .21 D3
Silver CI KT20 . . . . .97 E3
Silver Dr GU16 . . . . .66 C3
Silver Hill GU47 . . . . .64 E8
Silver Jubilee Way TW4 . . . .4 B5
Silver La Purley CR8 . . . . . .79 E7
 West Wickham BR4 . . . . . .63 D8
Silver Tree CI KT12 . . . . . . .54 A6
Silverdale SE23, SE26 . . . .23 C4
Silverdale Ave
 Oxshott KT22 . . . . .74 C5
 Walton-on-T KT12, KT13 . .53 F7
Silverdale CI
 Brockham RH3 . . . . .137 B5
 Cheam SM1 . . . . .58 F6
Silverdale Dr TW16 . . . . . . .35 B7
Silverglade KT9 . . . . .75 C7
Silverhall St TW7 . . . . .6 A4
Silverlea Gdns RH6 . . . . . .161 C2
Silverleigh Rd CR7 . . . . . . .42 A4
Silvermere Ave CR3 . . . . . .100 F3
Silvermere Rd 1 SE6 . . . . .24 B8
Silversmiths Way GU21 . . .69 C1
Silverstone CI RH1 . . . . . . .118 F3
Silverton Lodge SE19 . . . . .22 E1
Silverwood CI
 Beckenham BR3 . . . . .24 A1
 New Addington CR0 . . . . . .63 A2
Silverwood Dr GU15 . . . . . .66 A7
Silwood RG12 . . . . .26 E1
Silwood CI SL5 . . . . .29 D7
Silwood Park (Imperial
 Coll) SL5 . . . . .29 F6
Silwood Rd Ascot SL5 . . . . .29 F5
 Sunningdale SL5 . . . . .29 F5
Sim's Cotts KT10 . . . . .55 F4
Simkins CI RG42 . . . . .8 B2
Simmil Rd KT10 . . . . .55 E5
Simmonds CI RG42 . . . . . . .26 E8
Simmonds Cotts GU7 . . . .150 B4
Simmondstone La
 GU10 . . . . .167 D2
Simmons CI KT9 . . . . .56 C4
Simmons PI TW18 . . . . .12 E3
Simms CI SM5 . . . . .59 E8
Simon Lodge 31 SW19 . . . .19 D7
Simone Dr CR8 . . . . .80 C3
Simons CI KT16 . . . . .51 C4
Simons Wlk TW20 . . . . .11 C1
Simplemarsh Ct KT15 . . . .52 B6
Simplemarsh Rd KT15 . . . .52 B6
Simpson Rd
 Richmond TW10 . . . . .17 C4
 Twickenham TW4 . . . . .4 F2
Simpson Way KT6 . . . . .37 C3
Sinclair CI RH10 . . . . .202 C4

Sinclair Ct
22 Beckenham BR3 . . . . . .24 A1
2 Croydon CR0 . . . . .61 F8
Sinclair Dr SM2 . . . . .59 B2
Sinclair House SW12 . . . .21 D7
Sincots Rd RH1 . . . . .118 C1
Sine Cl GU14 . . . . .85 B8
Singlegate Prim Sch
SW19 . . . . .20 D1
Singleton Cl
Mitcham SW17, SW19 . . . .20 F1
Thornton Heath CR0 . . . . .42 C2
Singleton Rd RH12 . . . . .216 D3
Sinhurst Rd GU15 . . . . . . .65 B4
Sion Ct TW1 . . . . .17 B7
Sion Rd TW1 . . . . .17 B7
Sipson Cl UB7 . . . . .3 A8
Sipson La UB7 . . . . .3 A8
Sipson Rd Harlington UB7 . . .3 A7
Harmondsworth UB7 . . . . . .3 A7
Sipson Way UB7 . . . . .3 A7
Sir Cyril Black Way 2
SW19 . . . . .20 A1
Sir William Perkin's Ind
Sch for Girls KT16 . . . . .32 F1
Sirdar Rd CR4 . . . . .21 A2
Sirl Cotts SL5 . . . . .29 C5
Siskin Cl RH12 . . . . .217 E5
Sissinghurst Cl RH10 . . . .202 D7
Sissinghurst Rd CR0 . . . . .43 A3
Sistova Rd SW12 . . . . .21 B7
Siward Rd SW17 . . . . .20 C5
Six Cross-Roads GU21 . . .70 A5
Sixth Cross Rd TW2 . . . . .16 C5
Skeena Hill SW18, SW19 . . .19 E8
Skelbrook St SW18 . . . . . .20 C5
Skelmersdale Wlk RH11 . .200 E2
Skerne Rd KT2 . . . . .37 D8
Skid Hill La Biggin Hill CR6 . .82 F5
Fickleshole CR6 . . . . .82 F5
Skiff La RH14 . . . . .213 A1
Skiffington Cl SW2 . . . . . .22 A7
Skimmington Cotts RH2 . .138 D8
Skimpedhill La RG12 . . . . .27 B7
Skinners La Ashstead KT21 . .75 D1
Chiddingfold GU8 . . . . . . .191 D5
Heston TW5 . . . . .5 B6
Skipton Way RH6 . . . . . . .161 B5
Sky Bsns Pk TW20 . . . . . . .32 C7
Skyes Dr TW18 . . . . .13 B3
Skylark View RH12 . . . . . .217 D2
Skyport Dr UB7 . . . . .2 D7
Skyway 14 Trad Est SL3 . . . .1 F4
Slade Cl KT16 . . . . .51 D4
Slade House TW4 . . . . .4 F1
Slade Rd Ottershaw KT16 . .51 D4
Pirbright GU24 . . . . .87 D7
Slaidburn Gn RG12 . . . . . .27 E2
Slattery Rd TW13 . . . . . . .15 C7
Slaugham Ct RH11 . . . . . .200 F3
Sledmere Ct TW14 . . . . . . .14 E7
Sleets Rd RH12 . . . . .216 E3
Slim Cl GU11 . . . . .105 E7
Slim Rd GU15 . . . . .65 C7
Slines New Rd CR3, CR6 . .101 E7
Slines Oak Rd CR3, CR6 . .102 B6
Slinfold CE Sch RH13 . . . .215 D4
Slinfold Park (Golf &
Country Park) RH12 . . .215 A2
Slinfold Wlk RH11 . . . . . .201 C6
Slip Of Wood GU6 . . . . . .174 F4
Slipshatch Rd RH2 . . . . . .138 E5
Slipshoe St RH2 . . . . .118 A1
Sloane Hospl BR3 . . . . . . .44 D8
Sloane Wlk CR0 . . . . .43 F3
Slocock Hill GU21 . . . . . . .69 C2
Slough La Buckland RH3 . .117 A3
Headley RH5 . . . . .96 C2
Sloughbrook Cl RH12 . . . .217 F6
Slyfield Ct GU1 . . . . .109 E4
Slyfield Gn GU1 . . . . .109 E5
Slyfield Ind Est GU4 . . . . .109 E5
Small's La RH11 . . . . .201 C6
Smallberry Ave TW7 . . . . . .5 F5
Smallfield Rd Horley RH6 .161 D3
Horne RH6 . . . . .162 E3
Smallmead RH6 . . . . .161 B3
Smalls Hill Rd
Charlwood RH2, RH6 . . . .159 C6
Leigh RH2, RH6 . . . . .159 C6
Sidlow RH2, RH6 . . . . . . .159 C6
Smalls Mead RH11 . . . . . .201 C6
Smallwood Jun & Inf
Schs SW17 . . . . .20 D4
Smallwood Rd SW17 . . . . .20 D4
Smart's Heath La GU22 . . .89 A4
Smart's Heath Rd GU22 . . .89 B5
Smeaton Cl KT9 . . . . .56 D4
Smeaton Rd SW18 . . . . . . .20 A8
Smith Cl RH10 . . . . .201 D1
Smith Ct GU21 . . . . .70 D6
Smith Rd RH2 . . . . .138 F6
Smith Sq RG12 . . . . .27 D2
Smith St KT5 . . . . .37 F3
Smith's Yd SW18 . . . . .20 C6
Smitham Bottom La
CR5, CR8 . . . . .79 D7
Smitham Cty Prim Sch
CR5 . . . . .79 D4
Smitham Downs Rd
CR5, CR8 . . . . .79 E6
Smitham Prim Sch CR5 . . .79 C3
Smitham Sta CR5 . . . . .79 E4
Smithbarn RH13 . . . . .218 A2
Smithbarn Cl RH6 . . . . . . .161 B4

Smithers Cotts RH12 . . . .214 F7
Smithers House SE20 . . . . .23 D1
Smithers The RH3 . . . . . . .137 B7
Smithfield La GU35, GU10 167 A1
Smithwood Ave GU6 . . . . .174 B7
Smithwood Cl SW19 . . . . .19 E6
Smithwood Common Rd
GU5, GU6 . . . . .174 B7
Smithy Cl KT20 . . . . .97 F1
Smithy La
Headley Down GU10 . . . . .166 E2
Lower Kingswood KT20 . . . .97 F1
Smithy's Gn GU20 . . . . . . .48 D4
Smock Wlk CR0 . . . . .42 C3
Smoke La RH2 . . . . .139 B7
Smokejack Hill RH5 . . . . .196 D7
Smokescreen Hill RH5 . . .196 D7
Smolletts RH19 . . . . .205 C8
Smoothfield TW3 . . . . .5 A3
Smugglers' La RH5 . . . . . .197 E2
Smugglers' Way GU10 . . .126 E1
Snailslynch GU9 . . . . .125 D2
Snatts Hill RH8 . . . . .122 F6
Snelgate Cotts GU4 . . . . .111 D4
Snell Hatch RH11 . . . . . . .201 B6
Snellings Rd KT12 . . . . . . .54 C5
Snipe La GU27 . . . . .208 A1
Snow Hill Copthorne RH10 .183 F3
Domewood RH10 . . . . . . .183 F3
Snow Hill Bsns Ctr RH10 .184 A4
Snow House SE27 . . . . .22 B5
Snowdenham La GU5 . . . .151 E5
Snowdenham Links Rd
GU5 . . . . .151 D6
Snowdon Rd
Farnborough GU14 . . . . . . .84 E7
Harlington TW6 . . . . .3 C1
Snowdown Cl SE20 . . . . . .43 D8
Snowdrop Cl
Crawley RH11 . . . . .201 A2
2 Hampton TW12 . . . . . . .16 A2
Snowdrop Way GU24 . . . . .68 A2
Snowerhill Rd RH2, RH3 . .137 F6
Snowhill La RH10 . . . . . . .183 F5
Snows Paddock GU20 . . . . .48 B7
Snows Ride GU20 . . . . .48 B6
Snowy Fielder Waye TW7 . .6 B5
Snoxhall Field GU6 . . . . . .174 D2
Soames Wlk KT3 . . . . .38 E8
Soane Ct RH11 . . . . .200 E4
Soho Mills SM6 . . . . .41 B1
Sol-y-vista GU7 . . . . .150 D6
Solartron Rd GU14 . . . . . . .85 B3
Sole Farm Ave KT23 . . . . . .93 F2
Sole Farm Cl KT23 . . . . . . .93 F3
Sole Farm Rd KT23 . . . . . . .93 F2
Solecote KT23 . . . . .94 A2
Solent Rd TW6 . . . . .2 F1
Soloms Court Rd CR5, SM7 78 E2
Solway Cl TW4 . . . . .4 E4
Somborne House SW15 . . .19 A8
Somerfield Cl KT20 . . . . . . .97 E8
Somergate RH12 . . . . .216 F2
Somers Cl RH2 . . . . .118 A2
Somers Pl 1 Reigate RH2 .118 A2
Streatham SW2 . . . . .21 F8
Somers Rd Reigate RH2 . .118 A2
2 Streatham SW2 . . . . . . .21 F8
Somersbury
La GU6, RH12 . . . . .195 F7
Somersby Est SE20 . . . . . .23 C1
Somerset Ave
Chessington KT9 . . . . .56 D6
Wimbledon SW20 . . . . . . .39 B7
Somerset Ct Epsom KT19 . .57 E2
Hersham KT12 . . . . .54 B5
New Malden KT3 . . . . .38 E4
Somerset Ct 1 SW12 . . . . .36 A8
Somerset Gdns
Teddington TW11 . . . . . . .16 E3
Thornton Heath SW16 . . . .41 F6
Somerset House SW19 . . .19 E5
Somerset Rd Brentford TW8 .6 C8
Farnborough GU14 . . . . . . .85 C1
Kingston u T KT1 . . . . .37 F7
Reigate RH1 . . . . .139 D7
Teddington TW11 . . . . . . .16 E3
Wimbledon SW19 . . . . . . .19 D5
Somerset Waye TW5 . . . . . .4 E7
Somerton Ave TW9 . . . . . . .7 B4
Somerton Cl CR8 . . . . .80 A3
Somertons Cl GU2 . . . . . .109 A4
Somerville Ct SW16 . . . . . .21 D2
Somerville Dr RH10 . . . . .182 C1
Somerville Rd
Cobham KT11 . . . . .74 A5
Penge BR3, SE20 . . . . . . .23 D1
Sondes Farm RH4 . . . . . . .135 F7
Sondes Place Dr RH4 . . . .135 F7
Sondes Place Sch RH4 . . .135 F6
Sonia Gdns TW5 . . . . .5 A7
Sonnet Wlk TN16 . . . . .83 C1
Sonning Ct CR0 . . . . .62 A8
Sonning Gdns TW12 . . . . .15 E2
Sonning Rd CR0 . . . . .43 A3
Sonninge Cl GU47 . . . . . . .64 D8
Soper Dr CR3 . . . . .100 D4
Sopwith Ave KT9 . . . . .56 E5
Sopwith Cl 1 Biggin Hill TN16 .83 D3
Richmond TW10 . . . . .17 F3
Sopwith Dr KT13, KT14 . . .71 E7
Sopwith Rd TW5 . . . . .4 C7
Sopwith Way KT2 . . . . .37 E8
Sorbie Cl KT13 . . . . .53 D4
Sorrel Bank CR0 . . . . .62 E2
Sorrel Cl Crawley RH11 . . .201 A1
Farnborough GU14 . . . . . . .84 C5
Wokingham RG40 . . . . . . .25 E8

Sorrel Dr GU18 . . . . .66 F7
Sorrel House TW3 . . . . .5 C6
Sorrel Rd RH12 . . . . .217 E5
Sorrento Rd SM1 . . . . .59 B7
South Albert Rd RH2 . . . .117 F2
South Atlantic Dr GU11 . .105 C3
South Ave Egham TW20 . . .12 C3
Heath End GU9 . . . . .125 D6
Richmond TW9 . . . . .7 A5
Wallington SM6 . . . . .60 A3
Whiteley Village KT12 . . . .53 E1
South Bank KT6 . . . . .37 E3
South Bank Lodge 2 KT6 .37 E3
South Bank Terr KT6 . . . . .37 E3
South Bookham Cty Inf
Sch KT23 . . . . .114 C8
South Border The CR8 . . . .79 E8
South Cl Crawley RH10 . . .201 F7
Morden SM4 . . . . .40 A3
Twickenham TW13 . . . . . . .16 A5
Woking GU21 . . . . .69 C3
Wokingham RG40 . . . . . . .25 D4
South Close Gn RH1, RH2 119 B6
South Croxted Rd SE21 . . .22 D4
South Croydon Sta CR2 . . .61 D5
South Dr Banstead SM7 . . .78 E6
Beckenham BR3 . . . . .44 C4
Belmont SM2 . . . . .58 E2
Coulsdon CR5 . . . . .79 D4
Dorking RH5 . . . . .136 C7
Pirbright GU24 . . . . .87 C6
Wentworth GU25 . . . . .31 A2
Wokingham RG40 . . . . . . .25 C5
South Eden Park Rd
Beckenham BR3 . . . . .44 B4
West Wickham BR3 . . . . . .44 B2
South End
Croydon CR0, CR9 . . . . . . .61 C6
Great Bookham KT23 . . . . .94 B1
South Farm La GU19 . . . . .48 A2
South Farnborough Cty
Jun Sch GU14 . . . . .85 D2
South Farnborough Inf
Sch GU14 . . . . .105 D4
South Farnham Cty Jun
Sch GU9 . . . . .125 D1
South Gate Ave TW13 . . . .14 D4
South Gdns SW19 . . . . . . .20 D1
South Gr Chertsey KT16 . . .32 F3
Horsham RH13 . . . . .217 D1
South Hill Godalming GU7 .150 F4
Guildford GU1 . . . . .130 D7
South Hill Park RG12 . . . . .27 C2
South Hill Rd
Beckenham BR2 . . . . .44 E5
Bracknell RG12 . . . . .27 B3
South Holmes Rd RH13 . .218 B4
South La Ash GU12 . . . . . .106 B1
Kingston u T KT1 . . . . .37 D6
New Malden KT3 . . . . .38 D3
South La W KT3 . . . . .38 D5
South Lawn Ct GU7 . . . . .150 D6
South Lodge TW2 . . . . .5 C1
South Lodge Ave
CR4, CR7, SW16 . . . . . . .41 E5
South Lodge Rd KT12 . . . .54 B2
South Lynn Cres RG12 . . . .27 B4
South Mead Redhill RH1 . .118 F4
West Ewell KT19 . . . . .57 F3
South Mead Rd GU11 . . . .126 B8
South Meadow RG45 . . . . .45 D3
South Merton Sta 8 SW19 .39 F6
South Munstead La GU8 . .172 B7
South Norwood Country
Park SE25 . . . . .43 C5
South Norwood High Sch
SE25 . . . . .43 B4
South Norwood Hill
SE19, SE25 . . . . .42 F7
South Norwood Prim Sch
SE25 . . . . .43 A4
South Oak Rd SW16 . . . . . .21 F4
South Par RH5 . . . . .160 F4
South Park Cres SE6 . . . . .24 F7
South Park Ct 2 BR3 . . . . .24 A1
South Park Cty Inf Sch
RH2 . . . . .139 A6
South Park Gr KT3 . . . . . . .38 C5
South Park Hill Rd CR2 . . .61 D6
South Park La RH1 . . . . . .142 A4
South Park Rd SW19 . . . . .20 B2
South Pier Rd RH6 . . . . . .182 B7
South Pl Surbiton KT5 . . . .37 F2
Wokingham RG40 . . . . . . .25 D5
South Rd Ash Vale GU12 . .106 A4
Bisley GU24 . . . . .67 F3
Bracknell RG40, RG12 . . . .26 E1
Crowthorne RG45 . . . . . . .45 E3
Englefield Green TW20 . . . .11 D2
Feltham TW13 . . . . .15 D3
Forest Hill SE23 . . . . .23 D6
Guildford GU2 . . . . .109 B3
Hampton TW12 . . . . .15 F2
Merton SW19 . . . . .20 D2
Mitcham SW19 . . . . .20 D2
Reigate RH2 . . . . .139 B8
Twickenham TW2 . . . . . . .16 D5
Weybridge KT13 . . . . .53 B2
Weybridge KT13 . . . . .53 C5
Woking GU21 . . . . .69 C4
South Ridge KT13 . . . . . . .72 B8
South Rise SM5 . . . . .59 E2
South Side GU10 . . . . .126 F7
South St Dorking RH4 . . . .136 A7
Epsom KT18 . . . . .76 D5
Farnborough GU14 . . . . . . .85 E1
Farnham GU9 . . . . .125 C2

South St continued
Godalming GU7 . . . . .150 D4
Horsham RH12 . . . . .217 C2
Isleworth TW7 . . . . .6 A4
Staines TW18 . . . . .12 F3
South Station App RH1 . .140 F7
South Terr Dorking RH4 . .136 B6
Surbiton KT6 . . . . .37 E3
South Vale SE19 . . . . .22 E2
South Vale Rd 4 KT6 . . . . .56 E8
South View
Copthorne RH10 . . . . .183 E3
Wimbledon SW19 . . . . . . .19 D2
South View Ct SE19 . . . . . .22 C1
South View Rd Catford BR1 .24 D4
Headley Down GU35 . . . . .187 B5
Woldingham CR3 . . . . . . .102 B3
Southviews CR2 . . . . .62 D2
Southville Cl
East Bedfont TW14 . . . . . . .14 E7
West Ewell KT19 . . . . .57 C2
Southville Cres TW14 . . . . .14 E7
Southville Jun & Inf Schs
TW14 . . . . .14 F7
Southville Rd
East Bedfont TW14 . . . . . . .14 E7
Thames Ditton KT7 . . . . . . .37 B2
Southwark Cl RH11 . . . . . .201 B2
Southwater Cl BR3 . . . . . . .24 B1
Southway Camberley GU15 .65 B4
Guildford GU2 . . . . .108 F1
Wallington SM6 . . . . .60 C6
West Barnes SW20 . . . . . . .39 B5
Southway Ct GU2 . . . . . . .108 E1
Southways Pk RH10 . . . . .181 D3
Southwell Park Rd GU15 . .65 C5
Southwell Rd CR0, CR7 . . .42 A3
Southwick GU19 . . . . .47 E1
Southwick Cl RH19 . . . . . .185 D2
Southwick Ct RG12 . . . . . .27 E3
Southwick House RH19 . . .185 D2
Southwold RG12 . . . . .26 E1
Southwood Ave
Coulsdon CR5 . . . . .79 C4
Kingston u T KT2, KT3 . . . .38 C5
Knaphill GU21 . . . . .68 D1
Ottershaw KT16 . . . . .51 C3
Southwood Bsns Pk GU14 84 D4
Southwood Chase GU6 . . .174 F1
Southwood Cl KT4 . . . . . . .58 D1
Southwood Cres
The GU14 . . . . .84 D3
Southwood Ct GU14 . . . . . .53 B5
Southwood Cty Inf Sch
GU14 . . . . .84 D3
Southwood Dr KT5 . . . . . . .38 C1
Southwood Gdns KT10 . . . .56 A7
Southwood Golf Course
GU14 . . . . .84 E3
Southwood La
Farnborough GU17 . . . . . . .84 A3
Farnborough,
Southwood GU14 . . . . . . .84 D3
Southwood GU14 . . . . . . .84 E4
Sovereign Ct
East Molesey KT8 . . . . .35 F5
3 Richmond TW9 . . . . .6 F3
Sovereign Dr GU15 . . . . . .66 B7
Sovereign House
Ashford TW15 . . . . .13 E4
Wimbledon SW19 . . . . . . .19 E2
Spa Cl SE19 . . . . .42 E8
Spa Dr KT18 . . . . .76 A5
Spa Hill CR7, SE19 . . . . . . .42 D8
Spa View 6 SW16 . . . . . . .22 A3
Space Waye TW14 . . . . .4 B2
Spalding Rd SW17 . . . . . . .21 B3
Sparks Cl TW12 . . . . .15 E2
Sparrow Cl TW12 . . . . .15 E2
Sparrow Farm Dr TW14 . . .15 D8
Sparrow Farm Inf Sch
TW14 . . . . .15 C8
Sparrow Farm Jun Sch
TW14 . . . . .15 C8
Sparrow Farm Rd
KT17, KT4 . . . . .58 B6
Sparrow Row GU24 . . . . . .49 B4
Sparrowhawk Cl GU10 . . .124 D8
Sparrows Mead RH1 . . . . .119 A4
Sparvell Rd GU21 . . . . .88 B8
Sparvell Way GU15 . . . . . . .65 C6
Spats La GU35 . . . . .187 A8
Speaker's Ct 3 CR0 . . . . . .42 D1
Speart La TW5 . . . . .4 E7
Speedbird Way UB7 . . . . . . .2 C7
Speedwell Cl GU4 . . . . . . .110 C4
Speedwell House 5 RH1 119 A4
Speedwell Way RH12 . . . .217 E5
Speer Rd KT7 . . . . .36 F3
Speirs Cl KT3 . . . . .38 F3
Speke Rd CR7 . . . . .42 D7
Speldhurst Ct BR2 . . . . . . .44 F4
Spelthorne Coll TW15 . . . .13 F4
Spelthorne Cty Inf Sch
TW15 . . . . .14 E2
Spelthorne Gr TW16 . . . . .14 F1
Spelthorne La TW15, TW17 34 C8
Spelthorne Mus TW18 . . . .12 F3
Spelthorne Sports Club
TW15 . . . . .14 D1
Spence Ave KT14 . . . . .71 F5
Spencer Cl Frimley GU16 . .85 E6
Langley Vale KT18 . . . . . . .96 E8
Sheerwater GU21 . . . . .70 D5
Spencer Ct
Leatherhead KT22 . . . . . . .95 C4
Wimbledon SW20 . . . . . . .39 B8
Spencer Gdns
Englefield Green TW20 . . . .11 D3
Mortlake SW14 . . . . .7 C2

Spencer Hill SW19 19 E1
Spencer Hill Rd SW19 19 E1
Spencer House
24 Putney SW19 19 D7
Wimbledon SW19 19 D5
Spencer Mews SE21 22 D7
Spencer Pl CR0 42 D2
Spencer Rd Bracknell RG42 26 F8
Bromley BR1 24 F1
Carshalton CR4 41 A2
Caterham CR3 100 D6
Chiswick W4 7 C7
Cobham KT11 73 B4
East Molesey KT8 36 C4
Hounslow TW3, TW5, TW7 5 C6
Mitcham CR4 41 A6
South Croydon CR2 61 E5
Twickenham TW2 16 E6
Wimbledon SW20 39 B8
Spencer Way RH1 140 A4
Spencer's Rd RH12 217 B3
Spencers La RH6 159 F2
Spencers Pl RH12 217 B4
Spencers Rd RH11 201 D5
Spenser Ave KT13 53 A2
Spenser Ct 5 TW10 17 D4
Spiceall GU3 129 B3
Spicer Cl KT12 35 C3
Spicers Field KT22 74 E6
Spices Yd CR0 61 C6
Spiers Way RH6 161 B1
Spindle Way RH10 201 F5
Spindlewood Gdns
CR0, CR2 61 E6
Spindlewoods KT20 97 B4
Spinis RG12 26 F1
Spinnaker Ct 2 KT1 37 D8
Spinner Gn RG12 27 B4
Spinney Cl Cobham KT11 74 A8
Crawley Down RH10 204 C8
Horsham RH12 218 B6
New Malden KT3 38 E4
Worcester Park KT4 57 F8
Spinney Dr TW14 14 C8
Spinney Gdns SE19 22 F3
Spinney Hill KT15 51 F5
Spinney La SL4 9 B7
Spinney Oak KT16 51 D4
Spinney The Ascot SL5 29 E4
Burgh Heath KT18 97 B8
Cheam SM3 58 C6
Crawley RH11 201 B4
Frimley GU15 66 C6
Grayshott GU26 188 A4
Great Bookham KT23 94 B3
Haslemere GU27 208 C8
Horley RH6 161 A5
Oxshott KT22 74 C7
Purley CR8 80 B8
Ripley GU23 111 C8
Streatham SW16 21 D5
Sunbury TW16 35 A8
Spinneycroft KT22 74 D4
Spinning Wlk The GU5 133 A4
Spire Ct 10 TW10 6 E1
Spital Heath RH4 136 C8
Spoil La GU10 126 F7
Spokane Cl GU11 125 F8
Spook Hill RH5 136 B3
Spooner House TW5 5 A8
Spooner Wlk SM6 60 D5
Spooners Rd RH12 218 A4
Sportsbank St SE6 24 C8
Spout Hill CR0 63 A5
Spout La TW19 2 A3
Spout La N TW19 2 B3
Spratts Alley KT16 51 E4
Spratts La KT15 51 E4
Spread Eagle Wlk 2 KT18 76 D6
Spreighton Rd KT8 36 B5
Spring Ave TW20 11 F2
Spring Bottom La RH1 120 C8
Spring Cnr TW13 14 F5
Spring Copse
Copthorne RH10 183 C3
East Grinstead RH19 185 D3
Spring Cotts KT6 37 D4
Spring Ct Ewell KT17 57 F2
Guildford GU2 109 A5
Spring Gdns Ascot SL5 29 B5
Biggin Hill TN16 83 C1
Copthorne RH10 183 C3
Dorking RH4 136 A8
East Molesey KT8 36 C5
Farnborough GU14 85 A7
Frimley GU15 66 A5
Wallington SM6 60 C5
Spring Gr Brentford W4 7 A8
Farncombe GU7 150 E8
Fetcham KT22, KT23 94 B4
Hampton TW12 36 B8
Mitcham CR4 41 A8
Spring Grove Cres
TW3, TW5 5 C6
Spring Grove Jun & Inf
Sch TW7 5 D5
Spring Grove Rd
Hounslow TW3, TW5, TW7 5 C6
Richmond TW10 6 F2
Spring Hill SE26 23 C4
Spring Hill Wildfowl
Park RH18 206 A1
Spring House SW19 39 F8
Spring La
Croydon CR0, SE25 43 B3
Hale GU9 125 A7
Oxted RH8 122 D4
Slinfold RH13 215 C3
Spring La W GU9 125 A6
Spring Meadow
Bracknell RG12 27 D8
Forest Row RH18 206 F1
Spring Park Ave CR0 62 D8
Spring Park Inf Sch CR0 63 A7
Spring Park Jun Sch CR0 63 A7
Spring Park Rd CR0 62 D8
Spring Plat RH10 202 C6
Spring Plat Ct RH10 202 C6
Spring Rd TW13 14 F5
Spring Rise TW20 11 E2
Spring St KT17 57 F2
Spring Terr TW10 6 E2
Spring Way RH19 186 A4
Spring Woods
Sandhurst GU47 45 C1
Virginia Water GU25 31 B5
Springbank Rd SE13 24 E8
Springbourne Ct BR3 44 C8
Springclose La SM3 58 E4
Springcopse Rd RH2 139 C7
Springcross Ave GU17 64 D4
Springfarm Rd GU27 207 E5
Springfield
East Grinstead RH19 185 D4
Elstead GU8 148 D3
Lightwater GU18 67 D8
Oxted RH8 122 D5
South Norwood SE25 43 A6
Springfield Ave
Hampton TW12 16 B2
Merton SW20 39 F6
Springfield Cl GU21 68 E1
Springfield Cres RH12 217 B2
Springfield Ct
Horsham RH12 217 C2
9 Kingston u T KT1 37 E6
Wallington SM6 60 B5
Springfield Cty Prim Schs
TW16 34 F7
Springfield Drive KT22 94 F8
Springfield Gdns BR4 63 B8
Springfield Gr TW16 35 A8
Springfield Hospl SW17 20 E5
Springfield La KT13 53 B6
Springfield Meadows
KT13 53 B6
Springfield Park Rd
RH12 217 B2
Springfield Pl KT3 38 C5
Springfield Rd Ash GU12 106 A5
Ashford TW15 13 F3
Bracknell RG12 26 C8
Brands Hill SL3 1 B7
Crawley RH11 201 D5
East Ewell KT17 58 C1
Frimley GU15 66 B5
Guildford GU1 109 E1
Horsham RH12 217 C2
Kingston u T KT1 37 E6
Penge SE26 23 B3
South Norwood CR7 42 C8
6 Teddington TW11 17 A3
Twickenham TW2 16 A7
Wallington SM6 60 B5
Westcott RH4 135 C6
Wimbledon SW19 20 A3
Springfield Rise SE26 23 B5
Springfield Terr GU5 151 F6
Springfield Way GU8 148 E3
Springfields Cl KT16 33 B1
Springhaven GU8 148 E3
Springhaven Cl GU1 110 A1
Springhill GU8 148 E3
Springhill Ct RG12 27 B5
Springholm Cl TN16 83 C1
Springhurst Cl CR0 62 F6
Springlakes Est GU12 105 E3
Springmead Ct GU47 45 E1
Springpark Dr BR3 44 C6
Springwell Cl SW16 21 F4
Springwell Ct TW5 4 D5
Springwell Jun & Inf Schs
TW5 4 E7
Springwell Rd
Beare Green RH5 157 D3
Heston TW5 4 D6
Streatham SW16 22 A3
Springwood GU8 150 A1
Springwood Ct CR2 61 E6
Sprint Ind Est KT14 71 D8
Spruce Dr GU18 67 A7
Spruce Pk BR2 44 F5
Spruce Rd TN16 83 D3
Sprucedale Gdns
South Croydon CR0 62 D6
Wallington CR8 60 E2
Spur Rd Brentford TW7 6 B7
Feltham TW14 4 B3
Spur The GU21 68 B1
Spurfield KT8 36 B6
Spurgeon Ave SE19 42 D8
Spurgeon Cl RH11 201 C7
Spurgeon Rd SE19 22 D1
Spurgeon's Coll SE25 42 E7
Spurs Ct GU11 104 E2
Spy La RH14 213 A4
Square Dr GU27 208 B1
Square The Bagshot GU19 47 E3
Bracknell RG12 27 E5
Crawley RH10 201 D6
Guildford GU2 129 F7
Harmondsworth TW6 2 B6
Lightwater GU18 48 C1
Lingfield RH7 164 C4
12 Richmond TW10 6 D2
Rowledge GU10 145 E3
Square The *continued*
Tatsfield TN16 103 C7
Wallington SM5 60 A5
Weybridge KT13 53 C5
Wisley GU23, KT14 71 E3
Squarey St SW17 20 C5
Squire Ct 2 CR0 42 E1
Squire's Bridge Rd TW17 34 A5
Squire's Rd TW17 34 A5
Squires Bridge Rd KT17 33 F5
Squires Cl RH10 204 A8
Squires Ct Chertsey KT16 33 B1
Wimbledon SW19 20 A4
Squires Hill La GU10 147 C4
Squires Wlk TW15 14 D1
Squirrel Cl Crawley RH11 181 B1
Hounslow TW4 4 C4
Sandhurst GU47 64 B8
Squirrel Dr SL4 9 B7
Squirrel La GU14 85 A5
Squirrel Wood KT14 71 B7
Squirrel's Way KT18 76 D4
Squirrels Cl GU7 129 D1
Squirrels Ct KT4 57 F8
Squirrels Gn
Great Bookham KT23 94 A4
12 Redhill RH1 118 F2
Worcester Park KT4 58 A8
Stable Cl RH10 202 D3
Stable Croft GU19 47 D2
Stable Ct CR3 101 A5
Stable Mews Reigate RH2 118 A1
West Norwood SE27 22 C3
Stables The Cobham KT11 73 F5
Guildford GU1 109 D4
Stace Way RH10 202 E8
Stacey Ct RH1 119 C6
Stacey's Farm Rd GU8 148 D4
Stacey's Mdw GU8 148 C4
Stack House RH8 122 E5
Stackfield Rd RH11 200 E5
Staddon Ct BR3 43 E5
Staff Coll GU15 65 C7
Staff College Rd GU15 65 B6
Staff Rd GU12 105 C2
Staffhurst Wood Rd RH8 144 C6
Stafford Cl Caterham CR3 100 F4
Cheam SM3 58 E4
Stafford Gdns CR0 60 F5
Stafford Lake GU21 68 A1
Stafford Pl TW10 17 F8
Stafford Rd Caterham CR3 101 A6
Crawley RH11 181 B1
Croydon CR0 61 A6
Kingston u T KT3 38 C6
Wallington CR0, SM6 60 E4
Stafford Sq 2 KT13 53 D6
Staffords Pl RH6 161 B2
Stag Hill GU2 130 A8
Stag La SW15 18 F5
Stag Leys KT21 95 E7
Stag Leys Cl SM7 78 E4
Stagbury Ave CR5 78 E1
Stagbury Cl CR5 98 E8
Stagbury House CR5 98 E8
Stagelands RH11 201 C8
Stagelands Ct RH11 201 C8
Stags Way TW7 5 F8
Stainash Cres TW18 13 B3
Stainash Par TW18 13 B3
Stainbank Rd CR4 41 B6
Staines Ave SM3 58 D8
Staines By-Pass
TW15, TW18 13 C3
Staines Central Trad Est
TW18 12 E4
Staines La KT16 33 A3
Staines Lane Cl KT16 32 F4
Staines Prep Sch The
TW18 13 A3
Staines Rd Chertsey KT16 33 A5
East Bedfont TW14 14 D8
Feltham TW14, TW3, TW4 4 D2
Hounslow TW14, TW3, TW4 4 D2
Laleham TW18 33 B7
Staines TW18 33 B7
Twickenham TW13, TW2 16 C6
Wraysbury TW19 11 F7
Staines Rd E TW12, TW16 35 C8
Staines Rd W TW15 14 D1
Staines Sta TW18 13 A3
Stainford Cl TW15 14 D3
Stainton Rd SE13 24 D8
Stainton Wlk GU21 69 C1
Staiths Way KT20 97 B7
Stake La GU14 85 A4
Stakescorner Rd GU3 130 A2
Stambourne Way
South Norwood SE19 22 F1
West Wickham BR4 63 C7
Stamford Ave GU16 65 F1
Stamford Dr BR2 44 F5
Stamford Green Prim Sch
KT19 76 B7
Stamford Green Rd KT18 76 B6
Stamford Rd KT12 54 D7
Stan Hill RH6 180 D8
Stanborough Cl TW12 15 F2
Stanborough Rd TW3, TW7 5 D4
Stanbridge Cl RH11 200 E6
Standard Rd TW4 4 E4
Standen Cl RH19 185 A4
Standen (National Trust)
RH19 205 D4
Standen Pl RH12 218 A7
Standen Rd SW18 20 A8
Standinghall La RH10 203 A3
Standlake Point 1 SE23 23 D5
Standon La RH5 176 F2
Stane Cl SW19 20 B1
Stane St Ockley RH5 177 D4
Slinfold RH12, RH13 215 C4
Stane Way KT17 58 A1
Stanedge Ct SW16 21 E3
Stanford Cl TW12 15 F2
Stanford Cotts GU24 87 E1
Stanford Mid Sch SW16 41 D8
Stanford Orch RH12 216 F8
Stanford Pl RH7 164 D3
Stanford Rd SW16 41 E7
Stanford Way
Broadbridge Heath RH12 216 D3
Mitcham SW16 41 D7
Stanfords The KT17 76 F7
Stangate Mansions TW1 16 F5
Stanger Rd SE25 43 A5
Stangrave Hall RH9 121 B3
Stanhope Ave BR2 44 F1
Stanhope Cotts RH7 164 F3
Stanhope Gr BR3 43 F5
Stanhope Heath TW19 2 C1
Stanhope Rd
Camberley GU15 64 F4
South Croydon CR0 61 E7
Wallington SM5 60 A3
Stanhope Way TW19 2 C1
Stanhopes RH8 123 B7
Stanier Cl RH10 202 B5
Staniland Dr KT13 52 F1
Stanley Ave
Beckenham BR2, BR3 44 C6
West Barnes KT3 39 A4
Stanley Cl Coulsdon CR5 79 F2
Crawley RH10 201 E4
Stanley Cotts GU21 68 D2
Stanley Ct Belmont SM2 59 B3
Wallington SM5 60 A3
Stanley Ctr RH10 181 F2
Stanley Cty Inf Sch TW2 16 E4
Stanley Cty Jun Sch TW2 16 E4
Stanley Dr GU14 84 C3
Stanley Gardens Rd TW11 16 E3
Stanley Gdns
Hersham KT12 54 C4
Mitcham CR4 21 A2
Sanderstead CR2 81 A7
Wallington SM6 60 C4
Stanley Gr CR0, CR7 42 A3
Stanley Hill GU24 87 C5
Stanley Mansions SW17 20 F6
Stanley Park High Sch
SM5 60 A4
Stanley Park Inf Sch SM5 59 F3
Stanley Park Jun Sch SM5 59 F3
Stanley Park Rd SM5, SM6 60 A3
Stanley Rd Ashford TW15 13 E3
Hounslow TW3 5 C3
Mitcham CR4 21 A1
Morden SM4 40 A5
Mortlake SW14 7 B3
Sutton SM2 59 B3
Teddington TW11, TW2 16 E3
Thornton Heath CR0, CR7 42 A3
Twickenham TW2 16 D5
Wallington SM5 60 A3
Wimbledon SW19 20 A2
Woking GU21 69 F2
Wokingham RG40 25 E6
Stanley Sq SM5 59 F2
Stanley St CR3 100 C5
Stanley Tech High Sch
SE25 42 F6
Stanley Wlk RH13 217 D2
Stanleycroft Cl TW7 5 E6
Stanmore Cl SL5 29 A5
Stanmore Gdns
Richmond TW9 6 F4
Sutton SM1 59 C7
Stanmore Rd TW9 6 F4
Stanmore Terr BR3 44 A7
Stannet Way SM6 60 C6
Stansfield Rd TW4, TW5 4 B5
Stanstead Cl BR2 44 F3
Stanstead Gr SE23 23 F7
Stanstead Manor SM1 59 A4
Stanstead Rd
Caterham CR3, RH1 100 E2
Forest Hill SE23, SE6 23 E7
Stansted Rd TW6 2 F1
Stanthorpe Cl SW16 21 E3
Stanthorpe Rd SW16 21 E3
Stanton Ave TW11 16 E2
Stanton Cl Cranleigh GU6 174 A3
North Cheam KT4 39 D1
West Ewell KT19 57 B5
Stanton Rd Barnes SW13 7 F5
Thornton Heath CR0 42 C2
Wimbledon SW20 39 D8
Stanton Sq SE6 23 F4
Stanton Way SE26, SE6 23 F4
Stanway Sch RH4 115 B1
Stanwell Cl TW19 2 D1
Stanwell Gdns TW19 2 D1
Stanwell Moor Rd
Harmondsworth TW19,
TW6, UB7 2 B4
Stanwell TW19 2 B4
Stanwell New Rd
TW18, TW19 13 B5
Stanwell Rd Ashford TW15 13 E4
East Bedfont TW14,
TW19, TW6 14 B8
Horton SL3, TW19 1 C4
Stanworth Ct TW5 5 A7
Stanyhurst SE23 23 E7
Staple Hill GU24, KT16 49 E6
Staple La
East Clandon GU4 111 E2
Shere GU4 132 F8
Staplecross Ct 1 RH11 201 A3
Staplefield Cl 3 SW2 21 E7
Stapleford Cl
Kingston u T KT1 38 A6
Putney SW19 19 E8
Staplehurst RG12 26 E2
Staplehurst Cl RH2 139 C5
Staplehurst Rd
Reigate RH2 139 C5
Sutton SM5 59 E3
Stapleton Gdns CR0 61 A5
Stapleton Rd SW17 21 A5
Star and Garter Hill TW10 17 E8
Star Hill Churt GU10 167 D2
Woking GU22 89 D8
Star Hill Dr GU10 167 D2
Star La Aldershot GU12 105 F2
Hooley CR5 99 A6
Star Post Rd GU15 65 F8
Star Rd TW7 5 D5
Starborough Cotts RH7 185 F7
Starborough Rd TN8 165 E5
Starhurst Sch RH5 136 C5
Starling Wlk TW12 15 E3
Starmead Dr RG40 25 E5
Starrock La CR5 99 A7
Starrock Rd CR5 99 C8
Starwood Cl KT14 71 C8
Staten Gdns TW1 16 F7
Statham Ct RG42 26 E8
Station App
Ash Vale GU12 106 A7
Ashford TW15 13 F4
Beckenham BR3 44 A8
Beckenham, Lower
Sydenham SE6 23 F3
Belmont SM2 58 E3
Chipstead CR5 78 F1
Coulsdon CR5 79 D4
3 Croydon CR0 61 D8
Dorking RH4 115 C1
East Horsley KT24 92 E1
Epsom KT17, KT19 76 D6
Godalming GU7 150 D4
Guildford GU1 130 E8
Hampton TW12 36 A8
Haslemere GU27 208 B6
Hinchley Wood KT10 55 F7
Horley RH6 161 B2
4 Kingston u T KT1, KT2 38 A8
Leatherhead KT22 95 A6
6 New Malden KT4 39 A1
Oxted RH8 122 E6
Purley CR8 80 A8
Richmond TW9 7 A6
Shalford GU4 130 E3
Shepperton TW17 34 C4
South Croydon CR2 61 D2
Staines TW18 13 A3
Streatham SW16 21 D3
Sunbury TW16 35 A8
1 Surbiton KT6 37 E3
Sutton SM2 59 B1
Tadworth KT20 97 C4
Virginia Water GU25 31 D5
West Byfleet KT14 71 A7
Weybridge KT13 53 A4
Whyteleafe CR3 81 A1
Woking GU22 69 F2
Worcester Park KT19 58 A5
Station App E RH1 139 F7
Station App W RH1 139 F7
Station Approach Rd
Chiswick W4 7 C7
Coulsdon CR5 79 D4
Crawley RH6 182 B7
Station Ave Caterham CR3 101 A3
Kingston u T KT3 38 E6
Walton-on-T KT12 54 A6
West Ewell KT19 57 E2
Station Bldgs SW20 39 C7
Station Cl Hampton TW12 36 B8
Horsham RH13 217 D2
Station Cres TW15 13 E4
Station Est BR3 43 D5
Station Estate Rd TW14 15 B7
Station Flats SL5 30 B2
Station Gdns W4 7 C7
Station Hill Ascot SL5 29 A5
Crawley RH10 202 B7
Farnham GU9 125 C2
Station Ind Est RG40 25 B6
Station La
Enton Green GU8 171 A7
Milford GU8 171 A7
Station Par Ashford TW15 13 F4
Chipstead CR5 78 F1
East Horsley KT24 92 E1
Feltham TW14 15 B8
Richmond TW9 7 A6
Sunningdale SL5 30 A2
5 Upper Tooting SW12 21 A7
Virginia Water GU25 31 E4
Station Path TW18 12 F4
Station Rd Addlestone KT15 52 D6
Aldershot GU11 105 B2
Ashford TW15 13 F4
Bagshot GU19 47 E4
Barnes SW13 7 F5
Belmont SM2 59 A1
Betchworth RH3 116 E3
Bracknell RG12 27 B7

Station Rd *continued*
Bramley GU5 . . . . .152 A7
Bromley BR2 . . . . .44 E7
Carshalton SM5 . . . . .59 F6
Chertsey KT16 . . . . .33 A1
Chessington KT9 . . . . .56 E5
Chobham GU24 . . . . .69 B6
Claygate KT10 . . . . .55 E5
Cranleigh RH12 . . . . .195 C3
Crawley RH10, RH11 . . . . . .201 D5
Crawley Down RH10 . . . . . .204 B8
Croydon CR0 . . . . .42 C1
Dorking RH4 . . . . .136 A8
East Grinstead RH19 . . . . . .185 D1
Egham TW20 . . . . .12 A3
Esher KT10 . . . . .55 D8
Farnborough GU14 . . . . .85 B4
Farncombe GU7 . . . . .150 F7
Forest Row RH18 . . . . .206 F3
Godalming GU7 . . . . .150 D4
Gomshall GU5 . . . . .133 D4
Hampton TW12 . . . . .36 B8
Horley RH6 . . . . .161 B3
Horsham RH13 . . . . .217 D2
Hounslow TW3 . . . . .5 B3
Hydestile GU8 . . . . .171 D6
Kenley CR8 . . . . .80 C5
Kingston u T KT2 . . . . .38 A8
Leatherhead KT22 . . . . .95 A6
Lingfield RH7 . . . . .164 E4
Loxwood RH14 . . . . .213 A3
Merstham RH1 . . . . .119 C7
Merton SW19 . . . . .40 C8
Penge SE20 . . . . .23 C2
Redhill RH1 . . . . .118 F2
Rudgwick RH12 . . . . .214 D7
Shalford GU4 . . . . .130 E3
Shepperton TW17 . . . . .34 C4
South Godstone RH9 . . . . . .142 E5
South Norwood SE25 . . . . . .42 F5
Stoke D'Abernon KT11 . . . . .73 E3
Sunbury TW16 . . . . .15 A1
Sunningdale SL5 . . . . .30 A4
Teddington TW11 . . . . .17 A2
Teddington, Hampton
Wick KT1 . . . . .37 D8
Thames Ditton KT10 . . . . . . .55 D8
Thames Ditton, Weston
Green KT7 . . . . .36 F2
Twickenham TW1 . . . . .16 F8
Warnham RH12 . . . . .217 B8
West Barnes KT3 . . . . .39 B4
West Byfleet KT14 . . . . .71 A7
West Wickham BR4 . . . . .44 C1
Whyteleafe CR3 . . . . .80 F1
Wokingham RG40 . . . . .25 B6
Woldingham CR3 . . . . .101 F5
Wraysbury TW19 . . . . .1 A1
Station Rd E
Ash Vale GU12 . . . . .106 A7
Oxted RH8 . . . . .122 E6
Station Rd N
5 Egham TW20 . . . . .11 F3
Merstham RH1 . . . . .119 C7
Station Rd S RH1 . . . . . .119 C7
Station Rd W
Ash Vale GU12 . . . . .105 F8
Oxted RH8 . . . . .122 E6
Station Rise SE27 . . . . .22 B6
Station Row GU4 . . . . . . .130 E3
Station Terr RH4 . . . . .136 A8
Station View GU12 . . . . . .106 A8
Station Way
Cheam SM2, SM3 . . . . .58 E3
Crawley RH10, RH11 . . . . . .201 D5
Station Yd TW1 . . . . .17 A8
Staunton Rd KT2 . . . . .17 F1
Staveley Gdns W4 . . . . .7 D6
Staveley Rd Ashford TW15 . .14 D2
Chiswick W4 . . . . .7 D7
Staveley Way GU21 . . . . . . .68 E2
Staverton Cl RG40 . . . . .25 F6
Stavordale Rd SM4, SM5 . . .40 C2
Stayne End GU25 . . . . .31 A5
Stayton Rd SM1 . . . . .59 A7
Steadfast Rd KT1 . . . . .37 D8
Steam Farm La TW14 . . . . . . .3 F3
Steel's La KT11, KT22 . . . . .74 C5
Steele Rd TW7 . . . . .6 A3
Steele's Rd GU11 . . . . .105 B4
Steep Hill Chobham GU24 . .49 C3
South Croydon CR0 . . . . . . .61 E6
Streatham SW16 . . . . .21 D5
Steeple Cl SW19 . . . . .19 E4
Steeple Heights Dr TN16 . .83 D2
Steepways GU26 . . . . .188 B6
Steers Hill RH12 . . . . .199 C6
Steerforth Copse GU47 . . . .45 E2
Steerforth St SW18 . . . . . . .20 C6
Steers La RH10 . . . . .182 C4
Steers Mead CR4 . . . . .40 F8
Steetley Ct SM2 . . . . .59 C3
Steinman Ct TW7 . . . . .5 F4
Stella Rd SW17 . . . . .20 F2
Stembridge Rd SE20 . . . . . .43 B7
Stenning Ct KT22 . . . . .95 B5
Stennings The RH19 . . . . .185 C3
Stepgates KT16 . . . . .33 B2
Stepgates Cl KT16 . . . . .33 B2
Stepgates Prim Sch KT16 . .33 B2
Stephanie Chase Ct RG40 .25 D7
Stephen Cl Crawley RH11 .181 D1
Egham TW20 . . . . .12 C2
Stephen Ct 18 SW19 . . . . . .19 D7
Stephen Gould Ho GU14 .105 B8

Stephendale Rd GU9 . . . .125 D4
Stephenson Ct SM2 . . . . . .58 F3
Stephenson Dr RH19 . . . . .205 F7
Stephenson Pl RH10 . . . . .202 B6
Stephenson Rd TW4 . . . . . .16 A8
Stephenson Way RH10 . . .202 B6
Stepney Cl RH10 . . . . .202 C4
Sterling Ave TW17 . . . . . . .34 E6
Sterling Bldgs RH12 . . . . .217 C2
Sterling Pk RH10 . . . . .182 B3
Sternhold Ave SW12, SW2 .21 D6
Sterry Dr Thames Ditton KT7 36 E3
Worcester Park KT19 . . . . . . .57 E6
Steucers La SE23 . . . . .23 E7
Steve Biko La SE6 . . . . . . .24 A4
Steve Biko Way TW3 . . . . . .5 A4
Stevenage Rd RH11 . . . . . .200 E3
Stevens Cl Beckenham BR3 .24 A2
Epsom KT17 . . . . .76 E6
Hampton TW12 . . . . .15 F2
Stevens Cl SE3 . . . . .24 A2
Stevens' La KT10 . . . . .56 A4
Stevens Pl CR8 . . . . .80 B6
Stewart KT20 . . . . .97 D6
Stewart Ave TW17 . . . . .34 A5
Stewart Cl Hampton TW12 . .15 E2
Woking GU21 . . . . .68 F2
Stewart Fleming Prim Sch
SE20 . . . . .43 C6
Steyning Cl Crawley RH10 .201 E8
Purley CR8 . . . . .80 B3
Steyning Way TW4 . . . . .4 C3
Strathbrook Rd SW16 . . . . .21 F1
Stile Gdns GU27 . . . . .207 F6
Stile House GU4 . . . . .110 D2
Stile Path TW16 . . . . .35 A6
Stirling Cl Banstead SM7 . . .77 F2
Crawley RH10 . . . . .202 C5
Farnborough GU14 . . . . .85 A3
Frimley GU16 . . . . .65 E2
Mitcham SW16 . . . . .41 C8
Stirling Gr TW3 . . . . .5 C5
Stirling House 18 RH1 . . . .118 F1
Stirling Rd Guildford GU2 .108 E1
Stanwell TW19, TW6 . . . . . . .2 F1
Twickenham TW2 . . . . .16 B8
Stirling Way
East Grinstead RH19 . . . . . .186 B3
Horsham RH13 . . . . .217 E3
Stirrup Way RH10 . . . . .202 D7
Stites Hill Rd CR3, CR5 . . .100 C2
Stoatley Hollow GU27 . . . .208 A8
Stoatley House 10 SW15 . . .19 A7
Stoatley Rise GU27 . . . . . .208 A8
Stoats Nest Rd CR5 . . . . . . .79 E5
Stoats Nest Village CR5 . . .79 E4
Stock Hill TN16 . . . . .83 D2
Stockbridge Dr GU11 . . . .126 C6
Stockbury Rd CR0 . . . . .43 C3
Stockfield RH6 . . . . .161 B4
Stockfield Rd
Claygate KT10 . . . . .55 E5
Streatham SW16 . . . . .21 F5
Stockhams Cl CR2 . . . . .61 D1
Stocklund Sq GU6 . . . . . . .174 D3
Stockport Rd SW16 . . . . . . .41 D8
Stocks Cl RH6 . . . . .161 B2
Stockton Rd RH1 . . . . .139 A6
Stockwell Ctr RH10 . . . . . .202 A6
Stockwell Rd RH19 . . . . . .205 E6
Stockwell Works RH10 . . . .202 A6
Stockwood Rise GU15 . . . . .65 F5
Stockwood Way GU9 . . . . .125 D7
Stocton Cl GU1 . . . . .109 C2
Stocton Rd GU1 . . . . .109 D2
Stodart Rd SE20 . . . . .43 C8
Stoford Cl SW19 . . . . .19 E8
Stoke Brunswick Sch
RH19 . . . . .206 E7
Stoke Cl KT11 . . . . .73 F3
Stoke Fields 8 GU1 . . . . . .109 D1
Stoke Gr GU1 . . . . .109 D1
Stoke Hill Cty Prim Sch
GU1 . . . . .109 D1
Stoke Hills GU9 . . . . .125 C3
Stoke Hosp
(Almshouses) **6** GU1 . . . . .109 D1
Stoke Mews GU1 . . . . .130 D8
Stoke Park Ct 5 GU1 . . . . .109 D1
Stoke Rd Guildford GU1 . . .109 D1
Kingston u T KT2 . . . . .18 C1
Stoke D'Abernon KT11 . . . . .73 E3
Walton-on-T KT12 . . . . .54 C7
Stoke Rd Cotts KT22 . . . . . .94 D6
Stokeford Cl 8 RG12 . . . . . .27 F4
Stokes Cl RH10 . . . . .202 C4
Stokes Rd CR0 . . . . .43 D3
Stokes Ridings KT20 . . . . . .97 D4
Stokesby Rd KT9 . . . . .56 F4
Stokesheath Rd KT22 . . . . .74 C8
Stompond La KT12 . . . . . . .54 A8
Stoms Path SE6 . . . . .24 A3
Stonards Brow GU5 . . . . . .152 D4
Stondon Pk SE23 . . . . .23 E8
Stone Cres TW14 . . . . .14 F8
Stone Hatch GU6 . . . . .194 B3
Stone House Gdns CR3 . . .100 E2
Stone Park Ave BR3 . . . . . . .44 A5
Stone Pl KT4 . . . . .58 A8
Stone Rd BR2 . . . . .44 F4
Stone St Aldershot GU12 . .126 D8
Croydon CR0, CR9 . . . . .61 A5
Stone's Rd KT17 . . . . .76 E7
Stonebanks KT12 . . . . .35 A2
Stonebridge Ct
Crawley RH11 . . . . .201 C2
Horsham RH12 . . . . .217 A2
Stonebridge Fields GU4 . .130 D2

Stonebridge Wharf GU4 . .130 D2
Stonecot Cl SM3, SM4 . . . . .39 E1
Stonecot Hill SM4 . . . . .39 E1
Stonecourt Cl RH6 . . . . . . .161 C3
Stonecroft Way CR0 . . . . . . .41 E2
Stonecrop Cl RH11 . . . . . . .201 B3
Stonecrop Rd GU1, GU4 . . .110 C3
Stonedene Cl GU35 . . . . . .187 B4
Stonefield Cl RH10, RH11 .201 D5
Stonegate GU15 . . . . .66 C6
Stonehaven BR3 . . . . .44 B7
Stonehill Cl
Little Bookham KT23 . . . . . . .94 A2
Mortlake SW14 . . . . .7 D2
Stonehill Cres KT16 . . . . . . .50 E4
Stonehill Pk GU35 . . . . . . .187 C4
Stonehill Rd
Chobham GU24, KT16 . . . . . .50 D3
Headley Down GU35 . . . . . .187 C4
Lightwater GU18 . . . . .48 A1
Mortlake SW14 . . . . .7 D2
Ottershaw GU24, KT16 . . . . .50 D3
Stonehill's Mansions 3
SW16 . . . . .21 E6
Stonehills Ct SE21 . . . . .22 E5
Stonehouse Rise GU16 . . . .65 E1
Stoneleigh Ave KT17, KT4 . .58 A7
Stoneleigh
Broadway KT17 . . . . .58 A5
Stoneleigh Cl RH19 . . . . . .185 F1
Stoneleigh Cres KT19 . . . . .57 F5
Stoneleigh Ct KT19 . . . . . . .65 F1
Stoneleigh Fst Grant
Maintd Sch KT4 . . . . .58 B6
Stoneleigh Lodge 12 TW9 . . .6 F6
Stoneleigh Park Ave CR0 . .43 D3
Stoneleigh Park Rd
KT19, KT4 . . . . .58 A5
Stoneleigh Pk KT13 . . . . . . .53 C4
Stoneleigh Rd
Carshalton SM5 . . . . .40 E2
The Chart RH8 . . . . .123 C5
Stoneleigh Sta KT19 . . . . . .58 A5
Stonepit Cl GU7 . . . . .150 C4
Stoners Cl RH6 . . . . .181 E7
Stones La RH4 . . . . .135 C6
Stoneswood Rd RH8 . . . . . .123 B5
Stoneworth Ct SE25 . . . . . . .43 A3
Stoney Bottom GU26 . . . . .188 C3
Stoney Brook GU2 . . . . . . .108 E2
Stoney Deep TW11 . . . . . . .17 A4
Stoney La SE19 . . . . .22 F2
Stoney Rd RG42 . . . . .27 A8
Stoneybrook RH12 . . . . . . .216 F1
Stoneycroft Cl SE12 . . . . . . .24 F8
Stoneycroft Wlk 3 RH11 . .200 D5
Stoneyfield Ct CR5 . . . . .79 F2
Stoneyland Ct 6 TW20 . . . .11 F3
Stoneylands Rd TW20 . . . . .11 F3
Stonny Croft KT21 . . . . .75 F2
Stony Hill KT10 . . . . .54 F3
Stoop Ct KT14 . . . . .71 B7
Stoop Memorial Ground
TW2 . . . . .16 E8
Stopham Rd RH10 . . . . . . .202 C3
Stormont Way KT9 . . . . .56 C5
Storr's La GU3 . . . . .88 C3
Storrington Rd CR0 . . . . . . .42 F1
Stovold's Way GU11 . . . . . .125 F8
Stovolds Hill GU6, GU8 . . .193 D7
Stowell Ave CR0 . . . . .63 D7
Stowford Coll SM2 . . . . .59 C3
Strachan Pl SW19, SW20 . . .19 C2
Strachey Cl 1 RH11 . . . . . .201 B1
Strafford Rd Hounslow TW3 . .4 F4
Twickenham TW1 . . . . .17 A8
Straight Rd SL4, TW19 . . . . .11 C8
Strand Cl Crawley RH10 . . .202 A4
Langley Vale KT18 . . . . .96 D3
Strand on the Green Inf
Sch W4 . . . . .7 A8
Strand-on-the-Green Jun
Sch W4 . . . . .7 A8
Stranraer Way 1 TW6 . . . . . .2 E1
Stratfield RG12 . . . . .26 E1
Stratfield House 12 GU11 .105 A2
Stratford Ct
Farnborough GU14 . . . . .85 C4
Farnham GU9 . . . . .125 C1
New Malden KT3 . . . . .38 D5
Stratford Rd
Harlington TW6 . . . . .3 F7
Thornton Heath CR7 . . . . . . .42 B6
Strathavon Cl GU6 . . . . . . .174 B7
Strathcona Ave KT24 . . . . .113 E7
Strathcona Gdns
Knaphill GU21 . . . . .68 D1
Knaphill GU21 . . . . .88 C8
Strathdale SW16 . . . . .21 F3
Strathdon Dr SW17 . . . . . . .20 D5
Strathearn Ave
Harlington UB3 . . . . .3 F7
Twickenham TW2 . . . . .16 B7
Strathearn Rd Sutton SM1 . .59 A5
Wimbledon SW19 . . . . .20 A4
Strathmore Cl CR3 . . . . . . .100 E6

Strathmore Rd
Crawley RH11 . . . . .181 A1
Teddington TW11, TW2 . . . . .16 E4
Thornton Heath CR0 . . . . . . .42 D2
Wimbledon SW19 . . . . .20 A5
Strathmore Sch TW10 . . . . .17 D6
Strathville Rd SW18 . . . . . . .20 B6
Strathyre Ave CR7, SW16 . .42 A6
Stratton Ave SM6 . . . . .60 D2
Stratton Cl Heston TW5 . . . . .5 A8
Merton SW19 . . . . .40 A7
Walton-on-T KT12 . . . . .35 C1
Stratton Ct 10 KT6 . . . . . . .37 E4
Stratton Rd Merton SW19 . .40 A7
Sunbury TW16 . . . . .34 F7
Stratton Wlk GU14 . . . . .85 A7
Straw Cl CR3 . . . . .100 C4
Strawberry Cl GU24 . . . . . . .87 D7
Strawberry Fields GU24 . . .87 D7
Strawberry Hill Cl TW1 . . . .16 F5
Strawberry Hill Golf
Course TW2 . . . . .16 E5
Strawberry Hill Rd TW1 . . .16 F5
Strawberry Hill Sta TW2 . . .16 F5
Strawberry La SM5 . . . . .60 A7
Strawberry Rise GU24 . . . . .68 A6
Strawberry Vale TW1 . . . . . .17 A5
Stream Cl KT14 . . . . .71 E7
Stream Farm Cl
GU10, GU9 . . . . .146 D7
Stream Pk RH19 . . . . .185 A3
Stream Valley Rd GU10 . . .146 C6
Streatham Cl SW16 . . . . . . .21 E6
Streatham Comm N SW16 .21 F3
Streatham Comm S SW16 .21 F2
Streatham Common Sta
SW16 . . . . .21 D1
Streatham Ct SW16 . . . . . . .21 E5
Streatham High Rd
SW16, SW2 . . . . .21 E3
Streatham Hill SW2 . . . . . . .21 E8
Streatham Hill &
Clapham High Sch SW2 . .21 E6
Streatham Hill Sta SW2 . . . .21 E6
Streatham Pl SW2 . . . . .21 E8
Streatham Rd CR4 . . . . .41 A8
Streatham Sta SW16 . . . . . .21 D3
Streatham & Tooting
Adult Inst SW16 . . . . .21 F6
Streatham Vale SW16 . . . . .21 D1
Streathbourne Rd SW17 . . .21 A5
Streatham Wells Prim Sch
SW2 . . . . .22 A6
Streatleigh Par 4 SW16 . . .21 E6
Street End RH10 . . . . .202 E5
Street The Ashstead KT21 . .75 F1
Betchworth RH3 . . . . .116 E1
Capel RH5 . . . . .178 D6
Charlwood RH6 . . . . .180 E7
Compton GU3 . . . . .129 B2
Dockenfield GU10 . . . . .166 E6
East Clandon GU4 . . . . .111 E4
Effingham KT24 . . . . .113 D8
Ewhurst GU6 . . . . .175 E5
Fetcham KT22 . . . . .94 D5
Frensham GU10 . . . . .167 C2
Plaistow RH14 . . . . .211 E2
Puttenham GU3 . . . . .128 C4
Shackleford GU8 . . . . .149 C8
Shalford GU4 . . . . .130 E3
Slinfold RH13 . . . . .215 D4
Thursley GU8 . . . . .169 C4
Tongham GU10 . . . . .126 D6
West Clandon GU4 . . . . . . .111 B5
West Horsley KT24 . . . . . . .112 B7
Wonersh GU5 . . . . .152 A7
Wrecclesham GU10 . . . . . . .145 F6
Streete Court Sch RH9 . . . .121 E5
Streeters Cl GU7 . . . . .151 A6
Streeters La SM6 . . . . .60 D7
Streetfield GU8 . . . . .169 C4
Streetfield Rd RH13 . . . . . .215 E3
Streets Heath GU24 . . . . . . .67 F7
Stretton Rd Croydon CR0 . . .42 F3
Richmond TW10 . . . . .17 C6
Strickland Cl RH11 . . . . . . .200 E5
Strickland Row SW18 . . . . .20 D8
Stringer's Ave GU4 . . . . . . .109 D7
Stringhams Copse GU23 . . .91 A3
Strode House 3 SW2 . . . . . .22 A7
Strode St TW20 . . . . .12 A4
Strode's Coll TW20 . . . . . . .11 F3
Strode's Cres TW18 . . . . . . .13 C3
Strodes College La TW20 . .11 F3
Strood House 2 SE20 . . . . .23 C1
Strood La Warnham RH12 . .216 C7
Winkfield SL5 . . . . .9 C2
Stroud Cres SW15 . . . . .19 A4
Stroud Green Gdns CR0 . . .43 C2
Stroud Green Way CR0 . . . .43 C3
Stroud La GU5 . . . . .153 A3
Stroud Rd Croydon SE25 . . .43 A3
Wimbledon SW19 . . . . .20 A5
Stroud Way TW15 . . . . .14 B2
Stroude Rd Egham TW20 . . .12 A1
Thorpe GU25, TW20 . . . . . . .31 E6
Stroudes Cl KT4 . . . . .38 F2
Stroudley Cl RH10 . . . . . . .202 B5
Stroudwater Pk KT13 . . . . . .53 C4
Strudgate Cl RH10 . . . . . . .202 B4
Strudwicks Field GU6 . . . . .174 F4
Stuart Ave KT12 . . . . .35 C1
Stuart Cl Crawley RH10 . . .202 D5
Farnborough GU14 . . . . .85 A3
Stuart Cres Croydon CR0 . . .62 F7
Reigate RH2 . . . . .139 A6
Stuart Ct Godalming GU7 . .150 E4
18 Redhill RH1 . . . . .119 A2

Stuart Gr TW11 . . . . .16 E1
Stuart House RG42 . . . . . . .26 F7
Stuart Lodge
7 Epsom KT18 . . . . .76 D6
South Norwood SE25 . . . . . .42 E2
Stuart Pl CR4 . . . . .40 F8
Stuart Rd Reigate RH2 . . . .139 A6
Richmond TW10 . . . . .17 B5
South Norwood CR7 . . . . . . .42 C5
Warlingham CR3, CR6 . . . . .101 C2
Wimbledon SW19 . . . . .20 A5
Stuart Way
East Grinstead RH19 . . . . . .205 F2
Staines TW18 . . . . .13 B2
Virginia Water GU25 . . . . . . .31 A5
Stubbington House Sch
SL5 . . . . .29 B3
Stubbs Folly GU47 . . . . .64 D7
Stubbs La KT20 . . . . .118 A2
Stubbs Moor Rd GU14 . . . . .84 F5
Stubbs Way SW19 . . . . .40 D8
Stubfield RH12 . . . . .217 A3
Stubpond La RH19, RH7 . .184 D2
Stubs Cl RH4 . . . . .136 C5
Stubs Hill RH4, RH5 . . . . . .136 C6
Stubs Ind Site GU12 . . . . . .105 E5
Stucley Rd TW5, TW7 . . . . . .5 C7
Studios Rd TW17 . . . . .33 F6
Studland Rd Byfleet KT14 . .71 F7
Kingston u T KT2 . . . . .17 E2
Penge SE26 . . . . .23 D7
Study Prep Sch The SW19 .19 C3
Stumblets RH10 . . . . .202 C7
Stumps Hill La BR3 . . . . . . .24 A4
Sturdee Cl GU16 . . . . .65 E1
Sturges Rd RG40 . . . . .25 D5
Sturt Ave GU27 . . . . .207 F5
Sturt Ct GU4 . . . . .110 C2
Sturt Rd Frimley GU16 . . . . .85 F1
Haslemere GU27 . . . . .207 F5
Heath End GU9 . . . . .125 B3
Sturt's La KT20 . . . . .117 A8
Stychens Cl RH1 . . . . .120 C2
Stychens La RH1 . . . . .120 C2
Styles End KT23 . . . . .114 B8
Styles Way BR3 . . . . .44 C5
Styventon Pl KT16 . . . . .32 F2
Succomb's Hill CR3, CR6 .100 F1
Succombs Pl CR6 . . . . .101 A1
Sudbrook Gdns TW10 . . . . .17 E5
Sudbrook La TW10 . . . . .17 F6
Sudbrook Pk (Richmond
Golf Club) TW10 . . . . .17 E6
Sudbury Gdns CR0 . . . . . . .61 E4
Suffield Cl CR2 . . . . .81 D7
Suffield La
GU3, GU10, GU8 . . . . .128 B2
Suffield Rd SE20 . . . . .43 C7
Suffolk Cl Bagshot GU19 . . .47 E2
Horley RH6 . . . . .161 A2
Suffolk Ct 3 SW16 . . . . .22 A4
Suffolk Dr GU4 . . . . .110 B6
Suffolk House 4
Croydon CR0 . . . . .61 D8
Penge SE20 . . . . .43 C8
Suffolk Rd Barnes SW13 . . . .7 F7
South Norwood SE25 . . . . . .42 F5
Worcester Park KT4 . . . . .57 F8
Sugden Rd KT7 . . . . .37 B1
Sulina Rd SW2 . . . . .21 E8
Sullington Hill RH11 . . . . . .201 C4
Sullington Mead RH12 . . . .216 E3
Sullivan Cl
East Molesey KT8 . . . . .36 B5
Farnborough GU14 . . . . .85 A4
Sullivan Ct 4 CR0 . . . . .43 A1
Sullivan Dr RH11 . . . . .200 E3
Sullivan House Kenley CR8 .80 C5
Twickenham TW2 . . . . .5 F1
Sullivan Rd GU15 . . . . .65 A5
Sullivans Reach KT12 . . . . .35 A2
Sultan St BR3 . . . . .43 D7
Summer Ave KT8 . . . . .36 E4
Summer Gdns
Frimley GU15 . . . . .66 C5
Thames Ditton KT8 . . . . .36 E4
Summer Rd
East Molesey KT8 . . . . .36 D4
Thames Ditton KT7, KT8 . . . .36 E4
Summer Trees TW16 . . . . . .35 B8
Summer's Rd GU3, GU7 . . .151 A8
Summerene Cl SW16 . . . . . .21 C1
Summerfield KT21 . . . . .95 D8
Summerfield La
Long Ditton KT6 . . . . .56 D8
Rowledge GU10 . . . . .146 B2
Summerfield St SE12 . . . . . .24 F8
Summerfields Cl KT15 . . . . .51 F5
Summerhayes Cl GU21 . . . .69 E5
Summerhays KT11 . . . . .73 D6
Summerhill GU7 . . . . .150 E5
Summerhill Way CR4 . . . . . .41 A8
Summerhouse Ave TW5 . . . .4 E6
Summerhouse Cl GU7 . . . .150 D4
Summerhouse Ct GU26 . . .188 D3
Summerhouse La UB7 . . . . . .2 D8
Summerhouse Rd GU7 . . . .150 D4
Summerlands GU6 . . . . . . .174 E4
Summerlay Cl KT20 . . . . . . .97 E2
Summerleigh 5 KT13 . . . . . .53 D4
Summerley St SW18 . . . . . . .20 B6
Summerly Ave RH2 . . . . . . .118 A2
Summers Cl Belmont SM2 . .59 A3
Weybridge KT13 . . . . .72 A8
Summers La GU7 . . . . .150 A8
Summersbury Dr GU4 . . . .130 E3
Summersbury Hall GU4 . . .130 E3
Summersby Cl GU7 . . . . . . .150 F7

Summersell House SE27 . . .22 D3
Summerstown SW17 . . . . . .20 C4
Summersvere Cl RH10 . . .182 A1
Summerswood Cl CR8 . . . .80 D3
Summerville Gdns SM1 . . .58 F4
Summerwood Rd TW1, TW7 .5 F1
Summit Ave GU14 . . . . . . .84 C3
Summit Ctr UB7 . . . . .2 D7
Summit Pl KT13 . . . . .53 A3
Summit The 15 A1
Summit Way SE19 . . . . . . .22 E1
Sumner Cl KT22 . . . . .94 D3
Sumner Ct GU9 . . . . .125 C3
Sumner Gdns CR0 . . . . . . .42 A1
Sumner Pl KT15 . . . . .52 A5
Sumner Rd Farnham GU9 .125 C3
  Thornton Heath CR0 . . . . . .42 B1
Sumner Rd S CR0 . . . . .42 A1
Sun Alley 5 TW9 . . . . .6 E3
Sun Brow GU27 . . . . .208 A5
Sun Hill GU22 . . . . .89 A6
Sun Inn Rd GU8 . . . . .192 F5
Sun Life Trad Est TW14 . . . .4 A4
Sun Ray Est GU47 . . . . . . .64 A8
Sunbury Ave SW14 . . . . . . .7 D3
Sunbury Court
  Island TW16 . . . . .35 D6
Sunbury Court Rd TW16 . .35 C7
Sunbury Cres TW13 . . . . . .14 F4
Sunbury Cross Centre 9
  . . . . .14 F1
Sunbury Ct TW16 . . . . .35 D7
Sunbury Ct (Con Ctr)
  TW16 . . . . .35 D7
Sunbury Int Bsns Ctr
  . . . . .34 E8
Sunbury La KT12 . . . . .35 A3
Sunbury Manor Sch TW16 34 F4
Sunbury Rd Cheam SM3 . .58 E7
  Feltham TW13 . . . . .14 F4
Sunbury Sta TW16 . . . . . . .35 A8
Sunbury Way TW13 . . . . . .15 C3
Suncroft Pl SE26 . . . . .23 C5
Sundale Ave CR2 . . . . .62 C1
Sunderland Ct
  Dulwich SE22 . . . . .23 A8
  11 Stanwell TW19 . . . . .2 E1
Sunderland Mount SE23 . .23 D6
Sunderland Rd SE23 . . . . .23 D6
Sundew Cl Crawley RH11 .201 A2
  Lightwater GU18 . . . . .67 D8
  Wokingham RG40 . . . . .25 E7
Sundial Ave SE25 . . . . .42 F6
Sundial Ct KT5 . . . . .57 B8
Sundon Cres GU19 . . . . . . .31 C4
Sundown Ave CR2 . . . . . . .80 F8
Sundown Rd TW15 . . . . . . .14 C3
Sundridge Rd
  Croydon CR0, CR9 . . . . . . .43 A1
  Old Woking GU22 . . . . .90 A7
Sunkist Way SM6 . . . . .60 E2
Sunlight Cl SW19 . . . . .20 C2
Sunmead Cl KT22 . . . . .94 F5
Sunmead Rd TW16 . . . . . . .35 A6
Sunna Gdns TW16 . . . . . . .35 B7
Sunniholme Ct CR2 . . . . . .61 C5
Sunning Ave SL5 . . . . .29 E2
Sunning House Ascot SL5 .29 E2
  Windlesham GU20 . . . . .48 F8
Sunningdale Ave TW13 . . .15 E6
Sunningdale Cl 2 KT6 . . . .56 E8
Sunningdale Ct
  Crawley RH10 . . . . .201 D4
  13 Kingston u T KT2 . . . . . .18 A1
Sunningdale House SE26 .40 D7
Sunningdale Park (Civil
  Service Coll) SL5 . . . . . . .29 F4
Sunningdale Rd SM1 . . . . .58 F6
Sunningdale Sch SL5 . . . . .29 F3
Sunningdale Sta SL5 . . . . .30 A2
Sunninghill Cl SL5 . . . . . . .29 D5
Sunninghill Ct SL5 . . . . . . .29 D5
Sunninghill Lodge SL5 . . .29 C7
Sunninghill Rd Ascot SL5 .29 D5
  Windlesham GU20 . . . . .48 F8
  Winkfield SL4, SL5 . . . . .9 E2
Sunningvale Ave TN16 . . .83 D3
Sunningvale Cl TN16 . . . . .83 D3
Sunny Ave RH10 . . . . .204 A8
Sunny Bank Croydon SE25 .43 A6
  Epsom KT18 . . . . .76 C3
  Warlingham CR6 . . . . .81 E2
Sunny Down GU8 . . . . . . .170 E5
Sunny Hill GU8 . . . . .170 E6
Sunny Hill Rd GU11 . . . . .104 D2
Sunny Nook Gdns CR2 . . .61 D4
Sunny Rise CR3 . . . . .100 D3
Sunny View Cl GU12 . . . .105 C1
Sunnybank SL5 . . . . .29 A5
Sunnybank Mews GU12 .106 B3
Sunnybank Rd GU14 . . . . .84 D6
Sunnybank Villas RH1 . . .120 F3
Sunnycroft Rd
  Croydon SE25 . . . . .43 A6
  Hounslow TW3 . . . . .5 B5
Sunnydell La GU10, GU9 .146 A6
Sunnydene Rd CR8 . . . . . .80 B6
Sunnydene St SE26 . . . . . .23 E4
Sunnydown Boys'
  Sch CR3 . . . . .100 A6
Sunnyhill Cl RH10 . . . . . .204 A8
Sunnyhill Prim Sch SW16 .21 F4
Sunnyhill Rd SW16 . . . . . .21 E4
Sunnyhurst Cl SM1 . . . . . .59 A7
Sunnymead
  Crawley Down RH10 . . . . .204 B8
Sunnymead Ave
  CR4, SW16 . . . . .41 D6

Sunnymede Ave
  Sutton SM5 . . . . .78 D8
  West Ewell KT19 . . . . .57 E3
Sunnyside Knaphill GU21 . .88 B8
  Walton-on-T TW12 . . . . .35 C4
  Wimbledon SW19 . . . . .19 E2
Sunnyside Pl SW19 . . . . . .19 E2
Sunnyside Rd
  Headley Down GU35 . . . . .187 C4
  Teddington TW11 . . . . .16 D4
Sunray Ave KT5 . . . . .57 B8
Sunrise Cl TW13 . . . . .15 F5
Sunset Gdns SE25 . . . . . . .42 F7
Sunset Rd SW19 . . . . .19 B3
Sunshine Way CR4 . . . . . . .40 F7
Sunstone Gr RH1 . . . . . . .119 E6
Sunvale Ave GU27 . . . . . .207 D6
Sunvale Cl GU27 . . . . .207 D6
Surbiton Cres KT1, KT6 . . .37 E5
Surbiton Ct KT6 . . . . .37 D3
Surbiton Hall Cl KT1 . . . . .37 E5
Surbiton High Sch KT1 . . .37 E5
Surbiton High Sch Jun
  Sch for Girls KT1 . . . . . . .37 E5
Surbiton Hill Pk KT5 . . . . .38 A4
Surbiton Hill Rd KT6 . . . . .37 E4
Surbiton Hospl KT6 . . . . . .37 E3
Surbiton Prep Sch KT6 . . .37 E4
Surbiton Rd
  Camberley GU15 . . . . .47 A1
  Kingston u T KT1 . . . . .37 E5
Surbiton Sta KT6 . . . . .37 E3
Surrey Ave GU15 . . . . .65 A4
Surrey Bsns Pk KT17 . . . . .76 E8
Surrey Gr SM1 . . . . .59 D7
Surrey Heath Mus GU15 . .65 D6
Surrey Hills Ave KT20 . . .116 C4
Surrey Hills Way KT20 . . .116 C5
Surrey Inst of Art &
  Design KT17 . . . . .76 E7
Surrey Inst of Art &
  Design The GU9 . . . . . . .125 B2
Surrey Inst of Art & Tech
  KT18 . . . . .76 D5
Surrey Lodge KT12 . . . . . .54 B5
Surrey Mews SE27 . . . . . . .22 E4
Surrey Mount SE23 . . . . . .23 B7
Surrey Rd BR4 . . . . .44 B1
Surrey Research Pk The
  GU2 . . . . .129 D8
Surrey St CR0, CR9 . . . . . .61 C7
Surrey Tower 5 SE20 . . . . .23 C1
Surrey Towers KT15 . . . . . .52 C5
Surridge Ct GU19 . . . . .47 E2
Surridge Gdns SE19 . . . . . .22 D2
Sussex Ave KT9 . . . . .56 D4
Sussex Cl Knaphill GU21 . .68 C1
  New Malden KT3 . . . . .38 E5
  Reigate RH2 . . . . .139 D8
  4 Twickenham TW1 . . . . .6 B1
Sussex Ct Addlestone KT15 .52 C5
  Barnes SW13 . . . . .7 F5
  Horsham RH13 . . . . .217 E1
  Knaphill GU21 . . . . .68 C1
Sussex Gdns KT9 . . . . .56 D4
Sussex Ho TW9 . . . . .6 F5
Sussex Lodge RH12 . . . . .217 C4
Sussex Manor Bsns Pk
  RH10 . . . . .182 A2
Sussex Pl KT3 . . . . .38 E5
Sussex Rd Croydon CR2 . . .61 D4
  Knaphill GU21 . . . . .68 C1
  Mitcham CR4 . . . . .41 E4
  New Malden KT3 . . . . .38 E5
  South Croydon CR2 . . . . . .61 D4
  Wallington SM5 . . . . .59 F4
  West Wickham BR4 . . . . . .44 B1
Sutherland Ave
  Biggin Hill TN16 . . . . .83 E1
  Guildford GU4 . . . . .109 E7
  Sunbury TW16 . . . . .34 F7
Sutherland Chase SL5 . . .28 E7
Sutherland Dr
  Guildford GU1, GU4 . . . . .110 A4
  Mitcham SW19 . . . . .40 D8
Sutherland Gdns
  Mortlake SW14 . . . . .7 E4
  North Cheam KT4 . . . . .39 B1
  Sunbury TW16 . . . . .34 F7
Sutherland Gr
  Putney SW18, SW19 . . . . . .19 F8
  Teddington TW11 . . . . .16 E3
Sutherland House TW10 .17 C6
  Windlesham GU19 . . . . .47 F3
Sutherland Rd Chiswick W4 .7 E8
  Thornton Heath CR0 . . . . . .42 A2
Sutton Arc SM1 . . . . .59 B5
Sutton Ave GU21 . . . . .88 E8
Sutton Cl BR3 . . . . .44 B8
Sutton Common Rd
  Cheam SM3 . . . . .40 A1
  Sutton SM1, SM3 . . . . .59 B8
Sutton Common Sta SM1 .59 B8
Sutton Court Rd
  Chiswick W4 . . . . .7 C8
  Sutton SM1, SM2 . . . . .59 C4
Sutton Courtenay House
  SW17 . . . . .20 D4
Sutton Ct Chiswick W4 . . . .7 C8
  East Molesey KT8 . . . . .35 F4
  Penge SE19 . . . . .22 F1
  Sutton SM2 . . . . .59 C4
Sutton Dene TW3 . . . . .5 B6
Sutton Gdns
  Croydon CR0, SE25 . . . . . .42 F4
  Merstham RH1 . . . . .119 D6
Sutton Gr SM1 . . . . .59 D5
Sutton Gram Sch For Boys
  SM1 . . . . .59 C5

Sutton Green Rd GU4 . . . .89 F1
Sutton Hall TW5 . . . . .5 A7
Sutton High Sch For Girls
  SM1 . . . . .59 B4
Sutton Hospl SM2 . . . . . . .59 B1
Sutton La
  Abinger Common RH5 . . . .155 C8
  Banstead SM7 . . . . .78 B6
  Brands Hill SL3 . . . . .1 B8
  Hounslow TW3, TW4, TW5 . . .4 F5
Sutton La S W4 . . . . .7 C8
Sutton Lodge GU1 . . . . . .109 E1
Sutton Park Rd SM1, SM2 .59 B4
Sutton Pl Brands Hill SL3 . . .1 B8
  Peaslake RH5 . . . . .154 F8
Sutton Rd Camberley GU15 .47 A1
  Heston TW5 . . . . .5 A6
Sutton Sq TW5 . . . . .4 F5
Sutton Sta SM2 . . . . .59 C4
Sutton Way TW5 . . . . .4 F5
Swaby Rd SW17, SW18 . . .20 C8
Swaffield Prim Sch SW18 .20 C8
Swaffield Rd SW18 . . . . . .20 C8
Swail House 8 KT18 . . . . .76 D6
Swain Cl SW16, SW17 . . . .21 B2
Swain Rd CR7 . . . . .42 C4
Swains Rd
  CR4, SW17, SW19 . . . . . . .20 F1
Swale House 2 RH1 . . . . .119 A3
Swale Rd GU14 . . . . .84 E6
Swaledale RG12 . . . . .27 A4
Swaledale Cl RH11 . . . . . .201 C3
Swallands Rd SE6 . . . . . . .24 A5
Swallow Cl Staines TW18 . .12 F4
  Witley GU8 . . . . .170 E7
Swallow Gdns SW16 . . . . .21 D3
Swallow La RH5 . . . . .136 B1
Swallow Pk KT6 . . . . .56 F7
Swallow Rd RH11 . . . . . . .201 C8
Swallow Rise GU21 . . . . . .68 C2
Swallowdale
  New Addington CR2 . . . . . .62 D2
  Selsdon CR2 . . . . .62 D2
Swallowfield
  Dormansland RH7 . . . . . . .165 A2
  Englefield Green TW20 . . . .11 B2
Swallows Ct SE20 . . . . . . .23 D1
Swallowtail Rd RH12 . . . .217 E6
Swan Barn Rd GU27 . . . . .208 D6
Swan Cl Croydon CR0 . . . . .42 E2
  Feltham TW13 . . . . .15 E4
Swan Ct Guildford GU1 . . .109 D3
  Leatherhead KT22 . . . . .95 B5
Swan Ctr SW17 . . . . .20 C5
Swan House GU47 . . . . . . .64 B7
Swan La Charlwood RH6 . .180 F7
  Guildford GU1 . . . . .130 D7
  Sandhurst GU47 . . . . .64 B7
Swan Mill Gdns RH4 . . . .115 D1
Swan Pl SW13 . . . . .7 F5
Swan Rd TW13 . . . . .15 E4
Swan Sq RH12 . . . . .217 C2
Swan St TW7 . . . . .6 B4
Swan Wlk Horsham RH12 .217 C2
  Oatlands Park TW17 . . . . . . .34 C2
Swancote Gn RG12 . . . . . .27 B4
Swandrift TW18 . . . . .12 F1
Swann Ct 6 TW7 . . . . .6 A4
Swann Way RH12 . . . . . . .216 E3
Swanns Meadow KT23 . . .94 A1
Swans Ghyll RH18 . . . . . .206 E3
Swansea Rd TW14, TW6 . . .3 D1
Swansmere Sch KT12 . . . .35 C1
Swanton Gdns SW19 . . . . .19 D7
Swanwick Cl SW15 . . . . . .18 F8
Swanworth La RH5 . . . . . .115 B7
Swayne's La GU1 . . . . . . .110 E1
Swaynesland Rd RH8 . . . .123 F1
Swaythling House SW15 . . .7 F1
Swedish Sch SW13 . . . . . . .7 F8
Sweeps Ditch Cl TW18 . . .13 B1
Sweeps La TW20 . . . . .11 F3
Sweet La GU5 . . . . .154 E8
Sweetbriar RG45 . . . . .45 A7
Sweetwater Cl GU5 . . . . .152 D4
Sweetwater La
  Enton Green GU8 . . . . . . .171 B2
  Shamley Green GU5 . . . . .152 D4
Swievelands Rd TN16 . . . .83 C1
Swift Cl SM2 . . . . .59 B3
Swift La Crawley RH11 . . .201 C8
  Windlesham GU19 . . . . .47 F3
Swift Rd Feltham TW13 . . .15 E4
  Heath End GU9 . . . . .125 C7
Swift's Cl GU10 . . . . .126 B1
Swiftsden Way BR1 . . . . . .24 E2
Swinburne Cres CR0 . . . . .43 C3
Swindon Rd Harlington TW6 . .3 D4
  Horsham RH12 . . . . .217 B4
Swinfield Cl TW13 . . . . . . .15 E4
Swingate Rd GU9 . . . . . . .146 D8
Swinley County Prim Sch
  SL5 . . . . .29 A4
Swinley Forest Golf Club
  SL5 . . . . .28 F2
Swinley Rd SL5 . . . . .28 C4
Swiss Cl GU10 . . . . .146 A4
Swissland Hill RH19, RH7 .185 E7
Switchback La
  Rowledge GU10 . . . . .145 F4
  Rowledge GU10 . . . . .146 A3
Sycamore Ave RH12 . . . . .218 C6
Sycamore Cl
  Carshalton SM5 . . . . .59 F6
  Crawley RH11 . . . . .181 C1
  Feltham TW13 . . . . .15 A5
  Fetcham KT22 . . . . .94 F5
  Frimley GU16 . . . . .65 E1

Sycamore Cl continued
  Sandhurst GU47 . . . . .64 B8
Sycamore Ct
  Farncombe GU7 . . . . .150 E8
  Forest Hill SE26 . . . . .23 C4
  Hounslow TW4 . . . . .4 E3
  Ottershaw KT16 . . . . .51 C5
  Walton-on-T KT13 . . . . .53 F7
  10 West Norwood SW16 . . .22 A3
Sycamore Dr
  Ash Vale GU12 . . . . .106 A7
  East Grinstead RH19 . . . . .186 A1
  Frimley GU16 . . . . .65 E1
  Wrecclesham GU10 . . . . . .146 A6
Sycamore Gdns CR4 . . . . .40 D7
Sycamore Gr
  Kingston u T KT3 . . . . .38 E6
  Penge SE20 . . . . .43 A8
Sycamore Lodge 7 TW16 .14 F1
Sycamore Rd
  Farnborough GU14 . . . . . . .85 D2
  Guildford GU1 . . . . .109 D3
  Wimbledon SW19, SW20 . . .19 C2
Sycamore Rise
  Banstead KT17, SM7 . . . . . .77 D5
  Bracknell RG12 . . . . .27 D6
Sycamore Way TW11 . . . . .17 C2
Sycamore Wlk
  Englefield Green TW20 . . . .11 B3
  Reigate RH2 . . . . .139 C6
Sycamores The
  Blackwater GU17 . . . . .64 B5
  Farnborough GU14 . . . . . . .85 D3
Sydenham Ave SE26 . . . . .23 B3
Sydenham High Sch For
  Girls SE26 . . . . .23 B4
Sydenham Hill SE21, SE22,
  SE23, SE26, SE19 . . . . . . .23 B5
Sydenham Hill Sta SE26 . .23 C5
Sydenham House 16 KT6 . .37 D2
Sydenham Ind Est SE26 . .23 F3
Sydenham Park Mansions
  SE26 . . . . .23 C5
Sydenham Park Rd
  SE23, SE26 . . . . .23 C5
Sydenham Pk SE26 . . . . . .23 C5
Sydenham Rd Croydon CR0 42 D2
  Forest Hill SE26, SE6 . . . . .23 D3
  Guildford GU1 . . . . .130 E8
  Thornton Heath CR0 . . . . . .42 D2
Sydenham Rise SE23 . . . . .23 B6
Sydenham Sch SE26 . . . . .23 B5
Sydenham Sec Sch SE26 . .23 B4
Sydenham Sta SE26 . . . . . .23 C4
Sydenham Station App
  SE26 . . . . .23 C4
Sydmons Ct SE23 . . . . . . .23 C8
Sydney Ave CR8 . . . . .79 F7
Sydney Cl RG45 . . . . .45 C7
Sydney Cotts KT10 . . . . . .55 F4
Sydney Cres TW15 . . . . . . .14 B2
Sydney Pl GU1 . . . . .130 E8
Sydney Rd
  East Bedfont TW14 . . . . . . .15 A7
  Guildford GU1 . . . . .130 F8
  Merton SW20 . . . . .39 D7
  Richmond TW10, TW9 . . . . . .6 E3
  Sutton SM1 . . . . .59 A6
  Teddington TW11 . . . . .16 F3
Sydney Terr KT10 . . . . .55 F4
Sydney Wood Forest Wlks
  GU6 . . . . .193 C2
Sylva Ct 3 SW15 . . . . .19 D8
Sylvan Cl Limpsfield RH8 .123 B6
  South Croydon CR2 . . . . . .62 B1
  Woking GU22 . . . . .70 B2
Sylvan Gdns KT6 . . . . .37 D2
Sylvan Hill SE19 . . . . .42 E8
Sylvan Ridge GU47 . . . . . .45 A1
Sylvan Way Coney Hall BR4 .63 E6
  Redhill RH1 . . . . .140 A8
Sylvanus RG12 . . . . .26 F2
Sylvaways Cl GU6 . . . . . . .175 A3
Sylverdale Rd
  Croydon CR0, CR9 . . . . . . .61 B7
  Purley CR8 . . . . .80 B6
Sylvia Cl GU24 . . . . .68 A4
Syon Gate Way
  Brentford TW8 . . . . .6 B7
  Hounslow TW7, TW8 . . . . . . .6 A7
Syon Ho & Pk TW8 . . . . . . .6 C6
Syon La Brentford TW7 . . . .5 F8
  Brentford TW7, TW8 . . . . . . .6 A7
  Hounslow TW7 . . . . .6 A7
Syon Lane Sta TW7 . . . . . . .6 A7
Syon Park Cotts TW8 . . . . .6 C6
Syon Park Gdns TW7 . . . . .5 F7
Syon Pl GU14 . . . . .85 D4
Sythwood GU21 . . . . .69 B2
Sythwood Cty Prim Sch
  GU21 . . . . .69 B3
Szabo Cres GU3 . . . . .107 B1

T

Tabard House KT1 . . . . . . .37 C8
Tabarin Way KT17 . . . . . . .77 C3
Tabor Ct SM3 . . . . .58 F4
Tabor Gdns SM2, SM3 . . . .58 F3
Tabor Gr SW19 . . . . .19 F1
Tachbrook Rd TW14 . . . . . .14 F8
Tadlow KT1 . . . . .38 A6
Tadmor Cl TW16 . . . . .34 F5
Tadorne Rd KT20 . . . . .97 C5
Tadworth Ave KT3 . . . . . . .38 F4

Tadworth Cl KT20 . . . . . . .97 D5
Tadworth Cty Prim Sch
  KT20 . . . . .97 D5
Tadworth St KT20 . . . . . . .97 C5
Tadworth Sta KT20 . . . . . .97 C5
Taffy's How CR4 . . . . .40 E6
Tait Rd CR0, SE25 . . . . . . .42 E2
Talavera Cty Inf Sch
  GU11 . . . . .105 B3
Talavera Cty Jun Sch
  GU11 . . . . .105 B3
Talbot Cl Mytchett GU16 . .86 A4
  Reigate RH2 . . . . .139 B8
Talbot La RH12 . . . . .217 C1
Talbot Lodge KT10 . . . . . .55 A5
Talbot Pl GU19 . . . . .47 E4
Talbot Rd Ashford TW15 . . .13 E3
  Farnham GU9 . . . . .146 B8
  Isleworth TW1, TW7 . . . . . . .6 A3
  Lingfield RH7 . . . . .164 D4
  South Norwood CR7 . . . . . .42 D5
  Twickenham TW2 . . . . .16 F7
  Wallington SM5 . . . . .60 A5
Talcott Path 12 SW2 . . . . .22 A7
Taleworth Cl KT21 . . . . . . .95 D7
Taleworth Pk KT21 . . . . . .95 D7
Taleworth Rd KT21 . . . . . .95 E7
Talgarth Dr GU14 . . . . .85 D2
Taliesin Hts GU7 . . . . .150 D6
Talisman Sq SE26 . . . . . . .23 A4
Talisman Way KT17 . . . . . .77 C3
Tall Elms Cl BR2 . . . . .44 F4
Tall Trees Poyle SL3 . . . . . . .1 E6
  Thornton Heath SW16 . . . . .41 F6
Tallis Cl RH11 . . . . .200 F3
Tally Rd RH8 . . . . .123 E4
Talma Gdns TW2 . . . . .16 E8
Talmage Cl SE23 . . . . .23 C7
Talman Cl RH11 . . . . .200 E5
Tamar Cl RH10 . . . . .202 C5
Tamarind Cl GU2 . . . . . . .109 A6
Tamarind Ct 3 TW20 . . . . .11 F3
Tamarisk Rise RG40 . . . . . .25 C7
Tamerton Sq GU22 . . . . . . .89 E8
Tamesa Ho TW17 . . . . .34 A2
Tamesis Gdns KT4 . . . . . . .57 E8
Tamian Ind Est TW4 . . . . . .4 C3
Tamian Way TW4 . . . . .4 C3
Tamworth RG12 . . . . .27 D2
Tamworth La CR4 . . . . .41 B6
Tamworth Manor High
  Sch CR4 . . . . .41 D6
Tamworth Pk CR4 . . . . . . .41 B6
Tamworth Pl 3 CR0, CR9 . .61 C8
Tamworth Rd CR0, CR9 . . .61 C8
Tanbridge House Sch
  RH12 . . . . .216 F2
Tanbridge Pk RH12 . . . . . .217 B1
Tanbridge Pl RH12 . . . . . .217 B1
Tandem Ctr SW19 . . . . . . .40 D8
Tandridge Ct
  Caterham CR3 . . . . .101 A5
  Sutton SM2 . . . . .59 B4
Tandridge Gdns CR2 . . . . .81 A6
Tandridge Golf Course
  RH9 . . . . .122 B4
Tandridge La
  RH7, RH8, RH9 . . . . .143 B4
Tandridge Rd CR6 . . . . . .101 D8
Tandridge RH9 . . . . .122 B4
Tandridgehill La
  Tandridge RH9 . . . . .121 F6
  Woldingham RH9 . . . . .121 F6
Tanfield Ct RH12 . . . . .217 B2
Tanfield Rd CR0, CR9 . . . . .61 C6
Tangier Ct GU11 . . . . .104 C7
Tangier Rd Guildford GU1 .131 A8
  Mortlake TW10 . . . . .7 B4
Tangier Way KT20 . . . . . . .77 E1
Tangier Wood KT20 . . . . . .77 E1
Tangle Oak RH19 . . . . . . .184 E4
Tanglewood Cl
  Longcross KT16 . . . . .50 B7
  South Croydon CR0 . . . . . .62 C7
  Woking GU22 . . . . .70 D3
Tanglewood Ride GU24 . . .67 D7
Tanglewood Way TW13 . . .15 B5
Tangley Dr RG41 . . . . .25 B4
Tangley Gr SW15 . . . . .18 F8
Tangley La GU3 . . . . .108 F6
Tangley Park Rd TW12 . . .15 F3
Tanglyn Ave TW17 . . . . . . .34 B4
Tangmere Gr KT2 . . . . .17 D3
Tangmere Rd RH11 . . . . . .200 F5
Tanhouse La GU41 . . . . . . .25 A5
Tanhouse Rd RH8 . . . . . . .122 E4
Tanhurst House 2 SW2 . . .21 E8
Tanhurst La RH5 . . . . .155 E2
Tank Rd GU15 . . . . .64 F5
Tankerton Rd KT6 . . . . .56 F8
Tankerton Terr CR0 . . . . . .41 F3
Tankerville Rd SW16 . . . . .21 E1
Tanner House 1 SW19 . . .40 C8
Tanner's Ct RH3 . . . . .137 C5
Tanner's Hill RH3 . . . . . . .137 B8
Tanners Cl KT12 . . . . .35 B3
Tanners Dean KT22 . . . . . .95 D5
Tanners La GU27 . . . . . . .208 C2
Tanners Meadow RH3 . . .137 B5
Tanners Yd GU19 . . . . .47 E3
Tannersfield GU4 . . . . . . .130 E1
Tannery Cl
  Beckenham BR3, CR0 . . . . .43 D4
  Slinfold RH13 . . . . .215 D3
Tannery Cotts GU5 . . . . . .133 C4
Tannery La Send GU23 . . .90 E5

Tannery La *continued*
Send Marsh GU23 ....90 E5
Shalford GU5 ....151 F8
Tannery The RH1 ....118 F1
Tannsfeld Rd SE26 ....23 D3
Tansy Cl GU4 ....110 C3
Tantallon Rd SW12 ....21 A7
Tanyard Ave RH19 ....206 A8
Tanyard Cl Crawley RH10 .202 C3
Horsham RH13 ....217 E1
Tanyard Way RH6 ....161 B4
Tapestry Cl SM2 ....59 B3
Taplow Ct CR4 ....40 E5
Tapner's Rd RH2 ....137 F3
Tapping Cl 5 KT2 ....18 A1
Tara Ct BR3 ....44 B7
Tara Pk CR5 ....98 F7
Taragon Ct GU2 ....109 A5
Tarbat Ct 6 GU47 ....64 D8
Target Cl TW14 ....3 E1
Tarham Cl RH6 ....160 E5
Tarleton Gdns SE23 ....23 B7
Tarmac Way UB7 ....2 B7
Tarn Cl GU14 ....84 E2
Tarn Rd GU26 ....188 E3
Tarnbrook Way RG12 ....27 E2
Tarquin House SE26 ....23 A4
Tarragon Cl GU14 ....84 C4
Tarragon Dr GU2 ....109 A5
Tarragon Gr SE26 ....23 D2
Tarrington Cl SW16 ....21 D5
Tartar Hill KT11 ....73 B6
Tartar Rd KT11 ....73 C6
Tasker Cl UB7 ....3 C7
Tasman Ct TW16 ....14 E1
Tatchbury House SW15 ....7 F1
Tate Cl KT22 ....95 C4
Tate Rd SM1 ....59 A5
Tate's Way RH12 ....214 D7
Tatham Ct RH11 ....201 B1
Tatsfield Cty Prim Sch TN16 ....103 D6
Tatsfield La TN16 ....103 F6
Tattenham Cnr KT18 ....77 A1
Tattenham Corner Rd KT18 ....77 A1
Tattenham Corner Sta KT18 ....77 B1
Tattenham Cres KT18 ....77 B1
Tattenham Gr KT18 ....97 B8
Tattenham Way KT18, KT20 77 E2
Tattersall Cl RG40 ....25 E5
Taunton Ave
Caterham CR3 ....100 F4
Hounslow TW3 ....5 C5
Wimbledon SW20 ....39 B7
Taunton Cl SM3 ....40 A1
Taunton La CR5 ....100 B8
Tavern Cl SM5 ....40 E2
Tavistock Cl TW18 ....13 D1
Tavistock Cres CR4 ....41 E5
Tavistock Ct 1 CR0 ....42 D1
Tavistock Gdns GU14 ....85 B7
Tavistock Gr CR0 ....42 D2
Tavistock Rd
Beckenham BR2 ....44 F5
Carshalton SM5 ....40 D1
Croydon CR0 ....42 D1
Tavistock Wlk SM5 ....40 D1
Tavy House 3 RH1 ....118 F2
Tawfield RG12 ....26 E2
Tawny Cl TW13 ....15 A5
Tay Cl GU14 ....84 E6
Tayben Ave TW2 ....5 E1
Tayles Hill KT17 ....57 F1
Taylor Ave TW9 ....7 B5
Taylor Cl Hampton TW12 ....16 C3
Hounslow TW3 ....5 C6
Taylor Ct SE20 ....43 C7
Taylor House 10 SW2 ....22 A7
Taylor Rd Aldershot GU11 .105 D7
Ashstead KT21 ....75 D2
Mitcham CR4, SW19 ....20 E1
Wallington SM6 ....60 B5
Taylor Wlk RH11 ....201 C6
Taylor's La SE26 ....23 B4
Taylors Cres GU6 ....174 F3
Taylors Ct TW13 ....15 A6
Taymount Grange SE23 ....23 C6
Taymount Rise SE23 ....23 C6
Taynton Dr RH1 ....119 D6
Teal Cl Horsham RH12 ....217 C5
Selsdon CR2 ....81 D8
Teal Ct Dorking RH4 ....136 A8
Wallington SM6 ....60 C5
Teal Pl SM1 ....58 F5
Tealing Dr KT19 ....57 D6
Teasel Cl Crawley RH11 ....201 B3
Croydon CR0 ....43 D1
Teazlewood Pk KT22 ....75 A1
Tebbit Cl RG12 ....27 D7
Tebbs House 14 SW2 ....22 A8
Teck Cl TW7 ....6 A5
Tedder Cl KT9 ....56 C5
Tedder Rd CR2 ....62 D2
Teddington Cl KT19 ....57 D1
Teddington Memorial Hospl TW11 ....16 E2
Teddington Park Rd TW11 16 F4
Teddington Pk TW11 ....16 F3
Teddington Sch TW11 ....17 C2
Teddington Sta TW11 ....17 A2
Tedham La RH9 ....163 B7
Tees Cl GU14 ....84 E6
Teesdale RH11 ....201 C3
Teesdale Ave TW7 ....6 A6
Teesdale Gdns
Isleworth TW7 ....6 A6
South Norwood SE25 ....42 E7
Teevan Cl CR0 ....43 A2
Teevan Rd CR0, CR9 ....43 A2
Tegg's La GU22 ....70 F3
Tekels Ave GU15 ....65 D4
Tekels Ct GU15 ....65 E4
Tekels Way GU15 ....65 F3
Telconia Cl GU35 ....187 C4
Telegraph La KT10 ....55 F5
Telegraph Rd SW15 ....19 C8
Telegraph Track SM5, SM6 .60 A1
Telfei House 8 SE21 ....22 E4
Telferscot Jun Mix & Inf Sch SW12 ....21 D7
Telferscot Rd SW12 ....21 D7
Telford Ave
Crowthorne RG45 ....45 C8
Streatham SW12, SW2 ....21 E7
Telford Avenue Mansions SW2 ....21 E7
Telford Cl SE19 ....22 F2
Telford Ct 2 GU1 ....130 F8
Telford Dr KT12 ....35 C2
Telford Parade Mansions SW2 ....21 E7
Telford Pl RH10 ....201 E5
Telford Rd TW4 ....16 A8
Telham Ct 5 RH11 ....200 F3
Tellisford KT10 ....55 B6
Temperley Rd SW12 ....21 A8
Tempest Rd TW20 ....12 C2
Templar Cl GU47 ....64 A8
Templar Ct CR0 ....62 E2
Templar Pl TW12 ....16 A1
Temple Ave CR0 ....62 F7
Temple Bar Rd GU21 ....88 F8
Temple Cl RH10 ....202 D5
Temple Ct 9 TW10 ....6 E2
Temple Field Cl KT15 ....52 B4
Temple Gdns TW18 ....32 F8
Temple La RH5 ....178 F5
Temple Market KT13 ....53 B6
Temple Rd Biggin Hill TN16 .83 D2
Croydon CR0 ....61 D6
Epsom KT19 ....76 D7
Hounslow TW3 ....5 C3
Richmond TW9 ....6 F5
Temple Sheen SW14 ....7 C2
Temple Sheen Rd SW14 ....7 C3
Temple Way Bracknell RG42 26 E8
Carshalton SM1 ....59 D7
Temple Wood Dr RH1 ....118 F4
Temple's Cl GU10 ....126 C1
Templecombe Mews GU22 ....70 B3
Templecombe Way SM4 ....39 E4
Templecroft TW15 ....14 D2
Templedene BR2 ....44 D7
Templedene Ave TW18 ....13 C2
Templeman Cl CR8 ....80 B3
Templemere KT13 ....53 D7
Templeton Cl CR7, SE19 ....42 D8
Templewood House RH1 .118 F4
Ten Acre GU21 ....69 A1
Ten Acre La TW20 ....32 C7
Ten Acres KT22 ....94 D3
Ten Acres Cl KT22 ....94 D3
Tenbury Ct SW12 ....21 D7
Tenby Dr SL5 ....29 D4
Tenby Rd GU16 ....86 A8
Tenchley's La
Limpsfield RH8 ....123 D4
The Chart RH8 ....123 E2
Tenham Ave SW2 ....21 D6
Tenniel Cl GU2 ....109 B3
Tennison Cl CR5 ....100 B7
Tennison Rd Croydon SE25 .42 F4
South Norwood SE25 ....42 F4
Tennyson Ave
Twickenham TW1 ....16 F7
West Barnes KT3 ....39 B4
Tennyson Cl
Crawley RH10 ....202 B8
Feltham TW14 ....4 A1
Horsham RH12 ....217 E6
Tennyson Ct 3 TW10 ....17 D4
Tennyson Rd
Addlestone KT15 ....52 E6
Ashford TW15 ....13 E3
Hounslow TW3 ....5 C5
Penge SE20 ....23 D1
Wimbledon SW19 ....20 C2
Tennyson Rise RH19 ....205 C8
Tennyson's La
Haslemere GU27 ....208 E4
Lurgashall GU27 ....209 A2
Tennysons GU27 ....208 E4
Tennysons Ridge GU27 ....208 E5
Tensing Ct TW19 ....13 E7
Tenterden Gdns CR0 ....43 A2
Tenterden Rd CR0 ....43 A2
Tern Rd RH11 ....200 D5
Terra Cotta Rd RH9 ....142 C5
Terrace Gdns SW13 ....7 F5
Terrace La TW10 ....6 E1
Terrace Rd KT12 ....35 B3
Terrace The
Addlestone KT15 ....52 E5
Ascot SL5 ....29 D4
Barnes SW13, SW14 ....7 E5
Camberley GU15 ....65 A5
Crowthorne RG45 ....45 D5
Mortlake SW13, SW14 ....7 E5
Old Woking GU22 ....90 A6
Wokingham RG40 ....25 B6
Terrapin Ct SW17 ....21 B5
Terrapin Rd SW17 ....21 B5
Terrapins KT6 ....37 D2
Terry House SW2 ....22 A7
Terry Rd RH11 ....201 B1
Testard Rd GU2 ....130 C7
Testers Cl RH8 ....123 B3
Teviot Cl GU2 ....109 A4
Tewkesbury Ave SE23 ....23 B8
Tewkesbury Cl KT14 ....71 D8
Tewkesbury Rd SM5 ....40 D1
Thackeray Cl Isleworth TW7 .6 A5
Wimbledon SW19 ....19 D1
Thackeray Manor SM1 ....59 C5
Thackery Lodge TW14 ....3 D1
Thakeham Cl SE26 ....23 B3
Thames Ave KT16 ....33 A6
Thames Bank SW14 ....7 C5
Thames Cl Chertsey KT16 ....33 C2
East Molesey TW12 ....36 B7
Farnborough GU14 ....84 E6
Thames Ct KT8 ....36 B7
Thames Ditton Cty Fst Sch KT7 ....36 F3
Thames Ditton & Esher Golf Club KT10 ....55 D8
Thames Ditton Hospl KT7 .36 F2
Thames Ditton Island KT7 37 A4
Thames Ditton Jun Sch KT7 ....36 F2
Thames Ditton Sta KT7 ....36 F2
Thames Eyot 7 TW1 ....17 A7
Thames Haven KT6 ....37 D4
Thames Link House 6 TW9 6 E3
Thames Mead KT12 ....35 A2
Thames Meadow
East Molesey KT8 ....36 A6
Lower Halliford KT12, TW17 .34 E1
Thames Rd Brentford W4 ....7 B8
Chiswick W4 ....7 B8
Thames Side
Kingston u T KT1 ....37 D8
Laleham KT16, TW18 ....33 C4
Staines TW18 ....12 F2
Thames Ditton KT7 ....37 B3
Thames St
East Molesey TW12 ....36 B7
Kingston u T KT1, KT2 ....37 D7
Staines TW18 ....12 F3
Sunbury TW16 ....35 B6
Walton-on-T KT12 ....34 F2
Weybridge KT13 ....53 B7
Thames View House TW12 ....35 A3
Thames Village W4 ....7 C6
Thamesfield Ct TW17 ....34 C2
Thamesgate TW18 ....33 B8
Thamesgate Cl TW10 ....17 B4
Thameside TW11 ....17 D1
Thamesmead Sch TW17 ....34 D3
Thamespoint TW11 ....17 D1
Thamesvale Cl TW3 ....5 A5
Thanescroft Gdns CR0 ....61 E7
Thanet House 1 SE27 ....22 B5
Thanet Pl CR0 ....61 C6
Tharp Rd SM6 ....60 D5
Thatcher Cl RH10 ....201 D3
Thatchers Cl Horley RH6 ..161 B5
Horsham RH12 ....217 E4
Thatchers La GU3 ....108 E8
Thatchers Way TW7 ....5 D2
Thaxted Pl 7 SW20 ....19 D1
Thayers Farm Rd BR3 ....43 E8
Theal Cl GU47 ....64 D8
Thelma Gr TW11 ....17 A2
Thelton Ave RH12 ....216 D3
Theobald Rd CR0, CR9 ....61 B8
Theobalds Way GU16 ....66 C3
Thepps Cl RH1 ....140 F6
Therapia La
Thornton Heath CR0 ....41 E3
Wallington CR0, CR4 ....41 D2
Wallington CR0 ....41 E2
Theresa's Wlk CR2 ....61 D2
Therfield Sch KT22 ....95 A8
Thesiger Rd BR3, SE20 ....23 D1
Thetford Ct SE21 ....23 B6
Thetford Rd Ashford TW15 .13 E5
New Malden KT3 ....38 E4
Thetis Terr TW9 ....7 A8
Theydon Cl RH10 ....202 A4
Thibet Rd GU47 ....64 C8
Thicket Cres SM1 ....59 C6
Thicket Gr SE20 ....23 A1
Thicket Rd
Penge SE19, SE20 ....23 B1
Sutton SM1 ....59 C6
Thickthorne La TW18 ....13 C1
Third Cl KT8 ....36 C5
Third Cross Rd TW2 ....16 D6
Thirlmere Cl
Farnborough GU14 ....84 E4
Thorpe Lea TW20 ....12 B1
Thirlmere House TW1 ....5 F2
Thirlmere Rd
Crawley RH11 ....200 D4
Streatham SW16 ....21 D4
Thirlmere Rise BR1 ....24 F2
Thirlmere Wlk GU15 ....66 D4
Thirsk Rd Mitcham CR4 ....21 A1
South Norwood SE25 ....42 D5
Thistle Way RH6 ....162 C3
Thistlecroft Rd KT12 ....54 C6
Thistledene
Thames Ditton KT7 ....36 E3
West Byfleet KT14 ....70 F6
Thistledown Vale RH14 ..212 D3
Thistlewood Cres CR0 ....82 D7
Thistleworth Cl TW7 ....5 D7
Thistley La GU6 ....174 E4
Thomas Ave CR3 ....100 C6
Thomas Becket Jun Mix & Inf Sch SE25 ....43 A3
Thomas Bennett Com Coll Crawley RH10 ....201 D3
Crawley RH10 ....201 E2
Thomas Dean Rd SE26 ....23 F4
Thomas' La SE6 ....24 A8
Thomas Moore House RH2 ....118 C1
Thomas More RC High Sch CR8 ....61 A1
Thomas Pooley Ct KT6 ....37 E2
Thomas Rd GU11 ....105 D7
Thomas Wall Cl SM1 ....59 B5
Thompson Ave TW9 ....7 A4
Thompson Ct 16 RH11 ....201 B1
Thompson's La GU24 ....49 D2
Thompsons Cl GU24 ....87 D4
Thomson Cres CR0 ....42 A1
Thorburn Chase GU47 ....64 E6
Thorburn Way SW19 ....40 D8
Thorkhill Gdns KT7 ....37 B1
Thorkhill Rd KT7 ....37 B2
Thorley Cl KT14 ....71 A5
Thorley Gdns KT14 ....71 A5
Thorn Bank GU2 ....130 A7
Thorn Cl GU10 ....145 F4
Thorn Rd GU10 ....146 A5
Thornash Cl GU21 ....69 C4
Thornash Rd GU21 ....69 C4
Thornash Way GU21 ....69 C4
Thornbank Cl TW19 ....2 A2
Thornbury Ave TW7 ....5 D7
Thornbury Cl RG45 ....45 B5
Thornbury Ct Hounslow TW7 .5 E7
Whyteleafe CR3 ....100 F7
Thornbury Rd TW7 ....5 D6
Thorncombe St GU5, GU8 151 E2
Thorncroft TW20 ....11 C1
Thorncroft Cl CR5 ....100 A8
Thorncroft Rd SM1 ....59 B6
Thorndean St SW18 ....20 C6
Thorndon Gdns KT19 ....57 E6
Thorndown La GU20 ....48 D3
Thorndyke Cl RH10 ....202 D5
Thorne Cl Crowthorne RG45 45 A7
Littleton TW15 ....14 C1
Thorne St SW13, SW14 ....7 E4
Thorne's Cl BR3 ....44 C6
Thorneloe Gdns CR0, CR9 .61 B5
Thorneycroft Cl KT12 ....35 C3
Thornfield Gn GU17 ....64 F3
Thornfield Rd SM7 ....78 A2
Thornhill RG12 ....27 E5
Thornhill Ave KT6 ....56 E8
Thornhill Cres GU11 ....105 C3
Thornhill Rd
Aldershot GU11 ....105 D4
Surbiton KT6 ....56 F8
Thornton Heath CR0 ....42 C2
Thornhill Way TW17 ....34 A4
Thornlaw Rd SE27 ....22 B4
Thornleas Pl KT24 ....92 E1
Thornsbeach Rd SE6 ....24 C6
Thornsett Pl SE20 ....43 B7
Thornsett Rd Penge SE20 .43 B7
Wandsworth SW18 ....20 B7
Thornsett Terr SE20 ....43 B7
Thornton Ave
Streatham SW2 ....21 D7
Thornton Heath CR0 ....41 F3
Thornton Cl Guildford GU2 109 A4
Horley RH6 ....160 E3
Thornton Cres CR5 ....100 A8
Thornton Ct SW20 ....39 D4
Thornton Dene BR3 ....44 A7
Thornton Gdns SW12 ....21 D7
Thornton Heath Sta CR7 ....42 C5
Thornton Hill SW19 ....19 E1
Thornton Pl RH6 ....160 F3
Thornton Rd
Carshalton SM5 ....40 D1
Mortlake SW14 ....7 D4
Streatham SW12, SW2 ....21 D7
Thornton Heath CR0, CR7, CR9 ....41 F3
Wimbledon SW19 ....19 D1
Thornton Rd E
Wimbledon SW19 ....19 D2
Wimboldon SW19 ....19 D2
Thornton Row CR7 ....42 A4
Thornycroft Ct TW9 ....6 F5
Thornyhurst Rd GU16 ....86 A4
Thorold Cl CR0, CR2 ....62 D1
Thorold House 6 SW2 ....21 E8
Thorold Rd GU9 ....125 C3
Thoroughfare The KT20 ....97 A3
Thorpe By-Pass KT16, TW20 ....32 B6
Thorpe C of E Fst Sch TW20 ....32 B6
Thorpe Cl Forest Hill SE26 ..23 D4
New Addington CR0 ....82 C8
Wokingham RG41 ....25 A3
Thorpe Ind Est TW20 ....32 C8
Thorpe Ind Pk TW20 ....32 C8
Thorpe Lea Prim Sch TW20 ....12 D2
Thorpe Lea Rd
Egham TW20 ....12 C2
Thorpe Lea TW20 ....12 C2
Thorpe Park TW20 ....32 E5
Thorpe Rd Chertsey KT16 ..32 D4
Egham TW18, TW20 ....12 D3
Kingston u T KT2 ....17 E1
Thorpes Cl GU2 ....109 A4
Thorpeside Cl TW18, TW20 .32 E7
Thorpewood Ave SE23, SE26 ....23 B6
Thorsden Cl GU22 ....89 E8
Thorsden Ct 10 GU22 ....69 E1
Thorsden Way 2 SE19 ....22 E3
Thrale Almhouses SW16 ..21 E3
Thrale Rd SW16 ....21 C3
Three Acres RH12 ....217 A1
Three Arch Rd RH1 ....140 A5
Three Bridges Cty Fst Sch RH10 ....202 A7
Three Bridges Cty Mid Sch RH10 ....201 F6
Three Bridges Rd RH10 ..202 A6
Three Bridges Sta RH10 .202 B6
Three Gates GU1 ....110 C3
Three Gates La GU27 ....208 E8
Three Mile Rd GU6, RH5 .155 A2
Three Pears Rd GU1 ....110 E1
Three Stiles Rd GU9 ....124 F3
Three Ways GU10 ....166 D6
Threestile Rd RH12 ....197 F1
Threshfield RG12 ....27 A4
Thriffwood SE23, SE26 ....23 D5
Thrift Vale GU4 ....110 D4
Thrigby Rd KT9 ....56 F4
Throat Handpost Cnr The RG40 ....25 A1
Throwley Rd SM1 ....59 B5
Throwley Way SM1 ....59 B5
Thrupp Cl CR4 ....41 B7
Thrupps Ave KT12 ....54 D5
Thrupps La KT12 ....54 D5
Thundery Hill GU10 ....126 F4
Thurbans Rd GU9 ....146 A7
Thurbarn Rd SE6 ....24 B3
Thurbarns Hill RH5 ....157 E1
Thurlby Rd SE27 ....22 A4
Thurleigh Rd SW11, SW12 .20 F8
Thurleston Ave SM4 ....39 E4
Thurlestone Cl TW17 ....34 C3
Thurlestone Par TW17 ....34 C3
Thurlestone Rd SE27 ....22 A4
Thurlow Hill SE21 ....22 C6
Thurlow House 17 SW16 ..21 E5
Thurlow Park Rd
Dulwich SE21, SE24 ....22 C6
West Norwood SE21, SE24 ..22 C6
Thurlow Park Sch SE27 ..22 B6
Thurlow Towers SE27 ....22 A5
Thurlow Wlk GU6 ....174 E1
Thurlton Ct GU21 ....69 E3
Thurnby Ct TW2 ....16 E5
Thurne Way RH12 ....214 D7
Thurnham Way KT20 ....97 D7
Thursby Rd GU21 ....69 A1
Thursley Cres CR0 ....63 D3
Thursley Gdns SW19 ....19 D6
Thursley House
3 Kingston u T KT2 ....18 B1
13 Streatham SW2 ....21 F8
Thursley Rd
Churt GU10, GU8 ....168 C3
Thursley GU8, GU10 ....169 B6
Thurso St SW17 ....20 D4
Thurstan Rd SW20 ....19 B1
Thurston House BR3 ....24 B2
Thurza Ct TW7 ....5 F5
Thyme Ct
Farnborough GU14 ....84 C5
Guildford GU4 ....110 B4
Tibbet's Cnr SW19 ....19 D8
Tibbet's Ride SW19 ....19 D8
Tibbets Cl SW19 ....19 D7
Ticehurst Cl RH10 ....202 E6
Ticehurst Rd SE23 ....23 E6
Tichborne Cl GU17 ....64 D5
Tichborne Pl GU12 ....126 D8
Tichbourne Cl GU16 ....65 F3
Tichmarsh KT19 ....57 C1
Tidenham Gdns CR0 ....61 E7
Tideswell Rd CR0 ....63 A7
Tideway Cl TW10 ....17 C4
Tideway Yd SW13 ....7 E5
Tidwells Lea RG12 ....27 E8
Tiepigs La
Coney Hall BR2, BR4 ....44 F1
Hayes BR2, BR4 ....44 F1
Tierney Ct 1 CR0 ....61 F8
Tierney Rd SW2 ....21 E7
Tierney Terr SW2 ....21 E7
Tiffin Girls' Sch KT2 ....17 E2
Tiffin Sch KT2 ....37 F7
Tilburstow Cotts RH9 ....121 C3
Tilburstow Hill Rd
Blindley Heath RH9 ....142 D5
South Godstone RH9 ....142 D5
Tile Barn Cl GU14 ....85 A5
Tilehouse Rd GU4 ....130 E5
Tilehurst La
Betchworth RH3, RH5 ....136 F5
Dorking RH3, RH5 ....136 F5
Tilehurst Rd Cheam SM3 ....58 E5
Wandsworth SW17, SW18 ..20 D7
Tiler's Way RH2 ....139 C5
Tilford Ave CR0 ....63 C2
Tilford Gdns SW19 ....19 D7
Tilford House 11 SW2 ....21 F8
Tilford Rd
Beacon Hill GU10, GU26 ....188 E6
Farnham GU10, GU9 ....146 F7
Hindhead GU10, GU26 ....188 E6
Rushmoor GU10 ....168 C4
Tilford GU10 ....147 C4
Tilford St GU10 ....147 D5
Tilgate Comm RH1 ....120 C2

Tilgate Dr RH10, RH11 . . . .201 E2
Tilgate Forest Bsns Ctr RH11 . . . . .201 D1
Tilgate Forest Golf Course RH10 . . . . .202 A2
Tilgate Forest Recn Ctr RH10 . . . . .201 D1
Tilgate Par RH10 . . . . .201 E3
Tilgate Pk Ctry Pk RH11 .201 F1
Tilgate Pl RH10 . . . . .201 E3
Tilgate Way RH10 . . . . . . .201 E3
Tilgates Cotts RH1 . . . . . .120 C3
Tilletts La RH12 . . . . .216 E8
Tilley La KT18 . . . . .96 C4
Tillingbourne Cty Jun Sch GU4 . . . . .131 B2
Tillingbourne Rd GU4 . . .130 E3
Tillingdown Hill CR3 . . . .101 A5
Tillingdown La
Caterham CR3 . . . . .101 B2
Woldingham CR3 . . . . .101 B3
Tillman House 8 SW2 . . . .21 F7
Tillotson Cl RH10 . . . . . . .202 D5
Tilly's La TW18 . . . . .12 F4
Tilney Ct KT6 . . . . .37 D4
Tilson Gdns SW2, SW4 . . . .21 E8
Tilson House SW2 . . . . .21 E8
Tilt Cl KT11 . . . . .73 E3
Tilt Meadow KT11 . . . . .73 E3
Tilt Rd KT11 . . . . .73 D3
Tilthams Corner Rd GU7, GU7 . . . . .151 C8
Tilthams Gn GU7 . . . . .151 B8
Tiltview KT11 . . . . .73 C4
Tiltwood Dr RH10 . . . . . . .204 C8
Timber Bank GU16 . . . . . . .86 A6
Timber Cl
Great Bookham KT23 . . . . .114 C8
Pyrford GU22 . . . . .70 F5
Timber Ct RH12 . . . . .217 C3
Timber Hill KT21 . . . . .95 E8
Timber Hill Rd CR3 . . . . .101 A3
Timber La CR3 . . . . .101 A3
Timber Pl 18 GU9 . . . . . . .125 B2
Timbercroft KT19 . . . . .57 E6
Timberham Farm Rd RH6 . . . . .181 D8
Timberham Link RH6 . . . .181 E8
Timberham Way RH6 . . . .181 E8
Timberlands 14 RH11 . . . .201 B1
Timberling Gdns CR2 . . . . .61 D1
Timbermill Ct GU27 . . . . .207 F6
Timberslip Dr SM6 . . . . . . .60 D2
Timbertop Rd TN16 . . . . . .83 C1
Times Sq SM1 . . . . .59 B5
Timline Gn RG12 . . . . .27 F7
Timperley Ct RH1 . . . . . .118 E3
Timperley Gdns RH1 . . . . .118 E3
Timsbury Wlk 5 SW15 . . . .19 A7
Timsway TW18 . . . . .12 F3
Tina Ct SW16 . . . . .22 A5
Tindale Cl CR2 . . . . .80 D8
Tinsey Cl TW20 . . . . .12 B3
Tinsley Cl RH10 . . . . .182 A1
Tinsley Gn RH10 . . . . .182 B4
Tinsley La RH10 . . . . .182 A1
Tinsley La N RH10 . . . . . .182 B3
Tinsley La S RH10 . . . . . .202 A8
Tintagel Cl KT17 . . . . .76 F5
Tintagel Ct RH13 . . . . . . .217 D1
Tintagel Dr GU16 . . . . .65 F1
Tintagel Way GU22 . . . . . . .70 A3
Tintells La KT24 . . . . .112 B7
Tintern Cl SW19 . . . . .20 C2
Tintern Rd Carshalton SM5 .40 D1
Crawley RH11 . . . . .201 A4
Tippits Mead RG42 . . . . . . .26 D8
Tipton Dr CR0 . . . . .61 E6
Tiree Path RH11 . . . . .201 B3
Tirlemont Rd CR2 . . . . .61 C3
Tirrell Rd CR0 . . . . .42 C3
Tisbury Rd SW16 . . . . .41 E7
Titchfield Rd SM5 . . . . .40 D1
Titchfield Wlk SM5 . . . . . . .40 D2
Titchwell Rd SW18 . . . . . . .20 D7
Tite Hill TW20 . . . . .11 D3
Tithe Barn Cl KT2 . . . . .37 F8
Tithe Barn The GU4 . . . . .111 D4
Tithe Cl Thorpe GU25 . . . . .31 D3
Wentworth GU25 . . . . .31 D3
Tithe La TW19 . . . . .1 A1
Tithe Orch RH19 . . . . .184 E4
Tithepit Shaw La CR2, CR6 .81 B3
Titlarks Hill Rd SL5 . . . . . . .30 B1
Titmus Dr RH10 . . . . .201 F2
Titsey Cnr RH8 . . . . .123 B7
Titsey Hill CR6, RH8 . . . . .103 B4
Titsey Rd Limpsfield RH8 . .123 B8
Titsey RH8 . . . . .103 B1
Tiverton Rd TW3 . . . . .5 C5
Tiverton Way
Chessington KT9 . . . . .56 D5
Frimley GU16 . . . . .65 F1
Tivoli Rd Hounslow TW4 . . . . .4 E3
West Norwood SE19, SE27 . .22 C3
Toad La GU17 . . . . .64 E4
Tobias Sch of Art RH19 . .205 E6
Toby Way KT5, KT6 . . . . .57 B8
Todds Cl RH6 . . . . .160 E5
Toftwood Cl RH10 . . . . . . .202 C5
Toll Bar Ct SM2 . . . . .59 B2
Toll Gdns RG12 . . . . .27 F6
Tolldene Cl GU21 . . . . .68 E2
Tollers La CR5 . . . . .99 F8
Tollgate GU1 . . . . .110 D1
Tollgate Ave RH1 . . . . .139 F4
Tollgate Ct RH1 . . . . .139 F4
Tollgate Dr SE21 . . . . .22 E6
Tollgate Hill RH11 . . . . .201 C1
Tollgate Jun Mix & Inf Sch CR0 . . . . .43 C3
Tollgate Rd RH4 . . . . .136 B4
Tollhouse La SM6 . . . . .60 C2
Tolson Ho 2 TW7 . . . . .6 A4
Tolson Rd TW7 . . . . .6 A4
Tolvaddon GU21 . . . . .69 A2
Tolverne Rd SW20 . . . . .39 C8
Tolworth Cl KT6 . . . . .38 B1
Tolworth Girls' Sch KT6 . . .56 F7
Tolworth Hospl KT6 . . . . . . .57 A8
Tolworth Inf Sch KT6 . . . . .37 F1
Tolworth Jun Sch KT6 . . . . .37 F1
Tolworth Park Rd KT6 . . . . .56 F8
Tolworth Rd KT6 . . . . .56 E8
Tolworth Rise N KT5 . . . . . .38 B1
Tolworth Rise S KT5 . . . . . .38 B1
Tolworth Sta KT5 . . . . .57 B8
Tolworth Underpass KT5, KT6 . . . . .57 B8
Tomlin Cl KT19 . . . . .76 D8
Tomlin Ct KT19 . . . . .76 D8
Tomlins Ave GU16 . . . . .65 F2
Tomlinscote Sch GU16 . . . .66 A1
Tomlinscote Way GU16 . . .66 A2
Tompset's Bank RH18 . . .206 F1
Tomtits La RH18 . . . . .206 E1
Tonbridge Cl SM7 . . . . .78 F5
Tonbridge Rd KT12, KT8 . . .35 F5
Tonfield Rd SM3 . . . . .39 F1
Tonge Cl BR3 . . . . .44 A4
Tongham Meadows GU10 . . . . .126 F7
Tongham Rd
Aldershot GU12 . . . . .126 D8
Farnham GU10 . . . . .126 C4
Tonstall Rd Epsom KT19 . . .76 D8
Mitcham CR4 . . . . .41 A7
Tooting Bec Gdns SW16 . .21 D4
Tooting Bec Rd
Streatham SW16 . . . . .21 B4
Upper Tooting SW17 . . . . . . .21 B4
Tooting Bec Sta SW17 . . . .21 A5
Tooting Broadway SW17 . .20 F3
Tooting Broadway Sta SW17 . . . . .20 E3
Tooting Gr SW17 . . . . .20 E3
Tooting High St SW17, SW19 . . . . .20 E3
Tooting Mkt SW17 . . . . .20 F4
Tooting Sta SW17 . . . . .20 F2
Tootswood Rd BR2, BR3 . . .44 E5
Top Pk BR3 . . . . .44 E4
Topaz House KT4 . . . . .38 D1
Topiary Sq TW9 . . . . .6 F4
Topiary The Ashstead KT21 .95 E7
Farnborough GU14 . . . . .84 E3
Toplady Pl GU9 . . . . .125 C7
Topsham Rd SW17 . . . . .21 A4
Tor La KT13 . . . . .72 D8
Tor Rd GU9 . . . . .124 F2
Torcross Dr SE23 . . . . .23 C6
Torin Ct TW20 . . . . .11 C3
Torland Dr KT22 . . . . .74 D6
Tormead Cl SM1 . . . . .59 A4
Tormead Rd GU1 . . . . .109 F1
Tormead Sch GU1 . . . . . . .109 F1
Toronto Dr RH6 . . . . .162 A3
Torr Rd SE20 . . . . .23 D1
Torre Wlk SM5 . . . . .40 E1
Torridge Rd Brands Hill SL3 . .1 B8
Thornton Heath CR7 . . . . . . .42 B4
Torridon Cl GU21 . . . . .69 B2
Torridon Inf Sch SE6 . . . . .24 D6
Torridon Jun Sch SE6 . . . . .24 D6
Torridon Rd SE13, SE6 . . . .24 D7
Torrington Cl KT10 . . . . . . .55 E4
Torrington Ct SE26 . . . . . . .23 A3
Torrington Rd KT10 . . . . . . .55 E4
Torrington Sq CR0 . . . . .42 D2
Torrington Way SM4 . . . . . .40 A3
Torwood La CR3 . . . . .100 F8
Totford La GU10 . . . . .127 E4
Totham Lodge SW20 . . . . . .39 B8
Totland Cl GU14 . . . . .85 A6
Tottenham Rd GU7 . . . . . .150 E6
Tottenham Wlk GU47 . . . . . .45 D1
Totterdown St SW17 . . . . . .20 F3
Totton Rd CR7 . . . . .42 A6
Toulouse Cl GU15 . . . . .66 B7
Tournai Cl GU11 . . . . .105 E7
Toutley Rd RG41 . . . . .25 A8
Tovil Cl SE20 . . . . .43 B7
Tower Cl
East Grinstead RH19 . . . . .185 E2
Hindhead GU26 . . . . .188 E4
Horley RH6 . . . . .160 F3
Penge SE20 . . . . .23 B1
Woking GU21 . . . . .69 D2
Tower Cotts KT10 . . . . .54 F1
Tower Ct RH19 . . . . .185 E2
Tower Gdns KT10 . . . . .56 A3
Tower Gr KT13 . . . . .53 E8
Tower Hill Dorking RH4 . . .136 B5
Farnborough GU14 . . . . .85 A3
Tower Hill Cty Prim Sch GU14 . . . . .84 F3
Tower Hill Rd RH4 . . . . . . .136 B5
Tower Hill Rise GU5 . . . . . .133 C3
Tower Rd Crawley RH12 . . .218 F8
Hindhead GU26 . . . . .188 E4
Tadworth KT20 . . . . .97 C4
Twickenham TW1, TW2 . . . . .16 F5
Tower Rise TW9 . . . . .6 E4
Tower View CR0 . . . . .43 E2
Towerhill GU5 . . . . .133 C3
Towers Dr RG45 . . . . .45 B4
Towers Pl TW10 . . . . .6 E2
Towers The Kenley CR8 . . . .80 C4
1 Richmond TW9 . . . . .6 F3
Towers Wlk KT13 . . . . .53 B4
Towfield Ct TW13 . . . . .15 F6
Towfield Rd TW13 . . . . .15 F6
Town Barn Rd RH11 . . . . .201 C7
Town End Cl
Caterham CR3 . . . . .100 E5
Godalming GU7 . . . . .150 E4
Town End St GU7 . . . . . . .150 E4
Town Farm Cty Prim Sch TW19 . . . . .13 D8
Town Farm Way TW19 . . . .13 D8
Town Field Way TW7 . . . . . . .6 A5
Town Hill RH7 . . . . .164 E4
Town La TW19 . . . . .13 D7
Town Mead
Bletchingley RH1 . . . . .120 D2
Crawley RH11 . . . . .201 D7
Town Meadow TW8 . . . . .6 D7
Town Quay TW18 . . . . .33 C6
Town Sq Bracknell RG12 . . . .27 C7
Camberley GU15 . . . . .65 C6
3 Woking GU21 . . . . .69 F2
Town Tree Rd TW15 . . . . . . .14 A3
Townend CR3 . . . . .100 E5
Townend Ct BR1 . . . . .44 F8
Townfield Ct RH4 . . . . . . .136 A6
Townfield Rd RH4 . . . . . . .136 A6
Towngate KT11 . . . . .73 E4
Townmead Rd TW9 . . . . .7 B5
Townsend Cl RG12 . . . . .27 E4
Townsend La GU22 . . . . .90 B6
Townsend Rd TW15 . . . . . . .13 E3
Townshend Rd TW9 . . . . .6 F3
Townshend Terr TW9 . . . . . . .6 F3
Townshott Cl KT23 . . . . . . .94 A1
Townside Pl GU15 . . . . .65 D6
Towpath Way CR0, SE25 . . .42 F4
Towton Rd SE27 . . . . .22 C6
Toynbee Rd
Merton SW19, SW20 . . . . . . .39 E8
Wimbledon SW19, SW20 . . . .39 E8
Tracery The SM7 . . . . .78 B4
Tracious Cl GU21 . . . . .69 B3
Traemore Ct SW16 . . . . .22 A5
Trafalgar Ave KT4, SM3, SM4 . . . . .39 D1
Trafalgar Ct Cobham KT11 . .73 A6
Farnham GU9 . . . . .125 C1
Hounslow TW3 . . . . .4 F4
West Barnes KT3 . . . . .39 B6
Trafalgar Cty Inf Sch RH12 . . . . .217 B4
Trafalgar Dr KT12 . . . . .54 B7
Trafalgar Inf Sch TW2 . . . .16 D6
Trafalgar Jun Sch TW2 . . . .16 D6
Trafalgar Rd
Horsham RH12 . . . . .217 C4
Merton SW19 . . . . .20 C1
Twickenham TW2 . . . . .16 D6
Trafalgar Way
Camberley GU15 . . . . .64 F4
Croydon CR0, CR9 . . . . .61 A8
Trafford Rd Frimley GU16 . .85 D8
Thornton Heath CR7 . . . . . . .41 F4
Traherne Lodge 8 TW11 . .16 F3
Tramway Path CR4 . . . . . . .40 E5
Tranmere Ct SM2 . . . . .59 C3
Tranmere Rd
Twickenham TW2 . . . . .16 B8
Wandsworth SW17, SW18 . . .20 C6
Tranquil Dale RH3 . . . . . . .116 F3
Transport Ave TW8 . . . . .6 B8
Transport & Road Research Laboratory RG45 . . . . .45 C7
Trap La RH5 . . . . .176 F2
Traps La KT2, KT3 . . . . .38 E8
Trasher Mead RH4 . . . . . .136 C4
Travellers Way TW5 . . . . . . .4 C5
Travis La GU47 . . . . .64 C7
Treadcroft Dr RH12 . . . . . .217 E5
Treadwell Rd KT18 . . . . . . .76 F4
Treaty Ctr TW3 . . . . .5 B4
Trebor Ave GU9 . . . . .146 D8
Tredenham Cl GU14 . . . . . .105 C8
Tredown Rd SE26 . . . . .23 C3
Tredwell Rd SE27 . . . . .22 B4
Tree Ave GU27 . . . . .207 F8
Tree Cl TW10 . . . . .17 D7
Tree Tops CR6 . . . . .81 A1
Tree Tops Ave GU15 . . . . . .66 B8
Tree View Cl SE19 . . . . .42 E8
Treebourne Rd TN16 . . . . . .83 C1
Treebys Ave GU4 . . . . .109 D7
Treelands RH5 . . . . .136 C4
Treemount Ct KT17 . . . . . . .76 E6
Treen Ave SW13, SW14 . . . . .7 F4
Trees Sch The GU22 . . . . . .90 B8
Treeside Dr GU9 . . . . .125 E7
Treetops RH9 . . . . .142 E6
Treetops Ct CR7 . . . . .42 C4
Treeview RH11 . . . . .201 C1
Treeview Ct 3 RH2 . . . . . .118 D1
Treeway RH2 . . . . .118 B4
Trefoil Cl Horsham RH12 . .217 E5
Wokingham RG40 . . . . .25 E7
Trefoil Cres RH11 . . . . . . .201 A2
Trefusis Ct TW5 . . . . .4 B6
Tregaron Gdns KT3 . . . . . . .38 E5
Tregarth Pl GU21 . . . . .68 F2
Tregarthen Pl KT22 . . . . . . .95 C6
Treglos Ct KT13 . . . . .53 E8
Tregolls Dr GU14 . . . . .85 D3
Trehaven Par RH2 . . . . . . .139 B6
Trehern Rd 12 SW14 . . . . . . .7 D4
Treherne Ct SW17 . . . . .21 A4
Trelawn Cl KT16 . . . . .51 C3
Trelawne Dr GU6 . . . . . . .174 E2
Trelawney Gr KT13 . . . . . . .53 A4
Treloar Gdns SE19 . . . . . . .22 D2
Tremaine Rd SE20 . . . . .43 B7
Trematon Pl TW11 . . . . .17 C1
Tremayne Wlk GU15 . . . . . .66 C4
Trenance GU21 . . . . .69 A2
Trenchard Cl KT12 . . . . .54 C5
Trenchard Ct SM4 . . . . .40 A3
Trenear Cl RH13 . . . . .217 E2
Trenham Dr CR6 . . . . .81 C3
Trenholme Cl SE20 . . . . . . .23 B1
Trenholme Ct CR3 . . . . . . .101 A4
Trenholme Rd SE20 . . . . . . .23 B1
Trenholme Terr SE20 . . . . .23 B1
Trent Cl Crawley RH11 . . . .200 F4
Farnborough GU14 . . . . .84 E6
Trent Rd SL3 . . . . .1 B8
Trent Way KT4 . . . . .58 C7
Trentham Cres GU22 . . . . . .90 A6
Trentham Rd RH1 . . . . . . .140 A7
Trentham St SW18 . . . . . . .20 A7
Trenton Cl GU16 . . . . .66 A1
Treport St SW18 . . . . .20 B8
Treryn Hts GU7 . . . . .150 D6
Tresco Cl BR1 . . . . .24 E2
Tresidder House 10 SW4 . .21 D8
Tresillian Way GU21 . . . . . .69 B2
Tresta Wlk GU21 . . . . .69 A3
Trevanne Plat RH10 . . . . .202 D7
Trevelayan Rd SW17 . . . . . .20 F2
Trevelyan RG12 . . . . .26 E2
Trevelyan Ct KT3 . . . . .38 F2
Trevelyan House 6 TW1 . . .6 C1
Trevenna House 18 SE23 . . .23 D5
Trevereux Hill RH8 . . . . . .123 F4
Treversh Ct BR1 . . . . .44 F8
Treville St SW15 . . . . .19 B8
Treviso Rd SE23 . . . . .23 D6
Trevithick Cl TW14 . . . . . . .14 F7
Trevor Cl Hayes BR2 . . . . . .44 F2
Isleworth TW7 . . . . .5 F2
Trevor Rd SW19 . . . . .19 E1
Trevose Ave KT14 . . . . .70 F5
Trewenna Dr KT9 . . . . .56 D5
Trewince Rd SW20 . . . . . . .39 C8
Trewint St SW18 . . . . .20 C6
Trewsbury Rd SE26 . . . . . . .23 D3
Treyford Cl RH11 . . . . . . .200 F6
Triangle The
Kingston u T KT3 . . . . .38 C7
Woking GU21 . . . . .69 C1
Trickett House SM2 . . . . . . .59 B2
Trident Ind Est SL3 . . . . .1 E4
Trig St RH5 . . . . .178 F8
Trigg's Cl GU22 . . . . .89 D8
Trigg's La GU21, GU22 . . . . .89 D8
Trigo Ct KT19 . . . . .76 D8
Trilby Rd SE23 . . . . .23 D6
Trimmer Ct TW7 . . . . .5 F4
Trimmer Wlk 11 TW8 . . . . . .6 E8
Trimmer's Almshouses GU9 . . . . .125 A1
Trimmers Cl GU9 . . . . .125 C7
Trimmers Field GU9 . . . . .125 E1
Trimmers Wood GU26 . . . .188 E6
Trindles Rd RH1 . . . . .140 F7
Tring Ct TW1 . . . . .17 A4
Tringham Cl KT16 . . . . .51 C5
Trinity GU47 . . . . .45 E2
Trinity C of E Sch KT10 . . .55 A7
Trinity Cl Crawley RH10 . . .202 C8
Hounslow TW4 . . . . .4 E3
South Croydon CR2 . . . . .61 E2
Stanwell TW19 . . . . .2 C1
Trinity Cotts TW9 . . . . .6 F4
Trinity Cres
Sunningdale SL5 . . . . .30 A4
Upper Tooting SW17 . . . . . . .21 A6
Trinity Ct Croydon CR9 . . . .61 C8
Forest Hill SE23 . . . . .23 C5
Thornton Heath SE25 . . . . . .42 E3
Twickenham TW2 . . . . .16 E6
Trinity Fields GU9 . . . . . .125 A6
Trinity Hill GU9 . . . . .125 A6
Trinity Mews SE20 . . . . . . .43 B8
Trinity Par TW3 . . . . .5 B4
Trinity Rd Knaphill GU21 . . .68 B1
Richmond TW9 . . . . .6 F4
Upper Tooting SW17, SW18 . .20 E7
Wandsworth SW17, SW18 . . .20 E7
Wimbledon SW19 . . . . .20 A2
Trinity Rise SE24, SW2 . . . .22 B8
Trinity Sch CR9 . . . . .62 C8
Trinity St Mary's (C of E) Prim Sch SW12 . . . . .21 A7
Tristram Rd BR1 . . . . .24 F4
Tritton Ave CR0 . . . . .60 E6
Tritton Rd SE21, SE27 . . . . .22 D5
Trittons KT20 . . . . .97 D6
Triumph Cl UB7 . . . . .3 C6
Trodd's La GU1, GU4 . . . . .110 E1
Trojan Way CR0 . . . . .60 F7
Troon Cl RH11 . . . . .200 D5
Troon Ct SL5 . . . . .29 C4
Troston Ct TW18 . . . . .12 F3
Trotsworth Ave GU25 . . . . .31 E5
Trotsworth Ct GU25 . . . . . .31 D5
Trotters La GU24 . . . . .69 B7
Trotton Cl RH10 . . . . .202 C3
Trotwood Cl GU47 . . . . .45 E2
Trout Rd GU27 . . . . .207 E6
Troutbeck Wlk GU15 . . . . . .66 D3
Trowers Way RH1 . . . . . . .119 B4
Trowlock Ave TW11 . . . . . . .17 C2
Trowlock Way TW11 . . . . . .17 D2
Troy La TN8 . . . . .144 F4
Troy Rd SE19 . . . . .22 D2
Trumpeters Inn TW9 . . . . . . .6 C2
Trumpetshill Rd RH2 . . . .138 B7
Trumps Green Cl GU25 . . . .31 E4
Trumps Green Cty Fst Sch GU25 . . . . .31 D3
Trumps Mill La
Longcross GU25 . . . . .31 F4
Thorpe GU25 . . . . .31 F4
Trumpsgreen Ave GU25 . . .31 D3
Trumpsgreen Rd GU25 . . . .31 D3
Trundle Mead RH12 . . . . .217 C5
Trunk Rd GU14 . . . . .84 C5
Trunley Heath Rd GU5 . . .151 C8
Truslove Rd SE27 . . . . .22 B3
Truss Hill Rd SL5 . . . . .29 C4
Trust Wlk SE21 . . . . .22 B7
Trys Hill KT16 . . . . .51 A8
Trystings Cl KT10 . . . . .56 A4
Tucker Rd KT16 . . . . .51 D4
Tuckers Dr GU6 . . . . .174 B3
Tuckey Gr GU23 . . . . .90 F3
Tudor Ave Hampton TW12 . . .16 A1
North Cheam KT4 . . . . .58 B6
Tudor Circ GU7 . . . . .150 E7
Tudor Cl Ashford TW15 . . . . .13 E4
Banstead SM7 . . . . .77 E4
Cheam SM3 . . . . .58 E4
Chessington KT9 . . . . .56 E5
Cobham KT11 . . . . .73 F6
Coulsdon CR5 . . . . .80 A1
Crawley RH10 . . . . .202 D5
East Grinstead RH19 . . . . . .205 F8
Grayshott GU26 . . . . .188 D2
Hampton TW12 . . . . .16 C3
Hamsey Green CR2 . . . . .81 B4
Little Bookham KT23 . . . . . . .94 A3
Smallfield RH6 . . . . .162 B3
Wallington SM6 . . . . .60 C3
Woking GU22 . . . . .70 A2
Wokingham RG40 . . . . .25 F5
Tudor Ct Biggin Hill TN16 . . .83 E2
Farncombe GU7 . . . . .150 E5
Feltham TW13 . . . . .15 C4
12 Redhill RH1 . . . . .119 A2
Stanwell TW19 . . . . .2 E1
Teddington TW11 . . . . .16 F2
Tudor Dr Kingston u T KT2 . .17 E3
Walton-on-T KT12 . . . . .35 D1
West Barnes SM4 . . . . .39 E3
Tudor Gdns
Mortlake SW13, SW14 . . . . . . .7 E4
Twickenham TW1 . . . . .16 F7
West Wickham BR4 . . . . .63 C7
Tudor House
Bracknell RG12 . . . . .27 B4
Horsham RH13 . . . . .217 F3
Weybridge KT13 . . . . .53 A4
Tudor La SL4 . . . . .11 C8
Tudor Pl SW19 . . . . .20 E1
Tudor Prim Sch SM4 . . . . . .39 D2
Tudor Rd Ashford TW15 . . . .14 D2
Beckenham BR3 . . . . .44 C6
Croydon CR0, SE25 . . . . .43 B4
Farncombe GU7 . . . . .150 E7
Hampton TW12 . . . . .16 A1
Isleworth TW3 . . . . .5 D3
Kingston u T KT2 . . . . .18 A1
Penge SE19 . . . . .22 F1
Tudor Wlk
Leatherhead KT22 . . . . .94 F7
3 Weybridge KT13 . . . . .53 B7
Tudors The BR3 . . . . .44 B7
Tuesley Cnr GU7 . . . . .150 D3
Tuesley La
Godalming GU7, GU8 . . . . .150 D1
Milford GU7 . . . . .171 C7
Tufton Gdns KT8 . . . . .36 B7
Tugela Rd CR0 . . . . .42 D3
Tugela St SE6 . . . . .23 F6
Tuggles Plat RH12 . . . . . . .216 E7
Tulip Cl Croydon CR0 . . . . . .43 D1
Hampton TW12 . . . . .15 F2
Tulip Ct RH12 . . . . .217 C4
Tull St CR4 . . . . .40 F2
Tullett Rd RH10 . . . . .202 B2
Tulse Cl BR3 . . . . .44 C6
Tulse Hill SW2, SE24 . . . . . .22 A8
Tulse Hill Sta SE27 . . . . . . .22 B6
Tulsemere Rd SE21, SE27 . .22 C6
Tulyar Cl KT20 . . . . .97 B7
Tumber St KT18, KT22 . . . . .96 C2
Tumblewood Rd SM7 . . . . .77 E3
Tumbling Bay KT12 . . . . . . .35 A3
Tummons Gdns SE25 . . . . . .42 E7
Tunbridge Ct 1 SE26 . . . . .23 A5
Tunley Rd SW12, SW17 . . . .21 A6
Tunnel Link Rd TW6 . . . . . . .3 A2
Tunnel Rd E TW6 . . . . .3 B6
Tunnel Rd W TW6 . . . . .3 B6
Tunnmeade RH11 . . . . .200 E5
Tunsgate GU1 . . . . .130 D7
Tunsgate Sq GU1 . . . . . . .130 D7
Tunstall Ct 18 TW9 . . . . .6 F6
Tunstall Rd CR0 . . . . .42 E1
Tunstall Wlk 10 TW8 . . . . . . .6 E8
Tunworth Cres SW15 . . . . . . .7 F1
Tupwood Ct CR3 . . . . .101 A2
Tupwood La CR3 . . . . .101 A1
Tupwood Scrubbs Rd CR3, RH9 . . . . .121 A8
Turf Hill Rd GU15 . . . . .65 F8
Turfhouse La GU24 . . . . . . .49 E2
Turkey Oak Cl SE19 . . . . . . .42 E8

Turle Rd SW16 . . . . .41 E7
Turnberry RG12 . . . . .26 E2
Turner Ave Mitcham CR4 . .40 F8
  Twickenham TW2 . . . . .16 C5
Turner Cl Biggin Hill TN16 .83 C7
  Guildford GU1 . . . . .109 F4
Turner Ct
  East Grinstead RH19 . . . . .186 A3
  Godalming GU7 . . . . .150 D4
Turner House RH5 . . . . . . .157 C4
Turner Lodge 16 SW19 . . .19 D7
Turner Pl GU47 . . . . .64 D6
Turner's Hill Rd RH19 . . . .205 B6
Turners Cl TW18 . . . . .13 B3
Turners Hill CE
  (Controlled) Sch RH10 .204 A3
Turners Hill Rd
  Copthorne RH10 . . . . .183 F2
  Crawley RH10 . . . . .203 C5
  Crawley Down RH10 . . . . .204 A7
  Turners Hill RH10 . . . . . . .203 F5
Turners La KT12 . . . . .54 B3
Turners Mead GU8 . . . . . .191 C3
Turners Meadow Way BR3 43 F8
Turners Way CR0, CR9 . . . .61 A8
Turney Rd SE21 . . . . .22 D8
Turney Sch SE21 . . . . .22 C8
Turnham Cl GU2 . . . . .130 C5
Turnoak Ave GU22 . . . . . . .89 E7
Turnoak Cnr GU22 . . . . . . .89 E8
Turnoak La GU22 . . . . .89 E8
Turnpike La SM1 . . . . .59 C5
Turnpike Link CR0 . . . . . . .61 E8
Turnpike Pl RH11 . . . . . . .201 D8
Turnpike Rd RG42 . . . . . . .26 D7
Turnstone Ct CR0, CR2 . . .62 E1
Turnville Cl GU18 . . . . .48 A1
Turpin Rd TW14 . . . . .3 F1
Turpin Way SM6 . . . . .60 B3
Turpins Rise GU20 . . . . . . .48 B6
Turret Ct RH19 . . . . .185 C3
Turret House KT2 . . . . .17 E2
Turville Ct KT23 . . . . .94 B2
Tuscam Way GU15 . . . . . . .64 F4
Tushmore Ave
  RH10, RH11 . . . . .181 E1
Tushmore La RH10, RH11 .201 E8
Tushmore Rdbt RH11 . . . .201 D8
Tussock Ct RH11 . . . . .201 A4
Tuxford Cl RH10 . . . . .202 C4
Tweed Cl GU14 . . . . .84 E6
Tweed La Brockham RH3 .137 B5
  Rusper RH11 . . . . .180 F1
Tweed Rd SL3 . . . . .1 B8
Tweeddale Inf Sch SM5 . .40 D2
Tweeddale Jun Sch SM5 . .40 D1
Tweeddale Rd SM5 . . . . . . .40 D1
Tweedsmuir Cl GU14 . . . . .84 D3
Tweedy Rd BR1 . . . . .44 F8
Twelve Acre Cl KT23 . . . . .93 F3
Twelve Acre Cres GU14 . . .84 E5
Twickenham Bridge TW9 . .6 C2
Twickenham Cl CR0 . . . . . .60 F7
Twickenham Golf Course
  TW12 . . . . .16 B4
Twickenham Rd
  Feltham TW13 . . . . .15 F5
  Isleworth TW1, TW7 . . . . . .6 A4
  Richmond TW1, TW9 . . . . . .6 C3
  Teddington TW11 . . . . .17 A4
Twickenham Rugby
  Football Union Ground
  TW2 . . . . .5 E1
Twickenham Sta TW1 . . . .17 A8
Twickenham Trad Ctr TW1 .5 F1
Twilley St SW18 . . . . .20 B8
Twining Ave TW2 . . . . .16 D5
Twinoaks KT11 . . . . .74 A6
Twitten La RH19 . . . . .184 E4
Two Oaks KT13 . . . . .53 B6
Two Rivers Sh Ctr TW18 . .12 E4
Two Ways RH14 . . . . .213 A4
Twycross Rd
  Farncombe GU7 . . . . .150 D7
  Wokingham RG40 . . . . .25 E7
Twyford La GU10 . . . . .146 B6
Twyford Par KT6 . . . . .38 A1
Twyford Rd Carshalton SM5 40 D1
  Wokingham RG40 . . . . .25 B8
Twyhurst Ct RH19 . . . . . . .185 D3
Twyne Cl RH11 . . . . .200 F4
Twyner Cl RH6 . . . . .161 D4
Twynersh Ave KT16 . . . . . .32 F3
Tybenham Rd SW19 . . . . . .40 A6
Tydcombe Rd CR6 . . . . . .101 D8
Tyers House 11 SW16 . . . .21 C3
Tylden Way RH12 . . . . . . .217 F6
Tylecroft Rd SW16 . . . . . . .41 E7
Tylehost GU2 . . . . .109 A5
Tyler Gdns KT15 . . . . .52 C6
Tyler Rd RH10 . . . . .201 D3
Tylers Cl RH9 . . . . .121 B5
Tylers Path SM5 . . . . .59 F6
Tylney Ave SE19 . . . . .22 F3
Tymperley Ct RH13 . . . . . .217 E3
Tynamara KT1 . . . . .37 D5
Tyndalls Estate GU26 . . . .188 F4
Tyne Cl Crawley RH10 . . . .202 C5
  Farnborough GU14 . . . . . . .84 E6
Tynedale Rd RH3 . . . . .137 B5
Tynemouth Rd CR4 . . . . . .21 A1
Tynley Gr GU4 . . . . .109 D7

Tynwald House 14 SE26 . .23 A5
Tynwald Rd SM1 . . . . .59 F6
Tyrolean Ct SM7 . . . . .78 B4
Tyrols Rd SE23 . . . . .23 D7
Tyrrell Sq CR4 . . . . .40 E8
Tyrrell House BR3 . . . . .24 B3
Tyrrell Sq CR4 . . . . .40 E8
Tyrrell's Wood Golf
  Course KT22 . . . . .95 F2
Tyrwhitt Ave GU2 . . . . . . .109 B5
Tyson Rd SE23 . . . . .23 C8
Tythe The KT1 . . . . .35 B3
Tythebarn Cl GU4 . . . . . . .110 B6
Tythebarns La Ripley GU23 .91 A1
  Send Marsh GU23 . . . . . . .91 B1
Tytherton RG12 . . . . .27 C7

U

Uckfield Rd CR4 . . . . .41 A8
Udney Park Rd TW11 . . . . .17 A2
Uffington Dr RG12 . . . . . . .27 E5
Uffington Rd SE27 . . . . . . .22 A4
Ujima Ct SW16 . . . . .21 E4
Ujima House SW16 . . . . . . .21 E4
Ullathorne Rd SW16 . . . . . .21 C4
Ullswater RG12 . . . . .26 F2
Ullswater Ave GU14 . . . . . .84 E3
Ullswater Cl Bromley BR1 . .24 E1
  Hale GU9 . . . . .125 A6
  Kingston u T KT2, SW15 . . .18 D4
  Lightwater GU18 . . . . .48 B1
Ullswater Cres
  Coulsdon CR5 . . . . .79 E3
  Kingston u T SW15 . . . . . . .18 D4
Ullswater Rd
  Lightwater GU18 . . . . .48 B1
  West Norwood SE27, SW16 .22 B6
Ulstan Cl CR3 . . . . .102 A4
Ulster Ct KT2 . . . . .17 D2
Ulverstone Rd SE27 . . . . . .22 B6
Ulwyn Ave KT14 . . . . .71 E5
Underhill GU47 . . . . .150 D3
Underhill La GU10 . . . . . . .146 B7
Underhill Park Rd RH2 . . .118 A4
Underhill Rd
  Dulwich SE21, SE22 . . . . . .23 B8
  Newdigate RH5 . . . . .158 B1
Undershaw Rd BR1 . . . . . . .24 F5
  New Addington CR0 . . . . . .63 C5
Underwood Bracknell RG12 .26 E3
Underwood Ave GU12 . . . .105 F1
Underwood Cl RH10 . . . . .204 B8
Underwood Ct CR3 . . . . . .100 F2
Underwood Rd
  Caterham CR3 . . . . .100 E2
  Haslemere GU27 . . . . .207 F7
Undine St SW17 . . . . .20 F3
Unicorn Sch TW9 . . . . .6 F6
Union Cl GU47 . . . . .45 E2
Union Ct 2 TW10 . . . . .6 E2
Union Rd Farnham GU9 . . .125 C2
  Frimley GU16 . . . . .86 D8
  Thornton Heath CR0 . . . . . .42 C2
Union St Aldershot GU11 . .105 A2
  Farnborough GU14 . . . . . . .85 B4
  Kingston u T KT1 . . . . .37 D7
  Pirbright GU24 . . . . .87 A6
Union Terr 7 GU11 . . . . . .105 A2
  West Norwood SE19, SE27 .22 C3
Unity Cl New Addington CR0 .63 B1
Univ of Greenwich The
  SW15 . . . . .19 A8
University Rd SW19 . . . . . .20 D2
Unstead La GU5 . . . . .151 C2
Unstead Wood GU3 . . . . .130 C1
Unwin Ave TW14 . . . . .3 D2
Unwin Rd TW7 . . . . .5 E4
Upavon Gdns RG12 . . . . . .27 F4
Upchurch Cl SE20 . . . . . . .23 B1
Updown Hill GU20 . . . . . . .48 D4
Upfield Horley RH6 . . . . . .161 A1
  South Croydon CR0, CR9 . .62 B7
Upfield Cl RH6 . . . . .161 A1
Upfold Cl GU6 . . . . .174 B5
Upfold La GU6 . . . . .174 C5
Upfolds Gn GU4 . . . . .110 C5
Upgrove Manor Way 12
  SE24 . . . . .22 A8
Upland Rd SE23 . . . . .23 C6
Upland Rd Camberley GU15 .65 D7
  Croydon CR2 . . . . .61 D5
  Dulwich SE21, SE22 . . . . . .23 A8
  Sutton SM2 . . . . .59 D4
  Woldingham CR3 . . . . . . .102 B7
Upland Way KT18 . . . . .77 C1
Uplands
  Ashstead KT21, KT22 . . . . .95 D7
  Beckenham BR3 . . . . .44 A7
  Warlingham CR6 . . . . .81 F1
Uplands Cl
  Haslemere GU27 . . . . . . .208 D8
  Mortlake SW14 . . . . .7 B2
  Sandhurst GU47 . . . . .64 B8
Uplands Cty Prim Sch
  GU47 . . . . .64 B8
Uplands Dr KT22 . . . . .74 D5
Uplands Rd Farnham GU9 .125 C1
  Kenley CR8 . . . . .80 C2
Uppark Gdns RH12 . . . . . .217 F6
Upper Beulah Hill SE19 . . .42 E8
Upper Bourne La GU10 . . .146 B5
Upper Bourne Vale GU10 146 A5
Upper Bridge Rd RH1 . . . .118 F1
Upper Brighton Rd KT6 . .37 E2
Upper Broadmoor Rd
  RG45 . . . . .45 D5
Upper Butts TW8 . . . . .6 C8

Upper Charles St GU16 . . .65 C6
Upper Chobham Rd GU15 .66 B4
Upper Church La 11 GU9 .125 B2
Upper Cl RH18 . . . . .206 F2
Upper College Ride GU15 .65 E8
Upper Court Rd
  Epsom KT19 . . . . .76 C8
  Woldingham CR3 . . . . . . .102 A3
Upper Dr TN16 . . . . .83 C1
Upper Dunnymans 6 SM7 .77 F5
Upper Edgeborough Rd
  GU1 . . . . .130 F8
Upper Elmers End Rd BR3 43 E4
Upper Elms Rd GU11 . . . .105 A1
Upper Fairfield Rd KT22 . .95 B6
Upper Farm L Pk KT20 . . .115 F3
Upper Farm Rd KT8 . . . . . .35 F5
Upper Forecourt RH6 . . . .182 B7
Upper Gn E Mitcham CR4 . .40 F6
  Mitcham CR4 . . . . .41 A6
Upper Gn W CR4 . . . . .40 F7
Upper Gordon Rd GU15 . . .65 D5
Upper Gr SE25 . . . . .42 F5
Upper Grotto Rd TW1 . . . .16 F6
Upper Guildown Rd GU2 130 C6
Upper Hale Rd GU9 . . . . . .125 C6
Upper Halliford Rd
  Upper Halliford TW17 . . . . .34 E5
  Upper Halliford TW17 . . . . .34 E4
Upper Halliford Sta TW16 .34 E7
Upper Ham Rd KT2, TW10 .17 D4
Upper Harestone CR3 . . . .121 A8
Upper High St KT17 . . . . . .76 E6
Upper House La GU5 . . . .152 F1
Upper Manor Rd
  Farncombe GU7 . . . . .150 E6
  Milford GU8 . . . . .149 F1
Upper Mount GU27 . . . . . .189 F1
Upper Mulgrave Rd SM2 . .58 E3
Upper Nursery SL5 . . . . . . .30 A4
Upper Old Park La GU9 . .125 A5
Upper Park Rd
  Camberley GU15 . . . . .65 C6
  Kingston u T KT2 . . . . .18 A2
Upper Pillory Down SM5 . .79 A7
Upper Pinewood Rd
  GU12 . . . . .106 D3
Upper Queen St GU7 . . . .150 E4
Upper Rd SM6 . . . . .60 E5
Upper Richmond Rd SW15 .7 F3
Upper Richmond Rd W
  TW10, SW14, SW15 . . . . . .7 C3
Upper Rose Hill RH4 . . . . .136 B6
Upper Sawleywood 3
  SM7 . . . . .77 F5
Upper Selsdon Rd CR2 . . .62 A2
Upper Shirley Rd CR0, CR9 62 D7
Upper South View GU9 . . .125 C3
Upper Springfield GU8 . . .148 D3
Upper Sq Forest Row RH18 206 E3
  Isleworth TW7 . . . . .6 A4
Upper St GU5 . . . . .133 A4
Upper St Michael's Rd
  GU11 . . . . .126 B8
Upper Stanford Rd GU24 . .87 F1
Upper Sunbury Rd TW12 . .36 A8
Upper Sutton La TW5 . . . . .5 A6
Upper Teddington Rd
  KT1, KT8 . . . . .37 C8
Upper Tooting
  Independent High Sch
  SW17 . . . . .20 F6
Upper Tooting Park
  Mansions 11 SW17 . . . . . .21 A8
Upper Tooting Pk SW17 . . .20 F6
Upper Tooting Rd SW17 . . .20 F4
Upper Tulse Hill SW2 . . . . .21 F8
Upper Union St 11 GU11 .105 A2
Upper Union Terr 5
  GU11 . . . . .105 A2
Upper Vann La GU8 . . . . . .172 A1
Upper Vernon Rd SM1 . . . .59 D5
Upper Verran Rd GU15 . . . .65 D3
Upper Village Rd SL5 . . . . .29 D4
Upper Warlingham Sta
  CR6 . . . . .81 A1
Upper Way GU9 . . . . .146 B8
Upper West St RH2 . . . . . .117 F1
Upper Weybourne La
  GU9 . . . . .125 E7
Upper Wlk GU25 . . . . .31 E5
Upper Woodcote Village
  CR8 . . . . .79 D7
Upperton Rd GU2 . . . . . . .130 C7
Upshire Gdns RG12 . . . . . .27 F5
Upshott La GU22 . . . . .70 F2
Upton GU21 . . . . .69 B2
Upton Cl GU14 . . . . .85 D3
Upton Ct Penge SE20 . . . . .23 C1
  4 Wimbledon SW19 . . . . . .19 D1
Upton Dene SM2 . . . . .59 B3
Upton Rd Hounslow TW3 . . .5 A4
  South Norwood CR7 . . . . . .42 D7
Upwood Rd SW16 . . . . .41 E8
Urmston Dr SW19 . . . . .19 E7
Urquhart Ct BR3 . . . . .23 F1
Ursuline Convent Prep
  Sch SW19 . . . . .19 D1
Ursuline Convent Sch
  SW20 . . . . .39 D8
Usherwood Cl KT20 . . . . .116 C4
Uvedale Cl CR0 . . . . .82 D8
Uvedale Cres CR0 . . . . . . .82 E8
Uvedale Rd RH8 . . . . .122 F5
Uxbridge Rd
  Feltham TW13 . . . . .15 D6
  Hampton TW12, TW13 . . . .16 B3
  Kingston u T KT1, KT6 . . . . .37 D4

V

Vachery La GU6 . . . . .194 E7
Vaillant Rd KT13 . . . . .53 C6
Valan Leas BR2 . . . . .44 E6
Vale Cl Coulsdon CR5 . . . . .79 E5
  Farnham GU10 . . . . .146 C4
  Oatlands Park KT13 . . . . . .53 D7
  Twickenham TW1 . . . . .17 A5
  Woking GU21 . . . . .69 E3
Vale Cres SW15 . . . . .18 E4
Vale Croft KT10 . . . . .55 F2
Vale Ct KT13 . . . . .53 D7
Vale Dr RH12 . . . . .217 B3
Vale Farm Rd GU21 . . . . . .69 E2
Vale House GU21 . . . . .69 E2
Vale Lodge SE23 . . . . .23 C6
Vale Rd Ash Vale GU12 . . .106 A5
  Camberley GU15 . . . . .65 A4
  Claygate KT10 . . . . .55 F3
  Mitcham CR4 . . . . .41 D5
  Oatlands Park KT13 . . . . . .53 D7
  Sutton SM1 . . . . .59 B6
  Worcester Park KT19, KT4 . .57 F7
Vale Rd N KT6 . . . . .56 E8
Vale The Ashford TW16 . . .15 A2
  Coulsdon CR5, CR8 . . . . . .79 E5
  Croydon CR0 . . . . .62 D8
  Feltham TW14 . . . . .4 B1
  Heston TW5 . . . . .4 E8
Vale Wood Dr GU10 . . . . .146 D4
Vale Wood La GU26 . . . . .188 C4
Valens House 11 SW2 . . . .22 A7
Valentine Ct SE23 . . . . . . .23 D6
Valentyne Cl CR0 . . . . .82 E8
Valerie Ct SM2 . . . . .59 B3
Valewood Rd GU27 . . . . . .208 C5
Valley Cres RG41 . . . . .25 A8
Valley Ct CR3 . . . . .101 A3
Valley End C of E Inf Sch
  GU24 . . . . .49 A4
Valley End Rd GU24 . . . . . .49 B4
Valley Gardens The TW20 .30 E7
Valley Gdns SW19 . . . . . . .20 D1
Valley La GU10 . . . . .146 C7
Valley Mews TW1 . . . . .17 A6
Valley Pl KT6 . . . . .37 E3
Valley Prim Sch BR2 . . . . .44 F7
Valley Prospect 3 SE19 . .22 E2
Valley Rd Beckenham BR2 . .44 E7
  Frimley GU16 . . . . .86 B8
  Kenley CR3, CR8 . . . . .80 D4
  Streatham SW16 . . . . .21 F4
Valley The GU2 . . . . .130 C5
Valley View Biggin Hill TN16 .83 D1
  Godalming GU7 . . . . .150 D4
Valley View Gdns CR8 . . . .80 E4
Valleyfield Rd SW16 . . . . . .21 F3
Vallis Way KT9 . . . . .56 D6
Valnay St SW17 . . . . .20 F3
Valonus RH1 . . . . .119 B5
Valroy Cl GU15 . . . . .65 D6
Van Dyck Ave KT3 . . . . . . .38 D2
Vanborough Ct SM2 . . . . . .59 C4
Vanbrugh Cl RH11 . . . . . .200 E3
Vanbrugh Dr KT12 . . . . . . .35 C3
Vancouver Cl KT19 . . . . . . .76 C8
Vancouver Ct RH6 . . . . . . .162 A3
Vancouver Dr RH11 . . . . . .181 D1
Vancouver Rd
  Forest Hill SE23 . . . . .23 E6
  Richmond TW10 . . . . .17 C4
Vanderbilt Rd SW18 . . . . . .20 C7
Vandyke RG12 . . . . .26 E3
Vandyke Cl Putney SW15 . .19 D8
  Redhill RH1 . . . . .118 F3
Vanfame Ct KT3 . . . . .38 F6
Vanguard Cl CR0 . . . . .42 B1
Vanguard House
  7 Merton SW19 . . . . .20 C1
  5 Stanwell TW19 . . . . .2 E1
Vanguard Way SM6 . . . . . .60 E3
Vann Farm Rd RH5 . . . . . .177 E4
Vann La Chiddingfold GU8 .191 E4
Vann Lake RH5 . . . . .177 F4
Vann Lake Rd Ockley RH5 .177 F3
  Ockley RH5 . . . . .178 A4
Vanners RH10 . . . . .201 F3
Vant Rd SW17 . . . . .20 F3
Vapery La GU24 . . . . .87 D6
Varley Way CR4 . . . . .40 D7
Varna Rd TW12 . . . . .36 B8
Varney Cl GU14 . . . . .84 E5
Varsity Dr TW1, TW7 . . . . . .5 F1
Varsity Row SW14 . . . . .7 C5
Vaughan Almshouses
  TW15 . . . . .14 B3
Vaughan Rd KT7 . . . . .37 B2
Vaughan Way RH4 . . . . . .136 A7
Vaux Cres KT12 . . . . .54 A4
Vauxhall Gdns CR2 . . . . . .61 C4
Veals Mead CR4 . . . . .40 E8
Vectis Gdns SW17 . . . . . . .21 B3
Vectis Rd SW17 . . . . .21 B3
Vegal Cres TW20 . . . . .11 C3
Vellum Dr SM5 . . . . .60 A7
Venita Manor SE27 . . . . . .22 A3
Venner Rd
  Forest Hill SE20, SE26 . . . .23 C3
  Penge SE20, SE26 . . . . . . .23 C3
Ventnor Rd SM2 . . . . .59 B3
Ventnor Terr GU12 . . . . . .105 C1
Venton Cl GU21 . . . . .69 B2
Verbania Way RH19 . . . . .186 B1

Verdant Ct 3 SE6 . . . . . . .24 F8
Verdant La SE6 . . . . .24 E7
Verdayne Ave CR0, CR9 . . .62 D6
Verdayne Gdns CR6 . . . . . .81 C3
Vere Bank SW19 . . . . .19 F7
Vereker Dr TW16 . . . . .35 A6
Vermont Rd
  South Norwood SE19 . . . . .22 E2
  Sutton SM1 . . . . .59 B7
Verney House TW3 . . . . . . .5 C3
Vernon Ave SW20 . . . . .39 D7
Vernon Cl Horsham RH12 .218 A4
  Ottershaw KT16 . . . . .51 D4
  West Ewell KT19 . . . . .57 C4
Vernon Ct GU9 . . . . .125 A2
Vernon Dr Caterham CR3 .100 C5
  North Ascot SL5 . . . . .28 E7
Vernon Rd Feltham TW13 . .14 F6
  Mortlake SW14 . . . . .7 D4
  Sutton SM1 . . . . .59 D5
Vernon Way GU2 . . . . .108 F2
Vernon Wlk KT20 . . . . .97 D7
Verona Dr KT6 . . . . .56 E8
Veronica Gdns SW4, SW16 .41 C8
Veronica Rd SW17 . . . . . . .21 B6
Verralls GU22 . . . . .70 B2
Verran Rd Balham SW12 . . .21 B8
  Camberley GU15 . . . . .65 D3
Versailles Rd SE20 . . . . . . .23 A1
Verulam Ave CR8 . . . . .79 C7
Veryan GU21 . . . . .69 A2
Vesey Cl GU14 . . . . .85 A5
Vestris Rd SE23 . . . . .23 D8
Vevers Rd RH2 . . . . .139 C6
Vevey St SE23, SE6 . . . . . .23 F6
Vibart Gdns SW2 . . . . .21 F8
Viburnum Ct GU24 . . . . . . .67 E6
Vicarage Ave TW20 . . . . . .12 B3
Vicarage Cl Farnham GU9 .146 D7
  Kingswood KT20 . . . . .97 E3
  Lingfield RH7 . . . . .164 E4
  Little Bookham KT23 . . . . . .94 A2
Vicarage Cres TW20 . . . . . .12 B3
Vicarage Ct Beckenham BR3 43 E6
  East Bedfont TW14 . . . . . . .14 C8
  Egham TW20 . . . . .12 B2
  8 Roehampton SW15 . . . .19 A8
Vicarage Dr
  Beckenham BR3 . . . . .44 A8
  Mortlake SW14 . . . . .7 D3
Vicarage Farm Ct TW5 . . . .4 F7
Vicarage Farm Rd
  Heston TW3, TW4, TW5 . . . .4 E6
  Hounslow TW3, TW4, TW5 . .4 E6
Vicarage Fields KT12 . . . . .35 C3
Vicarage Gate GU2 . . . . . .130 A7
Vicarage Gdns Ascot SL5 . .29 A4
  Grayshott GU26 . . . . .188 C3
  Mitcham CR4 . . . . .40 E6
  Mortlake SW14 . . . . .7 D2
Vicarage Hill GU10, GU9 . .146 D7
Vicarage House 11 KT1 . . .37 F7
Vicarage La Capel RH5 . . .178 D6
  Farnham GU9 . . . . .125 B2
  Farnham, Middle
   Bourne GU9 . . . . .146 D7
  Haslemere GU27 . . . . .207 F6
  Heath End GU9 . . . . .125 C7
  Horley RH6 . . . . .160 F4
  Laleham TW18 . . . . .33 C6
  Leatherhead KT22 . . . . . . .95 B5
  Send GU23 . . . . .90 D1
  Wraysbury TW19 . . . . .11 F7
Vicarage Rd Ashford TW16 .14 F2
  Bagshot GU19 . . . . .47 C3
  Blackwater GU17 . . . . .64 E4
  Chobham GU24 . . . . .68 E8
  Crawley Down RH10 . . . . .204 A8
  Croydon CR0, CR9 . . . . . . .61 A7
  Egham TW20 . . . . .12 B3
  Kingston u T KT1, KT2 . . . . .37 D7
  Lingfield RH7 . . . . .164 D4
  Mortlake SW14 . . . . .7 D2
  Staines TW18 . . . . .12 E5
  Sutton SM1 . . . . .59 B7
  Teddington TW11 . . . . .17 A3
  Teddington, Hampton Wick
   KT1, KT8 . . . . .37 C8
  Twickenham TW2 . . . . .5 C1
  Twickenham, Strawberry
   Hill TW2 . . . . .16 E6
  Woking GU22 . . . . .89 F6
Vicarage Way SL3 . . . . .1 D7
Vicars Oak Rd SE19 . . . . . .22 E2
Viceroy Ct 5 CR0 . . . . .42 D1
Viceroy Lodge 6 KT6 . . . . .37 E4
Vickers Ct 9 TW19 . . . . .2 E1
Vickers Dr N KT13 . . . . . . .52 E1
Vickers Dr S KT13 . . . . . . .71 E8
Vickers Rd GU12 . . . . .105 F5
Victor Ct RH10 . . . . .182 D1
Victor Rd Penge SE20 . . . . .23 D1
  Teddington TW11 . . . . .16 E4
Victor Seymour Inf Sch
  SM5 . . . . .59 F6
Victoria Almshouses
  4 Redhill RH1 . . . . .119 A4
  11 Reigate RH2 . . . . .118 C1
Victoria Ave
  Camberley GU15 . . . . .65 A5
  East Molesey KT8 . . . . .36 B6
  Hackbridge SM5, SM6 . . . .60 A7
  Hounslow TW3, TW4 . . . . . .5 A2
  Kingston u T KT6 . . . . .37 D3
  South Croydon CR2 . . . . . .61 C1
Victoria Cl
  East Molesey KT8 . . . . .36 A6
  Horley RH6 . . . . .161 A3

Victoria Cl *continued*
Oatlands Park KT13 53 D7
Victoria Cotts 7 TW9 7 A6
Victoria Cres Merton SW19 19 F1
West Norwood SE19 22 E2
Victoria Ct Bagshot GU19 47 E1
Guildford GU1 130 D8
Horsham RH13 217 D2
Penge SE26 23 C2
Shalford GU4 130 E3
Victoria Dr
Blackwater GU17 64 C4
Putney SW15, SW19 19 D7
Victoria Entertainments Ctr The GU21 69 E2
Victoria Gdns
Biggin Hill TN16 83 C4
Heston TW5 4 E6
Victoria Jun Sch The TW13 15 B7
Victoria La UB7 3 D8
Victoria Lodge SW19 19 C1
Victoria Mews SW18 20 C7
Victoria Pl 5 Esher KT10 55 B6
Ewell KT17 76 E7
16 Richmond TW10 6 D2
Victoria Rd
Addlestone KT15 52 D6
Aldershot GU11 105 A2
Ascot SL5 29 A4
Coulsdon CR5 79 D4
Cranleigh GU6 174 D3
Crawley RH11 201 C6
Farnborough GU14 85 B4
Farnham GU9 125 C2
Feltham TW13 15 B7
Godalming GU7 150 E4
Guildford GU1 109 E1
Horley RH6 161 B2
Kingston u T KT1 37 F7
Kingston u T, Seething Wells KT6 37 D3
Knaphill GU21 68 E1
Mitcham CR4, SW19 20 F1
Mortlake SW14 7 D4
Oatlands Park KT13 53 D7
Redhill RH1 140 A8
Sandhurst GU47 45 E1
Staines TW18 12 E5
Sutton SM1 59 D5
Teddington TW11 17 A2
Twickenham TW1 17 B8
Woking GU22 69 F2
Victoria St
Englefield Green TW20 11 C2
Horsham RH13 217 D2
Victoria Terr RH4 136 A7
Victoria Villas TW9 6 F3
Victoria Way
East Grinstead RH19 205 F7
Oatlands Park KT13 53 D7
Woking GU21, GU22 69 E2
Victors Dr TW12 15 E2
Victory Ave SM4 40 C4
Victory Bsns Ctr The TW7 5 F3
Victory Cotts KT24 113 E7
Victory Park Rd KT15 52 C6
Victory Pl SE19 22 E2
Victory Rd Chertsey KT16 33 A1
Horsham RH12 217 B3
Merton SW19 20 C1
Victory Road Mews 5 SW19 20 C1
Vidler Cl KT9 56 C4
Vienna Ct GU14 85 A6
View Cl TN16 83 C3
View Terr RH7 165 A1
Viewfield Rd SW18 19 F8
Viggory La GU21 69 C4
Vigilant Cl SE26 23 A4
Viking RG12 26 E4
Viking Ct TW12 36 B8
Village Cl 3 KT13 53 D7
Village Ct SL5 29 C4
Village Gate TW17 34 B4
Village Gdns KT17 57 F1
Village Green Ave TN16 83 E2
Village Green Way TN16 83 E2
Village Rd TW20 32 C6
Village Row SM2 59 A3
Village St RH5 158 B1
Village The SL4 10 B5
Village Way Ashford TW15 14 A4
Beckenham BR3 44 A6
Sanderstead CR2 81 A6
Villas The RH7 163 E8
Villiers Ave Kingston u T KT5 37 F5
Twickenham TW2 15 F7
Villiers Cl KT5 37 F5
Villiers Gr SM2 58 D2
Villiers Mead RG41 25 A6
Villiers Rd Hounslow TW7 5 E5
Kingston u T KT1 37 F6
Penge BR3 43 D7
Villiers The KT13 53 D4
Vinall Gdns RH12 216 D4
Vincam Cl TW2 16 A8
Vincent Ave Sutton SM5 78 D8
3 Tolworth KT5 38 B1
Vincent Cl Chertsey KT16 32 E2
Esher KT10 55 B7
Fetcham KT23 94 B4
Harmondsworth UB7 3 A8
Horsham RH13 217 F2
Vincent Dr Dorking RH4 136 A6
Upper Halliford TW17 34 E6
Vincent House KT3 38 F5
Vincent La RH4 136 A7
Vincent Rd Chertsey KT16 32 E2
Coulsdon CR5 79 C3
Croydon CR0 42 E2
Dorking RH4 136 A7
Hounslow TW7 5 D6
Hounslow, Hounslow West TW4 4 D4
Kingston u T KT1 38 A6
Stoke D'Abernon KT11 73 E3
Vincent Rise RG12 27 E6
Vincent Row TW12 16 C3
Vincent Sq TN16 83 C6
Vincent Wks RH4 136 A7
Vincents Cl CR5 98 F7
Vine Cl Farnborough GU11 105 A6
Rowledge GU10 146 A4
Stanwell TW19 2 A2
Surbiton KT5 37 F3
Sutton SM1 59 C7
Worplesdon GU3 88 D1
Vine Cotts GU6 174 B3
Vine Ct KT12 54 C4
Vine House Cl GU16 86 A3
Vine La GU10 146 A5
Vine Pl TW3 5 B3
Vine Rd Barnes SW13, SW15 7 F4
East Molesey KT8 36 C5
Mortlake SW13, SW15 7 F4
Vine St GU11 105 A1
Vine Way GU10 146 A5
Vineries Cl UB7 3 A8
Viners Cl KT12 35 C3
Viney Bank CR0 62 F2
Vineyard Cl Forest Hill SE6 24 A7
Kingston u T KT1 37 F6
Vineyard Hill Rd SW19 20 A4
Vineyard Path SW14 7 D4
Vineyard Rd TW13 15 A5
Vineyard Row KT1, KT8 37 C8
Vineyard Sch The TW10 6 E1
Vineyard The TW10 6 E2
Vineyards The TW13 15 A5
Vinter Ct TW17 34 A4
Viola Ave Feltham TW14 4 C1
Stanwell TW19 13 E7
Viola Croft RG42 27 F8
Violet Cl CR4 41 A1
Violet Gdns CR0 61 B5
Violet La CR0 61 B5
Violette Szabo House 4 SE27 22 D4
Virginia Ave GU25 31 C4
Virginia Beeches GU25 31 C6
Virginia Cl Ashstead KT21 75 D1
Kingston u T KT3 38 C5
Laleham TW18 33 C6
Weybridge KT13 53 C4
Virginia Ct GU25 31 D5
Virginia Dr GU25 31 C5
Virginia Gdns GU14 85 C2
Virginia Pl KT11 73 A5
Virginia Rd CR7 42 B8
Virginia Water SL5 30 E6
Virginia Water Prep Sch GU25 31 D5
Virginia Water Sta GU25 31 E4
Viscount Gdns KT14 71 E7
Viscount Ind Est SL3 1 E4
Viscount Rd TW19 13 E7
Viscount Way TW6 3 E3
Vivien Cl KT9 56 E3
Vivienne Cl Crawley RH11 181 D1
Twickenham TW1 6 D1
Vivienne House TW18 13 A3
Voewood Cl KT3 38 F3
Vogan Cl RH2 139 B6
Volta Way CR0, CR9 41 F1
Voltaire 14 TW9 6 F6
Voss Ct SW16 21 E2
Vowels Forest Wlk RH19 204 E3
Vowels La RH19 204 E2
Vulcan Bsns Ctr CR9 63 E2
Vulcan Cl Crawley RH11 201 C2
Sandhurst GU47 64 A7
Wallington SM6 60 F3
Vulcan Way
New Addington CR0, CR9 63 E1
Sandhurst GU47 64 B7

W

Waddington Ave CR5, CR8 100 B8
Waddington Cl
Coulsdon CR5 100 B8
Crawley RH11 201 A3
Waddington Way CR7, SE19 42 D8
Waddon Cl CR0, CR9 61 A7
Waddon Court Rd CR0, CR9 61 A7
Waddon Inf Sch CR9 61 A5
Waddon Marsh Way CR0, CR9 41 F1
Waddon New Rd CR0, CR9 61 B8
Waddon Park Ave CR0, CR9 61 A7
Waddon Rd CR0, CR9 61 B7
Waddon Sta CR0 61 A6
Waddon Way CR0, CR2, CR9 61 B4
Wade's La TW11 17 A3
Wadham GU47 45 F1
Wadham Cl Crawley RH10 182 C1
Shepperton TW17 34 C2
Wadhurst Cl SE20 43 B7
Wadlands Brook Rd RH19 185 D5
Wagbullock Rise RG12 27 C3
Wagg Cl RH19 186 A1
Waggon Cl GU2 108 E2
Waggoners Hollow GU19 47 E2
Waggoners Way GU26 188 A4
Waggoners Wells La GU26 188 A2
Wagtail Cl RH12 217 D7
Wagtail Gdns CR2 62 E1
Waights Ct KT2 37 E8
Wain End RH12 217 D5
Wainford Cl SW19 19 D7
Wainwright Gr TW7 5 D3
Wainwrights RH10 201 D3
Waite Davies Rd SE12 24 F8
Wakefield Cl KT14 71 E7
Wakefield Gdns SE19 22 E1
Wakefield House SE22 23 B7
Wakefield Rd 19 TW10 6 D2
Wakehams Green Dr RH10 182 D1
Wakehurst Dr RH10, RH11 201 D3
Wakehurst Mews RH12 216 F1
Wakehurst Path GU21 70 C5
Wakelin House SE23 23 E8
Wakeling House 8 SE27 22 B5
Wakely Cl TN16 83 C1
Walburton Rd CR8 79 C7
Walbury RG12 27 E5
Waldby Ct RH11 201 A3
Waldeck Gr SE27 22 B5
Waldeck Rd Brentford W4 7 A8
Mortlake SW14 7 C4
Waldeck Terr SW14 7 C4
Waldegrave Ct 1 TW11 16 F3
Waldegrave Gdns TW1 16 F5
Waldegrave Pk TW1 16 F4
Waldegrave Rd Penge SE19 22 F1
Teddington TW11 16 F4
Waldegrave Sch for Girls TW2 16 D5
Waldegrove CR0 61 F7
Waldemar Rd SW19 20 A3
Walden Cotts GU3 107 A3
Walden Gdns CR7, SW16 41 F5
Waldens Park Rd GU21 69 C3
Waldens Rd GU21 69 D2
Waldenshaw Rd SE23 23 C7
Waldo Pl SW19 20 E1
Waldorf Cl CR2 61 B2
Waldorf Hts GU17 64 D3
Waldram Cres SE23 23 C7
Waldram Park Rd SE23 23 D7
Waldram Pl 6 SE23 23 C7
Waldron Gdns BR2 44 D6
Waldron Hill RG12 27 F8
Waldron Rd SW17, SW18 20 C6
Waldronhyrst CR0, CR2 61 B6
Waldrons The Croydon CR0 61 C6
Oxted RH8 122 F4
Waldy Rise GU6 174 E4
Wales Ave SM5 59 E5
Walesbeech RH10 202 A5
Waleton Acres SM6 60 C4
Waley's La RH5 177 C1
Walford Rd RH5 136 C3
Walham Rise SW19 19 E2
Walk The Ashford TW16 14 F1
Tandridge RH8 122 A2
Walkden Hall (Hall of Residence) KT2 18 D4
Walker Cl
East Bedfont TW14 14 F8
Hampton TW12 15 F2
Walker Rd RH10 202 C4
Walker's Ridge GU15 65 E5
Walkerscroft Mead SE21 22 C7
Walkfield Dr KT18 77 B2
Walking Bottom GU5 154 C6
Wall Hill Rd RH18, RH19 206 E5
Wallace Cl Fairlands GU3 108 C4
Upper Halliford TW17 34 D5
Wallace Cres SM5 59 F5
Wallace Fields KT17 77 A6
Wallace Fields Cty Inf Sch KT17 77 A6
Wallace Fields Cty Jun Sch KT17 77 A7
Wallace Wlk KT15 52 C6
Wallage La RH10 203 D6
Wallbrook Bsns Ctr TW4 4 B4
Walled Garden The
Loxwood RH14 212 F7
Tadworth KT20 97 D5
Walled Gdn The
Betchworth RH3 137 D8
Sunbury TW16 35 B6
Waller La CR3 100 F4
Wallingford Cl RG12 27 E5
Wallington Ct 10 SM6 60 B4
Wallington High Sch for Boys SM6 60 B6
Wallington High Sch for Girls SM6 60 B2
Wallington Rd GU15 47 A1
Wallington Sq 4 SM6 60 C4
Wallington Sta SM6 60 B4
Wallis Ct RH10 181 D2
Wallis House RH19 185 E1
Wallis Mews KT22 95 A5
Wallis Way RH13 218 A4
Wallner Way RG40 25 E5
Wallop Sch KT13 53 B5
Wallorton Gdns SW14 7 D3
Walmer Cl
Crowthorne RG45 45 C5
Frimley GU16 86 A7
Walmer House 11 SE20 23 C1
Walmsley House 1 SW16 21 C4
Walnut Cl Aldershot GU11 126 A8
Carshalton SM5 59 F5
Epsom KT18 76 F4
Walnut Ct RH13 217 E1
Walnut Dr KT20 97 E3
Walnut Gr SM7 77 D5
Walnut House RH2 139 C7
Walnut La RH11 181 B1
Walnut Mews SM2 59 C3
Walnut Tree Ave CR4 40 E6
Walnut Tree Cl Barnes SW13 7 F6
Belmont SM7 77 E7
Guildford GU1 130 C8
Walnut Tree Gdns GU7 150 E7
Walnut Tree La KT14 71 D7
Walnut Tree Pk GU1 109 C1
Walnut Tree Rd
Brentford TW8 6 E8
Charlton TW17 34 C7
Heston TW5 4 F8
Walpole Ave Chipstead CR5 98 F8
Richmond TW9 6 F5
Walpole Cres 7 TW11 16 F3
Walpole Ct TW2 16 E6
Walpole Gdns TW2 16 E5
Walpole House 3 GU11 105 B2
Walpole Pl 6 TW11 16 F3
Walpole Rd
Croydon CR0, CR9 61 D8
Mitcham SW19 20 D2
Old Windsor SL4 11 B8
Surbiton KT6 37 E3
Teddington TW11 16 F3
Twickenham TW2 16 E6
Walsh CE Jun Sch GU12 106 A1
Walsh Cres CR0 82 E7
Walsh Memorial C of E Inf Sch GU12 105 F1
Walsham Rd TW14 15 B8
Walsingham Gdns KT19 57 F5
Walsingham Rd
Mitcham CR4 40 F4
New Addington CR0 63 C1
Walstead House 2 RH10 201 D5
Walter Cty Inf Sch RG41 25 A6
Walter St 2 KT2 37 E8
Walter's Mead KT21 75 E2
Walter's Rd SE25 42 E5
Waltham Ave GU2 109 B5
Waltham Cl GU47 45 D1
Waltham Rd
Carshalton SM5 40 E1
Caterham CR3 101 B5
Walton Ave Cheam SM3 58 F7
New Malden KT3 38 F5
Walton Bridge Rd KT12, TW17 34 E2
Walton Comm Hospl KT12 54 C8
Walton Ct GU21 70 A3
Walton Dr Horsham RH13 218 C4
North Ascot SL5 28 F8
Walton Gdns TW13 14 F4
Walton Gn CR0 63 C3
Walton Heath RH10 202 D8
Walton La
Lower Halliford TW17 34 D2
Oatlands Park KT12 34 E1
Weybridge KT12, KT13 53 C8
Walton Leigh Special Training Sch KT13 53 F6
Walton on the Hill Cty Prim Sch KT20 97 B3
Walton Park La KT12 54 D8
Walton Pk KT12 54 D8
Walton Rd Ashstead KT18 96 C8
East Molesey KT8, KT12 36 B5
Walton-on-T KT12&KT8 35 E4
Woking GU21 70 A3
Walton St KT20 97 B3
Walton Terr GU21 70 B4
Walton Way CR4 41 C5
Wanborough Dr SW15 19 B7
Wanborough Hill GU3 128 C6
Wanborough La GU6 175 A3
Wanborough Sta GU3 107 C1
Wandle Bank Merton SW19 20 D1
Wallington CR0 60 E7
Wandle Cl Ash GU12 106 A1
Crawley RH10 202 C5
Wandle Court Gdns CR0 60 E7
Wandle Ct Wallington CR0 60 E7
West Ewell KT19 57 C6
Wandle House Catford BR1 24 D3
5 Redhill RH1 118 F2
Wandsworth SW18 20 B8
Wandle Lodge CR0 60 E7
Wandle Prim Sch SW18 20 B7
Wandle Rd
Croydon CR0, CR9 61 C7
Hackbridge SM6 60 B8
Morden CR4, SM4, SW19 40 D4
Upper Tooting SW17 20 E6
Wallington CR0 60 E7
Wandle Side Croydon CR0 60 F7
Hackbridge SM6 60 B7
Wandle Tech Pk CR4 40 F2
Wandle Trad Est CR4 40 F2
Wandle Valley Sch SM5 40 E2
Wandle Way Mitcham CR4 40 F4
Wandsworth SW18 20 B7
Wandsdyke Cl GU16 85 F8
Wandsworth Common Sta SW12 20 F8
Wansford Gn 3 GU21 68 F2
Wanstraw Gr RG12 27 E2
Wantage Cl Bracknell RG12 27 E4
Wantage Cl *continued*
Crawley RH10 202 C3
Wantage Rd GU47 64 D8
Waplings The KT20 97 B3
Wapshott Rd TW18 12 E3
War Coppice Rd CR3 120 D7
War Memorial Homes W4 7 D8
War Memorial Hospl SM5 59 F4
Warbank Cl CR0 63 E1
Warbank Cres CR0 63 E1
Warbank La KT2 18 F1
Warblers Gn KT11 73 F5
Warbleton House 6 RH11 200 F3
Warboys App KT2 18 B2
Warboys Rd KT2 18 B2
Warburton Cl RH19 206 A8
Warburton Rd TW2 16 B7
Warbury La GU21 68 C3
Ward Cl RG40 25 D8
Ward La CR6 81 D2
Ward St GU1 130 D8
Wardle Cl GU19 47 E3
Wardley St SW18 20 B8
Wardrobe The 3 TW9 6 D2
Wards Stone Pk RG12 27 E2
Ware Ct SM1 58 F6
Wareham Cl TW3 5 B3
Wareham Rd RG12 27 F4
Warenne Hts RH1 139 D7
Warenne Rd KT22 94 C5
Warfield Rd Bracknell RG12 27 C8
East Bedfont TW14 14 E8
Hampton TW12 36 B8
Wargrove Dr GU47 64 D8
Warham Rd CR0, CR2 61 C5
Waring St SE27 22 C4
Warkworth Gdns TW7 6 A7
Warlingham Cty Sec Sch CR6 81 A3
Warlingham Park Sch CR6 82 A3
Warlingham Rd CR7 42 B5
Warltersville Way RH6 161 C1
Warminster Gdns SE25 43 A7
Warminster Rd SE25 43 A7
Warminster Sq SE25 43 A7
Warminster Way CR4 41 B7
Warner Ave SM3 58 E8
Warner Cl Crawley RH10 202 C2
Harlington UB3 3 D7
Warner Ct SM3 58 E8
Warner House BR3 24 B2
Warner Rd BR1 24 F1
Warners La GU5 132 E2
Warnford House SW15 7 E1
Warnham CE (Controlled) Sch RH12 216 F8
Warnham Court Rd SM5 59 F3
Warnham Ct Sch RH12 216 F7
Warnham House 9 SW2 21 F8
Warnham Nature Reserve RH12 217 B6
Warnham Rd
Broadbridge Heath RH12 216 D4
Crawley RH10 202 B4
Horsham RH12 217 B5
Warnham Sta RH12 217 C8
Warpole Pk KT13 53 A3
Warramill Rd GU7 151 A5
Warren Ave Belmont SM2 58 F1
Bromley BR1 24 E1
Mortlake SW14, TW10 7 B3
South Croydon CR2 62 D3
Warren Cl Esher KT10 55 B6
Felbridge RH19 184 E3
Sandhurst GU47 64 A8
West Norwood SE21 22 C8
Warren Cnr GU10 124 C7
Warren Ct
18 Beckenham BR3 24 A1
6 Croydon CR0 42 E1
Weybridge KT13 53 A5
Warren Cutting KT2 18 D1
Warren Down RG42 26 E8
Warren Dr Crawley RH11 201 A8
Kingswood KT20 98 A4
Warren Dr N KT5, KT6 38 B1
Warren Dr S KT5 38 C1
Warren Farm Mobile Home Pk GU23 91 B8
Warren Hill KT18 76 D3
Warren House Rd RG40 25 D8
Warren La Oxshott KT22 74 C7
Oxted RH8 123 A1
Woking GU22, GU23 71 B1
Warren Lodge KT20 97 E3
Warren Lodge Dr KT20 97 E3
Warren Mead SM7 77 C4
Warren Mead Cty Inf Sch SM7 77 D4
Warren Mead Cty Jun Sch SM7 77 D4
Warren Park Rd SM1, SM2 59 E4
Warren Pk Kingston u T KT2 18 C2
Warlingham CR6 81 D1
Warren Rd Ashford TW15 14 E1
Banstead KT17, SM7 77 D5
Croydon CR0 42 F1
Farncombe GU7 150 E7
Guildford GU1, GU4 131 A8
Kingston u T KT2 18 C2
Mitcham SW19 20 E2
Purley CR8 80 B8
Reigate RH2 118 B2

Warren Rd *continued*
Twickenham TW2 . . . . .5 D1
Woodham KT15 . . . . .52 A1
Warren Rise Frimley GU16 . .65 F3
Kingston u T KT3 . . . . .38 D8
Warren Row SL5 . . . . .28 D7
Warren The
Aldershot GU11 . . . . .104 F1
Ashtead KT21 . . . . .95 F7
East Horsley KT24 . . . . . .112 F5
Heath End GU9 . . . . .125 E8
Heston TW5 . . . . .4 F7
Kingswood KT20 . . . . .97 E4
Oxshott KT22 . . . . .74 D6
Sutton SM3, SM5 . . . . . . .59 E4
Worcester Park KT19, KT4 . .57 D7
Warren Way KT13 . . . . . .53 C4
Warren Wood Cl BR2 . . . . .63 F8
Warreners La KT13 . . . . . .53 D3
Warrenhyrst GU1 . . . . . . .131 A8
Warrenne Rd RH3 . . . . . .137 C7
Warrington Cl RH11 . . . . .200 E2
Warrington Mews GU1 .125 E8
Warrington Rd
Croydon CR0, CR9 . . . . . . .61 B7
21 Richmond TW10 . . . . . . .6 D2
Warrington Spur SL4 . . . . .11 B8
Warwick GU12 . . . . .27 E3
Warwick Ave Staines TW18 .13 C2
Thorpe Lea TW20 . . . . . . .32 C8
Warwick Cl
Aldershot GU11 . . . . .126 C8
Frimley GU15 . . . . .66 B3
Hampton TW12 . . . . .16 C1
South Holmwood RH5 . . . .157 B7
Weybridge KT13 . . . . .53 A5
Warwick Ct Beckenham BR2 44 E7
Weybridge KT13 . . . . .53 A5
Warwick Deeping KT16 . . .51 C5
Warwick Gdns
Ashtead KT21 . . . . .75 C2
Thames Ditton KT7 . . . . . .36 F4
Thornton Heath CR7 . . . . .42 A5
Warwick Gr KT5 . . . . .37 F2
Warwick House 6 KT2 . .37 E8
Warwick La GU21 . . . . . . .89 A8
Warwick Lodge SM1 . . . . .58 F6
Warwick Quadrant RH1 ..119 A2
Warwick Rd
Ash Vale GU12 . . . . .106 A8
Ashford TW15 . . . . .13 E3
Coulsdon CR5 . . . . .79 D5
Hounslow TW4 . . . . .4 A4
Kingston u T KT3 . . . . .38 C6
Penge SE20 . . . . .43 B6
Redhill RH1 . . . . .118 F2
South Holmwood RH5 . . . .157 C7
Sutton SM1 . . . . .59 C5
Teddington KT1 . . . . .37 C8
Thames Ditton KT7 . . . . . .36 F4
Thornton Heath CR7 . . . . .42 A6
Twickenham TW2 . . . . .16 E7
Warwick Sch The RH1 . . .119 A2
Warwick Villas TW20 . . . .32 C8
Warwick Wold Rd
Bletchingley RH1 . . . . . . .120 A7
Caterham RH1 . . . . .120 A7
Warwick's Bench Rd
GU1 . . . . .130 E6
Warwicks Bench GU1 .130 D6
Wasdale Cl GU47 . . . . .45 D2
Washington Cl GU12 . . . . .118 A3
Washington Ct SW17 . . . . .20 F2
Washington Rd
Crawley RH11 . . . . .200 E4
Kingston u T KT1 . . . . .38 A7
North Cheam KT4 . . . . . . .39 B1
Washpond La CR6 . . . . . . .82 C1
Wasp Green La RH1 . . . .162 C8
Wassand Cl RH10 . . . . . . .202 A6
Wastdale Rd SE23 . . . . . . .23 D7
Watchetts Cty Jun Sch
GU15 . . . . .65 B2
Watchetts Dr GU15 . . . . . .65 C2
Watchetts Lake Cl GU15 ..65 D3
Watchetts Rd GU15 . . . . . .65 B4
Watchmoor Pk GU15 . . . . .65 A3
Watchmoor Rd GU15 . . . . .65 A4
Watchmoor Trade Ctr
GU15 . . . . .65 A3
Watcombe Cotts TW9 . . . . .7 A8
Watcombe Rd SE25 . . . . . .43 B4
Water La
Abinger Common RH5 . . . .155 B8
Albury GU4, GU5 . . . . . . .132 B5
Bisley GU24 . . . . .87 E8
Cobham KT11 . . . . .73 F5
Enton Green GU8 . . . . . . .171 B4
Farnborough GU14 . . . . . . .85 A7
Farnham GU9 . . . . .125 F4
Kingston u T KT1 . . . . .37 D8
Limpsfield RH8 . . . . .123 A8
Lingfield TN8 . . . . .165 D7
Little Bookham KT23, KT24 . .93 E1
Richmond TW10, TW9 . . . . .6 D2
South Godstone RH9 . . . . .142 D5
Twickenham TW1 . . . . .17 A7
Wormley GU8 . . . . .171 B4
Water Lea RH10 . . . . .202 A5
Water Mill Way TW13 . . . . .16 A6
Water Splash La SL5 . . . . .29 E8
Water Tower Hill CR0, CR2 .61 D6
Water View RH6 . . . . .161 C3
Waterbank Rd SE6 . . . . . . .24 C4
Watercress Way GU21 . . . . .69 D2
Waterden Cl GU1 . . . . .130 F8

Waterden Rd GU1 . . . . . .130 E8
Waterer Gdns KT20 . . . . . .77 E1
Waterer House SE6 . . . . . .24 C4
Waterers Rise GU21 . . . . . .68 D2
Waterfall Cl GU25 . . . . .31 A6
Waterfall Cotts SW19 . . . . .20 D2
Waterfall Rd SW19 . . . . . . .20 D2
Waterfall Terr SW17 . . . . . .20 E2
Waterfield KT20 . . . . .97 B7
Waterfield Cl RH13 . . . . . .217 E3
Waterfield Cty Fst Sch
RH11 . . . . .200 E4
Waterfield Ct DR6 . . . . . .101 C8
Waterfield Gdns
Crawley RH11 . . . . .200 E4
South Norwood SE25 . . . . .42 E4
Waterfield Gn KT20 . . . . . .97 B7
Waterfields KT22 . . . . .95 B8
Waterford Cl KT11 . . . . . . .73 E8
Waterford Way RG40 . . . . .25 C6
Waterham Rd RG12 . . . . . .27 B3
Waterhouse Ct 5 TW11 ..16 F3
Waterhouse La
Bletchingley RH1 . . . . . . .121 A3
Coulsdon CR8 . . . . .100 C8
Kingswood KT20 . . . . .97 E6
Waterhouse Mead GU47 ..64 D7
Waterlands La RH12 . . . . .196 E1
Waterloo Cl
Camberley GU15 . . . . .66 B7
East Bedfont TW14 . . . . . .14 F7
Waterloo Cres RG40 . . . . .25 E4
Waterloo Pl TW9 . . . . .7 A8
Waterloo Rd
Aldershot GU12 . . . . .105 C1
Carshalton SM5 . . . . .59 D5
Crowthorne RG45 . . . . . . .45 B4
Epsom KT17, KT19 . . . . . .76 D6
Wokingham RG40 . . . . . . .25 F5
Waterlow Rd RH2 . . . . . . .139 D8
Watermans Bsns Pk The
TW18 . . . . .12 E4
Watermans Ct 12 TW8 . . .6 D8
Watermead
East Bedfont TW14 . . . . . .14 E7
Tadworth KT20 . . . . .97 B6
Woking GU21 . . . . .68 F3
Watermead La CR4 . . . . . .40 F2
Watermead Rd SE6 . . . . . .24 C4
Watermeads High Sch
SM4 . . . . .40 D3
Watermen's Sq 1 SE20 ..23 C1
Watermill Cl TW10 . . . . . . .17 C5
Watermill Way SW19 . . . . .40 C8
Waterperry La GU24 . . . . . .49 F1
Waters Dr TW18 . . . . .12 F4
Waters Rd Catford SE6 . . . .24 E5
Kingston u T KT1 . . . . .38 B7
Waters Sq KT1 . . . . .38 B6
Watersedge KT19 . . . . .57 C6
Waterside Beckenham BR3 .44 A8
East Grinstead RH19 . . . . .186 B1
Horley RH6 . . . . .161 A5
Waterside Cl
Crawley RH11 . . . . .200 E4
Godalming GU7 . . . . .151 A5
Surbiton KT6 . . . . .56 E8
Waterside Dr KT12 . . . . . . .35 B4
Waterside La GU7 . . . . . . .150 C3
Waterside Mews GU1 . . . .109 C3
Waterside Rd GU1 . . . . . . .109 D4
Waterside Trad Est KT15 ..52 E6
Waterside Way
Wimbledon SW17 . . . . . . .20 C3
2 Woking GU21 . . . . .69 B1
Waterslade RH1 . . . . .118 E1
Watersmeet Cl GU4 . . . . .110 A6
Watersplash Cl KT1 . . . . . .37 E6
Watersplash Rd TW17 . . . .34 A5
Waterway Rd Fetcham KT22 95 A5
Leatherhead KT22 . . . . . . .95 A5
Watery La Chobham GU24 ..49 D1
Merton SW20 . . . . .39 F7
Watford Cl GU1 . . . . .109 F1
Wathen Rd RH4 . . . . .136 B8
Watlings Cl CR0 . . . . .43 E3
Watlington Gr SE26 . . . . . .23 E3
Watney Cotts SW14 . . . . . . .7 C4
Watney Rd SW14 . . . . .7 C4
Watneys Rd CR4 . . . . .41 D4
Watson Ave SM3 . . . . .58 E8
Watson Cl Crawley RH10 ..202 C3
Mitcham SW19 . . . . .20 E1
Watson House 3 SW2 . . .21 E8
Watson Rd RH4 . . . . .135 C6
Watt's La Tadworth KT20 . . .97 D5
Teddington TW11 . . . . .17 A3
Watt's Mead KT20 . . . . . . .97 D5
Wattenden Prim Sch CR8 .80 B3
Wattendon Rd CR8 . . . . . . .80 B3
Watts Cl KT20 . . . . .97 D5
Watts Lea GU21 . . . . .69 A4
Watts Rd Farnborough GU14 84 F5
Thames Ditton KT7 . . . . . .37 A2
Wavel Cl 7 SW16 . . . . . . .21 C5
Wavel Pl SE19, SE26 . . . . .22 F4
Wavell Sch The GU14 . . . .105 B7
Wavendene Ave TW20 . . . .12 C1
Waveney House 5 RH1 ..118 F1
Waveney Wlk RH10 . . . . . .202 B4
Waverleigh Rd GU6 . . . . . .174 E1
Waverley RG12 . . . . .26 E4
Waverley Abbey GU9 . . . . .147 B7
Waverley Abbey CE Jun
Sch GU10 . . . . .147 D5

Waverley Ave Kenley CR8 ..80 E3
Sutton SM1 . . . . .59 C8
Tolworth KT5 . . . . .38 C3
Twickenham TW2, TW4 . . . .16 A7
Waverley Cl Farnham GU9 125 D2
Frimley GU15 . . . . .65 F4
Waverley Ct
Horsham RH13 . . . . .217 B2
1 Woking GU22 . . . . .69 E1
Waverley Dr
Addlestone KT16 . . . . .51 D7
Ash Vale GU12 . . . . .106 A6
Camberley GU15 . . . . .65 F5
Virginia Water GU25 . . . . . .31 A5
Waverley Gdns GU12 . . . .106 A6
Waverley La
Farnham GU10, GU9 . . . . .147 C8
Farnham, Compton GU9 . . .125 E1
Waverley Pl KT22 . . . . .95 B5
Waverley Rd Bagshot GU19 .47 E3
Croydon SE25 . . . . .43 B6
Farnborough GU14 . . . . . . .85 D3
Oxshott KT11, KT22 . . . . . .74 B5
Stoneleigh KT17, KT4 . . . . .58 B5
Weybridge KT13 . . . . .53 A5
Waverley Way SM2, SM5 ..59 E4
Waverton Rd SW18 . . . . . . .20 C8
Wavertree Ct 9 SW2 . . . .21 E7
Wavertree Rd SW2 . . . . . . .21 F7
Way The RH2 . . . . .118 D2
Waye Ave TW5 . . . . .4 A6
Wayland Cl RG12 . . . . .27 F5
Waylands Mead BR3 . . . . .44 B8
Waylett Pl SE27 . . . . .22 B5
Wayman Rd GU14 . . . . . . .84 E8
Wayneflete Tower Ave
KT10 . . . . .55 A7
Waynflete Ave Croydon CR9, CR0 .61 B7
Waynflete La GU9 . . . . . . .124 F2
Waynflete St SW18 . . . . . . .20 C6
Ways End GU15 . . . . .65 E4
Wayside Capel RH5 . . . . . .178 D6
Crawley RH11 . . . . .200 E4
Mortlake SW14 . . . . .7 C2
New Addington CR0 . . . . . .63 B4
Wayside Ct Hounslow TW7 . . .5 E5
Twickenham TW1 . . . . .6 C1
Woking GU21 . . . . .68 E3
WC Lee's Resthouses
GU20 . . . . .48 D4
Weald CE Prim Sch The
RH5 . . . . .157 D3
Weald Cl GU4 . . . . .130 E3
Weald Day Hospl The
RH11 . . . . .201 C6
Weald Dr RH10 . . . . .202 A4
Weald The RH19 . . . . .185 F4
Weald View Cotts RH5 . . .156 D3
Weald Way Caterham CR3 .120 E8
Reigate RH2 . . . . .139 C5
Wealdon Cl 1 GU2 . . . . . .108 F1
Wealdstone Rd SM3 . . . . . .58 F8
Weare St Capel RH5 . . . . .178 B4
Ockley RH5 . . . . .177 F1
Weasdale Ct GU21 . . . . . . .68 F3
Weatherall Cl KT15 . . . . . .52 B5
Weatherhill Cl RH6 . . . . . .161 F3
Weatherhill Cotts RH6 . . .162 A4
Weatherill Rd RH6 . . . . . .162 A3
Weatherill Ct SE25 . . . . . . .43 B3
Weaver Cl RH11 . . . . .200 E4
Weaver Wlk SE27 . . . . .22 B4
Weavers Cl TW7 . . . . .5 E3
Weavers Gdns GU9 . . . . . .145 F7
Weavers Yd GU9 . . . . .125 B2
Webb Cl Bagshot GU19 . . . .47 E1
Crawley RH11 . . . . .201 B1
Webb Ct RG40 . . . . .25 E8
Webb House 2 SW12 . . . .21 C8
Webb Rd GU8 . . . . .170 C6
Webster Cl KT11, KT22 . . . .74 B5
Websters Cl GU22 . . . . . . .89 B7
Weddell Rd RH10 . . . . . . .201 F3
Wedgewood Ct BR2 . . . . . .44 F5
Wedgwood Way SE19 . . . .22 C1
Wedgwoods TN16 . . . . . . .103 C6
Weeks House TW10 . . . . . .17 C4
Weighbridge Rd KT15 . . . .52 B2
Weighton Rd SE20 . . . . . . .43 B7
Weihurst Ct SM1 . . . . .59 E5
Weihurst Gdns SM1 . . . . . .59 D5
Weir Ave GU14 . . . . .85 A3
Weir Cl GU14 . . . . .85 A3
Weir House 8 SW12 . . . . .21 C8
Weir Pl TW18 . . . . .32 E8
Weir Rd Chertsey KT16 . . . .33 B2
Streatham SW12 . . . . .21 C8
Walton-on-T KT12 . . . . . . .35 A3
Wimbledon SW18, SW19 ..20 B5
Weir Wood Resr
(Nature Reserve) RH19 .205 E2
Weirbrook RH10 . . . . .202 A3
Welbeck RG12 . . . . .26 E4
Welbeck Cl Ewell KT17 . . . .58 A3
Farnborough GU14 . . . . . . .84 F3
New Malden KT3 . . . . .38 F4
Welbeck Rd SM1, SM5 . . . .59 D8
Welbeck Wlk SM5 . . . . . . .40 D1
Welcome Cotts CR3 . . . . .102 A4
Welcome Terr CR3 . . . . . . .80 F3
Welcomes Rd CR8 . . . . . . .80 C3
Weldon Ct CR7 . . . . .42 B4
Weldon Dr KT8 . . . . .35 F5
Weldon Way RH1 . . . . . . .119 D6
Welford Pl SW19 . . . . .19 E4
Welham Rd SW16, SW17 . . .21 B2
Welhouse Rd SM5 . . . . . . .59 E8
Well Cl Camberley GU15 . . .65 B4

Well Cl *continued*
Streatham SW16 . . . . .21 F4
Woking GU21 . . . . .69 C2
Well Farm Rd CR3, CR6 . . .101 A8
Well House SM7 . . . . .78 B4
Well La Haslemere GU27 . . .208 D6
Mortlake SW14 . . . . .7 C2
Woking GU21 . . . . .69 C2
Well Path GU21 . . . . .69 C2
Well Way KT18 . . . . .76 A5
Welland Cl SL3 . . . . .1 B8
Wellburn Cl GU47 . . . . . . .64 B7
Weller Cl RH10 . . . . .202 D5
Weller Dr GU15 . . . . .65 C3
Wellesford Cl SM7 . . . . . . .77 F2
Wellesley Cl
Ash Vale GU12 . . . . .105 F7
Bagshot GU19 . . . . .47 C3
Wellesley Court Rd 1
CR0, CR9 . . . . .61 D8
Wellesley Cres TW2 . . . . . .16 E5
Wellesley Ct Cheam SM3 . . .39 E1
Twickenham TW2 . . . . .16 E5
Wellesley Garden GU9 . . .125 C2
Wellesley Gate 3 GU12 ..105 B1
Wellesley Gr CR0, CR9 . . . .61 D8
Wellesley Rd
Aldershot GU11 . . . . .104 E2
Croydon CR0 . . . . .42 C1
Rushmoor GU10 . . . . .168 C6
Sutton SM2 . . . . .59 C4
Twickenham TW2 . . . . .16 E5
Wellfield RH19 . . . . .206 C7
Wellfield Gdns SM5 . . . . . .59 E2
Wellfield Rd SW16 . . . . . . .21 F4
Wellhouse Rd
Beckenham BR3 . . . . .44 A5
Betchworth RH3 . . . . .137 D6
Wellington Ave
Aldershot GU11 . . . . .104 F2
Hounslow TW3, TW4 . . . . . .5 A2
North Cheam KT4 . . . . . . .58 C7
Virginia Water GU25 . . . . . .31 B4
Wentworth GU25 . . . . .31 B4
Wellington Cl
Crawley RH10 . . . . .182 E1
Sandhurst GU47 . . . . .64 C8
Walton-on-T KT12 . . . . . . .34 F1
Wellington Coll RG45 . . . . .45 A3
Wellington Cotts KT24 . . .112 C6
Wellington Cres KT3 . . . . . .38 C6
Wellington Ct
Stanwell TW19 . . . . .13 E8
5 Surbiton KT6 . . . . .37 E3
Teddington TW12 . . . . .16 D3
Wellington Ctr The GU11 105 A2
Wellington Dr
Bracknell RG12 . . . . .27 E4
Wallington CR8 . . . . .60 F1
Wellington Gdns
Aldershot GU11 . . . . .104 F1
Teddington TW12, TW2 . . . .16 D4
Wellington La GU9 . . . . . .125 D7
Wellington Pl
Cobham KT11 . . . . .73 C7
Farncombe GU7 . . . . .150 E7
Wellington Prim Sch TW3 ..4 F5
Wellington Rd
Ashford TW15 . . . . .13 E3
Caterham CR3 . . . . .100 C5
Crowthorne RG45 . . . . . . .45 C4
Hatton TW14 . . . . .3 E2
Horsham RH12, RH13 . . . .217 D2
Sandhurst GU47 . . . . .64 C8
Teddington TW12, TW2 . . . .16 D4
Thornton Heath CR0 . . . . .42 B2
Wimbledon SW19 . . . . . . .20 A6
Wokingham RG40 . . . . . . .25 B5
Wellington Rd N TW4 . . . . .4 F4
Wellington Rd S TW4 . . . . .4 F3
Wellington Rdbt GU11 . . .104 E2
Wellington St 8 GU11 . . .105 A2
Wellington Terr
6 Knaphill GU21 . . . . .68 E1
Sandhurst GU47 . . . . .64 C8
Wellington Town Rd
RH19 . . . . .185 D2
Wellington Way
Byfleet KT13 . . . . .52 F1
Horley RH6 . . . . .160 F5
Weybridge KT13 . . . . .52 F1
Wellingtonia Ave GU15 . . .52 A5
Wellmeadow Rd SE13, SE6 .24 E7
Wellow Wlk SM5 . . . . .40 D1
Wells Cl
Great Bookham KT23 . . . . .94 C3
Horsham RH12 . . . . .216 F2
Wells Cotts GU9 . . . . .146 A7
Wells La Ascot SL5 . . . . . . .29 B5
Normandy GU3 . . . . .107 C4
Wells Lea RH19 . . . . .185 D3
Wells Meadow RH19 . . . .185 D3
Wells Park Rd SE21, SE26 .23 B4
Wells Pl RH1 . . . . .119 B6
Wells Rd Crawley RH10 . . .201 E2
Epsom KT18 . . . . .76 B4
Guildford GU4 . . . . .110 C4
Wells The GU27 . . . . .208 C6
Wellside Gdns SW14 . . . . . .7 C2
Wellwood Cl
Coulsdon CR5, CR8 . . . . . .79 E5
Horsham RH13 . . . . .218 B4
Wellwynds Rd GU6 . . . . . .174 E2
Welwyn Ave TW14 . . . . .3 F1
Welwyn Cl RH11 . . . . .200 E1
Wembley Rd TW12 . . . . . . .36 A8
Wembury Pk RH7 . . . . . . .163 E1

Wend The CR5 . . . . .79 D5
Wendela Cl GU22 . . . . .69 F1
Wendley Dr KT15 . . . . .51 F1
Wendling Rd SM1, SM5 . . .59 D8
Wendover Dr Frimley GU16 .66 C3
New Malden KT3 . . . . .38 F3
Wendover Pl TW18 . . . . . . .12 D3
Wendover Rd TW18, TW20 .12 D3
Wendron Cl 2 GU21 . . . . .69 A1
Wendy Cres GU2 . . . . .109 A3
Wenlock Cl RH11 . . . . . . .201 A4
Wenlock Edge RH4 . . . . . .136 C5
Wensleydale RH11 . . . . . .201 C3
Wensleydale Dr GU15 . . . .66 D5
Wensleydale Gdns TW12 ..16 B1
Wensleydale Rd TW12 . . . .16 B1
Wentland Cl SE6 . . . . .24 D6
Wentland Rd SE6 . . . . .24 D6
Wentworth Ave SL5 . . . . . .28 C7
Wentworth Cl
Ash Vale GU12 . . . . .106 A4
Ashford TW15 . . . . .14 B4
Heath End GU9 . . . . .125 F6
Long Ditton KT6 . . . . .56 D8
Morden SM4 . . . . .40 A2
Ripley GU23 . . . . .91 B6
Wentworth Club GU25 . . . .31 A4
Wentworth Cres GU12 . . .106 A6
Wentworth Ct
20 Kingston u T KT6 . . . . . .37 E4
Twickenham TW2 . . . . .16 C1
Wentworth Dr
Crawley RH10 . . . . .202 D2
Wentworth GU25 . . . . .30 F5
Wentworth House KT15 . . .52 B6
Wentworth Rd CR0 . . . . . .42 A2
Wentworth Way
Hamsey Green CR2 . . . . . .81 A4
North Ascot SL5 . . . . .28 C7
Werndee Rd SE25 . . . . . . .43 A5
Wesco Ct GU21 . . . . .70 A3
Wescott Cty Inf Sch RG40 .25 D5
Wescott Rd RG40 . . . . .25 D6
Wesley Ave TW3 . . . . .4 F5
Wesley Cl Crawley RH11 . . .200 E3
Horley RH6 . . . . .161 A5
Reigate RH2 . . . . .138 F8
Wesley Dr TW20 . . . . .12 A2
Wesley Pl SL4 . . . . .9 B6
Wessels KT20 . . . . .97 D6
Wessex Ave SW19 . . . . . . .40 A6
Wessex Cl KT1, KT2 . . . . . .38 B8
Wessex Ct 4 TW19 . . . . . . .2 E1
Wessex Pl GU21 . . . . .125 C1
Wessex Rd TW19, TW6 . . . .2 C1
Wesson House 3 CR0 . . . .43 A1
West Ashtead Cty Prim
Sch KT21 . . . . .95 E7
West Ave Crawley RH10 . . .202 A8
Heath End GU9 . . . . .125 D7
Redhill RH1 . . . . .140 A3
Wallington CR0, SM6 . . . . .60 C5
Whiteley Village KT12, KT13 . .53 E2
West Bank RH4 . . . . .136 A6
West Barnes La
West Barnes KT3, SW20 . . .39 B6
Wimbledon KT3, SW20 . . . .39 E4
West Byfleet Cty Inf Sch
KT14 . . . . .71 B7
West Byfleet Cty Jun Sch
KT14 . . . . .71 B7
West Cl Ashford TW15 . . . .13 E4
Heath End GU9 . . . . .125 D7
West Cross Ctr TW8 . . . . . .6 B8
West Cross Way TW8 . . . . . .6 B8
West Croydon Sta CR9 . . .42 C1
West Ct Guildford GU4 . . . .110 D5
Hounslow TW7 . . . . .5 C7
West Down KT23 . . . . .114 B8
West Dr Belmont SM2 . . . . .58 E2
Burgh Heath KT20 . . . . . . .77 E1
Streatham SW16, SW17 . . .21 C4
Sutton SM5 . . . . .59 D1
Wentworth GU25 . . . . .30 E2
Woodham KT15 . . . . .52 B2
West Dulwich Sta SE21 . . .22 D7
West End Cty Inf Sch
GU11 . . . . .104 F2
West End Gdns KT10 . . . . .54 F5
West End Gr GU9 . . . . . . .125 A2
West End La
Chiddingfold GU27 . . . . . .190 E1
Esher KT10 . . . . .54 F4
Frensham GU10 . . . . .146 B1
Harlington UB7 . . . . .3 C7
West Ewell Cty Inf Sch
KT19 . . . . .57 D5
West Ewell Cty Jun Sch
KT19 . . . . .57 D5
West Farm Ave KT21 . . . . .95 D8
West Farm Cl KT21 . . . . . .95 C8
West Farm Dr KT21 . . . . . .95 D8
West Flexford La GU3 . . . .128 E8
West Gdns Ewell KT17 . . . .57 F1
Mitcham SW19 . . . . .20 E2
West Gr KT12 . . . . .54 B6
West Green Cty Fst Sch
RH11 . . . . .201 C7
West Green Dr RH11 . . . . .201 C6
West Hall Rd TW9 . . . . .7 B6
West Heath GU24 . . . . .87 D4
West Heath Rd GU14 . . . . .84 F4
West Hill Biggin Hill BR6 . . .83 F7
Dormans Park RH19 . . . . .185 E6
East Grinstead RH19 . . . . .205 D8
Elstead GU8 . . . . .148 C3
Epsom KT18, KT19 . . . . . .76 C6
Oxted RH8 . . . . .122 D5

West Hill *continued*
Putney SW15 . . . .**19** D8
South Croydon CR2 . . . .**61** E2
Woking GU22 . . . .**89** E8
West Hill Ave KT19 . . . .**76** C7
West Hill Bank RH8 . . . . . .**122** D5
West Hill Rd
Brookwood GU24 . . . .**88** B7
Elstead GU8 . . . .**148** C3
West Hill Sch KT22 . . . .**75** A1
West House Penge SE20 . .**23** D1
⑨ Streatham SW12 . . . . . .**21** C8
West House Cl SW19 . . . . .**19** E7
West La
East Grinstead RH19 . . . . .**205** D8
Wotton RH5 . . . .**134** D4
West Leigh RH19 . . . .**205** E7
West Mead KT19 . . . .**57** E4
West Mead SM RG40 . . . .**25** E6
West Meads GU2 . . . .**129** F8
West Middlesex Univ
Hospl TW7 . . . .**6** A5
West Mount GU2 . . . .**130** C7
West Norwood Sta SE27 . .**22** B5
West Oak BR3 . . . .**44** D8
West Palace Gdns KT13 . . .**53** B6
West Par RH12 . . . .**217** C4
West Park Ave TW9 . . . .**7** B6
West Park Cl TW5 . . . .**4** F8
West Park Hospl KT19 . . . . .**75** E7
West Pk
Domewood RH10 . . . .**183** F5
Epsom KT19 . . . .**75** F7
Horne RH7, RH10 . . . .**184** B7
Richmond TW9 . . . .**7** A6
West Pl SW19 . . . .**19** C3
West Ramp TW6 . . . .**3** A6
West Rd Bracknell RG40 . . .**26** D2
Camberley GU15 . . . .**65** D5
Chessington KT9 . . . .**75** C8
East Bedfont TW14 . . . .**14** D8
Farnborough GU14 . . . .**85** B8
Guildford GU1 . . . .**130** E8
Kingston u T KT2, KT3 . . . . .**38** C8
Reigate RH2 . . . .**139** B8
Weybridge KT13 . . . .**53** B3
West Ring GU10 . . . .**126** F7
West Sheen Vale TW9 . . . . . .**6** F3
West Side Comm SW19 . . . .**19** C3
West St Carshalton SM5 . . .**59** F6
Crawley RH11 . . . .**201** D5
Croydon CR0, CR9 . . . .**61** C6
Dorking RH4 . . . .**136** A7
Dormansland RH7 . . . .**165** A1
East Grinstead RH19 . . . . .**205** E8
Epsom KT18, KT19 . . . .**76** C6
Ewell KT17 . . . .**57** F1
Farnham GU9 . . . .**208** C6
Haslemere GU27 . . . .**208** C6
Horsham RH12 . . . .**217** C2
Reigate RH2 . . . .**117** F1
Sutton SM1 . . . .**59** B5
Woking GU21 . . . .**69** F2
West Street La SM5 . . . .**59** F6
West Street Pl ❶
CR0, CR9 . . . .**61** C6
West Surrey Estates TW15 **34** C8
West Sutton Sta SM1 . . . . .**59** A6
West Temple Sheen SW14 . . .**7** B2
West Thames Coll TW7 . . . . .**5** E6
West Thornton Prim Sch
CR0 . . . .**41** F3
West View TW14 . . . .**14** C8
West View Ave CR3 . . . .**80** F1
West View Gdns RH19 . . . .**205** E8
West View Rd
Headley Down GU35 . . . . .**187** C4
Warlingham CR6 . . . .**101** B8
West Way Crawley RH10 . .**202** A7
Croydon CR0 . . . .**62** E7
Heston TW5 . . . .**4** F6
Shepperton TW17 . . . .**34** D3
Slinfold RH13 . . . .**215** D3
Sutton SM2, SM5 . . . .**59** D1
West Wickham BR4 . . . .**44** E3
West Way Gdns CR0 . . . . . .**62** D8
West Wickham Sta BR3 . . . .**44** C2
Westacres KT10 . . . .**54** F3
Westbank Rd TW12 . . . .**16** C2
Westborough Cty Prim
Sch GU2 . . . .**108** F2
Westbourne Ave SM3 . . . . .**58** E8
Westbourne Dr SE23 . . . . . .**23** D6
Westbourne House
Heston TW5 . . . .**5** A8
⑨ Twickenham TW1 . . . . . .**17** B8
Westbourne Prim Sch
SM1 . . . .**59** A7
Westbourne Rd
Croydon CR0 . . . .**42** F3
Feltham TW13 . . . .**14** F5
Penge SE26 . . . .**23** D2
Sandhurst GU47 . . . .**64** C7
Staines TW18 . . . .**13** B1
Westbrook RH18 . . . .**206** E3
Westbrook Ave TW12 . . . . .**15** F1
Westbrook Gdns RG12 . . . .**27** D8
Westbrook Hill GU8 . . . . . .**148** C3
Westbrook Rd
Godalming GU7 . . . .**150** C5
Heston TW5 . . . .**4** F7
South Norwood CR7 . . . . . .**42** D7
Staines TW18 . . . .**12** F3
Westbury Ave KT10 . . . .**55** F4

Westbury Cl
Crowthorne RG45 . . . .**45** B6
Shepperton TW17 . . . .**34** B3
Whyteleafe CR3 . . . .**80** F1
Westbury Ct BR3 . . . .**44** B8
Westbury Gdns GU9 . . . . .**125** E4
Westbury House Sch KT3 . .**38** D4
Westbury Pl ❷ TW8 . . . .**6** D8
Westbury Rd
Beckenham BR3 . . . .**43** E6
Feltham TW13 . . . .**15** D6
New Malden KT3 . . . .**38** D4
Penge SE20 . . . .**43** D8
Thornton Heath CR0 . . . . . .**42** D3
Westcar La KT12 . . . .**54** B5
Westcombe Ave CR0 . . . . . .**41** F2
Westcombe Cl RG12 . . . . . .**27** E2
Westcoombe Ave SW20 . . .**38** F8
Westcote Rd SW16 . . . .**21** C3
Westcott C of E Fst Sch
RH4 . . . .**135** D5
Westcott Cl CR0 . . . .**63** B2
Westcott Rd RH4 . . . .**135** F7
Westcott St RH4 . . . .**135** B6
Westcott Way SM2 . . . .**58** C1
Westcroft Gdns SW20 **39** F5
Westcroft Rd SM5, SM6 . . . .**60** A6
Westdene GU7 . . . .**150** E1
Westdene Meadows GU6 **174** A3
Westdene Way KT13 . . . .**53** E7
Westdown Rd SE13, SE6 . . .**24** A8
Westende RG40 . . . .**25** D6
Westende Cty Jun Sch
RG40 . . . .**25** D6
Westerdale Dr GU16 . . . . . .**66** B3
Westerfolds Cl GU22 . . . . . .**70** C2
Westerham ❸ KT6 . . . .**37** E4
Westerham Cl
Belmont SM2 . . . .**59** A1
New Haw KT15 . . . .**52** C4
Westerham Lodge ❿ BR3 . .**24** A1
Westerham Rd RH8, TN16 **123** C6
Westerley Cres SE26, SE6 . .**23** F3
Westermain KT15 . . . .**52** C1
Western Apron Rd RH6 . . .**181** F8
Western Ave Chertsey KT16 **33** A6
Thorpe TW20 . . . .**32** B6
Western Cl KT16 . . . .**33** A6
Western Ctr The RG12 . . . . .**26** F7
Western Dr TW17 . . . .**34** D3
Western La SW12 . . . .**21** A8
Western Perimeter Rd
TW19, TW6, UB7 . . . .**2** B5
Western Perimeter Rd Rdbt
TW19 . . . .**2** C2
Western Rd
Aldershot GU11 . . . .**104** E1
Bracknell RG12 . . . .**26** F7
Mitcham CR4, SW19 . . . .**40** E7
Sutton SM1 . . . .**59** A5
Westfield Ashstead KT21 . . .**75** F1
Peaslake RH5 . . . .**154** E8
Reigate RH2 . . . .**118** A4
Westfield Ave
Sanderstead CR2, CR8 . . . . .**80** E6
Woking GU22 . . . .**89** E7
Westfield Cl SM1 . . . .**58** F6
Westfield Comm GU22 . . . . .**89** E6
Westfield Dr
Kingston u T KT6 . . . .**37** D4
New Haw KT15 . . . .**52** D1
Westfield Gr KT23 . . . .**94** B5
Westfield Gr GU22 . . . .**89** E7
Westfield La GU10 . . . .**145** E6
Westfield Par KT15 . . . .**52** D1
Westfield Prim Sch GU22 . .**89** E6
Westfield Rd
Beckenham BR3 . . . .**43** F7
Camberley GU15 . . . .**65** B2
Cheam SM1 . . . .**58** F6
Crawley RH11 . . . .**201** B6
Guildford GU1 . . . .**109** E5
Kingston u T KT6 . . . .**37** D4
Mitcham CR4 . . . .**40** F7
Thornton Heath CR0, CR9 . .**61** B8
Walton-on-T KT12 . . . .**35** E2
Woking GU22 . . . .**89** E5
Westfield Way GU22 . . . . . .**89** F5
Westfields SW13 . . . .**7** F4
Westfields Ave SW13, SW14 . .**7** E4
Westfields Sch SW13 . . . .**7** F4
Westgate Rd
Beckenham BR3 . . . .**44** C8
Croydon SE25 . . . .**43** B5
Westglade GU14 . . . .**84** D4
Westhall Pk CR6 . . . .**101** C8
Westhall Rd CR6 . . . .**101** B8
Westhay Gdns SW14 . . . .**7** B2
Westhumble St RH5 . . . . . .**115** B4
Westland Cl TW19 . . . .**2** E1
Westland Dr BR2, BR4 . . . . .**63** F8
Westlands RH13 . . . .**217** E3
Westlands Ct
East Molesey KT8 . . . .**36** E5
Epsom KT18 . . . .**76** C4
Westlands Way RH8 . . . . . .**122** D8
Westleas RH6 . . . .**160** E5
Westlees Cl RH5 . . . .**136** D4
Westleigh Ave CR5 . . . .**79** B3
Westmacott Dr TW14 . . . . . .**14** F7
Westmark Point ⓕ SW15 . .**19** B7
Westmead
Farnborough GU14 . . . .**85** B3
⑧ Farnham GU9 . . . .**125** B2
Putney SW15 . . . .**19** B8
Woking GU21 . . . .**69** B2
Westmead Dr RH1 . . . .**140** A1
Westmead Rd SM1 . . . .**59** D6

Westminster Ave CR7 . . . . .**42** B7
Westminster Cl
East Bedfont TW14 . . . .**15** A7
Teddington TW11 . . . .**17** A3
Westminster Ct
Old Woking GU22 . . . .**90** B6
South Norwood CR7 . . . . . .**42** C7
Westminster Rd
Carshalton SM1, SM5 . . . . . .**59** D8
Crawley RH10 . . . .**202** C5
Westmoat Cl BR3 . . . .**24** C1
Westmont Rd KT10 . . . .**55** E8
Westmore Rd TN16 . . . . . .**103** C7
Westmoreland Dr SM2 . . . .**59** B2
Westmoreland Rd
Barnes SW13 . . . .**7** F6
Beckenham BR2, BR3 . . . . . .**44** F5
Westmoreland Terr SE20 . .**23** B1
Westmorland Cl
Epsom KT19 . . . .**57** E2
❸ Twickenham TW1 . . . .**6** B1
Westmorland Ct ⓫ KT6 . . . .**37** D2
Westmorland Dr SM2 . . . . . .**59** B2
Westmorland Sq CR4 . . . . . .**41** E4
Westmorland Way CR4 . . . . .**41** E4
Weston Ave
Addlestone KT15 . . . .**52** B6
East Molesey KT8 . . . .**35** F5
Thames Ditton KT10, KT7 . . .**36** E2
Weston Cl Coulsdon CR5 . . .**99** F7
Farncombe GU7 . . . .**150** E6
Weston Ct Farncombe GU7 **150** E6
Weston Fields GU5 . . . .**132** D4
Weston Gdns Hounslow TW7 . .**5** E6
Pyrford GU22 . . . .**70** E3
Weston Gn KT7 . . . .**36** E1
Weston Gr Bagshot GU19 . . .**47** F2
Bromley BR1 . . . .**44** F8
Weston Green Prep Sch
KT7 . . . .**36** E1
Weston Green Rd KT7 . . . . .**36** E2
Weston Lea KT24 . . . .**92** D2
Weston Park Cl KT7 . . . .**36** E1
Weston Pk Kingston u T KT1 .**37** E7
Thames Ditton KT10, KT7 . . .**36** E1
Weston Rd Bromley BR1 . . . .**24** F1
Ewell KT17 . . . .**76** E8
Guildford GU2 . . . .**109** A2
Thames Ditton KT7 . . . .**36** E1
Weston Way GU22 . . . .**70** E3
Westons Cl RH12 . . . .**217** D7
Westover Cl SM2 . . . .**59** B1
Westover Rd SW18 . . . .**20** C8
Westow Hill SE19 . . . .**22** F2
Westow St SE19 . . . .**22** E2
Westpoint BR2 . . . .**44** D6
Westview ❺ **69** F1
Westview Cl RH1 . . . .**139** E6
Westville Rd KT7 . . . .**37** A2
Westward Ho GU1 . . . .**109** F3
Westwates Cl RG12 . . . .**27** D8
Westway Caterham CR3 . . .**100** D5
Copthorne RH10 . . . .**183** A3
Crawley RH6 . . . .**182** B7
Guildford GU2 . . . .**108** F3
West Barnes KT3, SW20 . . . .**39** C5
Wormley GU8 . . . .**190** F8
Westway Ave SW20 . . . .**39** B6
Westway Ct CR3 . . . .**100** D4
Westway Gdns RH1 . . . .**119** A4
Westways KT19 . . . .**57** F6
Westwell Rd SW16 . . . .**21** E2
Westwell Road App SW16 . .**21** E2
Westwick Gdns TW4, TW5 . . .**4** B5
Westwood Ave
South Norwood SE19 . . . . . .**42** C8
Woodham KT15 . . . .**70** F7
Westwood Cl KT10 . . . .**55** C7
Westwood Ct
❸ Forest Hill SE23 . . . .**23** C7
Guildford GU2 . . . .**108** F2
❼ Wimbledon SW19 . . . . . .**19** F3
Westwood Gdns SW13 . . . . . .**7** F4
Westwood Hill SE19, SE26 . .**23** B4
Westwood La
Flexford GU3 . . . .**107** A2
Normandy GU3 . . . .**107** A2
Wanborough GU3 . . . .**128** B7
Westwood Park Cty
Prim Sch GU2 . . . .**108** E1
Westwood Pk SE23 . . . .**23** B8
Westwood Rd
Coulsdon CR5 . . . .**79** D1
Mortlake SW13, SW15 . . . .**7** F4
Windlesham GU20 . . . .**48** E6
Westwood Sch SE19 . . . . . .**22** D1
Wetheral Ct SW17 . . . .**20** D4
Wetherby Cl SE25 . . . .**43** A6
Wetherby Gdns ❷ GU14 . . .**85** C1
Wetherby House GU15 . . . . .**65** D7
Wetherby Way KT9 . . . .**56** E3
Wettern Cl CR2 . . . .**61** E1
Wetton Pl TW20 . . . .**11** F3
Wexfenne Gdns GU22 . . . . .**71** B3
Wexford Rd SW12 . . . .**20** F8
Wey Ave KT16 . . . .**33** A6
Wey Cl Ash GU12 . . . .**106** A1
Camberley GU15 . . . .**65** B5
West Byfleet KT14 . . . .**71** B6
Wey Ct Farncombe GU7 . . .**151** A6
New Haw KT15 . . . .**52** D2
Wey Hill GU27 . . . .**208** A6
Wey House Sch GU5 . . . . . .**151** E8
Wey Manor Rd KT15 . . . . . .**52** D2
Wey Rd Godalming GU7 . . .**151** A5
Weybridge KT13 . . . .**52** F7

Wey Ret Pk KT14 . . . .**71** E7
Wey View Ct GU1 . . . .**130** C5
Weybank GU23 . . . .**71** E3
Weybank Cl GU9 . . . .**125** C3
Weybarton KT14 . . . .**71** F6
Weybourne Cty Inf Sch
GU9 . . . .**125** E6
Weybourne Pl CR2 . . . .**61** D1
Weybourne Rd GU11, GU9 **125** E6
Weybourne St SW18 . . . . . .**20** C6
Weybridge Bsns Pk KT15 . .**52** E6
Weybridge Hospl KT13 . . . .**53** A6
Weybridge House KT13 . . . .**53** D5
Weybridge Pk KT13 . . . .**53** B5
Weybridge Rd
Addlestone KT15, KT13 . . . . .**52** E6
Thornton Heath CR7 . . . . . .**42** A5
Weybridge KT15 . . . .**52** E6
Weybridge Sta KT13 . . . . . .**53** A4
Weybrook Dr GU4 . . . .**110** B6
Weycombe Rd GU27 . . . . . .**208** C8
Weydon Hill Cl GU9 . . . . . .**146** C8
Weydon Hill Rd GU9 . . . . . .**146** C8
Weydon La Farnham GU9 . .**146** A8
Wrecclesham GU9 . . . .**145** F8
Weydon Sch GU9 . . . .**145** F7
Weydown Cl
Guildford GU2 . . . .**109** A6
Putney SW19 . . . .**19** E7
Weydown Ct GU27 . . . .**208** B7
Weydown Ind Est GU27 . . .**208** B7
❸ Kingston u T KT1 . . . .**37** E6
Weydown La GU2 . . . .**109** A6
Weydown Rd GU27 . . . .**208** B7
Weyfield Prim Sch GU1 . . .**109** D4
Weylands Pk KT13 . . . .**53** D4
Weylea Ave GU1, GU4 . . . . .**110** A4
Weymead Cl KT16 . . . .**33** C1
Weymede KT14 . . . .**71** F7
Weymouth Ct Belmont SM2 .**59** A3
❶ Streatham SW2 . . . .**21** F8
Weyside GU9 . . . .**125** C2
Weyside Cl KT14 . . . .**71** F7
Weyside Gdns GU1 . . . .**109** C3
Weyside Pk GU7 . . . .**151** A5
Weyside Rd GU1 . . . .**109** B3
Weysprings GU27 . . . .**208** A6
Weyvern Pk GU3 . . . .**130** B1
Weyview Cl GU1 . . . .**109** C3
Weywood Cl GU9 . . . .**125** F7
Weywood La GU9 . . . .**125** D6
Whaley Rd RG40 . . . .**25** D8
Wharf Bridge Rd TW7 . . . . . .**6** B4
Wharf La Send GU23 . . . . . .**90** C4
Twickenham TW1 . . . .**17** A7
Wharf Rd Ash GU12 . . . . . .**106** A4
Frimley GU16 . . . .**86** A6
Guildford GU1 . . . .**109** C1
Wraysbury TW19 . . . .**11** D8
Wharf St GU7 . . . .**150** E4
Wharf Way GU16 . . . .**86** A6
Wharfedale Gdns
CR7, SW16 . . . .**41** F6
Wharfenden Way GU16 . . . .**85** F6
Wharncliffe Gdns SE25 . . . .**42** E7
Wharncliffe Rd SE25 . . . . . .**42** E7
Whateley Rd
Guildford GU2 . . . .**109** B5
Penge SE20 . . . .**23** D1
Whatley Ave SW20 . . . .**39** E6
Whatley Gn RG12 . . . .**27** B3
Whatman Rd SE23 . . . .**23** D8
Whatmore Cl TW19 . . . .**2** A1
Wheat Knoll GU15 . . . .**80** C3
Wheatash Rd KT15 . . . .**52** B8
Wheatfield Way
Horley RH6 . . . .**161** C4
Kingston u T KT1 . . . .**37** E7
Wheathill House SE20 . . . . .**43** B7
Wheathill Rd SE20 . . . .**43** B6
Wheatlands TW5 . . . .**5** A8
Wheatlands Rd SW17 . . . . . .**21** A5
Wheatley RG12 . . . .**26** E4
Wheatley House ❸ SW15 . . .**19** A8
Wheatley Rd TW7 . . . .**5** F4
Wheatley's Ait
Lower Halliford TW16 . . . . .**35** A4
Sunbury TW16 . . . .**35** A4
Wheatsheaf Cl
Horsham RH12 . . . .**217** E5
Ottershaw KT16 . . . .**51** D4
Woking GU21 . . . .**69** F3
Wheatsheaf La TW18 . . . . . .**12** F1
Wheatstone Cl
Crawley RH10 . . . .**182** B3
Mitcham SW19 . . . .**40** E8
Wheeler Ave RH8 . . . .**122** D6
Wheeler La GU8 . . . .**170** E6
Wheeler Rd RH10 . . . .**202** B4
Wheelers La
Brockham RH3 . . . .**137** C7
Epsom KT18 . . . .**76** C5
Smallfield RH6 . . . .**162** B3
Wheelers Way RH19 . . . . . .**184** E3
Wheelwrights La GU26 . . . .**188** A4
Wheelwrights Pl SL3 . . . .**1** C7
Whelan Way SM6 . . . .**60** D7
Wherwell Lodge GU2 . . . . .**130** C7
Wherwell Rd GU2 . . . .**130** C7
Whetstone Rd GU14 . . . .**84** C4
Whimbrel Cl CR2, CR8 . . . . .**80** D8
Whinfell Cl SW16 . . . .**21** D3
Whins Cl GU15 . . . .**65** B4
Whins Dr GU15 . . . .**65** B4
Whinshill Ct SL5 . . . .**30** A1
Whipley Cl GU4 . . . .**110** B6
Whistler Cl RH10 . . . .**201** F3
Whistler Gr GU47 . . . .**64** D6

Whistley Cl RG12 . . . .**27** E6
Whitby Cl TN16 . . . .**83** B1
Whitby Gdns SM1, SM5 . . . .**59** D8
Whitby Rd SM1, SM5 . . . . . .**59** D8
Whitchurch Cl GU11 . . . . . .**126** D6
Whitchurch Ct SW17 . . . . . .**20** D4
Whitchurch House SE6 . . . .**24** C5
White Acres Rd GU16 . . . . . .**85** F4
White Beam Way KT20 . . . . .**97** A6
White Bridge Cl TW14 . . . . . .**3** F1
White Bushes RH1 . . . .**140** A4
White City RG45 . . . .**45** D5
White Cottage Cl GU9 . . . .**125** D6
White Ct GU2 . . . .**109** A4
White Hart Ct
Horsham RH12 . . . .**217** C4
Ripley GU23 . . . .**91** C6
White Hart Ind Est GU17 . . .**64** E4
White Hart La
Mortlake SW14 . . . .**7** E4
Wood St V GU3 . . . .**108** A2
White Hart Meadows
GU23 . . . .**91** C6
White Hart Row CR3 . . . .**33** A2
White Heron Mews TW11 . . .**16** F7
White Hill Kingswood CR5 . .**98** D4
South Croydon CR2 . . . .**61** D1
Windlesham GU20 . . . .**48** B6
White Horse Dr KT18 . . . . . .**76** C5
White Horse La GU23 . . . . . .**91** C6
White House ❸ SW4 . . . .**21** D8
White House Ct BR3 . . . .**44** C8
White House La GU4 . . . . . .**109** D6
White House Prep Sch
RG41 . . . .**25** A3
White House Wlk GU9 . . . . .**125** D7
White Knights Rd KT13 . . . .**53** C3
White Knobs Way CR3 . . . .**101** A2
White La Ash GU10, GU12 . .**127** C7
Guildford GU4 . . . .**131** D7
Titsey RH8, TN16 . . . .**103** B3
Tongham GU10, GU12 . . . . .**127** C7
White Lodge Ashstead KT21 **95** E7
South Norwood SE19 . . . . . .**22** B1
White Lodge Cl SM2 . . . .**59** C3
White Lodge Gdns RH1 . . .**140** A1
White Lodge The Royal
Ballet Sch TW10 . . . .**18** D7
White Oak Dr BR3 . . . .**44** D7
White Post La GU10 . . . . . .**146** A4
White Rd GU15 . . . .**64** F6
White Rose La
Farnham GU9, GU10 . . . . . .**146** B7
Old Woking GU22 . . . .**90** A8
Woking GU22 . . . .**69** F1
White Way KT23 . . . .**94** B1
Whitebeam Dr RH2 . . . .**139** B6
Whitebeams Gdns GU14 . . .**84** C3
Whiteberry Rd RH5 . . . .**156** B7
Whitebines GU9 . . . .**125** D2
Whitecroft Cl BR3 . . . .**44** D5
Whitecroft Way BR3 . . . .**44** D5
Whitefield Ave CR8 . . . .**80** B3
Whitefield House CR8 . . . . . .**80** B3
Whitefoot La BR1, SE6 . . . . .**24** D5
Whitefoot Terr BR1 . . . .**24** F5
Whitegate Way KT20 . . . .**97** B7
Whitegates
Old Woking GU22 . . . .**89** F7
Whyteleafe CR3 . . . .**101** A8
Whitehall Cres KT9 . . . .**56** D5
Whitehall Dr RH11 . . . .**200** E6
Whitehall Farm La GU25 . . .**31** E6
Whitehall Gdns W4 . . . .**7** B8
Whitehall La Egham TW20 . .**11** F1
Horton TW19 . . . .**1** A1
Reigate RH2 . . . .**138** F6
Whitehall Park Rd W4 . . . . . .**7** B8
Whitehall Pl SM5 . . . .**60** B6
Whitehall Rd CR7 . . . .**42** A4
Whitehead Cl SW18 . . . .**20** C8
Whitehill Cl GU15 . . . .**65** D7
Whitehill La
Bletchingley RH1 . . . .**120** D6
Martyr's Green GU23 . . . . . .**92** C4
Whitehill Pl GU25 . . . .**31** E4
Whitehorse La SE25 . . . .**42** E5
Whitehorse Manor Inf Sch
CR7 . . . .**42** D4
Whitehorse Manor Jun
Sch CR7 . . . .**42** D5
Whitehorse Rd
Horsham RH12 . . . .**218** B6
South Norwood CR0,
CR7, SE25 . . . .**42** D3
Thornton Heath CR0,
CR7, SE25 . . . .**42** D3
Whitehouse Dr GU1 . . . . . .**110** A3
Whitelands Coll,
Roehampton Inst SW18 . . . .**19** E8
Whitelands Dr SL5 . . . .**28** D8
Whiteley House ❾ SW4 . . . .**21** D8
Whiteley House & Hospl
KT12 . . . .**53** F2
Whiteley Rd SE19 . . . .**22** D3
Whiteleys House TW13 . . . . .**16** A5
Whiteleys Way TW13 . . . . . .**16** A5
Whitelocke Cty Inf Sch
RG40 . . . .**25** D7
Whitely Hill RH10 . . . .**202** E6
Whitemore Rd GU1 . . . .**109** D5
Whiteoak House SE19 . . . . . .**22** C1
Whiteoaks SM7 . . . .**78** B6
Whitepost Hill RH1 . . . .**118** E1
Whitepost House RH1 . . . . .**118** E1

Whites Dr BR2 . . . . .44 F2
Whites Rd GU14 . . . . .85 E1
Whitethorn Ave CR5 . . . . . .79 B4
Whitethorn Cl GU12 . . . . .106 B1
Whitethorn Cotts GU6 . . . .174 B6
Whitethorn Gdns CR0 . . . . .62 B8
Whiteways St TW18 . . . . . . .13 B1
Whiteways End GU10 . . . . .126 D4
Whitewood Cotts TN16 . . . .103 C7
Whitewood La RH9 . . . . . . .163 B7
Whitfield Cl Guildford GU2 109 A4
Haslemere GU27 . . . . .189 C1
Whitfield Ct 🔢 SE21 . . . . . . .22 E4
Whitfield Rd GU27 . . . . . . .189 C1
Whitford Gdns CR4 . . . . . . .40 F6
Whitgift Ave CR2 . . . . .61 C5
Whitgift Ctr CR9 . . . . .61 C8
Whitgift House CR2 . . . . . . .61 C5
Whitgift Sch CR2 . . . . .61 C5
Whitgift St CR0, CR9 . . . . . .61 C7
Whitgift Wlk RH10 . . . . . . .201 D3
Whitland Rd SM5 . . . . .40 D1
Whitlet Cl GU9 . . . . .125 B1
Whitley Cl TW19 . . . . .2 E1
Whitlock Dr SW19 . . . . .19 E7
Whitmead Cl CR2 . . . . .61 E4
Whitmead La GU10 . . . . . . .147 E4
Whitmoor La GU4 . . . . .89 D1
Whitmoor Rd GU19 . . . . .47 F2
Whitmoor Vale Rd GU26 . . .188 A5
Whitmore Cl GU47 . . . . .45 D1
Whitmore Gn GU9 . . . . . . .125 E6
Whitmore La SL5 . . . . .30 A5
Whitmore Rd BR3 . . . . .43 F6
Whitmore Vale
  Grayshott RH18 . . . . .187 F6
  Headley Down GU26 . . . . .187 F6
Whitmore Vale Rd
  Grayshott RH18 . . . . .188 A4
  Headley Down GU26, GU27 187 E7
Whitmore Way RH6 . . . . . .160 E3
Whitmores Cl KT18 . . . . . . .76 C4
Whitstable Cl BR3 . . . . .43 F8
Whittaker Ave TW10, TW9 . . .6 D2
Whittaker Ct KT21 . . . . .75 D2
Whittaker Pl 🔢 TW10 . . . . . . .6 D2
Whittaker Rd SM3 . . . . .58 F7
Whittam House SE27 . . . . . .22 C3
Whittell Gdns SE26 . . . . . . .23 C5
Whittingham Ct W4 . . . . .7 E7
Whittington Coll RH19 . . . .185 A4
Whittington Ct SE20 . . . . . .43 B7
Whittington Rd RH10 . . . . .201 E3
Whittle Cl GU47 . . . . .45 A1
Whittle Cres GU14 . . . . .84 F7
Whittle Rd TW5 . . . . .4 C7
Whittle Way RH10 . . . . . . .182 A3
Whittlebury Cl SM5 . . . . . . .59 F3
Whitton Dene
  Isleworth TW2, TW3, TW7 . .5 D2
  Twickenham TW2, TW7 . . . . .5 D1
Whitton Manor Rd TW7 . . . . .5 C1
Whitton Rd Bracknell RG12 . .27 F6
  Hounslow TW3 . . . . .5 B2
  Isleworth TW3 . . . . .5 B2
  Twickenham TW1 . . . . .17 A8
Whitton Sch TW2 . . . . .16 B6
Whitton Sta TW2 . . . . .16 C8
Whitton Waye TW2, TW3 . . . .5 A1
Whitworth Rd
  Crawley RH11 . . . . .181 D2
  South Norwood SE25 . . . . . .42 F5
Whopshott Ave GU21 . . . . . .69 C3
Whopshott Cl GU21 . . . . . . .69 C3
Whopshott Dr GU21 . . . . . . .69 C3
Whynstones Rd SL5 . . . . . . .29 A4
Whyte Ave GU12 . . . . .126 D7
Whytebeam View CR3 . . . . .80 F1
Whytecliffe Rd N CR8 . . . . .80 B8
Whytecliffe Rd S CR8 . . . . .80 B8
Whytecroft TW5 . . . . .4 D7
Whyteleafe Bsns Village
  CR3 . . . . .80 F2
Whyteleafe Hill CR3 . . . . . . .80 F1
Whyteleafe Rd
  Caterham CR3 . . . . .100 F6
  Whyteleafe CR3 . . . . .100 F6
Whyteleafe Sch CR3 . . . . . .80 F1
Whyteleafe South Sta
  CR3 . . . . .101 A8
Whyteleafe Sta CR3 . . . . . . .80 F2
Wick House 🔢 KT1 . . . . .37 D8
Wick La TW20 . . . . .10 F3
Wick Rd
  Englefield Green TW20 . . . .11 B1
  Teddington TW11 . . . . .17 C1
Wickers Oake SE19 . . . . . . .22 F4
Wicket The CR0 . . . . .63 A5
Wickets The TW15 . . . . .13 E4
Wickham Ave
  Cheam KT4, SM3 . . . . .58 C5
  Croydon CR0 . . . . .43 E1
Wickham Chase BR4 . . . . . .44 E2
Wickham Cl Horley RH6 . . .160 F4
  New Malden KT3 . . . . .38 F4
Wickham Court Rd BR4 . . . .63 C8
Wickham Cres BR4 . . . . . . .63 C8
Wickham La TW20 . . . . .12 A1
Wickham Rd
  Beckenham BR3 . . . . .44 B6
  Camberley GU15 . . . . .65 E8
  Croydon CR0, CR9 . . . . . . .62 E8

Wickham Vale RG12 . . . . . .26 E3
Wickham Way BR3 . . . . .44 C4
Wickhurst Gdns RH12 . . . .216 E3
Wickhurst La RH12 . . . . . .216 E3
Wickland Ct RH10 . . . . . . .201 D3
Wicklow Ct SE26 . . . . .23 C3
Wide Way CR4, SW16 . . . . .41 D6
Widgeon Way RH12 . . . . . .217 C5
Widmer Ct TW5 . . . . .4 E5
Wiggie La RH1 . . . . .119 A3
Wigley Rd TW13 . . . . .15 D7
Wigmore La RH5 . . . . .157 C1
Wigmore Rd SM5 . . . . .40 E1
Wigmore Wlk SM5 . . . . .59 D8
Wilberforce Cl KT18 . . . . . . .76 D5
Wilberforce Way
  Bracknell RG12 . . . . .27 D4
  Wimbledon SW19 . . . . .19 D2
Wilbury Ave SM2 . . . . .58 F1
Wilbury Rd GU21 . . . . .69 D2
Wilcot Cl GU24 . . . . .68 A3
Wilcot Gdns GU24 . . . . .68 A3
Wilcox Gdns TW17 . . . . .33 F6
Wilcox Rd Sutton SM1 . . . . .59 B6
  Teddington TW11 . . . . .16 D4
Wild Acres KT14 . . . . .71 C8
Wildacre Cl RH14 . . . . .212 D3
Wildbank Ct 🔢 GU22 . . . . . . .69 F1
Wildcroft Dr Dorking RH5 . .136 D4
  Wokingham RG40 . . . . .25 A1
Wildcroft Manor SW15 . . . . .19 C8
Wildcroft Rd SW15 . . . . . . .19 C8
Wildcroft Wood GU8 . . . . . .170 D6
Wilde Pl SW18 . . . . .20 D8
Wilde Theatre RG12 . . . . . . .27 C2
Wilderness Ct GU2 . . . . . .129 F7
Wilderness Rd
  Frimley GU16 . . . . .65 E2
  Guildford GU2 . . . . .129 F7
  Oxted RH8 . . . . .122 E5
Wilderness Rise RH19 . . . .186 A6
Wilderness The
  East Molesey KT8 . . . . .36 C4
  Hampton TW12 . . . . .16 B4
Wilders Cl Frimley GU16 . . . .65 E3
  Woking GU21 . . . . .69 C1
Wilderwick Rd RH19, RH7 186 A5
Wildfell Rd SE6 . . . . .24 B8
Wildfield Cl GU3 . . . . .108 B2
Wildgoose Dr RH12 . . . . . .216 F3
Wildridings Cty Prim Sch
  RG12 . . . . .27 A5
Wildridings Rd RG12 . . . . . .27 A5
Wildridings Sq RG12 . . . . . .27 A5
Wildwood Cl
  East Horsley KT24 . . . . .92 F2
  Lewisham SE12 . . . . .24 F8
  Pyrford GU22 . . . . .70 F4
Wildwood Ct CR8 . . . . .80 D4
Wildwood La GU6 . . . . .194 C5
Wilford Rd CR0 . . . . .42 C2
Wilfred Owen Cl SW19 . . . . .20 C2
Wilfred St GU21 . . . . .69 D1
Wilhelmina Ave CR5 . . . . . .99 C8
Wilkes Rd 🔢 TW8 . . . . .6 E8
Wilkins Cl CR4 . . . . .40 E8
Wilkinson Ct
  🔢 Crawley RH11 . . . . .201 B1
  Upper Tooting SW17 . . . . . .20 D4
Wilkinson House TW7 . . . . . .5 F4
Wilks Gdns CR0 . . . . .43 E1
Will Miles Ct 🔢 SW19 . . . . . .20 C1
Willats Ct KT16 . . . . .33 A3
Willcocks Cl KT9 . . . . .56 E7
Willems Ave GU11 . . . . . . .104 F2
Willems Rdbt GU11 . . . . . .104 F2
Willerton Lodge 🔢 KT13 . . . .53 D4
Willett Pl CR7 . . . . .42 A4
Willett Rd CR7 . . . . .42 A4
Willetts RH4 . . . . .136 C4
Willey Broom La CR3 . . . . .100 A2
Willey Farm La CR3 . . . . . .100 C1
Willey La CR3 . . . . .100 D2
William Booth Rd SE20 . . . .43 A8
William Brown Ct SE27 . . . .22 B6
William Byrd Sch UB7 . . . . . .3 D8
William Cobbett Cty Jun
  Sch GU9 . . . . .125 E6
William Evelyn Ct RH5 . . . .134 F4
William Farthing Cl 🔢
  GU11 . . . . .105 A2
William Harvey House 🔢
  SW19 . . . . .19 E7
William Lilly House KT12 . .54 C5
William Morris Mid Sch
  CR4 . . . . .41 D6
William Morris Way
  RH11 . . . . .201 C1
William Rd Caterham CR3 . .100 D5
  Guildford GU1 . . . . .109 C1
  Merton SW19 . . . . .19 E1
  Sutton SM1 . . . . .59 C5
William Russell Ct 🔢
  GU21 . . . . .68 E1
William Sim Wood RG42 . . .8 B2
William Wood House
  SE26 . . . . .23 C5
Williams Cl
  Addlestone KT15 . . . . .52 B5
  Ewhurst GU6 . . . . .175 E5
Williams House 🔢 SW2 . . . .22 A7
Williams La Morden SM4 . . . .40 C4
  Mortlake SW14 . . . . .7 C5
Williams Terr CR0 . . . . .61 A4
Williamson Cl GU27 . . . . . .189 F1
Willingham Way KT1 . . . . . .38 A7

Willington Cl GU15 . . . . . . .65 B6
Willington Prep Sch SW19 19 F3
Willis Ave SM2 . . . . .59 E4
Willis Cl KT18 . . . . .76 B5
Willis Rd CR0 . . . . .42 C2
Willlows The CR0 . . . . .62 E8
Willmore End SW19 . . . . . . .40 B7
Willoughby Ave CR0 . . . . . . .60 F6
Willoughby Rd
  Bracknell RG12 . . . . .26 F6
  Kingston u T KT2 . . . . .37 F8
  Twickenham TW1 . . . . .6 D2
Willoughbys The SW15 . . . . .7 E3
Willow Ave SW13 . . . . .7 F5
Willow Bank GU22 . . . . .89 F6
Willow Brean RH6 . . . . . . .160 E5
Willow Cl
  Beare Green RH5 . . . . .157 C4
  Brentford TW8 . . . . .6 C8
  Catford SE6 . . . . .24 F7
  Colnbrook SL3 . . . . .1 C7
  Crawley RH10 . . . . .201 E8
  East Grinstead RH19 . . . . .185 D3
  Mytchett GU16 . . . . .85 E4
  Woodham KT15 . . . . .70 F8
Willow Cnr RH6 . . . . .180 F7
Willow Cotts
  Carshalton CR4 . . . . .40 F2
  Richmond TW9 . . . . .7 A8
Willow Cres GU14 . . . . .85 B7
Willow Ct Ash Vale GU12 . .106 A7
  Frimley GU16 . . . . .65 D1
  Horley RH6 . . . . .161 B6
  🔢 Streatham SW16 . . . . . . .21 F5
  Thornton Heath CR7 . . . . . .42 D4
  Wokingham RG41 . . . . .25 B6
Willow Ctr The CR4 . . . . . . .40 F3
Willow Dr Bracknell RG12 . . .27 C8
  Flexford GU3 . . . . .107 C1
  Send Marsh GU23 . . . . .91 A3
Willow End KT6 . . . . .37 E1
Willow Gdns TW5 . . . . .5 A6
Willow Glade RH2 . . . . .139 B6
Willow Gn GU24 . . . . .68 A6
Willow House TW14 . . . . . . .4 B2
Willow La Blackwater GU17 .64 D4
  Guildford GU1 . . . . .110 A2
  Mitcham CR4 . . . . .40 F3
Willow Lodge 🔢 TW16 . . . . .14 F1
Willow Manor SM1 . . . . .58 F6
Willow Mead Dorking RH4 136 A8
  🔢 East Grinstead RH19 . . .205 F8
  Witley GU8 . . . . .170 E5
Willow Mount CR0 . . . . .61 E7
Willow Pk GU12 . . . . .105 F2
Willow Rd Farncombe GU7 150 F8
  Horsham RH12 . . . . .218 B5
  Kingston u T KT3 . . . . .38 C5
  Poyle SL3 . . . . .1 E5
  Reigate RH1 . . . . .139 C6
  Wallington SM6 . . . . .60 B3
Willow Ridge RH10 . . . . . . .204 A3
Willow Tree Cl SW18 . . . . . .20 B7
Willow Vale KT23 . . . . .94 B4
Willow View SW19 . . . . .40 D8
Willow Way
  Aldershot GU12 . . . . .126 E8
  Forest Hill SE26 . . . . .23 C5
  Godstone RH9 . . . . .121 C3
  Guildford GU1 . . . . .109 B5
  Heath End GU9 . . . . .125 D5
  Sunbury TW16 . . . . .35 A5
  Twickenham TW2 . . . . .16 B6
  West Byfleet KT14 . . . . . . .71 C8
  West Ewell KT19 . . . . .57 D4
  Woking GU22 . . . . .89 E7
Willow Wlk Box Hill KT20 . .116 B5
  Cheam SM1, SM3 . . . . .58 F7
  Chertsey KT16 . . . . .33 B2
  Englefield Green TW20 . . . .11 C3
  Redhill RH1 . . . . .140 B7
Willow Wood Cres SE25 . . . .42 E3
Willowbank Gdns KT20 . . . .97 B5
Willowbrook Rd TW19 . . . . .13 E6
Willowdene Cl TW2 . . . . . . .16 C8
Willowfield 🔢 RH10 . . . . . .201 D5
Willowhayne Dr KT12 . . . . .35 B2
Willowhayne Gdns KT4 . . . .58 C6
Willowherb Cl RG40 . . . . . . .25 E7
Willowmead W18 . . . . .33 B8
Willowmead Cl GU21 . . . . . .69 A3
Willowmere KT10 . . . . .55 C6
Willows Ave SM4 . . . . .40 B4
Willows End GU47 . . . . .64 B8
Willows Path KT18 . . . . .76 B5
Willows The
  Beckenham BR3 . . . . .44 A8
  🔢 Bracknell RG12 . . . . .27 F5
  Byfleet KT14 . . . . .71 E6
  Chiddingfold GU8 . . . . . . .191 A4
  Claygate KT10 . . . . .55 E4
  Farnham GU10 . . . . .126 C4
  Guildford, Bushy Hill GU4 .110 D3
  Guildford, Pitch Place GU2 .108 F6
  Horsham RH12 . . . . .217 D5
  Lightwater GU18 . . . . .48 C1
  🔢 Redhill RH1 . . . . .139 F8
  Weybridge KT13 . . . . .53 A7
Willowtree Way SW16 . . . . .42 A8
Wills Cres TW3 . . . . .5 B1
Wilson Rd TW20 . . . . .11 B3
Wilmar Gdns BR4 . . . . .44 B1
Wilmer Cl KT2 . . . . .18 A3
Wilmer Cres KT2, TW10 . . .17 F3
Wilmerhatch La
  KT18, KT21 . . . . .76 B2
Wilmington Ave W4 . . . . .7 D7
Wilmington Cl RH11 . . . . . .201 C1

Wilmington Ct SW16 . . . . . .21 E1
Wilmot Rd Purley CR8 . . . . .80 A7
  Wallington SM5 . . . . .59 E5
Wilmot Way Banstead SM7 . .78 A5
  Frimley GU15 . . . . .65 F3
Wilmot's La RH1, RH6 . . . .162 E5
Wilmots Cl RH2 . . . . .118 C2
Wilna Rd SW18 . . . . .20 C8
Wilson Ave CR4, SW19 . . . .40 E8
Wilson Cl Crawley RH10 . . .202 D3
  Croydon CR0 . . . . .61 D5
Wilson Dr KT16 . . . . .51 B5
Wilson Hospl CR4 . . . . .40 F5
Wilson Rd Aldershot GU12 105 D1
  Chessington KT9 . . . . .56 F4
  Farnborough GU14 . . . . . . .84 F3
Wilson Way GU21 . . . . .69 D3
Wilson's Sch SM6 . . . . .60 E4
Wilsons KT20 . . . . .97 D6
Wilsons Rd GU35 . . . . .187 B5
Wilton Cl UB7 . . . . .2 D8
Wilton Cres SW19 . . . . .39 F8
Wilton Ct
  Farnborough GU14 . . . . . . .85 D3
  🔢 Richmond TW10 . . . . .6 E2
Wilton Gdns
  East Molesey KT8 . . . . .36 A6
  Walton-on-T KT12 . . . . .35 D1
Wilton Gr Merton SW19 . . . .39 F8
  New Malden KT3 . . . . .38 F3
Wilton Par TW13 . . . . .15 B6
Wilton Pl Beckenham BR3 . .44 C6
  New Haw KT15 . . . . .52 D2
Wilton Rd Camberley GU15 . .65 B3
  Hounslow TW4 . . . . .4 D4
  Mitcham SW19 . . . . .20 E1
  Redhill RH1 . . . . .139 F8
Wilton Wlk TW13 . . . . .15 B7
Wiltshire Ave RG45 . . . . . . .45 B5
Wiltshire Dr RG40 . . . . .25 D7
Wiltshire Gdns TW2 . . . . . . .16 C7
Wiltshire Rd
  Thornton Heath CR7 . . . . . .42 A6
  Wokingham RG40 . . . . .25 C7
Wimbart Rd SW2 . . . . .21 F8
Wimbledon Bridge SW19 . . .19 F2
Wimbledon Chase Mid
  Sch SW20 . . . . .39 E8
Wimbledon Chase Sta
  SW20 . . . . .39 E7
Wimbledon Cl
  Camberley GU15 . . . . .46 F1
  🔢 Wimbledon SW20 . . . . . .19 D1
Wimbledon Coll SW19 . . . . .19 D1
Wimbledon Common
  Prep Sch SW19 . . . . .19 D1
Wimbledon High Sch
  SW19 . . . . .19 E2
Wimbledon Hill Rd SW19 . .19 F2
Wimbledon House Sch
  SW19 . . . . .40 A8
Wimbledon Lawn Tennis
  Mus SW19 . . . . .19 E5
Wimbledon Park Ct SW19 . .19 F4
Wimbledon Park Prim Sch
  SW19 . . . . .20 B6
Wimbledon Park Rd
  Putney SW18, SW19 . . . . . .19 F7
  Wandsworth SW18, SW19 . .19 F7
Wimbledon Park Side
  SW19 . . . . .19 D7
Wimbledon Park Sta
  SW19 . . . . .20 A5
Wimbledon Rd
  Camberley GU15 . . . . .46 F1
  Wandsworth SW17 . . . . . . .20 C4
Wimbledon Sch of Art
  SW19 . . . . .39 E8
Wimbledon Sch of Art
  Annexe SW19 . . . . .20 A1
Wimbledon Sta SW19 . . . . .19 F2
Wimbledon Stadium
  SW17 . . . . .20 C4
Wimbledon Stadium
  Bsns Ctr SW17 . . . . .20 B5
Wimblehurst Ct RH12 . . . . .217 C4
Wimblehurst Rd RH12 . . . .217 C5
Wimboldon Windmill
  Mus SW19 . . . . .19 C5
Wimborne Ave RH1 . . . . . .140 A4
Wimborne Cl Epsom KT17 . .76 F6
  North Cheam KT4 . . . . .39 C1
Wimborne House
  Croydon CR0 . . . . .43 C4
  Upper Tooting SW12 . . . . . .21 C5
Wimborne Way BR3 . . . . . . .43 E5
Wimbourne Ct
  Mitcham SW19 . . . . .20 D1
  South Croydon CR2 . . . . . . .61 E4
Wimland Hill RH12 . . . . . . .199 D2
Wimland Rd
  Faygate RH12 . . . . .199 D1
  Rusper RH12 . . . . .199 C4
Wimlands La RH12 . . . . . . .199 E3
Wimpole Cl 🔢 KT1 . . . . .38 A7
Wimshurst Cl CR0 . . . . .41 E1
Wincanton Rd SW18 . . . . . .19 F8
Winchcombe Rd SM5 . . . . . .40 E1
Winchelsey Rise CR2 . . . . . .61 F4
Winchendon Rd
  TW11, TW12 . . . . .16 D4
Winchester Ave TW5 . . . . . . .4 F8
Winchester Cl
  Beckenham BR2 . . . . .44 F6
  Esher KT10 . . . . .55 A7
  Kingston u T KT2 . . . . .18 B1

Winchester Cl continued
  Poyle SL3 . . . . .1 E6
Winchester Pk BR2 . . . . . . .44 F6
Winchester Rd Ash GU12 . .106 A3
  Beckenham BR2 . . . . .44 F6
  Crawley RH10 . . . . .201 E2
  Feltham TW13 . . . . .15 F5
  Harlington UB3 . . . . .3 E7
  Rushmoor GU10 . . . . .168 B7
  Twickenham TW1 . . . . .6 B1
  Walton-on-T KT12 . . . . .35 A1
Winchester St GU14 . . . . . .105 C8
Winchester Way GU17 . . . . .64 C6
Winchet Wlk CR0 . . . . .43 C3
Winchfield House SW15 . . . .7 F1
Winchfield Rd SE26 . . . . . . .23 E3
Winchilsea Cres KT8 . . . . . .36 C7
Winchstone Cl TW17 . . . . . .33 F5
Windborough Rd SM5 . . . . .60 A3
Windermere Ave
  SM4, SW19 . . . . .40 B6
Windermere Cl
  East Bedfont TW14 . . . . . . .14 F7
  Farnborough GU14 . . . . . . .84 E3
  Stanwell TW19 . . . . .13 D6
  Thorpe Lea TW20 . . . . .12 B1
Windermere Ct
  Barnes SW13 . . . . .7 F8
  Purley CR8 . . . . .80 B1
Windermere House TW1 . . . .5 F2
Windermere Rd
  Coulsdon CR5 . . . . .79 E4
  Croydon CR0 . . . . .42 F1
  Kingston u T SW15 . . . . . . .18 E3
  Lightwater GU18 . . . . .48 B1
  Mitcham SW16 . . . . .41 D7
  West Wickham BR4 . . . . . . .63 E8
Windermere Way
  Hale GU9 . . . . .125 A6
  Redhill RH2 . . . . .118 E3
Windermere Wlk GU15 . . . .66 D5
Windfield KT22 . . . . .95 B5
Windfield Cl SE26 . . . . .23 D4
Windgates GU4 . . . . .110 C4
Windham Ave CR0 . . . . .63 D1
Windham Rd TW9 . . . . .6 F4
Winding Wood Dr GU15 . . .66 B3
Windings The CR2 . . . . .80 F8
Windle Cl GU20 . . . . .48 C4
Windlebrook Gn 🔢 RG42 . . .27 A8
Windlemere Golf Ctr
  GU24 . . . . .67 E8
Windlesham Ct GU20 . . . . . .48 C6
Windlesham Gr SW19 . . . . .19 D7
Windlesham House CR4 . . . .40 D7
Windlesham Rd
  Bracknell RG42 . . . . .26 F8
  Chobham GU24 . . . . .49 C3
  West End GU24 . . . . .67 F7
Windlesham Village Cty
  Inf Sch GU20 . . . . .48 B6
Windley Cl SE23 . . . . .23 C6
Windmill Ave KT17 . . . . .76 E8
Windmill Bridge
  House CR0 . . . . .42 E1
Windmill Bsns Village
  TW16 . . . . .34 E8
Windmill Cl Caterham CR3 100 C4
  Charlton TW16 . . . . .14 E1
  Ewell KT17 . . . . .76 F7
  Horley RH6 . . . . .161 B3
  Horsham RH13 . . . . .218 A4
  Long Ditton KT6 . . . . .37 C2
Windmill Ct RH10 . . . . .201 D8
Windmill Dr
  Headley Down GU35 . . . . .187 B6
  Leatherhead KT22 . . . . .95 C4
  Redhill RH2 . . . . .118 E3
Windmill End KT17 . . . . .76 F7
Windmill Field GU20 . . . . . .48 D4
Windmill Gr CR0 . . . . .42 C3
Windmill La
  Ashurst Wood RH19 . . . . .206 C7
  East Grinstead RH19 . . . . .185 D3
  Ewell KT17 . . . . .76 F7
  Thames Ditton KT7 . . . . . . .37 E2
Windmill Lodge TW16 . . . . .34 E8
Windmill Rd
  Aldershot GU12 . . . . .105 C1
  Bracknell RG42 . . . . .27 A8
  Brentford TW8 . . . . .6 D8
  Charlton TW16 . . . . .34 E8
  Hampton TW12 . . . . .16 C3
  Mitcham CR4 . . . . .41 C5
  Roehampton SW19 . . . . . . .19 B5
  Thornton Heath CR0 . . . . . .42 C2
Windmill Rd W TW16 . . . . . .34 E8
Windmill Rise KT2 . . . . .18 B1
Windmill Terr TW17 . . . . . . .34 E2
Windmill Trad Est TW16 . . .34 E8
Windmill Way RH2 . . . . . . .118 D3
Windrush Cl Bramley GU5 .151 F6
  Chiswick W4 . . . . .7 C7
  Crawley RH11 . . . . .200 F4
Windrush House 🔢 RH1 . . .118 F2
Windrush Hts GU47 . . . . . . .64 B8
Windrush La SE23 . . . . .23 D5
Winds Ridge GU23 . . . . .90 C2
Windsor Ave Cheam SM3 . . .58 E7
  East Molesey KT8 . . . . .36 A6
  Merton SW19 . . . . .40 C8
  New Malden KT3 . . . . .38 C4
Windsor Cl Crawley RH11 . .201 C2
  Guildford GU2 . . . . .129 F7
  West Norwood SE27 . . . . . .22 C4
Windsor Cres GU9 . . . . . . .125 B6
Windsor Ct Ashford TW16 . .15 A1
  Chobham GU24 . . . . .49 E2

Windsor Ct *continued*
Horsham RH13 217 F3
South Norwood SE19 42 E8
Windsor Dr TW15 13 D4
Windsor Gdns Ash GU12 105 F1
Wallington CR0 60 E7
Windsor Gr SE27 22 C4
Windsor Great Pk SL4 10 D4
Windsor House RH2 139 B4
Windsor Mews Catford SE6 24 C7
Forest Hill SE23 23 E7
Windsor Park Rd UB3 3 F7
Windsor Pk SW19 40 C8
Windsor Pl Chertsey KT16 33 A3
East Grinstead RH19 206 A8
Windsor Rd Ashford TW16 15 A2
Chobham GU24 49 D3
Cranford TW4, TW5 4 C5
Englefield Green
TW19, TW20 11 E6
Farnborough GU14 85 D1
Kingston u T KT2 17 E1
North Ascot SL5 29 A8
Richmond TW9 6 F5
South Norwood CR7 42 B7
Teddington TW11 16 D3
Worcester Park KT4 58 A8
Windsor Ride Bracknell SL5 28 C4
Sandhurst GU15 65 A8
Windsor St KT16 33 A3
Windsor Way
Aldershot GU11 105 B2
Frimley GU16 85 F8
Woking GU22 70 C3
Windsor Wlk
Walton-on-T KT12 35 D1
Weybridge KT13 53 B5
Windways GU8 192 F7
Windy Ridge Cl SW19 19 D3
Windy Wood GU7 150 C3
Windycroft Cl CR5, CR8 79 D6
Windyridge RH11 201 A5
Winern Glebe KT14 71 D6
Winery La KT1 37 F6
Winfield Ct RH5 158 B1
Winfield Gr RH5 158 B1
Winfrith Rd SW18 20 C7
Wingate Cres CR0 41 E3
Wingate Ct GU11 104 F2
Wingfield Cl KT15 52 B1
Wingfield Gdns GU16 66 D3
Wingfield Rd KT2 18 A2
Wingham House 3 SE26 23 A5
Wingrove Rd SE6 24 E6
Wings Cl Hale GU9 125 B6
Sutton SM1 59 A6
Wings Rd GU9 125 B6
Winifred Rd Coulsdon CR5 79 B4
Hampton TW12 16 A4
Merton SW19 40 A8
Winkfield Cl RG41 25 B3
Winkfield La SL4 8 D7
Winkfield Plain SL4 9 B8
Winkfield Rd Ascot SL5 29 B7
Windsor SL4 9 C8
Winkfield Row RG42 8 B3
Winkfield St SL4 8 C6
Winkworth Arboretum
GU8 172 C7
Winkworth Pl
Banstead SM7 78 A5
Farnham GU9 125 C3
Winkworth Rd SM7 78 A5
Winlaton Rd BR1, SE6 24 D4
Winner Way RH6 181 D6
Winnington Way GU21 69 C1
Winscombe RG12 26 E4
Winsford Rd SE6 23 F5
Winslade Way SE6 24 B8
Winslow Way
Feltham TW13 15 E5
Walton-on-T KT12 54 C7
Winstanley Cl KT11 73 B5
Winstanley Wlk KT11 73 B5
Winston Churchill Sch The
GU21 68 F1
Winston Cl GU16 85 F6
Winston Dr KT11 73 E3
Winston Way GU22 90 B7
Winston Wlk GU10 146 C6
Winter Box Wlk TW10 6 F2
Winterbourne RH12 217 F7
Winterbourne Ct RG12 27 D7
Winterbourne Gr KT13 53 C4
Winterbourne Inf Sch CR7 42 A5
Winterbourne Jun Boys' Sch CR7 42 A5
Winterbourne Jun Girls' Sch CR7 42 A5
Winterbourne Rd
Forest Hill SE23, SE6 23 F7
Thornton Heath CR7 42 A5
Winterbourne Wlk GU16 85 F8
Winterdown Gdns KT10 54 F4
Winterdown Rd KT10 54 F4
Winterfold RH10 202 A3
Winterfold Cl SW19 19 E6
Winterhill Way GU4 110 B5
Winters Rd KT7 37 B2
Wintersells Ind Est KT14 52 D1
Wintersells Rd KT13, KT14 52 E1
Winterstoke Rd SE23, SE6 23 F7
Winterton Ct RH13 217 D2
Winton Ct 15 KT6 37 D2
Winton House CR8 80 A3
Winton House Sch CR0 61 F8
Winton Rd Aldershot GU11 105 A1
Farnham GU9 125 D4
Winton Way SW16 22 A3
Wire Mill La RH7 184 F8
Wirrall House 15 SE26 23 A5
Wisbeach Rd CR0 42 D4
Wisborough Ct RH11 200 F3
Wisborough Rd CR2 61 F2
Wisdom Ct 5 TW7 6 A4
Wiseman Ct 12 SE19 22 E3
Wiseton Rd SW17 20 F7
Wishanger La GU10 167 B2
Wishbone Way GU21 68 F3
Wishford Ct KT21 75 F1
Wishmoor Cl GU15 65 E8
Wishmoor Rd GU15 65 E8
Wishmore Cross Sch
GU24 49 F1
Wisley Gdns GU14 84 D2
Wisley La GU23, KT14 71 E3
Wispers Sch GU27 189 C1
Wiston Ct RH11 200 F3
Witham Rd Hounslow TW7 5 D6
Penge BR3, SE20 43 C6
Wither Dale RH6 160 E4
Witherby Cl CR0, CR2 61 E6
Withers Cl KT9 56 C4
Witherslack Cl GU35 187 C4
Withey Brook RH6 160 D1
Withey Meadows RH6 160 D1
Witheygate Ave TW18 13 B2
Withies La GU3 129 C2
Withies The Knaphill GU21 68 E2
Leatherhead KT22 95 B6
Withy Cl GU18 48 C1
Withybed Cnr KT20 97 B4
Withypitts RH10 204 A3
Withypitts E RH10 204 A3
Witley CE Inf Sch GU8 170 F4
Witley Commons Visitor Ctr GU8 170 C6
Witley Cres CR0 63 C4
Witley House 5 SW2 21 F8
Witley & Milford Commons NR GU8 170 B6
Witley Point 8 SW15 19 B7
Witley Sta GU8 190 F8
Witney Path SE23 23 D5
Wittenham House KT3 38 D1
Wittenham Rd RG12 27 F8
Wittering Cl KT2 17 D3
Wittersham Rd BR1 24 F3
Wittmead Rd GU16 85 F4
Wivenhoe Ct TW4 4 F3
Wiverton Rd SE20, SE26 23 C3
Wix Hill KT24 112 B4
Woburn Ave
Farnborough GU14 85 D3
Purley CR8 80 A8
Woburn Cl Frimley GU16 66 A1
Merton SW19 20 C2
Woburn Ct Croydon CR0 42 C1
Richmond TW9 6 F4
Woburn Hill KT15 52 D7
Woburn Hill Pk KT15 52 D8
Woburn Rd Carshalton SM5 40 E1
Crawley RH11 201 A4
Croydon CR0 42 C1
Wodeland Ave GU2 130 B7
Woffington Cl KT1, KT8 37 C8
Woking Bsns Pk GU21 70 B4
Woking Cl SW15 7 F3
Woking Coll GU22 90 A7
Woking Comm Hospl
GU22 69 F1
Woking High Sch GU21 69 D4
Woking Nuffield Hospl The GU21 69 E5
Woking Rd GU1, GU4 109 D5
Woking Sta GU22 69 F2
Wokingham Hospl RG41 25 A6
Wokingham Rd RG42 26 F8
Wokingham Sta RG40 25 B6
Wokingham Theatre RG40 25 B8
Wold Cl RH11 200 F4
Wold The CR3 102 A5
Woldhurstlea Cl RH11 201 A4
Woldingham Rd CR3, CR6 101 C7
Woldingham Sch CR3 101 E2
Woldingham Sta CR3 101 D5
Wolf's Cnr RH8 123 A5
Wolf's Hill RH8 123 A4
Wolf's Rd RH8 123 B5
Wolfe Rd GU12 105 C1
Wolfington Rd SE27 22 B4
Wolfs Wood RH8 123 A3
Wolseley Ave SW18, SW19 20 A6
Wolseley Gdns W4 7 B8
Wolseley Rd
3 Aldershot GU11 105 A1
Carshalton CR4 41 A2
Farncombe GU7 150 F6
Wolsey Cl Isleworth TW3 5 C3
Kingston u T KT2 38 B8
Wimbledon SW20 19 B1
Worcester Park KT19, KT4 58 A6
Wolsey Cres
New Addington CR0 63 C2
West Barnes SM4 39 F2
Wolsey Ct BR1 24 F1
Wolsey Dr Kingston u T KT2 17 E2
Walton-on-T KT12 35 D1
Wolsey Gr 2 KT10 55 B6
Wolsey House 2 TW12 16 B2
Wolsey Inf & Jun Schs
CR0 63 D3
Wolsey Pl Sh Ctr GU22 69 E2
Wolsey Rd Ashford TW15 13 F4
Ashford, Felthamhill TW16 14 F2
East Molesey KT8 36 D5
Wolsey Rd *continued*
Esher KT10 55 B6
Hampton TW12 16 C2
Wolsey Way KT9 57 A5
Wolsey Wlk 4 GU21 69 F2
Wolstonbury Cl RH11 201 C4
Wolvens La
Coldharbour RH5 156 E5
Westcott RH4, RH5 135 B2
Wolverton Ave KT2 38 A8
Wolverton Cl RH6 160 F1
Wolverton Gdns RH6 160 F2
Wolves Hill RH5 178 C4
Wonersh Ct GU5 152 B7
Wonersh & Shamley Green CE Inf Sch GU5 152 D5
Wonersh Way SM2 58 D2
Wonford Cl King T KT2, KT3 38 E8
Walton on t H KT20 97 A1
Wonham La RH3, RH2 137 F8
Wonham Way
Gomshall GU5 133 D3
Peaslake GU5 133 D1
Wontford Rd CR8 80 B4
Wontner Rd SW12, SW17 20 F6
Wood Cl RH1 161 A8
Wood Ct GU2 109 B2
Wood End RH12 218 C5
Wood End Cl GU22 70 F3
Wood End The SM6 60 B2
Wood La Banstead KT20 77 F2
Bracknell RG42 26 E8
Caterham CR3 100 D3
Farnborough GU14 85 A3
Hounslow TW7 5 F7
Knaphill GU21 68 D1
Seale GU10 127 B5
Weybridge KT13 53 C2
Wood Lodge La BR4 63 C7
Wood Rd
Beacon Hill GU26 188 D6
Biggin Hill TN16 83 C1
Camberley GU15 65 B1
Farncombe GU7 150 F7
Heath End GU9 125 C7
Littleton TW17 34 A5
Wood Riding GU22 70 E4
Wood Rise GU3 108 E3
Wood St Ash Vale GU12 106 A6
Carshalton CR4 41 A2
East Grinstead RH19 185 D1
Kingston u T KT2 37 E8
Merstham RH1 119 C7
Wood Street Cty Inf Sch
GU3 108 C3
Wood Vale SE22 23 B8
Woodall House TW7 5 F4
Woodbank Rd BR1 24 F5
Woodbarn The GU9 125 C1
Woodbastwick Rd SE26 23 E3
Woodberry Cl
Ashford TW16 15 A2
Chiddingfold GU8 191 A5
Woodbine Cl
Sandhurst GU47 64 C7
Twickenham TW2 16 D6
Woodbine Cotts GU4 130 E2
Woodbine Gr SE20 23 B1
Woodbine La KT4 58 C7
Woodbines Ave KT1 37 D6
Woodbourne GU9 125 E7
Woodbourne Ave SW16 21 D5
Woodbourne Cl SW16 21 E5
Woodbourne Dr KT10 55 F4
Woodbourne Gdns SM6 60 B3
Woodbridge Ave KT22 75 A1
Woodbridge Ct RH12 218 A5
Woodbridge Dr GU15 65 D7
Woodbridge Gr KT22 75 A1
Woodbridge Hill GU2 109 B2
Woodbridge Hill Gdns
GU2 109 A2
Woodbridge Meadows
GU1 109 C2
Woodbridge Park Est
GU1 109 C2
Woodbridge Rd
Blackwater GU17 64 B5
Guildford GU1, GU2 109 C2
Woodbrook Sch BR3 43 F8
Woodbury Ave RH19 186 B1
Woodbury Cl
Biggin Hill TN16 83 F1
East Grinstead RH19 206 B8
South Croydon CR0 61 F8
Woodbury Dr SM2 59 C1
Woodbury House SE26 23 B5
Woodbury St SW17 20 E3
Woodby Dr SL5 29 F2
Woodcock Dr GU24 49 C3
Woodcock Hill RH19, RH7 184 F6
Woodcock La GU24 49 B3
Woodcombe Cres SE23 23 C7
Woodcot Gdns GU14 84 D4
Woodcote Artington GU2 130 B5
Cranleigh GU6 174 B4
Farncombe GU7 150 D6
Horley RH6 161 C4
Woodcote Ave
Thornton Heath CR7 42 B5
Wallington SM6 60 B2
Woodcote Cl Epsom KT18 76 D5
Kingston u T KT2 17 F3
Woodcote Dr CR8 60 D1
Woodcote End KT18 76 D4
Woodcote Gn SM6 60 C2
Woodcote Green Rd KT18 76 C4
Woodcote Grove Rd CR5 79 D5
Woodcote Hall
Epsom KT18 76 D5
Wallington SM6 60 B2
Woodcote High Sch CR5 79 D6
Woodcote House KT18 76 D4
Woodcote House Ct KT18 76 D4
Woodcote House (Sch)
GU20 48 B5
Woodcote Hurst KT18 76 C3
Woodcote Inf Sch CR5 79 D5
Woodcote Jun Sch CR5 79 D5
Woodcote La CR8 79 D7
Woodcote Mews SM6 60 B4
Woodcote Park Ave
CR5, CR8 79 C7
Woodcote Park Golf Club
CR5 79 B5
Woodcote Park Golf Course KT18 76 D2
Woodcote Park Rd KT18 76 C4
Woodcote Pl
North Ascot SL5 28 F8
1 West Norwood SE27 22 B3
Woodcote Rd Epsom KT18 76 D5
Epsom KT18 76 D5
Forest Row RH18 206 F2
Wallington CR8, SM6 60 C2
Woodcote Side KT18 76 B4
Woodcote Valley Rd
CR5, CR8 79 E7
Woodcott House 1 SW15 19 A8
Woodcott Terr GU12 126 D8
Woodcourt RH11 201 C1
Woodcrest Rd CR8 79 E6
Woodcrest Wlk RH2 118 E3
Woodcroft Rd
Crawley RH11 200 D4
Thornton Heath CR0, CR7 42 B3
Woodcut Rd GU10 145 F6
Woodend
Farnborough GU14 85 D3
Leatherhead KT22 95 C2
South Norwood SE19 22 C2
Sutton SM1 59 C8
Thames Ditton KT10 55 C8
Woodend Cl
Crawley RH10 202 A8
North Ascot SL5 28 E8
Woking GU21 89 A8
Woodend Dr SL5 29 B4
Woodend Pk KT11 73 D4
Woodend Rd GU16 86 C7
Woodenhill RG12 26 E1
Woodenhill Cty Prim Sch
RG12 26 E2
Wooderson Cl SE25 42 E5
Woodfield KT21 75 D2
Woodfield Ave
Streatham SW16 21 D5
Wallington SM5 60 A3
Woodfield Cl
Ashstead KT21 75 D2
Coulsdon CR5 99 C8
Crawley RH10 201 E7
Redhill RH1 118 E3
South Norwood SE19 22 C1
Woodfield Gdns KT3 38 F4
Woodfield Gr SW16 21 D5
Woodfield Hill CR5 99 B8
Woodfield House
11 Forest Hill SE23 23 D5
New Malden KT3 38 F4
Woodfield La KT21 75 E2
Woodfield Rd
Ashstead KT21 75 D2
Cranford TW4, TW5 4 B5
Crawley RH10 201 F7
Hinchley Wood KT10, KT7 55 F8
Rudgwick RH12 214 D7
Woodfield Sch RH1 119 E6
Woodfield Way RH1 118 E3
Woodfields Ct SM1 59 C7
Woodfields The CR2 80 F8
Woodford Gn RG12 27 F5
Woodgate Ave KT9 56 D5
Woodgate Dr SW16 21 D1
Woodgates Cl RH13 217 F3
Woodgavil SM7 77 F3
Woodger Cl GU1, GU4 110 C3
Woodgrange Ct BR2 44 F1
Woodhall Ave SE21 22 F5
Woodhall Dr SE21 22 F5
Woodhall La SL5 48 E8
Woodham La
New Haw KT15 52 B1
Sheerwater GU21, KT15 70 D7
Woodham KT15 52 B1
Woodham Park Rd KT15 51 F1
Woodham Park Way KT15 70 F8
Woodham Rd Catford SE6 24 C5
Woking GU21 69 F4
Woodham Rise GU21 70 A4
Woodham Waye GU21 70 B5
Woodhatch Rd
Redhill RH1, RH2 139 E5
Reigate RH1, RH2 139 E5
Woodhatch Spinney CR5 79 E3
Woodhaw TW20 12 B4
Woodhayes RH6 161 B4
Woodhayes Rd
SW19, SW20 19 C2
Woodhill GU23 90 D2
Woodhill La GU5 152 F4
Woodhouse La RH5 155 A8
Woodhouse St RG42 26 E8
Woodhurst La RH8 122 E4
Woodhurst Pk RH8 122 E5
Woodhyrst Gdns CR8 80 B4
Wooding Gr 15 RH11 201 B1
Woodland Ave GU6 174 F3
Woodland Cl
East Horsley KT24 112 F8
Horsham RH13 218 B4
West Ewell KT19 57 E4
West Norwood SE19 22 E2
Woodland Ct Cheam SM1 59 A4
Ewell KT17 76 F7
Oxted RH8 122 E7
Woodland Dr
Crawley Down RH10 204 B8
East Horsley KT24 112 F8
Farnham GU10 146 B6
Ockley RH5 178 A5
Woodland Gdns
Isleworth TW7 5 E4
Selsdon CR2 81 C8
Woodland Gr KT13 53 D6
Woodland Hill SE19 22 E2
Woodland Rd
Thornton Heath CR7 42 A5
West Norwood SE19 22 F2
Woodland Rise RH8 122 E5
Woodland View GU7 129 E1
Woodland Way
Caterham CR3 120 E8
Croydon CR0, CR9 43 E1
Horsham RH13 218 B4
Kingswood KT20 97 E4
Merton SM4 39 F5
Mitcham CR4 21 A1
Purley CR8 80 A6
Tolworth KT5 57 B8
West Wickham BR4 63 C7
Weybridge KT13 53 D5
Woodlands Beckenham BR3 24 B1
Chertsey KT15 52 E7
Crawley RH10 202 D8
Horley RH6 161 C4
Send Marsh GU23 90 F2
West Barnes SW20 39 D5
Woodlands Ave
Heath End GU9 125 F7
Kingston u T KT3 38 D8
Redhill RH1 139 F8
West Byfleet KT14, KT15 70 F7
Worcester Park KT4 58 A8
Woodlands Cl Ascot SL5 28 F3
Ash GU12 106 A5
Claygate KT10 55 F3
Cranleigh GU6 174 F2
Crawley Down RH10 204 B7
Farnborough GU17 64 E1
Ottershaw KT16 51 B1
Woodlands Ct Bromley BR1 44 F8
Dulwich SE22 23 B8
Sandhurst GU47 45 F1
7 Woking GU21 69 A1
Woking GU22 89 E8
Woodlands Dr
South Godstone RH9 142 E6
Sunbury TW16 35 C7
Woodlands Gr
Coulsdon CR5 79 B2
Isleworth TW7 5 E5
Woodlands House GU21 70 C5
Woodlands La
Haslemere GU27 207 F7
Stoke D'Abernon KT11 74 B2
Windlesham GU20, GU24 48 E3
Woodlands Par TW15 14 C2
Woodlands Pk
Addlestone KT15 51 F5
Box Hill KT20 116 B4
Guildford GU1 110 B2
Sheerwater GU21 70 C5
Woodlands Rd
Ashstead KT11, KT22 74 D1
Camberley GU15 65 B5
East Grinstead RH19 186 A4
Effingham KT23, KT24 113 F6
Epsom KT18 76 A4
Farnborough GU14 84 D6
Guildford GU1 109 D5
Hambledon GU8 171 D1
Isleworth TW7 5 E5
Leatherhead KT11, KT22 74 D1
Mortlake SW13 7 F4
Pyrford KT14 70 F5
Redhill RH1 139 F7
Surbiton KT6 37 D2
Virginia Water GU25 31 C5
Woodlands Rd E GU25 31 C5
Woodlands Rd W GU25 31 C5
Woodlands Ride SL5 29 A3
Woodlands Sch KT22 95 C5
Woodlands St SE13 24 D8
Woodlands The
Isleworth TW7 5 F5
Lewisham SE13 24 D8
Mitcham CR4 41 A6
Smallfield RH6 162 B3
South Norwood SE19 22 C1
Thames Ditton KT10 55 C8
Wallington SM6 60 B2
Woodlands Way
Ashstead KT21 76 B2
Box Hill KT20 116 C5
Woodlands Wlk GU17 64 E1
Woodlawn Cres TW2 16 B6
Woodlawn Dr TW13 15 D6
Woodlawn Gr GU21 69 F4
Woodlea Cty Prim Sch
CR3 101 F5

Woodlea Dr BR2 . . . . .44 E4
Woodlee Cl GU25 . . . . .31 C7
Woodleigh ❶ KT5 . . . . . . .37 F4
Woodleigh Gdns SW16 . . .21 C5
Woodley Cl SW17 . . . . .20 F1
Woodley House GU7 . . .150 E8
Woodley La SM1, SM5 . . .59 E7
Woodlodge Ashstead KT21 .75 E2
  ❹ Wimbledon SW19 . . . .19 F3
Woodman Rd CR5 . . . . .79 D4
Woodmancote Ct RH12 . .217 D5
Woodmancote Gdns KT14 .71 A6
Woodmancott Cl RG12 . . . .27 F3
Woodmancourt GU7 . . . .150 C8
Woodmans Hill RH11 . . . .201 C2
Woodmansterne Cty
  Prim Sch SM7 . . . . .78 F5
Woodmansterne La
  Banstead SM7 . . . . .78 D4
  Wallington SM5, SM6 . . . .79 A7
  Woodmansterne SM7 . . . .78 D4
Woodmansterne Prim Sch
  SW16 . . . . .41 D8
Woodmansterne Rd
  Coulsdon CR5 . . . . .79 C4
  Streatham SW16 . . . . .41 D8
  Sutton SM5, SM2 . . . . . . .59 C4
Woodmansterne St SM7 . .78 E4
Woodmansterne Sta CR5 .79 B3
Woodmere RG12 . . . . .27 E5
Woodmere Ave CR0 . . . . . .43 D2
Woodmere Cl CR0 . . . . . . .43 D2
Woodmere Gdns CR0 . . . . .43 D2
Woodmere Way BR3 . . . . . .44 D4
Woodnook Rd SW16 . . . . . .21 B3
Woodpecker Cl
  Cobham KT11 . . . . .73 E7
  Crondall GU10 . . . . .124 D8
Woodpecker La RH5 . . . .158 C2
Woodpecker Mount CR0 . .62 F2
Woodpecker Way GU22 . . .89 D3
Woodpeckers
  Bracknell RG12 . . . . .27 B5
  Witley GU8 . . . . .170 E7
Woodplace Cl CR5 . . . . . . .79 C1
Woodplace La
  Coulsdon CR5 . . . . .99 C7
  Hooley CR5 . . . . .99 C7
Woodridge Cl RG12 . . . . . .27 B5
Woodrow Dr RG40 . . . . . . .25 F6
Woodrough Copse GU5 . .152 A5
Woodroyd Ave RH6 . . . . .160 F2
Woodroyd Gdns RH6 . . . .160 F1
Woodruff Ave GU1 . . . . . .110 B4
Woods Hill Cl RH19 . . . . .206 D6
Woods Hill La RH19 . . . . .206 D6
Woodshore Cl GU25 . . . . . .31 B3
Woodside Blackwater GU17 .64 C3
  ❶ Farnborough GU14 . . . .85 B7
  Fetcham KT22 . . . . .94 B5
  Horsham RH13 . . . . .218 B4
  Hydestile GU8 . . . . .171 E5
  Lower Kingswood KT20 . .117 F7
  Sandhurst GU47 . . . . .64 F7
  Walton-on-T KT12 . . . . . .35 A1
  West Horsley KT24 . . . . . .92 C1
  Wimbledon SW19 . . . . . . .19 F3
Woodside Ave
  Croydon SE25 . . . . .43 B4
  Hersham KT12 . . . . .54 B6
  Thames Ditton KT10 . . . . .36 E2
Woodside Cl
  Caterham CR3 . . . . .100 E3
  Chiddingfold GU8 . . . . . .191 B4
  Knaphill GU21 . . . . .68 D2
  Tolworth KT5 . . . . .38 C2
Woodside Cotts GU8 . . . .148 C3
Woodside Court Rd
  CR0, CR9 . . . . .43 A2
Woodside Cres RH6 . . . . .162 A3
Woodside Gn CR0, SE25 . .43 A3
Woodside House SW19 . . .19 F2
Woodside Jun & Inf Sch
  CR0 . . . . .43 A2
Woodside La SL4, SL5 . . . . .9 C3
Woodside Park Est GU7 .150 F4
Woodside Pk SE25 . . . . . .43 B3
Woodside Rd
  Beare Green RH5 . . . . . .157 D3
  Chiddingfold GU8 . . . . . .191 B5
  Cobham KT11 . . . . .74 A6
  Crawley RH10 . . . . .201 F8
  Croydon SE25 . . . . .43 B3
  Farnborough GU11 . . . . .104 F7
  Guildford GU2 . . . . .108 F2
  Heath End GU9 . . . . .125 E7
  Kingston u T KT2 . . . . . . .17 E1
  Kingston u T KT3 . . . . . . .38 E7
  Purley CR8 . . . . .79 E6
  Sutton SM1 . . . . .59 C7
Woodside Way
  Croydon CR0 . . . . .43 C3
  Redhill RH1 . . . . .140 A3
  Redhill RH1 . . . . .140 A8
  Streatham CR4 . . . . .41 C8
  Virginia Water GU25 . . . . .31 B6
Woodsome Lodge KT13 . . .53 D4
Woodspring Rd SW19 . . . .19 E6
Woodstock
  East Grinstead RH19 . . . .185 C2
  West Clandon GU4 . . . . .111 B7
  Wokingham RG40 . . . . . . .25 C6
Woodstock Ave
  Cheam SM3, SM4 . . . . . . .39 F2
  Isleworth TW7 . . . . .6 A2

Woodstock Cl
  Cranleigh GU6 . . . . .174 F1
  Horsham RH12 . . . . .217 D5
  Woking GU21 . . . . .69 E3
Woodstock Ct KT17 . . . . . .76 D7
Woodstock Gdns BR3 . . . .24 B1
Woodstock Gr GU7 . . . . .150 E7
Woodstock La N KT6 . . . . .56 C8
Woodstock La S KT10, KT6 56 C6
Woodstock Rd
  Coulsdon CR5 . . . . .79 B3
  Croydon CR0, CR9 . . . . . .61 D7
  Wallington SM5, SM6 . . . .60 A5
Woodstock Rise SM3 . . . . .39 F2
Woodstock Way CR4 . . . . .41 C7
Woodstocks GU14 . . . . . . .85 D6
Woodstone Ave KT17, KT4 .58 A5
Woodsway KT22 . . . . .74 E5
Woodsyre SE19, SE26 . . . .22 F4
Woodthorpe Rd
  Ashford TW15 . . . . .13 D4
  Staines TW15 . . . . .13 D4
Woodvale Ave SE25 . . . . . .42 F7
Woodvale Ct SE25 . . . . . . .42 F6
Woodvale Wlk SE27 . . . . . .22 C3
Woodview KT9 . . . . .75 C8
Woodview Cl
  Hamsey Green CR2 . . . . . .81 B5
  Kingston u T SW15 . . . . . .18 D4
Woodview Ct KT13 . . . . . . .53 C5
Woodville Cl
  Blackwater GU17 . . . . . . .64 B5
  Teddington TW11 . . . . . . .17 A4
Woodville Gdns SK6 . . . . .37 D2
Woodville Pl CR3 . . . . . . .100 C5
Woodville Rd
  Leatherhead KT22 . . . . . .95 B7
  Merton SM4 . . . . .40 A5
  Richmond TW10 . . . . .17 C5
  South Norwood CR7 . . . . .42 D6
Woodville Sch The KT22 . .95 B7
Woodward Cl KT10 . . . . . .55 F4
Woodwarde Rd SE22 . . . . .22 F8
Woodwards RH11 . . . . . . .201 C1
Woodway Camberley GU15 .65 B5
  Guildford GU1 . . . . .110 B2
Woodyard La SE21 . . . . . . .22 E8
Woodyers Cl GU5 . . . . . . .152 B7
Wool Rd SW20 . . . . .19 B2
Woolborough Cl RH10 . . .201 E7
Woolborough La
  Crawley RH10 . . . . .181 F1
  Crawley, Three
    Bridges RH10 . . . . .202 A8
  South Nutfield RH1 . . . . .161 F8
Woolborough Rd RH10 . .201 E7
Woolford Cl RG42 . . . . .8 C1
Woolfords La GU8 . . . . . .169 B7
Woolhampton Way RG12 .27 D4
Woolhams SK3 . . . . .101 A1
Woollards Rd GU4 . . . . . .106 B4
Woolmead Rd GU9 . . . . . .125 C3
Woolmead The GU9 . . . . .125 C3
Woolmer Hill Rd
  GU26, GU27 . . . . .207 D7
Woolmer Hill Sch GU27 .207 D7
Woolmer View GU26 . . . .188 D3
Woolsack Way GU7 . . . . .150 F4
Woolstone Rd SE23, SE6 . .23 E6
Woosehill La RG41 . . . . . . .25 A5
Wootton Cl KT18 . . . . .76 F3
Wootton Grange GU22 . . .89 E8
Worbeck Rd SE20 . . . . .43 C7
Worcester Cl Croydon CR0 .63 A8
  Farnborough GU14 . . . . . .85 B7
  Mitcham CR4 . . . . .41 A7
Worcester Ct Ashford TW15 14 B3
  Walton-on-T KT12 . . . . . .35 C1
  Worcester Park KT4 . . . . .57 E7
Worcester Dr TW15 . . . . . .14 B3
Worcester Gdns KT4 . . . . .57 E7
Worcester Park Rd KT4 . . .57 D7
Worcester Park Sta KT4 . .39 A1
Worcester Rd Belmont SM2 59 B3
  Crawley RH10 . . . . .201 E2
  Guildford GU2 . . . . .108 F3
  Reigate RH2 . . . . .118 A2
  Sutton SM2 . . . . .59 B3
  ❶ Wimbledon SW19 . . . . .19 F3
Wordsworth RG12 . . . . . . .26 F4
Wordsworth Ave CR8 . . . .80 D4
Wordsworth Cl RH10 . . . .202 B8
Wordsworth Dr KT4, SM3 .58 C6
Wordsworth Mead RH1 . .119 B3
Wordsworth Pl RH12 . . . .217 E7
Wordsworth Rd
  Addlestone KT15 . . . . . . .52 D6
  Hampton TW12, TW13 . . . .15 F4
  Penge SE20 . . . . .23 D1
  Wallington SM6 . . . . .60 D4
Wordsworth Rise ❻
  RH19 . . . . .185 C1
Works Rd KT15 . . . . .52 B2
Worlds End Hill RG12 . . . .27 F3
Wormley La GU8 . . . . .171 B1
Worple Ave Isleworth TW7 . .6 A2
  Staines TW18 . . . . .13 B2
  Wimbledon SW19 . . . . . . .19 D1
Worple Ct SW19 . . . . .19 E2
Worple Prim Sch TW7 . . . . .6 A3
Worple Rd Epsom KT18 . . .76 D4
  Epsom KT18 . . . . .76 E5
  Isleworth TW7 . . . . .6 A3
  Leatherhead KT22 . . . . . .95 B4
  Staines TW18 . . . . .13 B1
  Wimbledon SW19, SW20 . .39 D8
Worple Road Mews SW19 .19 F2
Worple St SW14 . . . . .7 D4

Worple Way TW10 . . . . .6 E3
Worplesdon Cty Prim
  Sch GU3 . . . . .108 D4
Worplesdon Golf Course
  GU22 . . . . .88 D4
Worplesdon Hill Heath
  House Rd GU22 . . . . .88 D5
Worplesdon Rd GU2 . . . .109 A4
Worplesdon Sta GU22 . . . .89 B3
Worslade Rd SW17 . . . . . . .20 D4
Worsley Bridge Jun Sch
  BR3 . . . . .24 A1
Worsley Bridge Rd
  Beckenham BR3, SE6 . . . .24 A2
  Catford SE6 . . . . .23 F3
Worsley House SE23 . . . . .23 B6
Worsley Rd GU16 . . . . .85 F7
Worsted Gn RH1 . . . . .119 D6
Worsted La RH19 . . . . . . .206 B8
Worth Abbey & Sch
  RH10 . . . . .203 B1
Worth Park Ave RH10 . . . .202 C7
Worth Rd RH10 . . . . .202 C6
Worth Way RH10 . . . . . . .202 E5
Worthfield Cl KT19 . . . . . . .57 D3
Worthing Rd Heston TW5 . .4 F8
  Horsham RH12 . . . . .217 B1
Worthington Cl CR4 . . . . . .41 B6
Worthington House ❶❻
  SW2 . . . . .22 A8
Worthington Rd KT6 . . . . .37 F1
Wortley Rd CR0 . . . . .42 A2
Worton Ct TW7 . . . . .5 E3
Worton Gdns TW7 . . . . .5 D5
Worton Hall Est TW7 . . . . .5 E3
Worton Rd TW7 . . . . .5 E4
Worton Way TW3, TW7 . . . .5 D5
Wotton Dr RH5 . . . . .134 E3
Wotton Way SM2 . . . . .58 C1
Wrabness Way TW18 . . . . .33 B8
Wray Cl RH19 . . . . .206 D6
Wray Common Cty Prim
  Sch RH2 . . . . .118 D2
Wray Common Rd RH2 . .118 D2
Wray House ❶❶ SW2 . . . . .21 E7
Wray La RH2 . . . . .118 D4
Wray Mill House RH2 . . . .118 E4
Wray Mill Pk RH2 . . . . . . .118 E3
Wray Park Rd RH2 . . . . . .118 C2
Wray Rd SM2 . . . . .58 F2
Wrayfield Ave RH2 . . . . . .118 C2
Wrayfield Rd SM3 . . . . . . .58 D7
Wraylands Dr RH2 . . . . . .118 D3
Wraymead Pl RH2 . . . . . .118 B2
Wraymill Ct ❹ RH2 . . . . .118 D1
Wraysbury Cl TW4 . . . . .4 E2
Wraysbury Rd
  Staines TW18 . . . . .12 C5
  Wraysbury TW19 . . . . . . .12 C5
Wraysbury Sta TW19 . . . . . .1 A1
Wrecclesham Hill GU10 . .145 E5
Wrecclesham Rd
  Farnham GU10, GU9 . . . .145 F8
  Wrecclesham GU10, GU9 . .145 F8
Wrekin The GU14 . . . . .85 E1
Wren Cl Horsham RH12 . .217 D7
  Selsdon CR2 . . . . .62 D7
Wren Cres KT15 . . . . .52 D5
Wren Ct Ash GU12 . . . . . .106 B3
  Crawley RH10 . . . . .201 E3
  South Croydon CR0 . . . . . .61 D6
Wren House ❹ TW12 . . . .16 B2
Wren Way GU14 . . . . .84 F7
Wren's Hill KT22 . . . . .74 C4
Wrens Ave TW15 . . . . .14 C4
Wrenthorpe Rd BR1 . . . . . .24 E4
Wright Cl RH10 . . . . .202 C2
Wright Gdns TW17 . . . . . . .34 A4
Wright Rd TW5 . . . . .4 C7
Wright's Row SM5 . . . . . . .60 B4
Wrighton Ct SM1 . . . . .58 F4
Wrights Rd SE25 . . . . .42 E6
Wriotsley Way KT15 . . . . . .52 A4
Wrotham Hill GU8 . . . . . .192 E3
Wrotham House BR3 . . . . .23 F1
Wroxham RG12 . . . . .26 F4
Wroxham Wlk RH10 . . . . .202 B4
Wrythe Gn SM5 . . . . .59 F7
Wrythe Green Rd SM5 . . . .59 F7
Wrythe La SM1, SM5, SM4 . .59 F7
Wyatt Cl TW13 . . . . .15 D7
Wyatt Park Mansions ❶
  SW2 . . . . .21 E6
Wyatt Park Rd SW2 . . . . . .21 F6
Wyatt Rd TW18 . . . . .13 A3
Wyatt's Almshouses GU7 151 A6
Wyatt's Cl GU7 . . . . .151 A6
Wych Elm Rise GU1 . . . . .130 E6
Wych Hill GU22 . . . . .89 C8
Wych Hill La GU22 . . . . . . .89 D8
Wych Hill Pk GU22 . . . . . . .89 D8
Wych Hill Rise GU22 . . . . .89 D8
Wych Hill Way GU22 . . . . . .89 D8
Wyche Gr CR2 . . . . .61 D2
Wychelm Rd GU18 . . . . . . .67 C8
Wychwood SW19 . . . . .212 D3
Wychwood Ave
  Bracknell RG12 . . . . .27 F5
  South Norwood CR7 . . . . .42 C6
Wychwood Cl
  Aldershot GU12 . . . . .105 F2
  Ashford TW16 . . . . .15 A2
Wychwood Pl GU15 . . . . . .66 B8
Wychwood Way SE19 . . . . .22 D2
Wycliffe Bldgs GU2 . . . . .130 C7
Wycliffe Ct RH11 . . . . . . .200 E3
Wycliffe Rd Merton SW19 . .20 B2
  Wimbledon SW19 . . . . . . .20 B2

Wydell Cl SM4 . . . . .39 D3
Wydenhurst Rd CR0, CR9 . .43 B2
Wye Cl TW15 . . . . .14 B4
Wyecliffe Gdns RH1 . . . . .119 C5
Wyeth's Mews KT17 . . . . . .76 F6
Wyeth's Rd KT17 . . . . .76 F6
Wyke Ave GU12 . . . . .106 E3
Wyke Bglws GU12 . . . . . .106 D3
Wyke Cl TW7 . . . . .5 F8
Wyke Cty Prim Sch The
  GU3 . . . . .106 A4
Wyke Green Golf Course
  TW7 . . . . .5 F8
Wyke La GU12 . . . . .106 D2
Wyke Rd SW20 . . . . .39 C7
Wykeham Cl UB7 . . . . .3 A8
Wykeham House
  Farnborough GU14 . . . . .105 C8
  Merton SW19 . . . . .40 A8
Wykeham Rd
  Farnham GU9 . . . . .125 C3
  Guildford GU1 . . . . .110 D2
Wylam RG12 . . . . .26 F4
Wyleu St SE23 . . . . .23 E8
Wymering Ct GU14 . . . . . .85 D3
Wynash Gdns SM5 . . . . . . .59 E5
Wynbourne Ct SE20 . . . . . .43 B7
Wyncote Way CR2 . . . . . . .62 D2
Wyndham Ave KT11 . . . . . .73 A6
Wyndham Cl SM2 . . . . .59 A3
Wyndham Cres
  Cranleigh GU6 . . . . .174 A3
  Twickenham TW4 . . . . .5 A1
Wyndham Rd
  Kingston u T KT2 . . . . . . .17 F1
  Woking GU21 . . . . .69 B1
Wyndham St GU12 . . . . . .105 C1
Wyndhams GU22 . . . . .70 B3
Wynell Rd SE23 . . . . .23 D5
Wynfields GU16 . . . . .85 F3
Wynlea Cl RH10 . . . . .204 A8
Wynne Ct ❹ TW7 . . . . .6 A4
Wynnstow Pk RH8 . . . . . .122 F4
Wynsham Way GU20 . . . . .48 B6
Wynton Gdns SE25 . . . . . .42 F4
Wynton Gr KT12 . . . . .54 A7
Wyphurst Rd GU6 . . . . . . .174 E4
Wyresdale RG12 . . . . .27 F2
Wysemead RH6 . . . . .161 C4
Wythegate SE12 . . . . .11 F1
Wyvern Cl Ash Vale GU12 .105 F5
Wyvern Est The KT3 . . . . . .39 A5
Wyvern Pl KT15 . . . . .52 B6
Wyvern Rd CR8 . . . . .61 B1

Y

Yaffle Rd KT13 . . . . .53 C1
Yale Cl Hounslow TW4 . . . . .4 F2
  Sandhurst GU47 . . . . .45 F2
Yarborough Rd SW19 . . . . .40 D8
Yarbridge Cl SM2 . . . . .59 B1
Yard Mead TW20 . . . . .12 A5
Yardley RG12 . . . . .26 F4
Yardley Cl RH2 . . . . .118 B3
Yarm Cl KT22 . . . . .95 C4
Yarm Court Rd KT22 . . . . .95 C4
Yarm Way KT22 . . . . .95 C4
Yarmouth Cl RH10 . . . . . .202 A4
Yarnold Cl RG40 . . . . .25 F7
Yarrow Cl RH12 . . . . .217 E5
Yateley Ct CR8 . . . . .80 C5
Yatesbury Cl GU9 . . . . . . .145 F7
Yattendon Jun Sch RH6 .161 A4
Yattendon Rd RH6 . . . . . .161 B3
Yaverland Dr GU19 . . . . . .47 D2
Ye Market CR0 . . . . .61 D5
Yeats Cl RH1 . . . . .139 C6
Yeend Cl KT8 . . . . .36 A5
Yehudi Menuhin Sch
  KT11 . . . . .94 A8
Yellowcress Dr GU24 . . . . .68 A3
Yelverton Ct KT23 . . . . . . .94 A1
Yelverton Lodge TW1 . . . .17 C8
Yenston Cl SM4 . . . . .40 A3
Yeoman Cl SE27 . . . . .22 B5
Yeoman Ct TW5 . . . . .4 F7
Yeoman Way RH1 . . . . . . .140 B4
Yeomanry Cl KT17 . . . . . . .76 E7
Yeomans Cl
  Ash GU10, GU12 . . . . . . .126 F8
  Farnborough GU14 . . . . . .85 A5
Yeomans Mews TW7 . . . . . .5 D2
Yeomans Way GU15 . . . . . .65 E5
Yeoveney Cl TW19 . . . . . . .12 D6
Yeovil Cl GU14 . . . . .85 D1
Yeovil Rd Farnborough GU14 85 E1
  Sandhurst GU47 . . . . .45 E1
Yeovilton Pl KT2 . . . . .17 C3
Yetminster Rd GU14 . . . . .85 D1
Yew La RH19 . . . . .185 B3
Yew Pl KT13 . . . . .53 F7
Yew Tree Bottom Rd
  KT17, KT18 . . . . .77 C2
Yew Tree Cl Chipstead CR5 .98 F8
  Farnborough GU14 . . . . . .84 C3
  Horley RH6 . . . . .161 A4
  New Malden KT4 . . . . .38 E1
Yew Tree Cotts KT10 . . . . .55 D8
Yew Tree Ct SM2 . . . . .59 C3
Yew Tree Dr
  Caterham CR3 . . . . .100 F2
  Guildford GU1 . . . . .109 C6
Yew Tree Gdns KT18 . . . . .76 C4
Yew Tree House KT4 . . . . .38 E1

Yew Tree La RH2 . . . . . . .118 B4
Yew Tree Rd
  Charlwood RH6 . . . . .180 E2
  Dorking RH4 . . . . .115 A1
  Witley GU8 . . . . .170 D6
Yew Tree Wlk
  Effingham KT24 . . . . . . .113 D8
  Frimley KT16 . . . . .65 F1
  Hounslow TW4 . . . . .4 F2
  South Croydon CR8 . . . . . .61 C1
Yew Trees TW17 . . . . .33 F5
Yewbank Cl CR8 . . . . .80 C4
Yewdale Cl BR1 . . . . .24 E2
Yewens GU8 . . . . .191 B5
Yewlands Cl SM7 . . . . .78 C4
Yewlands Wlk RH11 . . . . .200 D4
Yews The TW15 . . . . .14 B4
Yewtree Rd BR3 . . . . .43 F6
Yewtrees TW19 . . . . .32 C6
Yockley Cl GU15 . . . . .66 D3
Yolland Cl GU9 . . . . .125 C7
York Ave
  East Grinstead RH19 . . . .206 A3
  Mortlake SW14 . . . . .7 C2
York Cl Byfleet KT14 . . . . . .71 E7
  Horsham RH13 . . . . .217 D1
  Morden SM4 . . . . .40 B5
York Cres GU11 . . . . .104 F1
York Ct Beckenham BR3 . . .44 B3
  Kingston u T KT2 . . . . . . .17 C2
  Wallington SM6 . . . . .60 C4
York Gdns KT12 . . . . .54 D8
York Hill SE27, SW16 . . . . .22 B5
York House Bracknell RG42 .26 E9
  Forest Hill SE26 . . . . .23 C3
  ❹ Kingston u T KT2 . . . . .17 F1
  Richmond TW9 . . . . .7 A6
  South Norwood SE25 . . . .42 E5
York Rd Aldershot GU11 . .104 F1
  Ash GU12 . . . . .106 A3
  Belmont SM1, SM2 . . . . . .59 A3
  Biggin Hill TN16 . . . . . . .103 E8
  Byfleet KT14 . . . . .71 E7
  Camberley GU15 . . . . .65 D7
  Crawley RH10 . . . . .201 E2
  Farnborough GU14 . . . . . .85 C1
  Farnham GU9 . . . . .125 C1
  Guildford GU1 . . . . .130 D8
  Hounslow TW3 . . . . .5 B4
  Kingston u T KT2 . . . . . . .17 F1
  ❸ Richmond TW10 . . . . . . .6 F2
  Selsdon CR2 . . . . .62 D1
  Teddington TW11 . . . . . . .16 E4
  Thornton Heath CR0 . . . . .42 A2
  Weybridge KT13 . . . . .53 C6
  Wimbledon SW19 . . . . . . .20 C2
  Woking GU22 . . . . .69 E1
York St Carshalton CR4 . . .41 A2
  Twickenham TW1 . . . . .17 A7
York Town Ind Est GU15 . .65 C4
York Way Chessington KT9 .56 E3
  Feltham TW13 . . . . .15 F5
  Sandhurst GU47 . . . . .64 B8
Yorke Gate Rd CR3 . . . . .100 C5
Yorke Gdns RH2 . . . . .118 A2
Yorke Rd RH2 . . . . .118 A2
Yorkshire Rd CR4 . . . . .41 E5
Yorktown Rd
  Sandhurst GU47 . . . . .64 C7
  Sandhurst GU47 . . . . .64 E7
Youlden Cl GU15 . . . . .66 A5
Youlden Dr GU15 . . . . .66 B6
Young St Fetcham KT22 . . .94 F3
  Leatherhead KT22 . . . . . .95 A3
Youngman RH7 . . . . .165 B4
Youngs Dr GU12 . . . . .105 F2
Yukon Rd SW12 . . . . .21 B8

Z

Zealand Ave UB7 . . . . .2 E7
Zennor Rd SW12 . . . . .21 C2
Zermatt Rd CR7 . . . . .42 C5
Zig Zag Rd Kenley CR8 . . .80 C3
  Mickleham KT20, RH4, RH5 .115 C7
Zinnia Dr GU24 . . . . .68 A3
Zion Pl CR7 . . . . .42 D5
Zion Rd CR7, SE25 . . . . . . .42 D5
Zodiac Ct CR0 . . . . .42 B1

NH	NJ	NK
NN	NO	NP
NS	NT	NU
NX	NY	NZ
SC	SD	SE	TA
SH	SJ	SK	TF	TG
SN	SO	SP	TL	TM
SS	ST	SU	TQ	TR
SX	SY	SZ	TV

Any feature in this atlas can be given a unique reference to help you find the same feature on other Ordnance Survey maps of the area, or to help someone else locate you if they do not have a Street Atlas.

The grid squares in this atlas match the Ordnance Survey National Grid and are at 500 metre intervals. The small figures at the bottom and sides of every other grid line are the National Grid kilometre values (**00** to **99** km) and are repeated across the country every 100 km (see left).

To give a unique National Grid reference you need to locate where in the country you are. The country is divided into 100 km squares with each square given a unique two-letter reference. Use the administrative map to determine in which 100 km square a particular page of this atlas falls.

The bold letters and numbers between each grid line (**A** to **F**, **1** to **8**) are for use within a specific Street Atlas only, and when used with the page number, are a convenient way of referencing these grid squares.

Example   The railway bridge over DARLEY GREEN RD in grid square B1

Step 1: Identify the two-letter reference, in this example the page is in **SP**

Step 2: Identify the 1 km square in which the railway bridge falls. Use the figures in the southwest corner of this square: Eastings **17**, Northings **74**. This gives a unique reference: **SP 17 74**, accurate to 1 km.

Step 3: To give a more precise reference accurate to 100 m you need to estimate how many tenths along and how many tenths up this 1 km square the feature is (to help with this the 1 km square is divided into four 500 m squares). This makes the bridge about **8** tenths along and about **1** tenth up from the southwest corner.

This gives a unique reference: **SP 178 741**, accurate to 100 m.

Eastings (read from left to right along the bottom) come before Northings (read from bottom to top). If you have trouble remembering say to yourself "Along the hall, THEN up the stairs"!

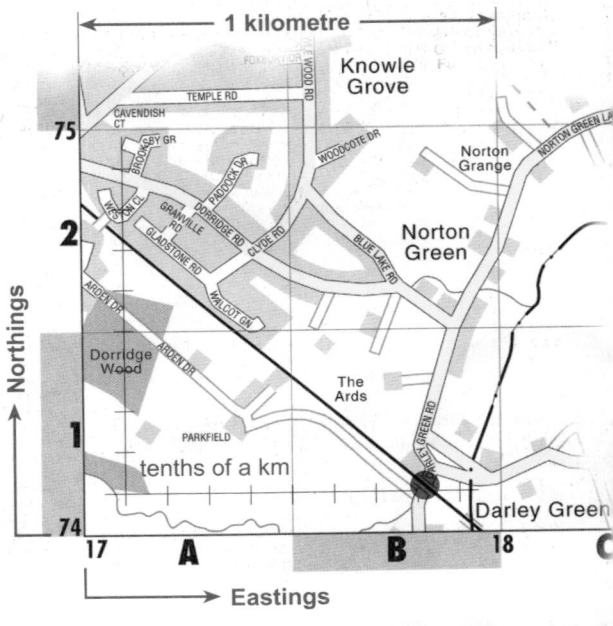

Street Atlases from Philip's

Philip's publish an extensive range of regional and local street atlases which are ideal for motoring, business and leisure use. They are widely used by the emergency services and local authorities throughout Britain.

Key features include:

◆ Superb county-wide mapping at an extra-large scale of 3½ inches to 1 mile, or 2½ inches to 1 mile in pocket edition

◆ Complete urban and rural coverage, detailing every named street in town and country

◆ Each atlas available in three handy formats – hardback, spiral, pocket paperback

'The mapping is very clear... great in scope and value'

★★★★ BEST BUY   AUTO EXPRESS

1 Bedfordshire
2 Berkshire
3 Birmingham and West Midlands
4 Bristol and Bath
5 Buckinghamshire
6 Cambridgeshire
7 Cardiff, Swansea and The Valleys
8 Cheshire
9 Derbyshire
10 Dorset
11 County Durham and Teesside
12 Edinburgh and East Central Scotland
13 North Essex
14 South Essex
15 Glasgow and West Central Scotland
16 Gloucestershire
17 North Hampshire
18 South Hampshire
19 Hertfordshire
20 East Kent
21 West Kent
22 Lancashire
23 Leicestershire and Rutland
24 London
25 Greater Manchester
26 Merseyside
27 Northamptonshire
28 Nottinghamshire
29 Oxfordshire
30 Staffordshire
31 Surrey
32 East Sussex
33 West Sussex
34 Tyne and Wear and Northumberland
35 Warwickshire
36 Wiltshire and Swindon
37 East Yorkshire and Northern Lincolnshire
38 North Yorkshire
39 South Yorkshire
40 West Yorkshire

How to order

The Philip's range of street atlases is available from good retailers or directly from the publisher by phoning 01903 828503